ENVIRONMENTAL
LAW

AUSTRALIA
The Law Book Company
Brisbane – Sydney – Melbourne – Perth

CANADA
Carswell
Ottawa – Toronto – Calgary – Montreal – Vancouver

Agents
Steimatzky's Agency Ltd., Tel Aviv
N.M. Tripathi (Private) Ltd., Bombay
Eastern Law House (Private) Ltd., Calcutta
M.P.P. House, Bangalore
Universal Book Traders, Delhi
Aditya Books, Delhi
MacMillan Shuppan KK, Tokyo
Pakistan Law House, Karachi, Lahore

ENVIRONMENTAL LAW

Richard Burnett-Hall, M.A. (Cantab.), C.P.A.
Solicitor, Head of the Environmental Law Group,
Bristows, Cooke & Carpmael

London
Sweet & Maxwell
1995

Published in 1995 by
Sweet & Maxwell Limited of
South Quay Plaza
183 Marsh Wall
London E14 9FT
Computerset by York House Typographic Ltd., London W13 8NT
Printed and bound in Great Britain by Hartnolls Ltd., Bodmin

No natural forests were destroyed to make this product; only farmed timber
was used and replanted

A CIP catalogue record for this book is available from the British Library

ISBN 0-421-47090-9

PREFACE

Public concern for improved protection of the environment has developed since the early 1980s from being the pre-occupation of a small minority to where it is now an almost daily news item. "The environment" is an important element of the policies of all the major political parties, and the government has since 1990 formally set out annual reports on its policies and achievements in this field. Though these may, perhaps inevitably, be less than wholly objective, such a public display of concern and commitment would have been un-imaginable ten years ago. The Water Act 1989 and the Environmental Protection Act 1990 have brought about a transformation of the substantive environmental law of Great Britain (most of the changes have yet to reach Northern Ireland), and their practical implementation through secondary legislation is largely complete.

Most of the major industrial firms now have or are developing active environmental policies. While this may have been largely led by those with experience of the dire consequences in the USA of failure to pay sufficient attention to environmental issues there, the culture change in industry is perceptibly taking root in the United Kingdom also, even though there is a considerable way still to go, particularly among smaller businesses. The United Kingdom Environmental Law Association has grown, from its foundation in 1987, when environmental law was considered by only a handful of firms to be a practice area in its own right, to a membership of one thousand, reflecting the spreading need for lawyers in all of industry and private practice, local government and academia, who have a proper understanding of the subject. The practice of environmental law in the United Kingdom can fairly be said to have come of age, and it is therefore an appropriate time to produce this survey of it.

Britain can be rightly proud of the pioneering legislation it introduced in the mid-19th century to protect public health and to control direct pollution of air and water (though rather less merit can be claimed for the much later development and enforcement of the laws on waste disposal). These laws and their immediate successors were operated largely independently of each other, separate regulatory bodies being developed to administer them, and this pattern of unco-ordinated regulation persisted right up to the 1980s. However with the introduction of integrated pollution control and the now imminent full amalgamation of the regulatory authorities, both our environmental law and the regime for its practical implementation have been brought towards a coherent whole.

Nevertheless, as has all too often been observed, having effective environmental legislation is of little value unless it is vigorously enforced, and enforcement in the United Kingdom has in the past undoubtedly been inadequate. While the previous legislation was theoretically capable of providing effective control and undoubtedly mitigated the worst excesses, its main defect to modern eyes lay primarily in the virtual absence of mandatory numerical standards, which both left a large degree of discretion in the hands of the regulators and also exacerbated the difficulties in obtaining a conviction except in the most blatant instances of non-compliance. To this was added a strong reluctance to take enforcement action in the Courts, partly through lack of resources, but at least as much from regarding (with the best of motives) a prosecution as a sign of failure by the regulators to induce compliance voluntarily. All this was coupled with a persistent failure by the courts to impose such penalties on those who were convicted as would operate as a serious deterrent both to them and others.

What appears not to have been sufficiently appreciated by those in a position to improve this record is that responsible industry – and much of it is so – has no objection to firm and fair enforcement against itself. A real concern is that, if it invests considerable money and management effort in securing good environmental behaviour on its part, its less responsible competitors who fail to do so may be able to get away with it. A culture of environmental responsibility within industry can only flourish if all those who cut corners are firmly dealt with – and not just those whose mere size gives them prominence. Furthermore the evidence is overwhelming that when organisations become committed to ensuring that their operations stay in compliance, far from this imposing extra costs as is often supposed, the improved management systems they set up almost invariably result in significant savings. The resourcing of the regulators by charging for permits, the declarations of increased willingness to prosecute, the recent reforms of the law, and the generally significantly greater penalties available to the magistrates courts, all create potential for effective change. Increased public access to environmental information will put additional pressure on the authorities to set demanding

vi

standards and to enforce them, and will facilitate the bringing of private actions, both criminal and civil.

Strong enforcement can however only be acceptable if the law itself is perceived to be reasonable. There will always be room for dispute in the setting of limits on permissible discharges to the environment. The effects of chronic exposure of man and other living organisms to low levels of chemical substances cannot be predicted with any precision from laboratory tests – and extensive testing on animals is in any event itself undesirable and discouraged by EC legislation. Limits that are always set on the basis of worst case assumptions will inevitably both burden the community with excessive costs and lead to undue fears when they are marginally exceeded; limits set on any other basis may perhaps prove in the long term to have been too lax. Ultimately a decision must be made that balances the publicly perceived risks against the publicly perceived benefits to be derived from the activity in question; unless made solely by reference to the use of best available technology (virtually irrespective of cost) it cannot therefore be a purely scientific assessment by technical experts alone, vital though their contribution is. While the US system arguably gives excessive weight to popular sentiment in determining environmental regulations, the tenuous degree of political accountability that there has been for standard setting in EC legislation – with the notable exception of the standards for small car exhaust emissions, which tends to prove the rule – is surely also hard to justify. Some development in this respect must be expected, as a result of the greater influence of the European Parliament following the Maastricht Treaty, leading to demands for increasingly stringent standards. To keep these standards realistic will require additional effort from industry to inform the public fully on the relevant risks and benefits, but this must be preferable to a paternalistic regime that is liable to result eventually in public cynicism and rejection of the real benefits that industry can give.

These issues are however matters of administrative detail by comparison with the fundamental issue with which virtually every country is faced, whether or not it chooses to make any effective response, namely how sustainable lifestyles – let alone sustainable *development* – are to be achieved world-wide. It can scarcely be contended that the present pattern of global economic activity is sustainable, but it is axiomatic that what is not sustainable must at some point come to an end. If that end is not planned for, it is likely to be nasty and brutish, though maybe unpleasantly long drawn out. Planning for it requires political, indeed moral, decisions on how limited resources are to be shared between richer and poorer countries and between present and future generations. The development of

vii

environmental law over the coming years will be increasingly influenced by how this over-riding issue is handled. The European Community's Fifth Action Programme on the environment is called "Towards Sustainability". Only time will tell whether the Community and its member states have the strength to make effective steps to that goal.

The present work

Environmental law is in essence the body of law concerned with the protection of living things (including man) from the harm that human activity may, immediately or eventually, cause to them or their species, either directly or to the media and the habitats on which they depend. The harm is usually incidental to the activity causing it, and in the past has usually been ignored when considering the activity's economic viability. It is this attribution of such harm to those who cause it that is at the heart of the polluter pays principle which now informs almost all modern environmental legislation.

The subject is so compendious that a book on it must necessarily be selective if it is to remain of manageable size. The approach adopted here has been to attempt to provide in one volume what the practising lawyer is most likely to need to know as a guide to the applicable law and its practical implications, as well as a reference source for those concerned with environmental law on a regular basis. Where specialist works exist that deal with individual topics in depth, notably John Bates' *Water and Drainage Law* and *U.K. Waste Law*, no useful purpose would be served in going over the same ground in as much detail. Also, although the most immediately relevant statutory provisions are quoted where appropriate, space does not permit full repetition of all that are mentioned: for these the reader is referred to the publishers' *Encyclopedia of Environmental Law* for the statutory sources, and to Steven Tromans' annotated version of the Environmental Protection Act 1990.

Much of the detail of the law is contained in secondary legislation. In some cases it is undoubtedly useful to treat this fairly fully, but in others, since a mere paraphrase of legislation is rarely helpful and may be dangerously misleading, only a relatively short description of salient features is given and the reader should resort to the statutory instrument itself for more. Inevitably the choice of when to amplify and when to mention briefly will not suit all requirements: it is hoped the balance is right, but if it is not the inconvenience is regretted. It may be possible to make adjustments on future occasions in the light of readers' experiences and needs.

This work is primarily about the law relating to pollution control, and its practical impacts. Neverthless pollution control is not an end in itself but a necessary indirect means of protecting the natural environment, and in particular man and other living organisms supported by the environmental media of air, water and land. Air includes air within buildings and thus there is a substantial overlap between environmental law and aspects of the law on health and safety at work. No attempt is made to give a comprehensive account of the latter, but the sections on the control of hazardous substances aim to mention any specific health and safety legislation that is relevant. The approach has been to cover the legislation on substances that are potentially harmful, both at work and elsewhere, but subject to that to omit legislation that is solely on the protection of the workplace.

Planning law is of course a vital element in the direct protection of the natural environment, and is consequently an important component of environmental law. However there is already an extensive literature on planning law, and here also no useful purpose would be served in going over the same ground in detail. A chapter is nevertheless included to explain planning law and practice in outline for those who are unfamiliar with it, and to lay the basis for the following chapters on environmental assessments and on wild-life and habitats conservation, which largely operate within the framework of planning law. These chapters do not however deal with issues of purely visual or aesthetic concern, such as landscapes, townscapes or traffic. Also, though reference is made to aspects of the law affecting farming practices where these have consequences for the environment, no attempt is made to address these in depth, since the space required would be disproportionate.

The significance of European Community legislation in determining the content of the substantive environmental law of the United Kingdom can hardly be overstated, particularly following the judgments of the European Court of Justice in *Marshall, Factortame* and *Francovich*.[1] Environmental law is of course administered almost entirely by government bodies and other "emanations of the state", who are required to give effect to European Community law, even where applicable United Kingdom law is or may be inconsistent. While there may be relatively few aspects where United Kingdom law is incontrovertibly in conflict with European Community law – most

---

[1] Case 152/84, *Marshall v. Southampton and South-West Hampshire Area Health Authority:* [1986] 1 CMLR 688; *R. v. Secretary of State for Transport, ex p. Factortame Limited and others (No. 2)* [1991] 1 AC 603; Cases C-6/90, C-9/90 [1991] E.C.R. I-5357, [1992] I.R.L.R. 84.

questions of non-compliance arise from matters of omission rather than commission – there are bound to be far more where interpretation of United Kingdom legislation could and should be determined by reference to the relevant European Community law and the policy objectives underlying it, not least the basic principles set out in Article 130R of the Rome Treaty. Indeed where the legislation is by EC regulation, which is now relatively frequent, this will generally be the only substantive law.

It has been necessary therefore throughout the book to discuss not only the domestic United Kingdom law but also, to some extent at least, such European Community law as is applicable, since both may potentially be equally relevant to any specific situation. Nevertheless, to keep the scope of the book within manageable bounds the emphasis is firmly on United Kingdom law, and European Community directives are dealt with primarily to put the domestic law in context (a matter of particular importance to those trading with other member states), and to point up any significant additional issues that they may raise.

After reviewing applicable United Kingdom and EC legislation, the next chapters address in outline how it is enforced, covering also the administrative statutory nuisance procedures and the vitally important civil remedies, notably in nuisance, of which, as the House of Lords has now confirmed in *Cambridge Water Company v. Eastern Counties Leather plc*,[2] the rule in *Rylands v. Fletcher* is but a branch. Much more could of course be said on criminal procedure, and the outline in Chapter 21 is merely intended to indicate what is likely to be of principal significance to those with little experience of it. The same chapter also deals with who may be held criminally liable, and considers the position of directors, parent companies and others who may in practice influence the conduct of a company's affairs.

The final part of the book is intended to provide a guide to the practical implications, principally for industry, of environmental law and the liabilities arising under it, as discussed earlier. Since this is essentially a textbook on the law, it is not appropriate to go into detail on how the numerous environmental issues that face business in their various operations and transactions may be addressed; indeed it could be counter-productive to do so, as the appropriate structures and drafting adopted are almost invariably dependent on the negotiating positions of the various parties to each transaction. Nevertheless, there are certain basic principles that apply to, for example, the acquisition of property and of the shares of companies owning property, and a chapter is devoted to the environmental aspects of

[2] [1994] 2 W.L.R. 53.

transactions involving land, and also of loan agreements which are frequently an integral part of them.

To an environmental lawyer these transactions tend to be dominated by the liabilities that may arise from the contamination of land. The costs of cleaning up contaminated land under the Superfund regime in the United States have been one of the main driving forces behind the development of the practice of environmental law there. Though in the United Kingdom the potential liabilities are almost as great, if somewhat less widespread, the absence of any official programme or automatic procedures for cleaning up historic contamination has in the past resulted in a neglect by both lawyers and their clients as to the risks that are run in acquiring interests (including charges by way of security) in potentially contaminated property. However since starting this book the issue has now come to the fore, starting with a Green Paper from the European Commission on remedying environmental damage, and a Council of Europe Convention on the same topic. These have prompted the introduction by the current Environment Bill of a potentially very effective regime for requiring remediation of historic as well as any future contamination; one that is likely to become a significant factor in nearly all property and corporate transactions.

In view of the extensive liabilities that environmental legislation may give rise to, insurance is a natural concern of any prudent business. This work is not the place to provide a textbook on insurance law, but again a chapter has been included to cover the aspects specific to environmental liabilities. Increasingly important, as a condition of obtaining insurance, in so far as it is offered at all, and of obtaining a loan, will be the adoption and implementation of suitable environmental management systems; a chapter is directed to this, with particular reference to the European Community eco-audit and management regulation. The final chapter is devoted to eco-labelling, and in particular the implementation of the EC eco-labelling regulation in the United Kingdom; despite the slow start this is an area that will undoubtedly be of considerable commercial importance in the future.

When this work was first conceived, it was intended to cover not only the law of England and Wales, but also that pertaining in both Scotland and in Northern Ireland, so as to provide a balanced coverage across the whole of the United Kingdom. So far as Scotland is concerned, it is hoped that this has been sufficiently achieved, and for this, I have relied almost totally on the contribution of Donald Reid of Morton Fraser Milligan W.S. in Edinburgh, for which I am most grateful. In many cases the law is essentially identical both sides of the border, so that little more has been required than to identify the applicable Scottish legislation and the Scottish administrative arrangements. However certain areas, particularly property law and court procedures, call for separate treatment, and where this is so, additional sections have been included.

It has not proved possible to deal with Northern Ireland in the same way, since the recent changes in the law on the mainland have generally not as yet been translated into law in the Province. There has usually been a time lag of some two years or more in replicating mainland environmental legislation in Northern Ireland, a delay that was criticised by the House of Commons Environment Committee in its report on Northern Irish environmental law, not least in respect of the implementation in due time of EC legislation. If the current Northern Irish law were to be properly described, it would require a substantial rewriting of the book, in effect to set out much of the old law as applied previously in England and Wales. This would not be realistic, and accordingly the bulk of the work does not attempt to cover this jurisdiction. By the time any further edition may be called for, it is to be hoped that the legislation in Northern Ireland will have been brought into line with that of the rest of the United Kingdom, and can be suitably dealt with.

My research has naturally included reading numerous articles and books by authors of eminence in this field. Inevitably few of my ideas and opinions are wholly original – they would probably be worth little if they were. What I have produced in this book therefore owes much to those who have already contributed to this area of the law. I have certainly aimed to make appropriate acknowledgment where I have placed direct reliance on the writings of others. Sometimes there may have been subconscious recollection, and if I have borrowed without due reference I apologise now. One work I am happy to acknowledge here, that has never been far from my desk, has been Nigel Haigh's *Manual of Environmental Policy:the EC and Britain*, which provides both an invaluable reference source and much interesting detail on the background to EC legislation and its implementation in the United Kingdom.

The scope of the book could not possibly have been as comprehensive as it is without the contributions of others who are far more expert than me in their fields. I would like to mention with particular gratitude Dr. George Black of George Black Associates, who provided virtually all the material of the chapter on nature conservation. His practical experience serving on The Nature Conservancy Council gave a dimension to the review of this area of the law that was invaluable. I also owe many thanks to Ian Gatenby for the chapters on the planning regime and environmental impact assessments, and to Carole Hooper for her patience in dealing with my no doubt tiresome queries on these matters. Equally I must especially thank Michael Langdon for his thought-provoking contribution on civil remedies, and generally acting as a sparring partner on numerous issues, and Caroline Day for her historical research and for providing nearly all of the opening chapter and additional help on civil remedies. Helen Harrison's ability to locate documents I needed (often having mislaid my own) has been of enormous help. Very special thanks are due to Mary Comiskey (now Stacey) and Maggie Maher for their valiant work not only in typing out for me the initial drafts of the chapters but also in their struggles to make sense of my amendments and to put them in their proper places. I have throughout been greatly helped by many others, too numerous to name, who have put up with my questions on what must often have seemed most obscure issues, and who have valuably extended my legal education. Finally, I owe a great debt to my wife for her continuing support, despite her having had much to endure while this book has been in preparation.

Every effort has been made to try to ensure that all details are correct and up-to-date, but if any are not the responsibility is mine. Any suggestions for improvement would be gladly received.

The law is mostly stated as at October 1, 1994, when the bulk of the text went to the printers. However developments since then, up to and including January 1995, have wherever possible been reflected either in the body of the text or in footnotes. Of these developments, particularly welcome are the decisions of the House of Lords in *NRA v Yorkshire Water Services Limited*[3] and of the Court of Appeal in *Attorney-General's Reference (No. 1 of 1994)*[4] which have helped to clear the confusion that had been developing in the case law in water pollution.

The implementation in the United Kingdom of the EC Habitats Directive 92/43, and in particular publication of the new PPG9 "Nature Conservation", which is essential to this, unfortunately came too late for detailed treatment in the present edition. The Environment Bill, introduced in the House of Lords in December 1994, will not only reorganise the administration of environmental regulation in Britain, but make several major changes to the substantive law. The provisions for remediation of contaminated land are likely to have the widest impact, but the present drafting of these raises so many issues requiring amendment of the Bill that comment here would be premature. Whatever the final form of the Bill, this feature at least makes it even more essential that liabilities under environmental

---

[3] [1994] 3 W.L.R. 1202.
[4] *The Times*, January 26, 1995; *The Independent*, January 31, 1995.

xiii

legislation be given due attention. Those affected (and especially perhaps their advisers) will neglect them at their peril.

Richard Burnett-Hall
Bristows, Cooke & Carpmael   February 1995

CONTENTS

xvii

Chapter 10
AIR POLLUTION   469

Chapter 11
WASTE ON LAND   519

TABLES OF CASES

U.K. CASES

E.C. COMMISSION DECISIONS

(in alphabetical order)

EUROPEAN COURT OF JUSTICE

(in numerical order)

EUROPEAN COURT OF HUMAN RIGHTS

TABLES OF LEGISLATION

U.K. Statutes

xlv

1

U.K. Secondary Legislation

E.C. Regulations

E.C. DIRECTIVES

E.C. Decisions

Treaties and Conventions

ciii

GUIDANCE AND INFORMAL INSTRUMENTS

TABLE OF ABBREVIATIONS

Å	Ångstrom (*q.v.*)
ACBE	Advisory Committee on Business and the Environment
ACDP	Advisory Committee on Dangerous Pathogens
ACGM	Advisory Committee on Genetic Manipulation
ACOP	Approved Code of Practice
ACOST	Advisory Council on Science and Technology
ACP	Advisory Committee on Pesticides
ACRE	Advisory Committee on Releases to the Environment (of micro-organisms) appointed under section 124 of the E.P.A.
ACTS	Advisory Committee on Toxic Substances
ADAS	Agricultural Development and Advisory Service
ADI	Acceptable Daily Intake (*q.v.*)
ADR	*Accord Européen relatif au transport international des marchandises Dangéreuses par Route* (European Agreement on the International Carriage of Dangerous Goods by Road)
AONB	Area of Outstanding Natural Beauty
AOX	Adsorbable organic halides
ASCOBANS	Agreement on the Conservation of Small Cetaceans of the Baltic and North Seas
ASTM	American Society for Testing and Materials
BAT	Best Available Technology
BATNEEC	Best Available Techniques Not Entailing Excessive Cost
BCME	bis (chlormethyl) ether
BOD	Biochemical (or Biological) Oxygen Demand (*q.v.*)
BPEO	Best Practicable Environmental Option (*q.v.*)
BPM	Best Practicable Means
Bq	Becquerel. A unit of radioactivity in the SI system

BREEAM	Building Research Establishment Environmental Assessment Method
BS	British Standard. BS 7750 is the specification for environmental management systems
BTU	British Thermal Unit (obs.)
C	Centigrade
CAS	Chemical Abstracts Service, a division of the American Chemical Society of Columbus, Ohio, USA. It has set up a classification system and information bank on millions of chemical compounds in which each compound is assigned a unique CAS number as described in the CAS Registry Handbook ISSN 0093-058X.
CAWR	Control of Asbestos at Work Regulations 1987
CFCs	chlorofluorocarbons (q.v.)
CGL	Comprehensive General Liability (insurance)
CHIP	The Chemicals (Hazard Information and Packaging for Supply) Regulations 1994 (S.I. 1994 No. 3247)
CHP	Combined Heat and Power
Ci	Curie. A unit of radioactivity (= 3.7×10^{10} Bq)
CIMAH	The Control of Industrial Major Accident Hazards Regulations 1984 (S.I. 1984 No. 1902)
CITES	Convention on International Trade in Endangered Species of Wild Flora and Fauna
CMTs	Carcinogens, Mutagens and Teratogens
CO/CO_2	carbon monoxide/carbon dioxide
COD	Chemical Oxygen Demand (q.v.)
COP	Code of Practice
COPA	Control of Pollution Act 1974
COSHH	The Control of Substances Hazardous to Health Regulations 1988 (S.I. 1988 No. 1657)
COT	The Committee on Toxicity of Chemicals in Food, Consumer Products and the Environment
COTC	Certificate of Technical Competence (in respect of the handling of waste)
COTIF	The Convention Concerning the Carriage of Goods by Rail (Cmnd.8535)
CPL	The Classification, Packaging and Labelling of Dangerous Substances Regulations 1984 (S.I. 1984 No. 1244)
CRI	Chemical Release Inventory
CRISTAL	Contract Regarding an Interim Supplement to Tanker Liabilities for Oil Pollution

CSD	The Commission for Sustainable Development; established under the UN ECOSOC to take responsibility for the implementation of Agenda 21
CTC	carbon tetrachloride (CCl_4)
dB	decibel
DBBT	dibromo benzyl toluene; monomethyl dibromo diphenyl methane.
DDT	dichloro diphenyl trichloroethane. An insecticide now generally banned due to its ability to bioaccumulate and non-biodegradability
DEMOS	[The] DTI's Environmental Management Options Scheme
DNA	deoxyribonucleic acid
DREF	Dose Rate Effectiveness Factor (a term used in toxicology)
DWI	Drinking Water Inspectorate
EA	Environmental Assessment
EAF	Environmental Action Fund. A DoE fund for supporting voluntary groups in the environmental sector
EC	The European Community/Communities (the EEC, the European Coal and Steel Community, and Euratom)
ECOSOC	(1) The (EC) Economic and Social Committee; one of the Community's institutions established under Article 193 of the Rome Treaty (2) The (UN) Economic and Social Council; a United Nations body under which the CSD (*q.v.*) has been established
EEC	The European Economic Community
ECN	The Environmental Change Network
EDC	ethylene dichloride; 1,2-dichloroethane
EH	English Heritage
EIA	Environmental Impact Assessment
EIL	Environmental Impairment Liability (insurance)
EINECS	European Inventory of Existing Commercial chemical Substances ([1990] O.J. C146A)
EIS	Environmental Impact Statement (also ES)
ELINCS	European List of Notified Chemical Substances (4th edition contained in [1994] O.J. C361)
EMAS	The EC Eco-Management and Audit Scheme
EMF	Electromagnetic field

EMS	Environmental Management System
EPA	(1) Environmental Protection Act 1990 (UK)
	(2) Environmental Protection Agency (the US Agency is sometimes referred to as the USEPA)
EQO	Environmental Quality Objective (*q.v.*)
EQS	Environmental Quality Standard (*q.v.*)
ERRA	European Recovery and Recycling Association
ES	Environmental Statement
ESA	Environmentally Sensitive Area
ETIS	Environment Technology Innovation Scheme
ETSU	Energy Technology Support Unit
EUCLID	European Chemicals Information Database; the database of all chemical substances notified to the European Commission pursuant to Directive 793/93
EWC	European Waste Catalogue
FAC	Food Advisory Committee
FEPA	Food and Environment Protection Act 1985
FGD	Flue Gas Desulphurisation
FOG	Fat, Oil and Grease
G	giga-. Used as prefix before units: 10^9
g, gm	gram
GDO	The Town and Country Planning General Development Order. The current (1988) Order is S.I. 1988 No. 1813
GEF	Global Environment Facility
GLP	Good Laboratory Practice
GMO	Genetically Modified Organism (*q.v.*)
GPR	Ground Penetrating Radar (used in surveys for underground objects)
GTAC	Gene Therapy Advisory Committee
HBFCs	hydrobromofluorocarbons (*q.v.*)
HCB	hexachlorobenzene
HCBD	hexachlorobutadiene
HCFCs	hydrochlorofluorocarbons (*q.v.*)
HCH	hexachlorocyclohexane (also sometimes HCCH); gamma-HCH is Lindane
HDPE	(see PE)
HEDSET	Harmonised Electronic Data Set; the computerised data on a chemical substance held by the European Commission pursuant to Directive 793/93 (see EUCLID)

HMIP	Her Majesty's Inspectorate of Pollution (England & Wales)
HMIPI	Her Majesty's Industrial Pollution Inspectorate (Scotland)
HSA	Hazardous Substances Authority
HSC	(1) Health and Safety Commission
	(2) Hazardous Substances Consent
HSE	Health and Safety Executive
HSWA	Health and Safety at Work etc. Act 1974
IARC	The International Agency for Research on Cancer (part of the WHO)
ICRP	International Commission on Radiological Protection
IMO	International Maritime Organisation
INCPEN	Industry Council for Packaging and the Environment
INES	International Nuclear Event Scale
IPC	Integrated Pollution Control (UK)
IPPC	Integrated Pollution Prevention and Control (EC)
IR	Infra-Red
IRPTC	International Register of Potentially Toxic Chemicals; a register operated by an office of UNEP based in Geneva
ISO	International Standards Organisation
IUCN	International Union for the Conservation of Nature
IUPAC	International Union of Pure and Applied Chemistry. The IUPAC nomenclature of organic compounds is generally regarded as definitive
LAAPC	Local Authority Air Pollution Control
LAWDC	Local Authority Waste Disposal Company
LC_{50}	Lethal Concentration: a measure of acute toxicity by reference to the concentration that kills 50 percent of the organisms under test
LCA	Life Cycle Analysis
LCP	Large Combustion Plant (*e.g.* the EC LCP Directive 88/609)
LD_{50}	Lethal Dose: a measure of acute toxicity by reference to the dose that kills 50 percent of the organisms under test
LDPE	(see PE)
LFG	Landfill Gas. The potentially explosive gas, consisting primarily of methane, resulting from the anaerobic decomposition of matter at landfill sites

LIFE	*L'Instrument Financiel pour l'Environnement* (the EC Financial Instrument for the Environment established by Regulation 1973/92)
LNG	Liquified Natural Gas
LNR	Local Nature Reserve
LPG	Liquified Petroleum Gas
m	milli-. Used as prefix before units: 10^{-3}
M	mega-. Used as prefix before units: 10^6
μ	(1) micro-. Used as prefix before units: 10^{-6}
	(2) micron. 10^{-6} metre, one thousandth of a millimetre
MAC	Maximum Allowable/Admissible Concentration
MEL	Maximum Exposure Limit (*e.g.* of hazardous substances at the workplace)
ml	millilitre
MNR	Marine Nature Reserve
MP	Melting Point
MPG	Mineral Planning Guidance
MRL	Maximum Residue Limit (*e.g.* of pesticides in foodstuffs)
MSDS	Material Safety Data Sheet (also simply SDS)
MTBE	methyl tertiary butyl ether
MW	(1) Molecular Weight
	(2) Megawatts
MWth/MW(th)	Megawatts thermal – used to express the rated thermal input of a power generator (see Input Rating)
n	nano-. Used as prefix before units: 10^{-9}
NAWDC	National Association of Waste Disposal Contractors
NCC	Nature Conservancy Council (now defunct)
NERC	Natural Environment Research Council
NFFO	Non-Fossil Fuel Obligation
NHA	Natural Heritage Area – a site designation under the Natural Heritage (Scotland) Act 1991
NIHHS	The Notification of Industries Handling Hazardous Substances Regulations 1992 (S.I. 1982 No. 1357)
NNR	National Nature Reserve
NO_x	Nitrogen Oxides. A general expression covering all the various oxides of nitrogen, *e.g.* N_2O, N_2O_3, NO_2
NOEL	No Observed Effect Level. The maximum level of a dose or exposure at which no effect is observed

NONS	The Notification of New Substances Regulations 1993 (S.I. 1993 No. 3050)
NRA	(1) National Rivers Authority (2) Nature Reserve Agreement (under the Countryside Act 1949)
NRPB	National Radiological Protection Board
NSA	Nitrate Sensitive Area
NTP	Normal Temperature and Pressure. Now obsolete, see STP
NVZ	Nitrate Vulnerable Zone, designated under the EC Nitrates Directive 91/676
OECD	Organisation for Economic Co-operation and Development
OEL	Occupational Exposure Limit
OES	Occupational Exposure Standard
OFWAT	Office of Water Services
p	(1) pico-. Used as prefix before units: 10^{-12} (2) para-. In organic chemistry used to denote substitution at the 1,4 positions in a benzene ring (*i.e.* on opposite carbon atoms)
PAH	polycyclic aromatic hydrocarbon(s)
PCB	polychlorinated biphenyl(s)
PCDD	polychlorinated dibenzo-dioxin(s)
PCDF	polychlorinated dibenzo-difuran(s)
PCH	polychlorinated hydrocarbons
PCP	pentachlorophenol
PCT	polychlorinated terphenyl(s)
PE	polyethylene. It may be made by polymerising ethylene in either a high pressure or a low pressure process, producing low density polyethylene (LDPE) or high density polyethylene (HDPE) respectively
pe	population equivalent (*q.v.*)
PEC	Predicted Environmental Concentration; relevant to risk assessments of potential releases of chemicals to the environment
PER	(1) perchlorethylene ($CCl_2:CCl_2$) (2) Polluting Emissions Register (EC)
PET	polyethylene terephthalate. A clear plastic, of which beverage bottles are often made.
PFA	Pulverised Fuel Ash

pH	(*pouvoir Hydrogène*) A measure of the acidity or alkalinity of an aqueous solution. pH7 is neutral, lower values being increasingly acidic, higher values being increasingly alkaline
PIC	Prior Informed Consent
PMN	Pre-Market Notication (of new chemical substances)
PNEC	Predicted No-Effect Concentration; relevant to, *e.g.* ecotoxicity assessments of chemicals
POST	Parliamentary Office of Science and Technology
PP	polypropylene
ppb	parts per billion
PPE	Personal Protective Equipment
PPG	Planning Policy Guidance
ppm	parts per million
psi	Pounds per Square Inch (a unit of pressure)
PVC	polyvinyl chloride
QA	Quality Assurance
RCEP	Royal Commission on Environmental Pollution
RDF	Refuse Derived Fuel
RPA	River Purification Authority (Scotland)
RPB	River Purification Board (Scotland)
RPG	Regional Planning Guidance
RID	Regulations concerning the International Carriage of Dangerous Goods by Rail
RIMNET	Radioactive Incident Monitoring Network
RSA	Radioactive Substances Act 1993
RWMAC	Radioactive Waste Management Advisory Committee
SAC	Special Area for Conservation, designated under the EC Habitats Directive 92/43
SDS	Safety Data Sheet (also MSDS)
SEPA	Scottish Environment Protection Agency
SIDS	Screening Information Data Set. The name given to an OECD chemicals testing programme
SNH	Scottish Natural Heritage
SNIF	Standard Notification Information Format. The format for information to be sent to the European Commission on new chemical substances and proposed releases of genetically modified organisms
SO_x	Sulphur Oxides. A general expression covering the various oxides of sulphur *e.g.* SO_2, SO_3

SOAFD	Scottish Office Agriculture and Fisheries Department
SORG	The Stratospheric Ozone Review Group
SPA	Special Protection Area, designated under the EC Birds Directive 79/409
SSSI	Site of Special Scientific Interest (designated under the Wildlife and Countryside Act 1981)
STEL	Short Term Exposure Limit (*e.g.* of hazardous substances at the workplace)
STP	(1) Standard Temperature and Pressure. The standard conditions used for comparing volumes of gases, *i.e.* 0°C and standard atmospheric pressure (760 mm mercury). The term is now used in preference to NTP (2) Sewage Treatment Plant
Sv	Sievert (*q.v.*)
SWQO	Statutory Water Quality Objective
T	tera-. Used as a prefix before units $= 10^{12}$
TBZ	thiabendazole. A fungicide – E233
TCB	trichlorobenzene
TCDD	2,3,7,8 – tetrachlorodibenzo-p-dioxin. Regarded as the most toxic of the family of dioxins and furans (see also TEQ)
TCE	trichlorethylene
TEQ	Toxic Equivalent (of TCCD). Used to define the toxicity of a mixture of dioxins and/or furans by ascribing a weighting factor to each relating their toxicity to that of TCCD
THM	trihalomethane (CHX_3 where X = any halogen)
TLV	Threshold Limit Value (a term used in the USA equivalent to MEL or OEL (*q.v.*) in the UK
TOC	Total Organic Carbon (*q.v.*)
TRI	Toxics Release Inventory (US)
TWA	Time Weighted Average
UCO	The Town and Country Planning (Use Classes) Order. The current (1987) Order is S.I. 1987 No. 764
UNCED	United Nations Conference on Environment and Development (at Rio de Janeiro in June 1992)
UN-ECE	United Nations – Economic Commission for Europe
UNED	United Nations Environment and Development
UNEP	United Nations Environment Programme
UST	Underground Storage Tank

UV	Ultra-Violet
VCM	Vinyl Chloride Monomer, a toxic substance which polymerises to PVC
VOCs	Volatile Organic Carbons
WATCH	Working Group on the Assessment of Toxic Chemicals
WAMITAB	Waste Management Industry Training Advisory Board
WCA	Waste Collection Authority
WDA	Waste Disposal Authority
WET	Whole Effluent Toxicity. A WET test considers the toxicity of an effluent stream as a whole as opposed to that of its individual components
WHO	World Health Organisation
WIA	Water Industry Act 1991
WMP	Waste Management Paper
WQO	Water Quality Objective
WQS	Water Quality Standard
WRA	(1) Waste Regulation Authority
	(2) Water Resources Act 1991

GLOSSARY[1]

Acid, acidic

(Strictly) anything having a pH (*q.v.*) below 7. Strongly acidic substances have a pH of 1–2 or less, and are substantially completely dissociated into hydrogen ions (positive) and anions (negative).

Acid Rain

Rain (including cloud, fog and snow) which has been acidified by SO_x and NO_x (*q.v.*) present in the atmosphere, leading in particular to damage to trees and other vegetation, the leaching out of essential nutrients from the soil, and acidifying and raising the concentration of metallic salts in rivers and lakes. The term is used in practice to extend also to the deposit of dry acids from the atmosphere.

Acceptable Daily Intake

The amount of a substance, *e.g.* a food additive, that can be ingested daily over a life-time without incurring an appreciable health risk. It may be calculated by dividing the relevant NOEL (*q.v.*) in mg per kg body weight per day by a safety factor, which is typically around 100.

[1] The explanations of the expressions in this Glossary are intended to assist the non-technical reader in understanding them in the context of environmental legislation and discussion of environmental issues. Accordingly while it is hoped there are no material inaccuracies, on occasion the precision and comprehensiveness to be found in scientific dictionaries have been eschewed in favour of intelligibility for the layman and relevance to the present subject.

Activated carbon	A form of carbon that has a high surface area per gram, used in water treatment and other processes to absorb unwanted substances in fluids passed over it.
Active ingredient/substance	The component of, *e.g.* a pharmaceutical or pesticide composition that provides the desired effect; the balance will consist primarily of an inert carrier or excipient, though there may also be *e.g.* wetting or solubilising agents and adjuvants.
Acute (exposure)	A single short-term (often high level) exposure; *cf.* "chronic (exposure)".
Aerobic	Requiring air, *e.g.* aerobic bacteria which can only function in the presence of oxygen.
Agenda 21	The programme of action agreed internationally at the UNCED (*q.v.*) at Rio de Janeiro in 1992, designed to lead towards sustainable development. So called as this issue was item 21 on the conference agenda.
Alkali	See "Base".
Alkane	A straight or branched chain fully saturated hydrocarbon, *e.g.* methane, propane, butane.
Ambient conditions	The normally existing state of potentially variable conditions at a particular location, *e.g.* the temperature and pressure, or the concentrations of pollutants or other substances in the air or water.
Anaerobic	Not requiring air, *e.g.* anaerobic bacteria which function in the absence of air. They produce for example methane in the decomposition of organic (*q.v.*) matter.

Ångstrom	A measure of length used in relation to distances between atoms and the wavelength of high frequency radiation, approximately 10^{-8}cm.
Aromatic compounds	Organic (*q.v.*) compounds containing one or more benzene rings or "condensed" ring structures (*e.g.* toluene, xylene, naphthalene, PCBs). They are to be contrasted with aliphatic compounds which are compounds containing a straight, branched or cyclic carbon chain but with no benzene or condensed ring structures.
Asbestos	Fibrous impure magnesium silicate. It exists in a variety of forms, all of which are highly toxic by inhalation of dust particles and carcinogenic. Amosite (brown asbestos) and crocidolite (blue asbestos) are particularly hazardous; chrysotile (white asbestos) and the amphibole forms (anthophyllite, tremolite and actinolite) somewhat less so.
Base, basic	Alkali, alkaline. (Strictly) anything having a pH (*q.v.*) above 7. Strong bases have a pH of 13–14 or more, and are substantially completely dissociated into hydroxyl ions (negative) and cations (positive).
Becquerel	A measure of radioactivity, being the number of nuclear transformations or disintegrations per second. Becquerel has replaced curie as the standard unit; 1 curie = 3.7×10^{10} becquerels.
Best Practicable Environmental Option	(For the purposes of IPC) the option which for a given set of objectives provides the most benefit or least damage to the environment as a whole, at acceptable cost in the long term as well as the short term, as a result of releases of substances from a process.

Bioaccumulate	The tendency of compounds, *e.g.* several types of pesticide and PCBs, to accumulate in animal tissues, and thus to increase in concentration in a series of animals up the food chain, prejudicing the survival of those at the top, either directly or indirectly by interfering with their reproductive cycle. The latter is the more lethal to a species, since toxic effects killing some only of the individuals in a population directly may merely remove weaker members or older ones that have already reproduced.
Biochemical Oxygen Demand	A measure of water quality, specifically its content of organic material, by reference to the amount of oxygen used by micro-organisms to break down the organic molecules in a sample of water. For any given content of organics, the figure is reduced by substances that inhibit the action of micro-organisms, such as heavy metals, chlorine and pesticides, and increased by the presence of ammonia and hydrogen sulphide which are themselves oxidised; *cf.* Chemical Oxygen Demand.
Biodegradable	The propensity of a substance to decompose under the action of biological organisms. Whether it in fact does so depends on the surrounding conditions being at least tolerable by the relevant organisms. In the absence of air (as is often so, deep in a landfill), aerobic (*q.v.*) bacteria will not be effective to degrade anything; nevertheless the anaerobic (*q.v.*) bacteria present will not necessarily decompose substances described as biodegradable. The ratio of COD to BOD (*q.v.*) may be used as measure of the biodegradability of substances in water.

Builder	A component of commercial detergents designed to improve their performance by associating with the deleterious metal ions present in hard water (*e.g.* calcium, magnesium), maintaining the detergent solution alkaline, keeping soil particles suspended and so preventing their re-deposition on the items being washed, and stabilising the physical properties of a washing powder. The most common builders are phosphates, in particular sodium tripolyphosphate, which can lead to eutrophication (*q.v.*). However their use enables less detergent to be used, and many alternatives available at comparable cost themselves have environmental and/or technical disadvantages.
Carcinogenic	Substances and preparations which, if they are inhaled or ingested or if they penetrate the skin, may induce cancer or increase its incidence (as defined in Directive 91/689/EEC). *cf.* mutagenic, teratogenic.
Chemical Oxygen Demand	A measure of water quality, specifically its content of organic material, by reference to the amount of potassium dichromate (an oxidising agent) required to oxidise the organic material in a sample of water after inorganic substances (such as ammonia and hydrogen sulphide) have been removed. Unlike the BOD (*q.v.*) test, it does not distinguish between biodegradable and non-biodegradable organic molecules, and so will not necessarily give closely similar results, but it is a relatively cheap and simple test to operate.

Chlorofluorocarbons

(CFCs). A range of alkanes (*q.v.*) in which all the hydrogen atoms are substituted by both chlorine and fluorine atoms. They are very stable and inert in normal circumstances but decompose in the stratosphere where the chlorine released combines with ozone in the ozone layer, so depleting it.

Chromatography

A general term for a variety of related methods of separating out the components of complex mixtures, typically by differential adsorption, prior to identifying the relative amounts present. Often of use in analyses of pollutants in samples of soil and groundwater.

Chronic (exposure)

Exposure (generally low level) over a long period; *cf.* "acute (exposure)".

Co-disposal

The mixing of different waste types in a landfill, desirably in order to promote a beneficial interaction between them that reduces or eliminates potentially harmful properties of one or more of the wastes. It is prohibited in several countries but favoured in the UK. It is an effective waste management option but must be properly conducted if release of pollutants is to be avoided.

Critical load

The maximum load of a defined pollutant or pollutants that a given ecosystem is known to be able to tolerate without suffering adverse effects. UK policy on the control of acid emissions to atmosphere is based to a large extent on seeking to avoid acid deposition on any site exceeding the critical load for that site.

Cryptosporidium	A microscopic parasite found in many environments, including animals and water, capable of causing ill-health in some circumstances. Its significance in water supplies was the subject of a report of the National Advisory Group (the Badenoch Report, 1990).
Diffuse source	See "non-point source".
Dioxins	A large family of highly toxic chlorinated organic (*q.v.*) compounds, the most toxic being TCDD. They are readily formed in the combustion products of mixed organic compounds and chlorine containing compounds; their formation in incinerators is generally thought to be minimised by very high temperatures, low residence times, and rapid cooling of emissions.
"Drins"	The chemically related chlorine-containing pesticides aldrin, isodrin, dieldrin and endrin.
Ecotoxic	Harmful to the environment.
Environmental Quality Objective	A classification of receiving waters by reference to their suitability for a specified purpose.
Environmental Quality Standard	An environmental quality specification defined by reference to numerical limit values for prescribed parameters, generally being concentrations of particular substances in water or air.
Epidemiology	The study of rates of disease among different population groups.

Eutrophication	Making a waterbody rich in nutrients. The consequence of excessive amounts of nutrients in water encourages undue growth of algae and aquatic plants. On the death of these, their decay under the action of aerobic bacteria may extract an excessive amount of dissolved oxygen from the water and make it uninhabitable for fish and other aquatic fauna. Following loss of the oxygen, anaerobic bacteria then continue the decay, mostly at the bottom of the water, producing toxins liable to kill any of the remaining fish and other fauna that have survived the loss of oxygen.
Flash point	The temperature at which the vapour formed by a liquid or volatile solid that is exposed to air will be capable of ignition.
Fugitive emissions	Uncontrolled leaks of gases and volatile liquids from, *e.g.* joints and valves of pipes, tanks and process plant.
Genetically Modified Organism	(Broadly) a reproducible organism of which the naturally occurring gene sequence has been modified by genetic engineering techniques. The UK Regulations on the contained use and deliberate release of GMOs (S.I. 1992 No. 3217 and S.I. 1992 No. 3280) contain more detailed definitions, which differ somewhat from each other.
GENHAZ	An adaptation of HAZOP (*q.v.*). A procedure designed to identify potential hazards resulting from the release of genetically modified organisms to the environment.
Geomorphological	Pertaining to the study of present-day landscapes and their origins.
Giga-	10^9.

Groundwater	Water contained in, and so capable of flowing (slowly) through, permeable underground strata (aquifers) lying over, and possibly also under, relatively impermeable strata. Since the planes of underground strata may be at wholly different angles to those of the ground surface above, and the groundwater subject to hydrostatic pressure, there is no necessary relationship between the direction of flow of (*e.g.* contaminated) groundwater and that of surface water above.
Half-life	A measure of the rate of decay of radioactive substances or of decomposition of relatively persistent substances. In the steady state (however fast or slow the actual rate), the time taken for half of any given quantity to decay or decompose (*i.e.* the half-life) is constant. The time for all of it to do so is theoretically always infinite; hence of the two only the half-life is a useful measure.
Halogen	Any of the elements forming Group VII of the Periodic Table: fluorine, chlorine, bromine, iodine.
Halons	A range of alkanes (*q.v.*) in which all the hydrogen atoms are substituted by halogen atoms. In distinction from the very similar chlorofluorocarbons (*q.v.*), the halogen atoms include both fluorine and bromine – chlorine may but need not be present. Bromine is an even more effective ozone-depleter than chlorine.
Hazard	A set of circumstances that may cause harm (from temporary minor harm to catastrophe); *cf.* "risk".

HAZOP	Hazard and Operability Study. A procedure for identifying the potential hazards of any operation, typically used in the designing of safe chemical manufacturing plant.
Heavy metals	Metals with an atomic number greater than that of sodium which form soaps with fatty acids (*e.g.* stearic acid). Most metals in fact come within this definition including *e.g.* copper, cobalt, cadmium, chromium.
Heterocyclic compounds	Organic compounds with a ring structure that includes an atom other than carbon, *e.g.* nitrogen, oxygen or sulphur, as a member of the ring.
Hydrocarbons	Organic compounds consisting exclusively of carbon and hydrogen, *e.g.* methane (CH_4), benzene (C_6H_6), polyethylene and the principal constituents of oils and petrol.
Hydrobromofluorocarbons	(HBFCs). A range of organic compounds analogous to HCFCs, but containing bromine in place of chlorine.
Hydrochlorofluorocarbons	(HCFCs). Organic compounds related to CFCs, but in which one or more hydrogen atoms remain unsubstituted by chlorine or fluorine.
In vitro	A term applied to experiments carried out on artificial systems such as cell cultures in, *e.g.* test tubes, rather than in vivo, *i.e.* on a live animal.
Input Rating	A generator may be rated by reference either to the energy it consumes (the rated input) or to the power it produces (the rated output), the ratio of the rated output to the rated input being its conversion factor. A thermal input rating is calculated from the maximum rate at which the intended fuel can be burned multiplied by the net calorific value of the fuel.

Latency Period	The lapse of time between exposure to the cause of a disease or other injury and its manifestation.
Leachate	The liquid emanating from underground strata. The term is most commonly applied to liquid derived from waste sites, when it is liable to contain toxic decomposition products and/or toxic materials from the waste, such as heavy metal compounds, pesticides, etc., and so pollute groundwater.
MARPOL	The 1973 international convention for the prevention of (marine) pollution from ships.
Mean	The arithmetical average of a set of figures obtained by dividing their aggregate by the number of figures in the set *cf.* "median".
Median	In a set of figures of varying amounts, the median is that amount which divides the set into equal halves, so that the number of figures in the set that are larger than it is the same as the number of those that are smaller. The median is often a more meaningful figure than the mean in a skewed sample where a few figures are markedly greater (or smaller) than the remainder.
Mega-	10^6.
Mesothelioma	Cancer of the lining of the chest, associated exclusively with exposure to asbestos, particularly crocidolite.

Metabolism	Biotransformation. The conversion of a foreign compound that has been absorbed by a biological system (*e.g.* an animal or plant) into other substances. The process operates in most cases to reduce or eliminate any toxic effects of the foreign compound (detoxication), but it may on occasion result in increased toxicity (toxication). The ability to metabolise a toxic substance may vary widely between species, and also between different strains and between the sexes of the same species. This can render it difficult or impossible to extrapolate to man with any certainty, still less precision, test results obtained from animals.
Metabolite	A substance to which a foreign compound is converted through metabolism (*q.v.*).
Methaemoglobinaemia	A rare blood condition (commonly known as "blue baby syndrome") affecting young babies, caused by excessive nitrate intake, *e.g.* from drinking water.
Micro-	10^{-6}
Montreal Protocol	A protocol to the Vienna Convention for the protection of the ozone layer, signed at Montreal, which laid down timetables for the global phasing out of CFCs, halons and other ozone depleting substances. The Protocol has been subsequently amended to accelerate the timetable, most recently at Copenhagen in 1992.
Mutagenic	Substances and preparations which, if they are inhaled or ingested, or if they penetrate the skin, may induce hereditary genetic defects or increase their incidence (as defined in Directive 91/689/EEC).
Nano-	10^{-9}

Natura 2000	A "coherent European ecological network" of special areas of conservation to be established under Article 3 of the EC Habitats Directive 92/43. The network is to include the special protection areas designated under the EC Birds Directive 79/409.
Nitrates	A term frequently used to signify the inorganic compounds, such as ammonium nitrate ($NH_4.NO_3$), used as agricultural fertilisers. Their presence in water in substantial quantities can lead to eutrophication (*q.v.*).
Non-point source	A diffuse source of pollutants, *e.g.* a field from which pesticides or fertilisers may seep into a watercourse, or a railway line; to be distinguished from a point source, *e.g.* an outfall from drains or a sewer, or a chimney stack.
Organic compounds	Carbon based compounds; in distinction from inorganic compounds. Organic compounds usually contain a stable chain of carbon atoms combined with at least some hydrogen atoms (as in hydrocarbons) but often also halogens, oxygen, nitrogen, etc.
Organohalogens	Organic compounds containing halogen atoms bound to carbon atoms (*e.g.* CFCs, HCFCs). Many organochlorine compounds in particular are highly toxic pesticides, *e.g.* dieldrin, DDT.
Ozone	A gas with a molecule consisting of three oxygen atoms, *i.e.* O_3 (oxygen gas consists of two, *i.e.* O_2). Low level ozone, liable to be formed by the action of the sun on mixtures of hydrocarbons and NO_x (typical components of vehicle exhausts) causes respiratory problems.

Ozone layer	The layer of ozone in the stratosphere that absorbs, and so filters out, ultra-violet rays that would otherwise reach the earth's surface. It is attacked by the chlorine and bromine atoms released from CFCs, halons, HCFCs and HBFCs.
Percentile	Literally, a one hundredth part. The term is used when setting limits to be met by a series of samples. Thus a 95 percentile limit must be met by 95 per cent of the samples. (In the absence of other conditions, this places no restraint on the amount by which the remaining 5 per cent may breach that limit).
Perch	Perching occurs where an isolated pocket of liquid, *e.g.* water, is held in a stratum over an impermeable layer that is itself set in or on a permeable stratum containing the local body of groundwater.
Percutaneous (absorption)	(Absorption) through the skin.
Perfluorocarbons	Organic compounds composed only of carbon and fluorine. They are possible substitutes for CFCs since they have similar properties but (having no chlorine) do not harm the ozone layer; however their global-warming potential is said to be substantially greater than that of CFCs.
Persistence	The property of a substance that remains chemically unchanged following release into the environment, *i.e.* it does not react with other compounds and is not metabolised on take-up by living organisms.
Pesticide	A generic term used to encompass, *e.g.* insecticides, herbicides, fumigants, fungicides and rodenticides.

Phosphates	Components of many standard formulations of both detergents, where they are used as builders (*q.v.*), and fertilisers. In water they act as nutrients for algae and plant life and in substantial quantities can thus lead to eutrophication (*q.v.*).
Photochemical reaction	A chemical reaction that is stimulated by the action of light, *e.g.* in the production of low level ozone from the components of vehicle exhausts.
Physiographical	A term used in some statutory definitions of nature conservation meaning geomorphological (*q.v.*).
Pica-	10^{-12}
Point source	See "non-point source".
Population equivalent	A term relating the polluting load of an organic discharge to the number of people who would normally cause an equivalent load. For the purposes of such a calculation, one person is assumed to produce daily a domestic effluent with a BOD of 60g of oxygen.
Radon	A radioactive inert gas, a decay product of radioactive substances such as uranium and thorium. It occurs naturally in many parts of Britain and is liable to accumulate at ground level in buildings in the absence of adequate ventilation.
Ringelmann Chart	A chart used for assessing the darkness of smoke, *e.g.* for the purposes of the Clean Air Act 1993. It consists of five squares, of which one is white and the remainder represent various shades of grey. These shades are produced by the effect of 20 equally spaced vertical lines crossing 20 equally spaced horizontal ones. The lines vary in thickness from one square to the next. The four grey shades produced thus define:

Ringelmann 1 – 20% obscured
Ringelmann 2 – 40% obscured
Ringelmann 3 – 60% obscured
Ringelmann 4 – 80% obscured
"Dark smoke" is at least as dark as Ringelmann 2; "black smoke" is at least as dark as Ringelmann 4. The chart is described in BS 2742C and its use in BS 2742.

Risk

The probability of an adverse effect occurring. In relation to a toxic substance, it is a function both of its toxicity to those at risk of exposure to it and of the duration, intensity and frequency of exposure.

Saturated

In organic chemistry, carbon atoms linked by a single bond or a molecule where all the carbon atoms in a chain are linked by single bonds only, *i.e.* there are no double or triple bonds; *cf.* "unsaturated".

Scrub

The treatment of flue gases to remove polluting components such as SO_x and NO_x.

Sievert

A measure of the dose of radiation received over a period of time adjusted to take account of the differing biological effects of different types of radiation. Natural background radiation in the UK provides an annual average dose of around 0.002 Sv, *i.e.* 2 mSv.

Synergy

Synergy is displayed when two (or more) substances together produce consequences greater than the aggregate of those produced by each of them separately.

Tera-

10^{12}

Teratogenic	Substances and preparations which, if they are inhaled or ingested or if they penetrate the skin, may induce non-hereditary congenital malformations or increase their incidence (as defined in Directive 91/689/EEC).
Total Organic Carbon	A measure of water quality, specifically its content of carbon in organic material, obtained by any of a number of different tests in which the carbon in the organic material is totally oxidised to carbon dioxide. It has greater sensitivity than the COD (*q.v.*) test, and is fast and convenient, but more expensive.
Toxicology	The study of harmful interactions between chemical substances and biological systems (including, but not limited to, humans).
Unsaturated	In organic chemistry, a pair of carbon atoms linked by a double or a triple bond or a molecule containing at least one such carbon pair. Hydrogenation, for example, may lead to one or two hydrogen atoms, as the case may be, becoming attached to each of these carbons; thus the bond becomes single and the molecule "saturated" (*q.v.*).
Vadose zone	The unsaturated stratum of ground between the surface and the water table.
Water table	The level of the upper surface of the saturated zone containing groundwater.

Chapter 1

THE DEVELOPMENT OF ENVIRONMENTAL LAW IN THE UNITED KINGDOM

Introduction

Britain's first recorded environmental regulation dates from 1273, in **1–001** the reign of Edward I (1272–1307), when the King issued a decree prohibiting the burning of "sea-coal" in order to protect the health of his subjects. Considerably later, Elizabeth I issued a proclamation forbidding the use of coal while Parliament was sitting. The matter was of such import that one 16th century violator of environmental regulation was executed for his wrong.[1] The next two centuries saw only modest legislation relating to environmental issues, of little long term significance. In 1661, John Evelyn, the diarist, presented his "Fumifugium or the Inconvenience of the Air and Smoke of London Dissipated", containing detailed proposals for a compulsory clean air programme. It pleased Charles II sufficiently for him to require it to be published by royal command, but it nevertheless came to nothing.

It was the industrial revolution, starting in the latter part of the 18th **1–002** century and gathering pace in the first half of the 19th, driven by steam generated from coal, that led the country eventually to develop a body of law that in today's terminology can properly be called "environmental". The 19th century was a time of metamorphosis for British society. The era of the industrial revolution brought with it urbanisation on a scale previously unimagined. Newly emergent industry, a myriad of mills, factories and workshops, concentrated in areas convenient for its raw materials and transport, drew to it a burgeoning workforce that settled alongside in cramped local communities. An agrarian society was now transformed and suffered the attendant problems of industrialisation: pollution, overcrowding and disease.

---

[1] David Vogel, *National Styles of Regulation—Environmental Policy in Great Britain and the United States* (Cornell University Press, 1986), p. 31.

Out of these conditions of potential social crisis emerged the first significant demands for environmental control.

1–003　　As the world's first industrialised nation, the United Kingdom was also the first to establish a nation-wide system of air pollution control, with the creation of the Alkali Inspectorate in 1863 as the world's first pollution control agency by the Alkali Works Regulation Act of that year. Legislation to deal with "nuisances", including waste deposits, was introduced in the late 1840s and strongly reinforced in 1875. Water pollution was the subject of an 1861 Act, and of more comprehensive legislation in 1876.

1–004　　By the 1880s a conservation movement had emerged, constituting what Vogel declares "an integral part of the backlash of the Victorian intelligentsia against the values of economic liberalism".[2] Led from the outset by prominent social philosophers such as John Ruskin and John Stuart Mill, its aims were to protect the values of traditional England, its remaining unspoilt countryside and its wildlife, from the clutches of the "base pursuits of trade and manufacture".[3] From out of this movement, in the era of the "social cause", emerged the British environmental movement as we might recognise it today.[4]

1–005　　It would be misleading, however, to suggest an environmentally aware nation promulgating protective legislation from a relatively early period, with a pioneering conservation movement leading the world in the introduction of pollution control measures, for this was not the case. The politics of environmental protection of that time were dominated by the demands of industry. The Alkali Inspectorate existed as a rare governmental body within a piecemeal system of environmental regulation and cannot be considered representative of the methods of pollution control, such as they were, employed during that period. A series of cholera epidemics beginning, so far as concerned Britain, in Sunderland in 1831 and which between 1849 and 1854 alone claimed 25,000 lives, caused widespread public alarm and highlighted the urgent need for improved public health and hence environmental reform. The "environmental law" of the 19th cen-tury—both common law and legislation—was motivated not by the

---

[2] *Ibid.*, p. 33.
[3] *Ibid.*, p. 33.
[4] For example, the Fur and Feathers Group was established in 1889 by a group of Manchester residents to protest against the use of birds' feathers in hats. It was from this small group of animals lovers that the Royal Society for the Protection of Birds eventually evolved. In the 1890s a few highly motivated individuals (including Beatrix Potter, who had eventually earned considerable wealth from her children's books) were moved by the threat of urban expansion to found the National Trust for Places of Historic Interest and Natural Beauty with the object of acquiring both land and buildings, in order to preserve them for the future from economic development. The National Trust was the self declared "national champion of the preservationist cause".

desire to protect and conserve the environment in the sense of the 20th century "green movement", but rather emerged (out of necessity) to temper the insanitary living conditions of a rapidly urbanising nation facing crisis.

Modern attitudes towards the environment are not to be read out of the environmental laws of the 19th century. At the time of the industrial revolution, man was perceived as the apex of the unchanging natural order of creation. Man's right, even his duty, to exploit nature for his own benefit was not in question. It was only, it may be suggested, after the significance of Charles Darwin's *The Origin of Species by Natural Selection*, which was published in 1859, had been generally accepted (a process that took many years), that there could develop a common awareness of man as being but one part of a global ecosystem, the balance of which he disturbs at his peril. The notion that the environment must be protected from man, if he is to continue to enjoy the benefits available from it in full measure, was inevitably slow to be accepted in an active industrial nation. The disadvantages of restraint to those with the power of decision were (and are) immediate and obvious, while the need for it was largely theoretical and any adverse consequences of current behaviour distant. It has taken until the end of the 20th century for these consequences to become closer and the need for protective action more widely recognised, most notably in the Conventions on Climate Change and on Biodiversity agreed at the UNCED Conference in Rio de Janeiro in 1992. **1–006**

This chapter examines the development of the common law of nuisance, both private and public, together with the introduction of national legislation on public health, air pollution and water pollution. These legal changes cannot be considered in isolation, but must be set against not only the backdrop of the industrial revolution but also the attitudes at that time to intervention by the state into what were regarded as private activities. **1–007**

Attitudes to Regulation

During the 18th century, the function of government was seen as essentially one of administration and not legislation, with the primary task of Parliament being to check the powers of the Executive. The government, therefore, possessed no coherent legislative programme, preferring instead to concentrate on foreign affairs and taxation.[5] The prevailing intellectual atmosphere has traditionally been regarded as **1–008**

---

[5] Edward Royle, *Modern Britain: A Social History (1750–1985)*, (Edward Arnold, 1987), pp. 189–190.

one of *laissez-faire*, a philosophy which demanded minimal state interference.[6] The bulk of legislation enacted during this period therefore issued from local and private members' bills. The government was, however, forced to act when necessity demanded it. As George Kitson Clark commented, although a policy of non-intervention may be appropriate in the economic sphere, it was "encouragement to error" if applied to social legislation.[7]

1–009 John Stuart Mill, in his Principles of Political Economy, declared that "the Earth itself, its forests and waters, above and below the surface . . . are the inheritance of the human race" and continued "What rights, and under what conditions, a person shall be allowed to exercise over any portion of this common inheritance cannot be left undecided. No function of government is less optional than the regulation of these things, or more completely involved in the idea of a civilised society".[8] Nevertheless his call for regulation was largely unheeded at the time. Indeed, so far as the United Kingdom was concerned, the existence of a coherent regulatory strategy at government level arguably only emerged following a speech of the Prime Minister, Margaret Thatcher, in 1988, in which she said "No generation has a freehold on the earth . . . All we have is a life tenancy, with a full repairing lease".

1–010 The transformation of society from agrarian to industrial, brought with it immense and rapid changes in population distribution and unprecedented social problems. The urbanisation of the nation, particularly around concentrations of new manufacturing industries in certain parts of the country, led to gross pollution, both atmospheric and water-borne. The over-crowded and insanitary conditions of those working in the new industries provided perfect breeding grounds for disease which rose to epidemic proportions. Changes in society had brought with them a new breed of philanthropist, motivated by the humanitarianism of the Enlightenment, who sought

[6] Recent writers have questioned the accuracy of the traditional labelling of the prevailing governmental philosophy as that of *laissez-faire*. They argue that the government pursued a philosophy of free trade rather than *laissez-faire*. On this basis, government interference by way of legislation (even social legislation) did not contradict this. By contrast it provided optimum conditions for the populace to pursue liberal aspirations of free trade. These arguments will not be considered here. The term *laissez-faire* is employed to describe the state's unwillingness to interfere with industrial and social activity. Whether government intervention was or was not in contradiction to this prevailing philosophy cannot change the fact that government intervention by way of legislation (albeit somewhat piecemeal) did in fact occur despite considerable reluctance of the government's part.

[7] N. Tonge & M. Quincey, *British Social and Economic History 1800–1900* (MacMillan, 1980) at p. 52.

[8] First published 1848; quoted at the beginning of the 1990 White Paper on the Environment "This Common Inheritance".

to provide minimum standards of sanitation and welfare for all. Influenced by the writings of Bentham, these reformers adopted two principles to achieve this end which ran counter to the nature of 18th century government: centralised administration and inspection. Prolonged periods of war with France had resulted in a much-increased executive created specifically for the administration of the war. These factors together encouraged changes in the nature of government intervention which were reflected in the subsequent development of environmental legislation.[9]

Vogel suggests that national regulatory styles indicate the relation- **1–011** ships between industry and government.[10] The modest extent of statutory reform in the early to mid-19th century, which took far greater account of the demands of manufacturing industry than of those suffering from its pollution, shows the reticence of the legislature to place even the most modest of restraints on the new industrial activities. This was justified in the name of free-market development and was reflected in the piecemeal nature of the legislation. Although the courts were also forced to address the problems of industrialisation, there was only minimal legal development; the case law clearly displays judicial unwillingness to utilise the law of nuisance as a control over industrial polluters. Pressure for statutory intervention followed, but legislation was slow to emerge and limited when it did, being constrained by the demands of industry. Initially its primary purpose was to maintain social stability, to encourage well-being and to reinforce the rectitude of property and station.[11] Later, as the environmental crisis became more acute, the government was forced to respond, reluctantly, with a wide range of interventionist legislation, which remained, however, in spite of considerable debate both at governmental and public level, largely unsupported by any coherent policy. The evolution of environmental law during this period directly reflects the conflicting political pressures from the polluters and the polluted.

The Common Law of Nuisance and Pollution

Nuisance is an ancient tort of mediaeval origin, the essence of which **1–012** is an act or omission that is an interference with, disturbance of or annoyance to a person in the exercise or enjoyment of either his ownership or occupation of land or of some easement, profit or other

---

[9] Royle, p. 191.
[10] *Ibid.*, p. 30.
[11] Tonge & Quincey, p. 53.

right used or enjoyed in connection with the land (private nuisance), or a right belonging to him as a member of the public (public nuisance).[12] It has three identifiable roots: the assize of nuisance, common or public nuisance, and action on the case.[13]

1–013   The Assize of Novel Disseisin, which was a seminal remedy designed to protect the possession of a freehold, had been introduced by Henry II for use in the King's Court to avoid the procedural burdens of the Writ of Right, so removing its jurisdiction from the feudal courts.[14] In Simon of Merston's case of 1201, Simon, a freeholder, laid a complaint against his neighbour, a miller, who had raised his mill pool, flooding Simon's land. Simon's remedy lay in the Assize of Novel Disseisin—the raising of the level of a pool of water on the miller's land had caused disadvantage to Simon and thus affected his right to free use and enjoyment of his property, *i.e.* disseised him of his land. It was adjudged that the pool be destroyed and that the miller pay Simon damages.[15] The Assize of Nuisance emerged during the 13th century to deal with those actions that did not amount to a disseisin,[16] by permitting an action for loss of profit arising from interference with incorporeal rights. It was, for that reason, essentially suppplementary to the Assize of Novel Disseisin. Both the Assize of Novel Disseisin and that of Nuisance enabled a line to be drawn around a freeholder's free use and enjoyment of land at that point at which his neighbour's use and enjoyment were impaired. The standards by which impairment was judged were rural, agricultural and conservative, with the guiding rule being the rights of the plaintiff.[17]

1–014   During the 15th and 16th centuries gaps in the relief available under the Assize were filled by the "Action on the Case", which consisted of specifically drafted writs that set out pleadings in much greater detail than the Assize. The Assize required actions to be brought by freeholders; Action on the Case, however, gave a remedy to non-freeholders also,[18] and extended the meaning of interference with enjoyment beyond the limited concept of disseisment to encompass the adverse effects of activities involving noxious trades. During these centuries the Action on the Case supplanted the Assize which lay

---

[12] Clerk and Lindsell on *Torts*, (Sweet & Maxwell, 16th ed., 1989), para. [1354].

[13] J. Cooke & D. Oughton, *The Common Law of Obligations* (Butterworths, 2nd ed, 1993).

[14] T.F.T. Plucknett, *Concise History of Common Law* (Little, Brown & Co, 5th Ed., 1956) pp. 358–9.

[15] J.F. Brenner, Nuisance Law and the Industrial Revolution (1974) 3 J. Leg. Stud. 403. This is an excellent study of the evolution of the law of nuisance during the 19th century.

[16] P.H. Winfield, *Nuisance as a Tort*, (1931) 4 Camb. L.J. 189 at 190.

[17] Brenner, at p. 404.

[18] *Ibid.*, p. 406.

largely unused until it was eventually abolished in 1833 by the Real Property Limitation Act.[19] Action on the Case lay only for damages and not for abatement, but it came to be preferred due to its procedural simplicity as compared with pursuing an action in equity. Although *Bush v. Western*[20] is the first known case of an enjoined nuisance, significant numbers of reports of plaintiffs seeking to enjoin industrial polluters do not appear until after 1850. The reasons appear to include the huge expense of pursuing proceedings in equity, the complex procedure, and considerable delay. Further, Equity Courts were reluctant to exercise their discretion to grant equitable relief except in the most extreme of cases.[21]

The Development of Private Nuisance

In 1610 *William Aldred's* case[22] laid down the doctrine which the common law courts constantly applied for the next two centuries. William Aldred brought an action on the case at the Norfolk Assizes against his neighbour, Thomas Benton, for building a pig sty "so near the house of the plaintiff that the air thereof was corrupted".[23] In his defence Benton argued that the pig sty "was necessary for the sustenance of man: and one ought not have so delicate a nose, that he cannot bear the smell of hogs."[24] The Court found in favour of Aldred: light and clean air were considered necessary for wholesome habitation, with ordinary comfort and necessity being the criteria.[25] The extent of a plaintiff's injury was measured in accordance with the contemporary standards of comfort rather than in accordance with the nature of the defendant's activity.   1–015

Thus, the necessity of the activity was irrelevant for this purpose.[26] Reasonableness, however, although not being an essential element of the tort of nuisance (unlike the tort of negligence) was an element that had to be considered. The notion of what activity was considered "reasonable" evolved during the industrial revolution with the expansion of industrial activity. Brenner describes nuisance as "the common law of competing land use", having a zoning function by which it allocates activities to appropriate areas.[27] This function was   1–016

---

[19] 3 & 4 Wm. 4, c.27, 36.
[20] (1720) 24 Eng. Rep. 237.
[21] Brenner, at pp. 406–407.
[22] (1610) 9 Co. Rep. 57b.
[23] *Ibid.*
[24] *Ibid.* at p. 58a.
[25] Brenner at p. 405.
[26] Although a tannery was necessary, this factor alone could be no defence to an action in nuisance *Jones v. Powell* (1628).
[27] Brenner at p. 407.

explicitly articulated in the case law with the onset of industrialisation. Although the basic rule of *Aldred's* case was not changed, its application became narrower. As factories became commonplace and their contribution towards the nation's economy regarded as crucial, so a standard of reasonableness was adopted by the Courts, demanding a greater degree of tolerance from the public of the activities of its industrial neighbours. Industrial growth brought with it a dramatic deterioration in the environment. However, increased air and water pollution were the price to be paid for the promotion of industry.

1–017   Despite the principles articulated in *Aldred's* case, the common law of nuisance had little impact on the advance of industrialisation or effect in protecting the environment. During the period of dramatic economic expansion in the 1850s and 1860s the law of nuisance was infiltrated by a standard of care that became a central feature of the tort, involving evaluation of the standard of amenity that the plaintiff may properly claim when regard is had to the importance of the offending activity and the manner in which it was carried out. The cases suggest, moreover, that the law was applied more leniently to industrial polluters than to private individuals, and that it was hardly applied at all to quasi-public enterprises.[28]

1–018   The reasonableness of a complaint was considered in the light of "plain and sober and simple notions among the British people" in *Walter v. Selfe*.[29] William Walter brought a motion for an injunction to restrain John Selfe, a brick and tile maker, from burning bricks on his land near to Walter's house on the basis that he was entitled to an untainted and unpolluted stream of air. The then Vice-Chancellor, Sir Knight Bruce, found in favour of the plaintiff, having articulated the principle on which his decision must be based: "Ought this inconvenience to be considered in fact as more than fanciful, more than one of mere delicacy or fastidiousness, as an inconvenience materially interfering with the ordinary comfort, physically of human existence, not merely according to elegant or dainty modes and habits of living, but according to plain and sober and simple notions among the English people?".[30]

1–019   In *Hole v. Barlow*[31] the standard of care was evaluated against the importance of the offending activity and the manner and place in which the defendant carried it out. This action for nuisance was again based upon the complaint of a neighbour burning bricks. It was held that the jury was correctly directed by the trial judge who declared that:

[28] Brenner at p. 408.
[29] (1851) 4 D.E.G. & S.M. 315.
[30] *Ibid.* at para. 322.
[31] (1858) 4 C.B. (NS) 334.

"it is not everybody whose enjoyment of life and property is rendered uncomfortable by the carrying on of an offensive or noxious trade in the neighbourhood, that can bring an action. If that was so . . . the neighbourhood of Birmingham and Wolverhampton and the other great manufacturing towns of England would be full of persons bringing actions for nuisances arising from the carrying on of noxious or offensive trades in their vicinity, to the great injury of the manufacturing and social interests of the community. I apprehend the law to be this; that no action lies for the use, the reasonable use, of a lawful trade in a convenient and proper place, even though someone may suffer annoyance from its being so carried on".

A different standard of (in)convenience was impliedly laid down for the industrialised areas from that appropriate to the neighbourhoods of Berkeley, Belgrave or Eaton Squares.[32]

The articulation of the rule in *Hole v. Barlow* was, however, expressly limited to its facts by the decision in *Bamford v. Turnley*.[33] *Bamford* stressed the difference between nuisance for the benefit of the public (justifiable) and a nuisance created for some private purpose (unjustifiable). This is the key to the development of the law during the industrial revolution. Two standards arguably existed, one for private convenience and another *pro bono publico*. In cases of personal discomfort from industrial nuisance the Courts were at their most reluctant to intervene.[34] It was in the decision in *St Helen's Smelting Company v. Tipping*[35] that this principle was expressly articulated.

1–020

William Tipping, a private land owner brought an action in nuisance against a copper smelting company, and its directors and shareholders,[36] for damages for injury to his trees and crops. It was pleaded that "the Defendant erected, used and continued to use certain smelting works upon land near to the said dwelling house and lands of the Plaintiff, and caused large quantities of noxious gases, vapours and other noxious matter, to issue from the said works, and diffuse themselves over the land and premises of the Plaintiff, whereby the hedges, trees, shrubs, fruit and herbage were greatly injured; the cattle were rendered unhealthy, and the Plaintiff was prevented from having so beneficial a use of the said land and premises".[37] The decision distinguished between "trifling inconveniences" (whereby

1–021

---

[32] *Ibid.* at para. 335.
[33] (1862) 3 B. & S. 67.
[34] Brenner p. 413.
[35] [1865] H.L.C. 642.
[36] This was of course some 40 years before the decision in *Salomon v. Salomon*, [1897] A.C. 22.
[37] *Ibid.*, at p. 643.

noxious vapours made life near the smelting works inconvenient and even uncomfortable) and material damage to property diminishing its value. In the former case, primary consideration had to be given to locality. In industrial areas the business of industry could not be made to suffer at the behest of an individual's discomfort. "If a man lives in a town, it is necessary that he should subject himself to the consequences of those operations of trade which may be carried on in his immediate locality, which are actually necessary for trade and commerce . . . and for the benefit of the inhabitants of the town and the public at large".[38] Although the outcome of the appeal was in favour of the plaintiff, the decision made actions in respect of nuisance not involving physical damage to property virtually impossible in industrialised areas. Once again the emphasis on locality was underlined. As was famously expressed somewhat later "What would be a nuisance in Belgrave Square would not necessarily be one in Bermondsey".[39] Thus was emphasised the difference between an individual polluter in a rural area and a group of factories which provided employment and prosperity for an area. "Strict nuisance liability would apply to John Doe down the street, but Doe Manufacturing Company Limited would be judged by a more lenient rule".[40]

1–022   The application of the law of private nuisance during the 19th century, narrowed by the application of tests of locality and the infiltration of a standard of care, enabled the Courts to distinguish between individual and industrial polluters and to lean in favour of the latter to such an extent that private nuisance became virtually ineffective in those areas where it was most needed.

Public Nuisances

1–023   Actions against public nuisances are the oldest means of public regulation of offensive activities. They are offences against public authority, *e.g.* encroaching on the Royal Domain, obstructing the King's highway or, more importantly for present purposes, emitting noxious vapours or fouling common water. The number of reported cases during the 19th century, however, suggests that public nuisance failed to play a significant regulatory role in the protection of the environment. Here also, where large corporations were indicted courts appeared to fear the economic consequences of enforcement. Prior to the industrial revolution, the courts had readily pursued their task without regard to any repercussions on the national economy. Later cases, however, illustrate a change in the courts' willingness to

---

[38] *Ibid.*, at p. 650.
[39] *Per* Thesiger L.J. in *Sturgess v. Bridgman* (1879) 11 Ch. D. 852.
[40] Brenner p. 415.

intervene. *R v. Medley*[41] considered an indictment against a private gas company following severe river pollution. The judge ruled that in spite of evidence of the destruction of river stock and the consequent unemployment of local fishermen, there was insufficient evidence to sustain a prosecution, fearing that all entrepreneurial speculation might end in prosecution.[42] Public and quasi-public bodies authorised by statute (such as railways and the utility companies) were in an even more advantageous position as they were protected from indictment, the only recourse against them being in negligence or *ultra vires*.[43]

A decision that would prove to be of long- term significance was *R. v. Stephens*,[44] holding that the owner of works is liable for a public nuisance caused by acts of his workmen in carrying on the works, even though done without his knowledge and contrary to his general orders. Liability was therefore strict and no *mens rea* needed to be proved. The judgments made clear that if the defendant would have been civilly liable in private nuisance, then the same facts would suffice for him to be criminally liable for a public nuisance, where public rights are injured, irrespective of the state of the defendant's knowledge or intent. The only issue was whether the nuisance was caused in the carrying on of the defendant's business. The judgment was subsequently referred to in *Sherras v. de Rutzen*[45] as showing public nuisances to be one of the exceptions to the general rule that *mens rea* is a necessary ingredient of a criminal offence. The latter case in turn was strongly relied on in *Alphacell v. Woodward*,[46] in which the House of Lords held that commission of the statutory offence of "causing" polluting matter to enter a stream required only, as in *R. v. Stephens*, the defendant's operations to have caused the entry, irrespective of his knowledge or intent.

1–024

The Rule in *Rylands v. Fletcher*

The rule in *Rylands v. Fletcher* has become so well-known in its own right that it is not always recognised that when Blackburn J. gave his famous judgment in 1866[47] he did not consider that he was making

1–025

---

[41] (1834) 172 Eng. Rep. 1246, 6 Car. & P. 292.
[42] Brenner at p. 421.
[43] Relator actions pursued by the Attorney-General on behalf of individuals were, however, facilitated by public health legislation from the 1840s onwards and so made it easier to take action against these bodies. Brenner at p. 423.
[44] [1866] L.R. 1 Q.B. 702. Stephens, a man of over 80, owned a slate quarry but did not supervise its day-to-day running; waste from the quarry stacked by the side of a river had fallen into it and obstructed navigation.
[45] [1895] 1 Q.B. 918.
[46] [1972] A.C. 824.
[47] [1861–73] All E.R. 1.

11

new law at all. The case and those based on it, in particular *Cambridge Water v. Eastern Counties Leather*, are discussed in Chapter 22.[48] It merits mention here nevertheless as demonstrating that the courts were prepared to hold a person liable for damage caused by the escape of anything he had brought on to or accumulated on his land, at least if the damage was foreseeable, however careful he may have been and whatever precautions he may have taken to prevent the damage. In such circumstances therefore there was no question of balancing the reasonableness or otherwise of the defendant's actions against the injury to the plaintiff.

The Introduction of Public Health Legislation

Setting the Scene—The Industrial Revolution

1–026   Between 1800 and 1850 the population in England and Wales doubled to more than 16 million people. By 1900 it had almost doubled again. In addition to expansion of the population, a mass migration of people to areas of increasing industrialisation such as the Midlands and the north of England resulted in a dramatic redistribution and concentration of the population. Prior to 1830, parish records indicated that movement of people had been over short distances due mainly to the rudimentary transport system and the diverse yet essentially agrarian economy that had not demanded a concentrated workforce. By 1830, however, rural counties began to experience an absolute population loss to industrialising counties; these not only experienced considerable population growth overall, but also within them people migrated from rural to industrial parishes. By the mid-19th century the emergence of the railways, together with the growth of industry as a mass employer, had changed the distribution of the population of Great Britain out of all recognition.

1–027   The growth and concentration of population led to urbanisation on a hitherto unknown scale, bringing with it intractable social problems for which the political institutions of the time were quite inadequate: the massed impoverished workforce formed vast insanitary urban slums rife with disease, while the new industries poured out noxious emissions into the air and poisonous waste into watercourses. The result was an environmental crisis of unprecedented dimensions. Fever, typhus and typhoid had been dogging the newly industrialised towns for some time, with little understanding, still less public

---

[48] At paras. 22–152 to 22–178.

awareness, of the causes of diseases or how they spread. However, the cholera epidemics (the first of which lasted for two years from autumn 1831 to summer 1833) heightened public fear and brought to a head the demand for government intervention in the field of public health. The inadequacy of the common law of nuisance to provide effective remedies against environmental pollution was everywhere evident. An alternative approach was urgently required. The government's first response to the cholera epidemic was to create a temporary central board of health with the somewhat limited powers to supervise and receive reports from local boards set up in large towns to contain the disease.[49] This heralded a new approach to environmental regulation.

Edwin Chadwick[50] was one of many who supported the view that disease was carried in the bad smells of a heavily polluted atmosphere. A Benthamite, he believed in centralised administration and inspection and, as such, was one of the motivating forces behind the early Victorian sanitary reform movement. Chadwick's desire was to introduce a coherent social philosophy and environmental engineering was just one aspect of this larger whole.[51] To Chadwick, poor standards of public health represented wastefulness, expense, pauperism and immorality. The fear of the cholera epidemics provided Chadwick with the ideal forum in which to investigate the connection between disease and the environment.   **1–028**

In 1831–1832 Charles Turner Thackrah, a Leeds doctor, had carried out a survey of occupational disease, morbidity and mortality. This was followed in 1832 by a study of Manchester cotton workers by James Phillip Kaye. The statistical societies of London and Manchester contributed further evidence of living conditions in parts of London and manufacturing districts and three parishes in Rutland. All were used by Chadwick to highlight the problems of the industrialised areas. The average life expectancy for England and Wales in 1841 was 41 years. This varied, however, substantially between different areas of the country. In London it was 37, in Liverpool 26 and in Manchester it dipped as low as 24 years.[52] A series of reports concluded overcrowding, poor ventilation, inadequate refuse disposal and bad water were major causes of disease (not the moral weakness and culpability of the poor that some moralists and politicians had previously indicated). The Poor Law Commission's annual report of 1838 officially endorsed Chadwick's plea to alleviate the conditions of pauperism by preventative medicine, in the wake of the typhus epidemic of   **1–029**

[49] Royle at p. 196.
[50] 1800–1890. He lived in Bentham's house, and was left a legacy by him.
[51] Wohl, p. 143.
[52] Brenner, p. 417.

the previous year. Especially influential in promoting political action was a report by the Select Committee on Burials in Towns which was published in 1842. These reports marked the onset of the first wave of sanitary reform.[53]

1–030   In 1842 Chadwick published his *Report on the Sanitary Condition of the Labouring Population of Great Britain*. This was a landmark in the British sanitary reform movement. It sought to portray the inadequacy of existing systems of sewerage, water supply and drainage, and connected the squalor of overcrowding with disease epidemics such as cholera, typhus and typhoid. Chadwick argued that "the various forms of epidemic, endemic, and other diseases caused or aggravated, or propagated chiefly amongst the labouring classes by atmospheric impurities produced by decomposing animal and vegetable substances, by damp and filth, and close and overcrowded dwelling prevail amongst the population in every part of the Kingdom".[54] He stated further that "the annual loss of life from filth and bad ventilation is greater than the loss from death or wounds in any wars in which the country has been engaged in modern times."[55] The report by its extensive use of comparative death rates and life expectancy tables[56] stressed the environmental causes of disease in the form of a compelling condemnation of the sanitary conditions of England and offered a programme for reform "that the primary and most important measures, and at the same time the most practicable, and in the recognised province of public administration, are drainage, the removal of all refuse of habitations, streets, and roads, and the improvement of the supplies of water."[57]

1–031   In 1844 the Duke of Buccleuch's Royal Commission on the Sanitary State of Large Towns and Populous Districts recommended that government should be given centralised powers to inspect and supervise local sanitary works and that local districts be founded with

---

[53] See also: *The History of the Cholera in Exeter in 1832* by Thomas Shapter with introduction by Robert Newton, (S. R. Publishers Ltd., 1971) (Shapter was a doctor who had come to Exeter in 1832—his account of the epidemic was first published in 1849); *A History of Epidemics in Britain* by Charles Creighton (1st ed., 1891). 2nd ed. with additional material by D.E.C. Eversley, E. Ashworth Underwood and Lynda Ovenall, 1965, London; and *King Cholera: the biography of a disease* by Norman Longmate, London, 1966.

[54] Wohl at p. 147.

[55] *Ibid.*

[56] Statisticians played a major role in the work of reformists during this period. William Farr who headed the Office of the Registrar-General aided Chadwick in stressing the need for environmental engineering to alleviate the spread of disease through the medium of statistics. By the presentation of apparently irrefutable facts as statistics, an element of objectivity was added to the moralising of evangelical reformists.

[57] Wohl at p. 148.

supervisory powers over drainage, paving, cleansing, dwellings and water supply. It marked, close to the mid-century, a realistic and Chadwickian appraisal of the sanitary state of the nation and the measures required to tackle the problem,[58] and paved the way for a series of statutes aimed at improving public health in Britain.

The Nuisances Removal Acts (the first of which was introduced in 1846[59]) gave petty sessional jurisdiction to justices to prosecute nuisances such as accumulations of filth, foul drains and cesspools. In addition they founded the Poor Law Authorities for rural areas. The Acts included in their definition of nuisance the phrase "injurious to health" but failed to define the precise meaning of this. It was interpreted so narrowly as to eliminate virtually all beneficial effect the legislation might have had on pollution, by requiring evidence of actual physical harm having resulted.[60] The Public Baths and Wash-houses Act of 1846 gave local authorities the power to provide those amenities, and in 1847 the Town Improvement Clauses Act and the Town Police Clauses Act set out the powers of towns to lay water supplies and main drainage systems. The Water Works Clauses Act, the Commissions Clauses Act and the Cemeteries Clauses Act, all of 1847, aided the introduction of private acts on a uniform basis by offering a standard legislative format for frequently used provisions.[61]

1–032

This first wave of public health legislation culminated in the Public Health Act of 1848, the first major statute directly dealing with public health in Britain. The Act established a General Board of Health in London together with local Boards of Health in places where the death rate exceeded 23 per 1000 living (by comparison with a national average of 21 per 1000 living). The local board had medical officers empowered to manage sewers, drains, water supplies, refuse and sewerage systems, to regulate offensive trades and to remove nuisances. These powers were backed up by the right to levy local rates and purchase land.[62] The Act placed great emphasis on local initiative, but despite this the General Board of Health represented to many the start of an era of intolerable state interference. Indeed the Board was itself reluctant to force unwilling communities to adopt the provisions of the Acts. Where the death rate was, by contrast, below 23 per 1,000 living, local boards might be established in response to petitions from at least 10 per cent of the inhabitants rated for poor relief. Between

1–033

---

[58] *Ibid.*
[59] 9 & 10 Vict., c. 96.
[60] Brenner, p. 426.
[61] Wohl at p. 149.
[62] A separate Act of 1848 applied to London, which was excluded from the scope of the principal Public Health Act.

1848 and 1853, however, the general board received applications from only 284 areas wishing to establish local boards of health, and by 1853 only some two million people were covered by local boards, out of a total population of nearly 20 million in England and Wales. In 1848, of the 187 incorporated towns in England and Wales only 29 had placed the powers of draining in one centralised body; in 30 towns the town corporation had no power over these functions at all and in 62 towns there was no public health authority whatsoever.[63] The fundamental problem with the General Board of Health was that it was reluctant to force unwilling communities to adopt the provisions of the Act and thus reignite the fears and hostility against centralisation.

1–034   The major contribution of the Board of Health, in spite of the opposition it attracted from many quarters, was however its influence in changing the attitudes of local authorities towards sanitary reform. The Board's inspectors were able to offer advice on sanitary engineering projects and generally assist authorities in relation to sanitary reform. In spite of this, however, it was far from popular — Chadwick's lack of tact and attacks on vested interests playing a significant part — and the Board was eventually dismantled in 1858.

1–035   The Nuisances Removal Acts of 1855, 1860 and 1863 attempted to deal with the problem of accumulations of excrement, refuse, industrial waste and smoke, polluted rivers and other threats to public health. They gave wide ranging powers of both inspection and seizure to local government, and extended the common law definition of nuisance to encompass many of the hazards produced by industry, in spite of the lack of clarity of definition experienced by the courts. The Sewage Utilisation Act of 1865 afforded councils and health authorities the power to dispose of sewage, and a subsequent Act of 1867 enabled authorities to purchase land together in order to dispose of sewage outside their boundaries. By 1868, 568 towns had elected to establish local boards of health. Although the piecemeal legislation and the powers it conferred were complex both in theory and practice, local authorities strove towards concentrated administration following the failure of the partial powers granted by local improvements acts. The growth of local boards indicated an increasing acceptance of the need for public health reform. This was aided by the apparent willingness of local authorities to accept the guidance of the Privy Council (which had taken over from the now defunct Board of Health) in matters of sanitary reform. Having played a significant role during the first cholera epidemic, the Privy Council appeared not to carry the same stigma for local bodies as Chadwick's General Board of Health had.

---

[63] Wohl at p. 150.

Wohl further suggests a more significant factor.[64] The Local Government Act of 1858 gave the Privy Council's medical department powers of inspection. Local authorities who required mortgages to finance public works—this was the method by which funds for public works tended to be raised—had to submit to inspection by the department. This put a new cast on the relationship between central and local government.[65]

During "the most exciting period in the history of public health"[66] from the 1830s to the mid-1850s the philosophy of sanitary reform was accepted not only by the leading sanitary reformers but rather extended to become one of the fundamental concerns of Victorian government; this development was one of the earliest strands of an emerging comprehensive public health movement. In 1866 the Sanitary Act[67] became the first public health act dominated by compulsory clauses giving powers to the Home Secretary to compel action rather than merely to advise local authorities, and marked a turning point in public health legislation.   1–036

In 1868 a Sanitary Commission was appointed which reported in 1871 after conducting "exhaustive investigation" advocating, among other things, the need for the unification and simplification of existing public health statutes. The Local Government Board Act 1871 having created the first unified public health administration, the great Public Health Act of 1875 laid the basis for all subsequent legislation in this area. It consolidated over 100 statutes, and continued in effect (amended by further Acts in 1907 and 1925) until replaced by the Public Health Act 1936. In Scotland, the Public Health (Scotland) Act 1867 was amended on several occasions over the next 30 years, and the legislation consolidated and further amended by the Public Health (Scotland) Act 1897, which with subsequent amendments remains in force today. A particularly notable feature of the 1875 Act was the imposition on local authorities, for the first time, of an express duty (as opposed to a mere   1–037

---

[64] Wohl at p. 151.
[65] John Simon was a major force in nurturing this new found co-operation. He was medical officer for the City of London from 1848 to 1855 and then had joined the General Board of Health until its dismantling in 1858. He was then appointed first medical officer of the Privy Council. During the 13 years of his time there he forwarded the cause of Public Health in Britain which culminated in the Sanitary Act of 1866. His philosophy was to encourage rather than enforce sanitary administration on local authorities by enquiring and reporting, and through epidemiological research developing a scientific base for the progress of sanitary law. By playing a leading role in the investigation of industrial diseases, the Privy Council generated a climate conducive to the passage of further legislation and encouraged the local authorities into introducing public health reforms voluntarily.
[66] Asa Briggs in Wohl at p. 155.
[67] 29 & 30 Vict. c. 90.

power) to inspect their areas for prescribed "statutory" nuisances, and to deal with such as they might find.

Air Pollution

1–038   The burning of domestic fuel had been an environmental problem since the 13th century, but by the 19th century deterioration of air quality had reached crisis point. 95 per cent of London's smoke was estimated to be produced by domestic fires. By the 1890s the United Kingdom as a whole was burning 110 million tons of coal annually, releasing into the atmosphere some 200 tons of fine soot every day, and 60,000 tons of carbolic acid (phenol) each year. Everything was dusted with a fine coating of black soot. In the 1840s the man charged with the unenviable task of ventilating the Houses of Parliament experimented by hanging a large veil to check the dust and soot particles in the air. He is claimed to have captured some 200,000 visible "particulates" in a single day. At the Horse Guards the deposits of soot were so great, he recounts "that it formed a complete and continuous film so that when I walked upon it I saw the impression of my foot left as distinctly on that occasion as when snow lies upon the ground". During this period "the Old Smoke" used to have a pall of smoke permanently extending for 20 to 30 miles around it.[68] Cleanliness of linen was considered a ready indicator of cleanliness of the town and it was remarked that linen became as dirty after it had been worn for two to three days in Manchester as after a whole week in the London suburbs.

1–039   With the emergence of industry, the problem was exacerbated. It was not only the larger factories that expelled noxious vapours in the atmosphere, so too the smaller unenviable trades of blood-boilers, bone-boilers, blood-dryers, tanners, glue-makers and gutscrapers contributed to the pollution with their pungent odours. The pollution of the atmosphere was not only unpleasant, it was harmful. At Northfleet the Thames became so engulfed by smoke from the local cement factories that it interfered with navigation on the river and residents complained of breathing irritations and nausea. In Battersea the sulphate and ammonia works caused loss of appetite to the local residents and as early at the 1840s Chelsea nurserymen complained of crop damage caused by the smoke from the factories and workshops. These reports were echoed throughout the country. Between 5 and 19 December 1891 during "ordinary" atmospheric conditions the annualised death rate in London was recorded at 18 per thousand living.

[68] Wohl at p. 209–210.

From December 20, 1891 to January 2, 1892 the annualised death rate had risen to 32 per thousand living, signifying an extra 829 people dying of respiratory diseases over those two weeks. The cause was a smog that enveloped the City on December 20, 1891 and lasted until December 25.[69] Though domestic coal burning was a major contributor to such smogs in all urban areas, it is arguable that the more densely industrialised areas of the north of England suffered more than London, having the additional pollution from an abundance of alkali and other chemical industry.

The Victorians were, however, slow to rise to the challenge of deteriorating air quality; from today's perspective surprisingly so, when one considers their prevalent belief in atmospheric theories of disease generation.[70] Wohl suggests that this was for several reasons. First, the popular belief was that smoke was associated with full employment and profits, a necessary by-product of industry and an outward symbol of social progress. Indeed, rather than constituting a nuisance, the smoke was a sign of the prosperity of the nation. Further, the issue was seen in black and white terms as one of a choice between economic stagnation or environmental pollution. "Noxious as are the vapours, St. Helen's cannot be said to be unhealthy. The large amount of high-priced labour which these works provide would cause the inhabitants to rise as one man to resist by every legitimate means any attempt on the part of the legislature to pass any bill which would have the effect of crippling so important a branch of the trade in this district".[71] Fear of the dramatic deleterious effect upon local industry had indeed been a powerful deterrent to environmental improvement in the application of the common law of nuisance. This fear was echoed in the reluctance to legislate. The Royal Commission on Noxious Vapours in 1878 concluded that the attitude of local authorities was to do nothing in the interest of those in their constituency, and in doing so sacrificed health and comfort in favour of the requirements of trade and industry. Legislation which was passed throughout the 19th century to curb pollution by smoke, fumes and gases remained subject to the paramount importance of industrial interests. "Thus England asked for profits and received profits. Everything turned to profit. The towns had their profitable dirt, their profitable smoke, their profitable slums, their profitable disorder, their profitable ignorance, their profitable despair. The Curse of Midas was on this Society: on its corporate life, on its common mind . . . "[72]

1–040

---

[69] *Ibid.*, p. 213.
[70] *Ibid.*, p. 215.
[71] *per* the Earl of Derby quoted Wohl at p. 216–217.
[72] From L. & B. Hammond *"The Rise of Modern Industry"* in Wohl at p. 215.

1–041   The Select Committee on Smoke Prevention (1843) was the first true study of air pollution. Despite concluding what was clearly already known: that smoking factory chimneys were causing widespread air pollution, the Committee fell short of advocating legislative measures requiring the installation of smoke consuming filters. Local byelaws and nuisance acts promoted cleaner air during the 1840s and 1850s but there still remained the reluctance to legislate on a national level. The Smoke Nuisance Abatement (Metropolis) Act 1853 and its amendment of 1856[73] governed smoke pollution in London and was administered by the Home Office appointed Inspector of Nuisances who worked in consultation with the Metropolitan Police. The Act extended to every smoke-producing furnace used for trade or manufacture within the metropolis. Industry avoided the Act by simply relocating outside the metropolitan area. In addition, the burning of domestic fuel was not covered by the legislation. Low fines, lax enforcement and ambiguous wording of the Acts, and difficulties in locating polluters precisely, all combined to minimise its influence on air pollution. The situation was similar outside London. Provincial towns operated under a series of Town Improvement Clauses Acts which also failed to improve environmental pollution effectively. Leeds, whose Improvement Amendment Act was introduced in 1856, never obtained more than nine convictions in any year between 1857 and 1866. In any event, dye works, iron works and brick works—all major polluters of the air— were not even covered by the Act.[74] A further inhibiting factor was that the Acts did not provide compulsory comprehensive regulation, but rather obligated manufacturers to instal smoke consuming devices "as far as practicable". This was in spite of the fact that an effective and inexpensive smoke reduction device had been patented (by Bodmer) as early as 1834 and adopted by several major firms; by the 1850s the Juke's furnace had also proved very successful. The irony was that those manufacturers who installed smoke consuming furnaces reported a significant saving in fuel consumption—an aspect of much basic environmental regulation that remains true to this day. Some improvement was achieved, however, and by 1861 there were over 8,000 smoke consuming furnaces in London.[75]

1–042   The Public Health Act of 1875,[76] in consolidating the existing Nuisance Acts, again required manufacturers to introduce smoke consuming furnaces only "as far as practicable", which phrase was, unsurprisingly, interpreted very generously by the Courts. Local authorities were empowered to sue outside their own districts but the

[73] 16 & 17 Vict. c. 128, 19 & 20 Vict. c. 107.
[74] Wohl at p. 221.
[75] *Ibid.*, p. 223.
[76] 38 & 39 Vict. c. 55.

expense was great and they had no powers of inspection outside their district boundaries. Even if prosecution was successful, the fines awarded rarely covered the expense suffered by the local authority of pursuing the prosecution. These factors combined, to use Wohl's phrase, "to give a quasi-immunity to polluting industry".[77] The argument for centralised inspection powers to enforce air pollution legislation continued into the 20th century.

The commercial manufacture of alkali (*i.e.* sodium carbonate) by the Leblanc process had commenced in England in 1823,[78] and by 1862 employed a workforce of in excess of 19,000 people. Among the particularly undesirable by-products of the process were hydrogen chloride and hydrogen sulphide, which not only smelt foul, but had considerable destructive properties.[79] The Royal Commission on Noxious Vapours of 1878[80] identified the damage done to properties adjoining the works and the violation of anti-pollution legislation by many of the manufacturers who allowed much gas to escape by night. Mr John Holder, a farmer living five miles out of St Helen's and two and a half miles away from the nearest works, had given evidence to the House of Lords Select Committee on Noxious Vapours (1862) of the injurious effect of the fumes from copper smelting works. His orchard bore no fruit, his clover meadows shrivelled and he had suffered a stunted hay harvest. Although his father had received eight pounds in compensation from the company previously, he told the Committee that the expense and low prospect of success made him reluctant to take any action. The Reverend Canon Hopwood felt that the pollution kept the health of his parishioners down, a view echoed by Dr McNicoll, the medical officer of health for St Helen's, who described hydrogen sulphide as a depressant that retarded recovery from illness.[81]

1–043

It was evident from the countryside surrounding alkali works of the destructive power of the emissions. The countryside was bare, with

1–044

---

[77] Wohl at p. 223.
[78] Before that it had been obtained by burning seaweed harvested on the west coast of Scotland. The Leblanc process was first operated on a commercial scale in 1792, in France.
[79] The process involved treating common salt with sulphuric acid, producing sodium sulphate (salt cake) and hydrochloric acid. The salt cake was then heated with coal and limestone (calcium carbonate) to give "black ash" containing the sodium carbonate, which was leached out with water, and unreacted coal, together with calcium sulphide. Production of alkali in this way peaked around 1880, when the more efficient Solvay process was introduced, and was virtually eliminated from the UK by the end of the first World War.
[80] Reports from Commissioners, Inspectors & Others: "Noxious Vapour" Vol. XLIV (1878).
[81] *Ibid.*

trees sometimes as much as five or six miles away from the nearest alkali works being stunted. Nearer the works, all vegetation was browned and bare by the release of hydrochloric acid from chimneys and hydrogen sulphide from sulphide waste heaps. In addition to polluting the atmosphere, the alkali works deposited its waste products not only in areas near the plant but also in the sea. "There is not a fence[82] from my place to St Helen's, nor a tree alive; — nobody can contradict me: not one coming up to a pear tree that has been planted for fruit. Here and there I see one alive, but they never bear." So attested Mr Thomas Boardman, a nurseryman of gardens some two and three quarter miles from St Helen's and one and a half miles from the nearest alkali works.[83]

1–045   The alkali industry was, however, invaluable to the national economy and the government remained cautious in its control of pollution. The industry, however, unlike other works, caused considerable damage to the property of surrounding land owners. The protection of private property and the interests of landowners remained of paramount importance. A great number of the members of Parliament were themselves part of this affected class. Wohl goes so far as to assert that the protection of private property rather than the protection of the nation's health was the true motive behind the early investigation of the alkali industry.[84]

1–046   The House of Lords Select Committee considered initially the extension of the Smoke Prevention Acts to the alkali industry. This was rejected following arguments from the manufacturers that, as a special industry, it required special legislation. The manufacturers demanded moderation on the basis that technology had only recently been developed to deal with the pollution from alkali works. As a result, the Alkali Works Act of 1863 was passed, aimed at "the more effectual condensation of Muriatic Acid [*i.e.* hydrochloric acid] gas in Alkali Works". Section 4 of the Act established a fixed standard of not less than 95 per cent condensation of "muriatic gases". Penalties were fixed at £50 for a first offence and £100 for subsequent offences. More significantly, perhaps, it provided for the appointment by the Board of Trade of an Alkali Inspectorate to enforce the standards laid down in the legislation. The first Chief Inspector, Robert Smith, was appointed with four sub-inspectors to work closely with the manufacturers and to persuade them that the control of pollution was in their own economic interest.

---

[82] The word was also used to mean a hedge.
[83] *Ibid.*, at para. 1233.
[84] Wohl at p. 228.

The Inspectorate set about investigating uses for the waste products **1–047**
of the alkali works, and considering whether they could be transformed into by-products for use by other industries such as commercial bleach for the textile industry. In doing so the Inspectorate found
itself providing an invaluable service to the alkali industry and
promoted co-operation within the industry. The initial five year period
after the introduction of the 1863 Act saw a significant drop in the
escape of hydrochloric acid from individual works. The increasing
number of alkali works, however, meant that the country enjoyed no
real decrease in the amount of air pollution. The Public Health Act of
1872 transferred the Alkali Inspectorate to the new Local Government
Board. At that time Smith called for more rigorous control. In 1874 a
further Alkali Works Act,[85] supplementing the 1863 Act, was introduced.
This declared that forming any sulphate in the treatment of copper ores
with chlorides, the process used in wet copper works, fell within the
controls of the 1863 Act, and extended the powers of inspection. It also
set an emission limit for hydrochloric acid gas, in addition to the
requirement for a 95 per cent condensation, namely " . . . in each cubic
foot of air, smoke or chimney gases escaping from the works into the
atmosphere, there is not contained more than one-fifth part of a grain
of muriatic acid".[86] Further, all alkali works were required to use "the
best practicable means" to prevent the escape of other noxious gases.

By 1876 most alkali works employed their own chemist to aid **1–048**
compliance with the legislation and seek profitable usage for the
works' waste products. In the period 1862–1876, however, the production of alkali works had doubled, seriously increasing the total amount
of gases being released into the atmosphere and so the complaints
from local land owners and pressure groups continued. The Royal
Commission on Noxious Vapours of 1878, following a brief overview
of "legislative interference (independently of enactments in the Public
Health and Nuisances Removal Acts)", recommended further inspection powers and the extension of the Alkali Acts to all noxious works, a
recommendation which was given effect in the Alkali, etc. Works and
Regulation Act of 1881. This continued the requirement for the
condensation of 95 per cent of hydrochloric acid gases and vapours
and introduced stricter controls on the release of sulphuric acid. The
Act extended its application to ammonia works, chlorine bleaching

---

[85] 37 & 38 Vict. c. 43. The 1863 Act was originally expressed to continue in force for a
fixed period of five years "and no longer" (s.19), but was made perpetual in 1868 (31 &
32 Vict. c. 36).
[86] s.4 of the Alkali Act 1874. 7,000 grains = 1lb (avoirdupois); 1 grain = 0.0648 gm. The
emission limit thus corresponds to approximately 458 mg HCl/m^3, which may be
compared with current BATNEEC emission limits for Integrated Pollution Control
processes producing hydrogen chloride of 10 mg HCl/m^3.

and gas works. Registration fees for all works falling within the ambit of the Act were introduced and payment of local inspectors' salaries (the staff doubling in numbers) was placed in the hands of the local authorities.[87] The Alkali, etc., Works and Regulation Act 1906 consolidated and extended the previous legislation, and remained the basis of air pollution control until its phasing out as the processes subject to it were brought under Part I of the Environmental Protection Act 1990.

1–049   The regulation of the alkali industry illustrates the progress of 19th century air pollution legislation. Other areas of industry, however, were not controlled in such a comprehensive manner. Real progress was only made once industrialists were convinced that profitability could in fact be increased by the installation of improved combustion furnaces, so that self-interest and national interest coincided. The nature of the Acts clearly marks, however, the nature of Victorian administrative reform. Piecemeal pragmatic legislative change gradually brought about improved public health protection without the adoption of a coherently articulated philosophy. Despite the eventual extensive nature of the Alkali Acts, air pollution control remained the domain of a wide range of legislation dealing with smoke abatement, public health and local nuisances. They were not enthusiastically enforced, and with their reliance on the requirement to use "best practicable means", uncertain in their application. The net result was that the remarkable growth of industry in the 19th century was largely unchecked by pollution controls despite its severe effect on the health of the people. How far the adverse consequences were counterbalanced, or even outweighed, by increased national prosperity cannot be examined here; this balance nevertheless remains of crucial significance to the numerous developing countries currently seeking to modernise their economies.

River Pollution

1–050   As the public health requirements of the towns increased with the introduction of sanitary reform legislation, an ever-increasing amount of waste, both human and industrial, was discharged into the rivers. Consequently, as public health in urban areas improved with the introduction of more efficient systems of drainage and waste disposal,

---

[87] Wohl at pp. 229–230.

the problems of water pollution were exacerbated.[88] Epidemiologists had already established the connection between cholera and polluted drinking water. However, the pollution of the rivers did not appear to be a great price to pay for the improvement in public health. Death rates were still declining, and so the pollution of water was not initially an unduly pressing issue. During the early part of the 19th century some 250 tons of faecal matter were being dumped into the Thames each day. By the end of the century and following the construction of sewerage systems, sewers were pouring approximately 150 million gallons a day into the River Thames which made up about one sixth of the total volume of the river water. The River Aire in Leeds was described in 1840 as "a reservoir of poison carefully kept for the purpose of breeding a pestilence in the town . . . it was full of refuse from water closets, cesspools, privies, common drains, dung hill drainings, infirmary refuse, waste from slaughterhouses, chemical soap, gas, dye-houses, and manufactures, coloured by blue and black dye, pig manure, old urine wash; there were dead animals, vegetable substances and occasionally a decomposed human body."[89]

One reason legislation was not introduced at an early stage to counter water pollution was primarily that it appeared to provide no imminent threat to public health (though the House of Commons was forced to suspend proceedings during a spell of hot weather in 1858, on account of the stench from the Thames). Only on rare occasions did any debate concerning river pollution arise. The collision of the *Princess Alice* with another boat on the Thames in 1878 near the sewer outfalls at Barking and Crossness was one such instance. Although few people drowned, out of 130 survivors, 14 people eventually died from poisoning by sewage. Dramatic tales abounded of victims having died from choking on floating sewage. The publicity served to strengthen the argument of the Thames Conservancy Board that outfall works needed to be improved.[90] The reforms demanded by environmentalists, however, would be at huge expense to the rate payer and industrialists, and once again, the economic argument defended the industrialists—that preventing pollution would cost industry and the manufacturers too dearly. When the legislation did

1–051

---

[88] The problem was nevertheless not new. Coleridge's poem "Cologne", written in 1828, includes the passage:

> Ye nymphs, who reign o'er sewers and stinks,
> The river Rhine, it is well known,
> Doth wash the city of Cologne.
> But tell me nymphs, what power divine
> Shall henceforth wash the river Rhine?

[89] Wohl at p. 235.
[90] Wohl at p. 240.

come, as with the sanitary reform and air pollution legislation, it was piecemeal, drafted in broad terms and weakly enforced.

1–052   Although an Act as early as 1388 had been introduced prohibiting the casting of animal filth and refuse into the rivers, river pollution was primarily controlled as a nuisance in common law and thus laboured under all the same limitations as discussed previously. From the early 1840s to the mid-1850s the dominant concern was for the immediate removal of all sewage from town centres. This resulted in its being channeled into the nearest watercourse. It was only in the 1870s that sanitary and environmental reformers came to regard the prevention of river pollution as a primary concern.

1–053   In 1847 the Towns Improvement Clauses Act was enacted, permitting local authorities to put sewage into rivers or the ocean and other non-tidal water. The Public Health Act of 1848 encouraged the construction of sewerage systems but permitted their emptying into such places "as may be fit and necessary". The General Board of Health did advocate sewage farms, but still retained a preference for pouring the sewage into rivers rather than accumulating it in stagnant heaps or cesspools. By 1860, however, epidemiologists began to connect diarrhoea with water pollution, and public attention finally focused with growing concern on the problem of river pollution. In 1868 the River Pollution Commission, following a series of investigations, directed its attention to the pollution arising from the woollen manufacturers in the River Aire and Calder Basin. Their report makes alarming reading.[91] The River Aire rose at Skipton. By Leeds it was being polluted by the sewage of 250,000 people and the waste products of one silk mill, 25 flax mills, 22 paper mills, 224 cloth or woollen mills, 28 tanneries, 29 chemical works, seven soap works, 10 carpet factories, three glue factories, 62 dye works and six dyewood mills.[92] By Bradford Beck, which carried the waste of approximately 140,000 people into the river, the Aire, which was up to that point still managing to support fish, left the area "black, filthy and offensive — even above the sewer outfall, it was, at the time of our inspection, emitting offensive gases and could scarcely be distinguished in appearance from the sewage itself".[93] To illustrate the extent of the pollution, the Report includes a facsimile of a memorandum written with the blackened water of the River Calder and "dedicated without permission to the Local Board of Health Wakefield."

[91] Third Report of the Commissioners, 12 Vol. XXV (1868).
[92] Third Report at p. 706. Sir Titis Salt of Bart, Sons & Co. a factory of some 3,500 employees related that he used annually 320,000 lbs dyewares, 15,000 lbs chloride of lime, ammonia and oil of vitriol, 40–50 tons of Gallipoli oil, 700,000 lbs of soap and 40,000 lbs alkali; ibid., p. 699.
[93] Third Report at p. 700.

In 1861 Parliament eventually bowed to the demands of the industry 1–054 and sport of fishing by passing a Salmon Fisheries Act forbidding the discharge of sewage into waters containing salmon.[94] As with much of the earlier legislation, it was difficult to enforce. Despite the deteriorating condition of the rivers in Britain, the government failed to effectively deal with the challenge of their pollution in spite of several condemning Royal Commission reports. Wider environmental issues again took second place to the demands of industry. In 1861 the Local Government Amendment Act introduced the requirement of purification of sewage prior to discharge into natural watercourses and the Sewage Utilisation Act of 1865 gave local authorities power to commence proceedings against river polluters, so introducing a phase of more general river pollution reform.

The Public Health Act of 1875 facilitated the building of sewage 1–055 farms by local authorities and made it an offence to dump untreated waste into watercourses. As with much of the air pollution legislation of an earlier era, the Act was weakened by the inclusion of the requirement to prove the polluter had not used the "best and available means" to control the sewage".[95] In 1876 after much debate which had diluted the effect of many of its substantive provisions, the Rivers Pollution Prevention Act was introduced. A Local Government Board was empowered to direct local authorities to take action against polluters, but with "regard to the industrial interest involved in the case and to the circumstances and requirements of the locality". Moreover, not only was the Board's consent to the taking of proceedings an essential pre-condition, but the statute expressly laid down that this consent was not to be given unless the Board was satisfied that "no material injury will be inflicted by such proceedings on the interests of such industry".[96] The Act made it obligatory for local authorities to allow manufacturers to connect into local authority sewers, although such could be refused if it was thought that it would overload or harm the sewers. The net effect of the Act was much reduced by its failure to give a central authority, comparable to the Alkali Inspectorate, or regional authorities, responsibility for enforcing anti-pollution measures. By leaving this in the hands of local authorities, the pressure of local industrialists discouraged much change; there was in any event little incentive for a local authority to enforce the law if its neighbours upstream were not doing so as well.

It was not until 1888 that the first effective water pollution legislation 1–056 was introduced in the form of the Local Government Act. This Act

[94] In fact, "all migratory fish of the *genus* salmon".
[95] Wohl at p. 247.
[96] s.6.

27

gave the new county councils as well as the Local Government Board powers to co-ordinate anti-pollution efforts, and the enforcement of river pollution measures was taken away from local bodies. Following this Act several river boards were established to deal with the enforcement of the legislation. They followed the prototype (but abortive) Lee and Thames Conservancy Board which had attempted, albeit ineffectually, to set standards of water purity. By the 1890s it was realised that the Rivers Pollution Prevention Act of 1876 had largely failed to achieve its objects, principally because of the influence it gave to industry to discourage enforcement. Eventually local authorities once again took the initiative, and petitioned Lancashire and Cheshire County Councils to have these matters removed from the control of local judges and local authorities, and put in the hands of bodies with responsibilities for entire river basins. The Mersey and Irwell Joint Committee Act of 1892 reflected this concern and represented an important departure from the previous legislation. It made it an offence to put any solid matter into the rivers and did not require that the solid matter interfere with the flow. In addition, it omitted the requirement that consideration be given to the circumstances and requirements of the locality, a standard that had persistently dogged not only river pollution legislation but also air pollution legislation and the common law. The Mersey and Irwell Joint Committee worked closely with the manufacturers and following lengthy negotiation it appeared that the Committee was making progress by the end of the century. The West Riding of Yorkshire Rivers Board was established in 1893 under the provisions of the West Riding of Yorkshire Rivers Act 1894.

1–057   Though the Boards represented a major advance in the control of river pollution, in spite of their vigour, the sheer volume of effluent being poured into the rivers was too much for them to cope with.

1–058   Other factors also operated against their success. The law remained ambiguous in the absence of a precise code of rules or national legislation, and even the wide regional efforts were only partially effective. No specific standards of pollution were set using chemical analysis to determine acceptable levels of pollution, even though a similar procedure had been introduced by the Alkali Acts. In particular, as today, the very substantial costs of constructing effective sewerage systems played a considerable part in the lack of river pollution control. The pollution of rivers was the price of the social and economic benefits of industrial and urban growth, and of preserving public health in the towns. As Wohl states "the prevention of river pollution must be viewed . . . as one of the least satisfactory chapters in the history of Victorian public health".[97]

[97] Wohl at p. 256.

Environmental Economics

The massive pollution caused by manufacturing industry through-   **1–059**
out the 19th century (and indeed most of the 20th also) is a classic
example of the excessive use that, in the absence of other restraints,
will inevitably be made of an economic good that is made available at a
price (in fact free) substantially below the benefit that it provides to the
user. Historically the unowned environment, air and water in particular, has been treated as though in limitless supply and accordingly as
having no cost. Nevertheless there are very real costs to society from
pollution caused by industrial emissions, at least when it reaches
significant levels (views will differ widely as what those levels are).
These may be perceived by most people primarily in terms of adverse
effects on human health and shortened life-spans, but they exist also
in, for example, harm to species of flora and fauna farmed for profit,
decreases in or losses of other species of importance to ecosystems of
economic significance, reduced fertility of soil, and loss of amenity
generally. No accurate figures can be put on such costs[98]; all that can
be said with certainty is that they not zero, and that an economic
regime that assumes they are will lead to a wasteful misallocation of
resources.

A legal treatise is not the place for an economic analysis of these   **1–060**
costs to society, still less for a review of the political and economic
issues involved in determining whether those who create them should
be restrained by conventional regulatory controls or by market
mechanisms that ensure the costs are paid by the polluter, or by some
combination of these.[99] Nevertheless, an account of environmental
legislation must necessarily make at least brief mention of the trend
towards the use of market mechanisms and the reliance that is already
being made of them, at least as a supplement to normal controls.

Environmental economics may be said to have been first developed   **1–061**
by Arthur Pigou at Cambridge in the 1920s, with his proposals for
environmental taxation. His ideas were not however taken up at the
time, though in the past two decades much greater interest has been
shown in the concept of using market forces to achieve environmental
goals. Dr Wilfred Beckerman and Lord Zuckerman argued for this in

---

[98] For a description of the approaches to assessing such costs, see "Values for the
Environment—A Guide to Economic Appraisal", J. T. Winpenny, HMSO London,
1991.

[99] Not charging the costs to the polluter itself involves a political decision to give him
what in economic terms amounts to a subsidy.

their minority report to the 1972 Third Report of The Royal Commission on Environmental Pollution.[1] The United Kingdom government signalled its intention to place greater reliance on economic instruments for environmental protection in its 1990 White Paper on the environment "This Common Inheritance",[2] and this has been reinforced by more recent announcements. At EC level the proposal for a carbon tax has been the subject of discussions for several years, though it has not in fact had the support of the United Kingdom. The somewhat uncertain principle now laid down in Article 130r(2) of the Rome Treaty that "the polluter should pay"[3] has underlain much EC legislation since the First Action Programme in 1973, and was formally incorporated into EC law by the Single European Act in 1985.

1–062   There are a wide variety of economic instruments available for adoption; many have already been put into practice in Britain and other countries. Thus pollution charges serve to discourage the consumption of scarce resources or polluting emissions—examples include the proposed EC carbon tax, the landfill levy suggested for the UK, charges on discharges to water as in France, charges on discharges to atmosphere up to prescribed emission levels as in Poland, and charges for the use of natural resources (which includes the emission of pollutants to air and water) as in Russia. Deposit refund systems encourage recycling, best known in relation to bottles, but also used for packaging generally in Germany (with less than ideal results, in the short term at least); they are to be introduced in the Netherlands for various consumer goods to bring about their eventual return at the end of their useful life, and to fund their dismantling and recycling of their component parts. Tradeable permits have been developed in the United States for sulphur dioxide emissions to air, and given statutory backing by the 1990 amendments to the US Clean Air Act. In theory these represent an efficient system for obtaining the greatest reduction in pollution for the least cost to the nation; the practice has not proved to be so ideal, but there is as yet insufficient experience to come to any firm conclusion. Subsidies may operate as inducements to environmentally benign behaviour. The reduced duty on unleaded petrol has had a powerful effect on the market share that this now enjoys; similar mechanisms may be seen in the recycling

---

[1] Reproduced with commentary in "Pricing for Pollution", Wilfred Beckerman, Hobart Paper 66, Institute of Economic Affairs, (2nd ed. 1990); see also: "Blueprint for a Green Economy", David Pearce, Anil Markandya and Edward Barbier (originally prepared as a report for the UK Department of the Environment), Earthscan Publications, 1989; IFS Commentary No. 19 "Taxation and Environmental Policy: Some Initial Evidence" Mark Pearson and Stephen Smith, Institute for Fiscal Studies, 1990; "Costing the Earth", Frances Cairncross, The Economist Books Ltd, 1991.
[2] See in particular its Annex A.
[3] See also paras. 2.018 to 2.020 below.

credits payable where waste is not sent for disposal, and in the non-fossil fuel obligation on the electricity generators that results in a higher price being paid for electricity derived from renewable sources. These and other economic instruments will undoubtedly play an increasingly large part in future policies for environmental control.

Chapter 2

SOURCES OF LAW AND ITS ADMINISTRATION

As described in Chapter 1, the basis of much current United **2–001** Kingdom environmental legislation was laid down in the 19th century. Thus the principal offences relating to pollution of water derive from the Rivers Pollution Prevention Act 1876; air pollution legislation has been based on the Alkali Acts since 1865, and statutory nuisance proceedings have been available for responding to deposits of waste that are "prejudicial to public health or a nuisance" since the Public Health Act 1875. All this was a purely national response to domestic issues.

However as public consciousness of environmental issues has **2–002** grown in recent years, so has the recognition that the impacts of industrial and other activities on the environment often extend beyond national boundaries, and that international cooperation is needed if there is to be effective control of the consequences of these activities. Nevertheless, where industrial activities produce goods for markets subject to international competition, there is inevitably reluctance to impose substantial environmental costs on a domestic industrial sector that do not have to be borne by competitors in other countries. While this aspect can be exaggerated, since strict controls are generally conducive to good management practice, which experience indicates often leads to significant cost savings and valuable precautionary measures, there is undoubtedly a point where environmental expenditures cease to produce positive returns to the organisation incurring them, however desirable they may be for the community as whole. International agreements to accept demanding standards in the general interest accordingly materially facilitate the adoption of such stricter measures by at least reducing to manageable proportions the extent of competition from organisations not subject to similar requirements.

The GATT

2–003   This issue has been a major factor in the development of environmental law at EC level, and is likely to be a major feature of the next round of negotiations of the General Agreement on Tariffs and Trade ("the GATT").[1] The broad purpose of the GATT is of course to avoid obstacles to and distortion of international trade. Thus Article XI forbids all prohibitions or restrictions on imports and exports, however achieved, otherwise than through duties, taxes or other charges, though this is subject to certain exceptions. Similarly, Article III requires all internal taxes and regulations of all kinds to be applied equally both to imported and domestic products. Breaches of these do of course occur in practice, particularly in relation to quantitative restrictions on imports and exports, for example those relating to ozone-depleting substances under the amended Montreal Protocol, and exports of waste to third world countries under the Basle Convention. However, where this occurs by multilateral arrangement, the GATT frequently takes no action; its prime concern is with unilateral actions by individual states.

2–004   Exceptions to the general rules prohibiting discrimination and trade restrictions are contained in Article XX. This does not in terms relate to the environment, but does permit the adoption or enforcement of any measures "necessary to protect human, animal or plant life or health" or "relating to the conservation of exhaustible natural resources if such measures are made effective in conjunction with restrictions on domestic production or consumption".[2] Article XX however is subject to the existence of certain pre-conditions, namely that any such measures must not be "applied in a manner which would constitute a means of arbitrary or unjustifiable discrimination between countries where the same conditions prevail, or a disguised restriction on

---

[1] It is sometimes argued that if a country is willing to set low values on its environment and to see it damaged in the interests of increased exports and economic development, that is a matter for that country alone, while the cheaper products it can consequently produce benefit consumers everywhere. This however ignores the adverse effects on manufacturing industry in more tightly regulated countries receiving the exports, which may put it at a long term competitive disadvantage even if the exporting country subsequently raises its environmental standards to a similar level. Additionally, as noted, certain environmental damage is legitimately of more than purely local concern, where it involves, for example, release of greenhouse gases or ozone depleting substances, loss of rain forest cover or unique wildlife habitats.

[2] Art. XX, paras. (b) and (g) respectively.

international trade". A similar exemption occurs in the GATT Standards Code, which relates to eliminating restrictions on trade arising through the application of national standards—subject to the same preconditions, the Code allows non-compliance with it on the ground of "protection of human health or safety, animal or plant life or health *or the environment*".

The main issue of contention is whether the references in Article XX(b) to "human, animal or plant life or health" and in Article XX(g) are exclusively concerned with conditions within the jurisdiction of the country seeking to apply the exception, or whether they also apply to conditions elsewhere, for example in the production and manufacturing processes of a third country exporter. The most notable decision in this regard related to US legislation prohibiting the importing of Mexican tuna that had been caught with nets.[3] Tuna fishing nets are liable to trap and kill dolphins; where tuna is fished on lines, the dolphin are not at risk. The GATT panel considering a complaint by Mexico held that the US legislation was a quantitative restriction prohibited by Article XI and that the prohibitions were discriminatory in that the imported tuna, as a product, was exactly the same, whether caught on a line or in a net.

2–005

The panel preferred the view that to come within the exception of Article XX(b) restrictions would have to be necessary to protect human, animal or plant life or health within the jurisdiction of the importing country, and not anywhere in the world, since otherwise any importing country could impose its own opinions and standards on those of any exporting country. The GATT panel likewise refused to allow the USA to rely on the exception of Article XX(g) on the ground that, here also, reference to measures relating to the conservation of exhaustible natural resources applied only to matters within the control of the country applying them. Even if that were not so, the US measures could not be regarded as being primarily aimed at the conservation of dolphins. Though the ruling in the *Mexican tuna* case is open to a variety of interpretations, it is clear that the effect of the GATT is severely to discourage contracting parties from imposing any trade restrictions designed to protect the environment anywhere outside their own jurisdictions, except through multilateral arrangements.

2–006

---

[3] The legislation required a ban on "the importation of commercial fish or products from fish which have been caught with commercial fishing technology which results in the incidental kill or incidental serious injury of ocean mammals in excess of United States standards".

International Conventions on the Environment

2–007   International conventions are often one of the principal motive forces behind new environmental legislation. Many of these have been promoted by the United Nations, through the United Nations Environment Programme ("UNEP"), the Organisation for Economic Cooperation and Development (the OECD), and the Council of Europe. There has been no uniform practice with regard to the manner of participation of EC Member States in these conventions. Individual states may be signatories to them, as may the European Community as a single body. In the latter case, the convention will then be implemented through EC legislation. The most significant international conventions for domestic United Kingdom environmental law are the following:[4]

Marine Pollution

2–008   (1) International Convention on Civil Liability for Oil Pollution Damage (1969);

(2) International Convention on the Establishment of an International Fund for Compensation for Oil Pollution Damage (1971);

The 1969 Convention makes ship owners strictly liable for oil pollution damage and makes insurance against civil claims compulsory. The fund established under the 1971 Convention increases the resources available for major pollution incidents. In addition to these, there are two voluntary schemes between tanker owners and cargo owners respectively, namely the Tanker Owners Voluntary Agreement Concerning Liability for Oil Pollution (TOVALOP) and the Contract Regarding an Interim Supplement to Tanker Liabilities for Oil Pollution (CRISTAL).

2–009   (3) The London Convention on the Prevention of Marine Pollution by the Dumping of Wastes and Other Matter (the London Dumping Convention) (1972);

(4) International Convention for the Prevention of Pollution from Ships (MARPOL) (1973);

(5) The Bonn Agreement for Cooperation in Dealing with Pollution of the North Sea by Oil and Other Harmful Substances (1983);

---

[4] For details of these and other conventions see *Encyclopedia of Environmental Law*, Part B.

(6)   The Paris Convention for the Protection of the Marine Environment of the North-east Atlantic (1992).

The 1992 Paris Convention consists of an amalgamation of earlier Paris (1974) and Oslo (1972) Conventions dealing with pollution of the North-East Atlantic (including the North Sea) from land-based sources and from dumping from ships and aircraft respectively. It was also updated in 1992 to cover, in addition, pollution from off-shore drilling, underwater pipelines, nuclear plants and artificial islands. It includes a prohibition on the dumping of radioactive substances, including wastes; there is however an exception in favour of the United Kingdom and France, who reserve options to resume such dumping in 2008. MARPOL and the London Dumping Convention address largely the same issues, but operate on a global scale. Mention may also be made of the UN Convention on the Law of the Sea agreed in 1982, which includes a section entitled "Protection and Preservation of the Marine Environment". The Convention is however still not in force.

Air

(1)   The Geneva Convention on Long Range Transboundary Air   2–010
Pollution (1979);
(2)   The Vienna Convention for the Protection of the Ozone Layer (1985);
(3)   The Framework Convention on Climate Change (Rio de Janeiro, 1992).

The Geneva Convention is concerned with controlling and reducing emissions to air of pollutants. It underlies the EC controls placed on SO_x and NO_x emissions in particular. The Vienna Convention is in fact most noted for the amendments to it introduced by the Montreal Protocol setting a staged programme for reducing or eliminating production of ozone depleting substances. This protocol has since been further amended, most recently in Copenhagen in November 1992; the EC controls over CFCs, halons and other ozone depleters, which are somewhat more demanding, are discussed in paragraphs 10.106 to 10.112.

The Convention on Climate Change, signed at Rio de Janeiro in June   2–011
1992,[5] and which came into effect on March 21, 1994, is directed to stabilising concentrations of greenhouse gases by the development of national programmes for action on emissions of and sinks for such gases. Many gases contribute to global warming, most notably carbon dioxide by virtue of the huge quantities released, but also CFCs,

---

[5] Approved by the EC in Decision 94/69, [1994] O.J. L33.

methane and nitrogen oxides which have far greater warming effect than carbon dioxide, weight for weight. The existence of global warming, whether carbon dioxide does indeed cause it or whether there are counterbalancing compensatory mechanisms, and the practical consequences of such global warming as there may be, all remain contentious issues. Nevertheless, this is generally accepted to be a clear case for the application of the precautionary principle—despite the uncertainty, the potential costs on a global scale of the warming taking place to a significant degree are such that precautions should be taken now to avert the risks.

Transport and Waste

2–012
    (1) The Basle Convention on the Control of Transboundary Movements of Hazardous Wastes and their Disposal (1989).

This forms the basis of EC Regulation No. 259/93, discussed in paragraphs 11.288 to 11.308. Both the United Kingdom and the EC became Parties to the Convention on May 8, 1994.

    (2) The European Agreement concerning the International Carriage of Dangerous Goods by Road (ADR) (1993 edition);
    (3) Regulations Concerning the International Carriage of Goods by Rail (RID) (1993 edition).

Heritage, Wildlife and Habitats

2–013
    (1) The Ramsar Convention on Wetlands of International Importance especially as Waterfowl Habitat (1971);
    (2) Convention for the Protection of the World Cultural and Natural Heritage (1972);
    (3) Convention on International Trade in Endangered Species of Wild Fauna and Flora (the CITES Convention) (1973);
    (4) The Berne Convention on the Conservation of European Wildlife and Natural Habitats (1979);
    (5) The Bonn Convention on the Conservation of Migratory Species of Wild Animals (1979);
    (6) Convention for the Protection of the Architectural Heritage of Europe (1985);
    (7) The Espoo Convention on Environmental Impact Assessment in a Transboundary Context (1991);
    (8) Convention on Biological Diversity (Rio de Janeiro, June 1992);
    (9) Agreement on the Conservation of small cetaceans of the Baltic and North Seas (1994).

The Convention on Biological Diversity was ratified by the United Kingdom on June 3, 1994.

The most notable recent international development was the United **2–014** Nations Conference on Environment and Development (UNCED) — the "Earth Summit" — at Rio de Janeiro in June 1992. This resulted in two conventions, on Climate Change and Biodiversity, referred to above, an agreed "Statement of Forest Principles" aimed at conserving the world's forests, and a lengthy document "Agenda 21" setting out bases for moving towards sustainable development. The United Kingdom government's strategy for achieving the commitments that it entered into at the Conference were published in early 1994.[6] Though criticised for not setting sufficient and measurable targets, these strategy documents will nevertheless undoubtedly play a significant part in future policy developments by providing a framework against which proposals may be assessed.

The European Economic Area

The Agreement on the European Economic Area[7] extends much EC **2–015** legislation and the relevant *acquis communautaire* to Austria, Liechtenstein, Switzerland, Norway, Sweden, Finland and Iceland. The Agreement includes provisions on the free movement of goods[8] corresponding to Articles 30 and 36 of the Rome Treaty[9] and also special provisions on the environment[10] that broadly correspond with those of Articles 130R (1) and (2) — (see paragraph 2–017). Article 75 however allows any contracting party to maintain or introduce more stringent protective measures "compatible with [the] Agreement", notwithstanding that they may interfere with trade with other countries.

European Community Law

The original Rome Treaty contained no mention of the environment **2–016** whatsoever. The first official mention of environmental protection

[6] Sustainable Development — The UK Strategy (Cm. 2426)
Climate Change — The UK Programme (Cm. 2427)
Biodiversity — The UK Action Plan (Cm. 2428)
Sustainable Forestry — The UK Programme (Cm. 2429).
[7] Brought into effect in the United Kingdom by the European Economic Area Act 1993. On the accession of Austria, Sweden and Finland to the European Community on January 1, 1995, these three countries of course ceased to be members of the EEA.
[8] Arts. 11 and 13.
[9] See also Protocol 12 and Annex II of the EEA Agreement.
[10] In Arts. 73 to 75 and in Annex XX.

came in a declaration made in October 1972 by the heads of the then six EC Member States:

> "Economic expansion is not an end in itself: its firm aim should be to enable disparities in living conditions to be reduced. It must take place with the participation of all the social partners. It should result in an improvement in the quality of life as well as in standards of living. As befits the genius of Europe, particular attention will be given to intangible values and to protecting the environment, so that progress may really be put at the service of mankind".[11]

2–017   It was only with the adoption of the Single European Act, which came into effect on July 1 1987, that specific provision was made in the Rome Treaty for environmental concerns. The principal amendments in this respect were the incorporation of a new Article 100A, providing:[12]

> "3. The Commission, in its proposals envisaged in paragraph 1 concerning health, safety, environmental protection and consumer protection, will take as a base a high level of protection"

and three new Articles 130R, 130S and 130T setting out the basic principles of Community action on the environment. These last three were revised by the Maastricht Treaty. The first paragraph of Article 130S(2) is central:

> "2. Community policy on the environment shall aim at a high level of protection taking into account the diversity of situations in the various regions of the Community. It shall be based on the precautionary principle and on the principles that preventive action should be taken, that environmental damage should as a priority be rectified at source and that the polluter should pay. Environmental protection requirements must be integrated into the definition and implementation of other Community policies."

2–018   The polluter pays principle, referred to here, is designed to ensure that the full costs of environmental damage caused by polluting activities are borne exclusively by the polluter. Historically, air, water and (to a degree) land have been treated as free resources that industry has been able to pollute at little or no cost to itself, and thereby pass on to the community, directly or indirectly, costs attributable to its own operations. The polluter pays principle aims to avoid such a mis-

---

[11] Quoted in the Introduction to the 1st Action Programme; [1975] O.J. C112 at p. 5.
[12] In para. 3.

allocation of economic resources by requiring these additional costs of an economic activity to be factored into the accounts of the relevant undertaking.[13] If an activity is not viable when required to bear its full costs then, provided that its competitors are subject to the same regime, it should not remain in business. In addition, the development of alternative clean technologies will be encouraged.[14]

Indiscriminate subsidies for waste disposal operations, or even for the installation of pollution abatement equipment, are consequently inconsistent with this. The principle is thus in essence an economic instrument and not a principle of law determining who should be ultimately liable for any damage; it is in no way inconsistent with the principle for a polluting undertaking to make a claim against a third party whose negligence or breach of contract, for example, is responsible for relevant environmental damage.   2–019

Detailed "Community guidelines on state aid for environmental protection" have been issued by the European Commission.[15] These distinguish between: 2–020

(i)   aid for adaptation of old plant and equipment to achieve mandatory standards, which is acceptable up to 15 per cent of capital costs (though a higher figure may be allowed in certain circumstances);

(ii)   aid for new plant and equipment, which is not acceptable, except where it replaces plant at least two years old and is no more than the cost of adapting the old plant;

(iii) aid for investment to attain significantly more than mandatory standards, which may be permitted up to 30 per cent of capital costs, and sometimes more;

(iv)   aid for information activities, which generally will be allowed in full;

(v)   aid for training and advice, which will be allowed up to 50 per cent for SMEs (in assisted areas aid may be given to all organisations);

(vi)   operating subsidies, which are normally unacceptable, except in special circumstances, e.g. some recycling activities and temporary relief from environmental taxes to maintain international competitiveness; and (vii) some measures to encourage purchase of environmentally friendly products.

---

[13] This is sometimes referred to as internalising external costs.
[14] Of course time may be needed to effect the transition, so as to avoid significant social and other costs. This is however good reason for planning ahead and adapting to new technology sooner rather than later, and not waiting until a deadline is reached.
[15] [1994] O.J. C72.

2–021   European Community law on the environment is shaped to some degree by international conventions; other pressures for change develop from political interaction within and between the Council of Ministers, the European Commission and the European Parliament. Legislation can only be initiated by the Commission, but it in practice will not develop proposals on its own initiative where it considers there is unlikely to be a sufficient consensus within the Council of Ministers for them to be adopted. It may however be requested to do so by the European Parliament.[16] The Commission works within a broad agenda laid down in the current "Action Programme on the Environment". There have been five such Programmes since 1973, the first four covering periods of four or five years each, as shown in Table 2/I. The 5th Programme runs for longer, from 1993 to 2000, though it provides for a review in 1995.

TABLE 2/I

Action Programme	Period	O.I. Reference
1st	1973–1976	[1973] O.J. C112
2nd	1977–1981	[1977] O.J. C139
3rd	1982–1986	[1983] O.J. C46
4th	1987–1992	[1987] O.J. C328
5th	1993–2000	[1993] O.J. C138

The Programmes, which are approved in general terms by the Council, only set out broad policy objectives, and justifications for these; there is no certainty that proposals will be brought forward to meet all of these objectives in full, and in fact matters are often carried over from one Programme to the next (if not abandoned).

2–022   The 1st Action Programme set out 11 "Principles of a Community Environment Policy" that continued to be supported in subsequent Programmes. These may be summarised as follows:

(1)   Pollution should be prevented at source rather than dealt with after the event;
(2)   Environmental issues must be taken into account at the earliest possible stage in planning and other technical decision making processes;
(3)   Abusive exploitation of natural resources is to be avoided;

---

[16] Rome Treaty, Art. 138B.

42

(4)   The standard of knowledge in the EC should be improved to promote effective action for environmental conservation and improvement;

(5)   The polluter should pay for preventing and eliminating "nuisances", subject to limited exceptions and transitional arrangements;

(6)   Activities in one country should not degrade the environment of another;

(7)   The EC and the Member States must in their environment policies have regard to the interests of developing countries and should aim to prevent or minimise any adverse effects on their economic development;

(8)   There should be a clearly defined long-term European environmental policy that includes participation in international organisations and co-operation at both regional and international levels;

(9)   Environmental protection is a matter for everyone in the EC, at all levels; their co-operation, and the harnessing of social forces, is necessary for success. Education should ensure the whole community accepts its responsibilities for future generations;

(10) Appropriate action levels must be established—local, regional, national, Community and international—for each type of pollution and area to be protected;

(11) Major aspects of national environmental protection policies should be harmonised. Economic growth should not be viewed from purely quantitative aspects.

The 5th Action Programme is entitled "Towards Sustainability" and **2–023** marks a departure from previous programmes in its approach. In particular, it concerns itself not with specific environmental media and how they should be protected, but with five sectors of economic activity: industry, energy, transport, agriculture and tourism. The programme addresses particular themes and sets out targets in several areas including climate change, acidification and air quality, protection of nature and bio-diversity, the management of water resources, the urban environment, coastal zones and waste management. In an important section,[17] the Programme reviews the range of instruments

[17] Chap. 7.

that are available to achieve environmental control and improvement, and deliberately aims to move away from the conventional "command and control" approach typical of the previous Action Programmes. It recognises that sustainable economic activity cannot be achieved simply by setting out controls that must be complied with.

2–024   Accordingly, it states that "environmental policy will rest on four main sets of instruments: regulatory instruments, market-based instruments (including economic and fiscal instruments and voluntary agreements), horizontal supporting instruments (research, information, education, etc.) and financial support mechanisms". The Programme states that the ultimate goal of sustainable development can only be achieved by concerted action on the part of all the relevant "actors" working together in partnership, and it thus seeks to implement the concept of "shared responsibility" involving, for example, a division of powers and responsibilities between the Community, the Member States, and regional and local authorities; in other cases, the relevant actors may be enterprises, the general public and consumers. There is thus a definite trend away from prescriptive legislation towards creating a framework providing economic and social encouragement and support for environmentally responsible behaviour.

2–025   The Action Programmes do not set out detailed proposals for legislation. Such proposals are usually issued by the Commission in draft form leading to a consultation among the Member States and relevant organisations.[18] The draft legislation is normally then followed by the text of a formal proposal.[19] The subsequent procedure depends on the Rome Treaty article under which the legislation is proceeding. Prior to the amendments made by the Maastricht Treaty legislation proceeding under Article 100A involved the so-called "co-operation" procedure, in which the European Parliament is actively

---

[18] The most effective time for influencing new legislation is before it has been crystallised in formal proposals. For those outside the normal network of consultees, it will often be highly desirable to have contacts in the European Commission, government departments or industry organisations, in order to be up to date with what consultations are in progress and on how the responses may have been reflected in drafts for legislation. The Commission and the Council have however now adopted a Code of Conduct (93/730) in respect of public access to their documents, allowing them to be more widely available. The procedures for applications for access are set out in Council Decision 93/731/EC and Commission Decision 94/90/ECSC, EC, Euratom ([1993] O.J. L340 and [1994] O.J. L46, respectively).

[19] Published in the C series of the Official Journal.

involved.[20] By contrast, where legislation proceeded under the unamended Article 130S, relating to environmental measures, the "consultation" procedure applied, in which the Parliament might express an opinion and recommend amendments but had no other power to change the legislation. The amendments made by the Maastricht Treaty give increased power to the European Parliament, and correspondingly reduce that of the Council of Ministers, broadly by applying the cooperation procedure[21] to environmental legislation proceeding under Article 130S, while harmonising legislation proceeding under Article 100A will, in most circumstances, be subject to a new "co-decision" procedure[22] giving the Parliament a right of veto. In a few reserved cases,[23] one of which relates to town and country planning, the consultation procedure still applies and a unanimous vote in the Council of Ministers will remain essential for environmental measures to be adopted, unless the Council itself otherwise determines.

In a number of cases, the issue has arisen as to whether certain proposed legislation is to be categorised as a harmonisation measure to be adopted under Article 100A, or whether it is an environmental measure to be adopted under Article 130S. In several of these, the Commission has proposed a measure under Article 100A, and it has been adopted by the Council under Article 130S.[24] While the Council's preference for Article 130S can be seen as illustrating a wish to keep as much influence as possible in its own hands, there is a further consideration in that by virtue of Article 130T, measures adopted under Article 130S do not prevent any Member State from maintaining or introducing more stringent protective measures compatible with the Treaty. By contrast, it is generally assumed, though the matter is by

2–026

---

[20] Having received a proposal on which the Council of Ministers has reached a common position, the Parliament may propose amendments (by an absolute majority). The amended proposal then goes to the Commission, which considers the amendments made by the Parliament, and decides which (if any) of them it approves and which should be rejected. The proposal is then returned to the Council of Ministers. Any of the Parliament's amendments that are approved by the Commission and so retained can only be rejected or further amended by the Council by unanimous vote. Where there is a majority in the Parliament in favour of a particular feature that is also approved by the Commission, there will almost inevitably in practice be at least one member of the Council also in favour. Consequently unanimity in the Council against such a feature is highly unlikely. The co-operation procedure first led to the adoption of an amendment contrary to the original wishes of a majority of Council members in the case of Directive 88/76 relating to the exhaust emissions of small cars—see para. 10–101 and note 26 thereto.

[21] As prescribed by Art. 189C.

[22] As prescribed by Art. 189B.

[23] Set out in Art. 130S(2).

[24] The European Parliament naturally is inclined to favour Article 100A wherever possible since this provides it with greater influence.

no means beyond doubt, that where a measure is adopted under Article 100A, Member States may not introduce measures conflicting with it, since this would destroy the very purpose of the intended harmonisation. There is a specific exception provided for in Article 100A(4), but this only applies where a harmonisation measure is adopted by a qualified majority, and allows a Member State to apply national provisions "on grounds of major needs referred to in Article 36, or relating to protection of the environment or the working environment". While it is open to argument that "applying national measures" extends to introducing new ones, the better view is probably that this exception is only applicable to national provisions already in existence at the time of the adoption of the harmonisation measure.[25] Nevertheless, despite Directive 91/173 (the 9th amendment to the marketing and use Directive 76/769, which relates to pentachlor-ophenol and its salts and esters), Germany was allowed by the European Commission to introduce more stringent controls than those of the Directive on the basis of the exemption of Article 100A(4).[26]

2–027   Where the environmental controls imposed by member states differ, this is liable to have an effect on trade between them, creating a direct conflict with the objectives of paragraphs (a) and (c) of Article 3 of the Treaty, namely: "the elimination as between member states, of customs, duties and quantitative restrictions on the import and export of goods, and of all other measures having equivalent effect" and "an internal market characterised by the abolition, as between member states, of obstacles to the free movement of goods, persons, services, and capital". The issue came before the European Court in the so-called "Danish Bottles" case[27] that concerned Danish legislation whereby beverage bottles (subject to certain minor exceptions) could only be used in Denmark if a satisfactory system for their re-use was established. It was argued by the Commission, and not seriously disputed by Denmark, that this legislation significantly hampered imports of beverages in glass bottles into Denmark from other member states. Nevertheless, it was held that national legislation aimed at protecting the environment but promoting the re-use of glass beverage containers was consistent with the environmental protection objectives that had been written into the Treaty by the Single

---

[25] See Krämer *Focus on European Environmental Law* (Sweet & Maxwell, 1992) pp. 180–182.
[26] This dispensation has been struck down by the European Court of Justice, but on procedural grounds that do not address the substantive questions. Case C-41/93, *France v. Commission*, (1994) 233 ENDS Report 43.
[27] Case 302/86, *Commission v. Denmark*, [1988] E.C.R. 460.

European Act. Accordingly these could be given effect, notwithstanding that they created obstacles to trade between Member States. In the case in point, the court found that the Danish legislation had in certain respects gone beyond what was reasonably necessary for environmental protection, and to that extent it was declared unlawful. Nevertheless, the basic principle was established that Member States may introduce reasonable measures for environmental protection, notwithstanding the consequences on trade within the Common Market.[28]

This case provided a precedent for *The Commission v. Belgium*,[29] which related to a prohibition by the region of Wallonia on the import of waste into its territory from outside. Following *Danish Bottles*, it was held that environmental considerations could have priority over internal market considerations, and that such a prohibition was legitimate if it was reasonably necessary for the purpose of protecting the environment.[30]

2–028

Imposition of measures designed to protect the environment must however respect the principles laid down in *Cassis de Dijon*, and accordingly where they create an effect on trade between Member States, this must be no more than is a necessary consequence of the environmental protection measures. Though the matter was never determined by the European Court of Justice, German legislation requiring deposits to be paid on mineral water bottles of plastics material had a disproportionate effect on imports of such bottled water from France. Proceedings were threatened against Germany by the

2–029

[28] See also Case 240/83 *Procureur de la République v. Association de défense des brûleurs d'huiles usagées*, ((1985) E.C.R. 531), concerning the compatibility with the Rome Treaty of Directive 75/439 on the disposal of waste oil, in which the court stated:

"The principle of freedom of trade is not to be viewed in absolute terms, but is subject to certain limits justified by the objective of general interest pursued by the Community, provided that the rights in question are not substantively impaired . . . The directive must be seen in the perspective of environmental protection, which is one of the Community's essential objectives."

[29] Case C-2/90, [1993] 1 C.M.L.R. 365.

[30] Though imports of hazardous waste could not be prohibited in this way, since Directive 78/319 was already in place harmonising national laws in this respect. The court relied on acceptance by the Commission of an assertion that "an abnormal, massive influx of waste had taken place from other regions for the purpose of dumping in Wallonia, thus constituting a genuine threat to the environment in view of the Region's limited capacity" (judgment, para. 31). Since Wallonia must be presumed to have control over its own waste disposal facilities and the transport of waste to them, the asserted threat to the environment seems improbable. Without this, a total ban on imports of non-hazardous waste—though permitting hazardous waste—would appear to be a plainly disproportionate measure for protecting the environment, and so impermissible. Even so, raising the price of disposing of waste in Wallonia, the normal market response to strong demand, would presumably also have prevented the "massive influx" in a far less restrictive way.

Commission, but not pursued, since the legislation was withdrawn on the introduction of the German law on packaging waste.

2–030   The question of which of the two articles is appropriate for an environmental measure was first taken to the European Court in a case concerning Directive 89/428 on titanium dioxide waste.[31] The Directive had been proposed under Article 100A but adopted unanimously by the Council after amendment of the basis to Article 130S. The European Court supported the position of the European Commission and held that in certain cases, such as the one in issue, both articles may be applicable. It pointed out that since paragraph 4 of Article 100A refers to harmonisation measures taking as their basis a high level of environmental protection, and that Article 130R states that environmental protection shall be a component of the Community's other policies, it is evident that the mere fact that a measure relates to environmental protection does not automatically mean that only Article 130S can be applicable. Where both Articles 100A and 130S apply, Article 100A with its associated co-operation procedure should have priority, since otherwise the European Parliament would be deprived of its legitimate role under the Rome Treaty. The Directive was thus declared void, and was re-introduced under the correct Article 100A as Directive 92/112.[32]

2–031   Shortly afterwards, the Commission started further proceedings in respect of Directive 91/156, which lays down a new basis for the definition and handling of waste. Again, this was proposed by the Commission under Article 100A, but adopted by the Council under Article 130S. On this occasion, however, the court found in favour of the Council, supporting adoption under Article 130S.[33] In an apparent withdrawal from the firm position adopted in the titanium dioxide case, it argued that although there were elements of harmonization contained in the waste directive, its predominant purpose was protection of the environment, for which Article 130S is intended. By contrast, Directive 91/689 relating to hazardous waste is clearly a harmonisation measure and was both proposed and adopted under Article 100A. While this conflict between the articles may become somewhat less intense given that the Parliament has increased influence in both cases following implementation of the Maastricht Treaty, it has to be accepted that currently the rationale for choosing one article rather than the other remains unsatisfactorily ill-defined. This can have significant practical consequences, given that not only is

---

[31] Case C-300/89, *Commission v. Council*, [1991] E.C.R. I-2867; [1993] 3 C.M.L.R. 359.
[32] [1992] O.J. L409, 31.12.92.
[33] Case C-155/91, *Commission v. Council*, so far unreported. Similarly also Case C-187/93, *European Parliament v. Council, Financial Times*, July 5, 1994, concerning Regulation 259/93 on shipments of waste.

an EC measure void that is adopted on the wrong legal basis, but so also is any implementing United Kingdom legislation that is based solely on section 2(2) of the European Communities Act 1972.

National Implementation of EC Legislation

EC environmental legislation is mostly in the form of Directives, though more recently it has increasingly turned to legislation by way of Regulation. Regulations have direct effect immediately on their coming into force and, in principle at least, require no domestic legislation to implement them. In practice, however, this is often needed in order to set up appropriate administrative structures and, for example, to provide for penalties for breach of a Regulation's requirements. A Directive, on the other hand, "shall be binding, as to the result to be achieved, upon each member state to which it is addressed, but shall leave to the national authorities the choice of form and methods".[34] Accordingly Regulations are used where uniformity is required, typically where international conventions are to be given effect.[35] They have also become used where there are strong reasons for ensuring identical implementation in all Member States, *e.g.* in relation to shipments of waste,[36] to overcome the quite frequent substantial delays and other failures by Member States to implement Directives in time or at all.

2–032

Unlike Regulations, a Directive cannot place legal obligations on individuals and most other legal persons unless and until it has been given effect in national law by implementing legislation—every Directive specifies a final date for this.[36A] Nevertheless, it is not uncommon for the requisite legislation either not to have been brought into effect by the implementation date, or else for it to have failed to give full effect to the Directive's requirements. In these circumstances, the doctrine of "direct effect" is of particular importance. The European Court of Justice has expressed this doctrine in the following terms:

2–033

"(W)herever the provisions of a Directive appear, as far as their subject matter is concerned, to be unconditional and sufficiently precise, those provisions may, in the absence of implementing measures adopted within the prescribed period, be relied upon

---

[34] Rome Treaty, Art. 189.
[35] For example the phasing out of CFCs, halons and other ozone-depleting compounds.
[36] See Reg. 259/93.
[36A] *Paola Faccini Dori v. Recreb Srl*, (E.C.J.), Case C-91/92, *The Times*, August 4, 1994.

... in so far as the provisions define rights which individuals are able to assert against the state."[37]

2–034   Consequently, a Member State that has failed to comply with the requirements imposed on it by a Directive within the prescribed period may not plead, as against individuals, its own failure to perform these obligations. Nevertheless the direct effect doctrine only gives individuals rights as against "the state" and not against other individuals. However for this purpose "the state" has received a wide interpretation in a series of decisions of the European Court,[38] and includes independent authorities responsible for the maintenance of public order and safety, and public authorities providing public health services. All such bodies are regarded as "emanations of the state" and accordingly capable of being directly subject to the obligations of a Directive. What constitutes an "emanation of the state" has been defined in the following terms:[39]

> "It follows from the foregoing that a body, whatever its legal form, which has been made responsible, pursuant to a measure adopted by the state, for providing a public service under the control of the state, and has for that purpose special powers beyond those which result from the normal rules applicable in relations between individuals, is included in any event among the bodies against which the provisions of a Directive capable of having direct effect may be relied upon."

2–035   In the case in question, British Gas Corporation (*i.e.* the publicly owned body before privatisation) was held to be directly subject to a Directive relating to equal treatment of men and women as regards retirement ages. The quotation from *Foster* makes it clear that the mere fact that a body may be in private ownership does not automatically exclude it from being an emanation of the state—the question is whether it has the special responsibilities and powers that the Court referred to. On receiving the judgment of the European Court, the House of Lords gave extensive consideration as to whether British Gas Corporation had the responsibilities and powers referred to and held that it had.[40] Conversely, the mere fact that the state may own a majority, or even all, of a company's share capital does not automatically make that company an emanation of the state. As was observed in

---

[37] Case 8/81, *Becker v. Finanzamt Münster—Innenstadt*: [1982] E.C.R. 53; [1982] 1 C.M.L.R. 499; Case 152/84, *Marshall v. Southampton and South-West Hampshire Area Health Authority*: [1986] E.C.R. 723, [1986] 1 C.M.L.R. 688.

[38] See the judgments cited in paragraph [19] of the judgment in Case C-188/89 *Foster and Ors. v. British Gas plc*: [1990] 1 E.C.R. 3313, [1990] 2 C.M.L.R. 833; [1990] 3 All E.R. 897.

[39] *Foster v. British Gas*, Judgment, para. [20].

[40] [1991] 2 A.C. 306; [1991] 2 W.L.R. 1075; [1991] 2 All E.R. 705.

Doughty v. Rolls-Royce plc,[41] a case which turned on whether a Directive was binding on Rolls-Royce by virtue solely of all its shares being owned by the government, the House of Lords in *Foster* would not have devoted the time they did to the responsibilities and powers of British Gas had the majority control held by the state been a sufficient criterion on its own. In *Doughty* it was held that, although 100 per cent owned by the state, Rolls-Royce plc behaved at all times as a commercial company and had no special responsibilities and powers such as to make directives directly binding on it. The question nevertheless still remains as to whether privatised industries subject to regulation, in particular the water and sewerage undertakers, are capable of being directly bound by directives on the basis of *Foster*; in view of the controls placed on them, by statute and through their Licences, it is at least clearly an arguable point.[41A]

The ability to claim damages was taken one stage further in the joined cases of *Francovich and Bonifaci and Others v. Italy.*[42] The plaintiffs were employed by a privately owned company that went into liquidation owing them wages. An EC Directive that would have ensured their being guaranteed at least three months wages in these circumstances had not been implemented by Italy by the due date. The case was referred to the European Court of Justice, which held that the Directive concerned did not have direct effect, since it was impossible to identify the institutions that might be liable under the guarantee to be given pursuant to the Directive. However the court went on to hold that a Member State is obliged to make good the damage to individuals caused by a breach of Community law for which it is responsible, provided three conditions are satisfied:

2–036

   (i)   The Directive confers rights on individuals for their benefit;
  (ii)   The content of these rights may be determined by reference to the provisions of the Directive;
 (iii)   There is a causal link between the breach of the obligation on the state and the damage suffered by those affected.

The court added that any conditions as to both substance and form for the recovery of damages laid down by the applicable national laws may not be less favourable than those relating to similar claims under national law, nor may they be so framed as to render the recovery of damages excessively difficult or impossible in practice.

---

[41] [1992] I.R.L.R. 126.
[41A] In *Griffin & ors v. South West Water Services* (August 25, 1994, unreported), an action concerning an employment directive, Blackburne J. applied *Foster* and held that the defendant, a water and sewerage undertaker, was a "state authority against which a person may rely upon provisions of EU directives in domestic courts and tribunals".
[42] Cases C-6/90, C-9/90, [1991] 1 ECR 5354, [1992] I.R.L.R. 84.

2–037   National courts must, where possible, give effect to European Community legislation. Thus in *Von Colson*, the European Court stated:

> "It is for the national court to interpret and apply the legislation adopted for the implementation of the directive in conformity with the requirements of Community law, in so far as it is given discretion to do so under national law."[43]

2–038   Similarly, in applying national law, the national court should interpret it, as far as possible, in the light of the wording and purpose of any relevant EC directive, whether the national law originated before or after adoption of the directive.[44] Though this is expressly stated in the European Court's judgment in *Marleasing*, it is strongly arguable that it is not within its powers to lay down rules for interpretation of national legislation. Courts in the United Kingdom will undoubtedly seek to give effect to domestic legislation in a manner that is consistent with a directive that it is intended to implement. Indeed where the domestic legislation is evidently intended to give effect to a directive, the Courts have a duty to give it a purposive construction, implying further words if necessary, to achieve that. In *Litster v. Forth Dry Dock & Engineering Co. Ltd.*[45] a construction of United Kingdom Regulations was thus adopted that it was said would be impermissible if they were to be read on their own.[46] A Court should not come to a decision that would result in the United Kingdom being in breach of its Treaty obligations "in the absence of the most compulsive context rendering any other conclusion impossible".[47] If it is compelled to do so in any such case, its proper course would be to acknowledge the inconsistency and apply the UK legislation (if it is valid), where either the Directive does not have direct effect or, if it does, it cannot be relied on in an action between private parties. An injured party may seek a remedy in damages from the government, following *Francovich*. In *R. v. Secretary of State for the Environment and others, ex p. Greenpeace Ltd.*[47A] it was held that there is a legal obligation to consider whether there is justification for any releases of radioactivity, before granting any authorisations under sections 13 and 16 of the Radioactive Substances Act 1993 that

---

[43] Case 14/83, *Von Colson and Kamann v. Land Nordrhein-Westfalen*: [1986] 2 C.M.L.R. 430.
[44] Case C-106/89, *Marleasing S.A. v. La Comercial Internacional de Elementacion S.A.*: [1992] 1 C.M.L.R. 305.
[45] [1990] 1 A.C. 546; [1989] 2 W.L.R. 634.
[46] *per* Lord Oliver at 576F.
[47] *per* Lord Oliver at 563C. See also *Webb v. EMO Air Cargo Ltd.*, [1993] 1 W.L.R. 49, at 59; [1992] 4 All E.R. 929, at 939.
[47A] [1994] Env.L.R. D10

would permit such releases, even though the statute is completely silent on this point. the statute had to be so construed in order to incorporate the justification principle contained in Articles 6 and 13 of the underlying Euratom Directive 80/836.[47B]

Nevertheless, a Directive cannot have the effect by itself, independently of national implementing legislation, of creating or extending criminal liabilities on those who fail to comply with it.[48] Consequently, if implementing national legislation does not clearly extend to a situation that is in fact within the scope of a Directive, it is not for the national court to attempt to stretch the national legislation in order to make it fit the Directive and thereby impose criminal sanctions that would not otherwise be imposed. As was argued by the Advocate-General in *Vessoso* and *Zanetti*,[49] it is for the national courts to consider if national legislation in question can be interpreted in accordance with any applicable Directives without recourse to an extensive interpretation that would be contrary to this principle that criminal liability should not arise by virtue only of the Directive.

2–039

The supremacy of EC law over domestic law is demonstrated by the series of cases involving the attempt of the UK government to legislate to give fishing rights to British registered fishing vessels but to exclude any such that were managed and controlled from Spain. Following a ruling by the European Court that if, in a case concerning Community law, the only obstacle to granting relief is a rule of national law, that rule must be set aside, the House of Lords held that, in an appropriate case, if a court finds that primary (or any other) UK legislation is contrary to the Treaty of Rome it may grant an injunction restraining enforcement of the legislation.[50]

2–040

The translation of international conventions and European Community legislation into United Kingdom law is effected in a variety of ways. By contrast with many other countries,[51] international treaties generally create no legal rights or obligations whatsoever within the United Kingdom, unless and until they are incorporated in UK or

2–041

[47B] [1980] O.J. L246.

[48] Case 14/86 *Pretore di Salo v. X*: [1987] E.C.R. 2545; Case 80/86 *Kolpinghuis Nijmegen*: [1987] E.C.R. 3969.

[49] Joint cases 206/88 and 207/88; (1990) 184 ENDS Report 30; material parts of the judgment are reproduced in Annex 7 of DoE Circular 14/92 (WO 30/92; SOEND 24/92) on The Controlled Waste Regulations 1992.

[50] *R. v. Secretary of State for Transport, ex p. Factortame Limited and others (No. 2)*, [1991] 1 A.C. 603; [1991] 1 All E.R. 70; for the principles to be applied to applications for interim relief, see *R. v. HM Treasury, ex p. British Telecommunications plc, The Times* December 2, 1993.

[51] Under whose constitutions international treaties may be self-executing, *i.e.* they form part of domestic law either immediately on ratification or by way of a formal vote of approval in their parliament.

binding EC legislation.[52] Accordingly, national obligations under an international convention may be complied with by way of government policies relating to the environment, including the provision or withholding of financial resources for particular activities or bodies and the issue of guidance or instructions to local authorities and other administrative organisations, often by way of Departmental Circulars.

2–042   Where EC legislation requires implementation into domestic law, however, the principle of legal certainty requires that this be done in a manner that permits legal challenge in the courts.[53] Nevertheless, even where appropriate implementing legislation is in place, official guidance, such as Departmental Circulars, is frequently issued to the administrative bodies concerned. This often provides valuable assistance to those affected by the legislation in ascertaining how it is likely to be applied to them in practice; such guidance may also form the basis of an application for judicial review of an unsatisfactory decision, where the guidance may be said to be inconsistent with the requirements of the underlying EC legislation.

2–043   The right to challenge, by way of judicial review, not only Ministerial and other decisions, but also the validity under EC law of United Kingdom legislation and of acts not amounting to decisions, has been established by the House of Lords in *R. v. Secretary of State for Employment, ex p. Equal Opportunities Commission and another*.[53A] Nevertheless, the holding in that case that the Equal Opportunities Commission had *locus standi* was on the basis of its "statutory duties and public law role",[53B] and so in terms that would *prima facie* exclude private bodies whose objects include the protection of the environment, such as the RSPB and Greenpeace (though extending to *e.g.* English Nature and, probably, the National Trust). In other cases both the RSPB and Greenpeace, as well as other private bodies, have in fact been regarded as having standing, and indeed the intervention of a body with both relevant expertise and the resources to meet any possible award of costs against it has been positively approved.[53C] It is however arguable that in these other cases they only obtained

---

[52] Nevertheless, treaties to which the EC is itself a party have sometimes been held by the European Court to have direct effect in national law, though the case law on this aspect is not consistent.

[53] See, *e.g.* Case 102/79, *EEC Commission v. Belgium*, [1980] E.C.R. 1473; [1981] 1 C.M.L.R. 282 and [1982] 2 C.M.L.R. 622; Case 145/82, *EEC Commission v. Italy*: [1983] E.C.R. 711; [1984] 1 C.M.L.R. 148.

[53A] [1994] 2 W.L.R. 409.

[53B] *per* Lord Keith of Kinkel, at p. 418.

[53C] *R. v. H.M.I.P. and M.A.F.F. ex p. Greenpeace*, [1994] Env.L.R. 76, at 100–102; *R v. Swale B.C. and Medway Ports Authority, ex p. R.S.P.B.*, [1991] J.P.L. 39. See also *R. v. Minister of Agriculture, Fisheries and Food ex p. Bell Lines and An Bord Bainne Co-operative Ltd.*, [1984] 2 C.M.L.R. 502; *Padfield v. Minister of Agriculture, Fisheries and Food*, [1968] AC 997, [1968] 1 All E.R. 694, [1968] 2 W.L.R. 924.

standing on the basis of their previous participation in relevant planning procedures, a basis that would not normally be available in any general challenge to the validity of legislation. Certainly there is consistent unwillingness to allow *locus* to individuals or *ad hoc* groups, except where they have been directly affected by the subject of the review.

The Three Jurisdictions of the United Kingdom

The United Kingdom consists of three distinct jurisdictions, namely   **2–044**
England and Wales, Scotland and Northern Ireland. Legislation, whether acts of Parliament or statutory instruments, may apply to the entire United Kingdom, or to the individual jurisdictions; quite frequently legislation may apply to all of Great Britain, *i.e.* England, Wales and Scotland, but excluding Northern Ireland. It is always essential therefore, when considering any individual piece of legislation, to establish the territory to which it applies. Thus, for example, the Environmental Protection Act 1990 generally applies to England, Wales and Scotland (though certain sections either do not apply to Scotland or apply exclusively there), whereas relatively few provisions apply to Northern Ireland.[54] By contrast, the bulk of the Water Act 1989, most of which was consolidated with other legislation into the Water Resources Act 1991 and the Water Industry Act 1991, among others, generally applied to England and Wales only, though two extensive schedules amended Part II of the Control of Pollution Act 1974, which continued thereafter to apply to Scotland only, instead of the whole of Great Britain, as previously.

England and Wales

The Legal System (England and Wales)

In England and Wales, civil and criminal cases are dealt with by   **2–045**
separate courts. Criminal cases are begun in the magistrates courts; following committal for trial they may remain there or be sent to the Crown Courts. Except in the larger conurbations, where there may be

---

[54] These include amendment of the radioactive substances legislation, and several of the miscellaneous controls contained in Part VIII; also certain provisions of Part VI, relating to the importation of genetically modified organisms, are applicable in Northern Ireland so as to ensure implementation of the relevant EC legislation.

a legally qualified stipendiary magistrate sitting alone, the magistrates' court consists of (normally three) lay people, advised on the law by a legally qualified court clerk. Appeals from the magistrates' courts are taken to the Crown Courts, though points of law may frequently be referred to a divisional court of the Queens Bench Division by way of judicial review. Civil cases, involving only moderate sums are normally heard in the County Courts[55]; the High Court has concurrent jurisdiction over these, but a matter started in the High Court that is within the jurisdiction of the County Court may either be transferred there, or, even if it is not, any award of costs may, if the court thinks fit, be calculated on the less generous County Court scale. The Court of Criminal Appeal hears appeals from the Crown Courts, while the Court of Appeal hears civil cases. In the High Court, the judges normally sit alone, whereas in the Court of Appeal there will normally be three judges, though frequently only two may sit, particularly on interlocutory applications. Cases may only be taken further on appeal to the House of Lords with leave. This may be granted by the Court of Appeal; if leave is refused at that stage, it is open to the party or parties to petition the Appellate Committee of the House of Lords, who will decide whether or not to grant leave.

The Regulatory System (England and Wales)

2–046   The first environmental measure involving national regulation was the Alkali Works Act 1863, which provided for an Alkali Inspectorate. The Inspectorate's function in practice was as much to provide technical information and instruction, assisting industrial organisations to comply with the air emission controls imposed on them, as it was regulatory. The Alkali Inspectorate retained its historical name for many years, during which the number and variety of "scheduled processes" covered by the Alkali, etc., Works Act 1906 increased substantially, but eventually it was transformed into the Industrial Air Pollution Inspectorate. After the Second World War the Radiochemical Inspectorate was established under the legislation controlling nuclear energy and radioactive substances, while the Hazardous Waste Inspectorate was formed as a central organisation to co-ordinate the controls over hazardous waste exercised by the waste disposal authorities at county and (in Wales) district level. These three inspectorates were combined into Her Majesty's Inspectorate of Pollution (HMIP) in 1987. HMIP, though part of the Department of the Environment, nevertheless operates as an independent inspectorate. Its principal responsibilities are the regulation of processes subject to

---

[55] The small claims courts have jurisdiction over minor matters.

"integrated pollution control", *i.e.* Part A processes subject to Part I of the E.P.A., the operation of the Radioactive Substances Act 1993, and in addition, the discharge of "special category effluent" (*i.e.* trade effluent containing certain hazardous substances) to sewer, under the Water Industry Act 1991. Its duties and responsibilities are described in its "Charter Statement"— "Pollution Prevention: Our Common Concern".[56]

Water was originally under the control of local authorities, whose primary concern in practice was to ensure effective drainage of their areas rather than to cope with the pollution of rivers and streams that was an inevitable consequence. Following the Local Government Act 1888, enforcement powers were transferred to County Councils, and also a number of river boards were set up. In the 1920s and 1930s, various Fishery Boards and Catchment Boards were established that did not necessarily conform with local authority boundaries, but were related to the areas of river basins. These boards formed the basis of 32 river boards created by the River Boards Act 1948. Further re-organisation followed the Water Act 1973, which created ten all-purpose water authorities throughout England and Wales, which had both operational and regulatory functions. Their regulatory functions were hived out into the National Rivers Authority (the NRA) by the Water Act 1989. The functions of the NRA are now laid down in the Water Resources Act 1991.[57] Broadly they relate to the management of water resources, the control of water pollution, flood defence and land drainage, and fisheries; it also acts as a navigation authority, harbour authority and conservancy authority. It is subject to broad duties to conserve and enhance the natural beauty and amenity of inland and coastal waters and land associated with them, the conservation of flora and fauna that are dependent on an aquatic environment, and the use of the waters and land for which they are responsible for recreational purposes.

2–047

These duties are reinforced by more specific obligations set out in sections 16 to 18 of the Water Resources Act 1991. These include requirements to have regard to the desirability of preserving freedom of access for the public to places of natural beauty, both inland and on the shore; to secure, so far as reasonably practicable and consistent with fulfilment by the NRA of its functions, that water and land to which it has rights are made available for recreational purposes; and to consult with any relevant authority before carrying out any activities likely to destroy or damage any of the flora, fauna or other features by reason of which a site is of special scientific interest, or likely to

2–048

[56] HMIP, February 1994.
[57] s.2.

prejudice significantly anything of particular importance in relation to such a site.

2–049   Essentially identical obligations are placed on the Secretary of State for the Environment, the Minister of Agriculture, Fisheries and Food, the Director General of Water Services, and every water and sewerage undertaker, by sections 3 and 4 of the Water Industry Act 1991, and on the Secretary of State, the Minister of Agriculture, Fisheries and Food, the NRA, internal drainage boards and local authorities by sections 61A to 61D of the Land Drainage Act 1991.[57A] These various bodies are required to observe any relevant codes of practice in respect of these obligations[58]; such a code of practice was issued under the corresponding provision of the Water Act 1989.[59]

2–050   Processes that did not come within the scope of the Alkali, etc., Works Act 1906, were subject to control by local authorities under statutory nuisance legislation. This division of responsibilities has been maintained under the Environmental Protection Act whereby HMIP is responsible for Part A processes, while local authorities are responsible for air pollution from Part B processes (see Chapters 10 and 11), and also continue to be responsible for taking enforcement action against statutory nuisances created by any others (see Chapter 23).

2–051   Legislation, the Environment Bill, is now in hand that will lead eventually to the NRA, HMIP and the waste regulation authorities being combined into a single Environment Agency for England and Wales. A Government consultation paper[60] initially canvassed four main options for the rôle and functions of the Agency:

(1) Combining HMIP and waste regulation (only) into a single body, leaving the NRA to operate separately.

(2) Creating a new umbrella body, co-ordinating the work of HMIP and the NRA, which would nevertheless remain separate. Waste regulation would either come under the control of HMIP or be administered by a third body under the umbrella.

(3) Forming a fully integrated Agency, combining the functions of HMIP and of the waste regulation authorities with all those of the NRA.

(4) Forming an integrated Agency as in (3), but taking in only the pollution control functions of the NRA, which would be left

---

[57A] As amended by the Land Drainage Act 1994.
[58] W.R.A., s.18; W.I.A., s.5; L.D.A., s.61E.
[59] Code of Practice on Conservation, Access and Recreation, July 1989.
[60] "Improving Environmental Quality—The Government's Proposals for a New Independent Environment Agency", October 1991.

with responsibility solely for operational matters, such as the management of water resources and responding to pollution incidents.

Eventually the Government decided in favour of option (3), so that **2–052** the new Agency will have all the operational functions of the NRA— there had been considerable pressure from some quarters, including the House of Commons Environment Committee[61] for option (4), and moving operational responsibilities to the control of the Ministry of Agriculture, Fisheries and Food. The Agency is likely to be built up on a similar structure to that of the NRA; perhaps the most substantial immediate change will be the bringing together of the 86 currently separate waste regulation authorities.

Scotland

The Legal System (Scotland)

An understanding of the detailed differences between Scots law and **2–053** that of England and Wales will not be required by practitioners of environmental law (a branch of legal practice displaying comparatively few differences of substance, particularly in technical aspects) but a few words on the Scottish court system and procedural differences may be of assistance.

The 1707 Treaty of Union ensured the preservation of Scotland's **2–054** distinctive legal system and while over the years there has been a considerable narrowing of the gap between legal systems north and south of the border, some differences remain, both in practice and procedure. Scots law (which is essentially a civil law system) owes much to Roman Dutch principles and for that reason it has in some instances a closer affinity to EC law (now the progenitor of so much environmental legislation) than does English and Welsh law. The principal sources of Scots law are judicial decisions, the writings of "institutional" authorities on the law, statute law and the law of the European Community.

Criminal Courts

The two main criminal courts are the High Court of Justiciary, which **2–055** deals with more serious offences, and the Sheriff Court, whose

---

[61] First report 1991–1992 "The Government's Proposals for an Environment Agency".

jurisdiction and sentencing powers are more restricted. The High Court which sits both in Edinburgh and "on circuit" around other Scottish cities has both trial and appellate functions, the latter being exercised as the Scottish Court of Criminal Appeal from which there is no appeal to the House of Lords. Criminal procedure is either *solemn*, involving trial before a jury of 15 lay members, when the jury decides on the facts and the judge pronounces on the law, or *summary*, where the judge decides questions of both fact and law. The Sheriff Court can hear cases initiated under both solemn and summary procedures, although most prosecutions are on the latter basis. Solemn procedure is initiated by a document called an Indictment, whereas summary procedure (environmental offences are usually brought on this basis) commence with the service on the accused of a Complaint.

2–056   In Scotland the Lord Advocate is responsible for the prosecution of criminal offences within an administrative framework provided by the Crown Office. Conduct of the Crown case in the High Court is at the hands of Advocates Depute, and in the Sheriff Court of Procurators Fiscal who are full time legally qualified civil servants. It is to Procurators Fiscal that most criminal offences involving environmental matters are referred for prosecution either by the police or by the regulatory agencies including Her Majesty's Industrial Pollution Inspectorate and the River Purification Boards. The latter have no power to initiate prosecutions, unlike the regulatory bodies in England and Wales, and private prosecutions are very rare as the judicial machinery to facilitate such action by members of the public is extremely cumbersome.[62]

Civil Courts

2–057   The Sheriff Court deals with most civil litigation in Scotland. There are six sheriffdoms sub-divided into 49 Sheriff Court districts, each district having its own court. Sheriffs who are legally qualified (either advocates or solicitors) hear cases on a very wide range of issues. Appeals may be taken to the Sheriff Principal or to the Court of Session.

2–058   The Court of Session is Scotland's supreme civil court. It sits only in Edinburgh and currently has 25 judges, in two branches—the Outer House containing 17 Lords Ordinary and the Inner House with two Divisions of four judges each. Most litigation originates in the former as a court of first instance; the principal business of the Inner House is to hear appeals from the Outer House, and from the Sheriff and other

---

[62] This has resulted in complaints of weaker enforcement of environmental controls in Scotland, due to the relative inexperience of the Procurators Fiscal in such matters by comparison with those handling similar prosecutions south of the border.

inferior Courts. The final Court of Appeal in civil matters in Scotland is the House of Lords which will take appeals from the Inner House of the Court of Session, theoretically on both law and fact, although cases on the latter are extremely rare.

In civil procedure the principal initiating writ is a summons and **2–059** thereafter pleadings are adjusted by both sides, the initiator of the action being referred to as the Pursuer and the other litigant as the Defender. If the action concerns disputed fact, the matter is resolved by the hearing of evidence (a Proof) by a judge who may sit on his own or with a jury (12 in number) in, for example, a damages action. Disputes on the law are dealt with by legal debate between opposing counsel. Procedure in the Sheriff Court is very similar. Until recently, one of the main differences was that while advocates had exclusive rights to appear in the Court of Session, most of the litigation in the Sheriff Court was conducted by solicitors. This has recently changed and suitably qualified solicitors (known as Solicitor Advocates) now have right of audience in the Higher Courts.

Other lesser Courts and those of Special Jurisdiction (few of which **2–060** have any relevance to environmental matters) include District Courts (which are the administrative responsibility of local authorities and which are presided over by lay justices of the peace) the Scottish Land Court (with jurisdiction over agricultural tenancy and crofting matters) and the Lands Valuation Appeal Court.

Administration of the Courts (particularly in respect of non-legal **2–061** matters) is the responsibility of the Secretary of State for Scotland through the Government Department known as the Scottish Courts Administration. The Supreme Courts establish their own procedural rules and those of the Sheriff Courts through the appropriate Rules Council. Development and reform of Scots law is entrusted to the Scottish Law Commission.

Precedent

Except in one case, the Scottish Courts are not bound to follow **2–062** decisions from Courts south of the border although facts in English cases may be persuasive and the Scottish courts would almost certainly follow a House of Lords decision on an English appeal if it related to the construction of UK statute. The exception is a decision set by the House of Lords in a Scottish appeal which the Court of Session could not disregard. In the area of environmental law which, as a discrete subject, is a relative newcomer to legal practice and which is developing rapidly but which has, as yet, built up relatively little case law, it is more than likely that the Court of Session would elect to follow a precedent set in an English appeal if it felt that it was a fair representation of general jurisprudence on the matter or if by doing so the Court took the view that it would be saving a litigant the expense of an appeal which he stood little chance of winning.

The Regulatory System (Scotland)

HMIPI

2–063   The underlying structure of enforcement of environmental legislation in Scotland is very similar to that in England and Wales and is based on the same combination of media specific agencies and local authority departments, with proposals for increasingly integrated control under the one roof. Her Majesty's Industrial Pollution Inspectorate (HMIPI) was set up in 1971 and sets emission limits for air pollution, and deals with radioactive substances and oil discharges. It also has input into hazardous waste management through the Hazardous Waste Inspectorate. In addition, it is one of the two enforcing authorities (the other being the River Purification Boards) responsible for implementing the Integrated Pollution Control provisions of the Environmental Protection Act 1990. HMIPI also has an appellate function, hearing a wide variety of appeals against refusal of licences, variation of onerous conditions, etc.

River Purification Boards

2–064   The River Purification Boards were set up under the Rivers (Prevention of Pollution) (Scotland) Act 1951 to establish control over water pollution and to ensure that water quality objectives are met. The seven mainland boards (the three Island Councils act as their own purification authorities) issue consents under Part II of the Control of Pollution Act 1974 (as amended by the Water Act 1989) for direct discharges into inland and coastal waters and also monitor consents, enforce consent conditions and issue reports to the Procurator Fiscal Service for the prosecution of offenders. Membership of the Boards to the extent of one half is from Local Authority representatives and the balance from nominees of the Secretary of State representing industry, local land owners, etc. The Boards, and the Regional and Island Councils in their capacities as water and sewerage authorities, are required to observe a code of practice[63] issued by the Scottish Office, under provisions in the Natural Heritage (Scotland) Act 1991, comparable to that issued for England and Wales for conservation of and access to the countryside—see paragraphs 2.048 and 2.049.

---

[63] "Conservation, Access and Recreation—Code of Practice for Water and Sewerage Authorities and River Purification Authorities", 1993.

Regional Councils

Regional Councils are responsible under the Water (Scotland) Act   **2–065**
1980 for the supply of "wholesome" water for domestic and other
purposes to consumers in their area. Unlike England and Wales, there
is no Drinking Water Inspectorate, policy and monitoring in this
respect being dealt with by the Scottish Office Environment Department. Regional and Island Councils also have a duty to provide
sewerage treatment works which themselves require discharge consents from the River Purification Boards.

District Councils

The District and Island Councils were waste disposal authorities   **2–066**
under Part I of the Control of Pollution Act 1974 and are waste
regulation, disposal and collection authorities under the new waste
management regime brought in under the Environmental Protection
Act 1990, Part II. There is no provision for the transfer of waste disposal
functions from local authorities to arm's length or private waste
disposal contractors, as there is for England and Wales. As well as
licensing the disposal of controlled waste, District and Island Councils
also control the handling of the potentially more harmful special waste
and administer the controls over noise.

The Scottish Office

Overall policy under which more local controls are administered is   **2–067**
set by the Scottish Office through the Environment Department in
Edinburgh. Other Government agencies such as the Department of
Agriculture and Fisheries, the Health and Safety Executive, Scottish
Natural Heritage (combining the functions of the Countryside
Commission and the Nature Conservancy Council in England) have
control functions for other aspects of pollution.

Scottish Environmental Protection Agency

Finally, the Government intends to establish a "one stop shop"   **2–068**
authority to be called the Scottish Environment Protection Agency
("SEPA"). Unlike the position south of the border where the Government originally offered four options, only the one approach is
proposed for Scotland—a fully integrated Agency incorporating the
functions of HMIPI, the River Purification Boards and the local
authorities—to include the latter's functions under the Local Authority Air Pollution Control system established for Part B processes
by Part I of the Environmental Protection Act 1990. Legislation is being

63

brought forward in the 1994/95 session of Parliament with the intention that the new Agency will commence operations in 1996. While the integrated approach to be applied by SEPA will generally be attractive to industry, there is still an underlying feeling in Scotland that there may not be that much at fault with the existing system that could not be remedied by, for example, improved liaison between the existing agencies.

2–069   Major criticisms of the proposal have been directed to a possible lack of accountability at local level and insufficient funding. The new Agency would, however, have its own legal staff and it is to be hoped that this development will greatly improve the existing enforcement record with a higher incidence of reported offences being pursued to conviction.

Northern Ireland

2–070   Northern Ireland is legislated for in a quite different a manner from that used for Great Britain. Since 1974 it has been governed directly under the provisions of the Northern Ireland Act 1974. The effect of this is that the bulk of the environmental (and other) legislation in the Province consists of Orders in Council issued under Schedule 1 to the 1974 Act. It is in the nature of an Order in Council (as it is for secondary legislation generally) that Parliament is not able to amend it, but must either vote for or against it in the form in which it is presented. Although this would appear to make it exceptionally easy for legislation to be introduced there, it has proved to be otherwise in practice, and there is frequently a delay of two or more years between the introduction of legislation in England and its equivalent in Northern Ireland.[64] This has also been the case as regards EC Directives, which have as a consequence frequently been implemented in Northern Ireland long after the due date. Much of the current environmental law in Northern Ireland therefore reflects the position in England and Wales before the new legislation of 1989 and 1990. In some respects, particularly in the field of conservation, the delays in introducing legislation in the province have been substantially longer. The principal legislation in relation to water is the Water Act (Northern Ireland) 1972, while air pollution controls are essentially the same as those operating in England before the implementation of Part I of the E.P.A., and waste disposal is controlled under the relevant Parts of C.O.P.A. 1974.

[64] Several items that have been in force in England for many years have never been introduced into Northern Ireland at all.

The European Environment Agency

Mention may also be made here of the European Environment   2–071
Agency. This was the subject of Council Regulation 1210/90,[65] but
owing to disputes within the Council of Ministers over the siting of the
European Parliament, it was only in late 1993 that it was eventually
decided that the Agency should be based in Denmark; the Regulation
came into force in October 1993 immediately following that decision.
The Agency however has no directly regulatory function, its tasks
being the collection and dissemination of information relating to the
quality of the environment, the pressures on the environment and its
sensitivity to those pressures. It is required to give priority to

- — air quality and atmospheric emissions;
- — water quality, pollutants and water resources;
- — the state of the soil, of the fauna and flora, and of biotopes;
- — land use and natural resources;
- — waste management;
- — noise emissions;
- — chemical substances which are hazardous for the
  environment;
- — coastal protection;

It is particularly required to address "transfrontier, plurinational and
global phenomena" and to take into the account the socio-economic
dimension.[66]

The European Parliament pressed strongly for the European   2–072
Agency to have a regulatory function also. This was not accepted by
the Council of Ministers, but the Regulation expressly provides for a
review of the agency's tasks within two years after its entry into force,
i.e. by October 1995.[67]

---

[65] [1990] O.J. L120.
[66] Art 3.
[67] Art 20.

Chapter 3

THE PLANNING SYSTEM

Introduction

For most individuals, the aspects of their environment of which they   **3–001**
are likely to be most immediately aware consist of the physical
appearance of their surroundings and of the impacts of the activities of
other people, whether at work, at home, at recreation elsewhere, or
travelling. If an environment is to be attractive, controls are necessary,
at least in a crowded island, to seek to preserve, and where possible to
enhance, the visual amenities of the towns and countryside, and to
limit the adverse effects on people of the way in which other members
of the community lead their lives.

Inevitably, many activities that are considered desirable, or indeed   **3–002**
essential, in a modern society are liable to damage the environment. At
least where no irreparable harm is involved, controls designed to limit
the damage from such activities must achieve an acceptable compromise between those adverse effects and maintaining or improving the
external environment.

The regulation of pollution and other hazards to the life or health of   **3–003**
humans and other living things from industrial activities is the subject
of later chapters. This and Chapters 4 to 7 review the controls that
enable the human environment to be protected from adverse impacts
on the senses, and the natural environment from activities liable to
destroy it or materially change its character. Whether, and if so the
manner in which, these controls are in fact exercised in any particular
instance is usually a matter for political decision on a case by case
basis. Except in relation to a relatively small number of designated
sites, their purpose is not automatically to restrain activities that may
damage the environment, or even those that are bound to do so, but to
try to ensure that such damage as otherwise desirable developments
are likely to cause is on balance acceptable, and is no more than is
reasonably unavoidable in achieving their benefits. These controls are
exercised very largely through the planning system, though other

legislation relating to nature conservation, water abstraction, land drainage and flood defences, is also vitally important.

3–004   Excellent works on the British planning legislation already exist[1] and no attempt is made here to duplicate them. Nevertheless an outline is included, since an appreciation of the system is essential to an overall understanding of how environmental protection is achieved in Great Britain. More particularly, a discussion of the law relating to environmental assessments[2] necessarily requires a background knowledge of the planning law of which, in Great Britain, it is nearly always in practice an integral part.

3–005   It should be noted that the development control regime in Northern Ireland, although it generally follows that of England and Wales, constitutes a separate legislative system. The main difference is that the Department of the Environment for Northern Ireland is the planning authority. This chapter does not deal with the detail of the Northern Ireland system although many of the general principles are substantially the same in practice. Likewise the Scottish system is based on separate legislation and guidance separate from that of England and Wales, although the main principles are the same.

The Planning System—General

3–006   "Planning control" is the regime of control over the use of land operated primarily by planning authorities. It has three distinct components:

(i)   the statutory framework;

(ii)   planning policies issued by the Department of the Environment, which also grants general planning permissions such as the Town and Country Planning General Development Order 1988[3] for limited types of developments;

(iii) the exercise of discretion by local planning authorities in their preparation of local plans and when considering and

---

[1] e.g. *Planning Law and Procedure*, Purdue, Young and Rowan-Robinson (Butterworths, 1989); *Urban Planning Law* Grant, Sweet & Maxwell, 1982, (updated by supplement); *Scottish Planning Law and Procedure*, Young and Rowan-Robinson (William Hodge, 1985); Blundell & Dobry's *Planning Appeals & Inquiries*, Carnwath (Sweet & Maxwell 4th ed., 1990); *Encyclopedia of Planning Law and Practice* (Sweet & Maxwell) (loose-leaf with regular updates). However all, with the exception of the Encyclopedia, are somewhat out of date and do not deal with the recently consolidated legislation.
[2] In Chapter 4.
[3] S.I. 1988 No. 1813 (as amended).

determining individual planning applications, imposing conditions on planning permissions, and negotiating agreements with landowners governing the use of land.

Planning control is therefore the product of a mixture of law, policy documents, and individual decisions by planning authorities; it is implemented at three levels, namely national, county and district.[4]

The modern planning system dates from July 1947 when the Town and Country Planning Act of that year came into force. This brought under control all new development by requiring that prior planning permission should be obtained for any "material change of use" or any "operations". Unlike previous legislative attempts to control development, which had tackled some aspects of planning, the 1947 Act was comprehensive. Agriculture and forestry were the only significant forms of activity which were left outside its control — that remains largely so. The primary statute is currently the Town and Country Planning Act 1990 (the "T.C.P.A."), which consolidates earlier legislation.

Planning permission does not necessarily deal with all aspects of a development; other consents may also be required, for example under the Environmental Protection Act 1990, the Planning (Hazardous Substances) Act 1990, the Planning (Listed Building and Conservation Areas) Act 1990, the Ancient Monuments and Archaeological Areas Act 1979, and, in the case of tree preservation orders, under Part VIII of the T.C.P.A.

The Department of the Environment issues national guidance from time to time in the form of planning circulars and, more recently, planning policy guidance notes ("PPGs"). These do not have the force of law, nor are they subject to independent scrutiny in the way in which, for example, local plans are scrutinised; nor can they be challenged in the courts. Nevertheless they exercise an enormous influence on the manner in which planning control is exercised. Effectively, they are politically determined ground rules within which planning authorities must operate.

Applications for planning permission are determined by the local planning authority for the site in question, this generally being the district council. An applicant who is dissatisfied with the decision on his application can appeal to the Secretary of State for the Environment. There is no right of appeal in respect of the grant of planning

3–007

3–008

3–009

3–010

---

[4] In some parts of the country, for example the Lake District, there are special planning authorities whose jurisdiction extends across administrative boundaries; the following comments do not deal with those special cases.

permission (except to the extent that an applicant can appeal in respect of conditions attached to a permission).[5]

3–011   An appeal in respect of a planning authority's decision is made to the Department of the Environment. The decision in well over 90 per cent of appeals is delegated to a planning Inspector, who is a full time official of the Planning Inspectorate, an Executive Agency in the Department of the Environment and the Welsh Office.

3–012   The role of the courts in the planning process is very circumscribed. It is possible to challenge planning decisions in the courts, but only by way of judicial review. Consequently such a challenge can be done only on very limited grounds[6] for example, a procedural irregularity, and the courts will not, save in very exceptional circumstances, review the merits of a planning authority's decision. Even if a court overturns a planning decision, this does not mean that the decision is reversed, turning a grant of planning permission into a refusal of planning permission or *vice versa*; the effect of a successful legal challenge is that the application is sent back to the authority to be re-determined. Anyone mounting a legal challenge to a planning decision, with a view to having it reversed, must therefore consider the practical chances of persuading the relevant authority to reach a different decision when it re-determines the application.

3–013   The courts are also concerned with enforcement of planning control, but generally only as a last resort. If all other remedies have failed, the planning authority can take court proceedings either to restrain action by an injunction or to prosecute a person for any offence under the planning legislation as may have been committed.

Scotland

3–014   Planning law in Scotland has not as yet been subjected to the same degree of consolidation as has its counterpart south of the border and the principal statute is still the Town and Country Planning (Scotland) Act 1972, establishing the underlying definition of development and providing for development plans, the procedure for applying and awarding planning permission, the enforcement of planning control and the use of planning agreements, amongst others. Important changes to the 1972 Act were made by the Planning and Compensation Act 1991, Parts II and IV of which apply exclusively to Scotland.

---

[5] This may be contrasted with the right of third parties with a legitimate interest to do so in most continental European jurisdictions.
[6] See para. 3–095.

Generally speaking, however, the substantive law is the same. The major difference as far as Scotland is concerned is that the P.C.A. did not affect the development plan system. There is a multitude of other planning statutes which require to be consulted in conjunction with the 1972 Act and the system is quite clearly crying out for further consolidation.

As far as subordinate legislation is concerned, there has been 3–015 considerable recent revision made in respect of both procedure and permitted development rights. Detailed procedures on applying for planning permission, appealing against a decision (or failure by the Authority to determine the matter) are prescribed by the Town and Country Planning (General Development Procedure) (Scotland) Order 1992.[6A] The control of permitted development is dealt with under the Town & Country Planning (General Permitted Development) (Scotland) Order 1992,[6B] replacing the 28 former "classes" of permitted development with 27 "parts".

As with other regulatory bodies, the Secretary of State for Scotland 3–016 exercises overall control through the Scottish Office Environment Department. Scottish policy has similarities with English/Welsh policy, but it is tailored specifically for Scottish circumstances. Regional Councils draw up Structure Plans and for those Regions with a two tier planning system the District Councils, as "District Planning Authorities" prepare and review the Local Plans. Borders, Dumfries and Galloway and Highland Regions and the three Island Councils operate a single tier system and are known as "general planning authorities".

There is a comprehensive series of policy statements giving advice 3–017 on the implementation of planning policy at all levels. National Planning Policy Guidelines provide statements of Government policy on nationally important land use and other planning matters. Circulars contain guidance on policy implementation through legislative or procedural changes and Planning Advice Notes give advice on good practice and other relevant information. Structure and Local Plans at the appropriate level also provide guidance.

As far as the law on "mainstream" planning procedures is con- 3–018 cerned, apart from some differences in terminology there is little of substance to differentiate the two systems. Indeed, English planning cases are often cited in Scottish appeals partly because of the comparative dearth of cases in point in Scotland. Decisions of the House of Lords in Scottish planning appeals are binding on the Scottish Courts. The Court of Session exercises a general supervisory

[6A] S.I. 1992 No. 24.
[6B] S.I. 1992 No. 223 (s.17).

control over the planning system in Scotland and "aggrieved persons" can appeal to it in respect of any decision by the Secretary of State in a planning matter or to challenge the validity of say a local plan. The Court of Session will also entertain applications for judicial review of planning authority decisions and the indications are that the Courts are taking a more relaxed view of who in addition to an applicant may have a justifiable right of complaint by this route and accept the relevance of environmental interests in determining this.

Environmental Protection through Planning Controls and Guidance

3–019   The help which the basic planning system can give to the protection of the natural environment is relatively limited. Its importance lies mainly in controlling new development by the requirement of the T.C.P.A. that development shall not take place without planning permission.[7] The Act defines development as:

> "the carrying out of building, engineering, mining or other operations in, on, over or under land, or the making of any material change in the use of any buildings or other land."[8]

There are thus two essentially distinct limbs to the control: over operations and over material changes of use.

3–020   Despite this comprehensive definition there are significant exceptions from the potential scope of the controls. First, certain operations and uses are specifically excluded from the definition of development, e.g. interior works and use of land for agriculture or forestry[9]. Secondly, some development has the benefit of general planning permissions, notably under the General Development Order[10] allowing it to proceed without any review as to impact and desirability from the environmental standpoint.[11] Although in theory such general permissions can be withdrawn or modified, in practice this is unusual. Sometimes extensive development can be undertaken under these

---

[7] T.C.P.A., s.57.
[8] T.C.P.A., s.55.
[9] T.C.P.A., s.55(2).
[10] See paras. 3–057 to 3–059.
[11] The Government is considering introducing requirements for environmental statements for the exercise of certain General Development Order rights.

general permissions and, hence, effectively without public scrutiny or control. Thirdly, development on Crown Land by Government Departments (except any health service body, which lost Crown immunity on April 1, 1991),[12] does not require planning permission and so is wholly outside the planning system as a matter of law. Fourthly, development on or in the seabed is normally outside planning control because local authority jurisdiction extends only as far as the low water mark.[13]

Additionally, not all changes of use require planning permission: **3–021** only a "material" change. It is often difficult to know when a change (which includes mere intensification of an existing use without any other alteration in its nature) becomes so marked as to amount to a material change of use. In practice, extensive changes can take place in this way without being effectively controlled by the planning system. Indeed the Use Classes Order[14] permits extensive changes between various types of use without the need to apply for planning permission. A factory might change from one producing effectively no emissions, save those from its heating system, and generating 10 vehicle movements per day, to a use producing large quantities of unpleasant, unsightly and perhaps noxious emissions, and generating perhaps 50 vehicle movements per day, and it is entirely possible that this would not amount to development requiring planning permission, nor involve any breach of planning control (*e.g.* breach of a planning condition). Such a change might perhaps be affected by controls under other legislation, and in severe cases it could give rise to liability at common law, for example enabling a neighbour to take action for nuisance. It could amount to a statutory nuisance (see Chapter 23), but even so, the planning system might be ineffective to prevent it.

Nevertheless, the planning system is unquestionably important in **3–022** at least two ways. First, it provides legal control over significant new development and significant changes of use. For example, planning permission will be required to build a new factory or a major factory extension. Planning permission is also generally required to change the use of an existing factory from light industrial use, *i.e.* a use which could take place within a residential area, to general industrial use, and from general industrial use to special industrial use (*i.e.* involving particularly unpleasant processes). Planning therefore has a role to play in the protection of the natural environment, but impact on the

---

[12] National Health Service and Community Care Act 1990, s.60.
[13] Local Government Act 1972, s.72.
[14] See paras. 3–060 to 3–063.

environment is only one of the factors which must be taken into account in determining a planning application: the planning authority must balance the protection of the natural environment with factors such as the needs for housing and employment and for a proper system of infrastructure, *e.g.* roads and power lines, and the legitimate requirements of businesses. It is stated Government policy that the planning system fails where it unnecessarily impedes the legitimate needs of business and economic activity—of course much turns on what is to be understood by "unnecessarily". There is no general presumption that planning authorities should favour protection of the natural environment over other considerations such as, for example, economic needs for a particular development.

3–023   A second significant feature of the planning system lies in its persuasive rather than legal force. National and local policy guidance can give indications of the weight to be given to the protection of the natural environment.[15] Local plans, in particular, can give importance to nature conservation in particular areas and in particular ways. Accordingly, if the local plan makes it clear that environmental considerations are to be given weight in certain areas, and this is reflected in the treatment of planning applications, this will be a potent influence on developers and landowners when preparing their development projects.

The Statutory Framework

3–024   The T.C.P.A. was the result of consolidating a large number of legislative measures. It did not of itself introduce any major reforms, but in the following year, the Planning and Compensation Act 1991 (the "P.C.A.") introduced some significant changes, most notably in the field of enforcement (see paragraphs 3–121 to 3–135 below), in providing for breach of condition notices and planning contravention notices. Other relevant statutes are the Planning (Listed Buildings and Conservation Areas) Act 1990 and the Planning (Consequential Provisions) Act 1990. These last two statutes, make up, with the

---

[15] *e.g.* PPG1 "General Policy and Principles", Annex A: Design Considerations, para A3: "Particular weight should be given to the impact of development on existing buildings and the landscape in environmentally sensitive areas such as National Parks, Areas of Outstanding Natural Beauty and Conservation Areas, where the scale of new development and the use of appropriate building materials will often be particularly important".

T.C.P.A. and the P.C.A. what are referred to collectively as "the Planning Acts".

The Role of the Secretaries of State

The Secretary of State for the Environment controls the planning system in England, and the Secretary of State for Wales exercises the same jurisdiction in the Principality. The system of planning control in Scotland is very similar to that in England and Wales although there are differences in law and procedure; regional and general, as well as district, planning authorities are involved in Scotland, and the system is controlled by the Secretary of State for Scotland. There is separate legislation for Scotland. For simplicity, where the following comments refer to the Department of the Environment, this should be taken to include the Welsh Office in relation to the Principality, and the Scottish Office in relation to Scotland.

3–025

The general functions of the Secretary of State for the Environment include:

3–026

— promoting planning legislation in Parliament;
— issuing general policy guidance in the form of circular and planning policy guidance notes; issuing planning guidance for each of the regions of the country;
— a general supervisory role over the system of planning control;
  examining plans and, if appropriate, seeking to influence their content or requiring that they be determined by him;[16]
— making and amending general planning permissions such as the General Development Order.[17]

In particular he can:

— determine planning appeals from decisions of local planning authorities on planning applications, and relating to enforcement notices[18];
— call-in and determine certain planning applications[19];

[16] Part II of the T.C.P.A.
[17] Part III of the T.C.P.A.
[18] T.C.P.A., ss.78 and 174.
[19] T.C.P.A., s.77.

- issue directions to restrict a planning authority's (or all authorities') ability to grant planning permission in certain circumstances (for example, until a certain category of planning application has been referred to the Department of the Environment for consideration)[20];
- serve completion notices[21];
- revoke or modify a planning permission in certain circumstances[22];
- make orders requiring discontinuance of use or alteration or removal of buildings or works in certain circumstances[23].

In practice, it is Government policy not to intervene in local planning decisions unless it is considered essential to do so.

Planning Policy

3–027   The application of the planning regime in practice is determined primarily by reference to national, regional and local planning policies. National planning policy is primarily made up from:

(i)   Department of the Environment circulars;
(ii) Planning Policy Guidance Notes ("PPGs");
(ii) Mineral Policy Guidance Notes ("MPGs");
(iv) Consultation papers.

In addition, national policy may be developed and promulgated through decisions by the Secretary of State on planning appeals and also through formal statements by him on policy issues.

3–028   Regional policy may be developed both by the Secretary of State at national level and also by groups of local authorities in a particular region. Thus the government issues Regional Policy Guidance Notes ("RPGs"), the first of which was issued in June 1989. In addition, other bodies in certain areas have issued non-statutory guidance on developments in their areas.[24]

3–029   Tables 3/I to 3/III list all the current PPGs, MPGs and RPGs.

---

[20] T.C.P.A., s.77.
[21] T.C.P.A., s.96.
[22] T.C.P.A., s.100.
[23] T.C.P.A., s.104.
[24] For example, the London Planning Advisory Committee ("LPAC"); the London and South East Regional Planning Conference ("SERPLAN").

TABLE 3/I

PLANNING POLICY GUIDANCE NOTES[25]

No.	Title	Date
PPG1	General Policy and Principles	January 1988 Revised March 1992
PPG2	Green Belts	January 1995
PPG3	Land for Housing	January 1988 Revised March 1992
PPG3 (Wales)	Housing (1992)	March 1992
PPG4	Industrial and Commercial Development and Small Firms	January 1988 Revised November 1992
PPG5	Simplified Planning Zones	January 1988 Revised November 1992
PPG6	Town Centres and Retail Development	January 1988 Revised July 1993
PPG7	Rural Enterprise and Development The Countryside and The Rural Economy	January 1988 Revised January 1992
PPG8	Telecommunications	January 1988 Revised December 1992
PPG9	Nature Conservation	October 1994
PPG10	Strategic Guidance for the West Midlands	September 1988 (Revision expected)
PPG11	Strategic Guidance for Merseyside	October 1988

---

[25] Most Welsh Office guidance relating to planning is issued jointly with the Department of the Environment. On some topics the Welsh Office has issued separate guidance; these separate guidance notes are listed below.

3–027

PPG12	Local Plans Development Plans and Regional Planning Guidance	November 1988 Revised February 1992
PPG12 (Wales)	Development Plans and Strategic Planning Guidance in Wales	February 1992
PPG13	Highway Considerations in Development Control	November 1988 Revised March 1994
PPG14	Development on Unstable Land	April 1990
PPG15	Planning and the Historic Environment	September 1994
PPG16	Archaeology and Planning	November 1990
PPG16 (Wales)	Archaeology and Planning	November 1991
PPG17	Sport and Recreation	September 1991
PPG18	Enforcing Planning Control	December 1991
PPG19	Outdoor Advertisement Control	March 1992
PPG20	Coastal Planning	September 1992
PPG21	Tourism	November 1992
PPG22	Renewable Energy	February 1993
PPG23	Planning and Pollution Control	July 1994
PPG24	Planning and Noise	October 1994

TABLE 3/II

MINERAL POLICY GUIDANCE NOTES

No.	Title	Date
MPG1	General Considerations and the Development Plan System	January 1988
MPG2	Applications, Permissions and Conditions	1988

MPG3	Coal Mining and Colliery Spoil Disposal	July 1994
MPG4	The Review of Mineral Working Sites	September 1988
MPG5	Minerals Planning and the General Development Order	December 1988
MPG6	Guidelines for Aggregates Provision in England and Wales	April 1994
MPG7	The Reclamation of Mineral Workings	1989
MPG8	Planning and Compensation Act 1991: Interim Development Order Permissions (IDOs) Statutory Provisions and Procedures	September 1991
MPG9	Planning and Compensation Act 1991: Interim Development Order Permissions (IDOs) Conditions	March 1992
MPG10	Provision of Raw Material for the Cement Industry	1991
MPG11	The Control of Noise at Surface Mineral Workings	April 1993
MPG12	Treatment of Disused Mine Openings and Availability of Information on Mined Ground	April 1994
MPGxx	Peat (draft)*	September 1994

*issued in draft as consultation paper.

TABLE 3/III

REGIONAL POLICY GUIDANCE NOTES

No.	Title	Date
RPG1	Strategic Guidance for Tyne and Wear	June 1989
RPG2	Strategic Guidance for West Yorkshire	September 1989
RPG3	Strategic Guidance for London	September 1989

RPG3 Annex A	Supplementary Guidance for London on the Protection of Strategic Views	November 1991
RPG4	Strategic Guidance for Greater Manchester	December 1989
RPG5	Strategic Guidance for South Yorkshire	December 1989
RPG6	Regional Planning Guidance for East Anglia	July 1991
RPG7	Regional Planning Guidance for the Northern Region	September 1993
RPG8	Regional Planning Guidance for the East Midlands	March 1994
RPG9	Regional Planning Guidance for the South East	March 1994
RPG10	Regional Planning Guidance for the South West	July 1994

The Development Plan—Structure and Local Plans

3–030   An integral part of the post-1947 planning system has been "the development plan". Generally, this is a plan prepared by a local authority to indicate the broad principles that are intended to govern land use within its area. The development plan has always been an important consideration in planning decisions. This is given statutory force by section 54A of the T.C.P.A., inserted by the P.C.A., which reads:

> "Where, in making any determination under the planning Acts, regard is to be had to the development plan, the determination shall be made in accordance with the [development] plan unless material considerations indicate otherwise".

A plan being out of date or inconsistent with national policy are examples of potentially material considerations which might lead to a plan not being followed.

3–031   The form of the development plan, and the means by which it is approved, have been sources of persistent problems since 1947.

80

Initially, there was a requirement that such plans should be on a 1:50,000 Ordnance Survey base and should all be approved by the Minister for Housing and Local Government. This proved completely unworkable, because it took many years for the plan to be approved, by when it would normally be substantially out of date. Following the conclusions of a review of the system,[26] it was changed in 1968 to one based on a combination of structure and local plans. Structure plans were prepared by county councils, and were intended to be primarily a written statement setting out the principles governing future development in the county. They were approved by the Minister of Housing and Local Government[27] (later the Secretary of State for the Environment), following examination by a panel appointed by him.[28] Local plans were then prepared, mostly by district councils, and were approved by the district itself following scrutiny of objections by an independent planning inspector at a public local inquiry. This system remains, with two recent variations. First, structure plans are no longer approved by the Secretary of State for the Environment, but by the county council itself,[29] although the Secretary of State still has extensive reserve powers to intervene.[30] Secondly, in metropolitan areas, each district council is required to prepare a unitary development plan for its district,[31] Part 1 of which is effectively a structure plan for the district, setting out general principles, and Part 2 of which is the local plan.

For most development control purposes it is the local plan which is the more important, since this spells out planning policies in the greater detail. Whereas a structure plan is basically a written policy statement with supporting diagrams, an essential part of a local plan is a map on an Ordnance Survey base which sets out the local authority's policies for individual parcels of land.   3–032

Unlike the regime in most of continental Europe, where a provision for specified activities in a development plan creates legally enforceable rights to carry on such activities in accordance with that plan, the British system has always given considerable discretion to the planning authority to depart from its plan. The legal requirement is   3–033

[26] White Paper entitled "Town and Country Planning", June 1967, Cmnd. 3333.
[27] From November 12, 1970, all the functions of the Minister were transferred to the Secretary of State for the Environment by the Secretary of State for the Environment Order 1970, (S.I. 1970 No. 168).
[28] Originally it was intended that structure plans should be considered at a public local inquiry. The examination in public procedure was introduced by the Town and Country Planning (Amendment) Act 1972.
[29] P.C.A., Sched 4, para. 17, which took effect, from February 10, 1992 by S.I. 1991 No. 2905.
[30] T.C.P.A., s.35A—power to direct that all or part of the structure plan proposals be submitted to the Secretary of State for approval.
[31] Introduced by the Local Government Act 1985, consolidated in T.C.P.A.

that the authority should consider each proposal on its merits: it is consequently free to decide whether or not to apply the policies of the development plan to the particular case. It is far from unusual for planning authorities to take decisions at variance with their development plans, for example because the development plan is out of date, or because some other reason is thought to outweigh its own development plan. The two key features of the British planning system are that it is very largely discretionary, and that the discretion is in almost all cases exercised by the elected district council. The Secretary of State for the Environment has extensive powers to intervene in the decision making process,[32] although as a matter of policy he rarely does so.[33]

3–034   There is no legal requirement that the draft development plan should be accompanied by any form of environmental statement, notwithstanding that the designation of a site in the plan for a particular form of development may effectively pre-determine a planning application for that development on that site, particularly having regard to section 54A of the T.C.P.A.[34] However it is now Government policy that development plans should undergo a form of environmental appraisal.[35]

3–035   While there is no general rule, structure plans are often reviewed every five years. The frequency of review of local plans varies considerably, but in many cases a five year review programme is adopted. The method for approval of structure and local plans is very similar. Each of the plans undergoes a three stage process following its preparation in draft. At the initial, *consultative*, stage, this first draft is published to enable any interested person to comment on it. Those comments are considered by the plan-making authority, which then prepares a final draft plan which is formally placed on deposit for objection, thus initiating the *objection* stage of the process. There is no limit to the issues which can be raised by way of representations or

---

[32] Part II of the T.C.P.A. — Secretary of State's powers to intervene in the development plan making process; Part III of the T.C.P.A. and Article 14 GDO — Secretary of State's powers of intervention for consideration of planning applications; see below for consideration in more detail.

[33] See the Government's statement in the White Paper "Planning: Appeals, Call-in and Major Public Inquiries", Cm. 43, (1986), "His [the Secretary of State's] general approach is not to interfere with the jurisdiction of the local planning authority unless it is necessary to do so and to require reference to him only where matters of more than local importance are raised by the application . . . Directions to refer applications to him will be relatively rare . . . The Secretary of State should intervene only where there are compelling reasons why the local authority ought not to be entrusted with the decision".

[34] See para. 3–030.

[35] See paras 3–053 to 3–055.

objections to a structure plan or local plan (even though one may not be allowed an oral hearing in relation to all objections). In particular, there is no limit to the representations and objections which can be made on environmental issues. However, the plans are concerned with land uses and, as noted above, deal in broad categories of use. Representations/objections which go beyond the traditional definition of land use planning are unlikely to be given weight in this context, especially if those controls can be exercised subsequently by other statutory bodies, for example HMIP, in relation to any particular proposed development. Nevertheless, both structure plans and (to a greater extent) local plans, do sometimes stray beyond strict land use planning matters.

The procedure differs at the objection stage between a structure   **3–036** plan and a local plan. With a structure plan, objections are considered by a panel, normally consisting of three persons appointed by the Department of the Environment, that conducts an "Examination in Public". There is no automatic right to appear before the panel. It is the panel which considers the objections and decides which topics it wishes to consider at its Examination in Public, and who will be invited to attend and speak on those topics. The form of the Examination in Public is in the nature of a round table discussion under the guidance of the chairman of the panel, although since it would be normal for 20 or 30 parties, including several planning authorities, to be represented at an Examination in Public, the extent to which one can effectively challenge arguments which are presented is somewhat limited.

At the objection stage of a local plan, the independent examination   **3–037** takes place at a public local inquiry conducted by an Inspector appointed by the Department of the Environment. In most cases, there is a statutory right for all who have properly objected to appear before him to present their objections; the exception relates to those parts of a local plan which are unchanged in the current review of the plan, where the Inspector has a direction whether to allow an oral hearing to objectors. Procedural control of the inquiry is for the Inspector, but normally local plan inquiries will be conducted in adversarial style, with witnesses being called and evidence cross-examined.

At the end of the objection stage, the Examination in Public panel   **3–038** considering the structure plan reports to the county council, and the local plan Inspector reports to the district council. In each case, the plan-making authority then considers whether to modify its plan in the light of the recommendations of the Examination in Public panel or the Inspector, as the case may be. If it decides to make modifications, these must be published formally for further objection, and this begins the third, *modifications*, stage of the process. Normally, objections to modifications will be considered by the plan-making authority without a further inquiry or hearing. The plan-making authority considers these further objections and takes its decision on the final form of the plan, which it then adopts formally and publishes.

3-039   The Government places considerable importance on the development plan system in relation to planning applications. In deciding planning appeals considerable weight will normally be given to the provisions of the development plan. Legally, it is only the approved development plan (*i.e.* the combination of relevant structure and local plans, or the unitary development plan, as the case may be) which is "the development plan" for planning purposes, although in practice at any time it would be normal for there to be both an approved development plan and also proposals under way for its modification and/or replacement, *e.g.* a draft replacement local plan. Although technically not part of the development plan until it is approved, a draft local or structure plan will be given some weight, the amount of which will depend on the stage which it has reached in the development plan procedure. For example, a local plan undergoing the first stage of its procedure will be given some weight as representing the more up to date views of the planning authority, but not a great deal of weight because those views have not yet been tested at a local plan inquiry; on the other hand, a local plan which is not yet adopted but which has been through its local inquiry and is at the modification stage, may well be given considerable weight even though it is not yet formally part of the development plan. In *Kissel v. Secretary of State for the Environment and Anor.*[36] The Secretary of State's decision on an appeal was quashed on the ground that the Inspector, whose decision had been appealed, had failed to give consideration to an emerging consultative draft local plan. Even though this was at its earliest stage, it was capable as a matter of law of being a material consideration, and the Inspector should have recognised its existence and indicated the extent to which it had influenced his decision.

3-040   Occasionally, there are subject local plans for special purposes, for example Green Belt plans or countryside plans. Additionally every county is now required to prepare waste local plans.[37]

---

[36] *The Times*, July 22, 1993.
[37] T.C.P.A., s.38, inserted by Sched. 4 of the P.C.A. from February 10, 1992. This applies only to non-metropolitan areas. There is no requirement on metropolitan authorities to prepare separate waste local plans; waste policies are included in the unitary development plan.

Waste Plans and Policies

Waste plans set out the land use planning elements of waste policies **3-041** *i.e.* those detailed policies relevant to development involving the disposal and/or recovery of refuse and other waste materials except minerals waste. The waste plan is part of the development plan. Waste policies may be included in the minerals local plan, rather than in a separate waste plan.

Before the 1992 reforms, county councils incorporated policies on **3-042** waste into the county structure plans or prepared separate subject plans on waste planning. These old-style plans will remain in effect until replaced by new-style plans; if "old" plans comply with the procedural and other requirements for "new" waste plans, then they will simply be treated as new plans.

In producing waste local plans, or formulating waste policies for **3-043** including in a minerals local plan, the local planning authority must have regard to any waste disposal plan for their area made under the E.P.A. and the reasons for any inconsistencies must be set out in the waste local plan.[38] The same procedures for adoption of waste local plans apply as for adoption of district local plans[39]. The Secretary of State's powers of intervention for district local plans also apply.

Whereas waste disposal plans are concerned with providing for all **3-044** wastes arising in the area of the relevant waste regulation authority, and in so doing take into account the availability of existing and expected sites for waste disposal under recovery, they do not address land use issues in the same way as a development plan, nor do they deal with issues specific to individual sites or planning criteria for new sites. These aspects are controlled by the relevant planning authority, which must *inter alia* have regard to the "relevant objectives" applicable to them as laid down in the Waste Management Licensing Regulations 1994.[40] Guidance on waste local plans is contained in PPG 23.[41] They must include detailed land use policies and proposals for all types of waste that may arise in each authority's area or require to be treated or disposed of in it, and must take account of:-

— the need for regions to aim for self-sufficiency in waste management facilities and the need to minimise the impact of waste transport;

---

[38] Town and Country Planning (Development Plan) Regulations 1991 (S.I. 1991 No. 2794), reg. 9.
[39] T.C.P.A., s.38(9).
[40] Sched. 4, Part I, para. 4.
[41] paras. 2.20 to 2.24.

- any relevant policies for waste minimisation and recycling affecting waste disposal requirements;
- the land-use and transport requirements of waste disposal and treatment facilities;
- opportunities for energy recovery; and
- the various methods for dealing with waste, by way of treatment or recycling that precede or avoid final disposal.

3–045   It is the function of the planning authority to identify existing and, where appropriate, new possible sites for waste management facilities, and to identify both broad areas which are likely to contain sufficient such sites, and also areas which are considered to be inappropriate for them having regard to environmental, physical and access constraints. They must set planning criteria to apply to applications for waste management developments covering, for example, the types of land that would be suitable, access routes, proximity to other developments, restoration and aftercare.

3–046   The planning authority must consider the various options for waste disposal, in particular landfill and incineration. PPG 23 draws attention to the likely increase in costs of landfill as the availability of suitable sites decreases and the stringency of applicable environmental standards rises, coupled with the increased demand for waste disposal on land by the ending of dumping of sewage sludge at sea; it emphasises the beneficial contribution that incineration of waste with energy recovery can make, and requires the planning authorities to set out in the waste local plan the appropriate criteria for the location of each method of treatment or disposal needed for their area, and to make adequate provision for suitable sites.[42]

3–047   Each waste regulation authority must draw up a waste disposal plan setting out its policies for the recovery, recycling and disposal of all controlled wastes for which it has responsibility, including those imported into and exported from its area. This necessitates establishing figures for present, and estimates of future, generation of different types of waste, and information on how these are currently dealt with and on what resources will be available for their recovery, recycling and disposal in the future. The waste regulation authority also defines priorities for waste treatment and disposal, and so derives the likely future requirement for waste management facilities of all types, set against existing capacity. Unlike the waste local plan, the EPA waste disposal plan is not itself part of the development plan, and cannot be the subject of a local plan inquiry in the same way as a development plan.

[42] PPG 23, para. 2.24.

The procedure and decision making process for any application for   3–048
planning permission involving waste disposal is the same as for any
other planning application; the waste local plan is another element of
the development plan and the waste disposal plan is a material
consideration to be taken into account.

Minerals Plans and Policies

Planning applications involving the winning and working of   3–049
minerals are also treated legally and procedurally in the same way as
any other planning application. The difference is that specific minerals
policies must be taken into account, both at national[43] and local level.

A minerals planning authority[44] is required to produce a minerals   3–050
local plan for its area[45], and this forms part of the development plan for
the area. Although some authorities had produced minerals local
plans before that date they had no statutory base and were not part of
the adopted development plan.

Similar procedural provisions apply for minerals plans as for waste   3–051
plans.[46] Minerals extraction sites are often suitable for the disposal of
other wastes, and minerals planning authorities may include waste
policies in the minerals local plan,[47] which must then be called a
minerals local plan "including waste policies".[48]

Certain mineral extraction rights were granted before the Town and   3–052
Country Planning Act 1947 came into force by virtue of "interim
development orders" under section 10 of the Town and Country
Planning Act 1932. A substantial number of these interim development orders were made during the last war, but though many lay
dormant thereafter, they were nevertheless liable to be activated at any
time. The P.C.A. provided[49] that, in the case of any site to which any
such interim development order made after July 21, 1943 applied, if
there had been no mineral extraction or deposit of mineral waste in the
two years ending on May 1, 1991, the rights under that order would be
extinguished, unless an application for its registration was made to the

---

[43] See Table 3/II Minerals Policy Guidance Notes.
[44] The minerals planning authority is the county planning authority in a non-
metroplitan area, and the local planning authority in a metropolitan area or London
Borough—T.C.P.A., s.1(4).
[45] T.C.P.A., s.37, inserted by Sched. 4 of the P.C.A. from February 10, 1992—in
metropolitan areas minerals policies are included in unitary development plans.
[46] T.C.P.A., s.37 and see paras. 3–041 to 3–043.
[47] T.C.P.A., s.38(2).
[48] Town and Country Planning (Development Plan) Regulations 1991 (S.I. 1991 No.
2794), reg. 4.
[49] In s.22.

relevant minerals planning authority within a six month period. On receiving such an application, the authority was entitled to impose appropriate conditions, relating for example to methods of working and subsequent site restoration. Provided application to register a site was duly made, however, the interim development order continues in force, subject only to these subsequent conditions, irrespective of the environmental consequences that any working of the site might now have.[50]

Environmental Considerations and the Development Plan

3–053   As already noted, there is no legal requirement for an assessment of the environmental consequences either of the policies of a structure plan, or of a local plan or of its detailed proposals, even though in practice a local plan may commit a site for development almost as much as a specific planning permission. There is a requirement that general policies of a development plan should be formulated having regard to environmental considerations, but this will apply only to structure plans and to that part of unitary development plans which contains general policies.[51] However, the Department of the Environment has issued policy guidance[52] in the following terms:

> "Most policies and proposals in all types of plans will have environmental implications, which should be appraised as part of the plan preparation process. Such an environmental appraisal is the process of identifying, quantifying, weighing up and reporting on the environmental and other costs and benefits of the measures which are proposed. All the implications of the options should be analysed, including financial, social and environmental effects. A systematic appraisal ensures that the objectives of a policy are clearly laid out, and the trade-offs between options identified and assessed. Those who later interpret, implement and build on the policy will then have a clear record showing how the decision was made; in the case of development plans this should be set out in the explanatory memorandum or reasoned justification. But the requirement to 'have regard' does not

---

[50] According to a report issued by Friends of the Earth, 573 sites were registered in this way, covering some 42,000 acres (*Daily Telegraph*, August 4, 1993).
[51] Art. 9 of the The Town and Country Planning (Development Plan) Regulations, 1991 (S.I. 1991 No. 2794).
[52] PPG12, para. 5.52.

require a full environmental impact statement of the sort needed for projects likely to have serious environmental effects".

The Department of the Environment has also published a guide **3–054** "Policy Appraisals and The Environment" which indicates how environmental considerations may be incorporated into the appraisal of policies. Also the United Kingdom strategy document "Sustainable Development" of January 1994 confirms[53] that planning guidance is being revised to incorporate concepts of sustainability.

Nevertheless this official guidance creates no binding obligations to **3–055** carry out any kind of environmental evaluation, which represents a significant lack in the ability of the British planning system to protect the environment.[54]

The General Development Order and the Use Classes Order

The T.C.P.A. empowers the Secretary of State[55] to issue general **3–056** orders and directions relating to planning control. These can include orders and directions granting general planning permissions. The best known and most extensive of these are the two orders known as the General Development Order (the "GDO") and the Use Classes Order (the "UCO").

The General Development Order

The GDO is the Town and Country Planning General Development **3–057** Order 1988[56] as amended by numerous subsequent amendment orders[57] and grants certain general planning permissions. It grants permission for material development falling within the various categories set out in the Order subject to conditions set out in relation to each type of development.

---

[53] para. 103.
[54] This lack may be addressed by proposals under consideration in the European Commission for revising Directive 85/337 on environmental impact assessments; however any such proposals seem likely to be strongly opposed on "subsidiarity" grounds.
[55] T.C.P.A., ss. 58–60 and 74(1).
[56] S.I. 1988 No.1813.
[57] S.I. 1988 No. 2091, S.I. 1989 No. 603, S.I. 1989 No. 1590, S.I. 1990 No. 457, S.I. 1990 No. 2032, S.I. 1991 No. 1536, S.I. 1991 No. 2268, S.I. 1991 No. 2805, S.I. 1992 No. 609, S.I. 1992 No. 658, S.I. 1992 No. 1280, S.I. 1992 No. 1493, S.I. 1992 No. 1563, S.I. 1992 No. 2450, S.I. 1994 No. 678.

3–058   By way of example, the GDO grants permission to enlarge, improve or otherwise alter a dwellinghouse, subject to certain conditions and limitations. It permits certain changes of use. It allows temporary use of land for any purpose ("temporary" generally meaning not more than 28 days, with a maximum of 14 days in certain cases). It permits the extension or alteration of an industrial building or warehouse, within certain limitations and subject to conditions.

3–059   This general planning permission can be withdrawn by a direction by the Secretary of State or the appropriate local planning authority made under Article 4 of the GDO, which can be done either by reference to a locality or to a particular site. Thus, in particularly sensitive conservation areas, householders' rights to carry out development to and near their houses might be limited; in sensitive countryside areas, rights to carry out development in the countryside might be limited. The normal rights of the Order can also be limited by conditions attached to a planning permission or by a planning agreement or undertaking. One should not therefore automatically assume that the rights exist, and the position needs to be checked in each case. In most circumstances, however, the Order authorises the development which it describes, without any reference to the planning authority being required. There is nevertheless a partial exception in relation to certain forms of agricultural development where, before exercising the GDO rights, a person must give notice to the planning authority, to give it the opportunity to intervene and to require that an application for express planning permission should be made. The Government is considering introducing requirements for environmental statements for the exercise of certain General Development Order rights.

The Use Classes Order

3–060   The UCO is the Town and Country Planning (Use Classes) Order 1987[58] as amended[59] and also grants a general planning permission. The rights under the UCO cannot be removed either generally or in relation to specific localities or sites by direction (by contrast with the GDO) although revisions, amendments or revocation of the UCO may be made by the Secretary of State by order, *i.e.* in the same way as the UCO itself was made.[60] However UCO rights can be excluded or modified by conditions attached to an individual planning permission

---

[58] S.I. 1987 No. 764.
[59] By S.I. 1991 No. 1576, S.I. 1992 No. 610, S.I. 1992 No. 657, S.I. 1994 No. 724.
[60] Under s.55(2)(f) of the T.C.P.A.

or by the terms of a planning agreement or undertaking. The UCO enables changes of use to take place between uses within the same class of the UCO (the GDO, in specific limited circumstances, grants permitted development rights for change between uses in certain different classes) without the need for express planning permission. For example, Class B1 includes (a) office use (b) research and development use, and (c) industrial use—provided that in each case the use can be carried out in any residential area without detriment to the amenity of that area by reason of noise, vibration, smell, fumes, smoke, soot, ash, dust or grit. Industrial use falling within that type is colloquially known as "light industrial use". Clearly, these forms of development could have wholly different impacts on the environment in terms of traffic, water requirements of both intake and discharge, power and heat requirements, noise and discharges to the atmosphere. Yet changes between these uses are permitted by the Order, regardless of the different environmental impacts, subject to any restrictions which may have been imposed on a particular site by planning conditions or planning obligations.

The UCO does not authorise any physical operations: only a change of use. However, works which affect only the interior of a building or which do not materially affect the external appearance (save works underground) are expressly excluded from the definition of development and so do not require planning permission in any event[61] and so it is normally possible for substantial physical adaptation to premises to take place for the purpose of a change of use, without planning permission being required.   3–061

As a matter of planning law, a use includes all ancillary uses. This has been accepted in numerous court decisions.[62] Thus, the right to use a building as an office would include the right to park the cars of the office workers and genuine visitors within the curtilage around it. The right to use a building as a factory would include the right to store outside it and within the curtilage of the premises materials used or produced in the factory. These ancillary uses may be controlled by, for example, planning conditions, but in the absence of express restrictions, no ancillary uses will breach planning control, regardless of their environmental consequences.   3–062

---

[61] s.55(2)(a); but note the Planning (Listed Building and Conservation Areas) Act 1990, which prohibits works (including interior works) for demolition, alteration or extension to any listed building which would affect its character as a building or its special architectural or historic interest, unless those works are authorised.

[62] See *e.g. Vickers Armstrong Ltd v. Central Land Board* (1958) 9 P. & C.R. 33; *G. Percy Trentham Ltd v. Gloucestershire County Council* [1966] 1 W.L.R. 506; *Brazil Concrete Ltd v. Amersham Rural District* (1967) 18 P. & C.R. 396.

3–063   As may be seen, a primary concern—and in many ways *the* primary concern—of planning is with the use made of a particular piece of land and only incidentally with the impact of that use on its surroundings. In deciding on the land use allocations of its local plan, a local planning authority will be mainly concerned with accommodating the perceived needs for new developments in its area in a manner that is politically acceptable to its electorate. In deciding whether to grant an application for planning permission, though the authority will take into account the impact of a proposed use on the area, the principal issue is the compatibility of the proposal with the local plan. Thus, once a development is permitted, it may well be possible to change that permitted use in a way which significantly affects the area, without a breach of planning control being involved, particularly as permitted uses are generally classified by reference to categories of use, *e.g.* shops or offices, deriving from their economic function rather than their environmental consequences. Though there are exceptions to these general propositions, they are few. Consequently, conventional planning controls are not in themselves adequate to ensure prevention or minimisation of harm to living organisms in the sense that this expression is used in the E.P.A.[63] For this, the procedures for environmental impact assessments (described in chapter 4) are of some assistance, though far from sufficient, and policy guidance, by incorporating concepts of sustainability, is increasing environmental awareness in planning decisions.

Applications for Planning Permission

3–064   The procedure for making applications for planning permission and subsequent appeals is contained in a mixture of statute[64], secondary legislation[65] and central Government guidance.[66]

3–065   Applications are made on forms obtainable from the relevant local planning authority (each authority has its own forms). There are

---

[63] Where "harm" means harm to the health of living organisms or other interference with the ecological systems of which they form part and, in the case of man, includes offence caused to any of his senses or harm to his property" E.P.A., s.1(4); similarly also ss.29(5), 107(6).

[64] Part III of the T.C.P.A.

[65] The main procedural provisions are set out in the GDO; Town and Country Planning (Fees for Applications and Deemed Applications) Regulations 1989, S.I. 1989 No. 193, as amended by S.I. 1990 No. 2473, S.I. 1991 No. 2735, S.I. 1992 No. 1817 and S.I. 1992 No. 3052; Town and Country Planning (Applications) Regulations 1988, S.I. 1988 No. 1912; Town and Country Planning (Inquiries Procedure) Rules 1992, S.I. 1992 No. 2039.

[66] DoE Circulars 22/88, 5/89, 20/91, 15/92, 24/92.

broadly two types of planning application: (i) for outline planning permission and (ii) for full planning permission. Applications for such permissions are often described as outline applications or full applications, respectively.

Outline permission is available only in relation to the erection of a **3–066** building.[67] An outline application enables the applicant to ask the planning authority to determine the principle of the development, while reserving for later approval all or any of specified "reserved matters", which are the siting, design, external appearance, means of access and landscaping.[68] The grant of outline planning permission is itself the planning permission. The subsequent approval of details on the matters reserved in the outline planning permission is not technically the grant of permission but simply approval of details. Depending on the terms of the permission and the wording of any conditions that have been imposed generally, the grant of outline permission will not put the developer in a position where he may proceed with construction or preparatory work. It is usual in practice for the conditions attached to the permission to require that key details be approved by the local planning authority before development can begin. In that situation it is probably the approval of those details which is the development consent for the purposes of the EC Directive 85/337 on environmental assessment (see chapter 4), which requires that any requisite environmental assessment must be made before development consent is given.

There is no legal requirement that key details have to be approved **3–067** before the developer begins; the position depends on the terms of the conditions in each case. However the extent to which the planning authority can control the reserved matters, in particular by the imposition of conditions, is constrained by the terms of the outline planning permission. Thus, once the principles are established in the outline permission it is not open to a planning authority when approving reserved matters to derogate from those principles. If the planning authority has for any reason failed to impose a planning condition at the outline stage relevant to what has been approved (as opposed to any reserved matters), then it may well be too late for it to do so at the detailed stage. An application for full planning permission does not ask for matters to be reserved for subsequent approval, although in practice this sometimes happens, as where the planning authority imposes conditions requiring the subsequent approval of certain details of the scheme.

[67] Art. 1 of the GDO defines "outline planning permission" as one "for the erection of a building, which is granted subject to a condition requiring the subsequent approval of the local planning authority with respect to one or more reserved matters".
[68] GDO, Art. 1.

3–068   Conditions can be attached to outline permission, detailed permission or, within considerable limitations, approval of reserved matters. Those conditions could require the submission of environmental information in connection with matters to be approved at a later date, although this is rarely done in practice.

3–069   When applying for planning permission for the erection, for example, of new industrial premises, it is not necessary for the applicant to give any details of the siting or design of the buildings, although he may choose to do so. In practice, many planning authorities ask for this kind of detail and the extent to which it is provided is a matter for discussion between the planning authority and the applicant. If the applicant believes that undue detail is being requested, he can appeal to the Secretary of State for the Environment.

3–070   There is no standard requirement for every applicant to give information about the environmental consequences of his proposal and, as will be seen, the requirement for an environmental statement is mandatory in only relatively few (though major) cases. Even when an outline planning application is accompanied by an environmental statement, there is no legal requirement that the submission of details for approval shall also be accompanied by environmental information. It is accordingly open to argument that the UK legislation in this respect fails to implement fully EC Directive 85/337.[69]

3–071   Planning applications are supposed to be determined within a prescribed period, although it is not unusual for planning authorities to request and receive extensions of time from the applicant.[70] The prescribed period is 8 weeks from the time of receipt of a valid application and fee by the local planning authority,[71] extended to 16 weeks from receipt of those papers and the environmental statement where one is required.[72] These periods may be extended by agreement with the applicant.[73] Applications may still be considered outside those periods, and valid permissions granted by the local planning authority. An applicant's remedy, if a decision is not made within the prescribed period, is to treat that non-determination as a refusal (usually called a deemed refusal) and submit an appeal to the

---

[69] See para. 4–026. Government advice is that, where there are significant risks of pollution, an outline planning application is not usually appropriate. There can in practice be formidable problems in submitting a full application for a complex scheme, however, and the advice is not always to be followed. See also paras. 3–107 to 3–120.

[70] T.C.P.A., s.78(2).

[71] Art. 23, GDO.

[72] Art. 16, Town and Country Planning (Assessment of Environmental Effects) Regulations 1988 (S.I. 1988 No. 1199).

[73] Art. 23, GDO.

Secretary of State.[74] From the time an appeal is submitted jurisdiction passes to the Secretary of State.

Every application for planning permission must be accompanied by   3–072
a certificate either confirming that no-one other than the applicant is an owner of the relevant land, or confirming that notice of the application has been served on every person other than the applicant who is an owner of the land, or confirming that an advertisement of the application has been put in the local press, where it has not been possible to trace all owners.[75] Similarly, every applicant must certify whether or not there is an agricultural tenancy on all or any part of the land and, if so, he must serve notice of the application on every agricultural tenant.[76] Owner is defined as "a person who for the time being is (a) the estate owner in respect of the fee simple in the land, or (b) entitled to a tenancy of the land granted or extended for a term of years certain of which not less than 7 years remain unexpired".[77] Those served with notices are given a period of 21 days from the date the notice was served in which to submit comments to the local authority. Submission of comments within that period gives certain limited procedural rights. As a matter of practice local authorities will almost certainly take into account representations made outside the statutory period, so long as they are received before the authority considers the application.

All planning applications are also publicised by the local planning   3–073
authority.[78] At the discretion of the authority, this can take the form either of a site notice or of notification to neighbours (in Scotland neighbour notification is undertaken exclusively by the applicant, not by the planning authority.[79]), save for an application accompanied by an environmental statement, or one which does not accord with the development plan, or which affects a right of way, in which cases the local authority has no discretion to exercise, and must publicise the application by posting a site notice and by local advertisement. Local advertisement is also required for any major development i.e. minerals workings or deposit, waste development, or development of more than 10 dwellings, or more than 1000 square metres floorspace or with a site area of more than one hectare (0.5 hectares if residential). The legal definition of neighbours for this purpose is somewhat limited and, broadly, involves only those whose land actually adjoins the

---

[74] s.78 of the T.C.P.A.
[75] T.C.P.A., s.65 and GDO Arts. 12 and 12A (substituted by S.I. 1992 No. 1493).
[76] T.C.P.A., s.5 and GDO Arts. 12 and 12A.
[77] T.C.P.A., s.65(8).
[78] T.C.P.A., s.65 and GDO, Art. 12B (substituted by S.I. 1992 No. 1493).
[79] See NPPG 1 issued by the Scottish Office Environment Department.

application site. In practice, planning authorities often choose to notify applications more widely. There is no statutory obligation to publicise changes to applications or to the submission of details pursuant to conditions, although as a matter of practice authorities do so where they think it desirable. Nevertheless, this discretion can result in quite significant alterations being made that may adversely affect neighbours, without their being made aware of them.

3–074   Guidance and advice on the scheme for publicity is set out in Department of the Environment Circular 15/92 (Welsh Office Circular 2/92). There are additional requirements for publicity in special cases such as applications for planning permission which affect the setting of a listed building or which fall within a conservation area.[80]

3–075   On receipt of the planning application, the local planning authority is statutorily obliged to consult various public bodies on the application depending on the description of development[81], for example, the local highway authority for development involving a new or altered access to a highway (other than a trunk road), or the NRA for development involving the deposit of waste or refuse.[82] It is the normal practice of most local authority planning departments to circulate details of applications to other departments of the same local authority who may wish to make observations on it. The planning authority may not determine the planning application until at least 14 days after the statutory consultees have been notified,[83] and it is obliged to take into account any representations made by these consultees.[84]

3–076   There is no obligation on applicants to supply details of their application to third parties, save that an applicant (or appellant) who has submitted an environmental statement must ensure that a reasonable number of copies are available, for which a reasonable charge may be made.[85] Details of planning applications are placed on a public register at the local authority's offices and the contents of that register are open to inspection by members of the public.[86]

3–077   Some local authorities delegate decisions on certain types of planning application to the chief planning officer. Normally, however, the planning officer will prepare a report to the authority's planning

---

[80] ss.67, 73 of the Planning (Listed Buildings and Conservation Areas) Act 1990 and DoE Circular 8/87.
[81] GDO, Art. 18(1).
[82] GDO, Art. 18(1), paras. (h), (q).
[83] GDO, Art. 18(4).
[84] GDO, Art. 18(5).
[85] Arts. 18 and 20, Town and Country Planning (Assessment of Environmental Effects) Regulations 1988, (S.I. 1988 No. 1199).
[86] T.C.P.A., s.69.

committee which will determine the application. It can approve the application, with or without conditions, refuse the application, in which case it must give reasons for doing so, defer consideration, for example if it requires further information, or resolve that it will grant planning permission subject to completion of a planning agreement or subject to some other matter.

There is no right for third parties to appeal in respect of the grant of   **3–078** planning permission or of conditions attached to it. Third parties can only challenge the grant of planning permission by way of an application for judicial review, for which leave must be obtained, and hence only on the limited grounds available in such proceedings.[87] Even where such grounds can be substantiated, which is comparatively rare, the court has discretion whether or not to quash the decision and, for example, might choose not to do so if it decided that the error of law or procedural defect was not material.[88] Anyone wishing to challenge a planning decision in the courts in this way must act with great promptness and apply to the High Court under R.S.C. Order 53 as soon as possible and in any event within three months, for leave to challenge the decision. The need for prompt action cannot be over-estimated and the courts will readily refuse an application for leave to challenge, or later exercise their discretion not to quash a planning decision, unless an applicant takes immediate action.[89]

Call-in of Applications

Section 77 of the T.C.P.A. gives the Secretary of State power   **3–079** exercisable by direction to call-in applications for his own decision, thereby removing jurisdiction from the local planning authority to himself. Such directions are rare and used mainly where further consideration is thought appropriate by the Secretary of State; they may relate to categories of proposed developments as well as to

---

[87] An error of law, procedural impropriety or manifest unreasonableness.

[88] As for example in the *Twyford Down* case, (*Twyford Parish Council v. Secretary of State for the Environment* [1992] 1 C.M.L.R. 276), where it was held that even if the requirements of EC Directive 85/337 had not been complied with (which the judge did not find) such failure had not materially prejudiced the applicants.

[89] In *R v. Swale Borough Council and Medway Ports Authority, ex p. the Royal Society for the Protection of Birds* [1991] J.P.L. 39; [1991] 1 P.L.R. 6, the failure to apply promptly was one principal ground for refusing to intervene, notwithstanding that the judge granting leave to make the application had considered the question of delay at that preliminary stage.

individual applications, usually where planning issues of more than local importance arise. The calling-in of an application is normally the result of representations by interested parties or following notification to the Secretary of State by the relevant local planning authority. The main criteria and procedures for the calling-in of an application are set out in the Town and Country Planning (Development Plans and Consultation) Directions 1992 (reproduced at Annex 3 of DoE Circular 19/92). Local planning authorities are required to notify the Secretary of State of any application not in accordance with the development plan, which they do not propose to refuse and which involves:

    (1) more than 150 houses or flats;

    (2) more than 10,000 square metres of retail floor space;

    (3) development of land of or for an interested planning authority, whether alone or jointly; and

    (4) any other development which, by reason of its scale or nature or the location of the land, would significantly prejudice the implementation of the development plan's policies and proposals.

3–080   The other notification requirements are set out in the Town and Country Planning (Shopping Development) (England and Wales) Direction 1986 (reproduced as Annex A to PPG6) whereby local authorities must notify the Secretary of State of any applications in relation to development involving more than 250,000 square feet (23,325 square metres) gross shopping floorspace, whether or not it is consistent with the development plan.

3–081   When an application is "called- in", this will almost invariably lead to a public local inquiry being arranged by the Secretary of State before he takes his decision. It is theoretically possible for the application to be considered by way of written representations or at an informal hearing, as with appeals (see below), but if a case is important enough to be called-in, it will in practice be dealt with by public inquiry. Those entitled to appear at such an inquiry are the same as those entitled to be heard at appeals by way of public inquiry (see paragraph 3–088).

3–082   The Secretary of State can also issue directions under Article 14 of the GDO restricting the right of a local authority to grant planning permission, either in respect of a particular development proposal or in relation to developments of a specified type or class, either for a specified period or indefinitely. He may, for example, require that before granting permission the local authority must refer the papers to the Department of the Environment so that it can decide whether to call-in the application, *i.e.* to "hold" the application. If he later decides not to call-in the application it remains with the local planning authority for decision in the usual way.

Appeals

The applicant for planning permission is entitled to appeal to the   3–083
Secretary of State in respect of the refusal of planning permission, the
imposition of conditions on the grant of planning permission, or the
failure by the planning authority to determine the application within a
period of 8 weeks (16 weeks where an environmental statement has
been provided) or such extended period as the applicant may have
agreed with the planning authority.[90]

An appeal to the Secretary of State can be dealt with by public local   3–084
inquiry, by written representations, or by informal hearing. The
written representations procedure can be used only if both the
planning authority and the applicant so agree; in other words, either
can elect not to proceed in this way.[91] An informal hearing takes place
where either party (or both) elects for a public inquiry, but in the
opinion of the Secretary of State the issues are relatively straightforward and can be dealt with by informal hearing. Both parties must
however agree to a hearing before this procedure can be used. It
generally takes the form of a round table discussion chaired by an
independent Inspector from the Planning Inspectorate, an Executive
Agency of the Department of the Environment.[92]

The written representations procedure, as its title suggests, involves   3–085
the exchange of written submissions between the applicant and the
planning authority. The planning authority may notify third parties of
a written representations appeal, so that they have the opportunity of
submitting representations, but whether it does so is a matter entirely
within its discretion; many planning authorities do not. Where they do
not, third parties have no other right to participate.[93]

Procedure by public local inquiry is somewhat more elaborate.   3–086
There are special rules for major inquiries[94] (not considered here) and
the following comments deal with the rules for ordinary inquiries.[95]
Shortly after the appeal documents are received by the Department of
the Environment, it will fix a timescale for submission of statements of

---

[90] T.C.P.A., s.78.
[91] The right to a hearing for the appellant or local planning authority is conferred by
s.79(2) of the T.C.P.A., or Sched. 6, para. 2(4) for called-in applications.
[92] See DoE "Code of Practice for Informal Hearings" reproduced as Annex 2 to DoE
Circular 10/88.
[93] Town and Country Planning (Appeals) (Written Representations Procedure) Regulations 1987, (S.I. 1987 No 701); DoE Circular 11/87.
[94] See the Town and Country Planning (Inquiries Procedure) Rules 1992, (S.I. 1992 No.
2038) and DoE Circular 24/92.
[95] See the Town and Country Planning (Determination by Inspectors) (Inquiries
Procedure) Rules 1992, (S.I. 1992, No. 2039) and DoE Circular 24/92. All references to
Rules in this section are to these Inquiries Procedure Rules.

case. From that time ("the relevant date"), the planning authority has six weeks in which to submit a statement of its case and the appellant nine weeks (*i.e.* three weeks longer than the planning authority) to submit a statement of its case. The statements must be accompanied by a list of the documents to which reference may be made. The time limits for submission of statements of case are not always observed and in practice sanctions are rarely applied to defaulters.

3–087   An inquiry date will be fixed by the Department of the Environment, in consultation with the appellants and the planning authority. Normally this will be several months after the appeal documents have been submitted. Three weeks before the inquiry date, the appellant and the planning authority must serve copies of their evidence on the Planning Inspectorate and on each other. Generally, third parties are not entitled to copies of the statements of case or evidence, although there are limited exceptions in special cases, *e.g.* owners or agricultural tenants of the site who have made representations to the planning authority in response to a formal notice of the application, or any person from whom the Secretary of State requires a statement of case under Rule 6(6). This requirement may be made where a person has notified the Secretary of State of an intention or wish to appear at an inquiry, and will give four weeks for a statement of case to be served.

3–088   Inquiries normally proceed in an adversarial manner, with witnesses being called to give evidence and to be cross-examined in turn. Each inquiry is conducted by an independent Inspector from the Planning Inspectorate. He will control the procedure and decide who may appear in addition to those who are entitled to do so. The appellant (or applicant for called-in applications) and the local planning authority have the right to appear at an inquiry,[96] to call witnesses to give evidence and to cross-examine other witnesses.[97] The appellant also has the right to give an opening statement and to make the final submissions; the order in which anyone else appears at the inquiry is in the inspector's discretion.[98] It is usual in practice for the local planning authority to be the first party to cross-examine the appellants' witnesses and to follow the appellants in presenting their case. The position of other parties at the inquiry depends upon the category into which they fall:

  (1) Statutory parties. Anyone who is an owner or agricultural tenant of the land to which an appeal relates and who responded to the notification within the prescribed 21 day

---

[96] r.11(1)(a) and (b).
[97] r.15(3).
[98] r.15(2).

period is a statutory party.[99] As such, they are entitled to appear, to call evidence and to cross-examine other witnesses.[1] The statutory right to appear includes an implied right to be heard and to have representations properly considered by the Inspector or Secretary of State in coming to a decision.[2]

(2) Parties entitled to appear under Rule 11(1) if the appeal site is situated in their area. These include county and district councils and other statutory bodies, *e.g.* a National Park Committee, an urban development corporation and a housing action trust. Anyone else has a statutory right to appear at the inquiry who has given notice of a wish to do so in accordance with Rule 6, has been required by the Secretary of State under rule 6(6) to serve a statement of case, and has done so within the four weeks allowed. All in this category have the right to be heard, to call witnesses, and to have their case considered. They can cross-examine at the Inspector's discretion, which must be exercised fairly, and in particular must take into account the risk of injustice or unfairness.[3] An objector would normally be given the right to cross-examine witnesses who had given evidence contrary to his case, provided his questions are directed to that evidence and are not repetitive, irrelevant or outside the purpose of the statute being considered.

(3) Other parties. Anyone may attend an inquiry and may listen to all oral evidence, which must be given in public, and may inspect any documentary evidence.[4] They may take part in the inquiry with the permission of the Inspector, but have no right to do so. The Inspector has a discretion whether or not to allow any party to appear, but permission to do so must not be unreasonably withheld.[5]

Anyone entitled or permitted to appear may present his case himself, or may be represented by counsel, a solicitor or some other person.

In practice, it is likely that all those who have a legitimate interest in the proposal will be allowed to present their views, even if not entitled to appear, although the extent to which they will be allowed to participate, for example in cross-examination, will be a matter for the

3–089

---

[99] s.79(4) of the T.C.P.A. applying s.71(2) of the T.C.P.A. to appeals. See Inquiries Procedure Rules, r.2.
[1] r.15(3).
[2] *Buxton v. Minister of Housing and Local Government* [1961] 1 Q.B. 278.
[3] *e.g. Nicholson v. Secretary of State for Energy* (1977) 76 L.G.R. 693; J.P.L. [1978] 41.
[4] T.C.P.A., s.321.
[5] r.11(2).

Inspector. The Inspector will always have in mind that a refusal to allow a person to make representations may provoke a subsequent application for judicial review of his decision for failing to have regard to a material consideration. He will not readily risk this, and as the principal participants will also generally prefer third parties not to have cause to challenge the outcome, the inquiries procedure is far more prone to allow in time-wasting irrelevant material than to exclude anything pertinent. In any event, anyone may make representations in writing to the Inspector before the end of the inquiry even where the Inspector has refused to hear such evidence orally.[6] Following the close of the inquiry the Inspector will make a formal inspection of the site and surrounding area, but no representations are permissible at that stage.

3–90   The determination of all planning appeals (and enforcement notice appeals) is delegated to the Inspector, except appeals by statutory undertakers relating to operational land.[7] However the Secretary of State retains the power to direct that he should recover jurisdiction to decide the appeal, and this is in practice done in a small minority of planning appeals (under 10%), which are of particular significance, either in planning terms or politically. Under the guidelines applicable to whether the decision should be made by the Secretary of State,[8] jurisdiction should be recovered in this way at least where an appeal is in respect of proposals:

(1)   for residential development of 150 or more houses;
(2)   for development of major importance having more than local significance;
(3)   giving rise to significant public controversy;
(4)   which raise important or novel issues of development control;
(5)   for retail development over 100,000 square feet;
(6)   for significant development in the Green Belt;
(7)   for the winning and working of minerals on a major scale;
(8)   which raise significant legal difficulties;
(9)   against which another Government Department has raised major objections;

or in cases linked to any such proposals.

3–091   The decision on an appeal determined by an Inspector is given by letter which will normally be available some weeks after the close of

---

[6] r.15(4).
[7] Sched. 6 of the T.C.P.A. and the Town and Country Planning (Determination of Appeals by Appointed Persons) (Prescribed Classes) Regulations 1981, (S.I. 1981 No. 804).
[8] "Planning: Appeals, Call-in and Major Public Inquiries", Cm. 43, 1986.

the procedure, *i.e.* inquiry, written representations or informal hearing. In other cases, where the Inspector sends a report to the Secretary of State for determination of the appeal, the Secretary of State will send out the decision letter; this process takes several weeks, and on occasion many months or even years.

Scotland

In Scotland, planning appeals, whether by way of written submission or public inquiry, are administered by Reporters chosen by the Secretary of State from a panel within the Scottish Office Reporters' Unit. The Reporter produces his report in two parts — Part I is a survey of his factual findings which is circulated to the parties for comment, and Part II which is subsequently sent to the Secretary of State and which contains the Reporter's recommendations.

3–092

Costs

The normal rule as to costs incurred on a planning inquiry relating to an appeal or a called-in application, or to a hearing on an appeal, is that each party must bear its own. However, there are provisions for the Secretary of State, on the application of one party to an inquiry or hearing,[9] to make an order for costs against another party on the basis that the latter's unreasonable conduct has led to costs being incurred unreasonably.[10] While this can be significant in relation to any appeal, in relation to a proposal involving an environmental assessment, where the costs can be particularly heavy, the provisions assume particular significance. An award of costs might be made, for example, where an applicant unreasonably fails to respond to requests for environmental information relating to his proposal.

3–093

The power to award appeal costs also applies following the late cancellation of an inquiry or hearing by either of the principal parties.[11] This could apply, for example, if an appellant withdraws an appeal without reasonable cause or if a local authority is forced to concede

3–094

---

[9] s.250(5) of the Local Government Act 1972 and s.320 and Sched. 6 of the T.C.P.A. (costs awards at inquiries); s.322 and para. 6(5), Sched. 6 of the T.C.P.A. (costs awards at hearings).

[10] Policy guidance set out in DoE Circular 8/93; see also DoE explanatory pamphlet "Costs Awards in Planning Appeals — A Guide for Appellants".

[11] T.C.P.A., s.322A, DoE Circular 8/93.

that a particular objection is not sustainable. Because of the very large costs often involved in environmental assessment, the penalty to an appellant who withdraws an appeal unreasonably or to a local authority who takes points on objection unreasonably, could be considerable. There is at the moment no power to award costs in written representation appeals, although that situation is being kept under review.

Legal Challenge

3–095   There is no appeal from a decision of the Secretary of State or of a planning Inspector, except on a point of law. In that event it is made to the High Court and must be lodged within six weeks from the decision.[12] Where grounds exist, an application for judicial review may of course be made.[13] However, given the substantial extent of discretion available to local authorities and the Secretary of State under the UK legislation in coming to planning decisions, the scope for legal appeal or judicial review is extremely limited, save only in respect of issues arising under EC Directive 85/337.

The Role of Environmental Issues in Dealing with Planning Applications

3–096   Broadly speaking, except where an environmental impact assessment or waste disposal or recovery is involved, the law does not distinguish between environmental and other issues. It is, and has been at all times since the inception of the modern planning system in 1947, the duty of a planning authority to take into account all material considerations, which certainly include environmental issues, before coming to a final decision on a planning application. Section 70 of the T.C.P.A. requires the local authority to have regard to all material considerations;[14] no further guidance is given in the T.C.P.A. as to what constitutes a "material consideration" but the issue has been considered by the courts of numerous occasions. It is normally

---

[12] T.C.P.A., ss.284, 288.

[13] Though leave to apply will not normally be granted in respect of a point of law which may be the subject of the statutory appeal procedure.

[14] ss.77 and 79 of the T.C.P.A. apply that section to decisions by or on behalf of the Secretary of State on decisions that are subject to call-in and appeal respectively.

interpreted broadly: thus in *Stinger v. Minster of Housing and Local Government*:[15]

" . . . any consideration which relates to the use and development of land is capable of being a planning consideration. Whether a particular consideration falling within that broad category is material in any given case will depend on the circumstances".[16]

Contaminated Land

The presence of contamination on any land is a material consider- **3–097**
ation that planning authorities must take into account when considering any proposal for the development of that land.[17] It is government policy that land which is already contaminated should be
brought to a standard where it is suitable for its actual or intended
use.[18] Guidance on the approach that planning authorities should take
to contaminated land is contained in Annex 10 of PPG 23. This spells
out that in preparing development plans, account must be taken of
possible effects on health and the environment of contaminated land,
and that these plans may include policies for its reclamation and
possible further use.[19] Local plans should set out detailed criteria to be
applied in determining applications for the development of land
which is or may be contaminated. Where any specific site is known to
be or considered likely to be contaminated, the local plans may also
make specific proposals for it.

There is no general legal obligation requiring a developer to **3–098**
undertake any investigations as to the presence and extent of
contamination on a proposed development site, nor to disclose such
information on this as he may have to the authority handling his
planning application. Nevertheless, where there is any significant
likelihood of contamination being present, a developer would be most
imprudent not to inform himself on the nature and extent of any
contamination that may be present, since it is likely to affect whether
or not spoil from the site is special waste, whether particular
precautions need be taken by those working on the site to meet health
and safety requirements, whether local surface waters and groundwater may become polluted in the course of the development, and, in

[15] [1971] 1 All ER 65 at 77, *per* Cooke J.
[16] See also *Great Portland Estates plc v. Westminster City Council*, [1985] A.C. 661, for a discussion of the general principles.
[17] See PPG 23, para. 3.2.
[18] PPG 23, Annex 10, para. 2.
[19] PPG 23, Annex 10, para. 4

particular, whether he can subsequently respond satisfactorily to inquiries by potential purchasers and/or occupiers, and their financiers, as to absence of contamination. Serious contamination can result in a site having negative value, *i.e.* the landowner has to pay a purchaster to take the site, and its liabilities, off his hands.

3–099   The local planning authority will frequently take the initiative, and notify a potential developer of the implications of the presence of contamination, should it suspect that it may be present. Further, authorities often include a question on contamination on their standard application forms. If it is known or strongly suspected that contamination is present to an extent that would adversely affect the development or infringe statutory requirements, an authority may insist upon an appropriate investigation by the developer, coupled with proposals by him for appropriate remediation, before the authority will determine any planning application. In such a case, the grant of planning consent is likely to be subject to remediation conditions. Where the likelihood of contamination is less strong, or where it is known that there is only modest contamination, then the authority may not insist on a prior investigation by the developer, but simply include conditions in the planning consent prohibiting the development from proceeding until the investigation and assessment of risks have been carried out, and the development adapted as needed to incorporate any necessary remedial measures. Planning consent may be given subject to conditions requiring the developer to notify the authority of the presence of any significant contamination that comes to light in the course of development.

3–100   Planning limitations, *e.g.* conditions or agreements, requiring the remediation of land will normally either set specific clean-up standards or require remediation to the satisfaction of the planning authority in consultation with some other body, normally the National Rivers Authority.[20] Where standards are set, these are frequently determined by reference to the Guidance Notes of the Inter-Departmental Committee on the Redevelopment of Contaminated Land (the ICRCL)—see Table 24/II for a list of current Guidance Notes. This guidance has however no legally binding effect, and planning authorities may apply different standards as they see fit.[21] Financial assistance for the redevelopment of contaminated land may be available through English Partnerships (the Urban Regeneration Agency), which administers the Derelict Land Grant. Such assistance

---

[20] This latter approach leaves indeterminate what action will be demanded of the developer, can lead to much subsequent dispute and delay and/or unexpectedly increased remedial costs, may be legally doubtful because it is not clear enough, and should only be accepted with great caution.

[21] See also paras. 24–027 to 24–030 on the remediation of contaminated land.

is however generally provided in relation to significant areas of contaminated land, and is not ordinarily directed at a single specific site.

Environmental Assessments

Where an environmental statement has been submitted with the planning application under the Town and Country Planning (Assessment of Environmental Effects) Regulations 1988, not only will that statement be a material consideration but the decision maker (whether local planning authority or Secretary of State) is required[22] to take environmental information (the statement and any other representations as to the environmental effects of the proposal) into account in reaching a decision. The weight to be given to those issues is a policy decision in the discretion of the local authority or, as the case may be, the planning Inspector or the Secretary of State, to be determined in accordance with national policy guidance, and also the development plan. This is consistent with the very discretionary nature of the British planning system. In practice, the increasing environmental awareness of recent years has caused environmental issues to be given greater prominence in planning decisions. This is broadly achieved by policy guidance, *e.g.* Department of the Environment Circulars urging greater environmental concern, or by discretionary policy decisions by the local authority, *e.g.* deciding that in their area or part of their area environmental matters should be given greater weight. The British planning system, in practice as well as in theory, therefore generally treats environmental issues as no different from others: except for waste disposal and recovery, Nature Reserves and Specially Protected Areas designated under the EC Birds and Habitats Directives,[23] they are factors to be weighed in the balance but no more than that.

3–101

Environmental Objectives

All planning authorities are required, when taking any action in respect of any of the matters listed below, in so far as they relate to the recovery or disposal of waste, to do so with the objectives set out in regulation 4 of the Waste Management Licensing Regulations 1994.[24]

3–102

---

[22] By reg. 4.
[23] 79/409 ([1979] O.J. L103) and 92/43 ([1992] O.J. L206) respectively; see paras. 5–245 to 5–257 and 5–262 to 5–275 below.
[24] S.I. 1994 No. 1056.

These are discussed more fully in Chapter 11 — they consist principally of:

(a) ensuring that waste is recovered or disposed of without endangering human health and without using processes or methods which could harm the environment (which includes adverse effects on the countryside and places of special interest);

(b) implementing so far as material any plan made under plan-making provisions; and, in relation to the disposal (only) of waste;

(c) establishing an integrated and adequate network of waste disposal installations, taking account of BATNEEC; and

(d) ensuring that the network enables (i) the EC as a whole to become self-sufficient in waste disposal and the United Kingdom individually to move towards that aim, taking account of geographical circumstances and any need for specialised installations, and (ii) waste to be disposed of in one of the nearest appropriate installations, by means of the most appropriate methods and technologies in order to ensure a high level of protection for the environment and public health.

The exercise of functions under plan-making provisions must have the further objectives of:

(e) encouraging the prevention or reduction of waste production and its harmfulness, in particular by the development of clean technologies, of products that make the minimum adverse impact on the environment during manufacture, use and final disposal, and of appropriate techniques for the final disposal of dangerous substances in waste destined for recovery; and

(f) encouraging the recovery of waste with a view to extracting secondary raw materials, and the use of waste as a source of energy.

To avoid duplication of controls, these objectives do not require a planning authority to deal with any matter that any pollution control authority has power to deal with.[25] For the same reason, authorities granting an authorisation under Part I of the EPA are not required to take account of these objectives, as they relate to the prevention of

---

[25] 1994 Licensing Regs., Sched. 4, para. 2(2).

detriment to the amenities of a locality, where planning permission for the relevant process has been granted on or after May 1, 1994.[26]

The functions to which these objectives apply are: 3–103

—   applications for planning permission and appeals in respect of such applications
—   considering the grant of planning permission in response to purchase notices and on determining appeals against enforcement notices
—   the deemed grant of planning permission to government departments and statutory undertakers
—   making and confirming discontinuance orders
—   all functions relating to development plans

Statutory and Other Consultees

With limited exceptions, no procedural advantages are given to   3–104
environmental interests. Nevertheless official bodies must be consulted in certain circumstances, as follows:

(1)   The Health and Safety Executive: on any proposed development on land which lies within an area it has notified to the local planning authority because of the presence in the vicinity of toxic, highly reactive, explosive or inflammable substances and which involves the provision of:
   (i)   residential accommodation;
   (ii)   more than 250 metres of retail floorspace;
   (iii) more than 500 metres of office floorspace; or
   (iv)   more than 750 metres of floorspace to be used for an industrial process or which is otherwise likely to result in a material increase in the number of persons working within or visiting the notified area;[27]
(2)   The National Rivers Authority: on development involving mining operations, works or operations in the bed of or on the banks of a river or stream, development for refining or storing mineral oils and their derivatives, development involving deposit of refuse or waste, development relating to

---

[26] 1994 Licensing Regs., reg.8(2).
[27] The Town and Country Planning General Development Order 1988 ("GDO") (S.I. 1988 No. 1813) Art. 18, para. (d), as amended by S.I. 1992 No. 658; see also DoE Circular 11/92 (WO 20/92) "Planning Controls for Hazardous Substances", March 1992.

sewage or waste treatment retention or disposal, development relating to use of land as a cemetery and development for the purposes of fish farming[28];

(3) The relevant waste regulation authority: on development within 250 metres of land which has been used for the deposit of waste or refuse within the previous 30 years, and in respect of which the waste regulation authority notifies the planning authority that it wishes to be consulted;[29]

(4) The Nature Conservancy Council or the Countryside Council for Wales: on development in or likely to affect a site of special scientific interest (an "SSSI"), or development within an area notified to the local authority by the relevant Council which lies within 2 kilometres of an SSSI;[30]

(5) The Minister of Agriculture, Fisheries and Food or the Secretary of State for Wales: on development not for agricultural purposes and not in accordance with the development plan which will involve or lead to a loss of 20 hectares or more of grade 1, 2 or 3a agricultural land.[31]

Otherwise, there is no statutory right of consultation for bodies concerned with the environment.

3–105   Nevertheless, a nature conservation body with recognised relevant expertise may, in a particular case, be held to have a legitimate expectation that it would be consulted, and in consequence may be given the right to challenge a planning decision by way of judicial review.[32] Although such bodies have been allowed to seek judicial review, the essentially discretionary nature of this procedure provides no enforceable right to be heard for those who have no clear property interest affected by a proposal, and most environmental groups will fall into this category. Nevertheless, on substantive issues it is as a matter of law wholly for the planning authority to give as much or as little weight to conservation interests as it thinks appropriate. For example, the fact of a site being contaminated will generally be a material consideration, but the extent to which the planning authority imposes conditions requiring the cleaning up of the contaminated land, and what those conditions should be, is wholly a matter for its discretion.

---

[28] GDO, Art. 18, paras. (j), (o) to (s) and (x) as amended by S.I. 1989 No. 1590.
[29] GDO, Art. 18, para. (w).
[30] GDO, Art. 18, para. (t).
[31] GDO, Art. 18, para. (v).
[32] e.g. the RSPB in R v. Swale Borough Council and Medway Ports Authority, ex p. the Royal Society for the Protection of Birds [1991] J.P.L. 39; [1991] 1 P.L.R. 6, where there had been previous communications between the parties giving the RSPB a legitimate expectation that it would be consulted in relation to the planning application in question.

There is no requirement that an applicant should provide environ- **3–106** mental improvement as part of any development, although some may choose to offer it. A planning authority may, in its discretion, seek it. But it is not a legal requirement; nor is there any policy requirement that it should be provided.

Inter-relationship between Planning and other Controls

The planning regime is only one of several that protect the **3–107** environment, and there is inevitably considerable potential overlap between them. It is Government policy, reflected in its guidance to the relevant authorities, that duplication of controls over any particular matter is to be avoided. The areas of competence of the various authorities are to be determined by reference to the specific objectives of the different control regimes and each authority must exercise its powers with a view to achieving its relevant objectives only. Thus, as a matter of law, a planning authority in the exercise of its planning functions is required to have regard to all relevant planning conside- rations, but to exclude from its mind all non-planning matters (other than the objectives laid down in the Waste Management Licensing Regulations[33] — see paragraphs 3–102 and 3–103). There is no clear definition of planning matters for these purposes but, historically, this has been interpreted as relating to land uses. The fact that a planning authority may have other duties as housing authority or as waste disposal authority is not relevant to the land use planning issues, so that a planning authority cannot use the powers given to it as planning authority to discharge functions given to it in another capacity.

The various forms of environmental control have developed in a **3–108** piecemeal fashion. Separate tasks are allocated to a variety of bodies but there has hitherto been no clarity on their proper inter-relationship and, except in special areas of the country such as National Parks, no formal co-ordination of the various interests in the preparation of their structure and local plans. This is exemplified in the Department of the Environment draft PPG on Nature Conservation, which invites planning authorities to have policies about nature conservation, but gives them no effective guidance on how to formulate these policies, nor on how they should conduct their consultations. They are, for example, invited to consult with English Nature on various matters, but no indication is given on the extent to which, if at all, they should

[33] At Sched. 4, para. 4.

111

consult with neighbouring local authorities. It appears from this that local planning authorities are not expected to perform a co-ordinating role, but nor is any other body.

3–109   The current guidance on the inter- relationship between planning powers and other powers is set out in PPG 1 in the following terms:

> "Decisions on individual applications should be based on planning grounds only, and must be reasonable. Planning legislation should not normally be used to secure objectives achievable under other legislation. This principle of non-duplication should be maintained even though the powers and duties resulting from other legislation may also be the concern of local authorities. But even where consent is needed under other legislation, the planning system may have an important part to play, for example in deciding whether the development is appropriate for the particular location. The grant of planning permission does not remove the need to obtain any other consents that may be necessary, nor does it imply that such consents will necessarily be forthcoming".[34]

As this implies, conflicts may quite properly arise between the objectives of different control regime. The differing requirements that they may impose on a proposed new development may well be inconsistent;[35] nevertheless liasion between the authorities can eliminate avoidable inconsistencies and unnecessary prejudice to the development.

3–110   The relationship between the two systems of control was at the centre of an appeal against refusal of planning permission for a clinical waste incinerator at Gateshead.[36] In that decision the Secretary of State makes it clear that while the planning system alone should determine locational issues of such facilities, according to the procedures and requirements of the planning system, it should not duplicate controls under the E.P.A. Where controls are available under the E.P.A., then those are the controls to be applied. The scope of these controls, and the possibility of imposing stricter standards (*e.g.* tighter emission limits), are not therefore legitimate concerns of a planning authority.

3–111   Conversely, if relevant planning permission is in force, the EPA prohibits a waste regulation authority that is considering an application for a waste management licence from rejecting it on the ground of

---

[34] para. 35.
[35] A typical example is a chimney stack that, to preserve visual amenity, should be short, but to avoid local pollution must have a substantial height.
[36] DoE Appeal reference APP/114505/A/91/177885 dated May 24, 1993. Decision quoted at length in [1994] Env. L.R. 11 (Q.B.D.).

preventing serious detriment to the amenities to the locality.[37] However to ensure the objectives of EC Directive 75/442 govern (see paragraphs 3–102 and 3–103), this only applies where the permission was granted after April 30, 1994.[38]

At Gateshead, one of the main issues was the impact of potential **3–112** emissions on neighbouring land uses; that was stated to be a proper matter to take into account when considering whether or not to grant permission. However the control of those emissions falls under Part I of the E.P.A., and these separate controls were considered adequate to deal with them. On an application for judicial review of the Secretary of State's decision it was upheld in the following terms:[39]

" . . . [T]he appropriate starting point is the Secretary of State's obligation to have regard to the development plan and other material considerations. It is clear beyond any doubt that the environmental impact of emissions to atmosphere is a material consideration at the planning stage. In support of that proposition one need look no further than the Town and Country Planning (Assessment of Environmental Effects) Regulations 1988. It follows, in my judgment, that the Secretary of State could not lawfully adopt a policy of hiving off all consideration of such environmental effects in their entirety to the EPA regime. But, just as the environmental impact of such emissions is a material planning consideration, so also is the existence of a stringent regime under the EPA for preventing or mitigating that impact and for rendering any emissions harmless. It is too simplistic to say 'the Secretary of State cannot leave the question of pollution to the EPA'.

It is accepted by the applicants[40] that there may come a point in the planning appeal process when the Secretary of State is entitled to be satisfied that, having regard to the existence of EPA controls, a residual difficulty or uncertainty is capable of being overcome, so that there is no reason to refuse planning permission. Whether that point has been reached is a question for the judgment of the decision taker on the facts of each individual case.

Where two statutory controls overlap, it is not helpful, in my view, to try to define where one control ends and another begins in terms of some abstract principle. If one does so, there is a very real danger that one loses sight of the obligation to consider each

---

[37] E.P.A., s.36(3).
[38] 1994 Licensing Regs., reg.9(7).
[39] [1994] Env. L.R. 11, at 23 (Q.B.D.). See also [1994] E.G.C.S. 92 (C.A.).
[40] *i.e.* the planning authority, which had applied for the judicial review.

case on its individual merits. At one extreme there will be cases where the evidence at the planning stage demonstrates that potential pollution problems have been substantially overcome, so that any reasonable person will accept that the remaining details can sensibly be left to the E.P.A. authorisation process.

At the other extreme, there may be cases where the evidence of environmental problems is so damning at the planning stage that any reasonable person would refuse planning permission, saying, in effect, there is no point in trying to resolve these very grave problems through the E.P.A. process. Between those two extremes there will be a whole spectrum of cases disclosing pollution problems of different types and differing degree of complexity and gravity. Reasonable people might well differ as to whether the proper course in a particular case would be to refuse planning permission, or whether it would be to grant planning permission on the basis that one could be satisfied that the problems could and would be resolved by the E.P.A. process. But that decision is for the Secretary of State to take as a matter of planning judgment, subject, of course, to challenge on normal *Wednesbury* principles.

It is clear that the Secretary of State does not operate a blanket 'leave it all to the E.P.A' policy. In certain cases . . . the Secretary of State has concluded that the potential pollution problems revealed at the planning stage are so serious that he should refuse planning permission. In this case, he has concluded that the controls available under the E.P.A. 'for this proposal' are such that there would be 'no unacceptable impact on adjacent land'."

3–113   This judgment was upheld by the Court of Appeal, which clearly stated that HMIP should not be inhibited by the grant of planning permission from refusing to authorise a process if in its discretion that appears the proper course. Unless therefore it had already become clear on consideration of the planning application that some discharges were bound to be unacceptable, it was within the competence and jurisdiction of HMIP to determine the issues in the application before it, and the matter could properly be left to it.

3–114   On a point of quite general application, the Court of Appeal also observed that

"Public concern is, of course, and must be recognised by the Secretary of State to be, a material consideration for him to take into account. But if in the end that public concern is not justified, it cannot be conclusive. If it were, no industrial development — indeed very little development of any kind — would ever be permitted".

114

Following the Gateshead decision, PPG 23 "Planning and Pollution   3–115
Control" was issued, which deals with the relationship between the
planning and pollution controls as they apply to proposed developments that are potentially polluting or are to be on contaminated land.
It confirms the need to avoid duplication of controls, and aims to
encourage close consultation to prevent this.[41] The PPG accepts that
the dividing lines between planning and pollution controls is not
always clear cut.[42] The function of the planning system is to regulate
the location of development and the control of operations to avoid or
minimise adverse effects on land use for the environment, and also
what happens after the development or use of land has ceased.[43] It
must however focus on whether a proposed development is an
acceptable use of the land rather than on the control of the process or
substances involved. Material (planning) considerations in this context include:

— Location
— Impact on amenity
— The risk and impact of potential pollution on the use of other
  land
— Prevention of nuisance
— Impact on transport networks and on the surrounding
  environment
— Restoration of the land to standards fit for an appropriate
  after use.[44]

In an important passage it is said: 3–116

"Planning authorities will need to consult pollution control
authorities in order that they can take account of the scope and
requirements of the relevant pollution controls. Planning authorities should work on the assumption that the pollution control
regime will be properly applied and enforced. They should not
seek to substitute their own judgement on pollution control issues
for that of the bodies with the relevant expertise and the statutory
responsibility for that control".[45]

This is reinforced by a further statement:

"Lack of confidence in the effectiveness of controls imposed
under pollution control legislation is not a legitimate ground for
the refusal of planning permission or for the imposition of

---

[41] paras. 1.3, 1.4.
[42] para. 1.34.
[43] para. 1.11.
[44] para. 1.33; see also para. 3.2.
[45] para. 1.34.

conditions on the planning information that merely duplicates such controls".[46]

3–117   Though few would argue in principle with this division of responsibility, there is room for argument, to put it no higher, that HMIP does not invariably impose standards as stringent as it might in setting conditions for processes subject to Integrated Pollution Control. Yet there is in practice little that those in the neighbourhood of such a process can effectively do if a development that is acceptable on pure planning grounds is given an authorisation to operate on relatively undemanding conditions, provided these are not so lax as to be manifestly unreasonable.

3–118   The requirement to consult extends also to proposed developments in the vicinity of a potentially polluting process. Where any of certain kinds of development is proposed, the planning authorities are recomended to consider consulting the regulatory authority, if the development is to be within 500m (measured from site boundaries) of a process subject to IPC or within 250m of a process subject to local authority air pollution control or of a site that has been used for depositing waste at any time within the previous 30 years. The types of development to which this recommendation applies include the construction of residential accommodation, any development which will attract people on a regular basis, including shopping centres, offices and open space, any other potential air polluting development which "gives rise to concerns" of a cumulative impact when taken with the first process, and the construction of tall buildings where they could be affected by emissions from neighbouring full chimneys.

3–119   The advice in PPG 23 in relation to applications for outline planning consent is that this is not usually appropriate for a development where the risk of pollution is significant. Accordingly the advice says that a full planning application should normally be required unless all matters relevant to assessing the risk of pollution can be considered at the outline stage.[47] Likewise, a waste management licence should not normally be issued until full planning permission has been granted for the activity. Nevertheless, it is also explicitly stated that it is recognised that in many instances an applicant does not have sufficient information to make an application for an IPC authorisation at the same time as his planning application, and staged applications for the IPC authorisation may in such instances be appropriate.[48] The effect of this guidance is that either the full planning application must be granted before the applicant has worked out his detailed engineering design,

---

[46] para. 3.23.
[47] para. 3.20.
[48] para. 3.7.

116

which in many cases will be out of the question, or he must develop detailed engineering drawings for the purposes of obtaining his authorisation with no certainty that planning consent will ever be granted, thus forcing him to risk substantial investments of time and money.[49]

There is no legal force behind the advice that a full planning   3–120
application should normally be required: it is policy guidance. In practice, it is often impractical to submit an application for full permission for a major scheme. Where an environmental statement is provided, it should contain sufficient information to enable the planning authority to deal with matters; if it does not, the authority has powers to require further information.[50] Where no environmental statement is provided, a planning authority can indicate that it requires further details, but there is no sanction to enforce the supply of that material:[51] failure to determine the application may simply result in an appeal to the Secretary of State, and in general he is more prepared than local authorities to deal with outline applications.

Enforcement

Enforcement of the planning system is almost entirely in the hands   3–121
of public authorities. In general, a member of the public or a neighbour is powerless to initiate direct action in the courts to enforce planning control. Breach of planning control is not in itself a criminal act liable to a penalty. It is open to the planning authority to take action in respect of that breach of planning control, but the authority has a complete discretion whether or not to do so. There is extensive policy guidance in PPG 18 on the approach which planning authorities should adopt, which emphasises that formal action to enforce planning control should not be taken unless it is essential and unless there is no other means available. If a planning authority decides not to take action in relation to breach of planning control, there is effectively nothing which any other person can do as a matter of law under the planning

---

[49] Overcoming the twin hurdles of obtaining both planning consent and IPC authorisation would be substantially simplified if the equivalent of outline planning permission were made available under the IPC regime, whereby an outline authorisation of a process would stipulate maximum emission limits, with full authorisation being available when the applicant has produced designs capable of complying with those limits and shown himself to be competent to operate the process.

[50] Town and Country Planning (Assessment of Environmental Effects) Regs. 1988, reg.21.

[51] GDO, Art. 7; Town and Country Planning (Applications) Regs. 1988, reg.21.

system. A breach of planning control only becomes an illegal action, giving rise to possible prosecution, when the authority has already taken steps to remedy that breach — typically by serving an enforcement notice or breach of condition notice — and when there has been a non-compliance by those against whom action is being taken. Although prosecution of the offence is not limited to the local authority, in practice only it would have the information needed to mount a prosecution, and only it can take the requisite preliminary steps. It is the experience of many planning authorities that enforcing planning control through the courts is unsatisfactory, partly because of the delay involved and partly because the criminal courts, which are not familiar with the operation of planning control, may decide that there is reasonable doubt as to the commission of an offence, and that penal sanctions should therefore not be imposed on the defendant.

3–122   The regime of enforcement of planning control has been the subject of much disquiet over its technicality and the delays in taking effective action. It has also been the subject of a great deal of litigation; not least because of the criminal sanctions which apply ultimately, and in some cases the very lucrative nature of the non-consented use. A number of statutory reforms have been attempted over the years, the last in the form of the PCA, which sought to implement some of the reforms recommended in a Government commissioned review, "the Carnwath Report".[52] The following main changes to the regime were made by the PCA, largely as a result of these recommendations:

(1) New rules on immunity from enforcement action through lapse of time. If enforcement proceedings are not taken within specified time limits, then a breach of planning control becomes lawful and cannot thereafter be restrained. These time limits are now generally four years in the case of change of use to use as a single dwelling, ten years in the case of other changes of use, four years in the case of operations carried out without planning permission, and ten years in the case of operations in breach of planning conditions.[53] Previously, changes of use were only immune if the change had taken place before the end of 1963 and the changed use had been maintained thereafter;

(2) The introduction of breach of condition notices, which enable summary enforcement of breaches of condition;[54]

[52] "Enforcing Planning Control" (HMSO), 1989.
[53] T.C.P.A., s.171B.
[54] T.C.P.A., s.187A.

118

(3) Placing on a statutory footing the power to obtain injunctions for breaches of planning control;[55]

(4) The introduction of a new procedure for obtaining information where an authority considers there may have been a breach of planning control, namely the planning contravention notice;[56]

(5) A new power of entry on to land to check if a breach of planning control has taken place or if any enforcement action has been complied with;[57]

(6) Amendments to the drafting and service of enforcement notices;[58]

(7) A requirement for leave of the Court in order to appeal to the High Court following an appeal against an enforcement notice, mirroring judicial review procedure.[59] Formerly such appeals were of right.

The principal means of enforcing planning control are enforcement notices and breach of condition notices. Other remedies are a stop notice or a court order for an injunction, although these remedies are seldom used.

3–123

Enforcement Notice

An enforcement notice may apply to any breach of planning control.[60] It must (1) state the matters which constitute the alleged breach of planning control, where it is sufficient if "it enables any person on whom a copy of the notice is served to know what those matters [*i.e.* the matters constituting the breach] are"; (2) state whether the breach is the carrying out of development without permission or the failure to comply with a condition; (3) specify the steps required to be taken to remedy the breach or any injury to amenity caused by the breach; (4) specify the date on which the notice is to take effect; (5) specify the period for compliance; (6) specify the reasons why the authority consider it expedient to issue the notice; (7) specify the

3–124

---

[55] T.C.P.A., s.187B.
[56] T.C.P.A., ss.171C and 171D; previously existing powers to obtain information under s.330 of the T.C.P.A. and s.16 of the Local Government Act 1972 are retained.
[57] T.C.P.A., ss.196A, 196B and 196C; more general rights of entry for certain purposes of the T.C.P.A. (except enforcement) are contained in s.324 of the T.C.P.A.
[58] T.C.P.A., ss.172 to 173A.
[59] T.C.P.A., s.289 (4A).
[60] T.C.P.A., s.172.

precise boundaries of the land to which the notice relates, whether by plan or otherwise; and (8) be accompanied by an explanatory note including a copy of relevant sections of the T.C.P.A., or a summary setting out the rights of appeal and the requirement to submit grounds of appeal.[61]

3–125   There is no restriction on what an enforcement notice may require in order to achieve its purposes, namely to remedy the breach complained of, provided it is not unreasonable. It may for example demand the discontinuance of any use, the restoration of the land to its condition before the breach took place,[62] or the remedying of any injury to amenity caused by the breach.[63] Other requirements may be the alteration or removal of any buildings or works; the carrying out of any building or other operations; the ceasing of any activity, save to the extent specified in the notice; and (where the breach complained of is demolition) construction of a replacement building.[64]

3–126   An appeal may be made to the Secretary of State for the Environment against an enforcement notice by anyone having an interest in the land to which a notice relates, or by anyone occupying the land by virtue of a licence, whether or not a copy of the notice has been served on them.[65] The appeal must be on one or more of seven statutory grounds:[66]

(a) that planning permission ought to be granted for the breach complained of;

(b) that the matters alleged have not occurred;

(c) that the matters alleged do not constitute a breach of planning control;

(d) that no enforcement action could be taken in respect of any breach caused by the matters complained of at the time the notice was served;

(e) that copies of the notice were not properly served;

(f) that the steps required by the notice are excessive; and

(g) that any period specified for compliance is too short.

An appeal must be made to the Secretary of State before the date for compliance specified in the enforcement notice.[67]

---

[61] T.C.P.A., s.173 and the Town and Country Planning (Enforcement Notices and Appeals) Regulations 1991, (S.I. 1991 No. 2804), regs. (3) and (4).

[62] T.C.P.A., s.173(5)(a).

[63] T.C.P.A., s.173(4)(b).

[64] T.C.P.A., s.173(5) and (6).

[65] T.C.P.A., s.174(1).

[66] T.C.P.A., s.174(2).

[67] T.C.P.A., s.174(4).

Both the appellant and the local planning authority have a right to **3–127** be heard at an appeal[68] save where either party fails to comply with certain procedural requirements.[69] That right is exercisable through a public local inquiry.[70] Inquiries procedure is set out in the Town and Country Planning (Enforcement) (Inquiries Procedure) Rules 1992,[71] which are largely similar in operation to the planning appeals inquiries procedure rules (see paragraphs 3–086 to 3–089 above). Both parties may agree that the appeal should be dealt with by way of written representations,[72] although in practice an appeal in respect of an enforcement notice is almost invariably heard at a public local inquiry. The operation of the enforcement notice is suspended while the appeal is outstanding and this could easily involve a delay of up to a year.

As with decisions on planning applications, there can be no appeal **3–128** from the decision of the Secretary of State on a contravention notice appeal except on a point of law, and again the appeal must be lodged within six weeks of his decision.[73] In this case however leave of the court to pursue the appeal must first be obtained.

Once the enforcement notice takes effect, there is a period for **3–129** compliance, which varies from case to case. If an enforcement notice has not been fully complied with at the end of the period for compliance then the owner of the land at that time is in breach of the notice[74] and therefore guilty of an offence.[75] Anyone who has control of or an interest in the land who continues, or permits or causes to continue, any activity which is required by the notice to cease, after the end of the compliance period is also guilty of an offence.[76] Such offences are triable either summarily (where the maximum fine is £20,000) or on indictment (where there is no limit to any fine that may be imposed);[77] in setting the level of the fine any financial benefit arising from the offence must be taken into account.[78] Alternatively, the local authority is empowered to enter on the land, take any necessary steps to end the non-compliance and to recover its costs from the owner;[79] however this is usually an unattractive option, not

---

[68] T.C.P.A., s.175(3).
[69] T.C.P.A., s.176(4).
[70] T.C.P.A., s.320 and Local Government Act 1972, s.250.
[71] S.I. 1992 No. 1903.
[72] See para. 3–085.
[73] T.C.P.A., ss.285, 289.
[74] T.C.P.A., s.179(1).
[75] T.C.P.A., s.179(2).
[76] T.C.P.A., s.179(4) and (5).
[77] T.C.P.A., s.179(8).
[78] T.C.P.A., s.179(9).
[79] T.C.P.A., s.178.

least because of uncertainties on whether costs will in practice be recoverable from the owner.

Breach of Condition Notice

3–130   A breach of condition notice ("BCN") does not apply to all breaches of planning control but, as the title suggests, only to breaches of conditions or limitations contained in a planning permission.[80] Where it applies, a breach of condition notice is an exceptionally powerful weapon since, unlike enforcement notices, there is no right of appeal to the Secretary of State. A BCN may be served on anyone who is carrying out or has carried out the development or anyone in control of the land, and may require that person (known as "the person responsible") to secure compliance with the conditions specified[81] by the carrying out of specified steps or stopping of specified activities. If this is not done by the end of the period allowed (which must be at least 28 days) then the person responsible is in breach of the notice[82] and liable on summary conviction to a maximum fine of level 3 on the standard scale.[83] There are two statutory defences to prosecution; that the defendant took all reasonable measures to secure compliance with the conditions in the notice[84] or, where the defendant was served with the notice on the ground that he had control over the land, that he no longer has control.[85] Government guidelines[86] advise that such notices should only be used where the specified condition is legally valid, satisfies the general criteria for conditions,[87] is enforceable and in force, and has clearly, on the evidence available, been breached. However these are not statutory requirements. This could lead to arguments over detailed planning law points being raised before the magistrates during a prosecution. Moreover the service of a notice does not prevent an application (and later appeal) to vary a condition — which could lead to applications for adjourned hearings pending the outcome of an appeal.[88] The validity of the notices may also be challenged by application for judicial review, in the normal way.

[80] T.C.P.A., s.187A.
[81] T.C.P.A., s.187A(1) and (2).
[82] T.C.P.A., s.187A(9).
[83] T.C.P.A., s.187A(12).
[84] T.C.P.A., s.187A(11)(a).
[85] T.C.P.A., s.187A(11)(b).
[86] DoE Circular 17/92, Annex 2.
[87] Set out in DoE Circular 1/85.
[88] See, *e.g. R. v. Polly Newland* (1987) 54 P. & C.R. 222; [1987] J.P.L. 851.

Planning Contravention Notice

A supplementary remedy for a planning authority is service of a   **3–131**
planning contravention notice.[89] This does not enforce planning
control, but it is a formal notice alerting the recipient to the possible
breach of planning control (and, hence, the possibility of enforcement
action), requiring the recipient to provide information about current
and previous activities on the land and inviting the recipient to come
forward with proposals for regularising the alleged breach of planning
control. Service of the planning contravention notice does not invoke
any penalties in itself, but it is a criminal offence not to respond
properly to the notice, by failing either to answer or to comply with
any requirement.[90] It is a separate offence knowingly or recklessly to
make a false statement in response.[91] Both offences are triable
summarily with a maximum fine at level 3 on the standard scale.

Stop Notice

A stop notice can only be served where an enforcement notice has   **3–132**
already been served. It has the advantage of producing an effectively
instantaneous enforcement of planning control, but it has two
disadvantages, at least as regards the planning authority. Firstly, the
authority may be liable to pay compensation where the preceding
enforcement notice is quashed, withdrawn or varied (except in
consequence of a later grant of planning permission), or where the
stop notice itself is withdrawn.[92] The compensation payable must
relate to any loss or damage directly attributable to the prohibition in
the stop notice and includes (by statute[93]) any sum in breach of
contract.[94] Secondly, it is not generally possible to use a stop notice for
limiting a breach, rather than stopping it completely; in many
instances a planning authority may not wish to stop an activity
completely but simply to control it, and a stop notice is inappropriate
for that. Procedurally, a stop notice can be served at the same time as

---

[89] T.C.P.A., s.171C.
[90] T.C.P.A., s.171D.
[91] T.C.P.A., s.171D(8).
[92] T.C.P.A., s.186.
[93] T.C.P.A., s.186(4).
[94] See *Graysmark v. South Hams District Council* [1989] 03 E.G. 75, for basis of assessment
of compensation.

an enforcement notice or at any time thereafter but before the enforcement notice takes effect.[95]

Injunctions

3–133   Applications to the court for injunctions to enforce planning control are seldom made, partly because the courts are reluctant to intervene except in a clear-cut case, and partly because an injunction is in any event a discretionary remedy and will not necessarily be granted, even in the face of a flagrant breach of planning control. The grant of injunctions in such circumstances has now been put on a statutory footing[96] and are an important addition to other enforcement powers in cases where urgent action is required, for example in circumstances where the continuing breach might cause permanent harm to land. Provision is expressly made for injunctions against unidentified persons, specifically to prevent environmental harm.[97] It is in the court's discretion whether or not an undertaking in damages will be required from the local authority seeking an interlocutory injunction.[98]

Obtaining Information

3–134   Quite apart from the constraints of the legal framework, it is frequently a difficult question of fact as to whether there has been a breach of planning control. In relation to changes of use, in particular, it is not every change which involves a breach of planning control but only a "material" change of use. The question whether a use can be carried out in a residential area without significant environmental detriment is necessarily a subjective one. In many cases there may be problems in finding out what exactly is happening on a piece of land, despite various powers available to local authorities to discover the relevant information. These powers include, in particular, the new provisions for use of a planning contravention notice;[99] the power to require an occupier or person receiving rent in respect of premises to provide certain information as to ownership and use of land, so as to

---

[95] T.C.P.A., s.183.
[96] T.C.P.A., s.187B.
[97] T.C.P.A., s.187B(3); R.S.C., Ord. 110 inserted by S.I. 1992 No. 638.
[98] *Kirklees Borough Council v. Wickes Building Supplies Limited* [1992] 3 All E.R. 717 (H.L.).
[99] See para.

enable a local authority (or the Secretary of State) to make, issue or serve any order, notice or other document under the T.C.P.A.[1] and the more limited power to obtain particulars of any person's interests in land from any owner, occupier or managing agent, which are required by a local authority for the purpose of carrying out any of its statutory functions.[2]

Local planning authorities (and the Secretary of State) also have the power to gain entry on to any land at all reasonable hours on production of appropriate written authority to investigate any alleged breach of planning control on that or any adjoining land, to establish what action should be taken to remedy the position, or generally in pursuance of the authority's role in the enforcement of planning control.[3] This is in effect a general power to enter on land for the purpose of finding information and may be supported by warrant from a justice of the peace. Compensation is payable by the local authority (or Secretary of State) for damage to any land or chattels. The disclosure of any information as to any manufacturing process or trade secret by anyone exercising this right of entry is a criminal offence (which can be tried summarily or on indictment with a maximum penalty of two years imprisonment and an unlimited fine) save where such disclosure was made for enforcement purposes.

3–135

The practical enforcement of planning control is far from easy and certainly not clear-cut.

---

[1] T.C.P.A., s.330—the matters on which information may be required are: (a) the recipient's interest in the land; (b) the name and address of anyone else with an interest in the land; (c) the purpose for which the premises are being used; (d) the time that use began; (e) the name and address of anyone who has used the premises for the existing purpose. Failure to respond or to respond properly are also offences carrying the same scale fine (level 3) on summary convention as under planning contravention notices.

[2] Local Government (Miscellaneous Provisions) Act 1976, s.16—the maximum fine in this case is set at level 5, again on summary conviction.

[3] T.C.P.A., ss.196A, 196B and 196C.

Chapter 4

ENVIRONMENTAL IMPACT ASSESSMENTS

Definitions

It is desirable to clarify at the outset of this chapter the terminology   4–001
that is used here and generally in the literature, at least so far as it
concerns UK law and practice:

— An "environmental impact assessment" ("EIA") or "environmental assessment" ("EA") is the process by which the
effects of projects on the environment are assessed. In
practice these two terms are used interchangeably, EA being
the more normal usage in the United Kingdom, and EIA
generally that found in EC documents.
— An "environmental statement" ("ES") is a document or
series of documents providing a statement of environmental
information relating to a development project, provided for
the purpose of assessing the likely impact upon the environment of the development proposed.

Introduction

Consideration of the environmental impact of a development, in its   4–002
widest sense, always has been an integral part of the English planning
system, since a planning authority is required to have regard to all
material considerations, of which the environmental impact is inevitably one. Consequently, for many years the United Kingdom Government took the view that formal environmental statements were
unnecessary, because of these general provisions in the planning
system. However, it was decided at EC level that more formal steps

should be taken to try to ensure consistent assessment of the effects of major projects on the environment. From the early 1970s, the EC Commission emphasised the need to prevent pollution and nuisances at source, rather than trying to counteract their effects subsequently, and the need to take the effects of proposed developments on the environment into account at the earliest possible stage in planning and decision making processes. This increasingly articulated concern eventually emerged in Council Directive 85/337 of June 27, 1985 on "the assessment of the effects of certain public and private projects on the environment"[1] (referred to throughout this chapter as "the Directive"), which has the objective that the environmental effects of the more significant developments should be fully considered before they are allowed to be started.[2]

4–003   Because the Directive, in so far as it is directly applicable, has directly binding effects on planning authorities (being "emanations of the State"),[3] in addition to the domestic law that has been enacted to implement its terms, it is proper to consider the objectives and requirements of the EC legislation before addressing the variety of UK regulations on the same topic. In the event of any discrepancy, the supremacy of EC law necessarily means that any failure to comply with its requirements, even though local law has been fully observed, may expose the validity of the ultimate planning decision to legal challenge.[4] Nevertheless, since in practice much is left to the discretion of member states, the occasions where material differences can arise are comparatively limited.

4–004   One problem that awaits definitive resolution in the European Court of Justice is the extent to which a planning decision which is "safe" in UK law, because it has not been challenged in the Courts within the UK prescribed time limits, can nevertheless be challenged by subsequent proceedings alleging non-compliance with EC law. English law has relatively short and reasonably clear time limits for taking action in respect of the need for an environmental assessment in relation to a planning application, and a planning decision by the Secretary of State, for example, cannot be questioned in the UK courts after six weeks from his decision. In some circumstances it may nevertheless be open to, *e.g.* the EC Commission, and possibly other

---

[1] [1985] O.J. L175.
[2] For a fuller account of the genesis of the Directive see N. Haigh *op. cit.*
[3] See paras. 2–033, 2–034.
[4] See paras. 2–037 to 2–040.

third parties, to intervene outside these time limits on grounds of failure to comply with obligations imposed by the Directive.[5]

The Purposes of Environmental Impact Assessment

Environmental impact assessment does not in itself require preven-   **4–005**
tive action, or indeed any mitigating steps, to be taken. It is a mechanism intended to ensure decision-making authorities are *aware* of the *relevant issues* relating to the environment. Provided that the authorities have made themselves aware, the Directive leaves it completely open to them to sanction any project, however damaging to the environment it may be.

The preamble to the Directive sets out its purposes, and its language   **4–006**
must be interpreted consistently with those purposes. These include:-

(a) the best environmental policy consists in preventing the creation of pollution or nuisance at source, rather than subsequently trying to counteract their effects;

(b) it is necessary to take effects on the environment into account at the earliest possible stage in all the technical planning and decision making processes;

(c) environmental assessment must be conducted on the basis of the appropriate information supplied by the developer, which may be supplemented by the authorities and by the people who may be concerned by the project in question;

(d) for projects which are subject to assessment, at least a certain minimum amount of information must be supplied, concerning the project and its effects;

(e) the effects of a project on the environment must be assessed in order to take account of concerns to protect human health, to contribute by means of a better environment to the quality

---

[5] Although procedural time limits under domestic law are in principle equally binding in relation to actions involving issues of EC law, the domestic law must not make it impracticable for those with a legitimate right to do so to invoke EC law before the courts. The restrictive rules as to who may challenge planning decisions, and as to who is to be regarded as having a sufficient interest to be allowed to apply for judicial review, arguably restrict unduly the ability to enforce the provisions of the Directive in the courts. See also articles on proceedings by the European Commission concerning the application of the Directive by the UK government referred to in n.23 below.

of life, to ensure maintenance of the diversity of species and to maintain the reproductive capacity of the ecosystem as a basic resource for life.

The Requirements of the Directive[6]

4–007　The preamble to the Directive indicates that it is concerned with projects likely to have a *major* effect on the environment. By Article 1 it is applied to projects "likely to" have "significant" effects on the environment. The word "significant" must be interpreted in the light of the word "major" in the preamble. Since the purpose of the procedure is to assess the environmental effects, the phrase "likely to" must be interpreted as meaning "potentially may", rather than "probably will".

4–008　The only one of the terms in this phrase which is defined in the Directive is "project" which means:

> "the execution of construction works or of other installations or schemes, [and] other interventions in the natural surroundings and landscape including those involving the extraction of mineral resources."[7]

In most cases these would require planning permission under UK law, although the second limb of the definition is sufficiently wide to include certain actions, *e.g.* involving agriculture and forestry, within the definition for the purposes of the Directive, which are outside the scope of "development" for the purposes of UK planning control.

4–009　The fundamental requirement of the Directive[8] is that member states must adopt all measures necessary to ensure that, before development consent is given, projects likely to have significant effects on the environment by virtue, *inter alia*, of their nature, size or location are made subject to an assessment with regard to their effects. "Development consent" is defined as the decision of the competent authority or authorities which entitles the developer to proceed with the project. Where several consents are involved, it may not be easy to determine which is a development consent for these purposes. The

---

[6] A proposal to amend the Directive so as to clarify the assessment procedure and to revise the lists of projects subject to it was published in [1994] O.J. C130.
[7] Art. 1(2).
[8] Art. 2.

UK Regulations giving effect to the Directive treat planning permission (including outline planning permission) as the development consent. Thus, for example, they do not require environmental assessment for a specific allocation in a local plan, nor do they require environmental assessment of details submitted pursuant to an outline planning permission, even though the development may not proceed until the full permission covering the details is granted; it is open to question whether this is proper implementation of the Directive.

Where authorisation under other legislation is also necessary, for example for a process subject to integrated pollution control, or a nuclear power station controlled under the Radioactive Substances Act 1960, it is likewise arguable that whichever consent is last — at least in so far as it addresses matters capable of having an impact on the environment — is the relevant consent for the purposes of the Directive. The Secretary of State has made it clear that planning control should not seek to duplicate integrated pollution control.[9] Control of emissions is not normally therefore a matter for planning control but for integrated pollution control or local authority air pollution control. In practice, IPC authorisation could be obtained before or after (but usually after) planning consent. In other jurisdictions development consent for such facilities may be administered exclusively through a regime distinct from that applicable to other developments such as housing or roads; there can therefore be no automatic presumption that the planning procedure in the UK is necessarily the one that is determinative of the proper application of the Directive. This again exposes the problems arising out of the independent operation of different permitting regimes in respect of a single proposed development.   **4–010**

It is expressly provided that environmental impact assessment may be integrated into existing procedures for consents. The information to be provided is that which is "relevant to a given stage of the consent procedure and the specific characteristics of a particular project or type of project and of the environmental features likely to be affected",[10] Annex III to the Directive listing, under seven category headings, the nature of the information to be supplied. There are powers[11] for specific projects to be exempted in whole or in part from the provisions of the Directive, but only in exceptional cases and after first informing the European Commission.   **4–011**

---

[9] PPG 23: Planning and Pollution Control (July 1994), paras. 1.34 to 1.37. See also paras. 3–107 to 3–120 above.
[10] Art. 5(1)(a).
[11] In Art. 3.

4–012   Projects authorised by specific acts of national legislation are exempted from the Directive.[12]

4–013   It is possible for planning permission to be granted by an Act of Parliament, which may be sponsored by the Government or promoted by other bodies. Any private or hybrid works bills[13] must be accompanied by an environmental statement, where the works have not otherwise been given planning permission.[14] Works bills will be less common than in the past, as many projects previously considered in this way are now dealt with under the procedure set out in the Transport and Works Act 1992. Under this 1992 Act the Secretary of State for Transport can make statutory orders authorising specific rail and water-related transport projects (being railways, tramways, trolley vehicle and other prescribed guided transport systems, inland waterways, and prescribed works interfering with navigation in territorial waters, *e.g.* harbours and dock facilities), and these orders have the same effect as an Act of Parliament. By regulations made under the 1992 Act[15] an application for a statutory order of this kind must be accompanied by an environmental statement, unless the Secretary of State grants total or partial dispensation from this requirement in the particular case. In certain very limited circumstances an absolute waiver may be given in respect of a class of applications for orders.

4–014   The Directive requires that certain classes of project, namely those listed in Annex I and constituting very substantial developments, must be the subject of EA. Other classes of somewhat less substantial projects, listed in Annex II to the Directive, require an EA where the relevant member state decides that their characteristics so require. Broadly, these correspond with Schedules 1 and 2 to the UK Regulations.[16]

---

[12] It appears to be the case that this exemption in the Directive was included expressly to address the situation in Denmark where parliamentary approval of projects is quite common, and is always accompanied by an EIA. Those drafting the Directive therefore considered it unnecessary to stipulate for an EIA in such circumstances. The penultimate recital and Art. 1(5) expressly state that projects adopted by specific national legislation can be and are exempted from the application of the Directive "since the objectives of this Directive, including that of supplying information, are achieved through the legislative process". It has accordingly been suggested that there would be a breach of the Directive if a project authorised by Parliament were to proceed if in fact no EIA had been undertaken. Since on principle derogations from broad rules are to be construed narrowly, it must be open to the European Court of Justice to hold that at least an Annex I project proceeding under an Act of Parliament must have an EIA.

[13] The proposed Channel Tunnel rail link bill is an example of a hybrid bill.

[14] Order 27A, Standing orders of the House of Commons Private Business 1991, HC (1990–91) 582.

[15] The Transport and Works (Applications and Objections Procedure) Rules 1992 (S.I. 1992 No. 2902).

[16] See paras. 4–090 to 4–109.

Article 5 of the Directive obliges Member States to adopt measures **4–015** to ensure that the applicant supplies the information specified in Annex III to the Directive in as much as the member state concerned considers that[17] (a) the information is relevant to a given stage of the consent procedure and to the specific characteristics of a particular project or type of project and of the environmental features likely to be affected, and (b) a developer may reasonably be required to compile the information having regard, *inter alia*, to current knowledge and methods of assessment.

Although Article 5 of the Directive allows an EIA to be provided in **4–016** parts, *e.g.* at various stages of the consent process giving the information relevant to that stage, the UK Government has not adopted that approach, but has required the whole EIA at the planning stage, so that all the Annex III information is required then. There is no requirement for an EIA on the submission of details pursuant to planning conditions, even though these can relate to major aspects of the proposal, *e.g.* the siting of buildings.

The central effect of the Directive is thus solely to prescribe steps **4–017** that must be taken to ensure consideration of an environmental assessment of projects liable to have a significant impact. Intentionally, it creates no control whatsoever over whether or not a project should proceed, provided the requisite procedures have been followed, even though the assessment may indicate that major environmental damage will inevitably be caused: such decisions are left entirely to local determination.[18]

UK Legislation

The broad effect of the UK regulations is to require that in certain **4–018** cases an environmental statement (ES) be provided by an applicant for planning permission, and that this be considered by the planning authority. The Department of the Environment and the Welsh Office publishes "Environmental Assessment—A Guide to the Procedures",

---

[17] This form of words clearly ensures that Member States have total discretion on the issues mentioned, precluding intervention by, *e.g.* the European Commission, provided that the factors are at least considered, and the decision is not wholly unreasonable.

[18] This practical application of subsidiarity is given explicit recognition in the amendment of Article 130 of the Treaty of Rome, agreed at Maastricht in December 1991. While this generally allows for environmental measures proceeding under Article 130S to be adopted by qualified majority in the Council of Ministers instead of by unanimous vote as hitherto, measures relating to land use planning remain subject to the unanimity requirement, so giving every Member State a right of veto.

which contains much useful guidance. It is referred to here as the "Blue Book".

4–019   The Directive required member states to take the necessary measures to comply with it by July 3, 1988. The United Kingdom nearly achieved this deadline and the principal Regulations for England and Wales came into effect on July 15, 1988, namely the Town and Country Planning (Assessment of Environmental Effects) Regulations 1988,[19] as subsequently amended.[20] Additional Regulations have been made to govern particular forms of project that for a variety of reasons fall outside the broad class of developments covered by the principal Regulations. Table 4/I lists all the Regulations made in pursuance of the Directive (with those revoked noted in italics); Table 4/II lists official guidance on the principal items.

TABLE 4/I

Legislation	
England and Wales	
(i)	Town and Country Planning (Assessment of Environmental Effects) Regulations 1988 (S.I. 1988 No. 1199);
(ii)	Environmental Assessment (Afforestation) Regulations 1988 (S.I. 1988 No. 1207);
(iii)	Land Drainage Improvement Works (Assessment of Environmental Effects) Regulations 1988 (S.I. 1988 No. 1217);
(iv)	Environmental Assessment (Salmon Farming in Marine Waters) Regulations 1988 (S.I. 1988 No. 1218);
(v)	Highways (Assessment of Environmental Effects) Regulations 1988 (S.I. 1988 No. 1241);
(vi)	Harbour Works (Assessment of Environmental Effects) Regulations 1988 (S.I. 1988 No.1336);
(vii)	*Town and Country Planning General Development (Amendment) Order 1988 (S.I. 1988 No. 1272)—revoked by S.I. 1988 No.1813, item (viii) below;*
(viii)	Town and Country Planning General Development Order 1988 (S.I. 1988 No. 1813), Article 14(2);

[19] S.I. 1988 No. 1199.
[20] By S.I. 1990 No. 367, S.I. 1990 No. 1494, S.I. 1992 No. 1494, S.I. 1994 No. 677.

(ix)	*Electricity and Pipe-line Works (Assessment of Environmental Effects) Regulations 1989 (S.I. 1989, No. 167)—revoked by S.I. 1990 No. 442, item (xii) below);*
(x)	Harbour Works (Assessment of Environmental Effects) (No. 2) Regulations 1989 (S.I. 1989 No. 424);
(xi)	Town and Country Planning (Assessment of Environmental Effects) (Amendment) Regulations 1990 (S.I. 1990 No. 367);
(xii)	Electricity and Pipe-line Works (Assessment of Environmental Effects) Regulations 1990 (S.I. 1990 No. 442);
(xiii)	The Harbour Works (Assessment of Environmental Effects) Regulations 1992 (S.I. 1992 No. 1421);
(xiv)	Town and Country Planning (Assessment of Environmental Effects (Amendment) Regulations 1992 (S.I. 1992 No. 1494);
(xv)	Town and Country Planning (Simplified Planning Zones) Regulations 1992 (S.I. 1992 No. 2414);
(xvi)	Transport and Works (Applications and Objections Procedure) Rules 1992 (S.I. 1992 No. 2902),
(xvii)	The Town and Country Planning (Assessment of Environmental Effects) (Amendment) Regulations 1994 (S.I. 1994 No. 677);
(xviii)	The Highways (Assessment of Environmental Effects) Regulations 1994 (S.I. 1994 No. 1002).
Scotland	
(i)	Town and Country Planning (General Development) (Scotland) Amendment Order 1988 (S.I. 1988 No. 977);
(ii)	The Environmental Assessment (Scotland) Regulations 1988 (S.I. 1988 No. 1221);
(iii)	*Town and Country Planning (General Development) (Scotland) Amendment No. 2 Order 1988 (S.I. 1988 No. 1249)—revoked by S.I. 1992 No. 224, item (iv) below;*
(iv)	Town and Country Planning (General Development Procedure) (Scotland) Order 1992 (S.I. 1992 No. 224);
(v)	The Environmental Assessment (Scotland) (Amendment) Regulations 1994 (S.I. 1994 No. 2012).
Northern Ireland (i)	Roads (Assessment of Environmental Effects) Regulations (Northern Ireland) 1988 (S.R. No. 344);

135

(ii)	Planning (Assessment of Environmental Effects) Regulations (Northern Ireland) 1989 (S.R. No. 20);
(iii)	Environmental Assessment (Afforestation) Regulations (Northern Ireland) 1989 (S.R. No. 226);
(iv)	Harbour Works (Assessment of Environmental Effects) Regulations (Northern Ireland) 1990 (S.R. No.181);
(v)	Drainage (Environmental Assessment) Regulations (Northern Ireland) 1991 (S.R. No. 376).
	Discharges to Water (Assessment of Environmental Effects) Regulations (Northern Ireland) (in preparation).

TABLE 4/II

	Guidance
(i)	"Environmental Assessment—a Guide to the Procedures", issued by DoE and Welsh Office, 1988 (the "Blue Book");
(ii)	DoE Circular 15/88 (Welsh Office Circular 23/88) "Environmental Assessment" dated July 12, 1988.;
(iii)	SDD Circular 13/88 "Environmental Assessment: Implementation of EC Directive: The Environmental Assessment (Scotland) Regulations 1988" dated July 12, 1988;
(iv)	Forestry Commission booklet "Environmental Assessment of Afforestation Projects" dated August 4, 1988;
(v)	"Environmental Assessment of Marine Salmon Farms", note by Crown Estate Office dated July 15, 1988;
(vi)	DoE Circular 24/88 (Welsh Office Circular 48/88) "Environmental Assessment of Projects in Simplified Planning Zones and Enterprise Zones" dated November 25, 1988;
(vii)	SDD Circular 26/88 "Environmental Assessment of Projects in Simplified Planning Zones and Enterprise Zones" (relates to Scotland) dated November 25, 1988;
(viii)	DoE Memorandum on "Environmental Assessment" dated March 30, 1989 to the General Managers of New Towns Development Corporations and to the Chief Executive of the Commission for the New Towns (advice on projects arising in new towns);
(ix)	DTp Departmental Standard notice HD 18/88 "Environmental Assessment under EC Directive 85/337" dated July 1989;

(x)	DoE free leaflet "Environmental Assessment";
(xi)	Welsh Office free leaflet "Environmental Assessment/ Asesu'r Amgylchedd" (bilingual);
(xii)	Scottish Office free leaflet "Environmental Assessment— a Guide";
(xiii)	DoE and Welsh Office joint Circular (DoE 7/94, W.O. 20/94) "Environmental Assessment: Amendment of Regulations" on the amendments made by the 1994 Regulations (S.I. 1994 No.677).

For simplicity, the following text deals only with the principal 1988   **4–020**
Regulations, as amended by the 1994 Amendment Regulations[21]
which apply generally, and references to the "1988 Regulations"
should be so understood; likewise, reference to a specific Regulation
by number is to the relevant one of the 1988 Regulations as amended.
The requirement for an environmental statement (ES) in respect of a
development within their scope is part of the process for obtaining
planning permission. The requirement is for a single ES, and not one
split between various stages of the consent procedure. Save as
specifically provided in the other Regulations mentioned above, there
is no requirement for an environmental assessment for development
which does not require an application for planning permission, e.g.
because permission is already granted by virtue of the General
Development Order,[22] or because it is a development authorised by an
Act of Parliament, a development by the Crown (which includes
Government Departments), a development below the high water
mark of the sea *e.g.* developments on the foreshore or on the sea-bed,
or an agricultural or forestry operation.

Since the 1988 Regulations do not faithfully reproduce the Directive,   **4–021**
it would be unsafe to assume that compliance with them will also
amount to compliance with the Directive.[23] At all stages, there should
be compliance with both and, in the event of any difference, there
should be compliance with the more stringent requirements. For
example, under paragraph 4 of Annex III to the Directive[24] it is a

---

[21] S.I.s 1988 No. 1199, 1994 No. 677.

[22] See paras. 3–057 to 3–059.

[23] See, *e.g.* "Environmental Assessment—the Question of Implementation" by J. R.
Salter, [1992] J.P.L. 313, considering the intepretation of the Directive by the UK
Government; European Commission Press Release: 92/51, July 31, 1992, and UK
Government News Release (No 549), July 31, 1992, reproduced in J.P.L. 913,
Proceedings by the European Commission concerning the application of the
Directive by the UK Government; "Environmental Assessment: The Challenge from
Brussels" by J. R. Salter, [1992] J.P.L. 14, looking at whether the Directive has been
properly implemented in the UK.

[24] See paras. 4–051 to 4–053.

mandatory requirement that where appropriate there should be given an outline of the main alternatives studied by the developer and an indication of the main reasons for his choice. Under the 1988 Regulations this requirement is optional. The environmental statement "may" include these matters; this appears to be an unduly liberal interpretation of the phrase "where appropriate" in the Directive. Also, under paragraph 4 of Annex III to the Directive it is mandatory that the description of the development should include secondary, cumulative, short, medium and long term, permanent and temporary, positive and negative effects of the project. In the 1988 Regulations this requirement is again optional.

4–022   A discrepancy which has received judicial comment is that between paragraph 1(f) of Schedule 2 to the Regulations concerning the "reclamation of land from the sea" and the corresponding provision in Annex II to the Directive. In both the Regulations and in the Directive this falls under the heading of agriculture, but all the categories within Schedule 2 are in addition prefaced with the words "development for any of the following *purposes*". The question of whether all land reclamation is included in this category in Schedule 2, or whether the Schedule is limited to land reclaimed "for the purposes of agriculture" was considered in the *R.S.P.B.* case.[25] Although the development in that case was for wholly non-agricultural purposes, the court was urged to hold that it fell within paragraph 1(f) of Schedule 2, and that the reference to agricultural purposes made nonsense of the underlying object of the Regulations and so should be ignored. However the court found this to be an impossible contention, torturing the construction of the Regulations beyond breaking point.

4–023   Annex II to the Directive does not use the opening words "for the purposes of", and merely lists numerous "Projects subject to Article 4(2)" grouped into 11 categories headed, apart from category 5, with the same main headings as Schedule 2. There is thus less reason to limit in the same way the construction to be given to the words "reclamation of land from the sea" in Annex II; further, given that reclamation of land for non-agricultural purposes is not listed in the Regulations, and that the purposes for which land is reclaimed from the sea are in principle irrelevant to the environmental impact of any such reclamation, it is hard to see how this case can be reconciled with the proper construction of Annex II to the Directive. (The problem has since been at least partly addressed by the inclusion in Schedule 2 to the Regulations, with effect from April 8, 1994 of coast protection works).

---

[25] *R. v. Swale Borough Council and Medway Ports Authority ex p. The Royal Society for the Protection of Birds* [1991] J.P.L. 39; [1991] 1 P.L.R. 6.

138

The court did not consider it appropriate to apply the provisions of **4–024** the Directive independently of the Schedule, and there does not appear to have been argument on whether it was directly applicable to and binding on the planning authority, being an "emanation of the State", and whether therefore the authority should have given it effect irrespective of anything in or omitted by the Regulations. It may well be right for a court to refrain from overturning a questionable (but not unreasonable) decision by a planning authority on whether an ES is needed for an Annex II project, where the Directive expressly provides for the exercise of discretion. It is however quite another matter in the case of a decision as to whether a project falls within Annex II (or indeed within Annex I) at all. If an authority misconstrues or fails to apply the law that is binding on it, whether the 1988 Regulations or the Directive, then it is not merely proper for a court to intervene but, at least in the case of a potential breach of Rome Treaty requirements, the court, also being an emanation of the State, arguably has a duty to do so.[26] In the *R.S.P.B.* case, it did note as curious that, on the construction of Schedule 2 it found necessary to apply, the draftsman of the UK Regulations appeared specifically to have omitted from the Schedule land reclamation for the purposes of any type of land use other than agriculture, even though it saw these other purposes as being expressly envisaged in the Directive. There are strong grounds for asserting that the court should, if it took the view that the development in question clearly fell within Annex II, even if not within Schedule 2, have been prepared to send the matter back for reconsideration by the planning authority, in the absence of cogent reasons for allowing the decision to stand.

Although national policy is now encouraging greater awareness of **4–025** environmental matters in formulating local policies, there is at present no legal requirement that proposals in the development plan shall have an ES, even though in practice the approval of a project in the development plan is very likely to commit the subsequent grant of planning permission, particularly having regard to section 54A of the Town and Country Planning Act 1990, which requires that where a development plan has provisions which are material to a planning application, that application shall be determined in accordance with

---

[26] Whether there is such a duty depends on whether the Directive has direct effect, at least in relation to Annex II projects. As to this see Rhiannon Williams, (1991) Cambridge Law Journal, pp.382–384, and the discussion by Richard Macrory, in J.E.L. Vol.4 No.2 (1992) 289 at 301–303, of the apparently conflicting judgments in the *Twyford Down* and *Kincardine and Deeside* decisions (*Twyford Parish Council and Others v. Secretary of State for Transport*; In the Petition of the *Kincardine and Deeside District Council*) reported in that issue of J.E.L. at pp. 273 and 289.

the development plan, unless material considerations indicate otherwise. It is anomalous in those circumstances that there should be no legal requirement to provide environmental information in the context of the development plan preparation.[27]

4–026 The implications of an ES on the British system of outline planning applications are uncertain. The view that an outline application is inappropriate where an ES is needed is incorrect as a matter of law.[28] However, to a degree, the ES will fix the scope of the outline permission: to the extent that the ES, for example, presupposes that access to a site will be constructed in a particular location, it could be unlawful for the planning authority to approve details permitting means of access where this would result in significantly different environmental implications in the absence of supplementary environmental information. As already noted, there is no legal requirement for additional environmental information relating to details submitted for approval pursuant to an outline planning permission, although such information could be required by a planning condition. This optional approach is to be contrasted with the positive requirement in Article 2(1) that, for projects covered by the Directive, before consent is given to them an assessment of their effects must be made. Consent is the final consent that entitles the developer to proceed with the project,[29] and clearly the assessment must be of all material effects, some of which at least may potentially arise out of matters reserved at the outline consent stage. It must be doubtful therefore whether the UK legislation complies properly with the Directive in this respect.[30]

4–027 Although it is normal to submit the environmental statement with the planning application, there is no legal requirement to do so. The 1988 Regulations provide that where an environmental statement is required, the planning authority shall not grant planning permission unless they have first taken the environmental information into consideration.[31] The environmental information includes not only the applicant's environmental statement but also:

(a) any representations made by a body entitled to be consulted on the application; and

---

[27] The first recital of the Directive (adopted unanimously — as was necessary in 1985 — by all the Member States) expresses the need "to take effects on the environment into account at the earliest possible stage in all the technical planning and decision making processes".

[28] The Gateshead planning appeal (see paras. 3–110 to 3–113) concerned a case where outline planning permission was granted for a large clinical waste incinerator, on a proposal which required an ES.

[29] Art. 1(2).

[30] See also paras. 4–009, 4–010.

[31] reg. 4(2).

(b) any representations duly made by any other person about the likely environmental effects.

For who is entitled to be consulted in relation to normal planning applications, see paragraph 3–075; statutory consultees in relation to applications proceeding under the Transport and Works Act 1992 are set out in Schedules 5 and 6 to the Transport and Works (Applications and Objections Procedure) Rules 1992.[31A]

This indicates that the planning authority is legally obliged to consider representations received from statutory consultees, whether or not made within the time limits prescribed under the T.C.P.A., whereas representations by other parties need be considered only if they are made within the time limits specified in a notice or advertisement inviting comment by a particular date. Although this is the strict legal position under the Regulations, a planning authority is in practice required under general law to have regard to all representations received in sufficient time to be considered before it takes its decision, whether or not made within a prescribed time limit.

4–028

When is an Environmental Statement Required?

The Regulations mirror the Directive by having two broad categories of project, namely those (Schedule 1 to the Regulations and Annex I to the Directive) where an ES is automatically required and those (Schedule 2 to the Regulations and Annex II to the Directive) where an ES is required only if the project is likely to have a significant effect on the environment.[32] In UK terminology a Schedule 1 application is an application for planning permission for carrying out a development of any description mentioned in that Schedule. A Schedule 2 application is defined to mean an application for planning permission for development of any description mentioned in that Schedule "and which would be likely to have significant effects on the environment by virtue of factors such as its nature, size or location". Whether on the particular facts a project requires an ES will depend not only on its size and characteristics, but on the sensitivity of the surrounding area. An incinerator sited in a rural area may not require an environmental statement whereas the same incinerator could require an environmental statement if situated near a residential area. The decision whether a project requires an environmental statement is for the local planning authority in the first instance, since as mentioned no planning application which falls within the Schedules

4–029

[31A] S.I. 1992 No. 2902.
[32] See paras. 4–033 to 4–037.

to the Regulations may be granted unless the planning authority has first taken the "environmental information" into consideration.

4–030   In the case of Schedule 1 applications, the position is relatively clear. The principal issue is simply whether a proposed project in fact falls within any one of the listed categories. Of course, if the relevant authority considers an ES should be provided anyway, even if the project properly falls into Schedule 2, then the issue becomes largely academic, since the developer is unlikely to find contesting the requirement for an ES fruitful in the case of a project that is at least on the margin of Schedule 1. A subsidiary issue, which applies also to Schedule 2 projects, is how to handle a proposed development that is in itself modest, but which is part of a series of other (modest) developments that together constitute one within the Schedule.

4–031   In the *R.S.P.B.* case, the development in question involved reclaiming 250 acres of land from the Lappel Bank in the Medway estuary, of which 125 acres were to form a business park providing a short-term cargo storage area that would be needed following completion of other developments at Sheerness Docks nearby. The planning application for reclamation was however proceeding independently of the other, more substantial, developments. It was held that:

> "The question whether or not the development was of a category described in either Schedule had to be answered strictly in relation to the development applied for, not any development contemplated beyond that. But the further question arising in respect of a Schedule 2 development, the question whether it 'would be likely to have significant effects on the environment by virtue of factors such as its nature, size or location', should be answered rather differently. The proposal should not then be considered in isolation if in reality it was properly to be regarded as an integral part of an inevitably more substantial development. This approach appears appropriate on the language of the Regulations, the existence of the smaller development of itself promoting the larger development and thereby likely to carry in its wake the environmental effects of the latter. In common sense, moreover, developers could otherwise defeat the object of the Regulations by piecemeal development proposals".[33]

4–032   Matters are much less easy in relation to Schedule 2 projects.[34] Significant effects on the environment may arise because of the development itself, or because of the areas which might be affected by

---

[33] [1991] J.P.L. at pp. 47, 48.
[34] See the definition of "Schedule 2 application" in reg. 1(1).

it, or both. The Department of the Environment has issued guidance to local authorities for consideration in deciding whether a proposed development requires environmental assessment.[35] The first step is to decide whether a project falls within Schedule 1—requiring environmental assessment in every case— and if not whether it falls within Schedule 2. Whether or not a project that is outside Schedule 1 is within Schedule 2 cannot be determined with precision. The guidance states that under the Regulations a project is to be taken as being likely to have significant environmental effects when the applicant and the local planning authority agree that this is the case, when the applicant volunteers an environmental statement which is expressed to be for the purposes of the Regulations, or when the Secretary of State directs that consideration of environmental information is required. In such cases planning permission may not be granted unless the person granting the permission has first taken the environmental information into consideration.

This test—whether a project is likely to have significant effects on **4–033** the environment—is described in the Blue Book as the "fundamental test" to be applied in each case, although regard should also be had to advice in DoE Circulars 15/88 and 7/94 and in the Blue Book (which repeats, in Appendix 2, Appendix A to the Circular).

The Circular suggests that, in general terms, there are three main **4–034** criteria of significance:

(i)   whether the project is of more than local importance;
(ii) whether the project is intended for a particularly sensitive location, for example, a national park or a site of special scientific interest (SSSI), and for that reason may have significant effects on the area's environment even though the project is not on a major scale;
(iii) whether the project is thought likely to give rise to particularly complex or adverse effects, for example, in terms of the discharge of pollutants.

Given the range of projects covered, and the need to consider **4–035** whether a particular development may have significant effects at the location proposed, the Department does not publish hard and fast limits above which an ES is required. However, broad criteria or thresholds are laid out, which in theory indicate only those projects to which indiviudal consideration must be given. These are set out in detail below, in respect of each type of Schedule 2 development (see

---

[35] DoE Circular 15/88.

paragraphs 4–092 to 4–109). In practice nearly all projects within these criteria will be made subject to EA. It is important to bear in mind that falling outside the criteria does not necessarily mean no EA is required; the basic test is whether significant effects on the environment are likely. Everything else is guidance only.

4–036   In considering whether EA is needed, all aspects of a project need to be considered, including the implications of construction activities, and any long term changes to the environment. The need to consider emissions of pollutants in relation to factory developments points up the substantial overlap between the planning regime and the granting of authorisations under IPC and air pollution control, and for discharges to water and/or to sewer. Though the conditions of any planning permission and of any authorisation should address only the matters properly for control by the relevant regime, as advised in PPG 23,[36] the decision on whether the development should proceed at all necessarily requires consideration of all aspects. Thus while a planning authority may not, through planning conditions, impose controls over potentially polluting operations that are properly exercisable by a regulatory body such as HMIP, this division of responsibility is quite irrelevant to the proper implementation of the Directive. Accordingly any EA of a potentially polluting development must necessarily take account of both the likely and the possible emissions from a plant, including emissions that may be made in breach of applicable controls, and the chances of such breaches occurring.

4–037   The guidance in respect of manufacturing industry and waste disposal is particularly relevant to the present context, and is set out here:

"Manufacturing Industry

New manufacturing plants requiring sites in the range 20–30 ha or above may well require EA.

In addition, EA may occasionally be required for new manufacturing plants on account of expected discharge of waste, emission of pollutants, etc. Among the factors to be taken into account are the following:

—   whether the project involves a process designated as a "scheduled process" for the purpose of air pollution control (these processes made up the bulk of those subject to Integrated Pollution Control under Part I of the EPA);

---

[36] See paras. 3–115 to 3–120.

—   whether the process involves discharges to water which require the consent of the water authority (now the National Rivers Authority);
—   whether the installation would give rise to the presence of environmentally significant quantities of potentially hazardous or polluting substances;
—   whether the process would give rise to radioactive or other hazardous waste.

Whether or not a project involving such a process requires EA will depend on the location, nature and significance of the emissions, etc., involved: in forming a judgment on this local planning authorities may find it helpful to consult the relevant authorities (HMIP, HSE, the water authority [now the NRA] or the environmental health authority). It should be noted that existing controls over hazardous and polluting substances will not be affected by the Regulations and the need for a consent under other legislation will *not* in itself be a justification for EA: authorities will need to consider with the relevant authority the likely significance, from the point of view of the possible need for EA, of the matters which give rise to the need for the consent.

Waste Disposal

Installations, including landfill sites, for the transfer, treatment or disposal of household, industrial and commercial wastes (as defined in the Collection and Disposal of Waste Regulations 1988)[36A] with a capacity of more than 75,000 tonnes a year may well be candidates for EA even when the special considerations relating to hazardous wastes do not arise. Except in the most sensitive locations, sites taking smaller tonnages of these wastes, Civic Amenity sites, and sites seeking only to accept inert waste (demolition rubble, etc.) are unlikely to be candidates for EA."

As indicated below, a decision that EA is required may be appealed **4–038** to the Secretary of State for the Environment. Decisions of the local planning authority and of the Secretary of State for the Environment may be challenged in the High Court on the basis of an error of law, but not on the merits. This approach was upheld in the RSPB case, where it was stated, *inter alia*, that:

"The decision whether any particular development was or was not within the scheduled descriptions was exclusively for the

[36A] Reference should now be made to the Controlled Waste Regulations 1992 (S.I. 1992 No. 588, as amended by S.I. 1993 No. 566).

145

planning authority in question, subject only to *Wednesbury* challenge. Questions of classification were essentially questions of fact and degree, not of law. . . . Even less was [the judge] persuaded that this court was entitled upon judicial review to act effectively as an appeal court and to reach its own decision so as to ensure that . . . EEC treaty obligations were properly discharged".[37]

For the reasons discussed earlier (in paragraphs 4–022 to 4–025), these views are open to challenge.

4–039   Uncertainty on whether an environmental statement is required can be resolved in five ways:

(a) A prospective applicant can ask the planning authority under Regulation 5 whether an environmental statement is required, and if he disagrees with their view he can apply to the Secretary of State for a direction on the matter under Regulation 5(6);

(b) The Secretary of State can issue directions requiring an environmental statement for a proposed development or class of developments. No such directions have yet been made;

(c) The legal consequences of a statutory environmental statement arise where one is volunteered—*i.e.* where a prospective applicant either agrees in writing that an environmental statement is needed[38] or he in fact submits one and expresses it to be for the purposes of the Regulations;[39]

(d) If a planning application is submitted without an environmental statement, the planning authority has three weeks in which to notify the applicant that they consider that a statement is required, *i.e.* that the application falls within Schedule 1 or Schedule 2.[40] The period can be extended by agreement.[41] Within three weeks from the planning authority's notification the applicant must take action. He can appeal to the Secretary of State against the local authority's ruling or he can confirm in writing that he will provide an ES[42] (see paragraph 4–044 below);

---

[37] [1991] J.P.L. at p. 47.
[38] reg. 4(4)(iii).
[39] reg. 4(4)(i).
[40] reg. 9(1).
[41] reg. 9(1).
[42] reg. 9(2).

(e) If an application comes before the Secretary of State without an environmental statement, he can determine that one is required.

Disputes on Whether an Environmental Statement is Required

A prospective applicant is entitled under Regulation 5 to ask the planning authority to state in writing whether an environmental statement is required. There is no form for such a request, but it must be accompanied by a plan identifying the land, a brief description of the nature and purpose of the proposed development and its possible effects on the environment, and any other material which the prospective applicant may wish to provide. The planning authority is entitled to request further information.[43]   **4-040**

The planning authority must respond to this request within three weeks from its receipt or such longer period as may be agreed in writing with the prospective applicant. If it determines that an environmental statement is required, it must provide a written statement giving clearly and precisely its full reasons for this conclusion.[44] The response and the reasons for it must be placed on the planning register.   **4-041**

If the applicant disagrees with the decision, or if the planning authority fails to give its decision within the relevant period, the prospective applicant may appeal to the Secretary of State for the Environment for a direction.[45] There is no time limit within which this "appeal" must be made. There is no form for the appeal but the applicant must provide a copy of his request with accompanying documents, a copy of any request for further information received from the local authority, a copy of the local authority's opinion and accompanying statements of reasons, and any other representations which the prospective applicant wishes to make. A copy of the application and any representations (including representations from the applicant to the Secretary of State) must be sent to the local planning authority. The Secretary of State may request further information from the prospective applicant or the local planning authority.   **4-042**

The Secretary of State's decision must be issued within three weeks from receipt of the application to him or such longer period as is   **4-043**

[43] reg. 5(3).
[44] reg. 5(4).
[45] reg. 5(6).

147

reasonably required. A copy of the direction is sent to the applicant and the planning authority and, where the decision is that an environmental statement is required, the direction must be accompanied by a written statement giving full reasons set out clearly and precisely.[46]

4-044   Where a planning authority receives a planning application and determines that an environmental statement is required, the applicant may within three weeks inform them in writing *either* that he accepts this position and will provide an environmental statement, *or* that he is applying to the Secretary of State for a direction on the point. Failure by the applicant to take either course of action within three weeks results in the penalty of a deemed refusal of the planning application with no right of appeal.[47]

Content and Scope of an ES

4-045   The formal requirements are set out in Schedule 3 to the 1988 Regulations (see paragraphs 4–111 to 4–114 for details). As mentioned above,[48] there are some significant differences between the 1988 Regulations and the EC Directive on what the environmental statement must contain and what is optional only. It is accordingly unsafe to rely solely upon the terms of the 1988 Regulations, and advisable to comply not only with them but also with the EC Directive.

4-046   The legal requirement for the content of the environmental statement is, necessarily, a broad indication of what should be considered. No indication is given of how it is considered and what parameters are chosen for the consideration. In practice, answering these questions gives rise to some of the most difficult questions in relation to environmental assessment. This exercise, of deciding what will be considered in an environmental statement and how it will be considered, is colloquially known as "scoping".

4-047   There is no requirement that the determining authority shall reach a separate conclusion on the ES or any part of it. The only requirement under the Directive is the Article 8 requirement that the information must be taken into consideration. There is a requirement that information gathered pursuant to an EIA must be made available to the public, and that the public must in turn be given the opportunity to express an opinion before the project is initiated.[49] This does not

---

[46] reg. 6.
[47] reg. 9(3).
[48] See paras. 4–021 to 4–024.
[49] Art. 6.2.

require further positive steps to ascertain public opinion before the development consent is issued, although the UK planning practice is such that this does in fact occur; it is up to the public to take the opportunity to express any views.

Article 10 of the Directive requires that it shall not override national laws and practices regarding industrial and commercial secrecy and the safeguarding of the public interest. **4–048**

The importance of discussing scoping with the planning authority and main consultees cannot be over-stated. There is no legal requirement that a prospective applicant should consult with anyone upon scoping, although such consultations are encouraged. The environmental statement is intended to deal with "significant" effects on the environment. A question of what is significant may in some cases be determined by reference to published criteria, *e.g.* recommended maximum levels of certain pollutants. But in many instances, the question of what is significant involves much subjective judgement. "The environment" is an interwoven continuum of living systems and the media that support them, and it is not possible to define with any precision what aspects should be considered and what need not be. In theory, it could require almost infinite resources to consider all effects on the environment, particularly since these are defined in Annex III to the Directive to include secondary, cumulative, short, medium and long term, permanent, temporary, positive and negative effects. **4–049**

The Department of the Environment guidance is that "developers and authorities should discuss the scope of an environmental statement before its preparation is begun".[50] It continues by saying[51] that environmental statements need not cover every conceivable aspect of a project's potential environmental effects at the same level of detail. The emphasis is on the "main" or "significant" effects to which a project is *likely* to give rise. In many cases only a few of the topics to be covered will need to be discussed in any depth. Other issues may be of little or no significance for the particular project in question, and will need only a very brief treatment—sufficient to indicate that their possible relevance has been considered. The DoE Blue Book contains a checklist of matters which should be considered for inclusion in an environmental statement. These are set out in paragraphs 4–115 to 4–121. **4–050**

In other jurisdictions there has been much discussion on how far an EA should take into account (a) alternative sites for the project in question, and (b) alternative projects that might utilise the site in question, dealing fully with the environmental aspects of all the **4–051**

---

[50] Blue Book, para. 24.
[51] *Ibid*, para. 25.

alternatives. In an ideal world these issues would no doubt be part of a system that ensured the minimum adverse environmental impact of all projects taken together, though such an approach, if taken to extremes, would create a massive additional burden for the applicant. It could also give rise to unnecessary alarm for members of the public, *e.g.* those living near sites identified as possible alternatives. The Directive says that "where appropriate" the ES should include an outline of the main alternatives studied by the developer and indication of the main reasons for his choice taking into account the environmental effects.[52] By contrast the 1988 Regulations do not impose so positive an obligation, but incorporate the information on alternatives in paragraph 3 of Schedule 3, which lists information that *may* optionally be included in an ES and includes as item (d):

> "(in outline) the main alternatives (if any) studied by the applicant [or] appellant . . . and an indication of the main reasons for choosing the development proposed, taking into account the environmental effects".

4–052   This contrasts with the right of the planning authority or Secretary of State or Inspector to require an applicant or appellant to provide (*inter alia*) information relating to any matter which may be included in an ES, being information reasonably required to give proper consideration to the likely environmental effects of the proposed development.[53] There is no guidance on when it is appropriate or reasonable to consider alternatives.

4–053   Where an applicant has in fact considered alternative sites or (more rarely) alternative projects, and the conclusions point to the chosen site on environmental grounds as well as on commercial ones, he may be willing to refer to these, but this will inevitably open up a comparative debate, the costs of which could be substantial. In many cases, disclosure of alternatives, will reveal development possibilities which the applicant regards as commercially confidential. Generally, in planning law it is not necessary to show that the site is the best one: simply that it is acceptable; an alternative is relevant normally only if it is so much better (and available for development) that its existence is an objection to the site in question. Alternatives may have greater relevance in law where there is need for a development on a single site, the selection of which would preclude comparable use of any others in the neighbourhood, *e.g.* in relation to motorway service

---

[52] Annex III, para. 2.
[53] reg. 21.

areas.[54] As already noted, reference to alternatives can cause anxiety and uncertainty for those affected by an alternative, particularly in the absence of an obvious mechanism for them to be consulted. The question of alternatives is therefore very sensitive and politically difficult.

Form of the Environmental Statement

No form is officially prescribed or recommended. The only legal requirements are that the statement shall be prepared by the applicant[55] and comprise a document or series of documents,[56] which shall contain the specified information and a summary in non-technical language of that information.[57]   **4–054**

An applicant may choose to engage consultants for some or all of the work, but he is under no obligation to do so. He is at liberty to write it all himself. In practice, it may well be the case that some aspects are appropriate for independent consultants whereas others are more appropriate for the applicant.[58] DoE guidance is that the environmental statement may embody or summarise the conclusion of more detailed work, but in that case sufficient information should be provided to identify the source of the information, so that the statement's conclusions can be verified.[59]   **4–055**

The degree of detail for each topic will depend on its importance. The relevant requirement of the Directive is that the information shall include, *inter alia* "the data required to identify and assess the *main* effects which the project is *likely* to have on the environment"   **4–056**

---

[54] *Edwards v. the Secretary of State for the Environment*, [1994] E.G.C.S. 60, C.A. See also *Greater London Council v. Secretary of State for the Environment and London Docklands Development Corporation* (C.A.) (1985) 52 P.&C.R. 158, [1986] J.P.L. 193; *Trusthouse Forte Hotels v. Secretary of State for the Environment and Northavon District Council* (1986) 53 P.&C.R. 293, [1986] J.P.L. 834, [1986] 2 E.G.L.R. 185.

[55] reg. 2(1).

[56] Sched. 3, para. 1.

[57] Sched. 3, para. 2(e).

[58] Since applicants naturally have a vested interest in the ES containing as little adverse matter as possible, their ES is likely to be more credible if prepared by independent consultants, and more advantageous if it is in fact innocuous. This can however raise difficult practical issues of professional ethics for such consultants where their conclusions seem likely to harm their client's interests in the project. There is no clear consensus as to whether their reports should be wholly objective and dispassionate, or whether they should (like the clients' lawyers) aim to present the facts and their opinions in the manner most favourable to the client, providing only that they act responsibly and do not mislead, perhaps leaving the authority to seek further information where the ES has not said quite as much as it might have. The law provides no guidance on this. While some individual firms of consultants have taken the view that their long-term professional and business interests dictate that their reports must be strictly objective, it remains up to each planning authority to determine how much reliance it can place on a report being impartial.

[59] Blue Book, para. 20.

151

(emphasis added). The detailed requirements of Annex III to the Directive make it clear that the description must include not only the likely *significant* effects (emphasis added) but also a description of the forecasting methods used to assess the effects on the environment. It follows from this that where there is uncertainty about the forecasting method, this should be indicated. It is considered acceptable, and government guidance reinforces this,[60] that where issues have little significance, they should at least be mentioned, even if only as a note that they have not been considered because they are not thought to be significant.

4–057   In practice, the content of environmental statements varies enormously, from relatively slim and relatively non-technical documents, to a weighty bible of reports extending to many hundred pages.[61] While there must be uncertainty until the courts have pronounced upon the point, it is at least very possible that a relatively slim environmental assessment is adequate as a matter of law, provided that it had addressed all the significant issues, and made an honest attempt to assess their impact. The fact that the outcome may be considered less than adequate as a matter of professional judgment will not necessarily make it inadequate as a matter of law. It is therefore considered that the Department of the Environment is correct in indicating in its Blue Book[62] that a planning authority cannot treat a planning application as invalid because it considers the environmental statement to be inadequate. Its remedy is to seek further information, under the powers mentioned below.

4–058   Although it may not be unlawful to provide a minimal environmental statement which observes the letter of the law rather than its spirit, this may be regarded as unreasonable behaviour in the context of any application for costs which may be made in the event of the proposal coming to a planning inquiry (see paragraphs 3–093, 3–094).

4–059   As important as the bare content of a statement is the manner in which it is assembled. Experience shows that treating environmental assessment as some procedural addition to an already formulated project—to be added at the end in order to comply with the Regulations—is frequently unsatisfactory to the point of being counter-productive. An environmental assessment will be most effective (not only in furthering the applicant's interests in the planning application, but equally in satisfying the objectives of the system, namely minimising adverse environmental impacts), where it is formulated as an iterative process while the development proposals

---

[60] Blue Book, para. 25.
[61] There is extensive literature on techniques of environmental assessment, a consideration of which is beyond the scope of this volume.
[62] para. 42.

are being designed, so that the environmental impacts of alternative options are taken into account as an integral part of the design process. Also, effective consultation by an applicant can be very beneficial in the formulation of the environmental assessment and a thorough and well managed consultation process is much to be recommended. The function of the entire process is to assemble and present environmental information in such a way as to enable the determining authority to take a proper decision and, so far as the applicant is concerned, it also has the function of helping to persuade the decision maker, local people, and others concerned, that the project is as environmentally acceptable as it feasibly can be.

Almost inevitably, an environmental statement will tend to give emphasis to some of the negative aspects of a proposal and ordinarily an environmental statement would not, for example, include information about the economic benefits of a proposal. Provided that the environmental statement contains what is required in the Regulations and the Directive, there seems no reason in principle why it should not include, or be accompanied by, additional material bringing out whatever positive aspects of the proposal that the applicant wishes to draw to the attention of those concerned with the proposal, *e.g.* how it might bring economic benefits to the local community. Indeed, there is merit in expanding or amending an environmental statement in this way, so as to present a balanced proposal.   4-060

Volunteering an Environmental Statement/Applicant's Right to Information

As indicated below, under the 1988 Regulations, there are specific legal consequences where an environmental statement is volunteered. This is so whether the development in question is within Schedule 2 to the Regulations, or is a proposal for erecting a single house.   4-061

An applicant may choose to volunteer an environmental statement for a number of reasons. He may believe that it is appropriate to provide this kind of information as a matter of business practice, or that the production of a statutory environmental statement will give him a better opportunity to persuade the planning authority, other interested bodies, and local people, that the development is acceptable. Most significantly however, anyone who indicates formally the intention to provide an environmental statement, by notice to the planning authority under regulation 22, is entitled to require the planning authority, and any of the statutory consultees in connection with the planning application, to enter into consultation with him to see whether they have information considered relevant to the preparation of the environmental statement. If so, then the planning   4-062

153

authority/consultee must make that information available to prospective applicants, unless it is of a confidential nature.

4–063   The process is initiated by written notice from a prospective applicant to the local planning authority pursuant to regulation 8(1). This notice must include the information and/or documents necessary to identify the land and the nature and purpose of the proposed development, and it must indicate the main environmental consequences to which reference is proposed in the environmental statement. The planning authority must notify statutory consultees of this and advise them of their obligation to provide information, and it must notify the prospective applicant in writing of the names and addresses of the bodies so notified.

4–064   The purpose of consultation is to determine whether the body has in its possession any information which it, or the prospective applicant, considers relevant to the preparation of an environmental statement; if they have such information, the body concerned must make it available to the potential applicant, unless it is of a confidential nature. Information is relevant if considered relevant by the prospective applicant or the consultee. Consultees cannot, therefore, simply answer the questions of the prospective applicant. They must positively volunteer any non-confidential information which they consider to be relevant; they must also answer the questions put to them on the matters which the prospective applicant considers to be relevant.[63]

4–065   The planning authority and consultees are not obliged to express any view about the merits of the proposal or the conclusions to be drawn from the factual material which they provide. As a matter of practice, however, many statutory consultees may be prepared to comment on the conclusions from the factual material.

4–066   Since this right to information is limited to the planning authority and statutory consultees, this can lead to anomalous situations where, for example, a development might have environmental consequences in the area of a neighbouring planning authority. Since adjacent planning authorities are not statutory consultees there is no right to information from them under the regulations.

4–067   The prospective applicant does not have to consult all or any these statutory consultees. He can consult only some, at his choosing; he may seek to consult any number of other bodies, and in particular prospective applicants might choose to consult with local people and local amenity bodies.

4–068   The Department of the Environment considers that the preparation of an environmental statement should be a collaborative exercise involving discussions with the local planning authority, statutory

[63] reg. 22.

consultees and possibly other bodies.[64] This implies that those bodies should be prepared not only to provide factual information but to discuss and if possible agree the conclusions to be drawn from that information. However, there is no legal requirement to that effect. In practice those hostile to a project may be reluctant to participate in consultation.

Those consulted under regulation 22 are entitled to make a reasonable charge reflecting the costs of making the relevant information available. There are divided opinions on whether this is limited to copying costs, or whether it can also include the time costs of people attending meetings. Policy guidance has not clarified the point. Probably the courts would incline towards a strict interpretation of this provision and allow direct expenses only. **4–069**

Planning Authority's Right to Further Information and Evidence

Under regulation 21(1) the planning authority can require the applicant who has provided an environmental statement to provide further information. This may be done by written notice to the applicant at any time, and may relate to any matter which is required to be, or may be dealt with in the environmental statement where in the opinion of the authority (a) the applicant could provide further information, having regard in particular to current knowledge and methods of assessment and (b) that further information is reasonably required to give proper consideration to the likely environmental effects of the proposed development. **4–070**

The applicant is under a legal duty to provide this information; there is however no time limit. There is no right of appeal in respect of a request for this information. The information is not restricted to information in the applicant's possession or which he can easily obtain; if the authority considers that it is reasonably required and the applicant could provide it (having regard to current knowledge, etc.) then he must do so. There is no express sanction if he fails to do so. In theory, a court order might be available to enforce the duty, but the more realistic sanction is that the application will not be determined or may be expressly turned down. **4–071**

Under regulation 21(2) the planning authority may also require an applicant to produce such evidence as it may reasonably call for to verify any information in the environmental statement. There is no **4–072**

---

[64] Blue Book, para. 19.

express legal duty on the applicant to provide this evidence; nor is there any express sanction on an applicant who fails to comply with such a request for information and/or evidence, although clearly the application is unlikely to succeed unless the material is provided.

4–073 Whether information can be requested under regulation 21(1) depends not on a objective test of reasonableness but on a subjective test depending on the opinion of the authority. On the other hand evidence can only be required under regulation 21(2) if it is reasonably called for, *i.e.* an objective test.

4–074 For planning authorities, the importance of these provisions can scarcely be over-stated. Particularly bearing in mind that there is no time limit, and no right of appeal in respect of a request under regulation 21, the powers give the planning authority substantial ability to obtain further information. It is not confined to what is in the ES, but can extend to what it might contain. The converse is that applicants submitting environmental statements should build into their budgets and programmes some allowance for dealing with requested information from the planning authority.

It can be time consuming and expensive to provide information of this kind. It is considered good practice, therefore, for a prospective applicant and a planning authority to discuss what information is to be provided, having regard to the cost and time required, in the hope of achieving reasonably adequate information for the authority without imposing excessive cost or delay on the applicant.[65]

4–075 The powers of a planning authority to request further information under regulation 21 apply also to the Secretary of State or an inspector, and apply when dealing with an appeal as they do when considering a planning application.

Applicant's Duties in relation to a Planning Application accompanied by an ES

4–076 As indicated above, where an environmental statement is to be provided, the applicant is responsible for its preparation (even though he may use consultants and other advisers).

The applicant must supply the planning authority with three extra copies of the environmental statement for transmission to the Secretary of State for the Environment, together with further copies to enable the planning authority to send them to the statutory consultees. Alternatively, the applicant is entitled to send copies of the

---

[65] In a field where the authority has such a high degree of discretion, it will in any event be prudent for an applicant to show himself as co-operative rather than confrontational, and so facilitate rational discussion on what can sensibly be provided and what cannot.

application and environmental statement direct to the statutory consultees or any other body, informing them that representations may be made to the local planning authority; in that event, he must inform the planning authority of the name of everybody whom he has so served, the date of service and which parts of the environmental statement had been sent to that body (where he does not send the entire statement to them). The applicant is required to notify the planning authority expressly whether he is sending material direct to other bodies, or whether he is leaving it to the local authority.[66]

Planning Authorities' Duties

Whether or not there is any mention of a possible environmental statement, it is almost certainly the duty of planning authorities, under EC law at least, to consider whether one is required. For an indication of the possible approaches by English courts to a legal challenge where this question is not asked, see *R v. Poole Borough Council, ex p. Beebee and others*.[67] In that case a proposed residential development at Canford Heath in Dorset, close to an SSSI but nevertheless in accordance with the development plan, had been granted planning permission. The grant was challenged on the basis that the planning authority had failed to consider whether an environmental statement was needed, and that the permission was therefore void in law. On the particular facts, it was held that even if there had been an error of law, discretion would not be exercised to quash the decision, because the substance of what would have been in an environmental statement had already been drawn to the Council's attention and considered.[68]   **4–077**

The court left open the question whether the planning authority   **4–078**
erred as a matter of law by failing to consider whether an environmental statement was required. Until the law is clarified it would be prudent to assume that a planning authority is under a legal duty positively to consider whether or not an environmental statement should have been provided, in relation to any development of significance. A grant of planning permission without an ES where one was required, would be a nullity in law.[69]

---

[66] reg. 14.
[67] [1991] 2 P.L.R. 27; [1991] J.P.L. 643; [1991] C.O.D. 264.
[68] Nevertheless the DoE subsequently intervened and revoked the planning permission.
[69] At least if promptly challenged. The issue of whether an unlawful act, *e.g.* for lack of *vires*, can be challenged at any time in a private action or must be held to be valid if not challenged promptly by way of judicial review is discussed in the Law Commission's Consultation Paper No. 126 "Administrative Law: Judicial Review and Statutory Appeals".

4-079   If the planning authority determines that an environmental state- ment is required it is still entitled to determine and refuse the application even without an ES, but it may not grant permission without one.[70] It must in any event (unless the application is "called- in" for determination by the Secretary of State) within three weeks from receipt of the application (or such longer period as may be agreed with the applicant in writing) notify the applicant that it considers the submission of an ES to be required, "giving [its] full reasons for [its] view clearly and precisely".[71] If the applicant fails to take any action within three weeks, then the application is deemed to be refused at the end of that period and the planning authority will have no further jurisdiction.[72]

4-080   If a planning authority fails to determine a planning application within a prescribed period, an applicant is entitled to appeal to the Secretary of State for the Environment as though the application had been refused. This is generally known as appealing the "deemed refusal" of the application. Normally, it is possible to appeal the deemed refusal eight weeks after submission of the application, or such extension of that period as may be agreed with the planning authority in writing, but where an environmental statement is supplied, this eight week period is extended to 16 weeks.[73] If the planning authority have notified the applicant that they consider an environmental statement to be required and that issue is eventually determined by direction of the Secretary of State (see paragraphs 4-042, 4-043), the 16 week period begins from the issue of the Secretary of State's direction.[74]

4-081   There is no requirement that an environmental statement should be served with or before a planning application. It can be served at any time. If an applicant indicates that he proposes to provide a statement in the course of planning procedures, the planning authority must immediately suspend consideration of the application until receipt of the documents (unless it intends to refuse the application anyway) and it may not determine it for 21 days beginning with the receipt of the environmental statement. It may seem curious that a planning authority should be obliged to suspend consideration of the applica- tion (except to refuse it) even in circumstances where the authority is prepared to continue its consideration. There will often be a number of respects in which an application could usefully be considered even in

---

[70] reg. 4(2).
[71] reg. 9(1).
[72] reg. 9(3).
[73] reg. 16(2).See para. 3-083. The period starts from the receipt of a complete and valid application.
[74] reg. 16(1).

the absence of an environmental statement. However, the legal provision is clear.[75]

When an environmental statement is received, whether with the application or later, the planning authority must serve copies of the environmental statement on statutory consultees, unless this has already been done by the applicant. The planning authority must also: **4–082**

(a) place a copy of the environmental statement on the planning register;

(b) send a copy of the application, accompanying documents, and the environmental statement to the Secretary of State for Environment;

(c) advise statutory consultees on whom the applicant has *not* served a copy of the statement that it will be taken into consideration. They must enquire of each of those bodies whether it wishes to receive a copy of the statement or part of it and must inform it of the right to make representations;

(d) inform the applicant of the copies required by statutory consultees, the names and addresses of the bodies concerned and enquire of the applicant whether he proposes to serve the copy of those bodies or to send the required copies to the local authority for service;

(e) serve on each statutory consultee a copy of the environmental statement supplied by the applicant;[76] and

(f) post at least one site notice on or near the land to which the application relates for at least 21 days and advertise the application in a local newspaper.[77]

The local planning authority may not determine the application until 14 days from the last date on which a copy of the environmental statement (or part of it) is served on statutory consultees.[78]

In summary, the time limits which a planning authority must comply with are as follows: **4–083**

(a) in all cases they must consider whether an environmental statement is required and if they consider that it is so required, must serve notice to that effect within three weeks from receipt of the application, or such longer period as may be agreed with the applicant in writing;

---

[75] This procedure would minimise the chances of a later assertion that permission was granted without proper regard having been given to the ES. Nevertheless it hardly seems necessary.

[76] reg. 14(2).

[77] G.D.O. 12B.

[78] reg. 14(4).

(b) the planning authority may not determine the application (by grant or refusal) until 14 days from the last date on which a copy of the environmental statement, or part of it, is served on a statutory consultee;

(c) where an environmental statement is submitted in the course of planning procedures, then from the moment that the applicant proposes to provide the statement, the planning authority must, unless disposed to refuse permission, suspend consideration of the application until receipt of the statement; once it is received, they may not determine the application, by refusal or by granting permission, within 21 days of receipt of the statement. This time limit is additional to, and not in substitution for, the 14 day time limit under item (b) above.

4–084   Once the environmental statement is received, the planning authority may seek additional information.[79] They must take into consideration the environmental statement, comments of the statutory consultees, and duly made comments from other parties regarding the likely environmental effects of the proposed development. There is no legal requirement that the environmental information must be analysed in any particular way. Nor is the planning authority legally required to take independent advice on that information, although in relation to technical aspects many local authorities will find it appropriate to do so. Additional information of this kind must be subjected to publicity and consultation.[80] The planning authority considering a Schedule 1 or Schedule 2 project must, when notifying their decision, state in writing whether they have taken environmental information into account.[81]

Planning Appeals and Inquiries

4–085   As indicated above,[82] a planning application may come before the Secretary of State for the Environment for determination either by appeal from a planning authority's decision, or from its failure to take a decision within the prescribed time limit, or because the Secretary of State issues a direction requiring that the application shall be referred to him for approval. In the case of a proposal which involves, or might involve, an environmental statement, where an application comes to

[79] reg. 21 see paras. 4–070 to 4–074.
[80] reg. 21(2)–(9), which came into effect on April 18, 1994.
[81] reg. 4(2).
[82] See paras. 3–079, 3–083.

the Secretary of State, he will almost invariably hold a public local inquiry.

Where an application reaches the Secretary of State, on appeal or because it is called in, he has powers[83] to require an environmental statement by direction. There is no appeal from such a direction. Unless within three weeks the applicant/appellant indicates in writing that he intends to provide an environmental statement, no further action will be taken on the application/appeal. **4–086**

The normal planning inquiries procedure rules apply to a planning inquiry where an environmental statement is involved.[84] In addition, it is open to the Secretary of State to apply the special rules dealing with major inquiries, which involve a somewhat more elaborate procedure including a possible pre-inquiry meeting and directions on procedure.[85] **4–087**

Where an environmental statement is received in the context of a proposal being considered by the Secretary of State, the rules on notifying statutory consultees[86] apply *mutatis mutandis*.

Where a matter goes to the Secretary of State on appeal or on call-in the applicant must supply the Secretary of State with a copy of the environmental statement unless the planning authority has already done so.[87]

Consultation with the Public

The requirement of the Directive on consulting the public is curious. Whereas the basic provision is that environmental assessment is considered before consent to the project is given,[88] so far as the public is concerned the requirement is that the request for development consent and any environmental information are made available to the public, and the public is given the opportunity to express an opinion before the project is initiated.[89] In theory, therefore, the public do not have to be consulted before the consent is given but simply before the project is initiated. Nevertheless if the purpose of the Directive is to be achieved, public consultation cannot be deferred to a point where in reality it would be an empty formality having no effect on whether the **4–088**

---

[83] regs. 10, 11.
[84] See para. 00 above.
[85] The Town and Country Planning (Inquiries Procedure) Rules 1992 (S.I. 1992 No. 2038), and DoE Circular 24/92.
[86] See paras. 4–076, 4–082.
[87] reg. 19.
[88] Art. 2.
[89] Art. 6(2).

project should proceed. Consequently where, as in the United Kingdom, planning consents cannot be revoked except on paying full compensation calculated on the basis that the developer is entitled to proceed with his project, the Directive should almost certainly properly be understood as requiring the public consultation to precede any action by the planning authority that would in practice significantly restrict its ability to determine the fate of a proposed project.

4–089   Considerable discretion is given to member states on how the public is to be consulted; under the UK regime the onus is placed on the local planning authority to publicise an application accompanied by an environmental statement by site notice and advertisement in a local newspaper.[90] The local authority must notify members of the public of the place where they may inspect copies of the environmental statement together with all other documents submitted with the application, and also inform them of the address from which copies may be obtained and the cost; such information is included within the prescribed form of site notice and newspaper advertisement.[91] Additional information under Regulation 21 must also be publicised.[92]

Projects Requiring Environmental Assessment

4–090   The Directive sets out those projects which always require EA in Annex I, and those that require EA if they are likely to have significant effects on the environment in Annex II. That approach is echoed in the 1988 Regulations, which list Schedule 1 (mandatory) and Schedule 2 (discretionary) projects, as follows. Where there are significant differences with the terms of the EC Directive, the relevant terms of the Directive are set out in italics.

4–091   Schedule 1 Projects

1.   The carrying out of building or other operations or the change of use of buildings or other land (where a material change) to provide any of the following:

(1)   A crude oil refinery (excluding an undertaking manufacturing only lubricants from crude oil) or an installation for the gasification and liquefaction of 500 tonnes or more of coal or bituminous shale per day;

---

[90] para. 4–082(f).
[91] See above, G.D.O., Art. 12B and Sched. 5.
[92] reg. 21(2)–(9).

(2) (a) A thermal power station or other combustion installation with a heat output of 300 megawatts or more (not being an installation falling within paragraph (b); and

    (b) A nuclear power station or other nuclear reactor (excluding a research installation for the production and conversion of fissionable and fertile materials, the maximum power of which does not exceed one kilowatt continuous thermal load).

(3) An installation designed solely for the permanent storage or final disposal of radioactive waste;

(4) An integrated works for the initial melting of cast iron and steel;

(5) An installation for the extraction of asbestos or for the processing and transformation of asbestos or products containing asbestos:

    (a) where the installation produces asbestos-cement products, with an annual production of more than 20,000 tonnes of finished products; or

    (b) where the installation produces friction material, with an annual production of more than 50 tonnes of finished products; or

    (c) in other cases, where the installation will utilise more than 200 tonnes of asbestos per year.

(6) An integrated chemical installation, that is to say, an industrial installation or group of installations where two or more linked chemical or physical processes are employed for the manufacture of olefins from petroleum products, or of sulphuric acid, nitric acid, hydrofluoric acid, chlorine or fluorine.

[Directive: "Integrated chemical installations"—not defined]

(7) A special road (*i.e.* a motorway, including a privately financed toll road); a line for long distance railway traffic [long distance not being defined]; or an aerodrome with a basic runway length of 2,100 metres or more.

[The Directive uses the word "airport", which has the same meaning for the purposes of the Directive as in the 1944 Chicago Convention setting up the International Civil Aviation Organisation (Annex 14)].

(8) A trading port, an inland waterway which permits the passage of vehicles of over 1,350 tonnes or a port for inland waterway traffic capable of handling such vessels.

(9) A waste disposal installation for the incineration or chemical treatment of special waste (see Chapter 11 for the definition of special waste, which is unique to the United Kingdom and

163

substantially narrower than the definition of hazardous waste in Directive 91/689.[93]

2.   The carrying out of operations whereby land is filled with special waste (see Chapter 11 for its definition and also item 1(9) above) or the change of use of land (where a material change) to use for the deposit of such waste.

[Directive: "Waste-disposal installations for the incineration, chemical treatment or landfill of toxic and dangerous waste"].

Schedule 2 projects

4–092   These are projects which require an ES only where, by virtue of factors such as their nature, size or location, there are likely to be significant effects on the environment (as to which see paras. 4–029, 4–032 to 4–034). The following summarises the Department of the Environment Guidance on the interpretation of the Schedule 2 projects and the criteria to be borne in mind when considering whether a particular project will require EA.[94]

Development for any of the following purposes:[95]

4–093   *(1) Agriculture*

    (a)   water management for agriculture;
    (b)   poultry-rearing;
    (c)   pig-rearing;
    (d)   a salmon hatchery;
    (e)   an installation for the rearing of salmon;
    (f)   the reclamation of land from the sea.

[Directive: "Agriculture

(a)   Projects for the restructuring of rural land holdings.
(b)   Projects for the use of uncultivated land or semi- natural areas for intensive agricultural purposes.
(c)   Water-management projects for agriculture.
(d)   Initial afforestation where this may lead to adverse ecological changes and land reclamation for the purposes of conversion to another type of land use.

---

[93] [1991] O.J. L377/20.
[94] DoE Circular 15/88, Appendix A.
[95] These opening words were taken in *R. v. Swale Borough Council and Medway Ports Authority ex p. R.S.P.B.* to require the individual "purposes " to be read as being limited to the main headings. Thus item 1(f) was construed as being limited to reclamation of land from the sea *for agricultural purposes* and so did not include reclamation in connection with the activities of a port (see para. 4–024).

    (e)   *Poultry-rearing installations.*
    (f)   *Pig-rearing installations.*
    (g)   *Salmon breeding.*
    (h)   *Reclamation of land from the sea."]*

In relation to pig-rearing, the DoE indicates that while new pig-   **4–094**
rearing installations will generally not require environmental assessment ("EA"), those designed to house more than 400 sows or 5,000
fattening pigs may require one. Similarly, the DoE indicates that new
poultry rearing installations will not require EA, unless designed to
house more than 100,000 broilers or 50,000 layers, turkey or other
poultry.

In relation to salmon farming, the environmental effects will need to   **4–095**
be considered in relation to the implications for the particular river
system but the DoE indicates that developments designed to produce
less than 100 tonnes of fish a year should not normally require EA.

Although new drainage and flood defence works are not included   **4–096**
within the headings under the category of agriculture in either the
Directive or the Regulations, they are included within that overall
category in Appendix A to Circular 15/88 which indicates criteria and
thresholds for Schedule 2 projects. It appears from this that land
reclamation may include also new drainage and flood defence works.

It is indicated that such works may merit EA where it becomes   **4–097**
apparent from the outcome of consultations between drainage bodies
(the relevant internal drainage boards and the NRA) and environmental interests under section 12 and 13 of the Land Drainage Act 1991. In
disputed cases the Secretary of State will decide on the need for EA
after taking into account the views of the relevant Agriculture Minister
according to that Minister's statutory responsibilities under the Land
Drainage Act 1991.

(2) Extractive industry.   **4–098**

    (a)   extracting peat;
    (b)   deep drilling including in particular:
        (i)   geothermal drilling;
        (ii) drilling for the storage of nuclear waste material;
        (iii) drilling for water supplies;
        but excluding drilling to investigate the stability of the soil;
    (c)   extracting minerals (other than metalliferous and energy
        producing minerals) such as marble, sand, gravel, shale, salt,
        phosphates and potash;
    (d)   extracting coal or lignite by underground or open cast
        mining;
    (e)   extracting petroleum ;

165

    (f)   extracting natural gas;

    (g)   extracting ores;

    (h)   extracting bituminous shale;

    (i)   extracting minerals (other than metalliferous and energy producing minerals) by open cast mining;

    (j)   a surface industrial installation for the extraction of coal, petroleum, natural gas or ores or bituminous shale;

    (k)   a coke oven (dry distillation of coal);

    (l)   an installation for the manufacture of cement.

4–099   Factors such as the sensitivity of the location, the size of the project, working methods, the proposals for disposing of waste, the nature and extent of processing and ancillary operations, the arrangements for transporting minerals away from the site, and the duration of the proposed workings are likely to be particularly relevant in deciding whether or not mineral workings would have significant environmental effects. Proposals in national parks and Areas of Outstanding Natural Beauty will normally require an environmental statement.

4–100   All new deep mines may well require EA. Opencast coal mines and sand and gravel workings of more than 50 hectares may well require an environmental statement and even significantly smaller sites could require one if they are in a sensitive area or subject to particularly obtrusive operations. For oil and gas extraction, the main considerations will be the volume to be produced, the arrangements for transporting it and the sensitivity of the area. Production of 300 tonnes or more per day may well attract a requirement for an ES, and lesser production may require an ES in sensitive areas. Exploratory deep drilling should not normally require ES unless the site is in a sensitive location. The possibility that exploratory drilling may eventually lead to production of oil or gas is not a reason for requiring an ES.

4–101   *(3) Energy industry*

    (a)   a non-nuclear thermal power station, not being an installation falling within Schedule 1, or an installation for the production of electricity, steam and hot water.

    (b)   an industrial installation for carrying gas, steam or hot water, or the transmission of electrical energy by overhead cables.

    (c)   the surface storage of natural gas.

    (d)   the underground storage of combustible gases.

    (e)   surface storage of fossil fuels.

    (f)   the industrial briquetting of coal or lignite.

    (g)   an installation for the production or enrichment of nuclear fuels.

(h)   an installation for the reprocessing of irradiated nuclear fuels.

(i)   an installation for the collection or processing of radioactive waste, not being an installation falling within Schedule 1.

(j)   an installation for hydro-electric energy production.

(k)   wind generators.

An EA may particularly be needed if the wind generator development is in a sensitive area, or more than 10 wind generators or a generation capacity exceeding 5 MW are involved.

(4) Processing of metals.   **4–102**

(a)   an ironworks or steelworks including a foundry, forge, drawing plant or rolling mill (not being a works falling within Schedule 1);

(b)   an installation for the production (including smelting, refining, drawing and rolling) of non-ferrous metals other than precious metals;

(c)   the pressing, drawing or stamping of large castings;

(d)   the surface treatment and coating of metals;

(e)   boilermaking or manufacturing reservoirs, tanks or other sheet metal containers;

(f)   manufacturing or assembling motor vehicles or manufacturing motor vehicle engines;

(g)   a shipyard;

(h)   an installation for the construction or repair of aircraft;

(i)   the manufacture of railway equipment;

(j)   swaging by explosive;

(k)   an installation for the roasting or sintering of metallic ores;

(5) Glassmaking   **4–103**

The manufacture of glass.

(6) Chemical Industry   **4–104**

(a)   the treatment of intermediate products and production of chemicals, other than development falling within Schedule 1;

(b)   the production of pesticides or pharmaceutical products, paints or varnishes, elastomers or peroxides;

(c)   the storage of petroleum or petrochemical or chemical products.

(7) Food Industry   **4–105**

(a)   the manufacture of vegetable or animal oils or fats;

(b)   the packing or canning of animal or vegetable products;

167

    (c)   the manufacture of dairy products;
    (d)   brewing or malting;
    (e)   confectionery or syrup manufacture;
    (f)   an installation for the slaughter of animals;
    (g)   an industrial starch manufacturing installation;
    (h)   a fish meal or fish oil factory;
    (i)   a sugar factory.

4–106   *(8) Textile, leather, wood and paper industries*

    (a)   a wool scouring, degreasing and bleaching factory;
    (b)   the manufacture of fibre board, particle board or ply wood;
    (c)   the manufacture of pulp, paper or board;
    (d)   a fibre-dying factory;
    (e)   a cellulose-processing and production installation;
    (f)   a tannery or a leather dressing factory;

4–107   *(9) Rubber Industry*

The manufacture and treatment of elastomer-based products.

4–108   *(10) Infrastructure Projects*

    (a)   an industrial estate development project;
          The DoE indicates that EA may be required where the site area exceeds 20 hectares or there are more than one thousand dwellings within 200 metres of the site boundaries.
    (b)   an urban development project;
          Redevelopment of previously developed land is unlikely to require EA, unless the project comes specifically within Schedule 1 or 2, or the project is on a very much greater scale than the previous use of the land. On land which had not previously been intensively developed EA may be required where the site is more than 5 hectares in an urbanised area, or where there are more than seven hundred dwellings within 200 metres of the site boundaries, or where the development would provide a total of more than 10,000 square metres (gross) of shops, offices or other commercial uses. The DoE indicates that high rise development is not in itself a cause for EA. In relation to major out of town shopping schemes, the DoE indicate that a threshold of about 20,000 square metres (gross) may be an indication of significance.
    (c)   a ski lift or cable car
    (d)   the construction of a road, a harbour, including a fishing harbour, or an aerodrome not being development falling within Schedule I;
          [Directive: "airfield"].

In relation to roads, motorways are already within Schedule 1; in the case of other roads, DoE indicates that outside urban areas the construction of new roads and major road improvements over 10 km in length (or over 1 km in length if the road passes through a national park or through or within 100 metres of a site of special scientific interest, in a national nature reserve or a conservation area), may require environmental statements; within urban areas, any scheme with more than 1,500 dwellings within 100 metres of the centre line of the proposed or improved road may require ES).

(e)   canalisation or flood-relief works;
(f)   a dam or other installation designed to hold water or store it on a long term basis;
(g)   a tramway, elevated or underground railway, suspended line or similar line, exclusively or mainly for passenger transport;
(h)   an oil or gas pipeline installation;
(i)   a long distance aqueduct;
(j)   a yacht marina;
(k)   motorway service areas.

An EA may well be required for a location in a sensitive area, or for developments exceeding five hectares;

(l)   coast protection works.

An EA may well be required where proposals are likely to have significant effects upon a sensitive area, *e.g.* an AONB, SSSI, heritage coast or marine nature reserve.

(11) Other projects   **4–109**

(a)   a holiday village or hotel complex ;
(b)   a permanent racing or test track for cars or motor vehicles;
(c)   an installation for the disposal of controlled waste[96] or waste from mines and quarries, not being an installation falling within Schedule I;
      [Directive: "Installations for the disposal of industrial and domestic waste"]
(d)   a waste water treatment plant;
(e)   a site for depositing sludge;
(f)   the storage of scrap iron;
(g)   a test bench for engines, turbines or reactors;
(h)   the manufacture of artificial mineral fibres;
(i)   the manufacture, packing, loading or placing in cartridges of gunpowder or other explosives;
(j)   a knackers yard.

---

[96] See Chapter 11 for definition.

(12) The modification of a Schedule 1 development, where permission for the modification is requested for one year or less, and where the development is exclusively or mainly for the development and testing of new methods or products.

Content of an Environmental Statement

EC Directive

4–110   The requirements of the EC Directive are set out in Article 5(1) and Annex III in the following terms:

> 1.   Description of the project, including in particular:
>   — a description of the physical characteristics of the whole project and the land-use requirements during the construction and operational phases;
>   — a description of the main characteristics of the production processes, for instance nature and quantity of the materials used;
>   — an estimate, by type and quantity, of expected residues and emissions (water, air and soil pollution, noise, vibration, light, heat, radiation, etc) resulting from the operation of the proposed project.
> 2.   Where appropriate, an outline of the main alternatives studied by the developer and an indication of the main reasons for his choice, taking into account the environmental effects.
> 3.   A description of the aspects of the environment likely to be significantly affected by the proposed project, including, in particular, population, fauna, flora, soil, water, air, climatic factors, material assets, including the architectural and archaeological heritage, landscape and the inter-relationship between the above factors. According to the EC Commission the effects on population include social impacts as long they stem directly from environmental effects of the proposed project.[97]
> 4.   A description[98] of the likely significant effects of the proposed project on the environment resulting from:
>   — the existence of the project;
>   — the use of natural resources;

---

[97] Answer to question from the European Parliament, [1992] O.J. C242.
[98] This description should cover the direct effects and any indirect, secondary, cumulative, short, medium and long-term, permanent and temporary, positive and negative effects of the project (Annex III, para. 4, footnote).

170

— the emission of pollutants, the creation of nuisances and the elimination of waste;

and the description by the developer of the forecasting methods used to assess the effects on the environment.

5. A description of the measures envisaged to prevent, reduce and where possible offset any significant adverse effects on the environment.

6. A non-technical summary of the information provided under the above headings.

7. An indication of any difficulties (technical deficiencies or lack of know-how) encountered by the developer in compiling the required information.

UK Requirements

The UK requirements are set out in regulation 2(1) and Schedule 3 as 4–111 follows:

1. An environmental statement comprises a document or series of documents providing, for the purpose of assessing the likely impact on the environment of the development proposed to be carried out, the information specified in paragraph 2 (referred to in this Schedule as "the specified information").

2. The specified information is: 4–112

   (a) a description of the development proposed comprising information about the site and design and size or scale of the development;

   (b) the data necessary to identify and assess the main effects which that development is likely to have on the environment;

   (c) a description of the likely significant effects, direct and indirect, on the environment of the development, explained by reference to its possible impact on:
   human beings
   flora
   fauna
   soil
   water
   air
   climate
   the landscape
   the interaction between any of the foregoing
   material assets

the cultural heritage;

(d) where significant adverse effects are identified with respect to any of the foregoing, a description of the measures envisaged in order to avoid, reduce or remedy those effects; and

(e) a summary in non-technical language of the information specified above.

4–113　3. An environmental statement may include, by way of explanation or amplification of any specified information, further information on any of the following matters:

(a) the physical characteristics of the proposed development, and the land use requirements during the construction and operational phases;

(b) the main characteristics of the production processes proposed, including the nature and quality of the materials to be used;

(c) the estimated type and quantity of expected residues and emissions (including pollutants of water, air or soil, noise, vibration, light, heat and radiation) resulting from the proposed development when in operation;

(d) (in outline) the main alternatives (if any) studied by the applicant, appellant or authority and an indication of the main reasons for choosing the development proposed, taking into account the environmental effects;

(e) the likely significant direct and indirect effects on the environment of the development proposed which may result from:

(i) the use of the natural resources;

(ii) the emission of pollutants, the creation of nuisances, and the elimination of waste;

(f) the forecasting methods used to assess any effects on the environment about which the information is given under subparagraph (e); and

(g) any difficulties, such as technical deficiencies or lack of know-how, encountered in compiling any specified information.

In paragraph (e), "effects" includes secondary, cumulative, short, medium and long term, permanent, temporary, positive and negative effects.

4–114　4. Where further information is included in an environmental statement pursuant to paragraph 3, a non-technical summary of that information shall also be provided.

172

DoE Checklist for Contents of Environmental Statement

In addition the DoE provides a checklist of matters to be considered **4–115** for inclusion in an environmental statement.[99] This checklist is not intended to constitute a prescribed framework but simply to act as a guide to the subjects that need to be considered in the course of preparing an environmental statement and in discussions with relevant authorities and bodies about the scope of the statement. It is unlikely that all the items in the list will be relevant to any one project.

The environmental effects of a development during its construction **4–116** and commissioning phases should be considered separately from the effects arising whilst it is operational. Where the operational life of a development is expected to be limited, the effects of decommissioning or reinstating the land should also be considered separately.

Section 1   4–117

Information describing the project

1.1 Purpose and physical characteristics of the project, including details of proposed access and transport arrangements, and of numbers to be employed and where they will come from.

1.2 Land use requirements and other physical features of the project:

   (a) during construction;
   (b) when operational;
   (c) after use has ceased (where appropriate).

1.3. Production processes and operational features of the project:

   (a) type and quantities of raw materials, energy and other resources consumed;
   (b) residues and emissions by type, quantity, composition and strength including:
      (i)   discharges to water;
      (ii)   emissions to air;
      (iii) noise;
      (iv)   vibration;
      (v)   light;
      (vi)   heat;
      (vii) radiation;

---

[99] *Blue Book*, Appendix 4.

(viii) deposits/residues to land and soil;

(ix) others.

1.4 Main alternative sites and processes considered, where appropriate, and reasons for final choice.

4–118 Section 2

Information describing the site and its environment

Physical features

2.1 Population—proximity and numbers.

2.2 Flora and fauna (including both habitats and species)—in particular, protected species and their habitats.

2.3 Soil—agricultural quality, geology and geomorphology.

2.4 Water—aquifers, water courses, shoreline, including the type, quantity, composition and strength of any existing discharges.

2.5 Air—climatic factors, air quality, etc.

2.6 Architectural and historic heritage, archaeological sites and features, and other material assets.

2.7 Landscape and topography.

2.8 Recreational uses.

2.9 Any other relevant environmental features.

The policy framework

2.10 Where applicable, the information considered under this section should include all relevant statutory designations such as national nature reserves, sites of special scientific interest, national parks, areas of outstanding natural beauty, heritage coasts, regional parks, country parks, national forest parks and designated areas, local nature reserves, areas affected by tree preservation orders, water protection zones, nitrate sensitive areas, conservation areas, listed buildings, scheduled ancient monuments, and designated areas of archaeological importance. It should also include references to structure, unitary and local plan policies applying to the site and surrounding area which are relevant to the proposed development.

2.11 Reference should also be made to international designations, *e.g.* those under the EC "Wild Birds" Directive, the World Heritage Convention, the UNEP Man and Biosphere Programme and the Ramsar Convention.[1]

---

[1] This list should now include the EC "Habitats" Directive.

Section 3

Assessment of effects

(Including direct and indirect, secondary, cumulative short, medium and long-term, permanent and temporary, positive and negative effects of the project).

Effects on human beings, buildings and man-made features.

3.1 Change in population arising from the development, and consequential environment effects.

3.2 Visual effects of the development on the surrounding area and landscape.

3.3 Levels and effects of emissions from the development during normal operation.

3.4 Levels and effects of noise from the development.

3.5 Effects of the development on local roads and transport.[2]

3.6 Effects of the development on buildings, the architectural and historic heritage, archaeological features, and other human artefacts, *e.g.* through pollutants, visual intrusion, vibration.

Effects on flora, fauna and geology

3.7 Loss of, and damage to, habitats and plant and animal species.

3.8 Loss of, and damage to, geological, palaeontological and physiographic features.

3.9 Other ecological consequences.

Effects on land

3.10 Physical effects of the development, *e.g.* change in local topography, effect of earth-moving on stability, soil erosion, etc.

3.11 Effects of chemical emissions and deposits on soil of site and surrounding land.

3.12 Land use/resource effects:

(a) quality and quantity of agricultural land to be taken;

(b) sterilisation of mineral resources;

(c) other alternative uses of the site, including the "do nothing" option;

(d) effect on surrounding land uses including agriculture;

(e) waste disposal.

Effects on water

3.13 Effects of development on drainage pattern in the area.

---

[2] Although impact on traffic is not required to be covered by an ES.

3.14 Changes to other hydrographic characteristics, *e.g.* ground water level, water courses, flow of underground water.

3.15 Effects on coastal or estuarine hydrology.

3.16 Effects of pollutants, waste, etc., on water quality.

Effects on air and climate

3.17 Level and concentration of chemical emissions and their environmental effects.

3.18 Particulate matter.

3.19 Offensive odours.

3.20 Any other climatic effects.

Other indirect and secondary effects associated with the project

3.21 Effects from traffic (road, rail, air, water) related to the development.

3.22 Effects arising from the extraction and consumption of materials, water, energy or other resources by the development.

3.23 Effects of other development associated with the project, *e.g.* new roads, sewers, housing, power lines, pipelines, telecommunications, etc.

3.24 Effects of association of the development with other existing or proposed development.

3.25 Secondary effects resulting from the interaction of separate direct effects listed above.

4–120   Section 4

Mitigating measures

4.1 Where significant adverse effects are identified, a description of the measures to be taken to avoid, reduce or remedy those effects, *e.g.*:

   (a) site planning;

   (b) technical measures, *e.g.*:
      (i) process selection;
      (ii) recycling;
      (iii) pollution control and treatment;
      (iv) containment (*e.g.* bunding of storage vessels).

   (c) aesthetic and ecological measures, *e.g.*:
      (i) mounding;
      (ii) design, colour, etc.;
      (iii) landscaping;
      (iv) tree plantings;
      (v) measures to preserve particular habitats or create alternative habitats;

     (vi) recording of archaeological sites;

     (vii) measures to safeguard historic building or sites.

4.2   Assessment of the likely effectiveness of mitigating measures.

Section 5   4–121

Risks of accidents and hazardous development

5.1   Risks of accidents as such are not covered in the Directive on EA or, consequently, in the implementing Regulations. However, when the proposed development involves materials that could be harmful to the environment (including people) in the event of an accident, the environmental statement should include an indication of the preventive measures that will be adopted so that such an occurrence is not likely to have a significant effect. This could, where appropriate, include reference to compliance with the Health and Safety at Work Act 1974 and its relevant statutory provisions such as the Control of Industrial Major Accident Hazards Regulations 1984.

5.2   There are separate arrangements in force relating to the keeping or use of hazardous substances and the Health and Safety Executive provides local planning authorities with expert advice about risk assessment on any planning application involving a hazardous installation.

5.3   Nevertheless, it is desirable that wherever possible the risk of accident and the general environmental effects of developments should be considered together, and developers and planning authorities should bear this in mind.

Chapter 5

NATURE CONSERVATION

Development of Nature Conservation in Britain

Introduction

Although statutory protection has been given to various individual   **5–001**
species and groups since Norman times, nature conservation, as it is
now practised, originated in a reawakening of interest in the natural
environment which began in the United States about 1865, and then
spread to much of Europe towards the close of the 19th century. In
Britain, this led to the establishment of voluntary organisations, such
as the (Royal) Society for the Protection of Birds in 1889 and the
National Trust in 1895, which aroused public interest and pressure for
legislation to protect both habitats and species.

Britain was not alone in developing an interest in conservation at   **5–002**
this time, for similar bodies with similar objectives were established
across Europe. Their efforts met with considerable success, with
Nature Conservation Acts being passed, for example, in Norway
(1910), Denmark (1917), Finland (1923) and Austria (1928). In Britain,
however, the development of a statutory basis for nature conservation
was not achieved until after the Second World War. Even so, the legal
and administrative framework was in place well before the United
Kingdom's accession to the European Community in 1973, and this
has so far been only moderately affected by EC legislation. The latter is
accordingly discussed after a review of UK domestic law, where its
potential future impact can be best assessed.

In the early 1940s, as part of the planning for the post-war   **5–003**
reconstruction of Britain, Governmental Special Committees were set
up to consider improvements in practically every aspect of life. Among
these were the Hobhouse and Huxley Committees, set up in 1945 to
consider, respectively, means to protect landscape for amenity and to
conserve habitats for scientific purposes in England and Wales; in
Scotland, their analogues were the Ramsey and Ritchie Committees.

5–004   In their reports,[1] these Committees set out the rationale for nature conservation, a rationale which still applies today. However, instead of proposing a unified approach to conserving the natural environment, they recommended powers and administrative structures for landscape conservation which differed extensively from those recommended for nature conservation.

5–005   Consequent on these reports, the Nature Conservancy was established in 1949 by Royal Charter to promote science-based nature conservation throughout Great Britain. Their recommendations were also implemented statutorily in 1949 by the establishment of a further organisation, in addition to the highly centralised Nature Conservancy, namely, the more decentralised National Parks Commission, to promote amenity-based landscape conservation in England and Wales. The enabling legislation, the National Parks and Access to the Countryside Act, 1949 ("the 1949 Act"), also gave statutory responsibilities to the Nature Conservancy, and the very different treatment it accorded to landscape and wildlife conservation has been a persistent characteristic of the British environmental scene ever since. Although the two branches of conservation were re-united in Wales in 1991, and in Scotland in 1992, the dichotomy between landscape and wildlife conservation still persists in England, at least while the current consultations continue.

          Only the powers and structures for nature conservation are discussed below; the statutory powers for the conservation of landscape have been outlined in Chapters 23 and 24.

5–006   For nature conservation, Part III of the 1949 Act enabled national and local government to establish nature reserves; the Act also laid a duty on the Nature Conservancy to inform local planning authorities of any land, other than any being managed as a nature reserve, of special interest by reason of its flora, fauna, or geological or physiographical features.[2] There was however no obligation on the planning authorities to take any action to protect any such land, though there has always been a duty laid on them by the applicable General Development Order[3] to consult with the Nature Conservancy (Council) before granting any planning consent in relation to the land. Section 23 thus provided the statutory basis for Sites of Special Scientific Interest ("SSSIs") discussed in paragraphs 5–061 to 5–133

---

[1] Cmd. 7121, 7122 and 7235 of 1947 and Cmd. 7814 of 1949.
[2] s.23, now re-enacted as s.28(1) of the Wildlife and Countryside Act 1981. "Physiography" is (and was in 1949) an obsolete synonym for "Geomorphology", the branch of physical science which studies present-day landscapes and seeks to explain their origin. It lies at the interface of geography and geology; in the present text "geology" has been taken to include "physiography".
[3] Now Art.18(1)(t) of the G.D.O. 1988.

below. However, as the Act came to be implemented, its powers were seen to be inadequate in two particulars: firstly, in achieving the effective conservation of endangered species (especially when these were mobile) and, secondly, in conserving fauna and flora in the face of operations, such as farming and forestry, which were exempt from planning control.

Some improvements in species protection were achieved by the Protection of Birds Acts, 1954–1967, and the Conservation of Wild Creatures and Wild Plants Act, 1975, but the problems posed by agriculture and forestry persisted until the passage of the Wildlife and Countryside Act, 1981.   5–007

This Act[4] forms the keystone of nature conservation as currently practised in Britain. It provides effective "off-site" powers to ensure the conservation of various endangered species, wherever they might be found and, at the same time, greatly expands the degree to which the government Conservation Agencies can restrict the rights of owners and occupiers and influence the management of designated sites.   5–008

The Wildlife and Countryside Act also remedied another weakness of the 1949 Act by making good the long-standing inability of the government's Conservation Agencies to meet the costs incurred by themselves and imposed on others in the interests of nature conservation. The 1949 Act had allowed management to be undertaken and compensation to be paid only on nature reserves declared under that Act; the Countryside Act, 1968, had made it possible to pay for the management of SSSIs; the 1981 Act introduced new provisions for the recompense of site owners and occupiers for profits foregone and for past expenditure on projects aborted in the interests of conservation. The Environmental Protection Act 1990[5] now allows payment for the management of land adjacent to SSSIs.   5–009

The policy statement "Nature Conservation in Great Britain", issued by the Nature Conservancy Council in 1984, outlines how the then Nature Conservancy Council intended to use the powers it had acquired under the 1981 Act. The policy chapters to be found towards the end of this statement make clear an intention to exercise the powers available to conservation in what was seen by some as a highly doctrinaire manner, rather than in co-operation with other landed interests.   5–010

---

[4] Which has been amended several times, principally by the Wildlife and Countryside (Amendment) Act 1985, the Wildlife and Countryside (Service of Notices) Act 1985 and the Wildlife and Countryside (Amendment) Act 1991; a series of Orders have also amended the Schedules.

[5] Sched.9, para. 4(2)(a).

181

5–011   In contrast, DoE Circular 27/87, which updates previous advice and
guidance to local authorities on the role they should play in implementing nature conservation legislation, advocates taking a balanced
view between the needs of the economy and the needs of conservation. In so doing, this Circular reflects the approach of the EC
directives that relate to nature conservation.

5–012   The implementation of the 1981 Act necessitated the reconsideration
of virtually all areas designated under the 1949 Act, the renotification
of those which met the new standards, and the notification for the first
time of numerous further sites. In all, the owners and occupiers of
some 1.9 million hectares (over 8 per cent of Britain) were made aware
that their land was considered to be of special interest to nature
conservation and that their activities were liable to be restricted
accordingly.

5–013   Perhaps not surprisingly, this provoked a growing demand for the
criteria used in the selection of SSSIs to be made public. For biological
sites, this demand was met, but very much in part, by the publication
in 1989 of "Guidelines for the selection of biological SSSIs", issued by
the Nature Conservancy Council for the instruction of its staff. Criteria
for the selection of geological SSSIs had been publicly available since
1976.[6]

Administration

5–014   The implementation of the 1981 Act under the 1984 policy also led to
structural changes in the governmental organisation of nature conservation. There had been a number of administrative changes since 1949,
for the original Royal Charter, which established the Nature Conservancy as a Body Corporate under the Privy Council, was superseded
by the Science and Technology Act, 1965, under which the Nature
Conservancy was incorporated within the newly formed Natural
Environment Research Council ("NERC") of the Department for
Education and Science. Later, the Nature Conservancy Council Act,
1973, transferred NERC's nature conservation functions to the Nature
Conservancy Council, a "quango" overseen by the Department of the
Environment, having jurisdiction over the whole of Great Britain.

---

[6] These criteria were first published in 1976 by the NCC in "Shetland: Localities of
Geological and Geomorphological Importance", p.58. An up-dated set of criteria
appears in the *Geological Curator*, vol. 5, pp.107–109, 1989, and the methodology
employed is set out in *Modern Geology* (in press).

Throughout these changes, the Nature Conservancy and the Nature   5–015
Conservancy Council continued to make all principal policy decisions
for Great Britain as a whole, although Scottish and Welsh headquarters had been set up shortly after the foundation of the Conservancy, and a headquarters for England in 1976. However, such very
modest devolution arguably did not properly reflect the diversity
across Britain, both socio-economic and in terms of nature conservation.[7] Thus when a single, uniform and confrontational policy for the
implementation of the statutory provisions for nature conservation
throughout Great Britain was introduced in 1984, this provoked strong
pressure for legislative change.

In 1989 and 1990 the House of Lords Select Committee on Science   5–016
and Technology, under the chairmanship of Lord Carver, considered
proposals that the Nature Conservancy Council had developed for
reorganising itself on a federal model. Their Report "Nature Conservancy Council"[8] observes that "on the same day [as the NCC met to
put the final touches to its proposals for a federal reorganisation] the
government announced, without consultation and to the surprise of
the NCC and everyone else, that the NCC would be split into three
autonomous country agencies". The Committee did not express a
preference as to possible alternative schemes for reorganising the
NCC, but largely confined itself to comments on the option selected by
the government. One of its main concerns was the maintenance of the
data and experience constituting the science base that, as has been
seen, had since 1949 been fundamental to the role of the NCC, after
this had been separated into three independent bodies. A joint
committee of the three new bodies was recommended to this end.

The Environmental Protection Act, 1990, consequently dismem-   5–017
bered the Nature Conservancy Council into its "country" units,
setting up in its stead the Nature Conservancy Council for England
(English Nature), the Nature Conservancy Council for Scotland, and
the Countryside Council for Wales; the last-mentioned Council also
assumed the responsibilities of the Countryside Commission in Wales.
A committee, the Joint Nature Conservation Committee, was set up to
provide a perspective over the whole of the United Kingdom and
brought in, for the first time, representation from Northern Ireland.
The remit of the Joint Committee is largely defined by the E.P.A.,
section 133, which sets out various "special functions" of the three

---

[7] A policy which is appropriate and acceptable in south-eastern England may well be
neither when applied to north-western Scotland. Similar contrasts elsewhere in
Europe (*e.g.* between the Netherlands and Norway) had long been recognised to
require the adoption of different, but nationally appropriate, conservation policies.
[8] H.L. Paper 33–I and II, Session 1989–90, Second Report, March 1990.

Councils that may only be discharged through the Joint Committee. These include:

(i) advising the UK government Ministers on policies relating to nature conservation for Great Britain as a whole or outside Great Britain;

(ii) providing advice and disseminating knowledge about nature conservation for Great Britain as a whole or outside Great Britain;

(iii) establishing common standards for Great Britain for monitoring and research into nature conservation; and

(iv) commissioning and supporting research relevant to any of these special functions.

5–018   In addition the Joint Committee may, pursuant to section 133(3), give advice or information to any of the individual Country Councils on nature conservation matters concerning Great Britain as a whole or outside it.

5–019   This reorganisation, dating effectively from April 1, 1991, was further modified by the Natural Heritage (Scotland) Act, 1991, which, from April 1, 1992, merged the Nature Conservancy Council for Scotland with the Countryside Commission for Scotland to form Scottish Natural Heritage.[9]

5–020   In other respects, the statutory provisions for nature conservation contained in Part VII of the Environmental Protection Act, 1990, which came into effect on 5th November 1990[10] were little changed from those previously existing. In contrast, the Natural Heritage (Scotland) Act, 1991, is more innovative in that it introduces, for the first time, provisions for appeals against decisions by Scottish Natural Heritage,[11] and reinforces a requirement, originally made in part in section 37 of the Countryside Act, 1968, that those responsible for the administration of nature conservation should take into account the needs of agriculture, fisheries and forestry, the need for social and economic development, the interests of the owners and occupiers of land, and the interests of local communities.[12] These requirements have been reflected in the decentralised internal structure adopted by Scottish Natural Heritage.

5–021   Nature conservation in Britain is at present in an unstable and transitional state. The re-unification of landscape and wildlife conservation has been achieved in Scotland and in Wales, but not in

---

[9] The organisational and other changes brought about in Scotland by the 1991 Act are the subject of Scottish Office Circular 4/1993.

[10] By the E.P.A. 1990 (Commencement No.1) Order 1990, S.I. 1990 No. 2226.

[11] s.12.

[12] s.3(1).

England.[13] In Scotland, the Conservation Agency is now decentralised, whereas its English analogue retains the traditional monolithic structure. Further, the remit of those who administer conservation in Scotland has now been significantly changed from that still current in England and Wales.[14] Finally, the growing body of EC legislation, the basic approach of which is to seek to balance the needs of nature conservation with demands for commercial development, is increasingly in conflict with the expectations of the voluntary wildlife organisations in Britain—this conflict will not easily be resolved. Currently the possible amalgamation of English Nature with the Countryside Commission is under consideration, and it would seem likely that this will lead to further legislation to complete the reorganisation begun in 1990.

All or any of the seven conservation bodies established by the 1949 Charter and the Acts of 1965, 1973, 1990 and 1991[15] are referred to below as "Conservation Agencies". The specific body or bodies to which reference is made will be apparent from the context. The expression "NCC" is used to indicate the Nature Conservancy Council.   5–022

For the sake of brevity, the National Parks and Access to the Countryside Act, 1949, will be referred to as the "1949 Act", the Countryside Act, 1968, as the "1968 Act", the Wildlife and Countryside Act, 1981, as the "1981 Act", the Wildlife and Countryside (Amendment) Act, 1985, as the "1985 Act", and the Environmental Protection Act, 1990, as the "1990 Act". Circular 27/87 of the Department of the Environment (also indexed as Circular 52/87 of the Welsh Office) is referred to as "27/87".   5–023

Habitat Conservation

In Britain, the conservation of habitats (that is the conservation of naturally occurring assemblages of plants and animals, as distinct   5–024

---

[13] The Secretary of State for the Environment at the time of the reorganisation of the NCC was decided upon, Mr Nicholas Ridley, is quoted in paragraph 1.6 of the House of Lords Select Committee Report (n.8) as saying that (in England) the NCC and the Countryside Commission would remain separate "in view of the much greater density of population and consequent pressure upon the land". The relevance of these factors to this decision is not explained.

[14] The basis of nature conservation in Northern Ireland differs substantially from that of the rest of the United Kingdom and is provided by The Nature Conservation and Amenity Lands (Northern Ireland) Order 1985 (S.I. 1985 No. 170) (N.I. 1).

[15] Namely the Science and Technology Act 1965; the Nature Conservancy Council Act, 1973; the Environmental Protection Act, 1990; the Natural Heritage (Scotland) Act, 1991.

from the conservation of individually identified, and often rare or endangered, species) and of features of geological and geomorphological significance, has been largely achieved by the creation and maintenance of a network of statutory site designations. The British legislation relating to each of these designations, and the procedures followed in its implementation, is described below; a conspectus of the system as a whole is provided in 27/87, paragraphs 1 to 6.

National Nature Reserves

5–025   The acquisition of rights in land so that it can be managed in the interests of wildlife has a long history, through which the underlying motive has gradually changed from field sports to nature conservation. Reserves specifically for the conservation of all nature (rather than a few game species) date back over 120 years[16] but, until the passage of the 1949 Act, their establishment fell to various private bodies set up for this purpose.

5–026   The 1949 Act allowed the establishment of what are now known as National Nature Reserves (NNRs) by the government's Conservation Agencies and on March 31, 1993, 259 had so far been declared; about half lie in England, three-tenths in Scotland, and one-fifth in Wales. Their total area is 185,201 hectares, three-fifths of which is in Scotland, more than three-tenths in England, and less than a tenth in Wales. NNRs thus account for rather less than 10 per cent of the total area designated for wildlife conservation.

5–027   The powers given to the Conservation Agencies for the establishment of NNRs derive almost entirely from sections 15 to 21 of the 1949 Act. Over the years, these sections have been much amended by subsequent legislation, including the Science and Technology Act 1965, the Nature Conservancy Council Act 1973, the Environmental Protection Act 1990, and the Natural Heritage (Scotland) Act 1991, but such amendments are principally concerned with the transfer of powers following organisational changes affecting the Nature Conservancy and its successor bodies. A more significant amendment, however, is to be found in section 35 of the 1981 Act which extends the powers of the Conservation Agencies under section 19 of the 1949 Act to declare as an NNR land which they do not control, but which is held and managed as a nature reserve by an "approved body" (*e.g.* a County Naturalists' Trust or the R.S.P.B.).

---

[16] The first were private ventures, with conservation organisations entering the field somewhat later. The National Trust, for example, acquired its first nature reserve at Wicken Fen, Cambridgeshire, in 1899.

The Definition of Nature Reserves

The expression "Nature Reserve" is defined in section 15 of the   **5–028**
1949 Act as meaning:
land managed for the purpose:

(a) of providing under suitable conditions and control special opportunities for the study of, and research into, matters relating to the fauna and flora of Great Britain and the physical conditions in which they live, and for the study of geological and physiographical features of special interest in the area; or
(b) of preserving flora and fauna or geological or physiographical features of special interest in the area;

or for both these purposes.

The 1949 Act refers only to "nature reserves" and, although the term   **5–029**
"National Nature Reserve" was much employed by the Nature
Conservancy and its successor bodies, it did not receive statutory
recognition until the 1981 Act. As mentioned below, section 21 of the
1949 Act also gave powers to local authorities to establish their own
separate nature reserves, thus creating the distinction between
"National" and "Local" nature reserves.

The 1949 Act set no qualitative standards for eligibility as an NNR;   **5–030**
its sole requirement is that the area declared should be managed for
scientific research and study and/or for the conservation of its features
of special interest. What was meant by "special interest" was nowhere
defined. Although Nature Reserve Agreements (NRAs—see below)
could only be concluded for land which the Nature Conservancy
considered should in the national interest be managed as a nature
reserve, there appears to have been no restraint on the Nature
Conservancy if it chose to declare any land it owned or leased as an
NNR. Indeed, by section 19(2), a declaration by the Conservancy that
land is being managed as a Nature Reserve is to be taken as conclusive
of the matters declared. Similarly, where the Conservancy is satisfied
that any land being managed as a nature reserve is of national
importance, a declaration of that land as a nature reserve is likewise
conclusive of the matters declared.

This lack of criteria was to some extent made good by the 1981 Act   **5–031**
which, in section 35, stipulates in effect that the Nature Conservancy
must be satisfied that land is of national importance before it can be
declared a NNR, whether it is owned, leased or established by
agreement. There is thus a presumption that NNRs will be of higher
quality than Sites of Special Scientific Interest (SSSIs; see paragraph 5–

079 below), for section 28 of the 1981 Act does not require the latter to be of national importance (although the contrary has often been argued by the Conservation Agencies)[17]

Management of NNRs

5–032   The very definition of "nature reserve" in both the 1949 Act and the 1981 Act,[18] requires that such reserves be managed. The 1949 Act proceeded on the basis that this management would be provided either directly by the relevant Conservation Agency owning or leasing the land, or indirectly through the creation of a "Nature Reserve Agreement" (NRA) relating to it. Thus section 16 of the 1949 Act provides for the conclusion of NRAs between the relevant Conservation Agency and every owner, lessee and occupier of land which the Agency considers it is in the national interest to manage as an NNR. Such agreements may, and in practice do, restrict the use of such land by its owners, lessees and occupiers within very broad limits set out in section 16(3) so as to provide for:

(a) the management of the land in such manner, the carrying out thereon of such work and the doing thereon of such other things as may be expedient for the purposes of the agreement; or

(b) any of the matters mentioned in the last foregoing paragraph being carried out, or for the cost thereof being defrayed, either by the said owner or other persons, or by the Conservancy, or partly in one way and partly in another.

The "purposes of the agreement" must be consistent with the purposes of management as set out in the section 15 definition of nature reserve, that is the study of and research into the fauna and flora and other features of special interest, and their preservation.

5–033   The powers to declare land as a nature reserve were extended by section 35 of the 1981 Act which permitted land already held by "an approved body" and managed as a nature reserve also to be declared as a NNR, but little use has so far been made of these further powers. In this situation there is no formal NRA, but the Conservation Agency may, if so requested, make byelaws to protect the reserve, as described below.

---

[17] The need for an NNR to possess "national importance" was demonstrated in 1990 when the Tring Reservoirs NNR, established in 1955, was "de-declared" as no longer meeting the required standard (17th Annual Report of the Nature Conservancy Council (for 1990-91), p.12).
[18] s.35(1).

Section 16 also provides for payments, both to defray management **5–034** costs and also by way of compensation for restrictions imposed. In practice, NRAs are concluded for a fixed term, typically of 21 years or more. They constrain the owner, lessees and all occupiers through restricting the uses to which the land can be put and the management techniques that can be employed, while promoting the interests of nature conservation and the related scientific research. Many provide for changes in access policy.

Compensation payments have in the past typically been at an **5–035** unrealistically low level, sometimes as low as 1p per hectare per annum. Section 50 of the 1981 Act, however, provides for Ministerial guidance on the level of such payments, which is contained in DoE Circular 4/83,[19] and for reference to arbitration in the event of dispute. On an appeal against an arbitration award, it was held that though a person affected by restrictions placed on land must seek to mitigate his loss, he is not necessarily required to pursue the most profitable solution and may also legitimately take into account considerations such as maintenance of amenity and aesthetic preference. Though profitability is obviously a relevant factor, whether a particular choice is reasonable is not to be determined solely in terms of the commercial optimum.[20]

Conservation Agencies are free to purchase or lease land, and where **5–036** an NNR is established in this way the normal law regarding tenure and ownership applies. On the other hand, those instances where the declaration of a NNR depends on the existence of an NRA require some further comment.[21]

National Nature Reserves established on the basis of NRAs re- **5–037** semble SSSIs in that the land restricted as to its use in the interests of nature conservation remains in private ownership. There are, how- ever, three important differences: firstly, the designation of NNRs requires the prior consent of every owner, lessee and occupier of the land and (save by use of compulsory purchase powers) cannot be imposed without such consent; secondly, their designation is not in perpetuity, but can be reviewed periodically at each expiry of the NRA; and, thirdly, the level of compensation payable by the Conserva- tion Agency to the owner, lessee and/or occupier does not depend on

---

[19] There have for a considerable time been indications of an intention to revise Circular 4/83, but as yet no new guidance has been issued.

[20] *Thomas and anor. v. Countryside Council for Wales, The Times*, August 23, 1993.

[21] NNRs subject to NRAs form over half the total area declared; as of March 31, 1993, 49 per cent of the total acreage of NNRs in Britain was owned or leased, 50 per cent was subject to NRAs, and less than 1 per cent was owned by "approved bodies" under s.35 of the 1981 Act. In Scotland, in particular, 67 per cent of all NNRs are dependent on NRAs.

future profits foregone in the interests of conservation but, following DoE circular 4/83, is fixed in advance for a significant term of years.

5–038   Since the passage of the 1981 Act, it has been the policy of the Conservation Agencies to notify all NNRs as SSSIs; in these circumstances, this difference as to the basis for compensation could well prove disadvantageous to the owners and occupiers, since the existence of an NRA may prejudice any payment of compensation under the very different provisions that apply in relation to SSSIs.

5–038   Powers for the compulsory purchase of land to be managed as an NNR are provided in sections 17 and 18 of the 1949 Act. Section 17 relates to land it is desired to manage as an NNR, but over which it has proved impossible to conclude an NRA; it is a precondition of the exercise of powers under section 17 that it is considered that a satisfactory NRA cannot be concluded on reasonable terms. Section 18 relates to land subject to an NRA but which it has proved impossible to manage satisfactorily as an NNR owing to a breach of the agreement. The use of these powers requires authorisation by the appropriate Minister and is subject to the dispute procedures of sections 18(3) and (4) and 103.

5–040   The Conservation Agencies have used these powers of compulsory purchase for the establishment of NNRs very sparingly since 1949, and principally to acquire rights in or over land where ownership has proved impossible to ascertain (*e.g.* turbary rights, the exercise of which would adversely affect the wildlife interest of a peat bog).

5–041   The procedures for the declaration of NNRs, which include an obligation to issue public notices, are set out in section 19 of the 1949 Act. This section, with section 35 of the 1981 Act, confers sufficient powers to allow the Conservation Agencies to establish NNRs without any consultation and without seeking approval, *e.g.* from Ministers.

5–042   Section 19(3) of the 1949 Act requires that, if an NNR ceases to be owned by or leased to the Conservation Agency, or if the NRA expires, the Conservation Agency must declare this fact, effectively withdrawing the status of NNR from the area once covered by the expired agreement. In practice, however, this duty is not invariably complied with.

Byelaws

5–043   The conclusion of an NRA also allows the Conservation Agencies, under section 20 of the 1949 Act, to introduce byelaws to protect the reserve and these, *inter alia*, can prohibit or restrict entry, pest control and shooting, and provide for licensing any of the controlled activities. Shooting of birds may also be controlled outside of the reserve within such area as may be requisite.[22] The byelaws may not however further restrict the rights of owners, lessees and/or occupiers, or interfere with public rights-of-way or with statutory undertakers. Should the introduction of such byelaws interfere with the rights of others, the Conservation Agency is required to pay compensation.[23] In practice, byelaws have been selectively applied to NNRs; their main utility appears to be to control wildfowling.

Conclusion

When originally devised in 1949, NNR status was of considerable utility to nature conservation for, under the provisions of the 1949 Act, it provided the only means whereby the original Nature Conservancy could manage land in the interests of nature conservation and incur expenditure in such management. It also provided a means whereby a Conservation Agency could acquire a right in land which would be of value in resolving problems arising from complex ownership situations, agricultural tenancies, and common rights for the benefit of conservation. Further, NNR status provided a much greater security against development or adverse forms of land use (including agriculture and forestry) than did the status of SSSI.   **5–044**

Over the years, however, the introduction of further statutory provisions for nature conservation have progressively eroded the unique status of the NNR. In particular, section 15 of the 1968 Act allowed payments to be made for the management of SSSIs in the interests of conservation, and other provisions for expenditure are made in sections 30 and 50 of the 1981 Act. Also, the 1981 Act allows rights in land to be established by the much simpler procedure of SSSI designation.   **5–045**

Further, forms of land use (*e.g.* many agricultural practices), which do not constitute development, but which are adverse to wildlife conservation, can now be controlled by the powers provided by sections 28 and 29 of the 1981 Act for areas notified as SSSIs. As all NNRs qualify for such notification, and are now notified as SSSIs in any event, the advantages they alone could once provide to conservation are now much more widely available.   **5–046**

The apparent advantages to be gained for conservation from declaring an area as a NNR have thus progressively diminished until they are now virtually confined to specialised matters such as public prestige, the provision of research facilities, the need for direct management, the control of access, or the ability to impose byelaws. In   **5–047**

[22] s.20(2)(c).
[23] By s.106(3) any authority having the power to make byelaws under the 1949 Act also has the power to enforce them.

response to changing circumstances, the declaration of extensive areas as new NNRs, so prominent in the years which followed the passage of the 1949 Act, now proceeds at a rate much reduced from its former levels. However, as recent EC Directives[24] now demand a guaranteed ability to manage conserved land positively, and as such management is difficult to achieve through the predominantly negative legislative provisions for SSSIs, the consequences of this long decline in enthusiasm for NNR declaration might prove, at best, to be a considerable embarrassment to British nature conservation. Recent figures suggest that this possibility has been recognised and that interest in declaring further NNRs is increasing, at least in England.

Local Nature Reserves

5–048   In addition to permitting the national Government's Conservation Agency to establish (national) nature reserves, the 1949 Act, by section 21, also gave counties and county boroughs in England and Wales, and burghs in Scotland, the power to provide, or to secure the provision of, nature reserves on any land in their area—not being land held by the Nature Conservancy or subject to an NRA—which they thought expedient to manage as a nature reserve. Before exercising this power, councils had first to consult with the Nature Conservancy. County districts received similar powers, but could only exercise these with the consent of both the relevant county council and the Nature Conservancy.

5–049   Section 184 of the Local Government Act, 1972, equalised the powers of district, county and local planning authorities and Schedule 30 to the same Act removed the need for the county districts to obtain the consent of their county and of the Nature Conservancy; in consequence of these changes, and of the re-organisation of the nature conservation agencies, district councils and county councils now have powers to establish nature reserves under section 21 of the 1949 Act, having first consulted the appropriate Conservation Agency. There is no requirement to obtain the approval of the Agency, mere consultation sufficing to meet the requirements of the Act.

5–050   Such nature reserves are customarily known as "Local Nature Reserves" (LNRs) to distinguish them from the "National Nature Reserves" (NNRs) established by the national Conservation Agency. Both types of reserve are governed by sections 15 to 21 of the 1949 Act but, in the case of LNRs, references in sections 16(1) and 17(1) to the national interest are to be taken to include references to the interests of

---

[24] The Birds and Habitats Directives—see paras. 5–245 to 5–257 and 5–262 to 5–275.

the locality.[25] The requirement in section 35 of the 1981 Act that new NNRs are to be of national importance does not apply to LNRs, so there is no explicit constraint on a council, other than the need to consult the appropriate Conservation Agency, as to the quality in nature conservation terms of any land that it may choose to declare as an LNR. In comparison with NNRs, the typical LNR is much smaller, much more likely to be found in an urban than in a rural setting, and much more likely to lie in lowland than in upland Britain.[26]

The statutory provisions for LNRs are *mutatis mutandis* the same as for NNRs. Thus the same definition of "nature reserve" in section 15 of the 1949 Act applies to both types, namely land managed to provide special opportunities for study and research, or to preserve the flora and fauna and/or geological features of special interest. Councils can negotiate NRAs for land they consider it is in the local interest to manage as a LNR. Powers for the compulsory purchase of land to be managed as a LNR are provided, as a last resort, in sections 17 and 18 and are subject to dispute procedures.[27] LNRs are likewise declared under the provisions of section 19; they may be established without any need for outside approval or consultation, although, in the case of LNRs, the appropriate Conservation Agency must be consulted; and councils may introduce byelaws for any LNR under section 20.

5–051

As noted above, section 35 of the 1981 Act extended the powers of the Conservation Agencies to enable them to declare as an NNR land held by an approved body and managed as a "nature reserve". A local authority could well be "approved" in this sense, so that land already declared as an LNR could also be declared as an NNR by a Conservation Agency. However, the reverse procedure is not possible, as the power to do this is expressly excluded by the terms of section 21(1) of the 1949 Act.

5–052

LNRs are evaluated and chosen in a purely local context and many do not attain the standards set for SSSIs. In these circumstances, it has been impracticable for the Conservation Agencies to notify all LNRs as SSSIs under the 1981 Act. Rather than seeking to conserve natural interests of high value, which is the function of the SSSI, the role of LNRs is seen as providing facilities for education and research, or for the informal enjoyment of nature by the public, on land which, while

5–053

---

[25] s.21(4).
[26] As at March 31, 1993, 365 Local Nature Reserves, totalling 20,458 hectares, had been declared under these provisions, all but 29 lying in England. Enthusiasm for LNRs is a relatively recent phenomenon. More were established in a single year (1990/91) than in the 25-year period which followed the passage of the 1949 Act, and the total further increased by more than half between March 31, 1991 and March 31, 1993.
[27] s.18(3), (4).

not necessarily of high value, is managed so that its biological or geological interests are preserved or enhanced or interpreted.[28]

Marine Nature Reserves

5–054   Marine Nature Reserves (MNRs) were introduced by sections 36 and 37 of the 1981 Act. They are unique among British nature conservation designations in their physical coverage, and may comprise any land covered, whether continuously or intermittently, by tidal waters or parts of the sea up to the seaward limits of British territorial waters.[29] By contrast all other possible conservation areas or sites are land-based and extend seaward only as far as the low water mark of neap tides in England and Wales, and of spring tides in Scotland.[30]

5–055   MNRs are also unique among British nature conservation designations in that they are designated, not by a Conservation Agency, but by the appropriate Secretary of State; in all other cases, the Agencies have sufficient powers to notify or declare conservation areas without the need to seek outside authority. In practice, the procedures for the establishment of MNRs (set out in Schedule 12 of the 1981 Act) have proved so difficult to complete that only two, Lundy and Skomer,[31] had been designated within ten years of the provision of the relevant powers, three more remain under negotiation.[32]

5–056   Under section 36(1), the Secretary of State may by order designate a MNR if he thinks it expedient that the land and water over it be managed by the relevant Conservation Agency for the purpose of conserving marine flora or fauna or geological or physiographical features of special interest in the area, or providing, under suitable conditions and control, special opportunities for the study of, and research into matters relating to this flora and fauna and these features. Following designation, the Agency must manage the MNR for either or both of these purposes.

5–057   The procedure has to be initiated by an application from the Conservation Agency, whereupon the steps set out in Schedule 12 must be followed. A draft of the order is prepared, published and

---

[28] A useful publication, "Local Nature Reserves in England" was issued by English Nature in 1991.

[29] s.36(1).

[30] This section deals with the creation of MNRs and the statutory powers available for their protection. For the protection of individual species that may be found in MNRs see: Seals, paras. 5–226 to 5–231.

[31] Islands off the coasts of Devon and south-west Wales respectively.

[32] Loch Sween, the Menai Strait, Bardsey and the Lleyn peninsula.

served on every relevant authority[33] in whose area the proposed MNR lies and, at the Secretary of State's discretion, on every person with an interest in the proposed MNR, and on such other bodies as he considers appropriate. If the draft order is unopposed, it can be made without delay; if, however, the draft order is opposed, a local inquiry ensues.

Section 37 of the 1981 Act gives the Conservation Agency powers to make byelaws for the protection of MNRs, subject to the consent of the Secretary of State. Section 36(2) requires that a copy of any proposed at the time of the initial application for the MNR order, and of any byelaws made or proposed by any relevant authority, must accompany the application; such byelaws, as approved or modified by the Secretary of State, are confirmed as part of the order. Any subsequently proposed are made in accordance with the procedures of sections 236 to 238 of the Local Government Act 1972 (in relation to England and Wales) or sections 202 to 204 of the Local Government (Scotland) Act 1973, as though the Conservation Agency were a local authority, subject to any modifications as may be made to those sections by statutory instrument.[34]

    5–058

Byelaws made under section 37 can prevent entry into the MNR, prohibit any interference with fauna, flora and any object within the MNR, and introduce a permit system. They cannot, however, interfere with the right of passage of any vessel other than a pleasure boat, and even pleasure boats cannot be excluded from all of the reserve for all of the year. They may not prohibit anything done for reasons of safety or preventing damage to vessels or cargo; discharges from vessels; or anything done more than thirty metres below the sea bed. Enforcement may only be undertaken by the Conservation Agency, unless the Director of Public Prosecutions otherwise agrees.

    5–059

In view of the number of conflicting interests which face the establishment of a MNR, it is not surprising that progress is slow. The Nature Conservancy Council, in its 17th Annual Report (for 1990/1991) recorded[35] that

    5–060

"Concern for the waters near Skomer began in the 1970s when a voluntary reserve was established. The process of formal notification as a Marine Nature Reserve involved several years of discussions and negotiations involving all individuals, organisations and official bodies with an interest in the area. Their

---

[33] "Relevant authority" is defined in section 36(7), and includes a local authority; the National Rivers Authority and a River Purification Board; navigation, harbour, pilotage and lighthouse authorities; and a local fisheries committee.

[34] s.36(5).

[35] At p. 14.

eventual conclusion owes much to the support of many of those who use the area for their livelihoods or for recreational and sporting purposes."

Even so, the Skomer MNR was not designated until July 1990, and such support cannot be assumed for all other potential MNRs.

Sites Of Special Scientific Interest

General Considerations

5–061   Sites of Special Scientific Interest (SSSIs) are areas of land of which the use is compulsorily restricted in the interests of nature conservation but which (excluding NNRs for which, though also SSSIs, the NNR status is over-riding) are not held by any Conservation Agency[36] and which cannot be required to be actively managed in the interests of conservation except with the consent of their owners and occupiers. In addition to the restrictions imposed on owners and occupiers in the day-by-day management of their land, the notification of an SSSI also requires the local planning authority, under Article 18(1) of the GDO, 1988, to consult the appropriate Conservation Agency before any development is permitted. It also activates various inter-departmental and other consultative procedures (*e.g.* with statutory undertakers) whenever any change in land use is proposed.

5–062   SSSIs are by far the most widespread statutory nature conservation designation.[37] They are by no means confined to the countryside, for many are found in urban and suburban areas.[38] The powers for their designation are limited to areas of land with a seaward limit of the low water mark of ordinary neap tides in England and Wales and the low water mark of ordinary spring tides in Scotland.

Despite the common misconception, SSSI status does not confer automatic and absolute protection against development; the purpose of the designation is, and has always been, to procure that nature

---

[36] Although there is no explicit legal prohibition on the Conservation Agencies holding land that is solely an SSSI, it is Government policy that acquisitions by them should only be of land meriting NNR status and to be declared as such.

[37] On March 31, 1993, the 5,959 notified sites covered over 8 per cent of Britain with a total area of 1,899,657 hectares. In terms of numbers 62 per cent lie in England, 23 per cent in Scotland, and 14 per cent in Wales, but the much larger SSSIs of the Scottish uplands, relative to those of the English lowlands, result in only 45 per cent of the total area being in England as compared with 44 per cent in Scotland and 11 per cent in Wales.

[38] In Greater London the density of SSSIs is somewhat higher than for England as a whole.

conservation considerations are taken into account before any decision affecting the future of an SSSI is made.

Origin and Development of the SSSI Concept

The concept of designating and controlling the use of land in the interests of nature conservation, while leaving it in private ownership, first found acceptance in the 1940s. The Government White Paper "Conservation of Nature in England and Wales",[39] still acknowledged to be the basis of current rationale for nature conservation, makes it clear that such sites are to be of the highest quality and that their selection is to be science-based; for instance, it recommends[40] that, for each local planning authority's area, such sites should be identified through inspection by "qualified scientists at the earliest date in order that a schedule may be drawn up setting out the precise features and sites within it which are considered to be of the greatest scientific value".   **5–063**

The White Paper also acknowledges a need to balance the requirements of nature conservation against those of other land uses and seeks to minimise any conflict through restricting the total area designated for nature conservation to the minimum judged to be necessary on the basis of the results achieved. Paragraph 128 anticipates current EC directives by many years in stating: **5–064**

> "Before passing to consider seriatim the economic interests affected [by the land-take for nature conservation], one general point should be stressed. It is because we give full weight to the increased competition which our proposals will engender that we have kept the list of National Reserves [now National Nature Reserves] to the lowest limit compatible with making certain that the system will pay its way in terms of practical results. Furthermore, we consider that the Biological Service [now the Conservation Agencies], in carrying out the preliminary inspections of Conservation Areas . . . recommended in paragraph 71, . . . should be instructed likewise to pay the closest attention to other economic requirements with a view to framing their minimum scientific proposals so that these can be dovetailed with other interests into a single pattern."

In Britain, one of these fundamental principles — that it is the best areas that should be sought out and conserved — continues to be stressed, for in the "Guidelines for the selection of biological SSSIs",   **5–065**

---

[39] Cmd. 7122 (1947).
[40] para. 71.

issued in 1989 by the Nature Conservancy Council,[41] its staff are advised that:

> "Within this rationale [*i.e.* the rationale of the 1947 White Paper] was enunciated a basic principle for site selection—that the series of sites as a whole should contain adequate representation, in the form of the best examples, of the countrywide range of variation in natural and semi-natural ecosystem types, with their associated assemblages of plants and animals, considered both as communities and as species."

5–066   The balancing principle, that economic requirements of land use are a legitimate consideration to set against the requirements of nature conservation, is liable to be resented by objectors to proposed developments affecting SSSIs, but it remains an essential element of the law. The 1968 Act expressed both requirements separately in different sections, without suggesting any inclination towards either one or means of reconciling them. Thus section 11 of that Act states:

> "In the exercise of their functions under any enactment every Minister, government department and public body shall have regard to the desirability of conserving the natural beauty and amenity of the countryside."

"The conservation of natural beauty" of an area must[42] be taken to include conservation of its flora, fauna and geological and physiographical features.

5–067   At the same time, section 37 of the 1968 Act (as amended) states:

> "In the exercise of their functions under this Act, the Act of 1949 and the Wildlife and Countryside Act 1981 it shall be the duty of every Minister, and of the [Countryside] Commission, the Nature Conservancy Council[43] and local authorities to have due regard to the needs of agriculture and forestry and to the economic and social interests of rural areas."

5–068   Such broad statements of desiderata were perhaps of more help in securing political acceptance of the legislation than they are in resolving inevitable conflicts that arise in practice. Nevertheless neglect by a decision-making body to take account of all of the matters spelled out in both sections 11 and 37 would expose the decision concerned to challenge.

---

[41] para. 4.4, p.14.
[42] By s.49(4).
[43] By the E.P.A. 1990, this now refers to the respective Councils for England, Wales and Scotland.

The balanced approach was effectively rejected by the policy   5–069
statement of the Nature Conservancy Council of 1984, and also largely
ignored in the Guidelines for the selection of biological SSSIs of 1989.
However, it has recently reappeared, in fuller form, as section 3 of the
Natural Heritage (Scotland) Act, 1991:

(1)   Subject to subsection (2) below it shall be the duty of SNH [*i.e.*
       Scottish Natural Heritage] in exercising its functions to take
       such account as may be appropriate in the circumstances of:
       (a)   actual or possible ecological and other environmental
             changes to the natural heritage of Scotland;
       (b)   the needs of agriculture, fisheries and forestry;
       (c)   the need for social and economic development in Scot-
             land or any part of Scotland;
       (d)   the need to conserve sites and landscapes of archaeologi-
             cal or historical interest;
       (e)   the interests of owners and occupiers of land; and
       (f)   the interests of local communities.
(2)   Paragraphs (b) to (f) of subsection (1) above shall not apply as
       regards any function exercised by SNH in pursuance of any
       of paragraphs (b) to (e) of section 133(2) of the Environmental
       Protection Act 1990 (special functions to be exercised through
       the Joint Committee).

Although the manner in which this Act will be implemented is still   5–070
unclear and it would be possible for the principles set out in section 3
to be paid no more than lip service, this list of considerations does at
least mean that in coming to any decision to which the section applies,
they must all be taken into account if the decision is not to be at risk of
challenge in the Courts.[44]

As may be noted from section 3(2) nevertheless, when making its   5–071
contribution to the work of the Joint Committee,[45] SNH is required to
have regard to ecological and environmental issues only. In that
context therefore it would be improper for it to give any weight to the
various economic and social interests set out.

The recommendation, advocated in the White Paper, to minimise   5–072
any conflict between nature conservation and other interests in the
land through restricting the total area designated for nature conservation to the minimum which can be judged to be necessary on the basis
of the results achieved remains without effective statutory backing.

[44] What weight is to be given to each is of course a proper matter for SNH's discretion.
[45] See para. 5–017.

Statutory Provisions—the 1949 Act

5–073   The first statutory provisions for the notification of SSSIs were made in section 23 of the 1949 Act which stated that:

> "Where the Nature Conservancy are of opinion that any area of land, not being land for the time being managed as a nature reserve, is of special interest by reason of its flora, fauna, or geological or physiographical features, it shall be the duty of the Conservancy to notify that fact to the local planning authority in whose area the land is situated."

5–074   The Act refers to land designated in this way as "Areas of Special Scientific Interest" and this usage has been continued in subsequent legislation. In general parlance, however, the more familiar term "Sites of Special Scientific Interest" is invariably used.

5–075   On this somewhat slender statutory basis, a network of just over 4,000 SSSIs was built up. Overall the system operated well enough, apart from the serious flaw, noted above, that it afforded protection only against "development" as defined in the Town and Country Planning Acts, and not against other changes in land use outside their control.

Transition from the 1949 to the 1981 Act

5–076   The 1981 Act repealed section 23 of the 1949 Act[46] and the Nature Conservancy Council commenced re-notification of all pre-existing SSSIs in accordance with section 28 of the new Act. However, sites already notified under section 23 of the 1949 Act retained their SSSI status. To facilitate this process, section 28(13) of the new Act removed any need for the Nature Conservancy Council to re-notify local authorities of these sites' existence, and section 28(14) made it unnecessary to consult their owners and occupiers when the sites were re-notified under the provisions of the 1981 Act.

5–077   It is important to note that, although the 1985 Act made extensive alterations to the provisions of section 28 of the 1981 Act, its section 3(10)(c) stipulated that these were not to apply to SSSIs notified under section 23 of the 1949 Act, but not renotified under the 1981 Act. These remaining section 23 sites were exempted from the changes the 1985 Act made to the procedures for the re-notification and confirmation of SSSIs and, for these sites alone, the procedures were to remain as

---

[46] By s.28(13).

originally specified in section 28(2), (4) and (14) of the unamended 1981 Act.[47]

The discussion which follows relates to SSSIs which have been notified under the 1981 Act, as amended.

Notification under the 1981 Act

The current provisions for the notification of SSSIs are to be found in section 28 of the 1981 Act, as very significantly amended by the 1985 Act and the Wildlife and Countryside (Services of Notices) Act, 1985. DoE Circular 27/87 provides guidance on the operation of the system of SSSIs as is now in effect and contains a brief summary of the provisions of the amended section 28.   5–078

Although the provisions of the 1981 Act are much more complex than those of the 1949 Act, section 28(1) of the new legislation follows its predecessor in retaining as the sole criterion for SSSI status the requirement that the Conservation Agency should be "of the opinion that any area of land is of special interest by reason of any of its flora, fauna, or geological or physiographical features".   5–079

In deciding whether or not to notify an SSSI, the "opinion" of a Conservation Agency is in itself sufficient; no approval from any outside body or person is required. The responsibility for formulating these all important "opinions" lies with the Chairman and Council of the Conservation Agency, who assess the case for the notification of each candidate site as put before them by their officers.   5–080

Neither the 1949 nor the 1981 Act provides any assistance to Council Members or their officers as to the basis on which "opinions" should be formulated. The guidance on SSSI selection,[48] given by the Nature Conservancy Council to its staff in 1989, suggests that the aim should be to select the smallest practicable areas of the best examples of all   5–081

---

[47] In 1985, no fewer than 2,591 SSSIs fell under these provisions, but the number was progressively reduced by renotification over the years until the 17th Report (for 1990/1991) of the Nature Conservancy Council could state that "The re-notification of SSSIs, begun after the enactment of the Wildlife and Countryside Act in 1982, was at last completed!" However, this statement does not accord with the figures (for March 31, 1991) which appear in the same Report; these show that 95 SSSIs notified only under s.23 of the 1949 Act still remained. This backlog, though subsequently reduced, has not yet been eliminated at least in England and Scotland; the returns for March 31, 1993 reveal the survival of 34 SSSIs in England, covering 45,953 hectares, and 10 SSSIs in Scotland, covering 2,516 hectares, which had been notified under just the 1949 Act. Thus although the number of such sites nowhere exceeds 1 per cent of the total number of SSSIs, the area yet to be re-notified in England is no less than 2.4 per cent of the whole.

[48] "Guidelines for Selection of Biological SSSIs", NCC, 1989.

British habitats for conservation, in accordance with the fundamental principles of Cmd. 7122.[49]

5–082   Once it has been decided to notify an SSSI, the Conservation Agency is subject to a duty under section 28(1) to notify its decision to the local planning authority, and to every owner and occupier of the land to be designated, and to the Secretary of State. At the same time details of the notification are also sent to the appropriate Agriculture Department, the Forestry Commission, the NRA, statutory undertakers and other relevant bodies. The notification procedures are laid down in the Wildlife and Countryside (Service of Notices) Act, 1985, which repealed section 28(3) of the 1981 Act.

5–083   The meaning of "owners" as used in Part II of the 1981 Act is defined by section 52(4) of the 1981 Act, but the meaning of "occupiers" is not. They were taken by the NCC to include lessees, tenants, licensees and others with rights to occupy the land, but to exclude commoners, those licensed just to enter the land, statutory bodies and persons exercising public rights. However it was stated on behalf of the Government during the passage of the Environmental Protection Bill through the House of Lords that commoners were to be regarded as occupiers.[50] In this somewhat "grey" area, there is a natural tendency for a Conservation Agency to notify anyone who could be considered an occupier but, even so, omissions have been known to occur.

5–084   By an amendment made in 1985 the area notified acquires the status of an SSSI immediately on receipt of the notification. In particular, the owners and occupiers of the area notified become subject to the provisions of section 28(5) and (7) at this time. Prior to this amendment owners and occupiers were given not less than three months notice of the intention to notify an SSSI on their land, to enable them time to lodge comments and objections. However this was also liable to enable anyone who would be adversely affected to take pre-emptive action, possibly nullifying the purpose of the proposal.

5–085   Even so in most cases there will have been previous signs of the Conservation Agency's taking an interest in and around the land which is subsequently notified. In particular, permission for access will have had to be sought to carry out surveys of flora, fauna and geological features, for officers of the Conservation Agencies have no powers of entry, except in the somewhat exceptional circumstances provided for in section 51 of the 1981 Act. Also, in many cases, there

---

[49] The "Code of Guidance for Sites of Special Scientific Interest", prepared under s.33 and published in 1982, provides guidance for those responsible for implementing ss. 28 to 32 of the 1981 Act. It makes no reference to how SSSIs should be selected but is concerned only with procedures for the notification (now out of date) and the provisions for the protection of SSSIs.

[50] Hansard October 17, 1990.

will have been previous correspondence or other contacts between owners and occupiers and the Agency, especially where the submission of a planning application is under consideration or has reached its preliminary stages.

Section 28(4) requires that the notification, sent to owners and occupiers under the terms of section 28(1)(b), must be accompanied by two further documents. One specifies "the flora, fauna, or geological or physiographical features by reason of which the land is of special interest"; and the other "any operations appearing to the Council[51] to be likely to damage that flora or fauna or those features".

5–086

There is no requirement in section 28(4) for these documents to be supplied to the local planning authority or to the Secretary of State, but section 2(8) of the 1985 Act requires them to be provided to local planning authorities in Scotland. By section 28(11) a notification to owners and occupiers under section 28(1)(b) is a local land charge, and so since many local planning authorities in England and Wales function as local land charge offices, they receive copies of these additional documents under the provisions of section 28(11).

5–087

The specification of the flora, fauna and physical features takes the form of a highly technical account of the entire site in nature conservation terms; in the case of sites in multiple ownership and/or occupation, no descriptions of the individual holdings are given. Characteristically, it begins by providing basic data about the size and location of the site, any previous history of SSSI notification (*e.g.* under section 23 of the 1949 Act) and other conservation designations considered applicable, and then goes on to list the various occurrences of biological and geological interest, identifying those considered to be of particular importance.

5–088

Little attempt is made in normal practice to present this information in a form comprehensible to the lay recipient or to explain the reasons for the SSSI notification even to a biologist or ecologist; the critical examination of these documents requires the services of experts who have specialised experience in the assessment of nature conservation values.

5–089

The second document required by section 28(4) lists the operations which are thought likely to damage the scientific interest of the SSSI. Such operations are known as "Potentially Damaging Operations" or "PDOs" and range from clearly defined activities such as ploughing to catch-all categories such as "recreational or other activities likely to damage or disturb features of interest". It must however be doubtful whether the latter circular definition represents proper compliance with the section 28(4)(b) requirement to "specify" operations.

5–090

---

[51] *i.e.* now the relevant Conservation Agency.

5–091   Most lists of PDOs are so comprehensive as to suggest a high degree of overkill; they are understood to be prepared from a master list from which only those PDOs which are manifestly impossible to carry out on the site in question are deleted.

Objection to Notification

5–092   Limited provision for the expression of views opposing notification is made in section 28(2), which directs that the Council of a Conservation Agency shall consider "representations or objections" to a notification made under section 28(1), provided these are made within a specified time (not less than three months from the date of the notification) and in a manner determined by the Agency. The deadline for the receipt of any such representations and objections will be specified on the notification letter issued under section 28(1).

5–093   Following consideration of these representations and objections, section 28(4A) requires the Conservation Agency either to withdraw the SSSI notification it has made under section 28(1) or to confirm it not later than nine months after the notification was made to the Secretary of State. If not withdrawn or confirmed within this time, the notification lapses. The Agency can modify the notification prior to its confirmation, but section 28(4B) prevents such modifications increasing the area notified or adding to the list of PDOs. Any withdrawals of, or modifications to, the notification have immediate effect.

5–094   The procedures under section 28 have significant shortcomings. Firstly, the Members of a Conservation Agency do not have access to all the relevant evidence at the time when they have to decide whether or not to notify an SSSI; their decision is made when only the case for notification is available.[52] Secondly, representations and objections to proposals to notify an SSSI are not put before an impartial third party, but before the Conservation Agency from which the proposals originated. Thirdly, the Conservation Agencies restrict all representations or objections to written submissions which they consider *in camera*. It is perhaps not surprising that the making of representations and objections under section 28(2) very seldom leads to any significant modification of proposals to notify an SSSI or of the restrictions this notification will impose.[53]

5–095   In these circumstances, the only effective, if costly, mechanism for challenging, or for testing the validity of an SSSI notification is to submit an application for planning consent under the provisions of

---

[52] For sound practical reasons, explained in para. 5–084, no advance warning of an intention to create an SSSI need be issued.

[53] Even so, failure to object at this stage is liable to be interpreted subsequently as tacit approval of an SSSI notification.

section 28(8). This section in effect allows operations that would otherwise be prohibited as a result of notification of an SSSI, if they have been authorised by a grant of planning permission. However, the Conservation Agencies have powers to request a "call-in" of a planning application affecting an SSSI, so that an applicant for planning permission on an SSSI can expect to be faced with a public planning inquiry. This means of contesting an SSSI is, of course, not available where development (as defined in the T.C.P.A.) is not intended.

In Scotland, these unsatisfactory aspects of section 28(2) of the 1981   5–096
Act have been addressed by section 12 of the Natural Heritage (Scotland) Act, 1991. This, although not amending the 1981 Act, empowers the Secretary of State to establish an Advisory Committee on SSSIs, whose members are independent of Scottish Natural Heritage. This committee considers, not only objections to the proposed notification of new SSSIs,[54] but also applications for the review of notifications which were unsuccessfully contested in the past or where more than ten years have elapsed since the notification was made.[55] There is currently little experience of the effectiveness of these new procedures. No equivalent provisions have yet been made in England or Wales.

Powers to Control Land Management

By sections 28(5) and (6) of the 1981 Act, as amended in 1985, owners   5–097
and occupiers must not carry out, or cause or permit to be carried out, within a notified SSSI any operations listed pursuant to section 28(4)(b) on its notification (i.e. the Potentially Damaging Operations), unless the Conservation Agency has been given written notice (after receipt of the SSSI notification), and the Agency has given its consent in writing. Operations which form part of a Nature Reserve Agreement under section 16 of the 1949 Act or a Management Agreement under section 15 of the 1968 Act have already in effect received the Conservation Agency's approval, and are accordingly exempt from this requirement.[56] If the Agency has not responded to the written notice given it within four months, the notified operations are in effect deemed to have been consented.[57]

---

[54] s.12(5).
[55] s.12(6).
[56] s.28(6)(b).
[57] 28.(6)(c), and see paras. 5–106 to 5–108.

5–098   Section 28(5) provides the means by which a Conservation Agency can prevent the carrying out of operations which, although not constituting permitted development, are considered likely to damage the interest of SSSIs. These controls, however, are not comprehensive for they extend only to operations carried out by, or with the consent of, owners or occupiers. The Act provides no remedy for or protection against any damaging operations carried out by third parties without such consent.

5–099   This was emphatically demonstrated by the House of Lords' judgment in a test case brought originally by the NCC and continued by English Nature.[58] The former Southern Water Authority had dredged, and thus damaged, the wildlife interest of a ditch within Alverstone Marshes SSSI without any consultation with English Nature. It was held that no breach of the 1981 Act by the Authority had occurred as it was not an occupier of the SSSI, notwithstanding its continued presence on the site for almost a month, as that term should be understood for the purposes of section 28 of the 1981 Act. The elaborate procedures for notification and waiting periods that the section applied to occupiers, as well as to owners:

> "showed that the occupier was someone who, although lacking the title of owner, nevertheless stood in such a comprehensive and stable relationship with the land as to be, in company with the actual owner, someone to whom the mechanism could sensibly be made to apply. A stranger who entered the land for a few weeks solely to do some work on it did not fall into that category. . . . Section 28 did not permit recourse against persons whose only connection with the part of the land in question was that they had entered on it to perform a proscribed operation." (*per* Lord Mustill).[59]

5–100   It was also argued that the Authority was itself an owner within the meaning of section 28, since it was fortuitously the owner of another part of the same SSSI, but this was held to be irrelevant. The prohibition in section 28(5) on an owner or occupier of any land is in respect of the carrying out on *that* land of the notified operations. Thus where, as is common, various parts of an SSSI are in different

---

[58] *Southern Water Authority v. Nature Conservancy Council,* [1992] 1 W.L.R. 775; [1992] 3 All E.R. 481.

[59] It seems that the two farmers reported as owning the land on either side of the ditch, and presumably the ditch itself, who asked the Water Authority to carry out the dredging to mitigate the flooding (and who had received the statutory notification of the SSSI), could have been successfully prosecuted for causing or for permitting the offending operations, but it was said the Council considered it to be "inexpedient" to proceed against them.

ownership, the obligations of section 28 apply to each owner separately in relation solely to his own land.[60]

Damage to an SSSI by third parties acting without the consent (or 5–101 without the need to obtain the consent) of owners or occupiers, is generally on a much smaller scale and arises from activities such as cross-country motor-cycling, horse riding, fires and fly tipping. Prevention of such damage depends almost entirely on an ability to control access. Where third parties can be effectively excluded, then such damage can be prevented but, on the other hand, where an SSSI is subject to rights of access, or *de facto* access, then the Act provides no powers (other than those provided by section 34 for limestone pavement[61]) to prevent or control such damage.

Further, there are no powers whereby a Conservation Agency can 5–102 carry out management to make good damage arising in this way (or to retain or enhance the wildlife value of any SSSI), without the consent of the owners and occupiers. This can result in a virtual impasse, with the Conservation Agency having powers to block all proposals which might damage the interest of an SSSI, while being unable to control or to make good its rapid deterioration whether from natural causes or from the activities of trespassers.[62]

When notice of an intention to carry out a PDO has been given 5–103 under the provisions of section 28(5), the Conservation Agency is required by section 28(6) to respond within a period of four months; section 28(6A) allows this time limit to be extended if the person who gave the notice under section 28(5) agrees in writing to such an extension. However, such agreements can be terminated on the owner or occupier giving the Conservation Agency at least one month's written notice under the terms of section 28(6B). Should no response be received from the Conservation Agency within the specified or agreed time limits, the owner or occupier is free to proceed with carrying out the PDO under the terms of section 28(5) and (6)(c).

The response of a Conservation Agency to a notice of a proposal to 5–104 carry out a PDO under section 28(5) will take one of several forms:

(i) If the Agency considers that the proposed operation will not damage the SSSI, a letter of consent will be issued; in some

---

[60] There could of course in principle be joint and several liability under contract where neighbouring owners enter into a Management Agreement under s.15 of the 1968 Act.

[61] See paras. 5–147 to 5–154.

[62] English Nature draw attention in their First Annual Report (for 1991/92) to the existence of "cases of chronic deterioration of special interest" and comment on the problems of "insufficient management" and of controlling recreational and other activities by third parties (pp 27–29).

circumstances the consent will be limited through the imposition of conditions.

(ii) If the Agency considers that the proposed operation, although damaging in its present form, could be rendered harmless if modified in some way, it will suggest that the original proposal should be withdrawn and that fresh proposals, incorporating the necessary modifications, should be submitted. Should these suggestions be accepted, a letter of consent for the modified proposals will be issued.

(iii) In cases where the Agency considers that a proposed PDO is necessarily damaging, or where the owner or occupier does not accept the modifications proposed by the Agency, a Management Agreement under section 15 of the 1968 Act, as amended by the 1981 Act, will be offered.

This will require the owner or occupier to abandon his intention to carry out the proposed PDO, but will provide compensation for any profits foregone under the guidelines of DoE Circular 4/83. Such Agreements can also provide compensation for the loss of various grants which have been withheld in the interests of nature conservation.[63] Any extension of the time limit needed for the conclusion of a Management Agreement can be provided through the provisions of section 28(6A).

(iv) Finally, if the Conservation Agency believes that the owner and/or occupier of an SSSI has no intention of concluding any agreement over the future use of his land and/or cannot be dissuaded from carrying out the proposed PDO, the Agency can apply for a Nature Conservation Order ("NCO")[64] under section 29 of the 1981 Act. The four month period is comparatively short for the necessary steps for making an NCO to be completed, but the NCC and its successors have developed streamlined procedures that enable this deadline to be met.

5–105   Nevertheless, an NCO intended to conserve "flora, fauna, or geological or physiographical features" may only be made in respect of land "of national importance" (see paragraphs 5–135, 5–136), and though the NCC have contended otherwise it is inherently highly improbable that this description can properly be applied to all SSSIs, having regard to the wider criteria on which their initial designation is

---

[63] The procedures for compensating owners and occupiers where grants have been refused in the interests of nature conservation are set out in paras 16 to 18 and 25 to 31 of the Code of Guidance produced under the provisions of s.33.

[64] See paras. 5–134 to 5–146.

based. Consequently the threat of an NCO against an owner/occupier proposing to carry out a PDO may quite possibly have no valid legal foundation. However in practice few are prepared to resist such a threat, which thus represents an effective enforcement weapon.

The need to issue consents under the requirements of section 28(5), (6), (6A), (6B) and (6C) has placed a very considerable administrative burden on the Conservation Agencies. However, many of the practices included in the PDO list, such as grazing, mowing, and manuring, are repetitive and not necessarily harmful and can be allowed to continue within set limits without there being any need for a separate consent being issued for each repetition or variation; some, indeed, may be essential to the retention of the scientific interest for which the SSSI has been notified. The burden of routine administration can thus be much reduced by offering standing consents (at the time of notification of the SSSI, or later) which allow the continuation of existing practices within specified limits for a period of years, and this practice has been adopted, at least for some SSSIs. It is important to note that such consents are issued at the sole discretion of the Conservation Agency and can be revoked without prior consultation at any time. If the consents offered are refused by the owner or occupier, the Agency has then to offer a Management Agreement under section 15 of the 1968 Act.   **5-106**

Since consents to carry out PDOs are intended to prevent damage to the scientific interest of SSSIs, it might be reasonable to expect that there would be some scientific basis to justify their provisions. In practice, however, many consents seem to have been issued, more to preserve the *status quo*, than to achieve any clear conservation objective. Further, conditions have been imposed which, for no stated reason, merely set the present level of some operation as the upper limit for its future conduct. For instance, where a pasture has been grazed by 20 cows, or where an owner has hitherto had only one boat on a loch, at the time of SSSI notification, this can become the upper limit for future usage, without any reason being given why, say, 25 cows or two boats would cause any significant additional damage.   **5-107**

Where an SSSI is in multiple ownership or occupation, consents may vary quite incongruously from one landholding to another. Even where the holdings are agriculturally similar, consents may set different stocking levels or may allow for one lamb per ewe in one holding and two lambs per ewe in its neighbour.[65]   **5-108**

---

[65] At Loch Insh in Speyside, a small loch, the consents issued for managing the fishery shared by six estates specified that the pike was to be treated as a game species in two, and as a pest species in two more, while its existence was ignored in the remainder.

Miscellaneous Provisions—Sections 28 and 32

5–109   As already noted, section 28(7) prescribes fines not exceeding level 4 on the standard scale for contraventions of section 28(5), but section 28(8) exempts operations which have been authorised by a grant of planning permission, and also those which have been carried out in an emergency, provided details of the emergency and the work which was carried out are given to the Conservation Agency as soon as practicable after the operations start. The Act does not define what constitutes an "emergency".

5–110   Section 28(9) empowers Conservation Agencies to enforce the provisions of section 28, but does not authorise them to initiate prosecutions in Scotland. By section 28(10), the consent of the Director of Public Prosecutions is required for any other person than a Conservation Agency to institute proceedings under section 28(7) in England and Wales.[66] In addition to criminal proceedings the NCC successfully sought injunctions in civil proceedings where the evidence indicated that criminal sanctions would not effectively deter damaging activities. In cases where damage is caused by removal of articles or material otherwise than by or with the consent of the owner, proceedings for theft may be appropriate.[67]

5–111   Section 28(11) establishes notification under section 28(1)(b) as a land charge in England and Wales. Sections 28(12), (12A) and (12B) apply solely to Scotland; section 28(12) requires the Conservation Agency to maintain a register of such notifications and section 28(12A) places a similar responsibility on local planning authorities.

5–112   Where land within an SSSI is included within an application for farm capital grant, section 32 of the 1981 Act provides that the Agriculture Minister must exercise his functions so as to further the conservation of its special scientific interest and must consider any objection from a Conservation Agency to the making of a grant. If grant is withheld in the interests of nature conservation, the Conservation Agency must offer a Management Agreement with compensation

---

[66] Although it is estimated that at least 5 per cent of all SSSIs are damaged each year, only 12 prosecutions in total had been instituted by the NCC and its successors under the 1981 Act by March 1, 1993 (none of which were in Scotland). This small number is due in part to much of the damage being by third parties who commit no offence under that Act; also to procedural problems prior to the two 1985 Acts, particularly difficulties in serving notices on *all* owners. Penalties have ranged up to £6,000, and costs orders to over £2,300.

[67] The NCC successfully prosecuted for theft in two instances of removal of fossil fish from sites in Scotland shortly before the 1981 Act provided for NCOs.

for the restrictions imposed, this offer to be made within a period of three months.

Modification of SSSIs

The statutory provisions for SSSIs relate entirely to *de novo* notification; there are no provisions for the denotification of SSSIs in whole or in part, or the extension of an already existing SSSI. It has, however, been the practice of the Conservation Agencies to remove the SSSI notification from land which, in their opinion, is no longer of special interest.   5–113

The denotification procedures employed follow those prescribed in section 28(2) and (4A) for notification. The local planning authority, all owners and occupiers of the land to be denotified, and the Secretary of State are informed in writing of the proposal by the Conservation Agency to denotify all or part of an SSSI and are invited to make representations and objections to this proposal. After a delay of four months, a further letter is sent to the same recipients confirming or withdrawing the denotification.   5–114

Where an already notified SSSI is to be extended, notification papers are sent by the Conservation Agency to the local planning authority, the owners and occupiers of the land within the extension, the appropriate Agriculture Department, the Forestry Commission, the NRA, statutory undertakers and other relevant bodies, and the Secretary of State in the usual way. "Representations and objections" can be submitted within four months under section 28(2), but these must relate only to the area of the extension and not to the land already notified.   5–115

As required by section 28(4), the notification papers will specify the flora, fauna, or geological or physiographical features of interest and a list of PDOs, but these will relate, not to the proposed extension, but to the entire SSSI as extended. Confirmation, modification or withdrawal of the extension has to be made by the Conservation Agency within nine months.   5–116

Present procedures for the extension of SSSIs are somewhat illogical in that the persons notified are required to limit their response to the land to be added to the site, whereas the Conservation Agency, instead of specifying the special interest which justifies the addition of the extension, merely gives an account of the interest of the site as extended. How far present practice can be considered to fulfil the requirements of section 28 or the guidance given in paragraph 6 of the Code of Guidance under section 33 has yet to be tested.   5–117

Consultations and Planning Procedures

5–118   The notification of an SSSI under section 23 of the 1949 Act had the effect[68] of requiring local planning authorities to consult with the Nature Conservancy (Council) before they granted permission for development within an SSSI; to allow time for this consultation, they were not allowed to determine any such planning application within 14 days of their notifying its receipt to the Nature Conservancy (Council). Advice to local authorities as to how they should implement section 23 appeared in various Ministry of Housing and Local Government and DoE Circulars, the latest of these being 108/77.

5–119   In addition, the Nature Conservancy (Council) was consulted by inter-departmental agreement, for example over the award of agricultural and forestry grants, and could request that cases in which it had an interest should be called-in for Ministerial decision. Involvement in activities of this sort exceeded the role anticipated in the 1949 Act.

5–120   Following the passage of the 1981 Act, local planning authorities continued to consult with the Nature Conservancy Council before they granted permission for development within an SSSI (whether notified under the 1949 or the 1981 Act), as required by Article 15(1)(g) and 15(5) of the Town and Country Planning General Development Order, 1977. The advice on nature conservation given to local authorities by DoE Circular 108/77 remained unchanged, as did the various consultative procedures under inter-Departmental agreement and other less formal arrangements; requests that cases should be called-in for Ministerial decision continued to be made and granted.

5–121   In 1987, Circular 108/77 was somewhat belatedly replaced by 27/87, which up-dated the advice to local planning authorities in the aftermath of the 1981 Act, the 1985 Act and EC Directive 79/409 on the Conservation of Wild Birds. Paragraph 1 of Annex A of 27/87 provides an abstract of government policies for the conservation of flora, fauna and their habitats in the following terms:

> "One of the essential tasks for Government, local authorities, and all public agencies concerned with the use of land and natural resources is to ensure effective conservation of the landscape, its wildlife and natural resources while making adequate provision for necessary development and economic growth. . . . The Government wishes to ensure that its commitment to the achievement of economic growth without detriment to wildlife and natural beauty is fully reflected in local decision making."

---

[68] By virtue of Art.9(9) of the then current Town and Country Planning General Development Order 1950, and its successors.

In linking together the need for nature conservation and the need **5–122** for economic development, the approach of Circular 27/87 is closely similar to that of recent EC legislation and raises echoes of the White Paper (Cmd. 7122) over the need for conservationists to frame "their minimum scientific proposals so that these can be dovetailed with other interests into a single pattern".[69]

Shortly thereafter, the Town and Country Planning General Deve- **5–123** lopment Order, 1977, was superseded by the Town and Country Planning General Development Order, 1988, and under the provisions of the latter's Article 18(1)(t), local planning authorities continued to consult with the Conservation Agencies before permitting development within an SSSI. The scope of such consultations had, however, been somewhat widened, for paragraph 35 of Circular 27/87 had recommended that planning authorities should also consult over planning applications which, in their opinion, seemed likely to affect a nearby SSSI.

The 40 years evolutionary development of these procedural **5–124** arrangements, was abruptly changed by the Town and Country Planning General Development (Amendment)(No. 3) Order 1991,[70] which came into force, with minimal publicity, on January 2, 1992. The Order amends Article 18(1)(t) of the GDO 1988 so that it requires local planning authorities to consult the appropriate Conservation Agency, not just about development proposals on SSSIs, but also over those which fall within a "consultation area" to be defined by the Conservation Agencies around each SSSI. This, at a stroke, more or less tripled the area over which consultation was required.

The concept of "consultation areas" is not new, for it merely **5–125** resurrects, in modified form, the "buffer land" concept promoted unsuccessfully by the Nature Conservancy Council in the years immediately following the passage of the 1981 Act. Then it was proposed to include land of no proven merit within SSSIs to protect the "core areas" from harmful external influences, but this proposal was deemed inappropriate as the 1981 Act allowed SSSIs to include only land of "special interest". From a planning viewpoint, the difference between the "buffer land" and the "consultation area" concepts is merely a matter of semantics, for their effects in extending the influence of the Conservation Agencies well beyond the areas of "special interest" are identical. At present, there are no provisions for notifying the owners and occupiers of these "consultation zones"; only the local planning authority need be notified.

[69] para. 128.
[70] S.I. 1991 No. 2805.

5–126   The practical consequence of the 1991 GDO (Amendment No. 3) Order, is to reverse section 28(13) of the 1981 Act,[71] for designation as a "consultation area" has the same effect as notification as an SSSI under the long repealed section 23 of the 1949 Act. The most significant difference between a pre-1981 section 23 SSSI and a post-1991 "consultation area", is that whereas the possession of "special interest" was the *sine qua non* of the former, this is not the case for the latter which need not have any merit whatsoever. The new regulations thus establish a network of SSSIs notified under the 1981 Act, each surrounded by an aureole, which might well be devoid of any merit, but whose status is virtually that given to SSSIs by the 1949 Act.

5–127   DoE Circular 1/92 (Welsh Office 1/92) explains that "consultation areas" can extend up to two kilometres from the SSSI boundary, but are normally not expected to measure more than 500 metres. However, a 500 metre "consultation area" around a one hectare SSSI will be nearly 100 hectares and a two kilometre "consultation area" will exceed 1,300 hectares.[72] Although the effects will be proportionately less for larger SSSIs, the areas concerned will be greater (*e.g.* at least 350 hectares and 2,000 hectares respectively for a 500 metre and a 2 kilometre consultation area around a 100 hectare site). Nationwide this amendment will increase the proportion of Britain subject to restrictions in the interests of nature conservation from about 8 per cent to perhaps 25 per cent.

5–128   Where no "consultation areas" have been defined, local planning authorities are advised by Circular 1/92 to consult the Conservation Agencies in cases where they are of the opinion that a planning application is likely to affect an SSSI. The Agencies are to give priority to defining "consultation areas" around those SSSIs which have been designated as Special Protection Areas for Birds[73] or which have been included in the Nature Conservation Review or the Geological Conservation Review;[74] the SSSI notification documents already show whether or not the site has been designated in any of these categories.

5–129   Circular 1/92 also advises that proximity of a proposed development to any such site should add further emphasis to the recommendations

---

[71] By which s.23 of the 1949 Act ceased to have effect except in relation to then existing SSSIs.

[72] A circle one ha in area will have a radius of approximately 56.5 metres. A circle with a radius of 556.5 metres (56.5 + 500m) has an area of 97 ha.

[73] See paras. 5–245 to 5–257.

[74] The Nature Conservation Review is an account of the most important biological SSSIs, originally published by the Cambridge University Press on behalf of the Nature Conservancy Council in 1977 and subsequently subject to unpublished updates. The Geological Conservation Review is the analogue for geology (and physiography); it commenced in 1977 and is currently being published as a part-work by Chapman & Hall.

given in Circular 15/88 (Welsh Office 23/88) regarding the need to obtain an environmental assessment.

The Town and Country Planning General Development (Amend-   **5–130**
ment)(No. 3) Order, 1991 also creates another precedent for nature conservation for it places further restrictions on war games, motor sports and clay pigeon shooting on SSSIs through withdrawing the permitted development rights under Part 4 of Schedule 2 to the 1988 GDO. Planning permission is now necessary before any land within an SSSI can be used for these recreations. It is uncertain how many SSSIs will be affected; for most, such activities should already have been proscribed under sections 28(5), (6) and (7), and 29, but there may well be implications for the payment of compensation.

In February 1992, the Department of the Environment issued a   **5–131**
consultation draft for a new Planning Policy Guidance note (PPG 24) on Nature and Conservation; parallel consultations were initiated by the Welsh Office. This new PPG is to set out "the principles and policies that apply to the reflection of nature conservation priorities in land use planning" as determined by international obligations and the requirements of domestic legislation. The draft text clearly owes much to 27/87; it restates the Government's desire "to ensure effective conservation of wildlife and natural features while making adequate provision for development and economic growth"[75] in accordance with recent EC legislation.[76] It also incorporates much of 1/92 which, with 27/87, the new PPG is intended to supersede.

Further consultation documents were issued by the DoE, Scottish   **5–132**
Office and DoE(NI) in October 1993 on proposed changes to domestic legislation for implementing EC Directive 92/43 on the Conservation of Natural Habitats and of Wild Fauna and Flora (the "Habitats Directive").[77] As with implementation of the Birds Directive,[78] much reliance is placed on the efficacy of the SSSI designation, despite the fact that this carries no automatic protection but merely confers the right to a more than usually favourable consideration of the needs of nature conservation. To overcome this obvious shortcoming, the Government proposes not only to continue with the draft PPG, but also to modify further the Town and Country Planning General Development Order 1988, and to amend yet again the Wildlife and Countryside Act 1981. In accordance with these proposals, a draft Statutory Instrument, the Conservation (Natural Habitats, etc.) Regulations 1994, was laid before Parliament in July 1994. This, though

---

[75] para. 2.
[76] *e.g.* the Habitats Directive, Article 2.3, see below para. 5–262.
[77] See paras. 5–262 to 5–275.
[78] See paras. 5–245 to 5–257.

based largely on pre-existing legislation, proposes a number of significant innovations (relating *inter alia* to the provisions for consented operations, the imposition of byelaws and marine conservation) and shifts of emphasis (relating *inter alia* to planning procedures, public interest and the revocation of existing planning consents).

5–133   This plethora of guidance, regulation, modification and amendment results from the current over-dependence of nature conservation in Britain on the SSSI concept, even although it is widely recognised that this designation, through its negative character, cannot provide the Conservation Agencies with adequate powers of practical and positive land management for those key sites whose conservation is required to meet international obligations. As such obligations have increased in the past, they have been met by an ever more elaborate shoring up of the SSSI powers. As they increase in the future, which they surely will, there would appear to be two possible alternatives. On the one hand, there could be a fundamental shift in conservation policy away from the notification of more and more bureaucracy-demanding but unmanageable SSSIs in favour of the more extensive declaration of NNRs which, although initially capital-intensive, can be effectively managed. Alternatively, innovative legislation could be introduced providing for positive management, and likely to create an upper tier of super-SSSIs where all rights in the land would be more restricted in the interests of nature conservation than under the present SSSI legislation.

Nature Conservation Orders

5–134   One of the most notable innovations of the 1981 Act was its provision, (in sections 29 to 32 and Schedule 11) of powers for the making of Nature Conservation Orders (NCOs) by the appropriate Secretary of State after consultation with the relevant Conservation Agency. These orders serve much the same function as an injunction in preventing or halting the destruction of flora, fauna, or habitats of value and are employed as a back-up to SSSI notification under section 28, especially where negotiations for a Management Agreement have failed. They differ from SSSI notifications in that:

(i)   they apply to land as soon as they are made and not, as with SSSIs, only following notification to specified individuals;

(ii)   the requirements to be met before an NCO may be made are (arguably) more demanding than those applicable to SSSIs;

216

(iii) they cannot be made by the Conservation Agency alone but require action by the Secretary of State; and

(iv) a more conventional appeals procedure is provided.[79]

Nature Conservation Orders may be made under section 29(1)   **5–135**
where this appears to the Secretary of State to be expedient, in order to
serve any of three purposes: firstly, to secure the survival in Great
Britain of any kind of animal and plant; secondly, to comply with an
international obligation; and, thirdly, to conserve any flora, fauna, or
geological or physiographical features. An Order can be in respect of
any land that the Secretary of State considers to be "of special interest
by reason of any of its flora, fauna, or geological or physiographical
features", save that if its purpose is their conservation, *i.e.* the third
category under section 29(1), the land concerned must also be "of
national importance" on their account.[80] Neither "special interest"
nor "national importance" are defined. In fact, all NCOs so far made
have belonged to this third category and, although there is no link
between sections 28 and 29 of the 1981 Act, all known NCOs have so
far been made on land which has previously been notified as an SSSI
under the provisions of section 28.

Whether or not all SSSIs are eligible for the imposition of an NCO   **5–136**
has been a matter of considerable debate. Section 28 of the 1981 Act
only requires SSSIs to be of "special interest", whereas section 29(2)(b)
explicitly adds to the "special interest" requirement of section 29(2)(a)
(which is itself in effect identical to that of section 28(1)) the extra
criterion that for NCOs in the third category the land must be of
"national importance". Despite this distinction—given that there are
no clear grounds for construing "special interest" differently in the
two sections of the Act—and despite the fact that biological SSSIs are
selected, not on a national basis, but on the basis of one out of over a
hundred "Areas of Search" into which Britain is divided, the Nature
Conservancy Council has argued that all SSSIs fulfilled the requirements for the making of NCOs on the premise that "every brick in a
wall has the same importance as the wall as a whole". This view,
however, has not been accepted by the Secretaries of State who have

---

[79] The first NCO was made on October 21, 1982 and the number made in each of the
following years has varied from zero (in 1991/92) to nine (in 1989/90). On March 31,
1993, of the 42 orders which had been made, 27 remained in force, 14 had been
withdrawn, and one had been revoked on appeal (West Mersea Meadow (Essex)
NCO, DoE file WLF 4958/ESSEX/1). Twelve further appeals against orders had failed,
as had a single challenge in the High Court (relating to Westhay Moor (Somerset)
NCO). However, the Secretary of State does not necessarily accept the advice he
receives from the Agency; at least five cases have been recorded where orders have
been refused in whole or in part.

[80] s.29(2).

rejected applications on the grounds that it had not been demonstrated that the SSSIs in question were of national importance. However, the Secretary of State for Wales has imposed a NCO on the grounds that the SSSI to which it was to apply had been shown to be of "national importance" in a Welsh, as distinct from a British, context. This reasoning appears misconceived: "national" must, in the context of a statute applying to Great Britain, mean at least all of that territory, and probably the United Kingdom as a whole, so as to result in an interpretation consistent with the reference to "international obligations" in section 29(1)(a).

5–137   Under section 29(3), NCOs specify prohibited operations which appear to the Secretary of State as likely to destroy or damage the biological and/or geological interest; in contrast to the blanket coverage of PDOs which forms part of a typical SSSI notification, those that are in practice specified under section 29 relate to damaging operations which are actually in prospect. This difference in practice would not appear to have any foundation in differences in the language of the two sections, (principally section 28(4)(b) and section 29(3)(a)). The most significant difference is that whereas the section 28 prohibitions apply only to owners and occupiers, section 29(3) states "no person" shall carry out the prohibited operations.

5–138   Nevertheless, sections 29(4) and (5) repeat sections 28(5) and (6) to enable the relaxation of any prohibition in favour of an owner or occupier[81] who gives the Agency written notice of a proposed operation. As section 29 of the 1981 Act was not amended by the Wildlife and Countryside (Amendment) Act, 1985, the Conservation Agency has to respond to a proposal to carry out a damaging operation within three, and not four, months.[82]

5–139   If, however, before the expiry of the three month period specified in section 29(5)(c), the Conservation Agency offers, either to acquire the interest of the owner or occupier who has given notice of his intention to carry out a damaging operation, or to negotiate a Management Agreement, section 29(6) extends the period which must elapse before the owner or occupier is free to carry out the intended damaging operation to either 12 months from the giving of the notice, or to three months from the date on which the offer of a Management Agreement was rejected or withdrawn, whichever is the later. Section 29(9) exempts from the prohibitions of section 29(3) operations which have been authorised by a grant of planning permission, and also those

---

[81] "Occupier" must be understood as excluding a person with merely a transient interest in the land: *Southern Water Authority v. Nature Conservancy Council (supra)*.
[82] s.29(5)(c).

which have been carried out in an emergency, provided details of the emergency and the work which was carried out have been given to the Conservation Agency.

Section 29(7) provides that, where a Conservation Agency uses its **5–140** powers of compulsory purchase to acquire the interest in land of owners or occupiers who give notice under section 29(4), the NCO will remain in force until the Agency enters the land, or the Compulsory Purchase Order is withdrawn, or the Secretary of State refuses to confirm the NCO.[83]

Section 29(8) prescribes penalties for contraventions "without **5–141** reasonable excuse" of section 29(3), providing for both summary proceedings and an unlimited fine on indictment. In addition the court may make an order under section 31 requiring a person convicted under section 29(8) to restore the flora, fauna and features on land subject to an NCO and prescribes penalties for the failure to carry out such a restoration.[84] Further, if a restoration order is not complied with within the period prescribed, the Conservation Agency may itself enter the land and carry out what was ordered, and recover its reasonable expenses from the person subject to the order.[85]

It is however a "reasonable excuse" for a person to carry out an **5–142** operation that contravenes the terms of an NCO if it has been authorised under a planning consent, or if it was an emergency operation and details of it and of the emergency itself were notified to the Agency as soon as practicable after the operation started. The making of an NCO is thus still no absolute protection of a site, if planning considerations favour damaging development on it.

When Conservation Agencies require to ascertain whether an NCO **5–143** should be made, or whether an NCO is being or has been breached, or to determine the amount of compensation payable under section 30, they have the power to enter land under section 51 of the 1981 Act.[86]

---

[83] These powers for the compulsory purchase of sites subject to an NCO remained unused for several years, although the threat of their employment had from time to time proved an effective stimulus to owners and occupiers. In 1990, however, a Compulsory Purchase Order was obtained over seven and a half hectares of Westhay Moor in Somerset as a final attempt to achieve conservation. Since in practice the Conservation Agencies only acquire land meriting NNR status, not every SSSI will in fact be at serious risk of a compulsory purchase order, though owners may well not be prepared to put that issue to the test.

[84] It is noteworthy that there is no provision for such remedial orders in relation to offences under s.28 in respect of SSSIs.

[85] s.31(6). This might well be necessary where the person convicted was neither an owner or occupier and had no right to enter on the land or to carry out works on it.

[86] These powers were first exercised in July 1987 to enter the land at Westhay Moor which eventually became subject to the Compulsory Purchase Order referred to above.

5–144   Section 30(2) of the 1981 Act requires Conservation Agencies to pay compensation to the owners and occupiers of land within an agricultural unit that has been made subject to an NCO where they can show that the value of their interest in that land has been reduced as a result of the making of the NCO. In that event the compensation is the amount of that reduction. They are also entitled to compensation under section 30(3) if they have reasonably incurred expenditure on projects which have been rendered abortive where an NCO is in existence and, following notifying the Agency of proposed prohibited operations under sections 29(4) and (5), the Agency has offered to enter into a Management Agreement or there has been a Compulsory Purchase Order made in favour of the Agency. In such cases any person with an interest in the relevant land is entitled to reimbursement of their reasonable expenses, and compensation for other loss and damages directly attributable through the making of the NCO, or that they have suffered loss or damage directly attributable to the making of the NCO. The making of claims under section 30 is governed by the Wildlife and Countryside (Claims for Compensation under Section 30) Regulations 1982.[87]

5–145   The provisions for compensation under section 30 of the 1981 Act are thus very different from payments made under Management Agreements negotiated under section 16 of the 1949 Act or section 15 of the 1968 Act, both of which are now governed by DoE Circular 4/83 and provide compensation on the basis of profits foregone. Should it be preferred to receive compensation under section 30 of the 1981 Act, it would appear quite practicable to provoke the making of an NCO under section 29.

5–146   The procedures relating to NCOs under section 29 (and also to Limestone Pavement Orders under section 34) are set out at length in Schedule 11. Orders come into force immediately on being made. The Secretary of State has to confirm all orders within a nine month period of their being made, otherwise they lapse. The area to which an order applies shall not be extended on its confirmation. A period of not less than 28 days is allowed for the making of representations and objections with respect to an order. Orders will be publicised in local newspapers but there is no absolute requirement to serve notice of an order on owners and occupiers. Where orders are opposed, the Secretary of State is required, either to arrange a local inquiry, or to afford any person who has made (and not subsequently withdrawn) a representation or objection a hearing before an Inspector. The validity of orders can be questioned in the High Court or the Court of Session,

---

[87] S.I. 1982 No. 1346.

as the case may be.[88] As mentioned earlier, land subject to an NCO will in practice also have been notified as an SSSI. When such dual status is challenged through a planning application, the NCO should only be sustained, where it was made to conserve flora or fauna or geological or physiographical features, if the area it covers can be shown to be of national significance or, in other words, to meet a higher standard than the minimum required for the SSSI notification, which need not have any national connotations. In NCO/SSSI cases, it may be appropriate to have two inquiries (preferably in tandem), the first (under Schedule 11) to consider the more vulnerable NCO and the second (a section 78 planning appeal) to consider the SSSI. To obtain a grant of planning permission will require, of course, a successful outcome to both.

Limestone Pavement Orders

Under the provisions of section 34 of the 1981 Act, Limestone   **5–147**
Pavement Orders (LPOs) are made, modified, revoked and confirmed by the Secretary of State, or by a local planning authority, following an application by one of the Conservation Agencies or by the Countryside Commission. These Orders are unique in conservation legislation in that they give special protection to one particular, narrowly specified habitat; no other habitat is singled out in this way. Paragraphs 11 to 14 of 27/87 give guidance on these provisions.

The origin of LPOs dates back to the 1960s when a "grey area" in   **5–148**
planning law became apparent. Stone merchants removing water-worn rockery limestone piece-meal from limestone pavements were required to apply for planning permission and, on their applications being refused, appealed on the grounds that the removal of "loose stone" from grazing land was not only a traditional agricultural practice but was also permitted development. In contesting these appeals, considerable difficulty was experienced in deciding how "loose stone" should be defined. Matters were not clarified by the 1977 General Development Order so that, when the 1981 Act came to be

---

[88] Up to March 31, 1993, NCOs had been opposed under these procedures on thirteen occasions and one NCO had been taken to the High Court. In this period, only one NCO was opposed successfully. This was very much a special case in which it was demonstrated that a very small but floristically rich area, which had been claimed to be of national interest as a relic of a "medieval meadow", in fact owed its interest to topsoil which had been brought on-site for disposal.

drafted, the working of "water-worn" rockery stone from limestone pavements was placed under specific controls.[89]

5-149   Section 34 of the 1981 Act is uniquely hybrid in character in that it conserves both landscape for amenity and habitat for science. In selecting sites, science is given priority, for section 34(1) closely follows section 28(1) in its terms; it lays a duty on the Conservation Agencies and the Countryside Commission to notify the local planning authority of any area of limestone pavement in the countryside which in their opinion "is of special interest by reason of its flora, fauna or geological or physiographical features". The initial applications for LPOs are thus made on the grounds of scientific interest, just as for SSSIs. To assist them in their responsibilities, Conservation Agencies have power, under section 51 of the 1981 Act, to enter land to ascertain whether a LPO should be made, or whether a LPO is being or has been breached.

5-150   The making of LPOs differs, however, from the notification of SSSIs in that it is a two stage process, the second stage of which lies outside the competence of any Conservation Agency or the Countryside Commission. By section 34(2) if either the Secretary of State or the relevant local planning authority consider that the "character or appearance" of land notified as just described under section 34(1) would be likely to be adversely affected by the removal of the limestone or its disturbance in any way whatever, either of them may make an LPO designating that land. Such endorsement brings the provisions of Schedule 11 to the 1981 Act into play.[90] These provisions, as seen above, allow for appeals against the imposition of LPOs, whereas there is no procedure for appealing against an SSSI designation in England and Wales.

5-151   The provisions for enforcement of LPOs are analogous to those for NCOs save that the restoration provisions of section 31 do not apply. Thus, any person removing or disturbing limestone without reasonable excuse on a site covered by a LPO commits an offence under section 34(4), rendering him liable to either summary conviction or an unlimited fine on indictment. As already noted, SSSI status places obligations only on the owner and occupier of a site. Consequently, a trespasser can remove loose stone from an SSSI without committing any offence under section 28,[91] but is liable to prosecution under section 34 if he does so from an area subject to an LPO.

---

[89] "Limestone pavement" is defined in s.34(6) as an area of limestone which lies wholly or partly exposed on the surface of the ground and has been fissured by natural erosion.

[90] Which also apply to Nature Conservation Orders.

[91] This may of course amount to theft or malicious damage, if done without the consent of the owner or occupier.

As in the case of SSSIs and NCOs, a grant of planning permission provides a "reasonable excuse" and so is effective to overcome an LPO; section 34 however, makes no provision for emergencies.

There is no explicit statutory link between LPOs and SSSIs; areas of   **5–152** pavement covered by LPOs do not have to be SSSIs, and SSSI status can be given to areas of pavement which are not covered by LPOs. On the other hand, it is difficult to envisage a Conservation Agency coming to the opinion that some particular area of limestone pavement fulfils the requirements of section 28(1) but not the identical requirements of section 34(1) or *vice versa*. It is clear from section 34(2), however, that the main purpose of an LPO is to retain, not the scientific values, but the "character and appearance" of the pavement. In other words, areas subject to LPOs are to be chosen for scientific merit but are to be conserved to preserve their visual amenity. Little confusion is likely to result, however, for it is understood that it is the intention of the Conservation Agencies that all limestone pavement SSSIs will also be covered by LPOs, although it remains unclear whether LPOs will be extended over areas which are not to be notified as SSSIs.

Because of the overlapping provisions of the two designations, such   **5–153** application of LPOs to sites already designated as SSSIs, will largely repeat, but will also to some extent reinforce, the constraints imposed by the SSSI notification. In particular, designation as a LPO invokes significant considerations of visual amenity in addition to the essentially science-based considerations which underlie SSSIs.

Specific procedures are laid down in section 34 of the 1981 Act for   **5–154** challenging the making of LPOs; these are set out in Schedule 11 of the Act. However, should a successful result be obtained, any SSSI notification will be left unscathed and will then require a further and quite separate challenge. To follow this procedure thus has the disadvantage that the removal of all conservation constraints requires a successful outcome from two public inquiries. However, as a grant of planning permission nullifies the restrictions imposed by both a LPO[92] and a SSSI designation,[93] a single successful section 79 appeal would overcome both the LPO and the SSSI status.

Land of Outstanding Scientific Interest

One of the categories of property granted conditional exemption   **5–155** from Inheritance Tax is "Land of Outstanding Scientific Interest"

[92] s.34(5).
[93] s.28(8).

(LOSI). Such land owes its outstanding scientific interest to its flora, fauna, or physiographical or geological features and is therefore likely also to have been declared as an NNR or notified as an SSSI. Additionally, some land which does not qualify for these designations can meet the standard set for LOSI.

5–156   Exemption from Inheritance Tax for LOSI is provided for by sections 30 to 35 of the Inheritance Tax Act 1984. These provisions make exemptions conditional on the new owner agreeing to maintain the scientific interest, to preserve the character of the land, including any scenic or historic features, and to provide reasonable public access, where this is appropriate. Where woodlands form an important part of the exemption, undertakings to manage these under a fixed plan will be required. Should a new owner fail to honour his agreement, or should the agreement not be renewed when the property changes hands, the tax which has been deferred will become payable and will be based on the proceeds of any sale or the market value at the time the agreement was breached.[94]

5–157   Sale of LOSI to the various bodies listed in Schedule 3 of the Inheritance Tax Act will normally be exempt from Capital Gains Tax, by virtue of section 258, Taxation of Chargeable Gains Act 1992. These bodies include the National Trust, the Conservation Agencies, universities and local authorities.[95]

5–158   In all cases, the decision to exempt tax liabilities arising from LOSI is the responsibility of the Inland Revenue; expert advice on the scientific value of the land is given by the Conservation Agencies. Since the concessions were first introduced by the Finance Act 1975, there have been many changes in the relevant regulations; it will always be advisable in any particular case for anyone affected to confirm the currently applicable terms of the LOSI regulations.

Species Protection

General Considerations

5–159   Statutory provisions for the conservation of particular species and groups of animals and plants in Britain date back to the Preservation

---

[94] More detail is provided in Inland Revenue booklet IR67 "Capital Taxation and the National Heritage".

[95] See also Inland Revenue leaflet IR88 "Capital Tax Relief for National Heritage Property : How to Make a Claim".

of Seabirds Act of 1869.[96] Since then, numerous further measures have been passed and, from time to time, have been consolidated by legislation such as the Protection of Birds Act 1954, which repealed and re-enacted no fewer than fifteen earlier statutes. The latest consolidation of the general legislation was effected in 1981 and forms Part I of the Wildlife and Countryside Act. This, however, was required to be more than a consolidation of earlier British legislation, for it also had to provide the statutory basis for the implementation of the EC Birds Directive 79/409 which became binding on all Member States on April 2, 1981.[97] The 1981 Act has itself been amended several times, most notably for the purposes of this section by the Wildlife and Countryside (Amendment) Act 1991 (the "1991 Act")[98] and by a series of orders amending the Schedules listing species to which provisions of Part I relate.

Part I of the 1981 Act provides for the protection of wild birds, their **5–160** nests and their eggs, for the protection of specified wild animals and plants, for the control of the introduction of non-indigenous species into the wild, and for the establishment of a licensing system to permit actions which would otherwise be illegal. Interpretation of the highly specialised sense in which Part I uses many everyday terms is provided in section 27; for example, the term "wild animal" is defined as: "any animal (other than a bird) which is or (before it was killed or taken) was living wild". By subsection (3), any reference in Part I of the Act to an animal of any kind includes, unless the context otherwise requires, a reference to an egg, larva, pupa or other immature stage of an animal of that kind. "Wild animal" is thus sufficiently wide a term to include the eggs of insects.

Much of the protection afforded to individual species by the 1981 **5–161** Act depends on their inclusion on the Schedules which accompany the Act. Under the provisions of section 22, species can be added to, or withdrawn from these Schedules by order of the Secretary of State, either to meet British needs or to comply with international requirements; for example, since 1988, over 250 species of animal and plant have been added to Schedules 5 and 8. As will be seen, the Schedules may, if appropriate, provide protection for a species only in particular areas or during particular times of the year, and orders made under section 22 may be likewise so limited. It is therefore necessary to

---

[96] The primary purpose of much of the earlier legislation was not the conservation of nature but the prevention of cruelty to animals. Present day measures, whose primary purpose is the conservation of species, still reflect this inheritance, as is clearly shown e.g. in ss.5, 8 and 11 of the 1981 Act.

[97] See paras. 5–245 to 5–257.

[98] 1991 (c.54).

confirm exactly which species are currently protected, and the extent of that protection, before attempting to apply the Act.[99]

5–162   Many of the actions defined as offences in Part I and under certain other legislation[1] can be carried out legally if the appropriate licence has first been obtained; section 16 sets out the legal basis for the issue of such licences, and the attachment of conditions to them, together with the purposes for which they may be granted. Obtaining a licence through making false statements is an offence under section 17. Their annual reports show that the Conservation Agencies alone issued over 2,600 licences under these provisions in 1991/92 and over 2,200 in 1992/3.

5–163   Provisions for the enforcement of Part I and for the prosecution of offences under its provisions are set out in sections 19 to 21. Section 18(1) makes an attempt to commit an offence subject to the same penalties as the actual offence. Similarly, under section 18(2) any person who, for the purposes of committing an offence under Part I has in his possession equipment capable of being used for the commission of the offence shall likewise be subject to the same penalties as are provided for the main offence. Some of the equipment which could be used in committing offences is of a very unspecialised nature (*e.g.* a spade or a garden trowel which could be used to uproot plants) and such equipment, including the cars used to transport it, has been confiscated by the courts when convicting offenders.

5–164   The duty of the Conservation Agencies to advise on the lists of species in Schedules 5 and 8 are set out in section 24 and those of the local authorities in relation to Part I in section 25; interestingly, the latter are instructed to bring Part I to the attention, not just of the public in general, but to the attention of schoolchildren in particular. Section 27(5) extends coverage of the legislation to the limits of territorial waters around Great Britain.[2]

5–165   Badgers and seals do not derive their principal protection from Part I of the 1981 Act. The former are the subject of the Protection of Badgers Act 1992, while seals are protected by the Conservation of Seals Act, 1970, as modified by the 1981 Act,[3] The management of deer is primarily governed by the Deer Act 1991 which consolidated previous legislation relating to means of killing deer, close seasons, poaching

---

[99] The following Orders amend the original Scheds: S.I. 1988 No. 288 (Scheds. 5, 8); S.I. 1989 No. 906 (Sched. 5); S.I. 1991 No. 367 (Sched. 5); S.I. 1992 No. 320 (Sched. 9); S.I. 1992 No. 2350 (Sched. 5) and S.I. 1994 No. 1151 (Sched. 4). Sched. 7 has been amended by Sched. 4 to the 1991 Act.

[1] The placing on land of poison and poisonous substances contrary to the Protection of Animals Act 1911 and the Protection of Animals (Scotland) Act 1912.

[2] Apart from a few minor exceptions, the 1981 Act does not apply to Northern Ireland; s.73(6).

[3] See paras. 5–214 to 5–231.

and related offences. However such activities are so influenced by commercial considerations as to fall outside the scope of nature conservation and are not therefore considered further here.[4]

Freshwater Fish

The conservation of freshwater fish and their habitats is largely an **5–166** aspect of the control of water pollution and the exercise by the National Rivers Authority (the NRA) of its powers and duties to set and to seek to maintain suitable water quality standards; these are largely considered in chapter 8 Water. These duties include the duty to maintain, improve and develop salmon fisheries, trout fisheries, freshwater fisheries and eel fisheries.[5] Brief mention must however be made here of the Salmon and Freshwater Fisheries Act 1975.

This Act has a long pedigree, being derived from the Salmon Fisheries **5–167** Acts 1861 and 1865.[6] The 1975 Act is concerned to a large extent with controlling the fishing of salmon, trout, eels and freshwater fish,[7] including the grant of fishing licences, prohibiting certain methods of taking fish, setting close seasons and making provision for the sale and transport of fish in such a manner as to facilitate control of poaching.

Environmental controls are contained in section 4(1) which **5–168** provides:

"Subject to subsection (2) below, any person who causes or knowingly permits to flow, or puts or knowingly permits to be put, into any waters containing fish or into any tributaries of waters containing fish, any liquid or solid matter to such an extent as to cause the waters to be poisonous or injurious to fish or the spawning grounds, spawn or food of fish, shall be guilty of an offence".

Prosecutions for polluting rivers and lakes, particularly where there **5–169** has been a fish kill, frequently charge an offence under this section as well as under section 61 of the Water Resources Act 1991. Trial may be summary or on indictment[8] with a maximum fine of £5,000 on conviction following summary trial, coupled with a daily fine of up to

[4] The principal issue, far from being conservation of deer stocks, is now to reduce their numbers to levels that can be properly supported by their territories without excessive damage to other interests, in particular the natural regeneration of woodland and other vegetation.
[5] W.R.A., s.114.
[6] The 1865 Act was replaced by the Salmon and Freshwater Fisheries Act 1923, which was amended in 1929 and followed by further Acts of the same name in 1935, 1965 and 1972. All five of these Acts were repealed and replaced by the 1975 Act.
[7] "Freshwater fish" being defined in s.41(1) as excluding salmon, trout, eels and any other fish migrating between fresh and tidal waters.
[8] See Sched.4, para. 1 and accompanying table.

227

£40 for so long as the offence continues after conviction. On conviction on indictment an unlimited fine may be imposed and/or a prison term of up to two years.

5–170   Unlike the offences of causing or knowingly permitting pollution under the Water Resources Act 1991, a prosecution for an offence under section 4(1) may only be instituted by the NRA or a person who has a material interest in the waters alleged to be affected.[9]

5–171   Section 4(1) is subject to section 4(2) which exempts anyone acting in exercise of a prescribed right or in continuance of a method in use at the same premises since July 18, 1923.[10] Further, by section 5(5), the use with the permission of the NRA of "any explosive substance, any poison or other noxious substance" for a scientific purpose or for the purpose of protecting, improving or replacing stocks of fish is also exempted from the effect of section 4(1).

5–172   Also exempted from section 4 is any entry of matter into any controlled waters (as defined in the Water Resources Act 1991) which is under and in accordance with a discharge consent under either the W.R.A. or (in Scotland) C.O.P.A. 1974, as amended, or which is the result of any act or omission under and in accordance with that consent.[11]

Sea Fish

5–173   The conservation of marine fish stocks is also largely based on commercial considerations and international quota agreements that are outside the scope of this book. Reference may nevertheless be made to the Sea Fisheries (Wildlife Conservation) Act 1992. This requires all relevant Government Ministers, any fisheries committee[12] or any other body exercising the powers of such a committee, when they are discharging any functions arising by virtue of the "Sea Fisheries Acts"

(a)   to have regard to the conservation of marine flora and fauna; and

(b)   to endeavour to achieve a reasonable balance between that consideration and any others to which they must have regard.[13]

"Sea Fisheries Acts" is widely and flexibly defined as any enactments for the time being in force relating to sea-fishing, including

---

[9] s.4(3). A certificate as to the existence of the relevant material interest must first be obtained before anyone other than the NRA may institute a prosecution.
[10] The date the Salmon and Freshwater Fisheries Act 1923 was passed.
[11] Sched.1, para.30, Water Consolidation (Consequential Provisions) Act 1991.
[12] Constituted under the Sea Fisheries Regulation Act 1966.
[13] s.1(1).

fishing in the sea for shellfish, salmon or migratory trout. Northern Ireland, atypically, is also covered by this 1992 Act. The duties under this Act are phrased so broadly that it would be virtually impossible to enforce them by mandatory injunction;[14] nevertheless a failure to take the stipulated considerations into account at all when discharging any of the functions the Act applies to would *prima facie* provide a basis for challenging the decision in question.

Conservation of Birds

Sections 1 to 8 of the 1981 Act protect wild birds, which are defined by section 27 to be "any bird of a kind which is ordinarily resident in or is a visitor to Great Britain in a wild state", but not poultry nor, generally, various specified game birds.[15] For the purposes of Section 1, "wild bird" also does not include any bird which is shown to have been bred in captivity.[16]   **5–174**

An evidential issue that is constantly liable to arise in enforcement of the 1981 Act is whether a particular specimen believed to be the subject of an offence is in fact wild within the meaning of the Act, or whether it has been bred in captivity. In all cases, the legislation creates a presumption in favour of the former, placing the burden of proof on a defendant to establish the contrary on the balance of probabilities. In the case of birds, section 27(2) further provides that a bird shall not be treated as bred in captivity unless (both) its parents were lawfully in captivity when the egg was laid. Thus, by section 1(6), section 1 applies to all wild birds unless they are shown to have been bred in captivity. Similarly sections 9(6) and 11(5) provide that in any proceedings for an offence under the relevant provisions of those sections the animal in question shall be presumed to have been wild unless the contrary is shown, and section 13(4) stipulates the like presumption in relation to offences under that section in respect of wild plants.   **5–175**

Section 1(1) makes it illegal, except under licence, to kill, injure or take any wild bird, or to take, damage or destroy their nests (but only while the nest is in use or being built), or to take or "destroy" (which is defined to include anything calculated to prevent hatching) any wild bird's egg. To "take" is to be understood as capturing a live wild bird.[17] To be in possession or control of a wild bird, whether alive or dead, any   **5–176**

---

[14] Few Courts would relish having to determine whether the Government had given sufficient regard to the conservation of fish when deciding not to exercise its powers under s.10 of the Conservation of Seals Act 1970—see paras. 5–226 to 5–231.

[15] "Game bird" is defined in s.27 as "any pheasant, partridge, grouse (or moor game), black (or heath) game or ptarmigan".

[16] s.1(6).

[17] *Robinson v. Everett & Another, The Times*, May 20, 1988.

part of a wild bird or anything derived from such a bird, or the whole or any part of a wild bird's egg, is an offence under section 1(2), unless the accused can establish any of the defences set out in section 1(3). This sub-section is available to a defendant who can show either that the bird or egg had not been killed or captured, or else that this had been done without breaching any provision of the 1981 Act or, in the case of a wild bird or part of or anything derived from a wild bird, any provision of the Protection of Birds Acts, 1954 to 1967, including any Order made under the 1981 Act or any of these earlier Acts.

5–177   In *Robinson v. Everett*, which concerned possession of a stuffed and mounted golden eagle, it was held on appeal that the effect of section 1(3) was to require an accused to show on the balance of probabilities that (a) the bird had neither been killed nor captured, or (b), if killed or captured by any person, that act was not intentional, or (c), if killed, no person was responsible. An accused would of course also be entitled to be acquitted if he could establish that the killing and capturing had occurred before the Protection of Birds Act 1954 came into force.

5–178   Offences relating to the birds listed on Part I of Schedule 1 attract "special penalties",[18] as do offences relating to the birds on Part II of this Schedule when these are committed during the close season. Disturbance (defined to include photography) of Schedule 1 birds, when building, occupying, or near a nest also attracts a special penalty.[19]

5–179   Some exceptions are made in section 2 to allow the shooting of the quarry species listed in Part I of Schedule 2 outside the close season[20] and to permit "authorised persons" to control the pest species on Part II of Schedule 2. The Secretary of State is given the power to vary the close seasons and, after consultation, to impose periods of "special protection" during which shooting is banned. "Authorised person" includes the owner or occupier of the land on which the relevant action is taken and anyone authorised by them; it also covers anyone authorised in writing by the relevant local authority and, in relation to

[18] A "special penalty" under Part I of the Act consists of a fine not exceeding level 5 on the standard scale; other offences under ss. 1 to 8 are subject to a maximum fine of level 3.

[19] Prosecutions for offences under s.1 are reported at frequent intervals in the Press. Many of those accused are, not unexpectedly, members of groups (*e.g.* egg collectors, taxidermists and falconers) whose specialist interests can run counter to the purpose of the legislation. There is however a growing trend to prosecute some sections of the general public, including amateur photographers and mountaineers, for disturbing Sched. 1 birds.

[20] The "close season" is defined in s.2(4) as being for most species the period from February 1 to August 31, inclusive; other periods are set for capercaillie and (outside Scotland) woodcock, snipe and wild duck and wild geese when in an area below high water mark.

wild birds (as opposed to other wild animals and plants), by the relevant Conservation Agency, the National Rivers Authority, statutory water undertakers, a district board of a Scottish fisheries district, and a local fisheries committee. A person who is deemed to be authorised for the purposes of Part I of the 1981 Act does not however, thereby acquire any right of entry on to the relevant land that he would not otherwise have.[21] A local authority nevertheless remains bound by this 1981 Act in any attempts it may make, under the powers available to it under section 74 of the Public Heath Act 1961, to abate or mitigate nuisance, annoyance or damage caused by flocks of house doves, pigeons, starlings or sparrows in built-up areas.

Section 3 grants powers to the Secretary of State to establish bird sanctuaries ("areas of special protection") by order, continuing powers under the Protection of Birds Act 1954 and earlier legislation. The section enables orders to make illegal not only acts that are prohibited by section 1, but also additional offences of disturbing a wild bird while building its nest or while at or near a nest containing eggs or young, and disturbing the bird's young. An order under section 3 may additionally prohibit entry to the whole or part of the protected area, either generally or during any specified period, subject to such exceptions as may be prescribed. It may be noted that whereas the offences under section 1 are, by virtue of section 2, subject to the right to kill birds listed in Schedule 2 (outside the close season, where applicable), this general exception does not apply to prohibitions made under section 3.[22] A section 3 order may also provide that contravention of any provision of Part I of the 1981 Act (or any as may be specified) shall be subject to a special penalty.

5–180

Section 3 orders can be made only with the consent of all owners and occupiers, thus restricting their employment outside statutory and non- statutory nature reserves. Although these orders have a long history, they have been little used in recent years; they have the advantage that, unlike the land-based SSSIs and the sea-based MNRs, they can be made over areas partly of land and partly of sea; they are thus an appropriate designation where the coastline is mobile. These section 3 areas are not to be confused with the Special Protection Areas

5–181

---

[21] s.27(1).

[22] This ironically could result in the killing of a magpie (listed in Part II of Schedule 2), that is attempting to take eggs from a rare bird's nest, being lawful outside a s.3 area but unlawful within it unless the relevant s.3 order is expressly restricted so as not to apply to all wild birds. It could even be an offence, unless the order is suitably drafted, actively to obstruct the thieving magpie, since s.3(1)(a)(iv), which refers to disturbing a wild bird near a nest containing eggs or young, does not in terms require that the nest belong to that bird, though no doubt that is what is intended.

for Birds, established by Directive 79/409, which are in practice notified as SSSIs (see paras. 5–245 to 5–257).

5–182   Exemptions from the provisions of both sections 1 and 3 are set out in section 4. These include cases where Ministers, under other legislation, require action to prevent damage to agriculture or the spread of disease, and provisions to allow the treatment and mercy killing of disabled birds. No offence is committed by an act which was "the incidental result of a lawful operation and could not reasonably have been avoided". "Authorised persons" commit no offence when they kill or injure any wild bird, provided that it does not belong to a species included in Schedule 1, to preserve public health or public or air safety, to prevent the spread of disease, or to prevent serious damage to livestock, fodder, crops, timber or fisheries. "Serious damage" is not defined, but the provisions of section 4(3) are in practice regarded as relating to emergencies, and not to routine actions, for which a licence should be obtained under section 16.[23]

5–183   Certain methods of taking or killing wild birds (including game birds) are prohibited by section 5. The list, which can be modified by the Secretary of State, is comprehensive and, in broad terms, includes mechanical and electrical traps, poisons, stupefying drugs, bird-lime, bows and cross-bows, explosives, automatic or semi-automatic weapons, over-large shotguns, spotlights, night sights, dazzling devices, gas, smoke, chemical wetting agents, sound recordings of birds or animals, live decoys and mechanically propelled vehicles.

5–184   However, no offence is committed if mechanical and electrical traps, poisons and stupefying drugs are used in the interests of public health, agriculture, forestry, fisheries or nature conservation and all reasonable steps are taken to prevent the equipment injuring wild birds. "Authorised persons" can use cage traps and nets to take the pest species listed in Part II of Schedule 2, nets can be used to take wild duck in certain duck decoys, and cage traps can be used to take game birds for breeding, but the use of nets to take birds in flight or on the ground is proscribed.

5–185   A significant amendment to section 5(1) of the principal Act, introduced by the Wildlife and Countryside (Amendment) Act 1991, creates the additional offence of knowingly causing or permitting any of the acts prohibited under (a) to (e) of that sub-section. There had previously been concern that some landowners had consented to or connived at repeated offences under section 5 on their land, but in the absence of cogent evidence as to the nature of their involvement, it

---

[23] See the 8th Annual Report of the Nature Conservancy Council (for 1981/82), pp. 138-139.

was virtually impossible to obtain a conviction against them. The new offence nevertheless still requires knowledge to be proved—this may however be satisfied by evidence of shutting eyes to the obvious.[24]

Trade in wild birds is regulated by section 6. Section 6(1) lays down, **5–186** *inter alia*, that the sale, offer or exposure for sale, or possession or transport for the purpose of sale, of any live birds (except those listed in Part I of Schedule 3, which have been ringed and bred in captivity), their eggs, or parts of their eggs (*e.g.* blown eggs), is an offence, as is the publication of any advertisements "likely to be understood as conveying" that the person concerned buys or sells such things or intends to do so. Section 6(2) makes the same acts offences in relation to dead wild birds other than game as defined in Part II of Schedule 3 and, in the open season, game as defined in Schedule 3, Part III. It is also an offence to exhibit live wild birds or birds *one* of whose parents was wild. Penalties are increased if the birds to be sold or exhibited belong to species listed in Schedule 1. Powers to enforce these provisions are conferred on the Secretary of State.

The registration and ringing of captive birds belonging to the **5–187** species listed in Schedule 4,[25] which include the species normally used in falconry, is required by section 7. By section 7(3) a conviction of any offence under Part I of the 1981 Act automatically debars the offender from keeping such birds for at least three years[26] and, should anyone else knowingly dispose of such a bird to him while the recipient is debarred or offer to do so, within the same period after the latter's conviction, that other person also commits an offence.[27] "Knowingly" in this context must, it is submitted, require knowledge of the previous conviction of the person to whom he is seeking to dispose of a bird, and at the least some knowledge that would suggest the relevant three or five year period was or at least might be still running. Powers for

---

[24] *James & Son v. Smee* [1955] 1 Q.B. 78 and *Westminster City Council v. Croyalgrange Limited* [1986] 2 All E.R. 353 (H.L.). The latter case is also authority for holding that knowledge may be imputed where the defendant has intentionally refrained from making enquiries where he might be embarrassed by their consequences—arguably this is simply restating what amounts to obvious facts that a person chooses to ignore. Reports of prosecutions for offences under s.5 are also to be found at frequent intervals in the press. These show such offences are almost invariably confined to members of specialist groups (some gamekeepers, hill farmers, and taxidermists, who may perhaps be joined in the future by pigeon fanciers). Where they involve popular and spectacular species, such as birds of prey, such offences can attract substantial adverse publicity.

[25] As amended substantially by S.I. 1994 No. 1151.

[26] Five years from conviction of an offence carrying a special penalty.

[27] s.7(4), which is ambiguous in its references to "that person" in paragraphs (a) and (b). However, comparison with the slightly different language in subsection (3) indicates that "that person" in those paragraphs is intended to mean the second-mentioned "any person" rather than the first.

authorised persons to enforce these provisions through entry to and inspection of premises are again provided.[28]

5–188   Section 8 prescribes minimum standards for the keeping of captive birds and makes all parties involved in the release of captive birds, so that they may be shot immediately after release, liable to prosecution. This applies to all birds, without exception, including game birds and those in Part II of Schedule 2 which "authorised persons" may kill at any time.

Conservation of Other Animals

5–189   Sections 9 to 12 provide protection to those wild animals ("animals" being defined very broadly so as to include mammals, reptiles, amphibians, fish, crustaceans, worms, sea anemones, insects, etc.,[29]) listed in Schedule 5. Species can be added to, or withdrawn from this Schedule by orders made under the provisions of section 22(3) and (4); several such additions and removals have been made, on the recommendation of the Conservation Agencies.[30] One species on the Schedule, the great crested newt, is understood to be included on Schedule 5 not because it is rare or endangered in Britain, but because of its rarity in Europe as a whole.[31]

5–190   There are now very significant variations in the degree of protection afforded by section 9 to the individual species included on Schedule 5, and the only almost consistent feature is that trade in all but two of the species[32] it lists is unlawful under section 9(5). For many of the species in the Schedule, including the common frog, the common toad and the rarer (but not the rarest) British butterflies, this is the only part of section 9 which applies. For some other species, for example the adder, the slow worm and the allis shad, there is additional protection from a partial application of section 9(1) so that these can lawfully be taken, but not killed, injured or traded. The protection given to the Atlantic stream crayfish, however, allows it to be killed or injured but not taken or sold, whereas that for the freshwater pearl mussel allows it to be taken and traded, but not killed or injured. The mire pill beetle receives even less security, for only the places that it inhabits are protected (under section 9(4)(a)) and not the animal itself. All the remaining

---

[28] Cases under ss.6 and 7 are relatively common, and very often are met with a defence that birds have been bred in captivity and not taken from the wild. (See paragraph 00 above). In recent cases DNA profiling has been successfully employed in refuting such a defence.

[29] See s.27(3) and para. 5–160.

[30] By S.I. 1988 No. 288, S.I. 1989 No. 906, S.I. 1991 No. 367 and S.I. 1992 No. 2350; see n. 99 above.

[31] See para. 5–259 and note 3 thereto.

[32] The freshwater pearl mussel and the mire pill beetle.

species on Schedule 5 are subject not only to the full provisions of section 9(1) and 9(5) but also to the more extensive protection afforded by sections 9(2) and 9(4), with the sole exception of the sea fan to which section 9(4) is not applied. In view of the very fluid nature of Schedule 5 and the range of permutations in the degree of protection it affords to individual species at any time, it is advisable to confirm the current contents of the Schedule with the Wildlife Division of the Department of the Environment (and its equivalents) before any potentially unlawful action is taken.

Section 9 makes it an offence, subject to the defences provided in the Act, principally in section 9 itself and section 10, intentionally to kill, injure or take any of the wild animals listed in Schedule 5 (the limited list), or to possess or control any live or dead animal of such a species, or any part of or anything derived from such an animal, unless it was obtained legally.[33] It is also an offence under section 9(4) to damage, destroy, or obstruct access to any "structure or place" which any such animal uses for shelter or protection or to disturb any such animal when it is in such a structure or place. Trade in all but two of the species listed on Schedule 5 is forbidden by section 9(5). An animal is presumed to be wild unless the contrary can be shown.[34]   **5–191**

The scope of section 9, and in particular section 9(4), is much less precisely defined than that of section 1, which confers the analogous protection on birds. Birds' nests are recognisable entities, and their protection under section 1 relates to an equally recognisable period when they are being built or are in use. In contrast, the "structures and places" used by animals for shelter vary greatly with the species and are virtually impossible to define; the 1981 Act seems to acknowledge this by making no attempt to do so. For some species, such as squirrels, the meaning is obvious, but for those species which do not build or inhabit structures, a distinction between the "home" in which they shelter and the "habitat" in which they live can be virtually impossible to make. The addition of the free-ranging dolphins, marine turtles, porpoises and whales to Schedule 5 in 1988 has not served to clarify the meaning of section 9(4).   **5–192**

Similarly, the precise manner in which an animal has to "use" a "structure or place" for "shelter and protection" is unclear. Although some species have a more or less permanently occupied home, others use a variety of "structures or places" during their lives. Bat colonies   **5–193**

---

[33] s.9(1), (2). Following *Robinson v. Everett* (see n. 17, above), this makes it an offence to possess any stuffed wild animal or the skin of any wild animal in Sched. 5, unless it can be shown it had been killed or sold otherwise than in breach of the "relevant provisions", namely those of the 1981 Act and of the Conservation of Wild Creatures and Wild Plants Act 1975, or before they came into force.

[34] s.9(6).

typically have a number of, often seasonally occupied, roosts, and amphibia require either water or land depending on the season of the year and the stage attained in their life cycle. Still others, like a squirrel treed by a dog, take to any available "shelter or protection" as expediency demands.

5–194   It is however suggested that the phrase should be understood as referring to a site that any particular animal habitually uses for shelter or protection, such that its pattern of behaviour would be significantly disturbed were that site to be damaged, destroyed or obstructed. It need not be the only such site that the animal uses for this purpose, but it must be more than whatever happens to be available and used on a purely opportunistic basis. It is not the purpose of this section to protect habitats generally, for example hedgerows or woodlands as such, even though these may be essential for the maintenance of a species, but specific sites within them in so far as they exist. Even so, there inevitably remains a substantial "grey area" in the interpretation of section 9(4), which can only be determined on a case by case basis.

5–195   Since the provisions of section 9 have obvious planning implications, and have long been used as grounds for objections to development proposals, allegations of the presence of a Schedule 5 species are often made to planning officers and to planning inspectors. The weight which has been attached to such evidence has varied widely but, in general, the proven presence of a large, breeding, resident colony of a protected species has led to a severe constraint, if not a total ban, on development, whereas a few sightings of single individual animals by the lay public have had little significant impact. In some cases, where suitable arrangements could be made, small colonies of protected species have been transferred to less threatened locations by conservation organisations holding the appropriate licences under section 16.[35]

5–196   The grant of planning consent does not of course carry any right to contravene the provisions of Part I of the 1981 Act. Accordingly an objection founded on the habitual use of a site by a Schedule 5 animal for shelter or protection is not properly one to be put in the balance with all other planning considerations relevant to the proposed development, but a basis for asserting that granting consent, and arguably consideration of the application at all, would in practice be futile for so long as the animal remains there. The planning authority does not itself have any power to authorise any action in contravention of section 9 (or indeed of any other provision of the Act); action

---

[35] No mention of s.9 would be complete without some reference to the claims, so far unconfirmed, that some occurrences of Sched. 5 species (often the great crested newt), which are timeously discovered on sites for which unwelcome development is intended, might owe more to human artifice than to natural dispersal.

prohibited by section 9(4) may be licensed by the relevant Conservation Agency under section 16(3) for the purposes of conserving wild animals or introducing them to particular areas. However in considering whether to grant any such licence, it would not ordinarily be appropriate for the Agency to have regard to the factors that might incline a planning authority to favour a proposed development: the Agency's concern must be solely the wildlife conservation objectives of section 16(3). While a licence might properly be granted therefore where the site used by a species was already under threat, such that the survival of that species there was at risk, it would not be proper to do so if the sole threat was the proposed development itself.[36]

Section 10 sets out the exemptions from the provisions of section 9 and follows section 4 more or less closely. Under Section 10(3), actions taken to meet Ministerial requirements to prevent damage to agriculture or the spread of disease, the treatment and mercy killing of disabled animals, and acts which were "the incidental result of a lawful operation and could not reasonably have been avoided", again do not constitute offences. Under section 10(4), "authorised persons" commit no offence when they kill or injure any wild animal of a species included in Schedule 5 to prevent serious damage to livestock, fodder, crops, timber or any other form of property[37] or fisheries. There is again no definition of "serious damage" but section 10(6) (which has no counterpart in section 4) disallows the defence provided by section 10(4) where it had previously become apparent that such action would be required and a licence under section 16 has been refused or has not been applied for.

5–197

An additional exemption is provided by section 10(2) that also has no counterpart in section 4, which permits any damage or destruction to, or obstruction of, structures or places, or the disturbance of any animal using such places, when this takes place within a dwelling house. However, in the case of all species of bats, this exemption is reduced by section 10(5) to the "living area" of a dwelling house,

5–198

---

[36] Public perceptions of the protection provided by Part I of the 1981 Act, and by ss.1 and 9 in particular, can extend beyond the requirements of the legislation. As already noted, there is inevitably uncertainty as to the legal extent of the provisions of s.9(4), and this can lead to exaggerated expectations, *e.g.* to claims that, because bats have been observed flying over an area, the land in question can not be developed because it falls within the scope of s.9. In some cases these expectations can inflame public opinion; for instance, where a migratory bird nests habitually in a particular tree, there would appear to be nothing in Part I of the 1981 Act to prevent that tree being felled during the bird's absence, but such an action is unlikely to escape highly adverse publicity. The protection under s.9(4) of any "structure or place" used by animals for shelter or protection may thus be somewhat wider than that provided for birds.

[37] Curiously, the corresponding provision in s.4(3)(c) relating to birds does not extend to actions to protect "any other form of property".

unless and until the relevant Agency has been notified of the proposed action and it has had a reasonable time to advise whether it should be carried out, and if so how.

5–199   Section 10(5) likewise removes the defence provided by section 10(3)(c) for acts that were the "incidental result of a lawful operation and could not reasonably have been avoided", where these affect bats, unless the relevant Agency's advice has first been sought. The drafting of this sub-section may raise some uncertainty as to the position where the Agency's advice has been obtained, but then disregarded. However there would not appear to be any reason to read the sub-section otherwise than as creating a purely temporary suspension of the defence of section 10(2) which ceases after the reasonable time for the Agency to give its advice has expired. Had it been intended to require the Agency to give a licence under section 16 before action could be taken against bats, this could easily have been provided. It is reasonable to assume that the legislation was not intended to enable homeowners to be forced to give space to bats, even outside the living area, but simply relies on the willingness of those affected in most cases to comply with expert advice; thus it provides no sanctions against any unwilling to do so.

5–200   It is evident from section 10(5) that "dwelling house" is used in section 10(2) to apply to more than those parts of a house in which the occupants may be regarded as "living"; a usage that is consistent with the judgment of Stamp L.J. in *Grigsby v. Melville*[38] that "dwelling house" includes a cellar. In *Batey v. Wakefield*[39] the Court of Appeal held that the term could apply to a group of two or more separate buildings, where they were in fact used together. The expression was defined in *Lewin v. End*[40] as being "a house in which people actually live or which is physically capable of being used for human habitation". While this would apply to a house that is immediately ready for occupation with little or no preliminary work, it may be distinguished from a derelict house in which animals, such as bats, have established themselves. It should also be distinguished from business premises, even where these have been created from what was originally a private house, or where they also have facilities for eating and sleeping, such as a position set aside for use by a caretaker.[41]

5–201   The reference in section 10(5) to the "living area" of a dwelling house must, it would seem, be taken to exclude not only the eaves and

---

[38] [1973] 3 All E.R. 455, at 462; [1974] 1 W.L.R. 80, at 87.
[39] [1982] 1 All E.R. 61, concerning the meaning of "dwelling house" for the purposes of the capital gains tax provisions of the Finance Act 1965.
[40] [1906] A.C. 299, at 304, *per* Lord Atkinson.
[41] See *Lewin v. End* at p. 302.

any cavity walls of a house, but also any cellar or garage, at least if used only for general storage and keeping a car under cover. Equally, it would appear to exclude an attic, in the absence of a loft conversion integrating it with the "living area" proper.

Certain methods of taking or killing wild animals are prohibited by section 11. The list, which can be modified by the Secretary of State, is again comprehensive. Self-locking snares, bows and cross-bows, explosives and decoys may not be used to take any wild animal, and snares and other mechanical and electrical traps, poisons, stupefying drugs, automatic or semi-automatic weapons, spotlights, night sights, dazzling devices, gas, smoke, sound recordings, live decoys and mechanically propelled vehicles may not be used to take or kill the species of wild animal listed on Schedule 6. Again there are some exemptions in the interests of public health, agriculture, forestry, fisheries or nature conservation, provided all reasonable steps are taken to prevent injury to the species listed on Schedule 6. The Wildlife and Countryside (Amendment) Act 1991, amended sections 11(1), (2) and (3) in the same way as section 5(1), so as to extend them to those knowingly causing or permitting the other acts prohibited by those subsections.[42]   **5–202**

Note may be made here of EC Regulation EEC No 3254/91[43] relating to leghold traps. Being a regulation it is directly applicable throughout the EC. Article 1 prohibits the use of leghold traps[44] in the Community by January 1, 1995 at the latest, while Article 2 prohibits, subject to a variety of qualifications, import into the Community of pelts of the animal species listed in Annex I[45] and also an extensive list of other goods incorporating pelts of some or all of the Annex I species. The European Commission may lift the import restrictions in relation to a particular country outside the Community if in that country the leghold trap is effectively prohibited or "internationally agreed humane trapping standards" are met for trapping the Annex I species.   **5 203**

Reports of prosecutions for offences under sections 9 and 11 have been less frequent than those under sections 1 and 5. This, however, may reflect the absence of any similarly specialised organisation with the resources of the Royal Society for the Protection of Birds to investigate complaints and instigate actions relating to the alleged   **5–204**

---

[42] See para. 5–185.
[43] [1991] O.J. L308. The Regulation came into effect on November 9, 1991.
[44] Defined as a device designed to restrain or capture an animal by means of jaws which close tightly upon one or more of the animal's limbs, thereby preventing withdrawal of the limb or limbs from the trap.
[45] Beaver, otter, coyote, wolf, lynx, bobcat, sable, raccoon, musk rat, fisher, badger, marten, ermine.

taking and killing of wild animals.[46] Almost all prosecutions, for offences under these provisions have related to bats, and most of these arise as a consequence of contractors spraying roof timbers with insecticides which prove to be just as lethal to the bats as to their intended target species. In many cases, the accused have claimed ignorance of the lethal nature (to bats) of the insecticide and of the existence of the bat colony; some difficulty has been experienced in obtaining convictions. Where prosecutions have succeeded, fines of up to £1,000 have been imposed, but in one case, where there were special circumstances, the fine represented less than 5p for every bat killed. Nevertheless, by section 21(5) where an offence relates to several individuals of a protected species, the maximum fine can be imposed in respect of each single individual that has been killed, injured, taken or disturbed. To disturb a large bat colony could thus increase the maximum fine to over £1 million.

Protection of Wild Plants

5–205   In contrast to the provisions for the protection of wild birds and other animals, those for the protection of wild plants are relatively simple. Section 13 makes it an offence for any person intentionally to pick, uproot or destroy any of the wild plants listed in Schedule 8, or for anyone other than an authorised person intentionally to pick, uproot or destroy any wild plant. It is also an offence to possess, transport, trade, or attempt to trade in any such plant, any parts of such plant, or any derivative of such plant. To "pick" is defined as "to gather or pluck any part of the plant without uprooting it".[47] Both from the language of this definition and from consideration of the purposes of the legislation, which includes protecting species so that they can successfully maintain themselves, it would be appropriate to construe "pick" as extending to the removal of seed from plants which are otherwise left undisturbed. Schedule 8 has been greatly extended under the provisions of section 22(3), so that it now applies to many more species than the 62 originally listed in 1981.

5–206   As in the case of birds and other animals, acts which are the "incidental result of a lawful operation and could not reasonably be avoided" do not constitute offences, and plants which are sold, or are

---

[46] In 1985, the Nature Conservancy Council successfully prosecuted in a case where heathland inhabited by sand lizards (a Sched. 5 species) had been bulldozed but, as the bulldozing also breached a Nature Conservation Order, no clear inferences can be drawn concerning the interpretation of s.9(4). In the following year, a pet shop owner was fined for possessing great crested newts (another Sched. 5 species), and for offering them for sale.

[47] s.27(1).

offered for sale, are presumed to have been wild plants unless the contrary can be shown.

Few prosecutions have been brought for offences against the provisions of section 13. However, the prohibited acts will generally also be offences under the Theft Act 1968, where not done by or with the consent of the owner of the land concerned. Charges of theft have thus been brought on occasion, particularly where the prosecutor has wished to use as a deterrent the possibility of a custodial sentence being imposed, as this is not available under the 1981 Act.[48]   **5–207**

The provisions of section 13 have also attracted attention as potential grounds of objection to development proposals, but to a lesser extent than those of section 9. Again the weight which has been attached to allegations of the existence of protected species has varied widely and, on several occasions, the translocation of colonies of protected species by conservation organisations holding the appropriate licences under section 16 has been carried out.[49]   **5–208**

Introduced Species

To protect indigenous species of birds, other animals and plants, and to prevent disturbance to existing ecological balances generally, section 14 prohibits the release of into the wild of non-native species of animals (including birds) and plants which are not found naturally in Britain, and to the further introduction of species (*e.g.* grey squirrels and Canada geese) which, although not native to Britain, were introduced some time ago and have now become established.   **5–209**

Specifically, it is an offence under section 14(1) to release or to allow to escape into the wild any animal which is either not ordinarily resident in and is not a regular visitor to Great Britain in a wild state, or is included in Part I of Schedule 9 as amended.[50] The general prohibition is thus not limited to species listed in Schedule 9—in distinction from the corresponding prohibition relating to plants (see below). It would extend therefore to transgenic animals produced by genetic engineering techniques notwithstanding that a consent to their release had been given under the Genetically Modified Organisms (Deliberate Release) Regulations 1992.[51] There must however be   **5–210**

---

[48] A moss gatherer was however successfully prosecuted under the 1981 Act for gathering 26 bags of moss without authority, British Wildlife, Oct. 1993, (vol. 5, no. 1) p. 62.

[49] See para. 5–162 on the grant of licences in such circumstances.

[50] The first prosecution under s.14, in April 1994, resulted in a gamekeeper being fined for releasing hybrid chukar partridges to the wild. All licences for such releases, once common, had been allowed to expire without renewal because of their harmful effects on the native red-legged partridge, *The Times*, April 20 and 22, 1994.

[51] S.I. 1992 No. 3280, see paras. 14–055 to 14–087.

some uncertainty as to whether the section 14 prohibition properly extends to animals where the genetic modification has been very slight, particularly if the result is no different from what might have been obtained by traditional breeding methods.[52]

5–211   For similar reasons, section 14(2) makes it an offence to plant or otherwise cause to grow in the wild any plant included in Part II of Schedule 9.[53] The limitation to scheduled species consequently renders section 14(2) inapplicable to the release of genetically modified plants, so that for this a consent under the 1992 Deliberate Release Regulations, referred to in the previous paragraph, would therefore be sufficient.

5–212   The offences under sections 14(1) and 14(2) are *prima facie* ones of strict liability. This follows both from the text of those subsections and also from section 14(3) which creates a defence for the accused to prove that he took all reasonable steps and exercised all due diligence to avoid committing the offence. Where, as in the typical case of an employer accused of such an offence as a result of the conduct of an employee, it is asserted by way of defence that another person was responsible for the act charged, the accused must by section 14(4), at least seven clear days before the hearing, serve a notice[54] identifying that other person or, where he is unable to do so, giving all information that he has that would assist in the identification.

5–213   Section 15 (as amended in 1990) and the very extensive Schedule 10 substantially amend the Endangered Species (Import and Export) Act, 1976; section 15 also gives the Conservation Agencies power to advise or assist in the enforcement of that Act.[55]

Protection of Badgers

5–214   Badgers are protected by the Badgers Act 1992, which consolidated the Badgers Act 1973, as amended by the 1981 and 1985 Acts, the Badgers Act 1991, and the Badgers (Further Protection) Act, 1991. In its original form, the 1973 Act proved inadequate in certain respects, and the 1991 legislation addressed the perceived deficiencies. Chief among

---

[52] The list in Part I of Sched. 9 consists almost entirely of non-native introduced species; it together with Part II of the Schedule has been amended under the provisions of s.22(6) by the Wildlife and Countryside Act 1981 (Variation of Schedule) Order 1992 (S.I. 1992 No. 320) to add a further substantial number of entries. A further recent amendment (S.I. 1992 No. 2674) controls the rearing and release to the wild of barn owls, by adding this unquestionably native species to Sched. 9 where it sits rather incongruously alongside the budgerigar, the Mongolian gerbil and the red-necked wallaby.

[53] Giant hogweed is probably the most familiar of the scheduled plants.

[54] In accordance with s.70A of the Act.

[55] So also implementing one aspect of the Berne Convention on the Conservation of European Wildlife and Habitats (see paras. 5–258, 5–259).

these was the ease of asserting the defence commonly used by those found digging a sett, that they were seeking foxes, not badgers.

Badgers are neither rare nor threatened in Britain and the intent behind the legislation is more to save the animals from cruelty than to protect them in the interests of nature conservation.[56] The present legislation, although generally similar in many of its provisions to Part I of the 1981 Act, thus descends from the Acts against bear baiting and cock fighting, rather than from those whose primary purpose is to safeguard wildlife. The scheme of the Act is to set out in sections 1 to 5 various prohibited acts; these are then followed by sections providing certain general exemptions and also specific exemptions from sections 1, 3 and 4, and, in section 10, a licensing regime operated by the relevant Conservation Agency. Sections 11 to 13 are directed to enforcement powers, penalties and other court orders.   **5–125**

It is an offence wilfully to kill, injure or take a badger, or to attempt to do so and if in any proceedings for this offence there is evidence from which such an attempt could reasonably be concluded, then this will be presumed to be the case unless the defendant can prove the contrary.[57] Similarly, it is an offence to dig for a badger, and if there is evidence from which it could reasonably be concluded that the defendant was doing this, the burden shifts to him to prove otherwise.[58]   **5–216**

To assist enforcement, section 1(5) entitles not only a constable but also the owner or occupier of any land (or any servant of his) to require anyone found committing any offence under section 1 of the Act (including an attempt, therefore) on that land to quit it and also to give his full name and address. Failure to comply with such requirements constitutes a further offence.   **5–217**

It is also *prima facie* an offence under section 4 to possess, to sell or offer for sale or to have under one's control a live badger; sale being widely defined as including hire, barter or exchange. Likewise, by section 1(3) it is an offence to possess or have under one's control a dead badger or any part of or anything derived from one. It is forbidden under section 5 to ring, tag or in any other way to mark a badger except by a person licensed to have it in his possession; to possess, or to control the possession of a live or a dead badger, or part of, or anything derived from a dead badger. It is also forbidden to ill-   **5–218**

---

[56] The 17th Annual Report of the Nature Conservancy Council (for 1990/91) included results of a survey showing that the badger population of Britain was approximately 250,000 individuals, living in about 43,000 groups. Access to 15.7 per cent of the main setts had been obstructed and digging had taken place at 10.5 per cent, so that interference was widespread. This survey pre-dates the Acts of 1991 and provides a baseline against which the effectiveness of the new legislation can be judged.

[57] s.1(1), (2).

[58] s.2(1), (2).

treat a badger, or to use badger tongs, or to use certain kinds of fire-arm against a badger.[59]

5–219 By provisions analogous to those of section 9(4) of the 1981 Act, section 3 makes it an offence intentionally or recklessly to damage or destroy a sett or part of a sett, to obstruct access to any entrance of a sett, to cause a dog to enter a sett, or to disturb a badger while it is occupying a sett. Setts are defined as "any structure or place which displays signs indicating current use by a badger".[60] This section is not, it will be noted, aimed exclusively at those intentionally interfering with setts in order to capture or kill badgers, but also anyone who in fact does so even if merely recklessly.[61] Such a situation can often arise in the context of agricultural or forestry operations, mineral extraction or other development. While this prohibition is subject to an exemption contained in section 8(3), whereby if a person is not guilty of damaging a badger set or disturbing a badger when in a sett or of obstructing access to a sett if he can show that his action was the incidental result of a lawful operation, he must also show that the interference of which he is accused could not reasonably have been avoided. Given that there is no relevant exemption at all to the offence of destroying a badger sett, and which can therefore only be done legitimately by virtue of a licence under section 10, the circumstances in which damage or other interference cannot reasonably be avoided will be rare.

5–220 Various exemptions are provided, for example, to allow mercy killing and the treatment of injured animals,[62] and the temporary stopping up of badger setts or interfering with them in the limited manner prescribed in section 8(4) to (9) for the purpose of fox hunting; in most cases unintentional lawful acts do not constitute an offence. Licences to carry out various acts, which would otherwise be an offence, may be granted under section 10 by the Conservation

---

[59] s.2(1).

[60] English Nature takes the view that a sett that is currently unoccupied but nevertheless still used intermittently falls within the definition, and clearly a purely temporary absence should not result in a sett becoming unoccupied for the purposes of the Act as this would allow its objects to be readily defeated. It would be a matter for evidence as to the period that must elapse since the last actual use (if that could be established with any precision) before a sett should be regarded as no longer in current (intermittent) use. To protect setts used intermittently would be consistent with the protection of any "structure or place" used by an animal for shelter or protection under section 9(4) of the 1981 Act (see paras. 5–193, 5–194).

[61] A person is reckless if he does an act which in fact involves obvious and serious risk of harmful consequences and either (i) he fails to give any thought to the possibility of there being any such risk, or (ii) having recognised that there is some risk involved, he nonetheless goes on to take it; *per* Lord Diplock in *R v. Laurence* [1982] A.C. 510 at 527; [1981] 1 All E.R. 974 at 982; also the *Metropolitan Police Commissioner v. Caldwell* [1982] A.C. 341 at 354, *sub nom R v. Caldwell* [1981] 1 All E.R. 961 at 967.

[62] ss.6 and 9.

Agencies and by the relevant Ministers responsible for agriculture. Subsections (1) to (3) of section 10 set out the purposes for which a licence may be granted; among what may be termed extraneous purposes are any development within the scope of the planning legislation (where the licence is granted by the relevant Conservation Agency)[63] and any agricultural or forestry operations involving water courses, flood defence or land drainage (where the licence is granted by the Minister of Agriculture or the relevant Secretary of State).[64] In those circumstances, a licence may only be granted by a Minister following consultation with and advice from the relevant Conservation Agency.

Licences may, and generally will be granted subject to appropriate conditions, and breach of any condition constitutes an offence.[65] Revocation of a licence may be made at any time, and is an appropriate sanction where a penalty for breach would be insufficient. By section 10(9), however, a licence shall not be unreasonably withheld or revoked. Nevertheless, in the case of withholding of a licence (which must, it is suggested, be understood as including refusing to grant a licence except on conditions that are unreasonable), no direct form of appeal is provided, and the only recourse therefore would be an application for judicial review, which would inevitably substantially delay any proposed development or other operations. This provision does however distinguish the grant of licences under the Protection of Badgers Act for the purposes of enabling or facilitating a development from the grant of licences under the Wildlife and Countryside Act 1981 where, as indicated above,[66] there is no provision for granting a licence in respect of actions prohibited by its section 9 in order to enable or facilitate a development if the only threat to the species involved arises or would arise from the carrying out of that development.

5–221

Where an application for a licence is made to carry out a development subject to planning control, English Nature requires extensive details to be provided with regard to the badger sett in question and stipulates as conditions:

5–222

(1) current detailed planning permission must be in force;
(2) a survey must have been commissioned to ascertain the status of any setts within the development area;
(3) the occupancy of the sett(s) has been established as well as can reasonably be expected;

---

[63] s.10(1)(d).
[64] s.10(2)(c), (d).
[65] s.10(8).
[66] para. 5–196.

    (4) the impact of the development on the sett(s) and on the badgers' social group(s) using them has being assessed;

    (5) appropriate mitigation works must have been agreed;

    (6) the methods to be used must deal with the sett effectively, legally and humanely;

    (7) the work must be carried out and supervised at all stages by suitably qualified experts.

5–223   Further, there is a presumption against the issue of licences to interfere with the sett during the breeding season of December 1 to June 30,[67] and it is in practice becoming increasingly common for licences to stipulate the creation of artificial replacement setts.[68]

5–224   The discovery that badgers could carry bovine tuberculosis is recognised by provisions exempting actions from the prohibitions of sections 1(1) and 3 if they are necessary for the prevention of serious damage to land, crops, poultry or other forms of property.[69] However, this exemption will not apply if the person concerned has had time to apply for a licence to kill or take a badger and either has failed to do so or his licence application has been determined.[70]

5–225   In addition to the usual powers of enforcement, courts may order the destruction of dogs used in committing an offence and disqualify offenders from keeping dogs.[71] They may also order the forfeiture of any weapon or article used in connection with the offence, and must order forfeiture of any badger or badger skin in respect of which an offence has been committed.[72]

Conservation of Seals

5–226   The conservation of the two British species of seal[73] is achieved by the Conservation of Seals Act, 1970.[74] This Act is unique among British conservation legislation in that, for the grey seal at least, earlier legislation had already raised numbers from a low level to well beyond the level at which the species could be considered endangered. The purpose of the 1970 Act is therefore to ensure the maintenance and management of the seal population at an appropriate level, rather than to reverse a decline in numbers and to prevent possible extinction.

---

[67] Which English Nature regards as potentially cruel ill-treatment within the prohibition of s.2(1) and as such incapable of being licensed.
[68] Which may cost up to £20,000.
[69] ss.7(1), 8(1).
[70] ss.7(2), 8(2).
[71] s.13(1).
[72] s.12(4).
[73] The grey seal and the common seal; the grey seal is in fact the more abundant.
[74] s.10 of which was amended by Sched. 7, para. 7, of the 1981 Act.

Section 1 of the Act forbids the poisoning of seals and the use of   **5–227**
certain types of firearm. Section 2 sets close seasons for both the grey
seal and the common seal, and section 3 empowers the Secretary of
State to establish sanctuary areas for seals by order. Offenders, their
vehicles and their boats may be searched and any seal, seal skin,
firearm, ammunition or poison found may be seized.[75] Where an
offence is committed at sea, the case will be taken to the court of the
place where the offender was found or first brought after committing
the offence.[76] The Secretary of State is empowered to make very
substantial modifications to the provisions of the 1970 Act[77] and these
powers have been used on an *ad hoc* basis from time to time.[78]

Exemptions are provided by section 9 to allow the mercy killing of   **5–228**
seals and the taking of injured seals so that they might be treated and
subsequently released. They also allow the killing of seals to prevent
damage to fishing nets or fishing tackle or to the fish within the net by
the owner of the nets or tackle or his agent. The "unavoidable killing
or injuring of any seal as an incidental result of a lawful action" is also
not an offence.

Licences to kill or take seals are issued by the Secretary of State   **5–229**
under the provisions of section 10 (as amended), after consultation
with the Conservation Agencies, for scientific or educational purposes
(including zoos), for the prevention of damage to fisheries, for the
elimination of population surpluses, for the use of such surpluses as a
resource, and for the conservation of the flora and fauna of any
designated conservation site. Licences may be revoked at any time;
their issue for any NNR, MNR, SSSI or any area subject to an NCO,
requires the consent of the Conservation Agency, unless the licences
relate to the prevention of damage to fisheries.[79]

The Secretary of State, after consultation with the Natural Environ-   **5–230**
ment Research Council (NERC), can authorise entry to any land for
the killing or taking of seals to prevent damage to fisheries. The NERC
is required to provide the Secretary of State with scientific advice on
the management of seal populations.[80]

---

[75] ss.4, 5 and 6.
[76] s.7.
[77] ss.1, 3, 10, 11 and 14.
[78] During the viral epidemic which affected common seals in the eastern North Sea in
1988, s.3 of the 1970 Act was invoked to prevent any killing of either species of seal in
England and Wales, and any killing of the common seal in Scotland, except under
licence.
[79] s.10(3), (4).
[80] The Nature Conservancy Council Act, 1973, by Sched. 1, para. 10, transferred the
responsibility under s.10 for advising on the issue of licences to NCC, but left the
responsibility under s.11 for advising on direct Government action in relation to seal
populations with the NERC.

5–231   As noted above, the 1970 Act and its predecessors, when seen purely from the viewpoint of wildlife protection, are unique among conservation legislation in that they have achieved their objective; in the case of the grey seal, the population in British waters has risen, more or less exponentially, from about 500 animals at the turn of the century to in excess of 100,000 today. However, success has brought its own problems, for it has long been argued that the protection of grey seals has been too successful. As early as 1962, when the population was only around 30,000 animals, it was accepted that control was required to keep the number of seals in balance with the competing fishery and other interests.[81] Accordingly, in that year, seal pups were culled on Orkney and, in 1963, the culling was extended to the Farne Islands. The Farne cull was more visible than that on Orkney and triggered off adverse public reactions which have become more hostile towards seal culling ever since.[82] This has created problems in the implementation of the 1970 Act for, over the years, it has become politically unacceptable to license action to prevent damage to fisheries or to eliminate population surpluses, as provided for by section 10(1)(c)(ii) and (iii), whatever the practical realities. Meanwhile the grey seal populations (and the problems they cause) have continued to rise.

Protection of Cetaceans

5–232   Cetaceans, that is the members of the whale and dolphin family, are given some protection by Regulation 348/81.[83] This makes imports of the commercially most significant products of cetaceans subject to an import licensing system, operated by a committee of representatives of the Member States and the Commission. The products thus controlled are listed in the Annex to the Regulation and include, for example, meat that is salted, in brine, dried or smoked, fats and oils, and a variety of forms of leather and leather goods. The list of products in the Annex may be extended by a qualified majority of the Council of

---

[81] "Report of the Nature Conservancy for the year ended 30th September 1962", p.52.
[82] The continued public concern with the culling of seal pups led to the issue of EC Directive 83/129 ([1983] O.J. L91) prohibiting the import into the EC of skins of whitecoat pups of harp seals and of pups of hooded seals, which had traditionally been hunted in Canada. The prohibition was of temporary effect pending the introduction of protective measures by the Canadian government, and the Directive only applied from October 1, 1983 to October 1, 1985. It was implemented in the UK by an Order (S.I. 1983 No. 1609) made under the Endangered Species (Import and Export) Act 1976, and which also ceased to have effect on October 1, 1985.
[83] [1981] O.J. L39.

Ministers. Member States may independently take measures concerning whales or other cetacean products not covered by the Regulation for the protection of the species.[84]

Dolphins and porpoises are protected under the Wildlife and Countryside Act 1981 against intentional killing, injury, capture and disturbance, as described earlier. Additional international conservation measures can be expected from the coming into effect of the Agreement on the Conservation of Small Cetaceans of the Baltic and North Seas (ASCOBANS).[85] The Government has announced that it and the Irish Government are liaising with a view to extending the Agreement to the Irish Sea.

5–233

EC and International Provisions for Conservation

General Considerations

Nature conservation originated, and for many years was operated, on a national basis. As interest in nature spread across Europe, national organisations, voluntary at first but later governmental, were established to secure the future of this aspect of each individual country's heritage. Each country, in turn, made what it considered to be the most appropriate statutory provisions for the protection of its own flora, fauna and geological features consistent with the interests of those living on and from the land, and reflecting the legal system, the structure of government, the nature of the wildlife resource, the threats to which this resource is subject, and the attitudes of the public towards wildlife, in the country in question.

5–234

Wildlife, however, pays no heed to national boundaries, so that its conservation in a piecemeal fashion, country by country, requires co-ordination if it is to be fully effective. For instance, many birds migrate annually through several countries, so that their protection cannot be secured by one country alone. For the same species to be rigorously protected as a rarity in Britain, while being enthusiastically hunted in the Eastern Mediterranean, is of little net benefit to the species. Although the need to solve such problems through international co-operation has long been recognised, little progress was made until recently, at least as far as species of no economic value were concerned. One reason of the delay no doubt lies in the need for the

5–235

---

[84] Art. 3.
[85] The UK ratified the Agreement in July 1993; it came into force on March 29, 1994.

widespread establishment of national organisations both willing and able to enforce conservation agreements with some consistency. Now, however, all governments in Western Europe support nature conservation and the statutory provisions for nature conservation in Britain have now to accommodate the requirements of a number of international conventions and EC legislation.

5–236   In Britain today, despite the existence of these broader measures, the rationale and, more especially, the mental attitudes which underlie the practice of nature conservation remain firmly based on the national perspective, with the European or international considerations being something of a "bolted-on" afterthought. Common continental species whose distribution just extends into Britain continue to be assessed as rarities (as if continental Europe did not exist) and, where a site has received multiple designations, it is the domestic designation which is still regarded as substantive, whereas the supra-national designation is seen merely as an additional mark of prestige. The status of the supra-national designations has not been enhanced by the procedures used in their application. Instead of being based on a single, systematic and Europe-wide reassessment of all candidate sites, it is in practice customary for such designations to be awarded through the piecemeal endorsement of nominations made by each of the participating countries almost entirely on the basis of purely national evaluations. This is however due to change somewhat as a result of the adoption of the EC Habitats Directive 92/43,[86] discussed below, which was to be implemented by May 21, 1994. At the time of writing, the Conservation (Natural Habitats, etc.) Regulations 1994 designed to implement the Directive are before Parliament.

5–237   In Britain, supra-national conservation designations originate in proposals made by the Conservation Agencies to the government; the Agencies themselves have no powers to designate such sites. The Agencies' role is to seek out candidate sites, bring them to the Government's attention, and make the best case for their designation. The candidate localities they put forward almost always already carry the British conservation designation of SSSI. However, the criteria for selecting such candidates can be pitched at any level, even one sufficiently low to allow a super-abundance of proposals.[87]

5–238   The role of the Government, however, is very different from that of the Conservation Agencies, for it has to take a broader and very much

---

[86] [1992] O.J. L206.

[87] Thus, each Member State must designate Special Protection Areas for Birds under paras 1 and 2 of Art. 4 of the Birds Directive 79/409 (discussed in paras. 5–245 to 5–257). A DoE press release of March 5, 1993 stated that 69 SPAs had been designated in the UK as at that date, covering over 194,000 ha, with a further 165 SSSIs under consideration for designation as additional SPAs.

more balanced view. Indeed, it is explicitly required to do so when considering the measures to be taken, including the designation of sites, under EC Directives, for these typically require Member States to "take the requisite measures [for conservation] . . . ., while taking account of economic and recreational requirements". Further, the Government, in coming to its balanced decision, inevitably sets very high standards, for designation under an EC Directive, once made, will be permanent and immutable and any breach of the obligations entailed is likely to lead to proceedings against it in the European Court of Justice.

Many of the areas quite properly put forward as candidates by the   **5–239**
Conservation Agencies will be seen by Government to be crucial for economic and social development (*e.g.* most of the undeveloped land along the Thames Estuary) so that their designation would create major practical and political problems. That is not however a sufficient reason for failing to make appropriate designations, if otherwise the survival and reproduction of a species would be put at risk. The balancing exercise is only legitimate in so far as a viable number of the relevant species and the habitats they require are maintained in any event. Other candidate areas will have little potential except for nature conservation and these can be designated without detriment to any other interest. In such circumstances, it is not surprising that, of the 310 definite and possible candidates for designation as Special Protection Areas under the Birds Directive, the Government, over the period 1980/91, saw fit to nominate only 40.

In consequence, sites proposed for supra-national designation are   **5–240**
much commoner than sites which have actually been designated, especially in those areas where conflicts between nature conservation and economic development are likely to arise.

There are currently no special provisions for the conservation of   **5–241**
supra-national sites; in Britain they are notified as SSSIs and so receive the same statutory protection as any other such site (and no more) under the powers given by sections 28 and 29 of the 1981 Act. Some, in addition, have been declared as NNRs. However, they differ from other SSSIs in that the Government is responsible to an outside body for ensuring their conservation. As will be seen, while the legal and administrative framework may in practice permit the supra-national obligations to be met, there are no binding constraints in UK domestic law that may be enforced to ensure this will happen; consequently the United Kingdom[88] is open to challenge for failure satisfactorily to implement its international obligations in domestic law.

---

[88] Along with many, if not all, other Member States.

Wetlands Protection—The Ramsar Convention

5–242   The Ramsar Convention[89] was signed by the UK Government in 1973, and ratified in 1976. The Convention was originally intended to be particularly directed towards wildfowl, but there has been subsequent pressure to apply it to wetlands of value for other groups, including amphibia, reptiles, fish and insects. The areas to which it can be applied include "marine water" to a depth of six metres at low tide, and this can be extended in certain cases, so that a designation under the Convention can extend further seaward than an SSSI designation.[90]

5–243   Under the Convention each participating country must "designate suitable wetlands[91] within its territory",[92] promote the conservation of the designated sites and, "as far as possible", the "wise use" of all their wetlands.[93] Each country must report any "changes" affecting its wetlands. Each country undertakes to promote the conservation of wetlands and waterfowl and where it "in its own urgent national interest, deletes or restricts the boundaries of wetlands" listed under the Convention, it must bring under protection replacement areas of wetland.[94]

5–244   The selection of candidate sites depends on criteria amplified by guidelines. These have been developed from Article 2(2) of the Convention and are revised at the three-yearly conferences of the representatives of the signatory Governments; in Britain, the minutes require ratification by the DoE. Most of the criteria are highly subjective and make much reference to the selection of "particularly good representative examples" of various types of wetland, "appreciable assemblages" of rare species, and habitats of "special value"; however some prescribe that either fixed numbers of waterfowl, or a fixed proportion of the population of a species should use a wetland before it becomes eligible. These latter criteria are susceptible to an *extensio ad absurdum* for virtually any area, provided it is large enough, will fulfil such numerical requirements. Moreover, the criteria cannot test an alleged need to extend a Ramsar site, for if they are met by the

---

[89] More properly, The Convention on Wetlands of International Importance Especially as Waterfowl Habitat, adopted at Ramsar in Iran in 1971.

[90] A DoE press release of July 28, 1994 stated that, as at that date, 90 SPAs had been designated in the UK, covering nearly 300,000 ha, and that 80 UK Ramsar sites, covering over 339,000 ha, had been listed, including one in the Turks and Caicos Islands.

[91] "Wetland" and "waterfowl" are defined in Art. 1.

[92] Art. 2.

[93] Art. 3

[94] Art. 4.

original site then they will automatically be fulfilled by the site when extended.

Special Protection Areas for Birds—The EC Birds Directive 79/409

Special Protection Areas ("SPAs") are designated under the provi-   5–245
sions of EEC Directive 79/409 on the Conservation of Wild Birds,[95]
commonly known as the Birds Directive. Compliance with its provisions is largely secured in Britain by Part I of the 1981 Act. Even though
UK legislation does not fully implement the Directive in every respect,
its requirements must largely be given practical effect by organs of
government, such as planning authorities and the Conservation
Agencies. It is directly binding on such bodies, who are accordingly
legally required to apply its provisions, even where—indeed particularly where—relevant UK legislation is lacking or arguably inconsistent. The full text of the Directive forms Annex C to DoE Circular 27/87
and its application to Scotland is defined in SDD Circular 1/88.
Paragraphs 20 to 27 of 27/87 relate to the Birds Directive and to Special
Protection Areas.

The Directive provides for the protection, management and control   5–246
of all species of naturally occurring birds in the wild state in the EC,
including their eggs, their nests and their habitats.[96] The Directive
thus goes further than Part I of the 1981 Act which makes no explicit
provision for the conservation of birds' habitats which, presumably, is
to be achieved by the operation of the SSSI system of Part II.

Article 2 requires Member States to "take the requisite measures to   5–247
maintain the population of the species referred to in Article 1 (*i.e.* all
those naturally occurring in the wild within the EEC) at a level which
corresponds in particular to ecological, scientific and cultural requirements, while taking account of economic and recreational requirements". Article 3 requires Member States to take "requisite measures
to preserve, maintain or re-establish a sufficient diversity and area of
habitats" for these species. Sites thus cannot be assessed in isolation,
but must be seen in the overall context to which they contribute. The
"measures" to be taken include the "creation of protected areas".

Article 4 imposes additional requirements for special conservation   5–248
measures for the habitats of 74 relatively vulnerable species of birds
listed in Annex I to the Directive to ensure their survival and
reproduction. In determining these measures account is to be taken of

---

[95] [1979] O.J. L103.
[96] Though Greenland was part of the EEC in 1979, it was specifically excluded from the
application of the Directive by Art.1(3).

species in danger of extinction, those vulnerable to specific changes in their habitat, those that are rare whether because of small populations or restricted local distribution, and other species requiring particular attention for reasons of the specific nature of their habitat. Article 4 further requires Member States to "classify in particular the most suitable territories in number and size as special protection areas for the conservation of these species, taking into account their protection requirements in the geographical sea and land area where this Directive applies". Paragraph (2) of Article 4 requires additional like measures to be taken for regularly occurring migratory species not listed in Annex I, that need protection in the EEC as regards "their breeding, moulting and wintering areas and staging posts along their migration routes". Particular attention is to be given to wetlands in this connection.

5–249   These sites to be designated under Article 4 are also not to be assessed in isolation, but the contribution each makes must be evaluated within an overall context; Article 4(3) requires the Commission to co-ordinate measures to ensure the SPAs set up under this Article "form a coherent whole which meets the protection requirements of these [Annex I] species" in the EEC. Within the SPAs, Member States must, by Article 4(4), take appropriate steps to avoid pollution, deterioration of habitats or any disturbances affecting the birds, in so far as these would be significant having regard to the objectives of Article 4. Even outside the SPAs, Member States "shall also strive to avoid pollution or deterioration of habitats". As will be seen, this Article 4(4) imposes very severe restraints on the subsequent activities that may take place in an SPA. In answer to a written question from a member of the European Parliament on the meaning of "disturbances" in the context of Article 4(4), the then (acting) Commissioner for the Environment Karel van Miert stated:[97]

> "Significant disturbances should be taken to mean any phenomenon entailing a substantial negative change in the population dynamics or eco-ethological characteristics of populations of sensitive bird species living in protected areas."

5–250   Unlike Ramsar sites, for which there are internationally agreed selection criteria, each country is free to determine the basis on which it chooses its SPAs. In Britain, criteria recently employed by the Nature Conservancy Council for selecting candidate SPAs require that a site should regularly hold 1 per cent of a species' world population, 1 per

---

[97] Written question 451/92; [1992] O.J. C289.

cent of its European population or 1 per cent of its biogeographical population; or should hold significant numbers of a globally threatened species; or be one of five most important sites in its region (there are 11 such regions in the UK), or one of the 100 most important in Europe for a species threatened in Europe. As noted above, these criteria for candidate SPAs are pitched at a sufficiently low level to allow a super-abundance of candidates. There have been strong suggestions that the Government would like more rigorous scientific justification of candidate sites.[98]

The Government's difficulties over the designation of SPAs were exacerbated by a case in the European Court of Justice[99] brought by the Commission against Germany for allowing development within an SPA. This case (generally known as the *Leybucht* case) concerned a wetland site in Lower Saxony of admitted importance—it had been listed by Germany as being of international importance under the Ramsar convention (Article 4(2) being applicable, therefore) as well as having been notified by Germany to the Commission as an SPA under Article 4(3). Various coastal defence works were undertaken involving the construction of a dyke within or adjacent to the SPA which would have the effect of reducing its area. The work additionally provided access to a port for some local fishing vessels. The principal issues raised were: **5–251**

(1) Can the area of an SPA ever be reduced, and if so in what circumstances and under what conditions?

(2) What discretion (if any) is available to a Member State to take into account interests other than achieving the objectives of the Directive when considering action that might conflict with those objectives?

(3) Can deleterious changes to an SPA be rendered permissible by making other beneficial changes?

In assessing these it must be noted that whereas Article 2 of the Directive invites Member States to take account of economic and recreational requirements in determining measures for conserving the populations of wild birds generally, Article 4, relating to conservation of the vulnerable species in Annex I, had no such qualification when adopted. Though one has now been inserted, the judgment remains very relevant. It was argued by Germany, which was supported by the **2–252**

---

[98] It is understood that the DoE has commissioned research on means to discriminate among the candidate sites for which SPA status is proposed.

[99] Case C-57/89, *The Commission of the European Communities v. Federal Republic of Germany*: [1990] 3 C.M.L.R. 651.

United Kingdom, that Article 4 should be understood as importing the same degree of discretion in relation to activities in SPAs designated under that Article. Although on the facts the Commission's case against Germany was not upheld, on this vital issue of discretion the Court rejected the German and British arguments.

In its judgment the court stated:

"18.   Thus, in order to resolve the present case, it is necessary to answer a number of questions of principle concerning Member States' obligations with regard to the management of special protection areas under Article 4(4) of the Directive. It must be established, therefore, whether, and if so under what conditions, Member States are entitled to reduce the size of a special protection area, and under what circumstances other interests may be taken into account.

19.   As regards Member States' powers to alter in this way a decision classifying a territory as a special protection area, no reduction in the size of a protected area is expressly envisaged in the provisions of the Directive.

20.   Although it is true that Member States enjoy a certain margin of discretion in selecting the most appropriate territories to be classified as special protection areas under Article 4(1) of the Directive, they cannot exercise a similar margin of discretion under Article 4(4) of the Directive in altering or reducing the size of such areas, since they themselves have acknowledged in their declarations that those areas offer the most appropriate living conditions for the species listed in Annex I to the Directive. Otherwise Member States could unilaterally evade their obligations under Article 4(4) of the Directive with regard to special protection areas.

21.   This interpretation of Article 4(4) is moreover confirmed by the ninth recital of the Directive, which stresses the special importance the Directive attaches to special conservation measures concerning the habitats of birds listed in Annex I in order to ensure their survival and reproduction in their area of distribution. This means that a Member State is entitled to reduce the size of a special protection area only in exceptional circumstances.

22.   Such circumstances must relate to a public interest which is greater than the ecological interest covered by the Directive. In this connection, the interests listed in Article 2 of the Directive, namely economic and recreational, cannot be taken into account. Moreover, as the court has stated in its Judgments of July 8, 1987,

256

Case 247/85, *Commission v. Belgium*: [1987] E.C.R. 3029, and Case 262/85, *Commission v. Italy*: [1987] E.C.R. 3073, this provision does not constitute an autonomous derogation from the system of protection laid down in the Directive.

23. As regards the grounds pleaded in the present case, it must be stated that the danger of floods and protection of the coastline provide sufficiently genuine reasons to justify the coastal and dyke improvement works provided such measures are kept to the strict minimum and involve only the smallest possible reduction in the size of the special protection area.

24. In this connection, however, it should be mentioned that as regards that part of the project which relates to the Leyhorn area, considerations relating not only to coastal protection but also to the desire to provide access to the port for Greetsiel fishing vessels influenced the line of the dyke. As regards the principles for interpreting Article 4(4) of the Directive set out above, taking such an interest into account is in principle incompatible with the requirements laid down in that provision.

25. It should be stressed, however, that that part of the project also involves specific positive effects for the birds' habitats. Indeed, the works will make possible the closure of two navigation channels which cross the Leybucht so that the area will enjoy complete peace. Furthermore, the planning decision provides for strict protection of the Leyhorn area. The dyke which formerly protected the site at Hauener Hooge will be opened up to re-expose a long stretch of land to tidal movement and thus lead to the formation of salt water meadows which will be of considerable ecological value.

26. Thus it was possible to take the wish to ensure the survival of the fishing port of Greetsiel into account in order to justify the decision regarding the line of the new dyke because there were the above-mentioned ecological compensations and only for that reason.

27. Lastly, it should be noted that the harm caused by the construction work itself has not exceeded what is necessary. The data on the number of avocets in this section of the Wattenmeer show, moreover, that there has been no significant alteration in the evolution of the population of this species within the meaning of Article 4(4) of the Directive during that period. The Commission has not provided any other material regarding the evolution of populations of protected species.

28. It follows the foregoing that the application must be dismissed."

5–253   This judgment thus provides the following answers to the three questions posed above (in paragraph 5–251) in relation to the Directive as originally adopted:

(1)   It may be permissible to reduce the size of an SPA designated under Article 4, but only to respond to an overriding public interest greater than the conservation interests forming the objective of the Directive. Flood prevention and public safety may in a particular case amount to such an over-riding interest; merely economic and recreational interests cannot (though since amendment of the Directive they can in most, but not all, circumstances). Even where there is an over-riding public interest the effects on the SPA in meeting that interest must be minimised.

(2)   In meeting a public interest, the fact that some other interest may also be served, which would not of itself justify the action in issue, is not relevant. That other interest may also be addressed therefore, provided that doing so has no additional impact on the SPA.

(3)   In principle the area of an SPA designated under Article 4 is sacrosanct. However, the requirement of Article 4(4) is to avoid impacts on the SPA "in so far as these would be significant" having regard to the objectives of Article 4. It may therefore in a particular case be that changes to the area are perceptible but not significant in terms of conservation of the relevant vulnerable bird species. In such a case there will be no breach of Article 4(4). Accordingly action that would be harmful to the SPA on its own may be legitimate if its impact is wholly counteracted by other operations made at the same time.

5–254   These effects of the Court's judgment were to some extent modified by Article 7 of the EC Habitats Directive 92/43 discussed below, which provides that obligations under the first, critical sentence of Article 4(4) are to be replaced by obligations arising from Article 6(2), (3) and (4) of the later Directive in respect of SPAs designated under Article 4(1) or recognised under Article 4(2). This change is to have effect from the date of implementation of the Habitats Directive, *i.e.* May 21, 1994. Although Article 6(2) itself substantially repeats the first sentence of Article 4(4) of the Birds Directive (adapted so as to apply to plant and animal species generally, though reference to "avoiding pollution" is omitted), it is subject to Article 2, paragraph 3 of which states:

"3.   Measures taken pursuant to this Directive shall take account of economic, social and cultural requirements and regional and local characteristics."

Thus the criteria of Article 2 of the Birds Directive have in effect been made applicable, and indeed somewhat extended.

While this change consequently gives wider discretion for Member   **5–255** States to approve projects affecting SPAs, the exercise of that discretion remains controlled by the other requirements of the Habitats Directive, notably that of Article 2, paragraph 2, namely:

"2.   Measures taken pursuant to this Directive shall be designed to maintain or restore, at favourable conservation status, natural habitats and species of wild fauna and flora of Community interest."

It is by no means clear what is to be understood by "measures taken   **5–256** *pursuant* to this Directive". On the face of it, it is difficult to see how a project intended purely to address economic, social or cultural requirements extraneous to any SPA could be such a measure. Nevertheless, Article 6(3) explicitly relates to "any plan or project not directly connected with or necessary to the management of [a designated site] but likely to have a significant effect thereon, either individually or in combination with other plants or projects". This paragraph requires such a proposal to be subject to appropriate assessment of its implications for the site having regard to the site's conservation objectives. The competent national authorities must have regard to the conclusions of the assessment, and only agree the proposed plan or project if they have ascertained that it will not adversely affect the integrity of the site (having obtained the opinion of the general public, if appropriate). In the United Kingdom, the requirements are to be met by regulations 48 and 49 of the Conservation (Natural Habitats, etc.) Regulations 1994.

Paragraph 4 of Article 6 provides for situations where a site will be   **5–257** adversely affected by proposed works, and sanctions these where the action must be carried out "for imperative reasons of over-riding public interest, including those of a social or economic nature". However, in such cases, the Member State is required to take compensatory measures "necessary to ensure that the overall coherence of Natura 2000 is protected".[1] Interests of a social or economic nature may therefore ordinarily be taken into account, provided always that they amount to "imperative reasons of overriding public

---

[1] "Natura 2000" is a coherent network of special areas of conservation to be set up under Art. 3 of the Habitats Directive.

interest" and suitable compensatory measures are adopted, but the second sentence of paragraph 4 of Article 6 disallows even this where the site concerns what is referred to as a priority natural habitat type and/or a priority species. Priority natural habitat types are those in danger of disappearance, and priority species are endangered species.[2] In such a case, the only considerations which may be taken into account are those relating to human health or public safety, beneficial consequences of primary importance for the environment or, subject to an opinion from the European Commission, "other imperative reasons of over-riding public interest". Consequently in such cases the decision in *Leybucht* is directly applicable in full.

The Berne Convention on the Conservation of European Wildlife and Habitats

5–258   The Committee of Ministers of the Council of Europe agreed the text of the Berne Convention in June 1979 and it came into force on June 1, 1982. The United Kingdom has both signed and ratified the Convention; the statutory provisions for compliance are made by the 1981 Act.

The Convention seeks to promote the conservation of wild flora and fauna and their natural habitats, especially where this requires the co-operation of several states; particular emphasis is placed on rare and endangered species. Article 2 follows that of the Birds Directive in requiring the signatory countries to maintain "the population of wild flora and fauna at, or adapt it to, a level which corresponds in particular to ecological, scientific and cultural requirements, while taking account of economic and recreational requirements"; Article 3 requires signatories to promote national policies for nature conservation, to have regard for conservation when devising policies for development or against pollution, and to inform the public of the need for conservation.

5–259   The habitats of the rare and endangered species listed in Appendices 1 and 2 have to be conserved under the provisions of Article 4 and in Articles 5 and 6 (which correspond to sections 9 and 13 of the 1981 Act), the plant species themselves are to be protected from being picked, collected, cut or uprooted, and the animal species from being killed, captured, or disturbed, especially in the breeding, rearing and hibernation seasons. Neither plants nor animals, whether alive or

---

[2] Excluding any whose natural range is marginal in the European Community, and which are not endangered or vulnerable in the Western Palaearctic region.

dead, are to be made the objects of trade. Article 10 urges co-ordination in the conservation of migratory species.[3]

World Heritage Sites

The Convention Concerning the Protection of the World Cultural and Natural Heritage was adopted by UNESCO on November 16, 1962, came into force on December 17, 1975, and was ratified by the United Kingdom in 1984. It established a World Heritage Committee to compile a list of the world's most outstanding localities ("World Heritage Sites") by reason of *inter alia* the "superlative values of international significance" of their plants, animals or rocks. Work on compiling the list has been slow and is still very much in progress.   5–260

Few British sites will qualify for designation as World Heritage Sites on nature conservation grounds. The procedure for designation commences with proposals made by the Conservation Agencies and their equivalents to the Government; these are then collated and considered and, if accepted, are passed on to the World Heritage Committee and UNESCO who have the powers to add proposed sites to the World Heritage List.[4] So far, in the United Kingdom, only St. Kilda and the Giant's Causeway have been designated as World Heritage Sites (as from January 1, 1987), but efforts have been made to induce the government to submit other areas to the Committee, including the Lake District, the Wash, the North Norfolk Coast and the Cairngorms. After six years of pressure, the Cairngorms were placed on a "tentative UK list" of proposals in 1990.   5–261

Special Areas Of Conservation—The EC Habitats Directive 92/43

The EC Council Directive on the Conservation of Natural Habitats and of Wild Fauna and Flora.[5] (the "Habitats" Directive) was adopted on May 21, 1992 and required national implementation by May 21,   5–262

---

[3] Experience suggests that this Convention is seldom cited in considering nature conservation issues. Perhaps its main claim to fame rests on its being the cause of the inclusion of the great crested newt, which is rare in Europe but not in Britain, in Sched. 5 of the 1981 Act.

[4] There are thus several categories of "Proposed World Heritage Site": firstly, those proposed to, but not accepted by the Government and, secondly, those proposed to, and accepted by the Government, but not accepted by the World Heritage Committee and by UNESCO. In addition, the Conservation Agencies themselves receive proposals from other bodies, thus creating a third category of even less significance. The status of any "Proposed World Heritage Site" thus requires careful investigation.

[5] [1992] O.J. L206.

1994.[6] The main aim of the Directive is described in the recitals as being "to promote the maintenance of biodiversity, taking account of economic, social, cultural and regional requirements". The Directive is also intended to make a contribution to the general objective of sustainable development, and recognises that "the maintenance of biodiversity may in certain cases require the maintenance, or indeed the encouragement, of human activities."

5–263   According to a further recital, since natural habitats are continuing to deteriorate and, since an increasing number of wild species are seriously threatened, often by "transboundary" threats, measures are required to conserve the Community's natural heritage. These are to provide for the creation of "a coherent European ecological network" of "Special Areas of Conservation" (SACs) into which all sites designated under European legislation, now or in the future, will have to be incorporated. These SACs will be designated by the Member States, but provision is made to allow the Community, in exceptional cases, to designate as SACs sites which have not been proposed for designation by the Member State in which they lie, but which the Community feels it is essential to conserve.

5–264   Provisions are made to share the financial burden of conserving this network, to establish a system of monitoring and inspection, to carry out conservation-related research and other scientific work, to establish a "regulatory committee to assist the Commission in the implementation of this Directive and in particular when decisions on Community co-financing are taken", for measures concerning the introduction and re-introduction of species, and for disseminating information about the Directive.

5–265   Article 1 defines the terms used in the Directive. Many of these, and their definitions, are somewhat unconventional when compared with British usage. Certain of the objectives of this Directive may be appreciated by reference to the definitions of when the "conservation status" of habitats and species are to be regarded as "favourable". Thus the conservation status of a natural habitat will be taken as "favourable" when:

—   its natural range and areas it covers within that range are stable or increasing; and
—   the specific structure and functions which are necessary for its long-term maintenance exist and are likely to continue to exist for the foreseeable future; and
—   the conservation status of its typical species is favourable.

[6] As to which see para. 5–132.

The conservation status of a species is to be taken as "favourable"   **5–266**
when:

- population dynamics data on the species concerned indicate
  that it is maintaining itself on a long-term basis as a viable
  component of its natural habitats; and
- the natural range of the species is neither being reduced nor
  is likely to be reduced for the foreseeable future; and
- there is, and will probably continue to be, a sufficiently large
  habitat to maintain its populations on a long-term basis.

Article 2 briefly defines the conservation and management object-   **5–267**
ives of the Directive and requires in paragraph 3 that "Measures taken
pursuant to this Directive shall take account of economic, social and
cultural requirements and regional and local characteristics". It is
noteworthy that this Directive follows its predecessors in requiring
that a balanced view be taken of competing interests in the land.[7]

Articles 3 to 11 relate to the conservation of natural habitats and the   **5–268**
habitats of species. Article 3 requires the setting up of a "coherent
European ecological network" (to be known as Natura 2000), whose
sites are to contain the habitat types set out in Annex I and the habitats
of the species listed in Annex II; the sites designated under the Birds
Directive will be incorporated within this new network. The sites in
the network will be designated as "Special Areas of Conservation";
selection will be by Member States and will reflect the proportion of
the particular habitats and of species populations within each state's
territory.

"Features of the landscape which are of major importance for wild   **5–269**
flora and fauna" are to be maintained and, where appropriate,
developed, as is required by Article 10. Particular mention is made in
Article 10 of features that are essential for the migration, dispersal and
genetic exchange of wild species, by virtue either of their linear and
continuous structure (such as river banks and hedgerows and other
field boundaries) or of their function as "stepping stones" (such as
ponds and small woods).

The requirement that the habitats of the protected species are to be   **5–270**
conserved, and not just the plants and animals themselves (and the
places where the latter shelter), goes beyond the provisions of section
9 of the 1981 Act, especially as the "habitat of a species" is defined[8] as
"an environment defined by specific abiotic and biotic factors, in
which the species lives at any stage of its biological cycle". Further,

---

[7] For a discussion on the implications of this paragraph for the Birds Directive 79/409,
see paras. 5–254 to 5–256.
[8] Art. 1(f).

there would seem to be no provisions in British conservation law relating to the further innovation of requiring the maintenance, and possibly the improvement, of "features of the landscape", other than section 16 of the 1949 Act which provides for such operations on NNRs.

5–271   Article 4 requires Member States to use the criteria set out in Annex III to select the SACs containing the habitats and species listed in Annexes I and II, which they propose incorporation into the coherent European ecological network. Such proposals, incorporating boundary maps and statements of interest, are to be submitted to the Commission within three years of May 21, 1994 and a draft list of sites of Community importance is to be adopted by the Commission within six years. All sites included in this list are to be designated as SACs within the six year period. Provisions for consultations by the Commission in cases where a Member State fails to propose some site of particular value are made in Article 5; should these fail, the matter will be referred to the Council. While Article 5 may assist in correcting deficiencies in "exceptional cases" (sic), the confrontation that invoking its procedures would make inevitable is unlikely to be conducive either to ready resort to this provision, or to successful management of any site designated pursuant to it.[9]

5–272   Although Annex III is entitled "Criteria for selecting sites . . . ", in fact it merely lists factors which have to be taken into consideration in site selection, such as "Degree of representativity (sic)", "Size and density of the population", and "Relative value of the site at a national level", and not criteria. No thresholds for acceptance or rejection are prescribed. As a result, the selection of SACs will be highly subjective, a characteristic they will share with a majority of SSSIs.

5–273   Article 6, which requires Member States to conserve their SACs through adopting appropriate statutory, administrative and contractual measures and through planning, has been considered in paragraphs 5–245 to 5–257 above in connection with the Birds Directive. Its most notable provision is the obligation, where an SAC has to be damaged for reasons of "overriding public interest, including those of a social or economic nature", to make appropriate compensation "to ensure that the overall coherence of Natura 2000 is protected". Article 9 provides for the "declassification" of SACs where the "surveillance" required by Article 11 reveals that they have lost their value to

---

[9] While perhaps unavoidable politically, it may prove unfortunate that the Directive retains the procedures whereby what is intended to be a coherent European network of conserved sites is once again to be selected piecemeal on the basis of site evaluations carried out within a national context. The whole British experience of nature conservation shows that, in the selection of sites, coherence is not promoted by this particular form of subsidiarity.

conservation through natural causes. In making such a provision, the Directive joins the 1949 Act which was previously unique in conservation legislation in making provision[10] for the de-designation of conserved sites.

Articles 12 to 16 are concerned with the protection of species and, in particular, with the "strict protection" of the species listed in Annex IV.[11] This section of the Directive contains broad prohibitions on the killing, taking, disturbance, etc., of protected animals and plants in a manner somewhat similar to Part I of the 1981 Act. In like fashion it follows, in Article 14, with provision for permitting procedures to allow, subject to conditions, the taking from the wild of the species listed in Annex V, and for enforcement. Article 15 proscribes the various methods of taking animals which are listed in Annex VI. Exceptions to some of the above provisions are set out in Article 16. The remaining Articles provide for the dissemination of information, the conduct of conservation-oriented research, the amendment of the Annexes, the establishment and the conduct of the advisory committee, and for consideration to be given to introductions and re-introductions. **5–274**

The Habitats Directive is by far the most comprehensive and far reaching supra-national conservation legislation with which the United Kingdom Government has had to comply. Though much of its content is inevitably as would be expected, and its so-called "criteria" for site selection are less than adequate, its implementation will ask much of the current SSSI system, even as strengthened by the draft Conservation (Natural Habitats, etc.) Regulations 1994, by the promised PPG, and by the intended amendment to the 1981 Act. **5–275**

International Trade in Endangered Species—The CITES Convention

The Convention on international trade in endangered species of wild fauna and flora, generally known as the CITES Convention, was signed at Washington on March 3, 1973. It was made part of the law of the EC Member States by Article 1 of Regulation 3626/82[12] of December 3, 1982, of which the Convention forms Annex A.[13] **5–276**

The Convention lists in separate Appendices three categories of species: **5–277**

---

[10] In s.19(3).

[11] The inclusion of all species of cetaceans in the Annex results in the prohibition of whale hunting, which poses a problem for Norway's accession to the EC.

[12] [1982] O.J. L384 amended by Reg. 3645/83 ([1983] O.J. L36]) amending Art. 4, and by Reg. 2295/86 ([1986] O.J. L201) amending Arts. 2 and 6(2).

[13] It was also published in the UK in Cmnd. 5459.

Appendix I—all species threatened with extinction which are or may be affected by trade. Trade in specimens of these species is to be authorised only in exceptional circumstances.

Appendix II—(a) all species which though not necessarily now threatened with extinction may become so unless trade in specimens of such species is subject to strict regulation; and

(b) other species that need to be regulated if trade in the specimens referred to in (a) is to be brought under effective control.

Appendix III—all species which any contracting party regulates within its own jurisdiction to prevent or restrict exploitation, and requires the co-operation of other parties for the control of trade.

5–278   Trade in the listed species is not to be allowed except in accordance with the provisions of the Convention.

Regulation 3626/82 in adopting the Convention sets out these three Appendices in Annex A and, in Annex B, parts or products of animals and plants listed in these Appendices trade in which is also controlled under the Regulation. There is a further Annex C, listing species given special treatment by the Community, which is divided into two parts. Part 1 lists species that are to be treated as though they were in Appendix I.[14] Part 2 lists species that require an import permit to be brought into the Community[15] that will only be issued if it is established that the capture or collection of the relevant specimen will not have a harmful effect on the species or the extent of its territory, and subject to further conditions to ensure responsible conduct.[16]

Appendices I, II and III in Annex A, and Annex C have been revised from time to time; Regulation 1970/92[17] sets out in full these lists as most recently revised.

5–279   The import, export, and any re-export, of specimens of all the listed species, of the parts and products of these in Annex B, and of all other goods that appear to be parts or derivatives of these species are brought under control, and, with certain exceptions, require either an import permit or import certificate, or an export permit or re-export certificate, as the case may be. Import permits are needed for specimens of any species in Appendix I and Annex C, Part 1, and for goods derived from them; import certificates certifying that the

[14] Art. 3(1).
[15] Art. 3(2).
[16] Art. 10(1)(b).
[17] [1992] O.J. L201.

formalities required by the Convention have been complied with suffice for the remainder.[18] Each Member State is required to recognise the decisions of the competent authorities of the others, and permits and certificates issued by any one must be accepted by the others.[19]

The specimens (including derivatives) of species in Appendix I and Annex C, Part 1, may not be publicly displayed, nor, subject to certain exceptions, may they be sold or kept, offered or transported for sale.

The CITES Convention was given effect in the United Kingdom by the Endangered Species (Import and Export) Act 1976.[20] This contains five schedules[21] which list respectively, "animals", "plants" and "items" "the importation and exportation of which are restricted", and "animals" and "plants" "the sale etc. of which is restricted". The Secretary of State has power to modify these schedules, both generally and also to give effect to any amendment to the CITES Convention. The Act extends throughout the United Kingdom, including Northern Ireland. In addition to prohibiting imports and exports of animals, plants and other items brought under control by the Convention, it permits derogations from this prohibition for those who are appropriately licensed by the Secretary of State under section 1.   **5–280**

The prohibitions on importation are reinforced by it being made an offence to sell, offer or expose for sale, to possess or transport for the purpose of sale, or to display to the public, anything imported contrary to the provisions of the Act, and any part of or anything which derives from, or which is made wholly or partly from, anything that has been unlawfully imported or is otherwise within the scope of either Schedule 4 or 5.[22]   **5–281**

Where a person is charged with any offence under these provisions, it is a defence to prove that at the time when the item concerned first came into his possession, he made such enquiries (if any) as in the circumstances were reasonable to ascertain whether it fell within the scope of the prohibitions of section 4, and that at the time the offence alleged was committed he had no reason to believe that it was something that fell within those prohibitions.[23] The requirement to make reasonable enquiries will be met if the defendant produces a signed certificate provided by the person who supplied him with the item concerned, stating that the supplier had made enquiries at the time the item came into his (the supplier's) possession to ascertain   **5–282**

---

[18] Art. 10(1), (2).
[19] Art. 9(2) — with the exception of a certificate issued under Art. 11(a) that a specimen was imported before the Regulation came into force (December 31, 1982) or was acquired before the Convention became applicable to it.
[20] 1976, c.72.
[21] Scheds. 4 and 5 being added by the Wildlife and Countryside Act 1981, s.15.
[22] s.4(1), (1A).
[23] s.4(2).

whether it came within the prohibitions, and that he had no reason to believe at the time he supplied the item on to the defendant that it was within the prohibitions.

5–283   The Secretary of State also has further powers under sections 5, 6 and 7 to determine the manner of import of any live animal within the scope of Schedule 1, and also the place of import. He may restrict movement of such animals after they have been imported, by requiring them to be kept at specified premises, and any duly authorised person may enter any such specified premises to establish whether they are suitable or to ascertain whether a particular animal is being kept there.

Introduction of Organisms Harmful to Plants

5–284   EC legislation on this topic is based on Directive 77/93[24] on "protective measures against the introduction into the Community of organisms harmful to plants or plant products and against their spread within the Community". The Directive is designed to harmonise the rules of the different Member States for preventing the import with plants (including fresh fruit and seeds), and products derived from them, of harmful pests and viruses, mycoplasmas or other pathogens. Set out in a series of Annexes are lists of harmful organisms, the import of which either must be or may be banned (Annex I, Part A and Annex I, Part B, respectively).

5–285   The scheme of the Directive may be seen from Table 5/I which sets out its principal features:

TABLE 5/I

Directive 77/93		
Article 3(1)	Harmful organisms, import of which must be banned	Annex I, Part A
Article 3(6)(a)	Harmful organisms, import of which may be banned by certain Member States	Annex I, Part B
Article 3(5)	Harmful organisms, import of which may be banned (subject to exceptions)	Annex II, Part A

[24] [1977] O.J. L26.

Article 3(4)	Plants/plant products, import of which shall be banned when contaminated with named organisms	Annex II, Part A
Article 3(6)(b)	Plants/plant products, import of which may be banned by certain Member States when contaminated with named organisms	Annex II, Part B
Article 4(1)	Plants/plant products, import of which shall be banned when originating from specified territories	Annex III, Part A
Article 4(2)(a)	Plants/plant products/other objects, import of which may be banned	Annex III, Part B
Article 5(1)	Plants/plant products/other objects, import of which shall be banned unless stipulated requirements are met	Annex IV, Part A
Article 5(2)(b)	Plants, import of which may be banned unless stipulated requirements are met	Annex IV, Part B

In addition Article 6 requires various plants, plant products and **5–286** other objects to be subjected to a plant health inspection, either at the place of production if originating within the Community (and in any event before any movement within the Community) or on import, if originating from outside the Community. The plants, plant products and objects which are subject to this control are listed in Annex V to the Directive; this was most recently amended by Directive 92/98,[25] which Member States were required to implement by May 16, 1993. Part A of Annex V lists controlled plants, plant products, and other objects originating within the Community, while Part B of the Annex lists controlled plants, plant products and other objects originating outside the Community. The controlled items of each Part are divided into two categories: those which are potential carriers of harmful organisms of relevance for the entire Community, and those which are potential carriers of harmful organisms of relevance for certain

[25] [1992] O.J. L352.

269

protected zones within the Community only. These controlled items must be provided with a phytosanitary certificate or "plant passport" (valid for the appropriate protected zone where relevant) not more than 14 days before they leave any Member State, and they may not be imported into any Member State from any other unless accompanied by a plant passport.[26] Unless however any of the circumstances listed in Article 8(2) applies, no import inspection may be required where a duly completed plant passport is provided.[27]

5–287   The Directive contains detailed rules for mandatory inspections of the plants, plant products and other objects listed in Annex V when coming from outside the EC. It also permits, subject to detailed qualifications, inspections of imports of goods controlled by the Directive to ensure the controls have been complied with. Derogations from the controls are allowed under Article 14, provided there is no risk of harmful organisms spreading as a consequence—these can apply, for example, to certain of the controls in the case of articles involved in moving house, or for consumption during transport.

5–288   The Directive is implemented in Great Britain by two orders made under the Plant Health Act 1967, namely the Plant Health (Great Britain) Order 1993 and the Plant Health (Forestry) (Great Britain) Order 1993.[28]

Other Arrangements of Incidental Benefit to Nature Conservation

Environmentally Sensitive Areas

5–289   Nature conservation is an incidental beneficiary of the system of Environmentally Sensitive Areas (ESAs) which is operated under the Agriculture Act 1986.[29] Where an ESA is designated, farmers in such areas may undertake to carry out a prescribed form of environmentally beneficial management appropriate to the particular characteristics of that area. In return they will receive payments reflecting the additional costs, or income foregone, as a result of the agricultural practices they have agreed to operate. The ESAs may thus promote the development and/or re-creation of habitats valuable for wildlife, in wetland areas,

---

[26] Art. 7(2).
[27] Art. 8(1).
[28] S.I. 1993 No.1320 and S.I. 1993 No.1283 respectively.
[29] Described by English Nature in its 1st Annual Report for 1991/2, p.48, as "one of the most valuable developments in agricultural policy in recent years . . . this is the only agricultural mechanism to support and promote regional diversity".

downland and other grassland, and upland landscapes. The Conservation Agencies may submit proposals for the designation of new ESAs to the Ministry of Agriculture, and advise on their boundaries, the value of the habitats and wildlife they contain, and on the management required to maintain and enhance this value.[30]

Set-aside

Under changes made to the European Community's Common Agricultural Policy in May 1992, farms are eligible for subsidy on the cereals they grow only if they take at least 15 per cent of their land out of production; an extra subsidy, set at a level sufficient to make this set-aside option attractive, is payable on such land. In Britain, the total area of land to be left uncultivated in this way is roughly equal to the total area currently notified as SSSIs. However, it is feared that, without appropriate management (for which there is no financial provision), the result will simply be large areas of poor quality wildlife habitat, of little benefit to nature conservation. The reduction in semi-natural habitats of wildlife value, which occurred during the Second World War and in the two or three succeeding decades, cannot readily be restored merely through ceasing to cultivate once-arable land. **5–290**

Conflicting Legislation

As might be expected, some legislation enacted before the spread of interest in nature conservation had been acknowledged, permits, encourages, or even requires actions which conflict with the requirements of the 1981 Act. **5–291**

Thus, section 260 of the Public Health Act, 1936, gives parish councils and local authorities the right to drain, cleanse or cover any pond, pool or ditch which contains drainage or stagnant water which might be prejudicial to health, and to carry out incidental works of maintenance and improvement. Such water bodies, although perhaps unsightly, are quite likely to contain species protected under Schedule 5 of the 1981 Act, so that the exercise of these powers can therefore be highly contentious. **5–292**

Similarly, the Prevention of Damage by Pests Act 1949, imposes the duty on every local authority to keep their district, so far as might be practicable, clear of rats and mice, but does not define the target species. Some species of mouse are none too common and what **5–293**

---

[30] As at August 31, 1994, 22 ESAs totalling 1,100,000 ha. had been designated.

survives of the Act is hardly consistent with the desire of some local authority officers to encourage mice in localities such as urban nature reserves and roadside verges where they provide food for predators.

5–294   The Weeds Act 1959, gives the Minister of Agriculture (in Scotland, the Secretary of State) powers to require occupiers to prevent the spread of a number of plant species which the Act regards as "injurious weeds". The same species, however, are often to be found growing on sites designated for their nature conservation value; here they can contribute to the scientific interest, and the prevention of their spread, as required by the Act, could be damaging. In this case, however, procedures for consultation before the Act is applied to conserved sites may operate to minimise such conflict.

Chapter 6

WATER RESOURCES MANAGEMENT

The management of water resources entails safeguarding both their **6–001** quantity and their quality. These two aspects are inextricably linked — a polluting discharge to a river at a time of drought will inevitably have far greater effects than the same discharge when the river is in spate, but, conversely, heavy rainfall may wash off fertiliser and pesticides into rivers that would otherwise migrate into water courses far more slowly. Nevertheless the legal controls are largely distinct, and it is convenient to treat those over abstraction and impounding of water, directly protecting natural resources, in this chapter; pollution controls are the subject of Chapter 8.

The statutory controls over the quantity of water resources in **6–002** England and Wales are mostly contained in Part II of the Water Resources Act 1991. This lays a duty on the NRA to take all such action as it may from time to time consider to be necessary or expedient for the purpose of conserving, re-distributing or otherwise augmenting water resources in England and Wales, and of securing their proper use.[1] Additionally the statutory water undertakers are required by section 37 of the Water Industry Act 1991 to develop water resources for the water supply systems within their respective areas. There is accordingly a necessary close liaison between the NRA and the water undertakers to ensure both a sufficient availability of water and suitable provision for its abstraction for eventual supply to the public. The maintenance of appropriate water levels is essential for the protection of conservation, agricultural and amenity interests. "Water Level Management Plans", which provides guidance on this to operating authorities was issued in June 1994 by the Ministry of Agriculture, the Welsh Office, the Association of Drainage Authorities, English Nature and the NRA.

In Scotland, where there is rarely a shortage of water, controls over **6–003** abstraction are far more limited. They consist essentially of (i) Water Orders, made under the Water (Scotland) Act 1980, which provide for

---

[1] s.19(1). All section references in this chapter are to the W.R.A., unless otherwise stated.

273

the compulsory acquisition of water rights for public water supply purposes, or approval of acquiring such rights by agreement, and (ii) controls over abstraction from both surface and ground waters for all commercial agricultural and horticultural irrigation, under the Natural Heritage (Scotland) Act 1991, whereby the Secretary of State for Scotland may approve abstractions for irrigation of specific areas. However proposals have been announced[2] for wider controls, to be exercised when and where necessary by the Scottish Environmental Protection Agency, subject to confirmation by the Secretary of State.

Low River Flows

6–004   Unacceptably low flows in a considerable number of rivers in England and Wales have been caused by excessive abstraction. The NRA has the power under W.R.A., s.21 to determine quantities that define the minimum acceptable flow at designated control points, which may then form the basis of remedial programmes by the NRA to improve the rivers and other waters adversely affected.[3] The Secretary of State may on his own initiative direct the NRA to address this issue in relation to any particular inland waters.[4] The minimum acceptable flow must be not less than that needed for safeguarding public health and for meeting (in respect of both quantity and quality of water) the requirements of existing lawful uses of the water concerned for any purposes, including agriculture, industry and water supply, and the requirements of navigation, fisheries and land drainage that are directly or indirectly affected.[5] In certain cases, for example reservoirs, it is more appropriate, and permitted, to determine the level or volume of water instead of, or possibly in addition to, flow.[6]

6–005   Where the NRA sees fit to make any such determination, it does so by way of a draft statement submitted to the Secretary of State, following notification of relevant water undertakers, drainage bodies and other statutory authorities, as prescribed by section 21, in

[2] "Abstraction Controls: A System for Scotland", Scottish Office Environment Department, April 1993.
[3] The NRA has identified the top 40 low flow rivers in England and Wales (some of which have ceased to exist in dry periods). Details of its progress in dealing with the problems represented by these are given in "Low Flows and Water Resources" issued by the NRA in March 1993. While the principal cause of low flows is excessive abstraction, some alleviation can be produced by lining river beds, by seasonal pumping of water from aquifers into the river at times of low flow, and recycling water from the lower stretches of a river to its upper reaches. Sometimes it may be sufficient for groundwater abstraction points to be relocated further downstream within the same catchment area.
[4] s.22.
[5] s.21(5).
[6] s.23.

accordance with procedures laid down in Schedule 5. Minimum acceptable flows, levels or volumes, as the case may be, that have been approved under this procedure are to be taken into account when considering any licence to abstract water.[7]

Avoidance of Waste of Water

The NRA's duty to secure the proper use of water resources and so to avoid waste and uneconomic use of water, inevitably impinges on the water undertakers, and the Office of Water Services (Ofwat), in the setting of charges, particularly as regards the use of water metering to provide the basis of charges imposed on domestic consumers. This constitutional conflict has not been legally resolved, but ultimately requires a political solution. The NRA set out its approach to water resource conservation policy in its report "Water Resources Development Strategy—A Discussion Document" published in March 1992, followed by "NRA Water Resources Strategy" published in 1993. The latter showed an overall surplus in England and Wales between available water resources and demand. However on making this comparison by each of the 10 regions, whereas Wales has, as might be expected, a very substantial surplus, the Thames region has a deficit, and the surplus in the Southern and Anglian Regions is very small. Since it is not possible in practice to use 100 per cent of available resources without damaging effects on the environment, the conclusion is inevitable that either the amount of water taken in the southeast of England must be limited, or substantial volumes must be transferred to there from areas in surplus. The NRA's most recent strategy document on managing demand for water resources is *Water: Nature's Precious Resource*.[8]

6–006

Abstraction Policy

NRA policy in relation to control of groundwater abstractions is stated in its strategy document "Policy and Practice for the Protection of Groundwater" in the following terms:

6–007

"The NRA will only authorise abstractions of groundwater within the scope of the Water Resources Act 1991 which would ensure that:

(a) total abstraction from any groundwater resource area does not exceed the long-term annual average rate of replenishment;

---

[7] s.40(3).
[8] March 1994.

    (b)   there is, in the view of the NRA, no unacceptable detriment to any watercourse or other environmental feature dependent upon groundwater; and

    (c)   any abstraction does not cause a deterioration of groundwater quality through the incursion of saline or polluted waters.

Abstraction Licensing

6–008   The right to abstract water first came under comprehensive statutory control in England and Wales through the Water Resources Act 1963, which introduced the requirement that abstraction be licensed. Where water had been abstracted within the five years immediately preceding the coming into force of the relevant provisions, the abstractor was entitled to a licence of right.[9] The provisions for licensing water abstraction were re-enacted in the Water Act 1989, the transitional provisions of which[10] provided that both licences granted under the 1963 Act and licences of right under that Act should continue, notwithstanding the repeal of the relevant provisions of the 1963 Act. In addition, the Water Act 1989 brought within the licensing system certain other abstractions that were permitted to continue unlicensed pursuant to section 24(2) and (3) of the 1963 Act[11] provided that water had in fact been abstracted under this right at any time within the five years preceding September 1, 1989 (the "transfer date", when the bulk of the provisions of the Water Act 1989 took effect), and an application for a licence under the 1989 Act was subsequently made in due time.[12] In 1993, the total number of abstraction licences in force in England and Wales was some 48,000.[13]

6–009   Except where a licence has been granted, and its terms complied with, there is a general prohibition on abstracting water from any source of supply, and on causing or permitting any other person to abstract any water.[14] It is likewise prohibited, in relation to water contained in any underground strata, (i) to begin, or to cause or permit any other person to begin, to construct any well or borehole or other work for abstracting water from those strata; (ii) to extend any such well, borehole or other work; or (iii) to instal or modify any machinery or apparatus for abstracting additional quantities of water.[15] Similarly,

---

[9] Water Resources Act 1963, s.33(1)(b).

[10] *i.e.* Sched. 26, Part IV, so far as concerns water resources.

[11] These roughly correspond to those permitted under W.R.A., s.27(3)–(5); see para 6.xx, items (j) and (k).

[12] Pursuant to the provisions of Sched.26, para. 30.

[13] "NRA Water Resources Strategy", p.4.

[14] s.24(1).

[15] s.24(2).

the construction or alteration of any impounding works is prohibited at any point in any inland waters which are not discrete waters. Breach of any of these prohibitions in the absence of a licence, or failure to comply with the terms of such licence as there may be, is an offence subject to a fine of up to £5,000 on summary conviction and to an unlimited fine on conviction on indictment.[16] Such a breach or failure does not of itself confer any right of action in civil proceedings.[17]

There are nevertheless certain exceptions to these prohibitions and licence requirements, including:

    6–010

(a) Abstraction under licences of right, whether deriving from the Water Resources Act 1963 or Schedule 26 to the Water Act 1989;[18]

(b) Abstraction in the course of or resulting from any land drainage operations;[19]

(c) Abstraction to prevent interference with any mining, quarrying, engineering, building or other operations, or to prevent damage to works resulting from any such operations.[20] However, where any well, borehole or other work is to be constructed or extended for this purpose, notice of the intention to do so must be given to the NRA before starting, and the NRA may serve a conservation notice requiring reasonable measures to be taken to conserve water.[21] There is a right of appeal to the Secretary of State against the terms of the notice;[22]

(d) Abstraction by machinery or apparatus on a vessel for use on that or any other vessel;[23]

(e) Abstraction in connection with fire fighting, including testing and training;[24]

(f) Abstraction to test for the presence of water in any underground strata or its quality or quantity or to ascertain the effect of abstracting water at one point on water abstraction or water levels elsewhere;[25]

---

[16] ss.24(5), 25(3).
[17] s.70.
[18] s.48, Sched. 7.
[19] s.29(1); "land drainage" includes coast protection, warping and irrigation, other than spray irrigation; s.29(5). Certain activities are excluded from "spray irrigation" by the Spray Irrigation (Definition) Order 1992; S.I. 1992 No.1096.
[20] s.29(2).
[21] s.30.
[22] s.31.
[23] s.32(1).
[24] s.32(2).
[25] s.32(3), (4).

(g) Impounding under an "alternative statutory provision" as defined in section 36(2) of the Water Resources Act 1963;[26]

(h) Abstraction and impounding by navigation, harbour or conservancy authorities in the course of performing their functions;[27]

(i) Abstraction of up to 5 cubic metres of water, not being part of a continuous operation or a series of operations by which, in either case, any larger quantity is abstracted;[28]

(j) Abstraction from inland waters by or on behalf of an occupier of contiguous land of no more than 20 cubic metres in any period of 24 hours, provided that the abstraction is for use on that land (whether or not with other land), for domestic purposes of the occupier's household or for agricultural purposes other than spray irrigation;[29]

(k) Abstraction from underground strata by or on behalf of an individual as a supply of water for his household's purposes, up to a maximum of 20 cubic metres in any 24 hours.[30]

6–011   The exceptions for the regular abstraction of small quantities, forming items (j) and (k) above (*i.e.* under sections 27(3) and 27(5)), create a "protected right" to abstract water.[31] In certain circumstances, the NRA may curtail a protected right in respect of abstraction from inland waters (item (j) above) to use on part only of the relevant land, having regard to the rights of other occupiers of land contiguous to the same waters.[32] The NRA must for this purpose serve a notice on the person concerned, and allow him at least 28 days to object by way of an appeal to the relevant County Court.[33]

6–012   Exemption may also be granted by order of the Secretary of State on the application of the NRA or any relevant navigation, harbour or conservancy authority as regards any one or more areas of inland waters or underground strata, if the prohibition on abstracting is not needed in relation to those waters or strata.[34] The prohibitions on abstraction and related activities in section 24(1) and (2) do not apply to any source of supply to which an exemption order relates, and any authorisations to abstract from that source under existing licences cease to have effect on the coming into force of the order.[35]

[26] s.25(5).
[27] s.26.
[28] s.27(1), (2).
[29] s.27(3), (4).
[30] s.27(5).
[31] s.26(6).
[32] s.28(1).
[33] s.28(2)–(5).
[34] s.33(1)–(3), Sched.6.
[35] s.33(6).

Applications for Licences

Applications may be made for abstracting water, for constructing or **6–013** altering impounding works, or for a combined licence in respect of both operations. The applicant for a licence to abstract must be the occupier of relevant land, or must have, at least when the licence takes effect, a right of access to that land. Where abstraction is to be from inland waters, the relevant land is that contiguous to the waters; in relation to abstraction from underground strata, it is the land consisting of or comprising those strata. In the case of abstraction from underground strata, a right to apply by virtue of a right of access only arises where the water level of the water to be abstracted depends wholly or mainly on water flowing from the strata (and not, therefore, by way of diversion of surface waters).

The procedures governing licence applications are contained in the **6–014** Water Resources (Licences) Regulations 1965.[36] These Regulations were introduced for the purposes of the new licensing provisions in the Water Resources Act 1963 and continue to have effect as though made under the Water Resources Act 1991. Applications are made to the NRA, and must be published,[37] with notifications being sent to specified bodies. A period of generally 28 days is allowed for lodging objections, and any representations made in consequence must be taken into account in considering the application, as well as the reasonable requirements of the applicant.[38] The NRA must also have regard to river flows[39]—where a minimum acceptable flow has been determined for any control point, then the flow at that point must not be reduced below the minimum; where the flow is already below the minimum, it must not be further reduced. If no minimum acceptable flow has been determined in accordance with sections 21 to 23, then the NRA must have regard to the same considerations as would have to be considered in determining the minimum acceptable flow for the relevant river or other inland waters.[40] Where an application is for the abstraction of not more than 20 cubic metres in any 24 hour period (and none of the exemptions in respect of small quantities apply) the NRA may nevertheless dispense with the statutory procedural requirements if it considers it appropriate.[41]

The NRA may not, except with the consent of the person affected, **6–015** authorise any abstraction of water or the obstructing or impeding of

---

[36] S.I. 1965 No. 534, as amended by SIs 1965 No. 2082 and 1989 No. 336.
[37] s.37.
[38] s.38(3).
[39] s.40.
[40] s.40(2).
[41] s.37(6).

the flow of any inland waters by impounding, if this will prevent the holder of a right to abstract water (whether under a licence, or the unlicensed right to abstract up to 20 cubic metres in 24 hours from inland waters or underground strata) from abstracting water up to the maximum limit to which he is entitled under that right.[42] In addition, where an application is to abstract from underground strata, the NRA must have regard to the requirements of existing lawful uses, including those for agriculture, industry and water supply.[43] It may treat any use as lawful unless it has been held not to be so in any legal proceedings by a decision that has not been quashed or reversed.[44] Nevertheless, the grant (or a variation) of a licence in breach of this duty not to derogate from existing rights will not be invalid, nor will it provide a cause of action against any person other than the NRA itself for breach of its statutory duty; even against the NRA the only relief lies in damages.[45] It is a defence for the NRA to establish that the derogation of which the plaintiff complains was wholly or mainly attributable to exceptional shortage of rain or to an accident or other unforeseen act or event not caused by, and outside the control of, the NRA.[46]

6–016   The Secretary of State may call-in licence applications, either on an individual basis or by reference to any class that may be specified, the procedure for dealing with such applications being set out in section 42. Appeals may be made to the Secretary of State[47] under the procedure laid down in sections 43 to 45, and regulation 12 of the Water Resources (Licences) Regulations 1965.

6–017   The NRA may attach such conditions as it thinks fit to any licences. To protect river flows, an abstraction licence may include conditions prescribing flows for neighbouring rivers at or below which there may be no abstraction. Specifically, a time limit may be imposed, and the NRA will favour this this where the consequences of the abstraction are uncertain.[48] The form of licence is largely at the discretion of the NRA, subject to the broad requirements of sections 46 and 47 and regulation 10(6) of the Licences Regulations 1965. Section 46(2) prescribes in particular the inclusion of provisions as to the quantity of water authorised to be abstracted during such a period or periods as may be specified, as to how that quantity is to be measured, and for

---

[42] s.39.
[43] s.39(2).
[44] s.39(2), (5).
[45] s.60(2), (3).
[46] s.60(5).
[47] s.43.
[48] "NRA Water Resources Strategy", p.12.

determining what quantity of water has in fact been abstracted during any specified period.

Revocation and Variation of Licences

Licences may be revoked or varied on the application of the holder. **6–018** An application to vary a licence will be treated in essentially the same manner as a new application for a licence, save that where the variation is by way of reduction of the amount of water to be abstracted, the provisions for publicity and consideration of representations do not apply.[49]

The NRA may revoke or vary licences on its own initiative or **6–019** pursuant to a direction given by the Secretary of State.[50] All such proposals must be published, and notice of them served on the licence holder. Any person may make representations with respect to the proposals and the holder may serve notice of objection. If the holder raises no objection, the NRA may determine the matter itself in the light of such representations as it may have received, but if he does object, the matter must be referred to the Secretary of State.[51] The Secretary of State may, if he thinks fit, set up a local inquiry or otherwise arrange for a hearing of the matter. His decision is declared by section 54(6) to be final.

Where fishing rights have been affected by a licensed abstraction of **6–020** water, and one year or more has elapsed since grant of the licence, the owner of those rights may be entitled to apply under section 55 for the relevant abstraction licence to be revoked or varied. "Fishing rights" for this purpose are rights which constitute or are included in an interest in land, or which are exercisable by virtue of an exclusive licence granted for valuable consideration, including rights held in common with one or more other persons.[52] An application under section 55 may however only be made where no minimum acceptable flow has been determined in relation to the waters in question[53]— accordingly, where it has been, no relief can be claimed whatever the actual flow. Such applications are determined by the Secretary of State, who may arrange for a local inquiry or a hearing. The licence may not be revoked or varied if he is satisfied that any loss or damage caused to the applicant by abstraction was wholly or mainly attributable to exceptional shortage of rain or to an accident or other unforeseen act or event not caused by and outside the control of the

[49] s.51(4).
[50] s.52(1)–(3).
[51] s.53(3), (4).
[52] s.55(5).
[53] s.55(2).

NRA.[54] Even where he does determine that a licence should be varied, the variation is to be limited to that which is requisite having regard to the loss or damage sustained by the applicant that is directly attributable to the abstraction of water.[55] Again, the Secretary of State's decision on the application is declared to be final.[56]

6–021   Revocation or variation of a licence under these provisions entitles the licence holder to compensation in respect of any directly attributable loss or damage, including wasted expenditure carrying out work that has been rendered abortive.[57] No compensation will however be payable if there has in fact been no abstraction under the licence concerned during the seven years immediately preceding service of notice of the proposals for revocation or variation on the holder.[58] The NRA is thus enabled to extinguish old unused licences.

6–022   Any dispute as to compensation is referred to the Lands Tribunal for determination in accordance with the Land Compensation Act 1961.[59] If the owner of fishing rights establishes that he has suffered loss and damage, but the abstraction licence is nevertheless not revoked or varied, he is entitled to compensation unless within 6 months the NRA has served a notice to treat for their acquisition, or has offered to acquire them on compulsory purchase terms.[60]

6–023   A licence to abstract water for spray irrigation, either alone or for other purposes, may be varied in a period of exceptional shortage of rain or other emergency so as to reduce the amount of water that may be abstracted.[61] However this will only apply in the case of abstraction from underground strata if this is likely to affect the flow, level or volume of any inland waters that are not discrete waters nor waters which are exempted from the licensing provisions under section 33. If there are two or more such licences for abstraction from the same point or from points that are "not far distant", proportionate reductions are to be required of each licence holder.[62]

6–024   A licence holder who has failed to pay the charges due in respect of his licence within 28 days of service of a notice demanding payment that complies with the requirements of section 58(2), may have his licence revoked. No compensation is payable either in these circumstances or where a licence to abstract for spray irrigation has been temporarily varied.

[54]   s.56(4).
[55]   s.56(5).
[56]   s.56(7).
[57]   s.61(1).
[58]   s.61(4).
[59]   s.61(5), (6)—specifically ss.2, 4 and 5 of the 1961 Act, so far as applicable.
[60]   s.62(4).
[61]   s.57.
[62]   s.57(4).

Succession to Licences

A licence to carry out impounding works is personal to the grantee   **6–025** exclusively. A licence to abstract may however be transferred in accordance with sections 49 and 50, and the Water Resources (Succession to Licences) Regulations 1969.[63] The provisions for succession are framed by reference to the land on which the water abstracted in pursuance of a licence is to be used, referred to as "the relevant land". Where, by reason of any act or event, including his death, the licence holder ceases to be the occupier of the whole of the relevant land and another person succeeds to him as the occupier of the whole of that land, the successor automatically becomes the new licence holder. However, he must give notice to the NRA of the change in occupation within 15 months of the relevant act or event, or the licence will lapse.[64] It will also lapse if, in any particular case, no-one succeeds to the licence.[65]

If two or more people (who may include the original licence holder)   **6–026** become occupiers of distinct parts of land previously occupied by a single licence holder, any one or more of the new occupiers may apply to become the sole licence holder,[66] or he may apply for a new licence pursuant to regulations 5, 6 and 7 of the Succession to Licences Regulations 1969. Applications for new licences must conform to the requirements of the Schedule to the Regulations. Where a new licence is applied for, it is a precondition that the original holder, if he remains in occupation of part of the land, or his successor to that other part, as the case may be, should also apply for a new licence, or for the revocation of the original licence, or for its variation in a manner that will permit the grant of appropriate rights to the other successor(s).[67] It follows that any contract for acquisition of a part of any land benefiting from an abstraction licence must contain appropriate provisions to ensure an orderly rearrangement of the rights under the licence. The provisions to be included in any new licence granted to a successor are laid down in regulation 7. In essence, where the original licence provided for abstraction for use on a particular part of the land, the person or persons in occupation of that portion after the division of the property will be authorised to abstract the same amount of water in aggregate as before, for use on that portion. Where the land on which the water abstracted is to be used is not spelled out in the licence, the NRA will make its own determination as to the proportions in which

[63] S.I. 1969 No. 976.
[64] s.49.
[65] s.49(5).
[66] s.50.
[67] reg. 5(3).

the original licence holder would have applied the abstracted water to the different portions of the land, and grant new licences accordingly.[68]

Registers of Abstraction and Impounding Licences

6–027   Section 189 of the WRA continues the requirement to maintain registers of abstraction and impounding licences introduced by section 53 of the Water Resources Act 1963. The particulars to be kept in these registers are set out in regulation 17 of the Water Resources (Licences) Regulations 1965; these include details of applications for such licences and the decisions made on them, of revocations and variations of granted licences, and of any succession to or transfer of licences. There must also be an index, normally in the form of a map, to enable entries to be traced. Registers must be kept available for public inspection at all reasonable hours.

Water Conservation

6–028   Several statutory provisions are aimed at conserving water, either by seeking to avoid its going to waste, or by restricting its use. Thus it is an offence to cause or allow any underground water to run to waste from any well, borehole or other work, or to abstract from any well, borehole or other work water in excess of the abstractor's reasonable requirements.[69] There are limited exceptions to this in respect of water running to waste to test the water supply, or for various cleaning and maintenance purposes, and for disposing of water that would otherwise interfere or threaten to interfere with underground works.[70] On conviction of this offence, the court may make any order that it considers necessary to prevent waste of water, including requiring that any relevant well or borehole be sealed.[71] Failure to comply with such an order is not only a contempt of court, but also entitles the NRA to apply to the court to be authorised to execute the order, and where this is done, its expenses are recoverable from the person convicted.[72]

6–029   Where a water fitting on any premises is out of order or in need of repair, or where, by its nature or as a result of its use, water provided by a water undertaker is or is likely to be wasted, misused or unduly

[68] reg. 7(2)(b).
[69] W.I.A., s.71(1).
[70] W.I.A., s.71(2), (3).
[71] W.I.A., s.71(5).
[72] W.I.A., s.71(6).

consumed, the owner or occupier of the premises concerned, if he negligently or intentionally causes or allows this, commits an offence, except where someone else is liable to maintain the fitting concerned.[73] It is likewise an offence to use any water supplied to premises for any purposes other than those for which it is supplied, except for extinguishing a fire. In any such case, the water undertaker concerned is entitled to recover a reasonable amount in respect of any water wasted, misused or improperly consumed as a consequence. Powers are granted to the Secretary of State under section 74 of the W.I.A. to make regulations with respect to water fittings for purposes including the prevention of waste or undue consumption, but none have in fact been made. Water undertakers may take action on their own initiative to avoid waste, misuse or undue consumption of water, including, among other things, disconnection in an emergency, and in any other case serving notice on any relevant consumer requiring appropriate steps to be taken.[74]

Hosepipe Bans

A general power is available to every water undertaker, when it considers that a serious deficiency of water available for distribution by it exists or is threatened, under which it may prohibit or restrict the use of any of its water drawn through a hosepipe for watering private gardens or washing private motor cars. A hosepipe ban may apply to the whole or any part of the undertaker's area and last for as long as it thinks necessary. Contravention of the ban is an offence; although the water undertaker is required to give public notice of any such ban in two or more newspapers circulating locally before it comes into effect, ignorance of the ban is no defence.[75]   6–030

Drought Orders

Where an exceptional shortage of rain has either led to a serious deficiency of water supplies in any area or threatens such a deficiency, the Secretary of State may make a "drought order" on the application of either the NRA or any water undertaker supplying water in that area.[76] A drought order may be either an "ordinary drought order" or an "emergency drought order". The latter allows slightly more   6–031

---

[73] W.I.A., s.73(1), (4).
[74] W.I.A., s.75(1),(2). The water undertakers themselves lose 29 per cent of their water through leakage from the mains; *Financial Times*, March 4, 1994, quoting Ofwat figures.
[75] W.I.A., s.76(2), (3).
[76] W.R.A., s.73.

extensive restrictions on the use of water, its maximum duration is shorter, and provisions as to compensation differ. Ordinary drought orders may differ according to whether they have been applied for by the NRA or by a water undertaker.

6–032   A drought order, whether ordinary or emergency, made on the application of the NRA may authorise the NRA, or those authorised by it, to take water from any specified source or to discharge water to any specified place; it may authorise the NRA to prohibit or limit the taking of water from any specified source, if that would otherwise seriously affect supplies available to any person; it may suspend or modify any restriction or obligation on any person as regards the taking or discharge of water, or its supply, e.g. as respects quantity, pressure or quality, or any treatment, such as filtration; and it may allow the NRA to suspend, vary or attach conditions to any effluent discharge consent.[77]

6–033   An ordinary drought order made on the application of a water undertaker may contain comparable provisions to those just set out, and in addition it may authorise the water undertaker to prohibit or limit the use of water for any purposes as have been specified in any direction given by the Secretary of State to water undertakers generally in relation to the content of drought orders. An ordinary order may also prohibit or limit the taking by the NRA of water from any specified source that would otherwise seriously affect supplies available to the water undertaker.[78] Ordinary drought orders may stay in effect for up to six months, subject to a possible extension by the Secretary of State to a maximum of twelve months in total.[79]

6–034   An emergency drought order may be made where the serious deficiency of water supplies that justifies an ordinary order is additionally such as to be likely to impair the economic or social well-being of persons in the area affected.[80] The powers that may be made available to the NRA are the same, whichever type of order is made; however, an order made on the application of a water undertaker may allow the undertaker to prohibit or limit the use of water for such purposes as the water undertaker thinks fit, without any restriction to those previously prescribed in a direction by the Secretary of State.[81] It may also authorise the undertaker to supply water by means of stand pipes or water tanks and to make provision for these in any street in its area. An emergency order may stay in effect for up to three months

[77] s.74(1).
[78] s.74(2).
[79] s.74(3), (4).
[80] s.73(2)(b).
[81] s.75(2).

only, subject to a possible extension by the Secretary of State to a maximum of five months in total.[82]

The powers that may be granted under an emergency order can be reinforced by directions given by the Secretary of State under section 75(5), imposing duties on anyone granted such powers as to how, or the circumstances in which, the powers are or are not to be exercised, and such a duty is enforceable under section 18 of the Water Industry Act 1991 by the Secretary of State (see paragraphs 8–049 to 8–051 for the significance of this provision as to enforcement). **6–035**

Any order that prohibits or limits the use of water may be made in relation to consumers generally, a class of consumer or a particular consumer. There is however a 72 hour grace period from publication of the relevant notice to those affected, or the sending to them of such a notice, as the case may be, before the restriction can take effect.[83] The manner in which the powers under a drought order are to be exercised, and certain consequential steps that may be taken are the subject of section 77. These include the right of a sewerage undertaker to modify any trade effluent consents or agreements so as to enable it to comply with any requirements or conditions that are imposed on that undertaker by way of a restriction of its effluent discharge from its sewers or other works.[84] **6–036**

The procedure for making the drought order is prescribed in Schedule 8 to the W.R.A. This provides for, among other things, the service of notices on various public authorities and persons affected by a proposed order, the lodging of objections and consideration of them by local inquiry or a hearing, unless the Secretary of State dispenses with that requirement because of the need for urgent action, and the publication of a drought order that has been made. Any action that contravenes a prohibition or limitation imposed by a drought order, or that breaches any condition or restriction imposed by or under an order, is an offence subject to a maximum fine of £5,000 on summary conviction, and an unlimited fine on conviction on indictment.[85] **6–037**

Compensation is payable to owners and occupiers of land, and to anyone else with an interest in land, in respect of loss or damage caused by the entry upon or occupation or use of land made by the applicant for the drought order.[86] Apart from this, no compensation is payable in respect of loss or damage caused by emergency drought orders, while compensation in respect of loss or damage caused by ordinary drought orders is only available to the extent provided for in **6–038**

[82] s.75(3), (4).
[83] s.76(1).
[84] s.77(5).
[85] s.80.
[86] Sched.9, para. 1.

Schedule 9, paragraph 2.[87] Claims for compensation must be made within 6 months from when the relevant drought order ceased to have effect.[88] A claim may also be made during the currency of any ordinary drought order, and in such a case, the Lands Tribunal may award a daily sum in respect of the loss or damage likely to be sustained by the claimant.[89]

[87] s.79(2).
[88] Sched. 9, para. 4(1).
[89] Sched. 9, para. 4(2)–(5).

Chapter 7

LAND DRAINAGE, FLOOD DEFENCE AND COAST PROTECTION

Land drainage law can be dated back to the reign of Henry VIII   **7–001**
when there was passed "A general Act concerning Commissions of
Sewers to be directed in all Parts within the Realm".[1] That Act and
numerous subsequent statutes[2] continued in force until comprehensive new legislation was brought into effect by the Land Drainage Act
1930. Since then, the law and the system of its local administration
have to a large degree remained unchanged. Some modifications were
introduced by the Land Drainage Act 1961, and a variety of minor
amendments by other legislation, which were consolidated into the
Land Drainage Act 1976. The 1991 consolidation of all water legislation
merely re-enacted drainage law, though divided it awkwardly
between the Land Drainage Act 1991 (the "L.D.A."), which deals with
essentially local drainage and its administration, and the Water
Resources Act 1991 (the "W.R.A."), which sets out the powers and
duties of the National Rivers Authority as regards flood defence
(which is substantially equivalent to drainage) and of the regional
flood defence committees through which the NRA acts.

The overall administration of land drainage has been through a   **7–002**
variety of changes since 1930, starting with catchment boards and
then, in turn, 29 river boards, river authorities, 10 water authorities,
with continuing responsibility for land drainage kept with regional
land drainage committees, and finally (so far) to the National Rivers
Authority and its 10 regional flood defence committees. The responsibilities of the NRA to be transferred to the proposed Environment
Agency will include those for flood defence and coast protection.[3]

---

[1] 23 Hen.8, c.5.
[2] Including a further one passed under Henry VIII and others under Edward VI, Mary
Stuart, Elizabeth I and James I.
[3] Notwithstanding a powerful campaign by the Ministry of Agriculture, Fisheries and
Food for these responsibilities to stay outside the remit of the new Agency,
supported in this respect by the House of Commons Environment Committee in its
report 'The Government's Proposals for an Environment Agency', 1991–92 First
Report, January 29, 1992.

7–003   Local administration however remains largely as set up in 1930, with locally elected "internal drainage boards" raising finance from those in their districts. Their administration and finance was reviewed and approved by the Tavistock Institute in 1982, and was also the subject of a government Green Paper in 1985.[4] Nevertheless, no action has been taken to give effect to any of the recommendations contained in that Green Paper notwithstanding the extensive water legislation that has been through Parliament since then. References to "drainage boards" in this chapter are to these internal drainage boards; references to the NRA having certain powers or taking certain action are to be understood, as appropriate, to references to the powers and actions of the relevant regional flood defence committee. For reasons of space, this chapter is largely confined to stating the law in England and Wales only. The Scottish statute law is based primarily on the Flood Prevention (Scotland) Act 1961.

Terminology

7–004   "Drainage", as used in the L.D.A., "includes defence against water (including sea water), irrigation, other than spray irrigation,[5] and warping."[6]

7–005   "Flood defence" is defined in the W.R.A. as meaning "the drainage of land and the provision of flood warning systems";[7] "drainage" is given the same definition in that Act as in the L.D.A. In most respects therefore "drainage" and flood defence" are synonymous.

7–006   "Main rivers" are those rivers, or stretches of rivers, shown as such on a "main river map".[8] Main river maps for each area of the regional flood defence committees must be kept available for public inspection at the principal office of each committee,[9] and may be varied by adding or removing rivers, or stretches of rivers, from them[10]—a process sometimes referred to as "maining" and "de-maining". The significance of whether a watercourse is a "main river" or not is that drainage responsibilities, and various powers to carry out drainage works, relating to main rivers may only be performed by the NRA, and not by

---

[4] 'The Administration and Financing of Land Drainage, Flood Defence and Coast Protection' Cmnd. 1449, 1985.
[5] Certain activities are excluded from "spray irrigation" by the Spray Irrigation (Definition) Order 1992 (S.I. 1992 No.1096).
[6] "Warping" is a term used for the deliberate flooding of low lying land by adjacent rivers and streams, with a view to its receiving alluvial sediments that improve its quality: L.D.A., s.72(1).
[7] W.R.A., s.113(1).
[8] Currently some 36,000 km of rivers are designated as main rivers ('NRA Flood Defence Strategy' 1993).
[9] W.R.A., s.193(1).
[10] W.R.A., s.194.

internal drainage boards (except by agreement). Main rivers also include watercourses subject to works schemes under W.R.A. 137(4), as mentioned below.

"Watercourse" is given a slightly different meaning in the provi- **7–007** sions in the Acts relating to drainage, from that used in the rest of the W.R.A. (apart from the sections on abstraction and impounding), being defined to include "all rivers, streams, ditches, drains, cuts, culverts, dykes, sluices, sewers and passages through which water flows, except a public sewer".[11]

Drainage Authorities

The NRA has a general supervisory duty over all matters relating to **7–008** flood defence.[12] It is expressly required to arrange for all its functions relating to flood defence under both the W.R.A. and the L.D.A. to be carried out by regional flood defence committees appointed for their respective areas, which largely correspond to those of the water authorities before privatisation and of the sewerage undertakers thereafter.[13] The NRA may nevertheless give directions to these committees where their operations seem likely to affect the NRA's management of water for purposes other than flood defence.[14] The NRA may also make arrangements with navigation and conservancy authorities, with a view to improving the drainage of any land:

(a) to transfer to the NRA the whole or any business of the navigation or conservancy authority or any of its property; or

(b) to alter or improve any of the works of the navigation or conservancy authority, and to arrange for payments between the parties in respect of any such matters.

The regional flood defence committees, though acting on behalf of **7–009** the NRA, are primarily under the control of the "relevant Minister", who is the Minister of Agriculture, Fisheries and Food, in relation to England, and the Secretary of State for Wales in relation to the principality.[15] A majority of each committee must be appointees of the relevant county, metropolitan district or London borough councils for the area, two members are appointed by the NRA, and the remainder by the relevant Minister.[16] The regional flood defence committees may

---

[11] W.R.A., ss.113(1) and 221(1)—the difference lies in the exception.
[12] W.R.A., s.105(1).
[13] W.R.A., s.106(1).
[14] W.R.A., s.106(3).
[15] W.R.A., ss.10(6), 221(1).
[16] W.R.A., ss.10(1), 11(6).

delegate their functions in respect of areas within their regions by making a local flood defence scheme for creating a local flood defence district and a local flood defence committee for that district.[17]

7–010 Drainage of land is administered at local level through "internal drainage boards", each of which is the drainage board for a corresponding "internal drainage district". The latter are such areas within those of the regional flood defence committees "as will derive benefit, or avoid danger, as a result of drainage operations".[18] The principles applied in determining whether an area falls within this description were established in a decision given in relation to a scheme for setting up the River Medway Catchment Board in 1933, referred as to "the Medway letter". These entail ascertaining the highest known flood level in an area under consideration: outside tidal areas, agricultural land up to eight feet above that level may be brought within a district, while in urban areas only land below the flood level will be so treated, save for areas that would otherwise by cut off by floods. In tidal areas, a district may include agricultural land lying five feet or less above spring tides, urban land being brought in where it is at or below the level of spring tides.

7–011 Drainage boards exercise a general supervision over all drainage matters within their district.[19] The boundaries of drainage boards may be amended by petition from time to time, though there is no obligation to do this more frequently than once every 10 years.[20] This re-organisation may also be brought about by the NRA itself, in respect of such matters as the alteration of the boundaries of any drainage district or an amalgamation of any district with another, the abolition or reconstitution of any internal drainage district, and of the drainage board for it, and also the constitution of new internal drainage districts. The NRA may take over the powers and responsibilities of a board,[21] it may itself be a drainage board for an internal drainage district,[22] and any functions that it may have as such may be transferred from the NRA to a drainage board.[23]

7–012 The NRA is entitled to give any directions it considers reasonable to guide internal drainage boards in relation to their powers and duties, so as to ensure efficient working and maintenance of existing drainage works and the construction of any necessary new ones.[24] The powers

---

[17] W.R.A., s.12.
[18] L.D.A., s.1(1).
[19] L.D.A., s.1(2).
[20] L.D.A., s.2(1).
[21] W.R.A., s.108.
[22] L.D.A., s.4.
[23] L.D.A., s.5.
[24] L.D.A., s.7(1), (2).

of the internal drainage boards are circumscribed,[25] in that they may not, except with the consent of the NRA, construct or alter any drainage works if this would affect any other drainage board, nor may they, otherwise by way of maintenance, construct or alter any structure, appliance or channel for the discharge of water from their districts into a main river, except on terms agreed with the NRA.

Where the NRA's consent is required it must not be unreasonably withheld, though it may be given subject to reasonable conditions.[26] In the event of any breach of these obligations, the NRA may take action to restore the situation, and to recover any costs incurred from the person occupying the property. If an internal board fails to exercise its drainage powers adequately, or at all, the NRA may exercise all or any of them itself, provided the board has had at least 30 days notice.[27] In the same circumstances a local authority may, with the agreement of the NRA, itself exercise these powers in lieu of the NRA.[28]

7–013

In the exercise of their functions under the L.D.A., the drainage boards and local authorities must comply with the same environmental and recreational duties, and with those relating to SSSIs, as are imposed on the NRA by virtue of sections 16 and 17 of the Water Resources Act, and likewise must observe relevant codes of practice,[29] as discussed in paragraph 2–048.

7–014

Flood Defence

The main objectives of the NRA in relation to flood defence are effective defence against flooding both from rivers and from the sea, and adequate arrangements for flood forecasting and warning. An essential element of this is the need to control development in flood plains. Policy in this respect is set out in Circular 30/92 on Development and Flood Risk, published jointly by the DoE, MAFF and the Welsh Office, which sets out guidance to planning authorities on the management of flood risk when formulating statutory and local plans. The NRA has a duty under section 105(2) of the WRA to carry out surveys of areas at risk of flooding, to provide information on land that is at risk in this respect, and to liaise with planning authorities in relation to proposals for development. Where appropriate, developers may be required to undertake works to mitigate the risk of flooding as a condition of planning permission. Nevertheless, decisions on

7–015

---

[25] By L.D.A., s.7(2).
[26] L.D.A., s.7(3).
[27] s.9(1), (2).
[28] L.D.A., s.10(1).
[29] L.D.A., ss.61A–61E, inserted by the Land Drainage Act 1994 to replace ss.12 and 13, now repealed.

development proposals are of course determined not by the NRA but by local authorities and, ultimately, by the Secretary of State for the Environment. Local authorities are inevitably tempted to sanction development in comparatively low lying areas that are readily accessible and most of the time—perhaps all of the time for many years— free from flooding. However, the more developed a catchment area becomes, and the more efficient its drainage, the more readily heavy rainfall flows directly into the local streams and rivers, creating rapid rises in water levels. Periods of prolonged and heavy rain, resulting in widespread flooding, provide some dramatic examples of unsuitable development in flood plain areas. One of the essential functions of the NRA is to provide a constant reminder of these longer term risks, that must be balanced against the short term and immediate advantages of development on low lying land.

7–016   The powers of drainage boards within their districts correspond to those given to the NRA to carry out flood defence and drainage works under W.R.A. section 165, namely the right to maintain and improve existing watercourses and drainage works, including removing or altering mill dams, weirs or other obstructions to watercourses, and to construct new watercourses or drainage works and to do anything else required for the drainage of any land.[30] These powers include the right to appropriate and dispose of any matter removed in the course of work on a watercourse and to deposit the matter removed in this work on to the banks of immediately adjacent land, provided this does not create a statutory nuisance.[31]

7–017   Local authorities may also carry out the same works, either to prevent flooding or to mitigate flood damage in their area, or pursuant to a drainage scheme. Where a district council does not exercise its powers under these provisions, they may be exercised by the relevant county council.[32] Any local authority, including a county council, that carries out any works of these kinds must, except in an emergency, obtain the consent of the NRA and comply with any reasonable conditions that it imposes. The NRA must in turn consult with the relevant drainage board. The NRA has an additional power to maintain, construct or improve drainage works for defending against sea water or tidal water, including below the low water mark, whether or not in connection with a main river.[33]

7–018   Construction of new drainage works or improvements to existing ones that are likely to have a significant effect on the environment will need an environmental assessment pursuant to the Land Drainage

[30] L.D.A., s.14(2).
[31] L.D.A., s.15(1), (3); W.R.A., s.167(1), (2).
[32] L.D.A., s.16.
[33] W.R.A., s.165(2).

Improvement Works (Assessment of Environmental Effects) Regulations 1988.[34] The improvement of drainage works will not ordinarily require planning permission since it will have deemed permission under the G.D.O. 1988.[35]

It is expressly provided that any person damaged by the exercise of any of these powers is entitled to compensation. However where this arises from the widening, deepening or dredging of a watercourse or the deposit of matter removed in the course of doing this, the compensation is only such as the NRA or the drainage board determines, unless the injury could have been avoided if the activities had been carried out with reasonable care, in which case compensation must be in full.[36]

7–019

Neither drainage boards nor the NRA have any right to enter on to any third party's land to exercise their general powers to improve existing works or to construct new ones except with agreement of the relevant owners or occupiers of the land concerned. Nevertheless, they may acquire land compulsorily, with the authorisation of the relevant Minister, to enable them to perform their functions.[37]

7–020

The NRA, drainage boards and relevant local authorities have powers to ensure that there is a proper flow of water in watercourses, and where this flow is impeded, a notice requiring appropriate action may be served on any person having control of the relevant part of the watercourse, any owner or occupier of adjoining land, or any person whose act or default has resulted in the impeded flow.[38] There is a right of appeal,[39] but subject to that, if the person served with the notice fails to carry out the works required within the period stipulated in the notice, the NRA, drainage board or local authority, as the case may be may carry out the works itself and to recover its expenses from the person served. Additionally, failure to comply with the notice is an offence liable to a fine of up to £2,500 on summary conviction.

7–021

The conditions of tenure of land may impose obligations on its owners or occupiers to maintain and repair watercourses, bridges and drainage works on or adjacent to it. Where these apply, either of the NRA and the drainage board may serve notice on the person concerned requiring him to do the necessary work with all reasonable and proper despatch.[40] Obligations re-enacted in either the L.D.A. or

7–022

[34] S.I. 1988 No. 1217.
[35] G.D.O., Sched. 2, P.6.
[36] L.D.A., s.15(4).
[37] L.D.A., s.62, W.R.A., s.154.
[38] L.D.A., s.25, W.R.A., s.107(3).
[39] L.D.A., s.27.
[40] L.D.A., s.21(2); by virtue of L.D.A., s.8 the NRA has concurrent powers in this respect with the drainage board.

the W.R.A. only continue so far as specifically provided for in either of those Acts, except in relation to any flood defence obligations contained in the W.R.A., which do not have the effect of releasing anyone from previous obligations of this kind.[41] Where a person is under such an obligation, the NRA or the drainage board, as the case may be, may make a proposal for its commutation, whereby the body concerned will take it over in consideration for payments as may be determined by the NRA or the drainage board, subject to arbitration if not agreed.[42]

7–023 A variety of statutory undertakings are protected from actions by the NRA, drainage boards and local authorities under either the W.R.A. or the L.D.A., in so far as these may prejudice them in the exercise of their functions or to interfere with works or property that will affect them adversely or interfere with the carrying on of their undertakings. These bodies include the water and sewerage undertakers, public gas suppliers, electricity undertakings, British Coal, navigation, harbour and conservancy authorities, airports and (in most respects) railways.[43]

7–024 Instead of constituting a new internal drainage district and board for a particular area, powers are available under sections 137 and 138 or the W.R.A. for the NRA to promote a drainage scheme where it appears to it that the interests of agriculture require drainage works to be carried out, improved or maintained. These powers derive from the Land Drainage Act 1961, but they have never been used.

7–025 Where either the NRA or a local authority other than a district council considers that any land is capable of improvement by drainage works, but that it would be impracticable—typically because the works are not substantial enough to justify it—to constitute an internal drainage district to carry them out, it may make a scheme under section 18 of the L.D.A., and in accordance with the provisions of Schedule 4 to that Act. The scheme must include an estimate of the expenses to be incurred, which are limited to at most £50 for each hectare in the area to be improved.[44] Costs incurred under any such scheme are recoverable from the owners of the land to which it relates; the scheme itself is made a local land charge. The £50 limit may be waived by the relevant Minister where the works are urgently required in the public interest.

---

[41] W.R.A., s.185(1).
[42] L.D.A., ss.33, 34; W.R.A., s.107(4).
[43] W.R.A., s.179, Sched. 22, paras. 1, 2; L.D.A., s.67, Sched. 4.
[44] Though the limitation is worded in this way, it is presumably intended to refer to the average expenses spread over the total area improved, and not that no single hectare could have more than £50 spent on it (provided that the average stayed below this figure), which could present severe accounting problems.

Where a person with an interest in land considers it capable of improvement by drainage works, but carrying them out requires action in relation to land of some third party, who either cannot or will not consent to this, an application may be made to the appropriate Minister for an order authorising the works to be carried out nonetheless. Notice of an application for such an order must be given to those whose land is likely to be affected, and also to the NRA and any relevant drainage board, all of whom are entitled to lodge objections. An order made on the application may give such persons as it authorises the power to carry out the works and to maintain them for ever thereafter.[45] Anyone having an interest in land affected by the order that is injured as a result of the works being carried out is entitled to compensation, to be determined in the event of dispute by the Lands Tribunal.[46]

7–026

Power to require the clearing and protection of ditches is vested in the Agricultural Land Tribunal by section 28 of the L.D.A. Where a ditch[47] is liable to cause injury to any land, or to prevent the improvement of its drainage, the owner or occupier of the land may apply to the tribunal, and it may order anyone who is an owner or occupier of land through which the ditch passes or which abuts on the ditch, and anyone else who has the right to carry out the work specified in the order, to carry out remedial work. This is defined as work for cleansing the ditch, removing from it any matter which impedes the flow of water, or otherwise putting it in proper order and for protecting it.[48] Where more than one person is required to carry out any work, the tribunal may specify how its costs are to be shared between them.[49]

7–027

Similarly, where the drainage of any land requires work in connection with a ditch passing through other land, or the replacement or construction of such a ditch, or the alteration or removal of any drainage work in connection with such a ditch, the tribunal may make an order for the appropriate work to be carried out. This will give a right to enter on the land, subject to the occupier having been given at least seven days notice, and to carry out the work specified.[50] If the work has not been carried out within three months or such longer period as may be specified in the order, the appropriate Minister, or any drainage body that he authorises, may carry out the work and

7–028

---

[45] No order may be made however to authorise work affecting streams, reservoirs or feeders supplying ornamental waters, except by consent of their owners.
[46] L.D.A., s.22(7).
[47] "Ditch" includes a culverted and a piped ditch, but not a watercourse vested in or under the control of a drainage body; L.D.A., s.28(5).
[48] L.D.A., s.28(5).
[49] L.D.A., s.28(4).
[50] L.D.A., s.29(1), (4).

recover reasonable expenses from the person required by the order to do it.[51] Again, if the work causes any injury to any person, he is entitled to full compensation, to be determined by the Lands Tribunal in the event of dispute.[52]

Offences and Enforcement

7–029   It is forbidden to erect, raise or otherwise alter any mill dam, weir or other like obstruction to the flow of any ordinary watercourse, or to erect or alter any culvert that would be likely to affect the flow of any ordinary watercourse, without the written consent of the drainage board concerned[53] or of the NRA, which has a concurrent jurisdiction as regards these issues.[54] Consent must not be unreasonably withheld, and is deemed to have been given if no determination has been made on an application within two months from when it was made or when any fee in respect of it was paid, whichever is the later.[55]

7–030   Anything done in contravention of this prohibition is deemed to be a nuisance (though not a "statutory nuisance" subject to Part III of the E.P.A.). In consequence, an abatement notice may be served on the person who erected, raised, or altered the obstruction, save that if he no longer has power to remove it, the notice is to be served on whoever does have that power. Failure to comply with a notice or contravention of its requirements is an offence subject on summary conviction to a fine of up £5000, and a daily fine of up to £40 for each day the failure or contravention is continued after conviction.[56] In addition, the drainage board or the NRA, as the case may be, may take such action as may be necessary and recover its costs from the person in default.[57]

7–031   Similar provisions in the Water Resources Act[58] prohibit:

(i)   the erection of any structure in, over or under a watercourse that is part of a main river, unless with the consent of and in accordance with plans and sections approved by the NRA;

(ii)   the alteration or repair of any such structure if the work is likely to affect the flow of water in the watercourse or to impede any drainage work, unless with the consent of the NRA; and

[51] L.D.A., s.29(2).
[52] L.D.A., s.29(5), (6).
[53] L.D.A., ss.23(1).
[54] L.D.A., s.8.
[55] L.D.A., s.23(3)(4).
[56] L.D.A., s.24(3).
[57] L.D.A., s.24(4).
[58] W.R.A., s.109.

(iii) the erection or alteration of any structure designed to contain or divert flood waters of part of a main river, unless with the consent of and in accordance with plans and sections approved by the NRA.

The first two prohibitions do not however apply to work carried out in an emergency, but in such an event, the person concerned must inform the NRA in writing as soon as possible. If anything is done in contravention of these prohibitions, the NRA is entitled to remove, alter or pull down whatever may have been constructed, and recover the expenses in doing so from the person who carried out the offending work. In these situations, therefore, the abatement notice procedure does not apply and the NRA may act forthwith. **7–032**

As under the L.D.A., consents must not be unreasonably withheld, and shall be deemed to be given if neither given nor refused within two months of an application for consent or payment of any fee due, whichever is the later. Any dispute as to whether a consent is unreasonably withheld or whether any condition is unreasonable may, by agreement, be referred to arbitration; failing agreement it will be referred to and determined by the relevant Ministers. **7–033**

Coast Protection

Coast protection is subject to separate legislation from flood defence, though inevitably there is substantial potential overlap. The statutory controls are contained in the Coast Protection Act 1949, which applies throughout Great Britain (*i.e.* excluding Northern Ireland). These controls are exercised by "coast protection authorities" which are the councils of each "maritime district", that is, a district any part of which adjoins the sea. In certain circumstances, these authorities may be replaced by a "coast protection board", appointed under section 2 of the Act (though none ever have been), and "sea defence commissioners" may be appointed under local Acts. **7–034**

To avoid conflict with the flood defence provisions of the Water Resources Act and the Land Drainage Act, the Coast Protection Act defines "sea" as excluding all the waters specified in the Fourth Schedule to the Act, and references to the seashore exclude the bed and shore of those waters. The Fourth Schedule sets out an extensive list of tidal waters, defining in each case the point below which the relevant coast protection authority has responsibility. **7–035**

Coast protection authorities have general powers under the Act to carry out coast protection work (both inside and outside their area) in order to protect any land in their area against erosion or encroachment **7–036**

299

by the sea.[59] To this end, they may maintain and repair existing coastal defences; if they propose any further coast protection work, they must publish these locally, and also in the *London Gazette* if the costs are greater than £50,000.[60] Notice of the proposed works must be served on neighbouring authorities, and they and any other person have the right to object. A hearing or a local inquiry must be held to hear objections on the grounds that the proposed work will be detrimental to the protection of any land specified in the notice, or will interfere with the exercise by the objector of any statutory functions laid on him (otherwise by the Coast Protection Act 1949 itself). The Minister[61] must make a determination, following expiry of the time for receipt of objections, and any subsequent hearing or inquiry. This procedure need not be followed in an emergency, but in such a case, the authority must give notice to the NRA and any relevant internal drainage board (in so far as these bodies are not represented on the Coast Protection Authority) of the nature of the work before it commences, or as soon as possible thereafter.[62]

7–037   Where a person is subject to obligations to carry out coast protection work independently of the coast protection authority, by reason of tenure, custom, prescription or otherwise, the authority may require him by notice to carry out such work as it considers desirable. If he fails to do what is required within the period stipulated the authority may carry out the work itself and recover its reasonable expenses from him.[63] Essentially the same provisions apply in relation to sea defence commissioners who have powers or duties to carry out any coast protection work that is considered by the coast protection authority to be necessary or desirable, and they have failed to exercise or perform them. In such a case, the Minister must give the commissioners an opportunity to make representations, but subject to that he may make an order authorising the coast protection authority to carry out the work and to recover its reasonable expenses from them.[64]

7–038   If compulsory powers are needed for coast protection work, or it is considered by the coast protection authority that persons with interests in land that would be benefited by carrying out coast protection work should pay charges under the Act, then the authority may prepare a "works scheme".[65] Such a scheme must indicate the nature of the work to be carried out by the authority on its own land or

---

[59] s.4(1). All remaining section references in this chapter are to the Coast Protection Act 1949.
[60] Coast Protection (Notices) Regulations 1950 (S.I. 1950 No.124), reg. 3.
[61] The Minister of Agriculture, Fisheries and Food.
[62] s.5(6).
[63] s.15(1)–(4).
[64] s.15(5).
[65] s.6(1).

land that it proposes to acquire for the purpose, and also any work to be carried out on any other land and specify the estimated cost of all the work to be undertaken. It may indicate "contributory land" in respect of which charges should be payable on the grounds that it will be benefited by the work to be carried out. These charges are calculated in a manner, laid down in the Act, designed to reflect the increase in value of the relevant interest, assuming that no future maintenance costs in respect of the coastal works would be chargeable to the person owning that interest.[66] A works scheme may only take effect when it has been confirmed by the Minister.

As with other coastal works, publicity must be given to works schemes in the local area, and also in the *London Gazette* if the costs will exceed £50,000. Copies of the scheme must be served on owners and occupiers of all land on which the work is to be carried out, on any person who would be subject to any levy under the scheme for coast protection charges, and also on owners of contributory land.[67] A period of at least 28 days must be allowed for objections to be made to the scheme, and if any are made on any of five stipulated grounds,[68] there must be a hearing or a local inquiry.[69] The Minister may either confirm the scheme or quash it; he may also modify it, but if he does so in a way that introduces additional contributory land or further persons upon whom a coast protection charge may be levied, then the procedure must be repeated to allow the owners of that land or those further persons to lodge objections. **7–039**

A scheme that has been confirmed by the Minister provides full powers to the coast protection authority to carry out the works concerned.[70] Nevertheless, if any owner of land that is neither vested in the authority nor proposed to be acquired by it, notifies the authority that he proposes to do the work himself, then the authority may not do it. However, if the owner then fails to do it, the authority may set a time limit on him to complete it, failing which it may do it itself.[71] **7–040**

Coast protection charges may be imposed followed implementation of a works scheme, and in any other case by serving on the person to be charged a notice specifying its amount. A charge may be payable by instalments over a period of up to 30 years, including interest at such reasonable rate as the authority may determine.[72] It is primarily **7–041**

---

[66] s.7.
[67] s.8(1), (2).
[68] Set out in s.8(4).
[69] s.8(3), (4).
[70] s.9(1).
[71] s.9(3).
[72] s.10(2).

chargeable on the person entitled to the relevant interest in the land in respect of which the charge was levied. Where that person is the owner, recovery may be made from the occupier, if different, who may deduct the charges from his rent; an occupier cannot however be required to pay any sum greater than that payable by him by way of rent. A charge is payable by a mortgagee in possession or who is in receipt of the rents or profits of the land, and not, in such circumstances, by the person entitled to the interest mortgaged.[73] Charges may also be recovered from any person who receives rents and profits of the land as agent for the person entitled to the interest, to the extent that such agent has had at any time relevant funds in his hands.[74]

7–042   Coast protection works that have been constructed, altered or improved under a works scheme, will be subject to obligations regarding their maintenance and repair in accordance with that scheme. In relation to other works, coast protection authorities have powers under section 12 to maintain and repair them and to recover their reasonable costs from the owner or occupier of the land on which the work is situated. Except in an emergency, prior notice of the proposal to carry out the works must be served on the owner, and on the occupier if different, specifying both the work to be done and a period after which the authority will carry out the work if it has not already been completed.[75] If at the end of that period the work has still not been done, the authority may take all necessary steps for to do it itself and recover its reasonable costs from the owner or occupier concerned. Where the owner and occupier are different persons the original notice must have specified from which of them the authority proposed to recover its costs. Within 21 days of service of the notice, either of them may refer the matter by way of complaint to the magistrates on a variety of grounds, including that the other should pay the whole or some part of the costs, or that the coast protection authority itself should do so. The complaint may also be based on the grounds that the work is not maintenance or repair at all, or that in all the circumstances the work should be done under a scheme. If the court holds that a scheme is the appropriate procedure for the works, then essentially the same procedure as set out above applies, save that the only grounds of objection that may be made are that any provision as to the charges is inequitable or unduly onerous.[76]

7–043   It is an offence to carry out any coast protection work other than maintenance or repair without the written consent of the relevant coast protection authority, or to carry out such work in contravention

---

[73] s.10(6).
[74] s.10(7), (8).
[75] s.12(1).
[76] s.13(6).

of any conditions to which any consent may have been granted.[77] Where any such offence has been committed, the coast protection authority may require the person concerned to remove the works or to alter them in such matter as it may specify, and stipulate a period of not less than 30 days for this. If the requirements of the notice are not complied with in due time the authority may do the work itself and recover its expenses from the person concerned.[78]

Since the excavation or other removal of materials from the sea shore may result in erosion, powers are provided under section 18 to enable coast protection authorities to make an order (in accordance with the provisions of Schedule 2 to the Act) applying that section to any portions of the sea shore within their area, including any portions of the sea shore within the three mile limit. The effect of an order is to make it unlawful to excavate or remove any materials (other than minerals more than 50 feet below the surface) on, under or forming part of any portion of the sea shore concerned, save to the extent that any exceptions to the prohibition are contained in the order. For the purposes of such an order, "materials" includes minerals and turf, but not seaweed.[79]   **7–044**

Where any portion of a sea shore is subject to such an order, a coast protection authoritity may grant licences to do anything that would otherwise contravene it, imposing such conditions as it thinks fit. There are no provisions for public involvement in this process save only that a drainage authority concerned with any relevant part must be consulted before any licence is granted. It is made an express duty of coast protection authorities to enforce the provisions of section 18;[80] consequently, any failure to take steps against a person offending against the prohibition may be made the subject of an action in the courts against the authority requiring it to perform its statutory duty.   **7–045**

Where any interest in land has been depreciated, or where a person's enjoyment of land has been disturbed, causing him damage, as a result of carrying out coast protection work by a coast protection authority under the Act the authority is liable to compensate him for that depreciation or damage.   **7–046**

Likewise, where a person has applied for consent to carry out protection work and the consent has been refused, or where conditions imposed on any such consent have caused him loss, he may seek compensation for any reduction in the value of his interest. Any   **7–047**

[77] s.16(1). This provision does not however apply to certain statutory bodies as defined in s.17.
[78] s.16(2), (3).
[79] s.49(1).
[80] s.18(8).

such claim must be made within 12 months of the completion of the relevant work or the refusal of consent or the imposition of conditions, as the case may be.[81] Disputes in respect of such claims must be determined by arbitration.[82]

[81] s.19(2).
[82] s.19(3).

Chapter 8

WATER

The potential for the transmission of disease through the public water supplies, and hence the need to safeguard their quality, was first recognised in Britain in the middle of the 19th century by Edwin Chadwick and others at the time of the outbreaks of cholera throughout the country. The immediate priority for the protection of public health was to ensure effective drainage away from drinking water sources, but the discharges of drains from urban areas and from industry into streams and rivers inevitably resulted in their becoming severely polluted, and increasingly unsuitable for use by those further downstream.[1] The first national legislation in respect of polluting discharges to water, namely the Salmon Fisheries Act 1861, was nevertheless aimed at the protection not of public health, but of fishing interests. It introduced the offence of causing or knowingly permitting polluting discharges, and 15 years later the Rivers Pollution Prevention Act 1876 extended this offence to all rivers. For the reasons outlined in paragraph 1–055, this legislation proved inadequate, by reason both of the broad defences available to those discharging polluting matter, and also of the lack of an effective administration to enforce the law against those breaches to which the defences did not extend. Inevitably the local authorities, who initially were primarily responsible for enforcement, could only control polluting discharges and water supplies in their areas; bodies with wider geographical responsibilities were required for proper management of the waters.

8–001

If rivers and streams are to be of high quality, readily capable of use for drinking water and supporting thriving populations of aquatic flora and fauna, there must be management of their whole catchment area, with sufficient control over the location of industry and over other developments and all actually or potentially polluting activities in the area, in particular over all discharges to water, and also the power to maintain a satisfactory balance between consumption of water and available supplies. This integrated system of controls is in

8–002

---

[1] See paras. 1–050 to 1–058, where the historical background is described more fully.

fact only now being put in place, and requires an acceptance of direction by regulatory bodies that would not have been contemplated 100 years ago.

8–003   There has also been increasing concern, both at official level and among the public at large over the effects of pollution of water, not only on public health but on the fish and other creatures that depend on the aquatic environment, in both inland waters, and also coastal and other marine waters. The decline of the otter may well have been partly due to loss of habitat, but it is also attributable to a lack of fish, as a result of pollution, in many of the rivers that it used to inhabit. Similarly, there has been concern over the fate of creatures at the top of the food chain, such as seals and certain sea birds, which are dependent on plentiful supplies of fish in the North Sea, which for many years received massive volumes of industrial wastes discharged into the major rivers that feed it.

8–004   Until very recently, there was no statutory definition of what quality of water was to be regarded as acceptable, drinking water merely being required to be "wholesome", without legally binding guidance as to the meaning of this term. For long after the need to avoid infectious pollutants in water, notably from sewage discharges, was recognised, there remained relatively little understanding, still less consensus, on what harmful effects other substances might have if regularly consumed at low concentrations, for example heavy metals, pesticides and nitrates. While such substances are today recognised to be at least potentially harmful, the appropriate maximum concentrations that should be permitted still remain highly debatable. These cannot but be somewhat arbitrary, arrived at by extrapolation from the results of experiments that necessarily involve consumption of atypical levels of the substances under test, by creatures with metabolisms that differ in uncertain ways from that of humans, and from the physical responses of often relatively few individuals who may be unusually sensitive or insensitive to the pollutants concerned. Even where a degree of risk is acknowledged, a determination of the acceptable extent of that risk has to have regard to the costs of any additional precautions. Setting the proper balance between those costs and the reduction in risk that they afford is not a scientific but a political question, albeit one requiring considerable scientific input and understanding.

8–005   The most widely accepted source of standards is the World Health Organisation, and its standards have in many cases formed the basis of those adopted in EC legislation. Nevertheless, the EC legislation imposes more stringent standards in a number of respects, and it is of course this latter that must be implemented in the United Kingdom, where mandatory.

306

Water legislation in the United Kingdom has historically been 8–006 divided between statutes broadly directed to the organisational structure and the relevant powers and duties for abstracting and supplying water to customers, land drainage, and the operation of sewerage systems, and statutes directed to controlling pollution of water. Until the recent wholesale revision of the legislation in England and Wales, the principal statutes were respectively the Water Act 1973 and the Control of Pollution Act 1974, part of which applied throughout Britain. Privatisation of the water industry in England and Wales in 1989 coincided, necessarily, with statutory implementation of several EC directives on water quality that had hitherto been given effect through administrative directions to the publicly controlled water authorities. The relevant legislative measures for both of these objectives were contained in the Water Act 1989, which additionally provided for the hiving out of the regulatory responsibilities of the water authorities (and also of HMIP in so far as it controlled the discharges of the water authorities' sewage treatment works), into a newly constituted National Rivers Authority (NRA). In 1991 all the water legislation was consolidated, and the Water Act 1989 was almost wholly repealed. The current legislation is now principally contained in the Water Industry Act 1991 and the Water Resources Act 1991, with further measures contained in the Land Drainage Act, the Statutory Water Companies Act and the Water Consolidation (Consequential Provisions) Act, all of 1991. Before considering these, however, it is appropriate to review the applicable and underlying EC legislation.

EC Legislation

The European Community was active in the promotion of water 8–007 quality controls from a comparatively early stage. The EC Directives of principal concern to water quality are set out in Table 8/I.

TABLE 8/I

Directive	O.J. Reference	Title
75/440	[1975] O.J. L194	The quality required of surface water intended for the abstraction of drinking water.
76/160	[1976] O.J. L31	The quality of bathing water

76/464	[1976] O.J. L129	Pollution caused by certain dangerous substances discharged into the aquatic environment
78/659	[1978] O.J. L222	The quality of fresh waters needing protection or improvement in order to support fish life
79/869	[1979] O.J. L271	The methods of measurement and frequencies of sampling and analysis of surface water intended for the abstraction of drinking water
79/923	[1979] O.J. L281	The quality required of shellfish waters
80/68	[1980] O.J. L20	The protection of groundwater against pollution caused by certain dangerous substances
80/778	[1980] O.J. L229	The quality of water intended for human consumption
82/176*	[1982] O.J. L81	Limit values and quality objectives for mercury discharges by the chlor-alkali electrolysis industry
83/513*	[1983] O.J. L291	Limit values and quality objectives for cadmium discharges
84/156*	[1984] O.J. L74	Limit values and quality objectives for mercury discharges by sectors other than the chlor-alkali electrolysis industry
84/491*	[1984] O.J. L274	Limit values and quality objectives for discharges of hexachloro-cyclo-hexane
86/280*	[1986] O.J. L181	Limit values and quality objectives for carbon tetrachloride, DDT, pentachlorophenol.
88/347*	[1988] O.J. L158	Limit values and quality objectives for isodrin, endrin, dieldrin, aldrin hexachlorobenzene, hexachlorobutadiene, chloroform
90/415*	[1990] O.J. L219	Limit values and quality objectives for 1,2 - dichloroethane, trichloroethylene, perchloroethylene, trichlorobenzene

91/271	[1991] O.J. L135	Urban waste water treatment
91/676	[1991] O.J. L375	The protection of waters against pollution caused by nitrates from agricultural sources
* daughter Directives to 76/464		

These Directives fall into three categories: **8–008**

(i) Directives specifying quality standards for waters to be used for specific purposes, (Directives 75/440, 76/160, 78/659, 79/869, 79/923 and 80/778);

(ii) Directives controlling the discharge of specific dangerous substances to surface waters or to groundwater (Directive 76/464 and its daughter Directives, and Directive 80/68); and

(iii) Controls over specific polluting activities (Directives 91/271 and 91/676).

The standards imposed by this EC legislation have in certain **8–009** respects been exceptionally stringent, and in some cases impossible to achieve.[2] Further, in the negotiations leading up to the Maastricht treaty concern was expressed, by the United Kingdom in particular, on the issue of subsidiarity and whether it was appropriate for the EC to be legislating for water quality, either at all, or at least to the extent that it already had done so. As mentioned below, the European Commission has announced that the bulk of the EC water legislation will be recast, and this is now in hand. It remains to be seen how far this will give increased discretion to Member States, and specifically increased discretion to reduce water quality, at least in certain circumstances.[3]

The European Commission announced proposals in late 1993 for **8–010** major revision of the EC water legislation, prompted at least in part by the emphasis on subsidiarity that is now part of the Rome Treaty following the Maastricht amendments. The drinking water Directive

[2] Notably in relation to the limit on total pesticides in drinking water, which can only be properly ascertained by measuring separately the concentrations of individual pesticide contaminants, several of which may be present in amounts below those at which they can be measured with any accuracy, if at all. There is an understandable but often misguided tendency to seek to prescribe as maximum levels of substances regarded as undesirable whatever is the limit of detection by current analytical techniques - if you can measure it there's too much - irrespective of the sometimes questionable environmental benefits obtained from the heavy expenditure that such an approach may require.

[3] Even if proposals along these lines are to be put forward, the change in the balance of power between the European Parliament and the other EC institutions following the Maastricht amendments to the Rome treaty may not allow proposals for repeal of the existing legislation in favour of anything noticeably less stringent an easy passage.

would be significantly amended, while the Directives on the quality of surface water for drinking, and on freshwater fish and shellfish waters would be replaced with a Directive on the ecological quality of surface waters[4] that sets out a number of objectives, in particular, that Member States should control pollution from point and diffuse sources and other anthropogenic factors affecting surface water quality. The Directive on bathing water would remain but amended so as to remove some parameters and to revise the applicable standards for the remainder. Proposals that have been in existence for some time for expansion or replacement of the groundwater Directive would also be implemented, to give one that addresses freshwater management and groundwater protection generally.[5]

8–011   Implementation by the United Kingdom of the current Directives was, until the Water Act 1989, purely by way of administrative direction to the water authorities. Though the European Commission issued a Reasoned Opinion in 1980 on the grounds that this did not constitute proper implementation, the matter was not pursued. The need for effective implementation came to the fore as a result of the proposals to privatise the water industry, coupled with uncertainty as to whether the EC Directives would be directly applicable to the newly privatised water companies.[6] The 1989 Act thus laid down for the first time provisions for establishing water quality standards and objectives that would express the obligations in the Directives in legally enforceable terms.

Dangerous Substances Directive 76/464

8–012   Several of the Directives set very demanding standards in respect of certain parameters, but possibly the most ambitious for the long term was Directive 76/464 on the discharge to water of various dangerous substances. This originally extended to the "aquatic environment" quite generally, including groundwater, but the subsequent ground-water Directive 80/68 provided that once member states had implemented it in their territories, the provisions of Directive 76/464 should no longer apply in that territory in so far as they relate to groundwater.[7]

8–013   Directive 76/464 sets out in its Annex a List I and List II of families and groups of substances, which have come to be known as the "black list" and the "grey list" respectively. Table 8/II sets out the Annex in its entirety.

[4] [1994] O.J. C222.
[5] DoE News Release 861, December 14, 1993.
[6] See paras. 2–034, 2–035 and n. 41A (Chapter 2).
[7] Directive 80/68, Art.21(3).

TABLE 8/II

Annex to Directive 76/464

List I of families and groups of substances

List I contains certain individual substances which belong to the following families and groups of substances, selected mainly on the basis of their toxicity, persistence and bioaccumulation, with the exception of those which are biologically harmless or which are rapidly converted into substances which are biologically harmless.

1. organohalogen compounds and substances which may form such compounds in the aquatic environment,
2. organophosphorus compounds,
3. organotin compounds,
4. substances in respect of which is has been proved that they possess carcinogenic properties in or via the aquatic environment (where certain substances in List II are carcinogenic, they are included in category 4 of this List),
5. mercury and its compounds,
6. cadmium and its compounds,
7. persistent mineral oils and hydrocarbons of petroleum origin,

and for the purposes of implementing Articles 2, 8, 9 and 14 of this Directive,

8. persistent synthetic substances which may float, remain in suspension or sink and which may interfere with any use of the waters.

List II of families and groups of substances

List II contains:

— substances belonging to the families and groups of substances in List I for which the limit values referred to in Article 6 of the Directive have not been determined,

— certain individual substances and categories of substances belonging to the families and groups of substances listed below,

311

and which have a deleterious effect on the aquatic environment, which can, however be confined to a given area and which depend on the characteristics and location of the water into which they are discharged.

Families and groups of substances referred to in the second indent:

1. The following metalloids and metals and their compounds:

1. zinc	6. selenium	11. tin	16. vanadium
2. copper	7. arsenic	12. barium	17. cobalt
3. nickel	8. antimony	13. beryllium	18. thalium
4. chromium	9. molybdenum	14. boron	19. tellurium
5. lead	10. titanium	15. uranium	20. silver

2. Biocides and their derivatives not appearing in List I.
3. Substances which have a deleterious effect on the taste and/ or smell of the products for human consumption derived from the aquatic environment, and compounds liable to give rise to such substances in water.
4. Toxic or persistent organic compounds of silicon and substances which may give rise to such compounds in water, excluding those which are biologically harmless or are rapidly converted in water into harmless substances.
5. Inorganic compounds of phosphorus and elemental phosphorus.
6. Non persistent mineral oils and hydrocarbons of petroleum origin.
7. Cyanides, fluorides.
8. Substances which have an adverse effect on the oxygen balance, particularly: ammonia, nitrites.

Member States are required to *eliminate* pollution of waters by the black list substances and to *reduce* pollution of waters by the grey list substances.[8] There must be prior authorisation of all discharges of black list substances, setting emission standards, including, where appropriate, standards for discharges to sewer.[9] These emission

[8] Art.2.
[9] Art.3.

standards must specify both the maximum permitted concentration in the discharge and the maximum quantity that may be discharged over prescribed periods, either in absolute terms or by reference to production levels of the activity giving rise to the discharge.[10] For grey list substances, programmes must be established for the reduction of water pollution by them, and there must likewise be prior authorisation of discharges to water, applying suitable emission standards based on quality objectives for the receiving waters.[11]

The European Commission is required by the Directive[12] to bring   **8–014**
forward proposals for limit values for emission standards for the black list substances, based mainly on their toxicity, persistence and bio-accumulation, together with proposals for quality objectives drawn up on the same basis. Provision for quality objectives was included at the instigation of the United Kingdom, which had traditionally applied water pollution controls by reference to the standards of the receiving waters rather than by emission limits on discharges, irrespective of the waters that they enter.

The European Commission proceeded to draw up a list of black list   **8–015**
substances contained in its Communication to the Council of June 22, 1982.[13] 1500 substances were identified as potential candidates for the black list; concentrating on those used in comparatively large quantities or which by reason of toxicity, persistence and bio-accumulation were of particular concern, produced the final list of 129 substances. Nevertheless, some 12 years later, only 17 of these had been made the subject of specific controls through daughter directives to Directive 76/464, as indicated in Table 8/I above.[14] As stated at the beginning of List II, the remainder are to be treated as though they were in the grey list until such time as limit values for them have been fixed.

Implementation of Directive 76/464 and its daughter directives in   **8–016**
the United Kingdom is to a large extent by way of individual authorisations of discharges, whether to surface waters or to sewer, through the consent systems described below. Water quality standards as prescribed by these directives are set out in the Surface Waters (Dangerous Substances) (Classification) Regulations 1989 for England and Wales, and the Surface Waters (Dangerous Substances) (Classification) (Scotland) Regulations 1990.[15]

---

[10] Art.5.
[11] Art.7.
[12] Art.6.
[13] [1982] O.J. C176.
[14] A proposal to set water quality objectives for chromium (a grey list substance) was also put forward, but it was never adopted, and has now been abandoned; [1985] O.J. C351 and [1988] O.J. C43.
[15] S.I. 1989 No. 2286 and S.I. 1990 No. 126 (S.15).

313

Groundwater Directive 80/68

8–017   It is in the nature of groundwater that it normally travels very slowly through the permeable strata in which it lies (the aquifer), and it is highly susceptible to contamination from both point and diffuse sources, depending on the permeability of the strata lying between these sources and the aquifer. Once contaminated, groundwater is exceptionally difficult, and in some circumstances virtually impossible, to clean up. Groundwater provides around 35 per cent of demand in England and Wales, and in some areas is the only available future resource.[16] Over the EC as a whole a much higher proportion, some 70 per cent, of all drinking water is abstracted from groundwater. As increases in the standard of living have resulted in disproportionate increases in demand for water, the pressures on water resources in many areas are now such that it is vital to protect reserves of groundwater to ensure they are available for future use, even if they are not already in use currently.

8–018   The Groundwater Directive is based on Directive 76/464, and inevitably has much in common with it. As with the earlier Directive, an Annex contains two lists of respectively "black list" and "grey list" compounds. These lists are very similar to the earlier lists, but differ in the following respects:

TABLE 8/III

Comparison of Directives 80/68 and 76/464	
Groundwater Directive 80/68	**Dangerous Substances Directive 76/464**
List I—'Black List' Substances	
7. Mineral oils and hydrocarbons	7. Persistent mineral oils and hydrocarbons of petroleum origin
8. Cyanides	8. Persistent synthetic substances which may float, or remain in suspension or sink, and which may interfere with any use of the waters

[16] *Policy and Practice for the Protection of Groundwater*, NRA, 1992, p.2.

314

List II—'Grey List' Substances	
3. Substances which have a deleterious effect on the taste and/or odour of groundwater, and compounds liable to cause the formation of such substances in such water and to render it unfit for human consumption	3. Substances which have a deleterious affect on the taste and/or smell of the products for human consumption derived from the aquatic environment.
6. Fluorides	6. Non-persistent mineral oils and hydrocarbons of petroleum origin
7. Ammonia and nitrites	7. Cyanides, fluorides 8. Substances which have an adverse effect on the oxygen balance, particularly ammonia, nitrites

The main changes therefore are that all mineral oils and hydrocarbons are in the black list of the groundwater Directive, whether persistent or not, and cyanides are in the black list of the groundwater Directive but in the grey list of Directive 76/464.

There are excepted from the scope of the Directive discharges of domestic effluents from isolated dwellings not connected to sewer and outside areas protected for abstraction of drinking water; the Directive also does not apply to matter containing radioactive substances. A further exception applies to discharges which contain either black list or grey list substances "in a quantity and concentration so small as to obviate any present or future danger of deterioration in the quality of the receiving groundwater".[17] This provision was considered by the European Court of Justice in *European Commission v. Germany*[18] in the following terms:

8–020

16. Article 2(b) of the Directive does not refer to discharges of substances in list I or II, whether or not in solution, but to discharges of other substances that contain substances in those two lists.

[17] Art.2(b).
[18] Case C-131/88, 1991 ECR I-825, at I-869, 870.

315

17. Substances in list I or II contained in such discharges must be present in quantities sufficiently small as to obviate *prima facie*, without there even being a need for an evaluation, all risk of pollution of the groundwater. That is why Article 2(b) of the Directive refers not to an evaluation by the competent authority of a Member State but to a simple finding.

18. Thus the meaning of that provision is that if the quantity of substances in list I (or II) contained in discharges of other substances is such that the risk of pollution cannot be automatically excluded, the Directive is applicable and, in that case, Article 2(b) cannot . . . . be taken in conjunction with the other provisions of the Directive in order to interpret them.

The United Kingdom now interprets this exception as applying to the disposal of waste only where the nature of the waste is such that any leachate from that waste can pose no danger in the quality of the receiving groundwater.[19]

8–021   The distinction between the black list and grey list substances is that in the former case, their introduction into groundwater must be prevented, whereas introduction of grey list substances and groundwater must merely be limited "so as to avoid pollution of this water by these substances".[20] To reinforce the preventative measures in relation to black list substances, Member States must prohibit all direct discharge of the substances (*i.e.* introduction of them into groundwater without percolation through ground or subsoil) and they must subject to prior investigation any disposal or tipping of them for the purpose of disposal which might lead to "indirect discharge" (being the introduction into groundwater of substances after percolation through ground or subsoil). Where there may be indirect discharge, the relevant activity must either be prohibited or all necessary technical precautions to prevent the discharge must be observed.[21] Additionally, Member States must take all appropriate measures to prevent any other indirect discharge of black list substances due to any activities other than disposal or tipping for the purpose of disposal. The only general exception from these prohibitions is where the groundwater is permanently unsuitable for other uses, and if all technical precautions have been taken to ensure that substances discharged into these groundwaters cannot reach other aquatic

---

[19] Circular 11/94, para. 7.9, which replaces previous unsatisfactory guidance based on whether unimpaired use of water from an aquifer would be possible without significant changes in its treatment.

[20] Art.3.

[21] Art.4(1).

systems and cannot harm other ecosystems.[22] There is also a specific exemption allowing re-injection into the same aquifer of water that has been pumped from it for geothermal purposes, water pumped out of mines and quarries, or other water pumped out for civil engineering works.[23] Essentially the same requirements apply in relation to grey list substances; however since the obligation is only to "limit" discharges of them, outright prohibitions are not called for, provided that appropriate technical precautions are taken to prevent pollution.

The Directive was relied on in a complaint made to the European   **8–022** Commission with regard to a landfill in Suffolk from which pesticide residues were found to be leaching, as disclosed by monitoring results released by the then Anglian Water Authority.[24] It remains however uncertain whether the Directive requires action to be taken in relation to closed, as opposed to active, landfill sites. The specific requirements in Articles 4 and 5 setting out prohibitions or controls over direct discharges and over other activities would appear to be clearly concerned with current and future operations only. Nevertheless the broad requirement in Article 3 is to take necessary steps to prevent or limit the introduction of the listed substances into groundwater, while paragraph 1 of Article 1 states that the purpose of the Directive is among other things "as far as possible to check or eliminate the consequences of pollution which has already occurred". The question resolves into whether the Directive requires the prohibition or limitation of discharges themselves, including in particular indirect discharges as by leachate from a closed landfill site, or whether it is confined to bringing about restrictions on such discharges by appropriate regulation of the activities that may give rise to them. It is relevant to note in this connection that the Directive was made under both Articles 100 and 235 of the Rome Treaty.[25] If the intention was to control activities solely, for the purposes of harmonising the relevant laws and ensuring proper functioning of the Common Market, Article 100 should have sufficed. Article 235 was relied on because of the intention to legislate in the sphere of environmental protection and improvement of the quality of life,[26] and this favours regarding indirect discharges by percolation from landfill sites as being within the scope of the Directive, however arising and notwithstanding that this does not result from any continuing operations of any kind. In any event, the Directive clearly must apply to any such discharges arising

---

[22] Art.4(2).

[23] Art.4(3).

[24] The matter was not however pursued to trial.

[25] In 1980 the current environmental provisions of Articles 130 R, S and T, introduced by the Single European Act, were of course absent from the Rome Treaty.

[26] Recital 4.

out of landfilling that took place after the Directive was due to be implemented, *i.e.* from December 19, 1981 onwards. In practice, it must be unlikely that the European Commission will itself take the initiative to resolve this uncertainty unless and until its own proposals with regard to liability for environmental damage have resulted in an agreed policy in relation to historic contamination.

8–023   In the United Kingdom, controls over waste disposal to landfill under C.O.P.A. and now the E.P.A., and over discharges to controlled waters under the W.R.A. have implemented the Directive in practice in relation to these activities, but until the Waste Management Licensing Regulations 1994[27] there was no attempt to introduce implementing legislation. Circular 4/82[28] issued guidance on the Directive's requirements, including advice as to determining whether substances should be regarded as in the black list or the grey list, and on the circumstances in which the Directive could be regarded as not applying at all by virtue of the amounts discharged being very small. The Circular was revised in these respects, principally by DoE Circular 20/90.[29]

8–024   Regulation 15 of the 1994 Licensing Regulations however gives the requirements a statutory basis.[30] This obliges waste regulation authorities, when considering an application for a waste management licence that might lead to a breach of the Directive, to undertake an appropriate investigation of the risks to groundwater of carrying on the proposed activity at the site in question, and to grant a licence only if it is satisfied that these can be effectively avoided, including by attaching appropriate conditions to any licence granted. Any licence for an activity that creates any risk of breach of the Directive must be for a limited period only and reviewed at least every four years. Existing waste management and C.O.P.A. waste disposal licences must also be reviewed and varied or revoked as necessary to give effect to the Directive.

The NRA has developed a policy for the protection of groundwater, set out in its 1992 strategy document; in particular, it is proposed that after the system of Statutory Water Quality Objectives (SWQOs) has been put in place for rivers (see paragraph 8–059 below) a similar set of SWQOs for groundwaters should also be established. Where SWQOs have been set, the NRA is under a statutory duty to ensure, so far as practicable, that these objectives are achieved at all times.[31] So far, however, no SWQOs for groundwater have been proposed.

---

[27] S.I. 1994 No. 1056.
[28] March 1, 1982; W.O. 7/82.
[29] October 29, 1990; W.O. 34/90.
[30] Discussed more fully at paras. 11–172 to 11–174.
[31] W.R.A. s.84(1).

Bathing Water—Directive 76/160

For the purposes of this Directive, bathing water is all running and **8–025**
still freshwaters, and sea water, in which bathing is either explicitly
authorised, or else is not prohibited and is in fact "traditionally
practised by a large number of bathers".[32] Water in swimming pools
(by which is presumably intended those replenished by piped water
supplies, and not man-made pools designed to be refilled by sea water
at high tide), and water used for therapeutic purposes, such as at
health spas, is excluded. An Annex to the Directive sets out 19
physical, chemical and microbiological parameters, and guide (G) or
imperative (I) values for each, as well as prescribing minimum
sampling frequencies and methods of analysis and inspection.
Member states are required to prescribe values for these parameters
for all its bathing areas that are at least as stringent as the I values, and
had to take all necessary measures to ensure that the quality of their
bathing waters conformed to these values within 10 years of the
Directive, *i.e.* by December 1986. Compliance with the values requires
compliance by either 95 per cent or 90 per cent of the samples,
depending on the parameter, except in the case of the "total coliform"
and faecal coliform parameters where compliance by 80 per cent of the
samples is sufficient; however the non-complying samples must not
deviate from the prescribed values by more than 50 per cent except in
the case of microbiological parameters, pH and dissolved oxygen, and
consecutive water samples taken at statistically suitable intervals must
not both deviate from the relevant values.

Non-compliance may be ignored if it results from floods, other **8–026**
natural disasters or abnormal weather conditions. Other derogations
are strictly limited to circumstances where certain defined parameters
are not met because of exceptional weather or geographical conditions, and when bathing water fails to comply as a result of natural
enrichment in certain substances received by the water from the
ground without human intervention. Even in these cases, public
health requirements must be maintained. Member states were also
entitled to grant derogations to provide for a longer period than the 10
years prescribed for bringing bathing waters into compliance, provided justification for this was communicated to the Commission
within six years of the directive, *i.e.* by December 1981.

As part of their implementation of the Directive, Member States **8–027**
were required to identify relevant bathing waters that would come
within the scope of the Directive. The United Kingdom initially
identified only 27 (as compared with 39 by Luxembourg, and 8,000

---

[32] Art.1(2).

throughout the EC in total), none of which were in Scotland or Northern Ireland. Following pressure from the European Commission[33] further bathing waters were identified, bringing the total up to around 450, including several in both Scotland and Northern Ireland.[34] Before privatisation of the water industry, the government relied on powers under the Water Resources Act 1963 and the Water Act 1973 to give effect to the Directive's requirements.[35] Following privatisation, the classification of bathing waters as required by the Directive has been required under the Bathing Waters (Classification) Regulations 1991 and the Bathing Waters (Classification) (Scotland) Regulations 1991.[36]

8–028   The United Kingdom was held to be in breach of the Directive by the European Court of Justice in relation to the quality of bathing water in the area of Blackpool, which had not been designated under the Directive,[37] The United Kingdom argued that the definition of "bathing water" in the Directive was too imprecise to be given legal effect, but this was dismissed by the European Court, in view of the Directive's underlying objectives as set out in the first two recitals, that include the protection of the environment and public health and the improvement of living conditions — accordingly excluding bathing waters from the Directive simply because the number of bathers was below a threshold set by the United Kingdom was not appropriate. An argument that the Directive merely required all practical steps to be taken to achieve compliance with the prescribed limit values was also dismissed, it being held that there was an explicit obligation to meet those values within the 10 years expiring at the end of December 1985. The Court suggested that an absolute physical impossibility to carry out the obligations imposed by the Directive might justify failure to fulfil them, but pointed out that the United Kingdom had not established the existence of any such impossibility.

8–029   In the recasting of the EC water Directives, the issue of subsidiarity arises particularly strongly in relation to controls over bathing water quality. Given that there is virtually no evidence of major public health

---

[33] The Commission was at the same time instituting proceedings, or threatening to do so, against all other Member States for failure to implement the Bathing Water Directive adequately, with the sole exception of Portugal, to which the Directive did not apply at all until 1993.

[34] In 1992, the last year for which figures are currently available, a total of 416 bathing waters had been identified in England and Wales for the purposes of the Directive; *Bathing Water Quality in England and Wales - 1992*, NRA, May 1993.

[35] Similar powers for Scotland were contained in the Rivers (Prevention of Pollution) Scotland Acts 1951 and 1965.

[36] S.I. 1991 No.1597 and S.I. 1991 No.1609 (S.144).

[37] *European Commission v. United Kingdom*, Case C-56/90, [1993] Env. L.R. 472.

hazards from bathing water in the designated bathing areas[38] (even though the waters may appear physically revolting and give rise to minor infections), the principal justification for EC controls would appear to be the harmonising of rules impacting on such an important economic activity as tourism. While this justification has considerable force in relation to, for example, Mediterranean beaches, it is far weaker in relation to many of those in the United Kingdom.[39]

Freshwater Fish and Shellfish Waters—Directives 78/659 and 79/923

These Directives both prescribe guide (G) and imperative (I) values for physical and chemical parameters that must be observed; the shellfish Directive has a considerably longer list of parameters, including in particular many more metals and faecal coliforms.   8–030

The freshwater fish Directive applies to waters designated by member states as needing protection or improvement in order to support fish life, excluding natural or artificial fish ponds used for intensive fish farming. The fish for these purposes are those of indigenous species and other species the presence of which is desirable for water management purposes. In fact the parameters given in this Directive relate solely to salmonid waters, which support or may be capable of supporting salmon, trout, grayling and white fish, and cyprinid waters, being waters which support or may be capable of supporting cyprinids and other species such as pike, perch and eel. Member States are required to set values for the waters concerned and establish programmes to reduce pollution and to ensure that designated waters comply with the prescribed values within five years following their designation. The values have to be read in conjunction with comments that are made against them in several cases which either impose additional requirements or allow some variation from the values in specific circumstances.   8–031

Compliance with the Directive can be achieved under the new water legislation through the system of statutory water quality objectives, and the accompanying programmes for water quality improvement   8–032

[38] House of Commons Select Committee on the Environment, Fourth Report 1989–1990 "Pollution of Beaches". A four year study, funded by the DoE, the Department of Health, the Welsh Office and the NRA, that formed the basis of a "Final Report into the Health Effects of Sea Bathing" (Water Research Centre, 1994), concluded that there is a correlation between levels of certain micro-organisms in the sea and gastro-intestinal symptoms, but that the likelihood of diarrhoea only became statistically significant at total coliform counts exceeding the imperative standards of the Directive.

[39] In principle, designation of 'bathing waters' should perhaps depend not on the number of bathers, but on the proportion of them who were not ordinarily resident in that Member State, impossible though that would be to administer.

that these involve. Similar powers are available in Scotland under the amendments to C.O.P.A. 1974 made by Schedule 23 to the Water Act 1989, and specifically sections 30B to 30D as inserted by that Schedule.

8–033   The appropriateness of EC legislation on this topic was questioned at the time of the Directive's introduction, and remains an issue that will be undoubtedly a matter for consideration in the recasting of the EC water legislation. The Directive is aimed specifically at the safeguarding of fish populations from harm deriving from pollution, and not public health as such. Indeed the public health aspects of the possible ingestion by edible fish of pollutants is the subject of a separate Directive 91/493[40] specifically concerned with these aspects; this is implemented in the United Kingdom by the Food Safety (Fishery Products) Regulations 1992 and the Food Safety Fishery Products on Fishing Vessels Regulations 1992.[41]

8–034   The shellfish Directive 79/923 follows essentially the same format as Directive 78/659. It applies to coastal and brackish waters designated by Member States as needing protection or improvement in order to support shellfish life and growth, and "thus to contribute to the high quality of shellfish products directly edible by man".[42] "Shellfish" covers both bivalve and gasteropod molluscs. Member States were required to designate shellfish waters within two years of notification of the Directive, and to establish programmes to reduce pollution and to ensure that designated waters conform with the prescribed values within six years following designation.

8–035   In the case of this Directive, although it is stated to be necessary to safeguard certain shellfish populations from harm resulting from discharge of pollutants into the sea, there is a hint that it is also drafted in part to protect public health, in that the final recital reads:

> "Whereas this Directive cannot, *by itself*, ensure protection of consumers of shellfish production; whereas proposals to this end should therefore be submitted by the Commission as soon as possible".

The Directive is certainly not sufficient in itself to secure such protection, since it neither covers all contaminants that may make edible shellfish dangerous to eat, nor does it of course address handling shellfish after they have been harvested. This latter aspect is the subject of the separate Directive 91/492,[43] implemented in the United Kingdom by the Food Safety (Live Bivalve Molluscs and Other

---

[40] [1991] O.J. L268.
[41] S.I. 1992 No. 3163 and S.I. 1992 No. 3165.
[42] Art. 1.
[43] [1991] O.J. L268.

Shellfish) Regulations 1992.[44] Nevertheless, it is clearly not only easier to sample shellfish waters than to take an adequate number of samples from shellfish, but also problems, particularly with sewage pollution, will come to light sooner by sampling the waters than the shellfish themselves.

Surface Water for Drinking—Directive 75/440

This Directive sets out 46 physical, chemical and microbiological parameters for assessing surface water to be used for drinking, and for classifying it into four categories, namely A1, A2 and A3, which may be used for drinking water when treated in the manner prescribed for that category, and other waters, which may not be used for drinking water except where suitable processes, including blending, are used to bring the standard up to that required for drinking water. "Appropriate" standard methods of treatment are given in Annex I for the three categories: Category A1, representing the purest water, requires simple physical treatment, such as rapid filtration, and disinfection, category A2 requires normal physical treatment, chemical treatment and disinfection, while category A3 requires intensive physical and chemical treatment, extended treatment and disinfection. These treatment processes are not however mandatory; reference to them in the Directive would appear to be essentially in order to provide a proper basis for establishing the values of the 46 parameters.

8–036

Annex II to the Directive that lists these parameters provides for both imperative (I) and guide (G) values to be prescribed for each parameter and for each category. In fact values have not been set in all cases, and for some parameters no values are set at all, though there is provision in the Directive for this to be done subsequently by the Commission. Methods of measurement of these parameters, and the frequencies of sampling and analysis are prescribed by the related Directive 79/869.[44A] These include the standard British approach of regarding water as complying if 95 per cent of tested samples comply though, unlike the traditional British approach, further qualifications are put on the non-complying 5 per cent, namely that (i) the deviation should not be more than 50 per cent (except for temperature, pH, dissolved oxygen and microbiological parameters), (ii) there must be no resultant danger to public health, and (iii) consecutive water samples taken at statistically suitable intervals should not deviate from the relevant parametric values.[45] However, where floods, natural disasters or abnormal weather conditions lead to high values these

8–037

---

[44] S.I. 1992 No. 3164.
[44A] [1979] O.J. L271.
[45] Dir.75/440, Art. 5(1).

may be ignored, and indeed the Directive itself may be disapplied.[46]
The Directive may also be disapplied in certain circumstances where
surface water undergoes natural enrichment causing it to exceed any
particular prescribed values, and also in the case of surface water in
shallow lakes or virtually stagnant water for certain parameters,
including nitrates and phosphates, BOD and COD.

8–038   Member States are required to take all necessary measures to ensure
continuing improvement of surface water, and especially any falling
within category A3. "Considerable improvements" were to be
achieved under these national programmes over the 10 years from
1975,[47] but in fact since the European Commission had no way of
monitoring any programmes or progress, this amounted to little more
than aspiration. Surface waters in England and Wales are classified in
accordance with the Surface Waters (Classification) Regulations
1989;[48] in Scotland the Surface Waters (Classification) (Scotland)
Regulations 1990[49] apply.

Drinking Water

8–039   Action to ensure constant availability of high quality drinking water
is fundamental to much of environmental legislation and its practical
implementation. Accordingly, though the supply of drinking water to
the public is arguably more of a commercial operation than an
environmental issue, an outline of the applicable controls is given
here.

8–040   The supply of drinking water to the general public is the responsibility of the statutory water undertakers appointed under section 6 of the
Water Industry Act 1991. For many parts of England and Wales, these
undertakers are the same as the sewerage undertakers who succeeded
to the 10 regional water authorities in September 1989. Nevertheless,
for historical reasons, there had for many years before that been
statutory water companies operating within defined areas of those
regions under a highly regulated statutory monopoly for the supply of
drinking water to the public. They might acquire the water either from
sources they had developed or acquired for themselves, or they might
purchase water from the local regional water authority. Essentially the
same structure for the water supply industry has been continued since
September 1989. Controls over the quality of drinking water are

---

[46] Dir.75/440, Art.5(3), Art.8.
[47] Art.4(2).
[48] S.I. 1989 No. 1148.
[49] S.I. 1990 No. 121 (S.13).

enforced by the Drinking Water Inspectorate, which is an independent arm of the Department of the Environment—it is planned that this should remain an independent regulator, following the absorption of the NRA into the new environment agency for England and Wales. In addition, a variety of relatively small scale supplies are made on a private basis, and private supplies (which include a supply provided for the purposes of the bottling of water, but not the bottled water itself) are also included in the quality controls of the W.I.A.

It is the duty of water undertakers, when supplying water to any premises for domestic or food production purposes, to supply only water which is wholesome at the time of supply. The undertaker is under a further duty to ensure, so far as reasonably practicable, that the sources from which it supplies water for these purposes that there is in general no deterioration in quality of the water supplied.[50] Accordingly, where a high standard has already been achieved, it must, so far as reasonably practicable, be maintained, notwithstanding that some deterioration would be possible without the water ceasing to be wholesome. The requirement to supply wholesome water continues up to where the water leaves the undertaker's pipes.[50A] Nevertheless the undertaker must take prescribed risk minimization measures to ensure the water does not thereafter cease to be wholesome while the water is in a pipe subject to mains pressure (or would be subject to mains pressure but for the closing of a valve).[50B] This provision principally relates to controlling the pH of the water so that it is not unduly acid—a pH value of greater than 6.5 is advised in the DoE guidance on Safeguarding the Quality of Public Water Supplies.[51] If the water is more acidic than this there is a risk of it attacking any lead, copper or galvanised iron pipes that it may pass through, leading to non-compliance with standards for lead, copper and zinc.

8–041

What is to be understood as "wholesome" for these purposes is defined in the Water Supply (Water Quality) Regulations 1989 as amended.[52] The corresponding regulations in respect of Scotland are the Water Supply (Water Quality) (Scotland) Regulations 1990, as amended.[53] These Regulations implement the EC Drinking Water Directive 80/778,[54] which required implementing legislation to be in place by July 18, 1982, and for this to be in effect by July 18, 1985. The

8–042

[50] s.68(1)(a), (b).
[50A] W.I.A., s.68(2).
[50B] W.I.A., s.68(3).
[51] (1989) p.41.
[52] S.I. 1989 No. 1147 as amended by S.I. 1989 No. 1384 and S.I. 1991 No.1837.
[53] S.I. 1990 No. 119 (S.11) as amended by S.I. 1991 No.1333 (S.129).
[54] [1980] O.J. L229.

Directive sets out in its Annex I various mandatory values for numerous parameters and also, in many cases, more stringent values referred to as "guide levels".[55]

8–043   Against certain parameters there are comments that qualify the prescribed figures. In relation to nitrates, for example, the maximum admissible concentration (MAC) is 50 mg/l, whereas the guide level is 25 mg/l. The obligation on member states is to fix values in their territories that are the same as or less than the MACs and in doing so they are to "take as a basis the values appearing in the Guide level column".[56] This leaves unclear what legal constraints, if any, are imposed by the Guide level figures, and in practice they appear to amount to no more than aspirations.

8–044   A notorious problem with the Directive is parameter 55 "pesticides and related products", which is defined to mean insecticides (persistent organochlorine compounds, organophosphorus compounds and carbamates), herbicides, fungicides, and PCBs and PCTs. The MAC for this parameter is 0.1 μg/l for each of the substances considered separately, and further, 0.5 μg/l for all these substances in total. While there is undoubtedly legitimate concern in relation to certain pesticides, many pesticides, particularly those developed more recently, are highly specific in their action and are subjected to very substantial testing before marketing to establish their lack of general toxicity or ecotoxicity. Accordingly, an indiscriminate MAC of 0.1 μg/l in relation to every single substance, even those established to be essentially harmless to humans, requires abandoning or substantial reduction in the use of numerous pesticides, or else highly expensive water treatment, without significant benefit. Further, the figure of 0.5 μg/l for the total of all these pesticides taken together is liable to be impossible to establish in practice, since, at least where there has been abstraction in agricultural areas, there are likely to be traces of numerous different substances, the concentrations of each of which must be measured and aggregated. The analytical techniques may well not be available in many cases for this to be done with sufficient precision, and the costs entailed would arguably be quite disproportionate. Accordingly, though the Directive's values for this parameter are faithfully repeated in the UK Regulations, there is little inclination on the part of the government to ensure compliance with them.

8–045   In proceedings brought by the European Commission against the United Kingdom[57] it was held that the nitrate levels in 28 supply zones

---

[55] The World Health Organisation publishes *Guidelines for Drinking Water Quality* (2nd ed., 1993), which indicate water quality standards over a range of parameters. The WHO figures differ from those of the EC Directive in a number of material respects.
[56] Art.7(3).
[57] Case C-337/89, [1993] Env. L.R. 299.

in England failed to conform with the MAC of 50 mg/l—no argument was based on the failure to meet the lower Guide level. The UK pleaded that it was entitled to rely on derogations in the Directive.[58] These derogations are available where compliance with the value(s) set for one or more parameters is due to (i) situations arising from the nature and structure of the ground in the area from which the supply in question emanates, (ii) situations arising from exceptional meteorological conditions, (iii) emergencies, and (iv) circumstances during which a Member State may for a limited period resort to surface water of an insufficiently high standard and when suitable treatment cannot be devised, provided this lasts for a limited period only. In addition, in exceptional cases and for geographically defined population groups, Member States may submit a special request for a longer period for complying with the Annex I values. Nevertheless, the European Court held that this request had to have been made within the five year period for giving effect to the requirements of the Directive, and the UK government had not done this. The UK sought to argue that the obligations to meet the MACs were not absolute but required all practicable steps to be taken to achieve compliance; it claimed to have done this and that failure to achieve the nitrate levels was due to extraneous factors relating to techniques used in agriculture, in fact the use of large quantities of fertilisers, and arguably, the consequence of ploughing up grassland many years previously, much of it during the 1940s in war time. The European Court held that the obligations on the UK were absolute, subject to the specific derogations that might be available but were not in this case, and that consequently the UK was in breach of the Directive in this respect.

The case against the UK also related to levels of lead in drinking water. Against this parameter in Annex I is the comment that: **8–046**

> "Where lead pipes are present, the lead content should not exceed 50 μg/l in a sample taken after flushing. If the sample is taken either directly or after flushing and the lead content either frequently or to an appreciable extent exceeds 100 μg/l, suitable measures must be taken to reduce the exposure to lead on the part of the consumer."

The MAC for lead is defined to be 50 μg/l *in running water*. The Court held that, having regard to the comment quoted above (as was required of it by Article 7(5)), the MAC value was for guidance only, and that in the absence of evidence that the 100 μg/l was exceeded

---

[58] Set out in Art.9.

frequently or to an appreciable extent, the case against the UK had not been made out.[59]

8–047   The Directive applies to all water intended for human consumption that is used for that purpose, whether it is supplied for consumption directly, or whether it is used in food production in activities affecting the wholesomeness of the foodstuff in its finished form.[60] It does not however apply to natural mineral waters or medicinal waters where these are recognised or defined as such by competent national authorities. The 1989 UK Regulations did not deal with water for food production; this omission was rectified by the Water Supply (Water Quality) (Amendment) Regulations 1991.

8–048   In addition to laying down prescribed values for the relevant parameters, the Directive and the Regulations also lay down minimum sampling frequencies, which vary in accordance with the volume of water distributed.[61]

Enforcement under W.I.A., s.18

8–049   The duty to supply wholesome drinking water and to avoid deterioration in the quality of water from drinking water sources is enforceable by the Secretary of State under section 18 of the W.I.A.[62] – in practice by the Drinking Water Inspectorate. Section 18 prescribes a procedure for enforcing a variety of obligations under the W.I.A.; by virtue of section 18(8), where any act or omission constitutes a contravention of a requirement that is enforceable under section 18, the only remedies for that contravention are those available under the section and such as there may be (if any) under any other enactment, though without prejudice to any remedies that may be available in respect of that act or omission that may exist otherwise than by virtue of its contravening the relevant requirement. This would not therefore preclude any action for, for example, negligence or under product liability legislation; nor would it preclude any proceedings for breach of EC legislation, such as the drinking water Directive.[63] The determination in *Griffith & ors. v. South West Water Services* that the defendant, a statutory water and sewerage undertaker, is an "emanation of the State" indicates that the provisions of the EC water (and indeed any

---

[59] The case also contained a complaint that the UK had failed to implement the Directive in time. Although there had been administrative circulars (DoE 20/82, 25/84; WO 33/82, 51/84) on the effect of the Directive, these did not amount to sufficient implementation.

[60] Art.2.

[61] Directive, Annex II, Table B; S.I. 1989 No.1147, Sched.3.

[62] s.68(5).

[63] Forcing plaintiffs to sue on the EC Directive is arguably evidence that it has not been sufficiently implemented into national domestic law.

other) directives, so far as they are precise and unconditional, can be enforced directly against all such undertakers. Any action based on EC law would however have to be by way of civil proceedings, and could therefore only be taken by a person with the necessary standing to sue. Subject to those considerations, and also of course the outcome of any appeal, this decision significantly reduces the protection of the statutory undertakers that section 18 was evidently intended to afford. It does not affect the possibility of recovering damages, where injury can be shown, for breach of the EC requirements, but these would now be due from the undertaker directly rather than from the government under the principles established in *Francovich*.[64]

8–050 Where a contravention is enforceable under section 18 the procedures set out in sections 18 to 21 apply. Briefly these entail the issue of an enforcement order, which may be either a final or a provisional order, requiring action by the person considered to be in breach to remedy it either forthwith or within such a period as may be stipulated. Before issuing any such order, the company to which it is to be addressed must have an opportunity to make representations on it or objections to it, and these must be taken into account before the order is in fact made. There is no obligation to make an enforcement order or to confirm a provisional order if any contraventions or apprehended contraventions are trivial or if a company has given a suitable undertaking and is complying with it.[65] Any undertaking given in such circumstances is to be treated as itself being a statutory requirement enforceable under section 18.[66] If a company to which an enforcement order relates is aggrieved, it (and only it) may challenge the order in the High Court on the basis either that its making was *ultra vires* section 18 or that the procedural requirements in section 20 have not been complied with. Save for this right of challenge, the validity of an enforcement order may not be questioned in any legal proceedings whatsoever.[67] The Drinking Water Inspectorate has issued a Code for Enforcement setting out its policy on enforcing the 1989 Regulations.[68]

8–051 Where an enforcement order has been made, this constitutes a statutory duty owed to any person who may be affected by a contravention of it, entitling him to damages for any loss or damage caused. It is a defence to any such action, with the sole exception of one brought in respect of failure to supply wholesome drinking water, that the company concerned took all reasonable steps and exercised all due diligence to avoid the contravention. Additionally, the order may

[64] See paras. 2–034 to 2–036 and n. 41A thereto.
[65] s.19(1)(a), (b).
[66] s.19(2).
[67] s.21(3).
[68] DoE, December 1993.

be enforced in civil proceedings by the Secretary of State or the Director General of Ofwat for an injunction or other relief.

Private Water Supplies

8–052   Private water supplies are subject to the same requirements as to quality, imposed by the Private Water Supplies Regulations 1991[69] as regards England and Wales, and by the Private Water Supplies (Scotland) Regulations 1992[70] as regards Scotland. A private water supply for the purposes of these Regulations will be either a "Category 1 supply" or a "Category 2" supply. The latter is a supply for food production purposes or for domestic purposes to premises used by significant numbers of people, for example staff canteens, hospitals, boarding schools, camp and caravan sites. Each of these categories is divided into five classes depending on the average daily volume of water supplied and, in the case of Category 1 supplies, the number of persons supplied. The differences in practical effect between the categories and classes is essentially in the frequency with which sampling for the various parameters must be undertaken.

8–053   A private supply is any supply of water provided otherwise than by a water undertaker. Where mains water from a water undertaker is supplied to premises and led directly to taps for use by those on the premises, this will not be a private supply. However, if any action is taken in relation to the water after it has left the water undertaker's pipes that might affect its quality, for example passing it through a water softener or an activated carbon filter, then the water emerging from any such treatment may be "water provided otherwise than by a water undertaker", and so a private supply by the person in control of the treatment process.

8–054   Enforcement of the statutory requirements in relation to private supplies is by way of service of a private supply notice by the relevant local authority on the owners or occupiers of the premises concerned, or where different, the owners or occupiers of the premises where the source of the private supply is situated and any other person who has the management or control of that source. The private supply notice may require appropriate action to be taken, and must stipulate a period within which that is to be done, as well specifying a period of not less than 28 days within which representations or objections may be submitted to the local authority.[71] The notice does not take effect until the end of the period specified for submitting representations or objections; if any are submitted, then it does not take effect until

[69] S.I. 1991 No. 2790.
[70] S.I. 1992 No.575 (S.64).
[71] s.80(1), (2).

confirmation of the notice by the Secretary of State or if the relevant representations or objections are withdrawn.[72] Failure to comply with a private supply notice is not of itself an offence, but entitles the local authority to take the requisite steps itself, and to recover its reasonable expenses from the person in default. Any requirement imposed by a private supply notice on the owner or occupier of any premises that is expressed to bind those premises in relation to the owners or occupiers from time to time is a local land charge binding successive owners and occupiers of the premises.[73]

Water Quality

In England and Wales the NRA has a responsibility for devising policies for maintaining and improving the quality of controlled waters, for monitoring that quality and enforcing the statutory controls (it is of course for the Government to decide between strategic policy options). The definition of "controlled waters" in section 104 of the W.R.A., which is the term applicable for the pollution control provisions in the Act, is completely comprehensive, covering territorial waters outside the three mile limit; coastal waters, being those within the three mile limit up to the limit of the highest tide and, in the case of rivers and other water courses, their freshwater limits; inland freshwaters, being lakes or ponds[74] and rivers or water courses above their freshwater limits; and groundwaters, being any waters contained in underground strata—this last expression is defined in section 221(3) to include, *inter alia*, water in a well or borehole. Though consideration of controls over water quality may for convenience treat surface waters and ground water separately, there is a very close relationship between the two;[75] surface waters may be transferred into groundwater aquifers, particularly under the influence of abstraction, but conversely the quantity and quality of groundwater may critically affect surface waters in any particular area. 8–055

In addition to the general functions of the NRA in respect of water pollution, it has more specific functions that include the protection against pollution of any waters belonging to it or any water undertaker or from which any of them may take water, including any reservoir and any underground strata from which the authority or any 8–056

[72] s.81(1), (2).
[73] s.82(5).
[74] Including certain reservoirs as defined in the Controlled Waters (Lakes and Ponds) Order 1989; S.I. 1989 No.1149.
[75] Emphasised by the NRA in its *Policy and Practice for the Protection of Groundwater*, p.7.

undertaker is authorised to abstract water.[76] Its strategy in relation to water quality includes setting water quality objectives for both surface waters and groundwater by reference to the uses to which these waters may be put, coupled with policies for the siting of actually or potentially polluting activities, and for the imposition of controls over such activities, such as will avoid any water pollution that would prevent the water quality objectives being attained.

8-057   This is not the place to discuss water policy in detail, but a brief review of the background to current legislation is in order. The first survey on the state of rivers in England was carried out in 1958 on an informal basis. The results of this were only published in 1970, in conjunction with those from a further survey conducted by the DoE in that year on rivers, canals and estuaries. Subsequently surveys have been carried out every five years, enabling the effectiveness of the pollution control regime to be assessed. A relatively imprecise system of classification was devised for the 1970 survey, but in 1978 a new system developed by the National Water Council (the NWC) was introduced, that enabled comparisons to be made across the country, and which was used up until 1994. The NWC Classes are now being replaced by "river ecosystem" classes, described below. It was proposed by the NWC at the outset that its classification should be used to define water quality objectives: this was coupled with a policy of "no deterioration", that has since become one of actively seeking steady improvement of polluted waters. This was in any event necessary in order to meet the quality standards prescribed by the various EC water directives, which thus, to a degree, determined applicable water quality objectives.

8-058   A House of Commons Select Committee Report on "Pollution of Rivers and Estuaries"[77] recommended developing a system of water quality objectives so as to allow priorities to be set, to ensure both regulators and the regulated kept to standards and practices compatible with achieving the objectives, and to allow investment needs to be identified and planned for. Following the provision of a statutory basis for such objectives by the Water Act 1989, the NRA issued a consultation document *Proposals for Statutory Water Quality Objectives* in December 1991,[78] discussing both why and how objectives should be set, and their implications. In June 1992 the Royal Commission on Environmental Pollution issued its Report *Freshwater Quality*,[79] which reviewed comprehensively water pollution, its sources and assessment, and means of controlling it. It reinforced the moves towards

[76] W.R.A. s.3(2).
[77] May 1987.
[78] Water Quality Series No. 5.
[79] RCEP 16th Report, Cm. 1966.

setting water quality objectives, advocating demanding standards and tighter discharge consents, while recognising that these should only be introduced in accordance with a "Best Environmental Timetable", so as to avoid imposing undue costs on dischargers.[80]

As mentioned, rivers and canals have hitherto been classified in accordance with the scheme devised by the National Water Council in the late 1970s. This classification was determined essentially by reference to the values for biochemical oxygen demand (BOD), dissolved oxygen, and ammonia. The quality of any particular river was assigned to one of five classes by reference to the values obtained, namely 1A and 1B (good), 2 (fair), 3 (poor), and 4 (bad), water within any of classes 1A, 1B and 2 being regarded as suitable for drinking water, at least after suitable treatment. This classification scheme was essentially administrative, and not underpinned by any requirements in UK legislation. It enabled programmes to be developed for improving the quality of rivers by setting targets for upgrading defined stretches of water. However, with a view to implementing fully the applicable EC water quality directives new regulations have now been issued, namely the Surface Waters (River Ecosystem) (Classification) Regulations 1994,[81] accompanied by an NRA procedures manual explaining how they will be put into effect. The Regulations, which are made under the general powers of section 82 that provide for statutory water quality objectives (SWQOs), lay down five "river ecosystem" (RE) classes, which bear a rough correlation with the previous grades. However, the new classes are determined by reference to additional parameters, and in some cases specify new test methods, which makes exact correlation impossible. The parameters to be used in determining the five RE classes are

8–059

(a) dissolved oxygen (10 percentile);
(b) BOD (90 percentile);
(c) total ammonia (90 percentile);
(d) un-ionised ammonia (95 percentile);
(e) minimum pH (5 percentile) and maximum pH (95 percentile);
(f) dissolved copper (95 percentile);
(g) total zinc (95 percentile).

Copper and zinc are the first two of the grey list compounds of EC Directive 76/464 on the discharge of dangerous substances to water — there remain however 18 substances in this grey list which, under the current proposals, would not be considered relevant for the purposes

[80] para.4.47.
[81] S.I. 1994 No. 1057.

of the new RE classification system. The Regulations require the frequency, location and methods of sampling, the methods of analysis of the samples and of determining percentile values, and any other question of compliance with the specified criteria, to be determined in accordance with an NRA document[82] *Water Quality Objectives: Procedures used by the National Rivers Authority for the purpose of the Surface Waters (River Ecosystem) (Classification) Regulations 1994.*[83] Notwithstanding the precision that this provides for many of the procedures, there are a number of situations where a subjective view will still have to be taken as to whether special circumstances exist, requiring or at least justifying the ignoring of certain sampling results when determining compliance with the applicable criteria.

8–060   It is proposed that, initially, a comparatively small number of catchment areas will be designated for the purposes of section 83 of the W.R.A., which will specify in each case one or more of the RE classes that must be attained by a prescribed date or dates. Such water quality objectives may be reviewed after five years for the catchment areas concerned, or earlier if the NRA so requests after consultation with water undertakers and anyone else it considers appropriate.[84] Once these objectives have been set for any waters, there is a duty on both the Secretary of State and the NRA to exercise their respective powers under the W.R.A. to ensure as far as practicable that the objectives are achieved at all times.[85]

Protective Measures

8–061   In addition to the system for consenting discharges to controlled waters backed by criminal sanctions for breach as described later (in paragraphs 8–153 to 8–172), there are a number of precautionary and other administrative measures available for reducing both the risk of pollution occurring at all, and also the amount of pollution in cases where the risks materialise or the pollution is authorised. These include, in particular:

(i)   powers to require works to be carried out and precautions to be taken in relation to persons holding matter that will pollute if it escapes;

(ii)   the designation of water protection zones in which prescribed activities may be prohibited or restricted;

---

[82] Dated March 30, 1994.
[83] Forming Annex B to the October 1993 consultation paper.
[84] s.83(3).
[85] s.84(1).

(iii) the designation of nitrate sensitive areas (NSAs) with a view to preventing or controlling the entry of nitrate into controlled waters from agricultural land; and

(iv) controls over the treatment of municipal and other waste water provided by sewage treatment plants, dependent on the sensitivity of the waters receiving their discharges.

Precautionary Works

The Secretary of State has power under section 92 to prohibit any person from having custody or control of any poisonous, noxious or polluting matter unless such works and precautionary measures as may be prescribed are taken to prevent or control the matter entering any controlled waters. He may likewise require anyone who already has custody or control of such matter to take the prescribed action. To date, the only exercise of this power has been to make the Control of Pollution (Silage, Slurry and Agricultural Fuel Oil) Regulations 1991, which apply in England and Wales, and the Control of Pollution (Silage, Slurry and Agricultural Fuel Oil) (Scotland) Regulations 1991.[86] Subject to certain limited exemptions, the effect of these Regulations is to prohibit any person having custody or control of:

8–062

(i) any crop being made into silage, unless kept in any silo meeting the requirements of Schedule 1 to the Regulations or unless it is compressed in sealed bales stored at least 10 metres from any inland or coastal waters which effluent escaping from the bales could enter;

(ii) slurry, unless it is stored in a slurry storage system meeting the requirements of Schedule 2 to the Regulations, except whilst it is stored temporarily in a tanker with a capacity not exceeding 18,000 litres used for transporting slurry on roads or about a farm; and

(iii) fuel oil, unless in a fuel storage tank within a storage area meeting the requirements of Schedule 3 or in drums within such a storage area, in an underground storage tank, or temporarily in a tanker used for transporting fuel oil on roads or about the farm.

The Regulations exempt silos, slurry storage systems and fuel storage tanks from these requirements if they were used or constructed before March 1, 1991, or their construction had been contracted for or commenced before that date, and was completed before September 1, 1991. This exemption may be lost or withdrawn in a number of

---

[86] S.I. 1991 No.324 and S.I. 1991 No.346 (S.35).

circumstances, including substantial enlargement or reconstruction of the structure or where a notice is served by the NRA on the person having custody or control of the relevant substance, where it considers there is a significant risk of pollution of controlled waters with the structure as it is. There is a right of appeal within the next following 28 days against such a notice to the Secretary of State. The Regulations permit the making of silage otherwise than in a silo or in compressed, sealed bales where the person concerned made the majority of his silage by such other method in the three years immediately before March 1, 1991; in this case also, the NRA may serve notice requiring appropriate precautionary work for other measures to be taken where it considers that the activity constitutes a significant risk of pollution of controlled waters.

8–063   The Regulations came into force on September 1, 1991, and any person proposing to have custody or control of any crop being made into silage, or of slurry or fuel oil that is to be kept or stored on a farm in a silo, slurry storage system or fuel storage area, as the case may be, which is constructed, substantially enlarged or reconstructed on or after that date must serve notice on the NRA specifying the type of structure to be used and its location, at least 14 days before it is used for that purpose.

8–064   Contravention of the prohibitions is an offence subject on summary conviction to a maximum fine of £5000 and an unlimited fine on conviction on indictment; failure to give the notice relating to the use of a new or enlarged or reconstructed structure is an offence liable to a fine of up to £500[87] on summary conviction.

8–065   Guidance on the handling of silage, slurries and fuel oil is included in the "Code of Good Agricultural Practice for the Protection of Water"; there is also an HSE Guidance Note GS 12 "Effluent Storage on Farms".

Water Protection Zones

8–066   The NRA has responsibility for the granting, varying and revocation of discharge consents and abstraction licences, and of the conditions attached to them. In making a determination it must have regard to the current quality of the surface and ground waters of the relevant catchment area and of any changes to their quality likely to occur in the future, to the river flows, and to the present and likely future demands for abstraction of water in that area. It is further able to have a positive, and not merely reactive, role by virtue of being a statutory consultee under the planning legislation and so exert influence both

---

[87] *i.e.* level 2.

336

on decisions on individual applications for new development, particularly where these entail an environmental assessment, and more generally on development plans for an area.[88] These functions allow the NRA to develop coherent policies for minimising water pollution from new developments, and, to a degree, for reducing pollution from existing activities. The controls over the quality and quantity of discharges and over the extent of abstraction are dealt with elsewhere; this section is concerned with the exercise of its powers to influence the location of activities in carrying out its duty to manage water resources. The NRA must have regard not only to the impacts of activities operating in compliance with applicable permits but also to the potential consequences of accidents and breaches of consent conditions, in particular spillages and emergencies such as a fire. There can never be foolproof protection against all errors and accidents, but their consequences for water pollution can be reduced by ensuring potentially polluting activities are located in areas where the consequences of accidents can best be contained, or cause least harm if not contained, in addition to imposing suitable conditions for all relevant consents and IPC authorisations.

For this purpose, the NRA has developed a system of source **8–067** protection zones (SPZs), each designed to protect a specific source of groundwater, and from which it is able to develop a coherent set of rules as to appropriate location of industrial and other potentially polluting activities. Currently, zones covering approximately half of the existing major potable water sources in England and Wales have been defined and it is intended to continue this programme, giving priority to sites for which proposals for development arise.

There are three categories of protection zone, namely Zone I (Inner **8–068** Source Protection), Zone II (Outer Source Protection) and Zone III (Source Catchment). Each of these zones is located around a groundwater abstraction source, with its boundaries defined by reference to the flow of water through the relevant aquifer to the abstracting point. Inevitably therefore, it requires assumptions to be made as to the aquifer's hydraulic characteristics and the flow rates of water in the aquifer. Flow rates may moreover vary if there are significant changes in the amount of water abstracted from elsewhere in the same aquifer. Accordingly, the zone boundaries are not fixed but best estimates that may change in the light of additional information.

The boundary of an Inner Source Protection Zone I represents **8–069** points in the aquifer where the water has a 50-day travel time to the abstraction point, subject to a minimum of 50 metres from that point.

---

[88] See in particular the NRA's *Guidance Notes for Local Planning Authorities on the Methods of Protecting the Water Environment through Development Plans,* January 1994.

This is a standard that is recognised internationally, since the 50-day travel time results in at least the bulk of the biological contaminants degrading. The boundary of an Outer Source Protection Zone II represents a 400-day travel time through the aquifer to the abstraction point. Not all contaminants will necessarily decay (if they decay at all) within 50 days, and the longer period allows for the decay of the more slowly degrading pollutants. A Source Catchment Zone III consists of the entire catchment area that in practice feeds the abstraction point. It represents the area sufficient to support the abstraction from long term annual ground water recharge. The larger the amount of water abstracted, the larger must therefore be the area.

8–070   In determining whether operation of a potentially polluting activity is acceptable at a particular proposed site, and if so on what conditions, consideration of its location in relation to any relevant source protection zone thus enables the NRA better to assess the degree of risk that it poses, and to act in a consistent manner on the basis of coherent policies. These are largely contained in its *Policy and Practice for the Protection of Groundwater*, which concludes with a series of groundwater protection policy statements relating to:

- Control of ground water abstractions;
- Physical disturbance of aquifers and ground water flow;
- Waste disposal to land;
- Contaminated land;
- Disposal of liquid effluents, sludges and slurries to land;
- Discharges to underground strata;
- Diffuse pollution of groundwater;
- Additional activities or developments which pose a threat to groundwater quality, in particular the protection storage and use of chemicals, the storage of farm waste and intensive livestock housing, graveyards and animal burial sites, sewage works, foul sewers and storm overflows, oil and petroleum storage and transport via pipelines, and major infrastructure developments.

8–071   While the impact of new development on water resources can be controlled under standard planning and regulatory procedures, existing activities cannot be so readily modified in the same way in a manner that will be perceived as operating fairly on all actual or potential polluters. Any attempt to achieve a significant upgrading of an area with many industrial sites on an individual basis is likely to lead to numerous appeals and be most laborious. Accordingly section 93 of the W.R.A. enables specified activities in a designated area to be prohibited or restricted. The section does not limit in any way what prohibitions and restrictions may be imposed, subject only to the

Secretary of State being satisfied that the exercise of his powers under it is appropriate with a view to preventing or controlling the entry of any poisonous, noxious or polluting matter into controlled waters. The only exclusion relates to the entry of nitrate into controlled waters to the extent this is capable of being controlled under the nitrate sensitive areas provisions of section 94[89] (see paragraphs 8–073 to 8–079).

No water protection zones have as yet been designated, but a consultation document was issued by the NRA in late 1993 proposing the creation of such a zone for the River Dee in North Wales.[90] The NRA has provided for wide consultation on these proposals before requesting the Secretary of State to act, though there is no statutory requirement for this, nor is there any obligation on the Secretary State either to invite representations or objections to any proposals that he may have in mind making or to consider any that may be made. The order designating a water protection zone may prohibit or restrict activities outright; it may also provide for a system of licensing such activities subject to conditions. In either case, it may provide for criminal sanctions for breaching any prohibition or contravening any licence condition, with penalties up to those prescribed for the pollution offences of section 85 referred to in paragraph 8–164. Any such licensing regime, including procedures for revocation or variation of licences and appeals, is to be made by regulations issued under section 96.

8–072

Nitrate Sensitive Areas

The EC drinking water Directive sets a MAC for nitrate of 50 mg/l. In some parts of the United Kingdom this is regularly exceeded in water abstracted for drinking water purposes, and treatment to reduce the concentration below the prescribed limit is expensive and leads to substantial quantities of brine effluent that is not always easily disposable. There has been public concern as to the health risks caused by ingesting excessive quantities of nitrates. While it does appear to be a cause of "blue baby syndrome" (methaemoglobinaemia), this is exceedingly rare.[91] There is some somewhat inconclusive evidence that nitrate may also lead to stomach cancer. Most authoritative

8–073

---

[89] s.93(3).
[90] Powers to designate water protection zones were in fact also available under C.O.P.A., but were never used.
[91] Only 14 cases have been recorded in the UK in the 35 years to 1991, the last being in 1972 from water from a private well; House of Lords Select Committee Report 'Nitrate in Water', Session 1988–89, 16th Report, July 18, 1989, para.23.

reviews of this evidence come to the conclusion that the link is unproven, but that it remains prudent on this ground to control nitrate levels in water to a maximum of around 50 mg/l, a level at which water would provide more than half the total normal human intake of nitrate.

8–074   Nitrates are used in very large quantities as agricultural fertiliser, and being highly soluble compounds, are liable to be washed away in periods of heavy rain into either groundwater or neighbouring surface waters. Waters that have high concentrations of nitrate, particularly when in combination with substantial quantities of phosphate, also suffer from eutrophication. The high concentrations of these compounds give rise to excessive algal growth; as the algae die off their decomposition extracts oxygen from the water. With high concentrations of algae, the water will be deprived of virtually all its dissolved oxygen, while the decomposition products of the algae are liable to be highly toxic. The results are accordingly potentially devastating to other forms of life in the waters affected. There has been considerable study of the effect of nitrates in water and of legislative proposals to control these. These include the Royal Commission on Environmental Pollution's 7th Report *Agriculture and Pollution*,[92] "Nitrate in Water"[93] and a report by the House of Lords Select Committee on the European Communities "Nitrate in Water" which was concerned with the draft EC proposals for what is now Directive 91/676. The subject is inevitably also dealt with in the Royal Commission on Environmental Pollution's 16th Report "Freshwater Quality".[94] In this last report, the RCEP concludes that there is little evidence that nitrate levels on their own have major effects on the freshwater environment, save as a component of nutrient enrichment.[95]

8–075   Section 94 of the W.R.A. provides for special powers to be taken in relation to designated "nitrate sensitive areas" (NSAs). It derives from the Water Act 1989, and in fact anticipated EC Directive 91/676. This Directive requires Member States first to designate waters which are or may be affected by pollution by nitrogen compounds (in fact principally nitrates and ammonium compounds, typically ammonium nitrate), and then[96] to designate as vulnerable zones all known areas of land in their territories which drain into such waters and which contribute to this form of pollution. In designating the waters, use is to

---

[92] Cmnd. 7644 (1979).
[93] A report by the Nitrate Co-ordination Group from both the DoE and MAFF, Pollution Paper No.26, 1986.
[94] Cm. 1966 (1992).
[95] See also para. on eutrophication.
[96] Within two years of December 19, 1991 when the Directive was notified; Art. 3(2).

be made, *inter alia*, of criteria spelled out in Annex I of the Directive, which essentially require consideration as to whether surface freshwaters and groundwaters already contain more than 50 mg/l of nitrates or may do so if preventive action is not taken, and whether relevant waters are found to be eutrophic or may become so in the near future if preventive action is not taken. Member States are required to review and revise as appropriate their designations of vulnerable zones at least every four years.[97]

Action programmes must be developed for the designated vulnerable zones, and these must be implemented within four years of their establishment. They must include the mandatory measures set out in Annex III to the Directive, relating for example to periods when the land application of certain types of fertiliser is to be prohibited, and to the capacity of storage vessels for livestock manure, and limiting the land application of fertilisers consistent with good agricultural practice having regard to the particular characteristics of the vulnerable zone concerned. Application of livestock manure to the land must be such that the nitrogen content applied must not exceed 170 kg per hectare (though this may be up to 210 kg per hectare for the first four years, and other amounts may be fixed if objectively justified — the Commission must be informed of any other amounts).

8–076

Member States must also apply a code of good agricultural practice for implementation on a voluntary basis; mandatory and voluntary matters for the contents of these codes are set out in Annex II to the Directive. Such a code has been prepared by MAFF and approved[98] under section 97 of the W.R.A.[99] Unlike the other codes of good agricultural practice, that for the protection of water has statutory force and a contravention of it, though not of itself giving rise to any criminal civil liability may be taken into account by the NRA in exercising its powers under section 86 (see paragraph) and under the 1991 Regulations relating to silage, slurry and agricultural fuel oil in respect of exempted structures.

8–077

Under section 94, the Minister has wide powers to designate land for the purpose of preventing or controlling the entry of nitrate into controlled waters as a result of, or anything done in connection with, the use for agricultural purposes of any land.[1] Having designated

8–078

---

[97] Art.3(4).
[98] By S.I. 1991 No.2285.
[99] 'Code of Good Agricultural Practice for the Protection of Water', MAFF, 1991, PB0587; this is one of three such codes, the others being in respect of air and soil. See also 'Fertiliser recommendations for agricultural and horticultural crops' (RB 209), MAFF, 6th edn.
[1] s.94(2).

land, any activities may be prohibited or restricted on or in relation to it, in so far as he considers this to be appropriate in order to give effect to the purposes of section 94. A designation order under section 94 may provide for the Minister to enter into agreements for payments to be made to the owner of the freehold of any agricultural land in return for his accepting obligations, in particular in respect to the management of the land. With the freeholder's consent, the agreement may be made instead with a tenant or any other person having an interest in the land.[2]

8–079   To date all actions in the United Kingdom designed to restrict use of nitrates have been voluntary, and have relied on compensation terms to encourage take-up. Ten NSA schemes were set up under the Nitrate Sensitive Areas (Designation) Order 1990[3] which covered comparatively large areas, and approximately 15,000 ha in total. The Order provided for both "basic scheme" agreements and for "premium" agreements, the latter requiring more substantial changes to farming practice coupled with considerably greater compensation payments. More recent proposals for NSAs are designed to cover smaller areas concentrated around water abstraction boreholes. It has however been estimated that as much as two million hectares of agricultural land may be due for designation under the Directive[4] so, if it is given full effect, the Directive will have an immense impact on British agriculture, and the present reliance on voluntary schemes is unlikely to suffice. A consultation document issued jointly by MAFF, the DoE and the Welsh Office "Designation of Vulnerable Zones under the EC Nitrate Directive (91/676)" proposes the designation of Nitrate Vulnerable Zones ("NVZs") as identified in the document that cover in aggregate about 650,000 hectares in England and Wales, and includes an Outline Action Programme as required by the Directive, to become compulsory at some date between 1995 and 1999.

Municipal Waste Water—Directive 91/271

8–080   Sewerage systems have always been major sources of pollution of rivers and coastal waters. Before privatisation of the water industry, the sewage treatment plants in England and Wales were operated by the water authorities (or by local authorities on their behalf), who were themselves the regulators in respect of all other discharges who

[2] s.95(1), (2).
[3] S.I. 1990 No. 1013.
[4] *The Independent*, June 15, 1991.

controlled waters in their respective areas. Their own discharges from the sewage treatment plants were subject to control by the Secretary of State, but in practice enforcement was far from stringent. To a large degree, their poor record was due to a long-standing failure to invest sufficient capital in the sewage treatment plants, and the sewerage systems generally, to provide for increased populations and greater through-puts, with the result that the principal consequence of strict enforcement would have been immediate demands for substantial sums of money either through the water rates or from the Treasury, neither of which was politically acceptable.[5] On privatisation, the NRA became responsible for enforcing the terms of all discharge consents, including those of the sewerage undertakers, in an even-handed manner. This, coupled with the development of the EC Directive 91/271 on urban waste water treatment, has required massive investments on the part of the sewerage undertakers, on a scale such that both the financing and the physical works must necessarily be spread over a considerable time.

The Directive is primarily concerned with the collection, treatment and discharge of waste-water from urban areas, including both domestic and industrial waste water. It also applies to certain industrial sectors that produce comparable waste water discharges (see paragraphs 8–088, 8–089). Its obligations are framed by reference to the size of the population served by any particular sewerage system; however for consistency the population size is not determined by a head count, but by reference to the organic biodegradable load in fact requiring to be treated. Thus one "pe" or "population equivalent" means an organic biodegradable load having a five day biochemical oxygen demand (BOD 5) of 60g of oxygen per day.[6] The Directive required implementing legislation to be in force by no later than June 30, 1993. Though the United Kingdom had by then issued in draft the Urban Waste Water Treatment (England and Wales) Regulations 1993, these in fact did not proceed in that year, and indeed currently remain outstanding.

8–081

Member States must identify "sensitive areas" of water by December 31, 1993:[7] for these areas, more stringent treatment is required before discharge to them. According to criteria for identifying sensitive areas set out in Annex II, a water body must be identified as a sensitive area it falls within any of the following groups:

8–082

---

[5] Indeed it is highly arguable that the entire privatisation process was driven at least as much by the political inability of the public sector to raise the capital needed, as by any consideration of the benefits of privatisation itself.

[6] Art. 2(6).

[7] Art. 5(1).

(a) natural freshwater lakes, other freshwater bodies, and coastal waters[8] which are found to be eutrophic or which in the near future may become eutrophic if protective action is not taken;

(b) surface freshwaters intended for the abstraction of drinking water which could contain more than the maximum concentration of nitrate (50mg/litre) prescribed by the Drinking Water Directive 75/440 if action is not taken; and

(c) areas where further treatment and the secondary treatment prescribed by the Directive is necessary "to fulfil Council Directives".[9] Compliance with these other EC Directives requires the relevant waters to have been designated under them. However where they have been designated, then compliance is of course called for irrespective of action under the Urban Waste Water Directive.

What is to be considered "eutrophic" is however a very subjective issue, in the absence of clear definition.[10] The so-called "criteria" in the Directive are far from precise and consequently Member States in fact have substantial discretion in classifying the waters concerned. In practice eutrophication will occur if there are present substantial quantities of both phosphorus and nitrogen in the water body. If one of these elements is present in abundance, but the other is lacking, substantial algal growth will not occur. If the nitrogen/phosphorus ratio falls below about 5:1, the extent of growth will be dependent on the nitrogen concentration, since there will be ample phosphorus for the purposes of such growth as occurs, which is then said to be nitrogen-limited. Similarly, where the nitrogen/phosphorus ratio is higher than about 12:1, the extent of growth will be determined by the phosphorus concentration since there will be ample nitrogen for the purposes of such growth as occurs—it is then phosphorus-limited. Generally speaking, in fresh waters phosphorus is the limiting factor; conversely, in marine waters it is nitrogen.[11]

8-083 Member States may at their option also identify "less sensitive" areas, in accordance with further criteria contained in Annex II, for which the standard requirements of the Directive may be relaxed. The

[8] "Coastal waters" is defined to mean all waters outside the low water line or the outer limit of an esturay, and does not have any outer three mile, or any other, limit.
[9] This refers, inter alia, to the Water Quality Directives such as those in respect of bathing water, surface water for drinking, shellfish water, etc.
[10] House of Lords Select Committee on the European Communities, Session 1990–91, Tenth Report "Municipal Waste Water Treatment", May 14, 1991, paras. 73–75; House of Lords, Select Committee on the European Communities, Session 1988–89, 16th Report "Nitrate in Water" July 18, 1989, para. 119.
[11] Royal Commission on Environmental Pollution, 16th Report "Freshwater Quality", June 1992, para. 6.2, Box 6.1.

government has identified in England and Wales 33 "sensitive areas (eutrophic)" or "SAs(E)",[12] and 58 "less sensitive" areas, referred to as "High Natural Dispersion Areas" or "HNDAs", the latter all being around the coastline.[13]

The Directive sets out a series of obligations that must be met, in nearly all cases, by December 31, of 1998, 2000 or 2005, as follows.   **8–084**

By December 31, 1998:

(1) Where urban waste water is discharged into sensitive receiving waters, collection systems for that urban waste water must be provided for all agglomerations of more than 10,000 pe;

(2) The sewage from agglomerations of more than 10,000 pe must be subject to tertiary treatment before discharge into sensitive areas;

(3) Disposal of sewage sludge to surface water by dumping from ships, discharge from pipelines or any other means, must be phased out.[14] Until the final date, Member States must ensure that the total amount of toxic, persistent or bio-accumulable materials in sludge disposed of in this way is both licensed, and progressively reduced.

By December 31, 2000:

(1) Collecting systems for urban waste water must be provided for agglomerations with a pe of more than 15,000;

(2) Secondary or equivalent treatment must be provided in sewage treatment plants serving agglomerations of more than 15,000 pe.

By December 31, 2005:

(1) Collecting systems must be provided for agglomerations with a pe of between 2,000 and 15,000;

(2) Sewage treatment works must provide secondary treatment where they serve agglomerations of between 10,000 and 15,000 in all cases, and also where they serve agglomerations of between 2,000 and 10,000 and discharge to fresh water and estuaries;

(3) Sewage treatment plants not otherwise required to provide secondary or tertiary treatment must provide "appropriate treatment" that allows the waters receiving the discharge to

---

[12] So-called to avoid confusion with Environmentally Sensitive Areas (ESAs).

[13] Press announcement, May 18, 1994. It appears that these designations may have been made after the time permitted for this by the Directive, which could affect the validity of the HNDA designations at least.

[14] Art. 14(3).

meet all relevant quality objectives, and relevant provisions of both this and other applicable EC Directives.[15] The remaining categories to which this requirement applies consist of discharges of fresh water and estuaries from agglomerations of less than 2,000 pe and discharges to coastal waters from agglomerations of less than 10,000 pe.

There are a number of exceptions to these requirements. In particular, instead of requiring tertiary treatment by December 31, 1998 for discharges to sensitive areas from agglomerations of more than 10,000 pe, this requirement is waived if it can be shown that the reduction in the overall load is at least 75 per cent of the total phosphorus and at least 75 per cent of total nitrogen.[16]

8–085   Where discharges from agglomerations of between 10,000 and 150,000 pe are to coastal waters, or are from agglomerations of between 2,000 and 10,000 pe to estuaries, and in each case are to "less sensitive areas", primary treatment only is sufficient provided "comprehensive studies indicate that such discharges will not adversely affect the environment" and the Commission is provided with all relevant information on these studies.[17] The same form of treatment may be applied to waste waters discharging into less sensitive areas from agglomerations of more than 150,000 in exceptional circumstances, if it can be demonstrated that any more advanced treatment will not produce any environmental benefits. Again the Commission must be given all relevant documentation in advance.[18]

8–086   Where the deadlines of December 31, 1998 or 2000 cannot be met, the Commission may in exceptional cases allow a longer period, provided the inability to meet the deadlines is due exclusively to technical reasons and is in respect of "geographically defined population groups"[19]—financial reasons will clearly therefore provide no justification for an exemption. In any event, relaxation of a deadline may not take the date for compliance beyond December 31, 2005 at the latest.[20]

8–087   The identification of sensitive areas must be reviewed at least every four years,[21] and where there are new areas identified as sensitive as a result, a period of seven years is given for the treatment plants discharging into the area to be upgraded to meet the Directive's requirements. Similarly, areas identified as less sensitive must be

---

[15] Art.2(9).
[16] Art. 5(4).
[17] Art. 6(2).
[18] Art. 8(5).
[19] Art. 8(1)–(3).
[20] Art. 8(3).
[21] Art. 5(6).

reviewed at least every four years, and for any areas no longer so identified, the same seven year period is allowed for upgrading any relevant sewage treatment plants.

The Directive is also applicable to a number of industrial sectors   8–088
where these produce discharges directly to receiving waters and not via sewage treatment plants. The industries concerned are:

- — Milk-processing
- — Manufacture of fruit and vegetable products
- — Manufacture and bottling of soft drinks
- — Potato-processing
- — Meat industry
- — Breweries
- — Production of alcohol and alcoholic beverages
- — Manufacture of animal feed from plant products
- — Manufacture of gelatine and of glue from hides, skin and bones
- — Malt-houses
- — Fish-processing industry

The selection of these particular processes has proved controversial— there is relatively little logic in applying the Directive's controls to these and not, for example, to intensive livestock rearing.

Article 13 of the Directive applies to all discharges from plants in the   8–089
listed industrial sectors which represent 4,000 pe or more. The controls are however relatively modest in that by December 31, 2000 the discharges must comply with regulatory controls set by Member States, and by December 31, 1993 "the competent authority of appropriate body in each Member State shall set requirements appropriate to the nature of the industry concerned for the discharge of such waste water".[22] Clearly in the United Kingdom these requirements are capable of being met under existing legislation, subject only to possible dispute as to what is an "appropriate" requirement to impose on a relevant discharge.

Pollution Offences

Section 85 of the W.R.A. lists a series of pollution offences that are   8–090
central to the water legislation.[23] They may most conveniently be set out as follows:

---

[22] Art. 13(2).
[23] There are also corresponding offences in Scotland under C.O.P.A. 1974, following the amendments to it made by Schedule 23 to the Water Act 1989.

A person contravenes this section if he causes or knowingly permits:

(1) any poisonous, noxious or polluting matter or any solid waste matter to enter any controlled waters;

(2) any matter, other than trade effluent or sewage effluent, to enter controlled waters by being discharged from a drain or sewer in contravention of a prohibition imposed under section 86 below;

(3) any trade effluent or sewage effluent to be discharged:
  (a) into any controlled waters; or
  (b) from land in England and Wales, through a pipe, into the sea outside the seaward limits of controlled waters;

(4) any trade effluent or sewage effluent to be discharged, in contravention of any prohibition imposed under section 86 below, from a building or from any fixed plant:
  (a) on to or into any land, or
  (b) into any waters of a lake or pond which are not inland freshwaters

(5) any matter whatever to enter any inland freshwaters so as to tend (either directly or in combination with other matter which he or another person causes or permits to enter those waters) to impede the proper flow of the waters in a manner leading, or likely to lead, to a substantial aggravation of:
  (a) pollution due to other causes; or
  (b) the consequences of such pollution.

It is also an offence under section 85(6) to contravene the conditions of any discharge consent. "Contravention" is defined in section 221 as including a failure to comply, and so offences under section 85 may be committed by a person even though he has taken no positive step with regard to the offending act. The holder of a discharge consent was accordingly guilty of an offence under section 85(6) where a breach of its conditions was due wholly to a non-complying discharge by a third party entitled to make a (complying) discharge under an agreement with the holder.[23A]

8–091   The offences most commonly charged are those under sections 85(1), (3)(a) and (6)—indeed an offence under section 85(3)(a) will almost invariably be an offence under section 85(1) also. The converse is not necessarily so, even in relation to, for example, trade effluent, in that a distinction can be drawn between *permitting* entry of matter into waters, which could be committed even though the offender was entirely passive, and a *discharge* of the same matter, which may be seen

---

[23A] *Taylor Woodrow Property Management Ltd. v. NRA, The Times,* July 14, 1994.

as an active operation designed to lead it to the waters concerned, *e.g.* through a pipe.[24] The reference to a pipe in (3)(b) may reasonably be seen as distinguishing the offence from one of discharging from a ship, which is subject to the controls of the Food and Environment Protection Act 1985 referred to below. It does not therefore require "discharge" in section 85(3) to be read as broadly as "entry".

8–092 The offences of sections 85(2) and (4) are only committed where there is a relevant prohibition under section 86. In the absence of such a prohibition, discharge from a drain or sewer of anything other than trade effluent or sewage effluent (typically surface water run-off) into controlled waters, and discharging trade effluent or sewage effluent on to or into any land or into any lake or pond other than inland freshwaters will not necessarily be an offence. However such actions may offend against the other provisions. If a surface water run-off brings with it any poisonous, noxious or polluting matter, then this will amount to an offence under 85(1) as in *NRA v. Egger* discussed below; similarly trade effluent or sewage effluent discharged on to or into any land may pass from there either into ground water or into surface waters, again being likely to result in an offence under 85(1). To control activities of this sort that represent a risk to controlled waters, the NRA is empowered under section 86 to issue a prohibition notice forbidding the discharge in question, or permitting it to continue on certain prescribed conditions; the offences under 85(2) and (4) will be committed if such prohibitions are ignored or any conditions imposed not complied with.

8–093 It is also an offence under section 4 of the Salmon and Freshwater Fisheries Act 1975 to cause or knowingly permit to flow, or to put or knowingly permit to be put, into any waters containing fish, or into any tributaries of waters containing fish, any liquid or solid matter to such an extent as to cause the waters to be poisonous or injurious to fish or the spawning grounds, spawn or food of fish. This offence, which may be prosecuted only by the NRA or by a person who has obtained a certificate that he has a material interest in the waters concerned, is frequently charged alongside offences under section 85 of the W.R.A., where there has been a fish kill.

8–094 The offences so far discussed relate to entry of matter into controlled waters. Section 90(1) makes it an offence to remove a deposit accumulated in any inland freshwaters by reason of a dam, weir or sluice holding back the waters by causing the deposit to be carried away in suspension in the waters, unless this is done with the consent of the NRA. Similarly, except with the consent of the NRA, it is an offence to cut or uproot a substantial amount of vegetation or to cause

---

[24] *National Rivers Authority v. Coal Products Ltd.*, ENDS, December 1993, Vol.227, p.45.

or permit this to be done, where this is in inland freshwaters, or so near that it falls into them, and to fail to take all reasonable steps to remove the vegetation from the waters.

8–095   There is a standing prohibition in respect of the discharge of "red list" substances, or, as the case may be, such substances in concentrations above the background concentration, and also in respect of discharges from certain prescribed processes involving these red list substances.[25] Accordingly, if any discharge as mentioned in section 85(2) or (4) contains any red list compound, at least where this is above the background concentration, or if it arises from a prescribed process of this type, there would be a breach of this section 86(2) prohibition, and hence an offence under section 85(2) or (4). Though the intention of section 86(2) was to enable controls to be made that would correspond to those over "special category effluent" under the W.I.A.,[26] no corresponding regulations have been made for the purposes of this provision.

8–096   Radioactive waste is *prima facie* excluded from the pollution control provisions of the W.R.A.,[27] being controlled by the R.S.A. 1993. However by the Control of Pollution (Radioactive Waste) Regulations 1989[28] made under the Water Act 1989, and having effect as though under W.R.A. section 98(2), such waste is subject to dual control, with discharges being controlled by the R.S.A. 1993 in so far as their radioactivity is concerned, but in all other respects by the W.R.A. 1991.

"Poisonous, Noxious or Polluting Matter"

8–097   The offence under section 85(1) requires poisonous, noxious or polluting matter or any solid waste matter to enter any controlled waters. There are no definitions in the W.R.A. of "poisonous", "noxious" or "polluting", which must therefore be given their natural meanings, so far as these can be ascertained. There has however been little judicial consideration of these terms.

8–098   What is poisonous is necessarily a matter of degree. It was stated by Paracelsus, who died in 1541: "All substances are poisons; there is none which is not a poison. The right dose differentiates a poison and a remedy". While obviously capable of numerous qualifications, as a broad statement of principle, this remains accepted by toxicologists

---

[25] s.86(2).
[26] Defined by reference to the Trade Effluents (Prescribed Substances and Processes) Regulations 1989, as amended.
[27] By s. 98(1).
[28] S.I. 1989 No. 1158.

today. There is no suggestion in the W.R.A. that "poisonous" should be considered by reference only to the effect on humans, and indeed there are sound reasons not to do so. The protection of water quality is of direct importance to farmers using it for their livestock, and equally so to those with fishing rights, albeit that these are also protected under the Salmon and Freshwater Fisheries Act 1975 as well. If "poisonous" is to apply to the effect of a substance on any of these other creatures, then it must logically extend to any living organism liable to come into contact with the water containing the matter in question. The way in which the offence is framed in section 85(1) however clearly refers to the nature of the matter that enters the controlled waters, and not to whether the controlled waters themselves are thereafter poisonous, noxious or polluting. For the reasons indicated, however, substances cannot necessarily be categorised as "poisonous" in the abstract, and in many situations the expression will only have meaning when considered in relation to organisms on which a substance may impact, and the amounts ingested, where it does. The best solution to this conundrum may be to regard as poisonous anything that may act as a poison on any organism into which it may come into contact as a result of its entry into any controlled waters, subject to a *de minimis* exception where the amount that enters is so trivial as not to be a poison to anything.

"Noxious" arguably is somewhat broader than "poisonous", if the latter is regarded as something causing substantial harm, in that noxious may cover effects which are physically unpleasant, without being necessarily dangerous in any respect. It would seem, however, that anything that is poisonous must necessarily also be noxious. **8–099**

"Polluting" appears to be the only term that has been the subject of significant judicial consideration, notably in *National Rivers Authority v. Egger UK Limited.*[29] The evidence, so far as appears from the judgment, was that there was a discharge into the River Tyne which produced a visible brown "stain" in the water for 100 metres, the effect of which had substantially disappeared within 150 metres of the discharge point.[30] There was no evidence of any physical damage to anything, and the question arose as to whether the mere discolouration of the water was sufficient to amount to the offence of causing or knowingly permitting "polluting matter" to enter the river. **8–100**

Matter that merely discoloured a stream was, if the discolouration was innocuous, expressly excluded from "poisonous, noxious or **8–101**

---

[29] Newcastle Upon Tyne Crown Court, June 15–17, 1992, unreported.
[30] It is understood that in fact the discharge was of mud and other surface 'rubbish' carried with surface water from the premises of the defendant, most of which will have sunk fairly rapidly to the bottom of the river.

polluting matter" by the Rivers (Prevention of Pollution) Act 1951,[31] which repeated a provision derived from the 1876 Act. No such exclusion is contained in the Water Resources Act 1991 (or its predecessor the Water Act 1989). While it is arguable that "polluting" in the water legislation has never extended to mere discolouration, and that the express exclusion of this in the 1951 Act was merely for clarity, the decision in *Egger* was to the contrary, and that discolouration is itself pollution.

8–102   The judgment in *Egger* also dealt at length with the question as to whether matter was polluting was to be assessed by reference to whether or not its entry worsened the quality of the receiving water. As to this, it was noted that the expression "poisonous, noxious or polluting" (without further qualification) has been contained in UK legislation since at least 1876. However, in the Public Health Act 1875, section 17 provided that nothing in the Act was to authorise any local authority

> "to make or use any sewer, drain, or outfall for the purpose of conveying sewage or filthy water into any natural stream or water course or into any canal, pond or lake, until such sewage or filthy water is freed from all excrementitious or other foul or noxious matter *such as would affect or deteriorate the purity and quality of the water in such stream or water course or in such canal, pond or lake"*.

The judge in *Egger* placed much reliance on the fact that Parliament could readily, in 1876 in the Rivers Pollution Prevention Act, and in the Water Act 1989 (the W.R.A.'s immediate antecedent), have incorporated words along the lines of those emphasised above, had they intended pollution to be considered by reference only to whether the quality of the receiving waters was made worse or not. It was accepted that "pollution", as a word, clearly has a relationship to what is polluted. However it was held that it does not follow that the words "polluting matter" can only be defined when it has been discovered whether, in fact, harm has been done to whatever the matter has come into contact with. What the statute is concerned with is the nature of the material being discharged into the controlled water, and to look at the question in relation to a natural, unpolluted river. Thus:

> "One looks at the nature of the discharge and one says, 'is that discharge capable of causing harm to a river, in the sense of causing damage to uses to which a river might be put; damage to

[31] s.11.

352

animal, vegetable or other—if there is such other life which might live in a river, or damaging that river aesthetically?' ".[31A]

Though the question is whether matter that is allowed to enter controlled waters, was potentially injurious before the entry, evidence as to its effect on the controlled waters is obviously also relevant. However it is sufficient to consider the receiving water at the point of entry, and not necessarily to review the overall effect on an entire river[32] If the statute is only concerned with the nature (and likely effect) of a substance entering controlled waters, and not with its actual effect, then it follows that it is unnecessary to show that any actual damage has been caused. In *Egger* this conclusion was also based at least in part on the difficulties that would otherwise be faced by a prosecutor.[33] Where there is an incident of gross pollution, then the evidence is likely to be readily available in the form of dead fish and other creatures. However where there is a lesser degree of pollution, it would be extremely difficult, in many cases, to establish whether any particular dead or weakened organisms that might be discovered were in that state as a result of the entry of the relevant matter, or whether there was some independent cause.

The effect of the decision in *Egger* is that adding any potentially   **8–103** polluting matter to a river would still amount to any entry of polluting matter contrary to section 85(1) of the W.R.A. even though the river was heavily polluted and the added matter was in so diluted a form that the quality of the river was in fact improved. Such a conclusion is entirely consistent with a policy of maintaining and upgrading river water quality, even though it may appear anomalous in cases where only very slightly contaminated water is discharged into a heavily polluted stream. But if the law were to the contrary, a charge of polluting could only be avoided with certainty if the discharge differed from the receiving water in dilution. If it contained any different contaminants in comparatively dilute form, the court would have to consider evidence and argument on whether the polluting effect (on what and where?) of the new contaminant was or was not outweighed by the diluting effect of the discharge as a whole. Moreover a discharge of constant composition might sometimes be lawful and

---

[31A] See also *Staffordshire County Council v. Seisdon Rural District Council,* (1907) 5 L.G.R. 347.

[32] *A.-G. v. The Birmingham, Tame and Rea District Drainage Board,* [1910] Ch. 48; *King v. The Chairman and Justices of Antrim,* (1906) I.R. (2) 298.

[33] It is debatable how far this line of argument is legitimate. The difficulties that may be faced in bringing a prosecution are arguably essentially a matter for Parliament to determine, and the interpretation of a statute should not depend on this consideration, except to prefer a construction where successful prosecutions were at least feasible to one where they would be virtually impossible.

sometimes not depending on how much rain had recently fallen in the area, and consequently whether existing pollutants in the receiving water were concentrated or well diluted. Though this would have some logic, it would make controls exceptionally difficult to maintain both for the discharger and the regulator.

8–104   What was, somewhat surprisingly, not discussed in *Egger*, was the definition of pollution in the Environmental Protection Act 1990. Thus in E.P.A. section 29(3) relating to pollution deriving from waste, pollution of the environment (which includes water) is defined by reference to the release or escape of substances or articles capable (by reason of the quantity or concentrations involved) of causing harm to man or any other living organisms supported by the environment. Harm is defined in turn[34] as meaning harm to the health of living organisms or other interference with the ecological systems of which they form part, and in the case of man *includes offence to any of his senses* or harm to his property. Similar definitions are contained in the other Parts of the Environmental Protection Act so far as material. Clearly for the purposes of that Act, pollution includes causing visual offence; the close relationship of the two statutes[35] provides strong grounds for adopting the same interpretation of the expression in the water legislation also, in the absence of compelling reasons to adopt any other.[36]

8–105   Since the W.R.A. 1991 and its predecessor the W.A. 1989 were clearly intended to implement EC legislation, the definition of "polluting" in the EC groundwater Directive 80/68[37] is also potentially relevant, though not (perhaps inevitably in the case of groundwater) directly to questions of discolouration, namely: "the discharge by man, directly or indirectly, of substances or energy into waters, the results of which are such as to endanger human health or water supplies, harm living resources and the aquatic ecosystem, interfere with the other legitimate uses of water". Nevertheless, it must be evident that any prolonged discolouration of water would most probably be such as to endanger aspects of the relevant aquatic ecosystem, and consequently the decision in *Egger* is consistent with the EC legislation.

---

[34] In E.P.A. s. 29(5).

[35] *e.g.* in Part I of the E.P.A., and in particular s.28, which provides for the imposition of controls over discharges to water on Part A processes subject to Integrated Pollution Control; also E.P.A. 33(1)(c) prohibits *inter alia* the disposal of controlled waste on land covered by waters (above the low water mark) 'in a manner likely to cause pollution of the environment'. Arguably Egger might have been charged under this section also.

[36] See also *Wyre Forest DC v. Secretary of State for the Environment*, [1990] 2 W.L.R. 517, per Lord Lowry.

[37] O.J. L 20, 26.1.80, Art.1(2)(d).

"Causing or Knowingly Permitting"

The offences under section 85 of the W.R.A. are committed by a **8–106** person who "causes or knowingly permits" a variety of forms of pollution of controlled waters. The framing of water pollution (and indeed other) offences in this way dates from the Salmon Fishery Act 1861;[38] it was repeated in the Rivers Pollution Prevention Act 1876, and is to be found in all subsequent UK legislation on the topic. Nevertheless, it was not until over 100 years later, in *Alphacell Limited v. Woodward*[39] that the House of Lords pronounced definitively on what is needed to make good a charge of "causing" pollution, and specifically on the relevance, if any, of the defendant's knowledge and intent, and the nature of his conduct.

Alphacell Limited were paper manufacturers whose premises were **8–107** on the banks of a river. Washing water from a relatively late stage in the paper making process was drained into two connected settling tanks by the river, one being higher than the other. The water from the lower tank was filtered and re-used. If the lower tank were to overflow, a channel directed the overflow into the river. Two pumps extracted water from the lower tank, one of which cut in automatically when the water rose beyond a certain level, while the second was operable manually. The company foreman inspected the tanks routinely, every two or three hours. On the day of the offence, he had noticed the water level in the lower tank rising and had switched on the second pump; a couple of hours later, he became aware that this had not reduced the level as it should have. Shortly after that, an inspector of the relevant river authority noticed liquid overflowing into the river, and took samples which showed a substantial breach of Alphacell's discharge consent condition relating to biological oxygen demand. At the material time, Alphacell was not aware of the overflow into the river. It was eventually established that various brambles, ferns and leaves had passed devices intended to prevent them from being sucked from the lower settling tank into the pumps, and had blocked the vents of both pumps rendering them ineffective. Alphacell was convicted of causing polluting matter to enter the river, contrary to the then applicable Rivers (Prevention of Pollution) Act 1951. It appealed on the ground that a person cannot be said to cause matter to enter a river if he is ignorant that he is doing so and has not been negligent in any respect, or alternatively that to cause something to happen denotes both knowledge and some positive act, or at least some positive omission.

[38] s.5.
[39] [1972] AC 824.

355

8–108   The case proceeded in the House of Lords on the basis that Alphacell had not been negligent in any respect. Nevertheless, the conviction was upheld on the ground that Alphacell, by locating and operating its factory where it did had undertaken a positive act that led to the pollution, and that knowledge of the specific polluting incident was not a necessary ingredient of the offence. Several of the speeches quoted with approval the judgment in *Sherras v. De Rutzen*,[40] in which it was said

> "There is a presumption that mens rea, an evil intention, or a knowledge of wrongfulness of the act, is an essential ingredient in every offence; but that presumption is liable to be displaced either by the words of the statute creating the offence or by the subject matter with which it deals, and both must be considered . . . [T]he principal classes of exceptions may perhaps be reduced to three. One is a class of acts which, in the language of Lush J. in *Davies v. Harvey*,[41] are not criminal in any real sense, but are acts which in the public interest are prohibited under a penalty . . . Another class comprehends some, and perhaps all, public nuisances: *Reg. v Stephens*[42] where the employer was held liable on indictment for a nuisance caused by workmen without his knowledge and contrary to his orders . . . ".

Thus Lord Pearson held that "mens rea is generally not a necessary ingredient in an offence of this kind, which is in nature of a public nuisance". In coming to the same conclusion, Lord Salmon[43] relied strongly on the underlying policy justification

> "The appellants contend that, even if they caused the pollution, still they should succeed since they did not cause it intentionally or knowingly or negligently. Section 2(1)(a) of the Rivers (Prevention of Pollution) Act 1951 is undoubtedly a penal section. It follows that if it is capable of two or more meanings then the meaning most favourable to the subject should be adopted. Accordingly, so the argument runs, the words 'intentionally' or 'knowingly' or 'negligently' should be read into the section immediately before the word 'causes'. I do not agree. It is of the utmost public importance that our rivers should not be polluted. The risk of pollution, particularly from the vast and increasing number of riparian industries, is very great. The offences created by the Act of 1951 seem to me to be prototypes of offences which

[40] [1895] 1 Q.B. 918, at 921, 922.
[41] Law Rep. 9 Q.B. 433.
[42] Law Rep. 1 Q.B. 702.
[43] At pp.848D–849A.

'are not criminal in any real sense, but are acts which in the public interest are prohibited under a penalty': *Sherras v. De Rutzen* [1895] 1 Q.B. 918, *per* Wright J. at p.922, referred to with approval by my noble and learned friends, Lord Reid and Lord Diplock, in *Sweet v. Parsley* [1970] A.C. 132, 149, 162. I can see no valid reason for reading the word 'intentionally', 'knowingly' or 'negligently' into section 2(1)(a) and a number of cogent reasons for not doing so. In the case of a minor pollution such as the present, when the justices find that there is no wrongful intention or negligence on the part of the defendant, a comparatively nominal fine will no doubt be imposed. This may be regarded as a not unfair hazard of carrying on a business which may cause pollution on the banks of a river. The present appellants were fined £20 and ordered to pay, in all, £24 costs. I should be surprised if the costs of pursuing this appeal to this House were incurred for the purpose of saving these appellants £44.

If this appeal succeeded and it were held to be the law that no conviction could be obtained under the Act of 1951 unless the prosecution could discharge the often impossible onus of proving that the pollution was caused intentionally or negligently, a great deal of pollution would go unpunished and undeterred to the relief of many riparian factory owners. As a result, many rivers which are now filthy would become filthier still and many rivers which are now clean would lose their cleanliness. The legislature no doubt recognised that as a matter of public policy this would be most unfortunate. Hence section 2(1)(a) which encourages riparian factory owners not only to take reasonable steps to prevent pollution but to do everything possible to ensure that they do not cause it."[44]

Having established that no mental element was called for, the question resolved into whether Alphacell had "caused" the pollution. This was approached by putting the question: "What other cause was there?" Possible answers that might have amounted to defences were the intervening act of a trespasser or an act of God.[45] "Cause" must be given its ordinary and natural meaning, and it consequently covers causing something not only intentionally or negligently, but also

---

[44] It may be noted that the obligation on EC member states to ensure compliance with the MAC for nitrates in the EC Drinking Water Directive 80/778 is likewise strict (or maybe even absolute). In *EC Commission v. United Kingdom* (Case C-337/89, November 25, 1992) the UK's argument that the directive only required all practicable steps to be taken to ensure this was rejected: Judgment, paras. 19, 20.

[45] *per* Lord Pearson at p.845 C/D. Similarly Lord Salmon at p.847 F.

inadvertently without negligence or intention.[46] As Lord Salmon put it:[47]

> "It seems plain to me that the appellants caused the pollution by the active operation of their plant. They certainly did not intend to cause pollution but they intended to do the acts which caused it. What they did was something different in kind from the passive storing of effluent which could not discharge into the river save by an act of God or, as in *Impress (Worcester) Limited v. Rees*,[48] by the active intervention of a stranger, the risk of which could not reasonably have been foreseen."

The presence of the expression "knowingly permitting" as well as "causing" was considered by Lord Salmon as being intended to ensure that the section also included an offence to deal with the type of case in which a man knows that contaminated effluent is escaping over his land into a river and does nothing at all to prevent it.[49] A possible inference from this, coupled with his earlier statement that he gave "cause" its ordinary and natural meaning, is that he understood the word to cover everything short of total inactivity. Lord Cross read out of the contrast that a man cannot be guilty of causing polluting matter to enter a stream unless at least he does some positive act in the chain of acts and events leading to that result.[50] It is not however necessary for a finding of having "caused" the result, that an accused should have known or have had the means of knowledge that his act might be expected to lead to the pollution.[50A]

8–109   These views were summed up in *Price v. Cromack*[51] by Lord Widgery C.J. in these terms:

> "It seems to me that the overwhelming opinion of their Lordships in that case [*i.e.* in *Alphacell*] was, that whatever else 'causing' might or might not involve, it did involve some active operation as opposed to mere tacit standing by and looking on."

8–110   A Scottish case, *Lockhart v. National Coal Board*,[52] applied *Alphacell* (though it is not strictly binding in Scotland), in holding the Coal Board liable for causing polluting matter to enter a stream by reason of

---

[46] *per* Lord Salmon at p.847 D.
[47] At p.847 G.
[48] [1971] 2 All E.R. 357.
[49] At 849 B.
[50] At p.846 C; similarly Lord Wilberforce at p.834E.
[50A] *R. v. CPC (UK) Ltd.*, (C.A.), *The Times*, August 4, 1994, where the defendant was held guilty of causing pollution arising from defects of which it was unaware that had been introduced by building work undertaken before its acquisition of the property concerned.
[51] [1975] 2 All E.R. 113; [1975] 1 W.L.R. 988.
[52] 1981 S.L.T. 161.

its failure to continue pumping and treating water accumulating in the mine workings after the mine had been closed. The Court adopted the argument of the Procurator Fiscal that everything stemmed from the original sinking of the mine in 1951. The ingress of air caused pyrite (iron sulphide—a very common mineral) present in the excavated workings to become oxidised. Constant pumping was necessary to remove water that would otherwise inevitably have accumulated in the mine. When the mine was closed, the pumping ceased, allowing the mine to fill with water that brought out with it to the surface the oxidised pyrite, polluting local streams that it flowed into. Thus there was a continuous chain of events carried out by the Coal Board which caused pollution of the streams. This pollution was bound to occur unless there were pumps of sufficient capacity to prevent this occurring. The Coal Board's decision to cease operations and stop pumping was held by the court to be a positive act. It was no defence that the lease of the property had expired, so that the Coal Board was not in a legal position to continue the pumping. A person could not be heard to say that he had put himself in a position where he could do nothing about a danger that he had created, and was therefore not to be held responsible for that danger.

On the other hand, in a case involving a mine in South Wales[53]   **8–111** where the cause of pollution was essentially the same, British Coal was acquitted, on the ground that the original sinking of the mine was by a third party, prior to nationalisation of the coal industry, and that the polluting water from the mine came from workings other than those developed since nationalisation. If British Coal had acquired the mine and done nothing further with it other than to stop pumping, then it would be *prima facie* liable for knowingly permitting pollution, when water from the abandoned mine entered controlled waters. However W.R.A. s.89(3) expressly excludes permitting such entry of water from an abandoned mine from the prescribed pollution offences of section 85. The exclusion is regarded as extending to matter dissolved or suspended in the water, since otherwise there would be no s.85 offence in the first place, at least under section 85(1).[54] Consequently liability in such a situation falls solely on whoever originally sank the mine (if still in existence) and, subject to relevant evidence regarding

---

[53] *R. v. British Coal Corporation*, ENDS, December 1993, Vol.227, p.44.
[54] On the wording of s.89(3) by itself this is open to question – had the intention been to extend the defence to polluted (and polluting) water the term 'effluent' could have been used, which is defined as any liquid, including particles of matter and other substances in suspension in the liquid. However the limitation by s.161(3) and (4) on the NRA's ability to recover costs of remedial work in relation to water from an abandoned mine indicates that 'water' includes pollutants dissolved or suspended in it.

the source of pollution, anyone who has carried on mining operations subsequently

"Knowingly Permitting"

8–112   In *Price v. Cromack* the defendant appellant, Price, was convicted of causing poisonous, noxious or polluting matter to enter a stream that ran by his land. He was in fact a director of a company that operated an abattoir and animal by-products plant on adjacent land, and had agreed to the discharge of effluent from those operations on to his own land. Some years previously, the company had constructed two lagoons on the defendant's land to receive the effluent. Polluting matter had escaped through breaches in the walls of the lagoons on to the surrounding land and thence into the stream. It was argued, following *Alphacell*, that the defendant had undertaken a positive act by entering into the arrangement whereby effluent was received on to his land from the company. Lord Widgery however did not accept that this was sufficient to justify a charge of "causing". He agreed that had the effluent been handed over to the defendant at the boundary of his land and that he had then been free to deal with it as he wished, the positive action justifying a charge of "causing" might well be justified. However in the particular case, the effluent came on to the land by gravity and found its way into the stream by gravity with no physical act on the part of the defendant whatever.

8–113   Lord Widgery accepted that in principle there should really be no great difference between the man who generates polluting matter on his own land and one who voluntarily agrees to accept somebody else's polluting matter and have it put on his land. It was, however, not so much a question of distinguishing between the culpability of those individuals, but in the precise nature of the offence committed. He could not accept that there was a "causing" of the entry of the polluting matter "merely because the landowner stands by and watches the polluting matter cross his land into the stream, even if he has committed himself by contract to allowing the adjoining owner so to act". There was no positive act on the part of the defendant.

8–114   Lord Widgery implied what Ashworth J. in the same case stated explicitly, that had the defendant been charged with knowingly permitting the pollution "I do not see what answer the present appellant could conceivably have had in circumstances of this case".[55] In coming to this conclusion, Ashworth J. referred expressly to Lord Salmon's comment that "the creation of an offence in relation to permitting pollution was probably included in the section so as to deal

---

[55] [1975] 2 All E.R. at 119.

with the type of case in which a man knows that contaminated effluent is escaping over his land into a river and does nothing at all to prevent it." He dismissed a suggestion that "knowingly permits" is limited to circumstances in which the knowledge and the permission occur after the discharge has started, arguing that if a man is guilty of knowingly permitting when he knows of an escape into a river and does nothing at all to prevent it, *a fortiori* this applies when he in fact enters into an agreement by which the discharge of the pollution over his land is expressly assented to by himself.

Proof of relevant knowledge on the part of the accused, is of course a **8–115** necessary element of a charge of "knowingly permitting" an event. However, if the prosecution is able to establish all the material surrounding facts, it is entitled to ask the court or the jury, as the case may be, to infer "that the accused acted with knowledge of the facts, unless there is some evidence to the contrary originating from the accused who alone can know on what belief he acted and on what ground the belief, if mistaken, was held".[56] In the case of a corporate defendant, the knowledge must be of someone responsible for the direction of the company, and not that of an ordinary employee.[57] On a charge under C.O.P.A. 1974 of knowingly permitting controlled waste to be deposited in contravention of an applicable waste disposal licence, it was held that the prosecution need only prove that the deposit has been knowingly permitted, and not knowledge of any breach of condition.[58] It was therefore sufficient to prove that there was in fact a breach of condition, notwithstanding ignorance of this on the part of the management of the defendant company. The reasoning would appear to apply equally to the offences under section 85 of the W.R.A. and section 33 of the E.P.A.

Convictions for "knowingly permitting" poisonous matter to be **8–116** discharged into controlled waters as a result of a spillage of oil that entered a nearby brook,[59] were overturned on appeal on the ground that "there was no finding and, as far as we can tell, no evidence that the Appellants could have prevented the escape of fuel oil into the brook sooner than they did, or that there was an escape during any period when they could have prevented but failed to prevent it". A charge of "knowingly permitting" in such circumstances must therefore be accompanied by evidence of knowledge of the pollution

---

[56] Per Lord Diplock in *Sweet v. Parsley* [1970] A.C. 132 at 164 F, cited with approval by Lord Bridge in *Westminster City Council v. Croyalgrange Limited* (H.L.) [1986] 2 All E.R. 353 at 358; see also *Kent County Council v. Beaney*, (Q.B.D.) [1993] 1 Env. L.R. 225.

[57] *Tesco Supermarkets v. Nattrass* [1972] A.C. 153; *James & Son Ltd v. Smee* [1955] 1 QB 78, [1954] 3 All E.R. 273. See also the discussion at paras. 21–003 to 21–006.

[58] *Ashcroft v. Cambro Waste Products*, [1981] 1 W.L.R. 1349; [1981] 3 All E.R. 699.

[59] *Schulmans Incorporated Limited v. NRA*; [1993] Env L.R. D1.

entering the relevant drains (independently of knowledge of the initial spillage), of when the pollution in the drainage system was cleaned up and whether that could have been done earlier, and of whether there was any alternative means of preventing the escape of oil into the brook. Evidence would also be essential on whether the management of the accused company knew that the contents of the drainage system would probably find their way into the brook before the system would have been cleaned out in the normal course of operations.

8–117   "Permitting" may mean either giving leave for an act which, without that leave, could not be legally done, or to abstain from taking reasonable steps to prevent the act, where it is within a man's power to prevent it.[60] This is an issue that directly affects lessors of premises who, in any normal lease, will reserve significant powers over the operations of the lessee, particularly in relation to breaches of the law. Where a lessor has the requisite knowledge, and fails to take reasonable steps to prevent such pollution as it is within his power to prevent, then he will be exposed to liability for knowingly permitting that pollution. It is probably not requisite to avoid liability that a lessor take active steps to ascertain whether or not the tenant is discharging polluting matter, but constructive knowledge will suffice,[61] and knowledge may be inferred from evidence of a defendant deliberately shutting his eyes to the obvious or refraining from inquiry because he suspected the truth but did not want to have his suspicion confirmed.[62]

General Defences

8–118   Although liability for "causing" pollution is "strict" in the sense that a mental element is not necessary, various defences are nevertheless available, including in particular the intervention of a third party or an act of God.[63] Certain statutory defences are provided by W.R.A., ss. 88 and 89; these do not however include a due diligence defence comparable to that found in many statutes imposing strict liability, for example in E.P.A. s. 33(7)(a):

> "that [the defendant] took all reasonable precautions and exercised all due diligence to avoid the commission of the offence".

---

[60] *Berton and Ors v. Alliance Economic Investment Co Ltd and Ors* (C.A.) [1922] 1 K.B. 742 at 759 *per* Atkin LJ.
[61] *Schulmans Incorporated Limited v. NRA.*
[62] *Westminster City Council v. Croyalgrange Limited*, at p.359 C.
[63] Other defences to strict liability offences were suggested by Lord Diplock in *Sweet v. Parsley* at 162 G–163 C: insanity, somnambulism, duress, inevitable accident and a belief, held honestly and upon reasonable grounds, in the existence of facts which, if true, would make the act innocent.

Lord Cross put it generically in *Alphacell*[64] that the appellants "could only escape being held to have caused the pollution if they proved that the overflow of the tank had been brought about by some other event which could fairly be regarded as being beyond their ability to foresee or control". The burden of establishing this defence is placed squarely on the person charged; the prosecution is only required to address it if the defendant produces cogent evidence to support such an argument.

In *Impress (Worcester) Limited v. Rees*[65] the defendants appealed **8–119** against a conviction for causing pollution as a result of a trespasser opening a valve at night time, thus causing oil to escape from the premises. There were no factory gates to prevent unauthorised entry nor any night watchman. There was also no interceptor in the storm water drains on the premises to retain any escaping oil. In the principal judgment, Cooke J. said:

> "Of course, in one sense the entry of oil into the river was the result of many causes, and it may be said that the mere fact that the appellants brought the oil on to their land was one of those causes. There were, however, a number of intervening causes, and in particular there was the opening of the valve by unauthorised persons who had entered the appellant's land. On general principles of causation, the question which the justices ought to have asked themselves was whether that intervening cause was of so powerful a nature that the conduct of the appellants was not a cause at all but was merely part of the surrounding circumstances.[66] If the justices had asked themselves that question, it seems to me that it would have been susceptible of only one answer, namely that it was not the conduct of the appellants but the intervening act of the unauthorised person which caused the oil to enter the river".

In *NRA v. Wright Engineering Co Ltd*,[67] where the facts were very similar to those of *Impress*, it was held by Buckley J. that foreseeability was one factor which a tribunal might consider in seeking to apply common sense to the question of who or what caused the result under consideration. Nevertheless, in his view, while reasonable foreseeability was clearly relevant to a charge of "knowingly permitting", it was

---

[64] At p.847A/B.
[65] [1971] 2 All E.R. 357.
[66] See also the comment by Denning LJ. in *Cork v. Kirby Maclean Limited* [1952] 2 All E.R. 402 at 407, cited by Lord Pearson in *Alphacell*: 'It is always a matter of seeing whether the particular event was sufficiently powerful a factor in bringing about the result as to be properly regarded by the law as a cause of it'.
[67] [1994] Env. L.R. 186.

less so to one of "causing". On the facts, it was open to the justices to find that vandals had "caused" the escape of oil and not the accused defendants.

8–120   Act of God was pleaded in *Southern Water Authority v. Pegrum*.[68] The defendant farmers had created a lagoon on their land to store pig slurry. A fissure in one side of the lagoon had developed and, after some heavy rain, liquid escaped through this, eventually entering a stream flowing into the River Medway. Though the rain had been very heavy, it followed a dry period, so that there had been only average rainfall for the preceding two weeks as a whole. A drain leading from the pig unit had become blocked, and water escaped from the drains at a manhole and ran into the lagoon which overflowed. Defining an act of God as "an operation of natural forces so unpredictable as to excuse the defendants all liability for its consequences" it was held that this did not apply either to the amount of rain, which though heavy, was not more than could reasonably have been contemplated, nor to blockage of the drain, which became and remained blocked due to the defendants' negligence. The blockage of the drain was moreover not an intervening act but part of the operations of the farm, comparable to those in *Alphacell*.

Multiple Parties

8–121   Difficult issues as to liability arise in attempting to apply *Alphacell* where two or more separate parties are involved in an activity that results in pollution, circumstances with which that case was not concerned. In *Northwest Water Authority v. McTay Construction Limited*[69] McTay had been appointed the main contractor for the construction of a road bypass for Greater Manchester Council. The Council's specification required ground to be compacted by vibro-flotation, a process that inevitably results in the displacement of a substantial amount of slurry, consisting of water heavily polluted with soil. Unless the slurry is taken into settling ponds, pollution of neighbouring water courses is virtually inevitable. McTay told the Council that it did not have the necessary expertise, and the Council supplied a list of approved specialist contractors from which McTay selected one called Bauer. Though some steps were taken to prevent the vibro-flotation slurry from entering controlled waters, in the event they proved ineffective, and McTay was charged with causing pollution of a brook. It was acquitted, and the acquittal upheld on appeal on the ground that McTay had not caused the pollution. It appears to have been

[68] (1989) Crim L.R. 442.
[69] Q.B.D. April 14, 1986, unreported.

found that McTay had no control over and were not in charge of the carrying out of the vibro-flotation process, including the process of settling the resulting slurry.[70] Although the pollution occurred as an adjunct to McTay's operations and could not have happened without them, Bauer's activities were regarded as sufficiently distinct. The point was raised in argument, and accepted by the prosecution, that on the general principles of *Alphacell*, if McTay were liable for the offence then the Council itself should also be liable on the same basis. This would be an perfectly logical conclusion, especially in view of the Council having required the use of vibro-flotation in its specification, but the Court was not prepared to go that far. In so deciding, it effectively exonerated McTay also.

Somewhat similarly, in *Welsh Water Authority v. Williams Motors*   **8–122**
(Cwmdu) Limited[71] the defendants were acquitted of causing diesel fuel oil to enter a canal, the acquittal being upheld on appeal, where the pollution derived from a spillage caused in the course of a delivery of oil by an independent supplier who overfilled a fuel tank. The court dealt with foreseeability by saying that "the question is not what was foreseeable by the defendants or anyone else: the question is whether any act on the part of the respondents caused the pollution." Its answer was that Williams Motors' function was purely passive and that the case came "on the *Price v. Cromack* side of the line rather than on the *Alphacell* side of the line".

In *Wychavon District Council v. NRA*[72] Wychavon had been acting as   **8–123**
agent for the statutory sewerage undertaker, Severn Trent Water Authority, to maintain various sewers in their area. A blockage formed in a sewer pipe, resulting in pollution of the River Avon by sewage effluent. The Council was charged with causing the pollution by failing promptly to discover the source of the discharge and failing to clear the blockage as soon as possible. The magistrates found that the Council had not brought about the blockage and could not be said to have caused sewage effluent merely by maintaining and operating the sewer as agents for the water authority. They nevertheless convicted on the ground that the Council had caused the overflow to continue and so enter controlled waters by failing within a reasonable time to discover and prevent this. The conviction was quashed on appeal, it being held there was neither a positive nor a deliberate act by the Council which could properly be said to have brought about the flow

---

[70] From the transcripts of the judgments in the Divisional Court, the magistrates seem to have accepted the defendants' submissions to this effect, though this is not wholly clear.

[71] Q.B.D. November 7, 1988, unreported.

[72] [1993] Env L.R. 330. The decision in this case was questioned by the Court of Appeal in coming to a contrary conclusion in *Attorney-General's Reference (No. 1 of 1994)*, *The Times*, January 26, 1995; *The Independent*, January 31, 1995.

of sewage effluent into the river.[73] Relying on the requirement in *Alphacell* that causing polluting matter to enter any controlled waters must involve some active operation or chain of operations bringing about pollution, in other words a positive act and not merely a passive looking on, the Council was entitled to be acquitted. Watkins LJ. said that there were facts which, in his opinion, could point to inactivity amounting possibly to negligence, and others which could amount to knowingly permitting the sewage effluent to be discharged, but the Council was not charged with that.

8–124   The difficulty that this decision highlights is that on the interpretations of "causing" and "knowingly permitting" that were applied, there is a distinct gap where a person may, as a result of some omission, in most people's eyes be culpable, but where there is neither a positive act nor a passive looking on. There is no reason in principle to construe the two expressions in the statute so restrictively; they are ordinary English words and not terms of art, and Parliament must be supposed to have intended to cover all normal situations where those responsible for actions that may result in pollution are given a sufficient deterrent to make sure this does not happen, for the policy reasons set out by Lord Salmon in *Alphacell*. It was not necessary, in order to establish the Council's guilt, to identify a specific act by it that had brought about the blockage that led to the pollution. The question should have been whether the entire operation conducted by the Council was itself an act that was liable to cause, and in the event did cause, pollution. *Alphacell* is distinguishable in that the only relevant activity by the Council was the maintenance and repair of the relevant sewers—it was not the owner of them at the material time, and there appears to have been no evidence as to whether it had any responsibility for the original construction. However the ownership of the relevant property cannot by itself be a material aspect of whether a person has caused pollution; if an organisation is operating a potentially polluting facility, that must in principle be capable of being a sufficient "positive act" on which to base a finding of causing pollution in an appropriate case. Indeed, if it were otherwise, the owners of facilities could avoid liability on the basis of the decision in *Welsh Development Agency* (see below), and possibly also *McTay*, while the operator could avoid liability on the basis of *Wychavon*.

8–125   It may be that the Council in *Wychavon* was in a special situation, entitling it to be absolved of liability by virtue of its acting as agent for a

---

[73] A further finding was that the facts were not capable of establishing that the Council created a (public) nuisance, which the Divisional Court defined (adopting the wording in *Stephen's Digest*, 8th Ed.) as 'an act not warranted by law or an omission to discharge a legal duty, which act or omission obstructs or causes inconvenience or damage to the public in the exercise of rights common to all His Majesty's subjects'.

sewerage undertaker, and so necessarily having to cope with whatever might be discharged to the sewers, the nature of which it, as opposed to the sewerage undertaker, had no control.[74] If so, the decision is dependent on these particular facts, and is not of general application.

National Rivers Authority v. Welsh Development Agency[75] related to an industrial estate created by the Development Agency on which it had established factory units that had been leased to various tenants. The industrial estate included a drainage system for effluent from the various units that had been designed and constructed by the Agency and was being maintained by it; this system discharged into a nearby stream pursuant to a consent granted to the Agency. All the tenancy agreements included a covenant by the tenant not to discharge effluent into the stream such as would cause pollution. Contrary to this, one of the tenants allowed polluting matter to be discharged into the drainage system and thence into the stream. The Agency was charged with causing the pollution but was acquitted; the acquittal was upheld on appeal. In the appeal judgment, Potts J. referred in particular to *Alphacell* and *Wychavon* and held that it was irrelevant that the Agency was responsible for the design and construction of the drainage system, in contrast to the situation in *Wychavon*, stating:

8–126

> "In my judgment there was nothing in the design of the drainage system which played a part in the discharge the subject matter of these proceedings. Nor was there anything inherent in the construction of the drains which played a part. To all intents and purposes, the position of the present respondent does not in any material way differ from that of the appellant council in the *Wychavon* case. . . . . In my view, neither the lease entered into by the respondent nor the consent [to discharge surface water into the stream] affects the position in any way."

The judge then cited the passage in *Impress* relating to causation (see paragraph 8–119), asking whether the intervening cause was of so powerful a nature that the conduct of [Impress] was not a cause at all but was merely part of the surrounding circumstances. In confirming the magistrate's decision, he held it was not the agency that had caused the pollution but the conduct of the tenant.

With respect to the judge in that case, by focusing on the design of the drains and the fact that there was nothing inherent in their

8–127

---

[74] See the discussion on this by Simon Ball, J.E.L., Vol 5, No. 1 (1993), pp.128–132. The argument, though appealing in relation to trade effluent, is less convincing where the issue relates to sewage effluent, which the operator must at all times have expected to have to dispose of.

[75] [1993] Env L.R. 407.

construction that played any part in the pollution, he appears not to have applied the broad approach adopted by the House of Lords in *Alphacell,* whereby regard is to be had to the totality of the operations of the defendant, in order to decide whether that as a whole constituted the cause. The fact that individual aspects of the Agency's activities, such as the design and construction of the drains, were perfectly in order is not relevant to that issue. Indeed if the drains had become blocked through inefficiency on the part of the Agency, presumably the pollutant would not have reached the stream, or at least not as quickly, and some remedial action might have been possible. What the Agency had done was to set up from nothing a complex of industrial activities near a river, equipped that complex with surface drains that would inevitably allow pollutants spilled on any part of the site to reach the river, and by letting out the factory units to known tenants it had created at least one, and possibly several potentially polluting operations on its land. The question that needed to be asked was whether this fell within the words of Lord Wilberforce in *Alphacell*:[76]

> "The whole complex operation which might lead to this result [pollution of the neighbouring stream] was an operation deliberately conducted by the appellants and I fail to see how a defect in one stage of it, even if we must assume that this happened without their negligence, can enable them to say they did not cause the pollution."

The facts in the *Welsh Development Agency* case were of course different from *Alphacell* in that third parties were involved, and it is certainly arguable that the ultimate decision was correct. Nevertheless the approach where third parties are involved was also addressed by Lord Wilberforce in these terms:

> " . . . [the decision in *Impress (Worcester) Limited v. Rees*] should not be regarded as a decision that in every case the act of a third person necessarily interrupts the chain of causation initiated by the person who owns or operates the installation or plant from which the flow took place. The answer to such questions is one of degree and depends on a proper attribution of responsibility for the flow of the polluting matter."[77]

The *Welsh Development Agency* decision is not easy to reconcile with Lord Widgery's comment in *Price v. Cromack* that if the effluent in that case had been handed over to the defendant at the boundary of his

[76] At p.834 H.
[77] At p.835 D/E. The evident rejection of *Wychavon* by the Court of Appeal in *Attorney-General's Reference (No. 1 of 1994)*, see n. 72 *supra*, effectively undermines the authority of the decision in *Welsh Development Agency* also.

land then he might very well have been guilty of "causing" the polluting entry. Furthermore, it is difficult to see in principle the distinction between the position of the Agency and that of the sewerage undertakers that have been held responsible for their discharges in numerous cases, for example, *Yorkshire West Riding Council v. Holmfirth Urban Sanitary Authority*[78] and *Rochford Rural District Council v. Port of London Authority.*[79] Under more recent legislation (currently W.R.A. s.87(1)) sewerage undertakers are deemed to be liable for their discharges of sewage effluent containing matter that they are bound to receive into their sewers or sewage treatment plant, as the case may be. It does not however follow that no liability would attach in the absence of the deeming provision.[80] While their remarks were *obiter*, both Viscount Dilhorne and Lord Salmon in *Alphacell* seemed to indicate that this provision was not strictly necessary, but served solely to deny a defence that might otherwise have been at least arguable. In both their judgments, it was made clear that the existence of this deeming provision should not affect in any way the meaning to be attached to "causes" in the principal pollution offences.

Circumstances can therefore readily be envisaged where a landlord might well be held liable under section 85(1) for the activities of a tenant, for example where a site has been deliberately developed and let out for the purposes of generating or using hazardous chemicals or, maybe, as a motorway service station, inevitably involving the storage and sale of vehicle fuels that are inherently liable to escape. The parent company of a group might acquire and retain ownership of land and lease it out to operating subsidiaries created as separate legal entities for their particular activities. While every case would depend on its particular facts, it is by no means self-evident that the organisation taking the initiative in such cases would be free from liability under section 85(1) in the event of pollution entering a nearby stream through a drainage system owned and operated by him. In any event, in view of the decision in *Taylor Woodrow Property Management Ltd. v. NRA*,[80A] any holder of a consent to discharge from drains serving third parties, as was the Welsh Development Agency, could be held strictly

8–128

---

[78] [1894] 2 Q.B. 843.
[79] [1914] 2 K.B. 916.
[80] Under s.87(1) a sewerage undertaker is deemed to have caused a discharge where (a) it is from any sewer or works vested in it, and (b) the undertaker did *not* cause or knowingly permit the discharge (but was bound to receive the matter in the discharge). In the light of the judgments in *Alphacell*, it must be doubted whether the conditions (a) and (b) can both exist at the same time, except where a defence such as act of God or third party intervention is available; however where it is, it presumably applies to the deemed offence under s.87(1) also.
[80A] See para. 8–090 and n. 23A thereto.

liable under section 85(6) for any breach of the consent conditions caused by a tenant of property served by the drains, notwithstanding that this constitutes a breach of the terms of the tenancy agreement.

8–129   Somewhat similarly, in *McTay* a crucial feature of the case would seem to be that the defendant company, to the knowledge of its principal, the Greater Manchester Council, took little or no responsibility for the day to day activities of the sub-contractor Bauer—though presumably it was responsible for the end-result of Bauer's operations being satisfactory. Moreover, Bauer was on the list of approved sub-contractors prepared by the Council itself, and not in the first instance prepared by McTay. It is readily conceivable that a building contractor might be held liable for pollution caused by a sub-contractor in circumstances where the delegation of work to the sub-contractor was entirely at the option of the main contractor and he had complete control over the choice of sub-contractor and the terms of the sub-contract. In such a case, the practical effect might be almost indistinguishable from the same work being undertaken by the main contractor's own employees.

8–130   The judgments in some of these cases involving two or more parties indicate an inclination to try to identify a single person who caused pollution, to the exclusion of the other or others involved. Neither the statute nor the authorities require any such restrictive approach.[80B] Though the basis of liability may well differ between different parties, this would not preclude two or more being held to have caused a single polluting incident. Lord Wilberforce recognised that the act of the third person does not necessarily interrupt the chain of causation initiated by the person who owns or operates the installation from which a pollutant has emanated.[81] Nevertheless, even though the chain is not broken, the fact that an operator is liable for pollution brought about by a third party, whether a vandal who has deliberately opened a valve or an incompetent contractor, cannot sensibly mean that the other party would not also be liable for causing the same pollution.[82] His liability will arise because of his responsibility for the specific incident that was the immediate cause; that of the operator of the polluting facility because of his responsibility for the conduct of the operations as a whole.

8–131   If Alphacell had hired an outside organisation to service or replace its pumps, and this had been done incompetently, resulting in a polluting discharge to the river, would Alphacell's liability be any different from where the servicing was by Alphacell's own

[80B] *R. v. CPC (UK) Ltd.*, see n. 50A to para 8–108; *Attorney-General's Reference (No. 1 of 1994)*, see n. 72 to para. 8–123.
[81] At p.835 D/E.
[82] See for example, the comments by Lord Pearson in *Alphacell* at p. 846D.

employees? Surely not. It is conceivable that a pipe might have been left disconnected, leading to a dispute with the outside contractor as to whether or not its reconnection was part of its job or not. To treat such detail as determinative would be to disregard the teaching of *Alphacell*. The legal relationship between the principal/employer and the contractor/employee cannot be the crucial issue, either on the authority of *Alphacell*, or on general policy grounds. If the policy spelled out by Lord Salmon is to apply (see paragraph 8–108), a riparian factory owner must do everything possible to ensure he does not cause pollution. He cannot therefore escape liability by the simple expedient of contracting out elements of his business to independent third parties largely irrespective of their competence. It is suggested that the proper approach should be to ascribe liability for independent contractors as in *Balfour v. Barty-King*.[83]

Where there is third party involvement — referring to "intervention" is liable to beg the question — a distinction is to be made between an intended involvement and one that is not. Where it is intended, as in *Williams Motors, McTay* and *Welsh Development Agency*, the question of causation by a party other than the one immediately responsible for the polluting incident is essentially an issue of remoteness. To apply the words of Cooke J. in *Impress* (with which the House of Lords appears to have agreed without reservation), the determining question is whether the act of the third party is of so powerful a nature that the conduct of the defendants is not a cause at all but merely part of the surrounding circumstances.   8–132

Conversely, where there is third party involvement that is unintended, the foreseeability of such intervention must be a critical issue in considering the question: who caused the pollution? In *Alphacell* Lord Salmon distinguished the operations of the defendant company from "the passive storing of effluent which could not discharge into the river save by an act of God or, as in *Impress (Worcester) v. Rees*, by the active intervention of an stranger, *the risk of which could not reasonably have been foreseen*"[84] (emphasis added). In some areas at least, vandalism is clearly a foreseeable hazard of operating any potentially polluting activity, possibly at least as much so as the intervention of natural forces causing clogging of the pumps, as in *Alphacell*, or the overflow of slurry as in *Pegrum*. It may be that the nature (though, it is suggested, not the precise consequences) of a vandal's intervention must be foreseeable, and not merely the intervention itself,[84A] but in most cases the distinction is unlikely to be of much significance.   8–133

---

[83] [1957] 1 Q.B. 496; similarly *Bower v. Peate*, (1876) 1 Q.B. 321 at 326.
[84] At p. 847G; see also Lord Cross at p. 847B, quoted above at para. 8–118.
[84A] As in *NRA v. Wright Engineering Co. Ltd.*; see para. 8–119.

8–134   In a sense, of course, wherever opportunities exist for people other than employees to gain access to vulnerable parts of a facility, even if only unlawfully, the possibility of damage by a third party creating pollution must in principle be foreseeable. If, in such a situation, the defence of third party intervention is to succeed, the operator must, it is suggested, have taken appropriate precautions to protect the facility, or at the least to prevent pollution resulting from any third party damage that may occur. Realistically, the precautionary measures should bear a sensible relation to the risk of damage and to how great a hazard pollution from the site might represent—large quantities of toxic chemicals such as pesticides clearly representing a greater potential hazard than, say, Alphacell's washwater effluent. Though this introduces reasonableness and negligence issues into what is otherwise one of strict liability, that is unavoidable but not necessarily out of place in a defence. Bearing in mind the origin of the statutory offences in public nuisance, and the relation of this with the rule in *Rylands v. Fletcher*, the decision in *Perry v. Kendricks Transport Ltd.*,[85] appears directly applicable.[86]

8–135   It is apparent from these cases that, where two or more parties are involved, the courts are extremely reluctant to apply with full rigour the strict liability imposed by the water pollution legislation. It is notable in this respect that, as mentioned above,[87] the W.R.A. does not include a due diligence defence. In *Tesco Supermarkets Limited v. Nattrass*,[88] which was concerned with such a defence,[89] Lord Reid noted that an offence that is held to be absolute leads to the conviction of persons who are entirely blameless, an injustice which brings the law into disrepute. He observed that Parliament had in many cases inserted defences intended to distinguish between those who are in some degree blameworthy and those who are not, and to enable the latter to escape from conviction if they can show that they were in no way to blame. The absence of an equivalent due diligence defence in the Water Resources Act is unfortunate, not only for reasons of fairness to defendants and those required to comply with that legislation, but also because of the distortions of the law that it would seem to have led to in decided cases.

8–136   Section 217(3) of the W.R.A. provides a possible solution to the difficulties encountered in some of these cases:

---

[85] [1956] 1 WLR 85.
[86] Indeed the language used by Lds Salmon and Cross in *Alphacell* at p.847 on this point suggests that they may have had this case in mind.
[87] See para. 8–118.
[88] [1972] AC 153 at 169; see also Chap. 21 below.
[89] In section 24(1) of the Trade Descriptions Act 1968.

" . . . .where the commission by any person of an offence under the water pollution provisions of this Act is due to the act or default of some other person, that other person may be charged with and convicted of the offence whether or not proceedings for the offence are taken against the first-mentioned person".

This provision is wide enough to catch anyone whose act or omission is culpable, provided that it is shown that another person can be held to have committed a pollution offence as a result of the incident. The prosecution would therefore have to establish the guilt of that other person to the satisfaction of the court—it would not be necessary for him to be charged. Where he is not, the Court might well consider such a procedure contrary to his interests and unsatisfactory, making it reluctant to find him guilty. However, in a clear case of a strict liability offence having been committed by a blameless person, the reasons for this approach should be accepted, if it would enable the court to dispense justice and convict someone whose act or default deserved punishment—particularly perhaps in cases where, as in *Wychavon*, the case law creates real uncertainty as to how to frame a charge of any of the primary pollution offences. Nevertheless, this roundabout approach, for which section 217(3) was surely not intended, and which would not always be available in any event, would be unnecessary if the Water Resources Act were to contain a proper due diligence defence, as it should.

Sewerage Undertakers

Sewerage undertakers are naturally held responsible for the compliance of discharges from their sewage treatment plants with applicable consents. Nevertheless, though they have some control over what they receive into their sewage treatment plants through the sewerage system by way of trade effluent consents, and general controls over what may and may not be discharged to sewer, inevitably they are liable from time to time to receive substances that cannot be handled in the receiving plant at all, or they receive them in such quantities that the treatment of them is inadequate and part of the substances is discharged with the remainder of the effluent from the plant. The W.R.A. places total responsibility on the sewerage undertaker for treating matter arriving at a sewage treatment plant in so far as he is required to receive it, whether unconditionally or subject to conditions which were observed—if the matter is included in the subsequent discharge, he is deemed to have caused that discharge for

8–137

the purposes of any offence under section 85.[90] In these circumstances, where a sewerage undertaker is bound to receive any matter, the person discharging it to the sewer, or otherwise to the sewage treatment works, is relieved of any criminal liability that could arise under section 85 from that matter being subsequently discharged from the sewage treatment works.[91]

8–138   A limited degree of protection is given to the sewerage undertaker who receives a discharge which he was either not bound to receive or was only bound to receive it on conditions which were not observed. In such a case, where (i) the sewerage undertaker's discharge contravenes conditions of his discharge consent, (ii) this is attributable to a discharge which another person caused or permitted to be made into the relevant sewer or sewage treatment works, and (iii) the undertaker could not reasonably have been expected to prevent the discharge into the sewer or works, then he will not be guilty of an offence under section 85.[92] In *National Rivers Authority v. Yorkshire Water Services Limited*[93] Yorkshire Water was charged with causing polluting matter to enter controlled waters contrary to section 107(1)(a) of the Water Act 1989, which corresponds precisely with section 85(1) of the W.R.A. Yorkshire Water owned and operated a sewage treatment works which discharged into controlled waters. One night, there was a single discharge of iso-octonal into a sewer leading to the sewage treatment plant. Once there it was inevitable that a significant proportion would pass through and be discharged into the controlled waters. The trade effluent consents granted by Yorkshire Water included conditions prohibiting discharge of iso-octonal into the sewer, and consequently it was not bound to receive it. On appeal to the Crown Court from conviction Yorkshire Water was held to have made good the defence contained in section 108(7) of the Water Act, which corresponds exactly with W.R.A. section 87(2).

8–139   A further appeal to the Divisional Court by the NRA succeeded in its turn, it being held that the wording of what is now section 87(2) was clear and that it provided a defence only to a charge of contravening the conditions of a consent. Since the charge against Yorkshire Water was causing polluting matter to enter controlled waters, the Divisional Court held that the defence was not available to that charge. The fact that Yorkshire Water could not reasonably have been expected to

---

[90] s.87(1).
[91] s.87(3); he would otherwise be at risk of a charge under both the W.R.A. of causing the polluting discharge and also under W.I.A. s.118(5) for an illegal discharge to sewer - see *Northumbrian Water Ltd. and National Rivers Authority v. Appletise Ltd.*, Environmental Law Brief, 1991, Vol.2(4), p.47.
[92] s.87(2).
[93] [1994] Env. L.R. 177.

know of the discharge, let alone prevent it, was relevant only to the question of penalty, but not to liability.

This decision, which self-evidently undermines the defence of section 87(2), is very questionable.[94] While it may be more convenient as a matter of pleading to charge an offence of contravening the conditions of a consent, any such contravention will almost invariably also represent causing or knowingly permitting poisonous, noxious or polluting matter to enter controlled waters in contravention of section 85(1). (As explained below, the existence of a consent is only a defence to such charge where the discharge is "under and in accordance with" that consent). It would be surprising therefore if, when drafting section 87(2), Parliament intended to limit the defence in the way the Divisional Court has held. Further, section 87(2) does not in terms provide a defence to a charge of contravening conditions of a consent, but states specifically that the sewerage undertaker shall not be guilty of *an* offence under section 85 by reason only of contravention of consent conditions, where the other limbs of the defence apply. The better interpretation of section 87(2) would seem to be that the undertaker "shall not be guilty of *any* offence under section 85", if the other features of that sub-section are established. This would both reflect what Parliament must surely be presumed to have intended to provide by way of a defence, and also correspond with the natural meaning of the existing language. Moreover, if section 87(2) should properly be so narrowly construed, then presumably so should the defences of sections 88(1) and 89(2), discussed in the next paragraphs, with the surprising consequence that they also would not be effective against a charge brought under section 85(1) of causing or knowingly permitting entry of polluting matter into controlled waters.

8–140

Statutory Defences

An offence under section 85 will not be committed by persons acting under and in accordance with a discharge consent given under the W.R.A.,[95] or under previous legislation and having effect as though under the W.R.A., an authorisation for the process subject to integrated pollution control, a waste management licence under Part II of the E.P.A. or a waste disposal licence under C.O.P.A. 1974, or under

8–141

[94] The House of Lords has now allowed Yorkshire Water's further appeal, ruling that the defence is available if the relevant facts are established, irrespective of the precise offence charged. [1994] 3 W.L.R. 1202.

[95] Discharge pursuant to a consent is also a defence to an offence under the Salmon and Freshwater Fisheries Act 1975, s.4, by virtue of the Water Consolidation (Consequential Provisions) Act 1991, Sched.1, para.30(1). The other defences contained in the W.R.A. are not however applicable.

Part II of the Food and Environment Protection Act 1985, which is concerned with the disposal of waste at sea, or under a variety of other statutory provisions.[96] The existence of a waste disposal licence under C.O.P.A. is however only a defence in relation to a charge of causing or permitting poisonous, noxious or polluting matter, or any solid waste matter, to enter controlled waters; it provides no defence to a discharge of trade or sewage effluent contrary to section 85(3), or to anything done in contravention of a section 86 prohibition that is contrary to sections 85(2) or (4).[97]

8–142   A defence is available in respect of all the offences under section 85 where:

(a)   the entry of any matter into any waters is caused or permitted, or any discharge is made, in an emergency in order to avoid danger to life or health;

(b)   the defendant takes all such steps as are reasonably practicable in the circumstances for minimising the extent of the entry or discharge and of its polluting effects; and

(c)   particulars of the entry or discharge are furnished to the NRA as soon as reasonably practicable after the entry occurs.[98]

This defence is not however a "due diligence" defence comparable to that contained in section 33(7) of the E.P.A. — it is limited to emergencies involving danger to life or health, and has no application to an inadvertent discharge despite all reasonable precautions and the exercise of all due diligence to avoid it. No guidance is available on what constitutes an emergency for this purpose, but it may well be that a foreseeable crisis brought about by the defendant's own activities will not be regarded as such, following *Perka et al. v. The Queen*.[99] Discharge of trade or sewage effluent from a vessel does not constitute an offence under section 85.[1] On the reasoning of the Divisional Court in *NRA v. Yorkshire Water Services* discussed above, this defence would appear applicable only to those offences under section 85 expressly referring to discharge of trade or sewage effluent, and not therefore to the events under section 85(1). For the reasons set out above, however, it must be doubtful whether this is how the defence should be construed. Such discharges from vessels are controlled under river bye-laws in the case of inland waters, and under

---

[96] s.88(1).
[97] s.88(3).
[98] s.89(1).
[99] Canada, (1985) 13 D.L.R. (4th) 1. See also *Waste Incineration Services Limited and Jacob v. Dudley Metropolitan Borough Council*, [1992] Env. L.R. 29.
[1] s.89(2).

the Food and Environment Protection Act 1985 in respect of discharges to sea.

It is not an offence under section 85 to permit water from an **8–143** abandoned mine to enter controlled waters.[2] The scope of this defence which, it may be noted, does not extend to the *causing* of water to enter controlled waters, is discussed above at paragraph 8–111.

A defence is also available in relation to the depositing of solid **8–144** refuse of a mine or quarry on any land if it falls or is carried into inland freshwaters, if this is done with the consent of the NRA, no other site for the deposit is reasonably practicable, and all reasonably practicable steps have been taken to prevent the entry of the refuse into the water.[3]

Dumping at Sea

The controlled waters to which the W.R.A. applies include coastal **8–145** waters from the fresh water limit of rivers and other water courses and territorial waters as far as the three mile limit. Accordingly the offences of sections 85(1), (2) and (3) all apply to the entry or discharge of matter into or to these marine waters. Part II of the Food and Environment Protection Act 1985 ("F.E.P.A.") controls the deposit of substances and articles in the sea, including the loading of vessels and other craft and containers in the United Kingdom with substances or articles for deposit anywhere in the sea. The sea, for the purposes of F.E.P.A., includes any area submerged at mean high water springs, up to the limit of tidal flow at mean high water springs in estuaries and rivers,[4] and extends to all "United Kingdom controlled waters", *i.e.* any part of the sea within the limits of an area designated under section 1(7) of the Continental Shelf Act 1964.[5] Since the definition of "sea" in F.E.P.A. overlaps with that of "controlled waters" in the W.R.A. certain actions will potentially be an offence under both Acts. Compliance with an licence under F.E.P.A. is however a defence to a charge under section 85(1) of the W.R.A.[6]

Part II of F.E.P.A. provides for the licensing of numerous activities **8–146** involving the deposit of substances and articles in the sea, and also for the incineration of substances or articles at sea, and makes it an offence to do any of these acts, or to cause of permit anyone else to do them,

---

[2] s.89(3).
[3] s.89(4).
[4] F.E.P.A. s.24(1).
[5] E.P.A., s.146.
[6] W.R.A. s.88(1).

except under and in accordance with the terms of a licence,[7] unless the activity is an operation exempted from the need for a licence by the Deposits in the Sea (Exemptions) Order 1985.[8] Carrying out any of these acts other than any benefiting from the Exemptions Order without a licence or in contravention of any provisions of a licence is punishable by a fine of up to £5000 on summary conviction and an unlimited fine and/or imprisonment for up to 2 years on conviction on indictment.[9] In any proceedings for an offence, it is a defence for the person charged to prove that he took all reasonable precautions and exercised all due diligence to avoid the commission of the offence.[10]

8–147   The acts prohibited, unless licensed, include:

    (1)   The deposit of substances or articles within United Kingdom waters or United Kingdom controlled waters,[11] either in the sea or under the sea-bed
        (i) from a vehicle, vessel, aircraft, hovercraft or marine structure
        (ii) from a container floating in the sea; or
        (iii) from a structure on land constructed or adapted wholly or mainly for the purpose of depositing solids in the sea.
    (2)   The deposit of substances or articles anywhere in the sea or under the sea-bed (so not confined to United Kingdom waters), from a vessel, aircraft, hovercraft or marine structure that is British, or from a container floating in the sea if the deposit is controlled from a vessel, aircraft, hovercraft or marine structure that is British.
    (3)   The loading of a vessel, aircraft, hovercraft, marine structure, or a floating container, in the United Kingdom or the United Kingdom waters, with substances or articles for deposit anywhere in the sea or under the sea-bed.
    (4)   The loading of a vehicle in the United Kingdom with substances or articles for deposit from that vehicle within United Kingdom waters, either in the sea or under the sea-bed.

8–148   F.E.P.A. also requires licensing for the scuttling of vessels and the towing or propelling from the United Kingdom of vessels for scuttling anywhere at sea. The effect of the 1992 Paris Convention for the protection of the Marine Environment of the North East Atlantic and the London Dumping Convention is that dumping of substances and

[7] F.E.P.A. s.9(1).
[8] S.I. 1985 No. 1699.
[9] F.E.P.A., s.21(2A), inserted by E.P.A., s.146(6).
[10] F.E.P.A., s.22(1).
[11] *i.e.* those designated under the Continental Shelf Act 1964.

articles at sea is not now carried out on any significant scale, save in relation to sewage sludge, which is being phased out by December 31, 1998 as provided for in the urban waste water Directive 91/271.

Incineration at sea is prohibited by F.E.P.A. unless licensed, where **8–149** this is within United Kingdom waters or United Kingdom controlled waters, or anywhere if on a British vessel or marine structure.[12] The prohibition extends to loading any vessel or marine structure in the United Kingdom or United Kingdom waters with substances or articles for incineration anywhere at sea.[13] In fact no licences will now be granted, incineration at sea as a waste disposal option having been phased out by the United Kingdom. Notwithstanding that incineration off-shore avoids all the intractable problems associated with finding locations for incinerators on land, the principal objections to it are the considerable difficulty of effectively enforcing compliance with emission and other controls, and the additional environmental hazards inherent in the loading of waste (especially hazardous waste) on to a ship and handling it at sea.

The operations exempted from the need for a licence by the **8–150** Deposits in the Sea (Exemptions) Order 1985[14] include numerous activities ordinarily carried out at sea, such as returning to the sea matter and items taken from the sea in the course of fishing or dredging operations, deposit of moorings and navigation aids, deposit of articles and substances in connection with harbour and coast protection works, and the launching of vessels and marine structures. In addition, however, there are several activities that represent disposal of waste originating from vessels, hovercraft and marine structures, including sewage, "victual or domestic waste" (not being bulky or industrial waste), any substance or article other than bulky waste deposited in the course of normal navigation or maintenance, and flaring off of hydrocarbons from oil and gas exploration and production. By virtue of new Articles 4 and 5 added to the 1985 Exemptions Order by the Waste Management Licensing Regulations 1994[15] all the exempted activities must, from December 31, 1994, be registered with the F.E.P.A. licensing authority, and the authority must keep its register open for inspection at all reasonable times. Further, in so far as any of the exempted operations involves waste disposal or recovery (as defined in the 1994 Licensing Regulations), the exemption only applies if any disposal takes place at the place of production, and if the type and quantity of waste involved and the method of disposal or recovery are consistent with the need to attain

---

[12] s.6(1)(a).
[13] s.6(1)(b).
[14] Made under F.E.P.A., s.7.
[15] S.I. 1994 No. 1056, reg.21.

the objective of ensuring that waste is recovered or disposed of without endangering human health and without using processes or methods which could harm the environment.[16]

8–151   The grant of licences is governed by section 8 and Schedule 3. In considering whether to grant a licence, the relevant Minister or Secretary of State must have regard, among other things, to the need to protect the marine environment, the living resources which it supports, and human health.[17] Further, the grant of a licence must include such provisions as are necessary or expedient for this protection.[18]

8–152   Registers of licences, including applications, variations and revocations, as well as convictions for offences under section 9 are to be held by the relevant Minister or the Secretary of State and made publicly available for inspection free of charge, copies being provided on payment of reasonable charges.[19] Information is to be excluded from the register if its disclosure there would be contrary to the interests of national security or would prejudice to an unreasonable degree some person's commercial interest. Exclusion of information on the latter ground, however, only continues for four years unless any person to whom the information relates applies for the exclusion to be continued.[20]

Consents to Discharge to Controlled Waters

8–153   The procedures for applying for a discharge consent, and for the revocation and variation of consents and the conditions attached to them are set out in Schedule 10 to the W.R.A., supplemented by the Control of Pollution (Consents for Discharges etc.) (Secretary of State Functions) Regulations 1989,[21] which have effect as though made under paragraph 4(9) of that Schedule in relation to applications transmitted to the Secretary of State, and under section 91(3) in relation to appeals. An application is made to the NRA (in fact to the appropriate regional office for the discharge point concerned) which must publish notice of the application in newspapers circulating in the locality of the discharge and any others that are in the vicinity of any controlled waters which might be affected, as well as in the London Gazette. Copies of the application must go to every relevant local

---

[16] Art.4(1).
[17] F.E.P.A., s.8(1).
[18] F.E.P.A., s.8(3).
[19] F.E.P.A., s.14, as amended by E.P.A., s.147.
[20] F.E.P.A., s.14(3).
[21] S.I. 1989 No.1151.

authority and water undertaker, and in the case of discharges to sea to the relevant Minister. Except in the last case, the provisions for publicity can be disregarded, if the NRA considers the discharge will have no appreciable effect. Where an applicant considers that publication of the details of the application would be contrary to public interest or would prejudice to an unreasonable degree some private interest by disclosing information about a trade secret, he may apply to the Secretary of State for a certificate disapplying the publicity provisions.[22] Objections to an application for a consent may be made in the six weeks beginning with the day of publication in the London Gazette, and the NRA is required to consider any made. The NRA has four months from the date of making the application to determine whether to grant the consent; an application still pending at that time will be deemed refused, unless the applicant agrees to a longer period.[23] The period will however cease to run if the NRA requests further information from the applicant in sufficient time before expiry of the four months to enable the applicant to respond within that period and he fails to do so. In such a case, the NRA is allowed a reasonable time to determine the application after the information requested is provided.[24]

When the NRA proposes to grant a consent it must notify anyone who has previously made representations or objections to it and allow them 21 days to request the Secretary of State not to grant consent. In such a case, the NRA must not proceed with the consent unless the Secretary of State decides not to comply with the objector's request.[25] Unless the Secretary of State decides to refuse the request, he must call in the matter for his determination; he also may do this on his own initiative at any time. In such a case, he may set up a local inquiry or otherwise arrange for the applicant, the NRA and any objectors to attend a hearing, before making his determination.[26]

8–154

The grant of a consent may, and invariably will, be made subject to conditions. These may be as to any matter that the NRA thinks appropriate; including in particular:

8–155

    (a) The place of discharge, and the design or construction of any outlets.

---

[22] Sched.10, para.1(7).
[23] Under the Deregulation Initiative failure to determine an application within 4 months (or any longer agreed period) will merely give the applicant a right of appeal, but will not result in a deemed refusal.
[24] Sched. 10, para. 2(4).
[25] Sched. 10, para. 3.
[26] Sched. 10, para. 4. Under the Deregulation Initiative the NRA will be able to proceed with a grant if it thinks fit, and merely notify objectors of this. The Secretary of State will continue to have the power to call-in applications and to direct the NRA to amend consents, *e.g.* in response to third party objections.

(b) The nature, origin, composition, temperature, volume and rate of the discharges, and the periods during which the discharges may be made.

(c) Any treatment or other process that should be applied, in order to minimise the polluting effects of the discharge.

(d) The provision of sampling facilities and the provision and maintenance of inspection chambers.

(e) The provision, maintenance and testing of meters for measuring and/or recording the volume and rate of discharges, and apparatus for determining their nature, composition and temperature.

(f) The keeping of records of the nature, origin, composition, temperature, volume and rate of the discharges, and also of meter readings and other recording apparatus.

(g) The making of returns to the NRA.

8–156   The consents that the NRA inherited from the water authorities displayed a wide variety of consent conditions, and little consistency across the country as to how they were formulated. One of its major tasks has been to bring some logical coherence to them. To this end it set up a working party, the conclusions of which were published in what is widely known as "the Kinnersley Report".[27] An issue that was highlighted in this Report was the conflict between having consent conditions that are technically the most appropriate for avoiding undue pollution of receiving waters in the most cost-effective fashion for the discharger, and framing the conditions in a manner that is both legally precise and capable of ready enforcement. It may, for example, be acceptable to have relatively high values for certain parameters for short periods, provided the average remains at a suitable level, and these values may well be capable of wide variation depending on the flow of the receiving waters. However, to frame the consent to take all these factors into account would render both compliance and enforcement exceptionally difficult. Similarly, if technically the most significant criterion is the total amount of a substance that is discharged over a lengthy period, framing a consent in these terms may mean that no offence is committed until almost the entire period has elapsed. This is not to say that such terms may not suitably be contained in a consent, but they are in practice likely to be insufficient for that consent to be readily enforceable.

8–157   A notable feature of discharge consents from sewage treatment plants was their use of 95 percentile limits backed by "look-up tables". The purpose of this approach was to allow for the occasional excess,

---

[27] 'Discharge Consent and Compliance Policy: a Blueprint for the Future', NRA, 1990, Water Quality Series No.1.

which would ordinarily be harmless on its own, since its avoidance might well require major extra expenditure on the part of the discharger, with little or no real benefit to the environment or otherwise to the public. A 95 percentile limit allows 5 readings in every 100 to be ignored; look-up tables prescribe how many out of a group of a smaller number of samples may be ignored in determining whether or not there has been compliance. Such a system can therefore allow very considerable divergences from the prescribed limit to occur without breach of the applicable consent condition, since (if there are no other conditions regarding that parameter) for those samples that can be ignored it does not matter how grossly they may have exceeded the prescribed limit.

One of the recommendations of the Kinnersley Report was accordingly that numeric consents of this type should contain absolute limits, as well as, if appropriate, other more demanding limits that should be met by a substantial proportion of all samples. Such an approach allows a variety of percentiles to be used in setting consent conditions—provided there is an overall cap, a 90 or 80 percentile limit may be technically more appropriate.[28]   **8–158**

Historically, there have been numerous discharges to controlled waters that should have been consented and have not. Many of these are in fact innocuous, and instead of using its enforcement powers against them, the NRA may, if it thinks fit, on its own initiative grant the discharger a consent on such conditions as it determines. The consent will nevertheless not be retroactive in effect, and consequently enforcement proceedings may be taken against the previous discharge, thus encouraging acquiescence to the NRA's action.[29] Any consent granted under these provisions must be publicised in the same manner as an application for a consent, and the NRA is bound to consider any representations or objections that may be made within the six weeks from publication in the London Gazette.   **8–159**

A discharge consent applies generally to all discharges complying with the terms of the consent, and is not limited to those made by any particular person.[30] Accordingly on any acquisition of a property benefiting from a discharge consent, the consent is automatically available to the new occupant. Nevertheless, as a practical matter, the outgoing occupant will undoubtedly wish to ensure that the NRA is made aware of his successor, so as to ensure that he ceases to be liable for the applicable charges.   **8–160**

[28] See in this respect the limits prescribed in the EC urban waste water Directive 91/271.
[29] Sched. 10, para.5(2).
[30] Sched. 10, para.2(6).

Revocation and Variation of Consents

8–161   The NRA is under an express duty to review all consents that have been granted and the conditions to which they are subject.[31] On any such review, it may revoke the consent or modify or add to its conditions. If no discharge has been made at all in pursuance of the consent within the preceding 12 months, the NRA may revoke it by notice served on the owner or occupier of the land from which the discharges under the consent would be made.[32] The Secretary of State also has independent power to direct the NRA to revoke a consent, or to modify or to add to its conditions, if it is appropriate to do so to give effect to any EC obligation or any international agreement to which the United Kingdom is a party, to protect public health or flora fauna dependent on an aquatic environment, or in consequence of any representations or objections that may be made.

8–162   Unless the NRA specifies some longer period, or the discharger agrees, it may normally only revoke or restrict a consent, without paying compensation, if two years or more have elapsed since grant of the consent or its most recent variation, as the case may be.[33] However the obligation to pay compensation will not arise if it is due to a direction from the Secretary of State given in consequence of a change of circumstances which could not reasonably have been foreseen at the grant of the consent or its latest variation, whichever is the later, or if it is in consequence of consideration by the Secretary of State of material information which was not reasonably available to the NRA at that time.[34] Information is material for this purpose if it relates to any discharge made or to be made by virtue of the consent, to the interaction of any such discharge with any other discharge, or to the combined effect of the matter discharged and any other matter.[35]

Appeals

8–163   Appeals may be made to the Secretary of State against a refusal of a consent, or in respect of the conditions attached, and against any revocation or variation of a consent.[36] An appeal in these respects may only be made by the applicant; there is no right of appeal for objectors to consents.[37] The procedure is laid down in paragraph 7 of the

---

[31] Sched. 10, para.6(1). Under the Deregulation Initiative it is proposed to remove this duty, leaving reviews to the NRA's discretion.
[32] Sched. 10, para.6(3).
[33] Under the Deregulation Initiative it is proposed to increase this period to 4 years.
[34] Sched. 10, para.6(5)(b).
[35] Sched. 10, para.6(6).
[36] W.R.A. s.91(1).
[37] s.91(2).

Control of Pollution (Consents for Discharges, etc.) (Secretary of State Functions) Regulations 1989, and allows three months for the serving of a notice of appeal, running from the day on which the NRA's decision to be appealed was notified or from when the application was deemed to have been refused; the Secretary of State may allow a longer period at his discretion. There is no provision for staying the effect of the decision appealed against, which accordingly operates unless and until it is reversed on the appeal.[38]

Enforcement of Pollution Controls

Summary offences under Part III of the W.R.A., all of which relates to control of pollution of water resources, may be tried if the relevant information is laid within 12 months after the commission of the offence.[39] This contrasts with the normal 6 months maximum for laying an information in the case of summary proceedings.[40] A person guilty of any of these offences under section 85 is liable on summary conviction to a fine of up to £20,000 and/or imprisonment for up to three months. On conviction on indictment, an unlimited fine may be imposed and imprisonment for up to two years. The offences under section 90 (see paragraph 8–094) are subject to a fine on summary conviction of up to £2,500.   **8–164**

Information to form the basis of a prosecution may be obtained either by direct sampling, normally by the NRA, or on the basis of information provided by the discharger and recorded by him in accordance with the provisions attached to his consent. In the latter case, the NRA is entitled by written notice to require any person to provide such information as it reasonably requires for it to carry out any of its functions, and failure to comply with such a request without reasonable excuse is an offence.[41] Any other person may also institute proceedings, and several actions have been started on the basis of information relating to discharges made publicly available through the pollution control registers prescribed by section 190.[42]   **8–165**

Wide powers may be granted to any person acting on behalf of the NRA, the Secretary of State or the Minister for Agriculture, Fisheries and Food to enter premises and any vessel to check on compliance   **8–166**

---

[38] Under the Deregulation Initiative it is proposed that modifications and revocations that are the subject of an appeal shall not take effect unless and until the appeal is dismissed.

[39] s.101.

[40] Magistrates' Courts Act 1980, s.127.

[41] s.202. Here also, up to 12 months is allowed for the laying of an information.

[42] see para. 8–173.

with the W.R.A. or any secondary legislation made under it, and to carry out inspections, measurements and tests, and to take away samples of water or effluent. The powers include a right to carry out experimental borings and to instal and to keep monitoring and other apparatus on any premises.[43]

8–167 Where, as is frequently the case, the NRA must proceed by way of evidence from samples of an effluent discharge, the requirements of section 209 apply. These stipulate that the result of any analysis of any sample taken on behalf of the NRA shall not be admissible in any legal proceedings in respect of any effluent passing from any land or vessel unless the person who took the sample

(a) on taking it notified the occupier of the land, or the owner or master of the vessel, of his intention to have it analysed;
(b) there and then divided the sample into three parts, and caused each part to be placed in a container which was sealed and marked;
(c) delivered one part to the occupier of the land, or to the owner or master of the vessel, and retained one part, apart from the one he submitted to be analysed, for future comparison.[44]

This procedure must be followed even in the case of a sample of river water taken for comparison purposes, if its analysis is to be admissible in proceedings in respect of effluent.[45] However, for a specimen of water to constitute a sample it must be separated physically from the water it comes from, and be isolated in a container. Section 209 does not therefore apply to analytical results obtained by apparatus (*e.g.* a phOX Systems mobile water monitor) that at no time creates any sample in this sense, and such results are admissible evidence.[45A]

Subsection 209(1)(a) requires notification "on taking" a sample; notification need not however precede either the taking or the division of the sample for the purposes of sub-section 209(1)(b). "There and then" in that sub-section means at or proximate to the site where the sample was taken, and on the occasion of taking the sample. Dividing the sample elsewhere would not satisfy the requirement.[45B]

8–168 Nevertheless, if it is not reasonably practicable for these require- ments to be complied with on taking of the sample, it will be sufficient if they were complied with as soon as reasonably practicable after it

---

[43] s.169.
[44] s.209(1).
[45] *National Rivers Authority v. Harcros Timber and Building Supplies Ltd.*, [1993] Env. L.R. 172, holding that s.209 differed in this respect from the previous requirement under s.113 of the Water Resources Act 1963.
[45A] *R. v. CPC (UK) Ltd.* (C.A.), *The Times*, August 4, 1994.
[45B] *Attorney-General's Reference (No.2 of 1994)*, (C.A.), *The Times*, August 4, 1994.

was taken.[46] It is not essential that samples be taken at a sampling point stipulated in a consent condition,[47] but if some other sampling point is chosen, it will be necessary to establish that the results are sufficiently determinative of the nature of the discharge at the prescribed sampling point. The sampling procedure just described is only applicable where samples are taken by or on behalf of the NRA. If the samples are taken by anyone else, and not on behalf of the NRA, then they need not necessarily conform with the tripartite procedure.[48] Accordingly, the results of analyses of samples taken by anyone else, typically the discharger himself in compliance with his consent conditions, will be admissible without the need for the tripartite procedure.[49]

The NRA has developed a variety of types of apparatus for **8–169** continuous or regular monitoring of discharges and receiving waters. One such system known as "Cyclops" is designed to capture samples automatically if it detects a significant change in the values of applicable parameters. In the nature of the system, these samples cannot be delivered forthwith to the discharger; the NRA's practice is nevertheless to deliver the sample as soon as practicable, and it must therefore rely on section 209(2) to justify such delay as may occur in this respect.[50]

Independently of any other right of action, including any criminal **8–170** proceedings that have been or may be taken, the NRA may take appropriate remedial works with a view to preventing any poisonous, noxious or polluting matter, or any solid waste matter, from entering any controlled waters. Similarly, where such matter appears to be or have been present in any controlled waters, the NRA may undertake remedial work to remove or dispose of the matter, to remedy or mitigate any pollution it has caused and, so far as reasonably practicable, to restore the waters, including any flora and fauna dependent on the aquatic environment of the waters, to their state immediately before the latter entered them.[51] Where it carries out any such work, it is entitled to recover its reasonable expenses from any person who caused or knowingly permitted the matter either to enter

---

[46] s.209(2).
[47] *Greenpeace v. Albright & Wilson*, LMELR Vol. 3(5), p. 170 and Vol. 4(1), pp 23–24.
[48] Even so, there will need to be tight procedural controls if evidence from such samples is to be convincing, and not open to challenge, *e.g.* for failure to ensure absence of confusion with other examples, or on the basis that contamination has been introduced in the analytical process.
[49] *National Rivers Authority v. Pasminco (Europe) Smelting Company*, ENDS Vol. 211, August 1992, p.38.
[50] For a general discussion on the issue of sampling, see "Monitoring Water Quality" Albert Mumma, J.E.L., Vol 5, No.2, 1993, pp. 191–201.
[51] s.161(1).

the controlled waters or to be where it was likely to enter them, except in the case of work in respect of water from an abandoned mine that has been permitted to reach a place where it was likely to enter controlled waters.[52]

8–171   It is an open question whether these remedial costs may be recovered from persons who caused or knowingly permitted pollution of water before the date when this provision came into effect, namely September 1, 1989,[53] or even January 31, 1985.[54] It is strongly arguable that it is immaterial when the relevant polluting act or omission occurred, provided the remedial work it gave rise to was after September 1, 1989. This would be consistent with an interpretation of the EC groundwater Directive that it applies to all indirect discharges after its implementation date of December 19, 1981, even from *e.g.* closed landfills (see paragraph 8–022), though this consideration is not conclusive.

8–172   No civil liability arises in respect of any breach of the pollution control provisions of the W.R.A. except as expressly provided, though the Act does not affect any other right of action or remedy that may otherwise be available.[55]

Pollution Control Registers

8–173   The NRA is required[56] to keep a pollution control register containing the particulars prescribed by the Control of Pollution (Registers) Regulations 1989.[57] These particulars consist essentially of notices served under W.R.A. section 83 specifying water quality objectives for specific waters, applications for discharge consents, consents granted and the conditions attached, particulars of samples, including an indication as to whether they were purely monitoring samples or whether they were taken in accordance with the tripartite procedure

---

[52] s.161(3), (4).

[53] When the equivalent provision in s.115 of the Water Act 1989 came into effect, by virtue of Sched.2, para.1(5) of the Water Consolidation (Consequential Provisions) Act 1991.

[54] When the equivalent provision in s.46(4) and (5) of C.O.P.A. 1974 commenced. Sched.26, para.23, of the Water Act 1989 provides for accrued rights under s.46(5) to be transferred to a water authority's successor company. By implication no other rights to recover costs under C.O.P.A. s.46(5) were transferred either to a successor company or to the NRA, but this does not preclude a right to recover costs incurred in the future in respect of past polluting activities.

[55] s.100.

[56] By W.R.A. s.190.

[57] S.I. 1989 No.1160.

of W.R.A. section 209, and details of certificates issued under paragraph 1(7) of Schedule 10 to the W.R.A., exempting certain information from publication. The registers are maintained by the NRA at its various regional offices, and are required to be available at all reasonable times for inspection free of charge, with the public being entitled to obtain copies on payment of reasonable charges. Similar requirements are imposed on the Scottish River Purification Boards by the Control of Pollution (Registers) (Scotland) Regulations 1993.[58]

Trade Effluent to Sewer

Under section 106 of the W.I.A., there is a general entitlement for the owner or occupier of any premises, and the owner of any private sewer that drains premises, to have the premises or sewer connected with the public sewers of the sewerage undertaker for the area, for the discharge of foul water and surface water. However, this does not entitle any person: **8–174**

    (a) to discharge directly or indirectly into any public sewer—
        (i) any liquid from a factory, other than domestic sewage or surface or storm water, or any liquid from a manufacturing process; or
        (ii) any liquid or other matter the discharge of which into public sewers is prohibited by or under any enactment; or

    (b) where separate public sewers are provided for foul water and for surface water,[59] to discharge directly or indirectly—
        (i) foul water into a sewer provided for surface water; or
        (ii) except with the approval of the undertaker, surface water into a sewer provided for foul water; or
    (c) to have his drains or sewer made to communicate directly with a storm-water overflow sewer.[60]

Additionally, except as authorised under the W.I.A., "no person shall throw, empty or turn or suffer or permit to be thrown or emptied   **8–175**

---

[58] S.I. 1993 No.1155 (S.172).
[59] As is the trend, so as to avoid foul water treatment systems becoming overloaded at times of heavy rainfall.
[60] W.I.A. s. 106(2). (All remaining section references in this Chapter are to the W.I.A. unless otherwise stated).

or to pass, into any public sewer, or into any drain or sewer communicating with a public sewer:

(a) any matter likely to injure the sewer or drain, to interfere with the free flow of its contents or to affect prejudicially the treatment and disposal of its contents; or

(b) any chemical refuse or waste steam or any liquid of a temperature higher than 110°F. if in any case (either alone or in combination with the contents of the sewer or drain in question) it is dangerous, the cause of a nuisance, or injurious or likely to cause injury to health; or

(c) any petroleum spirit;[61] or

(d) calcium carbide.''[62]

8–176   Nevertheless, subject to certain qualifications, there is a general right to discharge trade effluent[63] to the public sewers of a sewerage undertaker who has previously consented to this.[64] Apart from any civil liability that may arise, the discharge of trade effluent to sewer without this consent or any other necessary authorisation is an offence subject to a fine of up to £5000 on summary conviction and an unlimited fine on conviction on indictment.[65] EC Directive 92/271 on urban waste water treatment (see paragraphs 8–080 to 8–089) requires the discharge of industrial waste water into collecting systems and urban waste water treatment plants to be subject to prior regulations and/or specific authorisations, to ensure, inter alia, that discharges from the treatment plants do not adversely affect the environment, or prevent the receiving water from complying with EC directives.[66] However in the UK, the vast bulk of discharges to sewer were

---

[61] Defined in s.111(5) to mean any such (i) crude petroleum; (ii) oil made from petroleum or from coal, shale, peat or other bituminous substances; or (iii) product of petroleum or mixture containing petroleum; as when tested in the manner prescribed by or under the Petroleum (Consolidation) Act 1928, gives off an inflammable vapour at temperature of less than 73°F.

[62] s.11(1), (2).

[63] "Trade effluent" means: (a) any liquid, either with or without particles of matter in suspension in the liquid, which is wholly or partly produced in the course of any trade or industry carried on at trade premises; and (b) in relation to any trade premises, any such liquid which is so produced in the course of any trade or industry carried on at those premises; but does not include domestic sewage; s.141(1). "Trade premises" is defined as any premises used or intended to be used for carrying on any trade or industry, including any land or premises used or intended for use (in whole or in part and whether or not for profit) for agricultural or horticultural purposes or for the purposes of fish farming or for scientific research or experiment. Agriculture, horticulture, fish farming and scientific research for experiment are all regarded as trade or industry for the purposes of determining whether effluent from such activities is trade effluent; s.141(2).

[64] s.118(1).

[65] s.118(5).

[66] Art. 11 and Annex IC.

controlled for many years before the coming into effect of the Water Industry Act 1991, under the Public Health (Drainage of Trade Premises) Act 1937.

In Scotland, trade effluent to sewer is controlled by the Sewerage (Scotland) Act 1968, as amended by the Local Government (Scotland) Act 1973, which covers both the provision of sewers and a consent system for trade effluent discharges. The regime is in essentials similar to that in England.

Deemed Consents

Certain processes were entitled to deemed trade effluent consents **8–177** under the Public Health (Drainage of Trade Premises) Act 1937[67] and these deemed consents are entitled to continue in effect. However transitional provisions contained in Schedule 8 to the W.I.A. permit the holders of deemed consents to apply for actual consents for such discharges as were authorised by deemed consent; the sewerage undertaker concerned may itself require the substitution of an actual consent[68] on such conditions as the sewerage undertaker considers appropriate. Any dispute that may arise out of this procedure is referred to the Director General of Water Services for determination, unless otherwise agreed. His decision is final, save that he may refer a point of law by way of case stated for determination by the High Court.[69]

"Special Category" Effluent

Ordinarily, a sewerage undertaker will be expected to accept trade **8–178** effluent, subject to payment of appropriate charges to cover the costs of treating the trade effluent to a standard allowing discharge from the sewage treatment works that complies with its consent. However, where trade effluent contains certain highly toxic substances, it is designated "special category effluent", and not only can the sewerage undertaker not be expected to receive it, but he may not do so unless the matter has been referred to the Secretary of State for his determination, and he has determined not to prohibit the discharge.

---

[67] Set out in its Sched.8, paras.2–5.
[68] Sched.8 para.2(2).
[69] s.137.

(The powers of the Secretary of State in relation to special category effluent are in fact exercised by HMIP.) Special category effluent is any trade effluent which contains, in a concentration greater than the background concentration,[70] any of the substances listed in Schedule 1 to the Trade Effluents (Prescribed Processes and Substances) Regulations 1989 as amended,[71] or which derives from any of the processes listed in Schedule 2 to the Regulations if, in any case, either asbestos or chloroform is present in that effluent in a concentration greater than the background concentration. These prescribed substances and processes are set out in Table 8/IV below:

TABLE 8/IV

Special Category Effluent	
Prescribed Substances	
Mercury and its compounds	Dichlorvos
Cadmium and its compounds	1,2-Dichloroethane
gamma-Hexachlorocyclohexane	Trichlorobenzene
DDTA	Atrazine
Pentachlorophenol and its compounds	Simazine
Hexachlorobenzene	Tributyltin compounds
Hexachlorobutadiene	Triphenyltin compounds
Trifluralin	Aldrin
Fenitrothion	Dieldrin
Azinphos-methyl	Endrin
Malathion	Carbon tetrachloride
Endosulfan	Polychlorinated biphenyls

[70] reg.3.
[71] S.I. 1989 No. 1156, as amended by S.I. 1990 No.1629.

Prescribed Processes
Any process for the production of chlorinated organic chemicals Any process for the manufacture of paper pulp Any process for the manufacture of asbestos cement Any process for the manufacture of asbestos paper or board Any industrial process involving the use in any 12 month period of more than 100 kilograms of the product resulting from the crushing of asbestos ore.

Trade effluent from a process subject to integrated pollution control[72] is however not to be treated as special category effluent, since the relevant considerations will have been taken into account in the IPC authorisation process.

8–179

Consent Procedure

Except where it is proposed to enter into an agreement in relation to the discharge of trade effluent under section 129 (as to which see paragraph 8–192), the person wishing to make the discharge must serve a "trade effluent notice" on the relevant sewerage undertaker stating the nature or composition of the trade effluent to be discharged, the maximum quantity proposed to be discharged on any one day, and the highest rate at which it is proposed to discharge it.[73] The undertaker may make enquiries as to the sewers and other drains etc. that are proposed to be used for discharging the trade effluent, including requiring production of all relevant plans and other information.[74] Any consent may, and in practice will, be subject to conditions relating to the matters contained in the trade effluent notice and also to the sewer or sewers into which the effluent is to be discharged.[75] Numerous further conditions may be attached as listed in section 121(2), including in particular a requirement to eliminate or diminish any specified constituent of the effluent before it enters the sewer, where this would injure or obstruct the sewer or make the treatment or disposal of the sewage from the sewers especially difficult or expensive.

8–180

A further condition that will invariably be imposed will be for the payment, by the occupier of the premises from which the effluent is discharged, of charges for its reception. In determining the charges,

8–181

---

[72] *i.e.* excluding Part A processes in categories not yet brought under integrated pollution control, and those where applications for authorisation remain pending.
[73] s.119.
[74] s.204.
[75] s.121(1).

the undertaker must have regard to the matters specified in section 121(4), including any additional expense incurred or likely to be incurred by the undertaker in connection with the reception or disposal of that trade effluent.

8–182   Where an application is made for the discharge of any special category effluent, and the undertaker does not within the next two months refuse its consent, it is required within that period to refer the application to the Secretary of State to decide whether the discharges concerned should be prohibited and, if not, what conditions should be imposed on a consent to the discharge.[76]

Evidence and Enforcement

8–183   Meters or other apparatus provided in any trade premises for measuring, recording or determining the volume, rate of discharge, nature or composition of any trade effluent discharged, will be presumed to be accurate unless the contrary is shown.[77]

8–184   Quite apart from any remedy that may be available in civil proceedings brought by the undertaker, any contravention of a condition attached to a trade effluent consent constitutes an offence by the occupier of the premises concerned, who is liable on summary conviction to a fine up to £5000 and an unlimited fine on conviction on indictment.

Appeals and Charges

8–185   There is a right of appeal to the Director General of Water Services in the event of a refusal of an application for trade effluent consent, or the failure to grant one within two months from the date of the application, and also in respect of any condition that may be attached to such consent as is granted.[78] Pending any appeal, no discharge of trade effluent may take place, except in accordance with any existing consent. In the case of an application for discharge of special category effluent, the two month period that must elapse without a determination on an application before it is deemed to be refused, runs from the day after the Secretary of State receives the application referred to him.[79]

8–186   The approach of the Director to appeals is given in an Information Note of May 1993.[80] This is primarily concerned with consideration of

---

[76] s.120(1).
[77] s.136.
[78] s.122(1).
[79] s.123(1).
[80] Information Note No.21 "Trade Effluent Appeals".

the practical implications of conditions proposed to be attached to a consent or of the costs of meeting them. The note spells out that before considering any appeal, the Director expects to have had fully explained to him the reasons for any special conditions or costs the undertaker wishes to impose, and equally he expects the discharger to have explained fully the grounds for appeal and the substance of any negotiations that have taken place. Any determination will normally have regard to the practical and financial consequences for both the sewerage company and discharger, and will take into account health and safety requirements and intentions to discharge any substances likely to damage sewers or cause special difficulty or expense in subsequent treatment. The Director has a specific duty to have regard to the desirability of a sewerage company recovering its costs, including a reasonable return on capital. Thus conditions imposed by the sewerage undertaker should be related to those imposed on it by the NRA in relation to the discharge from the relevant sewage treatment plant. In addition, the Director will seek to establish and compare the long term cost implications for both the discharger and the sewerage undertaker of treating the effluent at minimum cost to meet environmental obligations. Evidence should be brought forward of all the consequences of proposed requirements, especially of any changes in necessary processes, together with evidence on sensible timetables for the achievement of changes. Where a sewerage undertaker has shortage of capacity in relation to standard effluent characteristics, such as suspended solids and oxygen demand, the Director will be inclined to order postponement of a discharge until a specified date by which the undertaker could reasonably be expected to have modified its plant in order to receive the effluent. Where a problem arises with non-standard characteristics which inhibit sewage treatment, the sewerage undertakers are expected to define any special conditions or special charges within a well-defined and even-handed overall policy. Ultimately, the Director's decision will involve a balance of the discharger's long term costs of complying with the standards proposed to be set against those reasonably estimated by the sewerage undertaker for treating the discharge to the same environmental standard at its works. If the discharger's costs are the lower, the appeal will normally be dismissed, and vice versa.

A sewerage undertaker may legitimately average out its trade effluent charges over the whole or part of its region, taking into account the fact that some of its sewage treatment plants may be more expensive to run than others. Where an average cost is used to set charges, then a refusal of a discharge, or the imposition of a limit, simply on account of the proposed discharge going to a relatively high cost sewage treatment plant, would not be viewed favourably by the

8–187

Director. Where a charges scheme[81] results in a significant mismatch between trade effluent charges and the costs of treatment in any respect, which amounts to undue preference or discrimination, the Director would look for a change in the charges scheme. Charges should not differentiate between new and existing discharges, as regards standard discharge characteristics, but where charges are not based on average costs, they may legitimately reflect different costs that a discharge may give rise to at different locations.

8–188   If the Director considers that a case appealed to him should have been referred to the Secretary of State on the ground that it relates to a discharge of special category effluent and the undertaker has not made that reference for whatever reason, the Director must make the referral himself, unless he determines in any event to uphold a refusal.[82]

Variation of Consents

8–189   The conditions of a trade effluent consent may be varied at any time; however, if this is done within two years from when the consent was first granted or from the latest of any variations, on the initiative of the sewerage undertaker, then the owner and occupier of the trade premises concerned may be entitled to compensation.[83] Any variation made outside the two year limit may not come into effect earlier than two months from when notice of the variation has been served on the owner and occupier of the trade premises concerned.[84] This notice must include information as to the right of appeal to the Director under section 126(1), within the two month period or at any later time with the Director's written permission. If an appeal is brought within those two months, the variation does not take effect until the appeal is withdrawn or finally disposed of,[85] with the exception of a variation in relation to charges, which may take effect on any date inside or outside the two months.[86]

8–190   Even though a sewerage undertaker directs that a variation of consent conditions is to take place earlier than two years from the initial consent or last variation, as the case may be, compensation will not be payable if the undertaker considers the variation to be in consequence of a change of circumstances since the beginning of the relevant two years that could not reasonably have been foreseen at the

---

[81] Made under s.143.
[82] s.123(2), (3).
[83] ss.124, 125.
[84] s.124(6)(b).
[85] s.126(2).
[86] s.126(3).

beginning of that period, and that it is required for reasons other than in consequence of other consents for discharges given since the beginning of that period.[87] Accordingly, if the undertaker has granted consents for more trade effluent than it handle at its sewage treatment works, it is not free to vary forthwith the conditions of these consents so as to bring the aggregate of the discharges within manageable bounds, but must, if it is to avoid paying compensation, wait for the relevant two year periods to expire.

Where a consent relates to special category effluent, the Secretary of   **8–191**
State may additionally review it as to whether the discharges authorised should be prohibited altogether or, if not, whether any conditions as to the discharges should be imposed. Such a review may be undertaken at any time, if carried out to enable the United Kingdom to give effect to any international agreement to which it is a party, or for the protection of public health, or of flora and fauna dependent on an aquatic environment. Except in these situations, the circumstances in which a review may be carried out are limited to those specified in section 127(2) — this requires two years to have elapsed since the time or the last time when notice of a determination by the Secretary of State of any reference or review relating to the consent was served.

Instead of applying for a trade effluent consent, the owner or   **8–192**
occupier of any trade premises may enter into an agreement with the sewerage undertaker for the discharge of trade effluent. Such an agreement has the effect of a consent granted under the notice procedure.[88] An agreement may typically be preferred where the sewerage undertaker has to instal additional or special effluent treatment facilities to cater for the particular discharge in question, thereby relieving the discharger of the need to instal suitable effluent treatment plant on his own premises. In such a case there is a need for commercial arrangements to cover payment by the discharger for the installation by the undertaker of the new facilities and, maybe, to bind the undertaker to continue accepting effluent of a defined nature for a period longer than the two years that it would ordinarily be committed to under a standard discharge consent. Any proposed agreement relating to special category effluent must be referred to the Secretary of State for his consideration, as in the case of a trade effluent notice for special category effluent. Here also no binding agreement is to be made with the discharger unless and until the Secretary of State has issued a determination allowing the discharge.[89] The Secretary of State

[87] s.125(2).
[88] s.129(3).
[89] s.130.

may review agreements relating to special category effluent as though they were consents to discharge special category effluent.[90]

8–193   The Secretary of State has wide powers under section 132 that he may exercise when considering trade effluent notices or agreements relating to special category effluent, or proposals to vary these, to prohibit discharges or to vary or add to conditions attached to the consents or agreements—in particular, the Secretary of State may revoke any applicable consent or agreement. Where the Secretary of State acts under these provisions, both the relevant undertaker and the Director must use their powers to secure compliance with whatever notice the Secretary of State may serve.[91] Where anything is done by the undertaker or the Director in order to comply with directions by the Secretary of State under his powers under section 132, no compensation is payable in respect of any loss or damage that may be caused.[92] However, the Secretary of State may be required to pay compensation in respect of loss or damage resulting from a notice issued by him under section 132 for the protection of public health or of flora and fauna, if the restrictions on the exercise of his powers contained in sections 127(2) (relating to special category effluent consents) and 131(2) (relating to special category effluent agreements) would otherwise have prevented him from exercising his general powers.[93] Even in this restricted case, the Secretary of State may not be liable to pay compensation if his determination was in consequence of a change of circumstances which could not reasonably have been foreseen when the relevant two year period first began, or was the result of his consideration of material information which was not reasonably available to him at the beginning of that two year period.

Trade Effluent Registers

8–194   Sewerage undertakers are required to keep available at their offices for inspection by the public at all reasonable times, free of charge, copies of every consent and direction given by the undertaker, every trade effluent agreement, and every notice served on the undertaker by the Secretary of State following the latter's determination of any reference made to him or any review by him relating to special category effluent.[94] Copies of or extracts from these must be obtainable

[90] s.131.
[91] s.133
[92] s.134(3).
[93] s.134(1).
[94] s.196(1).

at a reasonable charge.[95] Nevertheless, by section 206(1) no information with respect to any particular business which relates to the affairs of any individual and has been obtained under the W.I.A., including therefore the provisions relating to trade effluent consents and agreements, may be disclosed either during the lifetime of that individual or for so long as that business is carried on except with the consent of the relevant individual or person carrying on the business.[96] Accordingly, where any information protected in this way has been or is likely to be acquired by a sewerage undertaker or any public body under the powers in the W.I.A., the fact that it is sensitive information should be notified to those receiving it. Where trade effluent is from a process subject to integrated pollution control, then of course the much less comprehensive confidentiality restrictions of Part I of the E.P.A. apply, and then only for renewable periods of four years.[97] The distinction between these respective provisions in the two statutes has no logic.

Directors' and Officers' Liability

Both the W.R.A. and the W.I.A. have identical provisions in the usual terms whereby if a body corporate is guilty of an offence under either Act, and the offence is committed with the consent or connivance of any director, manager, secretary, or other similar officer, or any person who is purporting to act in any such capacity, or is attributable to any neglect on the part of any such person, then he as well as the body corporate is guilty of that offence. Further, in each case, where the affairs of a body corporate are managed by its members, those members are potentially liable for any offence by the body corporate on the same footing as if they were directors.[98] Additionally, where any offence is committed under the water pollution provisions of the W.R.A. that is due to the act or the fault of some other person, that other person may be charged with and convicted of the offence, whether or not proceedings are taken against the person who committed it.[99] Somewhat curiously, there is no corresponding provision in the W.I.A.

8–195

---

[95] s.196(2).
[96] s.206(1).
[97] E.P.A., s.22.
[98] W.R.A., s.217(1), (2); W.I.A., s.210.
[99] W.R.A., s.217(3).

Chapter 9

INTEGRATED POLLUTION CONTROL

Introduction

The Environmental Protection Act 1990 introduced Integrated **9–001**
Pollution Control ("IPC") into the United Kingdom environmental
regulatory system for the first time. Previously, all discharges to air
and to water, and the disposal of waste to land had been controlled
under independent legal and administrative regimes. Failure to co-
ordinate the controls can however lead merely to a diversion of
discharged pollutants from a medium subject to stringent regulation
to another where it is laxer. By scrubbing the gases in a stack,
emissions to air may be reduced, but at the cost of creating liquid
wastes. Filtering and precipitation steps applied to liquid wastes may
make them more acceptable for discharges, whether to sewer or
surface waters, but at the cost of creating solid wastes. Incineration of
solid wastes may reduce their bulk and/or toxicity, but can lead to
undesirable air emissions. The overall impact on the environment of a
process may thus not be significantly improved despite relatively
stringent control over any one medium; in some circumstances it
could even be made worse.

This issue was raised in 1976 by the Royal Commission on **9–002**
Environmental Pollution which, in its fifth report, recommended that
a body should be set up to be responsible for ensuring that polluting
releases should be carried out in a manner that minimised the effects
on the three environmental media (air, water, land) taken together, by
directing them to the environmental medium where the least environmental damage would be done. Accordingly for every process, the
"Best Practicable Environmental Option" (BPEO) should be determined, and the process then so conducted as to achieve that option.

It was this objective that led to the eventual creation in 1987 of Her **9–003**
Majesty's Inspectorate of Pollution (HMIP) in England and Wales. Her
Majesty's Industrial Pollution Inspectorate (HMIPI), which dates from
1971, fulfils similar functions in Scotland. These bodies became
responsible for air pollution, waste disposal (by way of supervision of

the various waste disposal authorities), and radioactive substances in their respective territories. Discharges to water were not however brought within the responsibilities of HMIP and HMIPI, except to the limited extent of supervising the activities (and specifically the discharges from sewage treatment plants) of the various water authorities in England and Wales, and the river purification boards (RPBs) in Scotland. Regulatory control over other discharges to water in their areas lay with these latter authorities. On the privatisation of the water authorities in England and Wales pollution control over the successor water companies has been exercised exclusively by the NRA. Practical implementation of IPC thus requires, as will be seen, close cooperation between HMIP and the NRA, and between the corresponding bodies in Scotland.

9–004   IPC is not simply a matter of having a single regulatory body responsible for setting and enforcing controls, though that is a virtually a prerequisite. It is the exercising of these controls in a manner leading to the BPEO that is the essence of the "integrated" regime. If IPC is understood in this sense, the United Kingdom is one of the first countries to have wholeheartedly embraced it and given effect to it in its environmental legislation.[1] The European Commission has itself been working for some years on a Directive on what it refers to as "integrated pollution prevention and control" (IPPC) for major industrial plants, modelled to a considerable degree on the British legislation.[2]

9–005 The Legal Framework

Part I of the E.P.A. and regulations made under it provide the legislative framework for the IPC regime.[3] By section 6(1) no person shall carry on a prescribed process after the relevant date for that process except under an authorisation granted by the enforcing authority and in accordance with the conditions to which it is subject.

9–006   "Process" is defined for the purposes of Part I as any activities carried on in Great Britain, (including relevant territorial waters as defined in Part III of the W.R.A. and (for Scotland) Part II of the Control of Pollution Act 1974—"C.O.P.A."), whether on premises or by means

---

[1] Denmark, France, and to some extent Germany, have all probably applied IPC earlier, but generally on a less comprehensive and systematic basis.

[2] The most recent version of which has been issued as COM (93) 423 final, [1993] O.J. C311.

[3] All section references in this chapter are to the E.P.A. unless otherwise stated.

of mobile plant, which are capable of causing pollution of the environment.

"Activities" is so defined as to be completely unrestricted in scope, and expressly extending to the keeping of a substance, with or without other activities. It appears therefore that anything done in the course of a trade or business, for example, however incidental or temporary, would be an "activity".

9–007

"Pollution of the environment" is likewise very broadly defined as meaning any such pollution due to the release into any environmental medium from any process of substances which are capable of causing harm to man or any other living organisms supported by the environment. "Substance" includes electricity or heat. "Harm" means harm to the health of living organisms or other interference with the ecological systems of which they form part and, in the case of man, includes offence caused to any of his senses or harm to his property. Pollution is thus treated as occurring on the release of a substance that is e.g. capable of causing any harm to any living organism, irrespective of whether such harm has in fact been caused — the potential for harm is sufficient.

9–008

The environmental medium into which a release is made is the medium into which it is directly released, and a release may be either within or outside Great Britain.[4] Shipping solid or liquid wastes for disposal outside Great Britain will not therefore evade the controls of Part I.[5] Releases to water include those to the surface of the sea-bed as well as to the sea, to any river, watercourse, lake, loch, pond or reservoir, and also to river beds and the land supporting all of such waters, and to ground waters.[6] Releases to water also include releases to sewer (within the meaning of the W.I.A. or, in Scotland, the Sewerage (Scotland) Act 1968), though in determining whether there is any pollution (as defined) at any instant the content of a sewer shall be disregarded.[7] "Ground waters" are broadly defined,[8] as including not only waters in underground strata but also in wells and boreholes in such strata, and in any adit or passage for facilitating collecting water in such wells, etc. They also include waters in any excavation in underground strata, where the water level depends wholly or mainly on water coming from the strata. A release to land however includes releases to land covered by any water other than the surface waters

9–009

---

[4] s.1(10).
[5] Different substances are prescribed under the E.P. (P.P. & S.) Regulations for releases to air, water and land respectively (see paras. 9–011 and 9–020), and, hence it may be critical to categorise a release correctly.
[6] s.1(11)(a).
[7] s.1(11)(c).
[8] s.1(12).

listed above[9] and to the water above such land, and releases to land beneath the seabed and beneath those surface waters.[10]

9–010 Sections 1(7) and 1(8) provide that the enforcing authority for IPC processes is, in England and Wales, the Chief Inspector, appointed under section 4, and, in Scotland, the Chief Inspector for Scotland or the relevant river purification authority determined pursuant to regulations made under section 5(1).[11] The Chief Inspector in each case is in practice the Director of HMIP and HMIPI respectively, and in Scotland, the relevant river purification authority has been designated to be the authority in whose area the prescribed process is carried out.

9–011 Schedule 1 to the Environmental Protection (Prescribed Processes and Substances) Regulations 1991[12] made pursuant to section 2(1)—the "E.P.(P.P. & S.) Regulations"—lists the prescribed processes. The broad categories of these processes are set out in Table 9/I. As from May 1, 1991 in England and Wales, and April 1, 1992 in Scotland, all the then prescribed processes became subject to IPC. These processes were largely those that required registration pursuant to the Alkali, etc., Works Regulation Act 1906, but there were also brought under these controls processes which produce significant quantities of special waste or discharge either prescribed quantities or, in some cases, any quantities at all of specified substances to air, water or land. These specified substances are listed in Schedules 4, 5 and 6 of the E.P.(P.P. & S.) Regulations—set out in Appendix 3.1A.

9–012 The principal effect of the two sets of Regulations made in 1994 (the later of which replaced the transitional provisions in Schedule 6 to the earlier) was to take a number of processes out of control altogether, to bring others under control for the first time, and to transfer yet others from IPC to the air pollution control regime (see below) and *vice versa*. Under complex transitional provisions these new arrangements take effect on various dates from June 1, 1994 to May 31, 1995.

---

[9] *i.e.* those set out in s.1(11)(a).
[10] s.1(11)(b).
[11] The Environmental Protection (Determination of Enforcing Authority, etc.) (Scotland) Regulations 1992; S.I. 1992 No. 530 (S.61).
[12] S.I. 1991 No. 472. These have been extensively amended by S.I. 1991 No. 836, S.I. 1992 No. 614, S.I. 1993 No. 1749, S.I. 1993 No. 2405, S.I. 1994 No. 1271 and S.I. 1994 No. 1329. A consolidated version of them has been issued by H.M.S.O. (August 1994).

TABLE 9/1

IPC Implementation Timetable for "Existing Processes" *England and Wales*		
Schedule 1 category	**Process**	**IPC applies from***
Section 1.3(a)	Combustion processes to produce > 50 MW energy (England & Wales only)	May 1, 1991
Chapter 1	All other fuel and power production and associated processes	July 1, 1992
Sections 2.1,2.3	Iron & steel production and processing; smelting processes	April 1, 1995
Section 2.2	Non-ferrous metals production processing	August 1, 1995
Sections 4.1, 4.2, 4, 7, 4.8	Petrochemical processes; organic chemicals; pesticides; pharmaceuticals	November 1, 1993**
Sections 4.3, 4.4, 4.6, 4.9	Acid processes; halogen, chemical fertiliser production; bulk chemical storage	February 1, 1994
Section 4.5	Inorganic chemical processes	August 1, 1994
Chapter 5	Waste disposal and recycling	November 1, 1992
Chapter 6	Paper & pulp manufacture; di-isocyanate, tar & bitumen, uranium and coating processes; coating manufacturing; timber processes; treatment of animal and plant matter	February 1, 1996

* or, for any specific process, the date on which a duly filed application is granted or refused

** postponed from August 1, 1993 by the Environmental Protection (Prescribed Processes and Substances) (Amendment) Regulations 1993 (S.I. 1993 No. 1749).

9–013

Existing Processes—Transitional Provisions

9–014   Transitional provisions provide for processes that were existing when Part I of the E.P.A. was brought into effect, and for these, IPC is to be phased in for the various processes at different dates up to February 1, 1996 set out in Schedule 3 to the E.P.(P.P. & S.) Regulations, as amended (see Table 9/I). To keep the phasing in programme manageable, an application for authorisation of an existing process must be made in the three month period immediately before the date IPC is to apply to existing processes of that category.

9–015   Where an application is filed in that period, the requirement that an authorisation be obtained before operating that process is postponed to the "determination date", *i.e.* the date of grant of the authorisation or the date of refusal of an authorisation (or if refusal is appealed, the date of affirmation of the refusal).[13]

9–016   What is an existing process for these purposes is defined in paragraphs 6 (for England and Wales) and 20 (for Scotland) of Schedule 3 to the E.P.(P.P. & S.) Regulations. Under these provisions, a process is an existing process if it was carried on at some time in the twelve months immediately preceding April 1, 1991 in England and Wales or April 1, 1992 in Scotland, or if it was to be carried on at a works, plant or factory or by means of mobile plant which was under construction or in course of manufacture or in the course of commission at the applicable date. Further, where construction or manufacture had not been begun before that date, if that construction or supply was the subject of a contract entered into before that date, then the process is still deemed to be an existing process.

9–017   There are however two exceptions. A process will cease to be an existing process if at any time between April 1, 1991 (or 1992 for Scotland) and the last date by which an application for authorisation for processes of that category is required to be made:

    (i)   the process ceases to be carried on, and is not started again at the same location or with the same mobile plant within the next following 12 months; or

    (ii) where during that period the process is subject to a substantial change and that change has not occasioned construction work already in progress on April 1, 1991/92, and is not the subject of a contract for construction work entered into before that date.[14]

---

[13] E.P. (P.P. & S.) Regs., Sched. 3, para. 8.
[14] E.P. (P.P. & S.) Regs., Sched. 3, paras. 3(1)(i), 7, 17(1)(i) and 21.

What is a "substantial change" is defined in subsection 10(7) as "a   **9–018**
substantial change in the substances released from the process or in
the amount or any other characteristic of any substance so released".
The same sub-section provides that the Secretary of State may give
directions to the enforcing authorities as to what does or does not
constitute a substantial change in relation to processes generally, to
any description of process or to any particular process. The guidance
issued by the DoE, the Welsh Office and the Scottish Office Environment Department[15] states that guidance on what constitutes a
substantial change for any particular class of process will be included
in the relevant Chief Inspector's Guidance Note issued or to be issued
in relation to that process. In the absence of a note covering a
particular class of process, a change will generally be regarded as
substantial if it results in an increase in the rate, concentration or
absolute quantity of a prescribed substance released, unless HMIP can
be satisfied that no significant environmental harm will result.[16]

The Processes Controlled

The processes prescribed for the purposes of Part I of the E.P.A. are   **9–019**
described in some detail in Schedule 1 of the E.P.(P.P. & S.) Regulations. This Schedule is divided into six chapters, and each chapter
consists of a number of sections. The sections are each divided into a
Part A and a Part B. Only the Part A processes are subject to IPC: they
constitute the processes "designated pursuant to section 2(4) for
central control". The Part B processes are "designated for local
control", and in such cases, by virtue of section 7(5), conditions
attached to authorisations granted by a local enforcing authority will
relate to releases to air but not to any other environmental medium.
Part B processes are considered in Chapter 10; nevertheless, most of
the concepts and procedures applicable to IPC, described in this
chapter, apply equally to the regulation of Part B processes also, and
references to them are made where appropriate in this chapter to
avoid undue repetition. The transitional provisions for existing Part B
processes prescribed a tighter time-table however, such that they all

---

[15] *Integrated Pollution Control : A Practical Guide*, (2nd ed.) 1993, referred to here as "the
IPC Practical Guide".
[16] Though not in any way decisive on the point, it is to be noted that comparable
language in Directive 86/280/EEC (which sets limit value and quality objectives on
discharges of certain chlorinated compounds), namely references to "substantially
increased" capacity, is construed by the UK Government as meaning an increase of
20 per cent or more (see DoE Circular 7/89, para. 22).

became subject to control under Part I of the E.P.A. with effect from October 1, 1992 in England & Wales and April 1, 1993 in Scotland.[17]

9–020   Regulation 4 of the E.P.(P.P. & S.) Regulations lists a series of exceptions to what would otherwise fall within the process descriptions of Schedule 1. The first of these relates to the lists of prescribed substances in relation to releases into the air, water and land respectively, contained in Schedules 4, 5 and 6.

9–021   If a Part A process cannot result in the release to air, water or land of any such substances (and, where relevant, in such amounts) as are prescribed for each of those media, then that process is not to be taken to be a Part A process, and hence not subject to IPC control.[18] Possible releases to air and land are to be ignored if there is no likelihood that any Schedule 4 or Schedule 6 prescribed substance will be released except in a quantity which is so trivial that it is incapable of causing harm or its capacity to cause harm is insignificant. In relation to releases to water, there was originally no allowance for "trivial" releases; this has now been addressed,[19] by setting, for each prescribed substance, a maximum quantity that may be released in any 12 month period. Accordingly, this exception applies if the process cannot result in a release of any of the Schedule 5 prescribed substances "except (a) in a concentration which is no greater than the background concentration"; or (b) in a quantity which does not, in any 12 month period, exceed the background quantity by more than the amount specified in relation to the description of substance in column 2 of Schedule 5. The background concentration is to be taken as the concentration of the relevant substances which could be present in the release, irrespective of any effect the process may have had on the composition of the release. In assessing the background concentration or quantity, as the case may be, it is necessary to look at all of the following, so far as relevant:

(i)   water supplied to the relevant premises;
(ii)   water abstracted for use in the process; and
(iii) precipitation on to the relevant premises.

9–022   For discharges to water, therefore, the issue is whether the process *cannot* result in release of more than the relevant prescribed amount of a Schedule 5 substance; for discharges to air and land there must be

---

[17] Except for existing processes the subject of an application for authorisation which was still in progress at the due date, having been neither granted nor refused, or else refused but the subject of a pending appeal.
[18] reg. 4(1).
[19] By the Environmental Protection (Prescribed Processes and Substances, etc.) Amendment Regs. 1994, (S.I. 1994 No. 1271) Sched. 5.

"no likelihood" of a more than trivial release—a less stringent test. If this is so in any particular case, the process is merely exempted from IPC; any discharges to controlled waters (and also to sewer) of Schedule 5 substances must still be granted consent by the relevant body. Since Schedule 5 permits a release of up to 1 kg of cadmium, for example, in any 12 months, such a consent cannot be taken for granted.

Regulation 4(2) sets out a corresponding exception in relation to Part B processes (those subject to local authority control for releases into air only), but the burden of proof is in effect reversed, in that a process will be taken to be a Part B process only if it will, or there is a likelihood that it will, result in the release into the air of one or more Schedule 4 substances in a quantity above that which is to be regarded as "trivial".   **9–023**

These two exceptions of regulations 4(1) and 4(2) are nevertheless subject to the qualification that neither will apply if any process as described in Schedule 1 may give rise to an offensive smell noticeable outside the premises where the process is carried on.[20]   **9–024**

Further exceptions are: processes carried on in a working museum or for educational purposes in a school; the running on any aircraft, vehicle or vessel of an engine which propels or provides electricity for it, or the testing of any engine before installation or during development; and a process carried on as a domestic activity in connection with a private dwelling.[21]   **9–025**

Inevitably not every process falls neatly within the descriptions in Schedule 1 to the Regulations. In that event and subject to any specific provision in Schedule 1, resort must be had to the interpretation rules contained in Schedule 2. These set out very detailed provisions for specific cases, covering a variety of process descriptions, some being in Part A only, some in Part B only, and some being combinations of Part A and Part B processes. As a general rule however, where a process falls within two or more descriptions within Schedule 1, the process is normally to be taken to be a process of the description that fits it most aptly.[22] Where a process falls equally aptly into more than one of the sections of Chapter 4 (the Chemical Industry), paragraph 4 sets out an order of priority of the constituent sections.   **9–026**

Similarly, various pairs of Part B processes are listed in paragraph 2C, and if a person operates both of a pair at the same location, then they are treated as a single process within the first mentioned section of the pair.[23] Originally there was liable to be difficulty in determining   **9–027**

---

[20] reg. 4(6).
[21] reg. 4(3), (4), (4A), (5).
[22] para. 4.
[23] ss. 2.1, 2.2; 3.1, 3.4; 3.6, 3.4; 6.5, 6.6; 6.7, 1.3(e) (waste wood burning only).

whether burning waste in a furnace that allowed the resulting heat to be beneficially used should be classed as a section 5.1 incineration process or a section 1.3 combustion process. The problem has now been alleviated by an amendment to paragraph 5 whereby the burning of waste oil, recovered oil or any fuel manufactured from or comprising any other waste in a furnace with a net rated thermal input of at least 3 MW, and as a process related to any Part B process, is to be treated as part of that Part B process.[24] Where any process involves the use, treatment or disposal of waste (whether as fuel or otherwise), by Schedule 2, paragraph 8, that use, treatment or disposal is to be regarded as being included in the relevant process description. The effect of this is to give the process the benefit of regulation 16(1)(a) and (b) of the Waste Management Licensing Regulations 1994,[25] so that no waste management licence under the E.P.A. is needed provided there is no final disposal by way of a deposit in or on land.

9–028   Which is the more apt description should not in principle affect the operating conditions to be imposed on the plant.[26] Of more immediate significance is that the controls under Part I of the E.P.A. apply to different categories of existing processes at different dates, and a wrong assumption by a process operator as to the category into which his process falls could lead to his failing to apply for authorisation by the stipulated date for the correct category, and so to his operating a process thereafter illegally.

9–029   Schedule 2 to the Regulations also sets out rules for determining whether various borderline situations fall within Part A or Part B as the case may be, and which section of the relevant Part applies when two or more processes are operated on the same site. Under paragraph 2, any description of a process is to include any other process carried on at the same location by the same person *as part of that process.* Consequently where a series of processes form an integral whole, then it is that whole process that is subject to IPC, and which must be placed in the most apt category, as described. However, the rule does not apply where there are two or more processes that fall into different sections of Schedule 1; they must be independently authorised, except in certain cases including:

—   Part A processes in different sections of Chapter 4 (the chemical industry) which are to be treated as if they were in the same section;[27]

---

[24] para. 5(e).
[25] S.I. 1994 No. 1056.
[26] Different approaches may well nevertheless be taken, depending on how the plant is categorised, since different Process Guidance Notes will apply, and there may be inconsistencies between these.
[27] para. 2(2).

- a combustion process within section 1.3, or one or more boilers, furnaces or other combustion appliances, that is or are operated as an inherent part of and primarily for a Part A process in section 1.1 (gasification and associated processes), in section 1.4 (petroleum processes), or in any section of Chapter 4, which is or are to be treated as part of that other process;[28] and
- a natural gas reforming process within Part A, paragraph (a), of section 1.1 used to produce a feedstock for any Part A process in Chapter 4, which is to be treated as part of the Chapter 4 process.[29]

Where two or more processes are carried on that fall within the same **9–030** section of Schedule 1 to the Regulations, or within different sections of Chapter 4, paragraphs 3 and 3A of Schedule 2 state that those processes shall be treated as requiring authorisation as a single process. Further, in such a situation, if one of the processes is in Part A and another in Part B, then the Part B processes are to be regarded as part of the Part A process and subject to HMIP/HMIPI/RPB central control only.

To allow for the need of manufacturers of specialty chemicals **9–031** operating on a relatively small scale to have a single authorisation for a variety of processes, by paragraph 3B of Schedule 2 where two or more processes in different sections of Chapter 4 are carried on at the same location by the same person, and it is not likely that more than 250 tonnes of relevant products will be made in any 12 month period, then they will be regarded as a single process.[30] "Relevant products" for this purpose means those resulting from the processes but excluding

- solid, liquid or gaseous waste;
- by-products, if their total value is insignificant in relation to that of the total output of the processes; and
- anything in the final product formulation that is not an active ingredient, *e.g.* a diluent, stabiliser or preservative.

Aggregation and Combined Processes

Many of the definitions of the Part A and Part B processes in the **9–032** E.P.(P.P. & S.) Regulations specify a minimum figure, *e.g.* an input or output, or a design rating. Where an operator runs two processes of

[28] para. 2A.
[29] para. 2B.
[30] Which process being determined in accordance with the rules of para. 4 of Sched. 2.

the same type, the question arises as to whether they should be treated as one for the purposes of the minimum figure in the relevant definition. Difficulties are liable to arise particularly in relation to boilers, which are often operated independently; in many cases certain boilers are kept operational on a standby basis only and as a practical matter only used as an energy supply when the principal boiler has been closed down—typically a standby boiler may use an alternative fuel, and be less efficient. The rules governing aggregation of boilers caused considerable uncertainty initially, but this has now been addressed by amendment of section 1.3 of Schedule 1, designed to ensure that the aggregation rules in relation to Part A processes are at least as wide as those of the Large Combustion Plants Directive 88/609.[31] Under the amended rules, in relation to Part A processes, where the boilers are "at the same location" (*i.e.* on the same site, even though physically separate), then there will be aggregation. However, in relation to Part B combustion processes, the Large Combustion Plants Directive is not relevant,[32] and for such processes, the Government has provided that there will be no aggregation. Boilers using normal fuels will be in Part A of section 1.3 if their aggregate net rated thermal input is 50MW or more and in Part B if the input is at least 20MW but under 50MW. The effect of the aggregation rules is that where a person operates four adjacent boilers with a net rated thermal input of 13MW each, they will be aggregated since their total comes to 52MW, and so they fall within Part A. However, if their net rated thermal input is, or is reduced to, 12MW each, they will not be aggregated, and they fall neither within Part A, nor, each individual input being below 20MW, Part B.

9–033　　Where there are two or more processes on a single site that fall within different sections of Schedule 1, then by paragraph 2 of Schedule 2, these processes will be treated separately and require distinct authorisations. If one such process is in Part A and another in Part B, then different enforcing authorities will be involved in independent regulation of each. This must, however, be read subject to sections 4(4) and (6) which empower the Secretary of State to transfer local authority powers over a Part B process to HMIP/HMIPI. This may be done either by a "general direction" relating to a class of processes carried on by all or by a prescribed category of persons, or by a "specific direction" relating to one specific process carried on by a

---

[31] [1988] O.J. L336. Art. 2(7) states: "Where two or more separate new plants are installed in such a way that, taking technical and economic factors into account, their waste gases could, in the judgment of the competent authorities, be discharged through a common stack, the combination formed by such plants is to be regarded as a single unit".

[32] It applies only to plants having a rated thermal input of 50MW or more.

specified person—generally no doubt at the latters' request. No criteria are given to govern when such a direction might appropriately be given, but the practice appears to be that it will not be given merely to avoid an operator having to go through two authorities, and that there will have to be some relationship between the processes that justifies taking control over the Part B process away from the local authority.

Authorisations and Conditions

In contrast with the relatively simple registration system of the Alkali, etc. Works Registration Act 1906, section 6 imposes a much more complex regime for obtaining prior authorisation. No process subject to it may be operated until an authorisation has been applied for, the proposed process assessed and, unless the application is refused at that stage, conditions determined and the application granted. Any authorisation of a prescribed process will invariably be made subject to conditions, as required by section 7. The primary purpose of the conditions is to secure the objective of "ensuring that, in carrying on the process, the best available techniques not entailing excessive cost (BATNEEC) will be used:

9–034

   (i)   for preventing the release of substances prescribed for any environmental medium into that medium, or where that is not practicable by such means, for reducing the release of such substances to a minimum, and for rendering harmless any such substances which are so released; and

  (ii) for rendering harmless any other substances which might cause harm if released into any environmental medium.

Further conditions must also be imposed where needed to bring about compliance with directions given by the Secretary of State to implement obligations under EC legislation or international conventions,[33] and also compliance with any limits or requirements or the achievement of any quality standards or quality objectives that are prescribed under any of the Clean Air Act 1993, the European Communities Act 1972, H.S.W.A. 1974, C.O.P.A. 1974, W.R.A. 1991 and E.P.A. section 3.[34] Further, where a plan has been made by the

9–035

---

[33] All the enforcing authorities, being "emanations of the State" are under a direct obligation to implement applicable binding EC Directives whether or not the Secretary of State has issued implementing directions.
[34] s.7(12).

Secretary of State under section 3(5), which may set limits for release of any substance or allocate quotas for release of any particular substances, then authorisation of any prescribed processes must contain such conditions as will bring about compliance with any requirements under such a plan. Section 7(8) empowers the inclusion of conditions imposing limits on the amounts or composition of any substance produced by or utilised in the process in any period[35] and, more significantly, requiring advanced notification of any proposed change in the manner of carrying on the process. This provision should reasonably be understood as enabling the imposition of a condition to prescribe a minimum period of advance notice sufficient to enable the enforcing authority to determine whether or not a "relevant change" is contemplated, with a consequent need for variation of the authorisation conditions in accordance with section 10 (see paragraph 9–085).

9–036   In so far as any prescribed processes (whether Part A or Part B) involve the disposal or recovery of waste, the relevant enforcing authority must exercise its powers, *inter alia*, for the purpose of achieving the waste management objectives derived from the waste Directive 75/442 as amended, and as set out in Schedule 4, paragraph 4, of the Waste Management Licensing Regulations 1994[36] (see paragraph 11–147 and note 87 to it). These require every relevant competent authority to ensure that waste is recovered or disposed of without endangering human health and without using processes or methods which could harm the environment, and in particular without

(i)   risk to water, air, soil, plants or animals, or
(ii) causing nuisance through noise or odours, or
(iii) adversely affecting the countryside or places of special interest.

It must also implement any applicable waste management plan.

9–037   Most of these matters are already taken fully into account in the course of authorising a process under Part I of the E.P.A.—the exceptions are essentially noise nuisance and the final item (iii), both of which issues are largely addressed, in the case of any new operation, when dealing with the necessary planning application. Nevertheless it is only since May 1, 1994 that planning authorities have been expressly required to meet these objectives; consequently enforcing authorities must observe all of them in relation to Part I

---

[35] This probably adds little to the broad provisions of section 7(2), but it confirms the power to impose such limits where, for example, the effects in a particular locality of a large or very intensive facility would otherwise be undesirable, notwithstanding full implementation of BATNEEC.
[36] S.I. 1994 No. 1056, Sched. 4, para. 8(1).

prescribed processes for which planning permission was granted before May 1, 1994, or where none was needed, *e.g.* because the relevant site had the benefit of an established use certificate. However, where the relevant planning permission is granted on or after that date, the enforcing authority is not required to take account of the objectives so far as they relate to preventing detriment to the amenities of the locality.[37] HMIP and HMIPI do not in any event have regard to purely visual amenity issues in controlling process operations, and the practical effect of the requirement is therefore for the earlier category of operations to be subject to control by HMIP and HMIPI over noise, to the extent that either of them considers this desirable having regard to any relevant planning conditions there may already be over the activity.[38] A Part B waste disposal or recovery process will also be subject to conditions imposed by its waste management licence (unless it is an exempt activity under regulation 17 and Schedule 3 of the Waste Management Licensing Regulations 1994). Overlap of controls is avoided by providing that, in controlling pollution of the environment, the local authority is not required to be concerned with discharges other than to air, while the waste regulation authority is not required to be concerned with discharges to air.[39]

Section 28 sets out certain important limits on the application of the IPC regime. Firstly, by section 28(1), no conditions are to be attached so as to regulate final disposal by deposit in or on land of controlled waste, for which a separate licence continues to be necessary, though there is an obligation on the enforcing authority to notify the appropriate waste regulation authority where the process is being carried on that there will be a final disposal of controlled waste by deposit in or on land.[40]   **9–038**

Conversely, by regulation 16 of the Waste Management Licensing Regulations 1994, no waste management licence under the E.P.A. is required for any recovery or disposal of waste, if this is an authorised Part A prescribed process, or for the disposal of waste in an authorised incineration process within paragraph (a) of Part B of section 5.1, provided in each case the process does not involve the final disposal of waste in or on land. Likewise, it is not an offence under section 85(1) of the Water Resources Act 1991 (pollution of controlled waters) if the entry of matter into the waters is in accordance with an authorised Part A process;[41] trade effluent will not be "special category trade effluent"   **9–039**

---

[37] Sched. 4, para. 8(2).
[38] See also Circular 11/94, paras.1.59–1.61.
[39] Sched. 4, para. 2(3), (4).
[40] In practice, any disposal to landfill may well take place outside the area of that waste regulation authority, so long as such authorities may be county and district councils.
[41] W.R.A. s.88(1)(b).

for the purposes of the Water Industry Act 1991 if it is produced, or to be produced, from a Part A process after the determination date for that process;[42] and Parts I to III of the Clean Air Act 1993 do not apply to any Part A or Part B process after its determination date.[43]

9–040   Secondly, as will be seen, in determining an application or varying authorisation conditions, HMIP/HMIPI/RPB is required to consider any representations that may be made by any of the prescribed bodies that it is required to consult.[44] These include the NRA for all Part A processes to be carried on in England and Wales, which by section 28(3) has the right to dictate conditions in every case where a prescribed process will entail the release of any substances into controlled waters. Thus, the enforcing authority must not grant an authorisation if the NRA certifies that in its opinion the release will result in or contribute to a failure to achieve any water quality objectives in force under the Water Resources Act 1991, and in any event, any authorisation that is granted shall, as respects releases to water, include such conditions as appear to the NRA to be appropriate for the purposes of achieving the objectives of the IPC regime, as a minimum—HMIP/HMIPI may impose more stringent conditions in this regard if it thinks fit.[45]

9–041   Finally, by section 28(2), where a process is regulated under both IPC and the Radioactive Substances Act 1993, then in the event of any inconsistency between the conditions imposed under the two separate regimes, the relevant R.S.A. condition will take preference.

BATNEEC and BPEO

9–042   The raison d'être of integrated pollution control is spelled out in section 7(7). This requires that the objectives to be achieved in granting an authorisation shall, in the case of any Part A process likely to involve the release of substances into more than one environmental medium, include the objective of ensuring that BATNEEC will be used for minimising the pollution which may be caused to the environment

---

[42] W.I.A., s.138(2).
[43] Clean Air Act 1993, s.41(1).
[44] Prescribed under the E.P. (A.A. & R.) Regs.
[45] Where a process will give rise to trade effluent, the consent of the sewerage undertaker or the relevant Scottish Regional or Islands Council—also statutory consultees—to the discharge to sewer, and the conditions on which that consent might be given, is an independent requirement, over which HMIP/HMIPI has no control. Such conditions will be likely to be set by reference as much to the ability of the relevant sewage treatment plant to handle the effluent without breaching the discharge limits it is or may become subject to, as to the exigencies of the applicant's process. See paras. 8–180 to 8–182 (trade effluent).

taken as a whole by the releases, having regard to the Best Practicable Environmental Option ("BPEO") available as respects the substances which may be released.

There is no definition of BPEO in the E.P.A., but it was the subject of the 12th Report of the Royal Commission on Environmental Pollution, to which further reference may usefully be made.[46] It includes the following description:

9–043

> "A BPEO is the outcome of a systematic consultative and decision-making procedure which emphasises the protection and conservation of the environment across land, air and water. The BPEO procedure establishes, for a given set of objectives, the option that provides the most benefit or least damage to the environment as a whole, at acceptable cost, in the long term as well as in the short term".

What amounts to BPEO in any particular case will often be difficult, if not impossible, to state with any degree of certainty. The determination of the various impacts on the environment that may occur could involve the same sort of considerations as those discussed below in relation to eco-labelling and the necessary life cycle analysis that may be applied to the products under consideration.

9–044

However the BPEO requirement is by section 7(7) limited to a consideration of the substances which may be *released* by the process— it is not a BPEO relating to the process taken as a whole.[47] Even limiting consideration to the particular releases, there must be a balance struck between the relative harm done by the alternative options on the different environmental media. This is a notoriously difficult operation, and may, in some cases, entail balancing substantial harm caused to plants or creatures of significance in their eco-systems but of no general wide appeal, against harm to other plants or creatures of less significance in ecological terms, but of greater political and perhaps economic importance, in the short term at least. This situation is further complicated where the harm, as from large combustion plants, is suffered as much, if not more, by populations in

9–045

---

[46] Cmnd. 310.
[47] Consideration of the total environmental impact of a process would have to include a review of the raw material inputs, and the environmental consequences of production of those materials, the energy consumption of the various components of the process, transport requirements for raw materials and for both the desired and the waste products, in addition to the environmental issues relating to the releases from the process, quite apart from the environmental impact of siting the process in the particular location used. Restricting the BPEO consideration to the releases may reasonably be regarded as the most that can realistically be undertaken in present circumstances. For a fuller review of BPEO in practice, see "IPC—A Practical Guide for Managers" Chap. 8, Turner, Brown, Vickers and Powell and the references there cited.

other countries, whereas the benefits, at least with certain options, are apparent more locally. There is no suggestion in the E.P.A. that only harm within the jurisdiction is relevant in assessing the BPEO. As inferring such a restricted approach would, at least in relation to air emissions, conflict with the UK obligations under the Geneva Convention on long-range trans-boundary air pollution, it would be wrong to do so, quite apart from issues of more general principle.[48]

9–046 References to "best available *technology* not entailing excessive cost" appear in EC legislation in the Air Framework Directive 84/360.[49] Neither this expression nor the corresponding UK term BATNEEC (where T = techniques) have however appeared in UK legislation before. BATNEEC is not comprehensively defined in the E.P.A., though section 7(10) states that, in relation to a process, the term includes, in addition to reference to any technical means and technology "references to the number, qualifications, training and supervision of persons employed in the process and the design, construction, lay-out and maintenance of the buildings in which it is carried on". It is therefore a very comprehensive term.

9–047 Apart from the extension from technology to techniques, it is a matter of inconclusive debate as to whether BATNEEC differs in any significant respects from the previous well-established expression "best practicable means" (BPM). The relevance of this latter expression is now being largely phased out, with the phasing out of the previous air pollution control regime under the Health & Safety at Work Act 1974.[50] As a matter of practice in construing "practicable" regard has always been had to the financial implications of any available option, as s. 79(9) now explicitly provides.[51] Accordingly, it is doubtful whether BATNEEC necessarily introduces any materially different standards from those previously required where BPM was to be employed. The reality, nevertheless, is that BATNEEC is likely to be given a more rigorous interpretation; it cannot safely be assumed that

---

[48] Flue gas desulphurisation provides a good example of the limitations of limiting BPEO analysis to releases only. The most common system used for removing SO_x is the limestone process, which is converted into gypsum, for which there is a market in plasterboard manufacture. The production of the large quantities of limestone however necessarily entails massive quarrying, often in scenic areas, and the transport of the limestone from the source to the FGD site. The Wellman-Lord FGD process does not require limestone, and converts the SO_x to sulphuric acid. There is however not a sufficient market for all the sulphuric acid that would be produced if every power station were to use this process.

[49] [1984] O.J. L188.

[50] Though BPM is somewhat anomalously retained by the E.P.A. in Part III, dealing with statutory nuisances; see paras. 23–032 to 23–035.

[51] In contrast with "as low as reasonably achievable (ALARA) used in implementing the UK radioactive substances legislation, where financial issues play a much less significant role. See also HMIP's Note on Best Practicable Means (BPM 1/81).

whatever may in the past have been accepted as meeting a BPM requirement will also be BATNEEC, even where there have been no relevant intervening advances in technology.

What amounts to BATNEEC for any particular process requires separate consideration of "best", "available" and "techniques", and of the cost implications of the process options that may be suggested set against their potential environmental benefits. To date, there is no case law, and indeed relatively little experience of HMIP decisions in respect of wholly new facilities. Nevertheless, in practice an essential first stage is a consideration of the Secretary of State's guidance issued under section 7(11). This section requires enforcing authorities "to have regard" to any guidance issued by the Secretary of State under it.[52] To provide some assistance when IPC was first brought in five general Guidance Notes (IPR 1 to 5) were issued covering whole industry sectors. These necessarily each covered a wide range of processes and were consequently not sufficient for a process operator to know precisely what standards he would have to comply with in any particular case. These notes are now supplemented by detailed Guidance Notes relating to specific processes, as listed in Table 9/II.

9–048

This guidance is nevertheless no more than that, and in any particular case, it will be open to either the operator or the enforcing authority to argue for less or more stringent conditions than it contains.[53] Operators may assert, for example, that features proposed in the guidance are technically excessively demanding or commercially impractical, while enforcing authorities may consider that a particular location requires more stringent controls, or that an advance in technology since preparation of the guidance allows tougher conditions to be fairly regarded as BATNEEC.

9–049

TABLE 9/II

Chief Inspector's Guidance Notes—Part A Processes	
(As published at June 1994)*	
(A) INDUSTRY SECTOR GUIDANCE NOTES	
IPR1	Fuel and Power Industry Sector
IPR2	Metal Industry Sector
IPR3	Mineral Industry Sector

[52] This function is in fact performed by the Chief Inspectors for England and Wales and for Scotland, respectively, in accordance with s.4(2).
[53] Even so, the statement in the IPC Practical Guide, at para. 7.22, that the Chief Inspector's Guidance Notes have no statutory force is a little misleading.

IPR4	Chemical Industry Sector
IPR5	Waste Disposal Industry Sector

(B) PROCESS GUIDANCE NOTES

CHAPTER 1: The Production of Fuel and Power and Associated Processes

IPR1/1	Combustion Processes Large Boilers and Furnaces of 50 MW(th) and over
IPR1/2	Combustion Processes Gas Turbines
IPR1/3	Combustion Processes Compression Ignition Engines of 50MW(th) and over
IPR1/4	Combustion Processes Waste and Recovered Oil Burners of 3MW(th) and over
IPR1/5	Combustion Processes Combustion of Solid Waste in Appliances with a Net Rated Thermal Input of 3 MW or more
IPR1/6	Combustion Processes Combustion of Fuel Manufactured from or Comprised of Tyres, Tyre Rubber or Similar Rubber Waste in appliances with a Net Rated Thermal Input of 3MW or more
IPR1/7	Combustion Processes Combustion of Solid Fuel Manufactured from or Comprised of Poultry Litter in Appliances with a Net Rated Thermal Input of 3MW or More
IPR1/8	Combustion Processes Combustion of Solid Fuel Manufactured from or Comprised of Wood Waste or Straw in Appliances with a Net Rated Thermal Input of 3 MW or more
IPR1/9	Carbonisation and Associated Processes Coke Manufacture
IPR1/10	Carbonisation and Associated Processes Smokeless Fuel, Activated Carbon and Carbon Black Manufacture
IPR1/11	Gasification Processes Gasification of Solid and Liquid Feedstocks
IPR1/12	Gasification Processes Refining of Natural Gas
IPR1/13	Gasification Processes The Refining of Natural Gas at Liquefied Natural Gas Sites

IPR1/14	Gasification Processes The Odorising of Natural Gas or Liquefied Petroleum Gas
IPR1/15	Petroleum Processes Crude Oil Refineries
IPR1/16	Petroleum Processes On-shore Oil Production
IPR1/17	Combustion Processes Reheat and Heat Treatment Furnaces 50MW(th) and over

CHAPTER 2: Metal Production and Processing

IPR2/1	Iron and Steel Making Processes Integrated Iron and Steel Works
IPR2/2	Ferrous Foundry Processes
IPR2/3	Processes for Electric Arc Steelmaking Secondary Steelmaking and Special Alloy Production

CHAPTER 3: The Mineral Industries

IPR3/1	Cement Manufacture and Associated Processes
IPR3/2	Lime Manufacture and Associated Processes
IPR3/3	Processes Involving Asbestos
IPR3/4	Glass Fibres and non-Asbestos Mineral Fibres
IPR3/5	Glass Manufacture and Production; Glass Frit and Enamel Frit
IPR3/6	Ceramic Processes

CHAPTER 4: The Chemical Industry

IPR4/1	Petrochemical Processes
IPR4/2	Processes for the Production and Use of Amines, Nitriles, Isocyanates and Pyridines
IRP4/3	Processes for the Production or Use of Acetylene, Aldehydes etc.
IPR4/4	Processes for the Production or Use of Organic Sulphur Compounds, and Production, Use or Recovery of Carbon Disulphide
IPR4/5	Batch Manufacture of Organic Chemicals in Multipurpose Plant
IPR4/6	Production and Polymerisation of Organic Monomers

IPR4/7	Processes for the Manufacture of Organo-Metallic Compounds
IPR4/8	Pesticide Processes
IPR4/9	Pharmaceutical Processes
IPR4/10	Processes for the manufacture, use or release of oxides of sulphur and the manufacture, recovery, condensation or distillation of sulphuric acid or oleum
IPR4/11	Processes for the manufacture or recovery of nitric acid and processes involving the manufacture or release of acid-forming oxides of nitrogen
IPR4/12	Processes for the sulphonation or nitration of organic chemicals
IPR4/13	Processes for the manufacture of, or which use or release halogens, mixed halogen compounds or oxohalocompounds
IPR4/14	Processes for the manufacture of, or which use or release hydrogen halides or any of their acids
IPR4/15	Processes for the halogenation of organic chemicals
IPR4/16	Processes for the manufacture of chemical fertilizers or their conversion into granules
IPR4/17	Bulk storage installations
IPR4/18	Processes for the manufacture of ammonia
IPR4/19	Processes involving the use, release or recovery of ammonia
IPR4/20	The production of and the use of, in any process for the manufacture of a chemical, phosphorus and any oxide, hydride, or halide of phosphorus
IPR4/21	Processes involving the manufacture, use or release of hydrogen cyanide or hydrogen sulphide
IPR4/22	Processes involving the use or release of antimony, arsenic, beryllium, gallium, indium, lead, palladium, platinum, selenium, tellurium, thallium or their compounds
IPR4/23	Processes involving the use or release of cadmium or any compounds of cadmium
IPR4/24	Processes involving the use or release of mercury or any compounds of mercury

IPR4/25	Processes for the production of compounds of chromium, magnesium, manganese, nickel, and zinc
CHAPTER 5: Waste Disposal and Recycling	
IPR5/1	Merchant and In-House Chemical Waste Incineration
IPR5/2	Clinical Waste Incineration
IPR5/3	Municipal Waste Incineration
IPR5/4	Animal Carcass Incineration
IPR5/5	The Burning out of Metal Containers
IPR5/6	Making Solid Fuel from Waste
IPR5/7	Cleaning and Regeneration of Carbon
IPR5/8	Recovery of Organic Solvents by Distillation
IPR5/9	Regeneration of Ion-Exchange Resins
IPR5/10	Recovery of Oil by Distillation
IPR5/11	Sewage Sludge Incineration

* Guidance Notes for processes contained in the remaining sectors are due to be published progressively at least three months before they become subject to IPC.

The European Commission is itself drawing up technical notes on **9–050** the interpretation of BATNEEC for the purposes of the Industrial Plants Directive 84/360. Although currently these technical notes are of no legal effect, they must be relevant to any UK operator of a process to which they apply, in so far as they differ in any material respects from what may be regarded as BATNEEC by the enforcing authority in this country, since if they are less demanding, this clearly provides valuable evidence that the UK requirements may be excessive, whereas if they are more demanding, this serves as a warning that the UK standards are liable to be tightened up at the next revision, a factor that it may be prudent to take into account at the process design stage.[54]

[54] It is of course entirely possible that the European Commission technical notes are themselves excessively demanding, and would be cut back at the time of any attempt to make them legally binding.

9–051   The following technical notes have been issued so far:

EUR

13001   Heavy metals emissions from non-ferrous industrial plant (lead, zinc and copper);
13002   Ammonia production;
13003   Manufacture, storage and handling of benzene;
13004   Nitric acid production;
13005   Cement manufacture;
13006   Sulphuric acid production;
13007   Hazardous waste incineration.[55]

It is understood that further notes are in hand in respect of oil refining, sinter plants, coke ovens, blast furnaces, basic oxygen steel making, and electric arc furnaces.[56]

9–052   The IPC Practical Guide contains the following comments[57] on each of the expressions "best", "available", and "techniques":

9–053   "Best" must be taken to mean most effective in preventing, minimising or rendering harmless polluting emissions. There may be more than one set of techniques that achieves comparable effectiveness—that is, there may be more than one set of "best" techniques.

9–054   "Available" should be taken to mean procurable by the operator of the process in question. It does not imply that the technique has to be in general use, but it does require general accessibility. It includes a technique which has been developed (or proven) at a scale which allows its implementation in the relevant industrial context with the necessary business confidence. It does not imply that sources outside the UK are "unavailable". Nor does it imply a competitive supply market. If there is a monopoly supplier the technique counts as being available provided that the operator can procure it.

9–055   "Techniques" is defined in section 7(10) of the Act. The term embraces both the plant in which the process is carried on and how the process is operated. It should be taken to mean the components of which it is made up and the manner in which they are connected together to make the whole. It also includes matters such as numbers and qualifications of staff, working methods, training and supervision and also the design, construction, lay-out and maintenance of buildings, and will affect the concept and design of the process.

9–056   "Available" is likely to give rise to the most argument in practice, given that many processes are being constantly upgraded, and it will

---

[55] Now the subject of a draft Directive [1994] O.J. C232.
[56] The NSCA 1993 Pollution Handbook, para. 1.5.1.
[57] At paras. 7.3–7.6.

often be a matter of opinion as to whether the experience to date with a particular process justifies an insistence on its use in what may be a significantly different context, and perhaps on a much larger scale. However the fact that a possible process is the subject of a patent, and can only be worked under licence from the patentee is not relevant, provided licences are in fact available to all who wish to have them. The refusal to grant or withdrawal of a licence to someone unwilling or unable to pay the royalty demanded should not prevent the licence from being "available", if the patentee is simply acting so as to maximise his return from the licence, and not discriminating between potential users. The level of the licence fees would be relevant to whether this particular technique entailed "excessive cost", but that is a separate question.

By including in "techniques" the concept and design of a process, **9–057** the intention is to avoid purely "end of pipe"solutions—with new processes at least—and so achieve a process design that inherently leads to the BPEO.

The IPC Practical Guide states[58] that in many cases, for new **9–058** processes, it is expected that BAT and BATNEEC will be synonymous. It sets out the following principles that should apply:

— the cost of the best available techniques must be weighed against the environmental damage from the process; the greater the environmental damage, the greater the costs of BAT that can be required before costs are considered excessive;
— the objective is to prevent damaging releases or to reduce such releases so far as this can be done without imposing excessive costs; if after applying BATNEEC serious harm would still result, the application can be refused;
— as objective an approach as possible to the consideration of what is BATNEEC is required. The concern is with what costs in general are excessive; the lack of profitability of a particular business should not affect the determination.

In relation to the last point, it should be noted that this regards as **9–059** irrelevant costs that might in practice be excessive only for the particular operator of an individual plant because of his financial circumstances. In considering therefore whether a particular technique amounts to BATNEEC, it would not be a relevant objection for the applicant operator to say that he personally could not afford to adopt

---

[58] para. 7.8.

it—he would have to show that his industry sector generally would find it unduly expensive to do so. Consequently, applicants wishing to raise this argument may need to consider both the UK market for the products of the process in question and how far it is supplied by imports, and also the international market for these products, if the UK industry sector affected is a significant exporter. If lower environmental standards are imposed on others, who compete in the UK or in any export market of importance to UK manufacturers, particularly in other EEC countries, so that they have a significantly lower costs burden, and the market for the products of the process is price sensitive, then this must be a relevant factor in determining what is BATNEEC.

9–060   In assessing BATNEEC for existing processes coming under the IPC regime in accordance with the phased programme, due consideration must be given to the timescale over which standards will be raised to those of new or substantially changed plant.[59]

9–061   The IPC Practical Guide states[60] that the Secretary of State considers that the approach of the EC Air Framework Directive 84/360 is helpful in coming to a decision on the speed of upgrading existing plants. Article 13 of this Directive (which applies only to processes in existence at the final date for the Directive's implementation, June 30, 1987) reads:

"In the light of an examination of developments as regards best available technology and the environmental situation, the Member States shall implement policies and strategies, including appropriate measures, for the gradual adaptation of [specified] existing plants to the best available technology, taking into account in particular:

—   the plant's technical characteristics;
—   its rate of utilization and length of its remaining life;
—   the nature and volume of polluting emissions from it;
—   the desirability of not entailing excessive costs for the plant concerned;

[59] This raises starkly the costs of environmental protection: if existing plant that cannot be economically upgraded has high standards imposed on it substantially before the end of its useful life, then there will be a significant waste of resources, possibly leading to elimination of domestic producers, to the benefit of competitors outside the United Kingdom. Conversely, for so long as existing operators are not required to bring their plant up to current BATNEEC standards, there will be a significant disincentive on all others from investing in new plant, with the result that available environmental improvements are not obtained.
[60] para. 7.10.

having regard in particular to the economic situation of undertakings belonging to the category in question."

Decisions on this will inevitably vary substantially from one industry to another. However the Chief Inspector's process guidance notes relating to Chapter 1 processes, other than large combustion plants in England and Wales which came under control in 1991, provide for upgrading periods of about four years for most of the simpler processes, rising to six years for more complex plants such as oil refineries, coal carbonisation and natural gas processing. According to the process guidance notes, any delay in upgrading beyond these four to six year deadlines will be allowed only in exceptional circumstances.

9–062

HMIP have published a (revised) Consultation Document[61] which sets out the approach to be used by HMIP inspectors on the technical assessment of environmental information provided by applicants for IPC authorisations, and also on the identification of the BPEO where there are two or more available processes. Though written as guidance for inspectors, the publication is also intended to help operators of relevant processes to understand the approach that will be taken to their applications, and so enable them to present their applications more effectively.

9–063

It is not possible here to give full details of the approach described in the publication, but an essential feature of it is the determination for each substance that might be released from a process, and for each of the media into which it might be released (air, water, land), a "predicted environmental concentration" ("PEC")—this consists of any background or ambient concentration of that substance in the relevant medium taken together with the long term contribution that is predicted to be made by emissions from the process to that medium. The potential for environmental harm from short term peak emissions, for example at start up or shut down, or in foreseeable emergency situations, and in particular from a combination of peak values, would be the subject of a separate study. Next, for each substance that may be emitted, and for each medium to which it may be emitted, an upper level for the PEC is determined. Where an applicable legally binding environmental quality standard ("EQS") exists, this will constitute the upper level; if there is no relevant EQS, HMIP will develop what it refers to as an "Environmental Assessment Level" ("EAL"). At the other end of the scale, for each substance that may be emitted to any one medium, a lower limit for the PEC, referred to as an "Action Level", is fixed, below which emissions would be regarded as

9–064

---

[61] "Environmental, Economic and BPEO Assessment Principles for Integrated Pollution Control", April 1994.

insignificant.[62] The fixing of the Action Level is relatively arbitrary; ideally it would be the "no observed effect level" (NOEL), but in many cases this will not be known and provisionally it is proposed that it should normally be set at 10 per cent of the EQS or EAL.

9–065   A process will not be authorised if the PEC for any substance is liable to exceed any statutory environmental quality standard; it is unlikely to be authorised if the PEC exceeds the EAL. In the latter case, the process would be regarded as *prima facie* unacceptable, but it would be open to the operator to seek to justify an authorisation for it on the basis that there was no other representing BATNEEC. The procedure involves considering what would be the Best Environmental Option (the "BEO")—questions of practicability are considered subsequently, if cost implications indicate this is necessary, in determining the BPEO.

9–066   Determining the BPEO involves a series of stages:

(i)   All releases to all media are individually identified, and separated into those that are "significant" and any that are not. As a rule of thumb, a release that causes the PEC to exceed the Action Level will be significant.

(ii)   Each significant release to any one medium is assessed against the relevant Action Level and the relevant EQS or EAL (as the case may be), and a substance "Environmental Quotient" calculated, being the ratio of the PEC to the EQS or EAL.

(iii) The substance Environmental Quotients calculated in this way for any one medium are added together to give an overall Environmental Quotient for that one medium.

(iv)   This exercise is repeated for each substance released to each of the other media in turn, and aggregates of the substance Environmental Quotients for the other media determined in the same way.

(v)   The resulting "media Environmental Quotients" for air, water and land are then compared, and their aggregate also calculated; this combined figure is termed "the Integrated Environmental Index" (the "IEI").

(vi)   This entire procedure is repeated for every other process option meriting consideration, to give comparable IEIs.

(vii) The releases of each process option are then assessed for

---

[62] Though an operator would still be required to prevent their release where possible, and to minimise and to render harmless any emissions that cannot be wholly prevented—however since they are regarded as insignificant if the PEC is below the Action Level, no substantial costs would need to be incurred to deal with them.

(a) their short term effects—most processes will not produce steady emission levels but ones that vary quite
widely from peaks to troughs, and the peak levels may
be damaging even though of relatively short duration
and having only minor impact on the total amount
released;

(b) their potential for global warming and for (low level)
ozone generation;

(c) the effects of disposal of waste arisings;

(d) any other relevant environmental factors, for example if
a PEC is close to, *e.g.* 80 per cent or more of, the
applicable EQS/EAL.

(viii) The various process (and abatement) options are then
ranked by reference to the results of the assessments to give
the BEO. Though the raw IEI figures are of particular
importance, they are not decisive—all other relevant factors
must be taken into account. This is not therefore a purely
mathematical exercise but involves professional judgment
as to the relative weightings to put on the impacts that have
been identified. Nevertheless, the ranking and the choice of
BEO must be fully justified. At this stage cost factors play no
direct part; the Consultation Document says "the only
economic consideration is that the options should be
viable". Presumably this means that an option that would
entail "excessive cost" in all circumstances is not to be
considered.

(ix) Finally, the site specific Best Practicable Environmental
Option must be determined. If the operator's preferred
option is also the BEO, then no further enquiry is needed.
Otherwise the issue turns on which option is BATNEEC for
the site, and requires the operator to show that the extra
cost(s) of the option or options giving better environmental
performance than the preferred one is or are excessive.

Whether the cost is excessive in any particular case cannot be   **9–067**
answered wholly objectively. A relevant consideration will be the
extra cost of one process over another compared with the reduction in
the Integrated Environmental Index, modified as appropriate by other
environmental factors, that is achieved with the extra cost. This
incremental cost generally increases with increasingly tight limits on
emissions, and at some stage extra environmental benefits are likely to
be obtainable only at a clearly disproportionate extra cost. However,
considerable difficulties arise in calculating cost levels on a consistent

basis, particularly where in one case the proposal may be for a new plant, but in another for the upgrading of an old one. Moreover, as a purely practical matter, accurate cost estimates for a variety of plants on a theoretical, pre-contract basis, will be difficult and probably impossible to obtain, so adding further uncertainties to the calculations.

9–068   It remains to be seen how this complex and very demanding approach to determining BPEO and BATNEEC will work out in practice. It clearly has the substantial merit of ensuring relative consistency between applications and between different HMIP inspectors. On the other hand, it depends heavily on the actual figures that are chosen for the "Action Level" and "Environmental Assessment Level", and the choice of these figures cannot avoid being quite subjective. Additionally, the process assumes a straight line relationship between environmental damage and the level of the PEC. It seems inherently unlikely that this is so in every single case. The aggregation of the various Environmental Quotients assumes they should all have equal weight, which may or may not be appropriate. Though a great deal of detailed work is necessary to calculate and assess all the relevant environmental impacts, ultimately their relative weightings and the final choice of BPEO necessarily require the exercise of subjective professional judgment, if determinations are not to be at risk of being struck down by the Courts for being overly mechanistic. While the approach represents in most respects a reasonable implementation of the requirements of Part I of the EPA, it is questionable whether those who drafted the Act, or for that matter the RCEP, realised the massive administrative burdens that BAT-NEEC/BPEO obligations would create.

9–069   Having determined what is BATNEEC for a particular process, this must be translated into a set of legally binding conditions attached to the authorisation. These conditions may be framed in a variety of ways. In certain circumstances a specific process or type of equipment may be made mandatory; for others it may be sufficient to specify release levels based on experience with particular technology, leaving it to the operator to choose that or any other technology that may get at least as good a result. This latter approach will normally be preferred, so as not to place undue restrictions on the operator. The framing of release limits requires careful attention by both regulators and operators if they are to be technically manageable, legally precise, so that there is no uncertainty as to whether or not a condition has been breached, and also capable of relatively straightforward monitoring and enforcement.[63]

A particular problem that faces some operators, particularly those in the speciality chemicals industry, is the need to be able to run a variety of quite different processes all subject to IPC, and to be able to switch from one to another rapidly, to suit customer demands, without administrative delays. The IPC Practical Guide recognises that processes involving frequent changes in inputs, throughput and outputs need to be able to operate within a regime that provides full environmental control but which allows the changes to take place without unnecessary delay.[64] It continues by saying that under IPC it is possible in appropriate cases to define an "envelope" of release limits for the process in question, within which the operator is able to make adjustments without the prior approval of HMIP; however the onus is on the operator to propose and justify such an "envelope" in his application (see also Guidance Note IPR4/5).

9–070

Even though conditions may have been specified for a wide variety of parameters relating to a process, a process operator must further use BATNEEC in respect of all other process features not specifically addressed in the consent.[65] Accordingly it will not be sufficient for an operator simply to ensure that all the specific conditions are complied with; he must also establish at the outset, and maintain updated, a policy in respect of all his process features, and ensure that BATNEEC is applied throughout. For this reason operators may well prefer to see conditions imposed in respect of a wide variety of their process operations, provided of course these set acceptable standards—in most other licensing situations, what is not subject to conditions is left free for an operator to handle or ignore at will, but under Part I of the E.P.A. all aspects of an operation are to be operated at BATNEEC standards, and where a process feature is not the subject of an explicit condition, the requirements on an operator are no less onerous, but simply less clear cut. This is all the more significant when taken in conjunction with section 25(1) that places the onus of proof that the BATNEEC requirement was complied with on the operator. Section 7(4) may be a residual requirement, but it is also very demanding.

9–071

---

[63] It is inevitable that compromise between at least the last two of these considerations will often be necessary. For example, where a condition relates to a substance that is not unduly harmful at any likely emission levels but is environmentally damaging in large quantities, the total released over a year may be the most significant measure environmentally, but a condition framed in such terms would, as a practical matter, make enforcement very difficult.

[64] para. 8.5.

[65] s. 7(4).

9-072   In any particular case, refusal of an application will ordinarily be on the grounds that the proposed techniques are not BATNEEC. However there is an overriding provision in section 6(4) that an application shall not be granted unless the enforcing authority considers that the applicant will be able to carry on the process so as to comply with the conditions that would be included in the authorisation. Thus if the inspector considers that an applicant simply has not got adequate financial resources or technical competence or environmental management systems, even though the applicant is willing to accept such conditions as the inspector thinks appropriate, the application must be turned down. Provided the enforcing authority has not acted unreasonably in coming to its view on the matter, its refusal on this ground will not be easily challenged.[66]

Applications for Authorisations

9-073   Applications for authorisations are governed by the terms of Schedule 1 to the E.P.A. and The Environmental Protection (Applications, Appeals and Registers) Regulations 1991[67] – the "E.P. (A.A. & R.) Regulations".[68] The requirements impose on an applicant responsibility for providing full details of the intended process, a list of all substances which might cause harm if released into any environmental medium, and which will be used in connection with, or which will result from, the carrying on of that process, being primarily, but not exclusively, the substances listed in Schedules 4, 5 and 6 of the E.P. (P.P. & S.) Regulations, and a description of the techniques to be used for preventing or minimising release of such substances and for rendering harmless any of them which are released. Where a release is proposed, there must be an assessment of the environmental con-

---

[66] The fact that the individual circumstances of an applicant are to be taken into account in applying section 6(4) reinforces the view that in assessing whether a process feature entails "excessive cost" it is proper to consider how the cost impact would affect the relevant industry sector as a whole, but not also its effect on the individual applicant.

[67] S.I. 1991 No. 507, as amended by S.I. 1991 No. 836, para. 3.

[68] Application forms and guidance on how to complete them are available from HMIP.

sequences,[69] and proposals must be made for monitoring such release; additionally, the applicant must himself set out how he intends to establish that he will achieve the objectives set out in section 7(2), including in particular the achievement of BATNEEC, together with appropriate evidence that the applicant will be able to comply with the general BATNEEC condition of section 7(4).

An issue that is as yet unresolved is the legal consequence of a failure by an applicant to make a full disclosure (whether intentionally or otherwise) as to the nature of the process it is proposed to operate. Where the authorisation itself is exhaustive in its detail, then a failure to disclose a material feature will result in the authorisation simply not covering it. However, given that there is a positive obligation under regulation 2(1) to disclose an extensive list of process features, a failure to comply with these requirements may lead to the resulting author-isation being a nullity. That would, however be a very harsh outcome where an applicant has in good faith attempted to meet the require-ments of regulation 2(1), particularly as those requirements are expressed in very broad terms such that in some circumstances precisely what is required will be far from certain.[70]

9–074

The E.P. (A.A. & R.) Regulations require the enforcing authority to give notice of any application to a series of statutory consultees consisting of the Health & Safety Executive; the Minister of Agricul-ture Fisheries & Food; the Secretary of State for Wales or the Secretary of State for Scotland, depending on whether the process is to be carried on in England, Wales or Scotland respectively; the National Rivers Authority for all processes to be carried on in England or Wales which may result in any discharge to controlled waters of any substance;[71] the sewerage undertaker, or the relevant regional or

9–075

---

[69] The requirement for an assessment of the environmental consequences was commented on in para. 6.2 of the 1st edition of the IPC "Practical Guide", where it was stated that "a detailed environmental impact statement relating to each process option considered and for all substances involved would be excessive. What is required is an assessment of the main areas where the process is likely to impact on the environment (whether globally, regionally or locally) and, against that, a justification of the process/technique to be used. For example, where a particular local environmental issue or sensitivity exists, the operator would need to demonstrate that his proposed process/technique takes adequate account of it. The assessment should demonstrate that the chosen combination of process and abatement techni-ques meets the objective set out in s.7 of the Act". There is no equivalent comment in the 2nd 1993 edition. See also PPG 23 "Planning and Pollution Control" and paras. 3–107 to 3–120 above.

[70] e.g. the requirement under (e) to list "any other substances which might cause harm if released into any environmental medium". Provided the enforcing authority itself investigates the proposed process in depth, this issue will rarely be a problem, but an applicant cannot prudently rely on this being done.

[71] The discharge is not qualified in any way; specifically it is not limited to the substances listed in Sched. 5 to the E.P. (P.P. & S.) Regs.

islands council in Scotland, where there may be any discharge of any substance into a sewer vested in any of these bodies; the Nature Conservancy Council for England, Scottish Natural Heritage or the Countryside Council for Wales if there may be release of any substance which may affect a site of special scientific interest within the relevant Council's area; and where there may be a release of any substance into a harbour managed by a harbour authority, that harbour authority.

9–076   In the case of processes designated for local control the only statutory consultees are the HSE, and also English Nature, the Countryside Council for Wales or Scottish Natural Heritage, as the case may be, if there may be a release of substances into air which may affect a site of special scientific interest within that body's area. The statutory consultees have 28 days from the date on which they were given notice to make representations in relation to that application.

9–077   Additionally, an applicant is required to advertise the application for the proposed process in one or more local newspapers, giving the applicant's name and the address of the premises for the intended process, together with a brief description of the process. The advertisement must also specify where any register containing particulars of the application may be inspected and that this inspection is free of charge;[72] it must further explain that any person may make representations in writing to the enforcing authority within 28 days of the date of the advertisement, giving the authority's address. The advertisement must itself be published within a period of 28 days beginning 14 days after the date of the application itself. For obvious practical reasons, these advertisement requirements do not apply in relation to a process intended to be operated by means of mobile plant.

9–078   A fee is payable on the making of an application for authorisation. This is currently calculated by reference to the number of process "components", and is subject to a discount where the process concerned was previously registered pursuant to the Alkali, etc., Works Registration Act 1906. HMIP intend in due course to move to a system where the charges are based more directly on the time required to handle each individual application, once experience operating the system permits this.[73]

9–079   The amount of information to be provided by an applicant is extensive; since almost by definition he is likely to be using recently developed process technology if he is to apply BATNEEC, there is a

---

[72] As required by s.20(7)(b) copies of all relevant documentation are available on request, on payment of reasonable charges (subject only to confidentiality exclusions).

[73] The level of fees for applications and annual renewal of authorisations, and also for variations, is designed to achieve a full cost recovery (but no more) by HMIP. A guidance note on IPC fees and charges is issued free by HMIP.

substantial likelihood that some of this will be confidential, either to the applicant or to a third party from whom he has licensed it. Section 22(2) provides some relief against disclosure by providing that where information is furnished to an enforcing authority for the purposes of an application for an authorisation or for varying an authorisation, or for the purpose of complying with any authorisation condition or with a notice requiring information pursuant to section 19, the person furnishing the information may apply to have that information excluded from the register on the ground that it is commercially confidential[74] either to himself or another person. The provisions of section 22 are discussed more fully in paragraphs 9–140 to 9–155.

Pending determination by the authority as to whether the informa- **9–080**
tion concerned is confidential, the application procedure, including notification of statutory consultees and advertisements is held up. Even where it is accepted that a process feature is confidential and should not therefore be included in the public register, it will still be provided to the relevant sewerage undertaker or Scottish Regional or Islands Council where it relates to the release of any substance into a sewer; to the relevant Conservation Agency where the information relates to the release of any substance which may affect an SSSI; and also to a harbour authority if it relates to information about the release of any substance into a harbour managed by that authority. It will be incumbent on the enforcing authority to ensure in these circumstances that the information transmitted to any such statutory consultee is designated as being confidential, since otherwise under the Environmental Information Regulations 1992 those bodies will be bound to provide the information to any member of the public at any time on request.

The enforcing authority is required to determine applications for **9–081**
authorisation within four months, or such longer period as may be agreed.[75] However, since failure to determine an application within that period results in a deemed refusal, the applicant has considerable incentive to agree to an extension. By paragraph 5(3) of Schedule 1, the Secretary of State may vary the four month period by Order to such other period as he considers appropriate. Thus, where a confidentiality issue has been raised, the four month period is postponed to the day on which the issue is finally disposed of, and again may be extended to such longer period as the parties may agree.[76] This power has also been used to specify various different periods in relation to certain Part B processes involving the burning of waste oil, where the

---

[74] Defined in s.22(11).
[75] Sched. 1, para. 5(1).
[76] The Environmental Protection (Authorisation of Processes) (Determination Periods) Order 1991, (S.I. 1991 No. 513), Art. 2.

new periods vary from 14 days to 18 months, depending on the precise circumstances.[77]

Determination by the Secretary of State

9–082   By paragraph 3 of Schedule 1, the Secretary of State may require any particular application or class of applications to be transmitted to him for determination. Where he does this, he may set up a local inquiry or afford both the applicant and the relevant enforcing authority an opportunity to be heard by a person appointed by him, and he must do so if either of the parties so requests within 21 days from the day on which the applicant is informed that the Secretary of State has called in the application.[78] Where an application has been called in under this paragraph 3, the four month period for determination of the application does not apply, and no time limit is set.[79] Where a public inquiry is held in respect of a called in application, subsections (2) to (5) of section 250 of the Local Government Act 1972 apply to such an inquiry as they do to an inquiry held under subsection 250(1) of the 1972 Act. Likewise in Scotland, subsections (2) to (8) of section 210 of the Local Government (Scotland) Act 1973 apply to inquiries held in Scotland as they do to inquiries there under section 210(1). Having called in an application, the Secretary of State may give the enforcing authority such direction as he thinks fit on the grant of the application and the conditions to be imposed on any authorisation to be granted.[80]

Variation of Authorisations, Authorisation Conditions

9–083   An authorisation may be varied both by the enforcing authority under section 10 and by the holder under section 11. Further, there is a requirement under section 6(6) that the enforcing authority carry out a review of the conditions of every authorisation for which it is

---

[77] The Environmental Protection (Authorisation of Processes) (Determination Periods) Order 1991, Art. 3.
[78] E.P. (A.A. & R.) Regs., reg. 8.
[79] It seems most likely that this power will be exercised where a planning application relating to a prescribed process has been called in and it appears appropriate to handle both the planning consent and the process authorisation concurrently.
[80] Sched. 1, para. 3(5).

responsible at least once every four years.[81] Action may be taken by the enforcing authority of its own initiative, and it is positively required to do so if it appears to it that an authorisation requires conditions to be included that are different from the subsisting conditions. Additionally, by section 28(4) where a prescribed process involves the release of any substances into controlled waters, if the NRA considers that conditions of the IPC authorisation should be varied, and so notifies the enforcing authority, then the authority is obliged to vary the authorisation conditions as required by the NRA.

Variation in these circumstances is initiated by service of a variation **9–084** notice on the holder by the enforcing authority, which specifies the variations it has decided to make and stipulating a date or dates on which these are to take effect. Unless the variation notice is withdrawn, the variation takes effect on the date or dates specified. Although there is a right of appeal against a variation notice, it is specifically provided by section 15(9) that the bringing of the appeal shall not have the effect of suspending the operation of the notice.[82]

A variation notice must, in addition to specifying the variations, **9–085** require the holder, within such period as is specified, to notify the authority what action, if any, he proposes to take to comply with the authorisation as varied; further, the holder must pay such fee as is prescribed to be due in these circumstances. Where the authority is of the view that any action to be taken by the holder to comply with the variation notice will involve a substantial change in the manner in which the process is being carried on, it must notify the holder of this opinion. What amounts to a "substantial change" is defined in section 10(7) as meaning "a substantial change in the substances released from the process or in the amount or any other characteristic of any substance so released" — this definition is subject to any directions that the Secretary of State may give as to what does or does not constitute a substantial change in relation to processes generally, any description of process or any particular process.[83]

Where the authority does consider that there will be a substantial **9–086** change, the provisions of Part II of Schedule 1 apply. These are amplified by the E.P. (A.A. & R.) Regulations, and require advertisement and notice to statutory consultees in essentially the same manner as is required in the case of an original application for authorisation, with the same periods allowed for the making of representations.

---

[81] Or such other period as may be prescribed by regulations under s.6(7).
[82] Cf. revocation of an authorisation, where an appeal does have suspensory effect.
[83] See para. 9–018, and n.15 thereto.

Variations by the Holder

9–087   It is virtually inevitable that over time the operator of a process will wish to make changes to it. These may be of major significance, as where the capacity is substantially changed, or possibly where a different raw material is used. On other occasions they may be minor, and perhaps have no or negligible environmental consequences. Even so, such minor changes may make the process different from that as described in the initial authorisation application. In such cases, it is likely to be a question of fact and degree as to whether operating the process with the proposed minor change will fall outside the authorisation. Section 11 of the Act accordingly entitles the holder to request the enforcing authority to determine whether a proposed "relevant" change would involve a breach of any condition of the authorisation, and if it would not, whether the authority would be likely to vary any of the conditions as a result of the change. "Relevant change" is defined in section 11(11) as being a change in the manner of carrying on the process which is capable of altering the substances released from it or of affecting the amount or any other characteristic of any substance so released. The question is thus whether the change is *capable* of affecting releases, and not whether, as a practical matter such changes will in fact occur; further, a wholly beneficial change, reducing emissions, will be a relevant change, even though another that has no actual or potential effect on the impact of the process on the environment will not be. The IPC Practical Guide expresses the view that in practice all but the most minor adjustments to the process are likely to fall within the definition, including possibly changes in the method of storing feedstock on site, or even the amount stored.[84]

9–088   Section 11 also provides for a request to the authority as to whether, if making the change would involve a breach of the original authorisation, the authority would vary the conditions so as to allow the change to be made. Finally, the holder may request a determination as to whether a proposed change would be a "substantial change" as defined in section 10(7). Where the holder is in no doubt that a proposed relevant change would require a variation of the conditions applicable to him, then he may simply apply in the prescribed manner for a variation of those conditions.[85] Where a holder wishes to have a condition varied independently of any relevant change to his process, perhaps because he is at risk of breaching it marginally, and he considers that some relaxation could be justified, he may apply for this, using a simpler procedure, under section 11(5).

[84] IPC Practical Guide, para. 8.6.
[85] s.11(6).

In circumstances where the enforcing authority considers that a   9–089
proposed change would involve a "substantial change" that would
lead to or require the variation of the authorisation conditions, then
the authority must so notify the holder, also informing him of the
variations which the authority would be likely to consider making.
The holder, if he wishes to proceed, must thereupon apply, in
accordance with the procedures of the E.P. (A.A. & R.) Regulations for
a variation. This will result in paragraph 7 of Schedule 1 becoming
applicable requiring, as with variations representing substantial
change initiated by the enforcing authority, the same procedures for
advertisement, notification of statutory consultees and giving them
the prescribed twenty-eight days for making representations, as set
out in the E.P. (A.A. & R.) Regulations.

Revocation of Authorisations

The enforcing authority may, at any time, revoke an authorisation   9–090
by notice in writing to the holder.[86] Further, an authorisation may be
revoked where the authority has reason to believe that a prescribed
process covered by an authorisation has not in fact been carried on
either at all or at least for a period of 12 months. Revocation must be by
notice in writing, and the notice must specify a date from which the
revocation will take effect, this date being not less than 28 days from
when the original revocation notice was served.

Appeals

An appeals procedure is provided by section 15 and paragraphs 9 to   9–091
14 inclusive of the E.P. (A.A. & R.) Regulations. This procedure is
available exclusively to those listed in sections 15(1) and (2) and
section 22(5), namely:

—   a person who has been refused an authorisation;
—   a person who is aggrieved by conditions attached to an
    authorisation to him;
—   a person who has been refused a variation of an authorisation
    on an application made by him under section 11;

---

[86] s.12(1).

- a person whose authorisation has been revoked under section 12;
- a person on whom a variation notice, an enforcement notice or prohibition notice has been served; and
- a person claiming that certain information is commercially confidential following a determination that it is not.

9–092   It will be seen that this list of potential appellants does not include independent third parties; neither environmental action groups nor immediate neighbours who fear adverse consequences have themselves any right of appeal. Certain third parties have an opportunity to make representations where an appeal is brought by any of the persons identified in sections 15(1) and (2) (see paragraphs 9–101, 9–102), but otherwise their recourse is limited to the possibility of an application for judicial review, if they can establish standing, or otherwise through the enforcement of common law rights, if any.

9–093   Paragraph 10 of the E.P. (A.A. & R.) Regulations sets out a variety of time limits within which an appeal must be brought, subject always, however, to the right of the Secretary of State to allow a late notice of appeal in any particular case. An appeal against refusal of an authorisation or against the conditions attached, or against a refusal of a variation, must be brought within six months from the date of the decision appealed against. An appeal against revocation must be made before the date on which the revocation is stipulated to come into effect. An appeal against a variation notice, an enforcement notice or a prohibition notice must be made within two months of the date of the notice, while an appeal against a determination that information is not commercially confidential must be brought within 21 days from the date of notice of that determination.

9–094   Generally an appeal will not defer the taking effect of the decision appealed against. However, in the case of an appeal filed in due time against the revocation of an authorisation, or against a decision of an enforcing authority that information is not commercially confidential, the effects of the decision concerned will be suspended until final determination or withdrawal of the appeal.[87]

9–095   On determining an appeal, the Secretary of State is given wide powers under sections 15(6) and (7) not merely to confirm or to quash the decision or notice appealed against, but to add to or to modify its terms. Thus, on overturning a refusal to grant or to vary an authorisation, or the revocation of an authorisation, he may give directions as to the conditions to be attached to the authorisation

---

[87] ss.15(8), (9) and 22(5), (6).

concerned. Similarly, on affirming a variation, enforcement or prohibition notice, he may make such modifications as he may in the circumstances think fit.

An initial issue that any person aggrieved and entitled to appeal will need to consider is the proper legal categorisation of the potential subject for appeal, and specifically whether or not it is in fact a nullity, rather than invalid. Where a decision is a nullity, then it has of course no legal effect whatsoever, and there is nothing on which to take an appeal to the Secretary of State.[88] A decision will be a nullity if it fails to comply with fundamental requirements of the Act; this is not necessarily so however because it has been arrived at improperly, if validly served in accordance with the statute. The most difficult issue arises where a condition attached to a decision is invalid. If the invalid condition is severable, it alone is of no effect and the remainder of the decision may be implemented without it. If it is not severable the entire decision falls along with it. There have been a number of cases in relation to conditions attached to planning consents that address this issue—see in particular *Pyx Granite Co v. Minister of Housing and Local Government, per* Hodson L.J.;[89] *Fawcett Properties Limited v. Buckinghamshire County Council per* Roxburgh L.J.;[90] *Hall & Co Limited v. Shoreham-on-Sea Urban District Council and Another,* (C.A.);[91] *Allnatt London Properties v. Middlesex County Council;*[92] *Kingsway Investments (Kent) Limited v. Kent County Council;*[93] and *R. v. Hillingdon London Borough Council, ex p. Royco Homes.*[94]

9–096

The effect of these numerous cases appears to be that it is relatively rare, at least in the context of planning permissions, that an invalid condition will be accepted as being severable; where this is so, it is only where the condition is of comparatively small importance. As to when a condition may be held to be void, grounds for such a finding will include unreasonableness[95] or uncertainty.[96] Further, a condition may not require the payment of money except to the extent expressly authorised by statute.[97] A condition that is impossible to enforce (as

9–097

---

[88] See *Miller-Mead v. Minister of Housing and Local Government* (1963) 2 Q.B. 196.
[89] (1958) 1 Q.B. 554.
[90] (1958) 1 W.L.R. 1161.
[91] (1964) 1 All E.R. 1
[92] (1964) 62 L.G.R. 304.
[93] (C.A.) (1968) 112 S.J. 1008; (H.L.) (1970) 1 All E.R. 70.
[94] (1974) 2 All E.R. 643.
[95] *CEG Newbury District Council v. Secretary of State for the Environment (1981)* A.C. 578, H.L.; *Hall & Co Limited v. Shoreham-on-Sea Urban District Council (supra); Allnatt London Properties v. Middlesex County Council (supra); Bradford Metropolitan City Council v. Secretary of State for the Environment* (1987), 53 P. & C.R. 55, C.A.
[96] See, *e.g. Fawcett Properties Limited v. Buckinghamshire County Council* (1961) A.C. 636, *per* Lord Denning; *Alderson v. Secretary of State for the Environment* (1984) 270 E.G. 225, C.A.
[97] *Att.-Gen. v. Wilts United Dairies Limited* (1921), 37 T.L.R. 884.

opposed to one for which enforcement is merely difficult) will likewise be invalid.[98]

9–098   If the effect of an invalid condition relating to an authorisation may be to nullify the decision as a whole, it is clearly vital to the applicant to be able to establish his legal position, since if he proceeds with the proposed process relying on severability of that condition, he is at risk of being held eventually to have been operating a controlled process without an applicable authorisation.[99] Unless therefore he can be confident that a condition objected to is severable, the prudent course must be to apply by way of judicial review for a declaration that the concession concerned is void and severable, or, in the alternative, a mandatory order requiring the authority to determine the application in a valid manner. Though inevitably inconsistent with an application for judicial review, it may well be advisable to enter a concurrent appeal to the Secretary of State, conditional on the outcome of the judicial review, as a precaution against a finding that the condition in issue and the authorisation as a whole are valid, and seeking a more favourable determination from the Secretary of State on that condition.

9–099   An issue that may well arise in the course of an appeal and is likely on occasion to be contentious is the extent to which an appellant may alter his case during the appeal, without the whole procedure for advertisement and notification having to be repeated. In particular, where an appeal is against the conditions attached to the grant of an authorisation or against the refusal of an authorisation altogether, an appellant may propose changes to his process in order to meet objections to it raised in the evidence on appeal. As a practical matter, it may be appropriate to determine whether or not such amendments amount to a "substantial change" as defined in section 10(7). Nevertheless, what is a substantial change in any particular case allows for considerable discretion on the part of the person determining it, and in the context of an appeal there could be considerable pressure to hold that a change was not "substantial", when in other circumstances the decision might well be that it was.

---

[98] *Bromsgrove District Council v. Secretary of State for the Environment* (1988) J.P.L. 257. For further reading on this general topic, see *Planning Controls and Their Enforcement*, (6th ed.), A. J. Little, Shaw & Sons.

[99] For example, it is conceivable that an enforcing authority may seek to impose a condition on the operation of a controlled process that relates exclusively to questions of amenity or other planning considerations and not to the control of pollution through the application of BATNEEC. It is open to question, for instance, whether requiring that there be "no visible plume" from a stack (as is proposed in certain of the Chief Inspector's Guidance Notes) is a legitimate subject of a condition on a Part I process, unless in the particular case there is a relationship between the visibility of a plume and the polluting potential of the emissions.

Appeals Procedure

The procedure to be followed on an appeal is largely set out in the   **9–100**
E.P. (A.A. & R.) Regulations. It is modelled closely on what is now well
established for planning appeals, save that there are no provisions for
appealing against decisions of the Secretary of State.[1] An appellant
must give the Secretary of State written notice of the appeal and a
statement of the grounds of appeal, together with copies of any
relevant application and any relevant authorisation, any relevant
correspondence between the appellant and the enforcing authority,
and any decision or notice which is the subject matter of the appeal.
Additionally the appellant must state whether he wishes the appeal to
be in the form of a hearing or to be disposed of on the basis of written
representations. At the same time, the appellant must send the
enforcing authority a copy of his notice of appeal together with the
statements of the grounds of appeal and as to whether he wishes a
hearing or disposal of the appeal by written representations.

Regulation 11 prescribes the persons on whom the enforcing   **9–101**
authority must serve a copy of a notice of appeal; this is to be done
within 14 days of its receipt by the authority. In the case of an appeal
relating to the revocation or to an enforcement notice or prohibition
notice, the authority must give notice to any person who appears to it
likely to have a particular interest in the subject matter of the appeal. In
all other cases, notice must be given to any person who made
representations to the authority with respect to the grant or variation
of the authorisation, and also to all relevant statutory consultees.

Regulation 11(2) spells out the information that must be given to   **9–102**
these third parties. Essentially it covers brief details of the appeal,
together with a statement that representations with respect to the
appeal may be made in writing within a period of 21 days from the date

---

[1] It is open to question whether the planning system provides an appropriate model
for challenges to decisions many of which have little or no political content.
Irrespective of the suitability of that system even in the planning context, decisions
under the E.P.A. (and for that matter under the water legislation) essentially involve
questions as to the proper interpretation of the law—including E.C. law— and its
application to specific factual situations, albeit often highly technical ones. It is a
matter for regret that such decisions, which may have very large financial
consequences for those affected, should not be capable of challenge in an
independent forum on their merits. Provided a decision is not wholly unreasonable
and there is no evident error of law, challenge by way of judicial review merely goes
to the question as to whether the decision making procedure was improper, and an
unsatisfactory decision may often be incapable of being effectively challenged in this
way. For a discussion of this issue see "Are the Judiciary Environmentally Myopic?",
Woolf L.J., Journal of Environmental Law, Vol. 4, No.1. The lack of an independent
forum for determining appeals on their merits may also be a contravention of Art.
6(1) of the European Convention on Human Rights.

of the third party notice, and that if a hearing is to be held wholly or partly in public, a person who makes such representations, and any of the relevant statutory consultees will be notified of the date of the hearing. In circumstances where a notice of the appeal is to be sent to persons who made representations with respect to the original grant or variation of the authorisation, they are to be informed that those representations will be sent to the Secretary of State and to the appellant, and will be considered on the appeal unless, within 21 days of the date of the notice, the person who made the representations requests that they should be disregarded. Copies of such representations are, in any event, to be sent to the Secretary of State within 14 days of issuing the third party notices.

9–103   An appeal will be dealt with by way of written representations only if both the appellant and the enforcing authority agree; even where they do, the Secretary of State may himself decide that the subject matter of the appeal is such that it should proceed by way of public hearing, notwithstanding the wishes of the two parties.[2] There is however no time limit laid down for requesting a hearing, and indeed the IPC Practical Guide (1st ed.) stated:[3]

> "if at any stage the written procedure appears not be to making sufficient progress it is open to either party or the Secretary of State to suggest the case be taken forward through a hearing".

9–104   By section 15(3), the Secretary of State may refer any matter involved in the appeal to a person appointed by him for the purpose. This is analogous to the appointment of inspectors to hear planning appeals who do not themselves make any final determination of the appeal but merely collect evidence, draw conclusions from it, and make recommendations to the Secretary of State.[4] However, section 15(3) also entitles the Secretary of State to direct that the appeal or any matter involved in it shall be determined by a person appointed by him for the purpose, and in those circumstances, the powers and obligations of the Secretary of State in relation to the further conduct of the appeal and its determination are devolved on to that appointee.

9–105   If it appears appropriate to the Inspector to visit the proposed site for the process in the context of the appeal, he may do so, if practicable (but not necessarily) at a time convenient to the other parties also.

---

[2] s.15(5).

[3] In para. 9.14.

[4] From "A Note about Appeals under Section 15 (REV 1)", issued by the Appeals Branch of the DoE and the Welsh Office (revised April 1994) it appears that this procedure is likely to be the norm.

Written Representations Procedure

Where the written representations route is followed, the enforcing   **9–106**
authority must submit its representations, if any, to the Secretary of
State within 28 days after receiving from the appellant a statement of
the grounds of appeal and of his wish to have it disposed of by way of
written representations. The appellant is entitled to make further
representations by way of reply to those of the enforcing authority
within 17 days after the latter have been submitted. The enforcing
authority and the appellant must each give to the other copies of
representations they submit to the Secretary of State.[5] Where the
Secretary of State receives representations from any of the third
parties entitled to notice of the appeal, he sends them to the appellant
and to the enforcing authority, and they each have at least 14 days in
which to respond to these.[6]

By regulation 12(6) the Secretary of State may require additional   **9–107**
exchanges of representations between the parties; as a practical
matter, it seems improbable that additional representations volunteered by either party on their own initiative would be rejected,
provided that the other had sufficient time to deal with them prior to
the Secretary of State's determination. Also, the Secretary of State is
entitled to set longer time limits than those prescribed, and where
there is no likelihood of any adverse impact on the public interest, and
the appellant is not unfairly prejudiced, then it seems likely that
extensions of time will be available.

Hearings

Where a hearing is to be held, the appellant and the enforcing   **9–108**
authority are given at least 28 days notice (unless a shorter period is
agreed) of the date, time and place of the hearing. The hearing is

---

[5] In reg. 12(4).
[6] reg. 12(5). The "Note about Appeals under Section 15" says that the Secretary of State
will send to both main parties copies of "any material third party representations" that
he receives. Undoubtedly he (or his Inspector) must at least consider representations
from anyone, whether or not they have had any previous connection with the case.
Since, however, the weight that the Secretary of State may put on any particular
evidence contained in written representations cannot be readily ascertained by the
appellant in advance, and given also that there is no opportunity to cross-examine
anyone making written representations, an appellant who may be content to deal with
the enforcing authority itself on the basis of written representations, may well be ill-
advised to do so should there be any serious risk of adverse representations of any
significance by third parties.

publicised by an advertisement placed in the locality of the process not less than 21 days before the hearing is due to begin. In the case of mobile plant also, advertisements are to be made of any appeals relating to revocation of an authorisation, or any variation, enforcement or prohibition notice, and these are to be in the locality in which the mobile plant was being operated at the time the relevant notice was served. Those who have made representations in respect of the appeal and the relevant statutory consultees must also be served with a notice of the hearing—no time is prescribed for doing this. Where the Secretary of State varies the date for the hearing at some later stage, the advertisement and notification requirements must be repeated; he may also vary the time and place, but in that event he is only required to give such notice of the variation as he thinks reasonable.

9–109   The advertisement and notification procedures however only apply where a hearing is to be held wholly or partly in public. In the case of an appeal relating to a claim in respect of confidentiality over certain information, a public hearing would be clearly inappropriate, and by regulation 13(5) the advertisement and notification procedures are expressly disapplied in such a case.

9–110   The conduct of a hearing is left almost entirely to the discretion of the inspector in charge of it. The only persons positively entitled to be heard are the appellant, the enforcing authority and any of the relevant statutory consultees.[7] Nevertheless, the inspector may permit any other person to be heard, and by regulation 13(7) such permission shall not be unreasonably withheld. Following the conclusion of the hearing, the inspector must make a report in writing to the Secretary of State including his conclusions and recommendations or, as the case may be, his reasons for not making any recommendations.[8] The following paragraphs from Chapter 9 of the original IPC Practical Guide were stated in that Guide to constitute a code of practice important for the smooth and efficient running of the appeals system. They have been omitted from the second, 1993, edition, but remain useful as a guide to what can be expected:

"An important element of the hearing procedure is that the appeals inspector, who will be appointed by the Secretary of State, must be fully aware of the issues and arguments likely to be made at the hearing so that he can properly lead the discussion. It is therefore essential that within six weeks of an appeal being lodged or at least 21 days before the hearing, whichever is the first, the appellant and the enforcing authority provide a written statement to the Department containing full particulars of the

[7] reg. 13(6).
[8] Reg. 13(8).

case they will wish to make at the hearing. The statements will be passed to the appeals inspector to enable him to prepare for the hearing. At the same time as sending their statement to the Department, the appellant and the enforcing authority should send a copy to each other. The statement should give details of any documents which it is proposed to submit.

The procedure at a hearing will be left to the appeals inspector. He may hear the parties in whatever order he thinks most suitable for the clarification of the issues. He may for instance review the case based on the papers already provided and then outline what he considers to be the main issues and indicate those matters which require further explanation or clarification. This will not preclude the appellant or the enforcing authority from referring to other aspects which they consider to be relevant. The approach that will be encouraged will be one of informality. For example, hearings may often take the form of a round table discussion, rather than a formal presentation of evidence.

Although there will be no formal procedure rules applying to the hearing, the rules of natural justice will apply. The appeals inspector will thus be concerned to ensure that interested parties who wish to give evidence have a fair opportunity to have their say. However, it will be open to him to refuse to hear evidence which is irrelevant or repetitious and is therefore wasting time. It is up to the parties to decide whether or not they wish to be professionally represented, although this will not normally be necessary in order to gain an effective hearing.

The exchange of written views prior to the hearing should normally obviate the need for this material to be read out at the hearing. It is important that the parties should make very effort to avoid introducing at the hearing new material or documents not previously referred to, as this may necessitate adjournment of the hearing to a later date. If documents are made available at the hearing, the appeals inspector will ask or allow questions on those points on which he, or others taking part in the hearing, require further information or clarification. Generally, the appeals inspector will wish to ensure that participants have an adequate opportunity to ask questions, provided those questions are relevant and the discussion proceeds in an orderly manner. The appellants will be given the opportunity to make any final comments before the discussion is closed.

The appeals inspector may adjourn a hearing to such time, place and on such terms as he thinks fit.

The appeals inspector may want to visit the process and will, if possible, arrange a date when both parties can be present.

The hearing, or part of a hearing, shall take place in public unless the appeals inspector otherwise orders on the application of either party (normally this would be because he was satisfied that commercial confidentiality would otherwise be prejudicially affected.

Although the procedures outlined above will be appropriate for the majority of appeals, there may be some, notably those which are particularly complex or controversial, where a more formal procedure would be appropriate. In such cases the hearing would be more akin to a public inquiry, including any appropriate pre-hearing procedures. The relevant part of the Town and Country Planning (Inquiries Procedure) Rules (SI 1988/944)[9] may be applied by analogy to this type of appeal."

9–111   The aim is to be as informal and as flexible as practicable and to avoid rigid procedural rules corresponding to those for court hearings.[10]

9–112   Following determination of an appeal, the Secretary of State must notify the appellant of it, and where there has been a hearing, the appellant is to be given a copy of the Inspector's report. Notification of the determination is also to be sent to the enforcing authority and relevant statutory consultees and to everyone who made representations with regard to the appeal, including any making representations at any hearing; of these the enforcing authority and relevant statutory consultees (only) receive a copy of the Inspectors' report.

Transfer of Authorisations

9–113   An authorisation for the carrying on of any prescribed process may be transferred by the holder to a person who proposes to carry on the

---

[9] S.I. 1980 No. 1676 for Scotland.

[10] This laudable aim nevertheless can lead, as it does in planning inquiries, unless the inspector is very confident as to his powers (and correct), to unnecessary difficulties for the participants by the introduction of additional evidence and submissions at a late stage. Either this results in inadequate time to deal with them properly or else the whole hearing must be postponed, which is obviously also highly undesirable. A positive requirement on all participants to lodge statements of case, a prescribed (reasonable) period in advance, coupled with a discretion to shorten the advance period or to waive it altogether (but only where it would be manifestly unfair to that party not to allow it to make its representations), and to put these rules into statutory requirements would lead to a much more efficient disposal of public hearings without, it is suggested, any significant reduction in their value.

process in the holder's place.[11] The transferee must however notify the enforcing authority in writing of the transfer within 21 days from its date; failure to do this is an offence under section 23(1)(b).[12] By section 9(3) a transferred authorisation shall have effect as from the date of the transfer as if it had been granted to the transferee, subject to the same conditions as applied immediately prior to the transfer; this provision of section 15(3) is not conditional on the notification of the transfer having been made within the prescribed 21 days.

Somewhat surprisingly, transfers are treated as a purely private **9–114** matter between the parties. Even though under section 6(4) the enforcing authority must not grant an authorisation unless it considers that the applicant will be able to carry on the process so as to comply with the conditions that would be included in it, the transfer of an authorisation is not in any way conditional on the enforcing authority being satisfied in these respects in relation to the transferee. This may be contrasted with the transfer of waste management licences, whereby under section 40(4) a waste management authority shall only effect the transfer of a licence to a proposed transferee if satisfied that he is a fit and proper person. If necessary, the authority could of course serve a revocation or prohibition notice.

Staged Applications

In all but the simplest cases, the design of a new process is **9–115** developed in a series of steps with modifications being made in the course of the design process to accommodate changed requirements, such as may be desirable to meet a revised product specification or to accommodate a particular piece of apparatus or to comply with requirements of regulatory, including planning, authorities. Where the final designs may take months or even years to develop, it is normal to seek outline planning permission so as to establish whether or not it is possible to proceed with a particular development, without incurring the major additional expense of finalising all its detail. In the case of prescribed processes under Part I, there is no explicit reference to outline authorisations, and the requirements of Regulation 2(1) are framed on the assumption that all the detailed engineering work has already been undertaken. The operator may be able to pursue informal

[11] s.9(1).
[12] Punishable on summary conviction by a fine not exceeding the statutory maximum or, on indictment, by an unlimited fine and/or up to two years imprisonment.

discussions with the enforcing authority, but in the absence of the equivalent of outline planning consent, he cannot have any legal certainty that whatever may be said to him in the informal discussions will be maintained when his full application is submitted and reviewed. Regrettably, no explicit provision for outline authorisations is made in the E.P. (A.A. & R.) Regulations,[13] though HMIP have developed what is referred to as a "staged applications" procedure.

9–116   In the IPC Practical Guide it is asserted[14] that for new processes with normal characteristics, and for which Chief Inspector's Guidance exists, it will generally be appropriate for applications to be made when full designs have been drawn up, but prior to construction commencing. The presumption is that it will only be in the case of "some novel and complex new processes, with long lead times for design and construction"[15] that the staged applications procedure will be appropriate. This procedure is available only with HMIP's agreement, and where this is forthcoming HMIP and the applicant agree a plan for the application and supporting information to be submitted in a number of tranches. The operator will submit his application either at the point at which he selects a primary process or when the outline of the process design is completed, providing as much information as he reasonably can at that stage. The application will be treated in the normal way, save that the standard four month period will not apply. In particular, the public consultation process will apply at the initial application stage and again with each additional tranche of process design information. By this means, observations by third parties can be taken into account as the designing of the process proceeds, rather than at a stage when any significant variations will be very time consuming and expensive to accommodate. This procedure will nevertheless not accelerate any formal determination of the application by HMIP itself, which is likely in most cases to be deferred until actual commissioning of the plant. Where the staged application procedure is used, fees will be charged by reference to time and resources spent, and not on the standard basis.

[13] It has been asserted on behalf of the DoE that no basis is available in the E.P.A. itself to enable this, but it is submitted that the powers of the Secretary of State under Sched. 1 are fully broad enough. It may be observed that outline planning permissions are granted, in England and Wales, pursuant to the Town & Country Planning (Applications) Regulations 1988 and the Town & Country Planning General Development Order 1988, and in Scotland pursuant to the Town and Country Planning (General Development Procedure) (Scotland) Order 1992, even though there is no mention of outline planning permissions in the primary legislation under which these Regulations and Orders were made.
[14] In para. 4.4.
[15] See para. 4.6.

Concurrent Planning Applications

A further difficulty facing applicants for authorisation for a new   **9–117**
process is the inconsistency between the procedures required under
Part I of the E.P.A. and those required for obtaining planning
permission.[16] These procedures are operated by independent authorities, and compliance in full with the requirements of either are often
only possible, or commercially practicable, if the other procedure has
already been completed. Thus planning permission will often only be
granted after an environmental assessment has been made pursuant
to the Town & Country Planning (Assessment of Environmental
Effects) Regulations 1988 or the Environmental Assessment (Scotland)
Regulations 1988, as the case may be.[17] These Regulations provide that
an environmental statement on which the assessment is based may
include further information on a variety of matters, for example:

> "the main characteristics of the production processes proposed
> . . . the estimated type and quantity of expected residues and
> emissions (including pollutants of water, air or soil, noise,
> vibration, light, heat and radiation) resulting from the proposed
> development when in operation . . . and the likely significant
> direct and indirect effects on the environment of the development
> proposed which may result from, *inter alia*, the emission of
> pollutants, the creation of nuisances, and the elimination of
> waste".

Self-evidently, there can be no adequate environmental statement
covering such matters unless an authorisation has already been
applied for and the conditions to be attached to the grant of an
authorisation are known. Conversely, neither an applicant for authorisation nor the enforcing authorities will wish to spend the very
substantial resources necessary to achieve authorisation, if it is
uncertain whether the development will be allowed to proceed at all as
a result of possible objections on planning grounds. What is the
appropriate solution is beyond the scope of this work, but it must
entail some systematic prior consultation procedure in relation to
proposed prescribed processes with the relevant enforcing authority
in most, if not all, cases, and not merely in what are evidently regarded
as the exceptional circumstances that would justify a "staged application" procedure; a systematic procedure, moreover, that operates
closely in parallel with that of the planning system.

---

[16] This conflict is discussed in paras. 3–107 to 3–120, but merits a mention here also.
[17] S.I. 1988 Nos. 1199 and 1221; see chapter 4.

Investigation, Enforcement and Remediation

9–118   Inspectors, whether appointed in relation to IPC processes, processes subject to local control or appointed in Scotland by a river purification authority, have extensive powers to enter premises in connection with any prescribed process, and to investigate as necessary to establish the state of affairs on those premises. The powers extend to any premises on which a prescribed process is, or is believed on reasonable grounds to be carried on, and also to any other premises on which a prescribed process has at some time in the past been carried on (whether or not it was a prescribed process at that time), where there are reasonable grounds for believing that the condition of those premises is such as to give rise to a risk of serious pollution of the environment.[18] The powers, set out in section 17(3) include power:

(a)   to enter any premises where the inspector has reason to believe it is necessary for him to do so;

(b)   on entering any premises, to be accompanied by any other person duly authorised by the relevant enforcing authority, and also a constable if the Inspector thinks he may be faced with serious obstruction, and to take any equipment or materials required for any purpose for which entry is being undertaken;

(c)   to make such examination and investigation as is necessary;

(d)   to direct that premises or any part of them or anything in them shall be left undisturbed for as long as is necessary to make any necessary examination or investigation;

(e)   to take measurements and photographs and make recordings;

(f)   to take samples of any articles or substances in or on the premises and of the air, water or land in or in the vicinity of the premises;

(g)   to cause any article or substance found in or on any such premises to be dismantled or subjected to any process or test, if it appears to have caused or to be likely to cause pollution (but not so as to damage or destroy it unless necessary); before taking any action under this power, the Inspector must consult whoever he considers appropriate to establish what dangers, if any, there may be in doing what he proposes to do. Further, any exercise of this power on any premises must, if so requested by a person with responsibilities for

[18] s.17(2).

452

these premises, cause anything which is to be done to be done in the presence of that person;

(h) to take possession of any such article or substance as is mentioned in (g) and to keep it for examination and/or to dismantle or subject it to any process; it may also be kept to ensure it is not tampered with, and to ensure that it is available for use as evidence. On taking possession of any article or substance, the Inspector must leave a notice giving particulars of what he has taken sufficient to identify it, and where practicable, he should provide a sample of any substance taken, and give a portion of that sample to a responsible person at the premises suitably marked so as to identify it;

(i) to require any person who may have relevant information to answer such questions as the Inspector thinks fit to ask, and to sign a declaration of the truth of his answers. Such questioning may be in the absence of anyone else other than the person(s) nominated to be present by the interviewee and any other persons whom the Inspector may permit. Although, under section 17(8) no answer given by a person in these circumstances is admissible in evidence against that person (in any proceedings in England and Wales and in any criminal proceedings in Scotland) this qualification would appear to be limited to proceedings against that individual personally, and not against the company employing him or of which he may be a director; additionally of course while the answers themselves may not be admissible, they may lead the Inspector to discover other evidence against that individual that would be admissible in proceedings against him personally;

(j) to require the production of any records, and to inspect and take copies of them or any entry in them;

(k) to require any person to give him such facilities and assistance as he needs and which that person is in a position to provide, so far as necessary to enable the Inspector to exercise his powers;

(l) any other power as may be conferred by regulations.[19]

All the above powers are equally available in relation to any mobile plant rather than premises, in so far as they are applicable. **9–119**

In addition to the powers under section 17, by section 19(2) the Secretary of State or any enforcing authority may, by notice in writing, **9–120**

---

[19] No such regulations have as yet been issued.

require any person to furnish such information as the Secretary of State or the authority requires to be provided in such form and within such period following service of the notice as may be specified. This additional power is available to assist in the discharge of any of the functions of the Secretary or State and the enforcing authorities under Part I of the E.P.A. and, in the case of the Secretary of State, the power may be exercised for the purposes of the discharge of any obligations on the United Kingdom under the Rome Treaty or any other of the Community Treaties or any other international agreement relating to environmental protection.

9–121   Failure to comply with any requirement imposed under section 17 or by a notice under section 19(2), preventing any other person from appearing before an Inspector or from answering any question which an Inspector is entitled to ask under section 17(3), and intentionally obstructing an Inspector in the exercise or performance of his powers or duties, are all criminal offences for which a person guilty is liable on summary conviction to a fine not exceeding the statutory maximum.[20] In addition, it is an offence under section 23(1)(h) to make any statement knowing it to be false or misleading in any material particular, or recklessly to make a statement which is in fact false or misleading in any material particular where this statement is made in purported compliance with a requirement to furnish any information under Part I of the E.P.A.[21]

Prevention of Imminent Harm

9–122   If an Inspector finds, on any premises which he has power to enter, any article or substance that he has reasonable cause to believe is a cause of imminent danger of serious harm,[22] he may seize it or cause it to be rendered harmless, by destruction or otherwise as he sees fit.[23] Where practicable to do so, the Inspector must take a sample of any

---

[20] s.23. Failure to comply with a request for information under s.19(2) is also triable on indictment, when it may lead to an unlimited fine and/or to imprisonment for a term for up to two years.

[21] This offence under s.23(1)(h) is quite general in its application, and is not confined to the information that an Inspector may require to be given to him under s.17(3)(i) (see above). The protection afforded to anyone under s.17(8), whereby no answer given in those circumstances is admissible in evidence against that person, could lead to the anomalous situation that it might be impossible to bring evidence to establish the commission of the offence of knowingly giving false information, notwithstanding that this was in fact the case and the person concerned signed a declaration of the truth of his (false) answers.

[22] As defined in s.1(4).

[23] s.18(1).

article that forms a batch of similar articles or a sample of any substance seized, and give a portion of it to a responsible person at the premises concerned, suitably marked so as to identify it; this is to be done before the article or substance is rendered harmless. After he has taken the steps to render an article or substance harmless, the Inspector is required to prepare and sign a written report on his actions and provide a signed copy of the report to a responsible person at the premises concerned, and also to the owner of the article or substance, if different. Where the owner is different, but the Inspector, after making reasonable enquiries, cannot establish his name and address, the owner's copy of the notice may also be served by giving it to the responsible person at the premises who was given the first copy of the notice.

Enforcement and Prohibition Notices

An enforcement regime analogous to that available in respect of planning controls is provided by enforcement notices under section 13 and prohibition notices under section 14. An enforcement notice may be served by the relevant enforcing authority on a person carrying on a prescribed process under an authorisation both if there is in fact a contravention of any condition of the authorisation, and also if it appears that the process operator is likely to contravene any such condition. An enforcement notice must contain at least: **9–123**

(i)   a statement of the opinion of the authority as to the existence or likelihood of a contravention;
(ii) it must set out the matters that constitute the contravention or make it likely that one will arise;
(iii) it must specify the steps that need to be taken to remedy the situation; and
(iv) it must stipulate a period for taking those steps.

The Secretary of State has reserve powers under section 13(3) to give directions to enforcing authorities in any particular case as to the service and contents of an enforcement notice; the power is sufficiently widely drafted to enable the Secretary of State to direct an authority to refrain from issuing an enforcement notice, if he were minded to do so. **9–124**

A closely similar procedure applies to the service of prohibition notices under section 14. However whereas the service of enforcement notices is discretionary, a prohibition notice must be served where the enforcing authority is of the opinion that continuing to carry on an **9–125** authorised prescribed process, either at all or in any particular manner, involves an imminent risk of serious pollution of the environment. It is irrelevant whether or not there is also a contravention of a condition of the authorisation, and the notice may relate to any aspect of the process and not merely aspects regulated by the authorisation conditions.[24]

9–126   A prohibition notice must contain:

(i)   a statement as to the authority's opinion;

(ii) a statement as to the risk involved in the process;

(iii) details of the steps that must be taken to remove the risk and the period for doing this; and

(iv) a direction that the process authorisation shall (until withdrawal of the notice) cease to have effect, either wholly or to such extent as may be specified in the notice. If part of the process only is prohibited, conditions may be prescribed for carrying on the remainder.

9–127   Again, the Secretary of State has reserve powers to give enforcing authorities directions as to the service and contents of prohibition notices.

9–128   When an enforcing authority is satisfied that the steps required by a prohibition notice have in fact been taken, it must serve a further notice on the person originally served withdrawing the prohibition.

9–129   An appeal may be entered against any enforcement or prohibition notice by the person on whom it was served within two months beginning with the date of the notice.[25]

9–130   A failure to comply with, or any contravention of any requirement or prohibition imposed by, an enforcement notice or prohibition notice is an offence for which the defendant is liable on summary conviction to a fine not exceeding £20,000 and on indictment to an unlimited fine and/or imprisonment for up to two years. However, where an enforcing authority is of the opinion that proceedings for such an offence would be ineffectual against a person who has in fact failed to comply with the requirements of an enforcement notice or prohibition notice, the authority may take proceedings in the High Court or, in Scotland, in any court of competent jurisdiction, in order to secure compliance.[26] This provision gives statutory recognition to the decision in *Mayor and Commonalty of the City of London v. Bovis Construction*[27] that recourse to the civil courts to reinforce implementation of the criminal law is available in any appropriate case, and that

---

[24] s.14(2).
[25] E.P. (A.A. & R.) Regs., reg. 10(1)(d).
[26] s.24.
[27] [1989] J.P.L. 263.

it is not necessary to establish that further breaches of the criminal law are bound to occur in the absence of a civil injunction.

Where there is an obligation under an authorisation to maintain certain records as to the observation of some further condition of the authorisation, and an entry has not been made in those records that should have been made, that fact is admissible in itself as evidence that the further condition has not been complied with.[28]   **9–131**

Remediation

Under section 26(1) the court has further powers where a person has   **9–132** been convicted of operating a prescribed process either without an authorisation or in contravention of applicable conditions, or of non-compliance with an enforcement or prohibition notice. In such cases, it may, either instead of imposing any other penalty or in addition to it, make such order as the court sees fit against the defendant, requiring him to take such steps as may be specified to remedy such matters in respect of which he was convicted as it appears to be in his power to remedy. The court will ordinarily impose a time limit for taking these steps, extendable on application made before expiry of this time. For so long as the time continues to run, the person concerned is freed from any further liability to prosecution under section 23 in respect of the matters the subject of the order. This section does not appear to empower the court to order general remediation of all *consequences* of the offence, such as the clean-up of land contaminated as a result of a failure to comply with an authorisation unless (as seems unlikely) clean-up was a condition of the authorisation and the defendant was convicted for its breach. Where contamination has resulted, then the remediation may be effected under section 27 (or a variety of other statutory provisions).[29]

Related powers are available under section 27 to the Chief Inspector   **9–133** in England and Wales and a river purification authority in Scotland against a person who has operated a prescribed process (Part A or Part B) either without an authorisation or without complying with applicable conditions, or who has failed to comply with an enforcement or prohibition notice.[30] In such a case, the Chief Inspector or river purification authority may arrange for any reasonable steps to be

[28] s.25(2).
[29] See Chapter 24 below.
[30] In theory a conviction is not a pre-condition for the exercise of such powers, but merely commission of an offence. It is virtually inconceivable that the enforcing authority would in practice act before a conviction had been obtained, where its costs are capable of being recovered.

taken towards remedying any harm which it is possible to remedy, and also to recover the cost of taking those steps from the person convicted. The powers under this section may however not be exercised without the written approval of the Secretary of State. Further, where any steps to be taken are on or will affect land in the occupation of anyone other than the person on whose land the prescribed process is carried on, the permission of that other person must also be obtained.

Registers

9–134   Unless protected for reasons of national security or commercial confidence, information regarding prescribed processes, the subject of applications for authorisation and of granted authorisations, is made publicly available in a series of registers held by the various enforcing authorities. In addition to each local enforcing authority maintaining a register of all Part B processes for which it is directly responsible, its register must also contain prescribed particulars of any Part A process carried on in its area.[31] Similarly in Scotland, each register held by a river purification authority is required to contain prescribed particulars of any process for which the Chief Inspector for Scotland is responsible carried out in that authority's area; however, in Scotland the Chief Inspector's register must also contain prescribed particulars of information held on the registers of the various river purification authorities.[32]

9–135   There is a general duty on each enforcing authority to make the registers it maintains available at all reasonable times for inspection by the public free of charge, and further to allow members of the public to obtain copies of entries on payment of reasonable charges.[33]

9–136   What is to be contained in the registers is prescribed by regulation 15 of the E.P. (A.A. & R.) Regulations, made pursuant to section 20(1). Broadly, this information extends across all applications for authorisations and granted authorisations and their enforcement, together with details of the relevant processes and monitoring information relating to them. More specifically, regulation 15 requires registers to contain:

(a) particulars of applications for authorisations, requests for further information and responses to such requests;

(b) representations made by statutory consultees in relation to initial applications and variations;

[31] s.20(2).
[32] s.20(3).
[33] s.20(7).

458

(c) particulars of all authorisations granted by the authority;

(d) particulars of variation, enforcement or prohibition notices issued by the authority, together with withdrawals of prohibition notices, and particulars of any revocation of any authorisation;

(e) particulars of any variation by the authority or applied for by a holder, wherever this entails a "substantial change";

(f) notices of appeal, together with decisions appealed against, statements of grounds and relevant correspondence, also the determination of appeals and any report of an inspector hearing an appeal;

(g) details of any convictions relating to the carrying on of the prescribed process under the control of the authority;

(h) monitoring information relating to the carrying on of a prescribed process under the control of the authority, whether this is obtained by the authority itself or furnished to it by the holder; in addition, where monitoring information is excluded from the register for reasons of commercial confidentiality, the authority must nevertheless, on the basis of monitoring information it has itself generated or received, include a statement as to whether or not there has been compliance with any relevant condition of the authorisation;

(i) any report assessing the environmental consequences of carrying on a prescribed process that is under the control of the authority;

(j) all particulars of any direction given to the authority by the Secretary of State under any provision of Part I of the E.P.A., other than a direction relating to the exclusion of information on grounds of national security.

To avoid the register being clogged up with out of date information, monitoring information need not be maintained for more than four years, and information that has been superseded by later information need not be kept for more than four years after that later information has itself been entered on the register. **9–137**

National Security

Section 21 provides broadly that no information shall be included in a register if and for so long as, in the opinion of the Secretary of State, the inclusion in the register of that information, or information of that description, would be contrary to the interests of national security. To that end, the Secretary of State may make directions to enforcing authorities specifying information which must either be excluded **9–138** from their registers or which must be referred to the Secretary of State for his consideration. Enforcing authorities must notify the Secretary of State of any information excluded from their registers in pursuance of such directions.

9–139   Where any person considers that information might be properly excluded from registers on grounds of national security, he may give notice to the Secretary of State specifying the information and indicating its apparent nature. Where he does this, he is to notify the enforcing authority of that fact, and unless and until the Secretary of State has otherwise determined, no information notified to the Secretary of State shall be included in any register.

Commercial Confidentiality

9–140   If information which will otherwise become publicly available on a register is commercially confidential, then it may be excluded from the register under section 22. This provides firstly, as a general exclusion, that no information relating to the affairs of any individual or business shall be included in a register without the consent of that individual or the person for the time being carrying on that business if and for so long as it is, in relation to him, commercially confidential, and provided it is not required to be included as a result of direction by the Secretary of State under section 22(7).[34] Nevertheless it is only treated as confidential if it is determined to be so by the enforcing authority, or on appeal, by the Secretary of State.

9–141   This subsection is thus limited to information that that individual or other person has a direct interest in keeping confidential; it does not appear therefore to extend to confidential information the property of a third party. Having regard to the different scope of section 22(2) discussed below, it is likely that the expression "information relating to the affairs of any individual or business" is intended to be directed to personal and business information, for example the identity of suppliers and customers, prices paid and charged, and the terms of technology licences, rather than to proprietary technology itself.

9–142   By contrast section 22(2) applies also to information that is commercially confidential to third parties. Where information is furnished to an enforcing authority for the purpose of an application for authorisation or for the variation of an authorisation, for the purpose of complying with any condition of an authorisation, e.g. the substances contained in a discharge, or for the purpose of complying with a notice under section 19(2),[35] the person furnishing the information may

---

[34] s.22(1).
[35] See para. 9–120.

apply under section 22(2) to the authority to have the information excluded from the register on the ground that it is commercially confidential, whether as regards himself or as regards someone else. The authority must then determine whether that information is or is not commercially confidential within fourteen days[36] from the date of applying to have the information excluded — failure to make a determination within the fourteen days results in the information being deemed to be commercially confidential. This deemed result only applies to determinations required to be made under this subsection 22(2) and not to those under 22(1) or 22(4) (see below).

Enforcing authorities may also acquire information that may be **9–143** commercially confidential in other ways, for example, as a result of an inspector entering premises under the powers available to him under section 17. Where an authority obtains any information in pursuance of any provision of Part I of the E.P.A. other than the circumstances set out in the previous paragraph, and it also appears to that authority that any such information might be commercially confidential — which could of course be as a result of a representation by the occupier of the premises concerned or the possessor of papers inspected — it must give to the person to whom or to whose business it relates notice that the information is required to be included in the register unless excluded for reasons of commercial confidentiality.[37] It must then give him a reasonable opportunity of objecting to its inclusion on that ground, and of making representations to justify his objection. It must take into account any representations that are made as a result, and determine whether the information concerned is or is not commercially confidential. In this case no specific time limit is prescribed.

Where in any of the circumstances described the authority does not **9–144** accept that the information is commercially confidential, it gives notice to the person concerned and it is not to put the information on the register until 21 days after the person has been notified. During that time an appeal may be lodged to the Secretary of State against the decision. Where an appeal is brought, the information must continue to be kept confidential pending the final determination or withdrawal of the appeal. In the event of an appeal, the procedures described above in paragraphs 9–100 to 9–102, apply so far as relevant, save that in the case of a confidentiality claim the requirement under section 15(4) to advertise the appeal does not apply. As normal, the appeal may be by way of a hearing or proceed on the basis of written

---

[36] Or such other period as the Secretary of State considers appropriate and substitutes for the 14 days by Order — s.22(10).
[37] s.22(4).

representations; if by a hearing, section 15(5) permits the person taking the hearing to hold it in whole or in part in private.

9–145   Information is to be regarded as commercially confidential in relation to any individual or person, for the purposes of section 22, if its being contained in a register would prejudice, to an unreasonable degree, the commercial interests of that individual or person.[38] This might be taken as being no more than an attempt at a statutory definition of all commercially confidential information, given the absence of any codified law on this topic.[39] However, the use of the expression "to an unreasonable degree" indicates a balancing of issues that arises in the case law on what is protectable by an action for breach of confidence only in relation to information that may properly be used and disclosed by ex-employees. Outside this area (which may in any event properly be regarded as an aspect of the special "public interest" exception), at least in relation to proprietary information not subject to any claims for disclosure in the public interest, it is a question of fact, and not of degree, as to whether information is entitled to the cloak of confidentiality.[40] The significance of any information may well be relevant to the appropriate remedy for breach of confidence, occasioned by its improper use or disclosure, but that is a quite separate issue.

9–146   It is relevant to note that by section 22(7) the Secretary of State can give enforcing authorities directions as to specified information or descriptions of information which is required to be included in registers in the public interest, notwithstanding that that information may be commercially confidential.[41] From this it is clear that registers may contain what was previously proprietary confidential information, so that it is quite consistent with this to view the definition of section 22(11) as not seeking to define confidential information for all purposes but merely to set out the balancing exercise necessary to

---

[38] s.22(11).

[39] Despite the publication by the Law Commission of its Working Paper No. 58 in 1974, and a full report "Breach of Confidence" (No. 110, Cmnd. 8388) including draft legislation in 1981.

[40] Cases on what may be disclosed in the public interest traditionally start from the basis that the information concerned is prima facie protectable: "public interest" issues are generally raised by way of a defence to a claim of improper use or disclosure. See *Initial Services Limited v. Putterill* (1968) 1 Q.B. 396; *R. v. Licensing Authority ex p. Smith Kline & French Laboratories Limited*, H.L. (1990) 1 A.C. 64; (1989) 1 F.S.R. 440. It may be that there is a trend towards the courts being asked to strike a balance in all "public interest" cases between the conflicting interests for and against disclosure or use, possibly even with a burden of proof resting on the party seeking to restrain it. See paras. 4.36 to 4.53 of the Law Commission Report (*supra*). Nevertheless the law is far from being so clear cut as to warrant any assumption that the definition in section 22(11) properly represents what should generally be regarded as protectable confidential information.

[41] To date no such directions have been given.

determine what may properly be excluded from the registers. Accordingly, although section 22(11) defines "confidential information" in a single phrase, in practice there are likely to be two stages in any application of this provision. Firstly, is the information properly protectable at all under the general law on breach of confidence since, if it is not, no legitimate objection can be made to its inclusion in a public register?[42] Secondly, if it is protectable under the general law, would the degree of prejudice caused to the commercial interests of the person concerned by disclosure in a public register pursuant to section 20 be "unreasonable"?

The first issue concerns essentially what sort of information is capable of protection by an action for breach of confidence, and for present purposes, this is likely to turn entirely on whether or not the information can properly be regarded as "secret" or whether it is in the public domain. It is clear law that where information has been deliberately disclosed by its owner, for example in the course of applying for patent protection, then no subsequent claim by him that it be protected as a trade secret can succeed.[43] It is however important to distinguish between what is contained in a single publication or in related publications (as where one cross-refers to the other), and what may be inferred or otherwise gathered, possibly by means of considerable assiduity, from what is in the public domain. Consequently, information which is only obtainable from something that is available in the public domain (typically a manufactured product) by the expenditure of a significant element of labour, skill or money will be protectable.[44] Similarly, even though all the information is potentially available from matter in the public domain, if this is distributed over a large variety of disclosures such that substantial effort would be needed for any third party to discover the sources and to put it all together, the courts protect the result.[45] Additionally, the fact that some, relatively few, people in the world are aware of the information, does not necessarily mean that it is incapable of being protected against disclosure to everyone else.[46]

9–147

In considering a claim that information is confidential, it is essential to analyse with precision wherein the secret (if any) lies. By way of

9–148

---

[42] This discussion is of course confined to commercial information; additional considerations might possibly apply in relation to personal information raising questions of privacy.

[43] *O. Mustad & Son v. Dosen* (1963) R.P.C. 41; (1964) 1 W.L.R. 109 — the decision dates from 1928.

[44] *Saltman Engineering Co. Ltd v. Campbell Engineering Co. Ltd* (1948) 65 R.P.C. 203; (1963) 3 All E.R. 413.

[45] *Schering Chemicals Limited v. Falkman Limited* (1981) 2 W.L.R. 848.

[46] *Vulcan Detinning Co. v. Assam* (1918) 185 N.Y. App. Div. 399, cited in the Law Commission Report (*supra*) at para. 4.20.

example, the process to be operated at a particular industrial facility may in itself be a known type of process. Nevertheless, the particular manner of operating that process, *e.g.* the precise raw materials and process parameters may well be unique to that facility. It does not follow from the fact that particular details might not be surprising to a third party competitor, that they would not be of interest and of commercial value to him. Depending on the circumstances therefore, obviousness in the sense appropriate to considerations of patent validity is not necessarily relevant to protectability of a secret. In principle also, the fact that one known process is being operated, rather than any other known processes or possibly some unknown one, is likewise capable of being protectable information. Since in such cases the value to a competitor of learning the secret, and the corresponding prejudice to the owner of the information if he does may both be quite modest, it is then appropriate to consider the second limb, as to whether disclosure on a register would cause unreasonable prejudice.

9–149   As to this, any public disclosure at all of commercially confidential information will, almost inevitably, prejudice the commercial interests of its owner to some degree. Such a disclosure must be unreasonable if in fact it does not relate to and further the objectives of Part I of the E.P.A. (including the enforcement of regulatory controls). Consequently, what is reasonable in this context must be judged by reference to the value to the public of having access to that information for the purpose of assessing the environmental consequences of the activities concerned or (though a conflict in this area seems less likely) assessing the conduct of the proprietor of the information in relation to his obligations under Part I of the E.P.A. In practice, the words "to an unreasonable degree" will be liable to place on the owner of information asserted to be confidential (or on the person furnishing it) the burden of proof that disclosure would prejudice him unreasonably since, for the reasons given, a mere assertion that the information is confidential will not suffice.

9–150   In a "Note about Applying for Commercial Confidentiality, and Appeals under section 22",[47] it is stated that the guiding principle is that information on processes controlled under Part I of the E.P.A. should be freely available. It is for an operator who wishes information to be withheld to show that its disclosure would negate or significantly diminish a commercial advantage. It will not be sufficient merely to claim that disclosure might damage the operator's reputation or, with a view to keeping back all process details, simply to say that its raw material is a trade secret. In certain cases it may be possible for an

---

[47] DoE and W.O., April 1994, REV 1.

operator to establish with the enforcing authority that the sensitive information need not be presented in the application for authorisation or variation, where it is not relevant to the emissions from the process or otherwise to the matters that must be taken into account in determining the application.

The first two cases in which these provisions were taken to appeal involved claims for confidentiality by each of PowerGen and by National Power. In the case of PowerGen, the Secretary of State dismissed its appeal, rejecting its claim that its forecast schedules of emissions of SO_x and NO_x for a year ahead should be kept confidential until the end of that year. The claim was made on the ground that knowledge of these forecasts would prove useful to a competitor or to a fuel supplier. At a hearing, the inspector recommended that these should be kept confidential, but the Secretary of State did not accept his recommendation. Having regard to the significance of the information to the application and authorisation process, and of its consequent importance to the public, he considered that its publication would not be prejudicial to an unreasonable degree to PowerGen's commercial interests. The National Power appeal was, on the other hand, successful. Consequently, it is not known exactly what the information related to, but it is believed to have related to types and/or quantities of fuel to be acquired. In this case, the Secretary of State determined that the information was not directly relevant to determination of the relevant applications for authorisation themselves or to any of the conditions which were likely to be imposed in the authorisations. Consequently, it was not necessary for the public to have access to the information to enable it to comment effectively on the applications. The information was provided "in excess of HMIP's normal requirements" and (in the opinion of the Secretary of State) was "not of the type intended by the legislation to be made available to the public". In view of the lack of relevance of the information for the purposes of IPC, it was determined that any prejudice to the company's commercial interests would in the circumstances be unreasonable.

9–151

It is relevant also to compare the definition under section 22(11) of what is to be regarded as commercially confidential with the provisions of Directive 90/313 on the Freedom of Access to Information on the Environment.[48] This provides in Article 3(2) that Member States may provide for a request for information relating to the environment to be refused where it affects, inter alia "commercial and industrial confidentiality, including intellectual property". As this is purely permissive and not mandatory, it does not create any necessary

9–152

[48] [1990] O.J. L158. See chapter 20.

limitation on the practical application of the commercial confidentiality provisions of the E.P.A. Nevertheless, in view of the manifest desirability of having substantially equal treatment of confidential information by the regulatory authorities throughout the EC, if and to the extent that it appears that other Member States give a wider protection to confidential information, then this would be a proper factor to take into consideration in determining whether disclosure would cause prejudice that was unreasonable.

9–153   Where information is treated as commercially confidential and consequently excluded from a register, this exclusion will continue only for four years beginning with the date of the determination that it was commercially confidential.[49] The person who furnished the information may nevertheless apply to the authority concerned for the information to remain excluded on the ground that it is still commercially confidential. No time is prescribed for making such an application, though it must necessarily be made within the four years if the confidentiality is not to be put at risk. The Act makes no provision for such an application to be made by anyone other than the person who furnished the information originally; this could create significant difficulties where the ownership of the information has changed in the meantime, for example, where a business has been purchased or, as a result of the restructuring of a company, the relevant technology is now exploited by some other legal entity, with the original one possibly having ceased to exist.

9–154   Where information was not originally furnished in the circumstances set out in section 22(2)[50] then, it is submitted, it is open to the authority concerned to exercise its powers under section 22(4), either on its own initiative or on the representation of any person interested — there is no reason to restrict the exercise of these powers to the first occasion on which the authority acquires the information. In the circumstances of section 22(2), however, there is no explicit grant of such powers. Nevertheless, justice could be achieved by equating "the person who furnished [the information]" with both the applicant for the authorisation and also the subsequent holder of the authorisation, and extending this to any transferee of the authorisation, though it has to be admitted that such an interpretation is straining the language of the statute. This restriction on who may apply for renewal of the exclusion could also severely prejudice a third party proprietor of technology who had licensed the operator of an authorised process in circumstances where the operator licensee had gone out of business.

---

[49] s.22(8).

[50] *i.e.* in applying for authorisation or variation, or complying with any condition or with a s.19(2) notice.

While this could and should result in revocation of the authorisation, it might well be that this step would not in fact be taken until well after expiry of the four year period, and in the meantime the information would be liable to have become publicly disclosed.

Where an application is properly made under section 22(8) for **9–155** information to remain excluded from the register, the authority must again determine whether or not the information is to be regarded as commercially confidential. If it determines that the information is not confidential, the provisions of section 22(5) apply as they do where the authority has acquired information that it considers might be commercially confidential. Thus it must notify the person who furnished the information or the person to whom or to whose business the information relates as to its determination, and not enter the information on the register for the next 21 days, during which time that person may appeal against the decision, the appeal having suspensory effect.

Chapter 10

AIR POLLUTION

National controls on air pollution have been in existence since the   **10–001**
Alkali Act of 1863. That Act, which was designed to control acidic
emissions (essentially hydrochloric acid) from caustic soda works, and
the succeeding Alkali Acts, formed the basis of air pollution control in
the United Kingdom up to the present day. The original Alkali Act
1863 set specific limits on the emissions from the works controlled, by
requiring *inter alia* that not more than 5 per cent of the offensive
emissions from the processes should be emitted to the atmosphere,
and the remainder therefore having to be arrested.[1] The Act was
replaced by the Alkali, Act 1874 which introduced for the first time the
concept of "Best Practicable Means" to prevent the escape of noxious
substances, a concept that underlay the regulatory controls on air
emissions up to the E.P.A. 1990, and indeed still continues to be the
basis of the technical defence available in actions in respect of
statutory nuisances under Part III of the E.P.A.[1A]

The Alkali, etc., Works Regulation Act 1906 consolidated all earlier   **10–002**
legislation. By a series of statutory instruments, its scope was
extended to cover an increasing variety of industrial processes, and
the administrative arrangements for exercising the controls were also
extended and consolidated. This regulatory system is however now
being phased out in Great Britain as the new controls introduced by
Part I of the E.P.A. in respect of both Part A and Part B processes, as
defined in the E.P.A. (P.P. & S.) Regulations 1990, are brought into
effect. A description of the older regulatory scheme is nevertheless
necessary, since it will continue to apply to certain industries
operating "existing processes".[2] In the case of Northern Ireland, the
old control regime still applies in full, since Part I of the E.P.A. does not
apply to it at all apart from sections 3(5) to (8) empowering the

---

[1] See para. 1–047 and n. 86 thereto.
[1A] See Chapter 23.
[2] See paras. 9–014 to 9–016 and Table 9/I.

Secretary of State to make plans in respect of emissions into the environment in all or any part of the United Kingdom.[3]

10–003   Other EC legislation and international conventions have also provided the basis for much recent development in the field of air pollution control. These will be dealt with more fully in the following sections of this chapter, but particularly important among these are the directives setting air quality standards in respect of sulphur dioxide and smoke (Directive 80/779), nitrogen dioxide (Directive 85/203), lead in air (Directive 82/884), and low level ozone (Directive 92/72), all of which are of general application across the country. The UK is also party to the UN-ECE NO_x protocol which requires the parties to it to reduce their NO_x emissions progressively. Thus the UK is required to reduce its total NO_x emissions by 1994 to 1987 levels, and to make further reductions thereafter. Proposals for an EC framework directive on air quality assessment and management have been published,[3A] which would be given effect through a series of daughter directives covering both the pollutants the subject of the existing directives and also additional substances, such as carbon monoxide, benzene and polyaromatic hydrocarbons, cadmium, arsenic, nickel and fluoride.

10–004   The Community and the Member States having accepted the objective of stabilising carbon dioxide emissions in the Community as a whole at 1990 levels by the year 2000, Council Decision 93/389[4] requires each of the Member States to "devise, publish and implement national programmes for limiting their anthropogenic emissions of CO_2".[5] These programmes, which are to be periodically updated, must include, at least from the first updating, inventories of these CO_2 emissions by sources and of their removal by sinks, details of national policies and measures contributing to limiting the emissions, measures being taken or envisaged to implement relevant Community legislation and policies, and an assessment of the economic impact of the constituent elements of the national programme. There is to be annual reporting to the Commission by each Member State of its CO_2 emissions and CO_2 removal by sinks. Additionally, Member States are to provide the Commission with information on emissions of greenhouse gases other than those controlled by the Montreal protocol (excluding therefore CFCs, halons, etc.), and a description of measures

---

[3] A statutory plan having been made for the purpose of implementing the EC Large Combustion Plants Directive 88/609, [1988] O.J. L336, issued as a daughter directive to the Industrial Plants Directive 84/360, [1984] O.J. L188.

[3A] COM (94) 109 final, [1994] O.J. C 126. The target date for bringing the framework directive into force is July 31, 1996, which is probably optimistic.

[4] [1993] O.J. L167.

[5] Art. 2.

being taken or envisaged for limiting emissions of these other greenhouse gases. National programmes for the limitation of these gases are to be established as policies in the light of developments decided pursuant to the United Nations Framework Convention on Climate Change.[6] The Council Decision, dated June 24, 1993, took immediate effect; nevertheless, no deadlines have been set for compliance with the various obligations it imposes.

Emissions of volatile organic compounds (VOCs) are the subject of a third protocol to the UN-ECE convention, which was laid open for signature in November 1991. It will oblige parties to it to secure by 1999 a 30 per cent reduction in their VOC emissions from their 1988 levels. In addition, new sources of VOCs (notably vehicles) will have to comply with emission standards based on control technologies referred to in the protocol, and measures will have to be applied to products containing solvents so as to promote those with low VOC content or none. **10–005**

Directives in respect of air emissions from municipal waste incinerators (89/369 and 89/429) together with a proposed Directive relating to emissions from hazardous waste incinerators will have a profound impact on the waste disposal industry, given that most existing incinerators are not in compliance with the prescribed standards, and many can only be brought into compliance, if at all, by highly expensive up-grading. The motor manufacturing industry must ensure its vehicles conform to the now numerous Directives on vehicle emissions, detailed in paragraphs 10–100 to 10–102. Likewise, the oil industry is directly affected by the Directives on sulphur content of petrol and diesel fuel, and the lead content of petrol. Last but not least, protection of the ozone layer has been the subject of a series of EC Regulations in respect of the production and marketing of CFCs and halons, first implementing and then accelerating the phase-out programme of the Montreal Protocol. **10–006**

As will be seen, the control of air pollution is brought about by attacking it from a number of different angles. Thus, fuels, whether for vehicles or solid fuel in areas controlled by the Clean Air Act 1993, may themselves be subject to specific control, hence indirectly reducing the overall polluting emissions that they give rise to. Secondly, specific equipment may be prescribed either directly as in the case of the Clean Air Act, or by reference to the polluting emissions they give rise to, as in the case of motor vehicles. Thirdly, polluting industrial processes within Part I of the E.P.A. are subject to prior authorisation, which will be given on conditions that will limit polluting emissions either directly or by reference to the use of prescribed technology and/or **10–007**

---

[6] Art. 7.

equipment. Other processes are also capable of being controlled both by local authorities and by individuals, under the statutory nuisance provisions of Part III of the E.P.A., discussed in chapter 23.[7] Finally, the binding air quality standards in respect of smoke, sulphur dioxide, nitrogen dioxide, lead and ozone oblige the regulatory authorities to use the various controls available to them if they are to ensure that these quality standards are not breached.

10–008 Responsibility for implementing air pollution controls has been historically divided between a central body, deriving from the original Alkali Inspectorate, in relation to the more polluting industries, and local authorities.[8] The central body has undergone a series of administrative transformations. The Alkali Inspectorate was set up to administer the Alkali Works Regulation Acts, and continued to do so until it was replaced by the Industrial Air Pollution Inspectorate (in England and Wales) and the Industrial Pollution Inspectorate (in Scotland). The controls were exercised under the aegis of the Health & Safety Executive when that was established under the Health & Safety at Work, etc., Act 1974, but in 1986 this responsibility was transferred to the Department of the Environment. When HMIP/HMIPI were set up these Inspectorates became components of them.

10–009 A further development putting pressure on the government to reduce acidic emissions is the concept of "critical loads" developed within the UN-ECE as a means of categorising the sensitivity of eco-systems to acid pollutants. By comparing the various critical load levels around the country with the known deposition rates from monitoring statistics, it becomes immediately apparent that deposition is already excessive in many parts of the United Kingdom, and this in itself gives added impetus to remedial action. The parties to the UN-ECE convention are now also working on a protocol on the control of sulphur dioxide emissions, likely to be ready for signature in late 1993, as well as a second protocol on NO_x.[9]

---

[7] A Part I process may also be proceeded against as being a statutory nuisance with the leave of the Secretary of State.

[8] For a history of these controls see Eric Ashby and Mary Anderson *The Politics of Clean Air*, Clarendon Press, Oxford, 1981.

[9] See the report to the DoE by the UK Critical Loads Advisory Group 'Critical and Target Loads Maps for Freshwaters in Great Britain', May 1992; the description of the earlier mapping work in "Acid Rain - Critical and Target Loads Maps for the United Kingdom", issued by the DoE in May 1991; also "Critical Loads of Acidity in the UK", DoE, March 1994.

Air Quality Standards and Monitoring

As already mentioned, EC Directives require the UK to maintain air **10–010** quality standards in respect of smoke, sulphur dioxide, nitrogen dioxide, lead and ozone. These are as follows:

80/779 ([1980] O.J. L229)—Sulphur Dioxide, Suspended Particulates

This sets out limit values and guide values for sulphur dioxide and **10–011** suspended particulates. The Directive's controls are so framed that the more there is of one of these pollutants the less is permitted of the other.[10]

The Directive imposes three separate sets of limits, namely on: **10–012**

    (i) the median of daily values throughout any one year;

    (ii) the median of daily values throughout the winter, defined as October 1 to March 31; and

    (iii) peak values (defined as the 98th percentile of daily values) which must not be exceeded throughout the year, though this is qualified in a footnote by a requirement that "Member States shall take all appropriate steps to ensure that [these peak values are] not exceeded for more than three consecutive days".

The effect of these limits is most easily understood from the **10–013** graphical representation of Figure 10/1, in which the concentrations of sulphur dioxide are represented on the vertical axis and those for suspended particulates on the horizontal axis. The Directive required these limit values to be met by April 1, 1993, having imposed various earlier dates for intermediate action. It additionally sets out what it terms "guide values" in respect of sulphur dioxide, namely 100–150μg/m^3 for any 24 hour mean, and 40–60μg/m^3 for a one year mean, these being values that Member States should seek to achieve wherever they are exceeded; values should be fixed for zones requiring special environmental protection that are generally lower than these guide values.

---

[10] There appears to be no good scientific basis for structuring the legislation in this way: the effects of each of the pollutants are unaffected by whatever levels there may be of the other. See the discussion on the formulation of this directive in N. Haigh, Manual of Environmental Policy, at Chapter 6.4.

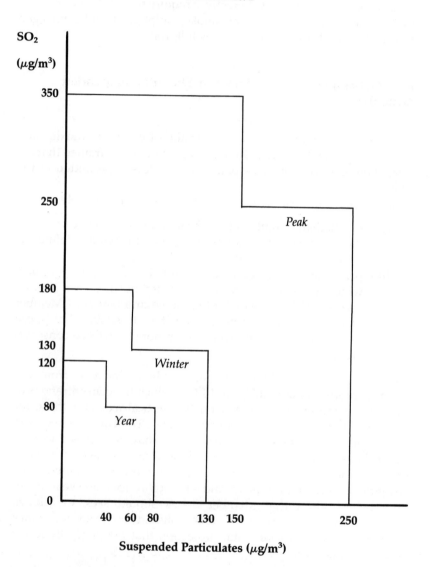

FIGURE 10/1

Directive 82/884 ([1982] O.J. L378)—Lead in Air

This Directive imposes a limit value for the annual mean concentration of lead in air of $2\mu g/m^3$, and requires compliance from December 9, 1987 at the latest.[11] It requires sampling points to be operated at places where individuals may be exposed continually for a long period and where there is a possibility that the limit value may be exceeded. **10–014**

Directive 85/203 ([1985] O.J. L87)—Nitrogen Dioxide

This imposes a limit value for nitrogen dioxide, expressed in terms of the 98th percentile of hourly means over a full year, of $200\mu g/m^3$. It also prescribes two guide values: (i) of $135\mu g/m^3$ for the 98th percentile of hourly means over a full year and (ii) of $50\mu g/m^3$ for the 50th percentile of hourly means over a full year. The directive was to be implemented by July 1, 1987. **10–015**

Directive 92/72 ([1992] O.J. L297)—Ozone

This Directive was adopted on September 21, 1992, and it is required to be implemented within eighteen months, *i.e.* by March 21, 1995. Excessive levels of low level ozone occur primarily in urban areas as a result of the action of light on the mixture of volatile organic carbon compounds and nitrogen oxides produced by vehicle exhaust emissions. The Directive requires ozone concentrations in ambient air to be measured so as to assess both the individual risk of exposure of human beings and the exposure of vegetation to values in excess of those prescribed. The Directive lays down four separate thresholds in order of significance namely: **10–016**

(i) a health protection threshold, being a level that should not be exceeded if human health is to be safeguarded in the event of prolonged pollution episodes;

(ii) a vegetation protection threshold, being a level above which vegetation may be affected;

(iii) a population information threshold, being a level beyond which there are limited, temporary effects on human health in the event of short exposure of particularly sensitive sections of the population and at which steps must be taken by the Member States in accordance with the Directive;

(iv) a population warning threshold above which there is a risk to human health in the event of short exposure and at which

---

[11] Being five years after notification of the Directive to Member States.

steps must be taken by the Member States in accordance with the Directive.

The figures set out in Annex I to the Directive for these threshold levels are as follows.[12]

Threshold	Mean Value
Health Protection	$110\mu g/m^3$ over 8 hours
Vegetation Protection	$200\mu g/m^3$ over 1 hour and $65\mu g/m^3$ over 24 hours
Population Information	$180\mu g/m^3$ over 1 hour
Population Warning	$360\mu g/m^3$ over 1 hour

Annex II requires measurement points to be located at geographically and climatologically representative sites where it is likely that either human beings or vegetation are exposed to ozone concentrations that risk approaching or exceeding a relevant threshold.

10–016　Where the information threshold is exceeded in the course of any calendar month Member States are required to give details of this to the Commission by the end of the following month, and similarly where the warning threshold is exceeded in the course of any week[13] Member States must give details to the Commission by the end of the following month at the latest.[14] Annual reports are also required to be given to the Commission from January 1, 1995 onwards.

10–017　All these Directives prescribe specific means of sampling for the pollutants concerned and for the methodology of measuring the concentrations in the samples. Given that the concentrations of these pollutants, particularly of lead and NO_2, are greatly affected by the extent of motor traffic, small variations in the locations of the sampling points in relation to roads can give dramatically different results, but there still remains uncertainty as to precisely what is required by the Directives in this respect. The United Kingdom bases its implementation on monitoring "areas" of highest emissions, rather than the points of highest pollution. A decision of the European Commission on this issue is pending.

10–018　Guidance to local authorities in respect of Directive 80/779 is contained in DoE Circular 11/81, and guidance in respect of Directive 82/884 is contained in DoE Circular 22/82. Directive 11/81 is however

[12] Expressed as micrograms of ozone/m³ at Standard temperature and pressure.
[13] From Monday to the following Sunday.
[14] Art. 6(2), (3).

476

mainly directed to smoke control and to encouraging local authorities to use their powers under the Clean Air Acts (1956 and 1968). Circular 22/82 is largely concerned with monitoring for lead; powers are of course available to control emissions of lead from industrial plants, but, at least until the widespread take-up of unleaded petrol, motor vehicles have been the principal source of airborne lead, this being controlled by regulation of the lead content of petrol.[15]

The Air Quality Standards Regulations 1989,[16] which apply throughout Great Britain, and the corresponding Air Quality Standards Regulations (Northern Ireland) 1990, aim to give effect to the first three of these air quality Directives.[17] The Secretary of State is required to ensure that the amounts of the various pollutants are measured and, as necessary, reduced to below the prescribed limits. The Regulations expressly exclude from the broad compliance requirement concentrations of lead and nitrogen dioxide at places of work and concentrations of nitrogen dioxide elsewhere within buildings. The Ozone Monitoring and Information Regulations 1994[18] implement Directive 92/72 in essentially the same manner; if the prescribed concentration values are exceeded the Secretary of State is required to take the necessary steps for the public to be informed as stipulated in the Directive. **10–019**

Monitoring of the atmosphere for these various pollutants is primarily achieved through the Government's Enhanced Urban Monitoring network. This consists of 12 sites in the United Kingdom providing hourly data on SO_2, NO_2 and ozone.[19] Each site is operated by the local environmental health department. A rural air quality network of 17 sites primarily monitors ozone levels. The separate UK smoke and sulphur dioxide monitoring network consists of some 280 sites. These sites are operated by a variety of bodies, including local authorities, on behalf of the DoE. Further information may be obtained from emissions statistics that those authorised under Part I of the E.P.A. may be required to provide. Additionally, local authorities have powers under Part V of the Clean Air Act 1993 and the Control of Atmospheric Pollution (Research and Publicity) Regulations 1977,[20] made under C.O.P.A., s.82, to obtain information on pollution and polluting activities in their areas (see also paragraph 10–069 below). **10–020**

Three committees of experts have been set up to advise the Government in connection with its urban air quality review, namely: **10–021**

---

[15] See para. 10–103.
[16] S.I. 1989 No. 317.
[17] Subject to temporary exemptions, now expired, for certain areas, mostly in respect of suspended particulates.
[18] S.I. 1994 No. 440.
[19] As at January 1994.
[20] S.I. 1977 No. 19.

(1) The Quality of Urban Air Review Group: responsible for UK monitoring networks and data, to recommend changes and to identify gaps in the understanding of urban pollution and its control;

(2) The Advisory Panel on Air Quality Standards: to advise on ambient air quality guidelines and targets for the UK;[21]

(3) The Committee on the Medical Effects of Air Pollution: to advise on the effects of the levels of UK air pollution on health, and to recommend any action for sensitive individuals.[22]

10–022 The air quality pollution monitoring results are made publicly available.[23] For this purpose the Government has defined categories of air quality in terms of the concentrations of nitrogen dioxide, sulphur dioxide and ozone as shown in Table 10/I.[24]

TABLE 10/I

	NO_2	SO_2	Ozone
Very Poor ppb $\mu g/m^3$	300 or more 564 or more	400 or more 1144 or more	180 or more 360 or more
Poor ppb $\mu g/m^3$	100–299 188–563	125–399 357–1143	90–179 180–359
Good ppb $\mu g/m^3$	50–99 94–187	60–124 172–356	50–89 100–179
Very Good ppb $\mu g/m^3$	under 50 under 94	under 60 under 172	under 50 under 100
Conversion factor ppb to $\mu g/m^3$	1.88	2.86	2.00

[21] The Panel issued in January 1994 a recommendation that an air quality standard for benzene be established, initially at a running annual average of 5 ppb, but reducing to 1 ppb by a target date to be fixed.

[22] DoE News Release 45, January 23, 1992.

[23] Obtainable over the telephone from the national air quality advice line on 0800 556677.

[24] The DoE figures, which are one hour averages, are given in parts per billion; conversion to $\mu g/m^3$ has been made on the basis of the indicated factors supplied by the DoE.

The Government's future strategy in relation to urban air quality is the subject of a discussion paper "Improving Air Quality".[25] It proposes the development of comprehensive health-related air quality standards, improvements in local air quality management and further action on vehicle emissions.

The Clean Air Act 1993

While the Alkali Acts served to control at least some of the worst excesses of industrial air emissions for many years, there continued to be gross air pollution, particularly in urban areas, as a result of the almost total dependence on the burning of coal for energy, both in industry and for domestic heating. The resulting emissions of smoke and sulphur oxides were liable, in certain geographical and climatological conditions, to produce the poisonous smogs for which Britain was notorious.   **10–023**

A particularly severe smog in December 1952, which was estimated to have brought about the deaths of some 4,000 people in London alone, caused a public outcry that led to the passing of the Clean Air Act 1956. This had two principal provisions, firstly a prohibition on the emission of dark smoke from chimneys of buildings (subject to exceptions that the Secretary of State might prescribe) and, secondly, the creation of smoke control areas within which it became an offence to emit smoke from the chimney of a building or which served the furnace of any fixed boiler or industrial plant. The Secretary of State was given power to authorise fuels for use within such areas, and to exempt approved classes of fireplace where they could be used to burn unauthorised fuels without producing any substantial quantity of smoke. In addition, it was made a requirement to inform local authorities of proposals to install any furnace, which enabled the authorities to approve the plans and specifications concerned for compliance with the legislation. The effects of the 1956 Clean Air Act were quite dramatic in the reduction of the incidence of smog in the country, as the number of smoke control areas extended to cover all the principal areas of substantial population density.   **10–024**

The 1956 Act was followed by the Clean Air Act 1968, which made a number of amendments, including providing specific limits on rates of emission of grit and dust from the chimneys of industrial furnaces and to require arrestment systems to be fitted to these furnaces to prevent grit and dust being emitted; it also contained provisions for approval   **10–025**

[25] DoE, March 1994.

of the height of chimneys serving furnaces.[26] The Control of Pollution Act 1974 included provisions relating to air pollution, and provided the Secretary of State with powers to make regulations on the composition and content of fuels for motor vehicles and heating oils. It also made it an offence to burn insulation from cables to recover the metal—an operation that is liable to produce particularly noxious fumes, and also to escape the other Clean Air Act controls since these are frequently not emitted from a chimney. The basic prohibition on emitting dark smoke required, as explained below, the use of a technique employing the so-called Ringelmann Chart, comparing the darkness of the smoke with shades of different depths on the chart. Inevitably this assessment was impossible after dark, which enabled the controls to be evaded until the Control of Smoke Pollution Act 1989 came into effect, which effectively allowed prosecutions on the basis that dark smoke was likely to be emitted from an activity, putting the burden of proof on the operator to show that that was not in fact the case.

10–026   These and numerous other legislative amendments since 1956 have now all been consolidated into the Clean Air Act 1993, which came into effect on August 27, 1993. It applies throughout Great Britain, but the only substantive provisions that extend to Northern Ireland relate to the power to make regulations on the composition and contents of fuel for motor vehicles. Because it is a consolidating Act no significant changes have been made to the substance of the earlier legislation. This was originally drafted using Imperial units for weight and energy production; although these have been converted to their metric equivalents, one has to refer back to the original legislation to find reasonably round numbers. Additionally, the previous legislation contained various transitional provisions for furnaces, etc. being installed at the time when relevant provisions of the 1956 and 1968 Acts were brought into force, and these have also been carried over into the 1993 Act.

10–027   The controls under the 1993 Act inevitably overlap to a considerable degree with both those of the Alkali, etc., Works Regulation Act 1906, and those under Part I of the E.P.A. 1990. Where there is such overlap, the main control provisions, namely those of Parts I, II and III of the 1993 Act, are generally disapplied in favour of the other legislation. Thus by s.41, these Parts I to III do not apply to any prescribed process under Part I of the E.P.A. from the "determination date" for that

---

[26] Extending chimneys, rather than reducing emissions, while protecting those in their immediate neighbourhood, of course simply ensures that pollutants are spread over a wider area and a larger population, a classic case of facilitating a polluter to pass on pollution costs to others.

process. This "determination date" is the date on which an authorisation is either granted or refused—in the case of an application that is refused initially but appealed, the relevant date is when the appeal is determined either by way of a direction to grant the authorisation or of an affirmation of the refusal.

Overlap with the Alkali, etc., Works Regulation Act 1906 will of course cease to apply as processes subject to that Act become controlled under the E.P.A. Part I instead, so that in the course of 1996 the 1906 Act will no longer apply to any processes, and will be repealed. When that happens, the relevant transitional provisions in section 66 and Schedule 3 of the Clean Air Act 1993 will also cease to have effect. In the meantime, that Schedule 3 applies to any "work subject or potentially subject" to the 1906 Act.[27] In the case of any such work, unless the Secretary of State has by order otherwise provided, Parts I to III of the 1993 Act will not apply to it. Where as a result of such an order these Parts of the 1993 Act are made applicable to a work, then it is a defence to any proceedings brought under any of sections 1, 2 or 20 to prove that best practicable means had been employed to prevent or minimise the alleged emission.[28] The prohibition on cable burning which is contained in Part IV of the 1993 Act is treated likewise—cable burning is an offence under section 33 unless the burning is part of a process subject to Part I of the E.P.A. or the place at which the cable burning is carried out is registered under section 9 of the 1906 Act, for so long as the latter remains in force. Schedule 3 contains further minor provisions applicable to works registered under the 1906 Act until such time as Part I of the E.P.A. applies to the process(es) concerned, and reference should be made to that Schedule in such a case.

10–028

Part I of the 1993 Act relates to dark smoke. By section 1(1) dark smoke may not be emitted from a chimney of any building, and by section 1(2) dark smoke may not be emitted from any other chimney which serves the furnace of any fixed boiler or industrial plant.[29] Under section 1(1) liability is on the occupier of the premises, and under section 1(2) it is on the person having possession of the boiler or plant. Chimney is defined to include structures and openings of any kind from or through which smoke, grit, dust or fumes may be emitted, and in particular, includes flues. If a chimney serves the whole or part of any building, it is immaterial that it may be structurally separate from that building. It follows that section 1(1) will

10–029

---

[27] Defined in Sched. 3, para. 1(i).
[28] Sched. 3, para. 4(a).
[29] Industrial plant includes any still, melting pot or other plant used for any industrial or trade purposes, and also an incinerator used for or in connection with any such purposes (s.64(1)).

generally apply to most situations, section 1(2) only being of relevance where a furnace is not within any building, for example a mobile furnace. "Furnace" is not defined anywhere in the legislation, but would appear to mean any apparatus for burning any combustible materials, whether liquid, solid or gaseous. Since "fireplace" is defined to include "any furnace, grate or stove, whether open or closed" a furnace does not, it seems, necessarily require to be a closed structure.

**10–030
–10–039** The Dark Smoke (Permitted Periods) Regulations 1958[30] made under the 1956 Act create limited derogations from the general prohibitions of section 1. These include provision for soot blowing, a recognised technique for removing soot deposits from inside industrial boilers. Under these Regulations, there may be disregarded for the purposes of the prohibitions of section 1 emissions of dark smoke[31] from any chimney for up to 10 minutes in total in any period of eight hours; if there is also soot blowing in that period, the permitted total is raised to 14 minutes. Where a chimney serves more than one furnace, these permitted totals are raised in stages up to a maximum of 29 minutes without soot blowing and 41 minutes with soot blowing, depending on whether there are two, three or four or more furnaces concerned. In calculating the number of furnaces, two or more that are used to fire a single boiler or unit of industrial plant are regarded as one furnace.[32] These permitted dark smoke emissions are qualified by regulation 4 which limits continuous emissions of dark smoke, caused otherwise than by soot blowing, to a maximum of four minutes on any one occasion, and also limits emissions of black smoke[33] (which is included within the definition of dark smoke) to a total of at the most two minutes in any period of 30 minutes. These exemptions do not apply to emissions of smoke from vessels, to which separate Regulations apply.[34]

10–040 In addition to the exemptions under the 1958 Permitted Periods Regulations, it is a defence to a prosecution under section 1 if it can be shown that:

(i) the emission was solely due to the lighting up of a cold furnace and all practicable steps had been taken to prevent or minimise the emission of dark smoke; or

(ii) the emission was solely due to some failure of a furnace or some connected apparatus and that the failure either could

---

[30] S.I. 1958 No. 498.
[31] Dark smoke is as dark or darker than Ringelmann 2 (see para. 10–044).
[32] Reg. 3; note that this deeming provision differs from that of s.64(6) of the 1993 Act, which deems all furnaces served by a single chimney to be one furnace.
[33] Black smoke is as dark as or darker than Ringelmann 4 (Reg. 2(2)).
[34] See paras. 10–051, 10–052.

not reasonably have been foreseen or could not reasonably have been provided against, and that the emission could not reasonably have been prevented by action taken after the failure; or

(iii) the emission was solely due the use of unsuitable fuel, that suitable fuel was unobtainable and that the least unsuitable fuel available was used and that all practicable steps had been taken to prevent or minimise the resulting emission of dark smoke.[35]

Prohibitions over emissions of dark smoke from industrial and trade premises otherwise than through a chimney to which section 1 applies are imposed by section 2(1). This is subject to the rule of evidence in section 2(3) that where material is burned on industrial or trade premises and the circumstances are such that the burning would be likely to give rise to the emission of dark smoke, then it is for the occupier or any person who caused or permitted the burning to prove that no dark smoke was in fact emitted. This latter provision, inserted in 1989 to deal with the problem of proving that dark smoke has been emitted at night, does not, it will be noted, apply to the prohibitions under s.1 on emitting dark smoke from a chimney of a building or a chimney serving a furnace of any fixed boiler or industrial plant.

10–041

"Premises" includes land[36] and "industrial or trade premises" means premises used for any industrial or trade purposes, or any other premises on which matter is burnt in connection with any industrial or trade process.[37] Where premises are used for any industrial or trade purposes, it is immaterial whether or not the burning of any matter is in connection with those particular purposes. Nevertheless, it is a defence to prove that the emission was inadvertent and that all practicable[38] steps had been taken to prevent or minimise the emission of dark smoke. The prohibitions of section 2(1) are subject to exemptions contained in the Clean Air (Emission of Dark Smoke) (Exemption) Regulations 1969,[39] which allows the burning of certain exempted materials, for example from demolishing buildings, road materials being burnt off prior to resurfacing, animal carcasses, etc. The exempted materials are subject to a variety of conditions, such as that there is no other reasonable, safe and practicable method, that the emission of dark smoke is minimised, and that the burning is

10–042

---

[35] s.1(4).
[36] s.64(1).
[37] s.2(6).
[38] For the meaning of 'practicable', see n.43, below.
[39] S.I. 1969 No. 1263.

carried out under supervision by or on behalf of the occupier of the relevant premises.

10–043   The offences under sections 1 and 2 consist of the emission of dark smoke in the prescribed circumstances "on any day", *i.e.* in any period of 24 hours beginning at midnight.[40] The effect of this is that emitting dark smoke in contravention of either section on consecutive days will amount to two (or more) offences, with consequent implications for the number of charges that may be brought and total fines that may be imposed.

10–044   "Dark smoke" and "black smoke" are defined by reference to shades on the Ringelmann Chart. This chart is the subject of British Standard BS 2742C. It consists of five squares of equal size (101mm square) printed on a white background. Four of these five squares are criss-crossed by 20 vertical and 20 horizontal parallel and equally spaced lines, the thickness of which varies from one square to the next. The thicknesses are selected such that in one square 20 per cent of the white background is obscured, and in the remaining three, 40 per cent, 60 per cent and 80 per cent of the background is obscured respectively. These squares are placed in a row, starting with the blank square, of increasing obscuration. The squares are held at a distance of more than 15 metres from the observer, where the lines merge into different shades of grey, enabling quite precise observations to be made of the degree of darkness of any smoke. The four cross-hatched squares of increasing obscuration represent Ringelmann 1, 2, 3 and 4 respectively, "dark smoke" therefore being anything as dark as or darker than the second square (Ringelmann 2) with 40 per cent obscuration, and "black smoke" anything as dark as or darker than Ringelmann 4, *i.e.* 80 per cent obscuration.

10–045   By section 3(2) it is made clear that it is not essential for the purposes of a prosecution to produce evidence of an actual comparison of smoke with the Ringelmann Chart and that the court may be satisfied that smoke is or is not "dark smoke" on the basis of other evidence, such as the use of the Miniature Smoke Chart.[41]

10–046   Proceedings for an offence under sections 1 or 2 (and also section 20, relating to emissions of smoke in smoke control areas) must be preceded by notice being given to "the appropriate person" by an authorised officer of the local authority of the offence that is being or has been committed. The "appropriate person" is either the occupier of the premises (where the prosecution is under section 1(1) or 20(1))

---

[40] s.64(1).

[41] The Miniature Smoke Chart (BS 2742) is of a more manageable size, 129mm x 69mm, on which the different shades of grey are printed directly. It is not intended as a substitute for the principal Ringelmann Chart, but when used by an experienced operator, essentially identical results can be obtained.

or the person having possession of the boiler or plant (where the prosecution is under section 1(2) or 20(2)). Unless the officer has reason to believe that notice has already been given by or on behalf of his authority he must give this notice, and if it is initially given orally he must confirm it in writing within four days next following the day on which he became aware of the offence.[42] It is a defence to any prosecution under sections 1, 2 and 20 to prove that this notice was not given, and that will be deemed to have been the case if notice was not given within the four days next following the day of the offence. The prosecution will then fail unless it can be proved that notice was in fact given within four days following the day on which the relevant officer in fact became aware of the offence.

Special Cases

Part VI of the 1993 Act provides for certain special cases to which the provisions in Parts I to III apply only partially or not at all. These cases consist of: **10–047**

Section 41 Prescribed processes under Part I of the E.P.A. (referred to in paragraph 10–027).
Section 42 Refuse from the mining or quarrying of coal or shale.
Section 43 Railway engines.
Section 44 Vessels.
Section 45 Exemptions for investigations and research.
Section 46 Crown premises.

Mines and Quarries

Section 42 is concerned exclusively with the combustion of refuse deposited from a mine or quarry from which coal or shale has been, is being or is to be got. Section 42(4) excludes the application of Part III of the E.P.A. (dealing with statutory nuisances) and of all the provisions of Parts I to III of the 1993 Act to any smoke, grit or dust from the combustion of such refuse. Instead, the owner of any relevant mine or quarry must employ "all practicable means"[43] for preventing combustion of refuse deposited from the mine or quarry, and for preventing or **10–048**

---

[42] s.51(1).
[43] 'Practicable' means reasonably practicable having regard, amongst other things, to local conditions and circumstances, to the financial implications and to the current state of technical knowledge, and 'practicable means' includes the provision and maintenance of plant and its proper use (s.64(1)).

minimising the emission of smoke and fumes from such refuse. Failure to comply with this requirement exposes the owner to summary proceedings and a fine not exceeding level 5 or cumulative penalties on continuance in accordance with section 50. For the purpose of this section 42, "mine", "quarry" and "owner" have the meanings ascribed to them in the Mines and Quarries Act 1954.[44]

10–049 By a transitional provision derived from the 1956 Act, the obligations under section 42(2) to prevent combustion and to avoid the emission of smoke and fumes do not apply to any deposit of refuse made before July 5, 1956 if at that date the deposit was neither any longer in use nor under the control of the owner of the relevant mine or quarry.

Railway Engines

10–050 Smoke, grit and dust from railway engines are exempted by section 43 from the application of the whole of Parts I to III of the 1993 Act with the exception of section 1, which applies in relation to railway locomotive engines as it applies in relation to buildings,[45] save that references to the owner of the engine are to be substituted in place of references to the occupier of a building. When prosecuting an offence consisting of the emission of dark smoke from a railway engine, the notice required under section 51 must be served on the owner of the railway engine.[46] In addition to this requirement not to emit dark smoke, the owner of any railway engine is required to use "any practicable means there may be"[47] for minimising the emission of smoke from the chimney on the engine,[48] and any offence under this provision leads to liability to cumulative penalties on continuance in accordance with section 50 or, alternatively, a fine not exceeding level 5 on summary conviction.

Vessels

10–051 References to vessels in section 44 are given the same meaning as in the Merchant Shipping Act 1894. The section applies to all vessels in waters that are not navigable by sea-going ships and also to vessels in UK territorial waters that are navigable by sea-going ships, where these are contained within any port, harbour, river, estuary, haven,

---

[44] Defined in ss.180 and 181 of the 1954 Act. 'Owner' is generally the person entitled for the time being to work the mine or quarry, but may be a contractor acting on behalf of that person, and includes the liquidator or receiver of any such owner.
[45] s.43(1).
[46] s.51(2).
[47] For the definition of practicable means, see n.43 above.
[48] s.43(3).

dock, canal or any other place where vessels entering or using facilities in it are made subject to charges under any statute.[49]

Any vessel in waters to which section 44 applies is exempted from all the provisions of Parts I to III of the 1993 Act in so far as they relate to smoke, grit or dust, with the exception of section 1, which applies to them as it applies in relation to buildings. In this case, references to the occupier of a building are to be replaced by references to the owner, and also to the master or other officer or person in charge of the vessel. Derogations from the section 1 prohibitions allowing limited emissions of dark smoke for varying periods depending on the circumstances are contained in the Dark Smoke (Permitted Periods) (Vessels) Regulations 1958.[50] A notice of an offence given under section 51 prior to proceedings must be given to either the owner or to the master or an officer or person in charge of the vessel.[51] The language of section 51(2) indicates that it is sufficient for a notice to be served on the owner of the vessel even though it is the master, for example, who is being prosecuted either alone or as well, and vice versa. References to a furnace include the engine of the vessel. Where an offence is committed by the emission of dark smoke from a vessel to which section 44 applies, this is triable summarily and subject to a fine not exceeding level 5.

10–052

Investigations and Research

A local authority may exempt any person from the operation of the main substantive provisions of the 1993 Act, and also from the application of the statutory nuisance provisions of the E.P.A., if satisfied that it is expedient to do so, in order to enable the conduct of investigations or research into air pollution.[52] An appeal lies to the Secretary of State from a local authority's decision on an application for such an exemption.

10–053

Crown Premises

The effect of Crown immunity is mitigated to some degree by section 46(1), which applies to premises which are under the control of any Government Department and are occupied for the public service of the Crown or for the purposes of any Government department. If any such premises emit dark smoke, grit or dust, or any smoke that

10–054

---

[49] Excluding light dues, local light dues and any other charges payable in respect of lighthouses, buoys or beacons and of charges in respect of pilotage (s.44(5)).
[50] S.I. 1958 No. 878.
[51] s.51(2).
[52] s.5(1).

creates a nuisance, or any smoke in a smoke control area, the relevant local authority may report this to the responsible Minister. He must then inquire as to whether there is cause for complaint and employ all practicable means for dealing with it and preventing any recurrence. Similar action may be taken if naval vessels emit dark smoke, and in relation to premises occupied by visiting forces.

Smoke, Grit, Dust and Fumes

10–055   Part II of the 1993 Act provides controls over the emission of smoke, grit, dust and fumes and is mostly concerned with non-domestic furnaces; domestic furnaces are treated separately, being defined as any furnace which is designed solely or mainly for domestic purposes, and used for heating a boiler with a maximum heating capacity of less than 16.12 kilowatts. Accordingly, a furnace used to heat a large block of flats, although serving residential purposes exclusively, is unlikely to be classed as a "domestic furnace". Further, for the purposes of this and other provisions relating to the capacity of furnaces, any furnaces which are in the occupation of the same person and are served by a single chimney are, for the purposes of the bulk of the provisions of Part II of the 1993 Act, to be taken to be one furnace.[53]

Non-domestic Furnaces

10–056   Before installing any non-domestic furnace in a building, or any fixed boiler or industrial plant, notice of the proposed installation must first be given to the relevant local authority,[54] and no such installation shall be made unless the furnace is so far as practicable capable of being operated continuously without emitting smoke when burning fuel of a type for which the furnace was designed.[55] Where an installation has been made in accordance with plans and specifications submitted to and approved for the purposes of section 4 by the local authority, it is deemed to comply with the latter requirements. The Clean Air Act (Emission of Grit and Dust From Furnaces) Regulations 1971[56] prescribe limits on the rates of emission of grit and dust from boilers, indirect heating appliances, and other furnaces in which the combustion gases are in contact with the material being heated but which does not itself contribute grit and dust to the combustion gases.

[53] s.61(3).
[54] s.4(1).
[55] s.4(2).
[56] S.I. 1971 No. 162.

The permitted emissions are set out in Schedules to the Regulations, and vary in accordance with the rating of the furnace and whether it is burning solid or liquid matter. Where these Regulations apply, it is a defence to any breach of the prescribed limits that the best practicable means had been used for minimising the emission.

For non-domestic furnaces to which the Regulations do not apply **10–057** that are contained in a building and served by a chimney, the occupier of the building is required to use "any practicable means there may be" for minimising the emission of grit or dust from the chimney.[57] The contrast between this expression and "best practicable means" in section 5(4) suggests that the former expression is less demanding. However "practicable" is defined[58] to mean "reasonably practicable" having regard, amongst other things, to local conditions and circumstances, to the financial implications and to the current state of technical knowledge, and "practicable means" includes the provision and maintenance of plant and its proper use. It was held in *Edwards v. National Coal Board*[59] that reasonably practicable is a narrower term than physically possible, and implies that a computation must be made in which the quantum of risk is placed in one scale, and the sacrifice, whether in money, time or trouble, involved in the measures necessary to avert the risk, is placed in the other. This judgment was approved by the House of Lords in *Marshall v. Gotham Co. Ltd*[60] where it was stated by Lord Reid "if a precaution is practicable it must be taken, unless in the whole circumstances that would be unreasonable". In that case, which involved physical dangers to life of those working in a gypsum mine, it was added that where men's lives may be at stake, it should not lightly be held that to take a practicable precaution is unreasonable. Even in those circumstances, however, it was held that such precautions as might have been taken would not have afforded anything like complete protection, and to require their adoption would have been unreasonable.

What amounts to "best practicable means", an expression that has **10–058** been in use in air pollution legislation since the Alkali, etc., Works Act 1874, has been the subject of non-binding guidance in Alkali Inspectorate reports and elsewhere.[61] In practice, the distinction between this and "reasonably practicable means" is likely to be more theoretical than real, since both include consideration of the balance of expense against the benefits of incurring that expenditure. The

---

[57] s.5(5).
[58] In s.64(1).
[59] [1949] 1 K.B. 704; [1949] 1 All E.R. 743 C.A.
[60] [1954] A.C. 360; [1954] All E.R. 937.
[61] *e.g.* Health and Safety booklet HS(R)6, (HMSO), 1980, para. 23.

circumstances where "best practicable means" are not also "reasonably practicable" must be very rare. Of much greater significance is that the burden of proof under section 5(5) that an occupier failed to use any practicable means is on the prosecutor, whereas under section 5(4) it is for the defence to show that best practicable means were used.

10–059   Arrestment plant for grit and dust must be fitted to all non-domestic furnaces in buildings used to burn pulverised fuel or to burn any other solid matter at a rate of 45.4kg (100lbs) an hour, or any liquid or gaseous matter at a rate equivalent to 366.4 kilowatts or more.[62] This obligation does not however apply to installations that were made, begun or contracted for before October 1, 1969.[63] Exemptions from these requirements are contained in the Clean Air (Arrestment Plant) (Exemption) Regulations 1969.[64] These generally apply to certain mobile or transportable furnaces for providing heat or power for agricultural purposes or for providing a temporary source of heat or power for other purposes. Other furnaces are exempted which by reason of their capacity or the materials they burn will not in fact contribute to the emission of grit or dust.

10–060   Where a building contains a furnace of a type to which these arrestment plant requirements apply, the relevant local authority may require the occupier to make and record measurements of the grit, dust and fumes emitted from his furnace, to provide and maintain appropriate apparatus, and to inform the local authority of the results obtained.[65] The local authority is entitled in certain circumstances to enter on to the premises during the taking of the measurements. The Clean Air (Measurement of Grit and Dust) Regulations 1971[66] set out notification and other procedures to be followed in implementing these requirements.

10–061   To avoid undue burdens on those operating relatively small furnaces, where a furnace to which the measuring and reporting requirements apply is used to burn solid matter, other than pulverised fuel, at a rate less than 1.02 tonnes an hour or to burn any liquid or gaseous matter at a rate of less than 8.21 megawatts, the occupier of the building may serve a notice on the local authority requiring it to make and record the relevant measurements.[67] There is no provision in the legislation for the authority to recover its costs incurred in doing this. Local authorities may supplement this information by seeking information from any occupier of any building as to the furnaces in the

---

[62] s.6(1).
[63] Sched. 5, para. 6(1).
[64] S.I. 1969 No. 1262.
[65] s.10.
[66] S.I. 1971 No. 161.
[67] s.11.

building and the fuel or waste burned in those furnaces as the authority may reasonably require. Failure to give the information as requested within the prescribed time (not less than 14 days) or to furnish information known to be false is an offence.[68]

10–062

The same controls as to the arrestment of grit and dust, and to the making and recording or measurements are applied by section 13 to the furnace of any "fixed boiler or industrial plant" as they apply in relation to a furnace in a building. "Fixed boiler or industrial plant" means any boiler or industrial plant which is attached to a building, or which is for the time being fixed to or installed on any land. This thus applies to outdoor furnaces the same controls as regards the fitting of arrestment plant and the recording and providing of information on emissions.

10–063

Under transitional provisions derived from the 1968 Act the provisions for domestic furnaces described in the next paragraph apply to non-domestic furnaces as though they were domestic furnaces, where the installation was made, begun or contracted for after June 1, 1958 in England and Wales, or November 15, 1958 in Scotland, but before October 1, 1969.[69]

Domestic Furnaces

10–064

A domestic furnace must be provided with approved plant for arresting grit and dust, and that plant must be properly maintained and used, if it either burns pulverised fuel or burns any solid fuel or solid waste at a rate of 1.02 tonnes an hour or more.[70] Approval may be by the local authority directly, or by way of approval of plans and specifications followed in the course of the installation. Appeals against refusal of approval may be made to the Secretary of State under section 9. Transitional provisions under the 1956 Act exempted from this requirement domestic furnaces where the installation was made, begun or contracted for before June 1, 1958 in England and Wales and before November 15, 1958 in Scotland.[71]

Height of Chimneys

10–065

Chimney heights are brought under control by section 14 in so far as the chimney serves a furnace used in a building:

(i) to burn pulverised fuel (whatever the rate of burning), or

[68] s.12.
[69] Sched. 5, para. 6(2), (3).
[70] s.8.
[71] Sched. 5, para. 6(3).

      (ii) to burn any other solid matter at a rate of 45.4kg. (100lbs.) or more an hour, or

     (iii) to burn any liquid or gaseous matter at a rate equivalent to 366.4 kilowatts or more.

It is an offence if the occupier of a building knowingly causes or permits any such use of a furnace in a building unless the height of the chimney serving it has been approved and any conditions to which the approval is subject are complied with. Likewise, a person having possession of any fixed boiler or industrial plant (other than one exempted by regulations) commits an offence if he knowingly causes or permits a furnace of that boiler or plant to be used in any of the three manners just set out, without prior approval.[72] Certain exemptions are made to the application of section 14 by the Clean Air (Heights of Chimneys) (Exemption) Regulations 1969.[73]

10–066   A local authority may only approve a proposed chimney height if it is satisfied that it will be sufficient to prevent, so far as practicable, the smoke, grit, dust, gases or fumes emitted from the chimney from becoming prejudicial to health or a nuisance having regard to the purpose of the chimney, the position and descriptions of buildings near it, the levels of the neighbouring ground, and any other matters requiring consideration in the circumstances.[74] Any approval may be granted subject to conditions on the rate and/or the quality of emissions from the chimney. Any application for approval to a local authority must be dealt with within four weeks, unless a longer period is agreed, otherwise the approval is deemed granted without qualification.[75] Essentially the same controls are applied to other chimneys of buildings outside Greater London or in an outer London borough other than a building used, wholly or in part as (a) a residence or residences; (b) a shop or shops; or (c) an office or offices, where it is proposed to construct a chimney, other than one serving a furnace, for carrying smoke, grit, dust or gases from the building. These controls are exercised by reference to the plans that must be deposited with local authorities in accordance with building regulations, and these plans must be rejected unless the authority concerned is satisfied that the height of the chimney is sufficient, having regard to the same considerations as relate to the approval of furnace chimneys under section 15.[76] Appeals from refusals under sections 15 and 16 may be made to the Secretary of State.

[72] s.14(4).
[73] S.I. 1969 No. 411.
[74] s.15(2).
[75] s.15(4).
[76] s.16(1), (2).

Finally, chimney heights are also subject to control under the **10–067** Building Regulations 1991.[77] These apply to solid fuel and oil burning appliances with a rated output of up to 45 kilowatts and to gas burning appliances with a rated input of up to 60 kilowatts.

Smoke Control Areas

The creation of smoke control areas was one of the principal **10–068** innovations of the Clean Air Act 1956, and the relevant provisions now form Part III of the 1993 Act (sections 18 to 29). Local authorities may by order declare the whole or any part of their districts to be a smoke control area; the Secretary of State has default powers under Section 19 to require them to do so. Such orders may be limited to, or have exempted from them, specified buildings or classes of building, and they may make exemptions in respect of certain fireplaces. Except where any relevant limitation or exemption applies, it is an offence in any such area to emit smoke (not only dark smoke) from a chimney of any building (for which the occupier of the building will be liable), or from any other chimney which serves a furnace of any fixed boiler or industrial plant (for which the person having possession of the boiler or plant will be liable).[78] It is however a defence to any proceedings to show that the emissions were not caused by the use of any fuel other than an authorised fuel.[79] Fuels may be authorised by regulations made by the Secretary of State under section 20(6) and numerous such regulations have been made. Further, section 21 empowers the Secretary of State to exempt any class of fireplace from the provisions of section 20, if he is satisfied that such fireplaces can be used for burning fuel other than authorised fuels without producing any smoke or a substantial quantity of smoke. Numerous fireplace orders have likewise been made under this section. Powers enabling local authorities to require the adaptation of existing fireplaces to avoid contraventions of section 20 are contained in section 24, while section 25, and more particularly Schedule 2, set out detailed provisions for providing financial assistance where such adaptions are required. Assistance is not however available in respect of private dwellings erected after August 15, 1964 or produced by the conversion after that date of other premises.[80] Local authorities may revoke or vary smoke

---

[77] S.I. 1991 No. 2768.
[78] s.20(1), (2).
[79] s.20(4).
[80] This provision applies only where the erection or conversion was begun after August 15, 1964.

control orders; however confirmation by the Secretary of State is needed where an order made before November 13, 1980 is involved.[81]

Air Pollution Information

10–069 Local authorities are given quite extensive powers under Part V of the 1993 Act to require occupiers of any premises to furnish information concerning air emissions from the premises, to measure and record such emissions and to enter on to the premises for that purpose. They may also enter into arrangements with occupiers of premises for the latter to measure and record emissions on behalf of the local authority. The provisions for measuring and recording emissions, however, do not apply to private dwellings or caravans[82] Those affected by notices requiring information to be furnished may appeal to the Secretary of State, in which event the provisions of the Control of Atmospheric Pollution (Appeals) Regulations 1977[83] apply. Regulations as to the manner in which and the methods by which local authorities are to carry out their functions of investigating and researching into and obtaining information about air pollution are contained in the Control of Atmospheric Pollution (Research and Publicity) Regulations 1977.[84] The obligations, other than rights of entry and powers to obtain information under sections 56 to 58, also apply to all premises used for and to persons in the public service of the Crown,[85] save in so far as they may be exempted by the Control of Atmospheric Pollution (Exempted Premises) Regulations 1977.[86]

Enforcement

10–070 Section 55 expresses it to be a duty of the relevant local authority to enforce the provisions of Parts I to III and VI of the Act and also section 33 (relating to cable burning). Additionally, a local authority may institute proceedings in respect of smoke emitted in a neighbouring area which affects any part of its own district. Where proceedings may only be effectually instituted by the service of a notice under section 51 by an authorised officer of the local authority, private prosecutions without the co-operation of the local authority are not possible. However section 55 enables private individuals, if they are so minded,

---

[81] s.18(3), (4); Sched. 5, para. 8.
[82] "Private dwelling" means any building or part of a building used or intended to be used as such (s.64(4)), and consequently excludes a caravan.
[83] S.I. 1977 No. 17.
[84] S.I. 1977 No. 19.
[85] s.36(6).
[86] S.I. 1977 No. 18.

to require local authorities to fulfil their duty to enforce, should there be any question of their failing to do so.

The 1993 Act contains the usual provisions for rendering directors and other corporate officers liable for offences of their company, where these have been committed with their consent or connivance or through their neglect. Parent companies may be liable, as though they were directors, by virtue of section 52(2). Additionally, where the commission by any person of an offence under the 1993 Act is due to the act of default of some other person, that other person shall be guilty of the offence, and may be charged with it, irrespective of whether any other proceedings are taken against anyone else.[87]

10–071

Registration of Works under the Alkali Acts

As explained above, prior to the implementation of Part I of the E.P.A., air pollution from industrial processes was primarily controlled under the Alkali, etc., Works Regulation Act 1906.[88] The 1906 Act was derived from previous Alkali Acts of 1863 and 1874 and was primarily directed to so-called "alkali works".[89] Owners of alkali works were required not only to reduce escapes of hydrogen chloride into the atmosphere to prescribed limits, but also to use "the best practicable means" for preventing the escape of noxious or offensive gases, for preventing the discharge, whether directly or indirectly, of such gases into the atmosphere, and for rendering such gases where discharged harmless and inoffensive.[90] For the purposes of the 1906 Act, "owner" includes any lessee, occupier or any other person carrying on any work to which the Act applies, and "best practicable means" "has reference not only to the provision and the efficient maintenance of appliances adequate for preventing such escape, but also to the manner in which such appliances are used and to the proper supervision, by the owner, of any operation in which such gases are evolved".[91]

10–072

---

[87] s.53; this provision, which is now generally applicable to the entire 1993 Act, was previously contained only in C.O.P.A. 1974, and applicable only to offences under that Act.

[88] In addition of course to the variety of statutory nuisance provisions, now consolidated into Part III of the E.P.A.

[89] Being works for the manufacture of sodium or potassium sulphate or the treatment of copper ores by sodium or other chlorides whereby any sulphate is formed and in which hydrochloric acid gas is evolved (s.27(1)).

[90] ss.1, 2.

[91] s.27(1).

10–073   The scope of the 1906 Act was extended by the requirement[92] that not only alkali works, but also other specified works should not be carried on unless they were certified to be registered. The specified works are now those listed in Schedule 1 to the Health & Safety (Emissions into the Atmosphere) Regulations 1983[93] as amended by the Health and Safety (Emissions into the Atmosphere) (Amendment) Regulations 1989.[94] Registration was normally for consecutive 12 month periods, but is now governed by the Control of Industrial Pollution (Registration of Works) Regulations 1989[95] whereby renewal of a registration is not required unless there has been a change to the registered work that is not an "exempt alteration", *i.e.* an alteration to a work which, in the opinion of the chief inspector, is not a substantial alteration.[96] Since the introduction of Part 1 of the E.P.A., however, any alteration that is not an exempt alteration will be a "substantial change" for the purposes of the E.P.A., and accordingly bring the process within the scope of the E.P.A. forthwith and outside that of the 1906 Act.

10–074   The 1983 Emissions into the Atmosphere Regulations contain an extensive schedule of chemical and other works prescribed for the purposes of the Health and Safety at Work, etc., Act 1974[97] (the "H.S.W.A."). Although the H.S.W.A. is primarily concerned with protecting the health and securing the safety of those at work, it also incidentally provides for controlling emissions into the atmosphere of noxious or offensive substances from premises of any class prescribed for the purposes of that Act.[98]. Section 5 is concerned with this aspect,[99] and reads as follows:

> "5.   (1) It shall be the duty of the person having control of any premises of a class prescribed for the purposes of section 1(1)(d) to use the best practicable means for preventing the emission into the atmosphere from the premises of noxious or offensive substances and for rendering harmless and inoffensive such substances as may be so emitted.
>
>   (2) The reference in subsection (1) above to the means to be used for the purposes there mentioned includes a reference to the manner in which the plant provided for those purposes is used

---

[92] In s.9(1).
[93] S.I. 1983 No. 943.
[94] S.I. 1989 No. 319.
[95] S.I. 1989 No. 318.
[96] Reg. 2.
[97] 1974 c.37.
[98] s.1(1)(d).
[99] The original intention was that the Alkali, etc., Act 1906 should be replaced *in toto* by C.O.P.A. 1974 and repealed, but this did not happen.

and to the supervision of any operation involving the emission of the substances to which that subsection applies.

(3) Any substance or a substance of any description prescribed for the purposes of subsection (1) above as noxious or offensive shall be a noxious or, as the case may be, an offensive substance for those purposes whether or not it would be so apart from this subsection.

(4) Any reference in this section to a person having control of any premises is a reference to a person having control of the premises in connection with the carrying on by him of a trade, business or other undertaking (whether for profit or not) and any duty imposed on any such person by this section shall extend only to matters within his control."

The 1983 Emissions into the Atmosphere Regulations serve two main purposes: first, they set out in Schedule 1 the prescribed classes of premises for the purposes of section 1(1)(d), and hence indirectly for the purposes of section 5(1), where best practicable means regarding emissions must be used; secondly, they list in Schedule 2 various substances that are deemed by virtue of section 5(3) to be noxious or offensive. While virtually all the substances listed in Schedule 2 are unquestionably noxious or offensive, at least when present in significant quantities, carbon dioxide is also listed, which is not of course inherently toxic at all, but which must be treated as such for the purposes of subsection 5(3). Its presence in the list enables controls to be placed over all the principal combustion products emitted from the prescribed classes of works.

10–075

Control over the works subject to registration under the 1906 Act was originally exercised by the Alkali Inspectorate, and is now undertaken by Her Majesty's Inspectorate of Pollution (HMIP) in England and Wales and Her Majesty's Industrial Pollution Inspectorate (HMIPI) in Scotland. The 1906 Act[1] made it a condition of registration that "the work is at the time of registration furnished with such appliances as appear to the Chief Inspector . . . to be necessary in order to enable the work to carry on in accordance with such of the requirements of" that Act or of Part I of the Health & Safety At Work, etc., Act 1974 as applied to the work. In consequence the Inspectorate developed extensive experience in determining what it considered to be best practicable means for preventing emissions and rendering them harmless and inoffensive. For several years appendices to the annual reports of the Chief Inspector contained "Notes on Best Practicable Means", and these were republished as a series of "BPM

10–076

---

[1] In s.9(5).

Notes" which provided guidance to the industrial operators concerned.

10–077   Though of considerable evidential value, the BPM Notes did not and do not have the force of law. Their main effect was to create various "presumptive limits", from which it could be presumed that BPM was not being applied if they were exceeded. Although the converse was not necessarily true, these presumptive limits were nevertheless of considerable practical value to those operating relevant processes, since by section 40 of the H.S.W.A. the burden is on any person accused of an offence under section 5(1) to show that there was no better practicable means than was in fact used to satisfy the duty. The presumptive limits in practice allow a person complying with them reasonable comfort that he will not be required to discharge this burden. Further, being considerably more general in their scope than the series of IPR and PG notes that have been produced for the purposes of the Part A and Part B processes controlled under Part I of the E.P.A., the BPM Notes could not in any event provide as much detailed guidance as the notes of the later series. With the introduction of the IPR and PG series, the BPM Notes are rapidly ceasing to have much relevance, particularly as they are nearly all a good many years old, and in many cases substantially out of date.

10–078   The Control of Industrial Pollution (Registration of Works) Regulations 1989[2] amended the registration procedure and, among other things, repealed the provisions in the 1906 Act requiring annual re-registration. Additionally, it made express provision for public access to applications, implementing Article 9 of EC Directive 84/360 (the Large Combustion Plants Directive).[3] By Regulation 10 of these 1989 Regulations, the owner of a registered work is required to give notice to the Secretary of State of any change in several of the particulars contained in the certificate of registration. Included in these are particulars as to the description of the nature of the work carried on and any change that may be required as to the maximum amount of any emissions that may be made when applying best practicable means, for example, where the capacity of the process is to be increased. If the alteration is not regarded as substantial, then the certificate of registration will be amended. Regulation 11(2) requires a application for a new certificate of registration to be made where the alternation is substantial; however since the bringing into force of Part I of the E.P.A., any such substantial alteration will inevitably mean the process will require authorisation as a Part A or Part B process, as the case may be, under Part I of the E.P.A. Where a registered process has

---

[2] S.I. 1989 No. 318.
[3] [1984] O.J. L188.

not been operated for 12 months or more, then its certificate of registration will automatically lapse; again any re-opening of the process will require authorisation under Part I of the E.P.A.

E.P.A. Part I—Part B Prescribed Processes

Chapter 9 has described the application of Part I of the E.P.A. to the processes to which it is applied, namely those in the Environmental Protection (Prescribed Processes and Substances) Regulations 1991 (the E.P. (P.P.&S.) Regulations), as amended. Since the legislation applicable to Part A and Part B processes is essentially the same, reference should accordingly be made to the discussion above relating to integrated pollution control. Nevertheless, at the risk of some repetition, it may be appropriate to re-state that Part B processes are exclusively concerned with emissions to air, and are subject to local, that is local authority, control as opposed to "central" control by HMIP/HMIPI.[4] The local authorities that exercise the controls over Part B processes are as set out in E.P.A., s.4(11), namely (outside Greater London) a District Council and the Council of Isles of Scilly, and also London Borough Councils, the Common Council of the City of London, the Sub-Treasurer of the Inner Temple and the Under-Treasurer of the Middle Temple; in Scotland the authority is an Islands or District Council as the case may be. An order may be made under section 2 of the Public Health (Control of Disease) Act 1984 designating a Port Health Authority, and where this has been done, that authority exercises the functions of a local authority within its district.[5]

10–079

The Part B processes controlled are those set out in the various Parts designated "B" in the E.P.(P.P.&S.) Regulations. As mentioned in paragraph 9–023 there is a presumption that (subject to the provisor referred to in paragraph 9–024 that there must be no offensive smell outside the premises) none of these processes is to be taken as a Part B Process, unless it will, or there is a likelihood that it will, result in the release into the air of one or more prescribed substances, being those listed in Schedule 4 to the same E.P.(P.P.&S.) Regulations, in a quantity greater than that which is so trivial that it is incapable of causing harm or its capacity to cause harm is insignificant. "Harm" has for this purpose the meaning given to it by section 1(4) of the E.P.A. (see paragraph 9–008).

10–080

Since only emissions to air are of concern in relation to a Part B Process, section 7(5), which deals with conditions to be attached to

10–081

---

[4] By s.4(4) of the E.P.A., the Secretary of State may direct that the or any local authority functions that may be exercisable in relation to a Part B process shall be exercised by HMIP.

[5] s.4(12).

authorisations, expressly provides that references in subsections (1) to (4) of section 7 to the release of substances into any environmental medium are to be read as references to the release of substances into the air. Further, the exclusive focus on emissions to air means that the concept of "Best Practicable Environmental Option" discussed in paragraphs 9–063 to 9–068 is not to be taken into account; the only consideration is what is BATNEEC for the process in question. For this, the same considerations apply as discussed earlier, and to assist the operators and the relevant authorities, a series of "Secretary of State's Process Guidance Notes" in respect of Part B processes has been issued, as listed in Table III/5.

TABLE 10/II

AIR POLLUTION CONTROL—PART B PROCESSES
List of Guidance Notes

10–082

PROCESS GUIDANCE NOTES	
Fuel and Power Industry Sector	
Reference	**Title**
PG1/1(91)	Waste oil burners, less than 0.4MW net rated thermal input
PG1/2(91)	Waste oil or recovered oil burners, less than 3MW net rated thermal input
PG1/3(91)	Boilers and furnaces, 20–50MW net rated thermal input
PG1/4(91)	Gas turbines, 200-50MW net rated thermal input
PG1/5(91)	Compression ignition engines, 20–50MW net rated thermal input
PG1/6(91)	Tyre and rubber combustion processes between 0.4 and 3MW net rated thermal input
PG1/7(91)	Straw combustion processes between 0.4 and 3MW net rated thermal input
PG1/8(91)	Wood combustion processes between 0.4 and 3MW net rated thermal input
PG1/9(91)	Poultry litter combustion processes between 0.4 and 3MW net rated thermal input

PG1/10(92)	Waste derived fuel combustion processes less than 3MW net rated thermal input
PG1/11(92)	Reheat and heat treatment furnaces, 20–50MW net rated thermal input

Metal Industry Sector

Reference	Title
PG2/1(91)	Furnaces for the extraction of non-ferrous metal from scrap
PG2/2(91)	Hot dip galvanising processes
PG2/3(91)	Electrical and rotary furnaces
PG2/4(91)	Iron, steel and non-ferrous metal foundry processes
PG2/5(91)	Hot and cold blast cupolas
PG2/6(91)	Aluminium and aluminium alloy processes
PG2/7(91)	Zinc and zinc alloy processes
PG2/8(91)	Copper and copper alloy processes
PG2/9(91)	Metal decontamination processes

Mineral Industry Sector

Reference	Title
PG3/1(93)	Blending, packing, loading and use of bulk cement
PG3/2(91)	Manufacture of heavy clay goods and refractory goods
PG3/3(91)	Glass (excluding lead glass) manufacturing processes
PG3/4(91)	Lead glass manufacturing processes
PG3/5(91)	Coal, coke and coal product processes
PG3/6(91)	Processes for the polishing or etching of glass or glass products using hydrofluoric acid
PG3/7(91)	Exfoliation of vermiculite and expansion of perlite
PG3/8(91)	Quarry processes including roadstone plants and the size reduction of bricks, tiles and concrete
PG3/9(91)	Sand drying and cooling
PG3/10(91)	China and ball clay
PG3/11(91)	Spray drying of ceramic materials
PG3/12(91)	Plaster processes
PG3/13(91)	Asbestos processes
PG3/14(91)	Lime slaking processes

Waste Disposal Industry Sector	
Reference	**Title**
PG5/1(92)	Clinical waste incineration processes under 1 tonne an hour
PG5/2(91)	Crematoria
PG5/3(91)	Animal carcase incineration processes under 1 tonne an hour
PG5/4(91)	General waste incineration processes under 1 tonne an hour
PG5/5(91)	Sewage sludge incineration processes under 1 tonne an hour

Other Industries	
Reference	**Title**
PG6/1(91)	Animal by-product rendering
PG6/2(91)	Manufacture of timber and wood-based products
PG6/3(91)	Chemical treatment of timber and wood-based products
PG6/4(91)	Processes for the manufacture of particleboard and fibre-board
PG6/5(91)	Maggot breeding processes
PG6/6(91)	Fur breeding processes
PG6/7(91)	Printing and coating of metal packaging
PG6/8(91)	Textile and fabric coating and finishing processes
PG6/9(91)	Manufacture of coating powder
PG6/10(92)	Coating manufacturing processes
PG6/11(92)	Manufacture of printing ink
PG6/12(91)	Production of natural sausage casings, tripe, chitterlings and other boiled green offal products
PG6/13(91)	Coil coating processes
PG6/14(91)	Film coating processes
PG6/15(91)	Coating in drum manufacturing and reconditioning processes
PG6/16(92)	Printworks
PG6/17(92)	Printing of flexible packaging
PG6/18(92)	Paper coating processes
PG6/19(92)	Fish meal and fish oil processes

PG6/20(92)	Paint application in vehicle manufacturing
PG6/21(92)	Hide and skin processes
PG6/22(92)	Leather finishing processes
PG6/23(92)	Coating of metal and plastic
PG6/24(92)	Pet food manufacturing processes
PG6/25(92)	Vegetable oil extraction and fat and oil refining processes
PG6/26(92)	Animal feed compounding processes
PG6/27(92)	Vegetable matter drying processes
PG6/28(92)	Rubber processes
PG6/29(92)	Di-isocyanate processes
PG6/30(92)	Production of compost for mushrooms
PG6/31(92)	Powder coating processes including sheradizing
PG6/32(92)	Adhesive coating processes
PG6/33(92)	Wood coating processes
PG6/34(92)	Respraying of road vehicles
PG6/35(92)	Metal and other thermal spraying processes
PG6/36(92)	Tobacco processing
PG6/37(92)	Knackers yards
PG6/38(92)	Blood processing
PG6/39(92)	Animal by-product dealers

GENERAL AND UPGRADING GUIDANCE NOTES	
GG1(91)	Introduction to Part I of the Act
GG1(91)	Authorisations
GG3(91)	Applications and registers
GG4(91)	Interpretation of terms used in process guidance notes
GG5(91)	Appeals
UG1 (92)	Revisions/additions to existing process and general guidance notes: No. 1

The application procedure for authorisation follows essentially the **10–083** same course as for a Part A process application. As mentioned in paragraph 9–076, the number of statutory consultees is however significantly less for a Part B process, being limited to the HSE and either English Nature, the Countryside Council for Wales or Scottish

Natural Heritage, as the case may be, if any emissions to the air may affect an SSSI within that body's area. In practice, local authorities have had considerable difficulty, firstly, in encouraging those requiring authorisation to put in their applications, and secondly, to process the applications that they have received. Accordingly, the Environmental Protection (Authorisation of Processes) (Determination Periods) Order 1991[6] extended the periods allowed for granting authorisations for Part B processes from four months to 12 months in most cases, and to 18 months[7] for certain waste oil burning processes. In essentially all other respects, the provisions relevant to Part A processes apply equally to Part B processes.

10–084   The requirements of section 5 of the H.S.W.A. cease to apply to any process that is a prescribed process for the purposes of Part I of the E.P.A., from the date that an authorisation under that Part I is granted or refused, or when, following any appeal against a refusal, there is a direction to grant the authorisation or an affirmation of the refusal.[8]

Statutory Nuisances

10–085   Processes that are neither prescribed processes under Part I of the E.P.A. nor come within the controls of the Clean Air Act 1993, may nevertheless be controlled under the statutory nuisance provisions contained in Part III of the E.P.A. These provisions are discussed in chapter 23, but it may be noted that among the matters that are declared to be statutory nuisances by section 79(1) are:

(b)   smoke emitted from premises so as to be prejudicial to health or a nuisance;

(c)   fumes or gases emitted from premises so as to be prejudicial to health or a nuisance;

(d)   any dust, steam, smell or other effluvia arising on industrial, trade or business premises and being prejudicial to health or a nuisance.

10–086   Nevertheless, by further provisions in section 79, the first of these three (item (b), smoke) excludes situations where the Clean Air Act 1993, would ordinarily apply, and the second item (c) (fumes or gases) is limited to private dwellings only, while item (d) is expressly stated not to apply to steam emitted from a railway locomotive engine.

10–087   A person who is charged with being responsible for a statutory nuisance is entitled in some circumstances to the defence that best practicable means were used to prevent, or to counteract the effects of,

---

[6] S.I. 1991 No. 513.
[7] In England & Wales; 15 months in Scotland.
[8] E.P.A., Sched. 15, para. 14.

the nuisance.[9] This defence is generally available in the case of the last of these three items, and also in relation to the first item (b) if, but only if, the smoke is emitted from a chimney. A person conducting investigations or research into air pollution may apply for an exemption under section 5(1) of the Clean Air Act 1993, and if granted this may also give exemption from liability under these statutory nuisance provisions.[10]

Agriculture

Agricultural practices and processes are generally subject to the same statutory provisions in respect of air pollution as other trade and business activities. Several of the processes prescribed for the purposes of Part I of the E.P.A. may be conducted on farms, and the provisions of the Clean Air Act 1993 and the statutory nuisance provisions of Part III of the E.P.A. are also normally applicable.[11] A Code of Good Agricultural Practice for the Protection of Air has been issued by the Ministry of Agriculture, Fisheries and Food and by the Welsh Office, Agriculture Department, which identifies many sources of air pollution that may arise on farms. Its provisions are however non-statutory, and though they might well be of some persuasive value to a court considering whether or not a statutory nuisance exists, compliance with its recommendations does not constitute any legal defence.

10–088

As a result of public concern over the extent of straw and stubble burning, provisions were included in the E.P.A., at section 152, to allow regulations to be made to restrict the burning, by persons engaged in agriculture, of crop residues on agricultural land, and also to provide exemptions from any such restrictions. Under this power, the burning of most crop residues has been phased out following the coming into effect on 29th June 1993 of the Crop Residues (Burning) Regulations 1993.[12] These prohibit the burning on agricultural land, by persons engaged in agriculture, of various crop residues, namely, cereal straw, cereal stubble, and residues of any of oil-seed rape, field beans harvested dry and peas harvested dry. Nevertheless, burning of these crop residues is permitted, by way of exception, for the purposes

10–089

---

[9] E.P.A., s.80(7), (8).
[10] See also para. 10–053.
[11] Though the Clean Air (Emission of Dark Smoke) (Exemption) Regulations 1969 exempt in certain circumstances the burning of carcasses of animals or poultry, and containers contaminated by any pesticide, at least where there is no other reasonably safe and practicable method of disposing of the matter other than by burning.
[12] S.I. 1993 No. 1366, which replaced the Crop Residues (Restrictions on Burning) (No.2) Regulations 1991 (S.I. 1991 No. 1590).

of educational research, disease control or the elimination of plant pests,[13] or in order to dispose of straw stack remains or broken bales.[14] Regulation 5 expressly permits the burning of linseed residues generally, and not only for the limited purposes applicable to the other residues. However, any burning of linseed, or of other residues under any of the exceptions to the general prohibition, must be conducted in accordance with the comprehensive conditions set out in Schedule 2 to the Regulations.

10–090   Schedule 2 sets out in detail how any burning must be conducted, and in particular where it may not be conducted, by prescribing distances from, *e.g.* buildings, roads, railways and hedgerows. In particular, burning is prohibited during the period between one hour before sunset and the following sunrise, and also on any Saturday, Sunday and Bank holiday. All persons concerned in the burning operation must be familiar with the provisions of the Regulations, and there must be supervision by at least two responsible adults, at least one of whom must have experience of burning crop residues and be in general control of the operation. Various fire precautions are stipulated, and notice must be given to the relevant fire authority and environmental health department, as well as to occupiers of all adjacent premises, and where appropriate to the air traffic control of any aerodrome that has a perimeter fence within 800 metres of the area to be burned.

10–091   Since the Clean Air Act provisions apply to stubble burning, it is essential to avoid the production of dark smoke. Guidance is given in the Code of Good Agricultural Practice for the Protection of Air on avoiding this. The ashes of burnt cereal straw and cereal stubble must not, without reasonable excuse, be allowed to remain on the soil for longer than 24 hours after commencement of the burning—they must be ploughed in either within that period or, if wind conditions would result in that creating a nuisance, as soon as conditions allow. To avoid inconsistent requirements being applied by local byelaws, the Burning of Crop Residues (Repeal of Byelaws) Order 1992, which came into force on April 2, 1992 repealed all local authority byelaws made under section 235(1) of the Local Government Act 1972 dealing with the burning of crop residues on agricultural land. Contravention of the provisions of the Regulations may lead to a fine on summary conviction not exceeding level 5.[15]

---

[13] Provided, in the last case, a notice has been served under art. 22 of the Plant Health (Great Britain) Order 1993 (S.I. 1993 No. 1320).
[14] Reg. 4.
[15] It is intended to bring in a general ban on the burning of crop residues, but limited exemptions are likely to be made to any such ban.

Equipment and Fuels

While controls over the conduct of various potentially polluting   **10–092**
processes form the bulk of air pollution legislation, controls over the
design and construction, and in particular over permitted emissions of
specified pollutants, of incinerators, power generation plant and
vehicles, and over fuel used for transport play a major part in practical
pollution control. These controls are not discussed here in depth, since
such detail is likely to be of interest to relatively few. The following is
therefore a brief account of the controls of principal significance.

Large Combustion Plants

EC Directive 88/609[16] places limits on emissions of sulphur dioxide   **10–093**
and nitrogen oxides from what it terms large combustion plants, being
principally electricity generating stations burning fossil fuels. The
Directive was to be implemented by the end of June 1990 and required
the drawing up and implementation by each Member State of national
programmes for the reduction of sulphur dioxide emissions in three
phases taking effect from 1993, 1998 and 2003 respectively, and
reductions of nitrogen oxides in two phases taking effect in 1993 and
1998. The Member States' emission ceilings and the timetables for
phased reductions are to be reviewed by not later than July 1, 1995. The
figures and percentages applicable to the United Kingdom are shown
in Table 10/III.

TABLE 10/III

		1980	1993	1998	2003
SO_2	UK emission ceilings (kilotonnes)	3,883	3,106	2,330	1,553
	% reduction	-	20	40	60
NO_x	UK emission ceilings (kilotonnes)	1,016	864	711	711
	% reduction	-	15	30	30

In addition, for new plants, being those authorised on or after July 1,
1987, specific emission limit values are set, for sulphur dioxide,
nitrogen oxides and dust, which vary in accordance with the fuel used
and, as regards sulphur dioxide, the thermal input rating of the plant.

[16] [1988] O.J. L336.

507

10–094   There are various escape clauses to cover certain contingencies making it difficult or impossible to meet the Directive's requirements. Where emission limits for new plants burning indigenous solid fuel (*e.g.* the high sulphur coal mined in Britain) cannot meet the SO_2 emission limits set without using "excessively expensive technology", such plants are excused from complying with those limits, but must at all events achieve prescribed rates of desulphurisation as laid down in Annex VIII to the Directive.[17]

10–095   The implementation of these requirements in the United Kingdom is brought about through the application of Part I of the E.P.A. Large combustion plants were the first category of process to be made subject to IPC.

Municipal Waste Incinerators

10–096   EC Directives 89/369[18] and 89/429[19] relate to emissions to air from new and existing municipal waste incineration plants[20] respectively. New municipal waste incineration plants are those for which authorisation to operate is granted on or after December 1, 1990, and existing plants those for which the first authorisation to operate was granted before that date. The New Plants Directive 89/369 sets out various emission limit values for such plants, relating to emissions of total dust, certain heavy metals, hydrochloric acid, hydrofluoric acid, and sulphur dioxide, these limits varying to some extent depending on the normal capacity of the incineration plant. In addition, all such plants must provide a residence time of at least two seconds at at least 850°C in the presence of at least 6 per cent oxygen—this requirement is particularly relevant in minimising production of dioxins. Special allowance is made for plants specifically designed to burn waste-derived fuels, which means, at least in this context, fuel manufactured from the combustible fraction of municipal waste, and which contains no more than 15 per cent ash prior to any addition of substances intended to enhance fuel properties. Member States may rely on this provision where compliance with the prescribed emission limits would entail excessive costs, or if these limits are otherwise inappropriate from a technical viewpoint. Nevertheless, plants benefiting from these derogations must not burn anything else, and the provisions of the Air Framework Directive 84/360[21] must be complied

[17] Art. 5(2).
[18] [1989] O.J. L163.
[19] [1989] O.J. L203.
[20] Defined to exclude plants used for the incineration of sewage sludge, chemical, toxic and dangerous waste, and clinical waste.
[21] [1984] O.J. L188.

with—specifically the requirement to use best available technology not entailing excessive cost.

The Existing Plants Directive 89/429 requires existing incineration **10–097** plants to be upgraded to meet the standards of the New Plants Directive by dates which depend on the nominal capacity of the plants concerned. Those with a capacity of six tonnes of waste or more per hour must meet these conditions by December 1, 1996. All other plants must be raised to the new plants emissions standards by December 1, 2000, and must meet intermediate standards laid down in the Existing Plants Directive[22] by December 1, 1995. These intermediate standards relate to emissions of dust and concentrations of carbon monoxide in the output gases. Additionally, by December 1, 1995, these existing plants of under six tonnes per hour capacity must be able to burn the waste at at least 850°C in the presence of at least 6 per cent oxygen; however in this case, the residence time is not required to be at least two seconds, and must merely be "a sufficient period of time to be determined by the competent authorities".

Implementation of these requirements is likewise to be brought **10–098** about by the application of Part I of the E.P.A. to such plants. The 17th Report of the Royal Commission on Environmental Pollution "The Incineration of Waste" lists the 30 municipal waste incinerators presently operating in the United Kingdom.[23] The most recent of these was opened in 1981, and none will comply with the requirements of the Existing Plants Directive without upgrading. It is generally accepted that for many of these plants upgrading will not be a commercially viable operation, unless they are also adapted to recover energy from the incineration process.

Hazardous Waste Incinerators

The incineration of hazardous waste is liable, in the absence of **10–099** effective preventive measures, to lead to emissions of a variety of toxic substances, including in particular dioxins and furans, and cadmium, mercury, lead and other heavy metals. Directive 94/67[24] on the incineration of hazardous waste which sets very tight limits for these and other substances and also prescribes detailed process and procedure controls. The dioxin/furan limit of $0.1ng/m^3$ [25] is of special note, being a level that had not been shown to be achievable on a commercial scale operation at the time it was first put forward in

---

[22] In Arts. 3 to 7.
[23] In its Table 3.4.
[24] [1994] O.J. L365.
[25] This being the aggregate of the amounts of 17 different dioxins and furans, adjusted by their appropriate toxic equivalence factors as set out in Annex I to the Directive.

earlier drafts. This is to apply from January 1, 1997, but will however only be a guide value unless the Commission has, by July 1, 1996, established the availability of harmonised measurement methods. The Directive's requirements will apply to all new hazardous waste incinerators granted "permit to operate" on or after December 31, 1996, and to previously permitted ones on June 30, 2000.

Road Vehicles

10–100   Transport is one of the industrial sectors on which the 5th EC Environmental Action Programme is focusing attention, and there have been numerous EC Directives and proposals for Directives in this area. In legislating for vehicle emissions, the Directives deal separately with light duty vehicles, being cars and vans under 3.5 tonnes, and heavy duty vehicles, being those over that limit, principally lorries and buses. Light duty vehicles are divided into various sub-categories, mostly based on whether they run on petrol or diesel fuel and on various bands of engine capacity. The principal Directives consist of:

Petrol Engines:	
Directive	*O.J. Reference*
70/220 as amended by	[1970] O.J. L76
88/76	[1988] O.J. L36
89/458	[1989] O.J. L226
91/441	[1991] O.J. L242
93/59	[1993] O.J. L186
94/12	[1994] O.J. L100
Diesel Engines	
Directive	*O.J. Reference*
72/306	[1972] O.J. L190
70/220 as amended by	[1970] O.J. L76
88/436	[1988] O.J. L214
91/441	[1991] O.J. L242
94/12	[1994] O.J. L100

Heavy Duty Vehicles	
Directive	*O.J. Reference*
72/306	[1972] O.J. L190
88/77	[1988] O.J. L36
as amended by	
91/542	[1991] O.J. L295
77/537	[1977] O.J. L220 (tractors)

It is inappropriate here to set out the full detail of these complex **10–101** Directives, for which reference should be made to them directly. They set out emission limits for carbon monoxide, hydrocarbons, NO_x, (sometimes hydrocarbons and NO_x jointly), VOCs and particulates. In certain cases, implementation dates are set for when the prescribed emission standards are to be met by new models, and a second date, following some six months to two years afterwards, for when the emission standards must be met by all new registrations in the relevant vehicle category. One such standard has the effect that all petrol driven cars first registered after January 1, 1993 should have been fitted with three-way catalytic converters. The UK nevertheless postponed the implementation of this requirement by twelve months in order to allow car manufacturers and dealers to clear their old stocks which were abnormally high due to the economic recession.[26]

Implementation of these EC Directives in the United Kingdom is **10–102** through a series of Motor Vehicles (Construction and Use) Regulations and Motor Vehicles (Type Approval) (Great Britain) Regulations, issued under the Road Traffic Acts 1972 and 1974.

Further controls over pollution created by transport are provided by **10–103** those governing the lead and sulphur content of fuels. Lead in petrol is

[26] As a matter of historical interest, Directive 88/76 provided the first occasion on which the European Parliament exercised the increased powers available to it following the amendment of the Rome Treaty by the Single European Act. The initial proposal for this Directive by the European Commission had been amended by the Council of Ministers when adopting their "common position" to apply a less stringent emission standard. When this common position was before the European Parliament, amendments were passed to tighten the emission standards in line with those present originally. The European Commission accepted these amendments, and accordingly when the amended proposal returned to the Council, the Ministers were unable, by virtue of Article 149 of the Rome Treaty, to re-amend the text back to their previous common position except by unanimous vote. Since Denmark at least was in favour of the stricter position, the Council's only options were to accept the amended proposal in its stricter form, or to fail to adopt the Directive at all, and this latter was in practice politically unacceptable. Directive 94/12 is one of the first environmental measures to have been issued since the coming into effect of the Maastricht Treaty. It proceeded under the co-decision procedure of Article 189B and is a joint Directive of both the Parliament and the Council.

the subject of Directives 85/210[27] and an amending Directive 87/416.[28] These have been implemented in the United Kingdom by the Motor Fuel (Lead Content of Petrol) Regulations 1981[29] as last amended in 1989. The effect of these Regulations has been to bring about a reduction of the permitted lead content of petrol from 0.84 grams per litre in the early 1970s to the present figure of 0.15 grams per litre. In addition, by virtue of The Road Vehicles (Construction and Use) (Amendment No. 6) Regulations 1988, Motor Vehicles (Type Approval) (Great Britain) (Amendment) Regulations 1988, and the Motor Vehicles (Type Approval for Goods Vehicles) (Great Britain) (Amendment) Regulations 1988, all new vehicles were required to be capable of running on unleaded petrol by October 1, 1989 for new type approvals and by October 1, 1990 for existing models. The amending Directive 87/416 entitled Member States to prohibit the sale of regular grade leaded petrol on not less six months notice.

10–104   The sulphur content of fuels for vehicles and combustion plants inevitably has a major impact on the creation of sulphur oxides and hence of acid rain. EC Directive 75/716 (as amended)[30] currently controls the sulphur content of gasoils (for example diesel fuel for vehicles and heating oil). A further Directive 93/12[31] is replacing the previous legislation on this topic, and imposes the following deadlines:

October 1, 1994	diesel fuels to contain 0.2 per cent maximum by weight of sulphur
October 1, 1994	gasoils, other than diesel fuels or kerosene for aircraft, to contain 0.2 per cent maximum by weight of sulphur
October 1, 1996	diesel fuels to contain 0.05 per cent maximum by weight of sulphur
July 31, 1994	a further proposal to be adopted by the Council for a second stage reduction, including prescribing a maximum limit for aviation kerosene to take effect by October 1, 1999.

To meet the October 1996 deadline for lower sulphur diesel fuels, such fuels must become increasingly available from October 1, 1995 in the Member States.

10–105   The Clean Air Act 1993 contains powers in sections 30 and 31 for the Secretary of State to impose controls over the composition and

---

[27] [1985] O.J. L96.
[28] [1987] O.J. L225.
[29] S.I. 1981 No. 1523, as amended by S.I. 1985 No. 1728 and S.I. 1989 No. 547.
[30] [1975] O.J. L307.
[31] [1993] O.J. L74.

contents of any fuel that may be used in motor vehicles and similarly to impose limits on the sulphur content of oil fuel used in furnaces or engines. These provisions, which derive from C.O.P.A. 1974, provided the basis of the Oil Fuel (Sulphur Content of Gas Oil) Regulations[32] and the Motor Fuel (Sulphur Content of Gas Oil) Regulations,[33] which give effect to the currently applicable Directive 75/716 as amended, setting a maximum sulphur content of 0.3 per cent for gas oils, whether used as motor fuel or as heating oil. Directive 87/219[34] permits Member States to impose a lower maximum figure of 0.2 per cent, but the United Kingdom has not made use of this.

Ozone Depleting Compounds

Stratospheric ozone serves to protect the surface of the earth from the full impact of the ultraviolet rays that are emitted by the sun. Excessive exposure to ultraviolet radiation leads to increased incidence of skin cancer, eye cataracts and various other pathological conditions. The discovery of a hole in the stratospheric ozone layer over the South Pole, and subsequently that this hole was expanding and that a similar hole existed over the North Pole, coupled with general acceptance in the scientific community as to the cause, has led to concerted international action with the aim of minimising any further damage. The principal factor in the depletion of the ozone layer has been identified as the chlorine in a variety of gaseous or volatile liquid organic compounds, and in particular those contained in chlorofluorocarbons—bromine has a similar effect. CFCs, although extremely inert chemically under normal conditions, and desirable for precisely that reason, are very volatile. If released into the atmosphere, they eventually rise to the stratosphere, where they dissociate under the action of sunlight, releasing chlorine atoms that attack the ozone. The process whereby releases of CFCs reach the ozone layer and attack it are extremely slow, and once this effect has occurred, it is thought it may take 100 years or more for the condition of the ozone layer to return to its original state, even without further effects of subsequent releases of more CFCs. CFCs are not however the only compounds that are liable to deplete the ozone layer—hydrochlorofluorocarbons, halons,[35] methyl chloroform, carbon tetrachloride, trichloroethane and methyl bromide are among the numerous other

10–106

---

[32] S.I. 1990 No. 1096
[33] S.I. 1990 No. 1097.
[34] [1987] O.J. L91.
[35] Compounds akin to CFCs but which contain bromine atoms in place of some (but not all) of the chlorine atoms, as well as fluorine atoms.

compounds that have been identified as potentially harmful ozone depleters.

10–107   The major uses of CFCs are, or at least have been, in aerosols, as the refrigerant in refrigerators, freezers and air-conditioning plant, as the blowing agent in polystyrene foam, and as a solvent for cleaning microelectronic components. Halons are widely used in fire extinguishers, being very effective and safe flame suppressants, and a wide variety of other chlorinated organic compounds are valuable as solvents, typically in dry cleaning. Methyl bromide is used for the fumigation of soil.

10–108   Following the recognition of the damage that was being done to the ozone layer, a meeting at Montreal in September 1987 resulted in the signing of a protocol to the Vienna Convention for the Protection of the Ozone Layer, termed "An Agreement on Substances Which Deplete the Ozone Layer" and commonly known as the "Montreal Protocol". This was ratified by some sixty nations, and required industrialised countries to phase out the principal ozone depleters. Subsequently the Protocol has been reviewed and revised so as to accelerate the phase out of the compounds and to add further compounds to the phase out programme. The original Montreal Protocol was given effect in the EC by EC Regulation 3322/88;[36] following an amendment to the Montreal Protocol agreed in London in June 1990, the Regulation was repealed and replaced by Regulation 594/91.[37] A meeting of the contracting parties in Copenhagen in November 1992 agreed a second amendment to the Protocol,[38] accelerating the phasing-out programme and introducing controls over certain additional substances recognised to be harmful to the ozone layer. This resulted in Regulation 3952/92[39] which significantly amended Regulation 594/91, and in fact imposes a still more rapid phase out of ozone depleters than is required by the second amendment.

10–109   Regulation 594/91 as amended applies to specified CFCs, halons and HCFCs as listed in Annex I to the Regulation together with carbon tetrachloride and 1,1,1-trichloroethane. These are all generically referred to as "controlled substances". The release into free circulation in the EC of these controlled substances is made subject to quantitative limits. The limits apply equally to virgin material as to recycled or used material or any imported from third countries.[40] Import quotas for named companies are allocated by Commission decision. Since

---

[36] [1988] O.J. L297.
[37] [1991] O.J. L67.
[38] Approved by the EC by Decision 94/68, [1994] O.J. L33.
[39] [1992] O.J. L405.
[40] Art. 3(1); Commission Decision 94/563 sets the limits for 1995, [1994] O.J. L215.

August 10, 1993,[41] all exports from the EC of controlled substances to any country not a party to the Montreal Protocol as amended have been prohibited,[42] and the release into free circulation in the EC of controlled substances imported from such non-parties prohibited, with the sole exception of HCFCs. Part II of the Regulation sets out detailed provisions for controlling production and supply to consumers of the various controlled substances, laying down phase out programmes for them. The effects of the amendments made by Regulation 3952/92 are as follows:

Controlled Substance	Revised Phase Out Programme
CFCs	85% cut by January 1, 1994 Phase out by January 1, 1995 *
Carbon tetrachloride	85% cut by January 1, 1994 Phase out by January 1, 1995 *
Halons	Phase out by January 1, 1994 *
1,1,1-trichloroethane	50% cut by January 1, 1994 Phase out by January 1, 1996 *

* Provision is made for possible exemptions from these phase out dates for essential uses.

As mentioned, the second (Copenhagen) amendment to the Protocol provided for controls over additional substances, by creating a phase out of HCFCs by 2030, a freeze on production and consumption of methyl bromide at 1991 levels, to take effect on January 1, 1995, and a phase out of HBFCs by January 1, 1996. A proposal for a further Council Regulation on ozone depleting substances was issued in August 1993.[43] **10–110**

Since these controls are the subject of EC Regulations, they are directly binding on all relevant producers and importers, and no implementing legislation is needed. Article 15 of Regulation 594/91 requires Member States to "take appropriate legal or administrative action in case of infringement of the provisions of this Regulation". No UK legislation has been made providing sanctions for infringements, **10-111**

---

[41] From January 1, 1993 for CFCs and halons.
[42] Subject to limited exceptions to certain countries as permitted by Reg. 2047/93: [1993] O.J. L185.
[43] [1993] O.J. C232; now issued as Reg. 3093/94, [1994] O.J. L333, which repealed Reg. 594/91.

but this is considered unnecessary since all the organisations concerned have co-operated in complying with the Regulation's requirements.

10–112   Nevertheless the Environmental Protection (Non-Refillable Containers) Regulations 1994,[44] made under section 140 of the E.P.A., prohibit the importation, supply and storage (subject to certain exceptions for the purposes of export, analysis, or research and development) of certain CFCs and HCFCs under pressure in non-refillable containers. Non-refillable containers, which have in the past been used for supplying refrigerants for use in air conditioning and refrigeration machinery, retain a "heel" of the refrigerant after release of the bulk of the contents that is in practice thereafter vented to the atmosphere. Powers of entry and search, and to request information and assistance, are given to the Secretary of State and to local authorities. Penalties for breach of the main prohibitions are a fine of up to the statutory maximum on summary conviction, and on conviction on indictment an unlimited fine and up to two years imprisonment.

Volatile Organic Compounds

10–113   Many volatile organic compounds (VOCs) are both precursors of low level ozone, and often also powerful greenhouse gases. Significant sources include vehicle exhausts, and the drying of solvent based products such as paints, glues and inks. Substantial fugitive emissions occur in the course of oil refining and petrochemical production operations, and also at petrol filling stations. There has been increasing concern to control emissions of VOCs, and in the United Kingdom relevant conditions may be attached to authorisations of processes subject to Part I of the E.P.A. A government strategy paper[45] has set out proposals for achieving a 30 per cent reduction in emissions of VOCs (on 1988 levels) by 1999. This would be designed to implement a protocol to the 1979 Convention on long-range transboundary air pollution concerning the control of VOC emissions, committing most of the parties to it to reduce their national emissions of VOCs by this amount. Additionally, the protocol requires national and international emission standards to be applied to new sources of VOCs and, among other things, to promote the use of products with low or no VOC content.

---

[44] S.I. 1994 No. 199.
[45] "Reducing Emissions of Volatile Organic Compounds and Levels of Ground Level Ozone—A UK Strategy", DoE, November 1993.

Two EC Directives are concerned with air pollution by VOCs. **10–114** Directive 91/441[46] (referred to above in paragraph 10–100) has among its objectives the reduction of VOC emissions from exhaust fumes and evaporation emissions from motor vehicles by some 80 to 90 per cent within ten to fifteen years. Directive 94/63[47] is directed at the control of VOC emissions from the storage of petrol and in the course of its distribution from terminals to service stations; these emissions are estimated to represent some 5% of total VOC emissions. The controls require storage installations at terminals and at service stations, loading and unloading equipment, and mobile equipment, all to be designed and operated as prescribed in the Directive. A draft of a further Directive, on VOC emissions occurring while refuelling vehicles with petrol at service stations, is expected to be formally published in 1995.[48]

[46] [1991] O.J. L242.
[47] [1994] O.J. L365.
[48] [1993] O.J. C125.

Chapter 11

WASTE ON LAND

Introduction

For many years public health legislation has not merely empowered, **11–001** but in fact required, local authorities to remove offensive accumulations of waste and other matter. These duties are now contained in the statutory nuisance provisions of Part III of the E.P.A., described in Chapter 23. Under these powers where a local authority becomes aware of "any accumulation or deposit which is prejudicial to health or a nuisance"[1] in its area, it must serve an abatement notice on the person responsible; any other person may seek an abatement order from the magistrates to deal with the problem. Precautionary controls over the deposit of waste on land are however of much more recent origin. Since 1948 a degree of prior control has been imposed through the Town and Country Planning Act 1947 and the planning legislation that followed it, which required, and still requires, as a pre-requisite for any deposit of waste on land, a planning permission for that deposit. Nevertheless, a planning consent, relating for example to the operations of a waste disposal site, cannot legitimately impose conditions that are not properly planning matters; moreover a planning permission, unlike a licence to dispose of waste, runs with the land, and cannot be revoked except on payment of compensation, however incompetent or dangerous the conduct of the landfill operation may be.

In the 1960s the government set up two groups to study toxic wastes **11–002** and refuse disposal; their reports, in 1970 and 1971 respectively,[2] laid the foundations of the subsequent 1974 legislation. However, as a result of public outcry following the discovery of several cyanide containing deposits, controls over toxic waste were introduced as a matter of urgency by the Deposit of Poisonous Waste Act 1972. This

---

[1] E.P.A., s.79(1)(e).
[2] "Disposal of Solid Toxic Wastes", DoE/Scottish Development Department, HMSO 1970; "Refuse Disposal", DoE, HMSO 1971.

established, for the first time, formal procedures for notifying the appropriate authorities before removing or depositing poisonous, noxious or polluting waste. Other non-toxic waste remained largely uncontrolled until implementation of the Control of Pollution Act 1974[3] ("C.O.P.A.") first brought the current extensive regulatory regime into effect. This regime was extended to "special", *i.e.* hazardous, waste in 1981, replacing that of the 1972 Act, which was then repealed.

11–003   Further seminal reports followed from the House of Lords Select Committee on Science and Technology in 1981, and the Royal Commission on Environmental Pollution in 1985.[4] The latter proposed the introduction of a duty of care in relation to waste, that has now been implemented by section 34 of the E.P.A. In 1989 the House of Lords Select Committee again reported on hazardous waste disposal in a critical report, while the House of Commons Environment Committee produced perhaps its most hard hitting report ever, lambasting the government for its failure to give effect to the existing legislation and in particular its failure to use its powers to control waste disposal practices.[5]

11–004   Two further reports were published by House of Commons Committees in early 1990, as the Environmental Protection Bill was passing through Parliament, on contaminated land and on toxic waste disposal in Wales.[6]

11–005   One feature of the waste controls under C.O.P.A. was their inadequacy against fly tipping. Even if the offender could be caught and convicted, the penalties imposed tended to be low and no serious deterrent, in view of the profits available on the occasions when prosecution was avoided. Due to delays in bringing forward the Environmental Protection Bill, legislation was introduced ahead of it that resulted in the Control of Pollution (Amendment) Act 1989, providing for registration (though not licensing) of carriers of waste, and for seizure of vehicles used for illegal waste disposal. This Act

---

[3] The principal operating provisions of which were brought into effect on June 14, 1976.
[4] "Hazardous Waste Disposal", House of Lords Select Committee on Science and Technology, First Report 1980–81, HMSO; "Managing Waste: The Duty of Care" RCEP 11th Report 1985, HMSO.
[5] "Hazardous Waste Disposal", House of Lords Select Committee on Science and Technology, 4th Report 1988–89, HMSO; "Toxic Waste", House of Commons Environment Committee, 2nd Report 1988–89, which opened with the words "Never, in any of our inquiries into environmental problems, have we experienced such consistent and universal criticism of existing legislation and of central and local government as we have during the course of this inquiry".
[6] "Contaminated Land" House of Commons Environment Committee, 1st Report 1989–90, HMSO; "Toxic Waste Disposal in Wales" House of Commons Welsh Affairs Committee, 1st Report 1989–90, HMSO.

came into full effect on April 1, 1992,[7] and is discussed more fully below (see paragraphs 11–266 to 11–287). It is intended to remain in full force alongside Part II of the E.P.A., which contains no comparable provisions.

Waste policy was also being developed at EC level over the same period, and in the mid 1970s EC Directive 75/442[8] issued, which required Member States to supervise and control the disposal of waste and to encourage the prevention, recycling and re-use of waste. It reflected in many respects similar provisions contained in the UK Control of Pollution Act that had become law the previous year. This Directive has now been totally rewritten by Directive 91/156,[9] which replaced all its substantive provisions.[10] In particular the amending Directive provides a definition of "waste", on the basis of which the Commission was required to draw up a list of wastes falling into the categories set out in that definition.[11] "Waste" as defined by the Directive is referred to in the UK legislation as "Directive waste"; its meaning is discussed at paragraphs 11–035 to 11–071.   **11–006**

The amendments made by Directive 91/156 were due to be implemented throughout the EC by April 1, 1993. The new text sets out a number of fundamental objectives, which must govern all waste disposal policies, thereby giving effect to EC waste disposal policy as proposed in a Commission Communication and defined in a Council Resolution on waste policy.[12] The Waste Management Licensing Regulations 1994[13] (the "1994 Licensing Regulations") made under the E.P.A. give these fundamental obligations statutory force in England, Wales and Scotland by defining them as "relevant objectives"[14] and requiring all authorities discharging waste regulatory functions, and preparing or modifying waste management plans, to do so with or for the purpose of achieving these relevant objectives.[15]   **11–007**

First, there must be a hierarchy of waste management options consisting of, in order of preference: **11–008**

---

[7] By the Control of Pollution (Amendment) Act 1989 (Commencement) Order 1991, S.I. 1991 No. 1618.

[8] [1975] O.J. L194.

[9] [1991] O.J. L78.

[10] References to "the Directive" and to "Directive 75/442" in this chapter are to Directive 75/442 as so amended unless otherwise stated.

[11] Annexed to its Decision of December 20, 1993, [1994] O.J. L5.

[12] [1990] O.J. L122. In *Comitato di Coordinamento per la Difesa della Cava and Others v. Regione Lombardia and Others*, Case C-236/92, [1994] Env. L.R. 281, the European Court of Justice held that the corresponding objectives of the original Directive were neither unconditional nor precise and so could not confer any enforceable rights on individuals.

[13] S.I. 1994 No.1056.

[14] Sched. 4, para. 4.

[15] Sched. 4, para. 2(1). The corresponding objectives in the Directive before amendment were never given legislative backing.

(1)   prevention or reduction of waste at source, and also of its harmfulness, by the development of clean technologies, by the technical development and marketing of products, which by the nature of their manufacture, use or final disposal would make the smallest possible contribution to the amount or harmfulness of waste and pollution hazards, and by the development of appropriate techniques for the final disposal of dangerous substances contained in waste destined for recovery;

(2)   the recovery of waste by means of recycling, re-use or reclamation, or any other process, with a view to extracting secondary raw materials, and also the use of waste as a source of energy.[16]

11–009   Secondly, there is the broad overall obligation on all Member States to take the necessary measures to ensure that waste is recovered or disposed of without endangering human health and without using processes or methods which could harm the environment.[17] In particular, such recovery is to be without risk to water, soil and plants and animals; without causing a nuisance through noise or odours; [and] without adversely affecting the countryside or places of special interest. In addition, Member States must also take the necessary measures to prohibit the abandonment, dumping or uncontrolled disposal of waste. The Directive has Annexes IIA and IIB listing "disposal operations" and "operations which may lead to recovery" respectively (see Tables 11/III and 11/IV), and "disposal" and "recovery" are used to mean any of those respective operations only.

11–010   Thirdly, and very significantly, Member States are required to establish "an integrated and adequate network of disposal installations, taking account of the best available technology not involving excessive costs". The network must enable the Community as a whole to become self-sufficient in waste disposal, and the Member States to move towards that aim individually, taking into account geographical circumstances or need for specialised solutions for certain types of waste.[18] As explicitly noted in the Council Resolution on waste policy, however, this requirement for self-sufficiency in waste disposal does not apply to waste recovery.

[16] Art. 3(1).
[17] Art. 4.
[18] Art. 5(1).

522

The competent authorities of the Member States are required to draw up waste management plans designed to achieve these objectives, covering among other things, the type, quality and origin of waste to be recovered or disposed of, general technical requirements, any special arrangements for particular wastes, and suitable disposal sites or installations.[19] Crucially, the Member States are permitted to take necessary measures to prevent movements of waste which are not in accordance with their waste management plans;[20] *prima facie*, therefore, they may prohibit imports of waste from other Member States that have not been allowed for in the relevant waste management plan. Whether such prohibitions are compatible with the free movement of goods provisions of the Rome Treaty has yet to be litigated. **11–011**

A conflict had developed between applying free market principles to the disposal of waste, seeing this as just another economic activity for which, in the single market, national boundaries should be irrelevant, and environmental principles whereby everyone should take direct responsibility for their own waste, with the incentives that that would be likely to create for preventing waste at source. This conflict came to a head in *The Commission v. Belgium*[21] in the European Court of Justice, in which the European Commission challenged rules laid down by Wallonia prohibiting the import of waste into that region from outside. The European Court held that environmental considerations should be given priority over free market considerations and that accordingly Wallonia was entitled to prohibit imports if this was in fact necessary for the purpose of protecting its environment.[22] **11–012**

The Directive lays down certain administrative requirements, a substantial number of which were already being met in the United Kingdom under C.O.P.A.; they are expressly provided for in the E.P.A. and the regulations made under it. In particular, there is a requirement for each Member State to draw up waste management plans, and to prevent movements of waste which do not conform with the applicable waste management plan; to provide for licensing of undertakings which carry out any disposal or recovery operations on waste; and to require registration or licensing of undertakings which either collect or transport waste on a professional basis or which, as **11–013**

---

[19] Art. 7(1).
[20] Art. 7(3).
[21] Case C-2/90.
[22] Though it could not prohibit imports of hazardous waste within the scope of Directive 78/319, as this had already provided for harmonisation of national laws on such waste. On the facts of that case it is hard to accept the reasoning of the Court that there was any significant threat to the environment in Wallonia that could not have been averted much less restrictively, for example by raising the price of the local waste disposal facilities.

dealers or brokers of waste, arrange for the disposal or recovery of waste on behalf of others.[23]

11–014   Under the waste regime of C.O.P.A. the growing trend towards recycling and re-use of waste came increasingly into conflict with the proper and effective enforcement of the statutory controls over the deposit and disposal of waste, which frequently tended to hamper such desirable activities. Article 11 of the Directive thus constitutes an important development in that it allows exemption from the licensing requirements of the preceding Articles for establishments or undertakings that carry out their own waste disposal and those that carry out waste recovery, provided (i) that the national competent authorities have adopted general rules for each type of activity laying down the types and quantities of waste and the conditions under which the activity in question may be exempted from the licensing requirements, and (ii) that the types and quantities of waste and methods of disposal or recovery are such that the conditions imposed under Article 4 to ensure environmental protection[24] are complied with. Although such activities are exempted from licensing, the establishments or undertakings concerned must still be registered.[25] The United Kingdom has taken the opportunity to exempt a substantial numbers of activities under this power, as listed in Part III of the 1994 Licensing Regulations.

11–015   The EC has also developed a series of rules in relation to hazardous waste through, firstly, Directive 78/319,[26] and now by Directive 91/689,[27] which will replace Directive 78/319 when it is brought into effect.[27A] The significance of the EC Directives on hazardous waste is considered more fully in paragraphs 11–114 to 11–118.

The Waste Regulatory Structure

11–016   Local authorities have been the natural basis for control of pollution arising from deposits of waste and noxious substances, originally through their responsibilities for protection of public health, and more

---

[23] Arts. 7, 9, 10, 12.
[24] See para. 11–147 and n.87 thereto.
[25] Art. 11(2).
[26] [1978] O.J. L84.
[27] [1991] O.J. L377.
[27A] Failure to prepare in time a definitive list of hazardous wastes has made it necessary to postpone the original implementation date of Directive 91/689 to June 27, 1995. This new date has been set by Directive 94/31, [1994] O.J. L 168.

recently under the Deposit of Poisonous Waste Act 1972 and C.O.P.A., subject to the general supervision of the Department of the Environment. A Hazardous Waste Inspectorate was set up in 1983, following a recommendation from the House of Lords Select Committee's report on "Hazardous Waste Disposal" in 1981. Though the recommendation was for this body to be part of the Health and Safety Executive, it was in fact put into the Department of the Environment, with the general remit to examine the management of hazardous waste, to advise the local waste disposal authorities on their duties under Part I of C.O.P.A., and to make recommendations to ensure, among other things, adequate protection of health and the environment. When Her Majesty's Inspectorate of Pollution (HMIP) was constituted, the Hazardous Waste Inspectorate formed an integral part of it, and HMIP (and the corresponding body in Scotland, Her Majesty's Industrial Pollution Inspectorate) remain currently the bodies with overall responsibility for waste management.

At local level, C.O.P.A. established waste disposal authorities **11–017** which, outside the major conurbations, were the County Councils in England and the District Councils in Wales. The disposal authorities had responsibility for preparing waste disposal plans for disposing of controlled waste that is or is likely to be in their areas, to issue waste disposal licences and to monitor and control the disposal of waste in their areas, including operating waste disposal facilities. C.O.P.A. also set up a network of waste collection authorities, being the District Councils in England and Wales and London Borough Councils. The collection authorities had and have the duty to arrange for the collection of all household waste (subject to certain minor exceptions) and to collect commercial waste on request, with the right to charge for this.

The waste disposal sites operated by the disposal authorities were in **11–018** practice generally viewed as a public service, for which charges were kept to a minimum, so as to encourage waste to be brought to them, rather than disposed of unlawfully. As the House of Commons Environment Committee's report on Toxic Waste recognised, however, this resulted in serious under-financing of the waste disposal operations, leading to frequent instances of poor practice or worse; moreover, the low charges of publicly run waste disposal sites meant that private organisations could not charge significantly more, as was desirable if they were to operate at the highest standards of good waste disposal practice. The waste disposal authorities' joint regulatory and waste disposal responsibilities led to concern, expressed in the Toxic Waste report, over the lack of effective regulation of waste disposal. Accordingly, and particularly with the experience of the earlier hiving out from the water authorities of their regulatory

functions into the National Rivers Authority, the government determined to bring about a similar division of responsibilities in relation to
waste disposal.[28] This was given effect by the E.P.A., whereby in
addition to waste disposal and waste collection authorities, there are
now waste regulation authorities, these latter taking over all the
regulatory controls previously exercised by the disposal authorities
including, somewhat contentiously, the preparation of waste disposal
plans in their areas.[29]

11–019   Section 31 of the E.P.A. provides for regional groupings of waste
regulatory authorities to be set up by the Secretary of State, thus giving
effect to a further recommendation of the House of Commons
Environment Committee. However as the authorities have voluntarily
formed themselves into regional groups, no formal action under this
section has been taken. It is likely that none will be, at least until the
shape and functions of the proposed Environment Agency for
England and Wales have been finally determined.

11–020   At the same time as the waste disposal authorities lost their
regulatory functions, their waste disposal functions were required to
be hived out into separate arm's length companies, commonly
referred to as LAWDCs ("Local Authority Waste Disposal Companies"). These companies must be self-financing and operate independently of their respective local authorities. The authorities are entitled
to retain 100 per cent ownership of their LAWDCs, but for many of
them the financial implications of doing so, particularly having regard
to the capital controls over the authorities, made that option less
attractive than selling off the business, either wholly or in part. Many
of the LAWDCs have in fact been turned into joint ventures with
private sector waste disposal organisations, with the local authority
equity involvement often being just under 20 per cent, to ensure
compliance with the conditions for "arm's length companies" specified in section 68(6) of the Local Government and Housing Act 1989.

11–021   The duties of waste collection authorities are not greatly changed by
the E.P.A., save that they have additional duties with regard to
recycling, referred to below (see paragraphs 11–224 to 11–233). The
duties of the waste disposal authorities, now without their regulatory
and waste disposal operation functions, are set out in E.P.A. section 51.
They are primarily concerned with organising contracts for the
disposal of waste collected by the collection authorities in their areas in
accordance with the conditions and procedures set out in Part II of
Schedule 2 to the E.P.A. These provide *inter alia*, for including in

---

[28] This division had already been established in London since 1986, following local
government reforms, where the London Waste Regulation Authority had been
created independently of the several disposal authorities for the region.
[29] E.P.A., s.50.

526

disposal contract terms provisions designed to minimise pollution of the environment or harm to human health and for maximising the recycling of waste under the contract. Accordingly disposal authorities are not obliged to accept the lowest tender, if policy considerations indicate that some other waste disposal route is to be preferred — indeed they are bound to take environmental considerations into account.[30]

Part II of Schedule 2 also spells out details of the required procedure **11–022** for putting waste disposal contracts out to tender. In framing terms and conditions of a contract for which it invites tenders, a disposal authority may not frame them in a manner that would create undue discrimination in favour of one description of waste disposal contractor and against other descriptions of such contractors.[31] Likewise where a disposal authority puts out disposal operations for tender, it may not, when reviewing bids, have regard to the fact that a bid may have come from the LAWDC for that area. Consequently, where a disposal authority had a reasonable policy favouring incineration over landfill, that was in itself legitimate, even if the costs were higher. However to require tenderers who offered to incinerate the waste to provide a site for the incinerator was (unduly) discriminatory in favour of the local authority's LAWDC, given that the disposal authority's own incinerator was to be made exclusively available to that LAWDC.[32] As was observed by Hobhouse L.J. in *Terry Adams*, E.P.A. Schedule 2 fails to give unequivocal guidance on how to rank the three (potentially) conflicting objectives of having regard to environmental considerations, divestiture by the local authority of their disposal undertakings, and making waste disposal open to fully competitive tendering.

In addition to organising waste disposal contracts, waste disposal **11–023** authorities must also arrange for places to be provided for household waste to be deposited (*i.e.* amenity sites) and for the disposal of waste left there. Again these amenity sites are to be operated by waste disposal contractors selected by tender arrangements as just described.

Table 11/I sets out the authorities that constitute the waste regula- **11–024** tion, waste disposal and waste collection authorities in Britain.[33]

---

[30] *R. v. Avon County Council, ex p. Terry Adams Ltd, The Times,* January 20, 1994, C.A.

[31] Sched. 2, para 18. As to what is "undue", see *South of Scotland Electricity Board v. British Oxygen Company,* [1956] 1 W.L.R. 1069 at 1076, *per* Lord Keith of Avonholm.

[32] *R. v. Avon County Council, ex p. Terry Adams Ltd.,* reversing in this respect the judgment at first instance.

[33] As defined in E.P.A., s.30.

TABLE 11/I

	Waste Regulation Authority	Waste Disposal Authority	Waste Collection Authority
English non-metropolitan counties	County Council	County Council	District Council
English metropolitan counties (save as otherwise indicated)	District Council	District Council	District Council
London	London W.R.A.	Inner London: East London Waste Authority North London Waste Authority West London Waste Authority Western Riverside Waste Authority City of London: Common Council Elsewhere: London Borough Council	London Borough Council City of London: Common Council Inner Temple: Sub-Treasurer Middle Temple: Under Treasurer
Greater Manchester	Greater Manchester W.R.A.	Greater Manchester W.D.A. Wigan District Council	District Council
Merseyside	Merseyside W.R.A.	Merseyside W.D.A.	District Council
Wales	District Council	District Council	District Council
Scotland	Islands/District Council	Islands/District Council	Islands/District Council

Waste Controls in the United Kingdom

Introduction

The basic regime of controls over waste on land established by Part I   **11–025**
of C.O.P.A. has in all material respects been re-enacted by Part II of the
E.P.A.; the E.P.A. has however introduced a number of very important
new features that considerably strengthen the practical implementation of the controls, and add greatly to their complexity. Initially,
only certain features of Part II of the E.P.A. were brought into full
effect; however, after a series of failures to meet target dates, virtually
all the remainder came into force on May 1, 1994[34] along with the
Waste Management Licensing Regulations 1994[35] ("the 1994 Licensing
Regulations"), though a transitional five months grace was allowed for
scrap metal dealers, subsequently extended to January 1, 1995.

The 1994 Licensing Regulations were accompanied by extensive   **11–026**
guidance in a Circular issued jointly by the DoE, the Welsh Office and
the Scottish Office Environment Department.[36] At the same time as
the EPA provisions came into force, the bulk of the remaining
provisions of Part I of C.O.P.A. were repealed though, so far as
material, they continued to apply to pending applications for a waste
disposal licence that had been filed before May 1, 1994. Under
transitional provisions contained in E.P.A., s.77, a subsisting disposal
licence under C.O.P.A. is, from May 1, 1994, to be treated as a site
licence under the E.P.A., and subject to the latter's provisions
applicable to site licences generally.

The 1994 Regulations additionally introduced numerous detailed   **11–027**
provisions designed to implement the amended Directive 75/442 at the
same time, notably creating legally binding obligations to comply with
its fundamental objectives and to observe the priorities it lays down
for waste treatment and in formulating waste management plans.[37]
These include the requirement to establish an integrated and adequate
network of waste disposal installations, and ensuring that the EC as a
whole and each Member State individually moves towards self-
sufficiency in waste disposal, and that waste is disposed of in one of
the nearest appropriate installations.[38] This requirement is no doubt
destined to give rise to considerable debate in the formulation of waste

---

[34] By the Environmental Protection Act 1990 (Commencement No.15) Order 1994, (S.I.
1994 No.1096) (C.18).
[35] S.I. 1994 No. 1056.
[36] "Environmental Protection Act 1990: Part II; Waste Management Licensing; The
Framework Directive on Waste"—DoE 11/94; WO 26/94 and SOED 10/94; April 19,
1994.
[37] See paras. 11–007 to 11–011.
[38] Sched. 4, para. 4(2).

management plans, the siting of waste disposal facilities and the granting of waste disposal licences, particularly when taken with the further requirements (applicable only to the making of plans) to encourage the prevention or reduction of waste production and its harmfulness, its recovery and use as a source of energy.[39] Planning authorities are not however bound by these obligations, so far as they relate to the recovery or disposal of waste, to the extent they bind waste regulation authorities.[40]

The Principal Controls

11–028   The structure of control consists of basic prohibitions over specified activities involving waste, coupled with a licensing system to permit authorised persons to conduct such activities, almost invariably subject to prescribed conditions. Certain types of wastes are regulated under legislation that is specific to them, and these will be covered in later sections. The great majority of wastes are however controlled under the E.P.A., and the system set up under this legislation will be considered first.

11–029   Section 33(1) of the E.P.A. reads:

> "33(1) Subject to subsections (2) and (3) below and, in relation to Scotland, to section 54 below, a person shall not—
> (a) deposit controlled waste, or knowingly cause or knowingly permit controlled waste to be deposited in or on any land unless a waste management licence authorising the deposit is in force and the deposit is in accordance with the licence;
> (b) treat, keep or dispose of controlled waste, or knowingly cause or knowingly permit controlled waste to be treated, kept or disposed of—
> (i) in or on any land, or
> (ii) by means of any mobile plant,
> except under and in accordance with a waste management licence;
> (c) treat, keep or dispose of controlled waste in a manner likely to cause pollution of the environment or harm to human health."

These various prohibitions, including in particular, the modified interpretation that they must be given as a result of the 1994 Licensing Regulations, are discussed at paragraphs 11–133 to 11–142. They build

[39] Sched. 4, para. 4(3).
[40] Sched. 4, para. 2(2).

on and expand similar prohibitions in C.O.P.A.;[41] unlike C.O.P.A., they are supplemented by section 33(6) that expressly makes it an offence to contravene any condition of a waste management licence. In addition subsection 33(1)(c) introduces a wholly new provision that is an exception to the general regulatory system in that it amounts to an absolute prohibition, which applies whether or not the treating, keeping or disposing of controlled waste has been licensed and, where there is a licence, whether or not the applicable licence conditions have been complied with. Accordingly any pollution of the environment or harm to human health caused by controlled waste will constitute an offence under the sub-section unless any of the defences provided under section 33(7) are available.

"Controlled waste" is the term used for the types of waste **11–030** (household, industrial and commercial) brought under control by the E.P.A. Its scope is discussed in paragraphs 11–079 to 11–087. Certain wastes are however expressly excluded from control under the Act, while an extensive list of recovery and other activities are exempted from the need for a licence, though registration of these is still required. In discussion of the controls, therefore a clear distinction is to be made between wastes that are *excluded* from them, and activities that are merely *exempted*. Additionally certain activities are also *excluded* from control under Part II of the E.P.A. since they are already covered by other legislation.

"Pollution of the environment" means pollution of any or all of land, **11–031** water and air, due to the release or escape from the land on which controlled waste is treated or kept, or from the land in or on which controlled waste is deposited, or from fixed plant by means of which controlled waste is treated, kept or disposed of, of substances[42] or articles constituting or resulting from the waste and capable (by reason of the quantity or concentrations involved) of causing harm to man or any other living organisms supported by the environment.[43] Hence

[41] C.O.P.A. s.3(1) reads:
"Except in prescribed cases, a person shall not—
　(a)　deposit controlled waste on any land; or
　(b)　use any plant or equipment, or cause or knowingly permit any plant or equipment to be used, for the purpose of disposing of controlled waste or of dealing in a prescribed manner with controlled waste,
unless the land on which the waste is deposited or, as the case may be, which forms the site of the plant or equipment, is occupied by the holder of a licence issued in pursuance of section 5 of this Act . . . which authorises the deposit or use in question and the deposit or use is in accordance with the conditions, if any, specified in the licence."
[42] "Substance" means any natural or artificial substance, whether in solid or liquid form, or in the form of a gas or vapour; E.P.A., s.29(11).
[43] E.P.A., s.29(2), (3).

the mere release of a substance *capable* of causing harm is pollution, irrespective of whether harm in fact ensues.

11–032 "Harm" is defined as meaning harm to the health of living organisms or other interference with the ecological systems of which they form part, and in the case of man includes offence to any of his senses, or harm to his property.[44] Thus, since living organisms are inevitably part of any eco-system, any interference with any eco-system (or at least anything that is more than *de minimis*) must be taken to be "harm". Further, "any of [man's] senses" includes sight, and anything visually offensive, perhaps the escape of some coloured material, may amount to harm, even though there is no evidence of any harm to the health of living organisms or any interference with any eco-system.

11–033 Carriage of waste is controlled under the Control of Pollution (Amendment) Act 1989, which makes it an offence, subject to certain limited exceptions, for any person who is not a registered carrier of controlled waste, in the course of any business of his or otherwise with a view to profit, to transport any controlled waste to or from any place in Great Britain. This Act is dealt with in paragraphs 11–266 to 11–287.

The Meaning of "Waste"

11–034 A fundamental issue that is dealt with only indirectly in the E.P.A. itself is what must be regarded as waste for the purposes of the legislation. Repeating wording used in C.O.P.A.,[45] the statute merely states that "waste" includes —

"(a) any substance which constitutes a scrap material or an effluent or other unwanted substance arising from the application of any process; and

(b) any substance or article which requires to be disposed of as being broken, worn out, contaminated or otherwise spoiled;"[46]

This inclusive definition is backed by an evidential provision that anything which is discarded or otherwise dealt with as if it were waste shall be presumed to be waste unless the contrary is proved.[47]

[44] E.P.A., s.29(5).
[45] C.O.P.A., s.30.
[46] E.P.A., s.75.
[47] E.P.A., s.75(3).

However, one of the principal effects of the 1994 Licensing Regula-   **11–035**
tions has been to ensure that, for the purposes of the statutory
controls, "controlled waste" is now given a definition identical in
scope with that of Directive 75/442 as amended. The term "Directive
waste" is used to mean any waste to which the Directive applies, that
is, "waste" as defined by the Directive other than wastes which are
expressly excluded from its scope by Article 2—as to which see
paragraphs 11–094 to 11–112. This definition is then in effect incorporated into Part II of the E.P.A. by two amendments:

(i)   Any reference to waste in the E.P.A. is to include a reference
      to Directive waste;[48] and
(ii) The Controlled Waste Regulations 1992[49] and also the Collec-
      tion and Disposal of Waste Regulations 1988[50] each have a
      new regulation 7A providing that waste which is not
      Directive waste is not to be treated as household, industrial
      or commercial waste, and is not therefore "controlled waste"
      at all.

"Directive waste" is defined as any substance or object in the   **11–036**
categories set out in Part II of Schedule 4 to the 1994 Licensing
Regulations which the producer or the person in possession of it
discards or intends or is required to discard—see Table 11/II below—
but with the exception of anything excluded from the scope of the
Directive by its Article 2.[51] "Producer" means anyone whose activities
produce Directive waste or who carries out pre-processing, mixing or
other operations resulting in a change in its nature or composition.
These definitions of "Directive waste" and "producer" are essentially
the same as those in the Directive. "Discard" is stated to have the same
meaning as in the Directive, which however contains no definition of
the term—its meaning is discussed below.

Directive Waste

Part II of Schedule 4 to the Regulations repeats verbatim the   **11–037**
categories of waste contained in Annex I of the Directive, as set out in
Table 11/II.

---

[48] 1994 Licensing Regs., reg. 19 and Sched.4, para.9(2).
[49] S.I. 1992 No.588, as amended by S.I.s 1993 No.566 and 1994 No.1056.
[50] S.I. 1988 No.819, as amended by S.I.s 1993 No.1968 and 1994 No.1056.
[51] reg. 1(3).

TABLE 11/II

Substances or Objects Which are Waste When Discarded, etc.	
(1994 Licensing Regulations, Schedule 4, Part II)	
1.	Production or consumption residues not otherwise specified in this Part of this Schedule
2.	Off-specification products
3.	Products whose date for appropriate use has expired
4.	Materials spilled, lost or having undergone other mishap, including any materials, equipment, *etc.*, contaminated as a result of the mishap
5.	Materials contaminated or soiled as a result of planned actions (*e.g.* residues from cleaning operations, packing materials, containers, *etc.*)
6.	Unusable parts (*e.g.* reject batteries, exhausted catalysts, *etc.*)
7.	Substances which no longer perform satisfactorily (*e.g.* contaminated acids, contaminated solvents, exhausted tempering salts, *etc.*)
8.	Residues of industrial processes (*e.g.* slags, still bottoms, *etc.*)
9.	Residues from pollution abatement processes (*e.g.* scrubber sludges, baghouse dusts, spent filters, *etc.*)
10.	Machining or finishing residues (*e.g.* lathe turnings, mill scales, *etc.*)
11.	Residues from raw materials extraction and processing (*e.g.* mining residues, oil field slops, *etc.*)
12.	Adulterated materials (*e.g.* oils contaminated with PCBs, *etc.*)
13.	Any materials, substances or products whose use has been banned by law
14.	Products for which the holder has no further use (*e.g.* agricultural, household, office, commercial and shop discards, *etc.*)
15.	Contaminated materials, substances or products resulting from remedial action with respect to land
16.	Any materials, substances or products which are not contained in the above categories

It will be seen that the list is of substances which are waste *when discarded*; a substance is not necessarily waste merely because it is in the list. The list, moreover, is completely comprehensive, by virtue of item 16, which covers all other materials, substances or products not contained in the previous categories. Anything falling within any of categories 1 to 15 is clearly likely either to have been or to be about to be discarded, and so be or about to be waste, but that is the most that can be said. The categories undoubtedly include products that may have a value or further utility, for example "products whose date for appropriate use has expired" (such as food, which may nevertheless be perfectly safe for further processing into, say, animal feedstuffs), and "substances which no longer perform satisfactorily (*e.g* . . . contaminated solvents . . .)". A comprehensive list of wastes within the scope of the Directive has been prepared by the Commission and annexed to its Decision, 94/3, of December 20, 1993.[52] This is subject to periodic revision and review. As with the list in Table 11/II, however, this list is likewise all inclusive; though it may well have a value for various regulatory and recording purposes, it provides no assistance in establishing the meaning of "Directive waste".

Reference to "waste" in the Directive must be seen in the context of the Directive's objects, which may be ascertained in part from its recitals, as well as from its substantive provisions. Thus recital 3 notes that "common terminology and a definition of waste are needed in order to improve the efficiency of waste management in the Community", and recital 6 that "it is desirable to encourage the recycling of waste and re-use of waste as raw materials; whereas it may be necessary to adopt specific rules for re-usable waste". **11–038**

The Directive defines the "management" of waste as meaning the collection, transport, recovery and disposal of waste, including the supervision of such operations and after-care of disposal sites. As mentioned, "disposal" and "recovery" mean any of the operations provided for in Annex IIA and IIB to the Directive. These are repeated, *mutatis mutandis*, in Parts II and IV of Schedule 4 to the 1994 Licensing Regulations and set out below in Tables 11/III and 11/IV respectively. For immediate purposes it is sufficient to observe that the fact that an item or substance is to be subjected to a recovery operation self-evidently does not affect whether or not it is waste—that has to be determined on other grounds. **11–039**

[52] [1994] O.J. L5.

535

11–040   The definition of "waste" in Directive 75/442 before its amend-ment[53] was the subject of two cases heard jointly before the European Court of Justice, *Vessoso* and *Zannetti*.[54] Italian legislation had implemented the Directive, and cases had been brought against Vessoso and Zannetti for breach of that legislation by transporting waste for third parties without a permit. Their defence was that the matter concerned was recyclable matter and therefore not waste, so that no permit was needed. The judgment of the court reads:

> "The concept of waste, within the meaning of Article 1 of Council Directives 75/442 and 78/319,[55] is not to be understood as excluding substances and objects capable of economic re-utilization. The concept does not presume that the holder disposing of a substance or of an object intends to exclude all economic re-utilization of the substance or object by others".

In its reasoning (paragraph 11) the court stressed that the definitions of the two Directives were quite general in referring to substances and objects that the holder disposes of, without making any distinction by reference to the intention of the holder making the disposal. Similarly, the court referred to the objectives of the Directives as being to protect human health and the environment and that this would be prejudiced if the application of the Directives depended on whether or not the possessor of waste intended to exclude an economic re-use by others of it. Hence, the meaning of waste should be determined objectively. Nevertheless the question put to the court was simply whether the concept of waste as defined in the two Directives required an intention on the part of the disposer to exclude further utilisation. In rejecting that, the court's judgment cannot, it is suggested, be read as saying that the intention of the disposer was wholly irrelevant, but merely that an intention on his part to re-use material could not be conclusive

---

[53] The relevant definitions in Directive 75/442 in its original form read:
> "(a) "waste" means any substance or object which the holder disposes of or is required to dispose of pursuant to the provisions of national law in force;
> (b) "disposal" means
> — the collection, sorting, transport and treatment of waste as well as its storage and tipping above or under ground,
> — the transformation operations necessary for its re-use, recovery or recycling."

The amended Directive now uses "disposal" in the sense of a final disposal, in contrast to "recovery". "Discard" in the amended Directive may be considered to have essentially the same meaning as "dispose of" in the original definition.

[54] Joint Cases 206/88 and 207/88; [1990] E.C.R. I-1461; material parts of the judgment are reproduced in Annex 7 of DoE Circular 14/92 (WO 30/92; SOED 24/92) on The Controlled Waste Regulations 1992.

[55] Concerning hazardous waste.

that it was *not* waste; consequently external factors must be considered to determine its status.

Indeed in the context of the Directive the intention of the disposer is undoubtedly a relevant objective fact to be taken into account in determining from all the circumstances whether there is a disposal—or a discarding—at all. To a bystander there may appear to be little or nothing to distinguish a sale of a second hand item from the discarding of it to someone who pays to take it off the discarder's hands. The distinction however lies essentially in the mind of the holder—if there is a sale and it falls through, he may be presumed to intend to keep the item, at least until he can sell it to another; conversely if he is discarding it, the payment may be welcome, but will not affect his intention to be rid of the item, for nothing if need be. As was memorably observed in *Edgington v. Fitzmaurice* "the state of a man's mind is as much a fact as the state of his digestion",[56] and this should be borne in mind in applying the ruling in *Vessoso* that the meaning of waste should be determined objectively. **11–041**

There has been no other case before the European Court on the meaning of "waste", and until the case law has developed further all views as to its meaning must necessarily be tentative. All that can so far be said with some certainty is that all materials, substances and products may constitute waste (having regard to the category 16 of Annex I and of Schedule 4, Part II) and that this may be so notwithstanding that they are capable of economic re-utilisation—*a fortiori* even where they are intended to be subjected to any of the recovery operations listed in Annex IIB. More generally, it is evident from the Directive, and required by *Vessoso*, that in assessing whether or not anything should be treated as waste for the purposes of the Directive, consideration must be given to whether it is desirable that waste controls should be applied to it in order to secure the objectives of the Directive, as set out principally in Articles 3 to 5, which are repeated in paragraph 4 of Schedule 4 to the 1994 Licensing Regulations. **11–042**

Although the previous case law of the English Courts on what is waste is no longer of any direct application—in any event, whether or not something is waste has always depended on the specific facts of each case—the issues considered in them remain extremely relevant. The manner in which waste was defined in C.O.P.A. allowed as wide an interpretation as the court thought fit. The English courts consistently held that the word should be taken in its ordinary sense, so far as that could be properly ascertained, and perhaps the one consistent theme throughout the various judgments is that the fact that a material **11–043**

---

[56] 29 Ch.D 459 at 483, *per* Bowen L.J.

retained some value did not prevent it from being waste for the purposes of the legislation, even if it was in fact re-used—an approach that is entirely consistent with the meaning to be given to Directive waste.

11–044   The following cases are illustrative of those in which the central issue has been whether or not something was waste, where it had a value and either was being or could be used in commerce.

1. *Long v. Brooke.*[57] This case was an appeal by a defendant who had been convicted of depositing waste contrary to section 3 of C.O.P.A. He was the occupier of a disused quarry. The sheer slopes had been re-graded, and he wished to cover the surface shale with soil which it was said he could not afford. He was, however, approached by Wimpey Limited who had substantial quantities of sub-soil they wished to dispose of from a nearby site. They paid the defendant £2.50 per load, which covered the cost of spreading the tipped sub-soil with a bulldozer, but no more. The Crown Court dismissed the appeal and held that "although one man's waste may be another man's valuable material", on its true construction C.O.P.A. defines waste from the point of view of the person discarding the material. As Wimpey Limited had disposed of the material as waste, the appellant required a disposal licence, and the fact that as occupier of the land he had a use for the discarded material did not prevent its constituting "waste" within the meaning of section 30 of C.O.P.A.

2. *Nottinghamshire County Council v. Berridge Incinerators.*[58] For present purposes it is sufficient to note the following part of the judgment:

> "It is, of course, a truism that one man's waste is another man's raw material. The fact that a price is paid by the collector of material to its originator is, no doubt, relevant; but I do not regard it as crucial. If I have an old fireplace to dispose of to a passing rag and bone man, its character as waste is not affected by whether or not I can persuade the latter to pay me 50 pence for it. In my judgment, the correct approach is to regard the material from the point of view of the person who produces it. Is it something which is produced as a product, or even as a by-product of his business, or is it something to be disposed of as useless? I notice that this was the approach adopted by His Honour Judge Chapman QC in the Crown Court (*Long v. Brooke*) and I respectfully agree with it."

[57] [1980] Crim.L.R. 109.
[58] Q.B.D., April 14, 1987, unreported.

3. *C. M. Ashcroft v. Michael McErlain Limited.*[59] The court considered whether waste was to be given any special or extended meaning for the purposes of C.O.P.A.; it decided against this and that the word should be given its ordinary meaning. In this case soil had been excavated from a field in order to reduce its level so that a road could be constructed. The defendant carted the soil from the field to a paddock in order to raise the level of the paddock. Having reviewed the meanings given to "waste" in the Oxford English Dictionary the court held that excavated soil was capable of being waste; whether it was waste in any particular case was a matter for the justices; and that in the case in question the court thought that the justices had been entirely correct in finding that the excavated soil was not waste.

4. *R. v. Rotherham MBC and Safety Kleen UK Limited, ex p. William Rankin.*[60] This case arose out of the grant of planning permission to Safety Kleen for a proposed distribution, waste extraction and recycling centre, which had been challenged on the grounds that it had not been appropriately advertised, because it came within a class of development to which section 26(2) of the Town and Country Planning Act 1971 applied. The relevant class consisted of:

"construction of buildings or other operations . . . or use of land for the purpose of the retention, treatment or disposal of sewage, trade waste or sludge" (GDO 1977, Art. 8).

A second application in respect of the same site raised the same issue under the GDO 1988, the relevant wording of which was effectively equivalent.

The material part of Safety Kleen's business consisted of supplying cellulose thinners and paraffin to industrial users for cleaning paint-spraying equipment and de-greasing mechanical parts. It leased certain equipment and these solvents to the users, and from time to time collected used solvent for recycling and re-use. The solvent and virtually all the equipment remained Safety Kleen's property at all times. The recycling process involved allowing solids to precipitate out from the used solvents, testing the solvents for contamination, and distilling them under low pressure to provide clean re-usable solvent. Before re-supply, the constitution of the distilled solvent was restored to a standard formulation by adding certain components as required (presumably the more volatile substances, which would tend to be lost disproportionately). The

---

[59] Q.B.D., unreported, but referred to in *R. v. Rotherham MBC and Safety Kleen, ex p. Rankin* (see n.60 below).
[60] Q.B.D. (Schiemann J.), (1990) 2 J.E.L. 250; *The Times*, November 6, 1989.

various residues from sedimentation and the distillation process would be disposed of to an authorised waste disposal company. The evidence was that, so far as Safety Kleen was concerned, the solvents, even when contaminated and being returned to them, were never regarded as waste; conversely, so far as the industrial users were concerned, they had no further use for the contaminated solvents which they needed to have replaced.

The judge held that he should construe the word "waste" in accordance with its ordinary meaning, and further that this meaning did not preclude the possibility that waste might have some residual value or utility. He considered that provisions of EC Directives, C.O.P.A. and regulations made under it were not relevant, maintaining that these were not legitimate aids to the construction of the GDO. The judge did however accept as relevant the decisions in other cases concerning the ordinary meaning of waste, and reviewed *Ashcroft v. Michael McErlain Limited* (see above). He also noted *Long v. Brooke* (see above), but did not find it helpful as it only concerned the meaning of waste under C.O.P.A.

He held that the planning authority "may have" erred in law on three grounds, two of which are material for present purposes. Firstly, it had assumed that the treatment of waste for the purposes of the GDO meant that it was concerned with matter that has no further use, and that therefore where there was a further use after recycling, it could not be waste. Secondly, the authority may have proceeded on the assumption that the ownership of the solvents was a relevant consideration. He held that, from the reference to sewage, the GDO itself did not preclude the possibility that there might be a further use for the materials. As to ownership, he held that this could not be a relevant factor in determining the operation of the planning system. He concluded that the used solvents could properly be regarded as both trade waste and raw materials at the same time. Since however they were in his view trade waste, he would have quashed the planning consent, but did not do so in the exercise of his discretion on other grounds.

5. *Kent County Council v. Queenborough Rolling Mill Company.*[61] This case involved an appeal by way of case stated. Contractors had been hired to clear a five acre site of Stelrad Limited at Queenborough, by removing from it material that had been used to provide a hard standing for storage purposes. At some previous time (at least 15 years previously) there had been a pottery on the site, and the material in the hard standing was evidently detritus from that

---

[61] Q.B.D. (Woolf L.J., Pill J), (1990) 2 J.E.L., Vol. 2, 257; *The Times*, February 2, 1990.

period. The contractors had divided this material into four categories:

1. Good rubble material suitable for making roads.
2. Household rubbish (disposed to a council operated landfill).
3. Material used for hard core including pieces of concrete.
4. A mixture of china clay, chalk, plaster of paris, broken china and pottery, as well as some concrete, ballast and stones— also used for road making.

The case was concerned exclusively with the material of the fourth category. 264 lorry loads of this material had been taken to a site, Coal Washer Wharf, on the Isle of Sheppey occupied by Queenborough that was prone to subsidence, and so required regular infilling. No payment passed between Stelrad and Queenborough in either direction. Queenborough were prosecuted under section 3(1) of C.O.P.A.; there was no dispute as to the facts, and the issue was solely whether the material concerned was waste for the purposes of the Act. The magistrates had held that it was not, having regard to the nature of the material and the use to which it was put. However on the appeal, the court held that it was waste, Pill J. (with whom Woolf L.J. agreed) saying:

"In my judgment the purpose to which the material was put is irrelevant in the present situation. The nature of the material must first be considered at the time of its removal from the Stelrad site. The material had earlier been discarded and had lain on the site for many years. When removed from the site it was waste within the meaning of that word in section 30.[62] It bore the same quality when it was deposited at Coal Washer Wharf. The usefulness, if it be so, of the deposit as fill on the receiving site did not change the character of the material.

Neither did the fact that the material was separated from another material before deposit deprive it of its identity as waste. Different considerations might apply if material is recycled or reconstituted before the deposit complained of. The material being waste material, it was not seriously disputed that it was or included industrial waste and, therefore, controlled waste under section 3 of the Act."

At least the following questions of particular significance are raised   **11–045**
by the cases reviewed above:

---

[62] *i.e.* the interpretation section of C.O.P.A..

541

1.   In the light of *Vessoso* and *Zannetti*, to what extent is the attitude of the person disposing of a material relevant at all as to whether it is waste or not?
2.   When is something resulting from a process other than the primary product to be regarded as waste despite having a value, and when may it properly be seen as a useful by-product in its own right?
3.   When waste is subjected to recycling, at what point in the recycling process does it lose its character as waste and become free thereafter from the legislative controls applying to waste?

1. The relevance of the disposer's intentions

11–046   As already noted, the European Court has determined that the concept of waste does not require the disposer to intend that there should be no further economic re-use of his waste. In its reasoning, the Court also referred to the fact that the definitions of waste in Directives 75/442[63] and 78/319 included material that the holder was required to dispose of. By implication, the holder may well have wished to retain the material but for some legal reason he had no option but to get rid of it. The definition in the amended Directive has two other limbs, material that the holder intends to discard, and material that he in fact does discard (whether he intends to or not). The latter might well apply where, for example, some toxic material is included in a load of inert waste by accident, and contrary to the wishes of the relevant management. It would be unrealistic not to regard the toxic material as waste merely because there was no intention on the part of its owner to discard it. Intention nevertheless is an essential element of the former limb of the definition; it would seem that this could first cause an accumulation of material on the site where it is produced to be waste, because it is intended to discard it, even though at that point no discarding has in fact occurred, other than to the accumulation itself.

11–047   An aspect emphasised by the European Court is that one of the objectives of both the EC Directives was the protection of human health and the safeguarding of the environment. Similarly, the amended Directive 75/442 refers to the amendments taking as a base a high level of environmental protection. Article 4 is of particular relevance in this context:

---

[63] The questions put to the European Court concerned the original version of the Directive before amendment. The judgment appears equally applicable to the amended version.

"Member States shall take the necessary measures to ensure that waste is recovered or disposed of without endangering human health and without using processes or methods which could harm the environment, and in particular:

— without risk to water, air, soil and plants and animals,
— without causing a nuisance through noise or odours,
— without adversely affecting the countryside or places of special interest.

Member States shall also take the necessary measures to prohibit the abandonment, dumping or uncontrolled disposal of waste."

Accordingly where it is not otherwise self-evident whether material is waste or not, it is pertinent to consider whether or not it is desirable that the waste legislation should apply in order to avoid risks of harm to human health or the environment, and that will apply quite independently of any attitude that the disposer of the material may hold.

In this connection, the value of the material is undoubtedly of significance. Where a material is completely useless and will cost money to dispose of, there is a clear potential risk of it being unlawfully abandoned or improperly handled. Even where a material does have a significant value when viewed objectively, it may not be a value of importance to the person producing it, and so be waste in his hands. He may have other priorities if he operates a quite different line of business from the management of the waste stream concerned, other lines of business may be substantially more profitable for him, or he may simply not be able to store the material, or at least not at any worthwhile cost. Another person may be quite prepared to hold on to low value material, if in his circumstances he is able to preserve it for little or no cost, and for him such material would therefore not necessarily be waste. He may indeed hold the material on a speculative basis if it is of a type (for example waste paper) where the market price is liable to fluctuate, and he may hold it until such time as he reckons he can obtain a worthwhile price for it—if the market turns against him and he decides keeping it is no longer good business, it may at that point (but only then) become waste in his hands also. **11–048**

In *Long v. Brooke*, it was said that "on its true construction the Act (C.O.P.A.) defines waste from the point of view of the person discarding the material".[64] Whether or not that is true of C.O.P.A., it would not be correct in the light of *Vessoso* to treat Directive waste as **11–049**

[64] This dictum can of course be read as saying no more than that the viewpoint of the recipient is irrelevant.

being defined exclusively in terms of the viewpoint of the original holder. Nevertheless, it is probably the best starting point, and only if, from that perspective, the conclusion is that the material in issue is not waste, need a more objective view to be taken as to whether the material should be treated as waste, notwithstanding the viewpoint of the original holder.

11–050   *Ashcroft v. McErlain* (see above) provides an instructive example. If the owner of the paddock that received the soil initiated the process because he wished to raise the level of his paddock, and found the owner of the field willing to part with the soil required because, coincidentally, a road was going to be put through his field, which could perfectly well run a few feet lower than it otherwise would, then the soil concerned cannot sensibly be categorised as waste. Conversely, if the owner of the field found it necessary to get rid of surplus soil because of the construction of the road, and the owner of the paddock was prepared to accept it, being content to have its level raised somewhat, then the soil could quite well be waste—a view that is incidentally wholly consistent with *Long v. Brooke* and *Kent CC v. Queenborough* (at least if the latter is understood as discussed below).

11–051   The fact that what to an outsider would appear to be identical transactions could in one case be seen to be a movement of soil outside the control of waste legislation, and in the other case to be a movement of waste, subject to all the controls over the movement and deposit of waste, can be explained on the basis that the legislation is only required where material might otherwise be abandoned or improperly disposed of in an undesirable manner. Where material is transferred in order to give a direct benefit to the recipient, the need for controls over (inert) waste disappears. (Planning legislation and controls over the handling of harmful substances may of course remain relevant, but those are quite separate issues.)

11–052   A separate matter that also concerns the intentions of the disposer arises from a consideration of the *Rotherham and Safety Kleen* case. It was held there (rightly, it is considered) that the contaminated solvent should be regarded as waste, since the customers who were sending it back to Safety Kleen had no further use for it, notwithstanding both its intrinsic value and that it was an essential asset of Safety Kleen. If one applies a similar approach to used protective clothing, for example laboratory coats and clothing used by hospital staff, the situation becomes somewhat more uncertain. If this clothing is of paper, intended to be used once and then disposed of, it would clearly be waste after use. Suppose, however, the garments were of cloth and let out on rental. If a supplier of such garments simply arranged to pick up, say, 100 used items each week and deliver 100 fresh ones at the same time, he would, on the *Safety Kleen* principles, be collecting waste. On the other hand, a person sending his own coat to be dry cleaned, clearly does not regard it as waste.

The distinction would appear to lie, in most cases, in whether or not the "disposer" expects to get that particular item back, or whether he will be equally satisfied with a replacement item. This question may well be determined by whether he owns the item but, as in *Safety Kleen*, the ownership of the "waste" cannot in itself be conclusive as to whether material is waste or not. The customers of Safety Kleen might, conceivably, have delivered their paint spray guns and other contaminated equipment to Safety Kleen for cleaning and return; this would not, on the reasoning indicated, be a disposal of waste. If Safety Kleen were to be in the business of supplying complete spray guns on rental, then conceivably one might come to the conclusion that their contaminated spray guns were as much waste as was the contaminated solvent, or as returned used laboratory coats might be.   **11–053**

A line must be drawn at some point, nevertheless, that takes into account the value of the "waste". Where a company leases a fleet of cars, on the basis that they will be replaced forthwith by equivalent vehicles in the event of any malfunction, it would be unrealistic to regard a car as waste when it was returned because the horn failed to work. If a line is to be drawn on this basis, then, it is suggested, the principal consideration should be whether or not the value of the goods concerned is such that there is a significant risk of their being abandoned or disposed of improperly in a manner that might cause harm to human health or the environment.   **11–054**

A separate point arises in the sending of contaminated materials for cleaning, where, in the circumstances, they are not to be regarded as waste. Since clearly the contamination associated with them is something that it is wished to dispose of, it seems proper to regard as waste for the purposes of C.O.P.A. and the E.P.A. only material that is capable of being handled separately from items that are not waste (disregarding associated containers or the packaging). A vacuum cleaner with a burnt out motor returned for servicing is not waste; nor, it is suggested, is its useless motor, until that has been removed and become capable of being thrown away or reconditioned, as the case may be. If it were to transpire at that point that the whole machine could not be economically repaired at all, then it would be likely to become waste as a whole then, but not before.[65]   **11–055**

---

[65] Most probably it would not be the person in possession of the machine who would determine the change of status to waste, but its owner, *e.g.* over the telephone on being told that a repair was uneconomic or impossible. The machine would thus become waste in the hands of the servicing organisation. Unless it was in a position to repair it, any further transfer would be a discarding by it of waste.

11–056   Annex 2 to Circular 11/94, which discusses how "waste" may be understood, proposes as the relevant—though not necessarily conclusive—test, whether an item or substance has fallen "out of the normal commercial cycle or out of the chain of utility", since if it has there may not be the self-interest necessary to ensure that the precautions needed to protect the environment will be taken. Where something is only capable of further beneficial use if subjected to what the Annex refers to as a "specialised recovery operation", then it will be waste. A "specialised recovery operation" is any of the recovery operations of Schedule 4, Part IV (*i.e.* Annex IIB to the Directive), other than those which are applied to products which have not fallen out of the commercial cycle and so are not waste. ("Recovery" as defined only occurs when applied to what is already waste). Burning a substance as a fuel, for example, is not necessarily recovery, nor is spreading farm manure on land to benefit the soil (see items 9 and 10 of Table 11/IV). While this approach may quite often be helpful, if applied too rigidly the definitions become circular: something is waste if it can only be beneficially used by being subjected to a recovery operation, but the operation is only a specialised recovery operation if what it is applied to is waste.

2. Valuable By-product or Waste ?

11–057   It is common in certain industries for there to be two or more products of a process all having a recognisable market value and contributing to the economic viability of the entire process. Since waste may well have a worthwhile market value, the question inevitably arises as to when any of the products are waste, and when just a less desirable product. By way of example, pulverised fuel ash (PFA) from coal fired power stations has some value in construction operations, despite the water pollution risks entailed, if only because so much of it is produced that an outlet has been sought for it, but it could quite well be regarded as waste by those operating the generating stations, being an unavoidable residue. The old gasworks on the other hand, produced not only gas as their primary product, but also large quantities of coke which had a very significant market value and could properly be regarded as a by-product. The manufacturer of dried milk may require the removal from his fresh milk input of at least some of the cream, which may be sold separately or converted into butter. Fish may be caught and processed primarily for use as food, but their remains may be converted into glue. There is no clear dividing line which can be used with confidence to distinguish waste from a by-product, but clearly a relevant consideration is whether, if the operator of the process were able to avoid making any or a substantial proportion of one of the products, he would choose to do so.

The problem is perhaps particularly acute in the chemical industry   **11–058**
where there may be a variety of separate processes, each aiming to produce separate products, but where several of the processes are so linked (though not necessarily in an integrated plant) that by-products of one are used or worked up in another. It must always be a question of fact and degree as to whether a process should be regarded as producing a single product and waste materials, or as producing two (or more) valuable products. In such circumstances, attention would no doubt be given to (a) whether the second product stream in question is directly useful as such as a raw material without further purification, concentration or sorting, (b) whether the whole process is intentionally structured so as to produce both the second as well as the first material to prescribed specifications and in defined quantities related to demand or predetermined production targets, and maybe (c) to the relative values of the two production streams to each other and to the business of the producer as a whole. It may well be that none of these considerations would be conclusive in itself, but it would be appropriate to have regard to them in coming to a conclusion in any particular case as to the status of a particular material.

Often of course, the question will not need to be asked, given that   **11–059**
waste recovery or disposal as part of a process controlled under Part I of the E.P.A.—which is the case for the more substantial chemical processes—is excluded from the Part II controls.[66] Similarly, the transport of waste (whether special waste or not) between different places within the same premises is excluded from the provisions of the Control of Pollution (Amendment) Act 1989.[67] Nevertheless, if the duty of care in respect of waste is to be observed, the proper categorisation of product and waste streams is essential.

Certain other activities inevitably give rise to products which are   **11–060**
incidental to the main purpose of the activity, but which are capable of being put to beneficial use in their current form, *i.e.* without applying any "recovery" process to them, though not necessarily by the operator of the activity. The issue arises as to whether, in such a case, the incidental product is to be regarded as waste. Typical cases are horse manure from riding stables, which will generally be of no direct use to the stables, and farm slurry, which (within limits) is likely to be capable of beneficial use by spreading it on the farm's land. Where there is an established market for the products which the operator can profitably use, then there is no discarding and no waste, but a

[66] 1994 Licensing Regs., reg.16(1)(a).
[67] By s.1(2)(a).

straightforward sale. Conversely, where a payment is made by the operator, there must normally be a rebuttable presumption that the product is waste. If the product is given away for use as such (or sold for a nominal amount) the particular circumstances of the transaction would be decisive. Following the guidance in Circular 11/94[68] relevant questions would be:

(i) whether the purpose of the intended use by the recipient was wholly or mainly to relieve the operator of the burden of otherwise disposing of the product; and

(ii) whether the recipient would be likely to seek a substitute for the product if the operator failed to supply it.

Where the operator uses the product himself, the question turns on whether the use is beneficial overall or whether there is merely a disguised disposal. Up to a certain extent, applying farm slurry to land is clearly beneficial. However beyond a certain point the returns from additional quantities may be small or non-existent, particularly where the costs of applying these extra quantities are set against such benefit as there may be. It may be proper to regard an application in such circumstances as a disposal.

3. Recycling—Change of Character

11–061   The judgment in *Vessoso* and the definition of "recovery" establish that the mere fact that a waste item or substance can be, even will be, re-used or recycled does not alter its character as waste. Thereafter, once it has been made ready for immediate re-use, or if the recycling process has created a product comparable to or better than virgin material, clearly it is no longer waste. At some point it loses its character as waste. Since the statutory controls over waste extend to its transport, under the Control of Pollution (Amendment) Act 1989, and to the treating and keeping of waste, requiring at least registration under the E.P.A., and since the duty of care under section 34 applies to all these activities and others, it is critically important for anyone handling a product that has been derived from waste, to know whether that point has been reached. There is no directly applicable case law. Even under C.O.P.A. there was very little—in *Queenborough* it was expressly stated that the mere separation of different categories of material found in the Stelrad hard standing was not sufficient to cause it to cease to be waste.[69] However if the separation had been of useable

---

[68] At paras. 2.34–2.38.

[69] This view may have been taken on the grounds that the material had to be seen as factory waste from the old pottery, and so under the C.O.P.A. definition would remain pottery waste whether separated out or not.

coal from an old slag heap (whether on its original site or after it had
been spread elsewhere, it would be unrealistic to regard the recovered
coal as waste if it was immediately usable as such.

Comparable questions arise in relation to, for example, the collec- **11–062**
tion of waste packaging materials and waste paper, which involve a
process of sorting and baling the sorted material, prior to use in a
paper manufacturing process or, possibly, incineration. The sorting
process will itself result in useful paper and cardboard being sorted
from less useful paper and outright rubbish (to a paper maker) such as
staples, paperclips and plastic covers and binders. In many cases
determination of exactly where a waste stream ceases to have the
character of waste will not be clear cut but will require an assessment
of the value of the product to the current holder. If it is such that:

(i)   there is no significant risk of its being abandoned, dumped or
      otherwise disposed of (in the sense of "disposal" in the
      Directive); *and*

(ii) any further recovery steps that may be needed to bring it to a
      point where it becomes usable as such without significant
      further cleaning, sorting or other processing, as a raw
      material or as a direct input, neither endanger human health
      nor risk harm to the environment,

then at that stage the Directive's objectives have been achieved, and
continued categorisation of the product as waste is neither necessary
nor desirable. Glass cullet for use in recycled glass products would, it
is suggested, cease to be waste as soon as the glass has been cleaned
and sorted to such extent as is normal to make it ready to be delivered
directly for recycling. On the other hand, where manufacture of refuse
derived fuel depends on a physical and/or chemical conversion of the
refuse into appropriate pellets, then the character of the waste may
only cease to exist on its being processed into the pellets.

The issue is addressed in Annex 2 of Circular 11/94[70] in broadly **11–063**
similar terms. The conclusion that recovery will "generally" have
occurred "when the recovered material can be used as a raw material
in the same way as raw materials of non-waste origin by a person other
than a specialised recovery establishment or undertaking" is arguably
unnecessarily demanding, and also suffers from the circularity in the
definition of "specialised recovery" (see paragraph 11–056).

A difficult question, that not infrequently arises, is when a waste **11–064**
product loses its character as waste if it can be put to further use
without any change in its nature or composition whatsoever, and
eventually this occurs. There are many old wooden railway sleepers

---

[70] Paras. 2.46–2.50.

up and down the country which may well have been regarded as waste when the railways had finished with them, but serve a useful purpose in providing hard standing, foot bridges and so on. Similarly, in *Queenborough*, the broken china and other detritus from the old pottery had been used for a good many years to provide a hard standing at the Stelrad site. In some cases, it may perhaps depend solely on the manner of storage. Waste oil for burning may continue to be waste until such time as it is delivered to a tank feeding the relevant oil burner. If the further use unchanged is to be by the next immediate transferee, and the transferor intends the transfer to be for that purpose, then the product has been gifted (if not sold) rather than discarded, and so is not waste at any point, even though the new use may be quite different from the original. The distinction may not always be easily drawn, but the guiding principle must be whether waste controls are needed to ensure the Directive's objectives are met. This would apply for example to horse manure given or sold to private individuals, and to cardboard boxes at supermarket checkouts (see also paragraph 11–060).

11–065   A transfer to a middleman who will not himself put the product to beneficial use will, by contrast, involve a discard of waste (unless of course it can properly be classed as a sale on the principles discussed earlier). Nevertheless in the hands of the middleman it may be a valuable asset and not waste at any time. If he has paid more than a purely nominal amount or has gone to appreciable expense to acquire it, this may reasonably be sufficient evidence of the change of character to rebut the presumption of waste under section 75(3) in the absence of any evidence to the contrary. Conversely, if he has not paid for it and not otherwise incurred appreciable expense, still more if he received money, the section 75(3) presumption must continue, unless and until there is evidence that there is no significant risk of his abandoning, dumping or otherwise "disposing" of it. This may well only occur on his selling the product on to a third party for that person's direct use. Carriage of that product, or of the relevant part of a larger bulk that has been appropriated to the sale contract, will not then be a carriage of waste. In cases of doubt as to motives, it may only be when such material has been put to its further use and, in appropriate cases, become fixed to the land in its new guise, that there will be convincing evidence of it having ceased to be waste. In *Queenborough* the Stelrad site was itself that of the old pottery, but it is entirely conceivable that the same hard standing material that was held (under C.O.P.A.) to be waste could have been brought on to the site from some distance away, and spread to provide a hard standing, whether legally, with the benefit of planning consent and an appropriate waste disposal licence, or illegally. It does not assist in protecting

550

the environment to make a distinction between such situations and one where material has simply stayed on the site where it was first thrown out, if in fact it has been put to worthwhile use. Accordingly in *Queenborough* the finding that the material taken to Coal Washer Wharf was waste would have been better based exclusively on the act of clearance of it from the Stelrad site causing the material to be waste, and this would have been so whether it was the detritus from an old pottery or completely fresh soil that had never been previously disturbed.

One of the principal objectives of the Directive is to encourage the recycling of waste and re-use of waste as raw materials;[71] this will not be furthered by placing waste controls unnecessarily on products destined for re-use or recycling, or on products that have been re-used. It must be for government to ensure that the rules in relation to waste intended for re-use and recycling are no more burdensome than is essential, which it has of course now sought to do by exempting Schedule 3 activities from licensing (subject to registration). In coming to any decision in a marginal case on whether a particular waste stream has or has not lost its character as waste, it would not be out of place for a court to have regard to the need to balance the issues of protecting the environment and encouraging recycling and re-use of waste, as one of the relevant factors.

11–066

The inevitable uncertainties as to whether waste has ceased to be such can lead to a practical difficulty for those who may receive it unaware, possibly, of exactly where it has come from and the circumstances in which it has been transferred. Provided everyone concerned is in full compliance with all legal requirements, then the recipient will be able to establish from the carrier who has supplied the material whether it is controlled waste. (Even this would not necessarily apply where waste has been imported from outside the EC.) If the evidential burden of E.P.A. section 75(3) is to be made good, those receiving what may be waste must ensure that they ascertain its provenance.

11–067

Government Guidance

Assistance on what is to be understood as "Directive waste" has been provided by Annex 2 of Circular 11/94, which reviews the issues at length. Since this Annex constitutes guidance to waste regulation authorities under section 35(8) of the E.P.A. to which they are legally

11–068

---

[71] Recital 6.

required to have regard, its contents are of direct practical importance, notwithstanding its caveat that interpretation of the law is a matter for the Courts.[72] The Annex concludes with a Summary in the following terms.[73]

Summary

11–069 *What is Waste?*

1. The following paragraphs are intended to provide a helpful summary of the Departments' guidance on the definition of waste; and to draw attention to some of the main questions which should be addressed in reaching a view on whether a particular substance or object is waste. *However, the Departments caution against reaching a view on whether any particular substance or object is waste until all of the relevant issues have been considered.* The main questions are:

   (a) does the substance or object fall into one of the categories set out in Part II of Schedule 4 to the Regulations; *and*
   (b) if so, has it been discarded by its holder, does he have any intention of discarding it or is he required to discard it?

11–070 *When is a Substance or Object Discarded?*

2. Waste appears to be perceived in the Directive as posing a threat to human health or the environment which is different from the threat posed by substances or objects which are not waste. This threat arises from the particular propensity of waste to be disposed of or recovered in ways which are potentially harmful to human health or the environment *and from the fact that the producers of the substances or objects concerned may no longer have the self interest necessary to ensure the provision of appropriate safeguards.* The purpose of the Directive, therefore, is to treat as waste those substances or objects which fall out of the normal commercial cycle or out of the chain of utility. To determine whether a substance or object has been discarded the following question should be asked:

   — has the substance or object been discarded so that it is no longer part of the normal commercial cycle or chain of utility?

3. An answer of "no" to this question should provide a reasonable indication that the substance or object concerned is not waste. A substance or object should *not* be regarded as waste:

---

[72] Annex 2, para. 2.12.
[73] Cross-references to earlier paragraphs of Annex 2 have been omitted, and the paragraph numbering has been simplified for present purposes.

(a) solely on the grounds that it falls into one of the categories listed in Part II of Schedule 4 to the Regulations;

(b) solely on the grounds that it has been consigned to a recovery operation listed in Part IV of Schedule 4 to the Regulations;

(c) if it is sold or given away and can be used in its present form (albeit after repair) or in the same way as any other raw material without being subjected to a *specialised recovery operation*;

(d) if its producer puts it to beneficial use;

(e) solely on the grounds that its producer would be unlikely to seek a substitute for it if it ceased to become available to him as, say, a by-product.

4. A substance or object *should* be regarded as waste if it falls into one of the categories listed in Part II of Schedule 4 to the Regulations and:

(a) it is consigned to a disposal operation listed in Part III of Schedule 4 to the Regulations;

(b) it can be used only after it has been consigned to a *specialised recovery operation*;

(c) the holder pays someone to provide him with a service and that service is the collection [and taking away] of a substance or object which the holder does not want and wishes to get rid of;

(d) the purpose of any [beneficial] use is wholly or mainly to relieve the holder of the burden of disposing of it and the user would be unlikely to seek a substitute for it if it ceased to become available to him as, say, a by-product;

(e) it is discarded or otherwise dealt with as if it were waste; or

(f) it is abandoned or dumped.

Can Waste Cease to be Waste?   11–071

5. A substance or object which is waste *does not* cease to be waste as soon as it is transferred for collection, transport, storage, *specialised recovery* or disposal; or as soon as it reaches a *specialised recovery establishment or undertaking*. A substance or object which is waste, and is not fit for use in its present form or in the same way as any other raw material, may cease to be waste when it has been recovered within the meaning of the Directive.

6. The recovery of waste occurs when its processing produces a material of sufficient beneficial use to eliminate or sufficiently diminish the threat posed by the original production of the waste. This will generally take place when the recovered material can be

used as a raw material in the same way as raw materials of non-waste origin by a natural or legal person other than *a specialised recovery establishment or undertaking.*

7. In a few cases, a change of intention by the person to whom waste has been transferred may be sufficient to result in the substance or object concerned ceasing to be waste. This is likely to occur only where it transpires that the substance or object which has been transferred as waste is in fact fit for use in its present form (albeit after repair) or in the same way as any other raw material without being subjected to a *specialised recovery operation.*

The Meaning of "Deposit"

11–072   The offence defined by section 33(1)(a) of the E.P.A. requires a "deposit", as did the corresponding offence under section 3(1)(a) of C.O.P.A. This term has been given different interpretations in conflicting decisions.

11–073   In *Leigh Land Reclamation Ltd v. Walsall Metropolitan Borough Council*[74] the defendants, Leigh, were charged with depositing waste in a landfill in a manner which was not in accordance with the conditions of the applicable site licence. Of the several informations laid, two were directed to depositing liquid wastes on the site (in one case half-buried, and in the other left for disposal after payment had been made) that were not within the categories of waste for which the site was licensed. The defendants were convicted but the Divisional Court upheld their appeal,[75] Bingham L.J. saying:

> "This statute is concerned primarily at least, with the manner in which waste is disposed of. Its provisions, and the conditions in the licence, are directed to the mode of final disposal and not to the intermediate processes. For the purposes of this Act, waste is, in my view, to be regarded as deposited when it is dumped on the site with no realistic prospect of further examination or inspection to reject goods of which deposit is not allowed under the licence".

This judgment caused consternation among the authorities responsible for regulating waste disposal, as it would mean that transfer

---

[74] Q.B.D.; [1993] Env. L.R. 16.
[75] The appeal succeeded on a further ground concerning whether a breach of condition created an offence under C.O.P.A. where it did not relate to the waste being deposited at the material time. It was held that it did not—this has been addressed by the E.P.A., s.33(6) of which provides that a breach of any condition is an offence independently of any depositing of waste.

stations, and much licensed activity that did not involve final deposits fell totally outside the control regime. It was subsequently disapproved in *R v. Metropolitan Stipendiary Magistrate, ex p. London Waste Regulation Authority and others*, and *Berkshire County Council v. Scott and another*,[76] which were heard together.[77]

In the first case, the London Waste Regulation Authority prosecuted **11–074** two defendants for operating an unlicensed waste transfer station. The magistrates had refused to commit the defendants for trial on the grounds that the materials on the site were not intended to be left there permanently, and accordingly were not, in the light of *Leigh*, a deposit. That decision not to commit was before the court by way of judicial review. In the second case, the defendants were operating a skip hire business, which involved an accumulation of substantial quantities of rubbish on the site. They were served with a notice under section 16 of C.O.P.A. requiring them to remove the waste at the site. The appeal against the notice was allowed on the grounds that the waste on the site had not been deposited, as that term had to be understood following *Leigh*, and the County Council appealed that decision. The Divisional Court reviewed the arguments that had found favour in *Leigh* very carefully, and held they were unsustainable, and that the decision in *Leigh* on the meaning of "deposit" was accordingly wrong.

The prosecution in respect of the waste transfer station was taken **11–075** under section 3(1)(b) which prohibits the use of "any plant or equipment . . . for the purpose of disposing of controlled waste . . .". The court rejected a submission that "deposit" bears the same meaning as "dispose of", but nevertheless held that if it were the case that "deposit" when used in section 3(1)(a) only applies to permanent deposits and not temporary ones, it could not be right that section 3(1)(b) should be construed in a manner that prohibited temporary disposals as well as permanent ones. Accordingly, if *Leigh* was rightly decided, section 3(1)(b) would have to be construed as being limited to the use of plant or equipment for the purpose of permanent, and not temporary disposals of controlled waste.

The court was presented with the argument used to distinguish **11–076** *Leigh* in *Nottinghamshire County Council v. Berridge Incinerators*,[78] namely that *Leigh* only applied where a site was licensed. This was rejected on

---

[76] Q.B.D., [1993] 3 All E.R. 113; Watkins L.J., Auld and Laws J.
[77] It had also been distinguished in *Nottinghamshire County Council v. Berridge Incinerators*, (1992) 204 ENDS Report 36, on the ground that *Leigh* was limited to licensed landfill sites, where the company had ample opportunity to inspect waste before its final committal to the ground. This distinction was itself disapproved in the *LWRA* and *Berkshire CC* cases.
[78] See n.77, above.

the grounds that "deposit" in the prohibition of section 3(1)(a) ("a person shall not deposit controlled waste on any land . . .") could not properly be given two separate meanings depending on whether the land was the subject of a waste disposal licence or not; at least a court should only come to such a conclusion if driven to it, because any other interpretation would produce wholly unacceptable consequences which could not possibly have been intended. That, it held, was not the case.

11–077   The court looked at the practical implications of the *Leigh* judgment, and in particular that it would result in the complete failure of C.O.P.A. to apply to quantities of waste being dumped (unlicensed) on a site with the firm intention that it be removed in due course. It could not see any basis on which it should hold that Parliament intended to create such a lacuna. It further held that in their ordinary senses, neither "deposit" nor "dispose of" necessarily required any finality — disposal occurs both when an article is destroyed and also when it is passed on from one person to another.[79] Thus C.O.P.A. section 4(3) explicitly referred to "any deposits which . . . are of such a temporary nature" [that they may be excluded from the controls of section 3(1)]. Clearly this implied that deposits within the meaning of section 3(1) need not be permanent. Consideration of certain provisions in the Control and Disposal of Waste Regulations 1988, made under section 3(1) (among others) suggested that these clearly envisaged purely temporary activities relating to waste being regarded as disposals (though it was doubted whether it was legitimate to treat these Regulations as an aid to construction of the statute under which they were made). The court thus held that neither deposit, as used in section 16 of C.O.P.A. (and, by necessary implication, also in section 3(1)(a)), nor disposal, as used in section 3(1)(b), required a final resting place or a final act of disposal, once and for all, of the controlled waste at the final resting place, and hence that the decision in *Leigh* was wrong.

11–078   As a matter of legal principle, there are now two conflicting decisions of the Queens Bench Division, both being of equal standing. Nevertheless, the detailed reasoning in the later case for rejecting the decision in *Leigh* is wholly persuasive, and argument that "deposit" requires a "final resting place" has, it may be hoped, itself now been finally laid to rest. Section 33(1)(a) of the E.P.A. is in effectively identical terms to C.O.P.A. s.3(1)(a) in this respect and these decisions remain equally relevant to interpreting "deposit" where it occurs in the E.P.A.

---

[79] This would appear to be equally true of "discarding".

"Controlled Waste"

Controlled waste is defined in the E.P.A. in the same terms as in   **11–079**
C.O.P.A., namely "household, industrial and commercial waste or any
such waste".[80] These three categories are then each defined in their
turn.[81] Power is given to the Secretary of State to make regulations
including further wastes in any of these categories or taking any
wastes out of them; hitherto the effect has generally been to move a
particular description of waste from one category to another, and to
take certain innocuous and/or desirable recycling activities out of the
licensing system. However, in the 1994 Licensing Regulations the
power has been used to bring about what is in the result a revision to
the substance of the E.P.A. itself, by substituting Directive waste for
the definition of waste in the statute. The distinctions between these
various categories are of significance primarily in relation to the
responsibilities and charging powers of waste collection and waste
disposal authorities: except where a type of waste is exempted from
the application of the controls, the basic prohibition and the licensing
regime apply equally to all forms of controlled waste.

In *Kent County Council v. Thanet District Council*[82] it was held that the   **11–080**
words "or any such waste", at the end of the definition of controlled
waste, do not serve to extend the meaning of the term, but merely
indicate that controlled waste is any one or more of the three
categories. Thus seaweed deposited on the beach by the wind and the
sea, being in none of the categories, was not controlled waste, and
could be collected and spread on land without a waste disposal
licence. Clearly it has not been discarded by anyone and is not
Directive waste.

"Household waste" means waste from a domestic property, a   **11–081**
caravan which usually and for the time being is on a caravan site, a
residential home, and premises forming part of a university, school or
other educational establishment or part of a hospital or nursing home.
"Industrial waste" means waste from any factory within the meaning
of the Factories Act 1961, any premises used for or in connection with
the provision of public transport, or the public supply of gas, water or
electricity or sewerage services and of postal and telecommunications
services. "Commercial waste" is then defined as waste from premises
used wholly or mainly for the purposes of a trade or business, or for

---

[80] E.P.A., s.75(4); C.O.P.A., s.30(1). The C.O.P.A. definition remains relevant since the
Collection and Disposal of Waste Regulations 1988 made under it determine the
scope of licences granted on applications made before May 1, 1994, that use any of
those expressions.
[81] E.P.A., s.75(5)–(7); C.O.P.A., s.30(3).
[82] [1993] Env. L.R. 391.

the purposes of sport, recreation or entertainment, but excluding household waste and industrial waste, waste from any mine or quarry and waste from agricultural premises.[83] The corresponding definitions in C.O.P.A.[84] are essentially the same, though there is no reference to caravans in relation to household waste, and the definition of industrial waste relates to nationalised industries, and did not envisage their privatisation.

11–082   No guidance is given on what is to be understood by the reference to using premises "wholly or mainly" for the purpose of a trade or business, etc. Any decision as to this will doubtless depend on the facts of each individual case, where the decision will ultimately turn on whether the main purpose of premises under consideration is for a trade or business or for sport, recreation or entertainment. Since "domestic property" is limited to a building (or a self-contained part of one) used wholly for the purposes of living accommodation, situations will arise where premises are neither private dwellings nor mainly used for a trade or business. However waste from a mixed heredita-ment is to be treated as commercial waste, by virtue of the 1988 Regulations.[85]

11–083   The Controlled Waste Regulations 1992[86] made under these powers define in Schedules 1, 3 and 4 waste that is to be treated for the purposes of the E.P.A. as household, industrial and commercial waste respectively.[87] The Collection and Disposal of Waste Regulations 1988[88] made under C.O.P.A., and the analogous but not equivalent regulations for Scotland, the Control of Pollution (Licensing of Waste Disposal) (Scotland) Regulations 1977, S.I. 1977 No. 2006, as amended by S.I. 1992 No. 1368], continue to apply to licences granted on applications made before May 1, 1994 and likewise define household, industrial and commercial waste in similar but by no means identical terms to those of the 1992 Regulations. Each of the 1992 and the 1988 Regulations have a Regulation 7A,[89] providing that waste which is not Directive waste is not household, industrial or commercial waste, so limiting all the statutory controls to Directive waste.[90]

11–084   As referred to later, the duty of care under E.P.A. section 34 does not apply to an occupier of domestic property as respects the household waste produced on that property. The 1992 Regulations include within

---

[83] E.P.A., s.75(5), (6), (7).
[84] s.30(3).
[85] Sched. 4, para. 3.
[86] S.I. 1992 No. 588, as amended by S.I. 1993 No. 566.
[87] Sched. 2 lists types of household waste for which a charge for collection may be made.
[88] S.I. 1988 No. 819.
[89] Inserted by regs. 24(8), 22(4) of the 1994 Licensing Regs.
[90] When taken with Sched.4, para.9(2), 1994 Licensing Regs.

"household waste", by virtue of Schedule 1, waste from any of the following:

- — hereditaments and premises exempt from local non-domestic rating by virtue of their being places of religious worship.
- — premises occupied by a charity and wholly or mainly used for charitable purposes.
- — any land belonging to or used in connection with domestic property, a caravan or a residential home.
- — a private garage which either has a floor area of 25 square metres or less or is used solely or mainly for the accommodation of a private motor vehicle.
- — private storage premises used wholly or mainly for the storage of articles of domestic use.
- — a moored vessel used wholly for the purposes of living accommodation.
- — a campsite.
- — a prison or other penal institution.
- — a hall or other premises used wholly or mainly for public meetings.
- — a royal palace.
- — the cleaning by local authorities of highways and roads of litter under E.P.A. s.89(2).

All waste, of any kind, that is imported into Great Britain is **11–085** industrial waste,[91] even though it would otherwise fall into the definition of household or commercial waste. Conversely, the following wastes are not household wastes but are to be treated as commercial waste by virtue of Schedule 4 (this list is not comprehensive), namely waste from:

- — an office or showroom.
- — a hotel (as defined in the Hotel Proprietors Act 1956 s.1(3) for England and Wales, and the Licensing (Scotland) Act 1976 s.139(1) for Scotland).
- — any part of a composite hereditament or, in Scotland, of part residential subjects, which is used for the purposes of a trade or business.[92]
- — premises occupied by a club, society or any association of persons in which activities are conducted for the benefit of the members.
- — a tent pitched on land other than a camp site.

---

[91] 1992 Regs., Sched. 3.
[92] Any self-contained part used wholly for the purposes of living accommodation is domestic property and its waste is household waste.

11–086   The prohibitions of E.P.A. section 33(1) do not apply in relation to household waste from a domestic property which is treated, kept or disposed of within the curtilage of the dwelling and with the occupier's consent.[93] However, this exception does not apply to any mineral or synthetic oil or grease, asbestos or clinical waste which, for the purposes of this exception only, are not to be treated as household waste.[94] These categories of waste are included among those listed in Schedule 2 to the 1992 Regulations as being types of household waste for which a charge for collection may be made.

11–087   Waste arising from construction (which includes improvement, repair or alteration) and demolition work, including any preparatory work, is industrial waste for all purposes of Part II of the E.P.A. except section 34(2). Where this waste comes from a domestic property, it would otherwise be household waste. The reference to section 34(2) however exempts occupiers of domestic property from the application of the duty of care in so far as it relates to such construction and demolition waste produced on their property. Anyone else concerned with that waste, for example, a builder, a carrier or someone disposing of the waste, will all be subject to the duty of care in the normal way.

Landed Ships' Waste

11–088   Under the MARPOL Convention (see paragraph 2–009) residues and mixtures containing oil or noxious liquid substances must not be dumped at sea but discharged from ships to reception facilities. This obligation is implemented by the Prevention of Pollution (Reception Facilities) Order 1984[95] which enables harbour authorities to provide such facilities, and requires both them and operators of terminals used by ships to ensure that the facilities they are responsible for are adequate. Annex V to the MARPOL Convention extended these provisions for preventing marine pollution to cover what is generically referred to as "garbage". Accordingly, the Merchant Shipping (Reception Facilities for Garbage) Regulations 1988[96] extend the obligation to provide adequate reception facilities, so that they are also suitable for receiving ships' garbage. Garbage is defined in these Regulations, and includes all kinds of food, domestic and operational waste generated during the normal operation of the ship, though excluding sewage and fresh fish and fish parts. Typically, garbage would include ropes and fishing nets made of synthetic materials and plastic garbage bags,

---

[93] s.33(2).
[94] Reg. 3(1).
[95] S.I. 1984 No. 862.
[96] S.I. 1988 No. 2293.

560

with which Annex V of the MARPOL Convention is principally concerned.

The keeping and disposing of the ships' waste that is thus received is the subject of the Control of Pollution (Landed Ships' Waste) Regulations 1987 as amended by the Control of Pollution (Landed Ships' Waste)(Amendment) Regulations 1989.[97] The effect of these Regulations is to prescribe under section 30(4) of C.O.P.A. that tank washings and garbage from ships is to be treated as industrial waste for the purposes of Part I of C.O.P.A., and so becomes subject to the provisions relating to controlled waste, except as provided in these 1987 Regulations.   **11–089**

For the purpose of these Regulations, "ship" is extremely widely defined as a vessel of any type whatsoever operating in the marine environment, including submersible craft, floating craft and any structure which is a fixed or floating platform. "Harbour area" is given the same meaning as in the Dangerous Substances in Harbour Areas Regulations 1987,[98] and covers all water within the statutory jurisdiction of a statutory harbour authority, any berth abutting any such areas of water, and any land within a harbour authority's jurisdiction or occupied by it that is used for loading or unloading vessels, as well as any monobuoy connected to storage facilities in a harbour area.[99]   **11–090**

Because the tank washings and garbage are to be treated as controlled waste, transport of the tank washings and garbage must be carried out by a registered carrier, and their disposal elsewhere must be carried out by a person with the appropriate waste licence. The storage of such waste, including any special waste, in the reception facilities for not more than seven days is exempted from the licensing requirements, so long as the amount from any ship does not exceed 20 cubic metres.[1] Registration under regulation 18 of this exempted activity is required, and the exemption is dependent on the storage being consistent with the objectives of Schedule 4, paragraph 4(1)(a).[2]   **11–091**

A similar exemption is available for the temporary storage of limited quantities of tank washings in reception facilities under the 1984 Reception Facilities Order.[3] Where special waste is moved from a harbour area, a special form of consignment note, as set out in Schedule 2 to the 1987 Landed Ships' Waste Regulations, is used so as to avoid undue delay to ships.   **11–092**

---

[97] S.I. 1987 No. 402, S.I. 1989 No. 65.
[98] S.I. 1987 No. 37.
[99] The previous definitions of "ship" and "harbour area" were significantly changed by the 1989 amending Regulations.
[1] Sched.3, para.36. It is arguable that the exemption also applies if the *average per ship* does not exceed 20 cubic metres.
[2] See para. 11–147 and n.87 thereto.
[3] S.I. 1984 No. 862.

11–093   Special rules apply to the landing at ports in England and Wales of waste food containing animal or poultry products. The import of animal and poultry products is generally prohibited unless licensed, by virtue of the Animal Products and Poultry Products Order 1980 (as amended).[4] General licences TAY-GEN/85/1186 and WOAD/GEN authorise the landing from ships of waste food containing animal or poultry products subject to:

(a) it being transported and kept in drip-proof containers;
(b) it being taken direct from the place of landing for disposal in accordance with arrangements approved by MAFF; and
(c) the containers used to transport the waste being cleaned and disinfected immediately after they have been emptied.

Any failure to comply with these requirements constitutes an offence under the Animal Health Act 1981.

Excluded Wastes and Activities involving Waste

11–094   An important series of exclusions from the scope of the Directive are listed in its Article 2, namely:

(a) gaseous effluents emitted into the atmosphere; and
(b) where they are already covered by other legislation
    (i)   radioactive waste;
    (ii) waste resulting from prospecting, extraction, treatment and storage of mineral resources and the working of quarries;
    (iii) animal carcases and the following agricultural waste: faecal matter and other natural, non-dangerous substances used in farming;
    (iv) waste waters, with the exception of waste in liquid form;
    (v)   decommissioned explosives.

Being thereby excluded from Directive waste, these categories are equally excluded from the application of the E.P.A. However the E.P.A. itself disapplies the controls of its Part II from a very similar list of wastes, namely:

    (i)   radioactive waste;[5]
    (ii) waste from any mine or quarry;[6]

---

[4] S.I. 1980 No. 14.
[5] s.78.
[6] s.75(7).

(iii) waste from premises used for agriculture;[7]

(iii) explosives;[8]

(v) sewage.[9]

In addition, the prohibitions of section 33(1) do not apply to certain activities involving waste which are the subject of other control regimes, by virtue of regulation 16 of the 1994 Licensing Regulations. These consist of:

(vi) Recovery and disposal of waste in the course of an authorised process subject to Integrated Pollution Control under Part I of the E.P.A. (*i.e.* a Part A process), not being an activity involving the final disposal of waste by deposit in or on land.

(vii) The disposal of waste where this is or forms part of an authorised Part B incineration process,[10] in so far as it results in emissions to air, not being an activity involving the final disposal of waste by deposit in or on land. Incinerators in this category may be exempt from the Part B controls in certain circumstances; if they are, then the E.P.A. Part II controls apply. An exempt incinerator that is designed to be moved on roads or other land is "mobile plant" for the purposes of section 33(1)(b),[11] and so requires a mobile plant licence.

(viii) Disposal of liquid waste under a discharge consent under the W.R.A. or, in Scotland, Part II of C.O.P.A.

(ix) Recovery and disposal of waste in the course of an operation that is licensed under Part II of F.E.P.A. (*i.e.* dumping at sea) or is exempted from the requirement for such a licence by an order under section 7 of F.E.P.A.

The exclusions from the Directive and the corresponding exclusions **11–095** from the E.P.A. are discussed in the following sections. Those from the Directive, other than that of gaseous effluents, are all subject to the proviso "where they are already covered by other legislation". It is unclear whether this expression applies to other national legislation or only to EC legislation. Circular 11/94 expresses the Government's view that the expression applies to both EC and national legislation.[12] Nevertheless, if national legislation is also intended, it has to be asked what the purpose of the expression is, since if national legislation in

---

[7] s.75(7).
[8] s.75(2).
[9] s.75(8).
[10] *i.e.* within section 5.1, Part B, (a), of the E.P. (P.P.&S.) Regs. 1991.
[11] 1994 Licensing Regs., reg.12.
[12] It is understood that this is also the informal view of the Commission.

respect of any of the listed matters is already in place that meets the requirements of the Directive, there is no reason to create an exclusion for it. The answer must be that "covered" by national legislation should be construed loosely as applying to equivalent legislation that provides environmental protection comparable to that provided by the Directive, but by different administrative means, and therefore not meeting its detailed requirements. Given that it was fully open to the Commission, when drafting the Directive, to identify all relevant EC legislation relating to the listed topics that would benefit from the exclusion, as it has done in other measures, the expression most probably applies to national legislation also in so far as it provides approximately equivalent environmental protection, even if by other administrative means.[13]

Gaseous effluents

11–096   "Gaseous effluents emitted into the atmosphere" is strictly construed by the Government as applying only to substances which are already gases at the time they become waste, and emitted from processes that are not themselves waste disposal or recovery operations, and which are consequently subject to the statutory controls over emissions to air. Gaseous emissions arising from waste disposal or recovery operations, and the venting of liquid compressed gases such as CFCs, are considered to be subject to the waste management licensing controls over those operations.[14]

Radioactive Waste

11–097   Comprehensive controls over radioactive waste are contained in the Radioactive Substances Act 1993, and regulations made thereunder[15] (see chapter 16), as well as in Council Directive 80/836/Euratom. Thus by virtue of E.P.A., s.78, except as provided by regulations made under that section, nothing in Part II of the E.P.A. applies to radioactive waste within the meaning of the Radioactive Substances Act 1993. Nevertheless, the Control of Pollution (Special Waste) Regulations 1980[16] provide in regulation 3 that section 17 of C.O.P.A., which deals with "special" (that is, hazardous) waste, applies also to waste that would be controlled waste but for the fact that it is radioactive waste.

[13] This is essentially the view expressed by the Government in Circular 11/94 at para. 1.16.
[14] Circular 11/94, Annex 1, para. 1.13; Annex 4 paras. 4.95–4.103.
[15] Or deemed to be made thereunder, having been made under the Radioactive Substances Act 1960.
[16] S.I. 1980 No. 1709.

Accordingly these 1980 Regulations, which define what is "special waste" will include any waste that is radioactive if it would otherwise fall within the criteria for special waste. In such cases both sets of controls apply, though in respect of different properties of the waste.

Mineral and Quarry Wastes

Waste from quarries and other mineral workings is controlled in the **11–098** UK under planning legislation and the Mines and Quarries (Tips) Act 1969. If it is correct to construe the Directive's exclusion as applying exclusively to mineral waste,[17] other waste that may be generated at mines and quarries remains within "Directive waste", for example waste from canteens or the equipment used in the mining or quarrying operations. However section 75(7)(c) of the E.P.A. excludes from commercial waste (and hence from "controlled waste") "waste from any mine or quarry", thus excluding also such non-mineral waste, and no regulations may be made in respect of such waste.[18] Further controls are to be expected in the United Kingdom in order to implement the Directive in respect of non-mineral waste.[19]

Waste from tunnelling or other excavations and also from dredging **11–099** operations is to be treated as industrial waste.[20] The deposit of waste from dredging of any inland water, either along the bank or towpath of the water from which it was dredged or along that of any other inland water so as to benefit agriculture or provide ecological improvement, and the keeping or deposit of excavated material from peat working are, in certain circumstances, exempt activities requiring only registration.[21]

Agricultural and Animal Waste

The Animal Waste Directive 90/667, and the Animal By-Products **11–100** Order 1992 that implements it in the United Kingdom, are regarded as providing corresponding controls over the disposal and recovery of animal carcasses, which consequently fall outside "Directive waste".[22] The remainder of this exclusion is limited in the Directive to faecal matter and natural, non-dangerous substances used in farming. Other wastes are inevitably generated in farming, for example machinery waste, waste oils and pesticides, which are also excluded from

---

[17] *Ibid*, para. 1.17(b).
[18] E.P.A., s.75(8).
[19] Circular 11/94, para. 28.
[20] Sched. 3 of the 1992 Regs.
[21] 1994 Licensing Regs., Sched.3, paras.25, 33.
[22] Circular 11/94, para.1.17(c).

"controlled waste" by E.P.A. s.75(7)(c). Here also, further waste controls are to be brought forward by the Government to give effect to the Directive.[23]

11–101 The E.P.A. exclusion under this head applies to all types of waste from premises used for agriculture within the meaning of the Agriculture Act 1947 or, in Scotland, the Agriculture (Scotland) Act 1948.[24] Again, no regulations may be made in respect of such waste.[25] Nevertheless, waste from premises used for the purposes of breeding, boarding, stabling or exhibiting animals is industrial waste.[26]

11–102 Animal by-products, being essentially materials produced by slaughterhouses that are not destined for human consumption, are often of inherent value, *e.g.* hides and offals. These are not regarded as waste when transferred for commercial use,[27] but where they are waste then supply and use is in most cases controlled under the Animal By-Products Order 1992.[28] Animal carcass waste, to the extent that it comes under the Order, may be regarded as within Article 2 of the Directive and so excluded from the standard waste controls of the E.P.A. It is nevertheless uncertain exactly what scope should be given to the reference to "animal carcasses" in the Directive.

11–103 Animal waste collected and transported in accordance with Schedule 2 to the 1992 Order is stated to be neither commercial nor industrial waste for the purposes of the duty of care under E.P.A. section 34.[29] Likewise anyone authorised to hold or deal with animal waste under the 1992 Order or who is the holder of a knackers yard licence is exempt from the requirement to register as a carrier of controlled waste under the Controlled Waste (Registration of Carriers and Seizure of Vehicles) Regulations 1991.[30] A carrier who is not so authorised must still be registered under these 1991 Regulations before carrying any animal waste. Keeping and treating animal by-products in accordance with the 1992 Order is exempted from the need for a waste management licence;[31] the usual requirement to register under

---

[23] Circular 11/94, para.28.
[24] By the Agriculture Act 1947, s.109(3), "Agriculture" includes horticulture, fruit growing, seed growing, dairy farming and livestock breeding and keeping, the use of land as grazing land, meadow land, osier land, market gardens and nursery grounds, and the use of land for woodlands where that use is ancillary to the farming of land for other agriculture purposes; "livestock" includes any creature kept for the production of food, wool, skins or fur, or for the purpose of its use in the farming of land.
[25] E.P.A., s.75(8).
[26] 1992 Regs., Sched. 3.
[27] Circular 11/94, para.4.91.
[28] S.I. 1992 No.3303.
[29] Controlled Waste Regs. 1992, reg.7(3).
[30] S.I. 1991 No.1624, reg.2(1)(i).
[31] 1994 Licensing Regs., Sched.3, para.23.

Regulation 18 is waived, the relevant registration authority being deemed to be aware of the activity.[32]

Explosives

The controls provided by the Explosives Act 1875, the Control of   **11–104**
Explosives Regulations 1991[33] and the Road Traffic (Carriage of
Explosives) Regulations 1989[34] cover, among other things, the disposal
and recovery of explosives. "Decommissioned", as applied to explosives in the Directive, would not appear to require any active steps to
have been taken to disable or dismantle the explosives—indeed it
would be strange if the exception applied only to explosives that had
been so treated—the term should be regarded as applying to all
explosives that have in fact been discarded.[35]

The E.P.A. excludes from the definition of waste any that is a   **11–105**
substance which is an explosive within the meaning of the Explosives
Act 1875 (whether "decommissioned" or not). Section 3 of that Act
provides that "explosive"

" (1) means gunpowder, nitro-glycerine, dynamite, gun-cotton,
       blasting powders, fulminate of mercury or of other metals,
       coloured fires, and every other substance, whether similar to
       those above mentioned or not, used or manufactured with a
       view to produce a practical effect by explosion or a pyrotech-
       nic effect; and
  (2) includes fog-signals, fireworks, fuzes (sic), rockets, percus-
       sion caps, detonators, cartridges, ammunition of all descrip-
       tions, and every adaptation or preparation of an explosive as
       above defined."

Orders in Council may be made under section 106 of the 1875 Act,
amending the scope of the term. Though explosives are excluded from
the E.P.A. controls, a waste derived from an explosive that is not itself
explosive is capable of being controlled waste.

"Waste Waters" and Sewage

The Directive's exclusion of "waste waters, with the exception of   **11–106**
waste in liquid form" is singularly obscure. Aqueous discharges to
controlled waters are subject to the controls provided by the Water

---

[32] 1994 Licensing Regs., regs.18(5), (10)(c).
[33] S.I. 1991 No.1531.
[34] S.I. 1989 No.615.
[35] cf. the Italian "i materiali esplosivi in disuso"; German "ausgesonderte Sprengstoffe";
French "les explosifs déclassés".

Resources Act 1991 (in Scotland by C.O.P.A.), and can properly be regarded as excluded from "Directive waste", though other consented discharges cannot. Waste waters from sewage treatment plants the subject of the EC Urban Waste Water Treatment Directive 91/271 are no doubt within this exclusion. "Waste in liquid form" is presumably intended to refer to aqueous solutions and suspensions, rather than to, *e.g.* non-aqueous organic solvents, which cannot in any circumstances be waste *waters*. A distinction may be intended between (consented) aqueous discharges, whether to controlled waters or to sewer, in which the concentration of any pollutants is very low and waste materials and products which are in fact relatively concentrated aqueous solutions or suspensions. If so, the latter would not be excluded and would accordingly be "Directive waste"; nevertheless discharge of such products to controlled waters may be consented under the Water Resources Act (or in Scotland Part II of C.O.P.A.) notwithstanding that they are "Directive waste". No waste management licence under the E.P.A. is required for such discharges by virtue of regulation 16(1)(c) of the 1994 Licensing Regulations, but the fact that Directive waste is involved will place responsibilities on the consenting authority equivalent to those laid on waste regulation authorities by the Directive. However even though the actual *discharge* from an effluent treatment plant may be excluded from the Directive's controls, if its *operation* on "wastes in liquid form" is a disposal or a recovery operation, as defined by the Directive, then it must be brought under control through licensing or an appropriate exemption, as required by the Directive, unless it is "covered by other legislation". In the United Kingdom, the only other relevant legislation is Integrated Pollution Control under Part I of the E.P.A. It follows that, except where it is a component of an IPC process, if an effluent treatment plant gives rise to substances that may be disposed of to, *e.g.* landfill or impounded in lagoons, then it is likely to involve physico-chemical and/or biological treatment of waste amounting to waste disposal (see items 8 and 9 of Table 11/III below).[35A]

11–107   The E.P.A. excludes sewage from commercial waste.[36] By regulation 1(4) of the 1992 Controlled Waste Regulations, references in those Regulations to waste do not include sewage, except so far as otherwise provided. Sewage, sludge or septic tank sludge which is treated, kept or disposed of (otherwise than by means of mobile plant) within the

---

[35A] Though the Directive permits (but does not require) exemption of waste disposal carried out at the place of its production, the exemption of para. 26(1) of Sched. 3 to the 1994 Licensing Regulations applies only when the disposal is an *integral part* of the process that produced the waste. A stand-alone effluent treatment plant will not necessarily be "integral" with the main process plant, and so may require a full licence.

[36] s.75(8).

curtilage of a sewage treatment works as an integral part of the operation of those works is not industrial waste or commercial waste. Likewise, sludge which is supplied or used in accordance with the Sludge (Use in Agriculture) Regulations 1989,[37] and septic tank sludge used in accordance with those 1989 Regulations are also neither industrial nor commercial waste.[38] Where septic tank sludge is used in accordance with these 1989 Regulations, it is to be treated as industrial waste. However septic tank sludge is to be regarded as household waste for the purposes of the duty of care, whereby the occupier of the relevant domestic property (but no one else) is exempted from the duty of care in relation to that sludge.

Sewage sludge is liable to contain various heavy metals, and if the sludge is used as agricultural fertiliser, these heavy metals can build up to dangerous concentrations in the soil. The Sludge (Use In Agriculture) Regulations 1989, as amended, which give effect to EC Directive 86/278,[39] are designed both to deal with this issue and also to prescribe minimum periods between using sludge on agricultural land and certain agricultural operations, to ensure safety from toxic substances contained in the sludge.[40] The Regulations impose obligations both on persons using sewage sludge and septic tank sludge on agricultural land, and also on sludge producers, defined to mean persons who manage a plant at which sludge is produced for disposal. The Regulations use "sludge" to refer to residual sludge from domestic or urban sewage treatment plants, and "septic tank sludge" to mean residual sludge from septic tanks and other similar installations. Where either form of sludge has been used on agricultural land, no person may cause or knowingly permit the grazing of animals or harvesting of forage crops from that land within the next three weeks, or the harvesting of fruit and vegetable crops which are grown in direct contact with the soil and normally eaten raw within ten months from that date.[41] Where any untreated sludge has been used on agricultural land without being injected into the soil, the occupier of that land must have the sludge worked into the soil as soon as reasonably practicable.[42] **11–108**

Regulation 3 sets out a series of requirements to control the build up of heavy metals in agricultural land by requiring that any sludge used must be tested in accordance with Schedule 1 to the Regulations, **11–109**

---

[37] S.I. 1989 No. 1263 as amended by S.I. 1990 No. 880.
[38] 1992 Regs., reg. 7(1).
[39] [1986] O.J. L181.
[40] Earlier studies on this topic include the 7th Report of the RCEP on "Agriculture and Pollution" (1979), and the Standing Technical Committee Report No. 20 on the disposal of sewage sludge to land (DoE, 1981).
[41] reg. 4(1).
[42] reg. 4(2).

including analyses for chromium, zinc, copper, nickel, cadmium, lead and mercury. The soil on the land itself must also be tested or assessed in accordance with Schedule 2 to the Regulations, which sets out, among other matters, specified maximum concentrations of the elements just listed. These concentrations vary, in the case of zinc, copper and nickel, with increasing pH of the soil from 5.0 up to 7.0.[43] The sludge must not be used on agricultural land if the pH of the soil is less than 5.0, and there is a general requirement that it be used in such a way "that account is taken of the nutrient needs of the plants and that the quality of the soil and of the surface and groundwater is not impaired".[44] This is designed to procure that no more than sufficient sludge is applied than can be usefully taken up by growing plants, since otherwise the remainder will leach away, creating dangers of eutrophication of waters that receive the surplus. Except for certain so-called "dedicated sites" (those that were dedicated to the disposal of sludge on June 17, 1986), the average annual rate of addition of any of the listed elements by means of the sludge must not exceed specified maximum figures, averaged over the preceding 10 years. Similarly, the concentration in the soil of any of these elements must at no time exceed the maxima prescribed in the table of Schedule 1 either before or after application of the sludge. Where sludge is being used on agricultural land, the occupier must give information to the sludge producer of where and when the sludge was used and how much of it was applied. Where any of the sludge was supplied to an intermediary, details of that person must also be given. The sludge producer is required to maintain a register containing the total quantities of sludge produced, the total quantity of sludge supplied for use in agriculture together with its composition and properties, and also quantities of treated sludge supplied and the type of treatment. Details of persons to whom sludge is being supplied and where it has been used must also be included. The register must also contain copies of every analysis or assessment made of agricultural soil. The contents of this register are to be made available for inspection by the Secretary of State at all reasonable times; there is no obligation under the Regulations to make this information available to the public generally.

11–110   The Regulations also contain detailed rules in relation to dedicated sites. For these, where the actual concentration of any of the elements in the soil exceeds the relevant maximum figure, no crop grown on it may be sold or offered for sale, except as advised by the relevant Minister or Secretary of State, nor may any commercial food crops be grown on it other than those intended for animal consumption. In

---

[43] The lower the pH, below 7.0, the more acidic the soil is, and the more likely it is for metals to form salts and be dissolved out.
[44] reg. 3(7).

such circumstances, the occupier must not use sludge on that site, except as advised by the relevant Minister or Secretary of State.

The Department of the Environment has issued a "Code of Practice **11–112** for the Agricultural Use of Sewage Sludge", giving guidance on this and on the necessary analyses. Two reports on, respectively, food safety and animal health and on the soil fertility aspects of using sewage sludge have been published by MAFF.[45] Both stress the importance of the precautionary principle in avoiding concentrations of heavy metals in soil; some reductions in certain limits for zinc, copper, nickel and cadmium are recommended.

Special and Other Hazardous Wastes

The properties of the wastes that are required to be disposed of have **11–113** an almost infinite variety. Inert wastes are by their nature likely to be relatively harmless to man or the environment, though in the wrong place can be major eyesores. Other wastes are putrescible, and not necessarily harmful when deposited, but liable on decomposition to give rise to leachate that may cause considerable environmental harm to water courses, as well as producing methane, which may create explosive mixtures with air, and is also a greenhouse gas. Heavy metals, pesticides and other organic compounds can result in extremely harmful pollution of groundwater, and certain wastes such as infectious clinical waste and PCBs are potentially so dangerous that incineration is generally the only appropriate disposal option. It is of course impossible to tailor the regulatory controls to correspond precisely to the degree of hazard represented by every particular consignment of waste. In the UK, the original Deposit of Poisonous Waste Act 1972 was only concerned with poisonous and other dangerous waste; the procedural rules over consignments of such waste that it introduced were followed by the more detailed rules set up under section 17 of C.O.P.A. Under this the Secretary of State is required to make special provision for the disposal of controlled waste of any kind that is or may be especially dangerous or difficult to dispose of. Although the E.P.A. contains an equivalent provision in

---

[45] Review of the Rules for Sewage Sludge Application to Agricultural Land: (1) Food Safety and Relevant Animal Health Aspects of Potentially Toxic Elements; (2) Soil Fertility Aspects of Potentially Toxic Elements, MAFF, 1993.

section 62,[46] this has not yet been brought into force due to difficulties in establishing a common definition of hazardous or dangerous waste at EC level. The procedures are dealt with below (see paragraphs 11–119 to 11–127) — this section will first deal with the nature of the wastes that are required to be given special consideration under EC and UK legislation by reason of the hazards that they represent.

11–114   Section 17 of C.O.P.A. was given effect by the Control of Pollution (Special Waste) Regulations 1980,[47] which apply throughout England, Wales and Scotland. The Regulations also implemented (though incompletely)[48] EC Directive 78/319 on Toxic and Dangerous Waste.[49] This Directive is due to be replaced by Directive 91/689 on Hazardous Waste[50] which should have been implemented by December 12, 1993. Failure to draw up in due time a list of wastes to which the Directive is to apply however delayed this, and a new implementation date of June 27, 1995, has now been sent.[51] Directive 78/319 set out a variety of requirements for dealing with hazardous waste, including keeping hazardous waste separate from other waste while being collected, transported, stored or deposited, imposed special packaging and labelling rules, and required comprehensive records to be kept of waste disposed of. Those producing, holding and disposing of such waste were required to keep records of the amounts and types of the waste, including its origin and methods and sites used for its disposal. Separately, consignment notes were required that must accompany any hazardous waste being transported in the course of disposal.[52] This 1978 Directive also explicitly required the "polluter pays" principle to be applied to the cost of disposing of toxic and dangerous waste, which (less any proceeds from treating the waste) must be borne by the person having waste collected, or any organisation carrying out the

---

[46] Though, in keeping with the wider controls in Part II of the E.P.A., s.62 extends also to the treating and keeping of such waste.

[47] S.I. 1980 No. 1709.

[48] The definition in the UK Regs. ignores risks solely to the environment, and excludes agricultural waste; waste produced by the Crown is not covered; there are no obligations reflecting those of the Directive to record the production and storage of waste.

[49] [1978] O.J. L84.

[50] [1991] O.J. L377.

[51] [1994] O.J. L168. The list of hazardous wastes was eventually published on December 31, 1994, in [1994] O.J. L356.

[52] "Disposal" being defined in Directive 78/319 to mean collection, sorting, carriage and treatment of the waste as well as its storage and tipping above or underground, in addition to transformation operations necessary for its recovery, re-use or recycling.

storage, treatment or deposit of waste, or previous holders or the producer of the product from which the waste came.

Directive 91/689 aims to apply the provisions of Directive 75/442 as amended to hazardous waste, subject to certain qualifications, and in addition to provide a clearer definition and classification of hazardous wastes than previously, where much was left to the discretion of Member States. The new definition will be applicable not only to hazardous waste disposal, but also to other EC rules on, for example, the landfill and incineration of hazardous wastes.[53] **11–115**

The definition of "waste" in Directive 75/442 applies equally to the Hazardous Waste Directive 91/689; what is to be regarded as a hazardous waste is to be determined by reference to a list drawn up on the basis of Annexes I and II to the Directive.[54] The Hazardous Waste Directive has three Annexes as follows: **11–116**

Annex I — categories or generic types of hazardous waste listed according to their nature or the activity which generated them. This Annex is divided into two groups A and B, group A being of wastes which will be hazardous for the purposes of the Directive if they display any of the properties listed in Annex III (see below), and group B consisting of (generally less dangerous) wastes which will be deemed hazardous if they both display any of the properties listed in Annex III and also contain in any of the constituents listed in Annex II.

Annex II — constituents of the wastes in Annex IB which render them hazardous when they have the properties described in Annex III.

Annex III — properties of wastes which render them hazardous.

The Annex III properties are in many respects very similar to those in EC Directive 67/548 (as amended) (see paragraphs 12–006 *et seq.*, in particular 12–102), namely:

---

[53] The transport of hazardous and other wastes is subject to EC Regulation 259/93 which applies a separate OECD classification of wastes into red, amber and green lists (see para. 11–293).

[54] This list was due to be drawn up by June 12, 1993 but is now contained in [1994] O.J. L356.

Explosive	Substances and preparations
Oxidising	which release toxic or very toxic
Highly Flammable	gases in contact with water, air or
Flammable	an acid
Irritant	
Harmful	Substances and preparations
Corrosive	capable by any means, after
Toxic	disposal, of yielding another
Carcinogenic	substance, *e.g.* a leachate, which
Teratogenic	possesses any of the
Mutagenic	characteristics listed above.
Infectious	
Ecotoxic	

The definition of "harmful" is exceptionally wide:

"Substances and the preparations which, if they are inhaled or ingested or if they penetrate the skin, may involve limited health risks".

Every remotely hazardous substance must be at least harmful, and accordingly this gives very wide scope to the Commission in compiling its list.

11–117   Annex II lists 51 categories of constituent—these include notoriously hazardous substances such as compounds of cadmium and of mercury, asbestos, PCBs and PCTs, and congeners of dioxins and furans. The list also includes numerous heavy metals and heavy metal compounds; organic compounds, including halogenated solvents, aromatic compounds and polycyclic and heterocyclic organic compounds; pharmaceutical and veterinary compounds; biocides and phyto-pharmaceutical substances, *e.g.* pesticides; and a variety of explosive compounds.

11–118   In addition to wastes which are on the hazardous waste list, any other waste may be added if a Member State considers that it shows any of the Annex III properties. The Member State must notify any such case to the Commission, and the substance will then be reviewed with a view to including it in the list. In exceptional cases, Member States may make provisions for determining that a waste on the list does not display any Annex III properties.

United Kingdom "Special Waste"

11–119   The United Kingdom Special Waste Regulations define "special waste" in a manner that is comparatively limited, namely any controlled waste which—

574

(a) consists of or contains any of the substances listed in Part I of Schedule 1 to the Regulations, and which by reason of the presence of such substances has any of the following properties:
  (i) the ability to be likely to cause death or serious damage to tissue if a single dose of not more than 5cm^3 were ingested by a child of 20kg body weight; or
  (ii) the ability to be likely to cause serious damage to human tissue by inhalation, skin contact or eye contact from exposure to the substance for 15 minutes or less; or
  (iii) a flashpoint of 21°C or less, or
(b) is a medicinal product, as defined in section 130 of the Medicines Act 1968, which is available only in accordance with a prescription given by an appropriate practitioner as defined in section 58(1) of that Act.

Radioactive waste is, as mentioned earlier, brought within the category of special waste, in so far as it would be special waste were it not radioactive.

To fall within the first limb of the definition, there must be one or **11–120** more of the listed substances. Part I of Schedule I, which details these, is comparable to Annex II of the Hazardous Waste Directive, though somewhat less extensive. Secondly, at least one of the three criteria must both be met and also be due to the presence of these substances, or any of them. These criteria apply to the waste itself, and not to the substances within it. Since it is of course impossible to carry out experiments to determine whether or not the first two criteria are met (death or serious damage on ingestion by a small child, and serious damage to human tissue on exposure for 15 minutes of less), whether these criteria are met in a relatively marginal case cannot be determined with precision. In practice, reference should be had to DoE Circular 4/81[55] "Control of Pollution Act 1974—Control of Pollution (Special Waste) Regulation 1980" and to Waste Management Paper No. 23 "Special Wastes—a Technical Memorandum providing Guidance on their Definition".[56] Circular 4/81 contains in its Annex 1 guidance notes on the application of the definition of special waste. It proposes that the properties of a waste should be approached in the following logical order:

(i) Is it within the category of medicinal products?
(ii) Does it contain any of the substances listed in Part I of Schedule 1 to the Regulations? If "yes" to (ii), then

[55] WO C8/81.
[56] HMSO, 1981.

(iii) Does it have a flashpoint of 21°C or less?

(iv) Is it dangerous to life as defined in the Regulations?

In considering toxicity to humans, the guidance recommends reference to the data published by the US National Institute of Occupational Safety and Health (NIOSH). Where human toxicity data are not available, estimates must be made from animal toxicity data, normally using the lowest dose, where dose data are quoted for several animal species. If data are not available at all, the recommendation is to consult with the relevant waste disposal authority. The guidance in Circular 4/81 additionally contains an Annex 2 which sets out worked examples showing how the definition of special waste applies to particular industrial waste arisings.

11–121   Where special and other wastes are mixed (a practice that is contrary to both Directives 78/319 and 91/156), paragraph 4 of Part II of Schedule 1 to the Regulations provides, in effect, that whether or not a whole consignment of waste is special waste will be determined by the toxicity of the most toxic 5cm^3 sample that may be taken from any part of the mixed waste. Accordingly, a small component of toxic material in a skip of otherwise inert waste can require the entire contents of the skip to be treated as special waste.

Transport of Special Waste

11–122   Regulations 4 to 7 of the Special Waste Regulations set up a system of consignment notes designed to ensure that all relevant authorities are aware of the movement of the waste before it takes place (so giving them a chance to control it); further copies of the consignment note travel with the waste to its point of final disposal, so creating an audit trail for use in checking procedures and investigating any incidents. The Special Waste Regulations set out the form of consignment note in Schedule 2—copies are available from waste disposal authorities. The note includes a producer's certificate setting out where the waste is to move from and to, and on behalf of whom. The waste itself must also be described, including its relevant chemical and biological components, and maximum concentrations. The form has further spaces for:

—   a certificate by the carrier that he has collected the waste and that the producer's certificate is correct (or setting out any respects in which it is not);

—   a further certificate by the producer, to be signed on collection of the waste, confirming that it has been collected by that carrier and verifying any amendments that the carrier may have made to the description;

— a disposer's certificate confirming, firstly that his waste disposal licence (which must be identified) authorises the treatment or disposal of the waste concerned at the address to which it has been delivered, and, secondly, details of who delivered the waste and when, and in what vehicle, and that proper instructions were given for where the waste was to be taken.

The blank consignment note is a multi-part form. The top copy is to be sent to the waste disposal authority for the area in which the proposed disposal site is situated, and must arrive at least three clear working days (but not more than one month) before the consignment leaves. The second copy which includes the carrier's certificate and any amendments to the description, must be sent by first class post forthwith on dispatch of the waste to the waste disposal authority for the area in which it was produced, if this is a different authority from that for the disposal site. The producer keeps the third copy, and hands the remainder to the carrier. On reaching the disposal site, the site operator will record receipt on the fourth form, which will be retained by the carrier. The fifth form should be sent by the disposal site operator to the waste disposal authority for the area in which the waste arose. This must be sent by first class post not later than one working day after the waste has been disposed of. The sixth and last form is retained by the waste disposal organisation for its records. Where more than one waste disposal authority is involved, it is the authority for the area in which the special waste is produced, or into which it is imported from abroad, that is responsible for ensuring that this procedure is complied with.

Where any special waste is imported or exported into or from Great **11–123** Britain, the importer is deemed to be the producer, while the exporter is deemed to be the disposer.

If more than one carrier is responsible for the waste in the course of **11–124** its journey, then a further consignment note needs to be created on transfer between the carriers. The first carrier will be deemed to be the producer of the waste for the purposes of the second consignment note. Where waste is disposed of by pipeline or within the curtilage of a factory or other premises at which it has been produced, then the consignment note procedure does not apply.[57] Circular 4/81 indicates[58] that the authorities should not be unduly strict about the precise meaning of "curtilage", so that the consignment note procedure would not be needed merely because, for example, a factory site is bisected by a public road and special waste is taken across that road,

[57] reg. 8.
[58] At para. 19.

577

or the site is divided into two "adjacent but not necessarily adjoining parts".

11–125   Where relatively frequent consignments of special waste of a similar composition are all taken to the same disposal site, the authority may agree to a pre-notification procedure, with batches of the relevant consignment notes being furnished at intervals not exceeding twelve months. In practice, such an arrangement will involve submitting three-monthly forecasts of consignments, repeated at three-monthly intervals, to the authority for the producer's area and to that for the disposer's area, if different. Where a producer or disposer of special waste wishes to operate such a system and the relevant authority has refused to allow it he may appeal to the Secretary of State.[59]

Registers and site records

11–126   Producers, carriers and disposers of special waste must all maintain registers of consignments that they have been responsible for. These registers may conveniently be made up from a compilation of the relevant consignment notes,[60] so that no transcription is necessary. Producers and carriers must each keep the relevant consignment notes in their registers for not less than two years from the date at which the relevant waste was removed from where it was produced. Disposers on the other hand must keep their registers for the full term of their disposal licence, and on its surrender or revocation, the registers must be given to the regulatory authority responsible for that site.

11–127   Disposal operators are required to keep detailed records of the location of each deposit of waste on their site. Again these are to be kept for the full term of the licence and on its termination they must be sent to the regulatory authority for that site.

Polychlorinated Biphenyl and Terphenyl Wastes

11–128   Wastes containing PCBs and PCTs in anything other than minute quantities will be special wastes. EC Directive 76/403[61] on the disposal of these compounds requires Member States to prohibit the uncontrolled discharge, dumping and tipping of PCBs ("PCB"s is used in the Directive to include PCTs), and of objects and equipment containing PCBs, to make compulsory the disposal of waste PCBs and PCBs contained in equipment no longer capable of being used, to

---

[59] reg. 11.
[60] reg. 13.
[61] [1976] O.J. L108.

ensure that PCBs are disposed of without endangering human health and without harming the environment, and to ensure as far as possible the promotion of the regeneration of waste PCBs. "Disposal" is defined to mean the collection and/or destruction of PCBs, and transformation operations necessary for regenerating them. There has been no legislation introduced in the United Kingdom specifically to comply with this Directive, though controls over waste oils containing PCBs and PCTs have been introduced by the 1994 Licensing Regulations,[62] as referred to below. A Commission proposal to replace the Directive was issued in 1988, and an amended version of this in late 1991.[63] This would prohibit regeneration of PCBs, require used PCBs and equipment containing them to be disposed of by undertakings licensed to do this, and set conditions for keeping PCBs still in use secure.

The application of the procedures applicable to special waste meet **11-129** the obligations imposed by Directive 76/403 to a considerable extent, but these are of course only concerned with such waste as is in fact transferred and disposed of, and they do not impose any obligations to collect or regenerate PCBs and PCTs. Waste Management Paper No. 6 on PCB wastes, which was published in 1976, contains a code of practice on handling these wastes; a revised draft was issued for consultation in November 1993. At the Third North Sea Conference in 1990, the participating states undertook to phase out all identifiable uses of PCBs and PCTs, to a large extent by 1995 and completely by 1999. PCBs and PCTs taken out of service are to be destroyed with as little delay as possible, and where practicable in the country of origin. As noted in paragraphs 12-155 to 12-160, no new PCBs should have been introduced to the United Kingdom market for some years, but there has been no obligation to eliminate plant and equipment containing PCBs and/or PCTs that remain in use.

Waste Oils

Waste oils may or may not be special waste, depending on the **11-130** impurities that they contain. Their disposal is the subject of EC Directive 75/439 as amended by Directive 87/101.[64] This lays down specific emission limits where waste oils are burnt in plants with a capacity of more than 3MW, and imposes various other requirements in relation to record keeping and the separate handling and storage of waste oils according to the contents of impurities, which are also not reflected in any UK legislation. Waste Management Paper No. 7

[62] reg. 14.
[63] COM (91) 373, [1991] O.J. C299.
[64] [1975] O.J. L194; [1987] O.J. L42.

"Mineral Oil Wastes" includes a code of practice with regard to these, and encourages their recovery. It does not however deal with all the matters covered by the Directive.[65]

11–131   Where a waste management licence (including a disposal licence granted under C.O.P.A.) authorises the regeneration of waste oil, it must include conditions to ensure that the regenerated base oils neither constitute a "toxic and dangerous waste" as defined in EC Directive 78/319, nor contain PCBs or PCTs in concentrations beyond a specified maximum of at most 50ppm. Where a licence authorises the keeping of waste oil, it must include a condition ensuring that it is not mixed with toxic and dangerous waste or with PCBs or PCTs.[66]

Clinical Waste

11–132   Clinical waste is given special treatment, both in the legislation and in practice. It is defined[66A] to be:

(a)   human and animal tissue or excretions, drugs and medicinal products, swabs and dressings, syringes and other sharp instruments, which unless rendered safe may prove hazardous to any person coming into contact with it; and

(b)   any other waste arising from various healthcare, veterinary, teaching or research activities or the collection of blood for transfusion, being waste which may cause infection to any person coming into contact with it.

Waste Management Paper No. 25 "Clinical Wastes" contains a memorandum on sources, treatment and disposal of clinical wastes, including a code of practice. Clinical waste will not ordinarily be "special waste", except where it is or contains a medicinal product available only on prescription. Nevertheless it is clearly potentially dangerous waste, and requires to be treated accordingly. A charge may be levied for removing clinical waste from a domestic property, a caravan or from a moored vessel used wholly for the purposes of living accommodation. Clinical waste from any other source is to be treated as industrial waste, except where it has been collected under the street cleaning provisions of C.O.P.A. or the E.P.A.[67]

---

[65] Even if it did so, being mere official guidance having no legally binding effect, it would not be sufficient implementation.

[66] 1994 Licensing Regs., reg. 14.

[66A] Controlled Waste Regs. 1992, reg. 1.

[67] The Controlled Waste Regulations 1992, Sched. 2, para. 4; Sched. 3, para. 8.

Prohibitions on Dealing in Waste

The prohibitions of section 33(1) of the E.P.A. and of section 3(1) of   **11–133**
C.O.P.A. have been set out at paragraph 11–029. The basic prohibition
in C.O.P.A. was that a person must not deposit controlled waste on
any land. The corresponding prohibition in the E.P.A. is that a person
shall not deposit controlled waste, or *knowingly* cause or knowingly
permit controlled waste to be deposited in or on any land. The
meaning of controlled waste has been discussed above. The case law
on "cause or knowingly permit" is discussed in paragraphs 8–106 to
8–136. The insertion of "knowingly" before "cause" has obscured the
position in that until there have been cases before the courts, it must be
uncertain what knowledge or other mental element is necessary to
create the offence. The knowledge could be as to (i) the activity that led
to a deposit, (ii) the act of depositing, or (iii) the composition of the
waste (in the case of a breach of condition). There might also need to
be an element of knowledge as to the absence of a relevant waste
management licence, though the position of the word before "cause"
and again before "permit" indicates that it is not used to qualify the
second limb of the prohibition starting "unless . . . ". It could be read
as merely requiring the act that produced the deposit to be intentional,
in which case it would not add anything (see the *obiter* observation of
Viscount Dilhorne in *Alphacell v. Woodward*),[68] though the very fact of
its new inclusion suggests that some additional meaning should be
given to it, if possible. The inclusion of "knowingly" does not appear
to have been preceded by any public discussion as to why this change
should have been made (it was not made in the corresponding
provision in the Water Act 1989 the previous year relating to pollution
of controlled waters). In most cases, the insertion seems likely to be
irrelevant, in that where a person might have been charged with
causing a deposit, he will usually also have actually deposited the
waste, and that offence remains without any qualification by way of
"knowingly".

However, where a person has not himself deposited waste but has   **11–134**
been responsible for a third party doing so, he may in such
circumstances only be liable (if at all) for having knowingly caused that
deposit. Knowledge is normally an essential ingredient of causing
another person to do or not to do something,[69] but by section 33(5)
where controlled waste is carried in and deposited from a motor
vehicle, the person who controls or is in a position to control the

---

[68] [1972] A.C. at p.840.
[69] *James & Son Limited v. Smee* [1955] 1 Q.B. 78, [1954] 3 All E.R. 273; *Ross Hillman v. Bond*
[1974] Q.B. 435, [1974] 2 All E.R. 287.

vehicle will be liable under section 33(1)(a) for having knowingly caused the deposit, whether or not he gave instructions for this to be done. In *Ashcroft v. Cambro Waste Products Limited*[70] it was held, in relation to a charge of knowingly permitting a deposit of controlled waste in contravention of a licence condition, that the prosecution needed to prove knowledge in relation to permitting the deposit, but not of the breach of condition itself. Since a condition can and often will relate to the nature of the waste that may be deposited, it must follow logically from this that knowledge of the nature or composition of the waste deposited is also not a necessary ingredient of the offence.

11–135   The definition of land in E.P.A. s.29(8) extends to all land covered by waters above the low-water mark of ordinary spring tides, whether or not a river or other body of flowing water, and by the same section a deposit on land is to be understood as a deposit on the surface of the land. There is thus an overlap in the offences created under the Water Resources Act 1991 and the E.P.A., in that a deposit of waste into a river may well result in pollution of controlled waters, contrary to section 85 of the Water Resources Act, in the absence of a consent under that Act, and if the waste has also settled to the bed of the river there may be an unlawful deposit contrary to section 33(1)(a) E.P.A. However section 33(1)(c) does not apply to a disposal of "liquid waste" under a discharge consent under either the W.R.A. or, in Scotland, C.O.P.A. Part II.[71]

11–136   The second principal prohibition in C.O.P.A. was that of section 3(1)(b) relating to the use of plant or equipment, or causing or knowingly permitting any plant or equipment to be used for the purpose of disposing of controlled waste. The corresponding provision in section 33(1)(b) of the E.P.A. is in most respects substantially broader. In this case, the offence is to treat, keep or dispose of controlled waste, or knowingly cause or knowingly permit controlled waste to be treated, kept or disposed of

(i)   in or on any land, or
(ii)   by means of any mobile plant,

except under and in accordance with a waste management licence.

11–137   The definitions section 29(6) provides that "disposal" of waste includes its disposal by way of deposit in or on land, and that, subject to any regulations that may be made under section 29(7), waste is "treated" when it is subjected to any process, including making it re-usable or reclaiming substances from it. Though "disposal" is thus a broader term than "deposit", and *prima facie* there would consequently

[70] [1981] 3 All E.R. 699, [1981] 1 W.L.R. 1349.
[71] 1994 Licensing Regs., reg.16(1)(c).

appear to be nothing falling within section 33(1)(a) that would not also come within section 33(1)(b), these terms must however now be read in the light of the definitions given in Regulation 1(3) of the 1994 Licensing Regulations, which materially modify the effect of section 33(1)and of corresponding provisions in other sections. "Disposal" is now defined to mean (and, by clear implication, is confined to) any of the operations listed in Part III of Schedule 4, and "recovery" any of the operations of Part IV,[72] as set out in Tables 11/III and 11/IV respectively.

TABLE 11/III

1994 Licensing Regulations, Schedule 4, Part III *(Directive 75/442, Annex II A)*		
Waste Disposal Operations		11–138
1.	Tipping of waste above or underground (*e.g.* landfill, *etc.*)	
2.	Land treatment of waste (*e.g.* biodegradation of liquid or sludge discards in soils, *etc.*).	
3.	Deep injection of waste (*e.g.* injection of pumpable discards into wells, salt domes or naturally occurring repositories, *etc.*).	
4.	Surface impoundment of waste (*e.g.* placement of liquid or sludge discards into pits, ponds or lagoons, *etc.*).	
5.	Specially engineered landfill of waste (*e.g.* placement of waste into lined discrete cells which are capped and isolated from one another and the environment, *etc.*).	
6.	Release of solid waste into a water body except seas or oceans.	
7.	Release of waste into seas or oceans including seabed insertion.	
8.	Biological treatment of waste not listed elsewhere in this Part of this Schedule which results in final compounds or mixtures which are disposed of by means of any of the operations listed in this Part of this Schedule.	

---

[72] reg. 1(3).

9.	Physico-chemical treatment of waste not listed elsewhere in this Part of this Schedule which results in final compounds or mixtures which are disposed of by means of any of the operations listed in this Part of this Schedule (*e.g.* evaporation, drying, calcination, *etc.*).
10.	Incineration of waste on land.
11.	Incineration of waste at sea.
12.	Permanent storage of waste (*e.g.* emplacement of containers in a mine, *etc.*).
13.	Blending or mixture of waste prior to the waste being submitted to any of the operations listed in this Part of this Schedule.
14.	Repackaging of waste prior to the waste being submitted to any of the operations listed in this Part of this Schedule.
15.	Storage of waste pending any of the operations listed in this Part of this Schedule, but excluding temporary storage, pending collection, on the site where the waste is produced.

TABLE 11/IV

1994 Licensing Regulations, Schedule 4, Part IV	
(*Directive 75/442, Annex IIB*)	
Waste Recovery Operations	
1.	Reclamation or regeneration of solvents
2.	Recycling or reclamation of organic substances which are not used as solvents
3.	Recycling or reclamation of metals and metal compounds
4.	Recycling or reclamation of other inorganic materials
5.	Regeneration of acids or bases.
6.	Recovery of components used for pollution abatement.
7.	Recovery of components from catalysts.
8.	Re-refining, or other reuses, of oil which is waste.

11–139

584

9.	Use of waste principally as a fuel or for other means of generating energy
10.	Spreading of waste on land resulting in benefit to agriculture or ecological improvement, including composting and other biological transformation processes, except in the case of waste excluded under Article 2(1)(b)(iii) of the Directive.[73]
11.	Use of wastes obtained from any of the operations listed in paragraphs 1 to 10 of this Part of this Schedule.
12.	Exchange of wastes for submission to any of the operations listed in paragraphs 1 to 11 of this Part of this Schedule.
13.	Storage of waste consisting of materials intended for submission to any operation listed in this Part of this Schedule, but excluding temporary storage, pending collection, on the site where it is produced.

11–140 Reference to "deposit" in section 33(1)(a) (and also sections 33(5), 54(1)(a), (2), (3), (4)(d) and 69(2)) is to *include* any such disposal or recovery operation that involves a deposit of waste in or on land.[74] By contrast, reference to the "treatment or disposal" or, as the case may be, to the "treatment, keeping or disposal", of controlled wastes in sections 33(1)(b), and also sections 54(1)(b), (2), (3), (4)(d) and 69(2), is a reference to those disposal and recovery operations (only), but excluding any that involve a deposit.[75] The combined effect of these is:

(i) Section 33(1)(a) applies to any deposit (temporary as well as permanent) of controlled waste including but not limited to those operations of Parts III and IV that involve a deposit;

(ii) Section 33(1)(b) applies to those operations of Parts III and IV that do not involve a deposit of controlled waste, and to no other.

Since a temporary deposit of waste is an almost inevitable accompaniment of virtually all the operations in practice, pending its treatment, a sensible distinction between "deposit" and "disposal" is only possible if reference is made exclusively to the operations themselves ignoring any storage of waste to be treated or of waste products from these operations.

11–141 Finally, section 33(1)(c) of the E.P.A. introduces the wholly new offence of treating, keeping or disposing of controlled waste in a

---

[73] *i.e.* natural, non-dangerous farming waste.
[74] Sched. 4, para. 9(3).
[75] Sched. 4, para. 9(4).

manner likely to cause pollution of the environment or harm to human health. Reference to treatment, keeping and disposal in this case (and also in section 35) *includes* a reference to the disposal and recovery operations of Parts III and IV of Schedule 4,[76] and is not therefore necessarily limited to them. It is reasonable therefore to read this sub-section as continuing to apply also to the keeping of controlled waste in a hazardous manner.[77] As noted earlier, unlike the two other prohibitions, which do not apply if the prohibited act is in fact authorised by and undertaken in accordance with a waste manage-ment licence, any action within section 33(1)(c) is an offence, even though it may not breach any condition of an applicable waste management licence.

11–142   In addition to these offences involving dealings with controlled waste, the E.P.A.[78] provides that it is also an offence to contravene any condition of a waste management licence.[79]

11–143   The following exceptions to these offences are provided:

(1) The prohibitions do not apply to household waste from a domestic property which is treated, kept or disposed of within the curtilage of the dwelling by or with the permission of the occupier of the dwelling.[80]

(2) Regulations may be made under section 33(3) of the E.P.A. to disapply any of the prohibitions of section 33(1) in prescribed cases. The exclusions from waste management licensing under Regulation 16 of the 1994 Licensing Regulations already referred to are made under this power. Likewise an extensive list of exemp-tions is made under regulation 17, as set out fully in Schedule 3— see paragraph 11–150. The exemptions are required to comply with Article 11 of the Directive—see paragraph 11–147. Broadly this limits them to activities carried out by establishments or undertak-ings which either dispose of their own waste where it was produced, or which carry out waste recovery. General rules must be laid down for each type of activity, and the types and quantities of waste must be such that the Article 4 conditions are observed.

---

[76] Sched. 4, para. 9(5).

[77] It would be ironic if amendments designed to ensure the protective provisions of the Directive were given effect should significantly cut back the scope of protection of the statute as enacted.

[78] By contrast with C.O.P.A., and nullifying the decision of the Divisional Court in *Leigh Land Reclamation Ltd. v. Walsall MBC* as to when a breach of condition may give rise to an offence.

[79] s.33(6).

[80] E.P.A., s.33(2). The corresponding provision in C.O.P.A., s.4(2) referred to "house-hold waste from a *private dwelling* which is deposited, disposed of or dealt with . . .". The references to "the dwelling" in the E.P.A. without any antecedent seem to have been inadvertently carried over from this corresponding provision in C.O.P.A.

Waste Management Licensing

Introduction

The activities prohibited by section 33(1)(a) and (b) of the E.P.A. may   **11–144**
be the subject of a waste management licence, of which there are two
categories: "site licences" authorising the treatment, keeping or
disposal of waste in or on land, and "mobile plant licences" authorising the treatment or disposal of waste by means of mobile plant.[81]
Under transitional provisions[82] existing disposal licences under
C.O.P.A. became site licences under the E.P.A. with effect from May 1,
1994, and from then on were wholly subject to its rules relating to
licences, and so capable of variation, transfer and surrender only in
accordance with the E.P.A., and subject to revocation and suspension
under that Act. Waste disposal plans prepared under section 2 of
C.O.P.A. became disposal plans for the purposes of section 50 of the
E.P.A.;[83] further transitional provisions relate to transfer of the duties
of the old waste disposal authorities and the conduct of their waste
disposal operations, to the new waste disposal authorities and to the
local authority waste disposal companies (LAWDCs).

Waste management licences are personal rights that are granted, in   **11–145**
the case of a site licence, to the person who is in occupation of the land
to which the licence relates, and in the case of a mobile plant licence, to
the person who operates it.[84] No site licence may be granted, however,
unless there is already in existence planning permission for all uses of
the land to be covered by the site licence (or, where appropriate, an
established use certificate in respect of such uses).[85] The licence is not
transferable to any third party, except under the provisions of section
14 (see paragraph 11–192). Once granted, a licence continues until it is
revoked or until it is surrendered. However, in the case of a site
licence, surrender is not effective unless and until it is accepted by the
waste regulation authority under section 39 (see paragraphs 11–193 to
11–197). This provision is a major departure from the procedures
under C.O.P.A., whereby a licence holder was able to surrender his
licence at any time, and thereby relieve himself of licence obligations
that were proving to be unduly onerous for him. Under the E.P.A. a
licence holder may be held bound by obligations in the licence to
monitor a closed landfill site for leachate and landfill gas, and to
respond appropriately to any causes for concern, for several decades

[81] s.35(12).
[82] Set out in E.P.A., s.77(2).
[83] s.77(4).
[84] s.35(2).
[85] s.36(2).

after closure, until these substances cease to be generated in significant quantities.

Exemptions from Waste Management Licensing

11–146   In addition to the activities which, being subject to alternative
control regimes, are excluded from waste management licensing
under Regulation 16 of the 1994 Licensing Regulations, a much longer
list of activities is exempted under Regulation 17 from the licensing
controls, *i.e.* from the prohibitions of ss.33(1)(a) and (b) only. These
exclusions and exemptions replace in their entirety the exclusions
from waste disposal licensing that were available under the Regulations made under C.O.P.A.[86] These exemptions are made under E.P.A.
section 33(3) and by virtue of section 33(4) whereby the Secretary of
State is required to have regard to the expediency of excluding from
the waste management licensing controls:

(a)   deposits which are small enough or of such temporary nature
that they may be excluded;

(b)   any means of treatment or disposal which are innocuous
enough to be excluded; and

(c)   cases for which adequate controls are provided by another
provision.

Nevertheless, in granting any exemptions under these powers, the
Secretary of State must have regard to Article 11 of the Directive which
in effect only allows exemptions of this kind for establishments or
undertakings carrying out their own waste disposal or carrying out
any waste recovery—"disposal" and "recovery" referring to the
operations listed in Parts III and IV of Schedule 4 to the Regulations,
respectively.

11–147   In respect of these operations, the Directive only permits exemptions where the competent authorities have adopted general rules for
each type of activity laying down the types and quantities of waste and
the conditions under which the activity may be exempted, and where
in any event the types and quantities of waste and the methods of

---

[86] The Control of Pollution (Licensing of Waste Disposal) (Scotland) Regulations 1977
(S.I. 1977 No.2006); The control of Pollution (Landed Ships' Waste) Regulations 1987
(S.I. 1987 No.402); The Collection and Disposal of Waste Regulations 1988 (S.I. 1988
No.819); The Control of Pollution (Landed Ships' Waste) (Amendment) Regulations
1989 (S.I. 1989 No.65); The Disposal of Controlled Waste (Exceptions) Regulations
1991 (S.I. 1991 No.508); The Controlled Waste Regulations 1992 (S.I. 1992 No.588 as
amended by S.I. 1993 No.566); The Control of Pollution (Licensing of Waste Disposal)
(Scotland) Amendment Regulations 1992 (S.I. 1992 No.1368).

disposal or recovery are such that the conditions of Article 4 of the Directive are met—these being repeated in the objectives of Schedule 4, paragraph 4(1)(a).[87] Accordingly, the exempted activities are in each case qualified in a variety of ways so as to give effect to these requirements. Since the general prohibition of section 33(1)(c) is as applicable to these exempted activities as it is to all licensed activities, a breach of the Article 4 conditions is likely in many cases also to be a contravention of section 33(1)(c). This is reinforced by the exemption of an activity only being available if the type and quantity of waste submitted to the activity and the method of disposal or recovery are consistent with the need to attain the objectives of Schedule 4, Part I, paragraph 4(1)(a), even where the specific conditions applicable to an exempted activity are complied with. In a number of cases, an activity is only exempted if it has the consent of the occupier of the land where it is carried on or where the person carrying on the exempt activity is otherwise entitled to do so on that land—these are marked with an asterisk in the list of Table 11/V. Of particular note is that, since it is essential that the exempted activities do not pose a threat to the environment, the exemptions do not apply to activities involving special waste except where otherwise indicated (and then only subject to observance of the applicable conditions).

The provisions for exemptions from waste management licensing **11–148** and the registration of exempt activities apply only where the activities are carried out by "an establishment or undertaking". These terms, which are taken from the Directive, are not defined, but should be understood as not extending to an individual acting in his private capacity. Nevertheless, an individual carrying on a commercial activity, even though entirely by himself, for example a sole lawyer acting in his professional capacity, may be regarded as an undertaking under EC law;[88] as may a company with a single employee.[89] Most cases on what is an undertaking have been concerned with the application of EC competition law, and so these are not necessarily authority for how the term should be understood in the context of Directive 75/442. However, with this *caveat*, an organisation carrying

---

[87] *i.e.* that waste is recovered or disposed of without endangering human health and without using processes or methods which could harm the environment, and in particular without (a) risk to waste, air, soil, plants or animals; or (b) causing nuisance through noise or odours; or (c) adversely affecting the countryside or places of special interest.

[88] Case 2/74, *Reyners v. Belgian State*: [1974] E.C.R. 631; [1974] 2 C.M.L.R. 305. See also, *e.g. Reuter/BASF*,]1976] O.J. L254, [1976] 2 C.M.L.R. D44; *RAI/UNITEL*, [1978] O.J. L157, [1978] 3 C.M.L.R. 306; Commission Decision 85/ 561 (Plant Breeders' rights—roses), [1985] O.J. L369.

[89] Case 392/92, *Christel Schmidt v. Spar- und Leihkasse der früheren Ämter Bordesholm, Kiel und Cronshagen*, The Times, May 25, 1994.

on any kind of commercial or economic activity is likely to be regarded as an undertaking, even though it is non-profit making; public bodies acting in a public law capacity may not be undertakings, but probably are when acting in any other.

11–149   The list of exempted activities is set out in Schedule 3 to the 1994 Licensing Regulations. Many of these activities are qualified by reference to maximum quantities that may be held on a site or dealt with in a given period. As is observed in Circular 11/94[90] if such a maximum quantity is exceeded, the exemption falls away altogether, and the activity, for so long as it is not licensed, is unlawful in relation to the entire quantities. References in Schedule 3 to waste being "intended to be" subjected to the activity are to be understood as confined to waste before they have been so dealt with, whereas references to waste being present "in connection with" an activity include waste resulting from it.

11–150   Reference must be made to Schedule 3 itself for full details of the exempted activities. The list in Table 11/V merely indicates the general subject matter of each exemption; in many cases storage of waste for use in the activity is also exempted. Each of the exempted activities is discussed in considerable detail in Annex 5 of Circular 11/94.[91] Exemptions of wide application meriting special mention are those of paragraphs 15, 17, 26, 28 and 41; the last in particular will be applicable to a great many organisations.

TABLE 11/V

Activities Exempted from Waste Management Licensing	
(1994 Licensing Regulations, Schedule 3)	

Paragraph	Activity
1.	Glass manufacture and production.
2.	Scrap metal furnaces.
3.	Burning as fuel, straw, poultry litter, wood, waste oil, waste-derived solid fuel, tyres.
4.	Treating packaging or containers for re-use.*
5.	Burning waste as fuel in small appliances.
6.	Burning waste oil as fuel in an engine.

[90] para. 5.39.
[91] paras. 5.43–5.249.

7.	Spreading of various wastes on agricultural land and of waste soil or compost, waste wood, bark or other plant matter on certain other land*.
8.	Spreading of sludge on land and septic tank sludge.
9.	Reclamation or improvement of land by spreading of waste soil, rock, ash, sludge, or dredging, construction or demolition waste.*
10.	Recovery operations in respect of sludge or septic tank sludge within sewage treatment works.
11.	Preliminary recovery operations on waste paper and cardboard, textiles, plastic, glass, steel and aluminum cans, aluminum foil, food and drink cartons.*
12.	Composting bio-degradable waste.
13.	Manufacture of various construction products from demolition, construction or excavation wastes, or from ash, slag, clinker, rock, wood, bark, paper, straw or gypsum.*
14.	Manufacture of finished goods from waste metal, plastic, glass, ceramics, rubber, textiles, wood, paper or cardboard.*
15.	The beneficial use of waste without further treatment and not involving its disposal.*
16.	Activities carried on pursuant to a licence under the Diseases of Animals (Waste Food) Order 1973 (S.I. 1973 No. 1936).
17.	The storage of various wastes for use as in paragraph 11 or any other recovery operation (also special waste). *
18.	Storage in a secure container or containers of waste oil or the wastes referred to in paragraph 17, other than waste solvents, refrigerants or halons, for use for the purposes of any activity described in paragraph 11 or any other recovery activity.*
19.	Storage of demolition, construction or excavation wastes, and of ash, slag, clinker, rock, wood or gypsum for use on the same site, and the storage of road planings for use elsewhere.*
20.	Laundering and other cleaning of waste textiles for recovery or re-use.
21.	Chipping, shredding, cutting or pulverising waste plant matter; sorting and baling sawdust or wood shavings.

591

22.	Recovery of silver from printing or photographic processing waste.
23.	Keeping or treatment of animal by-products in accordance with the Animal By-products Order 1992.
24.	Crushing, grinding or other size reduction of waste bricks, tiles or concrete.
25.	The deposit of dredging waste from inland waters or from clearing plant matter from inland waters on banks or tow paths; screening and de-watering such waste.*
26.	The recovery or disposal of any waste at the place where it is produced, as an integral part of the process that produces it.
27.	Baling, compacting, crushing, shredding or pulverising waste at the place where it is produced.
28.	The storage of returned goods that are waste by their manufacturer, distributor or retailer when intended for re-use or recovery; storage where the intention to discard them was formed pending disposal elsewhere.
29.	The disposal of waste where it is produced by the person producing it by burning in an exempt incinerator (see para. 11–094 at (vii)).
30.	Burning on most types of open land of waste consisting of wood, bark or other plant matter on the land where it is produced and by the person producing it.
31.	The discharge on to a railway track of waste from sanitary conveniences or sinks in passenger carriages.
32.	The burial of waste from a sanitary convenience with a removable receptacle on the same premises.
33.	The keeping or deposit of waste consisting of excavated materials arising from peat working where they arise.
34.	The keeping or deposit on operational land of a railway, light railway or tramway of spent ballast where it is produced.
35.	The deposited of excavated material from a bore hole or other excavation made for mineral exploration in or on the land where it is excavated.
36.	The temporary storage at harbour reception facilities of (i) garbage waste in accordance with the Merchant Shipping (Reception Facilities for Garbage) Regulations 1988 (S.I. 1988 No. 2293), and (ii) tank washings in

	accordance with the Prevention of Pollution (Reception Facilities) Order 1984 (S.I. 1984 No. 862) (also special waste).
37.	The burial of a dead domestic pet in the garden of the domestic property where it lived, so long as it is not hazardous (*i.e.* is not "clinical waste").*
38.	The deposit or storage of samples of waste intended for testing and analysis at any place where these are to be carried out, subject to certain limitations that would exclude deposit or storage of samples taken by a person considering acquiring but not yet the owner or occupier of relevant land (also special waste).
39.	The secure storage of waste medicines at a pharmacy pending their disposal; the storage at the premises of a medical, nursing or veterinary practice of waste produced in that practice (also special waste).
40.	The storage of non-liquid waste in a secure container or containers other than where it is produced; the temporary storage of scrap rails on operational land of a railway, light railway or tramway.*
41.	The temporary storage of waste, pending its collection, on the site where it is produced (also special waste).*
42.	*(Transitional provision allowing treatment, keeping and disposal of scrap metal and motor vehicles to be dismantled, where a disposal licence under C.O.P.A. was applied for before May 1, 1994) (also special waste).*
43.	*(Transitional provision in respect of any activity requiring a waste management licence under the E.P.A. that did not require a disposal licence under C.O.P.A., where an application for a waste management licence has been applied for on or before April 30, 1995) (also special waste).*
* Consent of the occupier of the relevant land is necessary for the exemption to apply, unless the operator is otherwise entitled to carry on the activity there (reg. 17(2))	

Registration of Exempt Activities

It is an offence to carry on any exempt activity involving the **11–152** recovery or disposal of waste without being registered with the appropriate registration authority.[92] Registration is intended to be a

---

[92] 1994 Licensing Regs., reg. 18(1). To provide time for registration, this only became an offence on January 1, 1995.

simple formality, merely requiring the provision of the name and address of the relevant establishment or undertaking, the exempt activity and the place where it is carried on.[93] Furthermore although, with certain exceptions, the obligation is primarily on the operator of the activity to effect the registration, the registration authority must in any event do so if it becomes aware of the relevant particulars, whether or not it receives notice of them from the operator. In a number of cases, the authorities are deemed to be aware of the exempt activity, so that no positive steps need to be taken by the operator at all; these are activities that are already subject to regulatory control, mostly by virtue of the Air Pollution Control provisions of Part I of the E.P.A., enforced by local authorities;[94] the deemed awareness also applies to processes licensed under the Diseases of Animals (Waste Food) Order 1973[95] and an activity licensed or registered under the Animal By-Products Order 1992 or licensed under the Slaughter-houses Act 1974 or the Slaughter of Animals (Scotland) Act 1980[96] Except for the activities just referred to that are subject to other controls, for which the appropriate registration authority is as set out in regulation 18(10), the authority is in every case the waste regulation authority for the area concerned.

11–153   There is a sole exception to the offence of carrying on an exempt activity without registration in the case of spreading waste on land used for agriculture within paragraph 7(3) of Schedule 3,[97] since this activity, to be exempt, requires specific details to be supplied to the relevant waste regulation authority as set out in paragraph 7(4).

11–154   The intention of the registration procedure is to comply with the Directive's requirements as simply as possible. Consequently, registration is automatic on the requisite information being made available; there is no right to refuse registration, nor is any renewal required. Registration therefore continues indefinitely - there is however no provision for removal of activities from the register when they have ceased or changed their character, which may create problems in the future. Registers must be open for inspection by members of the public free of charge at all reasonable hours; copies of entries must be obtainable on payment of reasonable charges.[98]

[93] reg. 18(3).
[94] 1994 Licensing Regs., Sched. 3, paras. 1, 2, 3, 24; also paras. 4 and 12 in certain circumstances.
[95] Sched. 3, para. 16.
[96] Sched. 3, para. 23.
[97] reg. 18(7).
[98] reg. 18(8).

Enforcement

A person guilty of carrying on an exempt activity without registra-   **11–155**
tion is liable on summary conviction to a fine not exceeding level 2 on
the standard scale.[99] Nevertheless, as soon as the relevant registration
authority has acquired the necessary information to establish the
offence, it also has the requisite information enabling it to register the
activity under regulation 18(4), and it must accordingly do so. In
practice, therefore, there will be no question of prosecuting a person
who is currently carrying on an exempt activity unregistered, but only
on a charge of having done so for some previous period.

Waste Management Licensees—"Fit and Proper Person"

A waste management licence may only be granted if the waste   **11–156**
regulation authority is satisfied that the applicant is a "fit and proper
person",[1] a term that is defined[2] negatively, in that a person shall be
treated as not being a fit and proper person if it appears to the waste
regulation authority that:

(a)   he or another relevant person has been convicted of a
      relevant offence;
(b)   the management of the activities which are, or are to be,
      authorised by the licence are not, or will not be, in the hands
      of a technically competent person; or
(c)   the person who holds, or is to hold, the licence has not made,
      and either has no intention of making or is in no position to
      make, financial provision adequate to discharge the obliga-
      tions arising from the licence.

In applying these tests, the authority is required to make its determination by reference to the carrying on by the applicant (or, after grant,
the licence holder) of the activities which are or are to be authorised by
the licence and the fulfilment of the requirements of the licence.[3] By
clear implication, it would be improper for regard to be had to any
other matters or circumstances than those just set out. Provided
however the determination keeps within these bounds when applying
the three tests, the authority is not necessarily limited to them.

---

[99] reg. 18(6).
[1] s.36(3).
[2] s.74(3).
[3] s.74(2).

Meeting any of the three criteria (conviction of a relevant offence, lack of technical competence, and inadequate financial provision), is simply conclusive that someone is not a fit and proper person. Guidance on the requirement for a "fit and proper person", to which every authority must have regard, by virtue of section 74(5), is contained primarily in Chapter 3 of Waste Management Paper No 4.[4]

"Relevant offence"

11–157   The relevant offences for the purpose of criterion (a) are prescribed in Regulation 3 of the 1994 Licensing Regulations,[5] and are offences under the following legislation:

TABLE 11/VI

"Fit and Proper Person" s.74(3)(a)
Prescribed Offences: Relevant Enactments
Section 22 of the Public Health (Scotland) Act 1897 Section 95(1) of the Public Health Act 1936 Sections 3, 5(6), 16(4), 18(2), 31(1), 32(1), 34(5), 78, 92(6) and 93(3) of the Control of Pollution Act 1974 Section 2 of the Refuse Disposal (Amenity) Act 1978 The Control of Pollution (Special Waste) Regulations 1980 Section 9(1) of the Food and Environment Protection Act 1985 The Transfrontier Shipment of Hazardous Waste Regulations 1988 The Transfrontier Shipment of Waste Regulations 1994 The Merchant Shipping (Prevention of Pollution by Garbage) Regulations 1988 Sections 1, 5, 6(9) and 7(3) of the Control of Pollution (Amendment) Act 1989 Sections 107, 118(4) and 175(1) of the Water Act 1989 Sections 23(1), 33, 34(6), 44, 47(6), 57(5), 59(5), 63(2), 69(9), 70(4), 71(3) and 80(4) of the Environmental Protection Act 1990 Sections 85, 202 and 206 of the Water Resources Act 1991 Section 33 of the Clean Air Act 1993

11–158   A licence applicant or holder will not be a fit and proper person, not only where he has been convicted of a relevant offence, but also if any other "relevant person" has been convicted of such an offence. These other persons are, broadly, those with whom the applicant or holder had business connections at the time the offence was committed that

[4] See Circular 11/94, Annex 4, paras 4,65 to 4.73.
[5] As amended by the Transfrontier Shipment of Waste Regulations 1994, reg. 19(3).

led to the conviction. The relationships are set out in the following Table 11/VII.

TABLE 11/VII

"Fit and Proper Person" s. 74(7) Conviction of Relevant Persons	
Status of applicant/licence holder at time of offence	**Relevant person convicted**
Employer	Any employee
Member of partnership (carrying on *any* business)	Any partner or other person convicted of an offence committed in the course of the partnership's business
Director, manager, secretary or other similar officer of a body corporate	That body corporate
Body corporate	(1) Any director, manager, secretary or other similar officer of the body corporate and (2) any other body corporate of which any person within (1) was a director, manager, secretary or other similar officer at the time of commission of the offence.

These provisions apply to offences whenever committed. Neverthe- **11–159** less, under the Rehabilitation of Offenders Act 1974, offences by individuals will be "spent" under the provisions of that Act after a number of years (mostly 5 years to 10, depending on the seriousness of the crime). However, the 1974 Act does not apply to offences by bodies corporate, for which, therefore, there will be no time limit, except in so far as the waste regulation authority itself imposes one. Official guidance however is that the authority should have regard to whether a conviction of a body corporate would have been spent if the offence had been committed by an individual.[5A]

The possibility that an applicant may not receive a licence, or that a **11–160** licence holder may lose a licence because of the past record of one particular person connected with him or it, means that considerable

---

[5A] WMP 4, para. 3.33.

care must be taken in choosing those to be involved in such ventures. Nevertheless the waste regulation authority has a discretion to disregard the fact that there has been conviction of the licence applicant or holder or of some other relevant person.[6] The factors that are to be taken into account in considering the implications of any conviction will include (1) whether it is the applicant (or licensee) who has been convicted, or some other "relevant person", (2) the number of offences committed; and (3) the nature and gravity of the relevant offence or offences.[7]

Technical Competence

11–161   The requirement of section 74(3)(b) that the management of the authorised activities must be in the hands of a technically competent person involves essentially two considerations, firstly, what degree of competence is called for and how this is to be evidenced, and secondly what position the competent person must hold—must there be such a person at every relevant site, or is it sufficient for him to be in charge of a number of sites, and only have general overall responsibility?

11–162   On the first point, regulation 4 of the 1994 Licensing Regulations prescribes the types of certificate of technical competence of the Waste Management Industry Training and Advisory Board (WAMITAB) that must be held in relation to different types of waste facility (and in some cases the capacity or throughput) to be licensed. Regulation 5 provides two transitional exemptions to these requirements. The first gives five years to August 10, 1999, for acquisition of an appropriate certificate to a person who applied by August 10, 1994 to WAMITAB for such a certificate and who was a manager of a relevant facility at any time in the 12 months to August 10, 1994. The second exempts for 10 years those who were over 55 on August 10, 1994 and who in the preceding 10 years had at least five years experience as a manager of a relevant facility. Those exempted will during those five or ten years, as the case may be, be regarded as technically competent for that type of facility and, depending on what that is, certain other facilities. The exemptions only apply to managers of sites duly authorised under C.O.P.A. or the E.P.A.,[8] which would prima facie operate against those whose experience has been outside the United Kingdom, hence raising questions of validity under EC law.

11–163   As regards the second point, the relevant technically competent person is regarded as the person in a position to control the day-to-day activities authorised by the licence that are carried out at the licensed

---

[6] s.74(4).
[7] See WMP 4, paras. 3.17–3.35.
[8] reg.5(3).

site.[9] The technically competent management is however not necessarily a single individual, and a group of several specialists may together provide this.[10] In appropriate cases—it being for the applicant/licensee to establish the facts—a technically competent individual may have day-to-day control over more than one site.

Financial Provision

Determining what financial provision may properly be required of   **11–164**
an applicant for a licence has proved to be particularly problematical. It
is however a feature of critical importance. There have been numerous
occasions where waste disposal sites have caused contamination and
the waste disposal authority has been minded to require the site
operator to clean it up. However, where the operator has inadequate
financial resources, it has been a common experience that he will
argue that if his licence is revoked he will lose his only source of
livelihood and will certainly be unable to afford any clean up
operations at all; conversely, if he is permitted to continue for this
reason, there can be no certainty that the contamination will not be
aggravated, still less dealt with. It is notable, nevertheless, that
whereas, as is described below, a licence can be suspended or revoked
on grounds that the holder is no longer a fit and proper person by
reason of a conviction of him or a relevant person or on grounds of
technical competence, no such right to suspend or revoke a licence
arises where the holder ceases to have adequate financial resources to
discharge the obligations under the licence, or it becomes apparent
that he never did.

All relevant guidance on what financial provision a fit and proper   **11–165**
person must make is contained in Waste Management Paper No. 4;[11]
there are no further statutory provisions in the E.P.A. or the 1994
Licensing Regulations. The main ways in which financial provision
may be made are by insurance with third parties, self-insurance, and
an adequate overdraft facility.[12] In so far as financial provision is to
cover the regular monitoring of the site after its closure, coupled with
the initial supply and maintenance and replacement of pollution
control and monitoring equipment, it must be adequate for 30 years or
more from closure. Financial schemes designed to cover this lengthy

---

[9] WMP4, para. 3.37.
[10] WMP4, para. 3.39.
[11] paras. 3.68–3.122.
[12] WMP4, para. 3.95.

period that are canvassed in WMP 4 include the use of a bond, an escrow account, and an independent or a mutual trust fund.

Licence Conditions

11–166   Waste management licences are issued subject to such terms and conditions as the waste regulation authority thinks fit, both as to the activities to be authorised, the precautions to be taken and any relevant works to be carried out. These may require actions not only during the licensed activities, but also before and after them, including monitoring for leachate and landfill gas after closure of a landfill site.[13] The relevant planning permission may also contain aftercare obligations; these cannot however continue for more than five years following restoration of the site, whereas there is no corresponding restriction on how long aftercare conditions contained in a waste management licence may last.[13A] Licences relating to disposal of waste must in any event cover the types and quantities of waste, the technical requirements, the security precautions to be taken, the disposal of site, and the treatment method.[13B] However no conditions may be imposed in any waste management licence for the purpose only of securing the health of persons at work within the meaning of H.S.W.A. 1974, Part I.[14] Conditions may even require works to be carried out by the licence holder that he has no legal right to do in the absence of the consent of some third party. In that event, section 35(4) requires that third party to grant or join in granting the licence holder such rights as may be required to enable the obligations under the licence to be complied with. The Secretary of State may give directions as to terms and conditions that are or are not to be included in a licence, which waste regulation authorities must give effect to, and may issue guidance on the grant of licences, to which the authorities must have regard.[15] Much of the relevant guidance made under this power is contained in the Waste Management Licensing Circular 11/94 and in particular in its Annexes which deal with the following matters:

---

[13] s.35(3).

[13A] TCPA 1990, Sched. 5, para. 2(7), as amended by P.C.A. 1991, Sched. 1, para. 14. See MPG 7 "The Reclamation of Mineral Workings" for guidance on conditions that may be imposed.

[13B] reg. 6, implementing Art. 9.

[14] reg. 13.

[15] s. 35(8); also s. 74(5) in relation to guidance on "fit and proper person".

Annex	Topic
1	The EC Framework Directive on Waste
2	The Definition of Waste
3	The Food and Environment Protection Act 1985
4	The Waste Management Licensing System
5	Exemptions from Licensing
6	The Registration of Exemptions
7	Protection of Groundwater
8	The Registration of Waste Brokers
9	Environmental Information: Public Registers and Annual Reports
10	Waste Management Licensing and Commercial Confidentiality Appeals
11	Other Provisions Related to Waste Management Licensing.

Further guidance issued under the same power, to which the authorities must have regard, is constituted by revised Waste Management Paper No. 4 "Licensing of Waste Facilities", and Waste Management Paper No. 26 "Landfilling Wastes", which covers, among other things, advice on after-care particularly relevant to the surrender of licences.

The full list of Waste Management Papers issued over the years **11–167** forms Table 11/VIII. Though several of these are now due for up-dating, they remain essential sources of guidance for those concerned with any of the particular topics covered.

TABLE 11/VIII

Waste Management Papers	
WMP1	A Review of Options (1992)
WMP2	Waste Disposal Surveys (1976)
WMP3	Guidelines for the Preparation of a Waste Disposal Plan (1976)
WMP4	The Licensing of Waste Facilities. 3rd Edition (1994)
WMP5	The Relationship between Waste Disposal Authorities and Private Industry (1976)
WMP6	Polychlorinated Biphenyl (PCB) Wastes (1994)

11–168

WMP7	Mineral Oil Wastes—a Technical Memorandum on Arisings, Treatment and Disposal (1976)
WMP8	Heat Treatment Cyanide Wastes—a Technical Memorandum on Arisings, Treatment and Disposal. 2nd Edition (1985)
WMP9	Halogenated Hydrocarbon Solvent Wastes from Cleaning Processes—a Technical Memorandum on Reclamation and Disposal (1976)
WMP10	Local Authority Waste Disposal Statistics 1974/75 (1976)
WMP11	Metal Finishing Wastes—a Technical Memorandum on Arisings, Treatment and Disposal (1976)
WMP12	Mercury Bearing Wastes—a Technical Memorandum on Storage, Handling, Treatment Disposal and Recovery (1977)
WMP13	Tarry and Distillation Wastes and other Chemical Based Wastes—a Technical Memorandum on Arisings, Treatment and Disposal (1977)
WMP 14	Solvent Wastes (excluding Halogenated Hydrocarbons)—a Technical Memorandum on Reclamation and Disposal (1977)
WMP15	Halogenated Organic Wastes—a Technical Memorandum on Arisings, Treatment and Disposal (1978)
WMP16	Wood Preserving Wastes—a Technical Memorandum on Arisings, Treatment and Disposal (1980)
WMP17	Wastes from Tanning, Leather Dressing and Fellmongering—a Technical Memorandum on Recovery, Treatment and Disposal (1978)
WMP18	Asbestos Waste—a Technical Memorandum on Arisings and Disposal (1979)
WMP19	Wastes from the Manufacture of Pharmaceuticals, Toiletries and Cosmetics—a Technical Memorandum on Arisings, Treatment and Disposal (1978)
WMP20	Arsenic Bearing Wastes—a Technical Memorandum on Recovery, Treatment and Disposal (1980)
WMP21	Pesticide Wastes—a Technical Memorandum on Arisings and Disposal (1980)
WMP22	Local Authority Waste Disposal Statistics 1974/75 to 1977/78 (1978)
WMP23	Special Wastes—a Technical Memorandum Providing Guidance on their Definition (1981)
WMP24	Cadmium Bearing Wastes—a Technical Memorandum on Arisings, Treatment and Disposal (1984)

WMP25	Clinical Wastes—A Technical Memorandum on Arisings, Treatment and Disposal (1983)
WMP26	Landfilling Wastes—a Technical Memorandum on Landfill Sites (1986)
WMP26A	Landfill Completion—a Technical Memorandum providing Guidance on Assessing the Completion of Licensed Landfill Sites (1994)
WMP27	Landfill Gas—a Technical Memorandum on the Monitoring and Control of Landfill Gas (1991)
WMP28	Recycling—A Memorandum for Local Authorities on Recycling (1991)

In imposing conditions on a licence, the waste regulation authority **11–169** will have regard to any conditions that may already be applicable to the site under the necessary relevant planning permission. Nevertheless, since the aims and objectives of the planning regime and of that for waste management licences are largely distinct, any excessive overlap of conditions may be open to challenge on the ground that the conditions are beyond the scope of the powers of the planning authority or the waste regulation authority, as the case may be.[16] Planning controls are appropriate for issues such as access, visual amenity, traffic, hours of operation, the potential for contamination, and the nature and type of restoration including planting. The focus of the licence conditions is on day to day detailed control of the operation, and should supplement those of the planning conditions.

The relationship of planning and waste management licence con- **11–170** ditions is the subject of Planning Policy Guidance (PPG) 23 "Planning and Pollution Control", discussed in paragraphs 3–107 to 3–120.[17] For Scotland it is proposed to issue corresponding advice in a National Planning Policy Guideline on land for waste disposal. The conflict between planning and pollution control regimes has also been judicially considered in *Gateshead Metropolitan Borough Council v. Secretary of State for the Environment and Northumbrian Water Group plc.*[18] referred to at paragraphs 3–110 to 3–113.

---

[16] DoE Circular 1/85 (WO 1/85), "The Use of Conditions in Planning Permission", states (Annex, paras. 18, 19) that duplication of planning and other controls is unnecessary, and that a planning condition conflicting with other controls "will be unreasonable and so *ultra vires*". This latter point would seem open to question if regarded as an absolute rule. Since the objectives of the planning and waste control regimes differ, it is entirely conceivable that the requirements for implementing each might conflict quite properly and legitimately.

[17] See also WMP 4, paras. 1.17 to 1.21.

[18] [1994] 1 Env. L.R. 11 (QBD); [1994] E.G.C.S. 92 (CA).

11–171   Specific aspects of the potential conflict with particular relation to implementation of Directive 75/442 are discussed in Annex A to Circular 11/94, at paragraphs 1.50 to 1.58. A combination of the regimes is likely to be relevant to give full effect to the Directive's objectives; where the licensing authority has the necessary power then it should exercise it, and the planning authority is not required to deal with the same issue also.[19] For new planning applications, *i.e.* made on or after May 1, 1994, relating to waste disposal or recovery, the planning authority should have regard to the objectives of avoiding harm to the environment, implementing any development plan, and establishing an integrated and adequate network of disposal installations.[20] Hence the licensing authority is not in such a case to reject an application in order to prevent detriment to the local amenities.[21] However in relation to installations with existing planning permission, or exempted from the need for it, a licence application may be rejected by the licensing authority, if necessary, for compliance with the Directive, thereby avoiding claims for compensation.[22]

11–172   Groundwater protection is the subject of EC Directive 80/68,[23] which is discussed in paragraphs 8–017 to 8–024. Although, in recent years at least, groundwater protection has been an issue of importance in the granting of waste disposal licences and in the conditions attached to them, the provisions of this Directive 80/68 have not hitherto been the subject of implementing legislation. This has been rectified by regulation 15 of the 1994 Licensing Regulations. The controls imposed by this regulation refer to substances in Lists I and II of the Directive, being respectively "black list" substances the introduction of which into groundwater must be prevented, and "grey list" substances, the introduction of which into groundwater must be limited "so as to avoid pollution of this water by these substances".[24] The requirements of the Directive are set out in paragraph 8–021.

11–173   A waste regulation authority must ensure that the activities the subject of an application for a waste management licence are subjected to prior investigation, where the licence would authorise any disposal, or tipping for the purpose of disposal, of a substance in either List I or List II which might lead to an indirect discharge into groundwater of such a substance, or any direct discharge into groundwater of any such substance.[25] This investigation must have regard to the hydro-

---

[19] Circular 11/94, para. 1.53.
[20] Circular 11/94, para. 1.54.
[21] s. 36(3); reg. 9(7).
[22] Circular 11/94, para 1.58; 1994 Licensing Regs., reg. 10.
[23] [1980] O.J. L20.
[24] Art. 3.
[25] reg. 15(1).

geological conditions of the area and the nature of the relevant soil and sub-soil, and the risk of pollution and alteration of the quality of the groundwater from any discharge. The authority must then establish whether the discharge of substances into groundwater is a satisfactory solution from the point of view of the environment;[26] this marks a sharp break from the dilute and disperse techniques that used to be standard practice. Additionally, the quality and other relevant features of the groundwater must be subject to appropriate surveillance, and no licence is to be issued unless the authority has checked that this will be carried out.[27] The authority is specifically required only to issue a waste management licence where it is satisfied that the requirements of Directive 80/68 will be complied with; these requirements are set out in regulations 15(4) and (5) in relation to List I and List II substances respectively.

Detailed terms to be included in any granted licence are set out in   **11–174** regulations 15(6) and (7) in relation to indirect discharges and direct discharges respectively. These include requirements to set conditions on the essential precautions to be taken, the maximum quantities of List I and List II substances either to be tipped or to be permitted in any effluent, and measures for monitoring groundwater. All such licences must be for limited periods only and are to be reviewed at least every four years.[28] Additionally, all licences granted under C.O.P.A. as well as under the E.P.A. that authorise any activity that is liable to give rise to a breach of the Directive 80/68 must be reviewed, and varied or revoked as may be necessary to give effect to the Directive.[29] Detailed guidance on the implementation of Directive 80/68 through the powers given by regulation 15 are contained in Annex 7 to Circular 11/94.

Attorney-General's Reference (No. 2 of 1988)[30] involved a challenge to   **11–175** the right of a waste disposal authority to impose a condition under section 6 of C.O.P.A. that:

> "The facility shall at all times be managed and operated so as to avoid creating a nuisance to the inhabitants of the neighbourhood".

The Court of Appeal held that the waste disposal authority's powers under C.O.P.A. did not permit a condition prohibiting public nuisances of any and all kinds (whether or not they polluted water

---

[26] reg. 15(2).
[27] reg. 15(3).
[28] reg. 15(8), (9).
[29] reg. 15(10)(11).
[30] C.A., [1989] 3 W.L.R. 397.

endangering public health or caused serious detriment to the amenities of the locality). If this was permitted, it would allow an authority
to create an indictable offence out of something that might be merely
a statutory nuisance, for example excessive noise, and that was, the
Court held, not what Parliament could have intended. Accordingly
any conditions must be sufficiently specific to relate to the achievement of the objectives of the statute; if for any reason these
objectives cannot be attained by any appropriate condition, then the
authority must revoke the licence altogether under the powers
available to it.

11–176 The European Commission has issued a proposal for a Directive on
the landfill of waste, an amended version of which, incorporating a
number of the European Parliament's amendments, was published in
1993.[31] This was in turn further amended by the Council in June 1994.
In view of the current status of the proposed Directive, it would be
premature to consider it in detail. Nevertheless it contains a number of
significant features that deserve mention, including:

- Various classes of landfill are defined, to which different
  types of waste are to be assigned, depending on their
  "eluate" criteria—"eluate" being the solution obtained by a
  simulated laboratory leaching test.
- No new sites for the co-disposal of hazardous and other
  waste may be opened. Existing ones must be closed down
  within five years of the Directive coming into force, unless
  they meet prescribed conditions designed to avoid environmental harm.
- Existing sites are to conform with requirements prescribed in
  the Directive as soon as possible and in any event within ten
  years of its coming into force, or else then close down.
- Closure procedures are to require the operator to maintain,
  monitor and control the closed landfill for so long as the site
  "could present hazards".
- The site operator must provide a financial guarantee or
  equivalent to cover estimated costs of closure procedures
  and aftercare operations.

---

[31] [1993] O.J. C212.

— The Member States are to establish one or more "landfill aftercare funds" to cover normal aftercare costs of closed landfills and any expenses for operations to prevent or cure damage to the environment produced by the disposal of waste, where this is not otherwise recoverable or covered by insurance or financial guarantee. The operators of all landfills are to contribute to this fund, in amounts reflecting the class of landfill, and the types and tonnage of the wastes landfilled.

Application Procedure

Applications for waste management licences are governed by **11–177** section 36 of the E.P.A. An application for a site licence must be made to the waste regulation authority for the area of that site; an application for a mobile plant licence is to be made to the authority in whose area the operator of the plant has his principal place of business.[32] Apart from having to be in writing, no standard form is prescribed and each authority is free to issue its own form; and there is inevitably also a prescribed fee. There is a presumption in favour of the grant of a licence, and accordingly provided that the regulation authority is satisfied that the application is a fit and proper person (the burden of showing this being thereby placed on the applicant), the application is not to be rejected unless it is necessary to prevent the pollution of the environment or harm to human health, or (where there is only an established use certificate and no grant of planning permission) to prevent serious detriment to the amenities of the locality.[33] If the authority proposes to grant a licence, it must, before doing so, consult with the National Rivers Authority or, in Scotland, the relevant river purification authority, and the Health and Safety Executive. In Scotland, if the regulation authority is not the district planning authority, then it must also consult the general planning authority for the area of the proposed site. These various bodies have 21 days to respond, unless a longer period is agreed, and the regulation authority must consider any representations these statutory consultees may make. Where the NRA or a river purification authority request the regulation authority not to proceed with granting the licence or disagree on any of the proposed conditions to

---

[32] s.36(1).
[33] s.36(3).

it, the dispute, if it cannot be resolved, must be referred to the Secretary of State for determination, and meanwhile no licence will be granted on the application. Where any part of the land to be used for licensed activities has been notified as an SSSI under section 28(1) of the Wildlife and Countryside Act 1981, a proposal to grant the licence must also be referred to the relevant conservation agency, namely the Nature Conservancy Council for England, the Nature Conservancy Council for Scotland or the Countryside Council for Wales, as the case may be, and the agency likewise has 21 days to respond with its observations. If the regulation authority has not taken an decision on an application for a waste management licence within four months then, unless a longer period is agreed, the application is deemed to be rejected at the end of the four months.[34]

11–178   An applicant may appeal to the Secretary of State, in the manner prescribed by regulation 6 of the 1994 Licensing Regulations, against any refusal to grant a licence or against any conditions attached to the grant of a licence, or against a determination under section 66(2) or 66(4) that information is not commercially confidential.[35] The Secretary of State may determine an appeal himself, after receiving the conclusions and recommendations of an inspector; he may alternatively give the inspector power to determine the appeal directly. Section 43 governs such appeals and also those against variation of licence conditions, suspension or revocation of a licence or the rejection of an application to surrender or to transfer a licence. No right of appeal is however available where the decision concerned gives effect to a direction by the Secretary of State. In the case of a rejected application, or a grant subject to conditions that are objected to, the appeal may be made by the applicant—third parties have no right of appeal against the grant of a licence or the conditions attached.

11–179   Regulation 6 of the 1994 Licensing Regulations prescribes the manner of making an appeal. Guidance on the procedure is contained in Annex 10 of Circular 11/94. Notice of appeal must, in most cases, be given within six months from either the date of the relevant decision or the date on which the application is deemed to have been rejected, unless the Secretary of State allows a longer period.[36] An appeal against a determination on confidentiality (which may be by the applicant or, if different, the person to whom or to whose business it relates) must be made within the next 21 days; no extension is available. The notice must have annexed to it a statement of the grounds of appeal and be accompanied by other related documents.

---

[34] s.36(9).
[35] As to which see paras. 11–222, 11–223.
[36] reg. 7.

Copies of the notice and all other related documents are also to be sent to the relevant authority.

Appeals may be dealt with either by way of written representations **11–180** or at a hearing. There will be a hearing if a party to the appeal (*i.e.* the appellant, any statutory consultee or, in a confidentiality case, a person to whose business the information in question relates) so requests, or the Secretary of State so decides.[37] Generally a hearing will be in public unless the person conducting it decides otherwise. However, hearing of appeals against a determination that information is not confidential will be in private unless the appellant requests it to be held in public.[38]

Modification of Conditions

A waste regulation authority may at any time modify the conditions **11–181** of a waste management licence to any extent that it thinks desirable, provided this is unlikely to require unreasonable expense on the part of the licence holder.[39] Further, the regulation authority must modify the conditions of a licence if and to the extent that, in its opinion, this is required to ensure that the licensed activities do not cause pollution of the environment or harm to human health or become seriously detrimental to the amenities of the locality affected by the activities.[40] Modification may also occur on the application of the licence holder,[41] with the consent of the authority. The Secretary of State may himself give directions to the authority on modifications to be made to any such licence, and in that event, the authority must comply with the directions.[42] In so far as there are any regulations issued under section 35(6) providing for what must or must not be included in a licence, then any modification of the conditions must not be inconsistent with those regulations; conversely, in the event of any new requirements being imposed by such regulations, the authority must modify the conditions of any licence to which the changes apply so as to give effect to them.

Where the authority proposes to modify the conditions of a licence **11–182** under these provisions, it must refer its proposal to the same statutory consultees as are required to be consulted for a fresh licence application, and again these consultees have 21 days to respond. If a decision has not been taken on an application by a licence holder to

---

[37] s.43(2)(c).
[38] Circular 11/94, Annex 10, paras. 10.24–10.27.
[39] s.37(1)(a).
[40] s.37(2)(a).
[41] Under s.37(1)(b).
[42] s.37(3).

modify his licensed conditions within two months, or such longer period as may be agreed, the application is deemed to have been rejected.

11–183   The licence holder may appeal against the rejection of an application by him to modify his licence conditions or against any decision by the authority to modify the conditions. The procedure is essentially the same as for an appeal in respect of an application for a licence, save that in relation to a decision by the authority to modify conditions, an appeal will normally have the effect of suspending that decision.[43] However if the notice of modification of the conditions includes a statement that, in the opinion of the authority, the decision is necessary for the purpose of preventing or, where that is not practicable, minimising pollution of the environment or harm to human health, the appeal will not suspend the operation of that decision. Nevertheless, if on determination of the appeal it is also determined that the authority acted unreasonably in issuing that statement and so preventing suspension of the decision, the licence holder is entitled to compensation for any loss suffered as a consequence. In the event of dispute as to whether a person is entitled to that compensation or as to quantum, the matter is to be referred to arbitration.[44]

Revocation and suspension of licences

11–184   Under the E.P.A., waste regulation authorities are given greater flexibility than was available under C.O.P.A. to deal with unsatisfactory performance by a licence holder. Whereas C.O.P.A. provided the ultimate sanction of revocation, and this is of course retained in the E.P.A. for appropriate cases (though with the added flexibility of being applicable to only some or all of the licensed activities, as thought appropriate), suspension is also made possible, whereby the permission to carry on some or all of the activities authorised under a licence can be temporarily withdrawn, while leaving the licence holder subject to the continuing obligations under the licence. As became apparent under C.O.P.A., the sole sanction of total revocation was liable to leave a thoroughly unsatisfactory site in the hands of the waste disposal authority, who would often then have to find the funds itself, if it could, to deal with the problems on the site. The grounds available under the E.P.A. for revocation and suspension respectively differ somewhat and are as follows:

[43] s.43(4).
[44] s.43(7).

11–185

Grounds for Revocation (s.38(1))	Grounds for Suspension (s.38(6))
(a) The licence holder has ceased to be a fit and proper person in that: (i) he has been convicted of a relevant offence; or (ii) management of the licensed activities is no longer in the hands of a technically competent person; or	(a) The licence holder has ceased to be a fit and proper person in that the management of the licensed activities is no longer in the hands of a technically competent person; or
(b) Continuation of the licensed activities would cause pollution of the environment or harm to human health or would be seriously detrimental to the amenities of the locality; and	(b) Serious pollution of the environment or serious harm to human health has resulted from or is about to be caused by either the licensed activities or the happening or threatened happening of an event affecting those activities; and
(c) The pollution, harm or detriment cannot be avoided by modifying the licence conditions.	(c) Continuing to carry on those activities or any of them will continue or will cause serious pollution of the environment or serious harm to human health.

The drafting of these provisions in sections 38(1) and (6) is **11–186** unsatisfactory, and in the case of the latter at least, ambiguous. In each case the structure is "(a) or (b) and (c)". This may be read either as [(a) or (b)] and [(c)], or as [(a) and (c)] or [(b) and (c)]. However, in the case of section 38(1) the words themselves make it clear that the two grounds are (i) ground (a) and (ii) grounds (b) and (c) jointly, since the words "the pollution, harm or detriment" in (c) can only refer back to (b). However in the case of the grounds for suspension under section 38(6) while there is possibly a marginally closer connection between (b) and (c) than there is between (a) and (c), the section would read perfectly well if interpreted either way. However, it is reasonable to interpret both sections in the same way, the two grounds in each case being ground (a) and ground (b) with (c).

It is to be noted that while a relevant conviction and technical **11–187** incompetence provide grounds for revocation or suspension of a licence, inability of a licence holder to make financial provisions adequate to discharge his licence obligations (where this is not already covered by some bond or other security) does not itself provide any grounds for either revocation or suspension, notwithstanding that the licence holder would as a result be likely to be held not to be a fit and proper person.

11–188   Revocation may take the form of either total revocation of the licence, leaving the licence holder with no further rights or obligations under it, or it may take the form of revocation of the authorisation to carry on either all or some of the licensed activities.[45] In the latter case, the revocation will not affect those requirements imposed by the licence which the authority, in revoking the licence, specifies as requirements which are to continue to bind the licence holder.[46] Though the wording leaves room for doubt, it would appear that unless the authority positively specifies the outstanding requirements that are continued to bind the licence holder, a partial revocation under section 38(3) would also revoke associated licence obligations. No doubt in practice, an authority choosing not to revoke a licence entirely will have clearly in mind what obligations it wishes to remain enforceable, and will expressly refer to these. Where revocation is on the grounds that the management of the licensed activities is no longer in the hands of a technically competent person, the authority does not have the right to revoke the licence entirely, but only in relation to some or all of the licensed activities.[47] If this power were to be exercised in relation to all the licensed activities, this would imply that the obligations of the licence would continue to be binding on the licensee automatically, since otherwise the effect would be the same as a total revocation under section 38(4), which is not permissible for this ground of revocation. It may be therefore that the final words of section 38(5) are unnecessary and by way of explanation only, merely indicating that the authority may, if it sees fit to do so, relieve the licensee of some of the licensed requirements, and leave only the remainder of them binding on him.

11–189   Suspension of a licence is designed to be temporary, and a notice of suspension must state the period at the end of which the suspension is to cease, or the event the occurrence of which will cause the suspension to cease. The intention is to bring some or all of the activities to a temporary halt while the licence holder deals with a particular problem, whether it be unsatisfactory conditions on the site or a lack of personnel or equipment. Accordingly the licence may suspend all or some of the activities and additionally the authority may require the holder to take such action to avert pollution or harm to

[45] s.38(4) and (3) respectively.
[46] s.38(5).
[47] s.38(2).

human health as it considers necessary. Such a requirement has the force of law directly, and non-compliance without reasonable excuse is an offence liable to a fine of up to £5,000 on summary conviction, and a fine and/or imprisonment of up to two years on conviction on indictment. Where the requirement that has not been complied with relates to special waste, the penalties are increased, in that imprisonment of up to 6 months may also be imposed on summary conviction, and up to five years on conviction on indictment.[48]

Overriding powers are given to the Secretary of State, who may in relation to any licence give directions to the relevant waste regulation authority as to whether and in what manner it should exercise it powers of modification and suspension; the authority has a duty to comply with any such directions.[49]   **11–190**

There is a right of appeal from any decision to revoke or suspend a licence under section 38, save where this is done to give effect to directions from the Secretary of State. The procedure is the same as for appeals relating to an application for a licence. An appeal against suspension will not itself have any suspensory effect; an appeal against revocation will however have suspensory effect unless (as in the case of a variation of conditions) the notice of revocation includes a statement that in the opinion of the authority the revocation is necessary to prevent, or where that is not practicable to minimise, pollution of the environment or harm to human health, and that an appeal should not have suspensory effect. Where in any case the relevant decision is not suspended, and on the appeal it is determined that the authority acted unreasonably either in suspending the licence or in excluding the suspensory effect of an appeal against revocation, then the licence holder is entitled to recover compensation. Any dispute as to the right to compensation or as to quantum is to be determined by arbitration.[50]   **11–191**

Transfer of Waste Management Licences

Transfers of licences are permissible at any time, including where a licence has been partially revoked or suspended. An application to transfer must be made in the manner prescribed under section 40(3) by both the current licence holder and the proposed transferee jointly. The waste regulation authority must satisfy itself that the proposed transferee is a fit and proper person, but subject to that shall effect the transfer to him by endorsing the licence. If no decision has been taken on an application for transfer within two months, it is deemed to have   **11–192**

---

[48] s.38(9) to (11).
[49] s.38(7).
[50] s.43(7).

been rejected. In the event of any rejection, only the proposed transferee[51] has a right of appeal. The procedures for any appeal by him are the same as those provided for an appeal in relation to a licence application; the decision to reject the application to transfer continues to have effect throughout any appeal.

Surrender of Waste Management Licences

11–193   Surrender of waste management licences is governed by the provisions of section 39. A holder of a mobile plant licence is entitled to surrender his licence at will at any time. In the case of site licences, however, the E.P.A. has introduced a highly significant change from the regime under C.O.P.A., and surrender is only possible if the waste regulation authority accepts it. Consequently, the holder of a site licence remains bound by the obligations contained in it until he obtains acceptance of the surrender (in the absence of earlier revocation).

11–194   Application to surrender a site licence must be made on the prescribed form and be accompanied by such evidence and other information as may be prescribed. The authority on receipt of the application is required to inspect the land to which the licence relates and may require the holder to provide further information or evidence. It must then determine whether it is likely or unlikely that the condition of the land will cause pollution of the environment or harm to human health, in so far as that condition is the result of the use of the land for the treatment, keeping or disposal of waste (irrespective of whether or not the treatment, keeping or disposal was in pursuance of the licence).[52] Guidance is given in relation to assessing completion of landfill sites in WMP 26A. This lists[53] the factors that need be addressed in considering whether a site is to be regarded as meeting the completion condition as:

(a)   the quality and quantity of leachate present;
(b)   the flow and concentration of gas;
(c)   the potential for polluting leachate or gas to be generated in future;
(d)   the potential for leachate or gas to reach sensitive targets;
(e)   the possibility of physical instability of the waste or retaining structures; and
(f)   the presence of particular problem wastes which could present a hazard in the future.

[51] s.43(1).
[52] s.39(5).
[53] para. 1.8.

These factors are discussed in Chapter 4 of WMP 26A, which **11–195**
includes an example of leachate criteria, setting values for some 36
determinands (*e.g.* pH, total organic carbon, and numerous anions and
cations) that should be met where leachate is likely to enter groundwater. An essential part of the post-closure programme is regular
monitoring and the waste regulation authority will impose conditions
on the licence to satisfy its requirements in this respect. Guidance on
monitoring is also included in WMP 26A.[54]

If, following this review, the authority is satisfied that the condition **11–196**
of the land is unlikely to cause pollution of the environment or harm to
human health, it must inform the National Rivers Authority or, in
Scotland, the relevant river purification authority and the general
planning authority (where the waste regulation authority is not also a
district planning authority), and consider any representations that
these bodies may make—they have 21 days to respond. If the National
Rivers Authority or, as the case may be, the river purification authority
requests that the surrender should not be accepted, then (unless, it
would seem, the regulation authority accepts this request) the matter
will be referred to the Secretary of State. Surrender of the licence will
not be accepted in the meantime and will occur only if the Secretary of
State's decision favours the licence holder's application. Where
surrender of the licence is accepted, the authority must issue a
certificate of completion to the applicant, along with its notice of
determination of the application to surrender. This certificate will state
that the authority is satisfied that the condition of the land is unlikely
to cause pollution of the environment or harm to human health, and
the licence will cease to have effect on the issue of the certificate.[55] If no
decision has been taken on the application to surrender a site licence
within three months of the application, then it is deemed to have been
rejected.[56]

The same appeal procedure is available in respect of a decision to **11–197**
reject an application to surrender a licence as is available in respect of
applications for a licence. A rejection of an application to surrender a
licence will continue to have effect throughout any appeal.

Closed Landfill Sites

The provisions as to surrender of a licence require to be seen in **11–198**
conjunction with the provisions of section 61 that sets out specific
duties of waste regulation authorities in relation to closed landfill sites

[54] paras. 3.18–3.56.
[55] s.39(9).
[56] s.39(10).

and, arguably, all contaminated land within its area. Section 61 (which has not been, and now will not be, brought into force)[57] applies to all land within a waste regulation authority's area other than land in relation to which a site licence is currently in force (over which it already has of course extensive powers of control). The authority has a duty to cause all other land in its area to be inspected from time to time to detect whether any of it is in such a condition that it may cause pollution of the environment or harm to human health by reason of the concentration or accumulation in the land, and emission or discharge from it, of noxious gases or noxious liquids caused by deposits of controlled waste in the land.[58] While the reference to "deposits of controlled waste in the land", which occurs in section 61(2), is clearly apt to cover a landfill site, the wide definition of what is waste, which includes anything which is discarded or otherwise dealt with as if it were waste, unless the contrary is proved, indicates that the expression would in fact apply to any deposits of pollutants in any land, whether deliberately placed there or not.

11–199   The application of the section is not limited to legal deposits of waste – indeed control of legal deposits may well be sufficiently achieved through other statutory provisions. Section 61(3) makes it clear that the provisions apply to, among other things, deposits of controlled waste that have not been made by virtue of a waste management licence or a C.O.P.A. waste disposal licence, even though these may have been made after January 1, 1976, when C.O.P.A. first came into effect. However if the section is read as covering illegal deposits, then there does not appear to be any point at which a line can be drawn between a systematic, though unauthorised, landfill operation and the occasional, one-off deposit of noxious waste, such as a drum of waste solvents or a container of an unwanted pesticide. If that be right, the only concern for the authority is whether the deposit of waste is giving or may give rise to noxious gases or noxious liquids such as may cause pollution of the environment or harm to human health. While "noxious gases" and "noxious liquids" are certainly apt terms for landfill gas and leachate from a landfill site, there is no reason to read into the section a limitation to those substances only.

11–200   The duty on the waste regulation authority to inspect its land also extends to keeping any contaminated land that it may find under

---

[57] The bringing into force of s.61, and also s.143 (registers of contaminative uses), was deferred, the latter indefinitely, while the Department of the Environment reviewed the whole question of liability for contamination of land. Both sections are to be repealed by the current Environment Bill and relpaced by new provisions, comparable to those applicable to statutory nuisances, for the remediation of contaminated land and for determining who may be held liable for the costs entailed.

[58] s.61(1), (2).

review,[59] and where any land appears likely to cause pollution of water it must consult the National Rivers Authority, or the appropriate river purification authority in Scotland, as to what remediation work may be called for. The duties on the waste regulation authority under this section extend further to an obligation to "do such works and take such other steps (whether on the land affected or on adjacent land, as appear to the authority to be reasonable to avoid [pollution to the environment or harm to human health]".[60]

By contrast with other provisions both in the E.P.A. and other environmental legislation, where the authority has carried out remedial work under section 61(7) it is entitled to recover all or any of the costs from "the person who is for the time being the owner of the land", except to the extent that the owner can show that any of these costs were incurred unreasonably. There is no definition of "owner" in Part II of the E.P.A., which leaves uncertain the position of, for example, a tenant holding on a relatively long lease or a mortgagee who may have taken property as security. Part III of the E.P.A. originally suffered the same defect; this has been cured, for the purposes of recovering expenses under section 81 in that Part, by the insertion of a definition in section 81A(9),[61] namely:

> "In this section—'owner', in relation to any premises, means a person (other than a mortgagee not in possession) who, whether in his own right or as trustee for any other person, is entitled to receive the rack rent of the premises or, where the premises are not let at a rack rent, would be so entitled if they were so let, and 'premises' does not include a vessel".

While there is no compelling reason to adopt the same definition when applying section 61, there is equally no strong reason not to and, considering the relatively close relationship between the purposes of the two sets of provisions and the circumstances to which they may apply, it must be desirable, and in the interests of owners and their lenders and insurers, for "owner" to be interpreted consistently in both Parts of the E.P.A.

There are two qualifications to the right to recover remedial costs from an owner. Firstly, where the waste in question was deposited under a waste management licence, and surrender of that licence has

11–201

11–202

---

[59] s.61(4).
[60] This may be contrasted with other clean up provisions under the E.P.A. and the Water Resources Act 1991, which merely grant powers and do not impose duties to take action.
[61] By the Noise and Statutory Nuisance Act 1993. This definition differs in certain significant respects from the corresponding definition in the Public Health Act 1936, s. 343. See also paras. 23–039, 23–040.

been accepted under section 39, so that a certificate of completion will have been issued, there will be no right to recover the costs from any owner for the time being of that site.[62] Secondly, in deciding whether to recover the cost, and if so how much, the authority is required to have to regard to any hardship which that might cause to the owner of the land.[63] This requirement does not however require the authority to abate any costs demand merely because hardship will be caused. The application of this requirement in practice may well turn on whether the owner was in any way responsible for the pollution, either directly by causing the deposit, or indirectly by failing to take steps that were reasonably open to him to prevent pollution, particularly where he may have bought the site, knowing its history, at a substantial discount precisely because of its condition. Conversely, where the owner was unaware of the condition of the site, or was in practice unable to do anything about it, for example the owner of one of numerous private houses built on an old landfill site, a decision by a waste regulation authority not to abate its costs demands might well be open to challenge on judicial review.

11–203   It is to be noted in conclusion that section 61 introduces two features into UK environmental law that mark a very significant change from previous practice:

> (i)   The waste regulation authority is both under a duty to inspect the land in its area, and also under a duty to clean up any contamination it may find that may cause pollution of the environment or harm to human health. In both cases these are duties and not merely powers. In these respects the legislation thus approximates to that relating to statutory nuisances.
>
> (ii) Costs incurred are recoverable from the owner for the time being, unlike the standard provision, for example that of section 59(8)(b) that permits recovery from the person who deposited or knowingly caused or knowingly permitted a deposit of waste. Whatever views one may have as to the fairness or otherwise of such a system, the introduction of owner liability will make it absolutely vital for purchasers of land to be fully aware of the nature of what they are acquiring and, given the *caveat emptor* rule, for them to make far more extensive enquiries before contract, compared with what has traditionally been the practice, and to stipulate for far more

[62] s.61(9).
[63] s.61(10).

protective contractual terms (unless the purchase price is suitably adjusted) to protect their legitimate interests.

Enforcement

Waste regulation authorities have a duty in relation to all licences that they have granted to take the steps needed to ensure that the conditions of the licence are complied with, and that the licensed activities neither cause pollution of the environment or harm to human health nor become seriously detrimental to the amenities of the locality affected by the activities.[64] They are expressly required to inspect periodically establishments and undertakings that carry out recovery or disposal of controlled waste.[65] If it appears to an authority that pollution of water is likely to be caused by any licensed activities, it must consult the National Rivers Authority or the relevant Scottish river purification authority with regard to carrying out this duty. If any duly authorised officer of the waste regulation authority considers that emergency measures are required, he may carry out work on the relevant land, or in relation to any plant or equipment on the land that the licence relates to, or in relation to the mobile plant, as the case may be. Any expenditure that is incurred in this way may be recovered from the holder of the licence, unless he can show either there was no emergency requiring the work, or to the extent that he can show any of the expenditure was unnecessary.[66]   **11–204**

In addition to breach of any of the prohibitions of section 33(1) being an offence, it is also an offence to contravene any condition of a waste management licence.[67] It is however a defence for the person charged to prove that   **11–205**

(a) he took all reasonable precautions and exercised all due diligence to avoid the commission of the offence; or

(b) he acted under instructions from his employer and neither knew nor had reason to suppose that the acts done by him constituted a contravention of subsection 33(1); or

(c) the acts alleged to constitute the contravention were done in an emergency in order to avoid danger to the public and that, as soon as reasonably practicable after they were done, particulars of them were furnished to the waste regulation

---

[64] s.42(1).
[65] Also those collecting or transporting waste on a professional basis, and waste brokers; 1994 Licensing Regs., Sched. 4. para 13(1).
[66] s.42(3), (4).
[67] s.33(6).

authority in whose area the treatment or disposal of the waste took place.[68]

11-206   The first limb of this defence is clearly closely connected with whether or not the person seeking to establish this complied with the duty of care under section 34. The common situation of depositing a load of waste that contains materials that should not be in it, and which are not authorised under the site licence, should become comparatively rare if all concerned comply fully with the duty of care. Conversely, where the situation does occur, there is likely to be a strong inference that one or more people in the chain of waste disposal failed to exercise the duty of care properly, who will be liable accordingly.

11-207   The second limb of the defence is designed to protect employees, who would otherwise be open to prosecution either directly for a contravention of section 33(1) or, where their employing company is charged with an offence under section 33, under section 158, which imposes liability on any person whose act or default led to the commission of an offence by another. This defence is not however absolute, and requires the employee to establish that he neither knew nor had reason to suppose that what he did was a contravention of subsection 33(1).

11-208   As regards the third limb, while this will prevent criminal liability arising under section 33, if there has been an unauthorised deposit of waste this may still give rise to civil liability, or to liability under Part III of the E.P.A. in so far as the deposit may be held to be a statutory nuisance, for example an accumulation or deposit which is prejudicial to health or a nuisance. In such cases, the person responsible for the deposit will also be financially liable for the consequences. It is probable that E.P.A., s.59 will also be available to the waste regulation authority to procure the removal of any deposit made in an emergency to which the third limb of the defence applies. The defence being a personal one available to the defendant means, it is submitted, that making it good does not mean that there has been no contravention of subsection 33(1), but merely that a prosecution of that defendant can be successfully resisted. If that is the correct approach, then the necessary pre-condition for the powers under section 59 to arise will exist notwithstanding that a prosecution for that contravention may fail.

11-209   The penalties for an offence under section 33 have been substantially increased from those available under C.O.P.A. Except where an offence relates to special waste, the maximum liability on summary

---

[68] s.33(7).

conviction is imprisonment for up to six months and/or a fine of up to £20,000, and on indictment imprisonment of up to two years or a fine or both. Where the offence is in relation to special waste, the maximum term of imprisonment on indictment is raised to five years.[69] A conviction under E.P.A., s.33 of the holder of a goods vehicle operator's licence, or of the holder's servant or agent, may also lead to the revocation or suspension of the licence, by virtue of section 69(4)(ffff)(iv) of the Transport Act 1968.[70]

In addition to the grounds for revocation and suspension under sections 38(1) and 38(6) referred to in paragraphs 11–184 to 11–191, the same sanctions are available in the event of any condition of a licence not being complied with. Where it appears to a waste regulation authority that this is the case, it may require the licence holder to comply with the relevant condition within such time as it specifies, and if in the authority's opinion the licence holder has not so complied within that time, it may revoke the licence entirely, revoke it in relation to any or all of the licensed activities, or suspend the licence in respect of all or any of the licensed activities.[71] As where a licence is suspended under section 38(6), in the event of suspension under section 42(6) the authority may require the licence holder to take such measures as it considers necessary to deal with or avert serious pollution of the environment or serious harm to human health, and any failure to comply with any such requirement is an offence.[72] Any decision to revoke a licence in whole or in part, or to suspend it under section 42, is subject to appeal in the same way as such a decision taken under section 38.

11–210

The Secretary of State has power to give such directions as he thinks fit as to whether and how a waste regulation authority should exercise its enforcement powers under section 42 in respect of any licence, with which the authority must comply.[73] As a last resort, the Secretary of State has default powers under section 72, whereby, if he is satisfied that a waste regulation authority has failed in any respect to discharge any function under Part II of the E.P.A. which it ought to have discharged, he may declare the authority to be in default. In that event, he may direct the authority to perform any function that he specifies, and how and when to do this, and in the event of the authority failing to comply with such a direction, he may transfer all or any of the functions of the authority to himself.[74]

11–211

[69] s.33(8), (9).
[70] Inserted by E.P.A., Sched. 15, para. 10(2)(b).
[71] s.42(5), (6).
[72] s.42(7).
[73] s.42(8).
[74] s.72(1)–(4).

11–212   Both the Secretary of State and any waste regulation authority may appoint inspectors under section 68. These inspectors have extensive powers, set out in sections 69 and 70, for the purpose, among other things, of determining whether any provision of Part II of the E.P.A. or of any regulations or other instruments made under it are being complied with. The powers are exercisable in relation to land on or in which, and vessels in or by means of which, controlled waste is being or has been deposited, treated, kept or disposed of, or where this is reasonably believed to be occurring or to have occurred, and also to land which is reasonably believed to be affected by any such activity on other land. An inspector may enter premises at any reasonable time, or at any time at all if there is an immediate risk of serious pollution of the environment or serious harm to human health, and he may make any examinations or investigations as may be necessary, including ordering premises or any part of them to be left undisturbed, and taking samples. An inspector may also require any person who may be able to give relevant information to answer questions, and to sign a declaration of the truth of the answers, to require the production of records, and to require any person to give the inspector such facilities and assistance as may be necessary to enable the inspector to exercise any of his powers. Where a person is required to answer questions under these powers, no answer that he gives will be admissible in evidence in England and Wales against that person in any proceedings or against the person in any criminal proceedings in Scotland. Where any person fails, without reasonable excuse, to comply with an inspector's requirements under these powers or prevents anyone else from appearing before the inspector or answering any of his questions, or otherwise intentionally obstructing the inspector, he will be liable to be fined up to £5,000 on summary conviction.

11–213   If an inspector, having entered any premises, finds any article or substance that he has reasonable cause to believe is a cause of imminent danger of serious pollution of the environment or serious harm to human health, he may seize it and have it rendered harmless. Where practicable, he must give a sample, suitably identified, of the substance to a responsible person at the relevant premises.[75] Intentional obstruction of an inspector exercising these powers is subject to a fine of up to £5,000 on summary conviction, or to a fine and/or imprisonment of up to two years on conviction on indictment.[76] The Secretary of State may require a waste regulation authority to provide him with information relating to its discharge of its

[75] s.70(1), (2).
[76] s.70(4).

functions under Part II of the E.P.A.[77] The Secretary of State and any waste regulation authority may by notice in writing require any person to provide such information as he or it reasonably considers to be needed, within such period as may be specified. Failure to comply with such a requirement, or knowingly or recklessly giving false or misleading information, may lead to a fine not exceeding £5,000 on summary conviction and, on indictment, a fine and imprisonment for up to two years.[78]

Removal of Unlawful Waste Deposits

Powers are given to both waste regulation authorities and waste collection authorities to deal with deposits of controlled waste that have been made in contravention of section 33(1), *i.e.* either without the benefit of any licence, or in breach of the conditions of a licence or, in either case, a deposit that is likely to cause pollution of the environment or harm to human health, thereby coming within section 33(1)(c).[79] (For the purposes of these paragraphs 11–214 to 11–217 "authority" is used to mean both a waste regulation authority and a waste collection authority, or either of them.) Where there has been an unlawful deposit of waste contrary to section 33(1) the authority can require the occupier of the relevant land to remove the waste within a specified period starting at least 21 days from the notice requiring this action, or to take any appropriate steps to eliminate or reduce the consequences of the deposit within a specified period. The person receiving such a notice has 21 days in which to appeal against it; he may appeal either on the ground that he neither deposited nor knowingly caused nor knowingly permitted the deposit of the waste or that there is a material defect in the notice. Thus, while the authority's powers only arise if there is an unlawful deposit, and it would therefore be for the authority to show that this pre-condition was satisfied, the burden of proof is on the occupier to show (on the balance of probabilities) that it was not him who committed the offence. Where the occupier can establish this, or otherwise that there is a material defect in the notice, the court must quash the original requirement; in any other case, for example an appeal against the terms of the requirement, the court may modify the requirement or dismiss the appeal as it sees fit. In the absence of a successful appeal, a failure to comply with the notice constitutes an offence subject to a fine of up to £5,000 and a daily fine of up to £500 for each day after conviction that the requirement is not complied with, unless and until

11–214

---

[77] s.71(1).
[78] s.71(2), (3).
[79] s.59.

the authority exercises its own clean up powers. These powers, under section 59(6), entitle an authority to do whatever a person has been required and has failed to do. Having done the work for themselves, the authority may recover their reasonable expenses from the person originally required to do the work.

11–215   In certain circumstances, instead of requiring an occupier to clean up unlawful deposits of waste, the authority may do the necessary work itself directly, namely if

>   (a)   it is necessary that the waste be removed forthwith, or other steps be taken to eliminate or reduce the consequences of the deposit in order to remove or prevent pollution of land, water or air or harm to human health; or
>   (b)   there is no occupier of the land; or
>   (c)   there is an occupier, but he neither made or knowingly permitted the deposit of the waste.[80]

11–216   Where an authority undertakes the work it may recover the cost incurred, including the cost of disposing of the waste,[81] either from any person who deposited or knowingly caused or knowingly permitted the deposit of any of the waste, or (where the action was taken to remove or prevent pollution or harm to human health), from the occupier of the land unless he proves that he neither made nor knowingly cause nor knowingly permitted the deposit of the waste. Liability to pay the costs does not extend to any that the person liable can show were incurred unnecessarily.

11–217   Since the liability is on any person who deposited or knowingly caused or knowingly permitted the deposit of *any* of the waste, where there is a substantial amount of waste it is only necessary for the authority to establish one person who has contributed to that, and he may be held liable for the total clean-up costs; the authority is not required to determine who is responsible for every part of the waste deposit before it can recover its costs in full.

Civil Liability

11–218   In addition to criminal liability for unlawful deposits of waste, section 73(6) provides that any person who deposits waste or knowingly causes or knowingly permits it to be deposited in or on

---

[80] s.59(7).
[81] s.59(8).

land so as to commit an offence under section 33(1) or section 63(2)[82] shall be civilly liable for damage caused by the waste. Damage in this connection includes the death of or injury to any person (including any disease and any impairment of physical or mental condition).[83] Since the liability arises where an offence has been committed under section 33(1) and not merely a contravention of that section, the civil liability should not arise where any of the personal defences under section 33(7) (due diligence, acting under instructions, emergency) are made good. This is confirmed by section 73(7), which specifically provides (though arguably unnecessarily[84]) that the defences under section 33(7) are also available to an action for civil damages under section 73(6). There is no liability however for damage due wholly to the fault of the person who suffered it or where that person voluntarily accepted the risk of the damage being caused.

Registers

The E.P.A. provides in section 64 for much more information to be made publicly available by way of registers held by waste regulation authorities than was previously the case under C.O.P.A.[85] Among the matters to be included in these registers in accordance with section 64, as supplemented by regulation 10 of the 1994 Licensing Regulations, are: **11–219**

— current or recently current licences and applications for licences;[86]
— applications for modifying the conditions of licences and notices of modification;
— notices revoking or suspending licences or imposing requirements on licence holders under section 38 or section 42(5);
— appeals under section 43 against decisions of the waste regulation authority;
— convictions of licence holders for any offence under Part II of the E.P.A. (whether or not in relation to a licence);

---

[82] Which provides for regulations to be made creating an offence of depositing, or knowingly causing or knowingly permitting the deposit of any waste that is not controlled waste.
[83] s.73(8).
[84] Where there has been no previous prosecution under s.33, the s.73(7) defence might be the more convenient defence to plead.
[85] Though this provision overlaps substantially with the requirements of the Environmental Information Regulations 1992 and the underlying EC Directive 90/313 (see paras. 20–006 to 20–025), the two regimes are not co-extensive.
[86] "Recently current" means current within the last 12 months, s.64(3).

>   — monitoring information relating to licensed activities;
>   — registers and records relating to special waste;
>   — applications for the surrender of licences and certificates of completion.

11–220   In addition, waste collection authorities in England are required to maintain a register containing particulars of the following information so far as it relates to the treatment, keeping or disposal of controlled waste in the collection authority's area:[87]

>   — current or recently current licences;
>   — notices modifying, revoking or suspending licences;
>   — certificates of completion.

Waste regulation authorities in England which are not waste collection authorities are required to provide the information to enable them to do this.

11–221   Information that has been superseded by later information need not be kept for more than four years after the later information is put on the register; similarly monitoring information need not be kept on the register for more than four years.[88] Guidance on the matters to be included in the registers is contained in Annex 9 of Circular 11/94. This includes a recommendation to delete information on convictions that have become spent under the Rehabilitation of Offenders Act 1974, and also on convictions of corporations that would have become spent if it had been of an individual.[89] The public has a right of access to these registers at all reasonable hours free of charge, with the right to obtain copies at a reasonable charge. Information may be excluded from a register if its inclusion would be contrary to the interests of national security.[90]

11–222   Information that is commercially confidential to any individual or business is not to be included in any register without consent of the relevant individual or person carrying on the business, except to the extent it is of a class of information prescribed by the Secretary of State for inclusion in the registers, whether commercially confidential or not.[91] The burden of proof that information is

---

[87] s.64(4); reg. 10(3).
[88] reg. 11(2).
[89] Annex 9, para. 9.24.
[90] s.65(1).
[91] s.66(7). No such information has however been prescribed.

commercially confidential is on the person requiring it to be so treated.

In determining whether information is commercially confidential **11–223** for the purposes of these provisions, the same criterion is applied as in Part I of the E.P.A., namely whether including the information in the register would prejudice to an unreasonable degree the commercial interests of any individual or person. The significance of defining confidentiality in this way is discussed in paragraphs 9–145 to 9–152 above; guidance on applying the test is contained in Annex 9 of Circular 11/94.[92] Where information is furnished to an authority for the purposes of an application for a licence, or for its modification, or in connection with complying with any licence condition or a notice requiring information from him served under section 71(2), the person furnishing the information may apply for it to be treated as commercially confidential. The determination must be made within 14 days, failing which the information is to be deemed to be confidential.[93] If an authority acquires information in any other way pursuant to Part II of the E.P.A. and it appears to the authority that it might be commercially confidential, the authority is required to serve notice that the information is to be included in the register, unless the relevant person can sustain an objection to that inclusion on grounds of commercial confidentiality. The person must be given a reasonable opportunity to make such an objection and to make representations in order to justify it.[94] Where an authority has determined that information is not commercially confidential it must nevertheless not enter the information on to a register for 21 days after that determination has been notified to the person concerned. If there is an appeal during that period to the Secretary of State against the determination, the information will continue to be kept off the register pending final determination or withdrawal of the appeal. Even where information has been determined to be commercially confidential, this protection will continue for four years only, running from the date of the determination unless the person who furnished it applies for the information to remain excluded thereafter; if this is not done the authority must put it on the register.[95] Any determination on that subsequent application is likewise subject to appeal to the Secretary of State.

---

[92] paras. 9.39–9.42.
[93] s.66(2), (3).
[94] s.66(4).
[95] Circular 11/94, Annex 9, para. 9.43.

Recycling and Other Recovery of Waste

11–224   It is part of the Community's strategy on waste that this should, so far as possible, be prevented at source. However to the extent this is not practicable, the strategy favours the recovery of waste by means of recycling, re-use or reclamation or any other process with a view to extracting secondary raw materials or the use of waste as a source of energy.[96] This is reflected in Waste Management Paper No. 28 "Recycling" which lists[97] the principal options available for waste management, in order of preference

- — waste minimisation;
- — re-use;
- — materials recycling;
- — energy recovery;
- — landfill/incineration (without energy recovery).

Pursuant to this strategy, the European Commission is developing a series of directives designed to promote recycling and re-use of products. Directive 94/62 98 is concerned with packaging and packaging waste; others in preparation relate to tyres and chlorinated solvents. Directives 91/157 and 93/86 on batteries and accumulators containing dangerous substances have been implemented in the UK by the Batteries and Accumulators (Containing Dangerous Substances) Regulations 1994.[99] These are described in paragraphs 12–168 to 12–173, since they relate primarily to the marketing and use and the marking of such items when containing prescribed amounts of heavy metals. The need for a packaging directive had become particularly urgent in view of the unfavourable impact on the relatively new recycling industries in many of the States of massive exports of waste from Germany, resulting from the German packaging legislation.[1] While recycling of certain particular hazardous materials can properly be regulated by legislation, achievement of

---

[96] Dir. 75/442, Art.3(1)(b); see also Council Resolution of May 7, 1990, [1990] O.J. C122, paras. 6 and 8.
[97] para. 2.3.
[98] [1994] O.J. L365. The Directive must be implemented by June 30, 1996.
[99] S.I. 1994 No. 232.
[1] The German legislation basically requires all suppliers (including importers from *e.g.* the UK) of packaged goods to take back their packaging free of charge. However if they contribute to the nationwide packaging recovery system "Duales System Deutschland", they may put a green spot on their packaging, which is then permitted to be collected in specially designated containers; the requirement to receive back the packaging then does not apply. Since incineration of the packaging is not permitted and the market for its re-use or recycling is far smaller than the quantities recovered in this way, there is a strong incentive to get rid of the recovered packaging by exporting it from Germany.

high rates of waste recovery are likely to be primarily dependent on cultural attitudes, reinforced to some degree by financial incentives. The United Kingdom's performance on recycling is noticeably lower than that of a number of other European countries; however the government has set a target of recycling half of all recyclable household waste by the end of the century, this being estimated to be around 25 per cent of all household waste.[2] Under Directive 94/62, by June 30, 2001, between 50 per cent and 65 per cent of all packaging waste must be recovered (including its use as a source of energy), and between 25 per cent and 45 per cent of all such waste must be recycled (with a minimum of 15 per cent for each packaging material).

Various provisions are included in Part II of the E.P.A. relating to the recycling of waste. In drawing up waste disposal plans, it is a duty of the waste regulation authorities to have regard to the desirability, where reasonably practicable, of giving priority to recycling waste.[3] The authorities are subject to a duty in preparing their waste disposal plans to consider, in consultation with the waste collection authorities in its area and any other persons what arrangements can reasonably be expected to be made for recycling waste, and what provisions should be included in the plan for that purpose.[4] Similarly, it is the duty of each waste collection authority as respects household and commercial waste arising in its area to prepare a waste recycling plan setting out arrangements made and proposed to be made both by the authority and any other persons for dealing with such waste by separating, baling or otherwise packaging it for the purpose of recycling.[5] There have been a considerable number of local initiatives aimed at encouraging recycling of household waste, trials mainly being directed to ascertaining the relevant costs and efficiencies of sorting recyclable matter from household waste at household level, and so collecting several streams of separated waste, and separating the recyclable material subsequently. All these schemes, however, have until recently suffered from the difficulty that there is no direct financial incentive on householders to operate in maximizing the recycling of waste, since charges for refuse collection are not based (as they are for commercial and industrial waste) on the amount of refuse collected.

11–225

The government has nevertheless introduced a financial incentive to recycle waste in the form of "recycling credits". These credits are

11–226

---

[2] A plan prepared by the Producer Responsibility Group (consisting of 28 major companies) at the request of the government, and welcomed by it, was issued in February 1994. It would aim to recover 58 per cent of Britain's packaging waste by the year 2000.

[3] s.50(4).

[4] s.50(7).

[5] s.49(1).

intended to reflect the savings made by waste disposal authorities in so far as waste that is recycled no longer requires to be disposed of at a cost to the disposal authority. When a waste disposal authority itself organises recycling of waste, there will be less waste for a waste collection authority to collect, with a consequent saving in its costs. Provisions for payment to the relevant authority organising recycling facilities of the savings made by the other authority or authorities are contained in section 52 of the E.P.A., and the Environmental Protection (Waste Recycling Payments) Regulations 1992[6] as amended by the Environmental Protection (Waste Recycling Payments) (Amendment) Regulations 1994.[7] These provisions are supplemented by Circular 4/92 (WO 10/92). They now provide for recycling credits to be calculated as the average cost per tonne of disposing of similar waste using the disposal authority's most expensive disposal method for waste collected in the relevant area.[8] These costs should include a proper allocation of overheads, for example the costs associated with developing a landfill site in the first place and subsequently closing it, and the after care costs. Higher credits may be paid if they can be justified on the basis of actual net savings of expenditure.

11–227   As calculation of the costs per tonne is far from straightforward, the 1992 Regulations set out figures that represent reasonable estimates of the figures for authorities in different areas.[9] The authorities are entitled under the Regulations to make use of these figures rather than to calculate their own, if there is insufficient information to let them do this, or if it can only be obtained at exorbitant cost.

11–228   Payments of recycling credits are not exclusively to the relevant waste disposal or waste collection authority; they may also be made to other organisations that themselves organise recycling, and there is power (as opposed to a duty) to do this under sections 52(3) and 52(4). Circular 4/92 says that the Secretary of State takes the view that there should be a presumption in favour of paying such credits unless there are good reasons for not doing so.[10]

---

[6] S.I. 1992 No. 462.

[7] S.I. 1994 No. 522.

[8] As an interim measure, prior to the 1994 Amendment Regs., payments were initially one half of the average cost.

[9] Ranging from £34.52 per tonne for an authority including an inner London borough to £16.72 per tonne for an authority outside all metropolitan districts, London, Greater Manchester and Merseyside (reduced to £9.42 per tonne if the authority incurs no transport costs in disposing of similar waste).

[10] para. 14.

A central issue, which is not easily resolved, is what in fact **11–229** constitutes recycling for the purposes of the E.P.A. An attempt at a definition appears in section 29(6), which reads as follows:

"(6) The disposal of waste includes its disposal by way of deposit in or on land and, subject to sub-section (7) below, waste is 'treated' when it is subjected to any process, including making it re-usable or reclaiming substances from it and 'recycle" (and cognate expressions) shall be construed accordingly".

This wording indicates that "recycle" means "making waste re-usable or reclaiming substances from it" — it must be presumed that it is not intended to be equated with treating waste, since that would not only be redundant but would cover, for example, conventional incineration without any attempt to recover anything, which would be a most perverse interpretation. If recycle means making waste re-usable or reclaiming substances from it, as opposed to including those activities, then the question arises as to whether incinerating waste in order to recover energy from it amounts to recycling. This is a critical issue, since the viability of a number of waste from energy schemes that have been promoted depends on their receiving recycling credits under section 52. Such energy from waste schemes almost invariably are used to generate electricity; they may also on occasion convert waste heat into hot water to provide heat to premises in the area.

Waste Management Paper No. 28 uses recycling to mean "the **11–230** collection and separation of materials from waste and subsequent processing to produce marketable products." Marketable products are then listed, namely materials such as paper and wood; finished products partly or totally consisting of recycled materials, fuel — solid, liquid or gaseous; energy — heat or electricity; and compost. All of these products, with the exception of "energy — heat or electricity" fall within the definition of "substance" in section 29(11), namely "any natural or artificial substance, whether in solid or liquid form or in the form of a gas or vapour". It would be stretching the language to breaking point, if not beyond, to regard producing heat and energy from waste as reclaiming a substance from it.[11] Using waste as a fuel to generate energy is certainly, in appropriate cases, a desirable recovery operation.[12] However, sections 55 and 56 appear to make a clear

---

[11] Mass may be equated with energy in nuclear physics, but this can hardly be what Parliament had in mind in legislating for recycling.

[12] It is listed as such in Annex IIB to Directive 75/442, at item R9; in that context also, where "recycling" is used it clearly is not intended to extend to incineration.

distinction between the recycling of waste, and the use of waste for the purpose of producing from it heat or electricity.[13]

11-231   Comparison of paragraphs (a) and (b) of section 55(2), and similarly of sub-paragraphs (i) and (ii) of section 56(1)(a) both appear to be making a clear contrast between the recycling of waste and its use for the purpose of producing heat or electricity or both from it. It may also be noted that section 55(2)(d) and section 56(1)(c) both use the broader expression "anything produced from such waste", which clearly could include heat and electricity, and do not refer to "reclaiming substances from it" (the expression used in the definition section 29(6)). Further, where a power is given to a waste collection authority to acquire waste with a view to recycling it, one must question whether it was intended that a collection authority, as opposed to a disposal authority, should be in the business of producing heat or electricity from waste. While it is arguable that this could be within a

---

[13] These sections read:

Powers for recycling waste.

55 (1) This section has effect for conferring on waste disposal authorities and waste collection authorities powers for the purposes of recycling waste.
    (2) A waste disposal authority may—
        (a) make arrangements with waste disposal contractors for them to recycle waste as respects which the authority has duties under section 51(1) above or agrees with another person for its disposal or treatment;
        (b) make arrangements with waste disposal contractors for them to use waste for the purpose of producing from it heat or electricity or both;
        (c) buy or otherwise acquire waste with a view to its being recycled;
        (d) use, sell or otherwise dispose of waste as respects which the authority has duties under section 51(1) above or anything produced from such waste.
    (3) A waste collection authority may—
        (a) buy or otherwise acquire waste with a view to recycling it;
        (b) use, or dispose of by way of sale or otherwise to another person, waste belonging to the authority or anything produced from such waste.
    (4) This section shall not apply to Scotland.

Powers for recycling waste: Scotland.

56 (1) Without prejudice to the powers of waste disposal authorities apart from this section, a waste disposal authority may—
        (a) do such things as the authority considers appropriate for the purpose of—
            (i) enabling waste belonging to the authority, or belonging to another person who requests the authority to deal with it under this section, to be recycled; or
            (ii) enabling waste to be used for the purpose of producing from it heat or electricity or both;
        (b) buy or otherwise acquire waste with a view to its being recycled;
        (c) use, sell or otherwise dispose of waste belonging to the authority or anything produced from such waste.
    (2) This section applies to Scotland only.

collection authority's powers, since it is always open to a waste disposal authority to exercise its right under section 48(4) to object to any recycling of waste by a waste collection authority, it is notable that if indeed a waste collection authority is entitled to use waste for the purpose of producing heat or electricity from it in the course of "recycling" it, it is surprising that it must do so itself, and is not empowered to make arrangements with waste disposal contractors to do so. The inference is thus strong that "recycling" in section 55(3)(a) is intended to be limited to relatively modest operations such as the collection and baling of specific waste streams, and the separation of materials from mixed waste streams.

Against this, it may be said that the reference to the meaning of **11–232** "recycle" in section 29(6) is intended merely to include making waste re-usable or reclaiming substances from it, rather than being limited to those activities. However that is certainly not the most natural way to read the language of that section. The head notes of sections 55 and 56 suggest that they are wholly concerned with recycling, though it is not normally permissible to refer to them on matters of interpretation.[14] The strongest argument for a wide construction is the arguably otherwise redundant section 55(1), though this is in no way inconsistent with giving further powers for the generation of heat or electricity. Moreover no corresponding provision appears in section 56, and there cannot have been any intention for "recycling" to have a different meaning in Scotland.

Article 3(1)(b) of Directive 75/442 as amended, in listing activities **11–233** Member States should encourage, sets out separately

(i) the recovery of waste by means of recycling, re-use or reclamation or any other process with a view to extracting secondary raw materials, or

(ii) the use of waste as a source of energy.

While it would be inappropriate to submit the language of EC legislation to the meticulous analysis sometimes necessary for UK legislation, the very clear contrast between "recycling, re-use or reclamation" on the one hand, and "the use of waste as a source of energy" on the other, is further support for the view that "recycling" is not normally understood to include substantially total destruction by incineration, even though this may be accompanied by harnessing of the energy produced.

---

[14] This rule may have been affected by the decision of the House of Lords in *Pepper (Inspector of Taxes) v. Hart* ([1992] 3 W.L.R. 1032) on statements made in promoting legislation.

The Duty of Care

11–234   In 1985, the Royal Commission on Environmental Pollution issued its 11th Report "Managing Waste; the Duty of Care".[15] This proposed a powerful reinforcement of the then current regulatory regime in the following terms:

> "The first task is for society to identify where the responsibility lies for ensuring that wastes are properly handled and disposed of. In our judgement this must rest with the individual or organisation who produces the waste. The producer incurs a *duty of care* which is owed to society, and we would like to see this duty reflected in public attitudes and enshrined in legislation and codes of practice."[16]

This proposal was reviewed by the House of Commons Environment Committee, and in its report "Toxic Waste"[17] it welcomed in principle the concept of a duty of care for waste producers, handlers and disposers, and continued:

> "We agree with both the Royal Commission on Environmental Pollution and the DoE that waste should be accounted for from the point of production to the point of disposal and subject to adequate evaluation of the disposal route. We would prefer that the liability be made strict liability and the waste producers should be responsible for their wastes from 'cradle to grave'. This more than anything else would ensure that producers consign their wastes to proper persons who in turn would be contractually responsible to them. It is slackness in the choosing of contractors or leaving the choice to brokers which have given rise to most of the abuses which have been reported to us".[18]

11–235   The duty was made law by section 34 of the E.P.A., subsection (1) of which reads as follows:

> 34   (1)   Subject to subsection (2) below,[19] it shall be the duty of any person who imports, produces, carries, keeps, treats or disposes of controlled waste or, as a broker, has control of such waste, to take all such measures applicable to him in that capacity as are reasonable in the circumstances —

---

[15] Cmnd. 9675, 1985.
[16] para. 3.5.
[17] Session 1988–89, 2nd report.
[18] para. 201.
[19] Whereby the duty of care does not apply to an occupier of domestic property as respects the household waste produced on the property.

(a) to prevent any contravention by any other person of section 33 above;

(b) to prevent the escape of the waste from his control or that of any other person; and

(c) on the transfer of the waste, to secure—

    (i) that the transfer is only to an authorised person or to a person for authorised transport purposes; and

    (ii) that there is transferred such a written description of the waste as will enable other persons to avoid a contravention of that section and to comply with the duty under this subsection as respects the escape of waste.

This duty thus applies to virtually everyone who has any involvement in the production, movement, disposal, or any other handling of waste, as well as waste brokers.

For the purposes of the third limb of the duty, item (c), an "authorised person" consists essentially of a waste collection authority; the holder of a waste management licence under the E.P.A. or of a waste disposal licence under C.O.P.A., as the case may be; any person registered as a carrier of controlled waste under the Control of Pollution (Amendment) Act 1989 (see paragraphs 11–266 to 11–282); and a waste disposal authority in Scotland. Certain people exempt from registration as carriers may also be authorised persons, namely charities and voluntary organisations, and British Rail when carrying waste by rail.[20]

11–236

If transfer of waste is made to anyone other than an authorised person, this may only be done for "authorised transport purposes". These consist of:

11–237

(a) the transport of controlled waste within the same premises between different places in those premises;

(b) the transport to a place in Great Britain of controlled waste that has been imported from elsewhere and has not been landed in Great Britain until it arrives at that place; and

(c) the transport by air or sea of controlled waste being exported from a place in Great Britain to elsewhere.

What is meant by "the same premises" in item (a) is not defined and not clear. It is a common situation that parts of a single building, or a collection of buildings or building units under common control, are leased to different tenants, and under a management agreement the

---

[20] Ship operators where waste is to be disposed of under licence at sea are also exempt from registration as waste carriers, but no new licences to dump at sea will now be available under the Food and Environment Protection Act 1985.

landlord or a management company will provide waste collection services for the various occupants, taking waste to a central disposal point. If these are all the same premises there is no problem, but if they are not, or if there is uncertainty, contract cleaners handling the individual parcels of waste will or may need to be registered carriers of waste, and the individual occupiers will need to ensure this. The same problem can arise on a large industrial site such as a major petrochemical plant, occupied by a variety of companies (possibly all part of a group, but that would be of no relevance), or a large hospital site with parts let off to different NHS Trusts.

11–238   In practice, the meaning of "premises" generally varies with its context.[21] Clearly anything that is, or is capable of being, the subject of a separate lease may constitute premises,[22] though common sense would suggest that a distinction could be drawn between a property some minor part of which has been temporarily let or sub-let by the occupier of the larger part, and a building designed (and in fact used) for multiple occupation. In a case under the Copyright Act 1956, however, "premises" was held for the purposes of that Act to extend over the whole of a camp site and its several detached chalets and amenity centre.[23]

11–239   The duty is supplemented by a code of practice issued under section 34(7) that provides practical guidance on how to discharge it. This code is admissible in evidence, and if relevant to any question as to breach of the duty, it is to be taken into account by the court determining that question.[24] Additionally, the Environmental Protection (Duty of Care) Regulations 1991[25] amplify the duty under section 34(1)(c) by specifying details of the records that are to be made and kept on the transfer of any controlled waste. Guidance to local authorities on the duty of care is contained in a joint Circular from the DoE, the Scottish Office and the Welsh Office (DoE 19/91; SO 25/91; WO 63/91).

11–240   The duty requires anyone subject to it to comply with all its
—11–249 elements, but the obligation is for the person concerned to take all such measures applicable to him, in whatever capacity brings him within the duty, whether producer, carrier, disposer or otherwise, as are *reasonable in the circumstances*. Acts required for compliance with the duty must be taken not only by a person who is passing on waste, but just as much by anyone receiving it. Since the duties under item (c)

---

[21] *Maunsell v. Olins*, [1975] 1 All E.R. 16 at 19, H.L., *per* Viscount Dilhorne.
[22] The word derives from the habendum of leases.
[23] *Phonographic Performance Ltd. v. Pontin's Ltd.*, [1967] 3 All E.R. 736.
[24] s.34(10).
[25] S.I. 1991 No. 2839.

only arise on the *transfer* of the waste, they do not apply where a person transports waste on his own account.

The first limb of the duty is extremely wide in requiring all **11–250** reasonable steps to be taken to prevent any contravention by any other person of section 33. To comply with the duty it is essential for all concerned to know just what waste there is that they are responsible for, and what it consists of. It is only with this knowledge that they can properly account for all their waste at any time, with information on how much may have been taken away and where to, and how much has been added to the waste and where from, so that the net balance accurately represents what is in fact on the ground. Secondly, only by knowing exactly what the waste consists of can appropriate steps be taken to ensure suitable security and a proper choice of appropriate disposal routes, and a transfer made safely to someone else with confidence that they will be able to handle it properly. Additionally, knowledge of the composition of the waste is essential to ensure that it is appropriately contained, and will continue to be appropriately contained at all times and under all foreseeable conditions that the waste may be subject to. In this connection, consideration must be given to possible mishandling of the waste by outsiders, whether by way of vandalism, children playing, and people (and for that matter animals) scavenging the waste. Among the obligations that the first limb of the duty gives rise to is to take steps to prevent any disposal of the waste by third parties in a manner likely to cause pollution of the environment or harm to human health, contrary to section 33(1)(c). Since the prohibitions of section 33(1) are strict liability offences, the question of fault does not arise. The fact that the third party may himself have a defence under section 33(7) does not in itself avoid a contravention of section 33(1) in the first place.[26]

The second limb of the duty requires the waste to be prevented from **11–251** escaping. Those under the duty must consequently attempt to foresee possible circumstances where this might happen, for example, through exposure to the weather, being blown away during transport, accidents or deliberate damage, corrosion and wear of containers, and poor handling on transfer.[27] It would appear that any leaks or other losses, even of substances that were not waste before they were lost, would breach this limb of the duty if in fact they cannot be fully retrieved. If a leaked or otherwise escaped substance can no longer be put to good use by its owner, it has presumably become waste. If then it escapes further, to ground, water or air, it will no longer be under control and the duty of care will be breached.

---

[26] See also the discussion on this point at para. 11–208 in relation to ss.59(1) and (5).
[27] Including, for example, the deliberate venting of refrigerant to the atmosphere.

11–252   One of the main reasons for introducing the duty of care was the common practice of many people who wished to dispose of their waste of getting several quotes, and giving the waste to the person with the cheapest offer and asking no further questions. As a matter of law, having transferred the property in the waste, they were not liable, except where the waste was special waste (so needing the consignment note procedure described) or otherwise in extreme circumstances, for what subsequently might be done with the waste. The registration of waste carriers, coupled with the duty of care, goes some way to meet that problem in that, although the principal responsibility for the fate of any waste transferred to a carrier is, as previously, with the carrier exclusively, the duty of care requires the transferor to take all reasonable steps to ensure the carrier is competent and suitably authorised, and does in fact deliver the waste to a suitably authorised disposal site. Further, if it emerges that the carrier appears to have acted in some way inconsistent with what was expected of him, for example if he returns from a journey to a waste disposal site significantly sooner than might be supposed possible, the transferor may be put on notice that there has been a contravention of section 33(1). If so, he should not only be cautious as regards using the same carrier in future, but should alert the relevant waste regulation authority to the grounds for concern. Particular care is therefore required in choosing a waste carrier in the first place—each waste regulation authority has a public register of registered carriers—and also in ensuring that the carrier's registration is in force; for this purpose, the carrier is required to provide the registration certificate itself or a certified copy of it—a mere photocopy is not sufficient to meet the requirements of the Code. Similarly, when sending waste for disposal or treatment, it is essential for the person responsible to check that whoever is to receive it is appropriately licensed (except to the extent there may be a relevant exemption from the licensing requirements). The carrier, who is of course also subject to the duty, should likewise satisfy himself that the recipient of the waste is appropriately authorised to deal with it.

11–253   Where there are repeated movements of essentially similar waste between the same points of origin and destination, the Code accepts that constant checking on these details is not essential, though as a minimum the relevant licences, registrations or other necessary documentation should be inspected at least once a year.

11–254   Compliance with the final limb of the duty will to a large extent be achieved through compliance with the Environmental Protection (Duty of Care) Regulations 1991. These stipulate the details to be contained in a transfer note that must accompany any waste, which include a description of the capacity of each of the transferor and the transferee; where either of them falls within one of the categories of "authorised persons" set out in section 34(3) they must identify which of these they belong to. A suitable form of transfer note is contained in Annex C to the Code of Practice. Though it is not compulsory to use this particular form it is clearly desirable to use one that is the same or closely similar, so as to ensure compliance with the duty. Where special waste or landed ships' waste is transferred, the requisite consignment notes must be used. The Code of Practice[28] says that the information on these will include almost that needed for the purposes of complying with the duty of care other than details relating to authorised persons. These may be added to the consignment notes so avoiding creation of additional paperwork.

To enable subsequent audits to be made of waste transfers, and checks on specific transfers, at least the written description of the waste and the transfer note, or copies of them, signed by both the transferor and the transferee of any consignment of waste, must be kept by each of them, for a period of two years from the date of the transfer.[29] Anyone who is under a duty to keep any documents under this requirement, and who has been required by a waste regulation authority to produce one must furnish the authority with a copy of the document within such period (of not less than seven days) as may be specified. Any non-compliance with the duty of care itself or with any requirement made under these Regulations is liable to a fine of up to £5,000 on summary conviction, and to an unlimited fine on conviction on indictment. A helpful "Summary Checklist" is contained in the Code of Practice, which is reproduced at Table 11/IX.

11–255

TABLE 11/IX

11–256

Summary Checklist

This section draws together in one place a simple checklist of the main steps that are normally necessary to meet the duty of care. As with the Code as a whole, *this does not mean that completing the steps listed here is all that needs to be done under the duty of care.*
 	
(a) Is what you have waste? if yes,
(b) is it controlled waste? if yes,
(c) while you have it, protect and store it properly,
(d) write a proper description of the waste, covering:
    — any problems it poses;
      and, *as necessary to others who might deal with it later,* one or more of:

[28] para. D.12.
[29] reg. 3.

— the type of premises the waste comes from;
— what the waste is called;
— the process that produced the waste; and
— a full analysis;

(e) select someone else to take the waste; they must be one or more of the following and must *prove* that they are:
— a registered waste carrier;
— exempt from registration;
— a waste manager licensed to accept the waste;
— exempt from waste licensing;
— a waste collection authority; or
— a waste disposal authority operating within the terms of a resolution (Scotland only);

(f) pack the waste safely when transferring it;

(g) check the next person's credentials when transferring waste to them;

(h) complete and sign a transfer note;

(i) hand over the description and complete a transfer note when transferring the waste;

(j) keep a copy of the transfer note signed by the person the waste was given to, and a copy of the description, for two years;

(k) when *receiving* waste, check that the person who hands it over is one of those listed in (e), obtain a description from them, complete a transfer note and keep the documents for two years.

(l) Whether transferring *or* receiving waste, be alert for any evidence or suspicion that the waste you handle is being dealt with illegally at any stage, in case of doubt question the person involved and if not satisfied, alert the waste regulation authority.

11–257 Among the people to whom the duty of care applies are those who produce waste. There is no definition of "produce" in the Act, and the Code of Practice advises starting by deciding how waste has become waste, and that where this is as a result of some action by a person, that person will be the waste producer. The Code continues "Where no action is involved the waste producer will be the person holding the object or substance who takes the decision that it is waste." This may of course not be a single person: in the example of a vacuum cleaner with a burnt out motor given earlier, the holder may be the repair shop, while the decision not to go ahead with the repair may be given by the owner over the telephone. Waste may also be produced without any action or decision whatsoever, as where a faulty valve or pipe seal allows a liquid to escape in a way that involves its loss as a useful material.[30] In such a case the producer would most probably be the person in possession and control of the material immediately before it escaped and ran to waste.

---

[30] Instead of, for example, escaping into a holding container from which it can be retrieved and used.

The Code considers in particular the circumstances of construction or demolition, and who is the producer of waste in such cases.[31] In a construction project involving, for example, the demolition of old buildings prior to some new construction, there can be a hierarchy of people all of whom may contribute to the production of the demolition waste, including:

    11–258

— The developer, who decides to clear the old buildings off the site.
— The main contractor, who draws up a plan of work for the entire project.
— A demolition sub-contractor.
— A company hiring out a crane with a ball and chain.
— A casual labourer with a pick-axe.

In the Code and the Circular, the view is expressed that:

    11–259

"The producer of waste may be regarded as the person undertaking the works which give rise to that waste, not the person who issues instructions or lets contracts which give rise to waste. The client for works, although he may take decisions as a result of which something becomes waste, is not himself producing the waste created by the works. Where there are several contractors and sub-contractors on site, the producer of a particular waste is the particular contractor or sub-contractor who (or whose employees) takes an action which creates waste, or, who begins to treat something as if it were waste."[32]

It is not clear why the client for works, who takes decisions that result in waste, should not be a producer of waste, when someone is to be regarded as a producer of waste when he holds an object or substance and decides that it is waste.[33] This guidance is written on the assumption that there can only properly be a single producer for the purposes of the duty of care. However there does not appear to be any reason for necessarily restricting the scope of who is subject to the duty in this way. The Circular continues:

"Where a client or contractor makes arrangements for the carriage or disposal of waste, for example by letting a disposal sub-contract to a haulier for waste produced on site by a demolition sub-contractor, then that client or contractor will be acting as a broker

---

[31] In para. B.3. The same considerations are dealt with in Circular 19/91 slightly more fully, at para. 17.
[32] Circular para. 17.
[33] Code para. B.2; Circular para. 16.

in respect of the transfer between the two sub-contractors; in such a case all three parties will be under the duty. In practice it is likely that every contractor involved on a site will either be producing or carrying away some waste and will be subject to the duty as producer or carrier and therefore liable to account for the measures they have taken to comply with the duty in respect of that waste."

This statement is unsatisfactory in its broad reference to a client or contractor acting as a broker, and is hardly consistent with paragraph 8.5 of Circular 11/94 relating to the registration of waste brokers which, correctly, regards main contractors, architects and civil engineers who arrange for disposal of waste to be doing so on their own behalf, if they are holders of the waste (and so do not need to register as brokers). As set out in the following paragraphs, a broker of waste is someone who does not handle waste on his own account, but on behalf of third parties. A client or contractor who becomes the holder of waste produced on site by one sub-contractor and arranges for it to be removed by another, which would be a typical situation, is not acting on behalf of third parties but for himself, and hence is not a broker. Nevertheless, the precise classification of the various parties is not critical for most purposes of the duty, but transfer notes must say whether or not the transferor is a producer, and it is in any event important for each to be aware whether or not they are subject to the duty of care at all. It is suggested that most if not all of them are, most probably as a producer.

Brokers of Controlled Waste

11–260   There is no definition of "broker" in the E.P.A., or in the Waste Management Licensing Regulations 1994, which require the registration of brokers;[34] the meaning of the term is to be taken from Directive 75/442, Article 12 of which requires brokers to be registered if not otherwise required to be licensed, in the following terms:

> "Article 12
> Establishments or undertakings which collect or transport waste on a professional basis or which arrange for the disposal or recovery of waste on behalf of others (dealers or brokers), where not subject to authorisation shall be registered with the competent authorities."

[34] For the purposes of this section "broker" and "dealer" are synonymous, and "broker" is used exclusively.

A consultation paper issued by the DoE on the implementation of this Article 12 listed three different categories of people commonly regarded as brokers and dealers:

(i) Companies which buy and sell scrap metal and other recoverables — or which arrange such deals for a commission (often referred to as traders or dealers);

(ii) Companies which arrange for the disposal of waste to an appropriate facility (may be referred to as brokers or environmental consultants);

(iii) Companies whose main business is either waste operator or carrier, but which may make alternative disposal arrangements for waste which they are unable to accept at their own sites.

The English language version of Article 12 of the Directive is unclear **11–261** as to whether "on behalf of others" qualifies only "arrange for the disposal or recovery of waste" or also the collection or transport of waste on a professional basis. However, reference to other language versions establishes that the former reading is correct.[35] Consequently, only category (ii) of the three listed in the DoE consultation paper mentioned are properly brokers in this sense; though a waste operator making alternative disposal arrangements for waste that it does not itself hold will also then be acting as a broker. A person buying and selling scrap metal will not on that account alone be a broker as the term is used in Article 12. The principal issue in every case is that the person should not himself hold the waste on his own account; there must also be an arrangement for waste disposal or recovery — mere buying and selling does not amount to this.

The Article 12 requirement for registration of brokers is given effect **11–262** by regulation 20(1) of the 1994 Licensing Regulations whereby it is an offence for an establishment or undertaking to arrange (as dealer or broker) for the disposal or recovery of waste on behalf of another after December 31, 1994, unless it is registered. A transitional exemption allows a person who has duly applied for registration as a broker before January 1, 1995 to act as such while the application remains pending.[36] The requirement is declared inapplicable to those who

---

[35] The German text leaves no room for doubt on this point: "Die Anlagen oder Unternehmen, die Gewerbemäßig Abfälle einsammeln oder befördern oder *die für die Beseitigung oder Verwertung von Abfällen für andere sorgen* (Händler oder Makler), müssen bei den zuständigen Behörden gemeldet sein, sofern sie keine Genehmigung haben." The Italian text supports this, having a comma following the Italian words for "on a professional basis". The French text is similar in structure and punctuation to the English.

[36] reg. 20(4)(d).

643

themselves[37] undertake the disposal or recovery under such an arrangement, if they are licensed for this purpose, whether under Part III of the E.P.A. or under any of E.P.A., Part I, the W.R.A., C.O.P.A. Part III and F.E.P.A., or if recovery of the waste is covered by a relevant exemption under the 1994 Licensing Regulations or the Deposits in the Sea (Exemptions) Order 1985.[38]

11–263   Also exempted from registration under regulation 20(1) are charities, certain voluntary organisations[39] and waste collection, disposal and regulation authorities.[40] These bodies still fall within the Article 12 requirement nevertheless, and so are made subject to the simpler registration obligation of Schedule 4, paragraph 12(2), to the 1994 Licensing Regulations.[41] The procedure for this, and applicable enforcement provisions, are laid down in the remainder of paragraph 12. In the case of these bodies registration is automatic, and not subject to any pre-conditions or possibility of revocation.

11–264   Registration under regulation 20(1) is governed by Schedule 5 to the 1994 Licensing Regulations. The applicable rules, including those relating to refusal to register in the event of conviction of a prescribed offence, duration of registration, revocation and appeals, are in all material respects the same as those governing the registration of carriers of waste, see paragraph 11–274 to 11–282. Combined applications for registration as both broker and carrier may be made, and also for renewal of such registrations.[42] The forms for an initial application and to renew a registration are set out in Parts II and III respectively of Schedule 5. Detailed guidance is contained in Annex 8 of Circular 11/94.

11–265   All establishments and undertakings which act as brokers of controlled waste must be inspected periodically by the relevant waste regulation authority.[43] The authority has powers to appoint inspectors, to enter premises and to obtain information.[44] Breach of the prohibition of regulation 20(1) is an offence punishable on summary conviction by a fine of up to £5000. Directors and other similar officers of a company may be liable for breach by it in accordance with section 157 of the E.P.A., as may its members.[45]

---

[37] In reg. 20(2).
[38] S.I. 1985 No. 1699.
[39] As defined in s.48(1) of the Local Government Act 1985 or s.83(2D) of the Local Government (Scotland) Act 1973.
[40] reg. 20(4).
[41] Unless they hold an applicable permit under Parts I to II of the E.P.A. (or a resolution under s.54), under F.E.P.A., Part II; W.R.A., Part III or C.O.P.A., Part II.
[42] Sched. 5, paras. 3(8), 3(9).
[43] Sched. 4, para. 13(1).
[44] reg. 20(8).
[45] reg. 20(6).

Carriers of Controlled Waste

The fly tipping of waste caused such concern that (as referred to in **11–266** paragraph 11–005) a private member's bill was introduced in Parliament to deal with the problems it represented. This was supported, subject to some fairly substantial amendments, by the Government, and led to the Control of Pollution (Amendment) Act 1989, ahead of the main reforms of environmental legislation brought about by the E.P.A. the next year. In practice nevertheless it forms an important part of the waste legislation of Part II of the E.P.A., and its substantive provisions were brought into effect on April 1, 1992, together with the duty of care. The 1989 Act was itself amended by Schedule 15 to the E.P.A., paragraph 31; detailed provisions for its implementation are contained in the Controlled Waste (Registration of Carriers and Seizure of Vehicles) Regulations 1991[46] ("the 1991 Regulations").

The 1989 Act has two principal objectives: to require registration of **11–267** all those in the business of carrying waste (with certain limited exceptions), and to provide for the seizure of vehicles used for the illegal disposal of waste. These objectives are not therefore in themselves intended to control the carriage or disposal of waste directly, but to enable the regulatory authorities to establish who is engaged in these activities, so that other controls can be exercised and enforced as appropriate.

The registration of carriers is made mandatory by section 1(1) of the **11–268** 1989 Act, which reads:

"Subject to the following provisions of this section, it shall be an offence for any person who is not a registered carrier of controlled waste, in the course of any business of his or otherwise with a view to profit, to transport any controlled waste to or from any place in Great Britain."

This requirement does not however apply to:

(a) the transport of controlled waste within the same premises between different places in those premises;

(b) the transport to a place in Great Britain of controlled waste imported into it from elsewhere that is not landed in Great Britain until it arrives at that place;

(c) the transport by air or sea of controlled waste from a place in Great Britain to elsewhere outside it.[47]

---

[46] S.I. 1991 No. 1624; amended by reg. 23 of the 1994 Licensing Regs., and by reg. 19 of the Transfrontier Shipment of Waste Regulations 1994, S.I. 1994 No. 1137.

[47] s.1(2).

Northern Ireland is thus treated as a separate territory for these purposes from England, Wales and Scotland.

11–269 Various organisations and other persons are exempted from the statutory requirement to register by regulation 2(1) of the 1991 Regulations,[48] including waste collection, waste disposal and waste regulation authorities, charities and certain voluntary organisations and, in particular, the producer of the relevant controlled waste, except where it is building or demolition waste.[49] As required by Article 12, the waste collection, disposal and regulation authorities, charities and voluntary organisations must still be registered,[50] and they are accordingly subject to the simplified and unconditional procedure of Schedule 4, paragraph 12, referred to in paragraph 11–263.[51]

11–270 It is however a defence to any offence charged under s.1(1)

(a) that the waste was transported in an emergency of which notice was given as soon as practicable thereafter to the relevant waste regulation authority; or

(b) that the person charged neither knew nor had reasonable grounds for suspecting that what was being transported was controlled waste, and he took all such steps as it was reasonable to take for ascertaining whether it was such waste; or

(c) that the person charged acted under instructions from his employer.[52]

"Emergency" for these purposes means any circumstances in which, in order to avoid, remove or reduce any serious danger to the public or serious risk of damage to the environment, it is necessary for the waste to be transported from one place to another without the use of a registered carrier.

11–271 A person guilty of an offence under these provisions is liable on summary conviction to a fine not exceeding £5,000. A conviction under section 1 of the 1989 Act of the holder of a goods vehicle operator's licence, or of the holder's servant or agent, may also lead to the

---

[48] Made under s.1(3).
[49] "Building or demolition waste" means waste arising from works of construction or demolition, including waste arising from work preparatory thereto (reg. 2(2)); "construction" means "improvement, repair or alteration" (Controlled Waste Regulations 1992, Reg. 10(1).
[50] Unless they hold an applicable permit under Parts I or II of the E.P.A. (or a resolution under s. 54), under F.E.P.A., Part II; W.R.A., Part III or C.O.P.A., Part II.
[51] Sched. 4, para. 12(1).
[52] s.1(4).

revocation or suspension of the licence, by virtue of section 69(4)(ffff)(iii) of the Transport Act 1968.[53]

In *Hallett Silberman Limited v. Cheshire County Council*,[54] it was held **11–272** that a road haulage company could properly be regarded as the "user" of a vehicle even though it was being driven by a self-employed driver who provided the tractor unit used to tow a trailer. That case was concerned with an offence under section 42(1)(b) of the Road Traffic Act 1988, whereby it is an offence to use on a road a motor vehicle or trailer which does not comply with any regulations made under section 41 of that Act or who causes or permits a vehicle to be so used. While the construction appropriate to one statute cannot of course automatically be applied to another dealing with quite separate subject matter, the reasoning in *Hallett Silberman* indicates that where a person is responsible for selecting the waste to be loaded on a lorry and determining the route to be taken to its destination, that person is transporting the waste, and should therefore be registered as a carrier, even though the vehicle may be driven by a self-employed driver and be owned by the driver or some other third party. It does not however follow that the self-employed driver in such circumstances is not also transporting waste; he must himself also be registered as a carrier.

The 1991 Regulations lay down the procedure for applying for **11–273** registration as a carrier and for renewing existing registrations. Except where a registration has been voluntarily terminated or revoked, or where an appeal against revocation is pending, registration lasts for a period of three years. Applications for renewal may be made at any time within the final six months of the three year period. Applications for renewal are treated on the same basis as initial applications for registration.

Applications for registration are made to the waste regulation **11–274** authority for the area in which the applicant has or proposes to have his principal place of business in Great Britain (if there is no principal place of business in Great Britain, then application may be made to any regulation authority).[55] An application on behalf of a partnership must be made by all the partners or prospective partners;[56] if any of the partners ceases to be registered, or if any person who is not registered becomes a partner, the registration automatically ceases to have effect.[57] An application to register a person about to join a partnership that is already registered may be made under regulation 4(5). Changes of circumstances affecting information in a register entry relating to

[53] Inserted by E.P.A., Sched. 15, para. 10(2)(b).
[54] [1993] R.T.R. 32; *The Times*, June 9, 1992.
[55] reg. 4(1).
[56] reg. 4(4).
[57] reg. 11(6).

any person, including therefore any resignation or appointment of partners, must be notified under regulation 8.

11–275   An application for registration must be made on a form that is essentially the same as that set out in Part I of Schedule 2 to the 1991 Regulations; an application for renewal is made on a form essentially the same as that set out in Part II of that Schedule 2. Copies are available free from the waste regulation authorities. Fees for applications are set out in the 1991 Regulations and are £95 for an initial application, £65 for a renewal application and £25 for an application by a registered broker for registration as a carrier also.

11–276   Except where there has been a failure to comply with the formal requirements of the application procedure, or the appropriate fee has not been paid, a regulation authority may only refuse to register an applicant if (i) he or another relevant person has been convicted of a prescribed offence and (ii) in the opinion of the authority it is undesirable for the applicant to be authorised to transport controlled waste.[58] Accordingly, even where there has been a conviction of a relevant offence, the authority must be of the opinion, arrived at on reasonable grounds, that it is undesirable for the applicant to remain on the register and therefore authorised to transport controlled waste. For individuals the Rehabilitation of Offenders Act 1974 will result in conviction being "spent" after a prescribed period; bodies corporate have no corresponding relief, though under official guidance waste regulation authorities should consider in their case whether conviction of the same offence would have been spent had it been committed by an individual.

11–277   The "prescribed offences" are offences under the following legislation:

TABLE 11/X

Prescribed Offences: Relevant Enactments
Section 22 of the Public Health (Scotland) Act 1897 Section 95(1) of the Public Health Act 1936 Section 60 of the Transport Act 1968 Sections 3, 5(6), 16(4), 18(2), 31(1), 32(1), 34(5), 78, 92(6) and 93(3) of the Control of Pollution Act 1974 Section 2 of the Refuse Disposal (Amenity) Act 1978 The Control of Pollution (Special Waste) Regulations 1980 Section 9(1) of the Food and Environment Protection Act 1985 The Transfrontier Shipment of Hazardous Waste Regulations 1988

---

[58] reg. 5(1).

The Transfrontier Shipment of Waste Regulations 1994
The Merchant Shipping (Prevention of Pollution by Garbage)
    Regulations 1988
Sections 1, 5, 6(9) and 7(3) of the Control of Pollution (Amendment)
    Act 1989
Sections 107, 118(4) and 175(1) of the Water Act 1989
Sections 23(1), 33, 34(6), 44, 47(6), 57(5), 59(5), 63(2), 69(9), 70(4),
    71(3) and 80(4) of the Environmental Protection Act 1990

As will be seen these are all environmental provisions, with the sole   **11–278**
exception of section 60 of the Transport Act, whereby it is an offence to
use a goods vehicle on a road unless the operator is duly licensed.
There has been no amendment to the 1991 Regulations to include
offences under the consolidating 1991 water legislation, though under
the Interpretation Act 1978 where an Act repeals and re-enacts, with or
without modification, a previous enactment, then, unless the contrary
intention appears, any reference in any other enactment to the
enactment so repealed must be construed as a reference to the
provision re-enacted. The provisions in the 1991 legislation most
nearly corresponding to those of the Water Act 1989 that are listed
are:[59]

Water Act 1989	1991 Consolidating Acts	**11–279**
section 107	W.R.A., section 85	
section 118(4)	W.R.A., section 202	
section 175(1)	W.R.A., section 206 W.I.A., section 207	

Who is a "relevant person", whose conviction of a prescribed   **11–280**
offence is material for this purpose, is set out in Table 11/XI.[60] The Table
applies equally to the registration of waste brokers, and it will be seen
that these are the same relationships as apply when considering
whether someone is a fit and proper person to be granted a waste
management licence — see paragraphs 11–158, 11–159 and Table II/VII.

---

[59] The corresponding list of enactments in reg. 3 of the 1994 Licensing Regs. (for a "fit
    and proper person") refers to W.R.A., ss. 85, 202 and 206 only.
[60] 1989 Act, s. 3(5); 1994 Licensing Regs, Sched. 5, para 1(3).

TABLE 11/XI

Registration of Waste Carriers and Brokers	
Conviction of Relevant Persons	
Status of applicant/registered carrier or broker at time of offence	**Relevant person convicted**
Employer	Any employee
Member of partnership (carrying on *any* business)	Any partner or other person convicted of an offence committed in the course of the partnership's business
Director, manager, secretary or other similar officer of a body corporate	That body corporate
Body corporate	(1) Any director, manager, secretary or other similar officer of the body corporate and (2) any other body corporate of which any person within (1) was a director, manager, secretary or other similar officer at the time of commission of the offence.

An appeals procedure is provided for contesting any refusal to register a person as a carrier or to renew his registration, as the case may be, or any revocation of a registration.[61]

11–282   On registration, a certificate of registration is issued free of charge, as is a copy of the entry in the register. Since either the certificate or official copies of it must be produced to ensure compliance with the duty of care, additional copies are available on payment of reasonable charges; the regulation authority must ensure that these copies are numbered and marked to show that they are copies and have been provided by the authority under the regulation requiring them to do so.[62] Where a registration has ceased to have effect or an amended certificate is issued, the person registered must immediately return the original certificate of registration together with any copies that the authority may have issued.[63]

[61] s.4 and regs. 15–18.
[62] reg. 9.
[63] reg. 13.

Enforcement

All establishments and undertakings which collect or transport **11–283** controlled waste on a professional basis must be inspected periodic- ally by the relevant waste regulation authority.[64] The authority has powers to appoint inspectors, to enter premises and to obtain information.[65] Powers are also provided under section 5 of the 1989 Act to both duly authorised officers of a waste regulation authority and to any constable to check whether an offence under section 1(1) is being or has been committed, if it reasonably appears to any such person that this is so. In such a case, the officer or constable may stop any person appearing to be or to have been engaged in transporting controlled waste and require him to produce his authority or his employer's authority for transporting it. However only a constable in uniform may stop a vehicle on a road. The officer or constable may search any vehicle that appears to be being or to have been used for transporting controlled waste contrary to section 1(1), carry out tests on and take away samples for testing of anything found. Where a person is required under these provisions to produce authority for transporting controlled waste, and he does not do so forthwith, he must send it to the office of the waste regulation authority of the area in which he was stopped within seven days.[66] The authority to be produced is either the certificate of registration as a carrier of controlled waste, applicable to the person concerned or his employer, as the case may be, or official copies of the certificate provided by the waste regulation authority, or evidence that the person concerned is not required to be registered as a carrier of controlled waste.

It is an offence intentionally to obstruct an authorised officer of a **11–284** disposal authority or constable exercising their powers under section 5 or to fail without reasonable excuse to comply with any requirement that they may impose in exercise of those powers, the burden of proof being on a defendant charged with any such offence to show that there was a reasonable excuse.[67] It is however a defence to a charge of failing to comply with a requirement that may have been imposed, if it is shown that the waste in question was controlled waste and if the person charged did transport it to or from a place in Great Britain. No such defence is available however in relation to a charge of intentional obstruction.[68]

---

[64] 1994 Licensing Regs., Sched. 4, para 13(1).
[65] 1994 Licensing Regs., Sched. 4, para. 13(3).
[66] reg. 14(1).
[67] s.5(4).
[68] s.5(5).

11–285   Detailed provisions are contained in section 6 and regulations 19 to 25 for the seizure of vehicles where there are reasonable grounds for believing that they have been used for illegal waste disposal, and for the sale of such vehicles and for the application of the proceeds of sale. The purpose of these provisions is essentially to enable the authorities to trace any person involved in illegal waste disposal—the seizure of a vehicle believed to have been used for this purpose provides a means for tracing the person who owns or keeps it, either directly through official records, or through anyone responding to a notice in a newspaper placed under regulation 23, giving details of the vehicle seized and its contents and inviting claimants to the vehicle and/or its contents to establish their entitlement within 28 days.[69] In addition to the requirement that there be reasonable grounds for believing that a vehicle has been used for illegal waste disposal, the vehicle may only be seized under the powers provided by section 6 if proceedings for that illegal waste disposal have not yet been brought against any person and the waste regulation authority has been unable to find out[70] the name and address of any person who can to provide them with the name and address of who was using the vehicle at the time the offence was committed. Where all these preconditions are satisfied, a magistrates' warrant may be issued to a waste regulation authority for the seizure of the vehicle concerned. Either a duly authorised officer of the authority or a constable may, armed with the warrant, stop the vehicle and seize it and its contents. However only a constable in uniform may stop the vehicle on a road, and the officer of the regulation authority may not seize any property unless he is accompanied by a constable.[71] Any intentional obstruction of the officer of the authority or the constable in exercise of their powers under the warrant is an offence triable summarily, and subject to a fine of up to £5,000.

11–286   The 1989 Act contains the standard provisions whereby in the event of an offence by a body corporate, any director, manager, secretary or other similar officer of the body corporate, or any person purporting to act in any such capacity, will also be liable if he consented to or connived at the offence, or if it was committed through his negligence. Further, where the affairs of the body corporate are managed by its members, for example a parent company, the members will be liable if they consented to or connived at the offence, or if their negligence led to it. Where the commission of an offence is due to the act or the fault of

---

[69] The property may be disposed of earlier, if its condition requires this (reg. 23(1)(c)(ii)).
[70] By steps prescribed in reg. 20.
[71] s.6(2), (3).

some other person, that other person is also guilty of the same offence.[72]

The proceeds of sale of any property sold pursuant to these provisions are to be applied first to meeting expenses incurred by the authority in exercising their powers under section 6; any balance is to be applied in meeting any claim to the proceeds of sale made under these statutory provisions by someone who can show that he would have been entitled to the return of the property if it had not been sold. **11–287**

International and Other Shipments of Waste— EC Regulation No. 259/93

Controls over the transfrontier shipment of hazardous waste within the EC were first laid down by Directive 84/631[73] (which has been amended several times). This provided a procedure for uniform consignment notes to be used in connection with hazardous waste, allowing each country of transit and destination to be aware of and to control imports of such waste, though not to prohibit them merely because of the waste having originated outside its own territory. The aims of the Directive were not fully achieved, partly because many countries failed to implement it by the due date, or indeed for many years after that date, and, more particularly, because there was no uniform definition of what constitutes "hazardous waste". **11–288**

Additionally, as referred to in paragraph 11–012, there was a conflict of principle between the aim to avoid any restrictions on trade between Member States, so allowing wastes to find their way to wherever they might be disposed of most cheaply, and the objective (now spelled out in amended Directive 75/442) of having every Member State self-sufficient in waste disposal, which in turn tends to reinforce the pressures to prevent production of waste at source. This conflict came to a head in the "Wallonia" case[74] the effect of which was to allow non-hazardous waste to be refused entry into Belgium but to prohibit similar restrictions on hazardous waste. Political pressures were also significant, as difficulties in locating new waste disposal sites in Germany led to substantial outflows of German waste, both to other EC Member States and beyond, exacerbated by the recent German laws on packaging, that produced a flood of packaging waste **11–289**

[72] s.7(5)–(7).
[73] [1984] O.J. L326.
[74] Case C-2/90, *The Commission v. Belgium.*

being sent to Germany's neighbours at knock-down prices, simultaneously undermining the indigenous recycling industries and at least partially defeating the objectives of the German legislation.

11–290   Though it was originally expected that the issue of definition would be addressed by the Hazardous Waste Directive 91/689, in fact this Directive is not of direct relevance as a new regime has been adopted that uses a quite different approach borrowed from the Basel Convention on the Control of Transboundary Movements of Hazardous Wastes and their Disposal, described below. This new regime is given effect by Regulation 259/93, as amended by Decision 94/721,[75] the substantive requirements of which, relating to the shipment of waste, came into force on May 6, 1994.

11–291   Making the new rules the subject of a Regulation has avoided the other principal problem that the previous Directive 84/631 faced, namely substantial failure of implementation by several Member States. Since regulations are directly binding, they have the force of law without requiring any implementation by Member States in their national laws. Nevertheless, certain domestic administrative rules are essential, as set out in the Transfrontier Shipment of Waste Regulations 1994,[76] which apply to the entire United Kingdom.

11–292   One of the principal objectives of the Regulation is to enable the EC to ratify the Basel Convention, and the rules it lays down closely follow the Basel Convention procedures. However it goes further than the Basel Convention, and also than the previous Directive 84/631, in that it applies to all wastes and not merely hazardous wastes. The significance of this arises in its implementation of the principles of "proximity, priority for recovery and self-sufficiency at Community and national levels" which are laid down in the waste framework Directive 75/442. It thus follows the Wallonia judgment and relies on these principles to derogate from the general Rome Treaty rule that national boundaries should not cause any interruption in trade between Member States, and expressly permits Member States to prohibit imports of waste from other Member States in order to give effect to those principles. The only explicit exception to this derogation is in the case of hazardous waste which is produced in a Member State in such small quantities that it would be uneconomic for that State to provide specialised facilities for its proper disposal.

11–293   The Regulation follows the Basel Convention in dividing up wastes into three categories of Green, Amber and Red wastes, which are listed in Annexes II, III and IV respectively to the Regulation. The Red list wastes are the most hazardous, including, *e.g.* PCBs and PCTs,

---

[75] [1993] O.J. L30; [1994] O.J. L288.
[76] S.I. 1994 No. 1137.

asbestos and waste tarry residues, and the Green list wastes are the least hazardous. A waste that has not been assigned to any of these lists is to be regarded as a Red list waste and therefore subject to the most stringent controls. It is therefore clearly in the interests of anyone liable to produce or to have to handle a waste that has not been assigned to any one of the three categories, to have it assigned to either the Green or the Amber list if possible.

The Regulation treats separately shipments within Member States, shipment between Member States, exports of waste from the Community and imports of waste into the Community. So far as concerns shipment within any one Member State and not destined for elsewhere, the Regulation essentially only requires that Member States establish an appropriate system for the supervision and control of such shipments. This is a notable step back from earlier proposals which would have been far more intrusive on the controls operated by individual Member States. **11–294**

The provisions relating to all other types of shipment deal separately in each case with waste intended for disposal and waste intended for recovery.[77] "Recovery" is given the meaning assigned to it in Directive 75/442, *i.e.* the recovery operations listed in Annex II B—see Table 11/IV. **11–295**

The detailed procedures of the Regulation are complex, and must be referred to directly if any particular type of waste shipment is under consideration. Guidance on it and on the UK implementing Regulations is contained in a Joint Circular issued by the Department of the Environment (13/94), the Welsh Office (44/94), the Scottish Environment Department (21/94) and the Department of the Environment, Northern Ireland (WM 1/94). This section merely attempts to outline the Regulation's principal effects. It is most convenient to consider it by reference to the three different categories of waste: Green, Amber, and Red. **11–296**

Green List Wastes

The wastes in the Green list are substantially non-hazardous. Except where a Member State has reason to treat a Green list waste as hazardous, where it is destined for *recovery* only it falls largely outside the scope of the Regulation. The only controls on shipments of such waste for *recovery* between Member States are those in Article 11 requiring simple formalities to be contained in a consignment note accompanying the waste. **11–297**

---

[77] In making this distinction, the Regulation in so far as it applies to hazardous wastes, is in clear breach of the Basel Convention which has no corresponding provision.

11–298   Where Green list wastes are exported from the EC for *recovery*, the importing country must first consent to accept the waste, and it must only go to an authorised facility for the recovery operation. The Commission is responsible for establishing what control procedures other countries wish to have applied to such shipments. Commission Decision 94/575[77A] gives the responses of a variety of non-OECD countries. For exports to Macau, Poland and Thailand of these wastes for recovery (whether all such wastes, or only specified categories, varies from country to country), the procedure for Amber list wastes is to apply, while for exports to 11 other countries, mostly in Eastern Europe and South America, the procedure for Red list wastes must be adopted.

11–299   Green list wastes being sent between Member States for *disposal* require prior notification to the authority of the destination country, and no shipment may take place unless that authority's consent has been given. This consent may be refused on the basis of the principles, already mentioned, of proximity, priority for recovery, and self-sufficiency at Community and national level(s). Furthermore, the person responsible for notifying the shipment of waste must make a contract with the consignee for its disposal, and this must include

  (i)   an obligation on the part of the notifier to take the waste back if the shipment is not completed as planned, and
  (ii)   an obligation on the part of the consignee to provide a certificate that the waste has been disposed of in an environmentally sound manner.

The party shipping the waste is responsible for giving the necessary notification and must also inform the competent authority in the country of dispatch, as this authority may itself raise objections to the shipment e.g. on the ground that the waste should be dealt with locally.

11–300   Exports of Green list, and indeed all, wastes for *disposal* outside of the EC are prohibited, except where they are to EFTA countries which are also parties to the Basel Convention. Exports to these countries may also be banned where the destination country either prohibits such imports or where it has not given its written consent to any specific import in question or if the relevant authority in the country of dispatch has reason to believe that the waste will not be managed in accordance with environmentally sound methods in the destination country.

11–301   Imports of Green list and of all other wastes, into the EC for *recovery* are generally prohibited. However an exception is made in respect of

[77A] [1994] O.J. L220.

imports from OECD countries other than Japan, and also imports from certain other countries which have made arrangements either with the EC as a whole or with individual Member States, as set out in Article 21 of the Regulation.

Substantially the same rules apply to imports into the EC of waste for *disposal*, though in this case the exception is limited to EFTA countries that are parties to the Basel Convention and the further countries that have entered into agreements either with the Community or with Member States in accordance with provisions of the Basel Convention. Such other countries, however, are only treated as a valid exception to the general prohibition where they can show that they do not have, and cannot reasonably acquire, the necessary technical capacity and other facilities to dispose of the waste concerned themselves in an environmentally sound manner.   **11–302**

Amber List Wastes

Amber list wastes are broadly treated in the same way as Green list wastes. However where they are being shipped between Member States of the EC for *recovery*, there must be prior notification to the competent authorities in the destination countries, and whose consent is deemed to be given if they have not raised any objection within 30 days. The rules for exports from and imports to the Community are the same as for Green list wastes, indicated above.   **11–303**

Red List Wastes

Red list wastes are generally subject to the same procedures as the Amber list wastes. However where they are being shipped between Member States of the EC for *recovery*, the deemed consent procedure if the destination authority has failed to respond within 30 days does not apply, and express written consent is needed.   **11–304**

Non-OECD Countries

One of the main concerns of those drawing up the Basel Convention, and even more so of the European Parliament, has been that wastes should not go to third world countries that have no proper facilities for dealing with them. Accordingly Article 18 of the Regulation expressly prohibits all exports of wastes to the so-called ACP states, *i.e.* the African, Caribbean and Pacific states who are party to the Lomé Convention. (This prohibition does not apply to Green list wastes for recovery, which are outside most of the controls of the   **11–305**

657

Regulation). At a meeting of the parties to the Basel Convention in March 1994 it was agreed to prohibit immediately all transboundary movements from OECD countries to non-OECD countries of hazardous wastes intended for disposal, and to phase out and to prohibit from December 31, 1997 all such movements for recycling or recovery.

Insurance/Guarantees

11–306   An essential feature of all the procedures is that there must be binding contracts to deal with any waste that is shipped, and if for any reason that contract is not completed, then the waste should go back to where it came from unless in fact it can be disposed of or recovered in an alternative and environmentally sound manner. Article 27 expressly requires all shipments of waste that are covered by the Regulation to be subject to an appropriate "financial guarantee or equivalent insurance", covering costs of shipment, which include the possibility of being shipped back to the country of destination where the disposal/recovery contract has not been completed, or if for any other reason the waste fails to comply with the regulation's requirements. Financial guarantees will continue until the certificate of disposal or recovery, as the case may be, has been issued. It is however not specified whether these guarantees must satisfy the exporting or the importing country or both. Banks have moreover proved reluctant on occasion to give guarantees that are available to more than one beneficiary, and these issues have resulted in significant practical difficulties, inhibiting waste movements.

Producer Liability

11–307   Article 34 places a general obligation on the producer of waste to take all the necessary steps to dispose of or recover or to arrange for disposal or recovery of his waste so as to protect the quality of the environment in accordance with the waste and hazardous waste Directives 75/442 and 91/689, and this obligation is irrespective of the point of disposal or recovery of the waste. Nevertheless, this is said to be without prejudice to Community and national provisions concerning civil liability — at this stage, while the issue of civil liability is under active consideration, it is not by any means clear what the effect of this provision is.

Documentation

11–308   The Regulations required the Commission to draw up by February 6, 1994 the appropriate documentation for shipments to be made in accordance with the Regulation, though it has failed to meet this deadline. Where a series of routine shipments of the same type of waste is to be made between the same people, then a general notification procedure will be possible. However this procedure may only apply to shipments made within a maximum period of one year.

Implementation in the United Kingdom

The Transfrontier Shipment of Waste Regulations 1994[78] (the "1994 Regulations") designate the waste regulation authorities in Great Britain and district councils in Northern Ireland as the competent authorities of dispatch and destination for the purposes of the EC Regulation, and the Secretary of State as the competent authority of transit. By so appointing himself, as well as simplifying the procedure, the Secretary of State has given himself the exclusive power under the EC Regulation to determine whether to object to the passage of a consignment of waste through the area of a waste regulation authority other than that of dispatch or destination.   **11–309**

A competent authority of dispatch may decide that it will itself transmit notifications of waste to competent authorities of destination, with copies to the competent authority of transit and the consignee.[79] Where a United Kingdom competent authority of dispatch so decides it must advertise that fact,[80] and its decision takes effect two weeks after the last of the advertisements. Notifiers of relevant waste shipments must then only notify that authority.[81] The documentation to be used is to be as prescribed by the Commission.[82]   **11–310**

A certificate must be obtained before any shipment of waste is made into or out of the United Kingdom that there is, or will be at the time of shipment, a sufficient financial guarantee or equivalent insurance in respect of that shipment meeting the requirements of Article 27 (reg.7). Various time limits are imposed on the competent authorities, ranging from 20 to 70 days depending on the type of shipment, for deciding on an application for a certificate.[83]   **11–311**

Competent authorities of dispatch are given powers to ensure return of waste to the United Kingdom, by serving notice on the   **11–312**

---

[78] S.I. 1994 No. 1137. Guidance on the Regulations is given in DoE Circular 13/94.
[79] Art. 3(8).
[80] In the London, Edinburgh or Belfast Gazette, as the case may be, and in a local newspaper.
[81] reg. 6.
[82] In its Decision 94/774, [1994] O.J. L310.
[83] reg. 7(4).

notifier, where this is required under Article 25(1) or 26(1),[84] and to ensure the environmentally sound disposal or recovery of waste, by serving notice on the consignee, where this is required under Article 26(3).[85] The Secre tary of State must prepare a waste management plan in accordance with Article 7 of Directive 75/442 as amended, setting out his policies for the import and export of waste for recovery or disposal into and out of the United Kingdom; any restrictions on imports or exports are to comply with Article 4(3)(a) of the EC Regulation.[86]

11–313   In so far as the EC Regulation controls imports and exports of special waste to and from the United Kingdom the corresponding provisions of the Control of Pollution (Special Waste) Regulations 1980 are disapplied.[87] The latter continue however in relation to imports and exports of special waste from and to Northern Ireland, which for this purpose remains treated as a separate country from Great Britain (and of course, countries outside the Community). Thus a person importing special waste from Northern Ireland into Great Britain is treated as its producer in Great Britain, and an exporter of it to Northern Ireland is treated as a disposer, and *vice versa* as regards importers and exporters based in Northern Ireland for the purposes of the Control of Pollution (Special Waste) Regulations (Northern Ireland) 1981.[88]

11–314   Regulation 12 lists numerous offences, including:

- contravening any provision of the EC Regulation so that a shipment of waste is "illegal traffic" for the purposes of Article 26;
- transporting, recovering, disposing of or other handling of waste in the United Kingdom in contravention of any condition imposed under the EC Regulation;
- failing to send a certificate of disposal or recovery when due, or sending one that is false in a material particular;
- shipping waste without a regulation 7 certificate;
- shipping waste not accompanied in the United Kingdom by the information required by Article 11;
- shipping waste from the United Kingdom without a contract with a consignee as required by the EC Regulation;
- mixing wastes the subject of different notifications during shipment.

---

[84] reg. 8.
[85] reg. 9.
[86] reg. 11(1), (2).
[87] reg. 18.
[88] S.R. 1981 No. 252.

The usual provisions are included rendering liable a person to whose act or default any offence under Regulation 12 is due, and also any director or other similar officer of a company that has committed such an offence with his consent or connivance or that is attributable to his negligence.[89] Likewise where a company is managed by its members, they may be liable on the same basis as the directors.[90] Similar provisions apply in relation to Scottish partnerships and unincorporated associations.[91]

Penalties for offences under the Regulation are in most cases a fine   **11–315**
of up to the statutory maximum on summary conviction or, on conviction on indictment, up to two years imprisonment and an unlimited fine.[92] Offences under the Regulations are also "prescribed offences" for the purposes of the grant of waste management licences and of the registration of waste carriers (see paragraphs 11–157 and 11–277).[93]

Regulation 20 sets out the procedure for registration of waste   **11–316**
dealers and brokers in the register kept under the Waste Management Licensing Regulations 1994.[94] Transitional provisions give until January 1, 1995 for applications for registration to be made, and continue thereafter in respect of applications made before that date, pending their determination.

[89] regs. 12(11), 13.
[90] reg. 13(2).
[91] reg. 13(3).
[92] reg. 15.
[93] reg. 19.
[94] *i.e.,* pursuant to Sched. 4, Part I, para. 12(5) of the Licensing Regs.

Chapter 12

CHEMICALS

Throughout most of the twentieth Century the chemical industry, in its various forms, has been one of the most vigorous participants in economic development. Major industries have grown up around petrochemicals, and polymers in particular, pharmaceuticals, and agrochemicals, both bulk fertilisers and pesticides. Numerous other products have been developed, often highly specialised for specific applications. Many are sold for use by the public, for example paints and adhesives, rubber and plastics, aerosols and pesticides, medicines and cosmetics, and food and fuel additives. Many others are used in industrial processes, for example in water treatment and food production, and as emulsifiers and wetting agents, dielectric and hydraulic fluids, degreasing agents and solvents generally, pigments and dyes.

12–001

The undoubted direct benefits of new chemical products often resulted in a ready take up by the market, and widespread application; only later were adverse effects on human health and the environment recognised.[1] The growing experience of the adverse aspects of apparently excellent products has led to an increasingly sophisticated regulatory regime, controlling both the introduction of new products, the manner in which they must be labelled when supplied to others, the conditions that must be complied with on their transport, and indeed over whether they may be exported at all, and in certain cases over their actual use. Several substances have of course long been recognised to be inherently hazardous, whether through their inflammability or explosive nature or through their toxicity, and controls in respect of them have been in place for many years. Nevertheless this

12–002

---

[1] The use of DDT as an insecticide, PCBs as a dielectric fluid in transformers and as a hydraulic fluid, tetra-ethyl lead as an anti-knock agent in petrol, and CFCs as refrigerants and in aerosols are perhaps among the most notable examples. All of these were, and indeed still are, excellent for the purposes for which they were intended, but their impact on the environment is such that these benefits are not now considered worthwhile. Nevertheless, the use of substitutes may well bring other disadvantages—the ban on lead in petrol has resulted in reformulations that have markedly higher contents of carcinogens such as benzene, toluene and xylene, as well as lower efficiency leading to higher emissions of carbon dioxide.

has tended to be on a somewhat piecemeal basis, and recently the whole system of chemicals regulation has been put on a much more coherent and comprehensive basis, within the EC and in the UK in particular.

12–003   A fully comprehensive description of the operation of all the controls would take up a disproportionate space in this work. The purpose here is to enable those affected to understand the nature of the various controls that may apply to their specific circumstances, but generally not to provide full detail, for which reference should be made to the relevant legislation and the often very extensive official guidance.

12–004   This chapter first describes the current controls over the putting of chemicals on to the market and the testing of chemicals. ("Chemicals" is used here to indicate broadly chemical compounds and mixtures of compounds[2] and also substances consisting of a single chemical element, such as lead or chlorine). It then covers the controls over certain particular substances which either are or may potentially be hazardous, including a survey of the statutory powers available to control specific products, generally by banning their import or sale. Later sections address the controls over the industrial handling of actually or potentially hazardous substances, in particular their transport and labelling and their storage. The regulatory regime controlling the use of pharmaceuticals, being of course essentially concerned with human health and not the environment more broadly, is not covered here; similarly, no attempt is made to cover the controls over food and substances for use in food. Pesticides and genetically modified organisms are the subject of Chapters 13 and 14 respectively.

12–005   The global trade in chemicals, whether as raw and intermediate materials or as finished products for sale to industry or through retail outlets, is so extensive that its regulation requires international harmonisation if significant distortions of that trade are to be avoided. Thus virtually all the substantive law in the United Kingdom in this area is derived from EC legislation (and significant elements of that are the implementation of global conventions); nevertheless, much of the administrative structure for applying the law is left to the discretion of the Member States. Accordingly, it is appropriate first to review the underlying EC Directives, as the corresponding UK legislation can be best understood in the context of the controls imposed on all Member States that it aims to implement.

---

[2] "Compound" is used to mean a substance having a particular molecular structure, as distinct from a composition which is a mixture of distinct compounds and/or elements, even though there may be some binding of these together, as in the composition of a car tyre.

EC Legislation

Classification, Packaging and Labelling—Directive 67/548

Background

Any regulation of chemicals must necessarily start by classifying the chemicals that are to be regulated by reference to relevant properties. The basis of EC chemicals regulation is Directive 67/548 concerning the classification, packaging and labelling of dangerous substances— referred to here as the "CPL Directive".[3] This Directive has been subject to a series of amendments whereby, among other changes, it applies in certain respects to all substances and not only those classed as dangerous. For present purposes it is sufficient to start with the Directive giving effect to the 6th Amendment,[4] which is generally referred to as "the 6th Amendment". The 6th Amendment replaced all the substantive provisions of the original Directive 67/548 and had an implementation date, for most purposes, of September 18, 1981. The 6th Amendment is now replaced by the 7th Amendment, namely Directive 92/32[5] which was due to be implemented by October 31, 1993. The 7th Amendment in turn replaces all the substantive provisions of the original Directive.[6] The main purpose of the Directive was originally the protection of the public, and particularly members of the workforce who might use the products as classified. The 6th Amendment also referred to protection of the environment among its objectives, and the 7th Amendment explicitly refers to the requirement of Article 100A(3) of the Rome Treaty that internal market measures concerning (among other things) health, safety and the protection of man and the environment must take as a basis a high level of protection.

12–006

"Substances" is defined in the now standard way as meaning chemical elements and their compounds in their natural state or obtained by any production process, as distinct from "preparations" which means mixtures or solutions composed of two or more substances. As defined, substances also includes any additive needed to preserve a product's stability and any impurity deriving from its

12–007

---

[3] To distinguish it, and the series of amending and adaptation Directives related to it, from Directive 76/769, and its series of related Directives, concerning the marketing and use of dangerous substances, discussed in paras. 12–152 to 12–154.

[4] 79/831; [1979] O.J. L259.

[5] [1992] O.J. L154.

[6] The reluctance of EC legislative draftsmen to repeal and replace out-dated legislation completely means that the 1967 Directive 67/548 (as amended) continues to govern chemicals regulation. However, it is generally more convenient to refer to the 6th and 7th Amendments of the CPL Directive, as appropriate.

production process. In essence, the system is intended to cover products that are put on the market or used commercially and not merely their pure constituents. Any solvents that may be present are however excluded, if they can be separated without affecting the stability of the substance or changing its composition in any other respect.[7]

The 6th Amendment

12–008   The original CPL Directive provided for the classification of dangerous chemical substances by degree of hazard and the nature of the risks entailed, and set out rules for packaging and labelling of these dangerous substances appropriate to the physical, chemical and health risk categories into which they had been classified. The 6th Amendment added an additional risk category "dangerous for the environment". In a departure from all previous versions of the Directive the 6th Amendment also provided that new substances should not be placed on the market either on their own or in admixture with one or more others—mixtures being termed "preparations"— unless the substances had previously been notified to the appropriate authority in one of the EC Member States, as well as being packaged and labelled in the prescribed manner. The notification procedure required the notifier (any manufacturer or importer into the Community of the substance, or a designated representative of a non-EC manufacturer) to submit to the competent authority, not less than 45 days before the substance was placed on the market, a technical dossier containing the information necessary to evaluate the foreseeable risks, setting out detailed information of the substance and a full description of the tests done on it and their results along with a declaration as to the unfavourable effects of the substances when used as proposed, the notifier's proposed classification and labelling of the substance and his proposals for any safety precautions to be recommended. To avoid wasteful duplication of effort the 6th Amendment contained an Annex I listing as potentially dangerous a number of chemical substances classified into specified risk categories, together with safety precautions to be applied in each case. Where a substance was on the Annex I list, certain of these notification requirements were waived; where the substance had been notified at least 10 years previously, then a later notifier was merely required to provide a much more limited amount of information relating to the identity of the substance and a limited amount of information on it, but excluding

---

[7] Art. 2.

information on its physico-chemical, toxicological and ecotoxicological properties.

EINECS and ELINCS

In addition to having to keep a list of new substances so notified after September 18, 1981, this being the date for implementation of the 6th Amendment, the Commission was required to draw up an inventory of substances that had been on the Community market by September 18, 1981. This led to (i) the inventory known as EINECS (the European Inventory of Existing Commercial Chemical Substances), being all substances deemed to have been on the EC market by September 18, 1981, and (ii) ELINCS (the European List of Notified Chemical Substances), being an additional list of substances that were first marketed after that cut-off date or, if marketed before, for which the relevant information was not provided within the time period provided for drawing up EINECS.   **12–009**

Guidance for drawing up EINECS was contained in Commission Decision 81/437.[8] This provided for the European Commission to prepare a European Core Inventory ("ECOIN") from data in its possession, which was to be supplemented by lists of additional substances provided to the Commission by way of declarations made by their manufacturer or any other person resident in the EC who had placed them on the market. Rules in an Annex to the Directive required that the substance must either (a) have been placed on the market "for genuine commercial purposes" between January 1, 1971 and September 18, 1981, or (b) be a monomer from which polymerisates, polycondensates or polyadducts, that had been on the market during that same period, had been manufactured. This resulted in EINECS listing slightly over 100,000 substances.[9]   **12–010**

ELINCS was prepared in accordance with Commission Decision 85/71.[10] Under this, it is for the competent authorities of the Member States—not individual manufacturers or those responsible for marketing goods—to notify the Commission of substances qualifying for inclusion in ELINCS. The Commission is required under Directive 85/71 to prepare a list of substances from such notifications as it receives between July 1 of any one year and June 30 of the next (inclusive), and to publish this list in the Official Journal by not later   **12–011**

[8] [1981] O.J. L167.
[9] [1990] O.J. C146A.
[10] [1985] O.J. L30.

than December 31, of that next year, *i.e.* within the following six months.[11]

12–012   The competent authority for the United Kingdom is the Health and Safety Executive, which originally obtained the relevant information for the purposes of Directive 85/71 from notifications to it made under the Notification of New Substances Regulations 1982[12] — referred to as "NONS 82". These Regulations have now been replaced by the Notification of New Substances Regulations 1993[13] ("NONS 93") discussed below at paragraphs 12–061 to 12–088.

The 7th Amendment

12–013   The 7th Amendment[14] strengthened a number of the provisions in the 6th Amendment, and included for the first time a positive requirement to supply safety data sheets to all recipients of dangerous substances at or before delivery of them.[15] The 7th Amendment likewise has an Annex I,[16] consisting of a lengthy list of 1338 chemical substances classified in accordance with the principles outlined in the 7th Amendment, together with their appropriate classification and labelling. This list includes a substantial number, but still a minority, of those in the EINECS inventory and also substances taken from ELINCS. The remaining substances in EINECS are to be reviewed, by methods prescribed in the 7th Amendment[17] and by procedures laid down by Regulation 793/93[18] (see paragraphs 12–052 to 12–055), to assess their properties and the appropriate risk category, and are then to be transferred to Annex I.[19]

12–014   There are thus in effect four broad classes of chemical substances that are subject to different requirements under the 7th Amendment:

(i)   Substances listed in Annex I (and also in EINECS or ELINCS).

[11] The 4th list, of substances notified up to June 30, 1993, was published (late) in [1994] O.J. C361.
[12] S.I. 1982 No. 1496.
[13] S.I. 1993 No. 3050.
[14] Directive 92/32/EEC, [1992] O.J. L154 and 154A.
[15] Art. 27.
[16] The most recent version of which is contained in Commission Directive 93/72, [1993] O.J. L258 and 258A, as amended by Directive 93/101, [1994] O.J. L13.
[17] In Art. 3 and Annex V to the parent Directive, the most recent version of which is set out in the Annex to the Adaptation Directive 92/69 [1992] O.J. L383 and 383A.
[18] [1993] O.J. L84.
[19] The European Commission has established a European Chemicals Bureau at the Joint Research Centre, Environment Institute, in Ispra, Italy, to provide the technical and scientific support for these and other tasks concerned with the regulation of chemicals (Commission Communication 93/C 1/02, [1993] O.J. C1). The Bureau will also operate the database known as EUCLID (see para. 12–043).

(ii) Substances in EINECS, but not yet listed in Annex I.

(iii) Substances that are not contained in EINECS (or Annex I) but have been previously notified — these are either already contained in ELINCS or should be included in the next edition of it.

(iv) Other substances that it is wished to place on the market in the EC which have not yet been the subject of any notification.

The 7th Amendment requires these categories to be treated in the following ways: **12–015**

(i) Substances in Annex I must be packaged and labelled, and safety data sheets prepared in respect of them, in accordance with their classification in Annex I and the requirements that follow from that classification as set out in the remainder of the Directive. This has the inevitable disadvantage that where the classification is based on relatively old data, it may not reflect more recently acquired information. However Member states may individually prescribe other classification and labelling requirements on a temporary basis, pending a decision at EC level, if they consider this to be necessary.[20] Compliance with a mandatory misdescription has evident product liability implications, and where a person responsible for a product is aware that the requisite labelling information fails to draw attention to a hazard, it must be advisable to seek immediate action at least at Member state level, to minimise the risk of an allegation of negligence.

(ii) There is a presumption that continued marketing of the remaining "existing" substances listed in EINECS is acceptable unless and until such time as review of them indicates otherwise. Consequently, in respect of these substances, manufacturers, distributors, and importers of them are merely obliged to make themselves aware of such relevant and accessible data as does exist concerning the properties of the substances, and must package and label the substances in the light of this information and in accordance with rules laid down in Articles 22–25 of the Directive. They are not however expected to conduct toxicological etc. studies of their own.

---

[20] Art. 31.

(iii) Notified substances that are neither in Annex I nor in EINECS must be classified, packaged and labelled in accordance with the requirements of the Directive, having regard to such adopted classification, and labelling and packaging requirements, as may appear in ELINCS; if these have not yet been determined then regard must be had to the properties of the substance as shown by the technical dossier supplied when notifying it to the authorities.

(iv) Substances that do not fall into any of the other categories may not be placed on the market until they have been notified to the competent authorities in one of the Member States in the manner required by the Directive, the prescribed period for consideration of the notification has elapsed, and no action has been taken requiring marketing to be postponed (see paragraphs 12–018, 12–019). This applies to all substances without exception, whether "dangerous" in fact or not.

Notification of New Substances (EC)

12–016   The obligation to notify a new substance, *i.e.* one not listed in EINECS, to be placed on the market in the EC falls on the manufacturer if manufacture takes place in any member state. If manufacture is outside the EC, notification must be made by every importer unless it has been made by that manufacturer through a designated representative of his within the EC, in which event the importers have no notification obligations—they must however provide information on their sales as is described in paragraph 12–077.

12–017   Where a substance has been notified, this notification can only be relied on to permit marketing of that substance in the EC by the following specific persons:

Notification by:	May be relied on by:
a manufacturer in the EC	that EC manufacturer
a designated representative in the EC of a manufacturer outside it	importers of that substance from that manufacturer
an importer into the EC	that importer

All other subsequent EC manufacturers and importers of the same substance must go through the notification procedure in respect of their version of it. Reference to the previous technical dossier is not permitted in the absence of consent from the previous notifier.

A full notification requires the provision of extensive technical information obtained from experimental data resulting from conducting the series of tests prescribed in the Directive. This may be submitted on disk in a precisely prescribed manner known as the Standard Notification Information Format (SNIF). The notifier must allow at least 60 days for the authority to consider the notification and may only start marketing the substance thereafter in the absence of any indication to the contrary from the relevant authority.[21] If the authority advises the notifier that further information is required, marketing may only take place sixty days after the authority has received that additional information.[22]

12–018

The Directive provides for reduced notification requirements where only relatively small quantities of a substance are to be marketed. Thus reduced requirements apply where a substance is to be marketed in quantities of less than one tonne per annum per manufacturer, and a still further reduced notification requirement is available where the quantity to be marketed is below 100kg per annum per manufacturer. Where the reduced notification requirements apply, marketing may begin after 30 days from notifying the relevant authority, again in the absence of any indication to the contrary.

12–019

Notifications must be supplemented where the amounts marketed rise above the levels permitting reduced notification requirements. Additionally, since notification may be made by one of several importers of the same substance, provision is made for aggregating the yearly tonnages to ensure additional notification is made when one of the relevant reduced notification levels is exceeded.

12–020

Every notifier of a substance that has already been notified must keep the authority concerned with the original notification informed of amounts of the substance marketed by him (and, in some cases, by others also), of new knowledge of the effects of the substance on man and on the environment of which he may reasonably be expected to have become aware, and also new uses for which the substance is

12–021

[21] This clarifies a grey area in the 6th Amendment which was unclear as to the right to market if the authority was unsatisfied with any aspect of the notification. Inevitably, also, the authorities in the different Member States tended to differ in their requirements for a satisfactory notification; the 7th Amendment spells out these requirements in more detail.

[22] It must of course remain open to a notifier to challenge an authority's requirement for further information, but the nature of the changes introduced by the 7th Amendment indicate that the marketing of a substance can legitimately continue to be prohibited pending resolution of that challenge. If the challenge succeeds the notifier might in some circumstances have recourse against the authority in respect of the delay caused, but only, at least if English rather than EC principles are determinative, in cases of malpractice.

marketed of which he may reasonably be expected to have become aware. These are therefore objective requirements placing a "reasonable" burden on the notifier to keep himself adequately informed; merely passing on what he in fact learns is not necessarily sufficient. Where a manufacturer outside the EC designates a person within the EC as his sole representative for the purposes of submitting a notification, all importers of the relevant substance produced by that manufacturer are to ensure that the sole representative is kept informed of the quantities he imports.

Testing

12–022   Tests on chemicals required pursuant to the 7th Amendment are to be conducted according to methods laid down in Annex V to the CPL Directive 67/548, as most recently revised by the Adaptation Directive 92/69.[23]

Good Laboratory Practice

12–023   Directive 87/18[24] sets common standards for the testing of chemicals by requiring testing for the purposes of Directive 67/548[25] to be in accordance with the principles of good laboratory practice, the subject of an OECD decision of May 12, 1981.[26] The objective is to ensure that the test results from laboratories anywhere in the EC are properly comparable and so can be accepted throughout it, thus avoiding duplicate testing. Article 5 expressly provides that where EC legislation requires the application of the good laboratory practice principles, member states may not interfere on grounds relating to laboratory practice with the marketing of chemical products if the principles applied by the relevant laboratory conform with those required by this Directive.

12–024   A further Directive 88/320[27] is directed to the inspection and verification of laboratories to ensure they are working to the OECD principles. Any laboratory claiming to comply with good laboratory principles in chemicals testing must be inspected by a designated body and its compliance (or otherwise) verified. Components of

---

[23] [1992] O.J. L383A.
[24] [1987] O.J. L15.
[25] See para. 12–022.
[26] Set out in Annex 2 to that decision. The decision and the principles are set out in Environment Monograph No. 45 "The OECD Principles of Good Laboratory Practice", OECD 1992; see also the HSE Approved Code of Practice COP 7.
[27] [1988] O.J. L145.

compliance monitoring procedures and guidance for the conduct of laboratory inspections and study audits are contained in Annexes A and B respectively to the Directive.[28] The laboratories inspected and the results of the inspections are not to be considered as confidential,[29] though disclosure of other commercially sensitive and confidential information is to be strictly limited. Where a member state considers a laboratory in its own territory is wrongly claiming compliance such that the integrity or authenticity of its studies might be compromised, the Commission must be informed and it will inform all the other member states.[30] Where a member state has reason to believe that a laboratory elsewhere in the EEC is not in compliance, it may request further information from the appropriate member state and a study audit.[31] In the absence of agreement between the member states, all the others and the Commission are to be informed of this with reasons.

There is a DHSS publication "The Good Laboratory Practice Compliance Programme" (1986) on the requirements of the OECD principles, and the principles are embodied in the HSE Approved Code of Practice COP 7.[32] Nevertheless, to date there has been no comprehensive implementation of these Directives by UK legislation notwithstanding that the implementation dates were June 30, 1988 and January 1, 1989, respectively.   **12–025**

Testing on Animals

One feature of the 7th Amendment is its concern to avoid duplicate testing on vertebrate animals, and Article 15 sets out procedures designed to minimise such testing. This gives effect to Directive 86/609[33] the object of which is to protect vertebrate animals used for experimental purposes. Among other measures, this 1986 Directive requires that no such use shall be made if another scientifically satisfactory experiment not entailing the use of any animal is reasonably and practicably available. It sets out a series of rules designed to minimise and where possible to avoid pain or distress to animals. In the United Kingdom these matters are covered by the Animals (Scientific Procedures) Act 1986, which came into force on January 1, 1987.   **12–026**

[28] Added by Adaptation Directive 90/18 [1990] O.J. L11.
[29] Art. 4(4).
[30] Art. 5.
[31] Art. 6(1).
[32] COP 8, 9 and 10 deal with methods for the determination of ecotoxicity, physico-chemical properties and toxicity, respectively.
[33] [1986] O.J. L358.

Confidentiality

12–027   Confidentiality in the data supplied in the course of a notification is respected where the notifier considers it to be commercially sensitive and that its disclosure might harm him industrially or commercially, provided that full justification is given. Nevertheless, none of the information can be kept secret from any of the national competent authorities or the Commission, and basic information as to the hazards that the substance may pose and appropriate safety precautions must of course be allowed to be made public. Inevitably, manufacturers will often consider commercially sensitive the chemical structure of the substances that they are proposing to market.[34] The Directive[35] thus provides that notified substances which are not classified as dangerous within the meaning of the Directive may be listed under their trade names (as opposed to their chemical nomenclature) if the relevant competent authority so requests. However this will normally be permitted for a maximum of three years only, unless the relevant authority considers that publication of the chemical nomenclature could reveal information concerning commercial exploitation or manufacture, in which event the use of the trade name in the list may be continued for as long as that authority sees fit. In the case of dangerous substances, the relevant competent authority may request listing under their trade names alone, and this may continue until such time as the substance is introduced into the Annex I list.

Packaging, Labelling, Safety Data Sheets, Advertising

12–028   The Directive sets out requirements as to the packaging of dangerous substances to be marketed,[36] and requirements as to labelling, and exemptions from these.[37] As previously mentioned, the 7th Amendment introduces a requirement for safety data sheets to be supplied on or before the first delivery of a dangerous substance to any recipient of it.[38] Community rules for the contents, format and distribution of these safety data sheets are contained in Directive 91/155.[39] Advertising of a substance that falls within any of the "dangerous" categories

---

[34] While such substances are likely to be capable of analysis once they are publicly available (though not always with total precision) a manufacturer may legitimately object to enabling his competitors to be informed as to his plans ahead of the actual launch of a product on the market.
[35] In Art. 19, para. 3.
[36] In Art. 22.
[37] In Arts. 23, 24 and 25.
[38] Art. 27.
[39] [1991] O.J. L76, as amended by Directive 93/112, [1993] O.J. L314.

set out in the Directive is prohibited unless mention is made in that advertisement of the relevant category or categories.[40]

Free Movement within the EC

It is fundamental to the purpose of the Directive that compliance **12–029** with it should enable a chemical product to be marketed in accordance with its notification throughout the entire Community (in the absence of specific controls imposed on its marketing and use under the separate EC and national legislation, as to which see paragraphs x to y below), and this is provided for by Article 30.[41] Nevertheless, where a Member State considers as a result of new information that there are justifiable reasons for considering a substance to be dangerous and/or that its existing classification, packaging or labelling is no longer appropriate, it may temporarily reclassify or, if necessary, prohibit the marketing of that substance in its territory, or make it subject to special conditions. The Commission and the other Member States must be informed immediately of any such action, and the Commission will take such further steps as it thinks appropriate.[42]

Exceptions

The following products when in the finished state intended for the **12–030** final user are excluded[43] from the scope of the Directive:

- medicinal products for human or veterinary use as defined in Directive 65/65 (as amended)
- cosmetic products defined by Directive 76/768 (as amended)
- mixtures of substances which, in the form of waste, are covered by Directive 75/442 and 78/319[44]
- foodstuffs
- animal feeding stuffs
- pesticides (being plant protection products, and not, *e.g.* pesticides intended for non-agricultural purposes or biocides)

---

[40] Art. 26.
[41] "Member States may not prohibit, restrict or impede the placing on the market of substances which comply with the requirements of this Directive, on grounds relating to notification, classification, packaging or labelling within the meaning of this Directive".
[42] Art. 31.
[43] By Art. 1(2).
[44] Directive 78/319 on hazardous waste was due to be replaced on December 12, 1991 (*i.e.* before the 7th Amendment) by Directive 91/689, but the latter is not yet in effect.

- radioactive substances as defined by Directive 80/836
- other substances or preparations for which equivalent Community notification or approval procedures and requirements exist. The Commission is required to establish a list of such substances and preparations and to revise it periodically.

The Directive also does not apply to the carriage of dangerous substances by rail, road, inland waterway, sea or air or to substances in transit under customs supervision.

12–031   Additionally, where comparable control procedures exist under EC legislation, the notification requirements of the 7th Amendment are to be waived. The Commission is required to establish a list of such other EC legislation and to revise it periodically.[44A] Specific mention is made in the 7th Amendment[45] of:

- additives and substances for exclusive use in animal feeding stuffs as covered by Directives 70/524 and 82/471
- substances used exclusively as additives in foodstuffs as covered by Directive 89/107
- substances used exclusively as flavourings in foodstuffs and which are covered by Directive 88/388
- active ingredients, other than chemical intermediates, used in medicinal products for human or veterinary use as defined in Directive 65/65 (as amended)

As will be apparent, there is considerable overlap between this list and that of the products in the finished state that are outside the scope of the Directive altogether. Where this is so, the practical effect of a waiver under Article 13(1) will be to avoid duplication of controls over products before they reach the finished state intended for the final user. It is to be observed that pesticide active ingredients (as opposed to final formulations) are not exempted, and are treated differently from the active ingredients of medical and veterinary products.

12–032   Further, the following substances are deemed[46] to have been notified, and are therefore exempted from initial notification requirements

- polymers unless they contain in combined form two per cent or more of any substance not within EINECS

[44A] See Directive 93/90, [1993] O.J. L277.
[45] Art. 13(1).
[46] By Art. 13(2).

- substances marketed in quantities of less than 10 kg per annum per manufacturer, subject to such requirements as any relevant Member State may see fit to impose[47]
- substances marketed in quantities not exceeding 100 kg per manufacturer per annum intended solely for scientific research and development[48] carried out under controlled conditions, subject to maintenance of prescribed written records
- substances marketed for the purposes of process-orientated research and development[49] with a limited number of registered customers in quantities limited to that purpose. This exemption will normally last for a maximum of one year though it may, exceptionally, be extended if justification can be shown. Individual Member States are entitled to impose, within limitations, their own controls on such research and development, and the substance concerned must not be made available to the general public at any time, either on its own or in a preparation.

The substances that benefit from the "deemed notification" procedure must however still be appropriately packaged and labelled as provided for in the Directive.[50]

Risk Assessment

New Substances

The 7th Amendment requires an assessment of the risks that each new substance may pose to be made on the basis of the technical dossier submitted with the relevant notification.[51] The principles to be applied in assessing these risks, both to human health and to the environment, are laid down in Directive 93/67.[52] A report on each assessment must be sent to the Commission (and updated on any

12–033

---

[47] But such requirements shall not exceed those provided for in Annex VII C I and II of the Directive.
[48] Defined in Art. 2(1)(f) as "scientific experimentation, analysis or chemical research carried out under controlled conditions"; it includes the determination of intrinsic properties, performance and efficacy as well as scientific investigation related to product development.
[49] Defined in Art. 2(1)(g) as "the further development of a substance in the course of which pilot plant or production trials are used to test the fields of application of the substance".
[50] Arts. 13(3), (4) and 22–25.
[51] Arts. 3(2), 16(1).
[52] [1993] O.J. L227.

revision of the assessment), and a copy supplied to the notifier on request.

Existing Substances—Regulation 793/93

12–034   Procedures for systematic review of existing substances (*i.e.* those in EINECS) to ascertain the risks that they may represent are the subject of Regulation 793/93.[53] This has been supplemented by official guidance issued by the HSE and the DoE "How to Report Data on Existing Chemical Substances".[54] Principles governing these risk assessments are laid down in Commission Regulation 1488/94.[55]

12–035   These risk assessment provisions being the subject of a regulation, the obligations are accordingly directly binding not only on national governments and, in the UK, the HSE (the body having the principal responsibility for ensuring the Regulation is given full effect), but also on companies and individuals who are required to comply with them by, most notably, the provision of information and the carrying out, where appropriate, of testing. Although the Regulation came into force on June 4, 1993[56] Member States were given one year from adoption of the Regulation, *i.e.* until March 23, 1994 to "establish appropriate legal or administrative measures in order to deal with non-compliance with the provisions of this Regulation".[57]

12–036   The Regulation is enforced in England, Wales and Scotland through the Notification of Existing Substances (Enforcement) Regulations 1994[58] which designate the Secretary of State and the HSE, acting jointly, as the competent authority in Great Britain for the purposes of Regulation 793/93. A separate enforcement regime is to be established for Northern Ireland. The Regulations make it an offence to fail to comply with the EC Regulation or, in connection with any purported compliance, to make any false or misleading statement knowingly or recklessly, intentionally to make a false entry in any document, or to use any such entry if known to be false with intent to deceive. Powers

---

[53] [1993] O.J. L84.
[54] HMSO, February 1994. There is substantial collaboration internationally, and particularly within OECD, with the objects of minimising the work that must be done in making such assessments on existing chemicals and of establishing internationally accepted harmonised hazard classification schemes (an absolute pre-requisite). The OECD has set up a voluntary chemicals testing programme known as SIDS (Screening Information Data Sets) aimed at sharing the costs of generating the data necessary for preparing technical dossiers on (currently 31) existing high production chemicals.
[55] [1994] O.J. L161.
[56] The 60th day following its publication in the Official Journal—see Art. 18.
[57] Art. 17.
[58] S.I. 1994 No. 1806.

of enforcement are given to both HSE inspectors and to HMIP/HMIPI.[59]

Enforcement may be by way of service of an enforcement notice specifying the matter constituting non-compliance, steps needed to remedy this, and a period for taking the required action. Appeals against an enforcement notice are made to an industrial tribunal and proceed as for appeals against improvement notices under H.S.W.A., section 21.[60] Twenty one days from service of the notice are allowed for bringing an appeal (subject to discretionary extension); the effect of an enforcement notice is suspended while an appeal is pending. It is also an offence to fail to observe any requirement of an enforcement notice or of an inspector acting under the Regulations, and also in various circumstances to obstruct enforcement. Proceedings may however only be brought by HMIP on the HSE, unless the Director of Public Prosecutions has consented to action by another prosecutor. Depending on the offence, penalties may be up to the statutory maximum on summary conviction; on conviction on indictment there may be an unlimited fine and up to two years imprisonment. The Court also has power to order remedial action by a defendant, either in addition to or instead of any punishment. The usual provisions apply rendering directors, other similar officers and the members of companies liable for offences of their companies due to their neglect, or committed with their connivance or consent. Likewise where any offence is committed due to the act or default of another person, that other person may also be convicted of the offence.

12–037

The broad objectives of the Regulation are the collection, circulation and accessibility of information on "existing substances", *i.e.* those listed in EINECS, and the evaluation of the risks that these may pose to man and the environment, so as to achieve better management of those risks within the framework of Community provisions.[61] It is divided into two principal parts dealing respectively with data reporting and with risk evaluation. The data reporting requirements are based on quantities that have been produced by any manufacturer or imported by any importer, whether as such or in a preparation in any of the three years preceding the adoption of the Regulation and the year following its adoption, that is each of the four years starting on March 23 in 1990 to 1993. If in any one of those four years a

12–038

---

[59] The powers of HMIP/HMIPI are expressly extended beyond enforcing Integrated Pollution Control by the new Regulations; the HSE has the necessary powers under the H.S.W.A. 1974.

[60] *i.e.* as set out in the Schedule to the Industrial Tribunals (Improvement and Prohibition Notices Appeals) Regs. 1974 and in the corresponding Scottish Regulations, S.I. 1974 Nos. 1925 and 1926 respectively. It is of interest that the usual provision for appeals to the Secretary of State is not applicable in this case.

[61] Art. 1.

manufacturer has produced or an importer has imported any existing substance, whether as such or in a preparation, in a quantity exceeding 1,000 tonnes in that year, then the full data reporting requirements of Article 3 apply.[62] Where the maximum quantity imported in any one of these four years is over ten tonnes but not exceeding 1,000 tonnes,[63] then the reduced data reporting requirements of Article 4 apply.

12–039   Annex II of the Regulation lists 67 substances and preparations, which are either naturally occurring or which are derived from naturally occurring materials, for example, glucose and sucrose, sodium stearate (a principal constituent of soap), limestone, a variety of common vegetable oils and fatty acids derived from them, and starch. These materials are exempted from the standard data reporting requirements of the Regulation, but information on them may be specifically requested.[64] For all other existing substances, the following timetable is prescribed[65] for the requisite data reporting:

Data Reporting Timetable	
Substance	**Data Reporting Date(s)**
In Annex I, and subject to **full** reporting requirements	by June 4, 1994
In EINECS but not in Annex I, and subject to **full** reporting requirements	by June 4, 1995
In EINECS (whether or not also in Annex I), and subject to **reduced** reporting requirements	from June 4, 1996 to June 4, 1998

12–041   The information required under the reduced reporting requirements of Article 4 consists simply of

(a)   the name of the substance and its EINECS number;
(b)   the quantity of the substance produced or imported;
(c)   the classification of the substance in accordance with Annex I of the CPL Directive 67/548 or its provisional classification, as

---

[62] The substances in this category are referred to as "High Production Volume" (HPV) substances.
[63] "Low Production Volume" (LPV) substances.
[64] Art. 5.
[65] Art. 3.

the case may be, including the class of danger, the danger symbol, the risk phrases and the safety phrases; and

(d) information on the reasonably foreseeable uses of the substance.

The full reporting requirements under Article 3 include the same four items as just set out and in addition: **12–042**

(e) data on the physico-chemical properties of the substance;
(f) data on pathways and environmental fate;
(g) data on the ecotoxicity of the substance;
(h) data on the acute and sub-acute toxicity of the substance;
(i) data on carcinogenicity, mutagenicity and/or toxicity for reproduction of the substance; and
(j) any other indication relevant to the risk evaluation of the substance.

This list of properties follows very closely the information required when notifying a new substance under Article 7 of the 7th Amendment as set out in Annex VII to the CPL Directive (which itself is set out in Annex 3 to the 7th Amendment).

The information to be supplied under the full reporting require- **12–043** ments of Article 3 is set out in more detail in Annex III, and that due under the reduced reporting requirements of Article 4 in Annex IV. All reasonable efforts must be made to obtain existing data regarding items (e) to (j), but there is no obligation to carry out tests on animals to create new data.[66] This information is to be supplied to the Commission using a special software package known as HEDSET (Harmonised Electronic Data Set), available on diskette free of charge from the Commission's various information offices.[67] The Commission stores the information supplied to it in a database called EUCLID (European Chemicals Information Database). Access to the full database is restricted in view of the confidential information that it is liable to contain (see also paragraph 12–056). However an edited version from which the confidential information has been excluded and which will include all relevant scientific and technical data is publicly available.

Even though the reduced reporting requirements of Article 4 would **12–044** otherwise apply to a particular substance, the Commission may, after consultation with the Member States, require manufacturers and importers of that substance to submit additional information within the scope of the full Article 3 reporting requirements.[68] Nevertheless,

---

[66] Art. 3.
[67] In the UK these offices are in London, Cardiff, Edinburgh and Belfast, their addresses, telex and fax numbers being set out in Annex V to the regulation.
[68] Art. 4(2).

no-one may be obliged to carry out further tests on animals by any such request for further information.

12–045 Where a substance is produced or imported by several people, the extra information required under Article 3 (*i.e.* categories (e) to (j) set out above), and any additional information that may be specifically requested by the Commission under Article 4(2), may be submitted by any one of the manufacturers and importers concerned acting by agreement on behalf of some or all of the others. Where this occurs, those others must nevertheless still give the information required for the purposes of the reduced requirements under Article 4, and also state whether the complete data set on the substance has already been submitted by another manufacturer or importer or if they are acting on behalf of another relevant manufacturer or importer. Information supplied to the Commission under these requirements will be automatically forwarded to all the Member States; Member States may, if they so wish, require manufacturers and importers established in their territory to submit simultaneously to their competent authorities the same information as is sent to the Commission under Articles 3 and 4.

12–046 Where information has been provided under either Article 3 or 4, Article 7 creates a standing obligation to keep that information updated. As regards production and import volumes, the broad obligation is to update the quantity figures every three years if there has been a change from the figures as previously reported. Since, inevitably, production and/or import figures will fluctuate to some extent from year to year, it is by no means clear when new and different figures should be supplied to the Commission before the end of the three years from when the information was previously given. Clearly minor variations should not require immediate reporting, but it would appear that any substantial increase in an annual figure should be reported, particularly if this were to take the figure for any one manufacturer or importer over the 1,000 tonnes per annum limit at which Article 3 first applies. Although for any one manufacturer or importer, a substantial decrease in quantities would not appear to need to be notified until the end of the three year period, the Commission will be maintaining statistics on aggregate figures prepared from those from all manufacturers and importers, and for this purpose a substantial decrease in the figures for any one person might well be highly material.

12–047 In addition to updating volume figures, Article 7 requires further information to be given on the notifier's initiative, in particular in relation to any new uses which may substantially change the type, form, magnitude or duration of exposure of man or the environment to the substance, and in relation to any new data on properties likely to be relevant to the risk evaluation of the substance, and to any change to the provisional classification under the CPL Directive 67/548. There is a specific obligation under Article 7(2) that any manufacturer or importer who acquires knowledge "which supports the conclusion that the substance in question may present a serious risk to man or the environment" must immediately report this information to the Commission and also to his own Member State where he is located. The words quoted make it clear that this information must be provided even though it is not conclusive as to the risk that the substance *may* pose—all that is required is that the information "supports the conclusion" that the substance may present a serious risk.

Priority Lists

The Commission has a duty under Article 8 to prepare priority lists **12–048** of substances to be reviewed. Preparation of these lists will be made on the basis both of information supplied under the Regulation, and also of lists of priority substances that may have been drawn up by individual Member States. The first such list published in May,[68A] 1994, and further lists are required to be drawn up regularly thereafter. The factors that are to be taken into account in preparing these lists are the effects of the substance on man or the environment, the exposure of man or the environment to the substance, any lack of data on these effects, work already carried out elsewhere, and other Community legislation and programmes relating to dangerous substances. Special attention is to be given to substances which may have chronic effects, especially substances known or suspected to be carcinogenic, toxic to reproduction and/or mutagenic, or which may or do increase these effects. Duplication of evaluations is to be avoided, and accordingly a substance that has already been evaluated under other legislation will not be put on a priority list under this regulation. This is particularly likely to apply to evaluations being carried out pursuant to the comparable OECD chemicals testing programme for developing SIDS data.[69]

Where a substance is on a priority list all manufacturers and **12–049** importers who have already submitted information on it under the Regulation must within six months of publication of the list submit all relevant available information and related study reports relevant to the risk assessment.[70]

Where information already supplied in respect of a priority list **12–050** substance lacks any of the data that must be given on full notification

[68A] Reg. 1179/94, [1994] O.J. L131.
[69] See n. 54 to para. 12–034.
[70] Arts. 9(1), 12(1).

of a new substance[71] the manufacturers and importers are obliged to carry out such testing as may be necessary to obtain the missing data and to provide the test results and test reports within twelve months.[72] The Directive does not state explicitly when the twelve month period starts—it is presumably the date of publication of the relevant priority list, which is the date from when the 6 months period referred to in Article 9(1) runs. A request may however be made to be exempted from any of the additional testing requirements on the ground either that the information concerned is not necessary or that it is impossible to obtain; in any event, a longer period than the twelve months stipulated can be asked for.[73]

12–051   The evaluation of substances on the priority lists is to be delegated to the Member States, and Article 10 provides that for each substance a Member State shall be designated to take responsibility for the conduct of the evaluation. The Member State must appoint one of its authorities to be what the regulation refers to as the "rapporteur" for that substance—in the United Kingdom, the rapporteur will be the HSE. It is accordingly this rapporteur that must receive the information required to be supplied for the priority list substances under Article 9(1) and the additional information following extra testing under Article 9(2); it is also this rapporteur who decides on whether any tests can be permitted under Article 9(3) or grants extensions of time for the test results to be provided. Nevertheless, the Commission must be informed of any decision in this respect by the rapporteur and it will pass this information on to the other Member States. Should any of them object to the rapporteur's decision, this may be put before a management committee constituted under Article 15. This Committee (referred to here as the "Article 15 Committee") is made up of representatives of each of the Member States, with a representative from the Commission acting as chairman. The national representatives' voting rights on the Committee are weighted in the same way as the weighted votes of the representatives of the Member States in the Council of Ministers, as provided for under Article 148(2) of the Rome Treaty. The Commission representative who is chairman has no voting rights.

Risk Evaluation

12–052   The rapporteur, appointed as just described, is responsible for evaluating all the information provided by manufacturers and importers on a substance, for deciding what further information and

---

[71] *i.e.* that required under Article 7 and Annex VIIA of the CPL Directive 67/548.
[72] Arts. 9(2), 12(1).
[73] Art. 9(3).

tests may be needed, and for making a risk assessment in the light of all the information eventually obtained. If it decides that more information and/or testing is needed, it must first consult the manufacturers and importers of this. If it maintains the need for more information and/or testing, it must inform the Commission, and a request from the rapporteur for further information and/or further testing is only to be made after approval by the Article 15 Committee, so providing some degree of uniformity across the EC as to the amount of extra work required.[74] Any such request must be complied with within the specified time.[75]

In assessing the real or potential risk to man and the environment, the rapporteur is to apply a set of principles laid down in Regulation 1488/94.[76] These principles will be regularly reviewed, and may be revised, by the Article 15 Committee.

12–053

The rapporteur forwards its risk evaluation and any recommendations for risk limitation to the Commission, and on the basis of this the Commission submits proposals to the Article 15 Committee for adoption by it.[77] In making recommendations, the rapporteur must analyse the benefits as well as the disadvantages of the substance, and have regard to the availability of substitute products.[78] The Committee has no power to amend the Commission's proposals directly, and if a compromise acceptable to both the Commission and the Committee cannot be found, the Commission must refer that proposal to the Council of Ministers, for it to decide on by a qualified majority. This procedure for resolving an impasse is, in most cases, subject to the further provision that if the Council of Ministers has not acted within two months from the Commission's proposal being submitted to it, the Commission's proposal shall be adopted. However where the issue concerns the results of the risk evaluation and any recommended strategy for risk limitation to be adopted under Article 11(2), or adaptations of the Annexes to the Directive to technical progress, the Council of Ministers may, by a simple majority, vote to reject the Commission's proposals within the two month period, without necessarily agreeing on any alternative proposals of their own.

12–054

To avoid duplicate and wasteful testing, where a substance is produced or imported by several manufacturers or importers, and additional tests are required in respect of a substance on the priority list or one to which Article 7(2) applies (that is where new knowledge

12–055

[74] Art. 10(2).
[75] Art. 12(1).
[76] [1994] O.J. L161.
[77] Art. 11(1), (2).
[78] Art. 10(3).

has been acquired that supports the conclusion that the substance may present a serious risk to man or the environment), the testing may be performed by one or more of the manufacturers or importers concerned acting on behalf of the remainder. In those circumstances, the others must make reference to the tests so carried out and "shall make a fair and equitable contribution to the cost".[79] It is nevertheless far from clear how this requirement to share costs is to be determined and enforced, particularly where manufacturers in different countries are involved.

Confidentiality

12–056   Confidentiality of information supplied is inevitably a sensitive issue in this area, particularly as all information supplied through the Commission will be forwarded to all Member States, whose attitudes to making information available to others are liable to vary quite widely. Article 16 provides for anyone supplying information, either under the general requirements of Articles 3, 4 or 7, or as a result of requests made under Article 12, to make a request for confidentiality if the information concerned is considered to be commercially sensitive, and disclosure might harm the manufacturer or importer concerned industrially or commercially. He must give full justification for his request for confidentiality. Article 16(1) sets out a list of matters that can in no circumstances be treated as secret. These include "summary results" of the toxicological and ecotoxicological tests, any information which, if withheld, might lead to animal experiments being carried out or repeated needlessly, and analytical methods enabling detection of the discharge of a dangerous substance or the determination of exposure of humans to it. Where information is accepted as confidential, if the person concerned should himself later disclose it, he must inform the relevant competent authority of this. Where the authority receiving information accepts it as being confidential, that decision must be followed by all other competent authorities.

Dangerous Preparations—Directive 88/379

12–057   A Directive closely related to the 7th Amendment of the CPL Directive is the so-called Preparations Directive 88/379.[80] Preparations, being mixtures (including solutions) of two or more substances, can

---

[79] Art. 12(3).
[80] [1988] O.J. L187.

take an infinite variety of forms,[81] and if each of these were to be required to be tested as though it were a new substance in order to evaluate any dangerous properties, and to classify those it may have, there would not only be a massive amount of duplicated work, which would be both inefficient and time wasting, but also repeated testing on animals which the Commission, as a matter of policy, seeks to avoid.[82] Accordingly, the purpose of the Preparations Directive is to set out procedures for establishing for any preparation which of the danger categories, as set out in the 7th Amendment, it should be regarded as belonging to, and to provide a set of principles applicable throughout the EC for deriving the appropriate classification from the properties of the component substances in the preparation, having regard in particular to their concentrations. The Directive sets out various labelling requirements, and it provides that suppliers must lodge details of their products with an appropriate body that can give advice in the event of medical emergencies. As with the 7th Amendment there are provisions for preserving confidential information, again subject to a variety of limitations and qualifications.

The Preparations Directive has been subject to three Adaptation Directives.[83] The first of these lowered the level of the lead content of paints and varnishes at which a warning label becomes obligatory, and also added some additional risk phrases for specific preparations containing active chlorine and certain cadmium alloys. The second stipulates concentration limits in terms of percentages by volume for use in applying the parent Directive to gaseous preparations. The third, which was due to be implemented by July 1, 1994, replaces both of Annexes I and II; the main changes (among several) replace references to "teratogenic" by "toxic for reproduction", and provide certain new risk phrases.

12–058

Safety Data Sheets (EC)

Both the 7th Amendment and the Preparations Directive require safety data sheets to be given to industrial users who are supplied with any dangerous substances or dangerous preparations, to ensure that industrial users have the information they need in order to take appropriate precautions against dangers to health, safety and the environment. The detailed contents of the data sheets are prescribed

12–059

---

[81] Including alloys, the properties of which may differ greatly from those of their individual components. Nevertheless alloys are assessed for the purposes of the Preparations Directive as though they were simple mixtures. A more useful approach would be to treat alloys as mixtures of the relevant eutectic mixture(s) and of the component(s) of any separate phase(s).

[82] See para. 12–026.

[83] Directives 89/178, [1989] O.J. L64; 90/492, [1990] O.J. 275; 93/18, [1993] O.J. L104.

in a separate Safety Data Sheets Directive 91/155, as amended,[84] and must be set out under sixteen obligatory headings listed in the Directive's Annex. The various obligations are given effect in the United Kingdom by regulation 6 of the Chemicals (Hazard Information and Packaging for Supply) Regulations 1994 (see paragraphs 12–089 to 12–127).

UK Legislation

12–060   The two principal sets of United Kingdom regulations of general application are the Notification of New Substances Regulations 1993,[85] (referred to as the NONS Regulations or sometimes as NONS 93 to distinguish them from the previous 1982 Regulations of the same name), and the Chemicals (Hazard Information and Packaging for Supply) Regulations 1994, referred to as the CHIP Regulations.[86] Notification of new substances, introduced by the 6th Amendment, was previously governed by the Notification of New Substances Regulations 1982;[87] the extensive additional provisions of the 7th Amendment and the other EC Directives outlined above led to the NONS and the CHIP Regulations; the 1982 Regulations have now been revoked. Official guidance to NONS 93 has been published jointly by the HSE and the DoE.[87A]

Notification of New Substances (UK)

12–061   The NONS Regulations apply to all "new substances", being defined as any substance except a substance listed in EINECS. Prima facie, therefore, they apply not only to new substances marketed following the date of coming into force of the Regulations,[88] but also any substance marketed since September 18, 1981, whether or not this is included in ELINCS. However, notifications made under NONS 82 are to be treated as notifications made under NONS 93,[89] and will be

---

[84] [1991] O.J. L76, amended by Directive 93/112, [1993] O.J. L314.
[85] S.I. 1993 No. 3050.
[86] S.I. 1994 No. 3247.
[87] S.I. 1982 No. 1496, as amended by S.I. 1986 No. 890 and S.I. 1991 No. 1914.
[87A] HS(G) 117, "Making Sense of NONS: Guide to the Notification of New Substances Regulations 1993."
[88] January 31, 1994.
[89] reg. 25(3).

subject to the same requirements, for example in relation to supply of further information, as apply to notifications made under NONS 93. A new substance that by reason of a certificate of exemption was not notified under NONS 82 (the certificate was available in respect of certain pesticides) had to be notified under NONS 93 by July 31, 1994. The terminology is used in the same sense as in the EC Directives already referred to; in particular, "substances" and "preparations" are given the same definitions as in the 7th Amendment, referred to above (see paragraph 12–007).

Because "substance" relates both to pure chemicals and also to the products of manufacturing processes including additives and impurities, there can on occasion be problems in determining whether an article proposed to be marketed is itself a substance, whether it incorporates one, or whether it is properly classed as a preparation. Examples[90] include carbonless copying paper and impregnated polymers. In the UK, the practice is to consider what may be released from the article: where a component is in fact merely an inert carrier, then it will be the active component supported by it that will be treated as the notifiable substance (or preparation). Alloys, though they often behave quite differently from their individual components (at least when consisting of a eutectic mixture), are treated as simple mixtures, and hence as preparations.[91] Salts, which may result from simple mixing of an acid and a base, are (undoubtedly quite rightly) regarded as separate substances and, if new, notifiable as such, irrespective of the status of the acid and base. The same applies *a fortiori* to organic esters.

12–062

Special rules apply to polymers, which, generally speaking, are accepted as being relatively harmless. Polymers can be in the form of complex molecules that are very difficult to categorise, and very small changes in their manufacturing process will lead to marginally different structures, if only in molecular weight. The rule that is applied is that if a "new" polymer contains below 2 per cent of a new monomer then it is not notifiable; the differences introduced by the monomer being assumed to be negligible. The practice in appropriate areas is to notify one or two representative members of a "family" of polymers that have essentially the same composition. Notification requirements in relation to these materials are accordingly set out separately, in Part D of Schedule 2 to the Regulations, which repeat *verbatim* the addition to Annex VII to the CPL Directive made by

12–063

---

[90] Cited by Dr John Davis of the HSE at an IBA Conference in December 1993 and gratefully adopted.
[91] See note 81 to para. 12–057.

Directive 93/105.[91A] The test results that must be provided depend on whether the polymer can be regarded as non-bioavailable by reference to criteria set out in paragraph C.2 of the Schedule; this depends essentially on whether it has a high number-average molecular weight, a low content of low molecular weight species, and low solubility/extractivity. Such polymers are allowed a "reduced test package", and hence are called "RTP polymers". The tests required also depend on the quantities placed on the Community market. For RTP polymers additional tests must be carried out if the amounts marketed are or exceed one tonne per annum or five tonnes in total; for other polymers additional tests are required at 100 kg per annum or 500kg in total, and one tonne per annum or five tonnes in total.

12–064   The exceptions from the application of the NONS Regulations, set out in regulation 3(2), follow those in the 7th Amendment. The Regulations accordingly do not apply to:

— a substance which is marketed exclusively as, or exclusively for use as an active ingredient in, either a medicinal product as defined in section 130 of the Medicines Act 1968[92] or a product to which that Act is made applicable by virtue of an order made under section 104 or 105;

— a substance which is marketed exclusively as, or exclusively for use in food within the meaning of section 1 of the Food Safety Act 1990[93] including any additives and flavourings;

— a substance which is marketed exclusively as or exclusively for use in an animal feeding stuff within the meaning of the Agriculture Feeding Stuffs Regulations 1991[94] including any additives;

— a substance which is marketed exclusively as or exclusively for use as an active ingredient in a pesticide which is covered by the Plant Protection Products Directive 91/414 (see Chapter 13);

— a substance in the form of waste covered by either Directives 91/156 or 91/689 (covering waste and hazardous waste respectively);

— a substance that is marketed exclusively as, or exclusively for use in, a cosmetic product within the meaning of the Cosmetic Products (Safety) Regulations 1989;[95]

[91A] [1993] O.J. L294.
[92] 1968 (c.67).
[93] 1990 (c.16).
[94] S.I. 1991 No. 2840.
[95] S.I. 1989 No. 2233.

- a new substance which is in transit through the United Kingdom under Customs Control and which does not undergo any treatment or processing within the United Kingdom;
- a substance intended exclusively for export to a country outside the EC (but subject to the provisions of EC Regulation 2455/92)[96] on the export of dangerous substances (see paragraphs 12–205 to 12–213).
- a new substance which is a substance "no longer polymer" — this expression relates to those materials that were within the definition of polymer under the 6th Amendment, and so benefited from the exemptions it provided, but which are no longer within the different definition of the 7th Amendment, and would otherwise require to be notified.

The Regulations apply throughout Great Britain, but generally do not extend to Northern Ireland, except in so far as they relate to the importation of new substances into the United Kingdom. However, in accordance with the free movement provisions of the 7th Amendment, where a substance has been duly notified in Northern Ireland or elsewhere in the EC, the Regulations do not apply to that substance when it is brought to Great Britain. The Regulations do however apply to those premises and activities offshore to which provisions of the H.S.W.A. 1974 apply by virtue of the Health and Safety at Work, etc., Act 1974 (Application Outside Great Britain) Order 1989 (SI 1989 No. 840).   **12–065**

The Regulations apply to all new substances that are placed on the market, either alone or in preparations. "Placing on the market" in relation to a substance or preparation is defined very broadly as supplying it or making it available to another person within the EC, and includes importation of it. This definition thus catches, among other activities, toll manufacture, where goods are supplied to a third party to carry out manufacturing operations on them, without the property in those goods passing to the third party.   **12–066**

Whether a new substance must be notified, and if so the amount of information that must be provided varies depending on the amount of that substance that is placed on the market in any one year. The differing requirements are set out in Table 12/I. For all but the very smallest quantities two criteria apply, namely the annual amount per manufacturer, and also the cumulative total amount that that manufacturer has placed on the market (anywhere within the EC).   **12–067**

---

[96] [1992] O.J. L251.

691

TABLE 12/I

12–068

Notification of New Substances Regulations 1993		
Quantity	**Applicable Regulation(s)**	**Information Requirements (except for polymers)**
Annually per manufacturer) under 10kg	6(4), maybe 6(5), 6(6)	Schedule 2, Part A, paras. 2.3, 2.4, 2.5; Part C, para. 2.3 may be required
Annually per manufacturer 10kg or more/ under 100kg or Total per manufacturer under 500 kg	6(2)	Schedule 2, Part C Reg. 4: (b) to (f)
Annually per manufacturer 100kg or more/ under 1 tonne or Total per manufacturer 500kg or more under 10 tonnes	6(1) 6(8)	Schedule 2, Part B Reg. 4: (b) to (f)
Annually per manufacturer 1 tonne or more or Total per manufacturer 10 tonnes or more under 50 tonnes	4(1)	Schedule 2, Part A Reg. 4: (a) to (f)
Annually per manufacturer 1 tonne or more/ under 1,000 tonnes or Total per manufacturer 50 tonnes or more/ under 500 tonnes	5(1)(a), 5(2)	Schedule 3, level 1 may be required
Annually per manufacturer 100 tonnes or more/ under 1,000 tonnes or Total per manufacturer 500 tonnes or more under 5,000 tonnes	5(1)(b), 5(2)	Schedule 3, level 1 shall be required
Annually per manufacturer) 1,000 tonnes or more or Total per manufacturer 5,000 tonnes or more	5(1)(c), 5(2)	Schedule 3, level 2

The full standard notification requirements apply when a manufac-   **12–069**
turer's annual quantity is one tonne or more. Where a manufacturer
has only had to supply a reduced notification dossier, relying on
regulation 6(2), he must provide the further information needed to
complete Part B of Schedule 2 before his annual total reaches 100 kg or
his cumulative total reaches 500 kg.[97]

The standard notification requirements include providing   **12–070**

— a technical dossier with information necessary for evaluating
the foreseeable risk that the substance may create for human
health and the environment, containing all available relevant
data including information and test results as set out in Part A
of Schedule 2 to the Regulations, together with a detailed and
full description of the studies conducted;

— a certificate in writing from the body that carried out the tests
being relied on, stating that the tests were carried out in
accordance with the principles of good laboratory practice
(see paragraphs 12–023 to 12–025);

— a declaration as to the unfavourable effects of the substance
by reference to the various foreseeable uses of it;

— if the substance is a dangerous substance, proposals for its
classification and labelling and for its safety data sheet for the
purposes of the CHIP Regulations 1993 (see paragraphs 12–
098 to 12–120);

— (where the substance is manufactured outside the EC) a
statement, where appropriate, that the notifier has been
appointed by the manufacturer for the purposes of submitting the notification as his sole representative, and that all
other importers from that manufacturer have been informed
of his name; and

— optionally, a request for exemption from the provisions of
regulation 13(4), under which a person notifying may be
required to share test results with later notifiers, where
necessary to avoid the duplication of testing on vertebrate
animals.

The notifier may, if he wishes, additionally include an assessment of   **12–071**
the real and potential risks created by the substance to human health
and the environment, in accordance with Article 3 of the 7th
Amendment (see paragraph 12–033). Further, at least where a full
notification has been made under regulation 4, and possibly in all

---

[97] reg. 6(8).

cases,[98] where additional testing has in fact been carried out, whether required under these Regulations or not, the notifier must forthwith provide the HSE with the results of those tests together with a certificate in writing from the body that carried them out stating that they were carried out in accordance with the principles of good laboratory practice referred to in Directive 87/18 and as required by regulation 14(1).[99]

12–072   As indicated in Table 12/I, where relatively small quantities are involved, the amount of information required is reduced. For under 100 kg annually per manufacturer or under 500 kg cumulative total per manufacturer, the information required is essentially purely factual relating to the product itself as opposed to its impact on man or the environment. Conversely, as the amounts involved increase, the provisions of regulation 5 become applicable, requiring significantly extended test results from physico-chemical, toxicological and ecotoxicity tests.

12–073   The NONS Regulations are primarily designed to ensure information is provided to the HSE, and through the HSE to the Commission, on all new substances being marketed. They are not in themselves intended to provide controls over the marketing. Nevertheless, to allow time for checking that the notification has been correctly made, regulation 8(1) stipulates that the notified substance may only be placed on the market if at least sixty days have elapsed from receipt by the HSE of a notification in conformity with the Regulations, and there has been no objection from the HSE in that period. If the HSE during that 60 day interval decides that the notification does not comply with the requirements of regulation 4, it must inform the notifier forthwith. In that event, the marketing of the substance may only take place 60 days after the HSE has received all the information necessary for the notification to comply with regulation 4.[1] Failure by the HSE to act within the 60 days to inform the notifier of any non-compliance with regulation 4 does not, it would seem, provide any implied consent to the marketing, and the HSE would be entitled to treat the original defective notification as a nullity. The purpose and effect of regulation

[98]   reg. 5(2) does not say in terms that it is limited to where notification has been made under reg. 4 (unlike reg. 5(1)), although the heading to reg. 5 indicates that the intention is to limit the whole of that regulation to substances notified under reg. 4. Applying the normal rule of interpretation that headings in statutes should be disregarded, reg. 5(2) would appear to apply to anyone who has submitted a notification, whether under reg. 4 or under reg. 6. The practical implications of this may however be small, unless the HSE attempts to enforce this provision against notifiers under reg. 6(1) or (2) also.

[99]   reg. 5(2); the principles are set out in Annex B to Directive 90/18 — see para. 12–024 and note 28 thereto.

[1]   reg. 8(2).

8(2) appears to be solely to stipulate that the 60 day period does not begin until all the notification requirements have been complied with, even though a substantially complete notification may have been made long before.

Where a notifier is entitled to take advantage of the reduced notification requirements of regulation 6, then he may market his substance after 30 days from receipt by the HSE of his regulation 6 notification in the absence of any objection from the HSE meanwhile.[2] Similarly, if the HSE within that 30 day period decides a notification is not in order it shall inform the notifier accordingly, and marketing may only take place after 30 days have elapsed following a notification that is fully in compliance with regulation 6. However, where regulation 6 applies, if the HSE informs the notifier in writing that his notification is accepted to be in order, the substance may be placed on the market at any time after 15 days have elapsed since the HSE received the notification—no corresponding provision is made where notification is made under regulation 4.

12–074

Where circumstances require it, the HSE may seek additional information in respect of a notified substance beyond that which is stipulated under the standard notification requirements applicable to the actual annual quantities and cumulative totals.[3] However a request for further information may only be made if the HSE is satisfied that this is reasonably required to evaluate the risks, or where it is acting to implement a decision of the Commission under Article 18(2) of Directive 67/548, as amended by the 7th Amendment.

12–075

Additionally, a notifier of a substance must inform the HSE of

12–076

- changes in the annual or total quantity of the substance marketed in the EC; where the notifier is acting on behalf of a manufacturer outside the EC, he must give this information in respect of both himself and all others importing that manufacturer's substance.
- new knowledge of the health and/or environmental effects of the substance that he may become aware of;
- new uses for the substance that he may become aware of (this presumably applies only to new uses actually made or likely to be made);
- any change in the composition of the substance from that notified;
- any change in the notifier's status as manufacturer, importer or sole representative.[4]

[2] reg. 8(3).
[3] reg. 9.
[4] reg. 10(1).

12–077   To ensure that sole representatives of a non-EC manufacturer are in a position to give the information they are required to supply, regulation 10(2) obliges any importer of a new substance made by that manufacturer to ensure that the sole representative is provided with up to date information on amounts marketed in the EC by that importer. Where there is no sole representative, cumulative yearly tonnages are to be determined by the Commission on the basis of information supplied to it by the various competent authorities of the Member States. Unless and until a sole representative is appointed, every importer of a substance in such circumstances is under the same obligation to carry out supplementary testing, where this is called for,[5] subject to the provisions of regulation 13, that seeks to avoid duplicate testing, so far as possible, particularly on vertebrate animals.

12–078   Where a new substance has been notified at least ten years previously, a subsequent notifier is only required to provide the basic information on the substance listed in paragaphs 1 and 2 of the relevant Part of Schedule 2.[6] In any other case a later manufacturer or importer is, in principle, under exactly the same obligations as the first notifier. However, where there are two or more notifications at different times, a later notifier may, if the first one consents, rely on the test results originally supplied, provided that the later can show that his substance is the same as the previous one, not only in its chemistry but also as regards the degree of purity and the nature of the impurities.[7] In order to trigger this provision, there is a positive obligation on all new notifiers of a substance to enquire of the HSE whether it has been notified previously, and if so the name and address of the first notifier. To avoid spurious requests, possibly made purely to elicit commercial information, they must be supported by evidence that the later notifier intends to place the same substance on the market and of the quantities involved, and the HSE must be satisfied as to these facts. If no exemption has been requested and granted under regulation 4(f) against disclosure of the relevant information, the HSE will provide the later notifier with the name and address of the first one, having however informed the first notifier of its intention to do this.[8]

12–079   It is not clear whether the first notifier has any right to seek an exemption under regulation 4(f) at any time other than in the course of his original notification. No other procedure is suggested, save by the mention in regulation 13(4) of the HSE informing the first notifier of his intention to disclose his name and address. It does not follow that

---

[5] reg. 12.
[6] reg. 11.
[7] reg. 13(1).
[8] reg. 13(4).

this mention is made to enable the first notifier to claim exemption belatedly, since the provision is consistent with simply warning him to expect an approach from the later notifier. Prudence suggests, therefore, that any first notifier of a substance must consider at that stage whether or not he is prepared to share his information on animal test results, and if not to claim the exemption at the outset where this can properly be done, and not hope to rely on seeking the exemption at some later stage.

Where a later notifier has received the name and address of the first, **12–080** the two of them are required to take all reasonable steps to agree to share information so as to avoid duplication of testing on vertebrate animals. If an agreement cannot be reached, the later notifier has to inform the HSE and must not commence testing on vertebrate animals for a further 30 days. Where agreement has been reached, and subsequently additional testing is required under regulation 5, the notifiers are required to take all reasonable steps to reach further agreement to share that information also.[9–10]

All testing must be in accordance with the principles of good **12–081** laboratory practice — see paragraphs 12–023 to 12–025. The test methods laid down by Directive 92/69 (see paragraph 12–022) are given effect in the United Kingdom by the adoption of the Annex to that Directive as an Approved Code of Practice.

Having received information on notified substances, the HSE must **12–082** carry out a risk assessment, including making recommendations on the most appropriate method for testing the substance and any risk reduction measures that may be appropriate. HSE advice on conducting risk assessments is contained in "Risk Assessment of New Substances: Technical Guidance Document". It must keep the Commission fully informed both of information supplied to it under the NONS Regulations and also of any risk assessment that it has made.[11]

Confidentiality

Part IV of the NONS Regulations is concerned with the extent to **12–083** which disclosure of information may be restricted. Under regulation 18(1), which is subject to the further provisions of that regulation, information notified under the NONS requirements is to be treated in the same way as information obtained or furnished under H.S.W.A. 1974, section 28 of which essentially requires it to be kept confidential, but allows limited use and disclosure without the consent of the person providing the information. Regulation 18(2) allows anyone

[9–10] reg. 5(5)–(7).
[11] regs. 16, 17.

making the notification to indicate information the disclosure of which might harm his competitive position and should be kept confidential. The HSE must then, if full justification for the request is given, decide what information is to be kept confidential and inform the notifier accordingly. No appeal procedure is provided, and in the event of an adverse decision, an aggrieved notifier would, having regard to the time constraints on him, have to proceed very rapidly with seeking an injunction against the HSE, if appropriate.

12–084   Regulation 18(3) sets out information that cannot in any event be kept confidential. This list mirrors that contained in the Risk Assessment regulation 793/93 (see paragraph 12–056). Similarly, if the manufacturer, an importer or the notifier himself subsequently discloses previously confidential information, regulation 18(4) requires him to inform the HSE accordingly, and that information shall no longer be treated as confidential for the purposes of the NONS Regulations. It must be presumed that a disclosure to which this paragraph applies is only relevant if it makes the information public (itself not always a straightforward issue), and is not one made under conditions maintaining confidentiality. How the obligation of this regulation 18(4) is to apply to a manufacturer or an importer other than the notifier himself is obscure, since there would not appear to be any necessary reason why anyone other than the notifier should be aware of exactly what he has requested should be kept confidential. It is also entirely conceivable that, where the notifier is separate from the manufacturer, the latter may have made a relevant disclosure of which the notifier is simply not aware.

12–085   Even where the HSE has agreed that certain information will be kept confidential, this information may be disclosed without the consent of the notifier

- to a competent authority of another Member State or to the Commission;
- to the extent necessary to evaluate the notification and to prepare the risk assessment; and
- for the purposes of legal proceedings.

Where confidential information is passed to other competent authorities and the Commission, they are to be informed of what has been agreed to be kept confidential. The converse equally applies where the HSE receives confidential information from the competent authorities of other Member States.[12]

12–086   To assist maintenance of confidentiality in the case of a substance that is not a dangerous substance, the European Commission may list

---

[12] reg. 19.

it in ELINCS in the form of its trade name for a maximum of three years if the HSE so requests.[13] It follows that a notifier wishing to benefit from this provision should ensure that a corresponding request is made to the HSE. Further, if the HSE considers the publication of the name of the substance in the IUPAC nomenclature could reveal information concerning the commercial exploitation or manufacture of the substance, then in those circumstances the substance may be recorded under its trade name for as long as the HSE sees fit. Where a notified substance is a dangerous substance, it may still be listed in ELINCS in the form of its trade name, but this limited protection will last only until it is introduced into Annex I of the Directive.[14]

Enforcement of the provisions of the NONS Regulations is the responsibility of the HSE. By way of reinforcement of the general controls, a new substance requiring notification under regulation 4 or 6 may not be brought into the United Kingdom until it has been duly notified.[15] Further, where the HSE has reasonable cause to believe that a person possesses a new substance requiring notification under the Regulations but which has not been duly notified, it may serve a notice on that person prohibiting him from marketing it or disposing of it for 60 days or 30 days, respectively, after it has been duly notified under regulation 4 or regulation 6, as the case may be.[16] **12–087**

The HSE may in its discretion, but subject to any provisions imposed by EC legislation, exempt any person or class of persons or any substance or class of substances from the controls of the NONS Regulations. However it may not do so unless having regard to all the circumstances of the case, including any conditions that may be attached and any other legal requirements, it is satisfied that neither the health and safety of persons who are likely to be affected by the exemption nor protection of the environment will be prejudiced as a consequence of it. **12–088**

Hazard Information and Packaging—the CHIP Regulations

The CHIP Regulations aim to implement the bulk of the 7th Amendment (other than the notification and risk assessment aspects), **12–089**

---

[13] reg. 20(1)(a).
[14] reg. 20(1)(b).
[15] reg. 22(1).
[16] reg. 22(3).

the Preparations Directive and the related safety Data Sheets Directive. As originally issued in 1993 they went further than these Directives and also addressed the transport of chemicals by road. However the transport aspects have since been hived out and applied also to carriage by rail—they are now contained in the Carriage of Dangerous Goods by Road and Rail (Classification, Packaging and Labelling) Regulations 1994 (the "Carriage Regulations"), supplemented by the Carriage of Dangerous Goods by Rail Regulations 1994.[17] The revised 1994 Regulations cover the classification, packaging and labelling of pesticides, and thereby give effect to Directive 78/631.[18] Official guidance on the CHIP Regulations consists of "Approved guide to the classification and labelling of substances and preparations dangerous for supply—Guidance on Regulations".

12–090   The CHIP Regulations do not stand alone: it is essential to read and use them in conjunction with:

(i)   The Approved Guide to the Classification and Labelling of Substances and Preparations Dangerous for Supply (L38) (the "Approved Labelling Guide");

(ii) Information Approved for the Classification and Labelling of Substances and Preparations Dangerous for Supply (the "Approved Supply List");

(iii) The Approved Code of Practice "Safety Data Sheets for Substances and Preparations Dangerous for Supply" (L37).

When used in conjunction with these documents, the CHIP Regulations as amended impose requirements to ascertain the hazards that the chemicals represent and to inform those who are supplied with the chemicals of these hazards by suitable labelling and the provision of safety data sheets. There are also general requirements on packaging; these are substantially supplemented by the Carriage Regulations.

Classification

12–091   Fundamental not only to the CHIP Regulations but also to other legislation concerned with hazardous substances, such as the CIMAH

---

[17] S.I.s 1994 Nos. 669, 670.
[18] [1978] O.J. L204; see also Chapter 13.

Regulations,[19] the COSHH Regulations[20] and the Carriage Regulations, is the comprehensive classification of all chemicals into a variety of risk categories. As explained above, a substantial start has been made to this by the preparation of Annex I to the 7th Amendment. This Annex I forms the basis of the Approved Supply List; like Annex I, the Approved Supply List is due to be updated periodically, so as to incorporate additional substances that have been notified to the relevant authorities or are in EINECS, and for which sufficient experimental data have been collected to enable a proper classification of the substance concerned.

The Regulations use "substances" and "preparations" in the same **12–092** sense as the EC Directives. Thus "substances" are defined as:

> Chemical elements and their compounds in the natural state or obtained by any production process, including any additive necessary to preserve the stability of the product and any impurity deriving from the process used, but excluding any solvent which may be separated without affecting the stability of the substance or changing its composition.

"Preparations" are defined to mean "mixtures or solutions of two or more substances".

"Supply" is defined to mean supply of the relevant substance or **12–093** preparation in the course of or for use at work, by way of—

   (i)   sale or offer for sale,
  (ii)   commercial sample,
 (iii) transfer from a factory, warehouse, or other place of work and its curtilage to another place of work, whether or not in the same ownership,
 (iv) whether as principal or as agent for another.

Subject to certain limited exceptions, this definition of "supply" **12–094** does not however apply to the supply of any dangerous substance in or from premises registered under the Medicines Act,[21] and also certain instances of supply directly to members of the public.[22] For

---

[19] S.I. 1984 No. 1902.
[20] S.I. 1988 No. 1657.
[21] Medicinal products themselves, and other substances or preparations that are deemed to be medicinal products under the Medicines Act 1968 are exempted altogether from the application of the Regulations (see reg. 3(1)(e)).
[22] In the circumstances set out in regulation 16(2)(b)— see para. 12–124.

these excluded situations, "supply" has the meaning given to it by section 46 of the Consumer Protection Act 1987.[23]

Exceptions

12-095   Regulation 3 lists a variety of materials to which the Regulations do not apply. These are essentially substances or preparations that are controlled by other statutory regimes, for example, radioactive substances, animal feeding stuffs, medicinal and cosmetic products, explosives, goods intended for use as food and in a finished state, pesticides and wastes covered by the applicable EC waste directives. In addition, the Regulations do not apply to a supply that consists of a transfer of a substance or preparation from one place of work and its curtilage to another place of work in the same ownership and in the immediate vicinity.[24]

Exemption Certificates

12-096   Notwithstanding any other provisions in the Regulations, regulation 15(1) permits the Health and Safety Executive to grant an exemption from all or any of their provisions either absolutely or subject to such conditions and to such time limits as it sees fit. This exemption may be in favour of any person or class of persons, or may relate to any dangerous substance or class of dangerous substances or article or class of articles. Such an exemption must be given by a

---

[23] s. 46 contains a very extensive definition in nine sub-sections. Subs. (1) reads:
Subject to the following provisions of this section, references in this Act to supplying goods shall be construed as references to doing any of the following, whether as principal or agent, that is to say —

    (a) selling, hiring out or lending the goods;
    (b) entering into a hire-purchase agreement to furnish the goods;
    (c) the performance of any contract for work and materials to furnish the goods;
    (d) providing the goods in exchange for any consideration (including trading stamps) other than money;
    (e) providing the goods in or in connection with the performance of any statutory function; or
    (f) giving the goods as a prize or otherwise making a gift of the goods;
and, in relation to gas or water, those references shall be construed as including references to providing the service by which the gas or water is made available for use, save that it additionally includes an offer to supply and exposing for supply.
    This extended definition may be contrasted with the prohibition in Art. 5 of the 7th Amendment against substances being "placed on the market" which is defined as "making available to third parties" and also importation into the Community customs territory. Though "supply" in the CHIP Regulations will doubtless cover the great majority of circumstances, it would not appear to be as comprehensive as the Directive's "placing on the market".
[24] reg. 3(1)(m).

702

certificate in writing; it may be revoked at any time by a further certificate in writing.

Nevertheless, no such exemption may be granted unless the **12–097** Executive is satisfied that in all the circumstances, including in particular any proposed conditions to be attached to the exemption and any other statutory requirements that may apply, the exemption will not prejudice the health and safety of any persons likely to be affected as a result.[25]

Classification of Substances and Preparations for Supply

The CHIP Regulations require substances and preparations danger- **12–098** ous for supply to be classified by prohibiting their supply unless they have been classified in accordance with the provisions of regulation 5.[26] Substances are "dangerous for supply" if they are listed in Part I of the Approved Supply List. Additionally, both substances and preparations are "dangerous for supply" if, on classifying them in accordance with regulation 5 of the CHIP Regulations they fall into one of more of the categories of danger specified in those Regulations.

The regulation addresses in turn: **12–099**

— a substance listed in the Approved Supply List—the classification must be in accordance with column 2 of Part V of that List

— a new substance as defined by regulation 2(1) of NONS 93 and which has been notified under regulation 4, 6(1) or 6(2) of those regulations— the classification must conform with that notification

— any other substance dangerous for supply: an investigation must be made into such relevant and accessible data as may exist. The substance is then to be classified into one or more of the danger categories set out in Part I of Schedule 1 (see Table 12/II) as corresponds to the properties of the substance, and appropriate Risk Phrases must be assigned on the basis of the criteria set out in the Approved Labelling Guide.

The first question facing anyone dealing with a substance is whether **12–100** it is to be regarded as "dangerous for supply" at all, and for this purpose reference must be made to the Approved Labelling Guide. In the case of preparations, reference must also be made to the classification provisions of Schedule 3 to the Regulations,[27] unless it is a pesticide that has not been approved under FEPA 1985, in which case reference

---

[25] reg. 15(2).
[26] reg. 5(1).
[27] reg. 5(5).

is to be had to the classification provisions in Schedule 4 to the Regulations.[28]

12–101   The supply classification for substances consists of a total of seventeen separate classes grouped into three distinct categories of danger as shown in the following Table:

TABLE 12/II

12–102

Categories of Danger	
Physico-chemical properties	explosive oxidizing extremely flammable highly flammable flammable
Health effects	very toxic toxic harmful corrosive irritant sensitizing sensitizing by inhalation sensitizing by skin contact carcinogenic—this being further subdivided into categories 1, 2 and 3 mutagenic—this being further subdivided into categories 1,2 and 3 toxic for reproduction—this being further subdivided into categories 1, 2 and 3
Environment	dangerous for the environment

12–103   These various classes are more fully described in Schedule 1 to the Regulations. Each class is assigned a particular "symbol-letter" and, in most cases, a symbol (such a skull and crossbones for the toxic classes and a leafless tree and dead fish for "dangerous for the environment") in Schedule 2 to the Regulations. Special rules are contained in Part II of Schedule I for the classification of chemicals to be supplied in aerosol dispensers. Part III of Schedule I stipulates the methods to be used for determining flashpoint. For substances which have not been assigned to the Approved Supply List, information as to the substance's properties will have been assembled for the purposes of notification of that substance. It is then necessary to assess the significance of those properties—specifically whether it is to be

---

[28] For a full definition of what is to be regarded as a pesticide for the purposes of the CHIP Regulations, see para. 1 of Sched. 4 to the Regulations.

regarded as dangerous at all within the meaning of the Regulations, and if so into which category it should be assigned—in accordance with Schedule 1 coupled with the detailed instructions set out in the Approved Labelling Guide. Though the principles may be simply stated, putting them into practice may well require expert assistance. The Approved Labelling Guide also sets out a series of "Risk Phrases" relating to each of the classes of danger; in addition, for each of the physico-chemical and health effects categories there are further risk phrases which may be applied as well as the phrases specific to the particular selected class.[29]

In the case of preparations, other than pesticides, Schedule 3 to the **12–104** Regulations sets out rules for classifying these by reference to the properties of the component substance(s). The properties of a preparation will naturally be dependent on the concentration of the dangerous substance component. Assessments of health effects in relation to concentrations differ somewhat from the classes used for substances—in particular, and anomalously, they omit "dangerous for the environment". They consist of:

— acute lethal effects
— non-lethal irreversible effects after a single exposure
— severe effects after repeated or prolonged exposure
— corrosive effects
— irritant effects
— sensitising effects
— carcinogenic effects
— mutagenic effects
— toxic for reproduction effects

Part II of Schedule 3 then sets out in a series of tables which of these **12–105** classifications should be given, having regard to the classification of the component substance and its concentration.

Pesticides are treated separately from other preparations, and are **12–106** classified into "very toxic", "toxic" and "harmful" in accordance with provisions set out in Schedule 4 to the Regulations.

All substances contained in the EINECS inventory have a unique **12–107** nine digit index number, referred to as its "EEC number". When a further substance is notified and added to the ELINCS list it is also given a unique seven digit EEC number (the first digit being 4). The approved supply list is based on Annex I to the CPL Directive and is organised by reference to the index numbers of the substances listed.

[29] A full list of all approved Risk Phrases (of which there are currently 59) is set out in Part III of the Approved Supply List. These Risk Phrases are followed by the approved wording to be used to express specific combinations of two or more particular risks.

Part I of the List consists of all the substances in alphabetical order with the relevant EEC number against each together with the relevant CAS number[30] where applicable. Part II of the List consists of the same substances as listed in Part I, but arranged in EEC number order. Part V, entitled "Classification under Labelling Information", contains the essential information against each substance in the List for its classification and labelling, and indicates the appropriate Risk and Safety phrases to be used. In addition, concentration limits are included where appropriate.

12–108   Pesticides are contained in Part VI of the List, where each is given a conventional oral LD50 value to be used for the purpose of classifying a pesticide preparation in accordance with the formula given in Schedule V to the Regulations.

12–109   Parts III and IV contain the approved Risk Phrases and Safety Phrases respectively. Each phrase is given a unique number, preceded by R for a Risk Phrase and S for a Safety Phrase. These parts also contain approved wordings for use where two or more such phrases are applicable.

Labelling

12–110   The labelling of substances and preparations dangerous for supply is controlled by regulation 9. Under this a substance or preparation dangerous for supply may not be supplied unless the prescribed particulars relating to it are clearly shown in accordance with the size and layout requirements set out in regulation 11, and summarised in Table 12/III. Such labelling must be contained both on the receptacle containing the substance or preparation and, where relevant, "on any such layer which is likely to be the outermost layer of packaging during the supply or the use of the substance or preparation"[31] unless the packaging, through transparent windows or the like, allows the particulars inside to be clearly seen. These labelling requirements are lifted in relation to small quantities of dangerous substances and preparations other than those classed as explosive, very toxic, toxic or sensitizing, such that there is no reason to fear danger to any person handling them or to anyone else.[32] In certain cases the prescribed risk and safety phrases need not be shown where the quantity involved is at most 125 ml.[33]

---

[30] In accordance with the Chemical Abstracts Service classification.
[31] reg. 9(1)(b).
[32] reg. 9(7). The drafting of this provision is confused, but its meaning would appear to be as set out here.
[33] reg. 9(8).

Regulation 10 stipulates additional labelling rules for certain specific **12–111** preparations set out in Part II of Schedule 6, which apply whether or not the preparations concerned would otherwise be regarded as dangerous for supply within the meaning of the Regulations. These preparations are essentially ones with particularly harmful properties that are liable, directly or indirectly, to reach people who may well not otherwise appreciate the hazards involved, and consist of:

(a) Preparations to be supplied to the general public, in particular those which are very toxic, toxic or corrosive.
(b) Preparations intended for use by spraying.
(c) Preparations containing a substance posing a danger of cumulative effects.
(d) Preparations containing a substance that may cause harm to breastfed babies.
(e) Paints or varnishes containing lead.
(f) Cyanoacrylate-based adhesives.
(g) Preparations containing isocyanates.
(h) Certain preparations containing epoxy constituents.
(i) Preparations intended to be sold to the general public that contain active chlorine.
(j) Preparations containing cadmium (alloys) intending to be used for brazing or soldering.

For preparations packaged in aerosol dispensers their classification **12–112** and labelling is subject to the rules of Part II of Schedule 1, applying special flammability criteria and designations.[34]

TABLE 12/III

Supply Labelling Requirements (Regulation 9)				**12–113**
Substances		**Preparations**		
Para. (2)		Para. (3)		
(a)	Name and full address and telephone number of the person in a Member State of the EC who is responsible for supplying the substance, whether it be its manufacturer, importer or distributor.	(a)	Name and full address and telephone number of the person in a Member State of the EC who is responsible for supplying the substance, whether it be its manufacturer, importer or distributor.	

---

[34] reg. 10(2).

(b)	The name of the substance as listed in Part I of the Approved Supply List or (if not so listed) by an internationally recognised name.	(b)	The trade name or other designation.
		(c)(i)	Identification of the constituents causing the preparation to be dangerous for supply.
(c)(i)	The indication(s) of danger and the corresponding symbols (if any).	(c)(ii)	The indication(s) of danger and the corresponding symbols (if any).
(c)(ii)	Risk phrases	(c)(iii)	Risk phrases
(c)(iii)	Safety phrases	(c)(iv)	Safety phrases
(c)(iv)	The EEC number if known. Where listed in Part I of the Approved Supply List, the words "EEC label"	(c)(v)	If a pesticide, information as specified in Schedule 6, Part I, paragraph 5
		(c)(vi)	If intended for sale to the general public, the nominal quantity (by mass or volume)
		(d)	If not fully tested and para. 5(5) of Part I of schedule 3 applies, the caution there prescribed

Any other health or safety information may be included but no statement indicating absence of danger, such as "non-toxic" or "non-harmful"

Records and Information

12–114   Anyone who supplies a substance dangerous for supply that is neither on the Approved Supply List nor has been notified under the Notification of New Substances Regulations 1982, or who supplies a preparation dangerous for supply, must keep a record of the information that was used for the purposes of classifying it for at least three years from the last date on which the substance or preparation was supplied. This record, or a copy, must be made available to an enforcing authority on request.[35]

Where a preparation is classified on the basis of one or more of its **12–115** health effects[36] to which the CHIP Regulations apply, the Poisons Advisory Centre must be notified of the information that must go into the relevant safety data sheet required by the Regulations.[37] This notification must be made before the preparation is first supplied; however where the preparation had already been previously supplied before the CHIP Regulations came into effect on January 31, 1995, the Poisons Advisory Centre must be notified at the latest on the first supply thereafter. In either case the information must be kept up to date thereafter.[38] Nevertheless, by virtue of the transitional provisions in regulation 17(4) these notification requirements will not apply until the Secretary of State has approved the Poisons Advisory Centre; having done so, a grace period of 6 or 12 months, depending on the relevant hazard indication, or such longer period as the HSE may approve, is given to allow time for notifications to be made. The Poisons Advisory Centre is under a duty to maintain confidential information it receives under this notification procedure, and may only disclose it to a registered medical practitioner who requests it in connection with the medical treatment of a person who may have been affected by the relevant preparation.[39]

Safety Data Sheets

Safety data sheets are documents designed to enable recipients of **12–116** substances and preparations that are "dangerous for supply" to take all necessary measures relating to protection of health and safety at work and to the protection of the environment.[40] Their immediate purpose is not therefore to provide warnings to those who may handle the substances and preparations—that is the purpose of the requisite labelling and hazard warning indications—though they may well assist usefully in that regard. The requirement to provide safety data sheets with substances and preparations dangerous for supply was first introduced by Article 27 of the 7th Amendment, as elaborated by the Safety Data Sheets Directive 91/155,[41] and is given effect in the United Kingdom by regulation 6 of the CHIP Regulations. Guidance in the form of an Approved Code of Practice issued under section 16(1) of

---

[35] reg. 13.
[36] Very toxic, toxic, harmful, corrosive, irritant, sensitizing, sensitizing by inhalation, sensitizing by skin contact, carcinogenic, mutagenic or toxic for reproduction.
[37] reg. 14(2).
[38] reg. 14(3).
[39] reg. 14(4).
[40] reg. 6(1).
[41] [1991] O.J. L76.

H.S.W.A. 1974 on regulation 6 has been issued by the HSC "Safety Data Sheets for Substances and Preparations Dangerous for Supply".[42]

12–117   The broad requirement of regulation 6(1) is that the supplier of a substance or preparation dangerous for supply shall provide the recipient of it with a safety data sheet containing information set out under obligatory headings specified in Schedule 5 to the CHIP Regulations. "Supply" is, for this purpose, given a more limited meaning that explicitly excludes aspects of the wide definition of "supply" in regulation 2(1). Thus it covers supply by way of sale or commercial sample, but does not include an offer for sale, or a transfer between two places of work in the same ownership, or the return of a substance or preparation to the person who supplied it provided that its properties have remained unchanged.[43] The supplier may be any of the manufacturer, importer or distributor of the substance or preparation, and he may act on his own account or as agent for another. In any particular instance, there may quite clearly be several "suppliers" within the statutory definition, and the obligations under regulation 6 will fall on all of them. Where there is a chain of supply and at intermediate stages goods are, for example, repackaged or sold for uses not foreseen by the original manufacturer, the persons responsible must apply their own minds to how the regulation should be given full effect. Though the primary obligation must necessarily fall on the manufacturer of the substance or preparation, all of those subsequently receiving the product must therefore in turn satisfy themselves as to the adequacy of the initial safety data sheet, and adapt it as appropriate, depending on who the product may be passed on to.

12–118   The information contained in the safety data sheet should be designed to allow the recipient to carry out a satisfactory COSHH assessment, and must be presented under a series of prescribed headings,[44] namely:

(1) Identification of the substance/preparation and company
(2) Composition/information on ingredients
(3) Hazards identification
(4) First-aid measures
(5) Fire-fighting measures
(6) Accidental release measures
(7) Handling and storage
(8) Exposure controls/personal protection

[42] August 2, 1993.
[43] A.C.O.P. para. 5, and reg. 6(2).
[44] In Sched. 5.

(9) Physical and chemical properties
(10) Stability and reactivity
(11) Toxicological information
(12) Ecological information
(13) Disposal considerations
(14) Transport information
(15) Regulatory information
(16) Other information

Full guidance on the contents of the safety data sheet to be given under these obligatory headings is given in Appendix 2 of the Approved Code of Practice. Safety data sheets must be in English. However where a substance or preparation is supplied to a recipient in another EC member state, the official language of that state may be employed.

The safety data sheet must be dated, and the supplier has an **12–118A** obligation to keep it up to date and to revise it forthwith if any significant new information becomes available regarding safety or risks to human health or the protection of the environment in relation to the substance or preparation concerned.[45] Any revised safety data sheet must be clearly marked with the word "Revision" and the date of that revision. The Approved Code of Practice states that the revision should be undertaken "when new information becomes available that may require users of the product to reassess the risks in their workplaces to health, safety or the environment". New information may become available from a wide variety of sources, and suppliers are under a clear obligation actively to keep themselves informed as to what new information may have become available relevant to their products; it is not sufficient merely to revise data sheets to reflect information that is passively acquired.

Each supplier of a substance or preparation must provide the **12–119** appropriate safety data sheet to the recipient, free of charge, no later than the date of the first supply . There is no requirement to continue supplying copies in respect of repeat orders, though in some circumstances, this may be a prudent step to ensure that no one is inadvertently left out. Where a safety data sheet is revised, a copy of the revised version must be provided free of charge to all those who have received the relevant substance or preparation in the preceding 12 months, and the changes drawn to their attention.[46]

Where substances or preparations dangerous for supply are sold to **12–120** the general public from pharmacies, any retail outlet or in any other manner, including by way of free sample, prize or mail order, safety

[45] reg. 6(3).
[46] reg. 6(4).

711

data sheets need not be provided with them, if sufficient information is furnished in any event to enable users to take appropriate precautionary measures.[47] Nevertheless, a safety data sheet must be given on request to any recipient intending to use a substance or preparation at work; where one is supplied in these circumstances, there is however no obligation to give that recipient any revised data sheets.

12–121   Manufacturers, importers and suppliers of any substance and any preparation, whether "dangerous for supply" or not, are under a general obligation by virtue of section 6(4)(c) and (d) of the H.S.W.A. 1974

(1) to take such steps as are necessary to secure that recipients of it are provided with adequate information about
— risks to health or safety to which its inherent properties may give rise
— the results of any relevant tests which have been carried out on it or in connection with it, and
— any conditions necessary to ensure that it will be safe and without risks to health at all times when it is being used, handled, processed, stored or transported by a person at work, or otherwise in premises to which section 4 of the H.S.W.A. applies, and also

(2) to provide revisions of that information where anything becomes known that gives rise to a serious risk to health or safety.

12–122   The obligations under regulation 6 to provide safety data sheets and to keep them up to date are supplemental to this general obligation under the H.S.W.A.; compliance with them may, in any particular case, also meet the H.S.W.A. requirements, but there can be no automatic presumption that it will.

Enforcement and Civil Liability

12–123   The requirements of the CHIP Regulations remaining after removal of those concerned with the carriage of goods, though made pursuant to section 2(2) of the European Communities Act, are to be regarded as though they were health and safety regulations made under section 15 of the H.S.W.A. 1974. Consequently, provisions as to enforcement, the approval of Codes of Practice, and the use of Codes of Practice as

---

[47] reg. 6(5) and A.C.O.P., para. 19.

evidence in criminal proceedings[48] apply as they do to other health and safety regulations. Further, any breach of EC derived provisions will potentially give rise to civil liability for breach of statutory duty.[49]

Enforcement will ordinarily be by the Health and Safety Executive. **12–124** However, where a dangerous substance is supplied in or from premises registered under the Medicines Act 1968, the enforcing authority is the Royal Pharmaceutical Society. Where a dangerous substance is supplied from a shop, mobile vehicle, market stall or other retail outlet, or in any other way to members of the public, whether by free sample or prize or mail order, the enforcing authority is the local weights and measures authority. In these circumstances, where the Health and Safety Executive is not the enforcing authority, the relevant provisions are to be enforced as if they were safety regulations made under the Consumer Protection Act 1987,[50] and the provisions of section 12 of that Act, relating to offences against safety regulations, will apply.

It is a defence to any alleged breach of the Regulations for any **12–125** person to prove that he took all reasonable precautions and exercised all due diligence to avoid the commission of the offence charged.[51]

The original CHIP Regulations came into force on September 1, **12–126** 1993, though their regulation 19(1) allowed a grace period of 12 months, to September 1, 1994, during which time any non-compliance with the Regulations was not an offence, provided that any relevant substance or preparation was classified, packaged and labelled in accordance with the Classification, Packaging and Labelling of Dangerous Substances Regulations 1984[52] as in force immediately before September 1, 1993.[53] Until March 1, 1995, substances and preparations packaged before September 1, 1994 in aggregate quantities per package or receptacle of not more than 25 litres need only comply with the then current CPL Regulations 1984; the safety data sheet requirements however apply.[54]

The CHIP Regulations do not apply to Northern Ireland, but they **12–127** are extended outside Great Britain in the same manner as health and

[48] By virtue of H.S.W.A., s.17.
[49] reg. 16(1)(b).
[50] 1987 (c.43).
[51] reg. 16(4); see paras. 21–002 to 21–006 on this defence.
[52] S.I. 1984 No. 1244, as subsequently amended by S.I. 1986 No. 1922, S.I. 1988 No. 766, S.I. 1989 No. 2208 and S.I. 1990 No. 1255.
[53] The wish to give industry a reasonable time to digest and adapt to the new regime is entirely laudable. Nevertheless, the obligation under Art. 3(1) of the 7th Amendment to bring its provisions into force by not later than October 31, 1993, means that any explicit waiver of that time limit in domestic legislation must necessarily involve a blatant breach of the EC Directive's requirements.
[54] reg. 17(3). Generally, until July 31, 1995, it will be sufficient compliance with the 1994 CHIP Regulations to comply with the original 1993 Regulations (reg. 17(8),(2)).

safety provisions are applied outside Great Britain in accordance with the Health and Safety at Work etc. Act 1974 (Application outside Great Britain) Order 1989.[55] They would therefore apply in relation to oil drilling and exploration vessels operating off-shore.

The Carriage of Dangerous Goods

12–128   The carriage of dangerous goods is governed by separate and very detailed provisions. As mentioned, the original CHIP Regulations spelled out "carriage requirements", but these were revoked with effect from April 1, 1994. Rules applicable to the carriage of dangerous goods by both road and rail are now contained in the Carriage of Dangerous Goods by Road and Rail (Classification, Packaging and Labelling) Regulations 1994[56] (referred to in this chapter as the "Carriage Regulations"). The Carriage Regulations are not based on any EC legislation, but on recommendations (known as the "UN List") prepared by the United Nations Committee of Experts on the Transport of Dangerous Goods.

12–129   The purpose of the Carriage Regulations is to introduce rules that are harmonised with international agreements, principally the UN Recommendations on the Transport of Dangerous Goods and the European-wide "ADR" agreement on the carriage of dangerous goods by road. The UN Recommendations set worldwide standards on the safe carriage of dangerous goods by sea, air and land (including road, rail and waterway), which have been widely adopted by various transport organisations as the basis of their own rules and codes of practice. The ADR agreement governs the international transport of dangerous goods within Europe. Although this is administered by the UN Economic Commission for Europe, there are significant differences between ADR and the UN Recommendations. The European Commission is itself working on a draft directive that would require member states to harmonise its carriage rules with ADR. It is expected however that there will be a derogation in favour of those member states that have legislation in place that is in line with the UN Recommendations, and the purpose of the new Carriage Regulations is to ensure that this is the case. As current UK rules are most closely aligned with the UN Recommendations,[57] the regulatory changes involved should thus be minimised.

---

[55] S.I. 1989 No. 840.

[56] S.I. 1994 No. 669.

[57] Prior to the opening of the Channel Tunnel, all international transport of goods had to go by sea or by air, and the international agreements relating to such transport are more closely aligned with the UN Recommendations than ADR.

An additional development has been prompted by the proposed **12–130** privatisation of British Rail. Hitherto, British Rail has imposed obligations on consignors by the conditions of acceptance of dangerous goods consigned to it for carriage. If a harmonised system of rules is to apply following privatisation, this must be by way of statutory requirements, and accordingly the government has taken the opportunity presented by the Carriage Regulations to make them applicable to rail as well as to road, and to supplement these with the Carriage of Dangerous Goods by Rail Regulations 1994[58] that set out additional requirements for all those involved in the transport of dangerous goods by rail.

Since, for the reasons indicated, the classification, packaging and **12–131** labelling requirements of the Carriage Regulations are not derived from the 7th Amendment or any other EC legislation, unlike the CHIP Regulations, the requirements in these respects that they lay down differ somewhat from those of the CHIP Regulations. As with the latter, the Carriage Regulations refer to a number of other documents, and regard must be had both to these and to relevant guidance for their practical implementation. Those of principal relevance are:

(i) Information Approved for the Classification, Packaging and Labelling of Dangerous Substances for Carriage by Road and Rail (L57) (the "Approved Carriage List");

(ii) Approved Methods for the Classification and Packaging of Dangerous Goods for Carriage by Road and Rail (L53) (the "Approved Methods");

(iii) The European Agreement Concerning the International Carriage of Dangerous Goods by Road ("ADR");

(iv) The United Nations Recommendations on the Transport of Dangerous Goods (the "UN Recommendations");

(v) The Regulations Concerning the International Carriage of Goods by Rail ("RID"), *i.e.* Annex 1 to Appendix B of the Convention concerning International Carriage by Rail ("COTIF");[59]

(vi) Technical Instructions for the Safe Transport of Dangerous Goods by Air, with Supplement;[60]

(vii) The International Maritime Goods Code ("IMDG") .[61]

---

[58] S.I. 1994 No. 670.

[59] Cmnd. 5897.

[60] Doc 9284-AN/905, obtainable from the Civil Aviation Authority, Printing and Publications Service, Greville House, 37 Gratton Road, Cheltenham, Gloucestershire, GL50 2BN.

[61] Vols I to V obtainable from the IMO, 4 Albert Embankment, London, SE1 7SR.

Guidance on the Carriage of Dangerous Goods by Rail Regulations is published by the HSE.

12–132 The Carriage Regulations apply to the carriage of any dangerous goods, subject to numerous exceptions set out in regulation 3. "Dangerous goods" is defined to mean (i) goods named individually in the Approved Carriage List, other than any that are so diluted or treated that they no longer have the "hazardous properties" of those goods, and (ii) any other goods which have one or more of the hazardous properties. The definition also extends the term to explosives and radioactive material, but explosives are then excluded from the application of the Regulations by regulation 3(1)(m) and most radioactive material is also excluded, by regulation 3(1)(s).

12–133 "Hazardous properties" is used to mean any such properties as are set out in Schedule 1 to the Carriage Regulations, an assessment of which is essential in order to determine the appropriate classification. For this assessment the Carriage Regulations merely refer to the Approved Methods,[62] and require the hazardous properties of any goods not named individually in the Approved Carriage List to be determined by the appropriate Approved Method.[63] "Goods" means articles or substances[64] — in this context, "substances" should not be given the restricted meaning derived from EC directives; the term is taken from the UN Recommendations, where is it is used in a comprehensive sense, and thus includes what, in EC parlance, are "preparations".

12–134 The extensive list of exceptions from the application of the Regulations consists essentially of circumstances where the goods are being carried in accordance with another set of rules applicable their packaging and labelling, for example COTIF, ADR, the International Maritime Dangerous Goods Code and the Technical Instructions for the Safe Transport of Dangerous Goods by Air, and *de minimis* circumstances where it would be inappropriate to make the Carriage Regulations applicable, for example where the vehicle in which the goods are being carried is not being used for or in connection with work,[65] such as after a private purchase, the carriage of fuel in a vehicle's tank,[66] and very short journeys carrying goods within a harbour area, factory, mine or quarry, or between two parts of private premises within the same vicinity.[67]

---

[62] reg. 4(1)(b).
[63] reg. 5(3)(a).
[64] reg. 2(1).
[65] reg. 3(1)(h).
[66] reg. 3(1)(q).
[67] reg. 3(1)(i), (l).

Classification of Dangerous Goods for Carriage

Dangerous goods may not be assigned for carriage unless their classification and the appropriate "Packing Group" and "Subsidiary Hazards", if any, have been ascertained in accordance with regulation 5.[68] Where dangerous goods are individually named in the Approved Carriage List, their classification must be as stipulated in the List, together with the Packing Group and Subsidiary Hazards, if any, associated with that entry. If there is no individual entry in the Approved Carriage list, then the classification must be as specified in column 1 of Part I of Schedule 1 to the Carriage Regulations. **12–135**

The classifications consist of: **12–136**

- non-flammable non-toxic gas
- toxic gas
- flammable gas
- flammable liquid
- flammable solid
- spontaneously combustible substance
- substance which in contact with water emits flammable gas
- oxidising substance
- organic peroxide
- toxic substance
- infectious substance
- corrosive substance
- other dangerous substance

Assigning one of these classifications to goods requires them to be assessed in accordance with the Approved Methods to determine whether they have any "hazardous properties", as set out in column 2 of Schedule 1. Having given goods the appropriate classification, Schedule 1 spells out a number of other matters relevant to that particular classification, including in particular a specific packing group and a danger sign unique to each classification, as well as optional lettering which, in most cases, repeats the wording of the classification itself. Similarly, the Approved Carriage List sets out against each of the entries the relevant classification, packing group and danger sign. **12–137**

Packaging

There are three packing groups graded in accordance with degree of danger which any particular substance presents. Packing group I applies to substances presenting great danger, group II is for medium **12–138**

---

[68] reg. 5(1).

717

danger, and group III for substances of minor danger. Detailed rules as to the packaging of dangerous goods to be consigned for carriage are set out in regulation 6, and the consignor may not consign any dangerous goods for carriage in packages unless the packages are suitable for that purpose and comply with the provisions of that regulation. These set out general requirements designed to ensure that the packaging retains the contents safely, and further that, subject to a variety of exceptions,[69] the consignor must ensure that the packaging used is of an approved and certified design type that has been allocated an ADR, RID, UN or joint ADR/RID mark by a competent authority, and bears that mark in a durable and legible form, sufficiently large to be readily visible. It is an offence to apply any of these marks to any packaging unless authorised to do so, or to apply any marks liable to be confused with them.[70]

Labelling

12–139   Dangerous goods for carriage may only be consigned in a package if it carries a label conforming in its dimensions and other physical properties with the requirements of regulation 11, and clearly showing all the particulars prescribed by regulation 8. These consist primarily of the designation of the goods themselves, the UN number (being a four digit number specified in the Approved Carriage List as a means of identification for dangerous goods), the relevant danger sign and the relevant subsidiary hazard sign, if any. Where the Approved Carriage List specifies for a particular item any additional labelling particulars, these must also be complied with. There are detailed rules designed to avoid conflict between the labelling requirements of the Carriage Regulations and those of the CHIP Regulations.[71]

Exemption Certificates

12–140   As with the CHIP Regulations, regulation 12(1) of the Carriage Regulations permits the Health and Safety Executive to grant an exemption from all or any of their provisions either absolutely or subject to such conditions and to such time limits as it sees fit. Nevertheless, no exemption may be granted unless the Executive is satisfied that in all the circumstances, including in particular any proposed conditions to be attached to the exemption and any other statutory requirements that may apply, the exemption will not

---

[69] In reg. 6(3).
[70] reg. 7.
[71] regs. 9, 10.

prejudice the health and safety of any persons likely to be affected as a result.[72]

Enforcement and Civil Liability

The Carriage Regulations are made under the H.S.W.A. 1974, and **12–141** accordingly the normal provisions as to enforcement, the approval of Codes of Practice and the use of Codes of Practice as evidence in criminal proceedings[73] apply as they do to other health and safety regulations. Any breach of the provisions will also potentially give rise to civil liability for breach of statutory duty.

It is a defence to any alleged breach of the Carriage Regulations for **12–142** the defendant to prove that he took all reasonable precautions and exercised all due diligence to avoid the commission of the offence charged.[74]

Lengthy transitional provisions provide potential further defences. **12–143** Although the Carriage Regulations came into force on April 1, 1994, it is a defence to any alleged contravention of them prior to July 1, 1995 to show that the goods concerned were classified, packaged and labelled in accordance with the "carriage requirements" of the 1993 CHIP Regulations immediately before their amendment.[75] Further, where a contravention of the Carriage Regulations is alleged to have taken place on or after July 1, 1995 and before January 1, 1999, it is a defence to show that the goods were classified, packaged and labelled for carriage before July 1, 1995 in accordance with these "carriage requirements", that since then neither had the goods been removed from their package or receptacle nor had the label been altered or removed, and further that is was not reasonably practicable either to re-package and re-label the goods before they were consigned for carriage, or to consign the goods for carriage on any earlier date than when they were in fact con signed.[76] Yet further specific transitional defences apply in relation to the consignment of goods for carriage in gas cylinders (up to July 1, 2005), the consignment of goods for carriage in metallic intermediate bulk containers or stainless steel or aluminium drums (if made within 15 years of the consignment and before July 1, 1995), and the consignment of goods for carriage in plastic packaging or other metal packaging (if made within five years of the consignment and before July 1, 1995).[77]

---

[72] reg. 12(2).
[73] By virtue of H.S.W.A., s.17.
[74] Reg. 13; see paras. 21–002 to 21–006 on this defence.
[75] reg. 14(1), *i.e.* in their form as at March 31, 1994.
[76] reg. 14(2).
[77] reg. 14(3)–(5).

Other Statutory Carriage Requirements

12–144   It is beyond the scope of this work to discuss in detail the other statutory requirements that may apply in various circumstances to the carriage of dangerous goods. The Carriage of Dangerous Goods by Rail Regulations 1994 have already been mentioned. These build on the Carriage Regulations and provide additional regulatory requirements in relation to carriage by rail. They place in particular a variety of duties on the consignor of dangerous goods and on the "train operator" (being the person having the management of the train for the time being). Every person engaged in the carriage of dangerous goods by rail must take all reasonable steps to ensure nothing is done to create hazards and that unauthorised access to the dangerous goods is prevented.

12–145   In addition to the requirements imposed by the Carriage Regulations, one or other of the Road Traffic (Carriage of Dangerous Substances in Packages etc) Regulations 1992 and the Road Traffic (Carriage of Dangerous Substances in Road Tankers and Tank Containers) Regulations 1992[78] will also apply in most cases, and regard must be had to their requirements. These prescribe detailed controls for the carriage of dangerous substances in or on vehicles, whether in receptacles, in bulk or in transformers or capacitors. Finally, where dangerous substances are to enter harbour areas, the Dangerous Substances in Harbour Areas Regulations 1987[79] must also be observed.

Specific Hazardous Materials and Products

Enabling Powers

12–146   While broad protection against hazards from chemical products may be obtained by suitable labelling, this does not necessarily ensure adequate protection of all individuals who may directly or indirectly come into contact with them. Further, even though all necessary precautions may be made to avoid harm to human health, other materials, such as PCBs, various heavy metals and their compounds, for example, organotin anti-fouling paints and certain wood preservatives, are potentially so damaging to the environment that it is considered desirable to restrict, and in some cases prohibit, the

---

[78] S.I.s 1992 Nos.742 and 743 respectively, each as amended by S.I.s 1992 No.1213, 1993 No.1746, 1994 No.669.
[79] S.I. 1987 No.37, as amended by S.I. 1993 No.1746.

marketing and use of them. Numerous powers are available to the government to impose controls to protect human health, whether at the workplace or elsewhere, and damage to the environment. The most significant of these, and the most widely used, are the powers under section 15 of the Health and Safety at Work Act 1974 to issue health and safety regulations.[80]

Additionally, safety regulations may be made under section 11(1) of the Consumer Protection Act 1987. These may ban, restrict, or allow subject to prescribed conditions, the importation and marketing of potentially harmful substances and articles. While the powers under this Act cannot be exercised exclusively for the purposes of environmental protection, which the Act is not intended to address, the fact that this result might incidentally be achieved through a safety regulation would not of course render it improper. **12–147**

Further wide powers are given by section 140(1) of the E.P.A. to the Secretary of State which he may exercise in relation to any substance or article, if he considers it appropriate, for the purpose of preventing it from causing pollution of the environment or harm to human health or to the health of animals or plants. Under these controls, he may prohibit or restrict the importation into, and the landing and unloading in, the United Kingdom of any specified substance or article, its use or supply for any purpose and its storage. Further, the controls may be limited to specific areas and/or persons; they may be made subject to conditions or be made contingent upon certain circumstances. **12–148**

Where a particular substance or article has already been produced in or brought into the United Kingdom the Secretary of State has powers under section 140(3) of the E.P.A. to procure that it is dealt with and/or disposed of in a suitable fashion. Under this section he may direct that the substance or article concerned is to be treated as waste or as any particular description of controlled waste, and he may either apply any provisions of Part II of the E.P.A. relating to waste, or simply direct that it be disposed of or treated as he sees fit. Provisions within Part II include section 70 which gives an inspector extensive powers to deal with any article or substance which he believes to be a cause of imminent danger of serious pollution of the environment or serious harm to human health. Further, where an article or substance has been brought into the United Kingdom the Secretary of State may require that it either be disposed of or treated in the United Kingdom or re- **12–149**

---

[80] The reader is referred to any of the standard works on health and safety for more detail. In the present work, health and safety regulations are only mentioned in so far as they relate to a substance that is liable to harm the environment more generally.

exported.[81] Where any other UK statute or any EC legislation imposes a prohibition or restriction on the importation into or the landing and unloading in the United Kingdom of anything, section 140(4) gives the Secretary of State powers to direct that he may treat such prohibition or restriction as having been imposed under section 140(1), thereby giving himself all the powers, such as having it treated as waste or re-exported, as just described.

12–150　Before the Secretary of State may exercise any of the powers available to him under section 140, he must consult an advisory committee set up under section 140(5).[82] Ordinarily the Secretary of State before making any regulations must, having consulted the advisory committee, give public notice of the regulations he intends to make, and leave at least fourteen days for written representations to be made.[83] The Secretary of State need not change his proposals, even though this might be contrary to the advice from the advisory committee and the sense of any representations received from the public. However if he does make modifications the effect of section 140(8) is that he should repeat the consultative exercise unless he is of the opinion that it is appropriate not to do so. Nevertheless any or all of the consultation and public notice provisions may be disregarded if observing them would, in the Secretary of State's opinion, result in an imminent risk that serious pollution of the environment would be caused.[84] Regulations made under this section may provide that contravention of any of their terms shall be an offence, and prescribe penalties of imprisonment of up to two years or, on summary conviction a fine not exceeding level 5 on the standard scale—fines may also be calculated on a daily basis.

12–151　Since it may not always be immediately apparent whether an article or substance is liable to cause pollution of the environment or harm to human health, section 142 enables the Secretary of State to issue regulations whereby he may make orders to secure any relevant information relating to such substances as may be specified by him. This section does not however apply to any substance first supplied in any EC Member State on or after September 18, 1981 (*i.e.* a substance

---

[81] The ability to order re-export does not apply to Northern Ireland, in view of the limited application of the E.P.A. to Northern Ireland—see s.164(4).

[82] The committee was first established by the Advisory Committee on Hazardous Substances Order 1991 (S.I. 1991 No. 1487). Schedule 12 to the E.P.A. governs the making of appointments to the committee, including the terms of any such appointment and any financial remuneration; this is supplemented by the Advisory Committee on Hazardous Substances (Terms of Office) Regulations 1991 (S.I. 1991 No. 1488).

[83] s.140(6).

[84] s.140(7).

which was not entitled to be included in the EINECS inventory).[85] Further, no order may be made in respect of any substance that is regulated for the purposes of statutes relating to explosives, radioactive substances, medicines, fertilisers and animal feeding stuffs, controlled drugs, pesticides and foodstuffs.[86] The powers potentially available to the Secretary of State under this section are also exceedingly wide and may require manufacturers, importers or suppliers to furnish information on specified substances, or on products or articles containing such substances and to carry out tests and to provide information as to the test results. Regulations under section 142 may create offences for non-compliance; in this case, however, no such offence is to be punishable with imprisonment. Before making any order under regulations made under this section, the Secretary of State must again consult the hazardous substances advisory committee set up under section 140(5).

EC Legislation

Marketing and Use—Directive 76/769

The purpose of the 7th Amendment to the CPL Directive is to **12–152** classify chemical substances, and having classified them to stipulate packaging and labelling requirements appropriate to the dangers, if any, that the substances represent. It is not designed to place controls on the marketing and use of any such substances, except in so far as such limitations necessarily follow from the manner of packaging and labelling that must be adopted. For controls in respect of marketing and use, a series of Directives has been developed, deriving from the parent Directive 76/769.[87] These Directives, a full list of which appears in Table 12/IV, are directed to specific substances and preparations, either as such or when sold for certain applications, and either prohibit them outright or impose specific conditions on their marketing and use, subject in some cases to transitional provisions for products

---

[85] There is a potential loophole here in that EINECS only includes those substances marketed before September 18, 1981 which were notified in due time to the European Commission. Additionally, compounds that were only marketed before January 1, 1971 in the EC were generally not included in EINECS. An order under s.142(1) could therefore be resisted if the relevant substance was in fact marketed in the EC before September 18, 1981 even though not listed in EINECS.

[86] s.142(2)(b) and (7).

[87] [1976] O.J. L262, relating to "restrictions on the marketing and use of certain dangerous substances and preparations". This Directive is sometimes referred to as the "Dangerous Substances" Directive but, to avoid confusion with the CPL Directive, not here.

currently being marketed. Where marketing subject to specified conditions is permitted, there is often overlap between the relevant Directives and packaging and labelling requirements of the 7th Amendment and of the Preparations Directive.

12–153   The Directives in this series had in several cases already been preceded in the United Kingdom by either legislation or voluntary agreements controlling the materials concerned; the effect of the Directives in such cases was to ensure a harmonised set of controls throughout the EC, and to replace voluntary arrangements by statutorily binding obligations.

TABLE 12/IV

12–154

Marketing and Use of Dangerous Substances and Preparations		
	Directive & O.J. Reference	Materials/Products Controlled
Parent Directive	76/769 [1976] O.J. L262	PCBs, PCTs, vinyl chloride monomer
1st Amendment	79/663 [1979] O.J. L197	Ornamental Objects
2nd Amendment	82/806 [1982] O.J. L339	Benzene in toys
3rd Amendment	82/828 [1982] O.J. L350	PCTs
4th Amendment	83/264 [1983] O.J. L147	Fire retardants and novelties
5th Amendment	83/478 [1983] O.J. L263	Crocidolite asbestos
6th Amendment	85/467 [1985] O.J. L269	PCBs and PCTs
7th Amendment	85/610 [1985] O.J. L374	Asbestos
8th Amendment	89/677 [1989] O.J. L398	Lead in paint; PCBs; mercury compounds in textile applications; mercury, arsenic and organotin compounds in industrial water treatment
9th Amendment	91/173 [1991] O.J. L85/34	PCP and its salts and esters
10th Amendment	91/338 [1991] O.J. L180	Cadmium

11th Amendment	91/339 [1991] O.J. L186	Ugilec 21 and 141, DBBT
12th Amendment	94/27 [1994] O.J. L188	Nickel in articles coming into contact with the skin
13th Amendment	94/48 [1994] O.J. L331	Flammable substances in aerosol generators for use in various novelties
14th Amendment	94/60 [1994] O.J. L365	Carcinogens, mutagens and teratogens Cresote Chlorinated solvents
(15th) Amendment (proposed)	COM(91) 7 final [1991] O.J. C46	Bromobiphenyl ethers
(16th) Amendment (proposed)	COM(94) 570 final [1994] O.J. C382	Hexacholorethane

UK Legislation

PCBs and PCTs

Polychlorinated biphenyls (PCBs) have historically been used as dielectric fluids in transformers and capacitors, for which their properties are excellent. They also have had widespread application as hydraulic fluids and plasticisers. Polychlorinated terphenyls (PCTs) have had a more limited but important application as tooling compounds. These compounds however represent major health hazards, and being extremely stable under normal conditions, persist almost indefinitely if released into the environment. The current legislation controlling them in the United Kingdom is the Control of Pollution (Supply and Use of Injurious Substances) Regulations 1986.[88] These regulations apply to any substance which is a PCB or a PCT or a waste oil that has a PCB or PCT content higher than 0.005 per cent by weight.[89] Regulation 3 provides that no person shall supply any PCB, **12–155**

---

[88] S.I. 1986 No. 902.
[89] This percentage figure having been reduced from 0.01 per cent by the Environmental Protection (Controls on Injurious Substances) Regulations 1992 (S.I. 1992 No. 31).

PCT, or waste oil containing more than 0.005 per cent of these, by way of sale for any purpose, or to use any of them in connection with any trade or business or manufacturing process. This broad prohibition is however subject to exemptions contained in regulation 4.

12–156 This regulation exempts the supply by way of sale or the use of any of these substances in any of the following activities:

(a) their transport, export to outside of the EEC or the mere holding of the substance in transit

(b) any process whereby the substance is destroyed

(c) any manufacturing process approved by the Secretary of State for converting such a substance into something else, which will not in his opinion constitute a danger to public health and the environment

(d) research and development, or

(e) analysis

12–157 Approval of a process by the Secretary of State for the purposes of (c) above must be sought at least three months before it is proposed to commence the process, unless the Secretary of State agrees to a shorter period.

12–158 Regulation 4(2) contains transitional provisions designed to allow an economic phasing out of certain uses of the substances, namely use as a dielectric fluid in any transformer or any large capacitor, use as a dielectric fluid in any small capacitor the PCB component of which contains at most 43 per cent of chlorine and 3.5 per cent of pentachlorinated or more highly chlorinated biphenyls; use in any hydraulic fluid in any underground mining equipment; and use in a heat transmitting fluid in a closed circuit heat transfer installation (other than those for processing foodstuffs, feeding stuffs or pharmaceutical or veterinary products) where the PCB content is at most 0.1 per cent by weight.

12–159 Such uses may, by virtue of regulation 4(3), continue if the relevant equipment, plant or fluid was in service prior to June 30, 1986 and has not reached the end of its service life. Broadly speaking, these uses represent contained uses that should not represent any significant danger to the environment merely by virtue of continuation of the use. Once any such use has come to an end the holder of the substances is not necessarily required to do anything further with them, unless at that point they are properly to be regarded as waste—in fact special waste—in which case a waste management licence would be needed in respect of the keeping of waste. However the holder may not part with the substance by way of sale, and consequently the expectation is that it will be disposed of as special waste in a suitable (and licensed) manner.

A government consultation paper[90] proposes a programme for the **12–160** collection and disposal of PCBs and PCTs, which would give effect to obligations in Directive 76/403,[91] as well as implementing a commitment made at the Third International North Sea Conference in 1990. Those possessing PCB-containing equipment would have to register with operators licensed to dispose of PCBs by the end of 1995, and the existing exemptions under regulation 4 of the 1986 Injurious Substances Regulations would be progressively withdrawn, ending with a complete ban on the supply, use and storage of PCBs from December 31, 1999.

"Polychlorinated biphenyls" is the subject of Waste Management Paper 6, and "Halogenated Organic Wastes" the subject of Waste Management Paper 15.

Ugilec 21/121, Ugilec 141, DBBT

A number of alternative compounds have been developed as **12–161** substitutes for PCBs and PCTs; many of these either do not in fact perform as well, or also represent environmental hazards. Three of these compounds, known as Ugilec 21 or 121, Ugilec 141 and DBBT (dibromobenzyltoluene) were made the subject of the 11th Amendment[92] to the marketing and use Directive, by reason of their hazardous properties. This has been implemented in the United Kingdom by The Environmental Protection (Controls on Injurious Substances) (No.2) Regulations 1992,[93] which were made under section 140 of the E.P.A. The effect of the regulations is to prohibit the marketing or use, other than for research and development or analysis purposes any of these compounds,[94] any substance of which any of them is a constituent, or any article containing any of them. For Ugilec 21/121 and DBBT these prohibitions came into force with the regulations in July 1992. For Ugilec 141 the prohibition first took effect on June 18, 1994, and is subject to an exception where plant or machinery

---

[90] "UK Action Plan for the Phasing Out and Destruction of PCBs and Dangerous PCB Substitutes", DoE, November 1993.
[91] [1976] O.J. L108. An amended proposal for replacing this Directive was published in [1991] O.J. C299.
[92] Directive 91/339, [1991] O.J. L186.
[93] S.I. 1992 No. 1583.
[94] Ugilec 21 and Ugilec 121 comprise the same chemical substance, a chlorinated organic compound.

was in service on June 18, 1994 to allow the marketing of Ugilec 141 or any substance that contains it, in a first hand condition (that is, not recycled), either for use in that plant or machinery or in its maintenance by the person whose equipment it is.

Pentachlorophenol

12-162   Pentachlorophenol ("PCP") and compounds derived from it (salts and esters) are very effective biocides and have been widely used in remedial treatment of timber and masonry infected by dry rot fungus and cubic rot fungi. It is highly toxic and dangerous to both man and the environment. The 9th Amendment[95] to the marketing and use Directive adds PCP to Annex I to that Directive. This Directive has been implemented by The Environmental Protection (Controls on Injurious Substances) Regulations 1993.[96] In these Regulations, references to PCP include references to its salts and esters. Regulations 3 and 4 prohibit the marketing and use, other than for research and development or analysis purposes, of PCP or any substance containing it in a concentration of 0.1 per cent by weight or more. By way of exception to the use prohibition, PCP or any substance containing it may be used in industrial installations for the impregnation of fibres of heavy duty textiles not intended for clothing or for decorative furniture and as a synthesising and/or processing agent in industrial processes, provided in every case, the content of hexachlorodibenzo-paradioxin (in all isomeric forms) is below 4 ppm. There is a corresponding exception to the marketing restriction, but any marketing of such a product for these purposes is subject to the conditions that only packages of twenty litres of more are used, clearly marked "reserved for industrial and professional use", that the material is not sold to the general public, and that it is not waste to which the EC waste and hazardous waste Directives 75/442 and 78/319[97] apply.

12-163   Additionally, the Regulations prohibit the use of wood treated with PCP inside buildings of any kind, other than as structural timbers or for the manufacture of containers intended for growing products for human or animal consumption or for packaging or other materials which may come into contact with or contaminate raw, intermediate and/or finished products intended for human or animal consumption, nor may the treated wood be used for the re-treatment of such containers, packaging or other materials.[98]

---

[95] Directive 91/173, [1991] O.J. L85.
[96] S.I. 1993 No. 1.
[97] To be replaced by Directive 91/689.
[98] reg. 5.

Regulation 2 contains general exemptions allowing the marketing **12–164** and the use of PCP, or any substance containing it, where the sale or supply or the use, as the case may be, has been approved under regulation 5(1) of the Control of Pesticides Regulations 1986, and is in accordance with that approval.

Guidance has been issued by the DoE, the Welsh Office and the **12–165** Scottish Office[99] on these Regulations. This notes that the industrial installations using PCP are or will be subject to Integrated Pollution Control and that processes taking advantage of the exemptions would have to avoid emitting or discharging PCP above the limits set out in the Surface Waters (Dangerous Substances) (Classification) Regulations 1989[1] and the Environmental Protection (Prescribed Processes and Substance) Regulations 1991[2] which establish an Environmental Quality Standard of $2\mu g/l$ for waters to which any such discharge might be made. As regards the exemption in relation to marketing and use approved under the Control of Pesticides Regulations 1986, approval might be given for in-situ remedial treatment of wood or masonry against dry or cubic rot in buildings of cultural, artistic or historic interest, or in case of emergencies. Each treatment would be considered on a case by case basis, and would have to be notified to the Building Research Establishment.

"Halogenated Organic Wastes" and "Wood Preserving Wastes" are the subjects of Waste Management Paper 15 and 16 respectively.

Vinyl Chloride Monomer

Vinyl chloride monomer (VCM) was brought partially under control **12–166** by the original parent Marketing and Use Directive 76/769, which prohibited its use as an "aerosol propellant for any use whatsoever". This was implemented by regulation 2 of the Dangerous Substances and Preparations (Safety) Regulations 1980,[3] which prohibits the supply, and also any offer, agreement, exposure or possession for supply, of any aerosol in which vinyl chloride monomer is used as a propellant.

---

[99] Circulars DoE 4/93, WO 8/93 and SDD 3/93.
[1] S.I. 1989 No. 2286.
[2] S.I. 1991 No. 472.
[3] S.I. 1980 No. 136.

Heavy Metals

12–167   It has long been known that various metals can constitute serious health hazards.[4] Space does not permit consideration here of all the legislation controlling exposure to metals and their compounds under health and safety and consumer protection legislation. Attention is therefore here primarily addressed to those controls which directly or indirectly promote environmental protection.

Batteries and Accumulators

12–168   Controls over batteries and accumulators that contain more than specified quantities of any of mercury, cadmium and lead, designed to facilitate their collection for recycling or safe disposal, and so avoid their contaminating conventional waste streams, are contained in the Batteries and Accumulators (Containing Dangerous Substances) Regulations 1994.[5] These implement Directive 91/157, as adapted by Commission Directive 93/86.[6]

12–169   There is a general prohibition on the marketing of alkaline manganese batteries that contain more than 0.025 per cent of mercury by weight. This prohibition does not however apply to alkaline manganese button cells or batteries composed of button cells; further, where an alkaline manganese battery is intended for prolonged use in "extreme conditions" the mercury content may be up to 0.05 per cent by weight. Neither "prolonged use" nor "extreme conditions" is defined, but the latter is said to include temperatures below 0°C or above 50°C, or where the battery is likely to be exposed to (presumably physical) shocks.[7]

12–170   The Regulations apply generally to both primary (non-rechargeable) batteries and secondary (rechargeable) cells[8] containing more than 25mg mercury per cell, or more than 0.025 per cent mercury by weight, more than 0.025 per cent cadmium by weight, or more than 0.4 per cent lead by weight. All such batteries must have printed on them or

---

[4] Those carrying out gilding work in 18th century France received higher wages because it was known that the mercury vapour given off shortened their lives. The use of mercury in the preparation of felt made poisoning by it an occupational hazard of hatters, causing them to go famously mad. It has been asserted that lead poisoning was a significant factor in the decline of the Roman empire.

[5] S.I. 1994 No. 232.

[6] [1991] O.J. L78; [1993] O.J. L264.

[7] reg. 3(2), (3).

[8] This distinction reflects the wording of the Directive 91/157, notwithstanding the recent availability of a device for recharging conventional, primary batteries.

on their packaging both a separate collection mark and a "heavy metal content mark", where they are either made in Great Britain for sale anywhere in the EC or made outside Great Britain and are to be marketed in Great Britain, and do not bear the requisite collection mark and relevant heavy metal content mark. (It may be noted that these controls are concerned with Great Britain, and not the entire United Kingdom—Northern Ireland will have to be the subject of separate legislation to implement the Directives.) Where relevant unmarked batteries are imported into Great Britain, the marking must be applied either by the manufacturer's authorised representative in Great Britain or by the person who is marketing the product in Great Britain.

The collection mark is a picture of a wheeled dustbin covered by a **12–171** diagonal cross, as illustrated in the Regulations. The heavy metal content mark consists of the chemical symbol for the metal concerned.[9] Details of how the marking is to be applied, including particularly size and positioning, are set out in Schedule 3 to the Regulations. Transitional provisions disapply the marking requirement for batteries marketed in Great Britain on or before December 31, 1995 where they were made in or imported into the Community before August 1, 1994.[10] Failure to mark the batteries is not an offence in itself, but liable to give rise to an enforcement notice pursuant to regulation 6. Such a notice is to be given to the manufacturer, where he is in Great Britain; in relation to a battery being marketed in Great Britain but made elsewhere, notice is given to the manufacturer's authorised representative in Great Britain or the person responsible for marketing it. An enforcement notice must specify the respects in which the marking of the battery fails to comply with the Regulations, and stipulate a period within which further batteries of the same type must be correctly marked. The marketing of an alkaline manganese battery containing more than the permitted amounts of mercury, contrary to regulation 3(1), and failure to comply with an enforcement notice are offences, subject to a maximum fine of £200[11] on summary conviction.

To facilitate the collection of batteries, regulation 5 requires manu- **12–172** facturers of all appliances (other than those specifically excluded from this provision), into which a battery or accumulator is or may be incorporated, to ensure that the battery can be readily removed by the consumer when it is spent. Schedule 1 to the Regulations lists categories of "excluded appliance" to which this requirement does not apply; these include appliances where batteries are permanently

[9] Mercury = Hg, cadmium = Cd, lead = Pb.
[10] reg. 4(3).
[11] *i.e.* level 1 on the standard scale.

attached to ensure continuity of the power supply, and certain situations where uninterrupted functioning is essential, *e.g.* heart pacemakers and other medical devices designed to maintain vital functions, or where removal and replacement of the batteries could present safety hazards or affect the operation of the appliance. Failure to comply with regulation 5 is also not in itself an offence, but again may be made the subject of an enforcement notice, as just described.

12–173   The Regulations contain the usual provisions[12] rendering directors and other officers and also parent companies potentially liable, where an offence is committed by a body corporate and they have either consented to or connived at it it is attributable to their negligence.[13] Also, where an offence is due to the act or default of some other person than the one who committed the offence, that other person may also be charged with it.[14]

Lead

12–174   The use of lead carbonate and lead sulphate in paints is effectively prohibited by regulation 3(1) of the Environmental Protection (Controls on Injurious Substances) Regulations 1992.[15] Thus the supply by way of sale of these lead compounds or of any substance containing them when intended for use as a paint is an offence, as is the use of these compounds or any substance containing them, when intended for use as a paint in connection with any trade or business or manufacturing process. These 1992 Regulations implement the 8th Amendment to the EC Marketing and Use Directive 76/769.

12–175   As a result of representations made by the United Kingdom, there are exceptions designed to enable the continuing use of lead pigments for use in the maintenance and restoration of works of art and historic buildings. These exceptions are reflected in paragraphs (2) and (3) of regulation 3. Under these, a person wishing to sell or use lead carbonate or lead sulphate in paint must make a declaration in the form set out in the Schedule. The declaration must set out full details of the relevant listed building or scheduled monument or work of art, as the case may be, and the reason why this paint needs to be used, and include an undertaking that the paint will be used solely for the purpose described. The declaration must be submitted to the Museums and Galleries Commission if it concerns a fine or decorative work of art; where it concerns a historic building, the declaration is submitted to the Historic Buildings and Monuments Commission in

---

[12] See chapter 21 for a fuller discussion.
[13] reg. 8.
[14] reg. 7(3).
[15] S.I. 1992 No. 31.

England, the Historic Buildings Council for Wales or the Secretary of State for Scotland, depending where the building is. The supplier of paint subject to the declaration must not supply it for at least three weeks after the declaration has been submitted; likewise a user must not use the paint until three weeks have elapsed from his having given his own further declaration. Any unused paint that may be left over from the work the subject of the declaration must not be used for any other purpose, unless a further declaration is made and no objection to it is raised.

Lead paint is liable to be both an environmental and a health hazard where it is removed by a blow torch. Exposure to lead at work is primarily controlled by the Control of Lead at Work Regulations 1980.[16] These define lead as including alloys and compounds of lead, and lead as a constituent of any substance or material, but are limited to lead in any such form as is liable to be inhaled, ingested or otherwise absorbed by persons; there is however a specific exclusion of lead from the exhaust of a vehicle on a road. In addition, the Approved Code of Practice on Control of Lead at Work must ordinarily be complied with. Section 74 of the Factories Act 1961 prohibits the employment of "a woman or young person"[17] in a variety of industrial operations in which lead is produced, treated or used, or in cleaning workrooms in which any of those processes are carried on. In addition section 131 of the Factories Act 1961 prohibits the employment of "a woman or young person" in painting any part of a building with lead paint. This is subject to the exclusion of certain apprentices in the painting trade and women or young persons in such special decorative or other work as may be excluded by an order of the HSE.[18] Section 132 provides a definition of lead paint which depends on an analytical method that has yet to be prescribed.[19] In view of the ban on the use of lead paint on buildings for all but historic monuments, the application of this section is now extremely limited in any event. **12–176**

Concern over the harm caused to wildlife, particularly swans, from ingesting lead weights lost or discarded by anglers resulted in the **12–177**

---

[16] S.I. 1980 No. 1248.
[17] "Woman" is defined in s.176(1) as any woman aged 18 or over, and "young person" as anyone under 18 who has ceased to be a child (*i.e.* a person not over compulsory school age). By s.128 however "young person" means, for the purposes of numerous sections including s.74, but not s.131, anyone under 18.
[18] Which has been substituted for the Minister referred to in s.131, for the purposes of the making of orders under that section.
[19] The prohibition on the employment of all women without exception would appear to be clearly invalid under EC law on sex discrimination. A ban on women of child bearing age might be valid under the principle of proportionality if it were shown that lead poisoning of an expectant mother might materially affect her unborn child. In fact there are many other sources of exposure to lead, particularly the tetra-ethyl lead in leaded petrol, which is soluble in body fat.

Control of Pollution (Anglers' Lead Weights) Regulations 1986.[20] These Regulations, which apply throughout the whole United Kingdom, prohibit the import of lead in the form of a lead weight (for any purpose), and the supply of lead in the form of a lead weight for the purpose of weighting fishing lines.[21] "Lead weight" is defined as split shot or any other thing suitable for weighting fishing lines, and which is neither incorporated and fully enclosed in the core of a fishing line, nor incorporated in the construction of a swim-feeder, a self-cocking float or a fishing fly. There is a presumption that a person supplying split shot shall be taken to be supplying it for the purpose of weighting fishing lines, as prohibited by regulation 4(1), unless the contrary is shown.[22] For the purposes of the Regulations, "lead" is not limited to the pure metal but includes any alloy or compound of it. The Regulations however only apply to lead weights of over 0.06 grams up to and including 28.35 grams (*i.e.* 1oz.) in weight.

Cadmium

12–178   Cadmium and its compounds are added to Annex I of the marketing and use Directive by the 10th Amendment,[23] which was due to have been implemented in the UK by December 31, 1992. Controls have now been imposed by the Environmental Protection (Controls on Injurious Substances) (No.2) Regulations 1993,[24] which came into effect on July 31, 1993. These prohibit certain uses of cadmium and the marketing of a variety of products containing cadmium. "Cadmium" for this purpose includes cadmium compounds.

12–179   The restrictions are essentially three-fold (subject to certain exceptions indicated below):

(1)   A ban with immediate effect, *i.e.* from July 31, 1993, (a) on the use of cadmium in pigments in finished products made from a variety of plastic materials, including polyvinyl chloride (PVC), low density polyethylene and epoxy resins, and (b) on placing on the market any finished products or components of products that have been made from any of these plastics in which cadmium pigments have been used, if the cadmium content (expressed as cadmium metal) exceeds 0.01 per cent by mass of the plastic material. These bans on the use of cadmium, and on marketing items with over 0.01 per cent of cadmium, are to be extended to items made from additional

[20] S.I. 1986 No. 1992.
[21] regs. 3, 4.
[22] reg. 4(2).
[23] Directive 91/338, [1991] O.J. L186.
[24] S.I. 1993 No. 1643.

plastics materials, including melamine-formaldehyde and urea-formaldehyde resins, PET, general purpose and high-impact polystyrene and polypropylene, with effect from December 31, 1995.[25]

From December 31, 1995 paints CN code nos. 3208 and 3209 may not be placed on the market if their cadmium content (expressed as cadmium metal) exceeds 0.01 per cent by mass. However this does not apply where these paints have a "high zinc content" (which is not defined in either the Regulations or the 10th Amendment), but in any such case the residual concentration of cadmium must be as low as possible and at most 0.1 per cent by mass.[26]

(2) The use of cadmium as a stabiliser in a variety of products made from PVC or vinyl chloride copolymers is prohibited from June 30, 1994. Likewise, from the same date, there may be no marketing of any of numerous listed finished products or components of such products made from PVC or vinyl chloride copolymers stabilised by substances containing cadmium, if the cadmium content (expressed as cadmium metal) exceeds 0.01 per cent by mass of the polymer.

(3) From July 31, 1993 the use of cadmium for cadmium plating a variety of metallic products or components of these products has been prohibited, as has the marketing of such products and components. This ban is extended to a further variety of other products and materials with effect from June 30, 1995.

The restrictions outlined do not extend to the use of cadmium for any research or development or analysis purposes, or to products covered by any EC legislation other than the 10th Amendment. The use of cadmium as pigment or as a stabiliser is exempted from the prohibitions indicated under (1) and (2) above where its use is for safety reasons. Likewise, the ban on use of cadmium for plating purposes in the marketing of cadmium plated products does not apply in certain listed technically demanding areas requiring high safety standards, in certain safety devices, or in electrical contacts in any sector of use where the cadmium is needed on account of the reliability required of the apparatus concerned. **12–180**

"Cadmium bearing wastes" is the subject of Waste Management Paper 24.

---

[25] reg. 2.
[26] reg. 3.

Mercury

12–181   Although in the past mercury represented an occupational hazard primarily,[27] its more recent uses in organo-mercury fungicides[28] and in the manufacture of, for example, plastics,[29] chlorine (by electrolysis of brine in mercury cells), and certain types of battery, has rendered it a potentially significant environmental hazard also.

12–182   By regulation 4 of the Environmental Protection (Controls on Injurious Substances) Regulations 1992, mercury compounds and substances containing them may not be used in the impregnation of heavy duty industrial textiles or the yarn intended for their manufacture, nor may they or any substance containing them be sold for this purpose.

12–183   By regulation 5 of these Regulations the use of mercury, arsenic or organostannic compounds and any substance containing any of them for the treatment of industrial waters, and the sale of such compounds and substances are prohibited. This regulation implements a further provision of the 8th Amendment to the Marketing and Use Directive.

"Mercury bearing wastes" is the subject of Waste Management Paper 12.

Tin Compounds

12–184   The use or sale of DBB (an organic compound containing tin and boron), or any substance containing DBB in a concentration of 0.1 per cent by weight or more, is prohibited by regulation 6(1) of the Environmental Protection (Controls on Injurious Substances) Regulations 1992. This prohibition does not however apply to DBB or any substance containing DBB if "that substance" (sic) is intended solely for conversion into finished products in which the concentration of DBB will be less than 0.1 per cent by weight.[30] It would seem that the reference to "that substance" is intended to include DBB itself.

12–185   As regards the prohibition on the use of organostannic compounds in the treatment of industrial waters, and their sale for that purpose, see paragraph 12–183. The prohibition in the 8th Amendment on the use of organotin compounds for marine anti-fouling agents does not appear in the 1992 regulations, and has yet to be implemented in the

---

[27] See n.4 to para. 12–167.

[28] Resulting in 5000 people affected, of whom 500 died, when treated grain was used for human consumption in Iraq in 1971/1972.

[29] The tragic "Minamata disease" in Japan was caused by discharges into the sea from a PVC factory using a mercuric chloride catalyst, which led to accumulations of methyl mercury in the fish and shellfish of Minamata Bay.

[30] reg. 6(2).

UK. However the Advisory Committee on Pesticides has advised[31] that:

— approvals for antifouling products containing free triorgano-tin should be revoked;

— approvals for antifouling products containing triorganotin copolymers should be allowed to continue, providing that the level of free organotin acting as a stabiliser does not exceed one percent, but that these products should be subject to a further review;

— additional guidelines for the painting and removal of anti-fouling products should be made available;

— the existing national monitoring programme for triorgano-tins should be continued and that the fresh-water environ-mental quality standard should be reviewed; and

— a review should be undertaken of copper-based alternatives to triorganotins.

Arsenic

As to the use of arsenic compounds in the treatment of industrial waters, and their sale for that purpose, see paragraph 12–183. "Arsenic bearing wastes" is the subject of Waste Management Paper 20.   **12–186**

Asbestos

The term "asbestos" is used to refer to a class of fibrous impure magnesium silicates. The most common forms to be used commer-cially were crocidolite (also known as blue asbestos), amosite (brown asbestos), chrysotile (white asbestos), anthophyllite, tremolite and actinolite. The material itself is highly inert, even at high temperatures, which makes asbestos an attractive product for use in numerous circumstances where the physical and chemical conditions are highly demanding. However a further property of asbestos is that it forms extremely fine dust particles with a particular length to thickness ratio that allows the particles to reach the remoter parts of the human respiratory system and become lodged there. Because of the inertness of the material the particles once lodged remain essentially unchanged, and are liable to cause asbestosis, lung cancer and mesothelioma. The principal, and certainly the most dangerous, form of ingestion is thus through the air.   **12–187**

---

[31] Following a review by the HSE of the effects of triorganotin compounds on the marine environment, announced in February 1993.

12–188   EC legislation on marketing and use of asbestos and asbestos products comprises the 5th and 7th amendments to the Marketing and Use Directive, listed in Table 12/IV, and also Commission Directive 91/659[32] adapting Annex I to the Marketing and Use Directive. The 5th Amendment bans the marketing and use of crocidolite and of products containing it, save that Member States may, optionally, permit its use in asbestos/cement pipes, certain acid and temperature resisting seals and the like, and torque convertors. Additionally, the 5th amendment specifies a form of label that must be used in the case of all products containing any of the normal forms of asbestos mentioned above.

12–189   The 7th amendment supplements the 5th Amendment, and applies to all the forms of asbestos other than crocidolite; it bans the marketing and use of these other forms of asbestos for use in a variety of specific applications. By the Adaptation Directive 91/659, the general ban on crocidolite is extended to all the other forms of asbestos except chrysotile. The Adaptation Directive further bans the marketing and use of products containing chrysotile for fourteen specified applications, including materials or preparations intended to be applied by spraying, finished products which are retailed to the public in powder form, filters for liquids and air filters, and filters used in the transport, distribution and utilisation of natural and town gas.

12–190   Directive 87/217[33] that is separate from the series based on the Marketing and Use Directive, is directed to minimising emissions of asbestos into the environment. Controls are required over various discharges to air; aqueous effluent from the manufacture of asbestos paper and board must be recycled, as must that from asbestos cement manufacture unless that is "not economically feasible";[34] and release of asbestos fibres or particles into the environment from transport, deposit and in particular landfill, of asbestos-containing waste is prevented.

12–191   Worker protection from asbestos is the subject of Directive 83/477,[35] which was made under the framework Directive 80/1107[36] on protection from risks related to exposure to chemical, physical an biological agents at work. This was amended by Directive 91/382.[37] In addition, Directive 90/394[38] on the protection from risks related to carcinogens at work relates in part to asbestos.

---

[32] [1991] O.J. L363.
[33] [1987] O.J. L85.
[34] A term implying that only practices which are prohibitively expensive are not required, but that those which are merely very expensive, but not crippling, may be.
[35] [1983] O.J. L263.
[36] [1980] O.J. L307.
[37] [1991] O.J. L206.
[38] [1990] O.J. L196.

UK legislation relating to asbestos falls into three categories: **12–192**

(i) Prohibitions on the marketing and use of various forms of asbestos and asbestos products, namely:

Regulation	S.I.
Asbestos Products (Safety) Regulations 1985	1985 No. 2042
Asbestos Products (Safety) (Amendment) Regulations 1987	1987 No. 1979
Asbestos (Prohibitions) Regulations 1992	1992 No. 3067

(ii) Regulations protecting those who may be exposed to asbestos at work, namely:

Regulation	S.I.
The Control of Asbestos at Work Regulations 1987	1987 No. 2115
The Control of Asbestos at Work (Amendment) Regulations 1988	1988 No. 712
The Control of Asbestos at Work (Amendment) Regulations 1992	1992 No. 3068

(iii) Regulations directed at those working with asbestos, including those engaged in its removal from buildings and elsewhere, namely:

Regulation	S.I.
The Asbestos (Licensing) Regulations 1983	1983 No. 1649
The Control of Asbestos in the Air Regulations 1990	1990 No. 556
The Trade Effluent (Asbestos) (Scotland) Regulations 1993	1993 No. 1446 (S.190)

The Asbestos Products (Safety) Regulations 1985, as amended by   **12–193**
the Asbestos Products (Safety) (Amendment) Regulations 1987, made under the Consumer Safety Act 1978, give effect to the 5th and 7th Amendments to the Marketing and Use Directive respectively, though they go further and prohibit the marketing and supply of amosite as

well as crocidolite asbestos and products containing them. As provided in the 5th Amendment, however, exceptions are made to allow the use of crocidolite (but not amosite) in torque convertors and brake bands for the repair of motor vehicles, if appropriately labelled as prescribed in the Regulations. As a result of the amendment made by the 1987 amending Regulations, the supply of certain products is banned where these contain any asbestos, of whatever form. These products include gas catalytic heaters, catalytic panels and insulation devices, toys, products to be applied by spraying, except for specified compounds for car undersealing, products in powder form intended for retail supply for private use or consumption, smokers' products such as pipes, and cigarette and cigar holders, and paints and varnishes.

12–194   The Adaptation Directive 91/659 is implemented by the Asbestos (Prohibitions) Regulations 1992. The practical effect of this is that the only form of asbestos that may now be used at all in the United Kingdom is chrysotile (white asbestos), and the permitted uses of even this material are very limited. A Schedule to these Regulations lists products containing chrysotile that may be neither supplied nor used, which in effect prohibits virtually all the main potential commercial applications other than asbestos cement pipes and brake linings. Regulation 7 however does permit transitional periods for certain of the prohibited products containing chrysotile, namely until December 31, 1994 for filters for medicinal use, and until December 31, 1998 for diaphragms for electrolysis processes. In addition, use of the prohibited chrysotile-containing products may continue for any such product that was already in use before January 1, 1993, provided that this use was not, immediately before that date, prohibited by the Asbestos (Prohibitions) Regulations 1985 as amended[39] (which were revoked by the 1992 Regulations). Any activity connected with the disposal of the prohibited products listed in the Schedule is however expressly allowed.[40]

12–195   By regulation 8 of the Asbestos (Prohibitions) Regulations 1992 the HSE may by a certificate in writing, exempt any person or class of persons or any product or class of products from all or any of these prohibitions. Such exemptions may be, and in practice are, made subject to various conditions; nevertheless they may only be made if the HSE is satisfied in all the circumstances that the health and safety of persons likely to be affected by any exemption will not be prejudiced.

---

[39] S.I. 1985 No. 910, amended by S.I. 1988 No. 711.
[40] reg. 7(2)(b).

The Control of Asbestos at Work Regulations 1987 as amended by **12–196**
the 1988 and 1992 Regulations,[41] govern all work with asbestos and are
designed to protect anyone at risk from work with that material.
Under these, an employer must not carry out any work which exposes
or is liable to expose any of his employees, or anyone else who may be
affected by the work,[42] to asbestos unless either, before commencing
the work he has identified the type of asbestos involved, or else he has
assumed that it is crocidolite or amosite (*i.e.* the most tightly controlled
forms) and treated it accordingly.[43] Further, no such work must be
carried out unless the HSE has been given details of the proposed
work at least 28 days beforehand.[44] There are further requirements
relating, *inter alia*, to assessment of the likely exposure, prevention or
at least minimisation of that exposure, the use and maintenance of
control measures, the provision and cleaning of protective clothing,
maintaining the cleanliness of premises and plant, air monitoring,
maintaining health records and medical surveillance, and providing
information, instruction and training to employees. "Action levels"
are set that bring into effect other measures in the Regulations, as are
"control limits" of air concentrations of asbestos, to which employees
must not be exposed unless they have respiratory protective equipment. There are two recently revised Approved Codes of Practice
relevant to asbestos namely "The Control of Asbestos at Work" (2nd
edition) and "Work With Asbestos Insulation, Asbestos Coating and
Asbestos Insulating Board" (2nd edition).[45]

The Asbestos (Licensing) Regulations 1983 prohibit any employer or **12–197**
self-employed person from any work with asbestos insulation or
asbestos coating unless he is licensed under the regulations and
complies with the terms and conditions of that licence. "Work with
asbestos insulation or asbestos coating" means work in which
asbestos insulation or asbestos coating is removed, repaired or
disturbed, and includes "such work in any supervisory or ancillary
capacity".[46] "Asbestos insulation" is defined in some detail; broadly it
covers any material used for thermal, acoustic or other insulation
purposes including fire protection, that contains asbestos, but

---

[41] The 1988 amendment revoked para. 8 of reg.16, relating to fees for medical
examinations, which are now regulated separately; the 1992 amendment makes
substantive changes to implement Directives 90/394 and 91/382 (see para. 12–191).
[42] reg. 3(1).
[43] reg. 4.
[44] reg. 6(2).
[45] HSE has issued a leaflet "Asbestos and You" outlining the substance of the Control of
Asbestos at Work Regulations 1987, which includes an "Asbestos Code" listing
precautionary measures for employees. The HSE has also issued a card "Asbestos
Alert For Garage Workers". This also includes a "Garage Worker's Asbestos Code"
setting out appropriate precautionary measures.
[46] reg. 2.

excludes asbestos cement or asbestos insulating board, and various bitumen and polymeric articles which contain asbestos but where the thermal and acoustic properties are incidental to their main purpose.

12–198 Exemptions to the requirement for a licence are set out in regulation 2, namely:

(i) where the amount of work is small, defined as the total time spent by all persons involved not exceeding two hours, and not more than one hour for any one person in any seven consecutive days;

(ii) the work is being carried out on premises occupied by the person whose employees are doing the work (or, in the case of a self-employed person, the individual who is doing the work), provided that, where the person concerned does not hold a valid licence, he is given at least 28 days notice of the work he intends to do to the HSE in accordance with regulation 5;

(iii) the work consists solely of air monitoring or collecting of samples for the purposes of identification.

12–199 A person taking advantage of the second exemption above who is given notice under regulation 5 must also provide adequate information to people in the neighbourhood who may be affected by the work, and appropriate instruction and training must be given to any employees doing it. There is a further obligation (which is reinforced by other asbestos Regulations) to ensure that everyone who may be in the neighbourhood, or who may be affected by the work, is exposed only to the lowest level of asbestos dust which is reasonably practicable.[47]

12–200 The HSE is given discretion under regulation 4 to grant licences for work with asbestos insulation or asbestos coating where it considers it appropriate to do so. An application for a licence must be made on a form approved by the HSE at least 28 before the date the licence needs to start. A licence will normally be made subject to conditions, and these may be varied at any time. The licence itself may be revoked by the HSE at any time if the licensee has breached any condition or restriction attached to any licence issued under the 1983 Regulations or has been connected of certain offences, principally the offence of carrying out work requiring a licence when unlicensed, or failing to comply with the various health and safety requirements relating to work with asbestos. Guidance on the operation of these Regulations has been issued by the HSE.[48]

---

[47] reg. 5(3).
[48] Booklet HS(R).

The Control of Asbestos in the Air Regulations 1990 are primarily **12–201** concerned with emissions of asbestos dust into the air, and in that respect implement EC Directive 87/217.[49] They apply to all commercial forms of asbestos. Regulation 2 applies to premises to which section 5 of the H.S.W.A. applies and from which asbestos is emitted through discharge outlets into the air during the use of asbestos. Such discharge outlets will normally to be ventilation ducts where the concentrations of any asbestos dust are likely to be highest. The Regulation requires the concentration[50] of asbestos to be at most 0.1 mg per cubic metre of air (at any time), and also that the concentration of asbestos emitted to be measured at regular intervals of not more than six months. This regulation 2 only applies to the emission of asbestos during "the use of asbestos" — an expression which is defined in regulation 2(2). It covers the production of raw asbestos from ore, and the manufacturing and industrial finishing of numerous products using raw asbestos, including asbestos cement, fillers, and filters, floor coverings, friction products, jointing, packing and textiles, among others, containing or made of asbestos.

Regulation 4 is expressed more broadly than regulation 2, and **12–202** requires any person undertaking activities involving the working of products containing asbestos to ensure that those activities do not cause significant environmental pollution by asbestos fibres or dust emitted into the air.[51] Additionally, the same obligation to ensure that significant environmental pollution is not caused by emission of asbestos fibres or dust into the air is imposed on any person undertaking the demolition of buildings, structures and installations containing asbestos and the removal from them of asbestos or materials containing asbestos.[52] Regulation 4 supplements regulation 2 by applying to the working of products containing asbestos, which is defined as activities other than the use of asbestos to which regulation 2 applies, and which are liable to release asbestos into the environment.

Asbestos processes are prescribed for the purposes of Part I of the **12–203** E.P.A. by the E.P. (P.P.&S.) Regulations - discharges from Part A processes to water (including sewer) and to air that contain asbestos are controlled by the relevant authorisations, as are discharges to air from Part B processes. Discharges to sewer that contain asbestos are prescribed under the Trade Effluents (Prescribed Processes and Substances) Regulations 1990, as amended, in England and Wales, and

---

[49] [1987] O.J. L85.
[50] As determined by procedures described in the Annex to Directive 87/217.
[51] reg. 4(1).
[52] reg. 4(2).

the Trade Effluent (Asbestos) (Scotland) Regulations 1993 in Scotland. Other discharges to water will be controlled by the normal discharge consent procedure.

12–204   "Asbestos Waste" is the subject of Waste Management Paper 18; in 1988, to up-date this, the Institute of Waste Management issued the "IWM Code of Practice for the Disposal of Asbestos Waste".

Export and Import of Dangerous Chemicals

12–205   The Marketing and Use series of Directives, and those relating to plant protection products, based on Directive 79/117, are only concerned with activities within the EC, and not with exports to third countries. The CPL series of Directives, though the rules they prescribe for the labelling of chemicals apply also to exports, do not attempt to control whether such exports should take place. While, in principle, control over exports of dangerous chemicals is properly the concern primarily of the importing country, incidents involving exports of chemicals that in the EC are either banned or severely restricted to countries not equipped to handle them have caused considerable disquiet on environmental grounds. Often in these incidents, the authorities in the recipient countries have not have full information on the chemicals being shipped and the dangers that they represent, and effective controls have not been exercised. To meet these concerns, EC controls over exports and imports of dangerous chemicals were introduced by Regulation 1734/88.[53] Under this, where chemicals that were banned or severely restricted under EC legislation were to be exported to a third country for the first time,[54] the importing country was to be notified of the reasons for the EC controls over it. This procedure did not in itself therefore restrict such exports, but merely gave the importing country an opportunity to respond as it thought fit to the proposed import.

12–206   Putting the burden on to the importing country to take restraining action has however been considered inadequate, and a so-called Prior Informed Consent ("PIC") procedure, which prohibits the export of specified dangerous chemicals unless express consent to import has first been given, has been developed, principally by the United

---

[53] [1988] O.J. L155.
[54] It was to be assumed that any export was for the first time unless the contrary was shown.

Nations Environment Programme ("UNEP") and the Food and
Agriculture Organisation ("FAO").[55]

Regulation 2455/92[56] which gives effect to the PIC procedure within   **12–207**
the Community, defines it as "the principle that international shipment of a chemical which is banned or severely restricted in order to
protect human health or the environment should not proceed without
the agreement, where such agreement exists, or contrary to the
decision of the designated national authority of the importing
country". It sets up controls for the export of such chemicals from the
EC, and also includes certain provisions relevant to the import of
dangerous chemicals into the Community. The regulation nevertheless does not apply to substances or preparations imported or
exported for the purposes of analysis or scientific research and
development, where the quantities involved are sufficiently small for
them to be unlikely to affect human health or the environment
adversely.[57] The previous regulation 1734/88 was repealed on the
coming into force of regulation 2455/92, on November 29, 1992.

The PIC procedure is co-ordinated on an international basis by the   **12–208**
International Register of Potentially Toxic Chemicals (the "IRPTC").
Each Member State is required to designate a competent authority for
receiving notification and information due to be provided under the
procedure. In the United Kingdom, the Health and Safety Commission (the HSC) has been designated for this purpose under The Export
of Dangerous Chemicals Regulations 1992.[58] Guidance on the regulation and the PIC procedure has been published by the European
Commission as "Informing the Importer" (1993). This includes full
details of the designated authorities in each Member State, and also a
list of recommended languages for the labelling of exports to 65
countries.

Exports of Dangerous Chemicals from the EC

Export controls are applied to a list of substances referred to as   **12–209**
"chemicals subject to notification" and set out in Annex I to the
Regulation.[59] The chemicals include an indication as to whether they
have been banned for all uses, or whether they are to be treated as

---

[55] See "London Guidelines for the Exchange of Information on Chemicals in International Trade", Decision 14/27 of the governing Council of UNEP of June 17, 1987, as
amended in May 1989; and FAO "International Code of Conduct on the Distribution
and Use of Pesticides", Rome 1986, as amended in November 1989.
[56] [1992] O.J. L251, as amended by Regs. 41/94, [1994] O.J. L8 and 3135/94, [1994] O.J.
L332.
[57] Art. 1(3).
[58] S.I. 1992 No. 2415.
[59] Amended by Reg. 3135/94, [1994] O.J. L332.

"severely restricted", the latter applying where, for health or environmental reasons, virtually all uses of a chemical have been prohibited but certain specific ones remain authorised.[60] In determining whether a chemical should be regarded as banned or severely restricted, reference is to be made to whether there is a ban or severe restriction on the use of the chemical in any of the categories consisting of plant protection products, industrial chemicals, and consumer product chemicals. If so, it is to be included in Annex I to the Regulation.[61] The Regulation applies not only to the chemical substances as listed, but also to any preparation containing any of these chemicals if it has a labelling obligation under any EC legislation as a result of the presence of the Annex I chemical. This provision will thus bring into the controls preparations required to be labelled under the Preparations Directive (see paragraphs 12–057, 12–058), and preparations required to be labelled under the EC pesticides legislation (see paragraph 13–067). "Chemical" is used in the Regulation and in this discussion of it, to indicate both the substances listed in Annex I, and relevant preparations.

12–210   Where a person is intending to export an Annex I chemical from the EC, he must give not less than 30 days notice of this to the designated authority in the Member State where he is established — thus, where establishment is in the UK, this will be to the HSC. The information must be given in the form set out in Annex III to the regulation. In addition to giving factual details as to the identity of the chemical, the information must include the intended country of destination and the expected date of first export; it must also give the EC labelling requirements for the chemical, including the appropriate risk phrases and safety phrases, together with a summary of the controls over it and the uses controlled, by reference to applicable EC legislation.

12–211   The relevant designated authority must notify the appropriate authorities in the country of destination of the proposed export, if possible, at least 15 days before the export takes place, and it must likewise provide the information as detailed in Annex III. The authority must also copy this notification to the European Commission, and the Commission in its turn forwards it to the corresponding authorities of the other Member States and also the IRPTC. The Commission assigns a unique reference number to each notification, and for every subsequent export of the same chemical from the EC to the same country of destination, the exporter must ensure that these exports also are accompanied by that reference number. If there are any major changes to EC legislation concerning the marketing use or

[60] Art. 2(4).
[61] Art. 11.

the labelling of the chemical, a new notification in accordance with the Annex III requirements must be made, indicating that it is a revised notification.[62]

The relevant authority of the exporting Member State must report back to the Commission as soon as possible on receipt of any "significant reaction" from the country of destination, and the Commission is to inform all other Member States of that reaction.[63] Where a country participating in the international PIC procedure does not make a response, or makes some interim decision that does not deal with importation, Article 5(5) requires the status quo with respect to imports of the chemical to continue. Consequently, the chemical should not be exported to that country without its explicit consent unless either it is a pesticide registered in that importing country, or it is a chemical the use or importation of which has previously been allowed by some other action of the importing country.   **12–212**

Exports of Annex I chemicals must be packaged and labelled in accordance with either the CPL Directive 67/548 or the applicable Directive on dangerous preparations,[64] as appropriate. The labelling will of course also need to comply with the requirements of the importing country, though the Directive itself only asks for compliance with the requirements of the importing country if these ensure that the label has all the health, safety and environment-related information that use in the EC would require. The information on the label must, as far as practicable, be given in the language(s) or in one or more of the principal languages, of the country of destination or of the area of intended use, as the case may be.[65]   **12–213**

Import of Chemicals

The Regulation contains a separate list of chemicals "subject to the PIC procedure" in Annex II. This is an international list of banned and severely restricted chemicals and includes a list of the countries participating in the international PIC scheme and the decisions of these countries (including the EC Member States) regarding the import of such chemicals. As with Annex I, the list of Annex II chemicals also extends to preparations containing them, unless the concentration is insufficient for a labelling requirement under any relevant EC legislation.[66] For the purposes of Annex II it is immaterial   **12–214**

---

[62] Art. 4(4). It is intended to publish information on when revised notifications should be made in the EC Official Journal.
[63] Art. 4(2).
[64] *i.e.* Directive 88/379, (as amended) or Directive 78/631 (as amended).
[65] Art. 7(2).
[66] Art. 2(2).

747

whether the chemical substance is obtained directly from nature or has been manufactured synthetically.

12–215 The Commission is required to evaluate the risks posed by the Annex II chemicals and to inform the IRPTC whether import into the Community of the chemicals, and if so which, is allowed, prohibited or restricted.[67] Where the import of a chemical into the Community is neither prohibited nor restricted, then import consent must not be normally refused. Nevertheless, where the chemical is one not produced within the EC, the Commission may impose import conditions on a case by case basis, if it considers that a proposal should be made for a Council Directive banning or severely restricting that chemical, and any such import conditions may be imposed on a temporary basis until such time as the Council has decided on the Commission's proposal.[68]

12–216 Under the Export of Dangerous Chemicals Regulations 1992[69] it is an offence to provide information for the purposes of the EC Regulation knowing it to be false or misleading in a material particular or being reckless as to this;[70] this prohibition and all requirements and prohibitions imposed by the EC Regulation are to be treated as though imposed by regulations under section 15 of the H.S.W.A. 1974 and enforceable accordingly.[71]

---

[67] Art. 5(2).
[68] Art. 5(2)(c).
[69] S.I. 1992 No. 2415.
[70] reg. 3.
[71] reg. 4(1).

Chapter 13

PESTICIDES

For many years the marketing of pesticides in the United Kingdom   **13–001**
was subject to a Government supported voluntary agreement
between the major pesticides manufacturers, the Pesticides Safety
Precaution Scheme. This ensured among other things that supplies
were only made to approved wholesalers, who were competent to,
and did, advise farmers on how best to use the pesticides and on the
risks attached. The arrangements however were liable to make it
difficult or impossible for parallel imports of pesticides from elsewhere
in the EC to be marketed in the United Kingdom, and for this and
other reasons the Scheme was eventually disbanded. The present
controls are based on Part III of the Food and Environment Protection
Act 1985[1] ("F.E.P.A.") as amended by the Pesticides (Fees and
Enforcement) Act 1989,[2] and regulations made under the 1985 Act.

The Food and Environment Protection Act 1985 is directed to a   **13–002**
number of relatively disparate subjects. The regulation of pesticides
forms Part III, which is very largely enabling legislation empowering
the Ministers (being the Minister of Agriculture, Fisheries and Food
and the Secretary of State) to make regulations and orders. The
Pesticides (Fees and Enforcement) Act 1989 replaced the whole of
section 18 of F.E.P.A. (relating to the charging of fees for applications
and other activities) and section 19(1) (relating to enforcement
powers), as well as making certain other relatively minor amendments.

The regulations of principal significance currently, for users at least,   **13–003**
are the Control of Pesticides Regulations 1986.[3] Proposals were issued
in 1993 for the amendment of these Regulations, providing for wider
public access to information relating to pesticides, and also updating
and clarifying certain aspects. However, action to implement these
proposals has been deferred until passage of necessary primary
legislation appropriately amending F.E.P.A.

---

[1] 1985, c.48.
[2] 1989, c.27.
[3] S.I. 1986 No. 1510.

13–004   Running in parallel with this regime is to be a separate one provided by the Plant Protection Product Regulations[4] (the "PPP Regulations"), which are designed to implement EC Directive 91/414, described below, and will apply to such pesticides as become approved for the purposes of that Directive. The new regime will apply to new pesticide active substances (*i.e.* those first marketed on or after July 26, 1993), and to products containing them, and also to pesticide active substances that were on the market before July 26, 1993, where these have subsequently been subjected to a review process and approved for marketing in the EC. This review process for existing active substances is expected to take some 10 years up to 2003, and possibly longer. Until they have been reviewed and either approved or have had existing approvals revoked they, and pesticide products containing them, will remain subject to the old regime of the 1986 Regulations, which accordingly requires discussion here.

13–005   At least since the introduction of the controls under the F.E.P.A., EC pesticides legislation prior to Directive 91/414 has been of little direct relevance to the marketing and use of pesticides in the United Kingdom. It consists of a series of Directives, namely Directive 79/117[5] and Directives amending it, which prohibit the marketing and use of "plant protection products" (which may be broadly equated with "pesticides") that contain any of the substances listed in an Annex to Directive 79/117 as amended. The UK legislation however operates by prohibiting virtually all marketing and use of all pesticides, unless and to the extent that they have received the requisite approvals and consents under the 1986 Regulations—these are not of course given to any activities involving the plant protection products prohibited under the amended Directive 79/117.

13–006   The pesticides legislation in the UK is primarily under the control of the Ministry of Agriculture, Fisheries and Food ("MAFF"), in England and Wales, and of the Welsh and Scottish Offices, as regards their jurisdictions. However since many of the activities involving pesticides are liable to be hazardous for those handling them or otherwise in the vicinity, the Health and Safety Executive also has responsibilities over the conduct of those activities under the H.S.W.A. 1974. Detailed expert advice to the Government on pesticides is provided by

---

[4] These Regulations were originally issued in draft in May 1993, together with the deferred proposals for amending the 1986 Regulations. At the time of writing the draft PPP Regulations have still not been laid before Parliament. The following description of their effect is based on a revised draft of August 3, 1994. Since the Regulations must implement the EC Directive, and are now to be based solely on the European Communities Act 1972 (unlike the original draft, which was to be based on F.E.P.A. also), the scope for major changes in the final version is slight.

[5] [1979] O.J. L33.

the Advisory Committee on Pesticides, which is set up under section 16(7) of F.E.P.A. MAFF's responsibilities used to be largely handled by its Pesticides Safety Division, but this has now been transformed into an agency, the Pesticides Safety Directorate.

The Current Controls under the 1986 Regulations

"Pesticide" is defined by F.E.P.A.[6] as "any substance, preparation or organism prepared or used for destroying any pest", "pest" being:　13–007

    (a) any organism harmful to plants or to wood or other plant products;
    (b) any undesired plant; and
    (c) any harmful creature.

"Creature" means any living organism other than a human being or a plant; and "plants" is defined as any form of vegetable matter, while it is growing and after it has been harvested, gathered, felled or picked, and includes:　13–008

    (a) agricultural crops;
    (b) trees and bushes grown for purposes other than those of agriculture;
    (c) wild plants; and
    (d) fungi.

The definition of "pest" appears to contrast "harmful organism" with "harmful creature" and "undesired plant", which might indicate an intention to limit the term "organism" to "micro-organisms". On the other hand, "creature" clearly includes larger organisms, for example, slugs, caterpillars and rodents, and hence "organism" in that definition has the same sense as it is given in relation to genetically modified organisms (see Chapter 14). Since there is no necessary reason to treat the three categories in the definition of "pest" as mutually exclusive, this wider meaning appears to be the more appropriate, both these and in the definition of "pesticide".[7]　13–009

Section 16(16) of F.E.P.A. in effect extends the definition of "pesticide" by providing that Part III of the Act applies to any substance, preparation or organism as if it were a pesticide, where it is not prepared or used for destroying anything (destroying being an essential element of the definition of "pesticide") but is used for a variety of specified purposes including protecting wanted plants and　13–010

---

[6] s.16(15).
[7] So the terrier used for rat catching is a pesticide for the purposes of F.E.P.A.; however the 1986 Regulations do not extend to organisms other than bacteria, protozoa, fungi, viruses and mycoplasmas.

controlling the activities of harmful organisms and creatures, or rendering them harmless.

13–011   The Control of Pesticides Regulations 1986 (referred to here as the "1986 Regulations") set out in regulation 4 a series of individual prohibitions on each of advertising, selling, supplying, storing and using a pesticide, unless the activity with the pesticide in question has received approval under regulation 5, and unless the so-called "basic conditions" of this approval and of the relevant consent granted under regulation 6 are complied with. (These prohibitions do not, it may be noted, extend to advising on the use or other dealing with pesticides, this being outside the "specified prohibitions" listed in section 16(3) of F.E.P.A. in respect of which regulations may be made). Approvals are the means used to impose conditions for controlling how any particular pesticide should be dealt with, while the consents are used to impose conditions on the activity to which each relates, irrespective of what pesticide(s) may be involved. Approvals for these various activities may be either provisional, that is, for a stipulated period with a view to satisfying outstanding data requirements, or full approval for an indefinite period. Additionally, supply, storage and use of pesticides may be subject to experimental permits to enable testing and development with a view to collecting data and providing it to the Ministers, such as for seeking an approval.[8] Whether or not approval is granted will depend on the properties of the pesticide concerned, and in considering whether or not to give approval, the Ministers will have regard to the broad objectives of Part III of the F.E.P.A., namely the protection of the health of human beings, creatures and plants, to safeguard the environment, and to secure safe, efficient and humane methods of controlling pests. On occasion a person may wish to use a pesticide that has a provisional or a full approval for one use for some other relatively similar use. Categories of minor "off-label" uses have been developed for which it is permitted to use any pesticide previously approved for a specified similar use.[9] No further approval is therefore needed for such a permitted use. Approval of any other off-label use must be specifically applied for and any approval may be subject to specific conditions.

13–012   Certain "commodity" chemicals have a variety of both pesticide and non-pesticide uses. Several such compounds have been approved for use as a pesticide, and any use of them for that purpose must conform

---

[8] reg. 5(2)(a). An experimental permit could not therefore be issued under this provision to enable data to be collected for supply to anyone else, *e.g.* a registration authority in another EC Member State. This would appear to be a potential source of conflict with Rome Treaty requirements.

[9] Set out in "Pesticides 1994" (HMSO), Chap. 3, Annex C.

with the conditions of approval.[10] However, the pesticides legislation only covers the sale and supply of any of these substances if and to the extent that it is sold or supplied as a pesticide.

The basic conditions of the consents to which each of the controlled activities is subject are set out in Schedules 1 to 3 of the 1986 Regulations. These relate respectively to the advertising of pesticides (Schedule 1), the sale, supply and storage of pesticides (Schedule 2), and the use of pesticides (Schedule 3). Reference to the full terms of these conditions is essential for those affected by them. Of particular note is the requirement, otherwise than in relation to advertising, for the involvement of a person who has a certificate of competence. Thus it is not permitted to sell or supply a pesticide approved for agricultural use, or to store such a pesticide for the purpose of sale or supply, unless the person doing so either has himself obtained a recognised certificate of competence or else is under the direct supervision of a person who has one. There is a further general obligation that any person who sells, supplies or stores a pesticide shall be competent for the duties which he is called upon to perform. Employers are under an express duty to ensure that any employees who may be required to sell, supply or store a pesticide receive the necessary instruction and guidance to enable them to achieve the requisite standard of competence and otherwise to comply with the requirements of the 1986 Regulations.[11]

13–013

Similar provisions apply to the use of pesticides approved for agricultural use. However, except where a pesticide is used "in the course of a commercial service", there is an exemption in favour of those born on or before December 31, 1964—this exemption was designed to avoid forcing practising farmers to obtain a certificate, but to make it compulsory for the next generation entering agriculture. A "commercial service" is the application of a pesticide by a person to land, buildings or the contents of buildings not in his or his employer's ownership or occupation, and includes the treatment of seed with the use of mobile or static equipment".[12] Whether, when a farmer does work for a neighbour, he is providing a commercial service and so

13–014

---

[10] The substances concerned are: ethylene dichloride, ethylene oxide, formaldehyde, methyl bromide, strychnine hydrochloride, urea and sulphuric acid. Several other substances have been approved for certain very restricted uses ("Pesticides 1994", Chap. 3, Annex D).

[11] Operators require a National Proficiency Testing Certificate. The Government supported BASIS (Registration) Ltd issues BASIS Storekeeper's Certificates and Certificates in Crop Protection. The crop protection certificates are general in scope; limited certificates in respect of horticulture, amenity horticulture, seed treatment and forestry are also issued.

[12] Sched. 3, para. 7

requires a certificate, must depend on the particular facts, but if it amounts to more than providing a helping hand in his spare time, and particularly if there is a deal whereby the neighbour does some other work for him, there must be a considerable risk of his committing an offence if he has no user's certificate.

13–015   The "basic conditions" relating to the use of pesticides include prohibitions on combining or mixing for two or more pesticides or the use of a pesticide in conjunction with an adjuvant, en either case except in accordance with the conditions of the approval given in relation to the relevant pesticides. Further, no person may use a pesticide in the course of business unless he has received adequate instruction and guidance in the safe, efficient and humane use of pesticides, and is competent for the duties that he is called upon to perform. A basic condition applying to every person who sells, supplies or stores a pesticide requires them to take all reasonable precautions, particularly with regard to storage and transport, to protect the health of human beings, creatures and plants and to safeguard the environment. A closely similar condition applies to users, which includes a specific mention of avoiding pollution of water.

13–016   Additional basic conditions apply where a pesticide is to be applied from an aircraft in flight. These include a requirement that an aerial application certificate granted under article 42(2) of the Air Navigation Order 1985[13] must be held by the person carrying out the application. There are lengthy requirements for prior consultation and notice, and there must be fixed warning signs on the ground. The application must not be conducted if the wind speed is over ten knots, unless the pesticide approval otherwise permits it; various minimum distances are set for the aircraft to keep away from buildings and other objects and areas, and relevant records must be kept for at least three years.

13–017   Official codes of practice may be issued under section 17 of F.E.P.A., and any such code (including any revisions) must be laid before Parliament. Failure to comply with the code is not of itself an offence, but the provisions of the code may be taken into account by a court conducting any criminal proceedings.[14] Current codes are: "Pesticides: Code of Practice for the Safe Use of Pesticides on Farms and Holdings"[15] and "Code of Practice for Suppliers of Pesticides to Agriculture, Horticulture and Forestry".[15A]

---

[13] S.I. 1985 No. 1643.
[14] s.17(6).
[15] Made under both s.17 of F.E.P.A. and also s.16 of H.S.W.A. 1974 in view of employers' duties with regard to the COSHH Regulations.
[15A] MAFF, 1990.

In addition to the statutory codes of practice, guidance notes have   **13–018**
been issued by the HSE on relevant aspects of the storage and use of
pesticides. These include:

CS/10	Fumigation using phosphine (rev.91)
CS/12	Fumigation using methyl bromide (rev.91)
CS/19	Storage of approved pesticides
MS/17	Biological monitoring of workers exposed to organophosphorus pesticides
L9	The safe use of pesticides for non-agricultural purposes
COP30	Control of substances hazardous to health in fumigation operations Remedial Timber Treatment in Buildings—A Guide to Good Practice and the Safe Use of Wood Preservatives

Pesticide wastes are the subject of Waste Management Paper No.21.
Information is made available to the public pursuant to Regulation   **13–019**
8.[16] This Regulation is expressed in permissive terms, but allows the
Ministers, following the grant of a provisional or full approval of a
pesticide or the modification of any applicable conditions, to make
available for inspection, on such conditions as they see fit, the
evaluation of the pesticide relevant to that approval or modification.
Any person receiving such an evaluation may seek further information if he can show that what he has been given is insufficient, and he
may then be entitled to see study reports and other date supporting
the pesticide's approval. It is expressly stipulated that no commercial
use may be made of the information contained in an evaluation or
study report by the person to whom it is made available under this
Regulation, nor may it be published without the written consent of the
Ministers. Whether these prohibitions provide enforceable protection
of the information, particularly where disclosure is to a company that
is part of a multi-national group, must be open to question.

Application Procedures

Approvals may be sought by any manufacturer, formulator, im-   **13–020**
porter or distributor or, on occasion, a user. Normally, approval will be
granted for a specific product (formulation) and generally only for
specific uses. An application must be supported by appropriate data

---

[16] See para. 13–003 relating to amendment of this Regulation in particular.

on safety, efficacy and humaneness. The procedures and the data required are set out in "Data Requirements for Approval Under the Control of Pesticides Regulations 1986" issued by the Pesticides Safety Directorate. The application procedures will necessarily be changing to some degree to reflect the requirements of the proposed Plant Protection Product Regulations. With the coming into effect of those PPP Regulations, a new application under the 1986 Regulations will only be appropriate in the case of new uses or formulations of pesticides of which the active ingredient has already been approved. Consideration of an application for approval is under the ultimate control of the Advisory Committee on Pesticides (the "ACP"). This has a Scientific Sub-Committee which meets to consider applications in respect of novel active ingredients, applications involving novel means of application, and other systems that may represent some new or additional hazard.

13–021   Where no special risk of this kind appears to be entailed, a Registration Department procedure is employed. Typically this procedure is appropriate for the approval of the minor use of a product already approved for use on one or more crops (known as an "off-label" approval) and for the approval of a product imported from elsewhere in the EC that is identical to a product already improved in the UK. For a product to be regarded as "identical" to another for this purpose:

  (i)   the active ingredient in the imported product must either be produced by the same company as that in the approved product, or else be produced by a directly associated undertaking and the active ingredient must also be substantially the same, that is, within the scope of variations accepted when the product was approved for the first time; and

  (ii) the relevant formulations must be produced by the same company or a directly associated undertaking, and in so far as there are any differences between the formulations, these must have no material effect on the safety of humans, animals or the environment generally.[16A]

13–022   If a pesticide is also a poison subject to the Poisons Act 1972, then the requirements of that Act and of the legislation made under it[17] must be complied with in addition.

[16A] "Data Requirements for Approval under the Control of Pesticides Regulations 1986", para. 36.
[17] The Poisons List Order 1982 and the Poisons Rules 1982.

Enforcement

It is an offence for a person, without reasonable excuse, to **13–023** contravene, or to cause or permit any other person to contravene any provision of, or any requirement imposed by, the 1986 Regulations, as amended, or any condition of approval of a pesticide.[18] In addition, a failure to provide information in response to certain requests and to provide false information may also be an offence.[19] The framing of these offences differs from those created under most other environmental legislation, which are generally strict, by the inclusion, as an essential element of the offence of "without reasonable excuse". What is a reasonable excuse in any particular circumstance is essentially a question of fact.[20] The terms of any statutory Code of Practice under section 17 will inevitably, so far as a point relevant to the particular case is addressed, be of very considerable significance in determining whether the defendant was operating in a responsible manner such as would provide a reasonable excuse. The offence extends to causing or permitting a contravention by any other person. Although this differs from the usual phrase "causes or *knowingly* permits" it must be doubtful whether the difference in language is material, given that to permit necessarily involves a knowledge of the facts permitted, or at least shutting one's eyes to the obvious, and possibly even recklessness as to whether or not an offence may be committed.[21]

There is a further general defence available in all proceedings taken **13–024** under F.E.P.A. that the defendant took all reasonable precautions and exercised all due diligence to avoid the commission of the offence.[22] A court must accept that this defence has been made out if the defendant proves that he acted under instructions given to him by his employer or that he acted in reliance on information supplied by another person without any reason to suppose that the information was false or misleading, provided that in either case he took all such steps as were reasonably open to him to ensure that no offence would be committed.[23] Where this defence is based on an allegation relating to an act or omission by another person, the defendant must, at least seven clear days before the hearing, give such information as he then may have that identifies or assists in the identification of the other person.[24]

---

[18] s.16(12)(a).
[19] s.16(11), (12)(b).
[20] *Leck v. Epsom R.D.C.* [1922] I K.B. 383, [1922] All E.R. Rep. 784.
[21] *James & Son Limited v. Smee* [1955] 1 Q.B. 78, [1954] 3 All E.R. 273.
[22] s.22(1).
[23] s.22(2).
[24] s.22(3).

13–025   The leading case on this general defence is *Tesco Supermarkets Limited v. Nattrass.*[25] This was concerned with an error made by a relatively junior employee, and it was held in that case that the reference to "another person" could apply to the employee of a company defendant, even though in other contexts, the acts of such a person may properly be taken to be the acts of the company. In that case, the defendant company was able to show that it had a system in operation designed to prevent misleading trade descriptions being applied to its products, and that the system had simply broken down on the occasion in question. It was able therefore to rely on the statutory provisions to establish that they had taken all reasonable precautions and exercised all due diligence. In principle, of course, that decision holds good for prosecutions under F.E.P.A. also. Nevertheless, in many situations, a person charged with an offence is likely to be operating on a much smaller scale than *Tesco Supermarkets*, and where those who are in charge of an organisation have opportunity for direct supervision of the activities of their subordinates, it may well be appreciably harder to establish the statutory due diligence defence.

13–026   The majority of offences under F.E.P.A. may be tried either summarily or on indictment; in the latter case, no maximum fine is stipulated. F.E.P.A. includes the standard provisions in respect of offences by corporations whereby directors and other similar officers may be held liable if they have consented to or connived at such an offence or it has been committed through their negligence. Further, parent companies and other shareholders may be held liable as though they were directors if they have managed the affairs of the defendant company.

13–027   Section 19 sets out extensive powers enabling any person authorised to enforce the Act to enter any land if he reasonably believes that any pesticide is being or has been applied to or stored on it, if he needs to do so for enforcement purposes; similar provisions apply in relation to the storage and transport of pesticides or their application, in relation to vehicles, vessels, aircraft and the like.[26] Further powers are available under section 19 to require information to be provided if an offence is being committed, or if one has been committed and it is likely to be repeated, and also if there appears to be a risk of the commission of an offence. In such circumstances, directions may be given that land, vehicles and other apparatus may be left undisturbed for so long as may be reasonably necessary and that other preventive measures should be taken. Where there is a risk of the commission of an offence, activities may be prohibited by notice until matters

[25] [1972] A.C. 153, [1971] 2 All E.R. 127, H.L.
[26] s.19(2), (3).

occasioning the risk have been remedied;[27] a public register of all such notices must be maintained by MAFF pursuant to the Environment and Safety Information Act 1988.[28]

Independently of any offence under F.E.P.A., there may well be offences committed under the H.S.W.A. 1974, where safe working conditions have not been provided.

Pesticide Residues[29]

Pesticide residues have been the subject of a series of EC Directives, consisting primarily of: **13–028**

Directive	O.J. Ref	Subject
76/895	[1976] O.J. L340	Residues in and on fruit and vegebles
86/362	[1986] O.J. L221	Residues in and on cereals
86/363	[1986] O.J. L221	Residues in and on foodstuffs of animal origin
91/132	[1991] O.J. L66	Undesirable substances and products in animal nutrition
93/57	[1993] O.J. L211	[1993] O.J. L211
93/58	[1993] O.J. L211	Amending the Annexes to 86/362 and 86/363 Amending the Annexes to 76/895 and 90/642 (see below)
90/642	[1990] O.J. L350	Maximum residue levels in and on products of plant origin, including fruit and vegetables

The first of the Directives, 76/895 has been amended on several occasions. It and the following Directives other than 90/642 set levels of pesticide residues that Member States must accept in any products covered by these Directives entering their jurisdiction from other Member States. Any state may, if it so wishes, allow higher residue levels in or on the product concerned without infringing any of those   **13–029**

---

[27] s.19(5), (6).
[28] 1988, c.30, s.1.
[29] Though not strictly an environmental issue, and more properly one of food law, a brief mention of the relevant legislation is included for completeness.

Directives. Directive 90/642, on the other hand, is a framework Directive designed to permit the setting of maximum residue levels which may not be exceeded by any Member State; daughter Directives fixing these levels for different food products will eventually supersede Directives 76/895 and 86/362.

13–030   In the UK, the issue is governed by the Pesticides (Maximum Residue Levels in Crops, Food and Feeding Stuffs) Regulations 1994.[30] These set out in Schedule 2 a chart of maximum levels of residues of numerous pesticides that are permitted in a variety of foods consisting of or derived from animals and plants. Part 1 of this Schedule stipulates the permissible qualities that may be left in products following the application of pesticide to the product or the land where it is grown, while Part 2 sets out the amounts permitted in products that are put into circulation. Schedule 1 specifies what substances should be taken into account in calculating quantities of pesticide residues, given that some pesticides exist as a group of related compounds, or may produce metabolites following application.

13–031   The levels set in Part 2 of Schedule 2 of the 1994 Regulations are taken from the relevant EC Directives. Those of Part 1 of this Schedule are the subject of advice from two government sponsored committees, the Food Advisory Committee ("FAC") and the Committee on Toxicity of Chemicals in Food, Consumer Products and the Environment ("COT").

Non-compliance with the prescribed levels may lead not only to a fine but also to the seizure and disposal of the offending product or other necessary remedial measure.[30A]

Regulation of Plant Protection Products

13–032   EC pesticides legislation has been totally recast by Directive 91/414[31] which introduces a prior authorisation regime of the type already in operation in the United Kingdom. The main purpose of the Directive is to ensure harmonisation of national systems for pesticides registration throughout the EC. Under the new regime, approved active substances will be contained in Annex I to Directive 91/414, and, subject to

---

[30] S.I. 1994 No. 1985. Excessive pesticide residues in food may also constitute an offence under the Food Safety Act 1990.
[30A] regs. 5(2), 6.
[31] [1991] O.J. L230.

certain limited exceptions, a plant protection product may not be authorised for marketing or use in any Member State, unless its active substance or substances is or are listed in that Annex. Authorisations are to be based on common standards for dossiers of technical data and for evaluation of that data, and Member States are required to authorise without qualification products that have been authorised in other Member States, unless local circumstances justify refusing an authorisation or applying particular conditions.

Substances will be listed in the Annex after being subjected to a full **13–033** review of their properties and approved for use. It is intended to review some 90 pesticides a year over 10 years, so that all existing pesticides of interest will have been reviewed by around 2003. In addition all new active substances that may be developed may only be used if they receive a favourable assessment following a review of their properties. They may receive limited approvals in a single Member State or in some only of the Member States for a limited period of time; thereafter, if they are to be approved for use they must be accepted for inclusion in Annex I.

It follows that until at least 2003 some existing pesticide products **13–034** will remain on the market that contain active substances not yet approved for inclusion in Annex I, and which will continue to be subject to national controls only. Further, national controls will continue to be applicable to new uses and new formulations of existing pesticides, for so long as their active substances are not included in Annex I.

The previous EC pesticides legislation based on Directive 79/117, **13–035** referred to in paragraph 13–005, that prohibits the use of specific substances, will continue in force at least until such time as all possible existing active substances of interest have been included in Annex I to Directive 91/414, and the transitional provisions of that Directive have ceased to apply.

Implementation of Directive 91/414 in the United Kingdom is to be **13–036** by new Plant Protection Products Regulations[32] (the "PPP Regulations"). These will follow the Directive very closely, and so will not have controls over advertising and use of products containing approved active substances corresponding to those of the 1986 Regulations, since these activities largely fall outside the scope of the Directive.

In view of the importance of the Directive to the harmonisation of **13–037** pesticides legislation across the EC, and in view of the likely close alignment of the UK PPP Regulations with it, the bulk of the following discussion is devoted to the Directive.

---

[32] See n. 4 above.

EC Directive 91/414

13–038   Directive 91/414 was adopted on July 15, 1991, and notified to the Member States on July 26, 1991. This latter date is used for the purposes of calculating the due date for implementation of the Directive by the Member States, namely July 26, 1993, and that in turn is the critical date for defining what may be termed "existing" active substances and "new" active substances, being those that were on the market in the EC before July 26, 1993, and those that were first marketed on or after that date. It has been amended by Directives 93/71, 94/37, 94/43 and 94/79, [33] which replace and expand parts of Annexes II and III, and insert a new Annex VI.

Definitions

13–039   The Directive is concerned with the marketing of plant protection products. Such products may consist exclusively of active substances or they may be preparations containing one or more active substances. In either case, the term applies to products "put up in the form in which they are supplied to the user" — in other words they will in most cases be formulated products, and an active substance will only be a plant protection product also if it is in the form as supplied to the user. "Plant protection product" includes not only conventional pesticides, herbicides, fungicides and rodenticides (in so far as these are used to protect plants or plant products), but also extend to products that "influence the life processes of plants, other than as a nutrient (*e.g.* growth regulators)" and those which preserve plant products (except in so far as these are subject to special EC provisions on preservatives). An "active substance" is any substance or micro-organism, including a virus, that has general or specific action against harmful organisms or on plants, parts of plants or plant products; "substance", in turn, includes any impurity that is an inevitable result from the manufacturing process of any chemical element or compound. This definition is important in relation to comparing one active substance with another, in seeking approval of the later substance. "Plant products" cover not only such products in the unprocessed state, but also those derived from plants that have "undergone only (*n.b.*) simple preparations such as milling, drying or pressing".

13–040   The core of the Directive is found in Articles 3 and 4, which broadly require that plant protection products may not be marketed and used in any Member State, unless that Member State has authorised the product in accordance with the Directive. Subject to transitional

---

[33] [1993] O.J. L221, [1994] O.J. L194 [1994] O.J. L227 and [1994] O.J. L354.

provisions for existing active substances, such a product must not be authorised unless its active substance(s) is or are listed in Annex I and any conditions applicable to the active substance(s) are fulfilled. Authorisation of a product based on a new active substance accordingly requires two separate stages. The relevant active substance must firstly be approved for inclusion in Annex I and only when this is done may a Member State proceed with authorisation of the plant protection product containing it. Approval of an active substance requires the provision of extensive details of the substance, together with appropriate details of at least one preparation (*i.e.* a mixture, and in practice a formulated product) containing that active substance. The extensive technical information requirements in relation to active substances are set out in Annex II, and in relation to preparations in Annex III.

Approval of Active Substances

Approval of active substances for inclusion in Annex I is determined at Community level by the Standing Committee on Plant Health[34] (the "Committee"). An applicant seeking the inclusion of a new substance in Annex I must forward the technical information to all Member States and to the European Commission. The Commission refers the technical dossier to the Committee who must decide within three to six months whether the dossier is complete in accordance with the requirements of the Directive. If assessment of the technical data shows that further information is needed, the Commission will seek this from the applicant; the Commission is also encouraged to invite representations from the applicant if an unfavourable decision is envisaged.[35] The decision on whether to approve or reject an application relating to a new active substance is determined in accordance with the procedure laid down in Article 19 of the Directive, which provides for qualified majority voting in the Committee (the chairman, a representative of the Commission, has no vote). It is for the Commission to propose measures to be voted on by the Committee, and to take appropriate action where its measures are approved. If the Committee does not agree with the Commission's proposal, or fails to deliver any opinion at all, the Commission is required to submit a proposal to the Council of Ministers. The Council, which also acts by qualified majority, must take a decision within three months, or else the Commission will adopt the measures as proposed to the Council.

13–041

Active substances are to be listed in Annex I for specific periods, not exceeding 10 years. The listing may be renewed for further periods of

13–042

---

[34] Set up by Council Decision 76/894—[1976] O.J. L340.
[35] Art. 6(4).

up to 10 years each, and any application for renewal must be made at least two years before the existing entry is due to lapse to provide time for sufficient review of the active substance concerned.[36] There must in any event be a review if at any time there are contra-indications suggesting that the basic requirements for a listing in the Annex are no longer satisfied.

13–043   Assessment of a substance must have regard to:

- — any harmful effects that any products containing them, or the residues of such products; may have human and animal health, groundwater and the environment
- — the ability to measure the residues in so far as they are of toxicological or environmental significance;
- — where relevant, what may be an acceptable daily intake for man, and acceptable operator exposure levels;
- — estimates of the fate and distribution of the substance in the environment and its impact on non-target species.[37]

13–044   The inclusion of an active substance in Annex I may be, and no doubt will be, made subject to conditions. These may relate to, *e.g.* minimum purity, the nature and amount of specific impurities, the types of product it may be used in, how it may be used, and any other conditions prompted by the evaluation of the substance.[38]

Review of Existing Active Substances

13–045   For new products containing active substances that were already on the market in the EC by July 26, 1993, Member States may operate their own national authorisation procedures, until such time as the active substance is either listed in Annex I or it has been decided that it is not to be so listed. In that latter case, any relevant authorisations must be withdrawn or varied as appropriate. A programme for review of all existing active substances is provided for by Article 8(2) of the Directive, as supplemented by Commission Regulation 3600/92.[39] This Regulation required producers[40] of existing active substances as listed in Annex I of that Regulation (consisting of 90 named substances) to have notified the Commission by August 1, 1993 that they wished to secure the inclusion of that substance (or any salts, esters or amines of

---

[36] Art. 5(5).
[37] Art. 5(1), (2).
[38] Art. 5(4).
[39] [1992] O.J. L366.
[40] Where a substance is manufactured outside the EC, the producer will be any person within the EC designated by the manufacturer to be his sole representative or, in the absence of any such designation, any importer(s) of the substance, whether as such or in a preparation.

it) in Annex I to the Directive. If for any of the 90 listed substances no producer has presented a notification, then individual Member States have the opportunity to seek its listing, failing which a decision will be taken not to include the substance in Annex I to the Directive.[41] Substances that have been notified are then to be reviewed by a designated Member State, in pursuance of a further Commission Regulation, which will also spell out a time limit for supplying the requisite information dossiers to the designated Member State (referred to in the regulation as the "rapporteur"), which will normally be 12 months.

The producer must provide both a summary dossier complying **13–046** with the requirements of Annex II to the Directive in respect of the active substance, and with those of Annex III in respect of at least one pesticide preparation that incorporates it. There must also be supplied a complete dossier which, in addition, contains the protocols and complete study reports of the trials that have been summarised for the purposes of the summary dossier. If the time limit for producing the technical information is not met, the rapporteur Member State must so inform the Commission giving any reasons for the delay that the notifier(s) may have pleaded; this will apply equally where some information has been put in in time, but is clearly inadequate.[42] In any such event, the Commission is required to present to the Committee a draft decision not to include the active substance in Annex I unless a new time limit has been set for the submission of information, or unless a Member State tells the Commission that it will take over responsibility for preparation of the technical information and to take on the duties of a notifier. An extension of time will however only be granted where the delay has been caused either by efforts by several notifiers to present information collectively, or where there has been force majeure. Producers will therefore have a powerful incentive to act promptly, since there is very little opportunity for the Commission to show any flexibility. Where 12 months is unlikely to be adequate, it will be important for producers to ensure a realistic timetable is specified in the first place.

The Member State that is acting as rapporteur for a particular active **13–047** substance must examine the dossiers submitted in the order in which they are received; if several dossiers are presented for a single active substance at different times, they will be treated as having been received when the last one is submitted. The rapporteur Member State must take a decision on the dossier, within at most 12 months from

---

[41] Reg. 3600/92, Art. 4.
[42] Art. 6(4).

receipt of the information, on whether to include the active substance in Annex I, or to remove the active substance from the market, to suspend the active substance from the market pending submission of further information, or to postpone any decision pending submission of further information.[43] During the examination, the Member State may seek further information from the notifier(s).

13–048 Other Member States and the European Commission are to be kept informed of the information supplied to the rapporteur. The Commission will decide what measures to propose to the Committee, following receipt of the rapporteur Member State's report and recommendations. Where further information is required, the Commission is to determine the time-limits for providing it, and also a further and shorter time limit for the notifiers to undertake that they will in fact supply the further information by the specified time limit. As previously, if no such undertaking is given, or in fact the further results are not submitted within the specified time-limit, the Commission is required to submit a decision to the Committee that the active substance shall not be included in Annex I.

13–049 Where further information is provided in time (unless yet further trials appear to be necessary, in which case this last stage is repeated), the rapporteur Member State must issue a report and recommendations on the entire application within the following nine months, whereupon the Commission must put a proposal to the Committee for the inclusion in or exclusion from Annex I, as the case may be, of the active substance. In any case where a substance is approved for inclusion in Annex I, this inclusion may be, and again it no doubt will be, made subject to any appropriate conditions, and these conditions may be varied following any review of the pesticide.[44]

13–050 The Commission may, in relation to any substance listed in Annex A to the Regulation present a proposal to the Council of Ministers for a total prohibition on use of such a substance, by way of a Directive amending Directive 79/117 (see paragraph 13–005). If the Council adopts such a proposal while a substance is being reviewed pursuant to the Regulation, all further steps in the relevant procedure will cease.

13–051 Following Regulation 3600/92, a series of additional Regulations will be issued setting out further lists of existing pesticides due for review, and this process will be continued until all existing pesticides have been reviewed, or at least decisions have been taken not to include them in Annex I to the Directive.

[43] Art. 7(1)(c).
[44] Art. 8(3).

Authorisation of Plant Protection Products

The authorisation of plant protection products, unlike that of active **13–052** substances, is organised on a national basis. Articles 3 and 4 of the Directive set out the substantive controls and procedures for authorisation, so harmonising these throughout the EC. The basic provision, that no plant protection product may be marketed or used in any Member State unless it has been authorised in accordance with the Directive,[45] is subject to two exceptions:

— for products being used for experimental or testing purposes within Article 22 of the Directive, in respect of which a separate Directive is to be proposed; and
— in an emergency involving an unforeseeable danger which cannot be contained by other means, an authorisation for a limited and controlled use for up to 120 days may be granted. Any extension of this period must be agreed at EC level.[46]

The authorisation procedure is laid down in Article 4, supplemented **13–053** by provisions in Article 13. These broadly require that no authorisation may be granted unless, firstly, the relevant active substance is listed in Annex I and any conditions laid down in respect of this are fulfilled, and, secondly, that the product is of an appropriate standard in respect of efficacy, absence of unacceptable effects on plants and plant products, absence of unnecessary suffering and pain to any vertebrates to be controlled, impact on human or animal health, whether directly or arising from residues, the fate and distribution in the environment of the product and its residues, the availability of appropriate analytical methods, both in respect of the impact of the active substance and any impurities, and also the pesticide residues, their physical and chemical properties, and residue levels in the agricultural products on which the pesticide may be used. An applicant must therefore normally provide full data on the properties of his product in relation to all these aspects. To assess a product's properties against these various criteria, a set of uniform principles has been developed which forms Annex VI to the Directive, inserted by Directive 94/43.[47]

Authorisations must set conditions relating to the marketing and **13–054** use of the product, and the holders of authorisations are to be required to notify "all new information on the potentially dangerous effects of any plant protection product, or of residues of an active substance on human or animal health or on groundwater, or their potentially

[45] Art. 3(1).
[46] Art. 8(4).
[47] [1994] O.J. L227.

767

dangerous effects on the environment".[48] Authorisations are to be granted for limited periods of not more than ten years, subject to renewal if the requirements to be taken into account on the first authorisation remain capable of being satisfied. Renewal may be limited to such period as is necessary for any necessary verification testing to be conducted. Additionally, authorisations may be reviewed at any time and revoked or modified in appropriate cases.

13–055   Member States are entitled to require applicants to provide samples of the proposed product and of its ingredients as part of the application procedure. Where this is required, applicants will need to consider whether any such material falls within the scope of any claim of a third party's patent effective in that jurisdiction, since supply to the authorities will be generally regarded as an infringing act not falling within any experimental use or other exemptions. Manufacturers of generic products may accordingly be unable to obtain authorisations in those countries operating such procedural requirements for so long as the product or any of its ingredients remain protected there by extant patents.[49]

13–056   Regulatory authorities considering an application may not make use of information provided by previous applicants except in certain strictly defined circumstances as set out in paragraphs 3 and 4 of Article 13. The first of these is where the first applicant agrees to such use. Secondly, in the case of a new active substance (one not on the market by July 26, 1993) the earlier information, in so far as it relates to the active substance ("Annex II information"), may be made use of after a period of 10 years from the first inclusion in Annex I of the Directive of that active substance; in so far as the information relates to a plant protection product ("Annex III information"), it may be made use of 10 years from first authorisation of the plant protection product in any Member State, provided that that authorisation is after the inclusion in Annex I of the active substance(s) that the product contains. Thirdly, where an existing active substance is concerned (*i.e.* one first marketed before July 26, 1993), Annex II information in respect of the active substance provided with the earlier application may be used after such period as each Member State determines, being at most 10 years from the date of the original approval in that Member State. Similarly, where a plant protection product has been authorised in any Member State before inclusion of the active substance(s) that it contains in Annex I, Annex III information relating to that plant protection product may be used after such period as each Member

---

[48] Art. 7. See para. 13–070 on the extent of this obligation.
[49] Art. 9(3).

State determines, again up to a maximum of 10 years from when the product was first authorised in that Member State.

Finally, where new information has been provided either to secure **13–057** the first inclusion of an active substance in Annex I, or to maintain its inclusion or to vary the conditions of maintained inclusion, the information relating to the active substance (and not, it would seem, merely the new information) may not be made use of for the benefit of a later applicant for a period of five years from the date of the relevant decision to vary the conditions for inclusion of an active substance in Annex I or to maintain its inclusion. However if the five year period expires before the 10 year period mentioned above in respect of use of Annex II information on active substances, then the five year period is deemed to be extended until expiry of the ten year period—in other words, the material date for the use of the earlier information is whichever is the later to expire of the ten and five year periods.

The drafting of these provisions is in the form of a ban on use of the **13–058** earlier information for the stipulated periods; it does not in terms provide that a later applicant is entitled to rely on the earlier information if the authorities are disinclined to assist him in this way (though, as referred to below, he may be able to avoid having to give duplicate information on the relevant active substance if he can show that his does not differ significantly from that of the product reviewed for the purposes of the initial inclusion of the substance in Annex I). It may be contrasted in this respect with Article 10(1), which requires Member States to authorise plant protection products that have been authorised in another Member State on evidence of comparability only, and also with Article 13(7) (referred to in the next paragraph below), which positively encourages the sharing of information. Similarly, Directive 65/65[50] on marketing approvals of proprietary medicinal products, as amended by Directive 87/21,[51] expressly states in Article 4(8)(a) that a later applicant "shall not be required to provide the results of [relevant tests and trials]" if his product is "essentially similar" to the one previously authorised and the relevant period (up to 10 years) has elapsed. However the reference to periods "not exceeding" 10 years in sub-paragraphs (3)(c) and (4)(c) carry a strong implication that it is intended that the earlier information should be used for the benefit of later applicants from then on, whenever appropriate. If that is right, it must follow that the same consequences follow expiry of the other periods referred to in these paragraphs (3) and (4).[52]

[50] [1965] O.J. L22.
[51] [1987] O.J. L15.
[52] See also paras. 13–071 to 13–073 with regard to the position in the UK.

13–059   Special rules provide for encouraging different applicants to co-operate in sharing test results in so far as this will avoid or reduce the need for experiments involving vertebrate animals. This also applies where existing active substances are under review for inclusion in Annex I and two or more persons are involved in the provision of relevant data. If agreement between the parties cannot be reached, Member States are permitted to oblige holders of previous authorisations located within their territory to share data with a later applicant to avoid duplicate testing on vertebrate animals.[53]

13–060   If an applicant who seeks approval of a product, of which the active substance is already listed in Annex I, can satisfy the authorities that his active substance "does not differ significantly in degree of purity and nature of impurities" from the active substance in the composition the subject of the dossier accompanying the original application, then he cannot be required to provide any further information in respect of that active substance.[54] This is however explicitly made subject to paragraphs 3 and 4 of Article 13, discussed above, which prohibit the authorities from using, for a limited period, information provided by an earlier applicant relating either to an active substance or to a formulated product. Where any such period is still running therefore, the later applicant must either repeat the trials concerned or wait for the period to expire (unless of course agreement can be reached with the earlier applicant on terms for using his information). These provisions, taken together, create a rough balance between the conflicting interests of the first applicant, on the one hand, who will have risked substantial sums in conducting often lengthy trials on his product and its active substance, and who would be unlikely to do so if others could readily take advantage of the work to compete with him, and those of the general public, on the other, in maximising price competition by not imposing the costs of duplicate trials on others who seek approval for comparable products.

13–061   Where the original manufacturing process is known, establishing that one active substance does not differ "significantly" from another may not prove unduly difficult, but in other circumstances there could be considerable dispute with the authorities and/or the earlier applicant as to whether the later applicant has made out an adequate case in this regard. As the provision stands, it seems that if a later product were to be significantly purer, or to have substantially less by way of deleterious impurities, this provision could not be relied on, even though the plant protection product concerned would presumably be safer in all respects. There would appear to be considerable scope for

---

[53] Art. 13(7).
[54] Art. 13(2).

differing views to be taken by the various authorities of the Member States.

Transitional Provisions

Because it is expected to take of the order of ten years to review all **13–062** existing active substances of commercial interest and to determine whether or not they merit inclusion in Annex I, lengthy transitional provisions are essential to allow existing controls to be maintained pending the full implementation of the new regime. These provisions apply where the active substances in any plant protection products were on the market before July 26, 1993, referred to here as "existing active substances". In any such case the marketing of plant protection products containing existing active substances may continue to be authorised by Member States up to July 26, 2003. Where an application is made for a product containing an existing active substance (such as would be the case with a product from a new manufacturer or a new formulation or a new application for a product from a manufacturer already holding an authorisation) Member States are entitled to maintain their previous national rules for data requirements, for so long as the active substance is not included in Annex I.[55] In the interim, these existing active substances are to be reviewed as described, the first list of substances and the procedures to be applied to them being set out in Commission Regulation 3600/92. The Commission is required to present a report by July 26, 2001 as to the progress it has made by then in this programme, and the transitional period may be extended. When considering applications for authorisation of plant protection products containing existing active substances, Member States are to have regard to the same issues as are relevant in the case of new active substances, but applying their own rules as to what data should be provided.[56]

Member States may also grant provisional authorisations, for **13–063** periods of not more than three years, for products containing new active substances not included in Annex I. Where they do so, they must provide information on the active substance to other Member States and the Commission, and hence to the Committee, and the Member State concerned is required to inform them of its assessment of the technical data provided and of the terms of the authorisation it grants. There is provision for the Member State to be required to withdraw the authorisation if the active substance is not approved at

[55] Art. 13(6).
[56] Art. 8(3).

EC level. The three year period may be extended, but any decision to do this must be taken at EC level and not nationally.[57]

13–064   To avoid obstacles to the free movement of goods, Member States are not allowed to impede the production, storage or movement of any plant protection product intended for use in another Member State, even though it is not authorised for use in their own territory, provided that it is in fact authorised in another Member State (presumably this must be read as the other Member State in which use is intended), and also that any inspection requirements are complied with that Member States may lay down to ensure there is no marketing or use of unauthorised products.[58]

13–065   Each Member State must accept an authorisation of a plant protection product granted by another Member State, and grant a like authorisation itself, provided that the applicant concerned can establish the necessary comparability of the products and data in question.[59] Thus the second Member State cannot require repetition of tests and analyses already carried out in the other except in so far as agricultural, plant health and environmental, particularly climatic, conditions relevant to the use of the product are not comparable in the two countries. Where the product consists solely of active substances listed in Annex I, and the uniform principles of Annex VI have been adopted, there is a requirement to authorise the marketing of the product in the second territory, again in so far as relevant agricultural, plant health and environmental conditions are comparable. Nevertheless, other conditions can be imposed on an authorisation to protect the health of those involved in handling the product, and there may also be restrictions on use to the extent that these are necessary to avoid risks of people exceeding an acceptable daily intake of pesticide residues, resulting from differences in dietary patterns between the Member States concerned. Where it will assist in obtaining an authorisation, an applicant may agree to the imposition of conditions of use which avoid issues that might arise out of differing agricultural plant health or environmental conditions between the two countries and, if he does, so imposing such conditions is permitted. Any dispute as to whether there is comparability between regions for the purposes of these provisions is to be decided at EC level under the procedure set out in Article 19, which provides for an initial decision by the Committee and, if the Committee does not adopt measures proposed by the Commission, an ultimate decision by the Council of Ministers.

---

[57] Art. 8(1), para. 4.
[58] Art. 3(2).
[59] Art. 10(1).

Member States are required to ensure that plant protection products **13–066** are used properly, which not only requires compliance with all applicable conditions and any requirements specified on labels, but also the principles of good plant protection practice and "whenever possible" the principles of integrated control. These latter principles essentially involve limiting to a minimum the use of chemical plant protection products, and combining them with other measures to maintain pest populations at levels below those causing economically unacceptable damage or loss.[60]

Active substances may not be marketed unless they are appropria- **13–067** tely labelled in accordance with the CPL Directive 67/548. Labelling of pesticides is in most cases subject to the provisions of Directive 78/631[61] as amended (see paragraphs 12–110 to 12–113); in so far as any plant protection products within the scope of Directive 91/414 are not covered by the pesticides labelling requirements of Directive 78/631, the packaging must comply with the requirements of Article 5(1) of 78/631.[62] In addition a series of labelling requirements are set out in Article 16(1). Among the matters to be shown on a label are the name and address of the holder of the authorisation and, if different, those of the person responsible for the final packaging and labelling of the product as marketed, any special risks and safety precautions, the uses for which the product has been authorised and conditions under which the product may be or should not be used, safety intervals between application and other later activities such as sowing or harvesting, and directions for safe disposal of the product and of its packaging. Certain (only) of these mandatory requirements may be met by using an accompanying leaflet, if the package itself is too small.

Experimental Permits

Authorisation for experimental use is generally outside the scope of **13–068** the Directive. Release of an unauthorised plant protection product into the environment still requires prior authorisation however, even for experimental purposes. Any such permit can only be granted for use under controlled conditions and for limited quantities and areas.[63] Harmonised conditions for the grant of experimental permits is to be the subject of a later Directive adopted under the Article 19 procedure. To the extent that any plant protection product consists of or contains

---

[60] Arts. 3(3), 2(13).
[61] [1978] O.J. L206.
[62] Art. 15.
[63] Art. 22(1).

a genetically modified organism, any release for experimental purposes will be governed exclusively by the Deliberate Release Directive 90/220.[64]

UK Plant Protection Products Regulations

13–069 The PPP Regulations are expected to correspond closely with EC Directive 91/414, and little additional description is necessary. The definitions in the draft of August 1994 follow those in the Directive, as referred to in paragraph 13–039. Marketing and using any plant protection product is to be prohibited unless an approval has been granted and all conditions of approval relating to the relevant activity are complied with.[65] In addition, use of a plant protection product must be "in accordance with the principles of good plant protection practice" and "whenever possible, . . . in accordance with the principles of integrated control"—these requirements being taken *verbatim* from Article 3(3) of the Directive. No further guidance is given in the draft legislation on what amounts to good plant protection practice, but "integrated control"[66] is defined as "the rational application of a combination of biological, bio-technological, chemical, cultural or plant-breeding measures whereby the use of chemical plant protection products is limited to the strict minimum necessary to maintain the pest population at levels below those causing economically unacceptable damage or loss".

13–070 Regulation 14 repeats the requirements of Article 7 (see paragraph 13–054), requiring the holder of an approval, and a person who has been granted an extension of an approved use, to notify the Ministers immediately of all new information on potentially dangerous effects of any plant protection product or of the residues of an active substance. It is not made clear whether this merely requires the holder to pass on such information as he happens to acquire, or whether it imposes any more stringent obligation to seek out "all new information" that ever becomes available independently of him. Though the wording is capable of bearing this latter construction, it could prove extremely onerous—unless the active substance is unique to the holder of the approval, he would have to keep himself informed of all information relating to the use or performance of products containing the active substance, whether his or anyone else's, presumably on a world-wide basis. Given that failure to comply with this obligation is a criminal offence, the narrower construction is probably to be preferred, requiring submission only of all new information of which the holder

---

[64] [1990] O.J. L117.
[65] reg. 3(1), (2).
[66] Recital 8 of the Directive refers to "integrated *pest* control".

774

in fact becomes aware. Even here there may be a grey area in respect of information that he should reasonably have learned of, but did not, either negligently or by deliberately turning a blind eye to a potential problem.

The system of consents in respect of marketing and use and the "basic conditions" attached to them, which are an essential part of authorisations under the 1986 Regulations, are maintained in the draft PPP Regulations.[67] Applications for approval of a plant protection product are made in accordance with the procedure and other provisions of regulations 5 and 6. As permitted by the Directive, provisional (i.e. for a period, which may be extended, of up to three years), emergency and experimental approvals may be granted in appropriate cases.[68] No experimental approval under the PPP regulations is however needed for experiments or tests involving genetically modified organisms that are covered by Part B of Directive 90/220, i.e. deliberate release into the environment otherwise than for marketing (see paragraphs 14–069 to 14–079). **13–071**

Additionally, marketing of any active substance is to be prohibited unless, in the case of any first marketed on or after July 26, 1993, an application for the inclusion of the active substance in Annex I has been made to the Minister of Agriculture, Fisheries and Food, a dossier of technical information has been provided to the Minister and the Commission that complies with the requirements of Annexes II and III of the Directive, and the person responsible has submitted a declaration that the active substance is intended for use in a plant protection product.[69] (Active substances marketed before July 26, 1993, are "existing active substances" and subject to the review process referred to paragraphs 13–045 to 13–051, and until included in Annex I (or banned) are controlled under the 1986 Regulations). **13–072**

Approvals for plant protection products are to be granted where the information provided by the applicant has been assessed in accordance with the requirements of the Directive, and these approvals may be granted for any fixed term up to a maximum of 10 years.[70] An approval must be granted for a product subject to an authorisation granted by another Member State, in line with the requirements of Article 10 of the Directive,[71] subject to the possible submission of further data where relevant conditions in Great Britain are not comparable with those used in assembling the data. Off-label uses of a **13–073**

[67] reg. 3(6).
[68] regs. 6–8.
[69] reg. 3(3).
[70] reg. 13(1).
[71] reg. 11.

plant protection product are provided for,[72] and such an extension of the approved use must be granted provided that the authorities are satisfied that this is in the public interest, all appropriate documentation and information has been submitted, painful or other harmful effects on vertebrates and other animals and unacceptable impacts on the environment are avoided, and the intended use is minor. Provision is made for renewal, review, revocation and amendment of approvals.[73] However, no formal procedures are set out, and specifically no positive requirement to apply for renewal at least two years before expiry of a current approval, as applies in the case of active substances approvals.[74]

13–074   As regards subsequent applications where it is sought to rely on information contained in earlier applications of third parties, the full provisions of Articles 13(3) and 13(4) (discussed in paragraphs 13–056 to 13–058) are incorporated by reference,[75] but without any clarification of whether later applicants have a right to the benefit of earlier information after expiry of the relevant periods (see paragraph 13–058). However as regards the United Kingdom at least the House of Lords judgment in *In re Smith Kline & French Laboratories Ltd.*[76] is pertinent. This case concerned whether the UK licensing authority, when considering an application for a product licence under the Medicines Act 1968 from a generic pharmaceutical manufacturer, might refer to information supplied by Smith Kline & French when obtaining a licence for their original product. Lord Templeman turned this round by holding that, since the authority had a duty to safeguard the health of the nation:

> "I am satisfied that it is the right *and duty* (emphasis added) of the licensing authority to make use of all the information supplied by any applicant for a product licence which assists the licensing authority in considering whether to grant or reject any other application, or which assists the licensing authority in performing any of its other functions under the Act of 1968. The use of such information should not harm the appellants and even were it to do so, this is the price which the appellants must pay for co-operating in the regime designed by Parliament for the protection of the public and for the protection of the appellants and all manufacturers of medicinal products from the dangers inherent in the introduction and reproduction of modern drugs."[77]

---

[72] reg. 10.
[73] reg. 13(2)–(4).
[74] Under Art. 5(5).
[75] reg. 13.
[76] [1990] 1 A.C. 64.
[77] At pp. 103, 104.

In the case of pesticides it is to be noted that recital 9 of the Directive   **13–075**
reads:

> "Whereas the provisions governing authorization must ensure a
> high standard of protection, which, in particular, must prevent
> the authorization of plant protection products whose risks to
> health, groundwater and the environment and human and
> animal health should take priority over the objective of improving
> plant production."

Further, the objectives of F.E.P.A.[78] include protecting the health of   **13–076**
human beings, creatures and plants, and safeguarding the environ-
ment. In these circumstances there are clearly strong arguments for
applying Lord Templeman's dictum to the use of information on
pesticides already held by the authorities. Nevertheless it does not
follow that later applicants necessarily have an enforceable right to
insist that they be relieved from supplying comparable information,
except in relation to an active substance where they can establish that
theirs does not differ significantly in "degree of purity and nature of
impurities" from that of the earlier product that supported the listing
of that substance in Annex I.

Packaging is required to be in conformity with regulation 8 of the   **13–077**
Chemicals (Hazards, Information and Packaging) Regulations 1993,[79]
while labelling must comply with the requirements of regulation 13
which, when coupled with Schedule 2, conforms in all material
respects with the requirements of Article 16 of the Directive.[80]

The issue of whether data may be required to be shared, specifically   **13–078**
to avoid duplicate experiments on any vertebrate animals, is dealt with
by simply repeating in regulation 16 the terms of Article 13(7) of the
Directive, including in particular the possibility of Ministers requiring
data to be shared. No indication is given as to whether or not this
option would be exercised, and if so how frequently. It is an offence (i)
to fail to make enquiries as to the existence of a previously approved
plant protection product the same as the applicant's, and as to the
holders of any relevant approvals, and (ii) not to comply with any
directions that may be given to share data.

If data submitted involves industrial or commercial secrets, these   **13–079**
will be treated as confidential if an applicant so requests and the
Ministers consider that the request is warranted.[80] It is clearly likely to
be so where an experimental permit is sought prior to a patent
application being filed. Full data will often provide useful information

---

[78] Set out in s. 16(1).
[79] reg. 18.
[80] reg. 17(1).

777

to competitors and a request for confidentiality should also be normally accepted as reasonable; nevertheless, as required by Article 14 of the Directive, confidentiality does not apply to certain basic information set out in Schedule 1,[81] and it will be a question of fact as to the extent to which it is reasonable to claim confidentiality in the comprehensive data when this basic information is in the public domain.

13–080   To avoid duplication of pesticides controls, it is provided, somewhat obscurely, that (except with regard to application of the basic conditions referred to in paragraphs 13–013 to 13–015) the 1986 Regulations (and also the Farm and Garden Chemical Regulations 1971[82]) shall not apply to the PPP Regulations.[83] Presumably this is intended to mean that in so far as the PPP Regulations govern any product, active substances or activity, then these 1986 and 1971 Regulations are disapplied.

13–081   F.E.P.A. contains the principal enforcement powers in respect of actual, prospective and suspected contraventions of regulations made under it. Nevertheless, the PPP Regulations provide additional powers to the Ministers to deal with contraventions by themselves seizing or disposing of any plant protection product involved in an offence and anything treated by it, or by requiring some other person to take such remedial action as appears to be necessary as a result of the contravention.[84] Where a product has been imported without the requisite authority, any of the owner, the importer and the person in charge of it can be required to re-export it from the United Kingdom.[85] Further ancillary offences, including, *e.g.* the making of false statements and intentional non-disclosure, are prescribed in regulation 21. The usual provisions are included rendering directors and other officers of a body corporate liable for any of its offences due or attributable to their consent, connivance or neglect; its members are potentially liable on the same basis where they managed the corporate body, as are the partners of a Scottish partnership.[86] A broad "due diligence" defence is however available under regulation 23, corresponding to that of F.E.P.A., s. 22, discussed in paragraphs 13–024 and 13–025.

[81] reg. 17(2).
[82] S.I. 1971 No. 729. These Regulations relate to the labelling of pesticides sold retail that contain any of a large variety of active substances, and require their labels to name those that are present.
[83] reg. 25.
[84] reg. 20(1).
[85] reg. 20(2).
[86] reg. 22(3)–(5).

Chapter 14

GENETICALLY MODIFIED ORGANISMS

Micro-organisms have been used by man for thousands of years in the production of food and drink, for example the leavening of bread with yeast, the fermentation of a variety of carbohydrate containing natural products to give alcohol, and the preparation of yoghurt from milk. The selective breeding and cross-breeding of animals and plants has also for many years been used to promote the production of particularly desired strains of genetic material. It was however only following the discovery of the molecular structure of such genetic material (the double helix, that is the principal characteristic of DNA[1]) and establishing the nature of the units of which it is composed, that it became possible to operate on these structures in a controlled way to produce intended changes in the replicating material.[2] The end products of many commercial processes involving genetic engineering are in many cases identical to those found in nature, save that they are in a pure form, and so safer and generally more suitable for commercial use.[3]

14–001

Thus in many cases, biotechnology is currently used to obtain no more than what may be achieved by traditional techniques with natural materials, but to do it with more precision and greater efficiency. Even where new products are produced, these are often only what might have been obtained by conventional selective breeding techniques, but the possibility of splicing into genetic material a new gene with an identified property eliminates to a considerable degree the randomness that is an unavoidable part of

14–002

---

[1] First postulated by James Watson and Francis Crick in 1953.

[2] The now standard DNA splicing techniques used in genetic engineering were first developed by Stanley Cohen and Herbert Boyer in around 1973.

[3] Biotechnology is now widely used in the pharmaceutical industry, for example, to manufacture naturally occurring products, such as hormones, that have previously only been produced by lengthy and expensive purification and concentration processes on naturally occurring raw materials. The ability of genetic engineering techniques to produce an identical product without impurities produces far greater predictability of performance and avoidance of uncertain side effects.

selective breeding.[4] However, genetic engineering techniques also undeniably make possible the creation of replicating organisms containing wholly novel combinations of genetic material, that would almost certainly never occur without human intervention.[5] These raise the inevitable possibility, albeit in the great majority of cases an extremely remote one, that such new organisms might, if allowed to escape, proliferate uncontrollably in the absence of any existing organisms that could compete successfully with them. The consequences could be severe, conceivably even fatal, disturbances to the eco-systems on which they might impinge.

14–003   It is this possibility of an adverse and conceivably catastrophic effect on humans and the environment generally from a newly created substance that demands that the handling, and in particular any deliberate release, of genetically modified organisms ("GMOs") capable of independent survival and reproduction be conducted with great care.

14–004   Commercial research using recombinant DNA techniques developed rapidly from the mid-1970s onwards.[6] After an initial period when those involved operated voluntary constraints, the first statutory controls in the United Kingdom that directly addressed these concerns were the Health and Safety (Genetic Manipulation) Regulations 1978.[7] These required notification to the Health and Safety Executive of any proposals to carry out genetic manipulation. As their title indicates, they were essentially aimed at protecting the health and safety of those working with genetic material; protection of the environment more generally was not the principal concern, and indeed the Health and Safety Executive responsible for administering the Regulations considered that it would be improper for them to exercise their powers for purposes other than health and safety. In the mid-1980s, however, official concern with the risks associated with the release of genetic material into the environment led to the issue of formal guidelines by the Advisory Committee on Genetic Manipula-

---

[4] Typical examples of such techniques are the production of horticulturally valuable plants with increased resistance to particular diseases; it is also possible to produce plants that are substantially resistant to selective weed killers, which then may be used on the weeds in a crop without destroying it.

[5] Such an approach has been used to develop uniquely effective delivery mechanisms for pharmaceuticals for treating specific parts of the body. Another example of the beneficial use of genetic manipulation (given in a question from a member of the European Parliament reported in [1992] O.J. C209), is the release into the environment in Belgium of baits containing genetically manipulated viruses with the intention of vaccinating foxes in the wild against rabies, a project that was supported by a grant from the European Commission.

[6] See n.2.

[7] S.I. 1978 No. 752.

tion (the "ACGM") that had been set up by the Health and Safety Commission in 1984.[8]

The ACGM guidelines were given statutory force in 1989 in the Genetic Manipulation Regulations 1989.[9] The purpose of these Regulations was to ensure prior notification took place of any activities involving genetic manipulation, whether contained within a laboratory or by way of intentional introduction into the environment. However, an intentional release required ninety days prior notification, as compared with thirty days for any other activity. The Regulations did not themselves contain any powers to prevent any such activity, provided it had been notified in the prescribed manner and appropriate risk assessments had been carried out where so required by the Regulations. Also in 1989, the Government issued a consultation paper "Proposals for Additional Legislation on the Intentional Release of Genetically Modified Organisms" and the Royal Commission on Environmental Pollution issued its 13th report "The Release of Genetically Engineered Organisms into The Environment".[10] At much the same time, the European Commission was developing its own proposals for control over genetically modified organisms which resulted, in April 1990, in Directives 90/219 and 90/220 relating respectively to the contained use of genetically modified micro-organisms, and the deliberate release into the environment of genetically modified organisms. The Environmental Protection Bill was also then in the course of its passage through Parliament, and Part VI of the eventual E.P.A. represented the first piece of primary legislation in the UK relating to the use of genetically modified organisms and concerned with the protection of the environment as well as human health.

14–005

The Royal Commission followed up its 13th Report in its 14th: "GENHAZ: A System for the Critical Appraisal of Proposals to Release Genetically Modified Organisms into the Environment".[11] GENHAZ is an adaptation of the procedure known as HAZOP (hazard and operability study) that is used, for example, in the chemical industry, for use in connection with the release of GMOs; the RCEP's 14th Report aimed to provide a handbook for those wishing to develop the procedure further. The Government's preliminary response,[12] though generally welcoming, was that the Commission's recommendations

14–006

---

[8] For a fuller account of the history of the various voluntary and statutory arrangements for controlling the use and release of genetically modified organisms, see Tromans, *The Environmental Protection Act 1990*, (2nd ed.), pp. 249–254.

[9] S.I. 1989 No. 1810.

[10] Cm. 720, July 1989; the Government response to which was published in 1993.

[11] Cm. 1557, June 1991.

[12] Published in August 1993; it is intended to supplement this once the results of two current studies on releases are available.

would tend to require an excessive amount of regulation for the great majority of GMOs, and it has, with the Advisory Committee on Releases to the Environment ("ACRE"), produced its own risk assessment procedure.

14–007   The issue of excessive regulation was a principal feature of a subsequent report issued by the House of Lords Select Committee on Science and Technology in October 1993 on the UK regulation of biotechnology. This severely criticised the regime set up by the two EC Directives as taking an unduly precautionary line. Its principal conclusions were: (i) except where pathogens are involved, separate regulation of GMOs in contained use is unnecessary over and above good laboratory practice; and (ii) deliberate release of GMOs is not inherently dangerous, except where bacterial or virus vectors, live vaccines or modification of the genome of animals are involved.

EC Legislation

14–008   The applicable EC legislation consists of Directive 90/219 on the contained use of micro-organisms (the "Contained Use Directive") and Directive 90/220 on the deliberate release into the environment of genetically modified organisms ("the Deliberate Release Directive").[13] Both Directives were due to be implemented by October 23, 1991. Simplified procedures applicable to releases of certain genetically modified plants are provided by Decision 93/584.[14] Directive 90/220 has been amended by Directive 94/15,[15] which divides its Annex II into two, reducing information requirements in relation to genetically modified higher plants. In addition, Council Decision 91/596 and Commission Decision 92/146[16] set out formats to be used for supplying information to the Commission.[17]

14–009   Directive 90/219 relates to micro-organisms only and not to genetically modified organisms generally, which reflects its essential purpose, namely the protection of the health and safety of those working in this field — large organisms are not considered to pose any comparable threat. The Directive provides for classifying the micro-organisms into either a Group I or a Group II in accordance with criteria set out in an Annex to the Directive, Group I micro-organisms posing the lesser

---

[13] Both contained in [1990] O.J. L117.
[14] [1993] O.J. L279.
[15] [1994] O.J. L103.
[16] [1991] O.J. L322; [1992] O.J. L60.
[17] The format of 91/596 has been amended, by Decision 94/211, [1994] O.J. L105, reflecting the fewer details required in the case of deliberate release of genetically modified higher plants.

hazard, and accordingly being subject to somewhat less stringent requirements.

The Directive also divides the types of activity with which the **14–010** contained use may be concerned into Type A and Type B operations. Type A operations are essentially small scale and for the purposes of teaching, research, development or for non-industrial or non-commercial purposes. The Directive illustrates "small scale" by stating, "*e.g.* 10 litres culture volume or less"; this aspect does not appear in the implementing UK Regulations, where the corresponding definitions are in purely functional terms relating to keeping the organisms under containment in accordance with good micro-biological practice and good occupational safety and hygiene and in a manner whereby they may be reasonably rendered inactive by standard laboratory decontamination techniques. All operations that do not fall within the Type A definition are regarded as Type B operations. Since the UK Regulations follow the EC legislation very closely, save that in relation to contained use they apply to GMOs generally and not merely micro-organisms, it is necessary to consider only the UK legislation in detail.

UK Legislation

The substantive UK legislation on GMOs consists essentially of: **14–011**

(i)   the bulk of Part VI of the E.P.A., namely Sections 106 to 127;[18]

(ii) the Genetically Modified Organisms (Contained Use) Regulations 1992[19] — the "Contained Use Regulations";

(iii) the Genetically Modified Organisms (Deliberate Release) Regulations 1992[20] — the "Deliberate Release Regulations";

(iv) the Genetically Modified Organisms (Contained Use) Regulations 1993[21] — the "1993 Contained Use Regulations"; and

(v) the Genetically Modified Organisms (Deliberate Release) Regulations 1993[22] — the "1993 Deliberate Release Regulations".

It may be noted here that regulation 13 of the Deliberate Release **14–012** Regulations inserts a subsection 6(A) into section 111 of the E.P.A., and makes a minor amendment to section 118, relating to offences, that

---

[18] Brought into force by the Environmental Protection Act 1990 (Commencement No. 7) Order 1991 (S.I. 1991 No. 1042) and by the Environmental Protection Act 1990 (Commencement No.12) Order 1992 (S.I. 1992 No. 3253).

[19] S.I. 1992 No. 3217.

[20] S.I. 1992 No. 3280.

[21] S.I. 1993 No. 15.

[22] S.I. 1993 No. 152.

reflects this additional subsection. Further, subsection 112(1) has also been amended to remove all constraints on the Secretary of State as regards the nature of the limitations and conditions that he may include in any consent (as to which see below).[23]

14–013   Both the Contained Use and Deliberate Release Directives require the Commission to set up a committee of national "competent authorities" to assist it in implementing the Directives.[24] The UK competent authorities are the HSE and the Department of the Environment jointly. Prime responsibility for contained use activities is nevertheless taken by the HSE, and for deliberate release activities by the DoE. The European Commission itself has also issued guidelines on the interpretation of various issues arising under the Directives which have been discussed and agreed in the committee, these guidance being reflected where appropriate in the official guidelines on the UK Contained Use and Deliberate Release Regulations.

14–014   In the UK, there are separate official committees that advise in relation to issues arising under the two sets of GMO Regulations. The Advisory Committee on Genetic Manipulation (ACGM), which was established in 1984 to advise the HSC and the HSE, and the relevant ministers, on aspects of genetic manipulation, continues to have responsibility for advising on human health and safety standards applicable to activities involving GMOs, and is responsible for advising in relation to the Contained Use Regulations. The Advisory Committee on Releases to the Environment (ACRE) was in existence before Part VI was brought into force, but its membership is now appointed under section 124 of the E.P.A. to advise the Secretary of State for the Environment on releases to the environment, as its name indicates, and on the exercise of other powers available to him under Part VI. His concern accordingly is essentially with potential harm to the environment that may be caused by GMOs, as opposed to considerations of human health and safety.

14–015   The structure of this legislation is somewhat complex since it must implement two EC Directives which differ as to the GMOs controlled, and also since environmental protection and health and safety are governed in the UK by largely distinct legal regimes with different regulatory authorities. Two types of activity require separate consideration, which between them are comprehensive in scope, in relation to the GMOs they apply to:

---

[23] By the E.P.A. 1990 (Modification of s.112) Regulations 1992, S.I. 1992 No. 2617.
[24] The deliberations of this committee are subject to the qualified majority voting procedure that obtains in the Council of Ministers, for example in respect of adopting measures proceeding under Article 100A of the Rome Treaty.

(1) Contained use of GMOs. The Contained Use Directive applies only to *micro*-organisms, but though the Contained Use Regulations also apply to other organisms (those referred to in Part III of Schedule 2 to those Regulations), controls over the latter are generally considerably less demanding. These Regulations are made under the H.S.W.A. 1974 (and also the European Communities Act 1972), but are nevertheless explicitly stated[25] to be also for the protection of the environment as well as from risks to health. They cover virtually every likely activity involving GMOs other than deliberate release (and marketing). Part VI of the E.P.A., which applies, *inter alia*, to the acquiring and importing of GMOs, therefore also governs contained use activities, except to the extent it is expressly disapplied, which is the effect in part of the 1993 Regulations.

(2) Deliberate release of GMOs. ("Release" in this context applies both to marketing and to other releases). The Deliberate Release Directive and Regulations both apply to the release to the environment of all GMOs (as defined), whether micro-organisms or not. Deliberate release is one of several activities which the Secretary of State may prescribe, under Part VI of the E.P.A., as prohibited unless made the subject of an express consent. It is so prescribed in the Deliberate Release Regulations.

Part VI of the Environmental Protection Act 1990

Part VI of the E.P.A. was designed to control (either directly or through regulations that may be made under it) the import,[26] acquisition, keeping, release and marketing of any GMOs "for the purpose of preventing or minimising any damage to the environment which may arise from the escape or release from human control of GMOs".[27] However, since controls over contained use of micro-organisms are contained in regulations made under the H.S.W.A. 1974, Part VI has been brought into force only so far as appropriate to

14–016

---

[25] In reg. 3(1).
[26] Import into any part of the United Kingdom (including therefore Northern Ireland) s.127(1).
[27] s.106(1).

control the release and marketing of (all) GMOs and the contained use of GMOs other than micro-organisms.[28] The following discussion of the E.P.A. accordingly relates only to those provisions of the E.P.A. that have been commenced (whether or not regulations have been made under powers that are in force).

14–017   Certain provisions of Part VI are stated not to apply to activities that are required to be consented to under section 111(1)(a) or (b),[29] as is the case for the releases and marketing prescribed under Regulations 5 and 10 of the Deliberate Release Regulations. A similar effect is achieved by the 1993 Contained Use Regulations which exempt many activities controlled under the Contained Use Regulations from the requirements of section 108(1)(a). Such provisions are accordingly in the nature of long-stop requirements that apply to the relatively few cases not subject to more specific controls.

14–018   "Acquire" is defined[30] for the purposes of Part VI as including any method by which GMOs may come to be in a person's possession, other than by their being imported. It is therefore comprehensive in its application and includes manufacture on a person's own premises. It neither requires any consideration nor does it necessarily entail the transfer of title. It would therefore include accidental acquisition, and even theft. It is however used in a manner that distinguishes acquisition from "keeping".

14–019   Section 108 (so far as in force) requires that, before any GMOs are imported or acquired, the person concerned must carry out an assessment of any risks that there may be of damage to the environment being caused as a result, and he must also, in such cases as are prescribed give advance notice to the Secretary of State of his intention to undertake any such activity, together with such further information as may be prescribed.[31] Similarly, a person who is keeping GMOs may be required in such cases or circumstances, and at such times or intervals, as may be prescribed, to give the Secretary of State notice of the fact that he is keeping the GMOs, together with such further information as may be prescribed.[32] Any person carrying out an assessment required by section 108(1)(a) must keep a record of his

---

[28] The following provisions have not been brought into force: ss.108(1)(a) (except in relation to contained use, *i.e.* import and acquisition of GMOs); 108(2), 108(3)(a); 108(4); 108(6); 108(8); 109; 112(3); and 112(4). Ss.110 and 116 are in force only in so far as they relate to the import, acquisition, release or marketing of GMOs, but not to keeping them. A number of others, that enable regulations to be made, have been commenced but not made use of.
[29] ss.108(7).
[30] s.127(1).
[31] s.108(1). No such cases have as yet been prescribed.
[32] s.108(3)(b).

assessment for 10 years.[33] Exemptions from these general requirements may be made by regulations under section 108(7). Subsection
108(9) provides for the making of regulations prescribing the scope
and frequency of risk assessments and how to conduct them, but as
yet none have been made.[34]

The scope of section 108(1)(a), in so far as it applies to the import or **14–020**
acquisition of GMOs, has been curtailed by the 1993 Contained Use
Regulations which exempt from its requirements:

— those relating to the protection of human health;
— those applying to:
  (a) micro-organisms as defined in the Contained Use
      Regulations;
  (b) all other organisms where these are non-pathogenic and
      naturally occurring, fulfil the criteria of Schedule 2, Part
      III, to the Contained Use Regulations, and are acquired by
      self-cloning of organisms other than GMOs; and
  (c) organisms consisting of or included in, an approved
      product under the Deliberate Release Regulations com-
      plying with all applicable limitations and conditions.[35]

Where a person releases or markets GMOs, he must use the best **14–021**
available techniques not entailing excessive cost (BATNEEC) for
preventing any damage to the environment being caused as a result.[36]
This expression is not defined in Part VI of the E.P.A., but it is to be
expected that it will be given the same construction as it is given in
relation to Part I of the Act, relating to integrated pollution control and
air pollution control.[37] As in Part I, where a person is charged with a
failure to comply with his duty to use BATNEEC, the burden of proof is
on the accused to show that there was no better available technique
not entailing excessive cost than the one that was in fact used to
comply with the statutory requirement.[38]

In addition, a control regime for GMOs is provided by sections 110 to **14–022**
112 of the E.P.A., which also applies to importing, acquiring, releasing
and marketing of GMOs. Section 111 empowers the Secretary of State
to require consents to be granted for all or any class of such activities or
for any such activities by any person or class or persons. Consents may
be granted subject to such limitations and conditions as may be

---

[33] s.108(5) and the GMOs (Contained Use) Regs. 1993, reg. 2.
[34] Though regs. 6(1)(c) and 11(2)(b) of the Deliberate Release Regulations also require
risk assessments, and Chap. 4 of the DoE Guidance on those Regulations sets out
what is required in detail.
[35] reg. 3.
[36] s.112(5).
[37] See paras. 9–046 to 9–052.
[38] s.119(1).

imposed or as are automatically implied in accordance with section 112; these may include conditions that continue to have effect even after the person concerned has completed or ceased the consented activities. Such consents may be revoked or varied at any time. The Secretary of State may serve a prohibition notice on any person he has reason to believe is proposing to import or acquire, release or market any GMOs, if he considers the activity would involve a risk of causing damage to the environment.[39] The essential content of the prohibition notice is set out in section 110(3); unlike section 111 there is no provision for imposing conditions on the activity concerned in place of an outright prohibition. Such a notice may be served even though a relevant consent relating to the prohibited activity is in effect.

14–023   The remaining sections of Part VI of the E.P.A. are largely concerned with obtaining information and enforcement. Inspectors, who may be appointed under section 114, have substantial powers of entry and inspection,[40] including powers to require any person to give any relevant information and to require the production of any records (other than any that may be legally privileged). Where information has been required under this power, no answer given by a person will be admissible in evidence against them; nevertheless, that does not exclude it being admissible in evidence against anyone else, for example their employer or another member of the workforce. These powers are exercisable both in relation to premises, other than domestic premises, where there is reason to believe GMOs are being or have been kept, or from which any have been released or have escaped, and also in relation to any premises where there is reason to believe that harmful GMOs may be present (whether being deliberately kept there or not) or where there is evidence of any damage to the environment caused by GMOs.

14–024   The inspectors' powers are reinforced by powers given directly to the Secretary of State to require information from any person who appears to him either to be involved, or to be about to be or to have been involved, in any of the importation, acquisition, release or marketing of GMOs.[41] Where an inspector considers that any GMOs present a cause of imminent danger or damage to the environment, he may seize the material and destroy it or otherwise render it harmless. Where an offence has been committed and the person convicted appears to the court to be capable of remedying any relevant matters, the court may in many circumstances order appropriate remedial action.[42] In the same circumstances the Secretary of State may instead

[39] s.110(1).
[40] Set out in s.115(3).
[41] s.116.
[42] s.120.

take steps to remedy the harm, and recover the cost from any person convicted of the offence.[43]

A public register is kept containing information concerning activi- **14–025** ties under Part VI. This includes directions requiring any person to obtain a consent before undertaking any activity, prohibition notices, applications for consent, advice on these given by ACRE, granted consents and relevant conditions, and "any other information obtained or furnished under any provision of this Part",[44] which is exceptionally wide in scope. Information may be kept out of the register on grounds of national security or where its inclusion might result in damage to the environment. It may also be excluded if it relates to the affairs of any individual or business and the Secretary of State has determined that the information is commercially confidential. The onus is on a person supplying information, and who wishes it to be excluded from the register, to apply for it to be treated as commercially confidential. However, certain basic information will always be included in the register, whether commercially confidential or not, including the description of any GMOs and their location, the purpose of the relevant activity, and the results of any risk assessment. Where information has not been furnished directly by a person but has been obtained in some other way and relates to him or his business, if it appears to the Secretary of State that this information might be commercially confidential, he shall give the person concerned a reasonable opportunity of objecting to its inclusion in the register, and any representations that he may make must be taken into account by the Secretary of State in any determination by him.[45]

Any determination that information is commercially confidential **14–026** will however only keep the information off the register for a period of four years from the date of the determination, though the person furnishing it, or to whom or to whose business it relates, may apply for the information to remain excluded thereafter.[46] Those affected must accordingly pay close attention to this provision if valuable secret information is not to emerge inadvertently.

Contained Use of Genetically Modified Organisms

The 1992 Contained Use Regulations are made under the Health and **14–027** Safety at Work Act 1974 and are administered by the Health and Safety

[43] s.121.
[44] s.122(1).
[45] s.123(6).
[46] s.123(8).

Executive. A person who performs genetic engineering techniques will acquire GMOs as a result, and very possibly have acquired them beforehand as well, and so (subject to his GMOs falling within the relevant definition in Part VI) he will come under the E.P.A. controls also. Nevertheless though the E.P.A. controls, so far as they apply to the acquisition of GMOs, might be used to regulate whether a person may undertake genetic engineering, and if so on what conditions, such activities are considered to be more aptly controlled under the H.S.W.A. 1974 by the HSE.

14–028   The 1992 Regulations define "organism" as "a biological entity capable of replication or of transferring genetic material; the term also includes a micro-organism. "Micro-organism" is defined as being a micro-biological entity, cellular, or non-cellular, capable of replication or of transferring genetic material; it is explicitly stated that the term includes animal or plant cell cultures. "Genetic modification" is also defined and means the altering of the genetic material in an organism by a way that does not occur naturally by mating or natural recombination or both. To assist in applying this definition, the Regulations set out in Part I of Schedule 1 examples of techniques that do constitute genetic modification, and in Part II of the same Schedule techniques which are considered not to result in genetic modification. Thus genetic modification includes:

(a)   the now standard recombinant DNA techniques whereby a new combination of genetic material is formed by the insertion of nucleic acid molecules into a vector system which is incorporated into a host organism, so that the whole is capable of continued propagation;

(b)   the direct introduction into an organism of heritable material; and

(c)   cell fusion or hybridisation techniques using methods that do not occur naturally.

14–029   Techniques which are considered not to result in genetic modification are

(a)   *in vitro* fertilisation;

(b)   conjugation, transduction, transformation or any other natural process; and

(c)   polyploidy induction

if these do not involve the use of recombinant DNA molecules or GMOs.[47]

---

[47] Sched. 1, Part II.

Regulation 3(3) excludes from the scope of the Contained Use   **14–030**
Regulations both the genetic modification of organisms solely by any
techniques listed in Schedule 1, Part II, provided they do not involve
the use of GMOs either as recipient or parental organisms, and also
organisms so modified. These techniques consist of:

(a) mutagenesis;
(b) the production or use of somatic hybridoma cells (*e.g.* the
     production of monoclonal antibodies);
(c) cell fusion (including protoplast fusion) of plant cells where
     the resulting organisms can also be produced by traditional
     breeding methods;
(d) self-cloning of non-pathogenic naturally occurring micro-
     organisms fulfilling the criteria of Group I for recipient micro-
     organisms (as to which the guidelines in Schedule 2, Parts I
     and II apply – see paragraph 14–035); and
(e) self-cloning of non-pathogenic naturally occurring orga-
     nisms other than micro-organisms which fulfil the criteria of
     Schedule 2, Part III.

The expression "traditional breeding methods" (which is also used   **14–031**
in Annex IB of each of the EC Directives) is the subject of an agreement
between the relevant competent authorities of the Member States in
the following terms:

"Traditional breeding refers to practices which use one or more of
a number of methods, including physical and/or chemical means
and control of physiological processes, which can lead to successful crosses between plants of the same botanical family."[48]

Notwithstanding that these Regulations are made under the   **14–032**
H.S.W.A. (and also the European Communities Act 1972), reg. 3(1)
spells out that the Regulations are to have effect not only with a view
to protecting the health of persons, but also the protection of the
environment. Consequently, the conditions that may be attached to
consents issued under these Regulations can properly take environmental considerations into account, and no question of *ultra vires*
would arise should this be done. Reflecting this wider scope,
regulation 4 extends the meaning of "work" as it is understood for the
purposes of the H.S.W.A., to include any activity involving genetic
modification, irrespective, therefore, of where and the circumstances
in which this takes place. Further, regulation 5 modifies section 3(2) of
the H.S.W.A., which places general health and safety duties on self-
employed persons to seek to avoid risks to themselves or to the

---

[48] HSE Guidelines, p. 10.

public,[49] such that where any activity involving genetic modification is conducted by any person who is neither an employer nor an employee, that person is made subject to the general duties. Thus those conducting private, non-commercial research would also be covered.

14–033   Nevertheless, regulation 3(4) provides that in so far as the Regulations relate to the protection of the environment they only apply to genetically modified micro-organisms, so making the Regulations co-extensive in this respect with the EC Contained Use Directive.

The Contained Use Control Regime in Outline

14–034   The broad structure of the Contained Use Regulations rests on regulation 6(1) which prohibits any operation in which organisms are genetically modified or in which GMOs are cultured, stored, used, transported, destroyed or disposed of, unless the operation is undertaken in conditions of contained use in accordance with the Regulations. The main requirements that must be complied with are: (1) assessing the risks created by the activity to human health and the environment; (2) notifying any use being made of premises for the first time for genetic modification; and (3) notifying the activity itself. In certain cases the activity may only be commenced if expressly authorised, in others it may be commenced after a stipulated period unless objected to, and in yet others, involving the least risks, notification of the activity is replaced by having to keep records and providing certain information annually. This prohibition does not however apply to any such operation with GMOs that are marketed, or that are contained in an "approved product", that is, a product that is marketed pursuant to a consent issued under section 111(1) of the E.P.A. or to a written consent issued by any other competent authority of any EC Member State (including, should it be relevant, the one for Northern Ireland) in respect of the deliberate release into the environment of GMOs, provided such operation is in accordance with any conditions or limitations attached to the relevant consent. To avoid overlap with section 111(1), the prohibition of regulation 6(1) does not extend to the release or marketing of GMOs; the circumstances in which release and marketing may occur are defined in the Deliberate Release Regulations discussed below.

---

[49] H.S.W.A., s.3(2) reads: "It shall be the duty of every self-employed person to conduct his undertaking in such a way as to ensure, so far as is reasonably practicable, that he and other persons (not being his employees) who may be affected thereby are not thereby exposed to risks to their health or safety".

Risk Assessment

Risk assessments are covered by regulation 7, which requires them to be undertaken both before the use for the first time of any premises for activities involving genetic modification and also before the undertaking of any such activity (whenever that may be). The assessment must be in respect of risks that may be created thereby both to human health and to the environment. An essential step is the classifying of any GMOs involved into either Group I or Group II, applying criteria that are set out extensively in Schedule 2 to the Regulations, and where appropriate deciding on the requisite level of containment for the activity. Conduct of the assessment must take into account the matters listed in Schedule 3 to the Regulations; which cover:

14–035

   (i)   characteristics of the donor, recipient, or, where relevant, parental organism;
  (ii)   characteristics of the modified organism;
 (iii)   health considerations; and
 (iv)   environmental considerations.

The HSE has issued guidance for the conduct of these assessments,[50] and by regulation 7(3)(b) these must be followed. There is an explicit requirement in regulation 7(4) to review the assessment forthwith if there is any reason to suspect that it is no longer valid or if there has been any significant change in the activity concerned. To try to ensure that risk assessments are undertaken in a professional and responsible manner, regulation 11 requires anyone undertaking such an assessment to establish a "Genetic Modification Safety Committee" to advise him on the conduct of that assessment.[51] The HSE Guidance suggests that where there is a sufficiently competent biological safety officer, an employer may wish to appoint that person to assist in procuring compliance with health and safety legislation as regards work with GMOs, for the purposes of regulation 6 of the Management of Health and Safety at Work Regulations 1992.[52]

14–036

The person making the assessment is required to make and retain a record of it, and of any subsequent review, and to keep that record throughout the activity concerned or the use of the premises, as the

14–037

---

[50] In notes 6 and 7 of the ACGM/HSE/DoE series; also note 5 in relation to eukaryotic viral vectors.
[51] ACGM/HSE/DoE Note 11 contains guidance on the constitution and functions of such committees.
[52] S.I. 1992 No. 2051.

case may be, and for a further ten years after that activity or use to which the assessment related has ceased.[53]

Notification of First Use of Premises for Genetic Modification Activities

14–038   Notification of the first use of premises must be made at least 90 days in advance of that use taking place, unless the HSE agrees a shorter period. Separate notifications are required in respect of Group I and Group II micro-organisms; where Group II micro-organisms are concerned, use of the premises may only be made with the express consent of the HSE, even after the 90 days. Nevertheless, by regulation 8(5) the HSE must take and communicate its decision within the 90 day period on whether it will grant the requisite consent. In any other case, the use may start at any time after the 90 day period has elapsed, unless the HSE has objected in writing beforehand.[54]

14–039   The information that must be given when making a notification under regulation 8(1) is set out in Schedule 4. In addition to details as to who is carrying on the activity and where, and a description of the activity, the information must include a summary of the risk assessment, details of the members of the notifier's Genetic Modification Safety Committee, and the comments made by that Committee on the local arrangements for risk assessment. It must also include the names of any biological and deputy biological safety officers and supervisory medical officer that there may be, as well as any arrangements made for health surveillance. The HSE is entitled to seek any further information in respect of a notification that it may require, and if it does so the running of the 90 day period is suspended until such time as the request has been dealt with to the satisfaction of the HSE.[55]

Notification of Activities Involving Genetic Modification

14–040   A separate notification is required under regulation 9 by anyone undertaking an activity involving genetic modification. The notification of activities must, with one exception, cover such details as are set out in Schedule 5 to the Regulations. The exception applies in the case of an activity which is a Type A operation[56] involving only a Group I micro-organism or a Schedule 2 Part III GMO.[57] In such a case, all that

---

[53] reg. 7(5).
[54] reg. 8(4).
[55] reg. 10(1).
[56] See para. 14–010 for the distinction between Type A and Type B operations.
[57] The criteria of this Part III are that the organism is a GMO which is not a genetically modified micro-organism and which is as safe in the containment facility as any recipient or parental organism.

is required is that a record be kept of all relevant activities and that the HSE is notified forthwith after the end of each calendar year:

(i)   of the total number of risk assessments undertaken during that year;
(ii) whether the notifier is intending to continue with the activities concerned; and
(iii) that the information notified under regulation 8 (in respect of the first use of the relevant premises) remains correct.

All other activities require prior notification, the amount of informa-   **14–041**
tion to be given depending on whether the activity is:

(i)   a Type B operation involving only Group I micro-organisms
(ii) a Type A operation involving Group II micro-organisms or any operation involving GMOs that are neither micro-organisms nor within the criteria of Part III of Schedule 2, or
(iii) a Type B operation involving Group II micro-organisms.

Nevertheless, if more than one activity is to be carried out in the   **14–042**
course of a connected programme of work, or if a single activity is to be carried on by the same person at more than one site, the HSE will accept a single notification.[58]

Where prior notification is required, this must be made at least 60   **14–043**
days before the activity is commenced, unless the HSE agrees to some shorter period. However, as in the case of a first use of premises notification involving Group II micro-organisms, where an activity is a Type B operation involving Group II micro-organisms, this activity may only be commenced with the express consent of the HSE, even after the 60 day period.[59] However, in this case the HSE must take and communicate its decision with regard to this notification within 90 days following its receipt.[60]

It is permissible, and indeed likely to be the practice, for a   **14–044**
notification of the first use of premises and a notification of the activity to be undertaken in those premises to be made at the same time. For the avoidance of doubt, regulation 8(6) makes it clear that the 90 day advance notice required under regulation 8 over-rides any shorter period available under regulation 9, and also applies even where the activity is exempted from prior notification under regulation 9 altogether.

Where consents are necessary under regulations 8 or 9, these may be   **14–045**
granted for a limited period and subject to such conditions as the HSE

---

[58] reg. 9(7).
[59] reg. 9(5).
[60] reg. 9(6).

sees fit, and the consent may be revoked and the conditions varied at any time.[61] However, in so far as any conditions relate to the protection of the environment, the HSE may not grant, vary or revoke consent, except with the agreement of the Secretary of State.[62] Similarly, where the running of the 90 or 60 day period of prior notification, as the case may be, has been stayed while the HSE seeks further information, HSE's approval to proceed, following receipt of that further information, again may only be given with the agreement of the Secretary of State, if that approval is dependent on matters relating to the protection of the environment.

14–046   Part III of the Contained Use Regulations stipulate certain procedures and principles that must be complied with in the conduct of activities involving genetic modification. These relate to the standards of occupational and environmental safety and containment,[63] emergency plans[64] and notification of accidents.[65] Containment provisions for Type B operations with Group II micro organisms are set out in Schedule 6 by reference to three containment levels, B2, B3 and B4, as explained in ACGM/HSE/DoE Note 6. These principles and procedures are discussed in the "Guidance on Regulations". Further information on aspects of containment are included in ACGM/HSE/DoE Guidance Notes 6, 8, 9 and 10.

14–047   The information supplied to the HSE in notifications will be treated as prima facie non-confidential, unless the person notifying indicates that its disclosure might harm his competitive position and should be kept confidential. In that event regulation 15(2) requires him to give full justification, whereupon the HSE will decide which information (if any) is to be kept confidential, after consulting the notifier, and will inform the notifier of its decision. Regulation 15(3) spells out that certain information shall not in any event be kept confidential, namely the name and address of the notifier, the location and purpose of the activity, the description of the relevant GMO, methods and plans for monitoring the GMO and for emergency response, and the valuation of foreseeable effects, particularly any that are pathogenic or ecologically disruptive. Nevertheless, temporary withholding from public access of any of this last class of information may be sought if the notifier requires this in order to protect his intellectual property rights. Specifically, this will allow the notifier to proceed with an activity to assemble data to support a patent application and to prepare and file

---

[61] reg. 10(2).
[62] reg. 10(3). The drafting of this provision is not very happy, but its intention would appear to be as stated here.
[63] reg. 12.
[64] reg. 13.
[65] reg. 14.

such an application.[66] Where a request has been made to keep information confidential, or that disclosure should be withheld to protect intellectual property rights, even where the HSE takes an adverse decision, it must not make any disclosure of the information for at least a further 14 days. The legislation does not contain any provisions for appeal from decisions of the HSE in this respect, but the 14 day period will enable a notifier to make further representations and, if necessary, take steps for applying for judicial review.

An issue that is relevant to the public disclosure of notified information is the extent to which it is subject to the Environmental Information Regulations 1992,[67] which implement EC Directive 90/313 on freedom of access to information on the environment.[68] These Regulations apply to any information which, *inter alia*, "relates to the environment". This expression is subsequently defined to mean information relating to, among other things, the state of any water or air, any activities or measures which adversely affect any water or air or are likely to do so, and any activities or administrative or other measures designed to protect any water or air. Although there is no further definition of "air" in these Regulations, the E.P.A. itself, in section 1(2), defines the environment as including air, and the medium of air as including "the air within buildings and the air within other natural or man-made structures above or below ground". It would be logical to give the same meaning to air for the purpose of the Environmental Information Regulations 1992. If "air" is thus broadly understood for the purpose of access to information acquired under the E.P.A., a corresponding construction would seem appropriate for information relating to air within buildings and man-made structures acquired under the Contained Use Regulations.[69]   **14–048**

The restrictions on disclosure of confidential information are limited in regulation 15(2) to information "the disclosure of which might harm the [notifier's] competitive position". It is instructive to compare this   **14–049**

---

[66] It is conceivable that where a notifier plans to work on an entirely new line of research, it could be a considerable time, even years, before he considers it appropriate to seek patent protection on such invention or inventions as he may have made. Inventors are often faced with the dilemma between filing early in order to get ahead of any possible competitors, but potentially risking throwing away all chances of protection because certain critical technical features have not been adequately researched, and filing later backed up by comprehensive data, but thereby risking losing priority to someone else. It remains to be seen whether the HSE will take a sympathetic line on non-disclosure of information belonging to someone adopting the latter course.

[67] S.I. 1992 No. 3240.

[68] See para. 20–004 *et seq.*

[69] Recourse to the underlying EC Directive 90/313 does not materially assist, since the Environmental Information Regulations 1992 repeat almost verbatim the Directive's definition of "information relating to the environment".

with section 123(3)(a) of the E.P.A., which governs the disclosure of information under the Deliberate Release Regulations, and states that no information relating to the affairs of any individual or business shall be included in the register (relating to Part VI matters) without the consent of the relevant individual or person currently carrying on that business, if the Secretary of State has determined that the information is in relation to him commercially confidential.[70] In determining whether information should be regarded as commercially confidential, it would certainly be highly material to consider whether or not disclosure would affect the competitive position of the owner of the information. Nevertheless, other factors might also be relevant which would justify a court finding for the owner of the information in a civil action for actual or threatened breach of confidence, and it is perhaps unfortunate that the Contained Use and the Deliberate Release Regulations should be subject to slightly different provisions in this respect, even if in the majority of cases, the distinction is likely to be academic.

14–050   A register of notifications is to be maintained that is to be open to inspection by members of the public at any reasonable time.[71] The register however only contains notifications requiring consent under the Regulations, and so is limited to those relating to first uses involving Group II micro-organisms and activities which are Type B operations with such Group II micro-organisms, these uses and activities being the only ones that require the explicit consent of the HSE before they may be undertaken. The HSE is required to enter information into the register within 14 days of its receipt, save where entry has been withheld on confidentiality grounds. Where, following the request of a notifier to withhold information, the HSE has decided not to accede to that request, it must enter the information concerned in the register not less than 14 days but not more than 28 days after that decision.[72]

14–051   Since the HSE will therefore be under a legal constraint to publish the information within 14 to 28 days, anyone aggrieved is likely to have to have obtained a temporary court order within two weeks restraining the HSE from entering information on the register. Obtaining such an order must necessarily entail an assertion that the

---

[70] This definition is not subject to the more stringent requirement of s.22(11) relating to information acquired under Part I of the E.P.A. which provides that information is commercially confidential for the purposes of that Part I if its being contained in the relevant register would prejudice to an unreasonable degree the commercial interests of the individual or person concerned.
[71] reg. 16(1).
[72] reg. 16(3).

HSE has failed to give proper effect to regulation 15(2).[73] Unlike the Deliberate Release Regulations, which are subject to Part VI of the E.P.A., and specifically section 123(8) which provides that information shall be treated as no longer commercially confidential after four years, unless an application is made and agreed to maintain confidentiality, no such four year limitation is automatic under the Contained Use Regulations. Nevertheless, since regulation 16(8) entitles the HSE to review any decision to maintain confidentiality, it is open to it to operate a procedure whereby such decisions are reviewed every four years. Nevertheless, the burden of proof that confidentiality should be lifted would be on the HSE under the Contained Use Regulations, whereas it is on the notifier under the Deliberate Release Regulations.

Information that is entered on the register in respect of Type B operations with Group II micro-organisms must be transmitted to the European Commission in accordance with Article 18(1) of the Contained Use Directive. Regulation 19 of the Contained Use Regulations provides for the HSE to do this and also to submit summary reports of the application of the Regulations as further required by Article 18 of the Contained Use Directive. **14–051A**

The HSE has the power under regulation 20 to grant exemptions from any of the requirements and prohibitions of the Contained Use Regulations, though it may attach conditions to such an exemption if it sees fit. Where the exemption relates to the environment, the Secretary of State's agreement must be obtained. No exemption may however be granted unless the HSE is satisfied that it would not prejudice the health and safety of anyone likely to be affected or the protection of the environment. The HSE is entitled to charge fees in respect of notifications under regulations 8 and 9.[74] **14–052**

The Contained Use Regulations came into effect on February 1, 1993. By transitional provisions contained in regulation 23, in certain circumstances, including where action had been taken under the now repealed Genetic Manipulation Regulations 1989[75] a few provisions of the new Regulations did not come into full effect until February 1, 1994. **14–053**

Enforcement of the provisions of the Contained Use Regulations is to be by the HSE.[76] Further, where any provision of regulations 6 to 14 is made under section 2 of the European Communities Act 1972, that is, those provisions relating to micro-organisms, implementing the Contained Use Directive, the enforcement provisions of the H.S.W.A. **14–054**

---

[73] This is an example of circumstances where judicial review is a most unsatisfactory procedure for what should be an appeal on the merits.
[74] reg. 22.
[75] S.I. 1989 No. 1810.
[76] reg. 21(2).

apply as though the Regulations had been made under its section 15. Also, where there has been any breach of the obligations relating to micro-organisms covered by the Directive, regulation 21(1)(b) provides a right of action in civil proceedings for damages for breach of statutory duty. The enforcement by criminal sanctions of the provisions of the Contained Use Regulations is likely therefore to be in accordance with normal HSE practice in respect of Health and Safety legislation. This frequently involves proceedings against relevant individuals in a company's workforce considered to be responsible for any non-compliance. It is by no means clear that the same position will obtain in relation to offences under the legislation relating to deliberate release and marketing where, historically, prosecutions have rarely been taken against individual members of a workforce, but against the employing organisation and on occasion its directors under E.P.A. s.157(1).

Deliberate Release and Marketing of Genetically Modified Organisms

14–055   Whereas contained use of GMOs is primarily controlled by the Contained Use Regulations made under the H.S.W.A., deliberate release and marketing of GMOs is controlled by Part VI of the E.P.A. (*i.e.* sections 106 to 127) so far as brought into force[77]) supplemented by the (1992) Deliberate Release Regulations[78] and the 1993 Deliberate Release Regulations.[79] The 1992 Regulations and the substantive provisions of Part VI of the E.P.A. came into force on February 1, 1993. However where a product subject to these controls was marketed in the United Kingdom before that date, the controls on marketing of GMOs under the E.P.A.[80] do not apply until February 1, 1995 unless that product is marketed by virtue of a consent granted under section 111(1) of the E.P.A. or by written consent of the competent authority of any Member State in accordance with Article 13(4) of the Deliberate Release Directive.

14–056   Guidance on this legislation has been published by the DoE on the advice of ACRE as "DoE/ACRE Guidance Note 1" under the title "The Regulation and Control of the Deliberate Release of Genetically Modified Organisms (GMOs)" — referred to in the rest of this chapter as "the Guidance" — to which anyone proposing to undertake any

---

[77] See n.28.
[78] S.I. 1992 No. 3280.
[79] S.I. 1993 No. 152, which correct an error in the 1992 Regulations.
[80] Contained in s.111(1)(a).

such activity should refer. It describes in detail how the various statutory provisions are intended to operate, and the Department's interpretation, often with examples, of most of the many, often highly technical, terms used.

Definitions

Part VI of the E.P.A. controls, among other things, the release and marketing of GMOs.   **14–057**

"Organism" is defined to mean any acellular, unicellular or multi-   **14–058** cellular entity in any form, other than humans or human embryos, and includes any article or substance consisting of or including "biological matter".[81] This latter term means anything consisting of or including tissue, cells, sub-cellular entities, or genes or other genetic material, capable of replication or of transferring genetic material.[82] These definitions apply equally to products of natural and of artificial reproduction; and biological matter does not need to have been part of a whole organism.[83]

Section 106(4) provides that an organism is "genetically modified" if   **14–059** its genes or other genetic material have been modified by means of any prescribed artificial technique, or if any of its genes or other genetic material have been derived in any way, through any number of replications, from genes or other genetic material which were modified by means of any such prescribed artificial technique. Such artificial techniques are prescribed in regulation 3 of the Deliberate Release Regulations in terms largely corresponding to, but not identical with, Parts I and II of Schedule 1 to the Contained Use Regulations. The main distinction of significance however is that the contents of these Parts of Schedule 1 are said to be merely examples of techniques that constitute genetic modification for the purposes of the Contained Use Regulations, whereas the techniques listed in regulation 3 of the Deliberate Release Regulations are the only prescribed artificial techniques for the purposes of the E.P.A., s. 106(4). Part III of Schedule 1 to the Contained Use Regulations sets out techniques to which those Regulations do *not* apply. This includes (as item (d)) self-cloning of non-pathogenic naturally occurring micro-organisms which fulfil the criteria of Group I for recipient micro-organisms. As is pointed out in the Guidance, such a procedure is clearly within the artificial techniques described in regulation 3(a) and/or 3(b) of the Deliberate Release Regulations.[84] It follows that there can be no

---

[81] s.106(2).
[82] s.106(3).
[83] s.106(3).
[84] para. 3.8.

automatic presumption that an organism that is not regarded as genetically modified for the purposes of the Contained Use controls will also fall outside the ambit of the Deliberate Release controls, and *vice versa.*

14–060   "Release" occurs where a person having an organism under his control deliberately causes or permits it to cease to be under his control or that of any other person and to enter the environment.[85] The term thus embraces "marketing"; nevertheless, in both the Deliberate Release Directive and the Deliberate Release Regulations marketing is treated separately from all other manners of release. Release is contrasted with "escape" which occurs where an organism ceases to be under a person's control or that of any other person and enters the environment otherwise than by being released.[86]

14–061   Organisms are under the "control" of a person where he keeps them contained by any system of physical, chemical or biological barriers (or any combination of these) that are used either to ensure that the organisms do not enter the environment or that they do not produce "descendants" that are not contained by such barriers, or else for ensuring that any organisms that do enter the environment or any of their descendants that are not so contained, are harmless. Merely using barriers to limit contact with the outside (*cf.* the definition of "contained use") will not therefore suffice. However, in contrast with the Contained Use Regulations, physical barriers are not essential. Generally of course a person proposing to release GMOs under the Deliberate Release Regulations must first be at least storing them, if not also culturing and transporting them under the provisions of the Contained Use Regulations, in which event the containment must include appropriate physical barriers, and so consequently the distinction between the two sets of Regulations will only rarely be relevant. However where a GMO is of a type that is only controlled by the Deliberate Release Regulations, then it is quite conceivable that it may be contained prior to release solely by chemical and/or biological barriers.

14–062   "Harm" is given the standard E.P.A. definition of "harm to the health of humans or other living organisms or other interference with

---

[85] s.107(10).
[86] It would be entirely feasible for an organism to be under the control of two or more distinct people simultaneously, such as a company that has developed it and is the legal owner and a third party who has physical possession of the organism, perhaps for safe keeping or for the purposes of carrying out experiments or for use in the manufacture of other material, on terms whereby the third party is required to keep it secure and deliver it up on demand (a common method of commercial exploitation of novel genetic material). In such circumstances, a deliberate but improper act by the third party might well represent a release by him, but would represent an escape in relation to the legal owner.

the ecological system of which they form part and, in the case of man, includes offence caused to any of his senses or harm to his property".

"Harmless" (and "harmful") are defined[87] in relation to GMOs by reference to their capability or otherwise of causing harm. A GMO may therefore be harmful even though it has not in fact caused any harm, if it is potentially capable of doing so. The ability of a particular organism under control to cause harm is not the only consideration. GMOs are deemed to be capable of causing harm when present in the environment not only if they are individually capable or are in such numbers that together they are capable of causing harm, but also if they are able to produce descendants which will be capable either themselves or which would be present in such numbers that together they would be capable of causing harm.[88]

"Descendant" is defined[89] as meaning any organism other than the original GMO, whose genes or other genetic material is derived, through any number of generations, from the original GMO by any process of reproduction. In the case of a self-replicating organism, the descendants will inevitably have the identical structure to the original GMO, in the absence of any mutation. However, by section 106(7) "reproduction" when used in Part VI of the E.P.A. means, wherever the context so permits, not only precise replication, but also the transfer of genetic material from one organism to another. Consequently, a "descendant" should be understood as including any organism which has genetic material derived directly or indirectly from the original organism. There may however be a *de minimis* situation where the amount of genetic material in an organism that has been derived from a parent organism is minuscule and has no noticeable effect on the properties of the organism containing that portion of genetic material. Where the properties of an organism are for all practical purposes determined by structures that owe nothing to the parent organism, it would, it is submitted, be inappropriate to regard these as "descendants" for the purposes of Part VI.

This approach is consistent with the definition in section 107(5)(b) that a GMO is capable of causing harm if it is able to produce descendants which are so capable. Most genetic material is capable of being spliced into some other genetic material presenting serious hazards, such that the novel material would as a result be "capable of causing harm". It would make nonsense of this definition in section 107(5) if the properties of "descendants" contributed by other genetic material should be taken into account in determining their capability

14–063

14–064

14–065

---

[87] In s.107(7).
[88] s.107(5).
[89] In s.127(1).

803

of causing harm. An alternative approach to section 107(5) is that reference to the ability of GMOs to produce descendants capable of causing harm is to the ability of such GMOs to produce such descendants without any outside interference or assistance. Having regard to the purposes of this legislation, at least one of which is to avoid adverse consequences as a result of the release or escape of GMOs into the environment beyond practical control, it is reasonable to read section 107(5)(b) as meaning:

> "(b) they are able *without deliberate external assistance or manipulation* to produce descendants which will be capable . . . of causing harm . . . ".

14–066   Nevertheless, where there is a risk that a released organism may become modified in some way as a result of interaction with other organisms in the environment to produce descendants capable of causing harm, then regard should be had to that possibility in determining whether the organism concerned is to be regarded as "harmful".

14–067   Though in general the purpose of the Deliberate Release Regulations is to prevent any harm to the environment from a release,[90] in certain circumstances harm to the health of certain living organisms or other interference with the ecosystems that contain them is specifically desired. This is recognised by regulation 4 of the Deliberate Release Regulations, which give effect to section 107(8) by prescribing GMOs which control (a) the number or activity or both of any organisms and (b) toxic wastes, as falling outside the scope of certain aspects (only) of Part VI. These aspects relate to prohibition notices under section 110(1), keeping properly informed on the nature of relevant risks, and the powers of an inspector where he fears imminent harm. Regulation 4 thus exempts in respect of the matters just mentioned (and no other) GMOs which control the number or activity or both of any organisms, or which control toxic wastes in so far as they cause harm of the type set out in paragraph (3) of regulation 4. This paragraph is limited to harm caused by GMOs which have been released or marketed in pursuance of a consent granted under section 111(1) or in pursuance of a written consent given by a competent authority of any EC Member State in accordance with Article 13(4) of the Deliberate Release Directive. It follows that the exemption is strictly limited in its scope—if such GMOs cause other harm, that will not be disregarded. The development of GMOs is thus encouraged for, for example, pest control and for decontaminating sites containing toxic waste. The provisions of sections 110(1), 112(5) and (7)(a) and

---

[90] See para. 14–062 for the definition of "harm".

117(1) referred to in regulation 4 are disapplied to the benefit of third parties who have acquired GMOs released or marketed for these purposes; the person responsible for the release or marketing will however remain responsible for complying with conditions attached to his consent, which will doubtless include requirements as to provision of information that do not apply to third parties by virtue of this exemption.

The Deliberate Release Control Regime in Outline

Control over the deliberate release and marketing of GMOs under Part VI of the E.P.A. and the Deliberate Release Regulations follows the normal pattern of a general prohibition of the controlled activities, followed by provisions for licensing these activities subject to conditions. The need for prior consent stems from section 111(1)(a) as a result of release and marketing being prescribed activities for the purposes of that subsection under regulations 5(1) and 10(1) of the Deliberate Release Regulations.   **14–068**

Deliberate Release of GMOs (otherwise than for marketing)

Procedures for obtaining consent to the release of GMOs otherwise than for marketing are contained in regulations 5 to 9 of the Deliberate Release Regulations. Save for certain transitional provisions all such releases require prior consent except where they are of an "approved product"[91] in accordance with all applicable conditions and limitations.   **14–069**

Applications are made to the Secretary of State and may relate either to one or more GMOs and releases on the same site for the same purpose or to one description of GMO to be released on one or more sites for the same purpose. In either case an application may be in respect of multiple releases of the one type; all applications must be for releases to be made within a defined period.[92] Except where an application is to repeat releases previously applied for, it must be accompanied by information as prescribed in regulation 6 and Schedule 1. Directive 94/15,[93] which was due to be implemented by June 30, 1994, reduces the information requirements in the case of   **14–070**

---

[91] *i.e.* one marketed pursuant to a consent under E.P.A., s.111 or a written consent given by a competent authority of another Member State in accordance with Art. 13(4) of the Deliberate Release Directive.

[92] reg. 5(2). The Guidance indicates (in paras. 3.21 and 3.22) that this period could be several years if, for example, the consent were to cover a full plant breeding programme, though in such a case regular, *e.g.* annual, reports might be required.

[93] [1994] O.J. L103.

releases of certain genetically modified higher plants. Reduced
information requirements already apply to applications to release (but
not to market) genetically modified plants, as described in detail in
DoE/ACRE Guidance Note 3. Except in these cases, the information,
which is to enable the Secretary of State, advised by ACRE, to assess
the degree of risk and the conditions that might appropriately be
imposed on a consent, must cover in detail:

- the applicant, and all individuals with responsibility for any
  aspect of the release;
- the GMO concerned, its derivation and characteristics;
- the nature of the proposed release;
- the behaviour of the GMO in the environment;
- monitoring techniques, control of the release, waste treatment and emergency response plans;
- information obtained from any previous relevant release by
  the applicant, and information from any previous application
  by him (whether made in the UK or elsewhere in the EC
  under the Deliberate Release Directive);
- an evaluation of impacts on and risks to human health and
  the environment;
- whether details of the GMOs and the purpose of the release
  have been published and, if so, relevant references;
- a summary of the foregoing information in the format
  prescribed by Council Decision 91/956 as amended.

Risk Assessment

14–071   An application to release a GMO must also be accompanied by "a
statement evaluating the impacts and risks posed to human health
and the environment by the release of the organisms".[94] This risk
assessment statement constitutes a separate document from the
information provided in accordance with Schedule 1. The Guidance
recommends that applicants should nevertheless prepare their
information and risk assessment statements as part of the same
exercise, since the level of detail required when providing information
will often depend on the degree to which a particular feature is
relevant to the assessment of risk, and the more significant it is in this
respect, the more information is likely to be required.

14–072   The Guidance sets out[95] a recommended approach to risk assessment, covering both the procedures for making the assessment and for
the presentation of a risk assessment statement. The statement is likely

[94] reg. 6(1)(c).
[95] In its Chap. 4.

in many cases to be technically complex; it should therefore be supplied together with a summary conclusion designed to be comprehensible to the layman,[96] since this information will be placed on a public register. Though the preparation of a risk assessment statement, and the format of the statement are left to individual applicants, the Guidance sets out some recommended practical steps, and includes a recommended format for the presentation of the assessment. The main steps in the assessment procedure are summarised in the Guidance in the following terms.

(1) Identify the hazards associated with the GMO. This will require consideration of its characteristics in at least the following respects:
  (i)   capacity to survive, establish and disseminate;
  (ii) potential for gene transfer;
  (iii) products of expression of introduced sequences;
  (iv) phenotypic and genotypic stability;
  (v)   pathogenicity to other organisms;
  (vi) potential for other environmental effects;
  (vii) potential for harm to humans.
(2) Identify how *each* hazard could be realised in the particular receiving environment(s).
(3) Estimate the magnitude of harm caused by each hazard, if realised.
(4) Estimate how likely and/or how often each hazard will be realised as harm.
(5) On the basis of 3 and 4, estimate for each hazard the risk of harm being caused by the release or marketing proposal.
(6) On the basis of 5, modify the release or marketing proposal, if necessary, until the lowest possible level of risk in relation to each hazard is reached.
(7) Evaluate the combined effects of 1 to 6 in terms of risks to the environment (including human health) from the release or marketing proposal.

The Guidance then continues with specific recommendations in relation to each of these items. Its suggested format for the assessment statement entails setting out in turn the conclusions of items (1) to (5) and (7) above, preceded by a summary of the overall risk of damage to the environment from the proposed activity the subject of the consent application. **14–073**

If, while an application is still pending a notifier becomes aware of any new information relevant to risks of damage to the environment **14–074**

[96] Guidance, para. 3.90(g).

being caused by release or marketing of the GMOs, he must notify it to the Secretary of State forthwith.[97]

14–075   The applicant may omit information if it is considered unnecessary or impossible to provide it.[98] Data and results from a third party's application for release may be contained in an application, if the third party's written consent is also included.[99]

14–076   The application must be publicly advertised in one or more newspapers circulating in the locality of the release between 14 and 28 days after receipt of the application has been acknowledged. The advertisement must include the name and address of the applicant, a general description of the GMOs to be released, and the location, general purpose and foreseen dates of the release. Within the same 14 day period, the applicant must give individual notice of his application and of the information required to be advertised to:

— the owner(s) of the site of the proposed release;
— the relevant local authority, being generally the district council in England and Wales outside London, or the London borough council, or the islands or district council in Scotland;

— the Nature Conservancy Council for England and the Countryside Commission if the release will be in England, or the Countryside Council for Wales, or Scottish Natural Heritage as the case may be;
— the Forestry Commission;
— The National Rivers Authority or, in Scotland, the relevant River Purification Board or Islands Council;
— the relevant water undertaker in England and Wales or, in Scotland, the relevant Regional or Islands Council;
— each member of the applicant's genetic modification safety committee.

14–077   No formal procedure is provided for those receiving a notice under regulation 8 to respond. Doubtless, concerns that any of the public authorities may have will be raised with the Secretary of State; it is not requisite however that the applicant be informed of any responses so made.

14–078   The Secretary of State must, within 30 days of receipt of an application, put in motion the procedure of Article 9 of the Deliberate Release Directive, by sending the Commission the summary of the

---

[97] s.111(6A), inserted by reg. 13(1).
[98] reg. 6(2).
[99] reg. 6(5).

notification.[1] The Commission then forwards this to the other Member States who have 30 days to comment. The Secretary of State must examine the application, assess any risks, carry out any inspections or tests, if appropriate, and consider any comments received under the Article 9 procedure. His decision on the application, which will include decision as to the conditions attaching to a consent, must be given to the applicant within 90 days calculated from the date of receipt of the application.[2] If further information is required of the applicant, the 90 day period is stayed until the information is provided. No consent to release (nor any variation or revocation of a consent) may however be given without the agreement of the HSE in so far as it relates to the protection of human health.[3]

A "fast track" procedure has been devised to allow applications for consent to release certain GMOs for research and development (only). This is available where (i) the GMOs concerned are recognised by ACRE as being low hazard, (ii) the release conditions for the GMOs in question are considered to provide for low risk, or (iii) certain GMO trials are to be repeated. The "fast track" approach is intended to enable the application to be handled by the ACRE secretariat within 30 days. Guidance on the procedure is contained in DoE/ACRE Guidance Note 2.   **14–079**

Deliberate Release for Marketing

Procedures for obtaining consent to the release of GMOs for marketing are governed by section 111 and are contained in Regulations 10 to 12 of the Deliberate Release Regulations. As with other releases prior consent for marketing is always required except for "approved products".[4] and where the transitional provisions in Regulation 12 apply which exempt from the application of section 111(1)(a) until February 1, 1995 the marketing of a product, not being an "approved product", by a person who marketed it in the United Kingdom before February 1, 1993. An application must be made both where the GMO has not previously been marketed under a consent from either the Secretary of State or from the competent authority of another Member State under Article 13(4) of the Deliberate Release Directive, and also where the GMO has been previously marketed   **14–080**

---

[1] reg 14(1). The Summary Notification Information Format (SNIF) to be used is laid down in Council Decision 91/596, [1991] O.J. L322, as amended by Decision 94/211, [1994] O.J. L105. See also n.9 to para. 14–084.
[2] reg. 15(2).
[3] reg. 15(1), (5).
[4] See n.91, above.

under such a consent, but is now intended for a different use from that previously consented.

14–081   The application must be accompanied by information as prescribed in regulation 11 and Schedules 1 and 2. With the exception of Schedule 2, the required information corresponds fairly closely with that required for other releases, and a risk assessment must likewise be provided with research and development information including that obtained from trial releases.[5]

14–082   Information required under Schedule 2 includes:

- the name of the product and of GMOs in it;
- details of its manufacturer or distributor in the EC;
- the specificity of the product and its exact conditions of use;
- the type of expected use and persons expected to use the product;
- measures to be taken in response to escape or nuisance;
- storage and handling instructions or recommendations;
- estimated quantities of production and import;
- proposed packaging and labelling.

14–083   Where an applicant considers that the marketing and use of the product concerned poses no risk, he may propose to omit any of the last four items.[6]

14–084   The procedure following the making of a marketing application differs significantly from that applicable to other releases. In such a case, the Secretary of State first decides whether to accept it and, if so, on what conditions,[7] and it is only thereafter, unless the application is rejected, that the Commission receives the summary information and also details of the conditions on which a consent is proposed to be given.[8] The Commission must be sent this within 90 days from receipt of the application, this period being extended by any time required to obtain further information from the applicant.[9] The Commission forwards the information it receives to the competent authorities of the other Member States, who have 60 days to respond.

---

[5] reg. 11(2)(c) requires "an assessment of any risks for human health or the environment related to the GMOs contained in the product". Though this wording differs from that of reg. 6(1)(c) relating to risk assessment for releases (see para. 14–071), there would not appear to be any real distinction in practice.

[6] reg. 11(5).

[7] As with other releases, the HSE's agreement is essential on matters relating to the protection of human health—reg. 16(8).

[8] reg. 16(2)(a).

[9] reg. 14(2), (4). The Summary Notification Information Format (SNIF) to be used for marketing releases is laid down in Commission Decision 92/146, [1992] O.J. L60. See also n.1 to para. 14–078.

If none of these competent authorities raises any objection, the **14–085** consent is to be granted. If they do object within the 60 days, and if agreement between the UK and the objecting State(s) cannot be achieved, then the Commission will itself act as arbiter and decide whether the objection should be upheld, or the application should be consented.[10] The Secretary of State is required to implement a favourable decision by the Commission.[11]

It is not immediately clear from the Directive whether the Commis- **14–086** sion has the power in such a situation to impose its own conditions on the proposed consent in order to accommodate objections, or whether it is simply to uphold the position of one State or that of the other. However, the procedure of Article 21 is to be followed which requires the Commission to propose to a committee of representatives of the Member States the measures to be taken—no restrictions on what measures may be proposed are suggested or implied. The committee has no right itself to amend the measures, but merely (by a qualified majority.[12]) to oppose or reject them. Since the Directive envisages the consenting and objecting Member States reaching agreement, which clearly could involve revision of the proposal conditions, and since Article 12(3) makes clear that the conditions to be included in the dossier to be forwarded to the Member States are merely proposed conditions, there would not appear to be any cogent reason to deny the Commission the right to impose such conditions as it sees fit.

Register of Information

Details relating to deliberate releases that must be shown in the **14–087** public register include:[13]

- applications for any consent under E.P.A., s.111(1), including evaluation of environmental impact, conditions and limitations subject to which each consent is granted, and the reasons for any refusal;
- information supplied pursuant to any condition or limitation, and any new information on risks to the environment furnished under section 111(6A) or 112(5)(b);
- revocations and variations of consents;
- prohibition notices under E.P.A., s.110;

---

[10] Deliberate Release Directive, Art. 13(3).
[11] reg. 16(7).
[12] *i.e.* 54 votes out of 76, with individual Member States having from two to ten votes as set out in Art. 148(2) Rome Treaty.
[13] reg. 17.

— convictions under E.P.A., s.118.

In nearly all cases these details must be put on the register within 14 days of the relevant event.

Chapter 15

RADIOACTIVE SUBSTANCES

Introduction

Radioactive substances may be broadly described as those that emit **15–001** ionising[1] radiation. This is constantly emitted by radioactive substances (both those which are naturally radioactive and those which have been made so artificially), and also by non-radioactive substances if bombarded with appropriate radiation. The atoms of radioactive substances contain unstable nuclei (radionuclides) that undergo spontaneous transformation, each transformation involving a release of energy in the form of radiation. Ionising radiation may take a variety of forms including:

— Alpha particles, which are positively charged helium atoms, *i.e.* helium nuclei, consisting of a pair of protons and a pair of neutrons. By comparison with beta particles, they are heavy. Though they may contain considerable energy, they are relatively easily absorbed. A substance emitting alpha particles is losing protons and neutrons from its nucleus, and accordingly changes its chemical character as it decays. Thus radium, on emitting alpha particles is converted into the radioactive inert gas radon.

— Beta particles, which are electrons ejected from the nucleus of a radioactive substance. They have a comparatively short range of just a few centimetres in air.

— X-rays. These are "pure" electromagnetic radiation, having a frequency of around 10^{18} Hz (Hertz). In the conventional depiction of the electromagnetic spectrum, the ultraviolet band stops and the X-ray band starts at around 3×10^{16} Hz.

— Gamma rays, which are also "pure" electromagnetic radiation, having a frequency of approximately 10^{21} Hz. They are capable of penetrating substances for considerable distances,

---

[1] *i.e.* removing electrons from atoms, so producing a charge on the remainder. An ion is a charged atom or group of atoms.

even several centimetres of lead, and accordingly effective screening requires substantial forms of protection.

— Cosmic rays. This is the term given to the forms of radiation that bombard the earth from outer space. They are absorbed to a considerable extent by the atmosphere, but form a significant component of the annual radiation dosage received by those who frequently fly at high altitudes in, for example, commercial passenger aircraft.

15–002　　Other forms of electromagnetic radiation (of lower frequency and non-ionising), some of which are discussed in chapter 17, are the radio waves used for broadcasting, microwaves as used in microwave ovens and radar, infra-red radiation, which is perceived as heat, and the visible light spectrum. All forms of electromagnetic radiation differ from each other only in their frequency and wavelength—frequency and wavelength always bearing a constant inverse relationship to each other.[2]

15–003　　The harm that radiation may do to humans, animals and other living things depends on the sensitivity of their tissues to the wavelength involved, which varies according to the particular tissue. Thus the lower frequencies pass through the tissues of living things without being absorbed, and so cause no perceptible damage. Consequently, in setting standard exposure limits, account needs to be taken both of the radiation energy received, and also of the biological effects of radiation of that particular frequency. The standard measure of radiation is the Becquerel (a unit that has replaced the older unit, Curie), which corresponds to the decay of one radionuclide, i.e. one nuclear transformation, per second.[3] The radioactivity of a substance is expressed in Becquerels per unit weight, normally one gram, of the radioactive substance concerned.

15–004　　To indicate the actual effect that radiation may have on a person, a different measure, the Sievert, is used, which represents the dose of radiation received over a period of time, adjusted to take account of the differing biological effects of different types of radiation. Inevitably this adjustment is somewhat arbitrary, since the exact effects of any particular dose of radiation will vary considerably depending on all the relevant circumstances. Nevertheless, as an approximation, the Sievert is accepted as being the appropriate unit when considering the protection of human health.[4] Natural background radiation in the UK

---

[2] Frequency in cycles per second (*i.e.* Hertz) multiplied by the wavelength in centimetres is a constant: 3×10^{10}.

[3] The Curie is defined by reference to the radioactivity of 1 gm of radium; 1 Curie = 3.7 $\times 10^{10}$ Becquerels.

[4] The Sievert being a large unit, in practice dosage limits are usually measured in milliSieverts (mSv) or even microSieverts (μSv).

provides an annual average dose of around 2 mSv, though the actual dose received by particular individuals may vary widely from this figure, depending on where they live and their occupation. For the purposes of setting acceptable levels of artificial radiation, so-called Generalised Derived Limits (GDLs) have been established, which are considered to represent an insignificant risk to members of the public. These GDLs are calculated such that, on very pessimistic assumptions, the radiation dose of people exposed should be no more than 1 mSv annually (in addition to the average natural dose of 2 mSv). Regulatory thresholds are mostly concerned with when a substance is sufficiently radioactive as to pose a significant risk of its making a material contribution to the dose of radioactivity that any one person may receive; such thresholds are therefore normally expressed in Becquerels per gram.

Guidance on safety standards in respect of radiation is issued by the International Commission on Radiological Protection (the ICRP). Its recommendations are widely accepted, and provide the basis of legislation made under the Euratom Treaty, and in particular Euratom Directive 80/836 as amended by Directive 84/467.[5] Within the United Kingdom, the National Radiological Protection Board (the NRPB) fulfils a similar role at national level. The NRPB was created by the Radiological Protection Act 1970, with the broad functions of advising, conducting research and providing technical services, in the field of protection against both ionising and non-ionising radiations. By Directions under that Act, it has been specifically required to advise on the acceptability to and the application within the United Kingdom of standards recommended by international or intergovernmental bodies, such as the ICRP, and to specify emergency reference levels of dose for limiting radiation doses in accidents.

15–005

Historical

The harnessing of nuclear energy for practical purposes dates from the development of the atomic bomb in the 1940s during the last world war. After the war, the Atomic Energy Act 1946 provided for control over the use of and research and development in nuclear energy, which at that time was essentially entirely for military purposes. The Atomic Energy Authority was set up by the Atomic Energy Authority Act 1954 with general powers of research and development in not only the military, but also civil fields. The civilian applications of nuclear energy were separated from military applications in the 1970s, with the setting up of the Radiochemical Centre at Amersham and the

15–006

---

[5] [1980] O.J. L246; [1984] O.J. L265.

transfer of other civil operations to British Nuclear Fuels Limited under the Atomic Energy Authority Act 1971, and research on military aspects being transferred to the Ministry of Defence under the Atomic Energy Authority (Weapons Group) Act 1973. Regulatory control over the handling of radioactive material was first under the Radioactive Substances Act 1948. This was followed by the Radioactive Substances Act 1960 (the R.S.A. 1960), which was variously amended in numerous respects by subsequent legislation, and in particular by the Environmental Protection Act 1990.[6] The legislation has now been consolidated, with minor improvements and corrections, into the Radioactive Substances Act 1993, referred to here as the R.S.A., or where appropriate for clarity, the R.S.A. 1993.

15–007   The generation of nuclear power is now primarily governed by the Nuclear Installations Act 1965 (the N.I.A. 1965), regulatory control over nuclear installations being the responsibility of the Nuclear Installations Inspectorate, which is a part of the Health and Safety Executive. It is not the intention in this chapter to review the legislation on the structure of the nuclear industry, and it would also occupy a disproportionate amount of space to discuss in detail the regulatory provisions governing nuclear installations under the 1965 Act. Accordingly this chapter is primarily concerned with the principal features of the R.S.A. 1993, coupled with a summary of the principal provisions of the N.I.A. 1965, as amended, of direct interest to the general public.

The Radioactive Substances Act 1993

15–008   The R.S.A. controls the keeping and use of "radioactive material" and of "mobile radioactive apparatus" (as defined in the R.S.A., in each case) and the accumulation and disposal of radioactive waste. Administration of the Act comes under the Department of the Environment, with the detailed regulation being the responsibility of HMIP in England and Wales and HMIPI in Scotland.

Definitions

15–009   The controls in the R.S.A. over keeping and using radioactive material relate to substances that are either or both of (i) a substance listed in Schedule 1 to the R.S.A. having a radioactivity per gram in excess of the figure prescribed for that substance in the Schedule, or (ii) a substance possessing radioactivity which is:

---

[6] Namely Part V (ss.100–105) and Sched. 5.

- wholly or partly attributable to a process of nuclear fission or other process of subjecting a substance to bombardment by neutrons or to ionising radiations (not being a process occurring in the course of nature);
- in consequence of the disposal of radioactive waste; or
- by way of contamination in the course of the application of a process to some other substance.[7]

The elements listed in the Schedule and the prescribed radioactivity for each are set out in Table 15/I.

"Radioactive material" is defined as anything which, not being waste, is any such substance, or an article made wholly or partly from or incorporating such a substance.[8]

TABLE 15/I

Radioactive Substances (R.S.A., Schedule 1)			
	Becquerels per gram (Bq/g)		
Element	Solid	Liquid	Gas or Vapour
Actinium	0.37	7.40×10^{-2}	2.59×10^{-6}
Lead	0.74	3.70×10^{-3}	1.11×10^{-4}
Polonium	0.37	2.59×10^{-2}	2.22×10^{-4}
Protoactinium	0.37	3.33×10^{-2}	1.11×10^{-6}
Radium	0.37	3.70×10^{-4}	3.70×10^{-5}
Radon	–	–	3.70×10^{-2}
Thorium	2.59	3.70×10^{-2}	2.22×10^{-5}
Uranium	11.10	0.74	7.40×10^{-5}

"Radioactive waste" is waste which consists wholly or partly of (a) **15–010** any radioactive material, as defined, or (b) any substance or article which has been contaminated in the course of the production, keeping or use of radioactive material, or by contact with or proximity to other radioactive waste within (a) above.[9] The use of the words "which consists wholly *or partly*" means that even if only a very small

[7] s.1(2).
[8] s.1(1).
[9] s.2.

component of a consignment of waste consists of radioactive waste as just described, the whole consignment is to be described as "radioactive waste".

15–011   Nevertheless, by virtue of the Radioactive Substances (Substances of Low Activity) Exemption Order 1986,[10] the controls over radioactive waste contained in sections 13(1) and 13(3) of the R.S.A. do not apply to waste that has a radioactivity below certain prescribed levels. The effect of this Order is to exclude insoluble solid waste, other than a closed source,[11] with radioactivity not exceeding 0.4 Becquerels per gram, organic liquids which are radioactive solely because of the presence of carbon 14 or tritium (often incorporated into organic molecules for purposes of tracing reactions in which they are involved) with a radioactivity not exceeding four Becquerels per ml, and gases with one or more radionuclides none of which have a half life greater than 100 seconds.

15–012   "Mobile radioactive apparatus" means anything which is radioactive material, including but not limited to "apparatus, equipment and appliances" which is constructed or adapted for being transported from place to place, or which is in fact portable and designed or intended to be used for releasing radioactive material into the environment or introducing it into organisms.[12]

Controls over Radioactive Material and Mobile Radioactive Apparatus

15–013   Section 6 imposes a general prohibition whereby no person may, on any premises used for the purposes of any undertaking carried on by him, keep or use, or cause or permit to be kept or used, radioactive material of any description, provided that he knows or has reasonable grounds for believing it to be radioactive material, unless he is registered under the Act in respect both of those premises and of the keeping and use on those premises of that radioactive material. However if the radioactive material is mobile radioactive apparatus for which he or anyone else is registered under section 10 or is exempted from registration under that section, then the section 6 prohibition

---

[10] S.I. No. 1002 as amended by the Radioactive Substances (Substances of Low Activity) Exemption (Amendment Order) 1992 (S.I. 1992 No.647).
[11] i.e., "an object free from patent defect which is radioactive material solely because it consists of one or more radionuclides firmly incorporated on or in, or sealed within, solid inert non-radioactive material so as to prevent in normal use the dispersion of any radioactive material" (1986 Order, Art. 1(3)).
[12] s.3.

does not apply.[13] This exemption would appear to be entirely general in application, and so extends not only to persons on whose premises the mobile apparatus has been brought or to whom it has been hired out, but also the owner of the apparatus itself. However, the DoE Guide to the R.S.A. 1960 states, in respect of the corresponding provisions in that Act, that "where the person who is lending or hiring out the mobile apparatus is registered in respect of that activity but also uses the apparatus on his own premises, he is required to register additionally in respect of his keeping or using radioactive material on his premises (*i.e.*, under section 6 of the R.S.A. 1993) also." Though this interpretation is open to question, those responsible for any such activity may need to have regard to the Department's understanding of the law. Nevertheless, the person who is lending or hiring out mobile radioactive apparatus may well do more than merely keep or use it on his own premises, for example maintenance or repair, and in such circumstances, registration under section 6 will be required.

Registration is also not required for the keeping of substantially insoluble solid radioactive material, other than a closed source, of which the activity does not exceed 0.4 Becquerels per gram, by virtue of regulation 2 of the Radioactive Substances (Substances of Low Activity) (Exemption) Order 1986. Numerous Orders also exempt specific articles and uses.[14] A series of exemptions are expressly set out in section 8 covering, subject to specific qualifications and conditions, holders of nuclear site licences under the N.I.A. 1965, and clocks and watches which are radioactive material, other than those manufactured or repaired by processes involving the use of luminous material. **15–014**

Applications for registration in respect of radioactive material are made on prescribed forms obtainable from the appropriate Inspectorate, and must give details of the relevant premises, the activities for which the premises are used, a description of the radioactive material in question and the maximum quantity likely to be kept or used at any one time, and the manner (if any) in which this material is proposed to be used on the premises. Copies are sent by the Inspectorate to the local authority for the area of the relevant premises. The registration may, and invariably will, be made subject to various conditions listed generically in section 7(6). These may relate to the premises, possibly including structural alterations, and to requirements on the person to whom the registration relates to provide information on any movement of radioactive material from the premises, and they may prohibit **15–015**

---

[13] s.6(c).
[14] Made under s.8(6). These are listed in the Encyclopedia of Environmental Law at para. D29–016, and in Garner's Environmental Law, Div. VII, para. 99.

any supply of radioactive material from the premises unless it is appropriately labelled. When imposing conditions regarding premises, regard may only be had to the amount and character of radioactive waste likely to arise from the keeping or use of the radioactive material in accordance with the registration on those premises.[15] (Safety precautions in respect of radioactive substances are imposed under the Ionising Radiation Regulations 1985 referred to in paragraph 15–047).

15–016   Registration in respect of mobile radioactive apparatus is required by section 9, which provides that unless they are registered (or are exempted from registration), no person shall keep, use, lend, or let on hire, any mobile radioactive apparatus, or cause or permit this, for the purposes of investigating (including testing and measuring) any characteristics of substances or articles or releasing quantities of radioactive material into the environment or introducing it into organisms. The requirement is waived for certain electronic valves and testing instruments by various exemption orders.[16] The procedure for registering in respect of mobile radioactive apparatus is essentially the same as for radioactive material; the application must specify the apparatus concerned and the manner in which it is proposed to be used, and a copy of the application is sent to each local authority in whose area the apparatus is likely to be kept or used for releasing radioactive material into the environment. In relation to mobile radioactive apparatus, the Inspectorate is entitled to impose such conditions as it thinks fit.

15–017   In either case, an application may be treated by the applicant as having been refused if it is not determined within four months or such longer period as may be agreed,[17] so entitling him to invoke the appeals procedure under sections 26 and 27.[18] A registration may be cancelled or varied at any time, by attaching or varying applicable limitations or conditions, without compensation.[19]

15–018   Registration in respect of radioactive material and mobile radioactive apparatus is personal to the applicant, and there are no provisions for transferring registration from one person to another. Consequently, in the event of any proposed transfer of ownership of radioactive material, whether by physical supply, or by the acquisition of an undertaking that is registered in respect of any radioactive material or mobile radioactive apparatus, the person registered must

---

[15] s.7(7).
[16] S.I.s 1967 No. 1797, 1985 No. 1049.
[17] ss.7(5), 10(4) and 47(1).
[18] See para. 15–035.
[19] s.12(1).

remain in control of the item until such time as the new owner is appropriately registered, and can take it over.

Radioactive Wastes

Radioactive wastes were the subject of a White Paper,[20] and the   **15–019**
Radioactive Substances Act 1960 was based on its recommendations.
A review of this White Paper by a group of experts led to a report[21] that
recommended that the radiological protection aspects of radioactive
waste management practices should be based on the system of dose
limitation recommended by the ICRP as expanded by the NRPB ASP
2.[22] These further recommendations were adopted by the government, and formed the basis of the 1982 Guide to the R.S.A. 1960, and
specifically its Part II[23]

In response to a recommendation in the sixth report of the Royal   **15–020**
Commission on Environmental Pollution, on Nuclear Power and the
Environment, there was set up what has become the Radioactive
Waste Management Advisory Committee (the RWMAC). The Committee's terms of reference are to advise the Secretaries of State for the
Environment, for Scotland and for Wales on (a) the technical and
environmental implications of major issues concerning the development and implementation of an overall policy for all aspects of the
management of civil radioactive waste, including research and development, and (b) on any such matters referred to it by the Secretaries of
State.

The management of radioactive waste in the UK is subject to certain   **15–021**
basic principles as set out in the 1982 Guide, namely:

(a) all practices giving rise to radioactive wastes must be justified
i.e., the need for the practice must be established in terms of
its overall benefit;

(b) radiation exposure of individuals and the collective dose to
the population arising from radioactive wastes must be
reduced to levels which are as low as reasonably achievable,
economic and social factors being taken into account; and

---

[20] Cmnd. 884 "The Control of Radioactive Wastes", 1959.
[21] "A Review of Cmnd. 884 'The Control of Radioactive Wastes' ". A Report by an Expert
Group to the Radioactive Waste Management Committee (1979).
[22] ICRP publication 26.
[23] This Guide in the process of being revised to take into account the amendments made
by the E.P.A. 1990, and the re-ordering of the various legislative provisions in the
R.S.A. 1993.

(c) the average effective dose equivalent from all sources, excluding natural background radiation and medical procedures, for representative members of a critical group of the general public is not to exceed 5 mSv in any one year.[24]

15–022 While the principles apply to the radiation that may be received by humans, the Guide recognises that exposure to other living things must also be taken into account. However in the case of other living things, it is the exposure to the population as a whole rather than to individual members of it that is generally of significance, and the ICRP's opinion is quoted that protection arrangements drawn up to ensure the health and safety of man will in general provide sufficient protection for other species. By way of application of these principles, the Guide sets out recommended limits for a variety of means of disposing of different types of radioactive waste, such as low level wastes in domestic refuse and high volume low activity wastes, incineration of radioactive waste, disposal at sea (a procedure that is currently subject to a moratorium), disposal of liquid wastes to surface waters and to sewer, and atmospheric discharges.

15–023 The R.S.A. deals separately with the disposal of radioactive waste, in section 13, and accumulation of radioactive waste with a view to its subsequent disposal, in section 14. In practice, the dividing line between these two procedures is not always clear cut—radioactive wastes are liable to be stored for a long time while attempts are made to organise suitable final disposal sites. In principle, however, storage of such wastes will be deemed to be an accumulation rather than disposal where it involves placing the wastes in a facility, with the intention of taking further action subsequently, in such a way and at such a location that further action is expected to be feasible. The further action might, for example, be recovery of the radioactive material in situ, or it could be a declaration that nothing further needs to be done, and that the material will be left where it is undisturbed, so converting the process into one of disposal.

15–024 "Waste" is given the same non-exclusive definition in the R.S.A.[25] as in the E.P.A., Part II, namely that it *includes:*

"any substance which constitutes scrap material or an effluent or other unwanted surplus substance arising from the application of any process, and also includes any substance or article which

---

[24] This maximum figure is considered to represent an average dose rated equivalent of less than 1 mSv per year of life-long whole body exposure from all sources, giving a lifetime whole body dose equivalent of not more than 70 mSv, which is regarded as acceptable. However it may be necessary to pay particular attention to this lifetime dose equivalent in certain cases.
[25] s.47(1).

requires to be disposed of as being broken, worn out, contaminated or otherwise spoilt."

Likewise, any substance or article which, in the course of the carrying on of any undertaking is discharged, discarded or otherwise dealt with as if it were waste shall, for the purposes of the R.S.A., be presumed to be waste unless the contrary is proved.[26] It is not at the time of writing known whether the new definition of "Directive waste" adopted for the purposes of the E.P.A. will be made applicable also to the R.S.A..

15–025

The "disposal" of waste includes its removal, deposit, destruction, discharge (whether into water or into the air or into a sewer or drain or otherwise) or burial (whether underground or otherwise).[27] The controls over disposal of radioactive waste apply:

15–026

— to its disposal on or from any premises which are used by a person for the purposes of any undertaking carried on by him;
— where it is received by a person for disposal by the recipient; and
— where it arises from any mobile radioactive apparatus kept for any of the purposes controlled under the R.S.A. (see paragraph 15–016),

provided, in the first two cases (only), he knows or has reasonable grounds for believing it to be radioactive waste. In each case, disposal of the waste (or causing or permitting it to be disposed of) requires prior authorisation under the relevant subsection of section 13, save only that where a person receives waste for disposal he does not need a specific authorisation if the relevant authorisation in respect of the premises or the mobile radioactive apparatus on or from which the waste arose provided for its disposal, and the disposal complies with its terms.

A person may not accumulate any radioactive waste (with a view to its subsequent disposal) on any premises used for an undertaking that he carries on, nor may he cause or permit this accumulation, if he knows or has reasonable grounds for believing it to be radioactive waste, except in accordance with an authorisation granted under section 14. A number of exceptions to this are nevertheless provided, namely:

15–027

— an authorisation to dispose of radioactive waste under section 13 may provide for its temporary accumulation, in

[26] s.47(4).
[27] s.47(1).

> which event no further authorisation under section 14 is needed;
>
> — the prohibition does not apply to the accumulation of radioactive waste on any premises situated on a nuclear site, since this will be controlled by the relevant site licence;
>
> — there are a series of exclusions applying both to accumulation and the disposal of radioactive waste, as listed below.

15–028   Inevitably, where radioactive waste is produced, it cannot necessarily be instantaneously disposed of, and as a matter of practicality, it must be kept for at least a brief period. Nevertheless, if any substance arising from the production, keeping or use of radioactive material is accumulated in a part of the premises appropriated for that purpose and is retained there for a period of not less than three months, the substance will be presumed to be radioactive waste and to be accumulated on the premises with a view to its subsequent disposal, unless the contrary is proved.[28] Exemptions to the prohibitions on disposal and accumulation of radioactive waste, unless appropriately authorised, apply to such waste arising from clocks or watches, except where it arises on premises on which the clocks or watches are manufactured or repaired by processes involving the use of luminous material. Additionally, there are numerous exemptions from either or both of sections 13 and 14 by virtue of section 15(1) and a series of exemption orders.[29]

15–029   Section 16 of the R.S.A. governs the grant of authorisations for the disposal or accumulation of radioactive waste, application for which is made to the appropriate Inspectorate.[30] In England, Wales and Northern Ireland, where an application relates to radioactive waste on or from premises on a nuclear site, the authorisation must be given jointly by the Inspectorate and the "appropriate Minister" namely, in England, the Minister of Agriculture, Fisheries and Food, in Wales, the Secretary of State for Wales and in relation to Northern Ireland, the Department of Agriculture for Northern Ireland.[31] In any such case, the Minister must consult with such local authorities, relevant water bodies,[32] and other public or local authorities as he thinks it proper to do so. In all cases, the Inspectorate will send a copy of the application to each local authority for the area in which the disposal or accumula-

---

[28] s.14(4).
[29] Made under s.15(2). These are listed in the Encyclopedia of Environmental Law at para. D29–030; also in Garner's Environmental Law, Div. VIII, para. 106
[30] On forms provided by the Inspectorates.
[31] s.16(3).
[32] *i.e.* water and sewerage undertakers and fisheries committees in England and Wales; river purification and water authorities and district salmon fishery boards in Scotland; and the Fisheries Conservation Board in Northern Ireland.

tion is to take place. Grant of an authorisation may, and invariably will, be made subject to such limitations and conditions as the Inspectorate (and the Minister, where applicable) sees fit. On grant, the Inspectorate must (except where disclosure is restricted on grounds of national security)[33] send a copy to each local authority for the relevant area, and also to any other public or local authority that may have been consulted by the Minister in respect of waste to be disposed on or from premises on a nuclear site. To give these bodies time to make representations, the authorisation will normally not come into effect until at least 28 days after the various copies have been sent to the local or other public bodies, unless it is considered necessary for it to come into effect sooner. It was held in *R. v. Secretary of State for the Environment, ex p. Greenpeace and Lancashire County Council*[33A] that sections 13 and 16 must be construed so as to be consistent with Euratom Directive 80/836, as amended, which the R.S.A. is intended to implement. Article 6 of this Directive sets out certain general principles, including:

> "(a) the various types of activity resulting in an exposure to ionising radiation shall have been justified in advance by the advantages which they produce".

Thus although there is no comparable language in the UK statute, there is nevertheless a binding obligation on the Inspectorate to be satisfied that any release of radiation that would result from a proposed activity is justified on this basis before authorising it.

Before granting any authorisation in circumstances where it appears that any local or other public authority or any relevant water body may need to take special precautions, there must be consultation with them.[34] Where such special precautions are taken by a local or public authority in accordance with an authorisation or with the prior approval of the Inspectorate (or the Minister where appropriate), the costs of so doing may be recovered from the person authorised.[35] If an authorisation to dispose of radioactive waste requires or permits radioactive waste to be removed to a place provided by a local authority for the deposit of refuse, that authority has an express duty to accept any radioactive waste taken to that place in accordance with the authorisation, and to deal with it in any manner as may be required by the authorisation.[36]   **15–030**

On grant of an authorisation, the Inspectorate must supply the applicant with a certificate containing all the material particulars of it.   **15–031**

---

[33] Under s.25.
[33A] [1994] Env. L.R. D11.
[34] s.18(1).
[35] s.18(2).
[36] s.18(3).

In so far as it relates to any premises in which radioactive material is kept or used, or used for the disposal or accumulation of radioactive waste, a copy of the certificate must be displayed at all times in a position where it may be conveniently read.

15–032   An application for authorisation may be treated by the applicant as having been refused if it is not determined within four months or such longer period as may be agreed,[37] so entitling him to invoke the appeals procedure under sections 26 and 27.[38] A granted authorisation may at any time be revoked or varied, by attaching or varying applicable limitations or conditions, without compensation.[39]

Overlap with Other Statutes

15–033   There is substantial potential overlap between the operation of the R.S.A. and that of various other statutes including Part III of the E.P.A. relating to statutory nuisances, numerous provisions of the Water Resources Act 1991, including those relating to pollution of water, and the provisions in the Water Industry Act 1991 relating to trade effluent. These and other statutory provisions, as listed in Part I of Schedule 3 to the R.S.A. continue to apply to radioactive substances, but in so far as they do apply, no account is to be taken of any radioactivity possessed by any substance or article, or by any part of any premises,[40] while the R.S.A. applies in respect of their radioactivity. Several of these other statutes likewise have provisions designed to avoid the overlap of jurisdiction. Thus, E.P.A., s.78 provides that Part II of that Act does not apply to radioactive waste within the meaning of the R.S.A., unless regulations otherwise provide. To date no such regulations have been issued. In relation to water pollution, the W.R.A. 1991 has a corresponding provision in section 98, but by virtue of the Control of Pollution (Radioactive Waste) Regulations 1989,[41] made under the corresponding provision of the Water Act 1989, its pollution controls are applied in respect of all matters other than radioactivity. Similarly, controls over the discharge of trade effluent under the Water Industry Act 1991 have been made applicable to matters other than radioactivity.[42]

---

[37] ss.16(7), 47(1).
[38] See paras. 15–035, 15–036.
[39] s.17.
[40] R.S.A., s.40(1), (2).
[41] S.I. 1989 No. 1158.
[42] S.I. 1976 No. 959.

Records

Anyone who has been granted an authorisation under any of the provisions of the R.S.A., may be required to maintain records as specified by the Inspectorate, and to retain these not only throughout the period of the activities or the authorisation, but also for such periods as may be specified thereafter. Additionally, the person may be required to supply the Inspectorate with copies of the records, in the event of his registration being cancelled, the authorisation revoked or in the event of his ceasing to carry on the relevant activities.[43]

15–034

Appeals

There is a right of appeal to the Secretary of State in respect of any refusal of an application for registration or authorisation, of any limitations or conditions attached to one, of any variations that may be made (other than revoking a limitation or condition), and of any cancellation of a registration or revocation of an authorisation. However in view of the pre-grant procedure for applications for of authorisation relating to disposal of radioactive waste on or from any premises on a nuclear site, there is no right of appeal from decisions on them, nor is there against any decision taken by the Inspectorate pursuant to a direction given by the Secretary of State, either in relation to any application or granted registration or authorisation, or the calling in of any application or applications generally.[44] Appeals are subject to detailed rules as set out in the Radioactive Substances (Appeals) Regulations 1990.[45] These provide, *inter alia*, that the appeals must generally be brought within two months of the relevant decision appealed against (or of when an application is deemed refused).[46] However an appeal against a decision by the chief inspector (*i.e.* HMIP/ HMIPI) to cancel a registration or to revoke an authorisation must be made within 28 days.[47] An appeal may be required to be advertised before it is dealt with,[48] and if either party so requests it must be in the form of a hearing;[49] otherwise a written procedure will apply. Where it takes the form of a hearing, the person hearing the appeal may decide that it should be held wholly or partly in private. The bringing of an appeal will not affect the enforceability of the decision or notice appealed against, save in the case of a cancellation or revocation of a

15–035

---

[43] s.20.
[44] s.26(3).
[45] S.I. 1990 No. 2504.
[46] reg. 3(1).
[47] reg. 3(2).
[48] s.27(2).
[49] s.27(3).

registration or authorisation, unless the Secretary of State otherwise directs.[50]

15–036   In the case of an application for an authorisation for the disposal of radioactive waste on or from any premises on a nuclear site, the applicant is entitled to a preliminary hearing prior to any decision to refuse application, and likewise before any decision to attach any limitations or conditions to an authorisation, to vary it (otherwise done by revoking a limitation or condition) or to revoke it.[51] In any such case, any local authorities or other bodies that the Secretary of State and relevant Minister consider appropriate may also be allowed to be heard.

Enforcement

15–037   Enforcement of the provisions of the R.S.A. may take the form of criminal prosecutions for breach of the various requirements of the R.S.A., or by the service of an enforcement or a prohibition notice under sections 21 and 22 respectively. Offences against the principal provisions of the Act, including a failure to comply with any requirement of an enforcement or prohibition notice, are subject to a fine not exceeding £20,000 and/or imprisonment for up to six months, on summary conviction, and to an unlimited fine and/or imprisonment for up to five years on indictment. Lesser penalties are provided for failure to display a certificate of registration or authorisation, or to comply with any obligations to retain or produce records.[52] Unlike most other regulatory offences, private prosecutions are excluded by an express prohibition against the taking of proceedings in respect of any offence under the R.S.A. in England and Wales except by the Secretary of State, the Chief Inspector of HMIP, or by or with the consent or the Director of Public Prosecutions.[53]

15–038   The standard provisions render directors liable who have consented or connived at an offence by their company or where it has been committed through their negligence.[54] Unusually, however, no corresponding liability is placed on the members of a body corporate that is managed by them, except where it is established by or under any enactment of the purposes of any nationalised industry.[55] The normal provision is provided for any other person to be charged with an offence where this is due to his act or default.[56]

---

[50] s.27(6).
[51] s.28.
[52] ss.32, 33.
[53] s.38.
[54] s.36(1).
[55] s.36(2).
[56] s.37.

Where a person has failed to comply with any limitation or **15–039** condition the subject of his registration or authorisation, or if the Inspectorate considers he is likely to do so, he may be served with an enforcement notice.[57] This must state the opinion of the inspector on which the notice is based, specify the matters constituting the relevant failure and also the steps that must be taken to remedy them, and the period in which they must be taken.[58] Where a local authority or other body has been sent copies of a registration or authorisation, a copy of the enforcement notice is to be served on them also.[59]

Where the Chief Inspector considers that there is an imminent risk **15–040** of pollution to the environment or of harm to human health due to any person continuing to keep or use radioactive material or mobile radioactive apparatus or to dispose or accumulate radioactive waste, he may serve a prohibition notice on that person.[60] This may be done whether or not the manner of carrying on the relevant activity complies with the requirements of the applicable registration or authorisation;[61] the procedure is not available if there is no registration or authorisation at all. A prohibition notice must likewise set out the opinion of the inspector on which the service of the notice is based, specify the matters giving rise to the risk involved, and the steps that must be taken to remove it, as well as the period in which they must be taken.[62] Additionally, it must direct that the registration or authorisation in question shall cease to have effect, either wholly or in part, until the prohibition notice is withdrawn. If the registration or authorisation is only partially suspended, limitations or conditions may be imposed in relation to the activity or activities that may still be carried on.[63] As with enforcement notices, copies of any prohibition notice must be sent to the relevant local authority and any other public bodies involved.[64] The prohibition notice must be withdrawn when the Chief Inspector (or where the relevant Minister was involve, the Minister also) is satisfied that the risk specified in the notice has been removed, and a copy of this withdrawal notice must likewise be sent to any authority or other body that was sent a copy of the prohibition notice originally.[65]

Anyone on whom an enforcement or prohibition notice has been **15–041** served and who requests a hearing within the period prescribed by the

[57] s.21(1).
[58] s.21(2).
[59] s.21(4).
[60] s.22.
[61] s.22(2).
[62] s.22(3).
[63] s.22(4).
[64] s.22(6).
[65] s.22(7).

notice is entitled to be heard by an inspector appointed for the purpose,[66] except where the notice was issued pursuant to a direction by the Secretary of State[67] or (where a Minister has joint control) by that Minister.[68]

15–042   Special powers are given to the Secretary of State to arrange for the safe disposal or accumulation of radioactive waste, if it appears to him that adequate facilities are not available.[69] He has further powers for disposing of radioactive waste on any premises where he is satisfied that it ought to be disposed of, but that it is unlikely for any reason that it will be lawfully disposed of unless extra powers are taken.[70] Where he takes such action, he may recover any expenses reasonably incurred from the occupier of the premises or, where they are unoccupied, from their owner, as defined in section 343 of the Public Health Act 1936 as regards England, Wales and Northern Ireland, and section 3 of the Public Health (Scotland) Act 1897 in relation to premises in Scotland, with certain qualifications.[71]

15–043   Extensive rights of entry and inspection are provided under section 31. Any intentional obstruction of any person exercising these powers, and any refusal to provide facilities or assistance or any information, or to permit any inspection reasonably required under those powers, or without reasonable excuse any failure to do any of those things, constitutes an offence subject to a fine of up to £5,000 on summary conviction and an unlimited fine on indictment.[72]

Public Access to Documents

15–044   There is general public access to all applications made to the Inspectorate under the R.S.A. and to all documents issued by the Inspectorate under it, as well as to any other documents that the Inspectorate may have sent to any local authority in pursuance of directions given by the Secretary of State and records of convictions, except to the extent that this would involve the disclosure of information relating to any relevant process or trade secret or where the Secretary of State has directed restrictions on grounds of national security.[73] Likewise, each local authority must both keep and make available copies of all documents that may be sent to it under any provision of the R.S.A., unless directed by the Inspectorate (with, in

[66] s.26(2).
[67] s.26(3)(b).
[68] s.26(4).
[69] s.29.
[70] s.30.
[71] Set out in s.13(3).
[72] s.35.
[73] s.39(1).

the appropriate cases, the relevant Minister) that all or any part of a document is not to be made available so as to prevent disclosure of relevant processes or trade secrets.[74] The public has a right to inspect copies of all such documents and to be provided with copies on payment of a reasonable fee.[75]

Scope

The Act extends throughout the United Kingdom including any **15–045** activities on the continental shelf. It is binding on the Crown, save in relation to premises occupied for military or other defence purposes or by or for a visiting force.[76] Nevertheless, any contravention by the Crown does not render it itself criminally liable, though the court may, if requested to do so, declare unlawful any contravention that it has found.[77] Though the Crown is not *per se* criminally liable, any persons in the public service of the Crown are potentially as liable as any other persons.[78]

Radiation Emergency Information

Information is to be supplied to the general public about health **15–046** protection measures required in the event of a "radiological emergency", by virtue of the Public Information for Radiation Emergencies Regulations 1992[79] which implement Euratom Directive 89/618.[80] This imposes obligations on both employers and self-employed persons who conduct an undertaking from which a radiation emergency is reasonably foreseeable to provide detailed information as set out in those Regulations. A "radiation emergency" is any occurrence which is likely to result in any member of the public being exposed to ionising radiation arising from that occurrence in excess of any of the doses set out in Schedule 1 to the Regulations. Schedule 1 sets out separately dose limits for (i) the whole body (ii) individual organs and tissues, and (iii) the lens of the eye. If any one or more of these limits is likely to be exceeded, then there is a potential radiation emergency. An emergency response facility, incorporating automatic monitors connected into an information network, known as the Radioactive Incident Monitoring Network (RIMNET), has been set up to collect

---

[74] s.39(2).
[75] s.39(5).
[76] s.42(1)(2).
[77] s.42(3).
[78] s.42(4).
[79] S.I. 1992 No. 2997.
[80] [1987] O.J. L357.

data and to raise an alert if any significant increase in radioactivity is detected.

Health and Safety at the Workplace

15–047   The health and safety at the workplace of those who may come into contact with ionising radiations is the subject of the Ionising Radiation Regulations 1985,[81] and an Approved Code of Practice: "The Protection of Persons against Ionising Radiation arising from any Work Activity". The Regulations largely implement Euratom Directive 80/836, as amended by Euratom Directive 84/467,[82] which are in turn based on recommendations by the ICRP on appropriate maximum radiation dose limits. These suggested a two to three fold reduction in the then existing dose limits, based on research results from studies of the survivors of the Hiroshima and Nagasaki nuclear bombs. Member states may impose stricter limits than those laid down in the Euratom Directives.[83] In addition, the Ionising Radiations (Outside Workers) Regulations 1993[84] which implement Euratom Directive 90/641[85] provide for radiation protection for outside workers who are brought on to a site operated by another employer where they may be exposed to ionising radiation. An Approved Code of Practice and guidance on these outside workers Regulations has also been issued.[86] Guidance on both sets of Regulations has been issued by the National Radiological Protection Board.[87]

Transport of Radioactive Substances

15–048   The transport of radioactive substances by road is primarily governed in the United Kingdom by the Radioactive Material (Road Transport) Act 1991, which provides extensive powers for the issue of regulations to control such transport. In addition to making failure to comply with any such regulations an offence, the Act also provides for prohibitions on the driving of any vehicle or the transport of any radioactive package or packaging component if, in any case, it does not comply with applicable regulations, and also for enforcement notices requiring specific action.[88] There are wide ranging powers

---

[81] S.I. 1985 No.1333.
[82] [1980] O.J. L246; [1984] O.J. L265.
[83] ECJ Case—376/90, *European Commission v. Kingdom of Belgium*, O.J. 337, 17.12.92.
[84] S.I. 1993 No. 2379.
[85] [1990] O.J. L349.
[86] L.49 "Protection of outside Workers against Ionising Radiations", 1993.
[87] "Co-operation between Employers", February 1994.
[88] ss. 3, 4.

exercisable at all reasonable hours to enter any relevant vehicle or premises; in certain circumstances, a warrant may be issued to carry out such actions, using reasonable force if need be. No regulations have been made directly under the 1991 Act, but the Radioactive Substances (Carriage by Road) (Great Britain) Regulations 1974, as amended by the Radioactive Substances (Carriage by Road) (Great Britain) (Amendment) Regulations 1985,[89] have effect as if made under the 1991 Act.[90]

Transport by rail is subject to the Carriage of Dangerous Goods by Rail Regulations 1994.[91] The definition of "dangerous goods" includes radioactive material, and regulation 21 sets out certain provisions that relate exclusively to its safe carriage.

Shipments of radioactive substances within the EC are governed by Euratom Directive 92/3[92] and Euratom Regulation 1493/93.[93] The Directive is implemented in the UK by the Transfrontier Shipment of Radioactive Waste Regulations 1993,[94] and sets up a system of prior notification and requirement for acceptance of shipments of radioactive waste. This procedure is supplemented by the Regulation, which prohibits the holder of such waste, and also of sealed sources, from exporting or arranging to export them to other member states until he has received from the intended recipient a written declaration stamped by the relevant competent authority in the recipient's country. The Regulation includes a standard declaration form that must be completed by a prospective consignee, stamped by his competent authority and sent to the holder, before the shipment may begin. The holder must provide the competent authorities in each member state with which he is concerned with information on the shipments of all radioactive substances made by him to that member state during each calendar quarter.

15–049

Nuclear Installations

The use of any site within the United Kingdom for the purpose of installing or operating any nuclear reactor or any other prescribed installation for (i) the production or use of atomic energy, (ii) the carrying out of any process which is preparatory or ancillary to the production or use of atomic energy, and which involves or is capable of causing the emission of ionising radiation, or (iii) the storage,

15–050

---

[89] S.I. 1974 No. 1735, S.I. 1985 No. 1729.
[90] s.2(6).
[91] S.I. 1994 No. 670.
[92] [1992] O.J. L35.
[93] [1993] O.J. L148.
[94] S.I. 1993 No. 3031.

processing or disposal of nuclear fuel or of bulk quantities of other radioactive matter produced or irradiated in the course of the production or use of nuclear fuel, requires a licence under the Nuclear Installations Act 1965 (the N.I.A.)[95]—a "nuclear site licence". Nuclear site licences may be granted only to a body corporate, and it is expressly provided that such a licence shall not be transferable.[96] Certain amendments were made to the 1965 Act by the Nuclear Installations Act 1969, and further amendments have been made by virtue of powers given to the Secretary of State under section 80 of the H.S.W.A. 1974.

15–051 Whether or not a nuclear site licence is in force, no one other than the Atomic Energy Authority (the A.E.A.) may extract plutonium or uranium from irradiated matter or treat uranium such as to increase the proportion of uranium 235, except pursuant with a written permit from the A.E.A. or relevant government department.[97] Fissile material produced under such a permit may be disposed of only as approved of by the grantor of the permit. Applications for a nuclear site licence are made to the Nuclear Installations Inspectorate. The Inspectorate may, where it considers it appropriate, require the applicant to give notice of his application, and such particulars as may be specified, to a variety of public authorities, including local authorities, water undertakers and local fisheries committees.[98] A licence must have attached to it such conditions as the Inspectorate considers necessary or desirable in the interests of safety, whether in normal circumstances or in the event of any accident or other emergency.[99] Further conditions may be added at any time with regard to the handling, treatment and disposal of nuclear matter, and any condition attached to a nuclear licence can be varied or revoked at any time. The Inspectorate is obliged to consider representations that may be made to it by any organisation representing persons having duties upon a site, in respect of which there is a nuclear site licence in force, with a view to the exercise by it of their powers in relation to licence conditions.[1] Copies of any conditions must be kept posted on the site in a manner enabling them to be conveniently read by those having duties on the site who may be affected.[2] Nuclear site licences may at any time be revoked by the Inspectorate, or surrendered by the licensee.[3] Notwithstanding revocation or surrender, a licensee continues to remain responsible under

[95] s.1(1).
[96] s.3(1).
[97] s.2(4).
[98] s.3(3).
[99] s.4.
[1] s.4(4).
[2] s.4(5).
[3] s.5(1).

the licence until the Inspectorate gives written notice that there has ceased to be any danger from ionising radiations from anything on the site. This duty will also cease if a new nuclear site licence is issued in respect of the same site, whether to the same licensee or someone else.[4]

Any holder of a nuclear site licence is under an express statutory duty to secure that no occurrence involving nuclear matter causes injury to any person or damage to any property of any person other than the licensee, whether this arises out of or results from the radioactive properties, or a combination of those and any toxic, explosive or other hazardous properties of the nuclear matter.[5] The licensee must also secure that there are no ionising radiations emitted from anything he has caused or permitted to be on the site that is not nuclear matter, or from any waste that may be discharged, in any form, on or from the site, that cause injury to any person or any damage to any property to any person other than the licensee. The duty in relation to nuclear matter applies not only to an occurrence on the site itself, but also, *inter alia*, to occurrences outside the site involving nuclear matter other than "excepted matter", and which at the relevant time is in the course of carriage on behalf of the licensee. (There are certain exceptions to this last duty, notably where the matter is on another licensed site in the United Kingdom). The duty does not however create liability in relation to a nuclear installation on the relevant site or other property on it that is there for use in connection with the operation or cessation of the operation of the installation or for constructing one. The same duties as just set out apply equally to the UK A.E.A. in relation to any premises that it currently occupies or has previously occupied.[6] Similarly, if a government department uses any site for a purpose that would require a nuclear site licence if the use were by anyone else, then the Crown becomes subject to the same liability as a nuclear site licensee throughout the duration of its occupation of the relevant site.[7]

15–052

A duty is also imposed on foreign operators in certain circumstances to secure that there is no injury to a person or damage to any property other than that of the operator, where this arises out of or results from the radioactive properties or a combination of those and any toxic, explosive or other hazardous properties of that matter.[8] This duty applies principally to nuclear matter, not being excepted matter, which is in the course of carriage on behalf of the foreign operator and is not

15–053

---

[4] s.5(3).
[5] s.7.
[6] s.8.
[7] s.9.
[8] s.10.

for the time being "on any relevant site in the United Kingdom". Similar duties are placed on anyone carrying nuclear matter within the territorial limits of the United Kingdom to avoid any occurrence involving that matter that causes injury to any person or property damage.[9]

15–054 The duties under these various provisions impose strict liability, irrespective of fault. The only exclusion of liability of general application is where the injury or damage or the causing of it is attributable to hostile action in the course of any armed conflict, including any within the United Kingdom.[10] It is expressly provided that the liability will apply even where the occurrence or the causing of the injury or damage is attributable to a natural disaster "notwithstanding that the disaster is of such an exceptional character that it could not reasonably have been foreseen", *i.e.*, an act of God.[11] Operators must therefore be prepared for earthquakes, or take the consequences. Certain other defences are set out in section 13 where the relevant injury or damage took place in certain other countries, and there is a provision for reduction in the compensation on account of the fault of the claimant, but only if and to the extent that the causing of his injury or damage is attributable to any act of his committed with the intention of causing harm to any person or property or with reckless disregard for the consequences of his act. This provision would therefore bite on terrorist action or, in some circumstances, anti-nuclear protesters, were they to take direct action against a nuclear installation.

15–055 Subject to the defences just indicated, provided that a claim is brought within time and no foreign court has jurisdiction over it under a relevant international agreement, compensation is due by virtue of section 12. There is an overall limit of £20 million capping the liability under these provisions in respect of any one occurrence, excluding payments in respect of interest and costs.[12] The N.I.A. includes detailed provisions aimed at ensuring there is appropriate financial cover for payments that may become due on any claims for breach of the statutory duties it imposes.[13] In general, there is a statutory bar on any claims made under these provisions after 30 years from the date of the relevant occurrence. However, where the occurrence was continuing one, or was one of a succession, all being attributable to a particular happening on a particular relevant site, or to the carrying out from time to time on a particular relevant site of a particular operation, the

[9] s.11.
[10] s.13(4)(a).
[11] s.13(4)(b).
[12] £5 million maximum in respect of such sites as may be prescribed by the Nuclear Installations (Prescribed Sites) Regulations 1983 (S.I. 1983 No. 1919).
[13] ss.18–21.

date of the last event in the course of that occurrence or succession of occurrences governs the calculation of the 30 year period. Nevertheless, where the occurrence involves nuclear matter that has been stolen from, or lost or abandoned by, the person subject to the duty, the period for bringing a claim is limited to 20 years from when the nuclear matter concerned was stolen, lost or abandoned.[14]

The compensation available under the N.I.A. is limited to compensation in respect of injury to any person or damage to property. This does not however, extend to economic loss. Thus, in *Merlin et al. v. British Nuclear Fuels plc*[15] the value of a house had been adversely affected because it was in an area of radioactive fall out resulting from a nuclear accident. However the house was still habitable, and it had not itself suffered damage, and the plaintiffs accordingly failed to recover under their claim brought under the N.I.A.

15–056

Where any dangerous occurrence occurs on a licensed site or in the course of the carriage of nuclear matter subject to any of the statutory duties imposed by the N.I.A. as may be prescribed, the relevant licensee or other person must report the occurrence forthwith to the Inspectorate and to anyone else as may be prescribed.[16] The occurrences subject to this requirement are prescribed in the Nuclear Installations (Dangerous Occurrences) Regulations 1965 as amended by the Nuclear Installation (Dangerous Occurrences) Amendment (Regulations) 1974.[17] Inspectors may be appointed by the Secretary of State in respect of most matters covered by the N.I.A., who may exercise such of the powers set out in section 20(2) of the H.S.W.A. 1974, as may be conferred on them, for example investigating any occurrence and the publication of reports on such investigations.

15–057

A system for the international reporting of nuclear incidents was introduced in 1990, with a view to achieving prompt informing of the media and the public on the safety significance of such incidents, graded on the International Nuclear Event Scale (the INES). The HSE is responsible for the United Kingdom's international reporting functions.

15–058

[14] s.15.
[15] [1990] 2 Q.B. 557; [1990] 3 W.L.R. 383; [1990] 3 All E.R. 711.
[16] s.22.
[17] S.I. 1965 No.1824; S.I. 1974 No.2056.

Chapter 16

HAZARDOUS OPERATIONS

From time to time major accidents at industrial installations have **16–001** attracted widespread notoriety and with it great public unease: Flixborough, Seveso, Bhopal, and the Sandoz fire at Basel.[1] Many more incidents have occurred which, although on a smaller scale, have been extremely damaging to their local communities. The damage may be essentially physical, as from an explosion and fire, it may arise from toxic emissions to the atmosphere, as with the release of dioxins at Seveso and the leak of methyl isocyanate at Bhopal, or it may be catastrophic environmental damage, where large quantities of pesticides and other toxic chemicals escape into a river. In virtually all cases the accidents that have arisen have been caused by a combination of failures; there must be numerous situations around the world where pure luck has saved similar combinations of failures from developing into comparable disasters.

Direct control over the conduct of hazardous activities, and over **16–002** products and materials used in the workplace, is exercised by the Health and Safety Executive giving effect to the Health & Safety at Work, etc., Act 1974 (the "H.S.W.A.") and the numerous regulations made under it. These controls are primarily concerned with protecting the health and the safety of those at work, and only indirectly minimising the risk of accidents having an impact outside the work site. These numerous and very important controls under the health and safety legislation are not however the subject of this work, where they are only touched on to the extent that they relate directly to those which may more properly be regarded as environmental controls. This chapter is accordingly primarily concerned with the legislation relating to hazardous installations that are liable to have an impact on the surrounding community and environment generally.

The major explosion at Flixborough in 1974,[2] in which 28 of the **16–003** workforce died, led to the setting up by the Health and Safety

---

[1] Chernobyl and Long Mile Island are also candidates for this list, but, being nuclear installations, are arguably a separate category.
[2] In a plant oxidising cyclohexane to cyclohexanone.

Commission of the Advisory Committee on Major Hazards. This Committee has issued three reports, many of the recommendations of which have now been incorporated into current legislation. The third[3] was particularly influential in defining the structure needed for legislation in this area. The first UK legislation was the Notification of Installations Handling Hazardous Substances Regulations 1982 ("the NIHHS Regulations"),[4] which preceded the Committee's third report. At essentially the same time, the so-called "Seveso" Directive 82/501/EEC[5] "on the major accident hazards of certain industrial activities" was also issued, which, as its colloquial name indicates, was developed in direct response to the explosion at the factory at Seveso that released a cloud of dioxins.[6] The Seveso Directive was implemented in the United Kingdom by the Control of Industrial Major Accident Hazards Regulations 1984 ("the CIMAH Regulations").[7] These Regulations, and the underlying Seveso Directive, have subsequently been significantly amended, as described below, following the fire at the Sandoz facility at Basel, so as to cover isolated storage facilities in addition to many manufacturing sites.

16–004   A further strand in the developing legislation concerned the interaction between planning control and the existence of significant quantities of hazardous substances on a site. The nature of the planning legislation is such that it cannot always control with sufficient precision whether particular hazardous substances are brought on to a site, or used there in a manner which ensures all appropriate safety precautions are taken, not merely to protect the workforce, but also the public living and working in neighbouring areas. This situation led to a recommendation from the Advisory Committee on Major Hazards in 1979 that planning controls should be made to apply also to the storage and use of hazardous substances. The recommendation was not acted on directly, but the General Development Order ("GDO") and the Use Classes Order ("UCO")[8] were amended so as to exclude developments from the general planning permissions granted by those Orders if they involved the presence of a hazardous substance in an amount notifiable under the NIHHS Regulations. Accordingly, any proposed operation or any material change of use that involved the presence of more than the

---

[3] "The Control of Major Hazards", 1984.
[4] S.I. 1982 No. 1357.
[5] [1982] O.J. L230.
[6] Despite the much feared toxic effects of dioxins, no fatalities were recorded due to dioxin poisoning (one person was killed in the explosion itself), though following an offer of compensation for animals killed by the dioxin release, the evidence is that other mammals are vastly more susceptible to dioxins than man!
[7] S.I. 1984 No. 1902 as subsequently amended—see paras. 16–013 to 16–028.
[8] See paras. 3–056 to 3–062.

notifiable amount of a hazardous substance required an individual planning application, and to some extent relevant safety conditions might be attached to any ensuing planning consent.

Nevertheless, for several years there was still no obligation on **16–005** planning authorities to consult the HSE in relation to the dangers that any proposed presence of hazardous substances might represent. These dangers might arise both from activities likely to give rise to substantial quantities of hazardous substances being on a site, and also from developments in the neighbourhood of a site on which substantial quantities of hazardous substances might be present. The former aspect was first addressed in Part IV of the Housing and Planning Act 1986. This Part IV was however never brought into effect and was re-enacted as the Planning (Hazardous Substances) Act 1990. That Act was in turn substantially amended by both the Environmental Protection Act 1990[9] and the Planning and Compensation Act 1991,[10] and was eventually brought into effect in England and Wales on June 1, 1992 with the Planning (Hazardous Substances) Regulations 1992,[11] and in Scotland on May 1, 1993 with the Town and Country Planning (Hazardous Substances) (Scotland) Regulations 1993.[12]

The NIHHS Regulations 1982

The Notification of Installations handling Hazardous Substances **16–006** Regulations 1982,[13] which are made under the H.S.W.A., are designed to ensure that the Health & Safety Executive is made aware of all sites where there is any hazardous substance in an amount equal to or greater than a "notifiable quantity". This is achieved by an express prohibition on the undertaking of any activity in which there is or liable to be at any one time a notifiable quantity or more of the hazardous substance at any site, or in any relevant pipeline, unless there has been at least three months prior notice in writing given to the HSE before that activity is commenced (or such shorter period as may be agreed).[14]

The Regulations do not allocate responsibility for giving the notice; **16–007** since the obligation they impose is not to undertake any relevant activity unless prior notice has been given, it is immaterial so far as

---

[9] Sched. 13 and Sched. 16, Part VII.
[10] Sched. 3, paras. 10 to 16, 30.
[11] S.I. 1992 No. 656.
[12] S.I. 1993 No. 323.
[13] S.I. 1982 No. 1357.
[14] reg. 3(1).

compliance is concerned, who notifies.[15] Non-compliance will constitute an offence by whoever is responsible for carrying on the activity. In practical terms, this will be the person in control of the site concerned.[16] However in some situations, if several parties are involved, such as where various related companies operate relevant activities in a large petrochemical works, or where both a lessor and a lessee have active responsibilities on a site, who has control will not always be readily apparent. As the HSE might, in the event of a failure to notify as required, take a different view from the parties as to who has control, it is essential for all the latter to be clear as to who is to be responsible for notifying.

16–008   What constitutes a hazardous substance for the purposes of these Regulations is set out in Schedule 1. This contains a list of some 30 substances in its Part I, while Part II lists categories of flammable gases, including liquefied gases, and low flash point liquids. The relevant "notifiable quantity" for these substances and categories is set out against each, being generally in the range from two to 100 tonnes, though 500 tonnes in the case of ammonium nitrate and certain solutions and mixtures of this and for "Site" includes not only areas of land but also any pier, jetty or other structure whether floating or not. Further, in calculating whether there is a notifiable quantity of any substance at a site there must be taken into the calculation any quantities that are:

    (a)   in any pipeline under the control of the person having control of the site, that is within 500 metres of that site and connected to it;

    (b)   at any other site under control of the same person which has any part of its boundary within 500 metres of the first site; and

    (c)   in any vehicle, vessel, aircraft or hovercraft under the control of the same person which is used for storage purposes either at the site or within 500 metres of it.

16–009   Nevertheless, quantities of hazardous substances that are in a vehicle, vessel, aircraft or hovercraft used for transporting it are to be excluded from the calculation. This last exclusion would appear on its face to apply to a road tanker used to transport a hazardous substance to a site, even though it may be left on the site indefinitely thereafter for the purpose of storing the same substance. To avoid this result, which could largely defeat the objective of item (c) above, it is arguable

---

[15] The HSE guidance on the Regulations is thus wrong in stating (in para. 2) that the Regulations require the person undertaking the activity to give the notification, though that may well be their practical effect.

[16] See para. 16–037 for commentary on "control".

that the final words of the exemption should read " . . . aircraft or hovercraft *which is being* used for transporting it". Even though any ambiguity in a provision creating a criminal offence should be construed in favour of a defendant, it would be imprudent, nevertheless, to rely on this exemption to use a vehicle for storage purposes. The Regulations contain no provision comparable to that in the Planning (Hazardous Substances) Regulations to the effect that where one company is a subsidiary of another, or where two companies are both subsidiaries of a third, the two companies are to be regarded as a single person (see paragraph 16–037). Consequently, where two adjacent sites are under the control of associated companies, for the purposes of the NIHHS Regulations these would be regarded as distinct from each other.[17]

When notifying the proposed presence of a hazardous substance, the notification should give the maximum quantity liable to be on the site, and not merely the precise quantity first intended to be introduced. Following a notification, the person in control of the relevant activity on the site is responsible for notifying any changes that may be appropriate to the details as originally notified, including any increase or reduction in the maximum quantity of any hazardous substance, and cessation of the relevant activity. However, where the maximum quantity of any one substance is to be increased to three times or more that of the originally notified quantity, then instead of a simple updating amendment under regulation 4, the activity must be re-notified completely.[18]   **16–010**

The enforcing authority for these Regulations is the HSE, and the provisions of the H.S.W.A. apply as they do to other regulations made under that Act. HSE guidance on the Regulations has been issued,[19] but is now out of print. Where any substance, and the quantities involved in any case, are such that not only is notification required under the NIHHS Regulations, but also a licence is required under the Petroleum (Consolidation) Act 1928 for the keeping of that substance, the HSE is empowered to grant that licence and to enforce any conditions attached to it, in lieu of the requirements of that Act.[20]   **16–011**

The provisions of the NIHHS Regulations are now largely superseded by those of the Planning (Hazardous Substances) Act and Regulations described below. Once the latter are running smoothly, the NIHHS Regulations are likely to be withdrawn.   **16–012**

---

[17] reg. 4.
[18] reg. 5.
[19] HS(R) 16–1983.
[20] reg. 7(2).

The CIMAH Regulations 1984

16–013   The Control of Industrial Major Accident Hazards Regulations 1984,[21] as amended by the Control of Industrial Major Accident Hazards (Amendment) Regulations 1988, 1990 and 1994, generally known as the "CIMAH Regulations", complement the NIHHS Regulations and implement the Seveso Directive 82/501,[22] as amended by Directives 87/216[23] and 88/610.[24] The objective of the Seveso Directive is to require those responsible for industrial activities that may result in major accidents with serious consequences for man and the environment, to take appropriate measures to prevent such accidents and to limit their consequences. This is to be achieved by the establishment of emergency plans, suitable training of the workforce on sites of these activities, and keeping the public outside the sites appropriately informed of safety measures and of action to be taken in the event of an accident. The industrial activities to which the Directive applies are defined by reference to various processes that may be carried on or may possibly involve one or more dangerous substances (as defined in Annexes), and are also capable of presenting major accident hazards, together with certain storage activities as defined.

16–014   Following the Bhopal disaster in India, the amending Directive 87/216 was adopted lowering, in respect of certain hazardous substances, the threshold levels that would bring industrial activities within the scope of the Directive,[25] and adding a few additional substances to the list. The further accident at the Sandoz facility at Basel, where large quantities of highly toxic substances were washed into the Rhine in the course of fire-fighting operations, led to Directive 88/610, which further amended the original Directive so as to make it applicable to off-site storage facilities, the source of the pollution from the Sandoz fire. The assumption was nevertheless made that off-site storage was generally less dangerous than the presence similar quantities of hazardous substances on a manufacturing site, and consequently the quantities brought under control are higher for off-site storage than for on-site use.

16–015   When the CIMAH (Amendment) Regulations 1990 were the subject of consultation, the HSE acknowledged that the resulting legislation

---

[21] S.I. 1984 No. 1902, as amended by S.I. 1988 No. 1462, S.I. 1990 No. 2325 and S.I. 1994 No. 118.
[22] [1982] O.J. L230.
[23] [1987] O.J. L85.
[24] [1988] O.J. L336.
[25] The limit for methyl isocyanate, the substance released in quantity at Bhopal was reduced from one tonne to 150kg.

was complex and difficult to follow, but it deferred any consolidating legislation at that time, because a complete overhaul of the Seveso Directive was expected imminently. In practice, that overhaul has taken much longer than expected, but a proposal for a new directive has now been published,[26] which makes many changes including the following:

- the list of 181 hazardous substances is cut back to 29 dangerous substances, coupled with a general definition of what is dangerous by reference to specific properties;
- the directive will apply to all establishments where there are, or likely to be in the event of an accident, any dangerous substances present in amounts at or above prescribed levels, without distinction between industrial activities and storage;
- current exemptions will be removed that relate to explosives, non-nuclear substances at nuclear installations and waste disposal sites;
- the properties that make substances dangerous will include "dangerous for the environment";
- provisions will be made for planning controls with a view to avoiding close proximity of hazardous installations and vulnerable community sectors (along the lines of the UK Planning (Hazardous Substances) Act and Regulations).

16–016 The current CIMAH Regulations as amended apply to certain specified industrial activities and also to storage of various "dangerous substances" in amounts at or above those prescribed for each substance. The industrial activities, which are listed in Schedule 4, are essentially installations for the production, processing or treatment of organic or inorganic chemicals, using any of a wide variety of chemical and physical processes. Since these include "mixing" there will be very few installations involving organic or inorganic chemicals that do not fall within this list. Other installations covered are those used for distillation, refining or processing of petroleum or petroleum products, incinerators, installations for the production, processing or treatment of gases such as LPG, LNG and SNG, those for the dry distillation of coal and those for the reduction of metals or non-metals by any wet process or using electricity, e.g. an electric arc furnace.

16–017 Such installations are only covered, however, where the operations concerned involve or are liable to involve one or more "dangerous substances", these being defined as substances which:

---

[26] [1994] O.J. C106; known as the "COMAH" Directive, being on the Control of Major Accident Hazards.

    (i)   satisfy any of the criteria of Schedule 1, which provide definitions of very toxic, other toxic, flammable, explosive and oxidising substances; and/or

    (ii) are any of the 181 substances listed in Schedule 3.

16–018   The operations include on-site storage and on-site transport activities associated with the operation. There is a qualification that an operation will fall outside these criteria if it is incapable of producing a "major accident" hazard. If all other criteria apply, proof of this would be bound to be exceptionally hard.

16–019   Certain activities are excluded, being the subject of other controls, specifically nuclear installations, military and explosives sites, and mines and quarries. Waste disposal sites operated by the relevant (C.O.P.A.) disposal authority were previously exempted, but the 1994 amending Regulations brought them under control with effect from various dates in 1994.[27]

16–020   "Major accident" is defined as an occurrence (including in particular a major emission, fire or explosion) resulting from uncontrolled developments in the course of an industrial activity, leading to a serious danger to persons, whether immediate or delayed, inside or outside the installation, or to the environment, and involving one or more dangerous substances.[28] What amounts to "serious danger" is of course subjective. The HSE guidance[29] indicates in this respect that, in relation to persons, "serious danger" would be death, serious injury, or harm to health, or the risk of any of these, whether immediate or delayed (as from a disease brought on by exposure to a chemical substance escaping as a result of an accident). Actual harm is not a necessary feature; mere risk of it is sufficient. As regards the environment, long term or permanent damage to rare or unique aspects of the natural or built environment or widespread loss or damage to the environment generally would be "serious". "Long term" damage for this purpose is regarded as damage requiring about 15 years for recovery for terrestrial habitats and about five years for aquatic habitats. Other relatively precise criteria are set out in the HSE guidance relating, for example, to the area of land of particular significance that may be affected or the percentage loss of a particular wildlife species. Precision in this context is however of only moderate value, since until an accident has happened accurate quantification of

---

[27] Following the reorganisation of local authority waste disposal operations in accordance with Part II of the E.P.A., this exemption was in any event about to become obsolete.

[28] This definition follows very closely that in the Seveso Directive.

[29] HS(R)21 (Rev) (1990).

the resulting damage is impossible. Nevertheless, these guidelines are of some help in indicating the levels of damage that an operator must be able to show cannot occur, if he wishes to assert that the Regulations are not properly applicable to him.[30]

The Regulations also apply to storage of certain dangerous sub-   **16–021**
stances and/or preparations, whether this is isolated or within some other establishment. Excluded from this separate category, however, is storage on the same site as an installation as just referred to, since in such a case, the amount of any hazardous substances stored on site is already taken into account. The substances relevant to storage are fewer than those relevant for the purpose of defining installations, and are set out in Schedule 2 to the CIMAH Regulations.[31] Part I of Schedule 2 lists specific named substances relevant for the purposes of storage; Part II lists substances by their properties, including "very toxic", "oxidising" and "explosive" and "highly flammable" and "extremely flammable".[32] The classification of substances into these various categories is to be made in accordance with the rules laid down for the purposes of the CHIP Regulations 1993,[33] or in accordance with the classification to which any pesticide may have been assigned. Substances in the course of transport that are on a site temporarily are excluded from any assessment of quantities, though if kept for any length of time or repackaged the Regulations would be likely to be applicable.

In some cases one of the named substances in Part I of Schedule 2   **16–022**
will also fall within one or other of the categories in Part II. In such circumstances, the relevant quantity for the purpose of the application of the Regulations is that set out in Part I against the individual substance, and not that appropriate to the broader Part II category into which it also falls. Where several substances all fall within any one of the categories in Part II, then their quantities are to be aggregated in determining whether any of the relevant threshold figures is met.

Schedule 2 has two columns of threshold figures for the various   **16–023**
substances and categories, those in the second column being substantially larger (of the order of 10 times) than those in the first, except in the case of methyl isocyanate and phosgene. Sites where there are quantities at or above any of the set of larger figures thus create a group of what are generally referred to as "top tier" facilities handling

---

[30] Further advice on criteria for determining what is a major accident is contained in the DoE publication "Interpretation of 'major accident to the environment' for the purposes of the CIMAH Regulations".
[31] Which was wholly replaced by the 1990 Amendment Regulations; see Sched. 3 to the latter.
[32] These latter expressions are defined in Sched. 1.
[33] See S.I. 1993 No. 1746, reg. 21(5)(b).

or storing very substantial amounts of hazardous substances: for these the requirements of the Regulations apply in full. Sites where the quantities exceed those in the first column, but do not reach those of the second, represent "bottom tier" facilities holding significant, but not very large, quantities of hazardous substances.

16–024   In calculating the total quantities of any substance for the purposes of the Regulations, there must be aggregated the maximum quantities liable to be present in any group of installations or stores, as the case may be, belonging to the same manufacturer, where the distance between the installations or stores is less than 500 metres. The "manufacturer" is the person having control of the relevant industrial activity,[34] which will normally be the operating company. However depending on the circumstances, a parent company could have the requisite control.

16–025   For the bottom tier facilities the main requirements of the Regulations are limited to:

  (i)   A requirement on the person having control[35] of the relevant industrial activity to be able to provide, and to do so on request, evidence (including documents) to show that he has identified the major accident hazards of the activity, and has taken adequate steps to prevent such major accidents and to limit their consequences to persons and the environment. He must also provide persons working on the site with the information, training and equipment necessary to ensure their safety.[36]

  (ii) Where a major accident does occur on a site, the person having control must forthwith notify the HSE of it, and the HSE will obtain from him full information of the accident, including the data available for assessing its various effects and the emergency measures taken. The HSE will also look for a statement of the steps envisaged to alleviate any medium or long term effects of the accident and to prevent any recurrence. Notification under this provision however is not required if it has already been made under the Reporting of Injuries, Diseases and Dangerous Occurrences Regulations 1985.[37]

16–026   Top tier facilities are subject to the obligations set out in regulations 7 to 12. These consist of:

---

[34] reg. 2(1).
[35] No definition of "control" is given. See para. 16–037 for commentary on this term.
[36] reg. 4(2).
[37] S.I. 1985 No. 2023 (see para. 16–029).

Written Reports

A requirement to prepare and provide a written report on the operations on the relevant site, including information relating to every dangerous substance that is present at or in excess of the threshold quantity for top tier facilities, information relating to the layout of the site, the processes or storage on it involving the dangerous substance(s), the number of people likely to be present, information on the management system used for controlling the activity, and information relating to potential major accidents, including preventive and emergency measures. This report must be sent to the HSE at least three months before the activity concerned is commenced, unless a shorter period is agreed. Where storage only is concerned, somewhat more limited information requirements apply in some cases. To the extent that the storage requirements were brought in by the 1990 Amendment Regulations, transitional provisions provide for an interim period for storage that was occurring on March 31, 1991, whereby relatively brief information would suffice for the period until June 1, 1994.[38] Subject to this transitional provision, further reports must be submitted within three years of each previous report taking into account any new technical knowledge relevant to safety and any new knowledge on hazard assessment. One further month is provided for submitting a copy of the further report to the HSE, unless it agrees a longer period.[39]

Where a report has been submitted, the industrial activity concerned may not be modified in any way that could materially affect what has been said in that report, unless at least three months previously a further report has been submitted taking account of the changes—again, a shorter period may be agreed by the HSE.[40] The HSE may require an operator to supplement information contained in a report, so far as this is reasonably required to evaluate the major accident hazards that the relevant activity creates.

Emergency Plans

A further requirement on those having control of top tier facilities is to prepare and keep up to date an adequate on-site

---

[38] reg. 7(3) as amended by Sched. 6 to the 1990 Amendment Regs.
[39] reg. 8(2).
[40] reg. 8(2).

emergency plan detailing how major accidents will be dealt with on the site. The plan must include the name of the person responsible for safety on the site, and the names of those authorised to take action under the plan in the event of an emergency. Everyone on the site affected by the plan must be informed of its provisions so far as relevant to them. The plan must be kept up to date, and in particular it must take into account any material changes that may be made in the activity on the site.[41] The emergency plan must be prepared before the activity itself is commenced.

Independently of the operator's emergency plan, the local authority of the area that includes the site concerned must also prepare and keep up to date an adequate off-site emergency plan, detailing how emergencies relating to any possible major accident on that site will be dealt with.[42] This must likewise be prepared before the activity is commenced. The operator must provide the authority with all information regarding the activity on the site as may reasonably be required. The authority must consult him (and also the HSE, and anyone else that the authority thinks should be consulted), and it must provide the operator with any information regarding the off-site emergency plan which relates to the preparation and updating of the on-site emergency plan, and also to the information that must be given to those affected by it. A local authority preparing an off-site emergency plan is entitled to recover its reasonable costs both for its preparation and for subsequently keeping it up to date.[43]

Guidance on the preparation of emergency plans has been issued by the HSE.[44]

Public Information

The third principal duty laid on the operator of a top tier facility is to make certain information publicly available before the activity commences;[45] he must moreover ensure that persons outside the site who are liable to be affected by a major accident on the site are supplied with this information without their having to request it. He has to take active steps therefore to communicate with these persons, and must

[41] reg. 10.
[42] For the purposes of regs. 11 and 15, relating to off- site emergency plans, the local authority is the County Council.
[43] reg. 15.
[44] HS (G) 25 (1985).
[45] reg. 12, as inserted by reg. 4 of the 1990 Amendment Regs.

endeavour to agree with the local authority for it to disseminate the information to them. In preparing the information,
the operator is required to consult the local authority[46] and
any other persons who seem to him to be appropriate.
Nevertheless, he remains responsible for the accuracy,
completeness and form of the information supplied. As to
who needs to be informed in this way, the regulation refers to
persons "who are likely to be in an area in which, in the
opinion of the Executive, they are liable to be affected . . . ".
There can clearly be no precision in determining the area,
since the consequences of an accident will vary greatly
according to its precise nature, and, often the prevailing
weather conditions. It is therefore essential for the operator
to consult closely with the HSE to establish what is appropriate in the circumstances.

There is no statutory provision on how the public should
be informed for the purposes of regulation 12. It is clearly a
matter that operators need to consider with considerable
care, with a view to avoiding undue alarm on the one hand or
complacency on the other. The information that must, as a
minimum, be communicated to the public is listed in
Schedule 8, and includes, in addition to general information
as to activities and substances on the site, information on
how people outside will be warned and informed in the
event of an accident and what they should do in such
circumstances. Inevitably, unless special steps are taken, the
vast majority of recipients are liable either to throw away
whatever they have been given, or else put it in a place where
they will not see it again until too late should an accident ever
in fact occur. If the Regulations are to achieve their purpose,
informing the public must be done in a way that is and
continues to be constructive. The guidance recommends the
use of durable cards giving summarised safety instructions.
Operators must bear in mind that individual members of the
public will be constantly moving away from the area while
others move in; and that many of those who stay will be
forgetful. There will therefore be a need for repetition of the
public information procedure from time to time; the guidance suggests this should be done at intervals of from 12 to
24 months. Obviously any changes in the activity or the

---

[46] For the purposes of reg. 12, the relevant local authority is the District Council. This
division of responsibilities for providing information to the public in the vicinity and
for preparing off-site emergency plans is inconvenient but must be recognised.

hazards will in themselves require new information to be disseminated among those in the vicinity.

Confidentiality

16–027   Information provided for the purposes of CIMAH Regulations to a local authority or to the HSE is required to be kept confidential under the normal provisions of the H.S.W.A.[47] Nevertheless, this must be read subject to the Environmental Information Regulations 1992,[48] so that information relating to an accident that has in fact affected the environment would, to the extent that those Regulations apply, be publicly available.

Enforcement

16–028   Enforcement of the CIMAH Regulations is by the HSE exercising their general powers of enforcement of health and safety regulations; their powers in this respect apply also in relation to activities that would in other respects come within the scope of the Petroleum (Consolidation) Act 1928 (Enforcement) Regulations 1979.[49]

Additional Controls

16–029   For completeness, mention may be made here of two further sets of Regulations that in practice need to be considered in conjunction with the NIHHS and CIMAH Regulations:

   (1) The Reporting of Injuries, Diseases and Dangerous Occurrences Regulations 1985[50] These Regulations, commonly
   known as "RIDDOR", as amended by the Reporting of
   Injuries, Diseases and Dangerous Occurrences (Amendment) Regulations 1989[51] require injuries and dangerous
   occurrences at work to be notified to the HSE, with a
   notification followed up by a fuller report. The injuries and
   occurrences that must be reported are spelled out in Regulation 3. Though these cover most normal workplace accidents,
   they will also include injuries and occurrences that may

---

[47] reg. 13(1).
[48] S.I. 1992 No. 3240.
[49] S.I. 1979 No. 427.
[50] S.I. 1985 No. 2023.
[51] S.I. 1989 No. 1457.

occur in the case of accidents giving rise to a significant environmental damage. Dangerous occurrences as spelled out in considerable detail in Schedule 1 must also be reported. Records must be kept of all matters the subject of the report. A consultation document containing proposals to revise RIDDOR was issued by the HSC in April 1994.

(2) The Dangerous Substances (Notification and Marking of Sites) Regulations 1990.[52] These Regulations set out details on how sites on which dangerous substances are present should be appropriately marked, primarily for the purposes of the fire services.

The Planning (Hazardous Substances) Act 1990

Under the CIMAH and the NIHHS Regulations described above, **16–030** operators who hold on their premises various prescribed hazardous substances, in quantities above limits prescribed for those substances, are required to take certain steps to prepare emergency plans as a precaution against accidents, and to notify the Health and Safety Executive of the activities carried on or to be carried on on the site. However, provided these requirements are complied with, the Regulations do not impose any direct control over the operator, either on the amount of hazardous substance or substances he keeps on the site, or how he handles them there. The Planning (Hazardous Substances Act 1990 (referred to here as the "Hazardous Substances Act") is designed to remedy this situation by requiring a "hazardous substances consent" (an "HSC") before any hazardous substance may be present on any site in more than the amount prescribed for that substance, called the "controlled quantity". This consent is obtained by a procedure closely modelled on that for obtaining planning consents, and is granted subject to appropriate conditions designed to safeguard both people on the site and those on neighbouring land.

When it was drafted, the Hazardous Substances Act was intended to **16–031** conform closely with the provisions of the T.C.P.A. 1990. Subsequent amendments have resulted in its departing in certain significant respects from the original format, but nevertheless the two are closely linked, and a number of provisions in the T.C.P.A. (referred to in the Hazardous Substances Act as "the principal Act") are incorporated by reference, notably those relating to contravention notices, and procedures relating to local inquiries, procedures for appeals, provisions for

[52] S.I. 1990 No. 304.

obtaining information and offences by corporations. Much of the detail of the new controls is contained in the Planning (Hazardous Substances) Regulations 1992,[53] referred to here as the "Hazardous Substances Regulations". DoE Circular 11/92[54] "Planning Controls for Hazardous Substances" provides a guide to the procedures involved, and (in Annex B) to the inter-relationship of these controls with those under other legislation concerned with hazardous substances.

This legislation does not apply to Scotland, but an equivalent regime is provided by the Town and Country (Scotland) Act 1972, as amended by the Housing and Planning Act 1986.

16–032 What constitutes a hazardous substance for the purposes of the legislation is defined in the Hazardous Substance Regulations.[55] The hazardous substances brought under control, together with the relevant "controlled quantity" for each substance are listed in Schedule 1 to the Regulations. They are divided into three groups: toxic substances, highly reactive and explosive substances, and finally flammable substances that are not otherwise within either of the first two groups. The majority of these substances and their controlled quantities are the same as those that require action under the NIHHS Regulations, but there are certain additional substances taken from the CIMAH Regulations, where these have significant potential for major accidents—for these latter the controlled quantities differ in some cases. The quantities concerned are comparatively large, in most cases being in the range of from 1 to 500 tonnes, the smallest being that for methyl isocyanate[56] at 150 kg. Special rules were made for setting the established quantity of ammonium nitrate fertilisers complying with EC Directive 80/86, for which no NIHHS notification was needed. For these the established quantity is in effect 200 per cent of the maximum previously held rather than the 150 per cent that would otherwise apply, so putting them on the same footing as other ammonium nitrate fertilisers requiring NIHHS notification.[57] The group of flammable substances includes liquefied petroleum gas, any other gas flammable in air and any liquid, flammable in air, that is held above its boiling point or which has a flash point of less than 21°.

16–033 The hazardous substances legislation aims to avoid duplication of controls, and accordingly controlled waste and radioactive waste are excluded[58] from the definition of "hazardous substance", being controlled under Part II of the E.P.A. (and some cases also under Part I

---

[53] S.I. 1992 No. 656. These and the 1990 Act came into effect on June 1, 1992.
[54] W.O. 20/92.
[55] reg. 3(1).
[56] The chemical responsible for the deaths and injuries at Bhopal.
[57] reg. 4(5); see also Circular 11/92, para. A-21.
[58] By reg. 3(2).

of the E.P.A.), and under the Radioactive Substances Act 1993 respectively. Likewise, explosives that are listed in Group 4 of Schedule 3 to the CIMAH Regulations are excluded, as they are already controlled by licences issued by the HSC under the Explosives Act 1875, in so far as this applies to factories and magazines, and under the Dangerous Substances in Harbour Areas Regulations 1987,[59] which controls the handling of explosives imports.

Further exemptions from the controls are set out in both section 4 **16–034** and Regulation 4.[60] These relate to:

Temporary presence

By section 4(3), the temporary presence of a hazardous substance while it is being transported from one place to another is not to be taken into account, unless it is unloaded. By regulation 4(1), even if it is unloaded, hazardous substances consent is not required for the temporary presence of a hazardous substance during the period between it being unloaded from one means of transport and loaded on to another while it is being transported from one place to another. There is no definition of "temporary", and so any particular case must be decided on its own facts. However, the critical wording in both these provisions is "while [the hazardous substance] is being transported from one place to another". This must be taken to be intended to connote a brief interruption in what can properly be seen as a single journey, for example an overnight stop or a break to pick up an additional load. Any significantly longer stop would run the risk of being regarded as temporary storage, and outside the exemption. Essentially the same considerations apply to temporary presence during transfer from one means of transport to another. Unless there is documentary evidence of an intention to transport the substance from its place of origin to its intended destination with no deliberate substantial delay in between, there must be a risk that any lengthy break in that journey would be held to be more than merely temporary. If at the transfer point the person in charge simply collects the substance until he has enough to make up a full load to send on, or alternatively if he receives a bulk load and splits it up otherwise than in accordance with pre-existing arrangements for disposal of the full load, then it is

[59] S.I. 1987 No. 37.
[60] All references to Regulations in this chapter are to the Hazardous Substances Regulations unless otherwise stated.

unlikely that the words of the exemption of regulation 4 (1) could properly apply. There does not, however, seem any reason in principle why breaking bulk should not take place as part of the unloading and reloading process, without the benefit of the exemption being lost.

Aerosol Dispensers

Two categories of aerosol dispensers are exempted under regulation 4(2). Firstly, aerosol dispensers with a capacity of not more than one litre are disregarded for the purposes of the controls, however many such dispensers there may be, and hence what total amount of hazardous substance may be contained by them. Additionally, the exemption extends to aerosol dispensers, whatever their size, if they do not contain any substances that are flammable within the meaning of the CPL Regulations 1984,[61] Schedule 1, Part III, paragraph 2, and also do not contain any of 14 substances listed in Schedule 1 to the Regulations — nevertheless, the presence of any of those scheduled substances can be ignored, if the aggregate quantity of them contained in aerosol dispensers with a capacity greater than one litre on the relevant site is less than the controlled quantity for that substance. The quantity contained in aerosol dispensers with a capacity of one litre or below would thus be ignored in any event in this calculation. It may also be noted that the calculation treats each substance separately, so that if there were to be several substances present simultaneously, each marginally below the relevant controlled quantity, then the Regulations do not apply.

Pipelines

Hazardous substances consent is not required for the presence of a hazardous substance contained in an "exempt pipeline" or a service pipe.[62] "Exempt pipeline" means a pipeline used to convey a hazardous substance to a far site, but excluded from this is the part of the pipeline within the boundaries of a site to which it has an outlet or inlet; the expression also excludes a service pipe. "Service pipe" is a pipeline used by a public gas supplier to supply gas to an individual consumer from a gas main. In this latter case, the

---

[61] S.I. 1984 No. 1244; so far this definition has not been amended to refer to the CHIP Regulations 1993.
[62] reg. 4(3).

fact that there is an outlet on the site, is not relevant and the contents of the pipe are ignored altogether. The effect of this exemption is to exclude from consideration all pipelines which cross a site but which have no outlet or inlet on the site, and also gas service pipes (only) that terminate on or have an outlet on a site. Controls over such pipelines are exercised under the Pipelines Act 1962.

Sea-going craft in emergencies

Regulation 4(4) provides a further exemption where any action taken in response to emergencies at sea has resulted in hazardous substance being unloaded from a craft without any or without adequate advance notice. In the emergencies to which this exemption applies, there is a grace period of 14 days beginning with the day on which the hazardous substance was unloaded, during which the substance may be stored without hazardous substances consent.

In addition, the Secretary of State has power to exempt from hazardous substances control the presence of a substance that would normally require a consent, if he considers that any part of the community is being or is likely to be deprived of an essential service or commodity, or that there is or is likely to be a shortage of such a service or commodity. Any direction giving effect to this may be withdrawn at any time, and will in any event not last more than three months, though further directions may be given to the same effect if appropriate.[63]   **16–035**

Although the scope of the Hazardous Substances Regulations is restricted in certain respects so as to avoid duplication with other controls, where there is potential overlap, both sets of controls apply cumulatively.[64] Further, if anything in the Hazardous Substances consent purports to require or permit anything to be done that contravenes any "relevant statutory provisions", then the consent is to that extent void, and must either be revoked if it is wholly void, or suitably amended, if partially so.[65] "Relevant statutory provisions" are as defined for the purposes of the H.S.W.A., Part I, and include that Part I and health and safety regulations made under it, including the NIHHS and CIMAH Regulations, the numerous statutory provisions listed in Schedule 1 to the H.S.W.A., and prohibition and improvement notices under any of the foregoing. If a hazardous substances   **16–036**

[63] s.27.
[64] s.29(1).
[65] s.29(2), (4), (5).

authority thinks that any consent or contravention notice that it has given or issued is rendered void for this reason, it must consult the HSE; if the HSE advises the authority that it is wholly void, the consent on it must be revoked, and if they advise that it is partially void, the authority must modify it.

16–037 In considering whether the controlled quantity of any substance is present on any site, there must be included in the calculation, not only all quantities on, over or under the land in question, but also all quantities on, over or under any other land which is within 500 metres of it and controlled by the same person or which is in or on a structure controlled by the same person, where any part of that structure is within 500 metres of the site in question.[66] For the purposes of the Hazardous Substances Act, two separate bodies corporate are to be treated as one person if one is a subsidiary of another or both are subsidiaries of the same body corporate ("subsidiary" being as defined in section 736 of the Companies Act 1985),[67] so that operations conducted by a group of companies are treated as one set of operations. The provisions also have the effect of discouraging any artificial splitting up of the ownership of a site into separate companies as a means of avoiding having to obtain hazardous substances consent. "Control" is not defined, but it may, in most cases at least, be equated with the management of a facility. It could also extend to the right (*de facto* as well as *de jure*) to instruct operators on a site, and so cover not only parent companies (who would of course be treated as the same "person" anyway), but also dominant shareholders and receivers. The actual ownership of the relevant land and facilities on it is accordingly not relevant; nor, for that matter, is the ownership of the hazardous substance itself.

16–038 The purpose of the legislation is twofold: to procure that hazardous substances are only held in appropriate areas, and not close to those that are for any reason particularly vulnerable, and also to ensure their safe storage. These separate planning and technical considerations are imposed by a new "hazardous substances authority" which is almost invariably the same as the planning authority for the area concerned. Before granting any consent, the authority must nevertheless consult with the HSE as well as a large number of other bodies, and for practical purposes it will be the HSE that determines the practical conditions on how consented hazardous substances are to be safely stored and used. Any decision on this aspect is ultimately for the authority alone (subject to any appeal) applied to 150 per cent of the maximum amount present in the 12 months preceding June 1, 1992,

[66] s.4(2).
[67] s.39(3).

when the legislation came into effect, provided this was not less that the controlled quantity for that substance. Deemed consents are automatically subject to the conditions set out in section 11 (7) of the Act and, more specifically, in Schedule 3 to the Hazardous Substances Regulations as interpreted by regulation 16. These automatic conditions apply to the temperature and pressure at which the substance may be held, with special rules in relation to moveable containers; their objective is very largely to maintain the status quo while permitting a limited degree of operational flexibility.

In addition to the deemed consents arising by virtue of the statutory transitional provisions, other deemed consents may be created at any time by the Secretary of State or a Government Department, when authorising certain types of development to be carried out by a local authority or by other statutory undertakers that would involve the presence of a hazardous substance requiring a consent. In any such case a direction may be given with the authorisation that a hazardous substances consent should be deemed to be granted; the direction will also lay down any applicable conditions.[68] The developments authorised by a Government Department to which this provision applies are set out in section 12(4). While the language is not wholly clear, the listing of five distinct situations as a means of construing the term "authorisation of a Government Department" indicates that this list is intended to be fully comprehensive, and that deemed consents may not be granted in any other situations under this power. This view is supported by the separate provisions enabling the Secretary of State, on granting any consent under section 36 of the Electricity Act 1989, for the construction of a generating station, to direct that a hazardous substances consent be deemed to be granted;[69] similarly, in connection with an order made under section 1 or 3 of the Transport and Works Act 1992.[70]

16–039

Express Consents

Application for a hazardous substances consent is made to the appropriate hazardous substances authority, which will normally be the local district council or London borough in which the relevant site is located.[71] Other bodies are however designated in special cases, namely National Parks, the Broads Authority, land used for mineral

16–040

---

[68] s.12(1).
[69] s.12(2).
[70] s.12(2A), inserted by s.18 of the Transport and Works Act 1992.
[71] s.1.

extraction or waste disposal, and land for which an urban development corporation or a housing action trust is the local planning authority. An application for HSC is made on the Form 1 described by regulation 5 and set out in Schedule 2. Completing the form requires information to be given as to the nature of the substance or substances, and the maximum quantity in tonnes proposed to be present; the nature of each storage vessel, and the storage conditions; and, where any such substances is to be used in an industrial process, the nature of that process and the physical conditions in which it is to be used. A site map and a substance location form must also be provided.

16–041   The procedure for obtaining consent is modelled closely on procedures for obtaining planning consent; indeed it will often be the case that planning and hazardous substance consents are sought substantially simultaneously. However, before a hazardous substances consent application is made, the intention to make the application must be publicised in a local newspaper during the preceding 21 days and there must also be a site notice, inviting representations on the application, on not less than seven of those 21 days, unless the applicant has no rights to the land that would enable this, even after having taken all reasonable steps to acquire sufficient rights.[72] A certificate of having posted the site notice or of inability to do so either for the full seven days or at all must be given on Form 4.[73]

16–042   So far as possible, owners are to be made aware of any application for consent that is being made in respect of their property. Accordingly, one of the certificates of Form 5 must also be lodged to the effect either that the applicant is the owner in respect of relevant parts of the land, or that steps have been taken to serve the appropriate notice on the owner and, if these have not been successful, what was in fact done. Form 6 is to be used to serve the notice on an owner. It is to be served within the 21 days preceding the application and invites the owner, if he wishes to make representations, to do so within 21 days of service of the notice. For the purpose of this notice, "owner" means a person having a freehold interest in the land, or a tenancy the unexpired term of which is not less than seven years.[74] For all purposes of the Hazardous Substances Act other than those of section 8, "owner" has the definition given to it in the T.C.P.A. 1990.[75] Having

---

[72] The provisions for publicity are detailed in reg.6.
[73] See Sched. 2.
[74] s.8(8).
[75] Where "owner", in relation to any land, means a person, other than a mortgagee, not in possession, who, whether in his own right or as trustee for any other person, is entitled to receive the rack rent of the land or, where the land is not let at a rack rent, would be so entitled if it were so let: T.C.P.A. 1990, s.336 (1).

posted a site notice and notified any owner, where relevant, the applicant must make a copy of his application available for inspection during the following 21 days within the locality of the application site.[76]

On receipt of the application, the hazardous substances authority is **16–043** required to consult numerous statutory consultees listed in Regulation 10(1), serving them with a copy of the application within seven days of its receipt by the authority. These consultees include the HSE, the relevant district or county council or London borough council, where such council is not also the hazardous substances authority, the NRA and the relevant waste disposal authority, as defined in section 30(2) of the E.P.A., where that authority is not also the hazardous substances authority. The authority is additionally advised to consult with all relevant pollution control authorities, and *vice versa*, before any of them grants any approval or serves any notice that might conflict with the requirements of any of the others.[76A]

The authority must not make a determination on an application **16–044** before expiry of the 21 day period for owners and others to make representations, nor before expiry of 28 days from the date the last of the various statutory consultees were served.[77] Nevertheless, the authority must, within eight weeks from its receipt of an application, give the applicant written notice of its determination or that the application has been referred by the authority to the Secretary of State for his determination. Failure to do so within the eight weeks, or within such longer period as may be agreed, results in the application being deemed to have been refused.[78] If an application is refused or granted subject to conditions, full reasons must be given and the applicant must be informed that he has six months to appeal to the Secretary of State from the date of the notice, or such longer period as the Secretary of State may allow.[79] The decision must also be notified to the HSE, the relevant district or county council or London borough council, where it is not the hazardous substances authority, and any other consultees or owners who have made representations.

In coming to its decision, the authority is required to have regard to **16–045** any material considerations, including any current or contemplated use of the land, the way in which land in the vicinity is being used or is likely to be used, any planning permission that has been granted for development of the land in the vicinity, the provisions of the

[76] reg. 8.
[76A] PPG 23 "Planning and Pollution Control", para. 3.14.
[77] reg. 11(1).
[78] s.21(2).
[79] reg. 11(4).

development plan,[80] and any advice that the HSE may have given as a result of the consultations.[81] The authority may attach such conditions as it thinks fit to any consent; these may include making the consent conditional on other works on the land being carried out, on how and where any hazardous substance is to be kept or used, and the times of day when it may be present. Provision may also be made for the permanent removal of such a substance on or by a specified date. Nevertheless, any conditions relating to how a hazardous substance is to be kept or used may only be imposed if the HSE has advised the authority that the consent should be subject to them. The authority may thus depart from advice given by the HSE, in the unlikely event that it is inclined to do so, but it may not usurp the HSE functions.

16–046   The Secretary of State has power to call-in an application for hazardous substances consent. Circular 11/92 indicates[82] that this should be very much the exception. Nevertheless, it would be logical to do so in circumstances where a planning application relating to a connected development on the same site was also being called in, and reasonable at least where the presence of substantial quantities of hazardous substances raised particularly sensitive political issues. Where a hazardous substances authority intends to go against advice given by the HSE, the Circular requires it to give at least 21 days notice to the HSE of that intention; during that time the HSE may ask the Secretary of State to call-in the application.[83]

Revocation and Variation of Consents

16–047   Hazardous substances consents will, unless any consent otherwise specifically provides, enure for the benefit of the land to which it relates and for all persons for the time being interested in the land.[84] However, a consent maybe revoked, or its conditions varied, by the hazardous substances authority at any time under section 14(1), if it appears to it expedient to do so "having regard to any material consideration". In that event, however, any person who has suffered damage as a consequence may claim compensation under section 16, to the extent that he can show depreciation of the value of any interest of his in the land or in minerals, in, on or under it, or otherwise by

---

[80] The Hazardous Substances Act is within the category of "planning Acts" as defined in T.C.P.A., s.336. Consequently, T.C.P.A., s.54A applies, the effect of which is that determinations under the Hazardous Substances Act shall also be made in accordance with the development plan (to the extent of course that this is relevant) unless material considerations indicate otherwise.
[81] s.9(2).
[82] In para. A-33.
[83] Circular, para. B-15.
[84] s.6(2).

being disturbed in his enjoyment of the land or such minerals. Further, anyone who carries out any works in order to comply with an order revoking or modifying a consent is entitled to recover from the authority his reasonable expenses. The general rules in relation to compensation under the T.C.P.A. 1990, contained in sections 117 and 118 of that Act, apply.

The hazardous substances authority may however revoke a hazar- **16–048**
dous substances consent, without payment of any compensation, if:

(a) there has been a material change of use of the land to which the consent applies;

(b) planning permission has been granted for developments that would entail a material change of use of the land concerned, and that development has commenced; or

(c) none of the substances to which the consent relates have been present on the relevant land for at least five years in an amount or amounts at or exceeding the controlled quantity for each substance.[85]

In the case of the first two of these three grounds, it is only a material **16–049**
change of use of the land to which the consent relates that is important. The fact that there may have been a material change of use of neighbouring land is not a matter justifying revocation of a consent without compensation. Where a consent relates to several substances, revocation under either of these first two grounds may apply to one or some only of the consented substances. As regards the third ground, in the case of a consent relating to several substances, revocation under this provision will not be possible if the controlled quantity or greater of any one or more of the substances has been present during the preceding five years.

Orders for revocation or modification of a consent under section 14 **16–050**
must be confirmed by the Secretary of State. The authority must submit its order to him therefore, and at the same time serve notice of it on anyone who is an owner of the whole or any part of the relevant land, on anyone else who appears to be in control of the whole or any part of the land, and on any other person who the authority considers will be affected by the order.[86] While this last item is expressed generally, in practice, it cannot refer to everyone in the vicinity who may be marginally affected; a realistic construction must be that anyone who has a commercial interest in the outcome and anyone who has any other interests that might be adversely affected should be

[85] s.14(2).
[86] s.15(3).

notified. It would also be appropriate to regard as affected for the purposes of this provision anyone who has shown active concern over the existence of the consent, or over the substances present on the site as a result—at the least anyone likely to have a "sufficient interest" to apply for a judicial review of the order.

16–051   These notices must give at least 28 days for any person served with them to seek an opportunity of appearing before and being heard by an appointee of the Secretary of State. Where this is requested, the Secretary of State may not confirm the authority's order unless and until that person and the hazardous substances authority have both had an opportunity to make representations.

16–052   Where the holder of a consent wishes to be relieved of a condition to which it is subject, he may apply for this under section 13. This procedure is likely to be used particularly by those holding deemed consents in view of the standard form of the conditions that they are subject to. On such an application the authority may only review the conditions of the consent[87] and decide whether the consent should be granted subject to different conditions or granted unconditionally. It may not therefore review the grant of the consent itself. Nevertheless, the authority is not in terms restricted from imposing more onerous conditions than previously applied, though if the consequence of doing so was that the consent was rendered commercially useless, this would be in clear conflict, firstly, with the evident purpose of the section in excluding the right to reconsider the grant of the consent itself and, secondly, with the right of the consent holder to compensation on a revocation under section 14(1). An application under section 13 is made on Form 2, and the procedure is essentially the same as the making of an original application (see paragraphs 16–040 to 16–044), including the publication in a local newspaper, the issue of site notices and notification of owners, giving 21 days to make representations.

16–053   Where one or a series of consents relates to several hazardous substances, and the application for variation does not relate to all of the substances, then the authority is not to take into account any consent relating to the substances not in issue, except in so far as this has implications for the one that is the subject of the application.[88]

16–054   Revocation of a consent is automatic if there is a change in the person in control of a part (only) of the land to which it relates, unless an application for the continuation of the consent has previously been made to the hazardous substances authority.[89] Since two companies

---

[87] s.13(2).
[88] s.13(5), (6).
[89] s.17(1).

within a group are to be treated as a single person,[90] this provision will not apply where land benefiting from a consent is subsequently divided between two or more associated companies. However, if land is parcelled out in that way and one of the owning companies then transfers the land to outside the group (even to a 50:50 joint venture), prior application for continuation of the consent will be essential, for the benefit not merely of the transferee, but also of the party retaining the remainder, since otherwise the consent will be lost. In the case of the sale of a facility, the purchaser will therefore wish to ensure that the application for continuation is made before completion.[91] This provision for automatic revocation will be of particular significance to anyone concerned with taking security on part only of land subject to a hazardous substances consent, since any entry into possession and assumption of control over that part by way of enforcement of the security will inevitably result in automatic revocation of the consent, in the absence of the requisite prior application for continuation.

Application for continuation of a consent is also made on Form 2, **16–055** and again the procedure is essentially the same as for making an original application (see paragraphs 16–040 to 16–044), including the publication in a local newspaper, issue of site notices and notification of owners, giving 21 days to make representations. The authority considering the application may nevertheless modify the consent in any way it considers appropriate, or revoke it.[92] However, if it does so, compensation is payable only to the person in control of the whole of the land before the change in control giving rise to the continuation application, if and in so far as that person has sustained any loss or damage directly attributable to the modification or revocation.[93] This provision for compensation is notably more limited than that under section 16 which allows any person damaged to seek to be compensated (see paragraph 16–047). A purchaser, or a lender who has enforced his security, may well suffer but will not be entitled to any compensation from the authority; any redress could only be achieved by contractual stipulations, if at all.

The authority considering a continuation application must have **16–056** regard to all material considerations, including those to which it must have regard when considering an initial application for consent;[94] and it must also have regard to any advice which the HSE may have given.

---

[90] s.39(3).
[91] Since automatic revocation occurs on a change of *control*, and property rights are not directly relevant, it should not ordinarily be necessary to make the application before contract.
[92] s.18(1).
[93] s.19.
[94] Listed in s.9(2) see para. 16–045.

Subsection 18(7) provides for a period to be prescribed within which a continuation application must be determined, failing which the application shall be deemed to have been granted. However, to date no such period has been prescribed.[95]

Appeals

16–057   Appeals lie to the Secretary of State under section 21 in respect of a variety of decisions by a hazardous substances authority, including refusal of any application for consent or in respect of the conditions attached to a granted consent. They must be made within six months of the date of the relevant decision, or such longer period as the Secretary of State may agree,[96] and are made on a prescribed form issued by the Planning Inspectorate. The procedural provisions of the Schedule to the Hazardous Substances Act govern appeals, and provide in paragraphs 1, 2 and 5 for determination of appeals by an appointed person; paragraph 3 provides for determination by the Secretary of State. However, it is indicated in the Circular that it is currently intended that all appeals will be decided by the Secretary of State with the benefit of recommendations from inspectors, rather than delegating such decisions to the inspectors themselves.

16–058   Appeals will normally be dealt with by public local inquiry, though in appropriate cases, the written representations procedure may be followed. Although they do not apply in terms, it is intended that the spirit of the Town and Country Planning (Inquiries Procedure) Rules 1998[97] will be applied to the conduct of local inquiries; where an appeal is dealt with by written representation it is intended that the procedure should follow the spirit of the Town and Country Planning (Appeals) (Written Representations Procedure) Regulations 1987[98]

16–059   The decision of the Secretary of State on any appeal under section 21 is final.[99] However, section 22 provides for the validity of any such decision to be reviewed by the court on the grounds either that it is *ultra vires* the Act or that any of the "relevant requirements" have not been complied with. "Relevant requirements" means requirements of the Hazardous Substances Act and also of the T.C.P.A. 1990, of the Tribunals and Inquiries Act 1971 and of any Order, Regulations or

---

[95] Notwithstanding that a period of eight weeks is prescribed by reg. 11(3) (*a*) for determining new applications, and the statement in the Circular (at para. A-61), explaining that there is no need for a right of appeal against the failure of an authority to determine a s.17 application within the prescribed period, because such failure would mean that the application will be deemed to be granted.
[96] reg. 13(1).
[97] S.I. 1988 No. 944.
[98] S.I. 1987 No. 701. Circular, para. A-36.
[99] s.21(6).

Rules made under any of those statutes. Application to the court must be made within six weeks of the Secretary of State's decision.[1] Additionally, the hazardous substances authority that made the decision may itself question the validity of any decision by the Secretary of State on the same limited grounds, by application to the court within the same six week period. The right of appeal is further circumscribed in that, except as provided by section 22, the validity of any decision of the Secretary of State on a called-in application or on an appeal "shall not be questioned in any legal proceedings whatsoever".[2] Where an appeal has been determined by a person appointed by the Secretary of State, his decision shall be treated as that of the Secretary of State, and again, except as provided by section 22, the validity of that decision also "shall not be questioned in any proceedings whatsoever".[3]

It is to be noted that this ouster clause is not qualified so as to protect third parties with an interest in the land concerned; this may be contrasted with the qualification to the corresponding ouster clause of section 285(2) of the T.C.P.A. as amended,[4] relating to hazardous substances contravention notices. In this latter case, the ouster does not apply to a person who is the owner or who is in control of land in respect of which a hazardous substances contravention notice is served where, among other things, he can satisfy the court that he did not know and could not reasonably been expected to know that the contravention notice had been issued, and that his interests have been substantially prejudiced by the failure to serve him with a copy of it.[5]   **16–060**

An issue that such an ouster clause inevitably raises is whether a decision of the Secretary of State, and any decision upheld by him on appeal, may be subsequently challenged on the ground that it is (and always has been) a nullity. A decision that is merely invalid will be subject to the ouster and so cannot be put in issue, but a nullity has in theory never existed, and a decision on it is arguably not being questioned by an assertion that it was an irrelevance. However, if a condition attached to a consent is a nullity, the question necessarily follows whether the consent itself is thereby rendered void. This will turn on whether the condition is severable, in which case the consent and any other conditions will continue to have effect, but if not then the consent itself will be void. Holders of consents will of course normally be concerned to establish severability, since otherwise they   **16–061**

[1] s.22(1).
[2] s.22(5).
[3] Hazardous Substances Act, Sched., para. 2(5), (6).
[4] Set out in Part 5 of Sched. 4 to the Hazardous Substances Regulations.
[5] So reversing the effect of *R v. Greenwich London Borough Council, ex p. Patel* (1985) 129 S.J. 654; (1985) 51 P. & C.R. 282.

will be immediately exposed to proceedings for possessing a quantity of a hazardous substance in excess of its controlled quantity without the requisite consent. Whether or not a condition is severable is largely dependent on its significance to the granted consent.[6]

Enforcement

16–062 There are three independent methods of enforcing the controls under the Hazardous Substances Act: criminal proceedings, a contravention notice and an injunction.

Criminal Proceedings

16–063 An offence is committed (i) if a hazardous substance is present in an amount in excess of its controlled quantity that is not consented, or (ii) if a condition of a consent is not complied with.[7] The offence is committed by the "appropriate person", defined to be:

(a) where there is an unconsented quantity of a hazardous substance, any person knowingly causing the substance to be present and any person allowing it to be so present; and

(b) in the case of breach of a condition, the person in control of the land to which the consent relates.[8]

16–064 It is a defence for an accused to prove that he took all reasonable precautions and exercised all due diligence to avoid commission of the offence, or that commission of the offence could be avoided only by the taking of action amounting to a breach of a statutory duty.[9] The existence of this defence indicates that the offence itself is one of strict liability.[10] The drafting of the definition of the "appropriate person" is somewhat unusual in referring to any person "knowingly causing . . . or allowing", in place of the more usual terminology "causing or knowingly permitting" found in much other legislation. As to what

---

[6] See, e.g. Hall & Co Limited v. Shoreham-on-Sea Urban District Council and another [1964] 1 All E.R. 1; Kingsway Investments (Kent) Limited v. Kent County Council [1968] 3 All E.R. 197 and sub nom. Kent County Council v. Kingsway Investments (Kent) Limited [1970] 1 All E.R. 70 (H.L.); R. v. Hillingdon London Borough Council, ex. p. Royco Homes [1974] 2 All E.R. 643; cf. Allnatt London Properties v. Middlesex County Council (1964) 62 LGR 304.

[7] s.23(2).

[8] s.23(3).

[9] s.23(5).

[10] See for example the judgment of Lord Reid in Tesco Ltd. v. Nattrass [1972] A.C. 153 at 169.

knowledge is to be proved in relation to a charge of "knowingly causing", it is relevant to note that section 23(6) provides that it shall be a defence if the accused proves that he did not know and had no reason to believe that the substance was present or, alternatively, that it was present in a quantity equal to or exceeding the controlled quantity. Similarly, if there is a charge that the amount of the hazardous substance exceeded the consented quantity, it is a defence to prove that the accused did not know and had no reason to believe that the substance was present in a quantity exceeding the consented maximum. It is likewise a defence to a charge that there has been failure to comply with a condition for the accused to prove that he did not know, and had no reason to believe, that there was a failure to comply with a condition subject to which hazardous substances consent had been granted.[11] It must follow that the knowledge required to constitute the offence does not need to be as precise as that spelled out by way of the statutory defences, since otherwise they would not of course be necessary.

It seems appropriate therefore to regard as sufficient knowledge to amount to "knowingly causing", to know that some substance was caused to be present. It would not be realistic to require knowledge as to what the hazardous substance was, especially since an essential element of one of the offences is that there is no hazardous substance consent at all. Schedule 1 to the Hazardous Substances Regulations, that lists the substances brought under control, sets out 71 different substances or categories of substances, and given the nature of the defence that is available, it is not unreasonable to construe the offence as simply requiring knowledge of any substance at all being caused to be on the site, leaving it to the defendant to establish his defence under section 23(6) if he can.[12] Such an approach is also consistent with construing "knowingly" as extending to situations where the defendant is reckless, or wilfully disregards facts that he would prefer not to find out.[13]   **16–065**

The offence of "allowing" a hazardous substance to be present that is not the subject of an appropriate consent or otherwise than in compliance with consent conditions, does not in terms require knowledge but by analogy with the cases on "permitting" (as to which   **16–066**

---

[11] s.23(7).
[12] Though it could be argued that the requisite knowledge was that a substance caused to be present was one controlled by the legislation (without knowing which one), this would be virtually impossible to prove, given the variety of substances covered – not that that is necessarily a sufficient reason for rejecting such a construction.
[13] *James & Son v. Smee* [1955] 1 Q.B. 78; *Westminster City Council v. Croyalgrange Ltd* [1986] 2 All E.R. 353, H.L. See also para. 8–117 on constructive knowledge.

see paragraphs 8–112 to 8–117)—and there is no reason to distinguish between the two words—one cannot allow something without knowledge of it. The extent of the knowledge would not, however, appear to be any more demanding than that required for the purposes of proving "knowingly causing".[14]

16–067   On summary conviction, the maximum fine is £20,000, with the possibility of a daily fine of £200 for each day on which an offence continues following conviction; on indictment, no maximum fines are stipulated. By an amendment inserted by the P.C.A.,[15] in determining the amount of any fine to be imposed the court is required to have regard in particular to any financial benefit that has accrued or appears likely to accrue to the person convicted in consequence of the offence.

Contravention Notice

16–068   A contravention notice procedure directly analogous to that used for breaches of planning control is provided by sections 24 to 26. In essence, such a notice spells out the alleged contravention of hazardous substances control and must require specified steps to be taken to remedy, wholly or partly, the contravention. It must also stipulate a date, at least 28 days from the date of service, as to when the notice is to take effect, it must identify the land to which the notice relates, and the period starting from that later date within which the required remedial steps are to be taken. Copies of the notice must be served on the owner of the relevant land and on any other person who appears to be in control of the land,[16] and all other persons having an interest in the land which in the opinion of the authority issuing the notice is materially affected by the notice.[17] The notice must also be accompanied by the authority's reasons for issuing it and set out the right of appeal to the Secretary of State, including in particular the time within which such an appeal may be brought. If a contravention notice requires that any hazardous substance be removed from the land, it may also, where relevant and appropriate, contain a direction that, at the end of the period for removal of the substance, any consent relating to the presence of that substance shall cease to have effect.[18] If any hazardous substances authority sees fit to do so, it may at any time after issuing a notice and either before or after it takes effect waive or

---

[14] See *Sweet v. Parsley* [1970] A.C. 132, [1969] 1 All E.R. 574, *per* Ld. Diplock; *Lomas v. Peek* [1947] 2 All E.R. 574, *per* Lord Goddard, C.J.
[15] s.23(4A).
[16] s.24(4).
[17] reg. 17(2).
[18] s.24(6), (7).

relax any requirement in the notice, or withdraw the notice altogether.[19] If that is done, everyone due to be served with the notice must also be served with a notice of the waiver, relaxation or withdrawal.

Appeals against contravention notices are subject to provisions set out extensively in Schedule 4 to the Hazardous Substances Regulations, which in Parts 1 to 4 amends various sections of the T.C.P.A. for the purposes of the hazardous substances legislation, and in Part 5 repeats those sections as amended. Briefly, they specify the grounds on which an appeal against a contravention notice may be brought and the procedures for determining the appeal, action that may be taken by a hazardous substances authority where steps required by the contravention notice have not been taken within the stipulated time, and provision for offences for non-compliance with a hazardous substances contravention notice.   **16–069**

As mentioned above, section 285(1) of the T.C.P.A., as amended for the purposes of the hazardous substances legislation, provides that the validity of a contravention notice shall not, except by way of an appeal in accordance with the T.C.P.A., be questioned in any proceedings whatsoever on any of the grounds on which such an appeal may be brought. However, subsection 285(2) states that this ouster clause shall not apply to proceedings for an offence consisting of non-compliance with a contravention notice against a person who, among other things, did not know and could not reasonably have been expected to know that the notice had been issued. Following a decision of the Secretary of State on an appeal against a contravention notice the appellant and the hazardous substances authority, and also any other person having an interest in the relevant land, may appeal to the court on a point of law or require the Secretary of State to state a case for the purposes of a judicial review.   **16–070**

Proceedings for an Injunction

A third course of action open to a hazardous substances authority, where it considers it necessary or expedient to deal with any actual or apprehended contravention is to apply by way of civil proceedings for an injunction. Section 26AA, giving this power, places no restriction on the persons against whom an injunction may be sought. An injunction being a discretionary remedy, it is left entirely to the court to determine whether or not any such order should be made and, if so, against whom and on what terms. The section specifically states that such an injunction may be sought whether or not the authority has   **16–071**

---

[19] ss.24(8), 24A(1), (2).

exercised or is proposing to exercise any other powers under the Act. Accordingly, while a court will be unlikely to grant an injunction where it thinks other remedies are clearly more appropriate, an application for an injunction should not be regarded as only available as a last resort. If a hazardous substances authority therefore reasonably considers that an injunction is at least as appropriate a means of ensuring effective hazardous substances control as any other available to it, then there would seem no reason why a court should refuse to grant the injunction sought, if in other respects it is reasonable to do so.

Rights of Entry

16–072   Extensive powers are granted to secure entry on to land for the purposes of surveying it in connection with any application for hazardous substances consent and also with any proposal to issue a contravention notice.[20] These powers may be exercised by any person duly authorised in writing by either the Secretary of State or the hazardous substances authority. The right to survey land includes a power to search and bore to ascertain the nature of the subsoil or the presence of any minerals in it. It is an offence wilfully to obstruct any person exercising a right of entry under these powers. Anyone entering land must however maintain confidentiality in respect of any information as to any manufacturing process or trade secret that he may obtain as a result. Any damage caused to land or chattels in exercising the right of entry or surveying the land (including making boreholes) a subject to a right of compensation.[21]

16–073   The Secretary of State has power[22] to direct that various of the enforcement provisions of the T.C.P.A. shall have effect in relation to contravention notices, and this has been given effect by regulations 18 and 20 to 22. Although the Secretary of State's powers include the right to provide for stop notices as under section 183 of the T.C.P.A., this has not been done and stop notices are not available for the purposes of hazardous substances control.

16–074   In addition to the sections of the T.C.P.A. that are applied with modifications as set out in Schedule 4 to the Hazardous Substances Regulations, several sections of the T.C.P.A. are made applicable directly.[23] These, and the matters to which they relate are as follows:

[20] ss.36, 36A and 36B.
[21] s.36B(6).
[22] Under s.25(1)(c).
[23] s.37.

s.320—local inquiries;

s.322—orders as to costs of parties where no inquiry has been held;

s.323—procedure on certain appeals and applications;

s.329—service of notices;

s.330—power to require information as to interests in the land;

s.331—personal liability of directors etc. for offences by corporations.

Section 331 of the T.C.P.A., which is incorporated by reference as **16–075** just described, contains the usual language whereby the director, manager, secretary or other similar officer of a body corporate and any person purporting to act in any such capacity will be held liable for any offence committed by their company where it is proved to have been committed either with their consent or connivance, or is attributable to any neglect by any of them. Unlike certain other statutes, however, no liability is placed on the shareholders of a company. Thus a parent company will not be held liable for the offences of its subsidiary under this provision, unless it held itself out to be an officer of the subsidiary.[24]

Public Registers

Public registers are to be kept which will show all hazardous **16–076** substances consent applications and decisions on these, including conditions attached to any consent, as well as details of revocations and modifications and any enforcement steps that may have been taken. These will include details of deemed consents.[25]

---

[24] Or, of course, if the subsidiary acted as agent for the parent in committing the offence.
[25] s.28, reg. 23.

Chapter 17

Non-Ionising Electromagnetic Radiation

Electromagnetic radiation is produced by numerous sources at frequencies ranging from the extremely low 50 Hz[1] of conventional power lines, through frequencies of the order of 20 kHz emitted by television sets and visual display units, the very high frequencies of around 100 mHz of FM radio, the ultra high frequencies from cellular telephones and microwave ovens (2.45 GHz) to higher frequencies still, up to 300 GHz (300×10^9 Hz), from radar and a variety of communications systems. Above these frequencies come the infra-red band, the visible spectrum, the ultra-violet band, and then X-rays at around 10^{18} Hz and gamma rays at around 10^{21} Hz. At frequencies below the ultra-violet band, the energy contained in the radiation is not sufficient to ionise[2] matter on which it impinges, by contrast with the radiation emitted from X-rays and gamma rays.[3] Radiation in this lower band of frequencies is thus referred to as non-ionising.

Unlike ionising radiation, where by far the largest exposure for most people is from natural sources, virtually all non-ionising radiation is man-made. The principal source of radiation is that emitted from cables conducting AC (alternating current) electricity which throughout Europe operates at 50 Hz. Exposure to this radiation occurs wherever there is mains electricity, though the main source of concern to the public is the radiation from high voltage power transmission lines, particularly where these pass over or close to residential areas and schools. The studies that have been carried out have resulted in conflicting conclusions as to what harm if any these may cause. For example, a study in Sweden, completed in October 1992, indicated children who lived near power lines have a 30 per cent increased risk of developing leukemia.[4] However a comprehensive review by the

17–001

17–002

---

[1] 1 Hertz (Hz) = 1 cycle per second.
[2] *i.e.*, to remove electrons from atoms, so producing a charge on the remainder.
[3] The change from non-ionising to ionising does not occur at a precise frequency, but gradually through the ultra-violet band as the frequency increases.
[4] International Environment Reporter, November 1992, p. 707.

National Radiological Protection Board on the biological effects of non-ionising radiation relevant to human health, which reported in 1992[5] contains among its conclusions:

"It cannot be concluded either that electromagnetic fields have no effect on the physiology of cells, even if the fields are weak, or that they produce effects that would, in other circumstances, be regarded as suggestive of potential carcinogenicity. In general, the available experimental evidence weighs against electromagnetic fields acting directly to damage cellular DNA, implying that these fields may not be capable of initiating cancer in a manner that parallels that of ionising radiation and many chemical agents. The results of some whole animal and cellular studies suggest the possibility that electromagnetic fields might act as co-carcinogens or tumour promoters[6] but, taken overall, the data are inconclusive."

17–003   The final conclusion reads:

"In the absence of any unambiguous experimental evidence to suggest that exposure to these electromagnetic fields is likely to be carcinogenic, in the broadest sense of the term, the findings to date can be regarded only as sufficient to justify formulating a hypothesis for testing by further investigation."

17–004   There is as yet no EC legislation designed to limit exposure of people to low frequency radiation, nor is there any in the United Kingdom.[7] However a proposed Physical Agents Directive has been issued in draft,[8] which would set minimum health and safety requirements in respect of, among other things, exposure to electric and/or magnetic fields with a frequency of up to 3×10^{15} Hz, *i.e.* essentially non-ionising radiation.[9] The European Parliament has also passed a detailed "Resolution on Combatting the Harmful Effects of Non-ionising Radiation" which, while recognising that the scientific evidence is inconclusive, nevertheless on the basis of the precautionary principle called on the Commission to propose measures aimed at limiting the exposure of workers and the public to electromagnetic fields (EMFs),

---

[5] "Electromagnetic Fields and the Risk of Cancer", Documents of the NRPB, Vol. 3, No. 1, 1992.

[6] *i.e.*, promoting the development of cancer, but not initiating it.

[7] By contrast, an Italian decree of April 23, 1992 provides for maximum limits of exposure to magnetic fields generated at 50 Hz, both out of doors and in residential areas, and specifies minimum distances between power lines and houses and other accommodation, dependent on the rating of the power line.

[8] COM (94) 284, [1994] O.J. C230, being an amended version of an earlier proposal.

[9] See also *Review of Occupational Exposure to Optical Radiation and Electric and Magnetic Fields with regard to the proposed CEC Physical Agents Directive*, NRPB, February 1994.

including making it mandatory to carry out environmental assessments on proposals for electricity transmission lines and transformer substances.[9A] In the United Kingdom, the location of power generators and overhead lines is essentially determined through the planning system.[10] DoE Circular 14/90[11] "Electricity generating stations and overhead lines" provides advice on the procedure for obtaining the views of planning authorities in relation to these matters, including advice on conducting environmental impact assessments in respect of generating stations and overhead lines. The concerns it deals with are however essentially those of visual intrusion, and not with any health implications arising from low frequency radiation. It has been held that Article 130R of the Rome Treaty, which requires Community policy on the environment to be based on, *inter alia*, the precautionary principle, does not impose any obligation on the Secretary of State, when carrying out his responsibilities under the Electricity Act 1989, to issue regulations or guidance to those responsible for underground electricity transmission lines, so as to define maximum permissible levels for the resulting electromagnetic fileds.[12]

Microwave ovens are the subject of a variety of British Standards,   **17–005** including British Standard 3456.[13] This requires microwave leakage to be limited to 50 Wm^{-2} at five cm from the external surface of the oven.

The Electromagnetic Compatibility Regulations 1992.[14]

These highly technical Regulations aim to avoid adverse effects   **17–006** from the interaction of different types of electrical and electronic apparatus. Certain protection requirements specifying both the relative immunity of apparatus from extraneous radiation, and also the extent of radiation that it itself emits, are specified in regulation 5, and apparatus covered by the Regulations may not be taken into service unless it conforms with these protection requirements.[15] Various procedural requirements are set out whereby apparatus may be assessed for its conformity with the protection requirements, a specific mark (the CE mark[16]) must be applied to the apparatus, and the

---

[9A] Resolution A3-0238/94, May 5, 1994.
[10] Consents are required under the Electricity Acts 1989 for the construction, extension or operation of large generators and overhead lines rated at over 20 kV.
[11] WO Circular 20/90; Dept. of Energy Circular 1/90.
[12] *R. v. Secretary of State for Trade and Industry, ex p. Lloyd Duddridge and others*, Q.B.D., *The Independent*, October 4, 1994.
[13] BS 3456: Part 102: 1988 "Appliances for Heating Food by Means of Microwave Energy" 1988.
[14] S.I. 1992 No. 2372, implementing EC Directive 89/336 as amended by Directives 91/263 and 92/31, [1989] O.J. L139; [1991] O.J. L128; and [1992] O.J. L126.
[15] reg. 29.
[16] Set out in Sched. 4.

manufacturer or his authorised representative must issue an EC declaration of conformity of the apparatus with the Regulations' requirements. Only if all these steps have been taken, and the apparatus complies with the protection requirements in fact, may the apparatus be supplied.[17]

17–007   The Regulations do not apply to any apparatus supplied or taken into service in the EEC before October 28, 1992, and until December 31, 1995, it is sufficient for any apparatus supplied or taken into service in the EEC if it complies with the requirements in force in the relevant member state at June 30, 1992. Until this date, it is thus sufficient within the United Kingdom for apparatus to meet the requirements set out in section 10 of the Wireless Telegraphy Act 1949 as set out in Schedule 1 to the 1992 Regulations.

[17] reg. 28.

Chapter 18

NOISE

Noise is not readily susceptible to control by legislation. What **18–001** constitutes unacceptable noise is often in practice a highly subjective issue. A neighbour's radio or choice of music may not bother one person but infuriate another. The regular crowing of a cock may seem a cheerful aspect of the rural scene at 200 yards but intolerable at 20. Some people become used to certain constant or frequent noises, such as cars, aeroplanes or trains; others never do. The acceptability or otherwise of a noise depends not only on its volume but also its pitch (very low frequency noise tends to be far more pervasive than high frequencies), its persistence, the time of day, and the presence or absence of other background noise that may mask its effect.

The difficulties in defining what is an acceptable noise and what is **18–002** unacceptable accordingly results in this issue generally being resolved in practice on a case by case basis.[1] Litigation between private parties over this issue will normally take the form of an action in nuisance or for an order to abate a statutory nuisance.[2] The most relevant of the statutory nuisances are those defined in section 79(1)(g) and 79(1)(ga) of the Environmental Protection Act 1990: "noise emitted from premises so as to be prejudicial to health or a nuisance"[3] and "noise that is prejudicial to health or a nuisance and is emitted from or caused by a vehicle, machinery or equipment in a street."[4]

Part III of the Control of Pollution Act 1974 ("C.O.P.A.") contains a **18–003** variety of statutory powers to control noise. These originally included[5]

---

[1] The DoE, with the Welsh and Scottish Offices, has issued (1992) a booklet for the general public "Bothered by Noise? What you can do about it".

[2] Considered in chapters 22 and 23.

[3] It is arguable that the statutory nuisance of s.79(1)(f) "any animal kept in such a place or manner as to be prejudicial to health or a nuisance" may also extend to noise made by such an animal, but this category of nuisance is probably intended to apply where an animal is kept in an inappropriate place or in an unsuitable manner. If so, it would not be properly applicable to, say, a dog that is merely excessively noisy but otherwise reasonably well looked after—guard dogs allowed to roam unaccompanied, or unsuitably sited kennels might be another matter.

[4] Inserted by the Noise and Statutory Nuisance Act 1993, s.2.

[5] ss.58, 59.

provisions for dealing with noise nuisances by way of abatement notices and abatement orders which now appear in Part III of the E.P.A. and are applicable to all statutory nuisances. Section 60 and 61 are concerned with the control of noise on construction sites, and section 62 with noise in streets. Sections 63 to 67 provide for the creation of noise abatement zones and enforcement powers relating to them, and section 68 allows the Secretary of State to make regulations limiting the noise caused by plant or machinery or resulting from the use of plant or machinery in factories.[6]

18–004   Under section 71, the Secretary of State may himself prepare and issue approved codes of practice setting out methods for minimising noise, and also approve suitable codes of practice issued by others. The codes do not have any legal status, but compliance or otherwise with them may nevertheless be of relevance in any consideration by a court as to whether particular conduct is reasonable. Codes issued by the Secretary of State under these powers are:[7]

> Code of Practice on Noise from Audible Intruder Alarms 1982
> Code of Practice on Noise from Model Aircraft 1982
> Code of Practice on Noise from Ice-Cream Van Chimes 1982

18–005   In addition the British Standard "Code of Practice for Noise Control on Construction and Demolition Sites" (BS 5228) has been approved.

18–006   Noise in the workplace is the subject of the Noise at Work Regulations 1989,[8] which implement EC Directive 86/188.[9]

18–007   Local authorities are the public bodies principally responsible for controlling noise. The planning system enables them, in their capacity as planning authorities, to take steps to minimise the adverse impact of noise, both in the consideration of individual applications and in the preparation of development plans. Guidance on this is contained in PPG 24 "Planning and Noise". As enforcement authorities they have a variety of statutory powers discussed in this chapter; specific noise nuisances being dealt with by their environmental health officers.[10]

---

[6] Though none have ever been made under this section.
[7] These three codes are the subject of DoE Circular 2/82 (WO 2/82).
[8] S.I. 1989 No. 1790.
[9] [1986] O.J. L137.
[10] The majority of their powers in this respect are usefully summarised in a guidance note used jointly by the Department of the Environment and the Home Office "Control of Noisy Parties" (September 1992).

Abatement of Statutory Nuisances[11]

Each local authority has a duty to inspect its area from time to time   **18–008**
to detect any statutory nuisances that require to be dealt with, and to
investigate complaints of any such nuisance in its area.[12]

Where an authority is satisfied that a statutory nuisance exists, it   **18–009**
must require it to be stopped or reduced by the service of an abatement
notice under section 80 of the E.P.A. In appropriate cases, an
abatement notice may be served before a nuisance has in fact arisen, if
the authority is satisfied that it is likely to occur. (In this respect, local
authorities have more extensive rights to deal with statutory nuisances
than are available, under E.P.A. section 82, to other persons). Evidence
of noise consisting of decibel measurements by an environmental
health officer is admissible and relevant and, at least if uncontested,
may be sufficient in itself, without evidence from persons aggrieved,
to establish the existence of a nuisance.[13] Although circumstances
amounting to a statutory nuisance must be "prejudicial to health or a
nuisance", for the purposes of determining whether that condition is
satisfied in relation to a noise, the only issue is the level of noise
concerned. If that is such as to be a nuisance, it is immaterial that those
affected by the noise are, by virtue of their legal relations with the
person responsible, estopped from taking proceedings in private
nuisance; they may accordingly apply for an order to abate the
statutory nuisance.[14]

Where an appeal is made against an abatement notice, its effect will   **18–010**
be suspended until the appeal has been abandoned or determined if
compliance with the notice would require expenditure on the carrying
out of any works before the hearing of the appeal, or (where the notice
is in respect of a noise nuisance under section 79(1)(g)) the noise
concerned is caused in the course of the performance of some duty
imposed by law on the appellant.[15] However if, as is in practice very
common, the local authority certifies in the abatement notice that the
nuisance concerned is injurious to health or is likely to last for so short
a time that suspension of the notice would make it ineffective in
practice, or that the expenditure that would be incurred before
determination of any appeal would not be disproportionate to the
public benefit from compliance in the meantime, then the effect of the

---

[11] The law relating to statutory nuisances is the subject of Chap. 23. This section outlines
its application to noise nuisances, notwithstanding some inevitable repetition, both
for completeness and since in certain respects noise nuisances are subject to specific
provisions more appropriately covered here.
[12] E.P.A., s.79(1).
[13] *Cooke v. Adatia*, The Times, November 3, 1988.
[14] *A Lambeth Flat Management Ltd. v. Lomas* [1981] 2 All E.R. 280.
[15] The Statutory Nuisance (Appeals) Regulations 1990, reg. 3(1).

notice is not suspended during any appeal.[16] There are no provisions for paying any compensation to the appellant where the appeal succeeds, notwithstanding that he may have been damaged by being required to comply with the terms of the abatement notice.

18–011   If an abatement notice has not been complied with, the local authority may itself abate the nuisance and do whatever may be necessary to secure execution of the notice,[17] whether or not it also takes proceedings for the non-compliance.[18] In exercise of its powers, a local authority may authorise any person to enter any premises at any reasonable time, both to ascertain whether or not a statutory nuisance exists and also for the purpose of taking any action authorised for the purpose of abating a statutory nuisance.[19] However, except in an emergency entry to premises used wholly or mainly for residential purposes cannot be demanded as of right without having given 24 hours prior notice to the occupier.[20]

18–012   An emergency for these purposes is "a case where the person requiring entry has reasonable cause to believe that circumstances exist which are likely to endanger life or health, *and* that immediate entry is necessary to verify the existence of those circumstances or to ascertain their cause and to effect a remedy".[21] The DoE/Home Office guidance note suggests that in the case of a noise nuisance it should be possible to argue that an emergency exists where the noise nuisance is widespread and/or people's health is being prejudiced through sleep disturbance. While this may be so in some circumstances, the second limb of the definition requires immediate entry to be necessary either to find out what is happening or to effect a remedy. These provisions apply to all statutory nuisances and in some cases, for example, temporarily unoccupied residential premises containing abandoned animals or rotting material attracting pests or creating offensive smells, the need for immediate entry may be very real. However, in the difficult case of neighbourhood noise nuisance, it will be all too clear what is the cause, and it may well be impossible to persuade a court that immediate entry is necessary to effect a remedy, except possibly after a series of repeated failures to respond to other legal sanctions.

18–013   Statutory nuisance proceedings may of course also be brought under E.P.A. s.82 by any person aggrieved. In *Southwark LBC v. Ince and*

---

[16] reg. 3(2), (3).

[17] s.81(3).

[18] Maximum penalties for non-compliance with an abatement notice are £5,000 together with a daily fine of up to £500 for so long as the offence continues or, where the offence occurs on industrial, trade or business premises, £20,000. See also paras. 23–029 to 23–031 on non-compliance generally.

[19] E.P.A., Sched. 3, para. 2(1).

[20] Sched. 3, para. 2(2).

[21] Sched. 3, para. 2(7).

another,[22] tenants of a local authority sought an abatement order against it for failing to insulate a block of converted flats adequately against traffic and railway noise. It was held that although the authority had no control over the source of the noise this did not prevent it from being the person "responsible" for the nuisance on account of its act or default. It was nevertheless observed by Woolf L.J. that the order should not place unreasonable burdens on the authority, and should have due regard to its resources. This case, which turned on the authority having carried out the conversion of the flats unsatisfactorily, indicates that similar liability might likewise attach to architects or builders responsible for the specifications of a property of which the occupants suffer from noise nuisance, if it is not reasonably insulated against foreseeable noise.[23]

Seizure of Equipment

The provisions set out above entitle local authorities to enter **18–014** premises to abate a nuisance in appropriate circumstances, if necessary under the authority of a warrant. Seizure of equipment may be the only practicable way of securing immediate abatement of the nuisance—such a step is likely therefore to be justified under E.P.A. s.81(3). Nevertheless, the step can only be taken where an abatement notice has already been served and not complied with. The guidance, "Control of Noisy Parties", recommends that although not strictly essential, local authorities would be well advised to obtain a warrant before seizing equipment. It also points out that if a warrant has to be sought to enter the premises, the issue of seizure can suitably be considered by the justice of the peace at the same time. The seizure of equipment in these circumstances does not in itself entitle the authority to retain it indefinitely, but there is no procedure for either ensuring orderly return of equipment or for its confiscation. Permanent removal of property may be achieved by way of a deprivation order under section 43 of the Powers of Criminal Courts Act 1973. However this only applies to property which has been lawfully seized at the time when the offender was arrested for an offence or at the time a summons for the offence was issued. The breach of an abatement notice is not itself an arrestable offence as defined in section 24 of the Police and Criminal Evidence Act 1984.

[22] I.L.R. April 19, 1989.
[23] See R. Macrory, ENDS Report 172, May 1989.

Injunctions under section 222 of the Local Government Act 1972

18–015   A local authority may seek an injunction to prevent or restrict a nuisance either before or, if it is likely to recur, after its creation, under the extensive powers provided by section 222 of the Local Government Act 1972. These entitle local authorities to act as they see fit in the promotion or protection of the interests of the inhabitants of their areas, including, *inter alia*, to prosecute any legal proceedings. An injunction may therefore be sought under this procedure where a nuisance is feared, and if the authority considers that proceedings for an offence would not afford an adequate remedy; the sanctions that may be imposed for contempt of court resulting from a breach of an injunction being frequently more respected than relatively modest criminal penalties. This is likely to be particularly apt in the circumstances described in the following paragraph. These powers were used in the *Bovis* case to restrain construction site noise.[24]

Licensing of Entertainments

18–016   The performance of music and dancing in public is subject to licensing controls under the Local Government (Miscellaneous Provisions) Act 1982 and (as regards Greater London) the London Government Act 1963. Accordingly, activities that require to be licensed and are not, or which are carried on in breach of conditions attached to the licence, constitute an offence, subject to a fine of up to £20,000 or six months imprisonment on summary conviction. However, outside Greater London, these licensing controls only apply to indoor events and hence public entertainment activities outdoors will not constitute any breach of the 1982 Act. What constitutes "public entertainment" is not defined with precision, but is the subject of guidance in Home Office Circular 95/84. The accepted test is not how many members of the public might participate in the entertainment but whether any reputable member of the public could do so, whether a payment is required or not.[25] Additionally, private events promoted for private gain are also subject to similar licensing controls under the Private Places of Entertainment (Licensing) Act 1967. However these controls only apply where they have been adopted by the relevant local authority in accordance with the procedure laid down in that Act.

---

[24] See paras. 18–028, 18–029.
[25] See the cases cited in paras. 51 to 53 of the DoE/Home Office joint guidance.

Planning Conditions

Extensive powers are also available to planning authorities to **18–017** impose conditions on planning permissions for new development, to impose restrictions on noise emissions from particular equipment or areas, and also to impose limits on the hours at which those activities may take place. Examples of model planning conditions for these purposes are given in Annex 4 to PPG 24 (which replace model conditions 5 to 10 of DoE Circular 1/85). Nevertheless, once a condition has been set as a term of a planning permission, no tightening of that condition can be insisted upon without compensation.

Byelaws

Local authorities have powers under section 235 of the Local **18–018** Government Act 1972 to make byelaws to suppress nuisances, breach of which is a criminal offence. Public use of radios and cassette players, and singing and playing musical instruments in the street, for example, may be controlled in this way.

Construction Site Noise

Construction sites are inherently liable to create noise nuisance. **18–019** While this can be mitigated to some extent by the use of appropriate muffling of equipment, and by requiring the equipment to comply with specific noise emission standards, construction work in built up areas will almost always be inconvenient for neighbours, and often may cause them serious disturbance. Nevertheless, it has been held that if the building work is carried out legitimately and reasonably, with all reasonable and proper steps being taken to ensure that no undue inconvenience is caused to neighbours, then no cause of action in private nuisance will arise at the instance of those neighbours.[26]

Section 60 and 61 of the Control of Pollution Act 1974 ("C.O.P.A.") **18–020** provide for controls to be imposed on those carrying out construction and demolition work and on any others who may be in control of it or otherwise responsible for it, and also for consents to such work being conducted under prescribed conditions. The types of construction work that the provisions apply to are set out in section 60(1) of C.O.P.A., and include demolition and dredging works. Where any construction works are being or going to be carried out, the local authority may serve a "section 60 notice" on the person who appears to be carrying them out or about to do so, and also on any other

---

[26] *Andreae v. Selfridge & Co Ltd.*, C.A. [1938] 1 Ch. 1.

persons that appear to the authority to be responsible for or to have control over the works. Section 60 is essentially permissive, therefore, in contrast with the duty on local authorities to take action in respect of noise amounting to a statutory nuisance. The section 60 notice will impose requirements on how the works are to be carried out, including specifying, for example, the plant or machinery which may or may not be used, the hours of working, and noise levels that may be emitted either generally or at any specified point on the premises or at particular times. The notice must be limited to specific identifiable works in contemplation at the time of the notice, and may not extend to other uncontemplated works at the same premises, for which a fresh notice should be issued if necessary.[27] Where a section 60 notice has been served and is complied with, then that will constitute a defence to any proceedings brought by a local authority under E.P.A., ss.80 or 81, in respect of a statutory nuisance—though not in proceedings brought under E.P.A., s.82, by persons aggrieved by the existence of a statutory nuisance.

18–021   In specifying any particular methods or plant or machinery, the authority must have regard to whether any other methods, plant or machinery would be substantially as effective in minimising noise and more acceptable to those subject to the requirements of the notice.[28] The authority must also have regard to the relevant provisions of any code of practice that may have been issued and approved under section 71 of C.O.P.A. The current code in this connection is that approved under the Control of Noise (Code of Practice for Construction and Open Sites) Order 1987,[29] i.e., British Standard BS 5228. The authority must further have regard to the need for ensuring that best practicable means are employed to minimise noise. For the meaning of this term, see paragraphs 23–034, 23–035.[30] Finally, the authority must, in exercising its powers under section 60 have regard to the need to protect any persons in the locality of the construction site from the effects of noise.[31] An HSE publication "Noise in Construction" provides guidance for workers and employers on limiting the effects of noise in the construction industry.

18–022   Any person served with a section 60 notice may appeal against it within 21 days from the date of service. The grounds of appeal and the applicable procedure are contained in the Control of Noise (Appeals)

[27] *Walter Lilly & Co Ltd v. Westminster City Council, The Times,* March 1, 1994.
[28] s.60(4)(c).
[29] S.I. 1987 No. 1730.
[30] For the purposes of these sections in C.O.P.A., the relevant definition of best practicable means appears in C.O.P.A., s.72. This definition is to all intents and purposes the same as that contained in E.P.A., s.79(9), which applies to the statutory nuisance provisions in the E.P.A.
[31] s.60(4).

Regulations 1975[32] ("the Appeals Regulations"). The grounds of appeal may include any of the following:[33]

(a) Section 60 does not justify the service of the notice;

(b) There has been some informality, defect or error in the notice;

(c) The authority has refused unreasonably to accept compliance with alternative requirements, or that the requirements with the notice are otherwise unreasonable in character or extent, or are unnecessary;

(d) The time or times given for compliance with the notice is or are not reasonably sufficient;

(e) Notice should not have been served the on appellant but on someone else instead who is carrying out or going to carry out the works or who is responsible for or who has control over the carrying out of the works;

(f) The notice might lawfully have been served not only on the appellant but also on someone else falling with category (e) above, and it would have been equitable for it to have been served on this other person;

(g) The authority has not had regard to some or all of the requirements of section 60(4) (*i.e.* the Code of Practice, the use of best practicable means, the specifying of other methods plant or machinery that is substantially as effective, and the need to protect persons in the locality).

Where an appeal is based on ground (e) or (f), the appellant must **18–023** serve a copy of his appeal on the other person referred to. Appeals are made to the local magistrates' court, who may quash the notice the subject of the appeal, vary it or dismiss the appeal.

Where an appeal is made against a section 60 notice, its effect will be **18–024** suspended until the appeal has been abandoned or determined either if the noise concerned is caused in the course of the performance of some duty imposed by law on the appellant, or if compliance with the notice would require expenditure on the carrying out of any works before the hearing of the appeal.[34] Nevertheless, if in the opinion of the local authority the noise concerned is injurious to health or is likely to last for so short a time that suspension of the notice would make it ineffective in practice, or if the authority considers that the expenditure that would be incurred before determination of any appeal would not be disproportionate to the public benefit from compliance in the

[32] S.I. 1975 No. 2116.
[33] reg. 5.
[34] The Control of Noise (Appeals) Regulations 1975, reg. 10(1).

887

meantime, the notice may (and in practice nearly always does) include a statement that it is to have effect notwithstanding any appeal.[35] There are no provisions for paying any compensation to the appellant where the appeal succeeds, notwithstanding that he may have been damaged by being required to comply with the terms of the notice.

18–025   It was held in *Johnsons News of London Limited v. Ealing London Borough Council*[36] (which was concerned with an action for statutory nuisance, but the reasoning of the case is equally applicable to a section 60 notice), that since the statutory provision in issue was administrative and not criminal in nature, the objective of the court should be to seek to secure appropriate conduct and was not to punish wrong-doing. Accordingly, the fact that the service of the notice may have been fully justified as at the date of service is therefore not material, if the appellant has since taken suitable measures to respond to it. Hence, on the hearing of an appeal against a section 60 notice, the magistrates' court should confine its consideration to the situation, including the likelihood of recurrence of any noise nuisance, as it exists at the time of the hearing of the appeal.

18–026   The fact that a local authority may have served a notice under section 60 does not create a defence against proceedings for an injunction to restrain a nuisance, notwithstanding compliance with the conditions of the section 60 notice. In *Lloyds Bank v. Guardian Assurance plc and another*,[37] the plaintiff obtained an injunction against the defendants which prohibited the use of certain drills and other tools during working hours on weekdays. At substantially the same time, the local authority served a section 60 notice prohibiting work within time limits that were somewhat narrower. On appeal against the injunction, the Court of Appeal held that the jurisdiction of the court in the tort proceedings were not ousted by section 60. In the case in point, the difference between the terms of the injunction and the section 60 notice were comparatively narrow, but in principle a court might impose a prohibition on working a construction site at night time so as to protect local residents, while the local authority might see fit, as in the case just referred to, to prohibit operations during working hours, so as to protect local business interests. In such a situation, it would appear that both sets of controls might operate simultaneously, effectively making it impossible to carry out any construction work at all. This situation could also arise where a person has sought relief for a statutory nuisance under E.P.A., section 82, where the existence of a section 60 notice is not relevant.

---

[35] reg. 10(2).
[36] *The Times*, July 26, 1989; also *Coventry City Corporation v. Doyle* [1981] 1 W.L.R. 1325.
[37] C.A., October 17, 1986, unreported.

Breach of the requirements of a section 60 notice is an offence that is   **18–027**
triable summarily, and subject to a maximum fine of £5,000 with a
possible further daily fine in respect of each day on which the offence
continues after the conviction.[38] The costs to a construction company
in not meeting a contractual deadline or, for that matter, in remaining
any longer on a site than is absolutely necessary, particularly when
there is other work to be done, are often many times the size of the fine
that it may be subject to for not complying with a section 60 notice
served on it, so that the deterrent effect of a fine on the company may
be largely lost.

In *City of London Corporation v. Bovis Construction Ltd*,[39] a section 60   **18–028**
notice had been served requiring operations causing noise outside the
boundaries of the construction site to be limited to 8.00 a.m. to 6.00
p.m. on weekdays, 8.00 a.m. to 1.00 p.m. on Saturdays, with no such
operations being permitted on Sundays and bank holidays. (Minor
exceptions were permitted of no direct relevance to the case.)
Informations were laid against the contractors for contravention of the
section 60 notice without reasonable excuse. The hearing was
adjourned on several occasions, and meanwhile the contractors
continued to contravene the terms of the notice. The local authority
issued a writ for an injunction under section 222 of the Local
Government Act 1972, and an interlocutory injunction was granted.
The contractors appealed on the ground that an injunction should not
be granted to prevent a breach of the criminal law unless it had been
established both that the person restrained not only had committed an
offence but also was deliberately and flagrantly flouting the law, and
that the criminal law provided an inadequate remedy. The grounds of
the appeal were based on speeches by Lord Templeman and Lord
Fraser of Tullybelton in *Stoke-on-Trent City Council v. B & Q Retail
Limited*,[40] which was concerned with unlawful Sunday trading. The
Court of Appeal held unanimously that civil proceedings for an
injunction could be resorted to in other circumstances than those
contended for by the contractors. Bingham L.J. held that the guiding
principles must be:

(i)   that the jurisdiction to grant an injunction is to be invoked
      and exercised exceptionally and with great caution;
(ii) there must certainly be something more than mere infringe-
      ment of the criminal law before the assistance of civil
      proceedings can be invoked and accorded for the protection
      or promotion of the interests of the inhabitants of the area;

---

[38] s.74(1).
[39] C.A., [1992] 3 All E.R. 697.
[40] [1984] A.C. 754 at 775 and 767; [1984] 2 All E.R. 332 at 341, 342 and 335, respectively.

(iii) the essential foundation for the exercise of the court's discretion to grant an injunction is not that the offender is deliberately and fragrantly flouting the law, but the need to draw the inference that the defendant's unlawful operations will continue unless and until effectively restrained by the law, and that nothing short of an injunction will be effective to restrain them.[41]

18–029 Applying those principles he held that the original grant of an injunction was justified and that the appeal should fail.

18–030 To enable contractors to establish in advance with the relevant local authority working hours and other conditions of operation that, if complied with, will avoid the service of any section 60 notices, section 61 entitles any person who intends to carry out construction works to apply to the local authority for a consent ("a section 61 consent"). An application for the consent must be made at the same time as or after the request for Building Regulations approval and must particularise the works to be undertaken, the methods that will be used, and also the steps that will be taken to minimise noise resulting from the construction works. The local authority must give its consent to the application if it considers that if the works are carried out in accordance with it it would not serve a section 60 notice. In granting the consent, the authority may attach conditions to it, it may limit or qualify the consent to allow for any changes in circumstances, and it may limit the duration of the consent. Anyone who knowingly carries out the works, or permits them to be carried out, in contravention of any conditions attached to a consent commits an offence. Provided however the consent and its conditions are complied with, it constitutes a defence under any proceedings for breach of a section 60 notice, and also any proceedings brought by a local authority under E.P.A. sections 80 or 81, in respect of an alleged statutory nuisance.

18–031 Applications for a section 61 consent should be dealt with within 28 days from receipt of the relevant application. Where the authority either does not give its consent within that period, or grants a consent subject to conditions that the applicant considers unacceptable, the applicant may appeal within 21 days from the end of the 28 day period. Appeals are subject to the provisions of regulation 6 of the Control of Noise (Appeals) Regulations 1975,[42] and may be based on any of the following grounds:

(a) any condition attached to the consent is not justified under section 61;

[41] [1992] 3 All E.R. at 714 g-j.
[42] S.I. 1975 No. 2116.

(b)   there has been some informality, defect or error in or in connection with the consent;

(c)   the requirements of any relevant condition are unreasonable in character or extent or are unnecessary;

(d)   the time or times within which the requirements of any condition are to be complied with is one not reasonably sufficient.

A practical difficulty in setting conditions on section 61 consents, in so far as these relate to noise levels, is the means by which, and where, these should be measured. The measurement of noise is a technically highly complex subject; where the extent of a condition is in fact uncertain, then an appeal will almost certainly succeed on the grounds that the requirements of the condition are unreasonable in character or extent.   **18–032**

Noise in Streets

A loudspeaker may only be operated in a street to the extent permitted by section 62 of C.O.P.A., as amended by section 7 of the Noise and Statutory Nuisance Act 1993. For this purpose "street" means a highway and any other road, footway, square or court which is for the time being open to the public.[43] Subject to exceptions set out in sections 62(2), (3) and (3A), loudspeakers may not be used for any purpose between 9.00 p.m. and 8.00 a.m.,[44] nor at any other time for the purpose of advertising any entertainment, trade or business. Nevertheless, a loudspeaker can be used between noon and 7.00 p.m. where it is fixed to a vehicle used for conveying perishable commodities and is solely operated to inform the public (otherwise than by means of words) that the commodity is on sale from the vehicle, and provided it is operated so as not to give reasonable cause for annoyance. This exemption is principally designed to allow the use of chimes on ice-cream vans. Detailed guidance on the operation of such chimes is contained in the "Code of Practice on Noise from Ice-Cream Van Chimes etc." (1982) issued by the Secretary of State under C.O.P.A., s.71.[45] (See paragraph 18–004 on other Codes of Practice under section 71.)   **18–033**

---

[43] s.62(1).

[44] s. 62(1)(a). These times may be amended by the Secretary of State by order under s. 62(1A) but not so as to include any time between 9.00 p.m. and 8.00 a.m.

[45] Approval for its issue being given under the Control Of Noise (Code of Practice on Noise from Ice-Cream Van Chimes etc.) Order 1981, S.I. 1981 No. 1828.

18–034   Exemptions from the general prohibitions of section 62(1) allow public authorities, including the police, fire brigade and ambulance services, to operate without this restraint, and also anyone else in case of emergency.[46] Car radios are also exempted, provided they are "so operated as not to give reasonable cause for annoyance to persons in the vicinity".

18–035   A number of additional controls over noise in the street have been introduced by the Noise and Statutory Nuisance Act 1993.[47] This generally tightens the controls, but at the same time makes them more flexible and capable of modification at the discretion of the local authority. Accordingly local authority consent may be given to any use of a loudspeaker that would otherwise be in contravention of section 62(1) of C.O.P.A., provided it is not for the purpose of advertising any entertainment, trade or business. This additional flexibility is only available to local authorities that have passed a resolution to the effect that Schedule 2 to the Act is to apply to its area. Any such resolution must be published in a local newspaper, and once the provisions of the Schedule have come into effect[48] any person may apply for a consent; the authority must determine any such application within 21 days.

18–036   Under E.P.A., s.79(1)(g) noise is only a statutory nuisance where it is emitted from premises. The Noise and Statutory Nuisance Act has created a further statutory nuisance,[49] namely "noise that is prejudicial to health or a nuisance and is emitted from or caused by a vehicle, machinery or equipment in a street". Action may consequently be taken against noise from, for example, car radios, diesel generators and parked refrigerator vehicles in the street.[50] Equipment is defined as including a musical instrument, and "street" is given the same meaning as it has in C.O.P.A., s.62(1).[51] The "person responsible", who may be made the subject of statutory nuisance proceedings in relation to noise in a street, is to include, in relation to a vehicle, the person in whose name it is registered and also any other person who is for the time being its driver, and in relation to machinery or equipment, any person who is for the time being the operator of it. The Act includes various consequential provisions for amending Part III of E.P.A. to provide for this additional statutory nuisance, including a requirement to serve the abatement notice by fixing it on the vehicle,

---

[46] s.62(2).
[47] With effect from January 5, 1994.
[48] Which must be at least one month after the date of resolution, s.8(2).
[49] As s.79(1)(ga), which came into effect on January 5, 1994.
[50] It was originally intended to cover also noisy political and other demonstrations, but these are now specifically excluded from being a statutory nuisance by E.P.A., s.79(6A)(c), inserted by s.2(3) of the 1993 Act.
[51] Inserted into E.P.A., s.79(7) by the 1993 Act, s.2(4).

machinery or equipment concerned where the person responsible for it cannot be found, or where the local authority in any event determines that this provision shall apply.[52] However, where a notice is served in this way, and the person can be found and served with a copy within one hour, it must also be served on him.[53] This requirement seems likely to discourage severely any significant use of this feature of the new law. Corresponding amendments are made to Part III of C.O.P.A. to give effect to the new legislation in Scotland.

Audible Intruder Alarms

Currently the noise created by burglar alarms is, outside London,   18–037
controlled by the use of the standard nuisance abatement procedures of the E.P.A., described in paragraphs 18–008 to 18–013. In addition there is the 1982 "Code of Practice on Noise from Audible Intruder Alarms", covering their installation and operation (including a suggestion that all such alarms should have a 20-minute cut-out). British Standard BS 4737 is the principal standard for these alarms; it includes a requirement to comply with the Code of Practice. Section 9 of the Noise and Statutory Nuisance Act (which has yet to be brought into force) enables local authorities to impose legally enforceable controls over burglar alarms. Schedule 3 to the Act sets out detailed provisions that they may adopt by resolution. These mirror very closely those of section 23 of the London Local Authorities Act 1991, which similarly allows London Borough Councils to adopt a set of rules that are largely based on the 1982 Code of Practice. Where the controls are adopted, "an audible intruder alarm on or in any premises"[54] may be required to comply with prescribed requirements, and operation of the alarm will be prohibited unless, in addition, the police have been notified of details of current key-holders and the local authority has been informed of the address of the relevant police station having this information. "Key-holders" is defined to mean either *two* persons other than the occupier of the premises, each of whom holds sufficient keys to obtain access, or else a company holding sufficient keys whose business consists of or includes holding keys for the occupiers of premises. An officer of the local authority may enter premises where an alarm has been operating for more than one hour and is giving reasonable cause for annoyance to those in the neighbourhood.

[52] s.80A(2).
[53] s.80A(3).
[54] Thus excluding car alarms from these controls.

However he may not enter the premises by force without a magistrate's warrant; in seeking issue of a warrant, it must be shown, among other things, that it has not been possible to get access to the premises by contacting current key-holders.

18–038   Existing burglar alarms will also have to comply with the prescribed requirements (typically the inclusion of a cut-off after a limited period such as twenty minutes). However whereas all the other provisions of Schedule 3 may come into force after four months or more from the date of the relevant resolution, the requirement that existing alarms comply with prescribed requirements cannot be imposed until at least nine months from the date of the resolution.

Noise Abatement Zones

18–039   The creation of noise abatement zones and procedures for securing compliance with them are the subject of sections 63 to 67 of C.O.P.A.[55] These provisions allow a local authority to designate by order the whole or any part of its area as a noise abatement zone, specifying in the order the classes of premises to which the noise abatement controls are to apply that will then operate within the zone. Where an order has been made, the then current levels of the noise from the specified classes of premises in the zone must be measured. These noise measurements are entered in a register of noise levels, and will form the reference levels against which noise from the same premises will be judged thereafter. The measurement and registration of noise levels are subject to the Control of Noise (Measurement and Registers) Regulations 1976.[56]

18–040   The procedure for designating a noise abatement zone is set out in Schedule 1 to C.O.P.A. Extensive detailed guidance on the use of the noise abatement zone powers under C.O.P.A. is set out in Appendix 2 to DoE Circular 2/76 (WO 3/76) "Control of Pollution Act 1974. Implementation of Part III—Noise". This advises that classes of premises should be specified broadly by function, e.g. industrial premises, places of entertainment of assembly, transport installations, etc., rather than by the particular trade or process that they may be carrying on. The guidance firmly recommends against classifying

---

[55] A survey conducted for the Department of the Environment in 1993 concluded that noise abatement zones had failed to meet their objectives and had fallen into virtual disuse. This followed a report by the Noise Review Working Party in 1990 that they were proving difficult to operate. The system is nevertheless in place and being operated by a few local authorities and therefore requires some description here.

[56] S.I. 1976 No. 37.

domestic premises since the numbers involved would make enforce-ment impracticable, and in any event control from domestic premises is more suitably dealt with as a statutory nuisance (or indeed in civil proceedings).

It is an offence to emit noise exceeding the noise level as recorded in the register[57] except with the local authority's consent, or to breach any condition attached to a consent. This consent may be given, for example, to allow excess noise to be made at certain times of day, possibly with a corresponding reduction at other times, and also to provide for circumstances where increased noise is unavoidable, for example where construction or demolition work is taking place. (Controls over the noise from construction and demolition work will be most appropriately controlled under sections 60 and 61, but such operations may nevertheless result in the registered noise levels being exceeded, even though the source of noise is quite different from that as measured for registration.) The grant of a consent will, if its terms are complied with, provide a defence in proceedings brought by a local authority for a statutory nuisance under E.P.A., s.79(1)(g), relating to noise; this defence is not available however in proceedings for a statutory nuisance abatement order under E.P.A., s.82 (or, in Scotland, under C.O.P.A., s.59).[58]

18–041

These provisions allow noise levels to be prevented from increasing, as may occur where the intensity of an activity increases as a business develops. An important further power is given[59] to local authorities to reduce existing noise levels by means of noise reduction notices. A noise reduction notice may be served on the person responsible for any noise (being the person to whose act, default or sufferance the noise is attributable[60]) where the level of noise from any premises is in fact unacceptable, even though within the registered limits, if a reduction in that level is practicable at reasonable cost, and would afford a public benefit.[61] The effect of a noise reduction notice is as though the level as recorded in the register has been reduced to the prescribed figure, so that after it takes effect, which will be at least six months from the date of service of the notice,[62] it will be an offence to exceed the reduced noise level without reasonable exercise except with consent.[63] However it is a defence to prove that the best

18–042

---

[57] s.65(1).
[58] E.P.A., s.80(9), C.O.P.A., s.65(8).
[59] By s.66.
[60] s.73(1).
[61] s.66(1).
[62] s.61(3).
[63] s.66(8).

practicable means had been used for preventing, or for counteracting the effect of, the noise.[64]

18–043   Appeals may be made against an initial entry in a noise level register, against a refusal to allow a registered noise level to be exceeded, against a noise reduction notice, and against a determination of the noise level from a new or converted building. Appeals against a noise reduction notice are made to the magistrates' court; all other appeals are made to the Secretary of State. These latter will normally be dealt with in writing, though a public local inquiry can be held if thought appropriate.

18–044   Where a new building is constructed, or an old one converted, that will perform a function bringing it within the classified premises of an existing noise abatement zone, it will also be covered by the relevant order, irrespective of whether or not the activities carried on in it will in fact be noisy. The local authority must determine what level of noise emanating from the premises would be acceptable, and will record that level in the noise level register. It may take this action either on its own initiative or on the application of the owner or occupier of the premises or of any other person who is negotiating to acquire an interest in them. It is in practice essential for whoever will be responsible for such premises to ensure that a satisfactory noise level is established, since if no action is taken to do this, or if an application to the authority for a level to be set is not determined, the person responsible for the building will be liable to have served on him a noise reduction notice, and he will not in those circumstances be entitled to rely on the best practicable means defence of section 66(9). Further, the right to serve such a notice is not dependent (as it is under section 66(1)(b)) on a reduction in noise level being practicable at reasonable cost. These relatively draconian measures are most likely to be applied where a new building has been erected or an old one converted in total disregard of the character of a noise abatement zone.

18–045   Where an appeal is made against a noise reduction notice, its effect will be suspended until the appeal has been abandoned or determined either if the noise concerned is caused in the course of the performance of some duty imposed by law on the appellant, or if compliance with the notice would require expenditure on the carrying out of any works before the hearing of the appeal. Nevertheless, if in the opinion of the local authority the noise concerned is injurious to health or is likely to last for so short a time that suspension of the notice would make it ineffective in practice, or if the authority considers that the expenditure that would be incurred before determination of any appeal would not be disproportionate to the public benefit from

[64] s.66(9).

compliance in the meantime, the notice may include a statement that it is to have effect notwithstanding any appeal. There are no provisions for paying any compensation to the appellant where the appeal succeeds, notwithstanding that he may have been damaged by being required to comply with the notice.

Controls over Equipment and Commercial/ Industrial Activities

There are numerous controls over the design and construction of **18–046** certain equipment to limit noise emissions, in particular motor vehicles, aircraft, construction plant and equipment, industrial machinery, household appliances and lawnmowers, all of which are based on EC directives. The requirements for industrial machines are based on health and safety considerations for operators.[65] The EC Directives on construction plant and equipment are designed as much for the protection of construction workers as for the benefit of the general public.[66] Further amendments will be made to the permitted noise levels of the earth-moving machinery referred to in Table 18/I, if a proposed amending directive issued by the Commission[67] is adopted. The principal items of EC legislation and the implementing UK regulations, other than those relating to motor vehicles and aircraft, are set out in this Table.

TABLE 18/I

	S.I.	EC Directive
Construction Plant and Equipment		
Construction Plant and Equipment (Harmonisation of Noise Emission Standards) Regulations 1985	1985 No. 1968	
Compressors		84/533, 85/406
Welding generators		84/535, 85/407
Power generators		84/536, 85/408
Hand held concrete breakers and picks		84/537, 85/409

---

[65] Dir. 89/392, Annex I.
[66] The controls over construction site noise generally are discussed in paras. 18–019 to 18–032 above.
[67] [1993] O.J. C157.

Construction Plant and Equipment (Harmonisation of Noise Emission Standards) (Amendment) Regulations 1989	1989 No. 1127	
Tower cranes		84/534, 87/405
Construction Plant and Equipment (Harmonisation of Noise Emission Standards) Regulations 1988	1988 No. 361	84/532
Construction Plant and Equipment (Harmonisation of Noise Emission Standards) (Amendment) Regulations 1992	1992 No. 488	
Excavators, dozers, loaders		86/662, 89/514
Household appliances		
Household Appliances (Noise Emission) Regulations 1990	1990 No. 161	86/594
Household Appliances (Noise Emission) (Amendment) Regulations 1994	1994 No. 1386	
Lawnmowers		
Lawnmowers (Harmonisation of Noise Emission Standards) Regulations 1992	1992 No. 168	
Rotary mowers		84/538, 87/252
Cylinder mowers		84/538, 88/180
Large cylinder mowers (120 cm. width)		84/538, 88/181

Motor Vehicles

18–048   There are two sets of controls over motor vehicles of relevance: these are made under the Road Traffic Act 1988 and consist of "construction and use" regulations, and type approval schemes, which require any manufacturer, before marketing a new type of vehicle in the United Kingdom, to have a sample tested by the Department of Transport. Regulations for these purposes were made under the legislation repealed by the 1988 Act, in particular the Road Vehicles (Construction and Use) Regulations 1986[67A] as amended, and these now have effect as though made under section 41 of that Act in relation to construction and use, and under section 61 in relation to type approvals. The permissible noise limits for motor vehicles have been progressively reduced. The basic EC Directive 70/157[68] has been twice amended and the current noise levels are those set by Directive

[67A] S.I. 1986 No. 1078.
[68] [1970] O.J. L42.

898

84/424[69] and the UK regulations that implement it. Directive 92/97[70] lowers all the maximum permitted levels, but these only become mandatory with effect from October 1, 1995 in respect of the vehicle certification procedures, and from 1st October 1996 for the entry into service of any vehicle in the EC (thus giving 12 months to sell off old stock). The permissible sound levels and exhaust systems of motorcycles are covered by Directive 78/1015,[71] as last amended by Directive 89/235[72] which took effect on October 1, 1989.

The applicability of the EC directives was called in question in **18–049** *Freight Transport Association Limited and others v. London Boroughs Transport Committee*,[73] in which conditions laid down by the Greater London Council were challenged, whereby heavy goods vehicles were banned from using residential streets in Greater London at night time, unless especially permitted to do so. The grant of special permits included a condition that vehicles over 16.5 tonnes which were capable of being fitted with an air brake noise suppressor must have one. On judicial review, the condition was quashed on the ground that it required technical features of the vehicles beyond those demanded by the relevant EC directives. Though upheld in the Court of Appeal, the decision was reversed by the House of Lords, on the grounds that the condition did not seek to determine the construction requirements of the vehicles, but was merely concerned with the proper regulation of local traffic. Given that the necessary suppressor only cost some £30, the condition could not be said to interfere with the operation of the single market. While this decision must surely be right, it does not constitute justification for widespread regulation of traffic throughout the country by reference to features of vehicle construction, if this were to present unreasonable obstacles to the use of the vehicles concerned.

Aircraft

Most types of aircraft[74] may only take-off or land in the UK if they **18–050** possess a noise certificate appropriate to its aircraft type. The standards that must be met to obtain a noise certificate are set out in the Air Navigation Noise Certification Order 1990[75] made under the

---

[69] [1984] O.J. L238.
[70] [1992] O.J. L371.
[71] [1978] O.J. L349.
[72] [1989] O.J. L98.
[73] [1991] 3 All E.R. 915; [1991] 1 W.L.R. 828.
[74] The principal exception being those with a take-off distance at maximum authorised weight under standard conditions of not more than 610 metres.
[75] S.I. 1990 No. 1514.

Civil Aviation Act 1982 which implements EC Directive 80/51 as amended by Directive 83/206[76] and Directive 89/629.[77]

18–051   Restrictions on the movement of aircraft, and particularly night landings at airports, are ultimately based on international agreements under the jurisdiction of the International Civil Aviation Organisation (the "ICAO"). These agreements are reflected in EC Directive 92/14, and the Aeroplane Noise (Limitation on Operation of Aeroplanes) Regulations 1993.[78] A consultation paper "Control of Aircraft Noise" was issued in August 1991, and conclusions following the consultation process were announced by the Department of Transport in March 1993. The principal proposal is for new primary legislation that will give those controlling aerodromes powers to prepare noise amelioration schemes and to penalise aircraft operators who do not comply with them. These schemes will replace the current less formal noise control arrangements. Where appropriate, the Secretary of State will be entitled to require an aerodrome to prepare a noise amelioration scheme. Local authorities are to have powers to ensure that those in control of aerodromes operate these schemes in an effective manner; the enforcement powers will correspond to those under a planning legislation and include the issue of notices requiring compliance with the scheme. These powers are to be applicable to all aerodromes from the very largest down to small sites used by helicopters.

18–052   Controls over the height at which aircraft may fly are contained in the Rules of the Air Regulations 1991,[79] rule 5 of which stipulates that, subject to a number of exceptions, aircraft should not fly at below 1500 feet over heavily populated areas or below 500 feet elsewhere, apart from when taking off or landing. No action, either in nuisance or in trespass, may ordinarily be taken in respect of the noise caused by an aircraft in flight, if (i) it is at a height above the ground which, having regard to wind, weather and all the circumstances of the case is reasonable, so long as the provisions of any relevant Air Navigation Order, and any orders under section 62[80] have been duly complied with, and (ii) the aircraft is not committing the offence of dangerous flying under section 81 of the Civil Aviation Act 1982.[81] In an appropriate case compensation is however payable under the Land Compensation Act 1973[82] where the value of an interest in land has been adversely affected by the noise from aircraft.

---

[76] [1980] O.J. L18; [1983] O.J. L117.
[77] [1989] O.J. L363.
[78] S.I. 1993 No. 1409, amended by S.I. 1994 No. 1734.
[79] S.I. 1991 No. 2437, made under art. 69 of the Air Navigation Order 1989, S.I. 1989 No. 2004, which is in turn made under the Civil Aviation Act 1982, ss.60, 61.
[80] Which provides for control of aviation in time of war or great national emergency.
[81] Civil Aviation Act 1982, s.76(1).
[82] s.1.

The effect of this exclusion of liability was challenged in *Powell and*   **18–053**
Rayner v. United Kingdom in the European Court of Human Rights.[83]
The applicants relied on Articles 6(1), 8 and 13 of the Convention of
Human Rights, which provide, *inter alia*, that everyone has the right to
respect for his private life and his home and that everyone whose
rights under the Convention are violated are to have an effective
remedy before a national authority. The applicants lived in the
neighbourhood of Heathrow Airport, and their respective properties
were directly under flight paths from the airport. However the court
dismissed the claims. While Article 8, providing for everyone to have
the right to respect for his private life and his home was a material
provision, regard had to be had to the fair balance that needed to be
struck between the competing interests of the individual and of the
community as whole. In view of the provisions of Article 8(2), which
allow for this balance to be struck, and the fact that relevant noise
abatement measures were observed at Heathrow, the claim could not
be sustained. Since there was no basis for a claim under Article 8, the
exclusion of access to the courts did not provide any breach of the
other provisions relied on, the court noting that the United Kingdom
Government had proceeded on the view that the problems posed by
aircraft noise were better dealt with by taking and enforcing specific
regulatory measures to minimise these, than to allow private claims in
nuisance.

[83] Case No. 3/1989/163/219; *The Times*, February 22, 1990.

Chapter 19

LITTER

The amount of litter on Britain's streets and public places became **19–001** the subject of increasing public comment and complaint during the 1980s. Street cleaning was an area in which local authorities had found it politically convenient to make economies, but trends in packaging and towards the use of disposable goods also aggravated the amount of litter created. Consequently, Part IV of the Environmental Protection Act 1990 was devoted to this issue, which addresses the problem in a variety of ways:

(1) It is an offence to deposit litter in any public open place and in a number of other places to which the public generally has access (sections 87, 88);

(2) An express duty is laid on local authorities and several other bodies, including occupiers of land within "litter control areas" to keep their land clear of litter and refuse. In addition, local authorities and the Secretary of State are required to keep clean the roads for which they are responsible. This duty may be enforced in a manner akin to statutory nuisances by way of "litter abatement notices" and "litter abatement orders" (sections 89 to 92);

(3) Local authorities may issue "street litter control notices" imposing requirements on occupiers of certain premises as to the clearing of litter or refuse from specified areas adjacent to those premises (sections 93, 94);

(4) Special provisions are made for dealing with abandoned shopping and luggage trolleys, including charging for their return to those claiming to own them (section 99 and Schedule 4).

The legislation is administered by what are referred to as "principal **19–002** litter authorities", namely, in England and Wales, county, district and London borough councils, the Common Council of the City of London and the Council of Isles of Scilly, and, in Scotland, regional and district or islands councils and joint boards.[1] The "Tidy Britain Group", a registered charity part-funded by the government, is recognised by it as its national agency for litter abatement. It forms part of the Litter Advisory Group, which advises the government in relation to the legislation on litter, and how well it is working.

Offences

19–003   Section 87 makes it an offence to throw down, drop or otherwise deposit in, into or from any place to which the section applies, and to leave it there, anything whatsoever in such circumstances as to cause, or contribute to, or tend to lead to, the defacement by litter of any such place. The section applies to a wide variety of places,[2] being any public open place,[3] and the following, in so far as they are not public open places:

- most roads and highways;
- land belonging to principal litter authorities that is open to the air, and under their direct control (including land designated as a litter control area under section 90[4]), to which the public are entitled or permitted to have access with or without payment, excluding land below mean high water springs.[5] Land is regarded as "open to the air", even though covered, if it is open on at least one side,[6] e.g. bus stations;
- "Crown land"[7] that is open to the air and to which the public are entitled or permitted to have access with or without payment, excluding land below mean high water springs;
- Land of a variety of statutory undertakers, in fact transport undertakings, that is under their direct control, again being land to which the public are entitled or permitted to have access with or without payment, and additionally certain types of "operational land" of these undertakings to which the public have no right or permission to have access, even with payment, which is within 100 metres of a railway station

---

[1] As defined in s.235(1) of the Local Government (Scotland) Act 1973. s.86(2).
[2] Set out in s.87(3).
[3] Defined in s.87(4) as being any place in the open air to which the public are entitled or permitted to have access without payment, including any covered place open to the air on at least one side and available for public use.
[4] s.86(12).
[5] By virtue of the Litter (Relevant Land of Principal Litter Authorities and Relevant Crown Land) Order 1991 (S.I. 1991 No. 476).
[6] s.86(4), (13).
[7] Defined in s.86(5).

platform in an urban area (as defined), including an embankment, cutting or siding, a viaduct or bridge, and the land within the rails or on the track sides, other than in a tunnel.[8] The transport undertakings affected consist of any person authorised by any enactment to carry on railway, light railway, tramway, road transport, canal, inland navigation, dock, harbour or pier undertakings, and also any relevant airport operator;[9]

— Land of a variety of educational institutions that is open to the air and under their direct control or that of the education authority responsible for its management. The institutions are all those universities and schools listed in section 98(2) and (3), with the sole exception of certain grant-aided schools in Scotland.[10]

The wording of the offence requires that the act that creates the litter **19–004** must take place on land to which the section applies, as well as in fact causing or contributing to litter on such land. Accordingly dropping litter anywhere else, even though it subsequently blows into, *e.g.* a public space, is not an offence under this section. Additionally, it is not an offence where the littering was authorised by law or done with the consent of the owner, occupier or other person or authority in control of the place concerned.

Enforcement may be by way of summary proceedings, where the **19–005** offence is subject to a fine not exceeding £2500.[11] However, an alternative system of fixed penalty notices is provided for by section 88 and The Litter (Fixed Penalty Notices) Order 1991.[12] The effect of these provisions is that an authorised officer of a litter authority may serve a fixed penalty notice on a person that he has reason to believe has committed an offence under section 87 in his authority's area. The form of notice is scheduled to the Fixed Penalty Notices Order; this repeats the statutory provisions to the effect that no proceedings for the offence will be instituted for 14 days following the date of the notice, and that there will be no conviction of that offence if the fixed penalty, which is set at £10,[13] is paid within that period. Litter authorities for this purpose are district and London borough councils, the Common Council of the City of London and the council of The

---

[8] s.86(6) and The Litter (Statutory Undertakers) (Designation and Relevant Land) Order 1991 (S.I. 1991 No. 1043 as amended by S.I. 1992 No. 406).
[9] As defined in the Airports Act 1986.
[10] By virtue of the Litter Designated Educational Institutions) Order 1991 (S.I. 1991 No. 561).
[11] s.87(5).
[12] S.I. 1991 No. 111.
[13] s.88(6).

Isles of Scilly, and, in Scotland, a district or island council; also any National Park Committee, any Park Board for any area in a National Park and the Broads Authority. Additionally, the Secretary of State may designate as the litter authority for any specific area the county council or, in Scotland, the regional council or joint board.

Litter Clearance Duties

19–006   A duty is laid on the authorities and other bodies whose land is mentioned in paragraph 19–003 to ensure that their land is, so far as practicable, kept clear of litter and refuse.[14] This duty also applies to local authorities in relation to highways and roads for which they are responsible, and to the Secretary of State as respects any trunk road which is a special road, and any relevant highway or relevant road for which he is responsible.[15]

19–007   Unlike the offence under section 87, which is concerned solely with litter, the clearance duty applies to both litter and refuse. By the Litter (Animal Droppings) Order 1991,[16] refuse is to be taken to include dog faeces on a wide variety of types of land, essentially that used by the public or to which it has access, not being heath or woodland nor used for the grazing of animals.

19–008   There is a further duty laid on every local authority and on the Secretary of State, as regards the highways and roads for which they are respectively responsible, to ensure that these highways and roads are, so far as practicable, kept clean.[17] The Secretary of State has power to transfer from local authorities their responsibilities in respect of specified roads to the highway or roads authority, which then becomes for all purposes of Part IV of the E.P.A. the responsible authority.[18] When cleaning roads, local authorities are required to place and maintain appropriate warning signs and barriers and to comply with any directions given to it by the appropriate highway or roads authority as regards these and also as regards when clearing or cleaning may not be done.

---

[14] s.89(1).

[15] "Highway", "special road", "trunk road", and "public road" being as defined (for England and Wales) in the Highways Act 1980, and (for Scotland) in the Roads (Scotland) Act 1984.

[16] S.I. 1991 No. 961.

[17] s.89(2).

[18] s.86(11); The Highway Litter Clearance and Cleaning (Transfer of Duties) Order 1991 (S.I. 1991 No.337).

It is expressly provided that in determining the appropriate stand- **19–009**
ard for discharging these duties of clearing litter and refuse and
cleaning roads, regard is to be had to the character and use of the land,
highway or road, as well as the measures which are practicable in the
circumstances.[19] Additionally, a Code of Practice on Litter and Refuse
has been issued under section 89 to which regard must be had by any
person subject to any of these duties.[20]

Litter Control Areas

Litter control areas may be designated by order by any principal **19–010**
litter authority (other than a County Council, Regional Council or joint
board) in respect of land in any of numerous categories if, and only if,
the authority considers that by reason of the presence of litter or refuse
the condition of the land is detrimental to the amenities of the locality,
and is likely to continue to be so unless an order designating it as a
litter control area is made.[21] The effect of such an order is to impose the
same duty on the occupier of the land concerned to keep it clear of
litter and refuse as applies by virtue of section 89(1) to the authorities
and other bodies mentioned in paragraph 19–003 in respect of their
land. The categories of land are set out in detail in the Litter Control
Areas Order 1991,[22] and include:

(a) Public car parks;
(b) Retail shopping developments with a floor space of 5,000
     square metres or more, excluding the retail floor space itself;
(c) Open areas to which the public have access forming part of
     business or office premises with a gross floor space of 5,000
     square metres or more;
(d) Land used for indoor or outdoor sports or recreations or as an
     amusement arcade or centre, *e.g.* cinemas, theatres and
     swimming baths;
(e) Any part of an inland beach or the seashore that is frequently
     used and managed as tourist resort or recreational facility;
(f) Any esplanade or promenade above mean high water
     springs;
(g) Certain aerodromes;
(h) Yachting marinas and the like above mean high water
     springs, other than boat repair yards;
(i) Motorway service stations;

---

[19] s.89(3).
[20] s.89(10).
[21] s.90(3), (4).
[22] S.I. 1991 No. 1325, reg. 2.

(j)　Open land to which the public are entitled or permitted to have access that is under the direct control of a wide variety of public bodies, including a housing action trust;

(l)　Land where markets are held, not being part of the highway or public road;

(m)　Camping or caravan sites used as such for more than 28 days a year;

(n)　A variety of picnic areas and picnic sites on trunk roads, and those provided by planning authorities.

19–011　　Where an authority proposed to designate any land as a litter control area, it must notify such persons as appear to it will be affected by the order, and give them an opportunity to make representations within 21 days within service of the notice. They must take into account when making a final decision any such representations as may be made as a result. The form of designation order to be used is set out in the Schedule to the Litter Control Areas Order 1991.

Enforcement

19–012　　Where any land is subject to the duty to keep it clear of litter and refuse, any person aggrieved by the defacement of it by litter or refuse may apply to the magistrates court for a litter abatement order.[23] Similarly, any person aggrieved may apply to the magistrates court in respect of any highway or road subject to the duty to keep it clean for an order requiring appropriate action to be taken. Persons aggrieved do not for these purposes include principal litter authorities,[24] whose remedy is to serve a litter abatement notice, as described in paragraph 19–014. Five days written notice of the intention to make such a complaint must be given to the defendant,[25] who is the person subject to the duty under section 89(1) or (2), as the case may be.[26] No order may be made if the defendant can prove that he has complied with the duty on him. Where an order is made, failure to comply with it without reasonable excuse[27] is an offence subject to a maximum fine of £2,500 on summary conviction, together with a daily fine of up to £125 for each day the offence continues after conviction. Similarly, it is a defence to any proceedings for non-compliance with a litter abatement order that the relevant duty was complied with. The Code of Practice is admissible evidence, and where it appears to be relevant to any

---

[23] s.91(1).
[24] s.91(3).
[25] s.91(5).
[26] s.91(4).
[27] See the discussion as to this defence at para. 23–036.

question before the court, it must be taken into account in determining that question.[28]

Where a complaint is made under these provisions, and the court is satisfied that when it was made it was in fact justified and that there were reasonable grounds for bringing it, the court must order a reasonable sum in respect of the complainant's costs to be paid by the defendant.[29] Appeals are possible in the normal way to the Crown court; or by way of judicial review where appropriate. In Scotland appeals may be brought on a point of law to the Court of Session against the making of a litter abatement order.   **19–013**

Litter abatement notices may be served by principal litter authorities (other than County Councils, Regional Councils or joint boards) in respect of somewhat fewer categories of land than those subject to the litter and refuse clearance duty, namely Crown land, land of a designated statutory undertaker and of a designated educational institution, and land within a litter control area.[30] Such a notice may be served where the authority is satisfied that the land in question is defaced by litter or refuse or that this defacement is likely to recur. The notice must impose a requirement that the litter or refuse be cleared within a specified time, or a prohibition on permitting the land to become defaced by litter or refuse, or both.[31] In the case of land within a litter control area, service of the notice must normally be on the occupier, but if the land is unoccupied, service is to be on the owner of the land.   **19–014**

An appeal may be lodged within 21 days from the date of service of the notice to either the magistrates' court, in England and Wales, or to the Sheriff in Scotland.[32] As with litter abatement orders, if the appellant proves that he has complied with the duty on him under section 89(1) his appeal must be allowed. If the person on whom the litter abatement notice is served fails without reasonable excuse to comply with any of its requirements or contravenes any prohibition, he is liable to a fine not exceeding £2,500 on summary conviction, coupled with a daily fine of up to £125.[33] It is a defence to a charge of non-compliance with or contravention of the litter abatement notice that the defendant complied with the duty laid on him by section 89(1); again the Code of Practice is admissible in evidence and any provision of the code that appears to the court to be relevant to any   **19–015**

---

[28] s.91(11).
[29] s.91(12).
[30] s.92(1); thus not extending to highways and roads nor, of course, the principal litter authority's own land.
[31] s.92(3).
[32] s.92(4).
[33] s.92(6).

question before it must be taken into account in determining that question.

19–016 In the event of non-compliance with an abatement notice requiring litter or refuse to be cleared away within the specified time limit, the relevant authority may (except in the case of Crown land) enter on the land, clear away the litter or refuse, and charge their reasonable expenses to the person subject to the duty.

Street Litter Control Notices

19–017 Certain types of activity are particularly liable to result in considerable quantities of litter, and street litter control notices allow additional controls to be imposed over them. The activities currently subject to these controls are set out in the Street Litter Control Notices Order 1991,[34] and consist of the following commercial and retail premises:

(1) Premises used wholly or partly for the sale of food or drink for consumption either off the premises or on a part of the premises forming open land adjacent to the street;

(2) Service stations and other premises for which fuel for motor vehicles is sold to the public;

(3) Premises used for indoor or outdoor sports or recreations or as an amusement arcade or centre, *e.g.* cinemas, theatres and swimming baths;

(4) Banks, building society offices and other premises with automated teller machines on an outside wall.

19–018 These controls may be exercised by any principal litter authority, other than a County Council, Regional Council or Joint Board, in relation to any of these premises that have a frontage on a street. The power to impose the controls arises if:

(i) there is in fact recurrent defacement by litter or refuse of any land in the vicinity of the premises that is either part of the street or open land adjacent to it;

(ii) open land in the vicinity of the frontage of the premises is detrimental to the amenities of the locality because of the presence of litter or refuse, and is likely to remain so if no notice is served; or

(iii) the activities carried on at the premises result in quantities of litter or refuse that are likely to cause the defacement of any

[34] S.I. 1991 No. 1324.

part of the street or open land adjacent to it in the vicinity of the premises.

If the authority is satisfied in respect of any of these matters, it may   **19–019**
serve a street litter control notice on the occupier of the premises or, where they are unoccupied, on their owner. The notice may impose requirements as to the clearing of litter or refuse from such area adjacent to the premises as it specifies, including in particular the provision or emptying of appropriate receptacles, either within a specified period or on a prescribed regular basis.[35] An order may be made in relation to any land which is part of a street other than a carriageway open to vehicles, "relevant land" of a principal litter authority (*i.e.* land open to the air and to which the public are entitled or permitted to have access, and which is under the direct control of the authority), and any land of any other local authority. The area of land that may be brought within a street litter control notice is limited to 100 metres from the relevant premises, except in the case of premises with automated teller machines, when it is at most 10 metres from the premises concerned.[36]

To avoid overlapping controls, no street litter control notice may be   **19–020**
made in respect of land that is within a litter control area.[37] Further, the authority, in determining what requirements to impose under the street litter control notice in respect of any area that is not part of the premises concerned must take account of its own duties generally (not only those imposed under Part IV of the E.P.A.) and of any similar duties of any other local authority relating to that land.[38] Thus the requirements must be commensurate with the litter expected to derive from the premises concerned, so that the person subject to them cannot be required to go beyond this and be made to perform duties properly the responsibility of that or any other local authority.

An authority proposing to issue a street litter control notice must   **19–021**
first inform the person on whom it is to be served of its proposals, and give him at least 21 days to make representations on them; it must take into account any such representations as may be made.[39] After the notice is served, an appeal may be made against it to a magistrates court in England and Wales, or to the Sheriff in Scotland, by way of summary application. The court may confirm or quash the notice, or vary its terms, whether by reducing or adding to the requirements. Failure to comply with any requirement imposed by a notice is not of

---

[35] s.94(4).
[36] The Street Litter Control Notices Order 1991, art. 3.
[37] s.94(3).
[38] s.94(5).
[39] s.94(6).

itself an offence, but entitles the authority to apply to a magistrates court or to the Sheriff, as the case may be, by way of summary application, for an order that the person comply with the requirement within such time as the order may specify. Failure to comply with that order without reasonable excuse is an offence, subject to a fine of £2,500 on summary conviction.

Public Registers

19–022   Each principal litter authority, other than County Councils, Regional Councils and Joint Boards, must maintain registers containing copies of all designations of land as litter control areas under section 90(3) and of street litter control notices (and variations of these) made under section 93(1). The copies may be deleted from the register after the relevant designation or notice has ceased to apply. The registers must be available at all reasonable times for inspection by the public free of charge, who may obtain copies on payment of reasonable charges.[40]

Abandoned Shopping and Luggage Trolleys

19–023   Local authorities (*i.e.* district and London borough councils, the Common Council of the City of London, the Council of the Isles of Scilly, and in Scotland, islands and district councils) are entitled, under section 99, to bring into effect in their area the provisions of Schedule 4 to the E.P.A. relating to abandoned shopping and luggage trolleys. This sets out a procedure for the seizure of trolleys that have been abandoned, for notifying the apparent owner of the seizure within not more than 14 days, and disposing of the trolley (by sale or otherwise) after six weeks, unless the owner has claimed it and paid an appropriate charge sufficient to cover the authority's costs. The authority is entitled to make a scheme with those who own shopping or luggage trolleys and provide them for use in the authority's area for the collection of the trolleys; where such a scheme is in force, no charge is to be made other than that provided for in the scheme itself.

---

[40] s.95.

Chapter 20

ACCESS TO INFORMATION

For many years the enforcement of environmental controls was treated as an essentially private matter between the regulators, on the one hand, who were (and remain) under statutory duties of confidence in respect of information acquired in the course of their duties, and the regulated, on the other, who generally have always had an entirely proper wish to keep close control of all disclosures of their activities. The sheltered relationship could be and generally was non-confrontational and, at its best, conducive to trust, allowing the authorities close access to key personnel in industrial organisations, so enabling effective encouragement of the adoption of pollution abatement techniques as needed, and avoiding the counter-productive hostility that enforcement litigation would be liable to cause. For so long as standards were not unduly demanding, and the public both accepted pollution as an inevitable aspect of industry, and had confidence that the regulators would deal with gross excesses, its exclusion from the regulatory system was not seriously challenged. Though the public had no direct role in it, the authorities were ultimately democratically accountable, and that sufficed.

However, with the growth of public consciousness of environmental issues, it became widely apparent that, inevitably, the best was not invariably attained, and moreover that the standards applied to industry did not provide the protection that a significant section of the public felt it needed. Frequently the cause could be seen to be not so much inherent inadequacies on the part of the regulatory system, but rather a failure by government to resource it adequately, coupled with a reluctance to enforce even moderate standards against polluting activities of public authorities, who would have to receive substantial capital injections to enable them to comply. The demand arose that the regulators be more openly accountable, and that the public should have the right to monitor for itself the performance of those authorised to carry on polluting activities. Awareness of the ability of individuals and groups in the United States to obtain the evidence needed to found actions for non-compliance with environmental controls, by

20–001

20–002

virtue of the US Freedom of Information Act of 1982, undoubtedly played a part in this development. Thus it was recommended by the Royal Commission on Environmental Pollution in 1984[1] that there should be a "presumption in favour of unrestricted access for the public to information which the pollution control authorities obtain or receive by virtue of their statutory powers".

20–003   The C.O.P.A. 1974 was the first statute to provide for any significant disclosures of environmental information, with section 41 requiring publication of registers of consented discharges to water and of monitoring results—though actual implementation of this had to wait for over ten years until July 31, 1985 when the Control of Pollution (Registers) Regulations 1985[2] first required the registers to be opened to the public. In the 1980s there was a change of attitude at government level in the United Kingdom favouring both disclosure and a more arm's length approach to regulation.[3] In its response to the RCEP report of 1984, the government accepted the recommendation quoted above. This change was reinforced by pressure from the European Commission, which had long espoused the harnessing of public opinion to bring about effective national implementation of EC policies. The first three action programmes on the environment all referred to public disclosure of environmental information, while the fourth, in 1987[4] called for ways to be devised to improve public access to information held by environmental authorities. The change of heart in the United Kingdom was registered in the government's 1990 White Paper "This Common Inheritance",[5] and has been given full expression in its more recent paper "Open Government".

20–004   In the United Kingdom there has resulted a widespread system of registers open to the public that are maintained by the various regulatory authorities in respect of virtually all regulated activities. Much of this was brought about by the EPA in 1990, while from the EC came Directive 90/313 on the freedom of access to information on the environment,[6] which was implemented in the United Kingdom by the

[1] RCEP 10th Report "Tackling Pollution—Experience and Prospects", Cmnd. 9149, 1984.
[2] S.I. 1985 No. 813.
[3] The previous attitude to public disclosure of information was nevertheless demonstrated by the hostility towards and attempts to kill off the private member's bill that eventually matured into the Environment and Safety Act 1988. This bill was motivated at least in part by a disastrous fire in Bradford football stadium, which was subsequently shown to be due to a failure by those in charge of it to respond to warnings by the fire authorities, of which there had been no previous public knowledge. It was only after a campaign in the media that parliamentary time was allowed for the bill to proceed.
[4] [1987] O.J. C70.
[5] Cmnd. 1200, para. 17.26.
[6] [1990] O.J. L158.

Environmental Information Regulations 1992[7] with effect from December 31, 1992. In addition the European Commission is currently working on a policy of public access to information available to the various European institutions.[8]

Since many of the administrative arrangements, in particular the system of registers, for providing public access to environmental information were set up before the 1992 Regulations, the information available from them is not necessarily entirely consistent with the requirements of the Regulations. In so far as the Regulations give rights to a wider class of information than is otherwise provided for, then these wider rights prevail.[9] Information that is contained in the public registers, and in any other records which are statutorily required to be made available for inspection by everyone who wishes to inspect them, is expressly excluded from the scope of the 1992 Regulations, which seek thereby to avoid duplication of duties. If that entails more information being made publicly available than is mandatory under the Regulations, then that additional information will continue to be provided under the applicable legislation. In these cases where the Regulations are disapplied, regulation 5 expressly imposes the same obligations on the authority holding the information as apply in relation to information that must be made available pursuant to the Regulations. Thus requests for information must be responded to as soon as possible, and at the latest within two months, any refusal to make information available must be in writing and specify the reasons for this, and any charges made for making the information available must be reasonable.

20–005

The Environmental Information Regulations 1992

The Regulations apply to any information which "relates to the environment". This is defined in terms closely following that contained in the underlying Directive as being information if, and only if, it relates to:

20–006

(a)   the state of any water or air, the state of any flora or fauna, the state of any soil or the state of any natural site or other land;

(b)   any activities or measures (including activities giving rise to noise or any other nuisance) which adversely affect anything mentioned in paragraph (a) or are likely adversely to affect anything so mentioned; or

---

[7] S.I. 1992 No. 3240.
[8] A preliminary report has been issued in a Communication "Public Access to the Institutions' Documents", [1993] O.J. C156.
[9] reg. 3(7).

(c) any activities or administrative or other measures (including any environmental management programmes) which are designed to protect anything so mentioned.[10]

20–007 Information includes anything contained in any records, which term includes registers, reports and returns, and non-documentary records such as those held on a computer.

20–008 In the great majority of cases, any relevant information will be held by public authorities, in relation to whom Directive 90/313 will be directly applicable. In an answer given on behalf of the European Commission to questions in the European Parliament regarding whether "activities or measures" (referred to in paragraph (b) above) would cover all projects subject to environmental impact assessment procedures pursuant to Directive 85/337, it was said:

> "Access to information refers to information held by public authorities concerning not only the state of the environment but also activities or measures which are damaging or potentially damaging to the environment. This information may relate to projects coming under Directive 85/337/EEC in so far as 'the execution of construction works or of other installations or schemes' constitutes activities which are potentially damaging to the environment. The concept of the environment contained in Directive 85/337/EEC is based on ideas such as material assets and the cultural heritage which are not explicitly contained in the definition of 'information relating to the environment' (Directive 90/313/EEC). If public authorities hold information relating to activities or measures which either aim to protect the environment or affect the environment, they must make it available to any person who requests access."[11]

20–009 Guidance from the DoE on the Regulations emphasises the broad scope to be given to "information relating to the environment".[12] This notes that the obligations apply to information collected before the Regulations came into force, and also information that may have been passed on to the Public Record Office for safe keeping.[13] The information does not have to be information collected by that body under any of its specific powers and duties—it is sufficient that the body holds it. Conversely, there is no obligation under the Regulations or the Directive for an authority to retain information if it does not wish to do so; the obligation is merely to provide such information as it

---

[10] reg. 2(2).
[11] Written Questions, nos. 212/92, 211/92, [1992] O.J. C317.
[12] Paras. 14 to 21.
[13] In such a case, the ownership remains with the providing body until such time as it is released for general public inspection.

does in fact hold. Similarly the public has no right of access to information held by a regulated facility on its site as a result of self-monitoring, *e.g.* of emissions, pursuant to a condition in a process authorisation. Accordingly, in such a case the regulatory authority will not itself have the emissions information but merely a right of access to it. The only publicly available information on the point may be solely whether or not the facility is in compliance with its authorisation.

There is no geographical limitation, and consequently information **20–010** that comes within the general definition must be disclosed, whatever part of the world it may relate to, subject only to the specified grounds of refusal referred to below. The guidance notes that the Regulations make no explicit reference to information relating to human health, but observes that the environment clearly impacts on human health, and to this extent information affecting it should be covered.[14]

It follows from the general obligation on authorities to disclose the **20–011** information that they hold, that they must provide this irrespective of its accuracy. They cannot therefore be expected to vouch for its accuracy, whether the information is derived from its own sources, or from third parties. Nevertheless, where the authority has developed a view as to the accuracy of that information—or even conflicting views—that additional material would also be part of the information that it has a duty to disclose.

The information is limited by the Regulations to that which is held **20–012** "in accessible form". It is not clear what these words add, and there is no directly corresponding qualification in the Directive. The expression presumably relates to physical accessibility, rather than to any legal constraints there may be on disclosure, considered below. It cannot however reasonably be intended to mean that the obligation does not apply to documents that have been locked away, where the key cannot be found. It would appear to be an attempt to interpret the Directive's reference to "available information in written, visual, aural or data-base form".[15] If so, it should be seen as requiring the authority to disclose such information as it has immediately available to it, as opposed to information that may be derived from it by further calculations, statistical analysis and the like.

Persons Subject to the Duty of Disclosure

The Regulations impose the duty of disclosure on all "relevant **20–013** persons", that is to say:

[14] para. 19.
[15] Art. 2(a).

917

    (a)   all such Ministers of the Crown, Government departments, local authorities and other persons carrying out functions of public administration at a national, regional or local level as, for the purposes of in connection with their functions, have responsibilities in relation to the environment; and

    (b)   any body with public responsibilities for the environment which does not fall within paragraph (a) but is under the control of a person falling within that paragraph.[16]

20–014   These definitions correspond to those in the Directive relating to "public authorities" and "bodies with public responsibilities for the environment and under the control of public authorities",[17] The Directive excludes from public authorities bodies acting in a judicial or legislative capacity; this limitation is transferred into the Regulations by excluding its application to information held "for the purposes of any judicial or legislative functions". While there is no definition of "judicial functions", it would be inappropriate to construe this as equivalent to functions in relation to all "legal *or other* proceedings" as defined in the Regulations, in view of the wide scope they give to this latter expression (see also paragraphs 20–021, 20–022). The DoE guidance[18] considers it to be unclear whether the Directive intends to distinguish between "public authorities" on the one hand, and publicly controlled "bodies with public responsibilities for the environment on the other". However the reference to the latter in article 6 must be intended to supplement the provisions of the previous articles 3, 4 and 5, which set out the duties of public authorities, as it would otherwise be superfluous. Further, the language of article 6 itself draws a distinction between "bodies with public responsibilities for the environment" and the competent public authorities that control them.

20–015   The guidance states that "control" means a relationship constituted by a statute, rights, contracts or other means, which either separately or jointly confer the possibility of directly or indirectly exercising a decisive influence on a body. It accepts this would be the case for most public-sector bodies, including government-owned companies, and that it could also be the case for private-sector bodies placed under some statutory duty. Among its examples are the N.R.A., English Nature, Scottish Natural Heritage and the Royal Botanic Gardens. It is questionable, though in the event immaterial, whether the first three of these examples should not more properly be regarded as "public authorities". The most sensitive question is whether the privatised

[16] reg. 2(3).
[17] Arts. 2(b), 6.
[18] para. 11.

bodies such as the water and sewerage undertakers, and possibly at least some of the privatised organisations within the electricity industry should be regarded as "bodies with public responsibilities for the environment and under the control of public authorities". As to this, the statutory obligations on these bodies and their terms of appointment must clearly be decisive; the point is certainly arguable, but there has as yet been no judicial determination of it.

In *Griffin and Others v. South West Water* it was held that South West   **20–016**
Water was an "emanation of the State" as defined by the European Court of Justice in *Foster v. British Gas* (see paragraphs 2–032 to 2–035). In so holding it was observed that the conditions laid down in *Foster* require only that the relevant public service be under the control of the State, and not that the body responsible for that service should be. While it is arguable that any body that is an "emanation of the State" should be equated with "public authorities" and so, if it has responsibilities in relation to the environment, fall within the first category (a) of relevant persons set out in paragraph 20–013, the language of the Directive suggests that this category may not be so broad. Consequently the second category also may properly exclude some emanations of the State where they are not "under the control" of a public authority, in the sense this expression was given in *Griffin*. However if "control" means not only, *e.g.* the control a parent company has over its subsidiary but also the control that may be exercised through enforcing the terms of appointment of a statutory undertaker, then the Directive and the Regulations will extend also to statutory undertakers that have public responsibilities for the environment.

Disclosure of Information

The broad obligation on those subject to the duty of disclosure is to   **20–017**
make information that they hold available to every person who requests it.[19] There is no explicit obligation on the bodies to say what information they do and do not hold, but the DoE guidance recognises that without this knowledge, the public may not be able to formulate a properly targeted request for information. It therefore recommends that all relevant bodies should review and state from time to time the principal areas in which they hold environmental information—it is also recommended that they should give publicity to the appropriate contact point for inquiries and assistance. Further, there is no duty to

[19] reg. 3(1).

919

publish information independently of express requests for it; nevertheless, the DoE itself has in recent years been publishing annual reports on the environment.

20–018   A notable feature of the Directive is that information must be provided to any natural or legal person at his request and "without his having to prove an interest." This is also the effect of regulation 3(1), which requires the subject of the duty to make information available to "every person who requests it." Though the guidance confirms that no interest need be proved, it is perhaps unfortunate that the Regulations do not spell this out, since practical experience suggests that the staff of at least some public sector bodies are reluctant to hand over information in the absence of clear justification on the part of the enquirer. It is the view of the European Commission that the Directive's stipulation that an applicant does not need to prove an interest means that he also may not be required to state his purpose in requesting the information.[20]

20–019   Every person subject to the duty must respond to every request for information as soon as possible, and in any event within two months. Any refusal to disclose information must be in writing and give the reasons for it.[21] Apart from the specific grounds for refusal discussed below, a request may be refused where it is manifestly unreasonable or is formulated in too general a manner.[22]

20–020   The Directive sets out[23] a variety of grounds on which refusal to provide information is legitimate, if national laws so provide. These grounds are given effect in regulation 4. This creates two categories of, firstly, information that may, but need not necessarily, be treated as confidential and, secondly, information which must be kept confidential. The first category, where maintaining confidentiality is a matter of discretion, consists of:

(a)   Information relating to matters affecting international relations, national defence or public security;

(b)   Information relating to any legal or other proceedings (whether actual or prospective), or to anything which is or has been the subject-matter of them;

(c)   Information relating to confidential deliberations of any "relevant person" (*e.g.* internal documents of a local authority or minutes of meetings to which the public has no right of access) and the contents of any internal communications of

---

[20] European Commission's answer to Written Question Number 211/92—see n.11 above.
[21] reg. 3(2).
[22] reg. 3(3).
[23] In Art. 3(2), (3).

corporate bodies and other organisations. Under the Local Government (Access to Information) Act 1985, the public has rights of access to council, committee and subcommittee meetings and to papers (including background papers, relating to these). Nevertheless under the Local Government Act 1972 certain information is defined to be "confidential"[24] and its disclosure is accordingly prohibited, and other information is defined as "exempt",[25] and will not be automatically released, if the public has been excluded from the relevant part of a meeting of the local authority. However, by virtue of regulation 3(7) these restrictions will not apply to information otherwise subject to disclosure pursuant to the 1992 Regulations.

(d) Information in documents or other records still in the course of completion (so including correspondence that may have taken place with a regulatory authority preliminary to a formal application for a consent or licence). A distinction is to be made between records which are incomplete, and those that relate to unfinished projects. The latter records, in so far as they are complete in themselves, are subject to the duty of disclosure.

(e) Information relating to matters to which any commercial or industrial confidentiality attaches or affecting any intellectual property.

The provision in the Directive corresponding to item (b) of this list **20–021** reads "matters which are, or have been, *sub judice*, or under enquiry (including disciplinary enquiries), or which are the subject of preliminary investigation proceedings".[26] However, the Regulations define "legal or other proceedings" as including not only disciplinary proceedings, but also "the proceedings at any local or other public enquiry and the proceedings at any hearing conducted by a person appointed under any enactment for the purpose of affording an opportunity to persons to make representations or objections with respect to any matter". It is open to question whether this does not unduly extend the exclusion in the Directive. As is argued by Krämer[27] the last sentence of Article 3(2) indicates that the context in which "enquiry" is mentioned suggests that it must be of a formal nature equivalent to a judicial proceeding and that its purpose must be to settle a conflict between opposing interests, ending with a formal

---

[24] By s.100A(3); Local Government (Scotland) Act 1973, s.50A(3).
[25] By Sched. 12A; Local Government (Scotland) Act 1973, Sched. 7A.
[26] Art. 3(2).
[27] *Focus on European Environmental Law*, p. 303.

decision. (By contrast, preliminary investigation proceedings, which may not end in a formal decision of this type are only protected while they are current).

20–022   In the United Kingdom local or public enquiries and other public hearings, for example appeals relating to applications for authorisation of a process subject to Integrated Pollution Control, are often not specifically judicial proceedings.[28] They are frequently held under the planning legislation, typically hearings on planning applications and on proposed structure plans, and there is no dispute that environmental information arising in the course of planning matters is subject to the Regulations (in the absence of any specific ground for refusing disclosure arising). Inspectors holding public enquiries are frequently not lawyers, nor need they be. Their role is either to assemble facts on which a recommendation to the Secretary of State is made, or they have delegated to them the power to make a policy decision on his behalf—clearly a matter of public administration. Since derogations from the broad provisions of EC legislation are to be construed restrictively, it is strongly arguable that this limitation has not been satisfactorily transposed from the Directive into the UK legislation.

20–023   Information must be treated as confidential, and therefore may not be disclosed, if it is:

(a) capable of being confidential and the disclosure would contravene any statutory provision or rule of law or would involve a breach of any agreement;

(b) personal information concerning an individual who has not consented to its disclosure;

(c) information held as a result of it having been supplied by a person who was not under any legal obligation to supply it, and could not have been put under any such obligation, where the body holding it would not otherwise have had a right to disclose it, and where the supplier has not consented to its disclosure; or

(d) information the disclosure of which would increase the likelihood of damage to the environment—this relates particularly to information on the location of rare species of flora and fauna.

20–024   There is a general presumption of a right to information, and in so far as a document contains both information that need not or must not be disclosed under the above provisions, and other information

---

[28] It might well be better if there were an environmental court to handle such matters, but the DoE attitude has been to regard them as purely administrative issues, requiring policy and not legal decisions.

disclosure of which cannot be refused, then the restricted information may be separated from the rest, so far as can be done, but subject to that, there must be a full disclosure. Only if the information subject to the duty of disclosure cannot be effectively separated out from legitimately restricted information, may its disclosure be refused.[29]

The duty of disclosure is a statutory duty owed to the person requesting the information,[30] and consequently any refusal may be made the subject of proceedings taken again the relevant body in the courts for an appropriate order. However, other steps may be sufficient to avoid court proceedings — if referring the matter to a senior level within the relevant organisation is not effective, in the case of a local authority, the issue may be taken to the local government Ombudsman on the grounds of maladministration giving rise to injustice. **20–025**

Information need only be made available in such form and at such times and places as is reasonable,[31] and its disclosure may be made subject to payment of a reasonable charge. The DoE guidance states that applicants for information should be advised of any likely charge before a request for information is met, and that it would be against the spirit of the Citizen's Charter to levy a charge when advising on the availability of information, explaining the grounds for withholding information or handling requests to reconsider refusals. Information available from public registers would not normally be made subject to a charge, and the guidance suggests that it may not be cost effective in some cases to charge for supplying information that is in fact readily available. In other circumstances, the charges may properly reflect resource costs including staff time, as well as the costs of copying, postage etc. **20–026**

Public Registers

There are numerous registers prescribed by statute for making information available to the public in respect of environmental matters, prepared by a variety of regulatory bodies, and held by them and, in some cases, other bodies also.[32] The more important registers have been mentioned, where appropriate, in earlier chapters. The **20–027**

---

[29] reg. 4(4).
[30] reg. 3(6).
[31] reg. 3(5).
[32] There is no central organisation holding all this information in one place, which would significantly ease searches in respect of particular organisations or sites; it may be that the new Environment Agency will provide some such facility.

following Table 20/I summarises the information available, the statutory basis, and by whom the registers are held in England and Wales.

TABLE 20/I

Public Registers (England & Wales)		
Information	**Statutory Basis**	**Held By**
Planning applications, consents Certificates for lawful use or development Environmental statement requests	Town and Country Planning General Development Order 1988, Art. 27	Local Authority (Part 3, Local land charges register)
Minerals planning applications, consents	(ditto)	Local Authority (Part 3, Local land charges register) County Minerals Planning Authority
Stop, enforcement and breach of condition notices	Town and Country Planning General Development Order 1988, Art. 28	Local Authority (Part 3, Local land charges register)
Tree preservation orders	T.C.P.A., ss.211, 214	Local Authority (Part 3, Local land charges register)
SSSIs	Wildlife and Countryside Act 1981, s.29	Local Authority (Part 4, Local land charges register)
Land drainage schemes	Land Drainage Act 1991, s.18	Local Authority (Part 12, Local land charges register)
Integrated Pollution Control—Part A processes	E.P.A., s.20	HMIP Local Authority N.R.A. regions
"Scheduled processes"	Alkali etc. Works Act 1906 H.S.W.A. 1974, s.5	HMIP
Air pollution—Part B processes	E.P.A., s.20	Local Authority
Chemical release inventory	–	HMIP

924

Water quality objectives	Water Resources Act, s.190	N.R.A. regions
Discharge consents to controlled waters	The Control of Pollution (Registers) Regulations 1989	
Monitoring results		
Abstraction, impounding licences	Water Resources Act, s.189	N.R.A. regions
Trade effluent consents	Water Industry Act, s.196	Sewerage Undertakers
Deposits/incineration at sea	Food and Environment Protection Act 1985, s.14	Licensing Authority
Waste management licences	E.P.A., s.64	Waste Regulation Authority
Registered waste carriers	Controlled Waste (Registration of Carriers and Seizure of Vehicles) Regulations 1991	Waste Regulation Authority
Radioactive substances	Radioactive Substances Act 1993, s.39	HMIP
Hazardous substances applications, consents	Planning (Hazardous Substances) Act 1990, s.28	Hazardous Substances Authority
Genetically modified organisms—deliberate release	E.P.A., s.122 The GMO (Deliberate Release) Regulations 1992, Reg.17	HMIP
Genetically modified organisms—contained use	The GMO (Contained Use) Regulations 1992, Reg.16	HSE
Pesticides—enforcement notices under FEPA 1985	Environment and Safety Information Act 1988, s.1	Ministry of Agriculture, Fisheries and Food
Litter control areas Street litter control notices	E.P.A., s.95	Litter Authorities

925

Noise abatement zones: Noise levels Noise reduction notices	C.O.P.A., ss.64, 66 Control of Noise (Measurement and Registers) Regulations 1976	Local authority noise level register
Sites registered under EMAS	EC Regulation 1836/93	Department of the Environment
Eco-labels	EC Regulation 880/92	European Commission

Chapter 21

CRIMINAL LIABILITY — DEFENDANTS AND DEFENCES

Where a corporation has committed an offence under environmen- **21–001**
tal legislation, normally only the relevant operating company is
prosecuted.[1] However it is quite common in prosecutions for breaches
of health and safety legislation to make an individual manager or
operator a further defendant, and there is an observable trend towards
seeking to impose such personal liability for environmental offences
also, at least in the more serious cases. In addition to members of the
workforce, there may, in certain cases, be reason to prosecute the
directors or other officers of the company, along with, possibly, a
parent company.

As has been seen,[2] the principal offences under environmental **21–002**
legislation are ones of strict liability, where absence of negligence or
other fault is irrelevant. Nevertheless, in most cases (the Water
Resources Act 1991 and the Radioactive Substances Act 1993 are
notable exceptions) a "due diligence" defence is provided for a person
who can show that he took all reasonable precautions and exercised all
due diligence to avoid the commission of the offence.[3]

Such a defence, contained in section 24(1) of the Trade Descriptions **21–003**
Act 1968 was analysed in *Tesco Supermarkets Limited v Nattrass*.[4] In that
case, a false trade description had been applied to some goods by a
relatively junior employee notwithstanding that, as was found, the
defendant company had, and had operated, a sound system of
supervision. The question at issue was whether the acts of any
employee must be equated with the acts of the company for the
purposes of a criminal statute: it was held that they should not be.[5] If it

---

[1] This is in notable contrast with many continental European jurisdictions where the
responsible company officers are frequently regarded as the appropriate defendants,
often to the exclusion of the company itself.
[2] See for instance paras. 8–106 to 8–111.
[3] See, *e.g.* E.P.A., s.33(7)(a).
[4] [1972] A.C. 153.
[5] See, *e.g.* Lord Reid at p.175A/B.

were otherwise, the due diligence defence would in practice be useless, since if an offence, which must necessarily result from acts or omissions of one or more natural persons, were committed, it would be impossible to say that *such* persons had taken all reasonable precautions and exercised all due diligence. Where an employer is himself a natural person, then the distinction between him and his employees is normally clear cut. Where however the employer is a corporate body, it may not be. As Lord Reid put it:

> "A living person has a mind which can have knowledge or intention or be negligent and he has hands to carry out his intentions. A corporation has none of these: it must act through living persons, though not always one or the same person. Then the person who acts is not speaking or acting *for*[6] the company. He is acting *as* the company and his mind which directs his acts is the mind of the company. There is no question of the company being vicariously liable. He is not acting as a servant, representative, agent or delegate. He is an embodiment of the company or, one could say, he hears and speaks through the persona of the company, within his appropriate sphere, and his mind is the mind of the company. If it is a guilty mind, then that guilt is the guilt of the company. It must be a question of law whether, once the facts have been ascertained, a person in doing particular things is to be regarded as the company or merely as the company's servant or agent."[7]

21–004   Lord Diplock asked the question "What natural person or persons are to be treated as being the corporation itself, and not merely its agents, for the purpose of taking precautions and exercising diligence?" In his view, the answer:

> "is to be found by identifying those natural persons who by the memorandum and articles of association or as a result of action taken by the directors, or by the company in general meeting pursuant to the articles, are entrusted with the exercise of the powers of the company"[8]

21–005   He continued by noting the provision in the statute in question as to the liabilities of directors and others, which corresponded to that of

---

[6] Emphasis added.

[7] p. 170E/G. See also *H. L. Bolton (Engineering) Co v. T. J. Graham & Sons Ltd* [1957] 1 Q.B.159, *per* Lord Denning; *Lennard's Carrying Co. Ltd. v. Asiatic Petroleum Co. Ltd* [1915] A.C. 705.

[8] At p. 200A.

E.P.A., s.157(1), set out in paragraph 21–009, drawing a distinction between "any director, manager, secretary or other similar officer of a body corporate" and other persons who are merely its servants or agents. Thus the persons in the category of "director, manager, secretary or other similar officer" correspond with those who exercise the powers of the company itself. Without a provision making such people liable, where they have consented to or connived at an offence or where it is attributable to their neglect, whose acts were in law the acts of the company itself, it would have been open to doubt whether they would have been guilty in their personal capacity also of the offence committed by the company. However in view of the special provision rendering them liable in certain circumstances, they should not be held liable merely by virtue of their position within the company for an offence by it.

A director who plays no part in a company's management may nevertheless be treated as its directing mind and will if he individually exercises power on its behalf, as by signing documents that commit it to involvement in a matter and making related financial arrangements. The fact that, in doing so, he may have been acting on proposals from others, for example non-resident directors, who do manage the company, is not relevant.[9]

21–006

Section 158 of the Environmental Protection Act reads:

21–007

"158. Where the commission by any person of an offence under Part I, II, IV or VI, or section 140, 141 or 142 above is due to the act or default of some other person, that other person may be charged with and convicted of the offence by virtue of this section whether or not proceedings for the offence are taken against the first-mentioned person."

In the typical case, where "the first- mentioned person" is a body corporate, the persons in the category of director, manager, secretary or similar officer, are thus not to be equated with "some other person", and there is consequently a precise line to be drawn with everybody involved in the activities of a company falling either on one side, as a director, manager, secretary or other similar officer, and liable under E.P.A., s.157(1), or on the other, and liable under E.P.A., s.158. Who falls which side of the line in any particular case is a question of fact, to be determined by, in Lord Diplock's words, identifying those natural persons who are entrusted with the exercise of the powers of the company, and those who are not.

21–008

---

[9] *El Ajou v. Dollar Land Holdings*, (C.A.), [1994] 2 All E.R. 685.

Directors' and Officers' Liability

21–009   Section 157 of the Environmental Protection Act 1990 reads as follows:

> "157. (1)   Where an offence under any provision of this Act committed by a body corporate is proved to have been committed with the consent or connivance of, or to have been attributable to any neglect on the part of, any director, manager, secretary or other similar officer of the body corporate or a person who was purporting to act in any such capacity, he as well as the body corporate shall be guilty of that offence and shall be liable to be proceeded against and punished accordingly.
>
> (2)   Where the affairs of a body corporate are managed by its members, subsection (1) above shall apply in relation to the acts or defaults of a member in connection with his functions of management as if he were a director of the body corporate."

21–010   Essentially the same provisions are contained in the Water Resources Act 1991, s.217. Virtually all modern regulatory statutes in the United Kingdom have a provision corresponding to section 157(1) and probably the majority also contain a provision corresponding to section 157(2), creating potential liability for parent companies.[10] As will be seen, a parent company that manages the affairs of a body corporate will be treated as though it were a director for the purposes of attracting criminal liability under the statutory provisions.

21–011   Although in many cases regulatory offences may be committed by bodies corporate without any fault or *mens rea*, for a director to be personally liable under the statutory provision he must either have consented to the offence or connived at it, or the offence must be attributable to some neglect on his part. He will not therefore be liable merely by virtue of his being a director, without more. He must be in breach of his duty as a director: this duty is however not absolute.

21–012   What amounts to consent and connivance were both dealt with in *Huckerby v. Elliott.*[11] Thus:

> "It would seem that where a director consents to the commission of an offence by his company, he is well aware of what is going on and agrees to it . . . Where he connives at the offence committed by the company he is equally well aware of what is going on but

---

[10] *e.g.* Health and Safety at Work Act 1974, s.37; Control of Pollution Act 1974, s. 87; Consumer Protection Act 1987, s.40; Medicines Act 1968, s. 124; Fire Precautions Act 1971, s.23(1); Food Act 1984, s. 94; Food and Environment Protection Act 1985, s. 21 (6), (7).

[11] [1970] 1 All E.R. 189 at 194.

his agreement is tacit, not actively encouraging what happens but letting it continue and saying nothing about it."

Connivance accordingly implies acquiescence in a course of conduct reasonably likely to lead to the commission of an offence. **21–013**

Negligence requires a breach of a duty. The duty of care owed by a **21–014**
director at common law is accurately stated in section 214(4) of the Insolvency Act 1986.[12] The duties of directors were dealt with at some length in *City Equitable Fire Insurance Company Ltd.*[13] A director of the company was convicted of fraud in relation to a shortage of funds, and the Official Receiver sought to make all of the directors liable, even though the articles of association stated that directors would not be answerable for the acts of fellow directors. The following principles are to be drawn from the judgment of Romer J.:[14]

(i)   The manner in which the work of a company is to be distributed between the board of directors and the staff is a business matter to be decided on business lines. The larger the business carried on by the company the more numerous and the more important the matters that must of necessity be left to the managers, the accountants, and the rest of the staff;

(ii) In ascertaining the duties of a director of a company, it is necessary to consider the nature of the company's business and the manner in which the work of a company is, reasonably in the circumstances and consistently with the articles of association, distributed between the directors and the other officials of the company;

(iii) In discharging those duties, a director (a) must act honestly, and (b) must exercise such degree of skill and diligence as would amount to the reasonable care which an ordinary man might be expected to take, in the circumstances, on his own behalf. But (c) he need not exhibit in the performance of this duties a greater degree of skill than may reasonably be expected from a person of his knowledge and experience; in

---

[12] *Re: D'Jan of London Ltd.*, [1993] B.C.C. 646 *per* Hoffmann L.J. S. 214(4) reads, so far as material:
   "The facts which a director of a company ought to know or ascertain, the conclusions which he ought to reach and the steps which he ought to take are those which would be known or ascertained, or reached or taken, by a reasonably diligent person having both—
   (a) the general knowledge, skill and experience that may reasonably be expected of a person carrying out the same functions as are carried out by that director in relation to the company, and
   (b) the general knowledge, skill and experience that that director has".
[13] [1925] Ch. 407.
[14] At pp. 426 to 430.

other words, he is not liable for mere errors of judgment; (d) he is not bound to give continuous attention to the affairs of his company—his duties are of an intermittent nature to be performed at periodical board meetings, and at meetings of any committee to which he is appointed, and though not bound to attend all such meetings he ought to attend them when reasonably able to do so; and (e) in respect of all duties, which having regard to the exigencies of business and the articles of association, may properly be left to some other official, he is, in the absence of grounds for suspicion, justified in trusting that official to perform such duties honestly.

21–015   Nevertheless, delegation was not a sufficient excuse in *Hirschler v. Birch*,[15] where a company and one of its directors were charged with offences of applying false trade descriptions to certain of its products. The purchasing director of the company had asked a co-director to check the legality of selling the products that he was importing from the Netherlands. This check was done incompetently, and goods were marketed on the basis they were fit for use in the UK, when they were not. The court considered both *Huckerby v. Elliott* and *City Equitable Fire Insurance*, but decided that the accused purchasing director could not rely on the fact that he had delegated enquiries as to the legality of the sales, and held that in the particular circumstances the director had neglected his duty. As it was put by Woolf L.J:

> " . . . it appears to me that, if the appellant [the defendant director] had pressed [his co-director] as to what enquiries he had made, it could well have become apparent to him that they were of a very superficial nature; and if further enquiries had then resulted at his instigation because he was dissatisfied (as he should have been) about [the co-director's] inquiries, this could indeed have avoided the offences being committed."

21–016   The general proposition may be drawn from the cases that a director can delegate the exercise of certain of his duties to another director or manager, provided that that other person has sufficient experience— indeed business cannot be conducted otherwise than on principles of trust.[16] Thus a director who properly delegates matters to management is entitled to expect that the work which he has delegated is carried out in accordance with his instructions, and it does not amount to neglect if he fails to check that the work is in fact carried out correctly. However where the delegatee does not have relevant

[15] [1986] Q.B.D. 151.
[16] *Huckerby v. Elliott*, [1970] 1 All E.R. at 194.

experience, and was not employed to do the sort of work that was delegated to him, then the director will have greater responsibilities to ensure that what is being done for the company is being done properly.

As to who falls within the category of "director, manager, secretary **21–017** or other similar officers of the body corporate or a person who is purporting to act in any such capacity", the leading case is *R. v. Boal*,[17] which was concerned with the application of section 23(1) of the Fire Precautions Act 1971, and is in essentially the same terms as E.P.A., s.157(1). It was held that the intended scope of this sort of provision was to fix with criminal liability only those who were in a position of real authority and who were responsible for putting proper procedures in place, namely the decision-makers within the company who had both the power and responsibility to decide corporate policy and strategy—"it is not meant to strike at underlings". Thus the defendant, the chief buyer of Foyles bookshop, was not caught by the provision. Although his title was "assistant general manager" he had had no managerial training, and in particular none in matters of health and safety or fire precautions, which was the subject of the prosecution. Similarly, in *Woodhouse v. Walsall Metropolitan Borough Council*,[18] it was not sufficient to find that the accused was "in a position of real authority", as this means nothing without a finding that he was a decision-maker having the power and responsibility to decide corporate policy and strategy.

A Scottish case, *Armour v. Skeen*,[19] was concerned with liability **21–018** under health and safety legislation following the death of an employee of a Regional Council, who fell when repainting a bridge. Both the Council and the Council's Director of Roads were prosecuted and convicted. Being a Regional Council, the Director of Roads was not a "director" under the Companies Acts, but it was held that his liability arose by virtue of his being a "similar officer", and his neglect of the duty flowing from his responsibilities in relation to the Council's Statement of Safety Policy, a duty imposed on him by the Council by virtue of their common law powers as employers. This decision indicates that where a board of directors apportions responsibility between its members for regulatory matters, a single individual may assume personal responsibilities in relation to statutory obligations which he would not otherwise have had directly imposed on him. Nevertheless, the conclusion cannot be that a board that had failed to allocate appropriate responsibilities would be safe—a failure by the

---

[17] C.A. [1992] 3 All E.R. 178.
[18] [1994] Env L.R. 30.
[19] [1977] S.L.T. 71, (not cited in *Boal*).

board as a whole to address in a responsible manner the proper compliance with regulatory obligations would expose all the members to an action based on their negligence.

21–019 Where a director has assumed relevant responsibilities, he must exercise them properly, and cannot allow himself to be pressurised by other directors against his better judgment, even where the others constitute a majority or even all of the remainder of the board. In *R. v. Roussel Laboratories Ltd and Good*[20] a pharmaceutical company and also its medical director were both accused of offences under the Medicines Act 1968 involving the issue of a misleading advertisement relating to a medicinal product. The director was said to have been very doubtful about the advertisement but had allowed himself to be overborne, and was found guilty on counts of consenting to and conniving at the company's offence.

21–020 An administrator has been held to be an officer of a company in administration for the purposes of the Companies Act 1985, s.727 (which allows the court to grant relief to an officer of a company in any proceedings against that officer, if he has acted honestly and reasonably and he ought fairly to be excused).[21] While it is not necessarily correct to give the same meaning to "officer" in other statutes, this case supports the contention that administrators are potentially liable for offences of the companies concerned, as though they were directors. The decision expressly followed that in In *Re X Company Limited*[22] in which it was held that a liquidator was an officer of a company in liquidation.

21–021 The reference to "a person . . . purporting to act in any such capacity" covers those who hold themselves out as directors, but who have not been formally appointed as such or whose appointment is for some reason invalid, *e.g.* because they have been convicted of an offence debarring them from being a director. If "purporting" is to be given its natural meaning, it is unlikely that the expression properly extends to persons who exert a powerful influence over a company from behind the scenes, where it is not clearly apparent to third parties that they are acting in the capacity of a director or other similar officer. Such people, for example, shadow directors,[23] and (in some circumstances) lenders who become closely involved in the running of a

---

[20] C.A., (1989) 153 J.P. 298; (1989) 88 Cr.App.R. 140.
[21] *Re Home Treat Limited* [1991] British Company Cases 165.
[22] [1907] 2 Ch. 92.
[23] Defined in the Companies Act 1985, s.741(2), as "a person in accordance with whose directions or instructions the directors of the company are accustomed to act". See *Hydrodam (Corby) Ltd.* (in liquidation), *The Times*, February 19, 1994, on the distinction between *de facto* and shadow directors.

company so as to protect their security, may however be vulnerable as being "managers".

Liability of Parent Companies

Where shareholders manage a company, as may typically happen **21–022** particularly in a parent/subsidiary relationship, the shareholders are treated for the purposes of the statutory provisions[24] as though they were directors or managers and liable accordingly. Hence, if the conduct of a subsidiary were to be materially affected by controls exercised by the parent company in such a manner that, to the knowledge of the parent company, it would or was liable to breach an environmental statute, then prosecution of the parent company could certainly be envisaged. Likewise, if a UK company were to be the subsidiary of a foreign parent that had assumed control over the environmental performance of all group companies, the foreign parent might, depending on the particular facts, be at risk in the event of the subsidiary committing a relevant offence.

"Other Persons"

Where a company has committed an offence, the relevant act or **21–023** omission must necessarily be attributable to one or more natural persons, who may as a result themselves be prima facie liable as principals for the same offence. Such persons will often not be a "director, manager, secretary or other similar officer", but rather a production manager or some hourly-paid employee. E.P.A., s.158 and W.R.A., s.217(3),[25] and similar provisions in other statutes, render such persons liable if the commission of the offence by the company is due to their "act or default". In *Tesco v. Nattrass*, it was said:

> " . . . the word 'act' is wide enough to include any physical act of the other person which is causative of the offence. But the use of the word 'default' instead of the neutral expression 'omission' connotes a failure to act which constitutes a breach of a legal duty to act. A legal duty to act may arise independently of any contract or it may be a duty owed to another person arising out of a contract with him."[26]

---

[24] *e.g.* E.P.A., s.157(2), W.R.A., s.217(2).

[25] W.R.A., s.217(3) reads: Without prejudice to subsections (1) and (2) above, where the commission by any person of an offence under the water pollution provisions of this Act is due to the act or default of some other person, that other person may be charged with and convicted of the offences by virtue of this section whether or not proceedings for the offence are taken against the first-mentioned person.

[26] Lord Diplock at p. 196G.

Acting under instructions

21–024   An individual may be entitled to a defence such as is contained in section 33(7)(b) of the E.P.A., namely "that he acted under instructions from his employer and neither knew nor had reason to suppose that the acts done by him constituted a contravention of [sub-section 33(1)]". In the case of deposits of waste, such a defence is unlikely to be capable of being made good in circumstances where any deposit would amount to an offence—it would however provide a safeguard where the person concerned was not aware of any particular hazardous nature that the waste might in fact have, and the deposit was unlawful by reason only of that special nature. This latter situation may be contrasted with that in *Ashcroft v. Cambro Waste Products*,[27] where the offence of knowingly permitting a deposit of waste was held to have been established despite a lack of knowledge on the part of the defendant company of the breach of a licence condition. It would appear in principle that this defence under section 33(7)(b) should be available to a self-employed sub-contractor, in circumstances where he was given little or no discretion on how he should act, following the reasoning in *Hallett Silberman Limited v. Cheshire County Council*.[28]

Due diligence

21–025   As already mentioned, a defence frequently provided to strict liability offences is that the defendant took all reasonable precautions and exercised all due diligence to avoid commission of the offence. For the reasons given earlier, where the defendant is a corporation it must be shown that its controlling officer or officers had exercised the requisite due diligence—the efforts or otherwise of members of the workforce closest to the offending acts are not necessarily material. What is needed to make good the defence was said by Lord Diplock in *Tesco* to depend upon all the circumstances of the business carried on by the defendant. It is a question of fact for the magistrates in summary proceedings or for the jury in proceedings on indictment.[29] He continued:

> "To exercise due diligence to prevent something being done is to take all reasonable steps to prevent it. It may be a reasonable step for an employer to instruct a superior servant to supervise the activities of inferior servants whose physical acts may in the

[27] [1981] 3 All E.R. 699.
[28] [1993] RTR 32.
[29] [1972] A.C. at 197H.

absence of supervision result in that being done which it is sought to prevent. This is not to delegate the employer's duty to exercise all due diligence; it is to perform it."

Although those in control of a corporation must themselves have taken appropriate action if a due diligence defence is to be available to it, it is not necessary for the prosecution to establish their personal involvement where the corporation is accused of a strict liability offence. In such a case the corporation will be vicariously liable for the acts of its employees and other agents unless an applicable defence can be made good.[30] In both *NRA. v. Alfred McAlpine* and in *R. v. British Steel*, where this was in issue, the Court held that any other conclusion would render the relevant legislation almost wholly ineffective. In the former case, which was concerned with water pollution, the judgments relied heavily on *Alphacell v. Woodward* as establishing vicarious liability for the policy reasons described by Lords Wilberforce and Salmon (see paragraphs 8–106 to 8–108). Similarly in the latter case, a prosecution under section 3(1) of the H.S.W.A. 1974, the Court of Appeal held that imposing absolute liability would promote a culture of guarding against risks to health and safety from hazardous industrial operations.

21–026

English Criminal Procedure

The rules of English criminal procedure are many and varied, and cannot be adequately covered in a short chapter. The intention of this section is simply to provide a brief description of the procedure that will normally apply in a prosecution for an offence in England under environmental legislation of medium gravity. (An outline of the Scottish criminal system is given at paragraphs 2–053 and 2–054).

21–027

Criminal offences may be divided into three categories: those triable on indictment only, those triable on summary trial only, and those which are triable "either way", *i.e.* triable on indictment or by way of summary trial. Indictment is reserved for the most serious criminal offences, involving trial before judge and jury in the Crown Court. In practice, no conventional environmental offences fall into this category. Summary trial involves trial in the magistrates courts, whose sentencing powers are strictly limited. Most of the principal offences under UK environmental legislation are triable either way. This allows

21–028

---

[30] *NRA (Southern Region) v. Alfred McAlpine Homes East Ltd,* [1994] Env. L.R. 198; *R. v. British Steel plc, The Times,* December 31, 1994.

the appropriate procedure to be adopted, depending on the gravity of the particular offence in question, and so caters for a range of offences which may go from very minor accidents, causing little or no harm to anyone, to deliberate or grossly negligent forms of pollution leading to extensive damage.

21–029 Unless a statute otherwise provides, any individual may start a prosecution for any crime.[31] In the environmental field, the most significant exception to this rule is perhaps the offence of failing to supply drinking water that is fit for human consumption, which may only be prosecuted by the Secretary of State or the Director of Public Prosecutions.

21–030 A private prosecutor has historically always had considerable difficulty in making any effective case for breach of environmental legislation, since his right of access to relevant evidence has been extremely limited or non-existent. However, with the introduction by C.O.P.A., 1974 of public registers relating to consents for discharges to controlled waters and the substantial expansion of environmental information made publicly available under more recent legislation, as described in Chapter 20, private prosecutions have been greatly facilitated, at least where the facts are not in dispute.

21–031 Nevertheless, the vast majority of prosecutions have been, and undoubtedly will continue to be, taken by the public regulatory authorities, who have regular access to monitoring information. Not every breach is made the subject of a prosecution. The principle that is applied remains as was stated by Lord Shawcross in a Parliamentary debate in 1951:

> "It has never been the rule of this country—I hope it never will be—that suspected criminal offences must automatically be the subject of prosecution. Indeed, the very first regulations under which the Director of Public Prosecutions worked provided that he should prosecute 'wherever it appears that the offence or the circumstances of its commission are of such a character that a prosecution in respect thereof is required in the public interest.' That is still the dominant consideration."

21–032 This criterion leaves wide scope for individual discretion and it is the case that the regulatory authorities are now very much more likely to prosecute than just a few years ago. The discretion on whether or not to do so gives considerable power to the regulators and a factor in

---

[31] Though where this is done, the Director of Public Prosecutions may decide to take the case over, and then may or may not proceed with it at his discretion.

coming to a decision in any particular case will undoubtedly be the past conduct of the potential defendant in dealing with such environmental problems as may have arisen previously.

Summary proceedings must generally be started within six months   **21–033** of the relevant offence.[32] This is the case also in Scotland notwithstanding there has been no explicit countermanding of the previous one year limit.[33] However among the exceptions to this rule are summary offences under the pollution control provisions of the Water Resources Act 1991, for which a period of 12 months is permitted.[34]

Trials of environmental offences will normally be started by way of   **21–034** the laying of an information; this states briefly (1) the act or omission said to constitute the offence, and (2) the statutory provision that is alleged to have been thereby breached. In practice, there may be a long list of separate informations covering a series of related acts, each of which independently constitutes a criminal offence. Where the offences charged are triable either way, as is normal, a hearing date will first be fixed in the relevant magistrates court. Before that date the defendant is served with a copy of the informations and also, in practice, with one or more witness statements setting out the evidence on which the prosecution intends to rely. The use of witness statements is not compulsory but is generally standard practice and entirely appropriate where there is no dispute as to most, if not all, of the facts of a pollution incident. The normal procedure is for the written statements to be read out to the court as the prosecution's evidence. The defendant is entitled to object to this procedure and will do so if he wishes to cross-examine the witness concerned, who otherwise does not need to be in court at all. Since in the great majority of environmental offences liability is strict, very few occasions arise where a significant challenge to the witness statements is appropriate. Most prosecutions are in circumstances where there is little or no doubt as to the guilt of the defendant, who accordingly pleads guilty and may simply seek to make a plea in mitigation. Pleas of not guilty are most often based on legal arguments rather than disputes as to fact. For this reason, although the use of witness statements is entirely voluntary, on both sides, it is the norm in prosecutions for environmental offences.

Where an offence is triable either way, the case will initially be   **21–035** brought before the magistrates who must first determine whether they will try the case summarily or whether it is to go to the Crown Court

---

[32] Magistrates' Courts Act 1980, s.127(1).
[33] *Friel v. Initial Contract Services Ltd.* [1993] Env. Liability C.S. 98.
[34] W.R.A., ss.101 and 202(5).

and be tried on indictment. The prosecution is likely to seek trial on indictment where it is considered the case requires a heavier penalty than the magistrates are able to impose, and particularly where it is wished to make an example of that defendant. Nevertheless, the magistrates, having heard a case, if they consider their own sentencing powers inadequate in relation to the conduct of the defendant as this has emerged at the trial, may still commit him to the Crown Court for sentencing. In other contexts, individual defendants quite often choose to be tried in the Crown Court, in the hope that juries are more likely to acquit them than magistrates. However, defendants charged with environmental offences generally have no wish to go to the Crown Court, where they will be exposed to heavier penalties and be appreciably more likely to receive widespread adverse publicity.

21–036   If an accused does not consent to summary trial of an offence triable either way, a trial on indictment must be held. Where the magistrates choose to hear a case summarily, they may, at any time before close of the prosecution case, change their mind. If they do, they may discontinue the trial and hold committal proceedings instead. Since the original decision to proceed by way of summary trial will have been taken before presentation of the evidence to the magistrates, it may only be later that they get a full appreciation of the offence of which the defendant is accused. This procedure is, however, only available where the defendant pleads not guilty; a guilty plea following a decision to proceed by way of summary trial will make that decision irrevocable. Conversely, if there is a decision for trial on indictment and the magistrates then move to the next stage of committal proceedings, at which the prosecution evidence is led, they may, having heard that evidence, and indeed at any stage during the committal proceedings, change their minds and invite the accused to elect for summary trial. Although the defendant is free to refuse, at least in environmental cases he is highly unlikely to object.

21–037   The maximum sentences that may be imposed for any offence are laid down in the relevant statutes, though frequently these permit fines of an unlimited amount on conviction on indictment. Nevertheless, the statutory maximum fines apply separately in respect of each offence of which the defendant is accused. Consequently if, as is quite normal, the prosecution case is based on a substantial number of informations, a conviction on each will expose the defendant to a corresponding multiple of the maximum fines. The mean level of fines has increased significantly over recent years due at least in part to the raising by the E.P.A. of the maximum fines on summary conviction for many offences from £2,000 to £20,000. This increase also reflects Government policy that fines should be realistic in relation to profits that may have been made by an offence or by failing to take appropriate precautionary measures.[35] Additionally the regulatory authorities normally seek orders for their costs; such awards can be for large sums and are rarely merely nominal amounts. Finally, compensation orders will often be sought to cover the costs of remedial work made necessary by the offence(s)—typically the cost of restocking a river following a fish kill resulting from pollution.

Appeals

A person convicted in a magistrates court following a plea of not guilty can appeal against both conviction and sentence. Where he has pleaded guilty, he may appeal only against the sentence. There are two standard routes for an appeal: to the Crown Court or to a Divisional Court by way of case stated.   **21–038**

Where an appeal goes to the Crown Court, it takes the form of a re-hearing, and the Crown Court may confirm, reverse or vary any part of the magistrates' decision, including findings of fact. It may indeed increase the sentence, though it rarely does so, provided it does not go beyond the maximum that could have been imposed by the magistrates themselves. More commonly in environmental cases an "appeal by way of case stated" is taken to the Divisional Court of the Queen's Bench Division of the High Court, under section 111(1) of the Magistrates Courts Act 1980. The only available grounds for such an appeal are that the decision of the magistrates court was wrong in law or in excess of jurisdiction, and the magistrates may be required to state a case on the question(s) of law or jurisdiction involved. Since in environmental offences disputes as to the facts will rarely be a significant element in a contested case, this route of appeal is generally more likely to be preferred to an appeal to the Crown Court.   **21–039**

Though not strictly an appeal, a decision of a magistrates court that is considered to have taken a mistaken view of the law may be questioned by way of an application for judicial review. Since there is provision for an appeal by way of case stated in such circumstances, judicial review would normally be inappropriate. It may however be apt where there has been some procedural irregularity in the conduct of the case before the magistrates.   **21–040**

Where a case has been tried by the Crown Court on indictment, or a defendant has been sentenced following committal to the Crown   **21–041**

---

[35] Crime, Justice and Protecting the Public, Cmnd. 965, para. 5.8. It is however notable that fines in the Scottish Courts are generally substantially lower than in England, which is frequently attributed to the fact that prosecutions are only conducted by Procurators Fiscal, who have no special environmental expertise, and not by the regulatory authorities.

Court by the magistrates for sentencing, an appeal may be taken to the criminal division of the Court of Appeal. Where there has been an appeal from a magistrates court to the Crown court, the decision of the Crown Court on that appeal may be made the subject of an appeal by way of case stated or of judicial review, in either case to a Divisional Court of the Queen's Bench Division, in the same manner as just described in relation to the decisions of magistrates courts.

Chapter 22

CIVIL LIABILITY

Introduction—Scope of Chapter

This chapter considers some aspects of tortious liability to others for **22–001** environmental damage, and primarily as they relate to land. It is thus principally concerned with the torts peculiar to land (nuisance, trespass, waste), though possible future developments in EC law are briefly considered first. It does not consider other torts of more general application (such as negligence, trespass to goods, trespass to person, or the economic torts); nor does it consider other than in passing defences, remedies, practice or procedure relating to remedies, statutory limitation periods, bars on equitable relief, equitable defences and such like, save where this is necessary or incidental to an explanation of the tort itself. These matters of general application are well covered in standard works and do not require special treatment here.

Plainly many other torts are capable of bearing upon "environmen- **22–002** tal law"—a category large enough to embrace many fields of human endeavour (and this is particularly so of negligence). Private nuisance is however the only tort pre-eminently and exclusively concerned with "land use" or "environmental" matters, and is in consequence the principal concern of this chapter. The torts of trespass to land and waste have in common with nuisance their application to damage to land. They are accordingly also considered in this chapter, though not at the same level of detail.

Statutory liability

Although this chapter is primarily concerned with civil liability **22–003** arising under common law, a variety of environmental statutes (although by no means all) expressly provide for civil remedies in the event of failure to comply with their requirements. The statutes are considered elsewhere in this work; accordingly the statutory remedies

are merely noted shortly here—reference should be made to the
appropriate chapter for further detail.

22–004

Statutory basis	Source of liability	Person liable
Environmental Protection Act 1990, s. 73(6).	Waste deposited in or on land.	Any person who deposited the waste or knowingly caused or knowingly permitted it to be deposited, so as to commit an offence under E.P.A., s.33(1) or 63(2).
Control of Pollution Act 1974 s.88(1).	Poisonous, noxious or polluting waste deposited on land.	Any person who deposited the waste or caused or knowingly permitted it to be deposited so as to commit an offence under C.O.P.A., ss. 3(3) or 18(2).
Water Resources Act 1991 s.208(1).	An escape of water, however caused, from a pipe vested in the NRA.	The NRA.
Water Industry Act 1991 s.209(1).	An escape of water, however caused, from a pipe vested in a water undertaker.	The water undertaker.
Nuclear Installations Act 1965 s.12(1).	Breach of any duty under ss.7 to 10, Nuclear Installations Act 1965.	The person subject to the duty.

22–005   In addition, a person may be held liable for the reasonable costs
incurred by a regulatory body in removing polluting matter or to
eliminate or reduce its consequences. These liabilities can arise under
the following heads:

Statutory basis	Source of liability	Person liable
Environmental Protection Act 1990 s.59(7)	A deposit of waste in or on any land in contravention of E.P.A. s.33(1).	The occupier (unless he can prove he was not responsible); the person who deposited or knowingly caused or knowingly permitted the deposit of the waste.
Environmental Protection Act 1990, s.61 (This section has not been brought into force. The Environment Bill will repeal it and substitute detailed provisions for the remediation of contaminated land.)	Any land in such a condition, due to noxious gases or noxious liquids caused by deposits of controlled waste in the land, that it may cause pollution of the environment or harm to human health.	The person who is for the time being the owner of the land. (Under the Environment Bill "the appropriate person" will be determined in accordance with government guidance.)
Environmental Protection Act Part III	Statutory nuisances under s.79(1), in particular any accumulation or deposit which is prejudicial to health or a nuisance.	The person responsible for the nuisance or the owner or occupier of the premises.
Radioactive Substances Act 1993 s.30	Radioactive waste located on premises.	The occupier or, if none, the owner of the premises.
Water Resources Act 1991 s.161	Any matter polluting or likely to pollute controlled waters.	Any person who caused or knowingly permitted the presence of the actual or potentially polluting matter.

Further, where a person has been convicted of a criminal offence, a **22–006** compensation order may be made against him under the Powers of the Criminal Courts Act 1973 (as amended).[1] Such orders may therefore be made following successful prosecutions under environmental statutes. They are particularly common in water pollution cases to pay for the costs of restocking after a fish kill, irrespective of whether anyone has a property interest in the lost fish (a rare example in English law of

---

[1] ss.35(1), 38.

liability for damage to the unowned environment). Although an order may be made in respect of personal injuries[2] the 1973 Act is not intended to provide an alternative route to substantial personal awards, particularly where the Defendant has an arguable case on civil liability and/or causation.[3]

European Developments

22–007   In the longer term, the United Kingdom civil liability regime in respect of environmental damage may be substantially altered as a result of two proposals being put forward at European level. These currently consist of a Convention on Civil Liability for Damage Resulting from Activities Dangerous to the Environment[4] promoted by the Council of Europe, and a consultative Green Paper on Remedying Environmental Damage[5] issued by the European Commission. The issues these raised were the subject of a full report by the House of Lords Select Committee on the European Community.[6]

22–008   The Convention (known as the "Lugano Convention") sets out a strict liability regime in respect of damage to the environment resulting from certain prescribed activities that represent significant environmental risks. "Environment" is defined to include property which forms part of the cultural heritage, and the characteristic aspects of the landscape. The Convention provides for actions to be taken not only by regulatory and other government bodies, but also by any organisation "which according to its statutes aims at the protection of the environment" and which complies with any further conditions of internal law of the country where the action is taken. The prescribed activities consist broadly of operations involving dangerous substances; those dealing with one or more genetically modified organisms or micro-organisms which pose significant risk for man, the environment or property; waste disposal (including incineration), treatment, handling or recycling facilities; and waste landfill sites. The damage for which compensation may be sought includes loss of life or personal injury, loss of or damage to property, impairment of the environment not within the previous two categories (though limited to the cost of reinstatement measures), and the cost of preventive measures, including any loss or damage these measures may cause. A

---

[2] In which event they will of course be taken in account in assessing damages that may be awarded in any civil proceedings.
[3] See Home Office Circular 53/1993, para. 8.
[4] Signed at Lugano June 21, 1993; European Treaty Series 150.
[5] COM (93) 47, March 1993.
[6] 3rd Report, Session 1993–4, "Remedying Environment (sic) Damage".

three year limitation period is provided, running from when the claimant knew or should have known of the damage and the identity of the operator defendant. However there is an overall long stop of 30 years from the date of the incident, after which no action may be bought in respect of that incident (unless it is part of a continuous occurrence or a series of occurrences) when the 30 year period will run from the end of the series.

The EC Commission's Green Paper covers very much the same **22–009** ground, although, being a consultation paper, it makes no firm proposals but merely debates the issues involved. Fundamental to these is the question of the application of the polluter pays principle and whether the liability should be fault-based or strict, and if strict subject to what defences. A further crucial issue is what constitutes damage to the environment and how this can be judicially assessed in a satisfactory manner. A particular concern is the insurability of the liability risks, an aspect which may well determine whether these ideas ever result in practical legislation, since if insurance is not available, as in many EC jurisdictions it is not, companies may prefer to avoid relevant hazardous activities and import products from outside the EC or else, if they can, carry on regardless, unable to meet any significant liabilities that may be awarded against them.

The EC Commission Green Paper was published in March 1993, and **22–010** invited responses within the next six months. The United Kingdom government, possibly stimulated by this, set up its own study into liability for contaminated land which, after some 12 months' gestation, resulted in two consultation documents being issued in March 1994. "Paying for Our Past", which related to England and Wales, was put out by the Department of the Environment, while "Contaminated Land Clean up and Control", which was very similar in content, was issued by the Scottish Office Environment Department. "Paying for Our Past" consisted very largely of a discussion of the problems of allocating liability for remedial work on contaminated land—despite its title, the paper was concerned not only with historic but also future pollution. The paper recognised in particular the multiplicity of different forms of statutory liability that exist, the variety of people who may be held liable, often under any of several statutory provisions, and the uncertainty as to what remedial work may reasonably be required. This paper, and the responses to it, formed the basis of Part II of the Environment Bill, currently before Parliament, which will set up a new regime, analogous to that for dealing with statutory nuisances, for assessing land for contamination, and for requiring its remediation where the contamination is "significant". Liability for remediation is intended to fall on the original polluter, in the first instance, but, where he "cannot be found", on the current owner or occupier. All others who may be held to have caused or knowingly permitted the contamination to be present, such as intermediate owners and occupiers (and including, possibly, those who have sent contaminating waste for disposal), are also to be potentially liable. Since many of the essential details, and crucially the ranking of those who are potentially liable where there are two or more, are yet to be determined (much will be prescribed in government guidance and not in legislation at all) a full review of this major development is not at present appropriate.

The Categories of Nuisance

Types of Nuisance

22–011   Three types of nuisance are generally recognised as actionable:

    (a)   Statutory nuisance, which is regarded as a quasi-criminal offence, in which the test for "nuisance" is equivalent to that in private nuisance at common law,[7] and which is considered at chapter 23, *post*.

    (b)   Private nuisance, which protects rights and interests in land and the ability to enjoy them, and (perhaps) some other proprietary interests related to them. It is considered at paragraphs 22–016 *et seq*.

    (c)   Public nuisance, which structurally has little in common with private nuisance (it is—and has evolved as—a crime with ancillary civil relief) but in its application to environmental matters shares certain features determinative of liability, if not its particular association with land. It is considered at paragraphs 22–186 *et seq*.

Examples of Nuisance

22–012   On the particular facts of particular cases, nuisances have been found in circumstances as varied as encroachment of tree roots,[8] noxious fumes from creosoted wood used as paving by a tramway company,[9] the presence of trespassing gipsies,[10] firing guns to disturb

---

[7] *e.g. NCB v. Thorn* [1976] 1 W.L.R. 543.
[8] *Solloway v. Hampshire County Council* [1981] 79 L.G.R. 449.
[9] *West v. Bristol Tramways Co.* [1908–10] All E.R. Rep 219.
[10] *Page Motors v. Epsom Borough Council* [1980] 78 L.G.R. 505; [1980] J.P.L. 396.

breeding fur foxes,[11] strong and offensive odours from stored veget-
ables,[12] smell from manure and swill-boiling in a piggery,[13] a steam
hammer interfering with worship in a Roman Catholic church,[14] noise,
dust and vibration from demolition and rebuilding works to the extent
that they were not reasonably carried on and without all reasonable
and proper steps to ensure no undue inconvenience,[15] clanging
churns,[16] crowing cocks,[17] oil refinery emissions and vehicular traffic
interfering with sleep, damaging drying clothes and the paintwork of
a car,[18] nocturnal use of a speaking trumpet,[19] pollution of air from
brick kilns,[20] damage caused by emissions from copper-smelting
works,[21] and specific damage and/or interference with enjoyment
provoked by any number of more or less common and more or less
modern domestic or industrial or agricultural uses.[22]

This is only a short list of a few randomly-selected examples. It   **22–013**
makes the point that nuisance is in modern and consumer terms an
environmental tort concerned with the indirect effect on the enjoyment of land by other (usually) land-users and with the common
media of the air and soil and water through which effects like heat,
noise, smell, dust, pollution and vibration may be transmitted.

Uses and Application

Apart from their historic connection with the problems which now   **22–014**
concern environmental lawyers, the torts of nuisance have other
advantages in modern contexts, when it comes to establishing liability
for and restraining particular types of damage caused by neighbours'
uses or activities.

In private nuisance neighbours owe a duty to each other, and that is   **22–015**
not a principle that needs establishing separately for each case as in
negligence. Other than in relatively limited circumstances (*e.g.* where

---

[11] *Hollywood Silver Fox Farm Ltd v. Emmett* [1936] 1 All E.R. 825; [1936] 2 K.B. 468.
[12] *Malcolm v. Brown* [1986] 16 C.L.T. Occ. N. 198 (CAN).
[13] *Bone v. Seale* [1975] 1 All E.R. 787; [1979] 1 W.C.R. 797.
[14] *Roskells v. Whitworth* [1871] 19 W.L.R. 804 L.J.J.
[15] *Andrea v. Selfridge & Co. Ltd* [1937] 3 All E.R. 259; [1938] C.H. 1.
[16] *Fanshawe v. London & Provincial Dairy Co.* [1988] 4 T.L.R. 694.
[17] *Leeman v. Montagu* [1936] 2 All E.R. 1677.
[18] *Halsey v. Esso Petroleum Co. Ltd* [1961] 2 All E.R. 145; [1961] 1 W.L.R. 683.
[19] *R. v. Smith* [1726] 93 E.R. 794 in which the defendant was convicted on an indictment
     for making great noises in the night with a speaking trumpet to the disturbance of the
     neighbourhood: which the court held to be a nuisance, and fined the defendant £5—
     in modern terms, a public nuisance.
[20] Numerous Victorian cases, but see especially *Bamford v. Turnley* [1862] 12 E.R. 27 Exch.
[21] *St Helen's Smelting Co. v. Tipping* [1869] 11 E.R. 1483, H.L.
[22] For a more comprehensive list the interested reader is referred to works such as The
     Digest, Volume 36(2) (2nd Reissue) (Butterworths 1990) where many such examples
     are cited or summarised.

the defendant is not the cause of the nuisance or where there is a special activity such as construction or there is a statutory authority defence—as to which see paragraphs 22–078 *et seq.* and 22–133 respectively—the extent to which the defendant has used reasonable skill and care will not usually be relevant. Even where it is, the onus of establishing it may well be on the defendant). In public and private nuisance, an injunction (subject to the usual factors affecting the exercise of discretion and to possible equitable defences) may in principle be available to restrain continuing or threatened nuisance, which—it would seem—may not be the case in negligence.[23]

Private Nuisance—General[24]

22–016   Private nuisance is principally a tort about conflicting *uses* of *land* in the occupation of particular plaintiffs and defendants. One traditional approach to the definition of private nuisance has been to say that it is not capable of exact definition.[25] That the circumstances amounting to a nuisance are not closed is plainly right. The nature, the location, the parties and the commercial and historic circumstances will be too diverse. In a system based on precedent, a tort whose function includes balancing these factors and others and which admits of intangible harm will generate a spectrum of particular applications which may not always be consistent with each other.

22–017   Words like "generic", "elastic" and "protean" feature in some descriptions of private nuisance. At other times its ambit is simply not addressed, or addressed only in a way which begs more questions ("unlawful act causing harm") or which is quite general such as:

> "It is the very essence of a private nuisance that it is the unreasonable use by a man of his land to the detriment of his neighbour"[26]

22–018   This last definition, by Lord Denning, is a good example of the difficulty in reconciling centuries of authority. Many of the older cases do not even admit that reasonableness of use or behaviour is a factor. The modern authorities are not always sure what type of detriment

---

[23] *Miller v. Jackson* [1977] 1 Q.B. 966 at 980 B-C, in which Lord Denning M.R. said:
    "But if he seeks an injunction to stop the playing of cricket altogether, I think he must make his claim in nuisance. The books are full of cases where an injunction has been granted to restrain the continuance of a nuisance. But there is no case, so far as I know, where it has been granted so as to stop a man being negligent."

[24] See paras. 1–015 to 1–022 for additional history of the tort.

[25] "I do not think the nuisance for which an action will lie is capable of any legal definition which will be applicable to all cases and useful in deciding them."
    Pollock CB's dissenting—and progressive—judgment in *Bamford v. Turnley* [1862] 122 E.R. 27 Exch.

[26] *per* Denning M.R., *Miller v. Jackson and Others* [1977] A.C. 966, 980D.

gives rise to a cause of action, or what part reasonableness has to play in cases of physical detriment. They largely suggest, however, that damage to land or its enjoyment is required, and that it must have been reasonably foreseeable.

Faced with these difficulties many writers still attempt a general definition. This book does not, but suggests that a definition of private nuisance will in most instances have to contend with the following factors: **22–019**

- An occupier of land (plaintiff) with a "neighbour" (defendant);
- Unreasonable use of land on the part of the defendant;
- Circumstances where the defendant knew or ought to have known that damage to the plaintiff might occur;
- Damage to or interference with the plaintiff's enjoyment of his land or an interest or right connected with it.

The following text gives what support it can to this suggestion though neither it nor any other is compatible with all the authorities in private nuisance.

The history of the tort of private nuisance (see paragraphs 1–015 to 1–022) and of the crime of public nuisance (see paragraphs 22–186 to 22–194) illuminates the genesis of the problem. The origins of private nuisance as a means of dealing with indirect interference with land are blurred—perhaps by association with public or common nuisance. Both types of nuisance have a common function as curbs on behaviour which from time to time and place to place might breach the bounds of what is acceptable (whether in relation to land and between individuals or whether in relation to "anti-social" behaviour generally). **22–020**

Although no definition of nuisance is consistent with all the authorities, and words like "reasonable" and "ought" give little practical guidance; the more consistent modern authorities enable the gamut of cases, descending from medieval agricultural society, through the confusion of a newly industrial economy, to today's relatively settled pattern of land use, to be assessed for reliability against a yardstick. **22–021**

This process shows how private nuisance is a part of commercial and land law, sensitive to the way in which commercial activity and patterns of land use have evolved. It illustrates the virtue of caution towards cases which—in terms of their facts—are not contemporaneous. A leading case like *St Helen's Smelting Co v. Tipping*[27] decided by **22–022**

---

[27] [1865] 11 H.L. Cas. 642.

the House of Lords in 1865, is plainly good law on what amounts to undue interference with enjoyment of land. Is it consistent with current trends when it comes to reasonableness and the relevance of "circumstances or place"?

22–023   It may in part be a consequence of the early reporting that medieval and late medieval actions of Novel Disseisin and on the case reflect a static and agricultural society with a limited range of land uses. In that society it may have been apparent to anyone what was and was not an appropriate (to use a neutral word) use to make of one's land in relation to that of one's neighbour, and what expectations the occupation of the neighbour's land conferred on him.

22–024   A judicial comment[28] that one cannot use one's land so as to damage another may not have been intended to hold unlawful *any* use which damages someone else's land. If doing something lawful on one's land caused a nuisance it was not necessarily actionable—the boundaries were recognised; the distinction between interference with a stream[29] and running a bakery[30] was well understood in a world of generally accepted norms. That world may have had clear views as to what rights attached implicitly to occupation of land. Once established that the bounds had been breached, liability was strict; hence a simplicity of definition—typically "unlawful"—which in modern terms seems at best unhelpful and circular.

22–025   The early attempts to grapple with conflicting land uses in a less static environment continued to assume that particular types of damage simply gave rise to a cause of action (*e.g.* brick pits in residential areas—when lack of transport must have made this difficult to avoid).[31] One finds little analysis of the use which generated them, and of its appropriateness in time and place. There is relatively little acknowledgement of a balance to be struck. However, whether in recognition of this sort of problem or not it is difficult now to tell, concepts of "reasonableness" surface for example in the minority judgment in *Bamford v. Turnley*. Another brick kiln, this time occupying a spot where bricks had previously been made was found to have been "emitting corrupted air upon the Plaintiff's house". The majority of the court found that the causing of a nuisance cannot be a reasonable use of land. Apart from circularity of definition, this shows a certainty and rigidity not found in many modern cases, but in his dissenting judgment Pollock C.B. said:

[28] *Rutland (Earl) v. Bowler* [1622] Palm. 290; 81 E.R. 1087.
[29] *ibid.*
[30] *Farmer v. Brooks Case* [1589] 1 Leon. 142; Owen 67; 74 E.R. 132.
[31] *Walter v. Selfe* [1851] 64 E.R. 849.

"The question so entirely depends on the surrounding circumstances—the place where, the time when, the alleged nuisance, what, the mode of committing it, how, and the duration of it, whether temporary or permanent, occasional or continual—as to make it impossible to lay down any rule of law applicable to every case, and which will also be useful in assisting a jury to come to a satisfactory conclusion; it must at all times be a question of fact with reference to all the circumstances of the case.

Most certainly in my judgment it cannot be laid down as a legal proposition or doctrine, that anything which, under any circumstances, lessens the comfort or endangers the health or safety of a neighbour, must necessarily be an actionable nuisance. That may be a nuisance in Grosvenor Square which would be none in Smithfield Market, that may be a nuisance at midday which would not be so at midnight, that may be a nuisance which would be no nuisance if temporary or occasional only . . . "

This is a worthy attempt to substitute, in relation to more fragmented and varied land uses, an objective list of local conditions for concepts of common knowledge.

That, broadly, is the way in which the authorities developed in one sense, though in others — cases for example of interference with "natural rights" to abstract clean water[32] or contamination of a well[33]—it was not considered necessary to address the point (perhaps because it was thought a generally acknowledged wrong or perhaps because tangible physical damage was considered to be involved). These two strands—the obvious and the analytical—did little to help the cause of clarity in the law of nuisance, which was further obscured by the development of negligence as a tort in itself and the pervasive trend to "duty of care situations". *Goldman v. Hargrave*[34] finds Lord Wilberforce reluctant even to acknowledge that the breach of a qualified duty for an occupier in relation to hazards present on his land through no fault of his own might be categorised as "nuisance". The Court of Appeal in *Leakey and Another v. The National Trust for Places of Historic Interest or Natural Beauty* had fewer inhibitions.[35]   **22–026**

As John P.S. McLaren pointed out in his article "The Common Law   **22–027** Nuisance Actions"[36] the tort of nuisance had by the 1970s reached a

---

[32] *e.g. Ballard v. Tomlinson* [1885] 29 Ch.D. 115.
[33] *Humphries v. Cousins* [1877] 2 C.P.D. 239, 46 L.J.C.P. 438 [1874–80] All E.R. Rep. 313.
[34] [1967] A.C. 645 at 656G.
[35] "I for my part should characterise that as a claim in nuisance" per Megaw L.J. [1980] 1 All E.R. 17, 26 a, b.
[36] (1972) Osgoode Hall L.J. 505, 520.

point where the English and Canadian authorities presented a most confused picture.[37]

22–028   What this introduction may have shown is the importance of chronology and context and the caution with which some earlier authorities should be treated. The case of *Cambridge Water Company v. Eastern Counties Leather Plc*,[38] having recently reintroduced some clarity to this area, reiterated the uniqueness of private nuisance, and affirmed its boundaries in relation to land. It may thus be helpful first to consider this case before attempting to summarise what principles of private nuisance can be deduced from it and from the authorities generally.

Cambridge Water Company v. Eastern Counties Leather plc

22–029   The Cambridge Water case was the first case for over 40 years in which the House of Lords had occasion to consider the rule in *Rylands v. Fletcher* directly and its relation to the law of private nuisance.

22–030   The defendant, Eastern Counties Leather plc[39] was a tannery using two chlorinated solvents, originally trichloroethylene (TCE) and subsequently perchlorethylene (PCE), for the degreasing of the leather to be tanned. Up until 1976, these solvents had been brought on to the site in drums; in using the solvent from these drums there had been over the years various spillages a considerable quantity of which had percolated through the soil to a chalk aquifer. From 1976 onwards, solvents were delivered in bulk by tanker, substantially eliminating the spillages. The

---

[37] "In the minds of many judges nuisance seems to conjure up a rather messy collage of strict liability and negligence, with no clear pointers to the applicability of either. The attempts at rationalisation by the courts are so abstract as to be useless as reliable precedent. When we are variously informed that liability in nuisance is strict[a], that proof of negligence is not required in nuisance[b], that nuisance and negligence are almost assimilated[c], that fault is nearly always present in nuisance[d], that foreseeability is the test for remoteness in nuisance[e], and that *Rylands v. Fletcher* is analogous to, but different from nuisance[f], Counsel might be forgiven for concluding that he is on his own."

NB: The footnotes in this quotation referred to the following cases:

    [a] *Read v. J. Lyons & Co.* [1947] A.C. 156; [1946] 2 All E.R. 471, *per* Lord Simonds at 183, 482.

    [b] *B.C. Pea Growers Ltd v. Portage La Prairie* [1966] S.C.R. 150, 54, W.W.R. 477, *per* Martland.

    [c] *MacMillan Bloedel (Alberni) Ltd v. B.C. Hydro* [1972] 22 D.L.R. (3d) 164 (B.C.S.C), *per* Rae J. at 181.

    [d] *Overseas Tankship (UK) Ltd v. The Miller S.S. Co.* [1967] 1 A.C. 617 (P.C., Aust.), [1966] 3 L.V.L.R. 498, *per* Lord Reid of 639, 508.

    [e] *ibid*, at 640, 509.

    [f] *J. P. Porter Co. v. Bell* [1955] 1 D.L.R. 62 (N.S.C.A.), *per* McDonald JA at 64, 65.

[38] [1994] 2 W.L.R. 53.

[39] At first instance there was a second defendant, Hutchings and Harding Limited, also a tannery, but that company took no further part in the litigation thereafter.

case proceeded exclusively on the basis of spillages occurring up to 1976.

In September 1976 Cambridge Water, a statutory drinking water **22–031** supplier, purchased a borehole at Sawston Mill a few miles from the tannery. It tested the water from the borehole before purchase and on a number of occasions thereafter to check that it was "wholesome" and so suitable for supply as drinking water. In 1980, the EC Drinking Water Directive was adopted; full compliance with the standards it set had to be achieved within five years, *i.e.* by September 1985. Implementation of the Directive was by DoE Circular 20/82 which set a maximum limit of 1 μg/litre of TCE and PCE, with effect from July 18, 1985. (Since 1989, the maximum value for PCE—the only solvent of present relevance—has been 10 μg/litre, a figure that corresponds with World Health Organisation guidelines.)

In 1983, Cambridge Water had its water analysed to check com- **22–032** pliance with the requirements of the EC Directive, and this analysis showed an average PCE concentration of 38.5 μg/litre in all the water it supplied; having identified the source of the contaminant as the Sawston Mill borehole, this was tested and showed concentrations in the range of 70 to 170 μg/litre, figures which are said in the judgment at first instance to be likely to have erred on the low side because the testing system was not well developed. As a result, the Sawston Mill borehole was shut down in October 1983. Very lengthy and detailed investigations traced the source of the contaminant at the borehole back to Eastern Counties Leather. Cambridge Water sued the company in nuisance, negligence and under the rule in *Rylands v. Fletcher*.

The evidence at first instance was that the defendants at the material **22–033** time, *i.e.* up to 1976, had not known of the harmful quality of the chlorinated solvents concerned, nor did they have any knowledge or reason to suppose that any solvents spilled would enter the aquifer and eventually reach the drinking water borehole. Indeed the assumption was that any spillages would simply evaporate. This was accepted at first instance, and not disputed in the higher courts, with the effect that both the negligence and nuisance claims were dismissed, and the judgment in this respect was not appealed.[40]

---

[40] Nevertheless, Lord Goff criticised a statement made in the first instance judgment to the effect that the common law would not entertain actions on these grounds for an award of damages in 1991 in respect of what was done 15 years before. He pointed out that the torts of negligence and nuisance are only complete when damage has been caused to the plaintiff; in the present case that was when the water at Sawston Mill borehole first became unsaleable by reason of the fact that it did not comply with the applicable standards relating to TCE and PCE, in other words in 1983. (There was no evidence that, even at the enhanced concentrations of PER, the water was actually harmful.) The mere fact that the solvents were spilled many years previously was not therefore to the point.

22–034   Though not strictly in issue by this stage of the case nuisance was nonetheless to the fore in practice because:

> "Since there is a close relationship between nuisance and the rule in *Rylands v. Fletcher*, I myself find it very difficult to form an opinion as to the validity of that submission [*i.e.* the relevance of knowledge to strict liability] without first considering whether foreseeability of such damage is an essential element in the law of nuisance."[41]

and

> "In order to consider the question in the present case in its proper legal context, it is desirable to look at the nature of liability in a case such as the present in relation both to the law of nuisance and the rule in *Rylands v. Fletcher* and for that purpose to consider the relationship between the two heads of liability."[42]

and (by way of conclusion):

> "It would moreover lead to a more coherent body of common law principles if the rule [in *Rylands v. Fletcher*] were to be regarded essentially as an extension of the law of nuisance to cases of isolated escapes from land . . . "[43]

22–035   Whether or not these comments on private nuisance by Lord Goff (who gave the sole reasoned judgment) should strictly be considered *obiter dicta*, the way in which he relates private nuisance to *Rylands* v. *Fletcher* means that his analysis of private nuisance cannot be ignored. This certainly succeeds in reconciling some diverse strands of authority, and as a long overdue attempt on the task at this level it is authoritative and merits the following consideration, whether technically *obiter* or not. It clarifies three distinct strands of the tort:

Land

22–036   The first point clarified is the significance of land as a component of private nuisance. Lord Goff cites with apparent approval Professor Newark's views[44] that the process through which nuisance — from being a tort associated with the plaintiff's enjoyment of rights over land — became distorted to embrace claims for personal injuries and produced adverse effects in the shape of cross-infection of nuisance by negligence. This approval, coupled with Lord Goff's explanation

---

[41] [1994] 2 W.L.R. 53, at 72G.
[42] *ibid*, 72 H.
[43] *ibid*, 80 F/G.
[44] "The Boundaries of Nuisance" (1949) 65 L.Q.R. 480.

of strict liability (see paragraphs 22–037 and 22–038), suggests that the primacy of land is being reiterated.

Reasonable Use

The second point clarified is how two concepts which from the cases   **22–037**
have not always seemed compatible—"strict liability" and "reasonab-leness"—are to be reconciled as a matter of general principle:

— If the user is reasonable, the defendant will not be liable for consequent harm to his neighbour's enjoyment of his land
— If the user is not reasonable, the defendant will normally be liable (subject to foreseeability of damage), even though he may have exercised reasonable care and skill to avoid that damage.[45]

Strict liability means no more than that, once it is established that   **22–038**
the defendant's use of land was not reasonable in itself, there will be no excuse for any reasonably foreseeable damage:

"It is still the law that the fact that the defendant has taken all reasonable care will not of itself exonerate him from liability, the relevant control mechanism being found within the principle of reasonable user".[46]

Foreseeability of Damage

The third point clarified is relevance of foreseeability; a defendant   **22–039**
should not be held liable for damage of a type which he could not reasonably foresee.

Overseas Tankship (U.K.) Ltd v. Miller Steamship Co. Pty (The Wagon   **22–040**
Mound) (No. 2)[47] is quoted as being widely accepted as settling the law to the effect that foreseeability of harm is a prerequisite to the recovery

---

[45] There are of course exceptions to this general principle—some of which are referred to in the judgment at 75D—*e.g.* natural causes, act of person for whom the defendant is not responsible), and also construction cases (*post* at 22–078) and statutory authority defences (*post* at 22–133).

[46] [1994] 2 W.L.R. 53, at 75 D/E.

[47] [1967] 1 A.C. 617. The headnote explains:
"The Respondents had two vessels undergoing repairs at a wharf in Sydney Harbour. The owners of the wharf in the course of doing the repairs were carrying out oxy-acetylene welding and cutting, work which was apt to cause pieces of hot metal to fly off and fall in to the sea. The appellant was charterer by demise of a vessel, *The Wagon Mound*, which in the early hours of 30 October, 1951, had been taking bunkering oil from another nearby wharf. By the carelessness of her engineers a large quantity of that oil overflowed from *The Wagon Mound* on to the surface of the water and drifted to and accumulated round the former wharf and the respondents' two vessels. On 1 November 1951 at about 2pm that oil was set alight. The fire spread rapidly and caused extensive damage to that wharf and to the respondents' two vessels."

957

of damages in private nuisance, as is the case in public nuisance. It is said to be regarded "essentially as one [*i.e.* a principle] relating to remoteness of damage".[48]

22–041   It may be that the principle is not confined entirely to remoteness of damage. Among the many authorities that speak of the balancing or give and take which the application of private nuisance requires,[49] there are suggestions that in some circumstances it might also be possible to view it as a component of liability. One might think, for example, that a use undertaken in circumstances where damage was not foreseeable (a cricket pitch not adjacent to cucumber frames) might be reasonable where it would not be if damage were foreseeable (cricket pitch adjacent to cucumber frames). The single distinguishing factor might then be the likelihood of the damage. The point is considered further below, at paragraph 22–072 *et seq.*

22–042   The analysis of private nuisance which *Cambridge Water* puts forward may not provide all of the answers to all of the questions to which this tort gives rise. Its reaffirmation of the role of land, its attempt to reconcile strict liability with the application of "give and take" principles, and its consideration of the part which foreseeability has to play nonetheless provide a convenient framework for the text which follows.

Interests in Land

Interest in Land as a Precondition for a Right of Action

22–043   It is fundamental to an action in private nuisance that the plaintiff should have a legal right connected with the occupation of land (or to the use of an interest in it) which has in some way been interfered with or damaged. Accounts of the genesis of private nuisance as a tort[50] stress its origins in the action on the case for indirect injury to the package of rights inherent in occupation or ownership of land—the indirect counterpart of trespass.

> "The assize of nuisance was a real action supplementary to the assize of novel disseisin. The latter was devised to protect the Plaintiff's seisin of his land, and the former aimed at vindicating the Plaintiff's right to the use and enjoyment of his land . . . with

---

[48] *Cambridge Water Company v. Eastern Counties Leather plc* [1994] 2 W.L.R. 53, Lord Goff at 76 C.

[49] *e.g.* Lord Wright in *Sedleigh Denfield v. O'Callaghan* [1940] 3 All E.R. Rep. 349 "A balance has to be maintained between the right of the occupier to do what he likes with his own and the right of his neighbour not to be interefered with".

[50] *e.g. Cunard v. Antifyre Ltd* [1933] 1 K.B. 551, 556–557; [1932] All E.R. Rep. 558. *Sedleigh Denfield v. O'Callaghan* [1940] 3 All E.R. Rep. 349.

certain possibly anomalous exceptions, not here material, possession or occupation is still the test".[51]

Emphasising the package of rights attaching to land may incidentally explain why interference with an easement—an incorporeal interest in land benefitting a dominant tenement—is actionable in its own right without proving damage.[52] It may also explain why the defendant in *Bradford Corporation v. Pickles*[53]—was not liable to the plaintiff for obstructing groundwater before it reached the Plaintiff's boreholes and streams and why his motives were irrelevant. The law does not recognise or protect a right to water percolating in undefined channels.[54] It is not part of the package of rights which an owner of land has, and cannot therefore be protected by an action in nuisance, regardless of the defendant's motives for abstracting the water to the detriment of the plaintiff in the first place.[55]

22–044

For a plaintiff to avail himself of the remedy of private nuisance the rights which he is trying to protect must be ones associated with land, and his cause of action must therefore be based on a right to use or occupy land or on an interest in it, whether in consequence of ownership or otherwise. The nature of that right is considered in the next section.

22–045

Who can Sue?

As the principal function of the tort of private nuisance is the protection of rights to use and enjoy land and perhaps—though not everyone classifies them in this way—rights to use easements,[56] it follows that a prospective plaintiff must have such a right or a right to possession though not necessarily an exclusive one. The lowest level of possible qualification is that of a licensee with exclusive possession of the land affected.[57] A licensee without

22–046

---

[51] *Sedleigh Denfield v. O'Callaghan* [1940] 3 All E.R. Rep. 349, *per* Ld. Wright at 364.
[52] *Nicholls v. Ely Sugar Beet Factory Limited* [1936] Ch. 343, 350.
[53] [1895] A.C. 587—the defendant's intention was alleged to have been to persuade the Corporation to buy his land or to give him some other compensation.
[54] See also *Stephens v. Anglia Water Authority* [1987] 3 All E.R. 379.
[55] Though in other cases, a plaintiff who has rights with which the defendant might be interfering, may be entitled to point to the defendant's motive as one of the factors to be considered in determining whether or not he is making a reasonable use of his land. See *Hollywood Silver Fox Farm Ltd v. Emmett* [1936] 2 K.B. 468; [1936] 1 All E.R. 825, where the plaintiff owner, who bred silver foxes, had set up notices on the edge of the highway advertising his business. He refused to remove them at the request of the defendant, a developer of adjacent land for housing, who thought they might deter prospective purchasers. Whereupon his son was instructed to shoot along the boundary of the fox farm, interfering—as he was aware it would—with breeding. The plaintiff was awarded damages and an injunction on his claim in nuisance.
[56] The cause of action for protecting a profit à prendre would seem to be trespass.
[57] *e.g. Foster v. Warblington U.D.C.* [1906] 1 K.B. 648.

exclusive possession cannot, it seems, succeed in private nuisance. Of the wife of the licensee manager of a company tenant it was said:

> "A person in the position of the plaintiff, who was in the premises as a mere licensee, had no right to dictate to [the defendants] which course they should take . . . it was a matter entirely for the tenant, and a person who is merely present in the house cannot complain of a nuisance which has in it no element of a public nuisance."[58]

22–047   It might perhaps have been different had all those entitled to possession as licensees put themselves forward as co-plaintiffs. It must be doubted whether a non-owning spouse—or indeed others with a lawful right to occupy—would be barred from action in the same way any more.

22–048   There may be more than one person who, in relation to any given piece of land and to actionable nuisance, can show a right to possession of the land and to the package of rights that goes with it. The landlord and tenant of a building whose quiet working environment is being disrupted by a new—and inappropriately sited—breaker's yard might be one example. The effect of the nuisance alleged is different for each of them. The tenant's day to day enjoyment of the building for which he is paying will be affected. Unless he decides to sell his interest the landlord may experience no immediate adverse financial consequences until his reversion falls in and/or the tenant decides to plead for a reduced rent at the next rent review and/or the landlord decides to sell it with the potential for those problems. Plainly, the tenant can in principle maintain an action in private nuisance. His ability to occupy the land and exploit the rights to which his legal interest in it gives him title has been interfered with. Receipt of money (or the reflection of the right to receive it) is however the only way in which a landlord not in occupation can enjoy his property.

22–049   The general view seems to be that a landlord whose reversion will be permanently damaged can sue—at least in circumstances where he can show that his right to possession (when it crystallises) will be damaged:

> "If the thing complained of is of such a permanent nature that the reversion may be injured, the question of whether the reversion is or is not injured is a question for the jury. I take 'permanent' in this connection to mean such as will continue indefinitely unless something is done to remove it. Thus a building which infringes ancient lights is permanent within the rule for, though it can be

---

[58] *Malone v. Laskey* [1907] 2 K.B. 141; [1904–7] All E.R. Rep. 304.

960

removed before the reversion falls into possession, still it will continue until it be removed. On the other hand, a noisy trade, or the exercise of an alleged right of way, are not in their nature permanent within the rule, for they cease of themselves unless there be someone to continue them."[59]

This quotation distinguishes between physical states and human **22–050** activities. That does not entirely explain why a landlord might be able to recover damages (though one can see why he might be given a *quia timet* injunction) before he actually suffers the loss when in possession. This is contrary to the usual pre-requisite of actual damage (see paragraph 22–088). One explanation might be that nuisances of a permanent nature could inflict immediate damage to value, which is considered to be either immediate economic damage to a proprietary interest or to an ability to enjoy a right associated with land (*e.g.* the right to receive rent), though not all the authorities look at the problem in this particular way.

Nuisance causing loss of tenants, is said not to be actionable at the **22–051** suit of a reversioner[60] even though the premises are only capable of being re-let at a lower rent. That, one would have thought, is capable of being permanent damage—though perhaps not within the special definition of *Jones v. Llanrwst UDC*—in that it is caused by an activity rather than a state.

It is difficult to see why the artificial distinction should survive in a **22–052** world where rent review is almost universal in commercial leases, and where tenants can be expected to point to recent (and perhaps actionable) deteriorations in the locality as a means of reducing rent.

Who can be Sued?

Other considerations apply to the choice of defendant—who is **22–053** liable in relation to a current nuisance? Lord Wright's speech in *Sedleigh-Denfield v. O'Callaghan* (a mine of useful quotations) provides this example:

"The ground of responsibility is the possession and control of the land from which the nuisance proceeds."[61]

As this quotation shows, the English Courts in private nuisance cases have shown an attachment, so far as defendants are concerned, to the entitlement to occupy land and the degree of control which it is

---

[59] *Jones v. Llanrwst UDC* [1911] 1 Ch. 393; [1908–10] All E.R. Rep. 922.
[60] *Mumford v. Oxford Worcester Wolverhampton Railway Co.* [1856] 57 E.R. 1107.
[61] [1940] 3 All E.R. 349, 364D.

considered to give to defendants over activities which occur there. In *Laugher v. Pointer*[62] the plaintiff tried unsuccessfully to fix with negligence the hirer of an independent contractor coachman; the position in nuisance was contrasted. Cases where land owners had been made liable for the acts of their independent contractors were distinguished by reference to the degree of control which a landowner has and the hirer of a coachman does not. In *St.Annes Well Brewery Co v. Roberts* Scrutton J. put it like this:

> "It appears to me that you are not able successfully to attack an owner no longer in occupation, because he has let the premises on which there is ultimately found to be a nuisance, unless you can show that at the time he let them there was then a nuisance on the premises and that he knew it." [63]

22–054   In Canada it seems that a defendant's activities need not be on private land which he occupies.[64] The subject of the tort is interference with the plaintiff's interest in land and this can occur without title to land on the defendant's part. There seems to be no reason in principle why an activity carried on in a public place or on a highway in such a way as to affect only one person's land should not be a private nuisance in England as well[65] — though it would conflict with the principle that liability is a consequence of control of land.[66] Some writers and dicta support the view[67] that a trespasser or licensee (even if not technically an "occupier") can be liable. These points must nonetheless both be regarded as uncertain.

22–055   Subject to possible anomalies like these it is generally the occupation of land and the control which that is said to confer which gives rise to potential liability for a private nuisance. Problems arise, however, where possession, control, ownership and occupation are stratified or

---

[62] [1824–34] All E.R. Rep. 368; 108 E.R. 204.
   "But supposing these cases [*i.e.* where defendants were owners of property] to have been rightly decided, there is this material distinction that there the injury was done upon or near and in respect of the property of the defendants of which they were in possession at the time"

[63] [1928] All E.R. Rep. 28 at 33 — where part of the ancient wall of the City of Exeter, on property occupied by a tenant of the defendants, had collapsed into the plaintiff's inn.

[64] *cf.* John P.S. McLaren *op. cit.* at 519.

[65] *cf.* the extension of statutory nuisances by the Noise and Statutory Nuisances Act 1993 to noise from the highway as well as from premises — see paras. 23–014 and 18–033 to 18–036.

[66] See quotation from Lord Wright at the beginning of paragraph 22–053.

[67] *e.g. Salmond & Heuston on the Law of Torts* (20th ed.), p. 60, " . . . even when it is on adjoining private land the defendant need not necessarily be the owner or occupier of that land" or *Clerk and Lindsell on Torts* (16th ed.) ss.24–17 "the interference need not emanate from the land of the defendant for a trespasser may be liable" and texts and authorities cited there.

dispersed among two or more of, say, landlord, tenant, licensee, trespasser, and independent contractor or simply owner and former owner. The position is far from clear, and there are by no means authorities on all of the possible permutations. The following commentary considers certain situations of frequent concern, where a person may be held liable for a nuisance the initial cause of which is due to someone else, or which arose through some accident of nature, and where the person who initially caused a nuisance is no longer in control of the land. It does not attempt to be comprehensive.

Liability for Nuisances Initiated by Others or by Nature

Where a private nuisance arises out of a state of affairs on a person's **22–056** land which the occupier can reasonably abate, liability will attach to him even though he neither created the offending state nor received any benefit from it. It is enough if he permitted it to continue after he knew or ought to have known of its existence.[68] This is so, whether the original cause was the act of a trespasser (as in *Sedleigh-Denfield v. O'Callaghan*), or of a previous occupier of the land (as in *Broder v. Saillard*[69]), or of nature (as in *Goldman v. Hargrave*[70]). In *Sedleigh-Denfield v. O'Callaghan*, Lord Atkin, in discussing decisions which imposed liability only where the defendant had "caused or continued" a nuisance said:[71]

> "In the context in which it is used 'continued' must indicate mere passive continuance. If a man uses on premises something which he found there, and which itself causes a nuisance by noise, vibration, smell or fumes, he is himself in continuing to bring into existence the noise, vibration, etc, causing a nuisance. Continuing in this sense and causing are the same thing. It seems to me clear that if a man permits an offensive thing on his premises to continue to offend, that is, if he knows that it is operating offensively, is able to prevent it, and omits to prevent it, he is permitting the nuisance to continue; in other words he is continuing it".

In that case a local authority had partially culverted a ditch on the **22–057** defendant's land without the defendant's knowledge and had left the culvert's opening unprotected by a grate. Over time, it became obstructed, and the ditch overflowed, flooding the plaintiff's adjoining land. The evidence showed that one of the defendant's functionaries

---

[68] *Sedleigh-Denfield v. O'Callaghan, per* Ld. Porter at p.919.
[69] 2 Ch. D. 692.
[70] [1967] A.C. 645.
[71] *ibid.* at p.897.

was aware of the ditch and of its unprotected state, but his superiors were not. They were in consequence found to have continued or adopted a nuisance and held liable in damages:

> "In my opinion, an occupier of land continues a nuisance if, with knowledge or presumed knowledge of its existence, he fails to take any reasonable means to bring it to any end, though with ample time to do so. He 'adopts' it if he makes any use of the erection, building, bank or artificial continuance which constitutes the nuisance".[72]

22–058   *Goldman v. Hargrave* was an Australian case in which a red gum tree on the defendant's land was struck by lightning and caught fire. He cleared a space around it of combustible material and sprayed it with water whilst help arrived. The tree was then cut down and continued to burn, the defendant taking no steps to stop it in the belief that it should be allowed to burn itself out. The fire spread and damaged adjoining property. The defendant, it was found, could have put the fire out by taking reasonable care and spraying it with water. Delivering the advice of the Board of the Privy Council Lord Wilberforce said that:[73]

> "On principle, therefore, their Lordships find in the opinions of the House of Lords in *Sedleigh-Denfield v. O'Callaghan*[74] and in statements of the law by Scrutton L.J.[75] and Salmond,[76] of which they approve, support for the existence of a general duty upon occupiers in relation to hazards occurring on their land, whether natural or man-made."

and[77]

> "the law must take account of the fact that the occupier on whom the duty is cast has, *ex hypothesi*, had this hazard thrust upon him through no seeking or fault of his own . . . In such situations the

---

[72] Viscount Maughan 358F, the other judges in the House of Lords expressing broadly concurring views, Lord Wright (365D) preferring to refer to "means of knowledge" rather than "presumed knowledge".

[73] [1967] 1 A.C. 645, at 661 G.

[74] [1940] 3 All E.R. Rep. 349.

[75] In the Court of Appeal in *Sedleigh-Denfield v. O'Callaghan*.

[76] Salmond's Law of Tort, (5th Ed., 1920) pp. 258–265 (being the edition referred to in the cited cases):
> "When a nuisance has been created by the act of a trespasser or otherwise without the act, authority, or permission of the occupier, the occupier is not responsible for that nuisance unless, with knowledge or means of knowledge of its existence, he suffers it to continue without taking reasonably prompt and efficient means for its abatement."

[77] [1967] 1 A.C. 645, at 663 B and E.

standard ought to be to require of the occupier what it is reasonable to expect of him in his individual circumstances."

These principles were later applied to a natural state of affairs in which the defendant had been quite passive, by the Court of Appeal in *Leakey and Another v. National Trust for Places of Historic Interest or Natural Beauty.*[78] The National Trust owned a large mound at the base of which the plaintiffs owned two houses. In consequence of a drought a large crack appeared at the base of the mound and was pointed out to the Trust which did nothing. Part of the mound duly collapsed on to the plaintiffs' land. Their case for the costs of clearing up was brought in nuisance alone, and the Trust was found liable; the suggestion that it should have been sued in negligence received short shrift.

22–059

Though it is clear law that an owner of premises cannot be said to have permitted the continuance of that which was not caused by him, and of which he had no knowledge,[79] liability does not depend exclusively on actual knowledge; constructive knowledge will suffice. So an absentee owner or an occupier oblivious of what is happening under his eyes is in no better position than the man who looks after his property.[80] A reasonable time must however be allowed for the relevant state of affairs to be discovered and remedied. Thus in *Barker v. Herbert* (a case in public nuisance, but where in this respect the same principles apply) a gap in railings dividing the area of the defendant's house from the highway was created by trespassers, and a child that got through the gap fell and was injured. On the facts it was found that the defendant, who was not living in the house which was vacant at the time, did not know of the gap in the railings at the time of the accident, and that such a time had not elapsed between the creation of the gap and the accident that with reasonable care he should have known of it. Although there are statements in *Sedleigh-Denfield v. O'Callaghan* that suggest liability may attach even though the defendant is wholly ignorant of the existence of the offending state of affairs,[81] and this appears to have been the case in *Broder v. Saillard* and

22–060

---

[78] [1980] 2 All E.R. 17.
[79] *Barker v. Herbert*, [1911] 2 K.B. 633 at 642, *per* Fletcher Moulton L.J.
[80] *Sedleigh-Denfield v. O' Callaghan, per* Ld. Maugham at p.887.
[81] See Ld. Atkin at p.898 and in particular Ld. Porter at p.919 who said (*obiter*) that an occupier may be liable even though he is wholly blameless, not only ignorant of the existence of the nuisance but also without means of detecting it, and entered into occupation after the nuisance had come into existence. In *Tarry v. Ashton*, (1876) 1 Q.B.D. 314, however, though two judges seemed to impose a strict liability, Blackburn J. clearly indicated his preference for knowledge of a defect to be a pre-requisite to liability, though the issue did not fall to be decided in that case.

was expressly held to be so in *Humphries v. Cousins*,[82] it would now appear to be the law that actual or constructive knowledge is an essential element of liability. Such a requirement would moreover be consonant with the trend towards applying negligence standards in nuisance and with the need for damage to be foreseeable where the state of affairs is known, if liability is to attach, as recently stressed by Lord Goff in *Cambridge Water*.

22–061 In observing that it was not appropriate to make a defendant liable for a continuing nuisance, damage having only become reasonably foreseeable since the conditions were originally created,[83] Lord Goff in *Cambridge Water* appears to introduce a test of whether the conditions are now beyond the defendant's control—which on the face of it extends the indulgence granted by *Sedleigh-Denfield v. O'Callaghan* and *Goldman v. Hargrave* from circumstances not caused by the defendant to ones which he did cause (though at the time blamelessly) but can no longer control. It is interesting to consider where this principle might end if developed. Though the evidence on which this observation was based does not emerge from the reports[84]—and one can only speculate, therefore—if further escape of solvent from the defendant's land might have been prevented or at least appreciably reduced by suitable pumping, the decision on this point may well have turned on its being unreasonable to spend the money required, or, to put it more positively, on its being reasonable to take no action.

22–062 In the *Cambridge Water* case there was of course a long period of latency before damage occurred. Lord Goff said that foreseeability applies to the time of the act or default in question, so that during the latency period there is liability only if the defendant can reasonably do something to retrieve the situation.

22–063 A separate issue, where a defendant did not initially create the offending state of affairs, is the extent to which his personal means are relevant to what may be required of him to abate a nuisance that he discovers to be on his land. In *Goldman v. Hargrave* it was held that where the occupier found himself responsible for a hazard through no seeking or fault of his own, the law would only require of him what it

---

[82] (1877) 2 C.P.D. 239; [1874–80] All E.R. Rep. 313.
[83] [1994] 2 W.L.R. at 53, at 81.
[84] Indeed it appears that the lost solvent is far from irretrievable, and that the defendant, Eastern Counties Leather, has agreed with the NRA to pump and treat contaminated water from the acquifer.

was reasonable to expect in his individual circumstances.[85] On principle the same approach should apply where an owner or occupier has acquired an interest in land—whether the purchase of a freehold, or the taking of a new lease or the assignment of the residue of one—and it is only subsequently that the existence of some offending state of affairs comes to light. Nevertheless, in view of the requirement that he should use reasonable diligence in establishing his property is not liable to interfere with the enjoyment of neighbouring property, a distinction may be drawn between cases where the problem should reasonably have come to light during pre-contract investigations, and cases where despite reasonable diligence at that stage, no problem was then ascertained. In the latter, if the *Goldman v. Hargrave* principle applies, the means of the defendant would be relevant to whether any remedial action could be required of him, and if so how much.

Conversely, in the former situation, the defendant had, or must be **22–064** presumed to have had, the opportunity not to proceed with the acquisition, and if he nevertheless did so, it may be argued that there is no good reason why the neighbour, whose property has been harmed, should as a matter of law have to accept a lesser remedy than if he faced a better resourced defendant. Moreover, where the defendant has proceeded with his acquisition, it may be presumed that the contract would have taken into account the potential liability of the purchaser to abate any nuisance and to compensate his neighbours, whether by way of reduction in the purchase price or through appropriate warranties and indemnities, or both. If the law makes such a presumption, then purchasers of property will be all the more inclined to put pressure on sellers to establish the absence of potential nuisances, such as pollution that may spread to neighbours or through groundwater, and so encourage property owners to avoid pollution and other nuisances in the first place. By making such a presumption the common law would be acting in support of the objectives of

---

[85] *Goldman v. Hargrave*, from which it is apparent that it is the involuntary nature of responsibility for circumstances not of his own making which confers on a defendant a "measured" duty and allows his means, circumstances and conduct to be taken into account:

> "Thus, less must be expected of the infirm than of the able-bodied: the owner of a small property where a hazard arises which threatens a neighbour with substantial interests should not have to do so much as one with larger interests of his own at stake and greater resources to protect them: if the small owner does what he can and promptly calls on his neighbour to provide additional resources, he may be held to have done his duty: he should not be liable unless it is clearly proved that he could, and reasonably in his individual circumstances should have done more."

per Lord Wilberforce, [1967] 1 A.C. at 663.

environmental legislation, and in particular the principles contained in Article 130R(2) of the Rome Treaty that preventive action should be taken, the environmental damage should as a priority be recitifed at source, and that the polluter should pay.

22–065 Although an occupier may for these reasons become liable for a nuisance that exists on his property, this does not exonerate the person who was in fact responsible for creating the state of affairs that constitutes or has resulted in the nuisance. An occupier, once liable for his existing act or omission cannot usually relieve himself of the liability by parting with control of the land and/or seeking to pass the liability on to a successor.[86] The mere fact that by contract with another he may have put it out of his power to remedy the nuisance will not relieve him of liability in damages, subject to the possible right to claim a contribution from the current occupier in appropriate circumstances. Since a cause of action in nuisance only arises when the plaintiff suffers damage, the potential liability of a person who has created a latent or a continuing nuisance on land which he has ceased to occupy may in principle last indefinitely, at least until the hazard materialises and the damage is caused—the limitation period will only then begin to run—and maybe thereafter. In the case of a nuisance, for example a leaking drain or a contaminated site from which pollutants constantly leach out, that causes continuing damage, there will be a fresh cause of action each day in respect of new damage. The long-stop period, provided by the Latent Damage Act 1986, of fifteen years from the original act or default that eventually created the damage, will not however afford any relief against an action in nuisance, as it is restricted to claims in negligence.

Liability as between Landlords and Tenants/Licensees

22–066 An occupier's liability may extend not merely to acts and omissions perpetrated by him, and those directly employed by him, but also to those of persons lawfully on his land—this liability probably also

---

[86] *Roswell v. Prior* [1701] 12 Mod. 635; *Esso Petroleum Co. Ltd v. Southport Corporation* [1956] A.C. 218; *Brew Bros v. Snax Ross* [1970] 1 Q.B. 612 in which a landlord who had let premises with a defective wall to a tenant who covenanted to repair was found liable for the nuisance caused by the wall; perhaps *Pemberton and another v. Bright and others* [1960] All E.R. 792, provides an analogy for what might happen in some cases. There a county council which had culverted a stream below a highway in 1926 (but was not the landowner) was found liable in nuisance to pay 75 per cent of the damages to a plaintiff whose land flooded in 1956 for want of a grate to keep the mouth of the culvert free of debris. The "occupier" of the offending culvert (who had been there since 1934) was found liable to pay 25 per cent.

extends to those not lawfully on the land but over whom the occupier might be expected to have some control.[87]

It is trite law that if a person is liable to a third party for a private nuisance, he cannot, by contractual means with a third party, escape his liability to the person injured by the nuisance.[88] As where a person has parted with his entire interest in land may remain liable for a nuisance on it for which he was originally responsible, so a landlord may likewise continue to be liable, notwithstanding that he may be unable to take remedial action without a breach of the terms of the lease.[89]   **22–067**

The liability of a landlord for the acts or omissions of his tenant, on   **22–068** the other hand, will ordinarily depend on whether or not he has authorised the tenant to behave in such a way as to cause a nuisance.[90] Where a nuisance is an "ordinary and necessary" consequence of the purpose for which an occupier lets or licences his land to another, he will be taken to have authorised it and thus to be liable.[91] However if the nuisance is merely a possibility, as where the tenant is allowed to carry out a potentially, though not necessarily, polluting activity, it may be that there will be no presumption of authorisation.[92] The landlord's position will be strengthened in this respect if he has obtained appropriate covenants barring nuisance or the particular use complained of, as he will not then be taken to have authorised the

---

[87] *Page Motors Ltd v. Epsom & Ewell Borough Council* [1981] 80 L.G.R. 337 and *DuPont v. Avon County Council* [1993] Q.B. (unreported)—both cases involving trespassing travellers, though cases like this are probably best analysed in terms of the occupier's responsibility for states of affairs natural or otherwise not actually created by him, considered above at para. 22–056 *et seq.*

[88] Thus with regard to a tenancy agreement providing that the tenant should deal with any pre-existing nuisance for which the landlord was responsible it was said:
"any bargain made by the person responsible to his neighbour or to the public that another person should perform that obligation may give rise to rights as between the two contracting parties but does not, in my judgment, in any way affect any right of third parties, who are not parties or privy to such a contract."
St Anne's Well Brewery Co. v. Roberts [1928] All E.R. Rep. 28.

[89] *Spicer and Another v. Smee,* [1946] 1 All E.R. 489 at 493F, *per* Atkinson J., applying *dictum* of Scrutton L.J. in *Job Edwards Ltd. v. Birmingham Navigations,* [1924] 1 K.B. 341 at 355.

[90] Pennycuick V.-C. in *Smith v. Scott* [1972] 3 All E.R. 645, [1973] 1 Ch. 314 at 648–649, 320–321:
"In general, a landlord is not liable for nuisance committed by his tenant, but to this rule there is, so far as now in point, one recognized exception, namely, that the landlord is liable if he has authorised his tenant to commit the nuisance . . . The exception is squarely based in the reported cases as express or implied authority."

[91] *Tetley v. Chitty* [1986] 1 All E.R. 663.

[92] There seems to be no authority directly on point (in *Smith v. Scott* the issue was complicated by the covenant) but the conclusion appears consistent with the building cases.

nuisance[93] even if it was foreseeable. Conversely, if the creation of the nuisance was "objectively foreseeable" and there are no such covenants, the landlord may be held liable.[94] This seems to be the rationale of at least some of the building cases discussed below. However, where the landlord has let his land on a basis which gives him continuing responsibility over an aspect of its maintenance (*e.g.* a landlord's repairing covenant) he may be taken to have authorised his tenant not to maintain the property in that particular way, and thus himself to be responsible for any nuisance resulting.[95]

Landowner and Building Contractor

22–069   As discussed below (see paragraphs 22–081 to 22–083), building cases often raise exceptions to the normal rules of liability, since it has long been accepted by the Courts that though a temporary disturbance or neighbours is often an inevitable part of building operations, yet such operations must be allowed to proceed, at least if they are conducted with due skill and care. Where a building contractor nevertheless causes a nuisance, *prima facie* the landowner employer will not be liable for the contractor's tort because the latter will ordinarily be an independent contractor.[96] However where an independent contractor carries out an operation that is inherently likely to cause danger, then the standard rule is disapplied and the employer made liable.[97] This exception to the standard rule, which was developed in negligent cases, was adopted for the purposes of a claim in nuisance in *Matania v. The National Provincial Bank Ltd and The*

---

[93] *e.g. Smith v. Scott* [1972] 3 All E.R. 645. It would not appear from the cases that there need be any practical steps taken to ensure compliance by the tenant with his obligations under the lease. Conversely, if such steps are taken and the lease permits remedial action to be demanded of the tenant, where appropriate, it may be that the cases of n. 95 apply. It will doubtless be a question of fact and degree.

[94] See dicta of McNeill J. in *Tetley v. Chitty* [1986] All E.R. 663, at 671 D/E. "Authority elsewhere points to objective foreseeability as the proper test."

[95] *Wringe v. Cohen* [1940] 1 K.B. 229 as explained in Salmond and Heuston, *op. cit.* at p. 73. See also *St Anne's Well Brewery Company v. Roberts* [1928] All E.R. Rep. 28.

[96] As to the broad principle of liability for an independent contractor, see *Bower v. Peate*, (1876) 1 Q.B.D. 321 at 325, 326, *per* Cockburn C.J.:

"A man who orders a work to be executed, from which, in the natural course of things, injurious consequences to his neighbour must be expected to arise, unless means are adopted by which such consequences may be prevented, is bound to see to the doing of that which is necessary to prevent the mischief, and cannot relieve himself of his responsibility by employing someone else — whether it be the contractor employed to do the work from which the danger arises or some independent person to do what is necessary to prevent the act he has ordered to be done from becoming wrongful."

See also *Laugher v. Pointer*, [1824] All E.R. Rep. 368; 108 E.R. 204. Nevertheless, the landowner's degree of control, and the foreseeability or otherwise of nuisance, must remain relevant.

[97] *Honeywill & Stein v. Larkin Bros*, [1934] 1 K.B. 191.

Elevenist Syndicate Ltd.[98] It was there held that if the act done is one which in its very nature involves a special danger of nuisance being complained of, then it is one which falls within the exception for which the employer of the contractor will be responsible if there is a failure to take the necessary precautions that the nuisance shall not arise.[99] In that case, the plaintiff, a singing teacher, sued in respect of excessive dust and noise arising from construction works carried on on the floor of the building immediately below his premises, though the most immediate danger of nuisance appears to have been that his own floor might have collapsed. Though Finlay J. was concerned as to whether the construction works were so out of the ordinary to justify an exception to the general rule of liability, he eventually held that it was "a case where unless precautions were taken there was a great and obvious danger that nuisance would be caused, as indeed it was caused".[1]

Liability for Contributing to Aggregation Causing Nuisance

As well as vertical divisions of liability (*e.g.* landlord and tenant) issues also arise in relation to "horizontal" divisions as where, for example, it appears that more than one discharging riparian owner may have contributed to contamination of a river and thus to interference with fishing rights, or where in an industrial area it is the cumulative effect of smoke and fumes from different sources which is interfering with an occupier's enjoyment of his premises. **22–070**

It now seems settled that where an aggregation of acts not in themselves a nuisance and committed by several defendant results in a nuisance, individual contributors to the problem are liable for the consequences. The liability of the individual tortfeasor in these cases would appear to extend to that part of the whole of the damage suffered attributable to him.[2] **22–071**

---

[98] [1936] 2 All E.R. 633.
[99] *Ibid.*, at p.646, *per* Slesser L.J.
[1] *Ibid.*, at p.651.
[2] See, *e.g. Pride of Derby and Derbyshire Angling Association Limited v. British Celanese Limited* [1952] 1 All E.R. 1326. As to apportionment of liability, Harman J. appears to have decided in that case that it was open to him in principle to apportion the damages and did so, although not stating explicitly that in principle each defendant was only liable for what he caused (*i.e.* severally rather than jointly and severally). Perhaps this follows from the fact that the acts of each of them were one of a series of separate acts which, combined, caused damage, rather than originating in some common purpose. This type of case is, however, obviously different from one in which each individual's act might itself amount to a tort.

Reasonableness of Use

22–072   What in modern parlance might be described as determining the reasonableness or otherwise of the defendant's use of his land would seem to equate with the well established principle of balancing conflicting uses and aspirations in context—the process of "give and take" as it is frequently described.[3] The list of factors to be balanced is not necessarily closed (see the references to "all the circumstances of the case" or words to that effect[4] in many of the cases). Traditionally they have included time and place,[5] duration and object,[6] severity of harm,[7] temporary or permanent.[8] It may now also be that foreseeability of damage should now be grouped with the surrounding circumstances as a relevant factor in determining liability.[9]

22–073   Though many modern cases suggest that the reasonableness of the use to which the defendant puts his land is a principal factor in determining liability for private nuisance, the position is less clear when it comes to establishing (through consideration of the authorities generally) whether that applies only to cases of interference or also to cases of encroachment on land and actual physical damage. Lord Goff in *Cambridge Water* is perhaps more the exception than the rule in explicitly citing reasonableness as relevant to liability. Many authorities which do cite reasonableness involve interference, and applying the concept where there is actual physical damage is by no means free from difficulty. *Clerk and Lindsell* indeed remarks[10]:

> "In nuisance of the first two kinds [encroachment and physical damage] liability for the nuisance is established by proving the encroachment or the damage to the land, as the case may be. The situation of the land affected, the character of the neighbourhood and the surrounding circumstances are not matters to be taken into consideration"

---

[3] See, *e.g.* Lord Goff in *Cambridge Water*, [1994] 2 W.L.R. at 74, equating "the principle of reasonable user—with the principle of give and take between neighbouring occupiers of land, under which "those acts necessary for the common and ordinary use and occupation of land and houses may be done, if conveniently done, without subjecting those who do them to an action".

[4] *e.g.* the passage from *Bamford v. Turnley* cited at para. 22–025.

[5] Including the "character of the neighbourhood" discussed at paras. 22–108 *et seq.*

[6] As to the relevance of the motive see para. 22–045 and n.55, as well as the discussion at paras. 22–078 *et seq.*

[7] See discussion at para. 22–105.

[8] *Matania v. National Provincial Bank* [1936] 2 All E.R. 633.

[9] See also the discussion at paras. 22–094 *et seq.*

[10] 16th ed. (1989) Sweet & Maxwell.

Salmond & Heuston on the Law of Torts seems to suggest that it may only
be the situation of the land which is not relevant[11]

Cases such as *Watt v. Jamieson*[12] and *Halsey v. Esso Petroleum*[13] and the   **22–074**
passage from *St Helens Smelting Co. v. Tipping* quoted at paragraph 22–
092, may be taken to suggest that the occurrence of "sensible" physical
damage (in the appropriate circumstances) displaces questions of
reasonableness and give and take. It is significant, however, that the
Cambridge Water case itself (which was arguably about physical damage
or at least about inability to enjoy land for physical reasons) made no
explicit distinction. Lord Goff on the contrary drew attention to a
"similarity of function" between the principle of reasonable user as
applied in the law of nuisance and the principle of natural use of the
land in *Rylands v. Fletcher*, a notion generally applying to cases of
physical damage or encroachment. He observed that:[14]

> "—although liability for nuisance has generally been regarded as
> strict, at least in the case of a defendant who has been responsible
> for the creation of a nuisance, even so that liability has been kept
> under control by the principal of reasonable user . . . if the user is
> reasonable, the defendant will not be liable for consequent harm
> to his neighbour's enjoyment of his land."

Though this case and many others refer to harm to the plaintiff's   **22–075**
enjoyment, the boundary between the two sorts of damage—physical
and encroachment and interference is not clear-cut.[15] Making the
plaintiff's property a less pleasant or less productive place to occupy
might interfere with enjoyment not only in a non-material way, but
cause financial damage by reducing its value or its productive
capacity. Equally the flooding of plaintiff's property causing to
physical damage or encroachment might also remove it temporarily
from use, and thus from the enjoyment of the plaintiff.

---

[11] See also comments in *Salmond & Heuston on Torts* (20th ed., 1992) Sweet & Maxwell at
p. 63 "the rule that the standard is determined by the locality where the nuisance is
created is limited to those cases where the nuisance complained of its productive of
sensible personal discomfort. A different principle applies where the nuisance causes
a material injury to property, or sensibly reduces its value". This comment appears
confined to the relevance of "character of the neighbourhood".

[12] [1954] S.C. 46, a Scottish Court of Session case in which the water vapour discharged
from the defender's fire caused damage to the pursuers and was found to be a
nuisance. Of the suggestion that the user was usual, familiar, and normal it was said:
"any type of use which in the sense indicated above subjects adjoining
properties to substantial annoyance, or causes material damage to their property
is prima facie not a reasonable use".

[13] [1961] 1 W.L.R. 683.

[14] [1994] 2 W.L.R. 53 at 74.

[15] See, *e.g. Salmond and Heuston on the Law of Torts* (20th Ed.), p.61.

22-076   That there may be no distinction in principle but only of degree between different types of damage, when it comes to assessing the relevance of reasonableness, seems to derive some support from— admittedly brief—general statements of principle at the highest level[16], and from a case like *Miller v. Jackson*,[17] where all of the judgments make it clear that it was being considered (among other things) as a case of physical damage or potential physical damage whilst equally stressing the need to balance the conflicting interests of plaintiff and defendant to use their properties as they please.[18] Perhaps this was just another case in which the boundaries between different types of damage were blurred. Both the prospect and the reality of cricket balls damaging one's property may of course be an interference with enjoyment, as well as a cause of more tangible damage.

22-077   It cannot in short be regarded as clear that reasonableness will be determinative of liability in cases of encroachment or physical damage as it is in cases of interference, though there is a significant degree of support for the view that it is. It may be that the way in which to reconcile the authorities in this respect is to accept that those of them which do not explicitly acknowledge the role of reasonableness in determining liability for physical damage are implicitly putting forward the proposition that in any process of give and take, the extent of damage and the ability to foresee damage will be the predominant factors—though not necessarily the only ones—where physical damage is caused.[19]

Object or Duration or Motive

22-078   In certain circumstances, these factors may all justify an otherwise unjustifiable activity. They provide an example of an apparently clear

---

[16] *e.g.* "There must be something more than the mere harm done to the neighbour's property to make the party responsible," *per* Lord Aitken at 360 B in *Sedleigh Denfield v. O' Callaghan*, which is a case about either physical damage or encroachment or enjoyment, or all of them depending on how one views flooding, and fault of some kind is almost always necessary, and fault generally involves foreseeability" *per* Ld. Reid in *The Wagon Mound No. 2* [1967] 1 A.C. 617, at 639F.

[17] [1977] 1 Q.B. 966 where the complaint was a familiar one. New residents of a new development adjacent to a pitch on which cricket had been played for upwards of 70 years were objecting to having cricket balls hit onto their property.

[18] *e.g.* the tenor of the judgment of Denning MR which, in a case where physical damage was caused and was likely to be repeated, explicitly considers reasonableness and Geoffrey Lane L.J. (though dissenting) still considers a balancing exercise to be relevant—"where as here the damage or potential damage is physical, the answer is more simple."

[19] *Clerk & Lindsell on Torts* (16th ed.) (1988) comments that Lord Westbury's statement in *St Helen's Smelting Co v. Tipping* cited at para. 22–092 may perhaps be seen as a presumption against judging by locality in damage cases.

criterion (the public benefit of the use complained of is not a defence to an action in private nuisance)[20] being qualified by the application of a similar concept under another name. The object of the activity complained of is, for example, of particular relevance in building and demolition cases.[21] A degree of disturbance is unavoidable and the consequences would be unacceptable but for the social respectability of the aim.

Provided the duration is relatively short and the defendant's object **22–079** socially respectable (*e.g.* development), whether there is an actionable nuisance depends on the care and skill employed by him, contrary to the normal rules.

The converse may apply in relation to an objective not as socially **22–080** respectable or necessary.[22] The reasons for an activity which might otherwise be considered legitimate become relevant and may lead to a finding of nuisance. Of course, in cases like this, it can equally be said that it was open to the defendant to avoid the nuisance complained of by acting in a less disruptive way or simply choosing to desist — a choice not open to a developer.

In building cases, it would seem that a land owner who ensures that **22–081** a method of working which avoids nuisance is prescribed and relinquishes control of his site to a contractor may be able, in appropriate circumstances (*e.g.* where he could not reasonably have foreseen that a nuisance was likely to result) to avoid or share liability for any nuisance which is not a necessary consequence of the work which he has authorised. The particular circumstances and relationships will of course be crucial, but it may be that there is some relationship here with the division of liability between landlords and tenants (see paragraph 22–068).

---

[20] *e.g. R. v. Pierce* [1683] 2 Shaw 327; 89 E.R. 967.

[21] " . . . a man who pulls down his house for the purpose of building a new one no doubt causes considerable inconvenience to his next door neighbours during the process of demolition; but he is not responsible as for a nuisance if he uses all reasonable skill and care to avoid annoyance to his neighbour by the works of demolition. Nor is he liable to an action, even though the noise and dust and the consequent annoyance be such as would constitute a nuisance if the same instead of being created for the purpose of the demolition of the house, had been created in sheer wantonness, or in the execution of works for a purpose involving a permanent continuance of the noise and dust. For the law, in judging what constitutes a nuisance, does take into consideration both the object and duration of that which is said to constitute a nuisance."
Harrison v. Southwark & Vauxhall Water Company [1890] 2 Ch. 409, 414.

[22] *e.g.* disturbing breeding fur foxes — *Emmett v. Hollywood Silver Fur Fox Farm*, see n. 55 *ante*.

22–082   It is the normality of the use of the land[23] implicit in building operations (coupled with their temporary nature) which, it seems, can justify their being tolerated as a necessary evil, provided that they are conducted "with all reasonable skill, and taking all reasonable precautions not to cause annoyance to its neighbours". Methods of building and the nature of "an ordinary use of land are not to be considered stabilised for ever.[24]

22–083   It is considered an inevitable use of urban land that it should, from time to time, have building operations upon it. Adjoining sites are expected to extend tolerance to each other, provided the process is relatively short-lived, and no more irksome than reasonably necessary.[25] There is therefore an onus on the builder/occupier to take precautions and establish a proper and reasonable way of working from the outset, rather than by way of response to criticism. To the extent he does not and a nuisance results he will still be liable to damages, or an injunction, however normal his use might be.[26]

Third Party Actions and Natural States

22–084   In *Cambridge Water* Lord Goff points out[27] that in cases of nuisance which have arisen through natural causes, or by the act of a person for whose actions the defendant is not responsible "the applicable principles in nuisance have become closely associated with those applicable in negligence", referring to *Sedleigh Denfield v. O'Callaghan*[28] and *Goldman v. Hargrave.*[29]

---

[23]   "Whether, from other points of view, that is a matter which is desirable for humanity, is neither here nor there; but it is part of the normal use of land to make use, upon your land, in the matter of construction, of what particular type and what particular depth of foundations and particular height of building, may be reasonable, in the circumstances and in the development of the day."
   Andreae v. Selfridge & Company Ltd [1937] 3 All E.R. 255, 264F.
[24]   *Ibid.*, at 260 E-F.
[25]   *Andreae v. Selfridge, ibid*, which remains the leading case, provides some flexible guidance
   "All those questions [the relation between expense and avoiding disturbance] are matters of common sense and degree, and quite clearly it would be unreasonable to expect people to conduct their work so slowly or so expensively for the purpose of preventing a transient inconvenience, that it would make it a prohibitive operation. It is all a question of fact and degree, and must necessarily be so."
   per Greene M.R., at 267 G.
[26]   He will of course also be subject to the construction noise provisions of C.O.P.A., ss. 60, 61, as to which see paras. 18–019 to 18–032.
[27]   [1994] 2 W.L.R. 53, at 75 D.
[28]   [1940] A.C. 880.
[29]   [1967] 1 A.C. 645.

Another way of looking at it might be to say that in the particular   **22–085**
circumstances considerations of knowledge, the ability to acquire such
knowledge, the ability to avert the consequences, the means available
to the defendant to avert them, are all relevant to the reasonableness of
allowing a particular state of affairs to persist and cause damage.
Spelling out the criteria in this way, incidentally, also emphasises the
way in which (in these particular cases of nuisance and perhaps in
others) foreseeability of damage may be relevant as a component of
the tort itself.

The distinction between these types of case and those where the   **22–086**
defendant caused the nuisance, and the different considerations of
conduct and ability to act which apply to it, are coherent when one
considers the original justification for fixing occupiers with "strict"
liability for what they, or those acting on their behalf, do on their land,
though it may not be expressed like this in the cases. Their status is
presumed to give them control over what goes on there (see paragraph
22–053). Where the activity or state of affairs complained of is not
carried on by them or on their behalf, but is a natural state or a
consequence of activities of third parties not directly under the
occupier's control, that same presumption cannot be made. The
occupier's degree of control has to be established, by reference, we are
told in *Leakey*, to whether or not he has done "that which is reasonable
in all the circumstances, and no more than what, if anything, is
reasonable, to prevent or minimise the known risk of damage or injury
to one's neighbour or to his property".[30]

Though the case law on the duty of an unwitting defendant is not   **22–087**
entirely consistent, there emerges from the cases reviewed here the
possibility that foreseeability of damage (coupled with a presumed or
real ability to control) and the practicability of avoiding problems (also
a function of control, and akin to the reasonableness test in building

---

[30] *Ibid., per* Megaw L.J., [1980] 1 All E.R. at 35, at in a passage that is worth quoting in full:
"The considerations with which the law is familiar are all to be taken into account
in deciding whether there has been a breach of duty, and, if so, what that breach
is, and whether it is causative of the damage in respect of which the claim is
made. Thus, there will fall to be considered the extent of the risk. What, so far as
reasonably can be foreseen, are the chances that anything untoward will happen
or that any damage will be caused? What is to be foreseen as to the possible
extent of the damage if the risk becomes a reality? Is it practicable to prevent, or
to minimise, the happening of any damage? If it is practicable, how simple or
how difficult are the measures which could be taken, how much and how
lengthy work do they involve, and what is the probable cost of such works? Was
there sufficient time for preventative action to have been taken, by persons
acting reasonably in relation to the known risk, between the time when it became
known to, or should have been realised by, the defendant, and the time when the
damage occurred? Factors such as these, so far as they apply in a particular case,
fall to be weighed in deciding whether the defendant's duty of care requires, or
required, him to do anything, and, if so, what?"

cases) could be components of reasonableness of use. Whether they are of material relevance, in any particular case may well depend simply upon the degree of technical, legal and physical control which the defendant has over the source of the nuisance complained of.

Damage

As a Condition of Liability

22–088   It is, as *Cambridge Water* has recently reaffirmed, an essential element of private nuisance that the plaintiff should have been damaged by the acts or omissions complained of:

> "It is not to be forgotten that both nuisance and negligence are historically actions on the case; and accordingly in neither case is the tort complete, so that damages are recoverable, unless and until damage has been caused to the plaintiff."[31]

Hence in *Cambridge Water*, the cause of action only arose in 1983 when the plaintiff became subject to the drinking water limits for TCE and PCE and so could no longer use the water from the Sawston borehole.

22–089   Plainly this does not hold for an application for a *quia timet* injunction—where by definition the plaintiff is trying to restrain a threat or intention on the defendant's part to cause him damage which has not yet occurred—or to the special case of interference with an undoubted easement appurtenant to the plaintiff's interest.[32]

22–090   Why anyone should wish to attempt recovery of damages in nuisance without actual damage is perhaps clearer if one considers a case like *Midland Bank v. Bardgrove Property Services Limited*.[33] The leasehold property of the plaintiff's Bank ended in an earth bank from which the defendant's contractors, in the course of developing the defendant's land, had withdrawn support (temporary restraining works having proved inadequate), in breach of the plaintiff Bank's natural right to have its land supported by that of the defendant. They had tried to make this good by—among other things—putting up a retaining wall. The plaintiff thought this wall inadequate. There was evidence to show that the wall would probably collapse within 10 to 15 years, resulting in a wholesale removal of support to the plaintiff's land.

---

[31] [1994] 2 W.L.R. at 70C.
[32] *Young v. Bankier Distillery* [1893] A.C. 691 at 698.
    "Every riparian proprietor is entitled to the water of his stream, in its natural flow, without sensible diminution or increase and without sensible alteration in its character or quality."
[33] [1992] 2 E.G.L.R. 168.

The Bank took steps to reduce the future risk to itself by instructing **22–091** sheet piling works. It then tried to reclaim the costs incurred. The Court decided that at the time when the Bank embarked on its remedial works, its land was still being still supported for better or for worse. It had suffered no damage and that its right of support had not been interfered with. There was therefore no nuisance and so no recoverable loss. In some such cases and in appropriate circumstances it might be that a *quia timet* injunction against the likelihood of future actionable injury and indirectly compelling the defendants to do the work which they themselves had done would be available, or equitable damages in lieu.[34] It is interesting to speculate whether or not the plaintiff's landlord, had the Bank done nothing, might have been able to make out a claim simply based on the loss in value of its land—though arguably that would have been pure economic loss with the considerations and difficulties which that may entail (see paragraphs 22–124 to 22–126).

Types of Damage to Land

The law of private nuisance recognises broadly two sorts of damage **22–092** to land: firstly, physical damage to the land itself and things which are part of it and, secondly, interference with the enjoyment of land. A commonly quoted passage in which the distinction is drawn comes from the speech of Westbury L.C. in *St Helen's Smelting Co v. Tipping*[35]:

> " . . . in matters of this description it appears to me that it is a very desirable thing to mark the difference between an action brought for a nuisance upon the ground that the alleged nuisance produces material injury to the property, and an action brought for a nuisance on the ground that the thing alleged to be a nuisance is productive of sensible personal discomfort. With regard to the latter, namely, the personal inconvenience and interference with one's enjoyment, one's quiet, one's personal freedom, anything that discomposes or injuriously affects the senses or the nerves, whether that may or may not be denominated a nuisance, must undoubtedly depend greatly on the circumstances of the place where the thing complained of actually occurs. If a man lives in a town, it is necessary that he should

---

[34] Whether a *quia timet* injunction would have been granted in this case is an open question. Normally the applicant must show a threat of imminent harm, which on the facts would have been difficult for the plaintiff Bank; it is to be hoped that requirement will be relaxed in situations where pre-emptive action is likely to be the most cost-effective option.

[35] [1865] 11 H.L.C. 642, at 650, where emissions from an established copper smelting works in an established industrial neighbourhood damaged trees on the plaintiff's newly-acquired agricultural estate.

subject himself to the consequences of those operations of trade which may be carried on in his immediate locality, which are actually necessary for trade and commerce, and also for the enjoyment of property, and for the benefit of the inhabitants of the town and of the public at large. If a man lives in a street where there are numerous shops, and a shop is opened next door to him, which is carried on in a fair and reasonable way, he has no ground for complaint, because to himself individually there may arise much discomfort from the trade carried on in that shop. But where an occupation is carried on by one person in the neighbourhood of another, and the result of that trade, or occupation, or business, is a material injury to property, then there unquestionably arises a very different consideration. I think, my Lords, that in a case of that description, the submission which is required from persons living in society to that amount of discomfort which may be necessary for the legitimate and free exercise of the trade of their neighbours, would not apply to circumstances the immediate result of which is sensible injury to the value of the property."

22–093   Whether that passage can still be relied upon as showing that the test for liability in nuisance which directly causes damage to land is different from that where there is only interference with its enjoyment, and whether it actually means that, is not clear (as to which see paragraphs 22–072 *et seq.*). It serves nonetheless to illustrate the two types of actionable harm to land for which a private nuisance action is generally considered to provide a remedy. Some commentators add a third—encroachment—though for most practical purposes this can be viewed as a form of physical damage.

Knowledge and Foreseeability

22–094   It is not a new proposition that knowledge (or at least reasonably available means of knowledge) that an activity or a state of affairs is causing or is liable to cause harm to an occupier of land may be a necessary ingredient for liability in private nuisance.

22–095   In *St Anne's Well Brewery Company v. Roberts*[36] lack of knowledge of a state of affairs liable to cause nuisance to the plaintiffs was explicitly stated to prevent a defendant being found liable in nuisance:

"In those circumstances it appears to me that the cardinal thing which would have to be proved to establish any liability against anybody would be, namely, knowledge of the defect which

[36] [1928] All E.R. Rep. 28 at 33, *per* Scrutton L.J.

ultimately resulted in the fall of the wall and/or failure to acquire that knowledge because you had failed to use reasonable care to ascertain what you should have ascertained."

Similarly in *Sedleigh-Denfield v. O'Callaghan*[37]:

> "If he is to be liable, a further condition is necessary—namely, that he had knowledge, or means of knowledge, that he knew or should have known, of a nuisance in time to correct it and obviate its mischievous effects."

It might be said that these examples say that if the defendant has no knowledge of the state of affairs amounting to a nuisance, he cannot be liable and that knowledge (or lack of it) is a component in determining the reasonableness of the defendant's use of his land. A distinction, however, is to be made between having knowledge of *both* a state of affairs *and* the potential of that state of affairs to cause damage, on the one hand, and having knowledge of the state of affairs, not knowing that it is liable to cause damage, on the other. **22–096**

Previous authority, as *The Wagon Mound (No. 2)*[38] points out, was inconsistent on this point. Whilst Lord Reid in that case is not explicit as to whether knowledge of or the ability to foresee damage is a component of liability or simply part of the test relating to remoteness of damage, or as to whether he thinks the distinction material, he does explain: **22–097**

> "And although negligence may not be necessary, fault of some kind is almost always necessary and fault generally involves foreseeability, *e.g.* in cases like *Sedleigh-Denfield v. O'Callaghan* the fault is in failing to abate the nuisance of the existence of which the defender is or ought to be aware as likely to cause damage to his neighbour."[39]

Lord Goff in *Cambridge Water* starts by considering foreseeability of damage as a component of liability (" . . . the question whether foreseeability of harm of the relevant type is an essential element of liability . . . in nuisance") and concludes by saying that: **22–098**

> "It is unnecessary in the present case to consider the precise nature of this principle; but it appears from Lord Reid's statement of the law that he regarded it essentially as one relating to remoteness of damage."

---

[37] [1940] A.C. 880 at 904, *per* Lord Wright.
[38] [1967] 1 A.C. 617.
[39–41] *ibid.* at 639F.

22–100   Does it matter whether foreseeability/knowledge is a component of liability or merely a test relating to remoteness? In most cases (as in *Cambridge Water*) if the plaintiff cannot establish the foreseeability it now appears that he will not get his damages in any event, whether he is barred on grounds of remoteness, having established nuisance in principle, or for failing to establish a nuisance at all.

22–101   But what if two sorts of damage result from any given state of affairs or activity? Take the favourite case of a cricket ground and imagine that there are cucumber frames on the mid-wicket boundary and a brick-built summer house at long leg, both in vulnerable positions and belonging to the same plaintiff. Successive sixes are hit through the cucumber frames and through a defective slate on the roof of the summer house damaging the plaintiff's tea service.

22–102   The defendant might reasonably say that damage to cucumber frames is foreseeable but the fact that the summer house had a defective roof which would admit a cricket ball was not. If foreseeability is a component of liability, playing cricket on that ground might then be a nuisance so far as the owner of the cucumber frames is concerned, but not so far as the owner of the summer house is concerned, which seems rather strange. If foreseeability bears simply on remoteness, then the activity is in itself a nuisance (the cucumber frames being part of the surrounding circumstances), but the owner of the summer house cannot recover because the damage to him is too remote. That seems more coherent, though the result is no different.

22–103   Equally if, as suggested in the discussion at paragraph 22–077 above—there may be grounds in practice for assimilating foreseeability of damage in the general criterion of reasonableness of use, and thus for making it an element of liability, a difficult question might arise of how different plaintiffs suffering different consequences from the same general activity might be treated where it is thought that one ought to be entitled to recover and the other not.

22–104   Circumstances affecting different plaintiffs differently, as in the examples above, could be analysed by saying that particular types of harm (*e.g.* to someone owning a summer house with a defective roof) are not harms to the use of property according to the "ordinary notions of mankind" and/or in that particular case are concerned with plaintiffs of abnormal sensitivity, so that in practice any type of damage which qualifies as actionable would be from a limited range and likely to be foreseeable.

Physical Damage—Standard and Sensitivity

It is clear that it is not any physical damage which will suffice to **22–105** ground a case in nuisance. "Sensible injury" is the phrase used in *St Helen's Smelting Co v. Tipping*. The transient nature of any damage will also be a factor though if the damage is substantial the fact that it is transient or occasional is irrelevant.

> "It appears to me that nothing can be deemed to be fleeting or evanescent which results in substantial damage, and that the question, therefore, is to be answered not by time but by the effects on the plaintiff."[42]

This affirms the point that to be actionable, a nuisance resulting in **22–106** physical damage need not be the consequence of a state of affairs but can be the consequence of a one-off incident. *Sedleigh-Denfield v. O'Callaghan*[43] (where the consequence of the nuisance was a flooding of the plaintiff's land) and *Goldman v. Hargrave*[44] (where fire spread to the plaintiff's property) and indeed *The Wagon Mound (No. 2)*[45] (where the plaintiff's property was also burnt) are examples.[46]

The land in relation to which damages can be recovered is land **22–107** being used in an ordinary way and not by especially sensitive people or for especially sensitive purposes. Interference with rights relating to it will be actionable so far as they are the ordinary rights enjoyed by any piece of land in those circumstances. An act which would not interfere with the ordinary enjoyment of property cannot constitute a legal nuisance if the activity of the injured party is of abnormal sensitivity.[47] Once that basic level of ordinary damage has been established, however, it may be that damages can be claimed in relation to the effect of a nuisance on particularly sensitive uses[48] or particularly outstanding attributes of the land affected which are not otherwise actionable in themselves.[49]

---

[42] Fry J. in *Fritz v. Hobson* [1880] 4 Ch.D. 542 (see also *Gaunt v. Fynney* [1872] L.R. 8 Ch.8).

[43] [1940] A.C. 880.

[44] [1967] 1 A.C. 645.

[45] [1967] 1 A.C. 617.

[46] It follows that Lord Goff's suggestion in *Cambridge Water* that the rule in *Rylands v. Fletcher* be regarded as an extension of the law of nuisance to isolated escapes from land would seem to be unnecessary. If the rule in *Rylands v. Fletcher* is to have separate existence, this must be justified on other grounds.

[47] *e.g.* *Robinson v. Kilvert* [1889] 41 Ch.D.88.

[48] *e.g.* The Canadian Privy Council case of *McKinnon Industries Ltd v. Walker* [1951] W.N. 401; 3 D.L.R. 557 where emission of sulphur-dioxide fumes damaged orchids.

[49] *e.g.* a fine view lost in consequence of an actionable interference with the right to light—*Carr Saunders v. Dick McNeil & Associates* [1986] 2 E.G.L.R. 181.

Interference — Character of the Neighbourhood and Standards

22–108   If he wishes to establish that the particular interference with his enjoyment or use of land amounts to "damage" so as to found a claim in private nuisance where there is no physical damage, the plaintiff has to establish that he is experiencing undue interference from a particular use. One of the most important factors will be whether or not the degree of interference complained of is appropriate to the character of the neighbourhood.

22–109   One of many statements of the importance of neighbourhood is in *Sturges v. Bridgman*[50]:

> " . . . whether anything is a nuisance or not is a question to be determined not merely by an abstract consideration of the thing itself, but in reference to its circumstances; what would be a nuisance in Belgrave Square would not necessarily be so in Bermondsey."

22–110   As to standards and undue interference *Walter v. Selfe*[51] contains a much-quoted statement of "undue" interference — in that case to air from the intended burning of bricks — the plaintiff being entitled to:

> " . . . air not rendered to an important degree less compatible, or at least not rendered incompatible, with the physical comfort of human existence, a phrase to be understood of course with reference to the climate and habits of England."

22–111   Different cases apply different criteria to different localities accordingly — village life in *Miller v. Jackson*, the people of Fulham in *Halsey v. Esso Petroleum*,[52] a case where a particular type of noise and interference were considered to be acceptable during the daytime (which dealt with the appropriateness of the use to the character of the neighbourhood) but not to the same degree at night (the interference then being excessive). A similar distinction emerges from *Polsue & Alfieri Limited v. Rushmer*[53] where it was said:

> "It does not follow that because I live, say, in the manufacturing part of Sheffield I cannot complain if a steam hammer is introduced next door, and so work as to render sleep at night

---

[50] [1879] 11 Ch.D. 852.
[51] [1851] 64 E.R. 849.
[52] [1961] 1 W.L.R. 683; [1961] 2 All E.R. 145, where the acid smuts from an oil refinery in a residential area damaged the plaintiff's drying clothes and his car, and where the "pungent and nauseating smell of oil" and the noise and vibration of nocturnal operations interfered with his enjoyment of his property and were found to constitute a private and (in the case of the car which was parked on the highway) a public nuisance.
[53] Court of Appeal at [1906] 1 Ch. 234.

almost impossible, although previously to its introduction my house was a reasonable comfortable abode, having regard to the local standards; and it would be no answer to say that the steam hammer is of the most modern approved pattern and is reasonably worked."

This case being, as it was, about printing and associated trades in the area around Fleet Street in London (where such trades are now largely displaced by less noisy users like large office blocks) prompts consideration of what happens when the character of a neighbourhood changes. Suppose, for example, the industrial component of an area of mixed residential and industrial uses is growing in intensity, and a person wishes to carry on activity which, even when taking all due precautions, would at one time have been held to be a nuisance to their residents. At what point can he successfully resist an action in private nuisance by an incoming resident and require the plaintiff to accept the area as he finds it, and not be defeated by the accusation that he is seeking to rely on the bad defence that the plaintiff came to the nuisance?[54] **22–112**

In all cases of progressive change, there must be a point at which one circumstance displaces the other—that point being either where the use complained of has become anomalous (in a neighbourhood going up in nuisance terms—Fleet Street) or where the use complained of has come to represent the norm (in a neighbourhood going down in nuisance terms—eg. the neighbourhood of Chatham Dockyard in the case of *Gillingham BC v. Medway*).[55] **22–113**

Miller v. Jackson[56] is again a good example of a case where different judges in the Court of Appeal concentrated on different sides of this same coin. Denning M.R. concluded that the use of the land in a village as a cricket pitch was reasonable having regard to the character of the neighbourhood and that the plaintiffs new to the area could not complain about it. The other judges, holding themselves bound by **22–114**

---

[54] *e.g. Miller v. Jackson ibid*, and *post* at para. 22–129.
[55] [1992] 3 W.L.R. 449 in which the defendant dock company had obtained planning permission to develop land as a commercial port and did so. The resulting heavy vehicle movements adversely affected local residential roads. The plaintiff local authority sought injunctions on behalf of the residents sought injunctions to restrain a public nuisance. The judge held that the balance of conflicting private and public interests had already been struck in the decision to grant planning permission, that the character of the neighbourhood had therefore changed as a given fact, and that there was in consequence no actionable nuisance.
[56] See n. 17 to para. 22–076.

Sturges v. Bridgman[57] and *Bliss v. Hall*,[58] decided in favour of the plaintiffs that the fact that they had come to the nuisance was not relevant as a defence.

22–115   Some of the reasoning in the *Gillingham* decision might be taken to suggest that a local planning authority has it in its power to change the character of the neighbourhood by the way in which its development plans and planning permissions granted by it permit the area to develop and to strike the balance between competing interests to the exclusion of the courts. On the authorities it has hitherto been regarded as settled law that a planning consent merely sanctions what would otherwise be unlawful under the planning legislation, but does not, and indeed cannot, affect the civil rights of third parties at common law; if third party rights are to be adversely affected, this can only be done by Parliament. Neighbourhoods do change in character over time—inner London residential areas often became light industrial first, and have now been "gentrified". Authorisation of developments may reflect and consolidate *previous* changes but (pre-*Gillingham*, at least) could not create that change to the detriment of third parties.

22–116   Applied to a plaintiff moving to an area after a planning permission has been granted, or after a new development plan has been adopted but before its implementation, this aspect of *Gillingham* might bar him from characterising his neighbourhood as, say, a residential one because the possibility of the future use of part of it for a conflicting purpose has been sanctioned by the local planning authority. That plaintiff would then find it more difficult to establish a cause of action in nuisance when the permission was implemented. A plaintiff who had built his house before the planning permission or development plan might not. This seems perplexing given that at either time nothing had actually happened on the ground.

22–117   The ambit of the *Gillingham* decision has, however, been much circumscribed by the subsequent case of *Wheeler v. J.J. Saunders Limited* in which the Court of Appeal, in judgments more akin to the *status quo ante* gave qualified approval to those parts of the reasoning in Gillingham which adopted previous authority, but doubted other

---

[57] [1879] 11 Ch.D. 852.
[58] [1838] 4 Bing N.C. 183; [1839] 132 E.R. 758.

parts.[59] The conclusion seems to be that a planning authority in general has no jurisdiction to authorise a nuisance as such. If it can do so at all, it is only indirectly, by permitting a change in the character in the neighbourhood and so in the criteria against which a nuisance is to be assessed.

Types of Damage—Land, Injuries to Person and Chattels, Economic Loss

The basic principle for assessing damages in nuisance is to award to the plaintiff such sum as will put him in the position which he would have been in had the wrong not been committed.[60] That is a feature which private nuisance shares with other torts and is limited by rules about remoteness of damage.[61] A distinctive feature of nuisance, however, is its role in protecting land and the rights which English law recognises as appurtenant to its occupation. **22–118**

One might therefore expect the fact that private nuisance is pre-eminently concerned with protection of rights in land to circumscribe the other categories of loss for which damages can be recovered, limiting them to damage to land in consequence of whatever right appurtenant to it has been affected. As Professor Newark pointed out: **22–119**

> "A sulphurous chimney in a residential area is not a nuisance because it makes householders cough and splutter but because it prevents them taking their ease in their gardens."[62]

Since a true nuisance is a tort to the enjoyment of rights in land it should follow that damage to the person or chattels of the plaintiff may not *by itself* amount to a nuisance. This is not the apparent conclusion **22–120**

---

[59] *The Times*, January 6, 1995. In deciding that the consequences of erecting two new pig weaning sheds could not be described as a change in the character of the neighbourhood, and generally accepting that a planning permission was in no sense equivalent to statutory authority and could not in itself authorise a nuisance, each Judge expressed himself with a slightly different emphasis.

Staughton L.J. accepted that it may be (but expressed no concluded opinion) that *some* planning decisions—seemingly ones of strategic significance affected by considerations of public interest—*might* authorise some nuisance. Peter Gibson L.J. stressed that the Court should be slow to acquiesce in the extinction of private rights without compensation as a result of administrative decisions which cannot be appealed and are difficult to challenge. Sir Peter May reiterated that planning is concerned with public interest rather than private.

[60] *e.g. Armstrong v. Sheppard & Short* [1959] 2 Q.B. 384.

[61] A subject which is beyond the scope of this work but see, *inter alia Overseas Tankship (UK) Ltd v. The Miller Steamship Co. Pty* [1967] A.C. 617.

[62] The Boundaries of Nuisance [1949] 65 L.Q.R. 480. 9

of some older cases, some of which stress the difference which a defendant's control of land makes to his liability, and others of which award damages for personal injuries in consequence. A factor rarely considered in them from the plaintiff's point of view are the limits on recoverable loss to which the cause of action ought to make him subject. These limits are however generally recognised in the more modern cases. In *Read v. J. Lyons & Co. Limited*[63] for example Lord Simonds said:

> " . . . only he has a lawful claim who has suffered an invasion of some proprietary or other interest."

This was an early protest against the intrusion of concepts of personal duty and reasonable foreseeability upon a land-based tort, but cited with approval now by Lord Goff in the *Cambridge Water Case*. It may be that one can expect to see the principles on which damages are assessed re-examined in this light.

22–121   It is still not clear whether damage to interests which are not plainly part of the plaintiff's property rights can be recovered in association with such damages. Salmond and Heuston[64] for example observes that there is no case which definitely either affirms or denies the right to recover for personal injuries in an action for private nuisance — excepting the reference to "whatever form the injury takes" in *Cunard v. Antifyre Limited*.[65] The want of authority may be because the point has not been explicitly addressed in most cases.[66]

22–122   There seems no reason in principle why the direct (and foreseeable) consequences of damage to the plaintiff's property rights — *e.g.* having to move — should not be compensated for in nuisance, as seems to have been assumed, for example, in the case of *Grosvenor Hotel v. Hamilton*[67] — though subject to rules about remoteness. The rationale for this (which in the light of *Cambridge Water* is persuasive) would presumably be that it is the damage to land which is a basic ingredient of liability. Once it is established, the "usual rules" as to

---

[63] [1947] A.C. 156 at 183.
[64] *op. cit.* p. 67.
[65] [1933] 1 K.B. 551, 567 — though the Court declined to treat this case (in which the plaintiff had been injured and property damaged by the defendant's gutter falling through her glass roof) as one of nuisance and applied authorities based on negligence; which might equally suggest that the case affirms the proposition that nuisance is limited to damage to land, and this dictum should be limited to negligence.
[66] But see, *e.g. Read v. J. Lyons & Co. Ltd* [1947] A.C. 156 — a case on the rule in *Rylands v. Fletcher.* where Lord MacMillan said that an allegation of negligence was in general essential to an action of reparation for personal injuries (170) and Lord Simonds left the point open (181).
[67] [1894] 2 Q.B. 13; [1891–4] All E.R. Rep. 1188.

recoverable loss might apply. The point, must, however be viewed as undecided.

So far as actual physical damage to real property itself is concerned, 22–123 compensation has been traditionally been based on the diminution of its market value[68] or, if this produces an unfair result, the reinstatement value of the property.[69] Where the claim is for interference with enjoyment, the plaintiff's loss may be measured in terms of the diminution in value of the property for letting over the relevant period,[70] or by analogy with damages in personal injury cases.[71]

As to economic loss, in *Andreae v. Selfridge*[72] it was said that there was 22–124 damage "both by personal inconvenience (which is not such an important matter) and by the unfortunate result upon her [the plaintiff's] guests and the reputation of their hotel".

Damages, however, were based solely on the actionable part of the 22–125 loss of custom. It does not appear to have been argued that this was a consequence of the personal inconvenience, though clearly a consequence of the activities causing this. It was essentially pure economic loss, though equally capable of being described (in relation to commercial premises) as a consequence of inability to enjoy one's property to the full, measured as much in terms of the plaintiff's ability to extract money from it as anything else.

In *Bone v. Seale*[73] it seems to have been accepted that the plaintiffs 22–126 could have, in principle, recovered purely for any diminution in value caused by nuisance from an adjacent pig farm. They failed to prove it, however, and recovered only for loss of amenity. Ultimately, it is difficult to imagine circumstances where economic loss caused by a nuisance is not going to be associated with the loss of amenity or of the ability to enjoy property or rights associated with it, which is a right in land that the law does recognise, and it may be that there are few cases of "pure" economic loss in the sense in which that term is used in negligence cases.

Defences

This account of private nuisance suggests that some of what are 22–127 traditionally viewed as defences to the tort can be seen as cases where a material circumstance or factor in creating the tort is missing. The

---

[68] *Moss v. Christchurch RDC* [1925] 2 K.B. 750.
[69] *O'Grady v. Westminster Scaffoldings* [1962] 2 Lloyds Reports 238 or *Dodds Properties (Kent) v. Canterbury City Council* [1980] 1 W.L.R. 433.
[70] *Grosvenor Hotel Co. v. Hamilton* [1894] 2 Q.B. 13.
[71] *Bone v. Seale* [1979] 1 All E.R. 787.
[72] [1937] 3 All E.R. 255.
[73] [1975] 1 All E.R. 787.

converse may be the case with some of what are sometimes categorised as unsuccessful defences or as ones which are not available in this tort. The following paragraphs consider some possible defences, by way of illustration, without attempting to cover comprehensively all those raised and discussed as such in cases and textbooks.

22–128   Some Act of God or Act of Third Party defences might for example have been put on the basis that the defendant did not have the requisite degree of control over land and knowledge of the relevant circumstances to give rise to liability in the first place. Victorian cases concerning exceptional rainfalls are good examples.[74] Similarly perhaps, the defences of necessity[75] or self-protection against extraordinary danger[76] which can be viewed as occurring in cases in which the extreme and weighty nature of one of the factors to be balanced was arguably such as, in all the circumstances, to make reasonable conduct which would not in any other circumstances have been reasonable.

22–129   Despite some early authority to the contrary[77] it is not however a defence to an action in nuisance to say that the plaintiff contributed to his own problems by choosing to locate himself within the sphere of an established use which is known to be a nuisance.[78] The reasonableness or otherwise of the defendant's use of his land is to be ascertained objectively "having regard to the fact that he has a neighbour"[79] and to the fact that the neighbour too is entitled to make use of his land from time to time in whatever way the law permits without being unduly

---

[74] e.g. *Nichols v. Marsland* [1875] [1874–80] All E.R. Rep. 40, a case of bursting banks to which the principles canvassed in *Sedleigh-Denfield v. O'Callaghan* could perhaps be applied, along with more modern considerations as to reasonableness of user, to give the same result.

[75] See e.g. *Southport Corporation v. Esso Petroleum Co. Ltd.* [1953] 2 All E.R. 1204 at 1209, *per* Devlin J., and on appeal at [1954] 2 Q.B. 182 at 194, *per* Singleton L.J.—claims in nuisance and trespass would not lie in respect of pollution of the foreshore caused by the jettisoning of 400 tons of oil, if necessary, to save the lives of the crew, in the absence of negligence. (The decision of the Court of Appeal was reversed in part by the House of Lords, [1955] 3 All E.R. 864, where nuisance was not however in issue).

[76] Such as cases about water and the reasonableness of flood defence works conducted with "reasonable care and skill and adopting reasonable and usual means for the purpose", e.g. *Maxey Drainage Board v. Great Northern Railway Company* [1912] 10 L.G.R. 248. The value of cases like this as direct authority on the points which they decided might now be questioned in the light of improved engineering techniques and greater options (see *Tate and Lyle Industries Ltd v. Greater London Council* [1983] 2 A.C. 509 for a case in which it was thought that necessary works could have been done better). There seems to be a relationship with construction-nuisance cases, which also exonerate defendants with "necessary" works to the extent that they are reasonably carried out—see paras. 22–078 to 22–083.

[77] "If a party set up a noxious trade remote from habitations and public roads, and after that new houses are built and new roads constructed near it, the party may continue his trade though it be a nuisance to persons inhabiting such houses or passing along such roads". *R. v. Cross* (1826) 2 C.&P. 483.

[78] *Miller v. Jackson* [1977] Q.B. 966; [1977] 3 All E.R. 338.

[79] *Kennaway v. Thompson* [1981] Q.B. 88; [1980] 3 All E.R. 329.

constrained by adjoining uses.[80] The relative time at which adjoining owners decide to exploit their land to best lawful advantage is not, in short, a relevant consideration because it conflicts with their general right to do so. Plainly, however, this interacts—in ways which have not always been satisfactorily explained —with the "character of the neighbourhood" criteria, as to which see paragraphs 22–108 to 22–117.

If an activity or state of affairs is otherwise a nuisance it is no defence **22–130** to liability to say that it benefits the public in some way.[81] This may be another illustration of the fact that the reasonableness of the defendant's land use has to be assessed by reference to land use considerations alone which exclude its beneficial effects on persons other than neighbours (see also paragraphs 22–143 to 22–147, concerning the availability of injunctions). The disturbance caused by building and demolition operations, if reasonably minimised, may not be an actionable nuisance because it results from a reasonable use of the land (see paragraphs 22–081 to 22–087). Clearly the public benefit perceived to result from development in urban areas is a factor which favours the treatment of such uses as reasonable, but its influence is indirect only.

The defendant's use of reasonable care and skill is likewise not a **22–131** defence[82] other than, in a small category of cases such as statutory authority, construction sites in appropriate circumstances, and preservation from extraordinary danger. In cases in these categories, the use for the purpose concerned and any inevitable nuisance which it causes being deemed necessary, the defendant is required to show that he did apply reasonable skill and care, and that any residual nuisance is therefore inevitable. In other cases, one explanation of its lack of

---

[80] *Sturges v. Bridgman* [1879] C.A. 852, 867:
"It would be on the one hand in a very high degree unreasonable and undesirable that there should be a right of action for acts which are not, in the present condition of the adjoining land, and possibly never will be, any annoyance or inconvenience to either owner or occupier; and it would be on the other hand in an equally (*sic*.) degree unjust, and, from a public point of view, inexpedient that the use and value of the adjoining land should, for all time and under all circumstances, be restricted and diminished by reason of the continuance of acts incapable of physical interruption, and which the law gives no power to prevent."
and at 866
". . . the negation of the principle would lead even more to individual hardship, and would at the same time produce a prejudicial effect upon the land for residential purposes."
[81] *e.g. Shelfer v. City of London Electric Lighting Company* [1894] C.A. 300.
"Neither has the circumstance that the wrongdoer is in some sense a public benefactor (*e.g.* a gas or water company or a sewer authority) ever been considered a sufficient reason for refusing to protect by injunction an individual whose rights are being persistently infringed."
per Lindley L.J. at 316.
[82] *Midwood v. Manchester Corporation* [1905] 2 K.B. 597.

relevance may perhaps be that the reasonableness of the use is judged by reference to its effects on the plaintiff, having regard to all the relevant—objectively ascertainable —circumstances.[83]

22–132   A nuisance cannot be justified by the existence of other nuisances of a similar character if it can be shown that the inconvenience is increased by the nuisance complained of[84]—which is again consonant with the principle that a nuisance is a nuisance if in consequence of an unreasonable use of land and having regard (among other things) to the existing character of the neighbourhood it interferes unduly with the plaintiff's enjoyment of his land.[85]

22–133   Of particular relevance to environmental law, the defence of statutory authority is available only where the statute concerned authorises a nuisance expressly or by necessary implication. The criteria are now conveniently set out—"in broad terms"—in the judgment of Webster J. at first instance in *Department of Transport v. North West Water Authority*[86] and approved on appeal in the House of Lords[87] as follows (but omitting the authorities cited):

   " (1) In the absence of negligence, a body is not liable for a nuisance which is attributable to the exercise by it of a duty imposed on it by statute:

   (2) It is not liable in those circumstances (*i.e.* those of (1) above) even if by statute it is expressly made liable, or (expressly) not exempted from liability from nuisance . . .

   (3) In the absence of negligence, a body is not liable for a nuisance which is attributable to the exercise by it of a power conferred by statute if, by statute, it is not expressly either made liable or not exempted from liability for nuisance . . .

   (4) A body is liable for a nuisance by it attributable to the exercise of a power conferred by statute, even without negligence, if by statute it is expressly either made liable, or not exempted from liability for nuisance . . .

   In these rules, references to absence of negligence are references to 'the qualification, or condition, that the statutory powers are exercised without negligence—that word being used in a special sense so as to require the undertaker, as a condition of obtaining

---

[83] *e.g. Watt v. Jamieson* [1954] S.C. 96. The "best practicable means" defence, available in many statutory nuisance cases, is thus of much wider application.

[84] *Crosskey & Sons Ltd v. Lightower* (1867) 2 Ch. App. 478.

[85] See paras. 22–108 *et seq.*

[86] [1984] 1 A.C. 336 at 334 A-D.

[87] [1984] 1 A.C. 351 at 359 E-H—though the appeal was allowed on another point.

immunity from action, to carry out the work and conduct the operation with all reasonable regard and care for the interests of other persons . . .''[88]

Broadly, this appears to mean that: **22–134**

(1) if a nuisance is attributable to a statutory duty, the defendant can only be liable if it has been "negligent" in the special sense in which that word is used here;
(2) if a nuisance is attributable to the exercise of a statutory power (as opposed to the carrying out of a duty) the defendant will only be liable if either:
    (a) it has been negligent (in the same special sense); or
    (b) the statute expressly makes it liable or expressly declares it not to be exempt from liability or nuisance.

The underlying justification appears to be that things which a   **22–135**
defendant has a lawful right to do cannot be actionable.[89] The difficulty in most nuisance cases of course lies in establishing the limits of lawfulness by reference to the relevant circumstances. In cases of statutory authority this has already been painlessly achieved by a benevolent legislature but only to the extent that what is complained of is an inevitable consequence of what has been authorised. In establishing what is inevitable and what not, whether or not the defendant has used reasonable regard and care for the interests of others is the determining factor.[90]

It may be an effective defence to an action in private nuisance that   **22–136**
the plaintiff has consented to, acquiesced in or even licensed the nuisance in question. It also seems from *Bliss v. Hall*—though the defendant in that case did not succeed in establishing it—and from other cases, that a right to commit a nuisance can in principle be acquired by prescription. In *Crump v. Lambert*,[92] for example, the

---

[88] See *Allen v. Gulf Oil Refining Ltd* [1981] A.C. 1001, 1011, *per* Lord Wilberforce.
[89] *e.g. Bradford Corporation v. Pickles* [1895] A.C. 957 and obstruction of groundwater.
[90] *e.g. Tate & Lyle v. Greater London Council* where the predecessor Council of the GLC in exercise of powers in the London County Council (Improvements) Act 1962 built two new terminals in the Thames for the Woolwich Ferry, causing silting up of a channel and berth used by Tate & Lyle. It was found that the terminals could have been so designed as to reduce the incidence of the problem. The House of Lords affirmed that to rely on statutory authority as a defence to an action based on nuisance the defendants must show that they had carried out the work and conducted the operation in questions with all reasonable regard and care for the interests of other persons and that the Council was accordingly liable in public nuisance.
[91] [1838] 4 Bing N.C. 183; (1839) 132 E.R. 758.
[92] (1867) L.R. 3 Eq. 409.

owner of a dominant tenement was found was found, in view of the lack of resistance to it for over 20 years by the servient owner, to have established a right of "discharging the gases or fluid, or sending smoke or noise from his tenement over the tenement of his neighbour".

22–137 Presumably the basic criteria for acquisition and existence of an easement would still have to be satisfied.[93] In relation to phenomena and variable as evanescent and inconsistent as most types of nuisance (water pollution, smoke, dust, noise or vibration) it will not be common for those criteria to be satisfied in practice over the relevant period. It is not sufficient merely that the particular activity complained of must have been carried on for the relevant period. It must have been carried on as a nuisance — an activity which the plaintiff would have been entitled to take steps to prevent — during the whole of the relevant period. If, as in *Sturges v. Bridgman* the activity only becomes a nuisance in consequence of a change in circumstances — the extension to the doctor's consulting rooms affected by noise from the confectioner's pestle and mortar was a late addition — time for establishing prescription under the Prescription Act of 1832 does not start to run until then.

Remedies

Remedies — Limitation and other time constraints[94]

22–138 The limitation period which applies to claims founded on private or public nuisance (other than in cases where damages in respect of personal injuries are claimed) is generally six years from the date on which the cause of action accrued, which (unless postponed due to special circumstances) is when damage was caused to the plaintiff.[95]

22–139 By contrast, actual damage is not required for the tort of trespass to be actionable, and the limitation period runs from the date of the trespass itself. Where, however, there is a continuing trespass, *e.g.* a

---

[93] See Gale on Easements (15th ed.) p. 6 *et seq.* for essential characteristics of an easement, and p. 150 *et seq.* for acquisition by prescription.

[94] These issues are mentioned in a summary way and for completeness only. They are very complex, and for a fuller treatment readers should consult specialist texts on Tort, Limitation of Actions, Equitable Remedies and the Limitation Acts themselves.

[95] Limitation Act 1980, s.2. For some comments on the arising of a cause of action in private nuisance, see Lord Goff in the *Cambridge Water* case [1984] 2 W.L.R. 53 at 70c;

> "It is not to be forgotten that both nuisance and negligence are historically actions on the case; and accordingly in neither case is the tort complete, so that damages are recoverable, unless and until damage has been caused to the plaintiff".

permanent deposit of the defendant's polluting matter on the plaintiff's land, the tort is created afresh each day so that a new limitation period starts to run in relation to each day of damage, while the trespass lasts.[96]

In cases where damages claimed consist of or include damages in **22–140** respect of personal injuries to any person, the basic limitation period is three years, but there are complex rules for determining when that period starts to run, and provisions giving the courts power to "disapply" the usual rules in particular circumstances.[97]

The statutory limitation periods for actions founded on tort does not **22–141** apply to equitable remedies such as injunctions, though section 36 of the Limitation Act 1980 leaves some limited scope for applying them by analogy. A party seeking equitable relief must however always act with reasonable diligence. This is likely to mean that access to equitable relief is likely to be barred more swiftly than access to a legal remedy. Promptness in seeking equitable relief will always be relevant (particularly at an interlocutory stage), and section 36 also preserves expressly equitable defences such as acquiescence or laches.

Remedies Generally

Damages, injunction or damages in lieu of injunction, and a highly **22–142** qualified and circumscribed right of abatement, may in appropriate circumstances be available in principle as remedies for private nuisance. Though certain principles relating to damages have been considered in this chapter where it was necessary to explain the basis of liability, consideration of these remedies and the relevant rules, practice and procedure, restrictions and relevant time limits governing their application are beyond the scope of this work. The reader is accordingly referred to the relevant specialist texts.[98]

Injunctions and Public Benefit

It is appropriate briefly to mention, however, particular conside- **22–143** rations relating to nuisance and the availability of injunctions, as from time to time it has been suggested that in deciding whether to restrain

---

[96] For further details see Limitation Act 1980, ss. 11, 14, 33 and specialist texts; as to private and public nuisance and damages for personal injury see paras. 22–121 and 22–194 respectively.

[97] *Winterbourne v. Morgan* (1809) 11 East 395.

[98] *e.g.* Clerk & Lindsell, Salmond & Heuston for torts and remedies generally, O.29 R.S.C. and notes in *Supreme Court Practice, Snell on Equity; Spry on Equitable Remedies* for injunctions, and Clerk & Lindsell, Salmond & Heuston for abatement and restrictions on it.

an admitted private nuisance by injunction the court should take into account the potential public benefit of the continuing use—public benefit not of course being of itself a defence to liability in nuisance. Thus in *Miller v. Jackson* sympathy for the English summer game prompted Lord Denning M.R. to say:[1]

" . . . I am of the opinion that the public interest should prevail over the private interest. The cricket club should not be driven out. In my opinion, the right exercise of discretion is to refuse an injunction; and of course to refuse damages in lieu of an injunction."

22–144   Similarly Cumming-Bruce L.J.[2] said (in reference to the fact that the plaintiff had "come to the nuisance"):

" . . . These are here special circumstances which should inhibit a court of equity from granting the injunction claimed."

22–145   In *Shelfer v. City of London Electric Lighting Company*[3] the vibration of the defendant's generating plant was found to constitute a nuisance in relation to the plaintiff's public house. The point was taken that the defendants were authorised by law to carry on their business and had done all that skill and care could effect to prevent any nuisance. The Order on which the defendants relied was found expressly to preserve liability for nuisance, and the statutory authority defence failed. It was then suggested that Lord Cairns' Act[4] had interfered with the plaintiff's prima facie right to an injunction, and that the public benefit of the defendant's operation should sway the court in favour of damages in lieu contrary to previous authority. The Court of Appeal rejected the suggestion, Lindley L.J. observing:

" . . . the Court has always protested against the notion that it ought to allow a wrong to continue simply because the wrong-doer is able and willing to pay for the injury he may inflict. Neither has the circumstance that the wrongdoer is in some sense a public benefactor (*e.g.* a gas or water company or a sewer authority) ever been considered a sufficient reason for refusing to protect by injunction an individual whose rights are being persistently infringed. Expropriation, even for a money conside-ration, is only justifiable when Parliament has sanctioned it."

---

[1] [1977] 1 Q.B. 966, at 982 C.
[2] *ibid* at 989 E.
[3] [1895] 1 Ch. 287.
[4] Which conferred upon the Courts of Equity jurisdiction to award damages in lieu of an injunction.

He comments that the jurisdiction to award damages instead of an injunction ought not to be exercised in cases of continuing actionable nuisances "except under very exceptional circumstances".[5]

The public benefit of the defendant's activity is not, in short, a **22–146** ground on which the court will refuse an injunction to prevent an admitted or established violation of the plaintiff's rights. It was *Shelfer*, rather than *Miller v. Jackson* that the Court of Appeal followed in *Kennaway v. Thompson and another*.[6]

In this last case, Lawton L.J. said that there was nothing in *Miller v.* **22–147** *Jackson* that was binding on the Court of Appeal that qualified what was decided in *Shelfer's* case. It is not clear whether he was suggesting that Cumming-Bruce L.J.'s statement, that the plaintiff's purchase of a house knowing it to be next to a cricket ground was relevant to discretion, was not in accordance with authority. This seems still to be something of an open question

Scotland

Civil Liability

The basis for liability most frequently resorted to under the common **22–148** law is the law of nuisance as a branch of the general law of delict (analogous to tort in England). Nuisance has been judicially defined as when one person "so uses his property as to occasion serious disturbance or substantial inconvenience to his neighbour or material damage to his neighbour's property" (*Watt v. Jamieson*).[7] Scots law

---

[5] He goes on to give examples of exceptions, "trivial and occasional nuisances: cases in which a plaintiff has shown that he only wants money; vexatious and oppressive cases; and cases where the plaintiff has so conducted himself as to render it unjust to give him more than pecuniary relief". See also the "good working rule" adopted *ibid* at 322 by A.C. Smith L.J.

> " (1) If the injury to the plaintiff's legal rights is small,
> (2) and is one which is capable of being estimated in money,
> (3) and is one which can be adequately compensated by a small money payment
> (4) and the case is one in which it would be oppressive to the defendant to grant an injunction . . . then damages in substitution for an injunction may be given."

[6] [1981] Q.B. 88.
"Lord Denning M.R.'s statement that the public interest should prevail over the private interest was counter to the principles enunciated in Shelfer's case and does not accord with Cumming-Bruce L.J.'s reason for refusing an injunction." *per* Lawton L.J. at 93F when granting to a plaintiff who had purchased a house by a lake used by a motor boat racing club a limited injunction to restrain excessive noise. This decision in turn was followed; in *Tetley v. Chitty* [1986] 1 All E.R. 663, see *ante*, in preference to *Miller v. Jackson* [1981] 1 Q.B. 88.

[7] [1954] S.C. 56.

does not distinguish between public and private nuisance and accordingly all actions which cause offence or degrade the quality of life whether occasioned to the public generally or as part of the more localised law of neighbourhood come within the definition. The same criteria for successfully proving liability require to be met in Scotland as under English law, *e.g.* a sufficient causal link between the damage and the perpetrator, proving a degree of damage sufficient for it to be actionable. It has, however, been clearly established that fault is a necessary prerequisite to establishing liability in terms of the rule in *Rylands v. Fletcher* which has not found favour with the Scottish Courts. Indeed Lord Fraser in commenting on the *Rylands v. Fletcher* rule stated:

> "(It) has sometimes been referred to as if it were authoritative in Scotland. In my opinion, with all respect to eminent judges who have referred to in that way, it has no place in Scots law, and the suggestion that it has, is a heresy which ought to be extirpated."[8]

Notwithstanding this distinction, failure to take adequate precautions to guard against damage arising from some object or substance with hazardous potential does lead to a strong presumption of fault.

Remedies for Civil Liability

22–149   The two principal remedies available under the law of delict are those of damages and interdict. The principles applying to a claim for damages are little different from those under English law, and requirements of reasonable foreseeability and proof that the pursuer has actually suffered loss, apply equally in Scotland.

22–150   Interdict, which is the Scottish equivalent of an injunction, can either be granted on an interim basis with virtually no investigation of the facts (provided the Court is convinced that there is a very real risk of further damage occurring if the offending action is not stopped and the balance of convenience favours granting the interdict) or final, following an in-depth consideration of the facts and law as affecting both sides.

22–151   A third remedy, that of specific implement, is also available under Scots law which, unlike interdict, is a Court decree requiring the defender to carry out some positive act such as cleaning up contaminated land to eliminate the nuisance. It corresponds therefore to the mandatory injunction in English practice.

---

[8] *RHM Bakeries (Scotland) Ltd v. Strathclyde Regional Council* [1985] S.L.T. 214.

The Rule in Rylands v. Fletcher

The Basic Principle

The nature and extent of the rule in *Rylands v. Fletcher* has been the   **22–152**
subject of much judicial and academic debate since the two principal
decisions in that case of 1866 and 1868.[9] In essence the rule as
originally formulated by Blackburn J. in 1866 held that where a person
brings on to his land an inherently hazardous thing (whether an
animal, a noxious substance, or large quantities of water for example)
if it then escapes he is strictly liable for all damage that results.
Subsequent cases have often applied the rule in an inconsistent
manner; in those that have reached the House of Lords, including
Rylands v. Fletcher itself, there have been dicta that have in practice
served to confuse rather than clarify. The tendency during the present
century, reinforced in particular by the decision of the House of Lords
in *Read v. J Lyons & Co. Ltd*,[10] has until now been to restrict the scope of
the rule to the point where it became unclear whether anything
significant remained. However in *Cambridge Water v. Eastern Counties
Leather plc*,[11] the House of Lords, in its first major review of the rule for
nearly 50 years, has both affirmed its existence and established it as an
extension of the law of nuisance. It has thus made possible its future
development on a more certain basis, freed from some of its
unsatisfactory accretions and qualifications.

In *Rylands v. Fletcher* the defendants (Rylands and Horrocks) who   **22–153**
were mill owners, made arrangements with Lord Wilton to construct a
reservoir on his land to provide water for their mill,[12] and proceeded to
do so. Unknown to them, beneath the site of the reservoir there were
old shafts running down into disused coal workings. The plaintiff,
Fletcher, was working a mine extracting coal from under neighbouring
land, and in doing so communicated with the disused workings under
the reservoir site. In the course of constructing the reservoir, the old
shafts were noticed, but it was not known or suspected that they were
connected with mining coal beneath the reservoir site, and were not
filled up as they should have been. When the reservoir filled with
water, this burst into the old shafts and found its way into the
plaintiff's mine, causing damage. At first instance it was held that
Rylands and Horrocks were not negligent in relation to the selection of

---

[9] [1861–73] All E.R. Rep. 1; [1866] 1 Exch. 265 and [1868] L.R. 3, H.L. 330, H.L.
[10] [1947] A.C. 156.
[11] [1994] 2 W.L.R. 53, summarised at paras. 22–029 to 22–035.
[12] Apparently under some form of lease, though the nature of their interest in the land
concerned is not clear from the reports.

the site or the construction of the reservoir. Although those who constructed it were held not to have used reasonable and proper care to ensure that the old shafts would not give way under the water, this did not render the defendants liable, in view of their lack of knowledge of the communication of these shafts with the plaintiff's mine workings. This decision was reversed on appeal, where Blackburn J. in his famous judgment addressed the question: "What is the liability which the law casts upon a person who, like the defendants, lawfully brings on his land something which, though harmless while it remains there, will naturally do mischief if it escape out of his land?" Specifically: is the duty an absolute duty to keep it on his land at his peril, or is it merely a duty to take all reasonable and prudent precautions in order to keep it in but no more? Giving the unanimous judgment of seven judges of the Court of Exchequer Chamber, he answered the questions in the classic statement:

> "We think that the true rule of law is that the person who, for his own purposes, brings on his land, and collects and keeps there anything likely to do mischief if it escapes, must keep it in at his peril, and, if he does not do so, he is prima facie answerable for all the damage which is the natural consequence of its escape. He can excuse himself by showing that the escape was owing to the plaintiff's default, or, perhaps, that the escape was the consequence of vis major or the act of God; . . . The person whose grass or corn is eaten down by the escaped cattle of his neighbour, or whose mine is flooded by the water from his neighbour's reservoir, or whose cellar is invaded by the filth of his neighbour's privy, or whose habitation is made unhealthy by the fumes and noisome vapours of his neighbour's alkali works, is damnified without any fault of his own; and it seems but reasonable and just that the neighbour who has brought something on his own property which was not naturally there, harmless to others so long as it is confined to his own property, but which he knows will be mischievous if it gets on his neighbour's, should be obliged to make good the damage which ensues if he does not succeed in confining it to his own property. But for his act in bringing it there no mischief could have accrued, and it seems but just that he should at his peril keep it there, so that no mischief may accrue, or answer for the natural and anticipated consequences. On authority this, we think, is established to be the law, whether the thing so brought be beasts or water, or filth or stenches."

In formulating this rule, Blackburn J. did not consider he was making any new law. A few years later he said: "I wasted much time in the preparation of the judgment in *Rylands v. Fletcher* if I did not succeed in showing that the law held to govern it had been law for at least 300 years".[13]

The judgment distinguished between such liability and liability **22–154** arising on the highway, which "cannot be conducted without exposing those whose persons or property are near to it to some inevitable risk; and, that being so, those who go on the highway, or have their property adjacent to it, may well be held to do so subject to their taking upon themselves the risk of injury from that inevitable danger." In such cases, therefore, a plaintiff must prove negligence if he is to recover.[14] Conversely, in *Rylands v. Fletcher* there was:

> "no ground for saying that the plaintiff here took upon himself any risk arising from the uses to which the defendants should choose to apply their land. He neither knew what there might be, nor could he in any way control the defendants, or hinder their building what reservoirs they liked, and storing up in them what water they pleased, so long as the defendants succeeded in preventing the water which they there brought from interfering with the plaintiff's property".

An appeal to the House of Lords was dismissed.[15] Lord Cairns **22–155** quoted in full the "true rule of law" as spelled out by Blackburn J. saying "In that opinion, I must say, I entirely concur". Similarly, Lord Cranworth concurred in thinking that the rule of law was correctly stated by Blackburn J. Lord Cairns however chose to set out in addition his own understanding of the applicable legal principles in the following terms:

> "The principles on which this case must be determined appear to me to be extremely simple. The defendants, treating them as the owners or occupiers of the close on which the reservoir was constructed, might lawfully have used that close for any purpose for which it might, in the ordinary course of the enjoyment of land, be used, and if, in what I may term the natural user of that land, there had been any accumulation of water, either on the surface or underground, and if by the operation of the laws of nature that accumulation of water had passed off into the close occupied by that plaintiff, the plaintiff could not have complained that result had taken place. . . . On the other hand, if the defendants, not stopping at the natural use of their close, had

---

[13] *Ross v. Fedden* (1872) 26 L.T. 966 at 968.
[14] This has not prevented actions based on dangerous "things" in or under the highway, *e.g.* creosote flocks, and mains gas pipes.
[15] Only two members of the House of Lords gave judgment, and it is not apparent from the report that any others were present, notwithstanding the need for three to make a quorum.

desired to use it for any purpose which I may term a non-natural use, for the purpose of introducing into the close that which, in its natural condition, was not in or on it—for the purpose of introducing water, either above or below ground, in quantities and in a manner not the result of any work or any operation on or under the land, and if in consequence of their doing so, or in consequence of any imperfection in the mode of their doing so, the water came to escape and to pass off into the close of the plaintiff, then it appears to me that which the defendants were doing they were doing at their own peril; and . . . for the consequence of that, in my opinion, the defendant would be liable".

Non-Natural Use

22–156   By so expressing the principles, Lord Cairns added the concept of "non-natural use" to the principles as set out by Blackburn J. It is perhaps now generally accepted that he did not intend thereby to qualify the earlier judgment, but to clarify that the liability would not arise where the damage was brought about by natural forces. Nevertheless, this feature of Lord Cairn's judgment has formed the basis of much subsequent litigation and its effect has been to introduce a further element into the rule which is now inescapably part of it. Thus in *Rickards v. Lothian*[16] where damage had been caused by a washbasin overflowing as a result of a third party deliberately turning on a tap and blocking the waste pipe, Lord Moulton said:

> "It is not every use to which land is put that brings into play that principle [*i.e.* the rule in *Rylands v. Fletcher*]. It must be some special use bringing with it increased danger to others, and must not merely be the ordinary use of the land or such a use as is proper for the general benefit of the community".

22–157   Lord Moulton also quoted with approval the statement of Wright J. in *Blake v. Woolf*[17]:

> "The bringing of water on to such premises as these and the maintaining of a cistern in the usual way seems to me to be an ordinary and reasonable user of such premises as these were; and, therefore, if the water escapes without any negligence or default on the part of the person bringing the water in and owning the cistern, I do not think that he is liable for any damage that may ensue."

[16] [1913] A.C. 263, at 280.
[17] [1898] 2 Q.B. 426.

Interestingly, on very similar facts, Blackburn J. himself held, some **22–158** six years after his judgment in *Rylands v. Fletcher*:

"I think it is impossible to say that defendants as occupiers of the upper story of a house were liable to the plaintiff under the circumstances found in the case. A water-closet and the supply pipe are for their convenience and use, but I cannot think there is any obligation on them at all hazards to keep the pipe from bursting or otherwise getting out of order."[18]

It may be interpolated here that though a defendant may be strictly **22–159** liable for the consequences of an escape where he is making a "non-natural" use of his land, it does not follow that he will not be under any liability for an escape resulting from purely natural phenomena affecting his land.[19]

There have been numerous cases on what is and what is not a non- **22–160** natural use of land but, in view of the decision in *Cambridge Water*, discussed below, those holding particular operations to be a natural use must now be regarded as of uncertain authority. Among the matters that have been held to be a "non-natural" use of land, in addition to water in bulk, which formed the subject of *Rylands v. Fletcher* itself, are mains water pipes under pressure,[20] mains gas;[21] mains electricity;[22] sewage in bulk;[23] colliery spoil;[24] a vehicle with fuel in its tank[25] and one without fuel;[26] creosoted wood blocks used for tramlines, creating noxious fumes[27] and a blowlamp.[28] Explosives were admitted to be within the rule in *Rainham Chemical Works v. Belvedere Fish Guano Co*[29] and consequently the issue was not up for decision, but in *Read v. J. Lyons & Co. Limited*[30] it was indicated that this admission might not have been appropriate and that the House of Lords would not be bound to say that the making of munitions in a factory at the Government's request in time of war for the purpose of helping to defeat the enemy was a "non-natural" use of land, adopted

---

[18] *Ross v. Fedden* (1872) 26 L.T. 966; (1871–72) 7 Q.B. 661.
[19] *Leakey v. National Trust for Places of Historic Interest or Natural Beauty* [1980] 1 Q.B. 485, applying *Goldman v. Hargrave* [1967] 1 A.C. 645, P.C. and *Sedleigh-Denfield v. O'Callaghan* [1940] A.C. 880, H.L.
[20] *Charing Cross Electricity Supply Co. v. Hydraulic Power Co.* [1914] 3 K.B. 772.
[21] *Northwestern Utilities Limited v. London Guarantee & Accident Co.* [1936] A.C. 108; *Hanson v. Wearmouth Coal Co.* [1939] 3 All E.R. 47.
[22] *National Telephone Co. v. Baker* [1893] 2 Ch. 186.
[23] *Smeaton v. Ilford Corporation* [1954] Ch. 450.
[24] *A.-G. v. Cory Bros* [1921] 1 A.C. 521
[25] *Musgrove v. Pandelis* [1919] 2 K.B. 43.
[26] *Perry v. Kendrick's Transport Limited* [1956] 1 W.L.R. 85.
[27] *West v. Bristol Tramways Co.* [1908] 2 K.B. 14.
[28] *Balfour v. Barty-King* [1959] 1 Q.B. 496.
[29] [1921] 2 A.C. 465.
[30] [1947] A.C. 156, at 169, *per* Viscount Simon.

by the occupier "for his own purposes". Cases where the rule has been considered to be applicable, though arguably incorrectly so, have included a flagpole;[31] caravans and their occupants[32] and vibrations caused by pile-driving.[33] Cases that have been held to be outside the rule by reason of their presence constituting natural use of land have included water in a cistern[34]; gas pipes used by a landlord in tenanted domestic property[35]; electric wiring[36] and metal foil used for manufacturing electrical capacitors.[37]

22–161   It is difficult, if not impossible, to discern any clear principle underlying these various decisions as to what is and what is not a natural use of land. They are certainly particularly hard to reconcile with the statement by Blackburn J. in *Rylands v. Fletcher* (with which Lord Cairns "entirely concurred") that the rule should apply to cattle (though animals may properly be seen as forming a special category on their own) or "the filth of his neighbour's privy".

22–162   In *Cambridge Water* (see paragraphs 22–029 *et seq.* for a summary of the facts of this case) the use of organochlorine solvents in a tannery was held at first instance to be a natural use of land in an industrial estate, providing employment to the local community. In the House of Lords, where the decision turned on the issue of foreseeability of harm, the question was not strictly in issue, but Lord Goff nevertheless commented on it in these terms:

"It is a commonplace that this particular [natural use] exception to liability under the rule has developed and changed over the years. It seems clear that, in *Fletcher v. Rylands*[38] itself, Blackburn J.'s statement of the law was limited to things which are brought by the defendant on to his land, and so did not apply to things that were naturally upon the land. Furthermore, it is doubtful whether in the House of Lords in the same case Lord Cairns, to whom we owe the expression 'non-natural use' of the land, was intending to expand the concept of natural use beyond that envisaged by Blackburn J. Even so, the law has long since departed from any such simple idea, redolent of a different age; and, at least since the advice of the Privy Council delivered by Lord Moulton in *Rickards*

---

[31] *Shiffman v. Order of St. John* [1936] 1 All E.R. 557.
[32] *A.-G. v. Corke* [1933] Ch. 89.
[33] *Hoare & Co. v. McAlpine* [1923] 1 Ch. 167.
[34] *Rickards v. Lothian* [1913] A.C. 263.
[35] *Miller v. Addie & Son's Collieries* [1934] S.C. 150.
[36] *Collingwood v. Home and Colonial Stores* [1936] 3 All E.R. 200.
[37] *British Celanese Limited v. A.H. Hunt Limited* [1969] 2 All E.R. 1252.
[38] Though Fletcher was the plaintiff mine owner, Rylands was the appellant in the House of Lords; hence the reversal of the names.

v. Lothian, natural use has been extended to embrace the ordinary use of land".

After quoting Lord Moulton's statement in *Rickards v. Lothian* (in paragraph 22–156), saying it had lain at the heart of the subsequent development of this exception, he continued **22–163**

"*Rickards v. Lothian* itself was concerned with a use of a domestic kind, viz. the overflow of water from a basin whose runaway had become blocked. But over the years the concept of natural use, in the sense of ordinary use, has been extended to embrace a wide variety of uses, including not only domestic uses but also recreational uses and even some industrial uses.

It is obvious that the expression 'ordinary use of the land' in Lord Moulton's statement of the law is one which is lacking in precision . . . A particular doubt is introduced by Lord Moulton's alternative criterion— 'or such a use as is proper for the general benefit of the community'. If these words are understood to refer to a local community, they can be given some content as intended to refer to such matters as, for example, the provision of services; indeed the same idea can, without too much difficulty, be extended to, for example, the provision of services to industrial premises, as in a business park or an industrial estate. But if the words are extended to embrace the wider interests of the local community or the general benefit of the community at large, it is difficult to see how the exception can be kept within reasonable bounds. A notable extension was considered in your Lordships' House in *Read v. J. Lyons & Co. Limited* . . . . where it was suggested that, in time of war, the manufacture of explosives might be held to constitute a natural use of land, apparently on the basis that, in a country in which the greater part of the population was involved in the war effort, many otherwise exceptional uses might become 'ordinary' for the duration of the war. It is however unnecessary to consider so wide an extension as that in a case such as the present. Even so, we can see the introduction of another extension in the present case, when the judge invoked the creation of employment as clearly for the benefit of the local community, viz. 'the industrial village' at Sawston. I myself, however, do not feel able to accept that the creation of employment as such, even in a small industrial complex, is sufficient of itself to establish a particular use as constituting a natural or ordinary use of land.

Fortunately, I do not think it is necessary for the purposes of the present case to attempt any redefinition of the concept of natural or ordinary use. This is because I am satisfied that the storage of

chemicals in substantial quantities, and their use in the manner
employed at ECL's premises, cannot fall within the exception. For
the purpose of testing the point, let it be assumed that ECL was
well aware of the possibility that PCE, if it escaped, could indeed
cause damage, for example by contaminating any water with
which it became mixed so as to render that water undrinkable by
human beings. I cannot think that it would be right in such
circumstances to exempt ECL from liability under the rule in
Rylands v. Fletcher on the ground that the use was natural or
ordinary. The mere fact that the use is common in the tanning
industry cannot, in my opinion, be enough to bring the use within
the exception, nor the fact that Sawston contains a small industrial
community which is worthy of encouragement or support.
Indeed I feel bound to say that the storage of substantial
quantities of chemicals on industrial premises should be regarded
as an almost classic case of non-natural use; and I find it very
difficult to think that it should be thought objectionable to impose
strict liability for damage caused in the event of their escape. It
may well be that, now that it is recognised that foreseeability of
harm of the relevant type is a prerequisite of liability in damages
under the rule, the courts may feel less pressure to extend the
concept of natural use to circumstances such as those in the
present case; and in due course it may become easier to control
this exception, and to ensure that it has a more recognisable basis
of principle."

The last sentence from this quotation is of particular significance, with
its clear implication that some at least of the decided cases (and
notably *Read v. J. Lyons & Co. Limited*) are no longer sound authority.

22–164   As to what should constitute natural use of land, it is, necessarily
very tentatively, suggested that this should extend only to things that
would be likely to be brought on to land in the event of any human
occupation of any kind, and so would include a conventional
plumbing system with its mains cistern, and the standard mains
services of water, electricity, gas and sewerage. Most people would
probably regard also parking and garaging one or two cars as a natural
appurtenant use of most property, and common forms of recreation.
In principle, however, it would not seem either necessary or appropriate to extend the concept to things brought on to land specifically for
the purpose of an activity that is not an inherent part of every
occupation, including therefore one carried on for profit. Firstly this
would be consistent with Blackburn J.'s reasoning that a person who
cannot control the risks he may be exposed to by his neighbour should
be entitled to compensation for all resulting damage irrespective of

fault, if that neighbour allows a harmful substance to escape. Additionally in so far as such an approach required economic undertakings to include in their costings appropriate sums to cover such liabilities in full it would, to a large extent, incorporate into the common law one of the basic principles of environmental protection in the Rome Treaty the polluter pays principle.[39] A "natural use" exception for non-economic activities only would be consistent with this. As an economic instrument in essence, the principle operates primarily to influence economic activities in favour of environmental protection. Imposing it rather than a negligence standard on non-economic activities is unlikely to be relevant to this—whether or not it is right to do so may therefore be determined by reference to other principles, of fairness and equity.

The polluter pays principle would even so not be fully reflected by applying the rule to all economic activities, unless liability under the rule extended to all damage caused by the escape that the polluter may properly be expected to pay for in accordance with the principle. There is currently no consensus on what this in fact is—whether it extends to damage to the unowned environment for example, and, if it does, how quantum is to be assessed.[40]   **22–165**

Foreseeability in Rylands v. Fletcher

The *Cambridge Water* case was the first case for over 40 years in which the House of Lords had occasion to consider the rule in *Rylands v. Fletcher* directly and in particular the relevance of foreseeability. By the time it reached the House of Lords the action turned solely on the scope of the rule in *Rylands v. Fletcher*, and specifically whether it applied even though it was not foreseeable to the defendant that what he had brought on to his land was likely to cause mischief if it escaped.   **22–166**

After reviewing the history of the rule Lord Goff, giving the sole substantive speech, concluded that it was simply an extension of the tort of nuisance, having regard among other things to the fact that Blackburn J. himself did not believe he was creating new law but stating existing law on the basis of existing authority. Such distinction as there is with nuisance is that whereas nuisance is concerned with reasonable user of land, *Rylands v. Fletcher* was concerned with the   **22–167**

---

[39] Art. 130, r.(2).
[40] See, for example, the EC Commission's Green Paper on Remedying Environmental Damage (COM(93) 47 final), the report on the same subject of the House of Lords Select Committee on the European Communities (December 1993); and the Council of Europe Convention on civil liability for damage resulting from activities dangerous to the environment.

situation where the defendant collects things upon his land which are likely to do mischief if they escape. The central basis of liability was this collection, and its consequence was a strict liability in the event of damage caused by escape of the things collected, even if the escape was an isolated event. Even so, the rule in *Rylands v. Fletcher* has in practice become qualified in a manner comparable to the "reasonable user" requirement in nuisance, by the principle that the rule will not apply where the defendant has made only natural use of the land. Basing his opinion on the judgment in *The Wagon Mound (No. 2)*[41] Lord Goff confirmed that that judgment settled the law to the effect that foreseeability of harm is a prerequisite for the recovery of damages in private nuisance as in the case of public nuisance. He further held, having reviewed relevant cases concerning the application of the rule in *Rylands v. Fletcher*, that foreseeability of damage of the relevant type should be a prerequisite of liability in damages under the rule also. This conclusion is entirely consistent with the original judgment of Blackburn J. in which he referred to "the neighbour who has brought something on his own property . . . *which he knows will be mischievous if it gets on his neighbour's.*"

22–168   In concluding his survey of the applicable principles, Lord Goff observed that "it would lead to a more coherent body of common law principles if the rule were to be regarded essentially as an extension of the law of nuisance to cases of isolated escapes from land, even though the rule as established is not limited to escapes which are in fact isolated".[41A] In the case in issue, he recognised, the escape was not isolated but a continuing one resulting from an accumulation of PCE forming at the base of the chalk aquifer underneath Eastern Counties' premises. This, as he pointed out, would classically have been regarded as a case of nuisance, and it would be strange if the liability would be rendered any the more strict by characterising the case as one falling under the rule in *Rylands v. Fletcher*.

22–169   In his speech Lord Goff recognised that it would in principle be possible to develop the rule in *Rylands v. Fletcher* into a principle of strict liability for damage caused by ultra-hazardous operations, as has perhaps to some extent happened in the United States, though *Read v. J. Lyons* had effectively precluded this in England. While this would be consistent with applying the polluter pays principle, which *Cambridge Water* had pressed for, by making the person responsible for any damage build into his overheads the relevant costs (or more probably the applicable insurance premiums), this accountancy response cannot in practice happen except where the damage is foreseeable

---

[41] *Overseas Tankship (UK) Limited v. Miller Steamship Co. Pty.* [1967] 1 E.C. 617.
[41A] On this point see para. 22–106 and n. 46 thereto.

—otherwise, clearly, the operator has no way of knowing what figures to apply. In holding that foreseeability is an essential element of the rule in *Rylands v. Fletcher*, Lord Goff emphasised that the protection and preservation of the environment is now perceived as being of crucial importance to the future of mankind, and that there are numerous bodies developing legislation promoting this. In his view, this tended to strengthen his inclination not to develop the common law in a similar direction, but to leave any major changes to new legislation.

There remain accumulations of PCE in the aquifer within the **22–170** boundaries of Eastern Counties' property, that continue to escape. As to liability for these it was said that the:

> "PCE has so travelled down through the drift and the chalk aquifer beneath ECL's premises that it has passed beyond the control of ECL. To impose strict liability on ECL in these circumstances, either as the creator of a nuisance or under the rule in *Rylands v. Fletcher*, on the ground that it has subsequently become reasonably foreseeable that the PCE may, if it escapes, cause damage, appears to me to go beyond the scope of the regimes imposed under either of these two related heads of liability. . . . Indeed, long before the relevant legislation came into force, the PCE had become irretrievably lost in the ground below. In such circumstances I do not consider that ECL should be under any greater liability than that imposed for negligence. At best, if the case is regarded as one of nuisance, it should be treated no differently from, for example, the case of the landslip in *Leakey v. The National Trust*."

Accordingly, there should be no liability for "historic pollution" in **22–171** such circumstances. The assumption that the PCE was "irretrievably lost" must be open to question. It is not apparent what evidence was before the court on the issue, but it is standard practice in such circumstances to drill a borehole into the contaminated aquifer and pump out its contents. This would tend to alter locally the direction of flow in the aquifer, and discourage or stop altogether any movement of PCE-containing water away from Eastern Counties' land and also, over time, reduce the quantities of remaining PCE to negligible levels.[42] Though this aspect of the judgment may have been justified on the evidence in that case, it cannot be considered to be a safe statement of the law in relation to contaminated sites generally.

Cambridge Water has now clarified the nature and extent of the rule in **22–172** *Rylands v. Fletcher* and brought some coherence to the numerous cases that purport to have applied it. The clear finding that "the storage of

---

[42] It appears that Eastern Counties is indeed now doing just this.

substantial quantities of chemicals on industrial premises [is to] be regarded as an almost classic case of non-natural use" and that there should be strict liability for damage caused in the event of their escape will be of widespread application. Moreover, while Eastern Counties may reasonably have been ignorant up until 1976 of the dangerous qualities of their chlorinated solvents, the far more extensive amount of information available regarding toxicity of chemical substances today, and the need to supply safety data sheets under the 7th Amendment to the CPL Directive 67/548 (see paragraphs 12–116 to 12–122) means that few if any people will in future be able to rely on ignorance of the potential for harm of any chemical substances that they may have on their premises. Although therefore *Cambridge Water* means that those responsible for historic pollution will not invariably be held accountable for the damage it may have caused or will cause in the future, they will be liable if that damage was at the material time foreseeable. Further, they will be liable for contamination in the soil of their property or in the water in aquifers below their property, if such pollutants can be retrieved, at least where this can be done at reasonable cost, to be judged, it must be presumed, by reference to the extent of foreseeable damage that may be caused in the absence of effective remedial action.

The Plaintiff

22–173   The rule as stated by Blackburn J. is that the person bringing the dangerous thing on to land shall, if it escapes, be "prima facie answerable for all the damage which is the natural consequence of its escape". Hitherto at least this has not been limited, as is the case in nuisance, to interference with the use or enjoyment of other land. It is open to question whether a claim may be made under the rule for personal injuries, though there is nothing in the rule itself which would preclude this. The right to do so was doubted by the House of Lords in *Read v. J. Lyons & Co. Limited*, though that case was decided on a separate ground, namely that in the absence of damage caused by an "escape", liability under the rule would not arise at all. There appears no other reason to doubt that there should be liability in respect of personal injuries as well as damage to land and personal property,[43] though it may be that only those with a relevant interest in neighbouring land can recover under the rule for personal injuries, all others (such as the plaintiff in *Read v. J. Lyons*) having to prove negligence. If the applicable principles were the same as in nuisance, as it now appears that they are following *Cambridge Water*, then a plaintiff

---

[43] See *e.g. Perry v. Kendrick's Transport Co.* [1986] 1 W.L.R. 85, *per* Ld., Parker C.J.

seeking to recover for personal injuries would have to show negligence on the part of the defendant; though this would not be consistent with the general application of the rule, and with all the previous authorities in *Rylands v. Fletcher*.[44]

The Defendant

Liability under the rule is on "a person who, for his own purposes, brings on his land, and collects and keeps there anything likely to do mischief if it escapes".[45] This is not however limited to those who bring things on to their own land but whoever owns or controls the thing and has brought it on to his or anyone else's land. He may have no more than a licence to use the land or to enter on it.[46] Where the person who owns or controls the dangerous thing is not the owner or occupier of the land, then the owner and/or the occupier may also be liable if either of them have consented to the bringing of the dangerous thing on to the land. However an owner of land who has let it out on terms that do not allow him to control the bringing on to the land of the dangerous thing should not be liable under the rule. The words "for his own purposes" in Blackburn J.'s statement of the rule should be seen as distinguishing the case from where the thing has been brought on wholly or partly for the purposes of the plaintiff. Thus where the thing is brought on by the defendant pursuant to a contract with a third party who will benefit from the action, the owner of the dangerous thing remains liable. Similarly, where the action is taken by a local authority under statutory requirements.[47]

22–174

Defences

Defences to the application of the rule in *Rylands v. Fletcher* are essentially act of God, the intervention of a third party and statutory authority. The limited application of the rule has not produced the same category of defences which can now be viewed as a missing ingredient of the tort (see paragraphs 22–127 to 22–141). In addition, where the plaintiff himself has participated in or consented to the defendant's actions then he will be unable to rely on the rule.[48] Where the plaintiff or his property is exceptionally sensitive and damaged to a degree that

22–175

---

[44] *e.g. Miles v. Forest Block Granite Co.* (1981) T.L.R. 500 and *Hale v. Jennings Bros.* [1938] 1 All E.R. 579.

[45] *Northwestern Utilities Limited v. London Guarantee and Accident Co.* [1936] A.C. 108.

[46] See *e.g. Rainham Chemical Works v. Belvedere Fish Guano Co.* [1921] 2 A.C. 465, and *National Telephone Co. v. Baker* [1893] 2 Ch. 186.

[47] *Smeaton v. Ilford Corporation.* [1954] Ch. 450.

[48] He may also have his damages reduced where he has been contributorily negligent.

is out of the ordinary, then he will not be entitled to recover the excess damage.[49]

22–176 Though act of God is an exception recognised by Blackburn J. himself to the rule, in practice it appears to have been recognised in a single case only.[50] The cases where act of God has been relied on to deny liability under the rule have all involved exceptionally heavy falls of rain; in all cases but the one exception, it has been held that these falls were not so exceptional as to be unforeseeable. Occasional extremely heavy rainfalls are part of the British climate, and a person who is doing anything that brings him within the rule can properly be expected to guard against even such exceptional events. It is of the essence of this defence that the occurrence must be extraordinary and such as could not reasonably be anticipated.[50A] Given the much greater extent and sophistication of the weather records that are now available, as compared with the 19th century when most of the usually cited cases on the point were decided, any future cases are likely to turn on argument as to statistical probabilities and the costs of guarding against wholly exceptional but not totally unforeseeable events, unless they involve such inherently improbable disasters as a major earthquake (in Britain) or the falling of a meteor.

22–177 Third party intervention is also a potential defence where this was without the consent of the defendant and he has taken all reasonable steps to guard against escape being brought about in this way. This defence was successful in *Rickards v. Lothian*, where the escape of water was the result of a third party who deliberately plugged a waste pipe and turned on a tap. Similarly in *Box v. Jubb*[51] the defendant's reservoir overflowed because of the sudden emptying into it of a third party's reservoir, and he was held liable. The burden of proof is on the defendant to show that the escape was the result of the intervention of the third party. If he establishes that, the plaintiff must show, if he can, that the defendant could reasonably have foreseen the third party intervention and taken appropriate steps to prevent the escape.[52] It is of the essence of this defence that the third party is not under the control of the defendant, whether as employee or independent

---

[49] *Eastern & SA Telegraph Co. Ltd. v. Cape Tramways Co. Ltd* [1902] A.C. 381.

[50] *Nichols v. Marsland* (1876) 2 Ex. D. 1, and the correctness of even that decision was subsequently doubted by the House of Lords in *Greenock Corporation v. Caledonian Railway Co.* [1917] A.C. 556; 1917 2 S.L.T. 67.

[50A] See, *e.g. Nitro-Phosphate and Odam's Chemical Manure Co. v. London and St. Katharine's Docks Co.*, (1878) 9 Ch. D. 503, *per* Fry J. at pp. 515, 516. "Anticipate", as used in this and other cases of that period, should probably be understood in the sense of taking pre-emptive action or forestalling, rather than merely expecting (at any undefined future time).

[51] (1879) 4 Ex. D. 76.

[52] *Perry v. Kendrick's Transport Limited* [1956] 1 All E.R. 154; [1956] 1 W.L.R. 85.

contractor,[53] and further that the act is not merely negligent, as negligence is foreseeable.

The defence of statutory authority is of general application, and is **22–178** discussed at paragraphs 12–133 to 12–135. Where the issue has arisen in relation to the rule in *Rylands v. Fletcher* the plaintiff must show negligence on the part of the defendant,[54] provided always that the bringing by the defendant of the dangerous thing on to land is required by the statute, either expressly or by necessary implication.

Scotland

The strict liability rule in *Rylands v. Fletcher* does not form part of the **22–179** law of Scotland. In the important 1985 Scottish case of *RHM Bakeries (Scotland) Limited v. Strathclyde Regional Council*[55] Lord Fraser stated[56] in the House of Lords that any suggestion that *Rylands v. Fletcher* was part of Scots law is "a heresy which ought to be extirpated". As a result of *RHM Bakeries* it is now clear that in Scotland a pursuer may only recover damages under the common law of nuisance against a defender if he can prove that such damage arose as a result of fault on the part of the defender.

In *RHM Bakeries* the pursuer's bakery flooded as a result of a **22–180** collapsed main brick sewer which was under the operation and control of the local authority. RHM claimed damages from the local authority under nuisance but did not aver that their loss was caused by any fault on the part of the local authority either in maintaining or repairing the collapsed sewer. Instead they argued that the local authority was strictly liable under the law of nuisance for their loss. Lord Fraser noted[57] that the issue is:

> "whether the local authority are liable at common law for the damage caused by flooding even if it occurred without fault on their part, or whether they are only liable if they were to some extent at fault."

Lord Fraser then examined the nineteenth century Scottish case of **22–181** *Kerr v. Earl of Orkney*[58] which appeared to suggest that the defender, the Earl of Orkney, was held strictly liable under the law of nuisance for damage caused to an owner of land downstream as a result of the

---

[53] *Balfour v. Barty-King* [1957] 1 Q.B. 496; [1957] 2 W.L.R. 84.
[54] *Green v. Chelsea Waterworks Co.* (1894) 70 L.T. 547; *Dunne v. North Western Gas Board* [1964] 2 Q.B. 806.
[55] 1985 S.L.T. 214.
[56] *ibid.* at 217.
[57] *ibid.* at 215.
[58] (1857) 20 D. 298.

collapse of a dam that the Earl of Orkney had built on his land. In that case, the Lord Justice-Clerk Hope stated[59] that:

> "[The] principle is—that if a person chooses upon a stream to make a great operation for collecting and damming up the water for whatever purpose, he is bound, as the necessary condition of such an operation, to accomplish his objective in such a way as to protect all persons lower down the stream from all danger: He must secure them against danger. It is not sufficient that he took all the pains which were thought at the time necessary and sufficient."

22–183   After considering the opinions of each judge however, Lord Fraser stated that in his opinion, the true basis of the decision in *Kerr v. Earl of Orkney* was culpa (*i.e.* fault) on the part of the defender. After a consideration of other Scottish nuisance cases and *Rylands v. Fletcher* he went on to say that under the law of nuisance in Scotland "liability has, I think, always depended on culpa".[60]

22–184   One situation where strict liability may still arise in Scotland is when a person interferes with the course of a natural stream and thereby occasions damage to another. In *RHM Bakeries* the House of Lords distinguished its earlier decision in *Greenock Corporation v. Caledonian Railway Company*,[61] where the defenders, Greenock Corporation, had altered the course of a burn to make a paddling pool. Heavy rainfall caused the burn to flood with the result that damage was caused to the railway company's property. The House of Lords held the defenders liable, and Lord Fraser in *RHM Bakeries*[62] acknowledged that the basis of the Court's decision may have been acceptance of a rule of strict liability. Lord Fraser did not however consider *Caledonian Railway* to be directly applicable to the facts of *RHM Bakeries*, and stated[63] that:

> "It may be that *Caledonian Railway* should be regarded as laying down a special rule [of strict liability] applicable only to the case of a person who interferes with the course of a natural stream. If so, it is contrary to a general principle of the law of Scotland and, in my opinion, the rule should not be extended beyond the precise facts of that case."

22–185   In England therefore, as a result of *Rylands v. Fletcher*, strict liability attaches to damage caused by the non-natural use of land and the

---

[59] *ibid.* at 302.
[60] 1985 S.L.T. 214, at 217.
[61] [1917] A.C. 556; 1917 2 S.L.T. 67.
[62] 1985 S.L.T. 214, at 217.
[63] *ibid.* at 218.

escape of a dangerous thing from it. In Scotland however, with the possible exception of interfering with the course of a natural stream, fault is a pre-requisite for liability under the law of nuisance. While there are consequently major theoretical differences in the law between the two jurisdictions on this point, in practice the difference is probably very slight. This is because Scottish courts will readily infer fault on the part of a person causing damage in such circumstances, with the result that the onus will then be on that person to explain events in such a way as to show that he was not at fault. As Lord Fraser stated in *RHM Bakeries*,[64] when the onus of proof has been so switched, "as a general rule the defences available will be limited to proving that the event was caused either by the action of a third party for whom he was not responsible . . . or by a *damnum fatale*. Even so, in *Logan v. Wang (UK) Limited*,[65] the lower proprietor of a burn, which suffered from an increasing rate of flow and chemical pollution, failed in his action after the Court held, *inter alia*, that he had insufficiently specified in his written pleadings how the upper proprietors were at fault.

Public Nuisance

It might be thought inappropriate to include consideration of public nuisance in this chapter, as it is in origin and still in essence a criminal offence. However its principal interest to lawyers practising in the environmental field is the ancillary relief that the courts may grant, both by way of an injunction at the relation of the Attorney-General, and also the remedies in tort that are available to a plaintiff who has suffered special or particular damage, whatever that may consist of. The criminal offence is triable either way and is committed by a person "who (a) does an act not warranted by law, or (b) omits to discharge a legal duty, if the effect of the act or omission is to endanger the life, health, property, morals or comfort of the public, or to obstruct the public in the exercise or enjoyment of rights common to all Her Majesty's subjects".[66]   **22–186**

Deriving, as it does, from days long before the European Convention on Human Rights, the offence encompasses virtually any activity that, by the standards of the day, the courts have considered it proper   **22–187**

---

[64] *ibid.* at 219.
[65] 1991 S.L.T. 580.
[66] Archbold, *Criminal Pleading, Evidence and Practice*, (1994), para. 31–50, and see references there cited. See also the discussion of earlier cases on public nuisance by Romer L.J. in *Att.-Gen. v. P.Y.A. Quarries Ltd.*, [1957] 2 Q.B. 169 at 180–184; [1957] 1 All E.R. 894; [1957] 2 W.L.R. 1770.

to prevent.[67] Many of the cases have concerned obstructing the highway or endangering those on it, but the offence ranges far more widely, and there are numerous cases on interference with the public comfort and health by pollution, including noise,[68] and acts endangering public safety or offending against public decency, morals or order. As J.R. Spencer points out in a comprehensive account of its origins, "everything in public nuisance runs contrary to modern notions of certainty and precision in criminal—and indeed, in civil law as well".[69] Although the offence continues to be charged where no statutory offence is readily to hand, the vast majority of matters that have been held to be public nuisances are now subject to statutory regulation of the relevant activity, and those that are not directly regulated are very largely encompassed by the "statutory nuisances" the subject of Part III of the E.P.A. and which are discussed in the next chapter. Nevertheless, although for practical purposes the offence is no longer needed in the vast majority of situations, it remains available and may be charged instead of or in addition to the statutory offences, in appropriate cases. Being a common law offence, there are no statutory restrictions on the fines and periods of imprisonment that may be imposed, other than those applying generally to the jurisdiction of particular courts.

22–188   Since the offence is designed to protect public rights, private individuals have no standing in proceedings in respect of a public nuisance, except in so far as they have suffered special damage.[70] Subject to this exception, and apart from certain circumstances where local authorities may take proceedings in their own name under

---

[67] A quite recent case, *Holme*, reported in 1984 Current Law Year Book, No. 2471, reads: "The defendant was the subject of a rare common law prosecution for public nuisance following a series of incidents which included "purposefully following people, approaching and threatening children on the public highway and in the school playground, banging on the roofs of cars, walking in a public highway without regard for the safety of traffic, blocking the public highway, behaving in an intimidating manner on a public highway, imitating an ape, persistently provoking dogs to bark in the early hours of the morning, shouting and screaming in a public place and various other acts". Among these "various other acts" were failing to keep his back garden in a sanitary condition, repeatedly playing a single chord on the piano throughout the entire night, suspending a radio on a rope from his bedroom window and playing it loudly at all times of the day and night, obstructing the progress of persons on the highway, peering through windows, causing a disturbance in a post office, kicking a dog along the street, and assault. The defendant was found guilty and sentenced to fifteen months' imprisonment, part of which was suspended, in order to prevent any repetition of the offence."

[68] *Halsey v. Esso Petroleum Co. Ltd.*, [1961] 1 W.L.R. 683. Also *R. v. Shorrock*, *The Times* March 11, 1993, *The Independent*, March 22, 1993 (permitting land to be used for an "acid-house party").

[69] "Public Nuisance—a Critical Examination", J.R. Spencer, (1989) 48 (1) Camb. L.J. 55.

[70] *Gouriet v. Union of Post Office Workers* [1978] A.C. 435; [1977] 3 All E.R. 70.

section 222 of the Local Government Act 1972 in the interests of the inhabitants of their areas, only the Attorney-General can sue on behalf of the public for the purpose of preventing public wrongs. Nevertheless, this in no way excludes the possibility of individuals or bodies from instigating proceedings; they must however do so by way of a relator action brought in the name of the Attorney-General, provided he gives his consent.[71] Proceedings for an injunction can therefore be brought on behalf of a community or class of people, and not therefore necessarily at the expense of any one individual. Further, there is no need for the plaintiff(s) to have any interest in land, and it is clear that public nuisance may exist in the case of a single act, whereas private nuisance normally requires a degree of repetition.

Liability in public nuisance is strict, though not absolute. Actual knowledge by a defendant that his actions would lead to the commission of a public nuisance is not required, if he ought to have known this.[72] As explained by Denning L.J., as he then was, in *Southport Corporation v. Esso Petroleum Co. Ltd.*,[73] one of the principal differences between an action for a public nuisance and an action for negligence is the burden of proof. In an action for a public nuisance, once the nuisance is proved and the defendant is shown to have caused it, then the legal burden is shifted on to the defendant to justify or excuse himself. If he fails to do so, he is held liable, whereas in an action for negligence the legal burden in most cases remains throughout on the plaintiff. In that case, the steering gear of an oil tanker was defective, and the tanker had become stranded in a river estuary. To prevent the tanker breaking up the captain had jettisoned 400 tons of oil, a considerable part of which reached the foreshore belonging to Southport Corporation. Though it was accepted that having become stranded it was necessary to discharge the oil to get the tanker off, and that lives might have been lost had this not been done, this was not a sufficient excuse. As Denning L.J. put it:

22–189

"Must the Southport Corporation prove that the ship was at fault in getting on to the wall, or must the ship prove that she herself was not at fault? In my opinion the burden is on the ship. She does not justify herself in law by necessity alone, but only by unavoidable necessity, and the burden is on her to show it was unavoidable . . . [He then reviewed earlier cases] . . . Applying these cases, I am of opinion that the defendants can only escape

---

[71] The procedure for relator actions is governed by R.S.C., O.15, r.11. The Attorney-General has total discretion over the giving of consent, and is answerable only to Parliament as to his exercise of it—*Gouriet v. Union of Post Office Workers* [1978] A.C. 435, at 524.

[72] *R. v. Shorrock*, n.68 *supra*.

[73] [1954] 2 Q.B. 182, at 197; [1954] 2 All E.R. 561.

liability if they can prove that the discharge of oil was an unavoidable necessity; that is, a necessity which arose utterly without their fault. In other words, that they committed no negligence to give occasion to it."

Relationship with Private Nuisance

22–190   The relationship between public and private nuisance is historically almost accidental, and the concepts are very largely distinct. Indeed at one time it was a defence in an action for private nuisance to establish that it was in fact a public nuisance, and the common law courts hearing the case would have no jurisdiction over the action. It was only subsequently that the common law courts accepted that a person who had suffered special damage from a public nuisance might bring a personal action in respect of it.[74] In *Att.-Gen. v. P.Y.A Quarries Limited*, Romer L.J., having reviewed of the case law, stated that:

> "Any nuisance is 'public' which materially affects the reasonable comfort and convenience of life of a class of Her Majesty's subjects. The sphere of the nuisance may be described generally as "the neighbourhood"; but the question of whether the local community within that sphere comprises a sufficient number of persons to constitute a class of the public is a question of fact in every case. It is not necessary, in my judgment, to prove that every member of the class has been injuriously affected; it is sufficient to show that a representative cross-section of the class has been so affected for an injunction to issue."

22–191   Later in the same case, when dealing with the evidence necessary to prove a public nuisance, he said:

> "Some public nuisances (for example, the pollution of rivers) can often be established without the necessity of calling a number of individual complainants as witnesses. In general, however, a public nuisance is proved by the cumulative effect which it is shown to have had on the people living within its sphere of influence. In other words, a normal and legitimate way of proving a public nuisance is to prove a sufficiently large collection of private nuisances."

22–192   Denning L.J. also dealt in that case with the question: what is the difference between a public nuisance and a private nuisance? Having pointed out that it does not help much to say that a public nuisance affects Her Majesty's subjects generally, whereas a private nuisance

---

[74] *Crowder v. Tinkler*, (1816), 19 Ves. Jun. 618, 34 E.R. 645; affirmed by the House of Lords in *Boyce v. Paddington Corporation*, [1903] 1 Ch. 110, [1906] A.C. 1.

only affects particular individuals, he continued with the often quoted statement:

> "So here I decline to answer the question how many people are necessary to make up Her Majesty's subjects generally. I prefer to look to the reason of the thing and to say that a public nuisance is a nuisance which is so widespread in its range or so indiscriminate in its effect that it would not be reasonable to expect one person to take proceedings on his own responsibility to put a stop to it, but that it should be taken on the responsibility of the community at large."

Inevitably any public nuisance that emanates from a single source will most greatly affect those nearest to it. The fact that such a nuisance has an uneven effect in no way prevents it from being a public nuisance, provided the effect is sufficiently wide.[75]   **22–193**

Special Damage

A private individual, to maintain a claim in public nuisance must show that "he has sustained a particular damage or injury other than and beyond the general injury to the public and that such damage is substantial".[76] The categories of damages that a plaintiff may recover are—it would seem—wider than those which probably apply in private nuisance, though the matter is far from clear. Spencer[77] notes that few points in civil law are more obscure than the meaning of "special damage" in the context of public nuisance. Though most kinds of harm will be relevant damage, such as personal injury, physical damage to property and economic loss, it is not clear whether inconvenience that is not directly translatable into financial loss will suffice. It is also uncertain whether a plaintiff can be said to have suffered special damage if there are a large number of others who have suffered equally. In a Canadian case, *Hickey v. Electric Reduction Company of Canada Ltd.*,[78] the plaintiff, a fisherman, failed to recover damages arising from the defendant's pollution that had killed the fish in the locality, because the other fishermen in the area were likewise affected. It is also unsettled whether the mere fact that the defendant has created a public nuisance automatically enables a plaintiff who has   **22–194**

---

[75] *R. v. Lloyd*, (1802) 4 Esp. 200, where an indictment for a public nuisance for noise failed as only three members of Clifford's Inn were affected—the proceedings ought to have been for a private nuisance; see *Att.-Gen. v. P.Y.A. Quarries Ltd.*, *per* Romer L.J. [1957] 2 Q.B. at 182, and *per* Denning L.J. at 191.
[76] *Benjamin v. Storr*, [1874–86] All E.R. Rep., Ext. 2000.
[77] *op. cit.*, p. 74.
[78] (1970) 21 D.L.R. (2nd) 368.

suffered special damage to succeed, or whether the plaintiff must show that the damage was foreseeable[79]

Trespass to Land

Definition

22–195 "Every unlawful entry by one person on land in the possession of another is a trespass for which an action lies, even though no actual damage is done".[80]

A person trespasses upon land if he wrongfully enters it, or drives over it or takes possession of it, or expels the person in possession, or destroys or removes anything permanently fixed to it, or places or fixes anything on it or in it, or if he erects or leaves anything on his own land which invades the airspace of another, or if he discharges water or filth upon another's land.

22–196 Trespass may, therefore, be distinguished from nuisance as involving direct rather than indirect injury to an interest in land; unlike nuisance, it is actionable without proof of damage. The distinction between trespass and nuisance is drawn by comparing the action of a man who flushes stagnant water from his own yard into his neighbour's cellar (trespass, and only possibly nuisance) with a man whose privy is out of repair with the consequence that the filth from it flows into his neighbour's cellar (nuisance, but not trespass).[81] The trivial nature of the trespass is no defence — arguably a policy decision on the basis that acts of direct interference with another's possession, left unchecked, may lead to breaches of the peace.[82]

22–197 The action of trespass became common in the reign of Edward I where it followed the style of a criminal proceeding. The defendant was punished by the Court in addition to the plaintiff being compensated for the wrong. Maitland's "fertile mother of actions" continued to evolve as a misdemeanour and gave rise also to the action of extended trespass on the case with the result that where the injury was

---

[79] *Dymond v. Pearce*, [1972] 1 Q.B. 496.
[80] Halsbury *Laws of England* (4th Ed., 1985) at para. 1384. Trespass literally means "to pass beyond."
[81] Compare *Preston v. Mercer* (1656) Hardr. 61 with *Reynolds v. Clark* (1725) 2 Ld.Ray. 1399 and *Tenant v. Goldwin* (1704) 2 Ld.Ray. 1089.
[82] Clerk and Lindsell at para. 23–07 [1308].

immediate, trespass lay; where it was consequential an action of trespass on the case lay.

A Question of Possession

Trespass lies at the suit of the person in possession of the land. What amounts to possession is a question of fact and twofold: **22–198**

(1)   There must be an intention to possess the land; and
(2)   The person in possession must exercise control over the land to the exclusion of other persons.[83]

Intention to Possess

Possession, in its most general sense, is enjoyed by the person who is in occupation or physical control of the land at the time the trespass occurs. Thus, if a person (other than the owner) is lawfully in possession of the land at the time of the trespass, the owner has no right to sue in trespass. Mere right of property without possession is consequently not sufficient to support the action.[84] A lawful tenant has the right to sue for trespass as against the land owner. If the land is vacant, however, the owner will have sufficient interest to pursue an action for trespass.[85] Possession, therefore, is ultimately indicated by the conduct applicable to the type of land. Thus where land consists of buildings, possession may be sufficiently evidenced by occupation of the buildings. Where the land is not built upon, however, possession may be shown by acts of enjoyment over the land such as its cultivation.   **22–199**

It is not necessary for possession to be lawful to maintain an action for trespass. Actual possession is good against all those who cannot show a better right to possession.[86] A person claiming possession against the true owner, however, cannot do so unless the true owner has been lawfully dispossessed.   **22–200**

The owner of the land is considered, prima facie, to have possession of the land in the absence of evidence to the contrary. Thus a trespasser who expels the person in possession does not obtain   **22–201**

---

[83] Halsbury, p. 636, para. 1394.
[84] *Wallis v. Hands* [1893] 2 Ch. 75 followed what it cited as "settled law", ruling that a person with a mere *"interesse termini"* cannot bring an action for trespass. He must first bring an action for recovery of possession.
[85] The doctrine of possession by relation is the legal fiction whereby the person with the right to possession is extended the remedies allowed to those with actual possession, the right to immediate possession being converted into actual possession by entry upon any part of the land. In doing so, the person is deemed to have been in possession of the land from the date when his right of entry accrued.
[86] *Asher v. Whitlock* [1865] L.R. 1 Q.B.I.

sufficient possession to enable him to maintain an action for trespass against the evicted person unless the owner has been dispossessed.[87]

22–202　　Distinction must be made between a voluntary act of entry and an involuntary one. It is no defence that the person in question was mistaken as to the extent of his own land provided that the actual act of entry was voluntary, even if unintended. There is no liability, however, if the act is involuntary. In *Smith v. Stone*[88] the defendant was held not to be liable where he was thrown onto the plaintiff's land. So too, falling on to railway tracks in an epileptic fit is no trespass.[89]

22–203　　Negligent entry will amount to trespass, as in *The League Against Cruel Sports Limited v. Scott*[90] where the Master of Hounds negligently failed to prevent his pack entering on to prohibited land. It is probably not trespass to make an unintentional non-negligent entry — inevitable accident seems to be a defence.[91] So a chemical tanker leaving the road in an accident due entirely to another would not seemingly constitute a trespass, but *quaere*, if the driver deliberately swerved in order to avoid an accident.

Possession to the Exclusion of Others

22–204　　The possession enjoyed by the plaintiff in an action for trespass must be exclusive. A lodger cannot bring an action for trespass because possession, by definition, remains with the landlord with whom he continues to share the property. A sub-tenant who has exclusive possession of specific rooms in a house may do so.

22–205　　The subject matter of trespass to land is real or corporeal property. Land with its subsoil and superstructures may be divided horizontally so that one person may be in possession of the surface and another in possession of the minerals below it. The owner of a *profit à prendre* can accordingly maintain an action for trespass in respect of interference with the subject matter of his profit. The grantee of an exclusive right to fish has a right of action in trespass against a person who wrongfully discharges sediment-loaded water into a river, driving away the fish.[92]

---

[87] Note that a person may only bring an action to recover land within 12 years of the date of dispossession after which time his title will be extinguished — see the Limitation Act 1980, s.17.

[88] (1647) Sty.65. Compare *National Coal Board v. J.E. Evans & Co (Cardiff) Limited and Maberley Parker Limited* [1951] 2 K.B. 861.

[89] *Public Transport Comm. of New South Wales v. Perry* (1977) 14 A.L.R. 273.

[90] [1986] Q.B. 240.

[91] Clerk & Lindsell at 23–05 [1307].

[92] *Fitzgerald v. Firbank* [1897] 2 Ch. 96. By comparison, the owner of an easement cannot maintain an action for trespass.

Defences

Entry on to land will not be a trespass if it is lawful, that is justifiable   **22–206**
either by operation of law, by the act of the plaintiff or his predecessors
in title, or under a licence.

Justification by Operation of Law

The law may in certain circumstances entitle entry on to land   **22–207**
without the consent of the person in possession of it. Examples
include the licence to go upon adjoining land to abate nuisance, to
restrain against goods, to go upon the plaintiff's land to return goods
wrongfully deposited by the plaintiff on the defendant's land, and to
enter another's land to recapture goods if taken and put there by the
plaintiff himself. Certain statutes may also afford licence to enter
without the consent of the possessor, *e.g.* the National Parks and
Access to the Countryside Act 1949 and the Police and Criminal
Evidence Act 1984.

Justification under Right of Way

The exercise of a right of way, whether private or public, may be a   **22–208**
defence against an action for trespass. The extent of this right will vary
according to its terms. Private rights of way may arise by express grant
or by Act of Parliament in accordance with the terms of the grant. The
right of way in respect of a public highway is limited to its use for the
purpose of passing and re-passing on the highway and for other
reasonable purposes ancillary to this. There is no general right of way
with regard to passing over the foreshore to bathe in the sea or to tow
on the banks of a navigable river.

In the case of both public and private rights of way any use in excess   **22–209**
of the right renders the user a trespasser on the land; anyone seeking
to rely on a right of way should be aware of its exact extent. There may
be justification of trespass under easements entitling a person to do
some act on the land of another without giving him exclusive
possession of the same, such as right of entry and repair. By custom
the inhabitants of a locality may be entitled to exercise rights such as
fetching water from a spring or using land for recreation. Custom must
be certain as to the nature of the user and the locality to which it
applies[93] if it is to afford a defence to trespass.

---

[93] *Hall v. Nottingham* (1875) 1 Ex.D. 1.

Licences

22–210   It is a defence to an action of trespass to show that the person is on the land with the leave and licence (either express or implied) of the owner.

22–211   A licensee exceeding the terms of his licence by acting beyond the authorisation given to him, or the time in which he may remain on the land after a reasonable "packing up" time will be a trespasser. In *Winter Garden Theatre (London) Limited v. Millennium Productions Limited*[94] the question of the revocability of a contractual licence was considered. Where the licensor expressly or impliedly promised by contract not to revoke the licence, he may not do so until the licensee gives him just cause to withdraw his promise. Thus the licensee does not turn into a trespasser until that time. A licence coupled with an interest is also irrevocable and therefore the grant cannot be defeated to which it is incident.

Limitation period

22–212   The general rule is that an action for trespass to land must be brought within six years from the date upon which the cause of action accrued.[95] Time begins to run from the date upon which the act of trespass is committed unless it was fraudulent or secret — then it runs from the date upon which the injured party discovers the trespass or should reasonably have discovered it. Where the defendant's article or substance remains on the plaintiff's land, this constitutes a new trespass each day — it is thus a continuing tort and a new limitation period likewise starts afresh each day in relation to the damage caused by that day's trespass, though time continues to run in relation to that caused on previous days. Further, no person can bring an action to recover land unless it is within 12 years after the time at which the right to bring such action first accrues.[96] After 12 years adverse possession by the person with possession of the land extinguishes the title.[97]

Remedies

22–213   The law provides several remedies in respect of a trespass. These include, in particular, damages, injunction and declaration, expulsion, and distress damage feasant.

---

[94] [1948] A.C. 173.
[95] Limitation Act 1980, s.2.
[96] Limitation Act 1980, s.15.
[97] Limitation Act 1980, s.17.

Damages

As illustrated above, a successful plaintiff does not have to show **22–214** that he has suffered actual loss and so may always recover at least nominal damages. If he shows actual damage to have been suffered, he is entitled to receive damages to compensate him for his loss. The measure of damages varies according to the trespass, which may be one of three kinds. In general, the tortious measure of damages is calculated to put the plaintiff in the position he would have been if the damage had not been incurred.

(i) Trespass which results in a benefit to the defendant but without damage being suffered by the plaintiff. The damages recoverable will be the sum that is payable for the manner of right exercised by the defendant in the area, *e.g.* the standard for a bailee.

(ii) Trespass which results in physical damage to the land, so that the plaintiff suffers actual loss. The measure of damages in this instance will be either the diminution in value (as a general rule) or the costs of repair and reinstatement of the land so exceeding diminution in value where those expenditures are reasonable[98]; and

(iii) Severance and removal of things attached to the soil, *e.g.* felling of timber. The measure is again the diminution in the value of the land.

Further, exemplary damages may be awarded in cases where the **22–215** wrong is an oppressive, arbitrary or unconstitutional action by the government or where the tortfeasor's conduct has been calculated on the basis of profit that he could make exceeding the compensation ordinarily payable to the plaintiff. Aggravated damages may also be awarded where the trespass inflicts injury on the plaintiff's pride and dignity or is accompanied by noise and disturbance. Damages are not, however, to be calculated so as to punish the trespasser.

Injunction and declaration

An injunction may be granted to prevent a continuing trespass or a **22–216** repetition of a trespass or where a trespass is threatened.[99] An injunction will not be awarded where the trespass is considered to be of a trifling nature or where damages are sufficient remedy so that an

---

[98] *Heath v. Keys* [1984] C.L.Y. 3568.
[99] So in *Kelsen v. Imperial Tobacco Co (Great Britain and Ireland) Limited* [1957] 2 Q.B. 334 it was held to be proper to grant a mandatory injunction to remove an advertising sign whose invasion of a neighbouring shop's airspace amounted to a trespass.

injunction would be oppressive. An injunction may, however, be coupled with an award of damages, and a declaration may be made concerning the claim.

Expulsion/Ejectment

22–217   Expulsion is the right of a person entitled to possession of the land to remove a trespasser, using no more force than reasonably necessary. If the trespasser enters peaceably, the trespasser must first be requested to leave. If, however, he enters with force or violence, the person in possession may remove him without first requesting him to do so. If excessive force is used, a trespass upon the person of the trespasser may be committed. The common law principle that a person entitled to immediate possession of land may enter and use such reasonable force as is necessary to effect entry is now limited by the Protection from Eviction Act 1977 and the Criminal Law Act 1977.

22–218   Ejectment is an action for recovery of land whereby the plaintiff out of possession claims immediate possession of the land by virtue of his title to the land.

Distress Damage Feasant

22–219   If a chattel is unlawfully on the land of another, the person entitled to possession of the land may instead of bringing an action for trespass, distrain the chattel which is doing the damage. His right to recover damage by action is, however, suspended so long as the distress continues.[1]

Waste

Definition and Origins

22–220   The law of waste is concerned with injuries to an interest in land committed by persons in possession of the land, *i.e.* those persons with a limited interest as against the reversioner, remainderman or heir. Thus it may be distinguished from trespass to land in that it is concerned with injury to the land in the defendant's possession, not neighbouring land.

22–221   An action for waste lies in the law of tort. Originally an action for waste lay against a tenant in dower and tenant by courtesy of

[1] *Boden v. Roscoe* [1894] 1 Q.B. 608.

England.[2] No action lay against a tenant for life or years on the basis that his demise came from the owner of the land who could in the actual demise make provision for action against waste by his tenant. The tenancy in dower and tenancy by courtesy were creatures created by law and therefore law had to provide the remedy.

The statute of Mortbridge[3] extended the common law liability to **22-222** "fermors" holding by lease for life, or for years with or without deed. The Statute of Gloucester[4] provided the remedy of a writ of waste and awarded treble damages and recovery of the land wasted to the successful plaintiff, but, as with many proceedings originated by way of writ, it was very narrow in application— *locus standi* being limited to the owner of a vested estate of inheritance immediately expectant on the estate in possession.[5] The action was, therefore, for practical reasons, superseded by separate actions at common law for damages (action on the case)[6] and in equity by way of injunction. The ancient writ of waste was abolished in 1833.[7]

In strict terms, waste is any act altering the nature of the land, **22-223** whether deleterious or not. There are four basic categories:

Categories

    (1) Ameliorating;   **22-224**
    (2) Permissive;
    (3) Voluntary; and
    (4) Equitable waste.

The evolution of the law of waste has led to the requirement that **22-225** injury to the inheritance must be shown and that nominal damages will not be awarded. An action for waste, will not, therefore, lie in every category of waste.

(1) Ameliorating waste

As the title suggests, this consists of alterations to the land which improve it, such as the conversion of dilapidated buildings into dwellings.[8] No action for damages can lie, as no damage has been

---

[2] A tenant in dower was a widow who enjoyed for the term of her life her husband's lands after his death for her sustenance and the nurture and education of her children. Dower was abolished by the Administration of Estates Act 1925. A tenant by courtesy of England was a widower's life estate in the land of his deceased wife provided he had children by her capable of inheriting the land. This form of tenancy was also abolished by the Administration of Estates Act 1925.

[3] c.23, 52 Hen. 3.

[4] 6 Edw. 1, c. 5.

[5] Megarry & Wade, *The Law of Real Property* (5th Ed., 1984) p. 96.

[6] *Woodhouse v. Walker* [1880] 5 Q.B.D. 404.

[7] *Lowndes v. Norton* [1864] 33 L.J. Ch. 583.

[8] 3 & 4 W.M. 4, c. 27, s.36.

suffered. The Court may, however, (albeit in rare cases) award an injunction if it thinks it appropriate.[9]

(2) Permissive waste

This is waste by omission, or non-feasance, *i.e.* by failing to carry out repairs in cases where a duty or an obligation to do so exists. Actions for permissive waste most frequently arise in landlord and tenant relations and, in practice, are dealt with on the basis of an action for breach of contract. No action will lie against a tenant for life unless he is expressly required to keep the premises in repair[10] and fails to do so.

(3) Voluntary waste

This is waste by way of misfeasance, *i.e.* doing that which ought not to be done, such as the opening and working of mines in the land,[11] the felling of timber (except for the purpose of estover or bote[12] and on timber estates, *i.e.* estates cultivated merely for the production of timber where the proceeds of sale from the timber are treated as part of the annual profits of the land). "Timber" consists of oak, ash and elm trees at least 20 years old[13] together with other trees which rank as timber by local custom, *e.g.* willow in Hampshire, birch in Yorkshire. Local custom may also prescribe some other qualification, *e.g.* that the tree has a minimum age of 24 years or a specified minimum girth. Unless the instrument granting the tenant his interest expressly exempts him from liability for voluntary waste, that is, a grant "without impeachment of waste", the tenant will be liable for voluntary waste.

(4) Equitable waste

Equitable waste is waste by way of misfeasance and is that which a prudent man would not do in the management of his own property.[14] Even if a tenant is not liable for voluntary waste, it would be inequitable to allow him to ruin the property unhindered, *e.g.* for stripping a house of all its fixtures or felling timber

---

[9] *Doherty v. Allman* [1878] 3 App. Cas. 709.

[10] *McIntosh v. Pontypridd Improvements Co. Ltd* [1891] 61 L.J. Q.B. 164.

[11] Clerk & Lindsell at para. 23–71 [1352].

[12] The mineral rights of a tenant for life depend on whether the mine is open when the tenancy begins and whether he is "impeachable of waste". If these conditions are not met he cannot work the mine as this would be voluntary waste. By s.41–42 and 45–43 of the Settled Land Act 1925 a tenant for life is authorised to grant mining leases for 100 years or less, whether the mine is open or not.

[13] The basic rule is that a tenant for life can take reasonable botes or estovers from the land for repairing the house or burning (house-bote), for making repairs to agricultural implements (plough-bote) or for repairing fences (hay-bote). This, however, does not entitle the tenant to cut down timber in excess of his reasonable needs.

[14] *Honywood v. Honywood* [1874] L.R. 18 E.Q. 306 at p. 309.

planted to provide shelter. The tenant will thus be liable for equitable waste (unless the vesting deed indicates otherwise).

Remedies

The measure of damages is, in general, the diminution in the value **22–226** of the reversion and not necessarily the sum it would cost to restore the property to its condition before the waste.[15]

In *Whitham v. Kershaw*, an action was brought by the landlord **22–227** against his tenant for waste for the "very monstrous act" in which the tenant had removed 600 cartloads of soil from an already shallow allotment to enrich his own neighbouring plot. Lord Esher M.R. distinguished between the implied covenant not to commit waste and the covenant to deliver up the premises in the condition in which it was received. The true measure of damages in the case of waste is the diminution in the value of the reversion (less a discount for immediate payment) and not the sum it would cost to restore the property to its condition before the waste.

Where "vindictive" damage has been caused, punitive damages **22–228** may be awarded.[16]

---

[15] *Turner v. Wright* [1860] 2 D.E. G.F. & J. 234, Megarry & Wade at p. 98.
[16] *Whitham v. Kershaw* [1885–86] 16 Q.B.D. 613.

Chapter 23

STATUTORY NUISANCES

A duty to deal with "statutory" nuisances was first imposed on local **23–001** authorities by the Public Health Act 1875, replacing the merely permissive power that they previously enjoyed. The nature of the nuisances to which this duty has applied has been progressively expanded and refined over the years, and different procedures developed for dealing with them. The Environmental Protection Act 1990[1] consolidated the list of nuisances with minor amendments and set out a uniform procedure applicable to all of them. The Noise and Statutory Nuisance Act 1993 has however added a further category of statutory nuisance covering noise emitted or caused in a street (noise could previously only be a statutory nuisance where it was emitted from premises), and necessarily created special procedures for dealing with this particular problem.

The following circumstances constitute a statutory nuisance:[2]   **23–002**

- (a) any premises in such a state as to be prejudicial to health or a nuisance;
- (b) smoke emitted from premises so as to be prejudicial to health or a nuisance;
- (c) fumes or gases emitted from premises so as to be prejudicial to health or a nuisance;
- (d) any dust, steam, smell or other effluvia arising on industrial, trade or business premises and being prejudicial to health or a nuisance;
- (e) any accumulation or deposit which is prejudicial to health or a nuisance;
- (f) any animal kept in such a place or manner as to be prejudicial to health or a nuisance;
- (g) noise emitted from premises so as to be prejudicial to health or a nuisance;

---

[1] In ss.79 to 83.
[2] s.79(1).

1031

(ga) noise that is prejudicial to health or a nuisance and is emitted from or caused by a vehicle, machinery or equipment in a street;

(h) any other matter declared by any enactment to be a statutory nuisance.

"Prejudicial to Health or a Nuisance"

23–003   It will be seen that all of the specific nuisances are qualified by the expression "prejudicial to health or a nuisance". These are two quite separate considerations, either of which will suffice.[3] "Prejudicial to health" means "injurious, or likely to cause injury, to health", and consequently evidence of actual injury is not needed. In a case brought under the Public Health Act 1936, it was held that a nuisance coming within the meaning of that Act must be either a private or a public nuisance as understood by common law.[4] In so deciding, a public nuisance was defined as "an act or omission which materially affects the material comfort and quality of life of a class of Her Majesty's subjects", and it was said that "private nuisances, at least in the vast majority of cases, are interferences for a substantial length of time by owners or occupiers of property with the use or enjoyment of neighbouring property".[5] Hence if what has taken place affects only the person or persons occupying the premises where the nuisance is said to have taken place, this cannot be a statutory nuisance (though see paragraph 18–013).

23–004   It was also argued in the same case that not only must a statutory nuisance be either of a private or public kind at common law, but the act of nuisance itself must be such as to come within the spirit of the 1936 Act, that is, it must in some way be concerned with the health of the person who claims to be or who has been affected by the nuisance. That proposition was considered "attractive, though no decision was called for on the point". However, whereas the long title of the 1936 Act is "an Act to consolidate with amendments certain enactments relating to public health", that of the E.P.A. 1990, so far as relevant, is "an Act . . . to *restate* the law defining statutory nuisances and improve the summary procedures for dealing with them". By contrast the latter also refers to it being "an Act . . . to *re-enact* the provisions of [C.O.P.A.] relating to waste on land with modifications . . . ". Accordingly, it is probably no longer appropriate, if it ever was, to

---

[3] *Bishop Auckland Local Board v. Bishop Auckland Iron and Steel Company Ltd* (1882) 10 Q.B.D. 138, where it was observed that the 1875 Public Health Act definition did not refer to "an injurious nuisance" but had the two quite distinct limbs.

[4] *National Coal Board v. Neath Borough Council* [1976] 2 All E.R. 478 at 482.

[5] [1976] 2 All E.R. at 481.

construe the references to statutory nuisances as necessarily being coloured by public health issues. There seems no reason to put any particular gloss on the normal meaning of the words, but in so far as the legislative context is material, it must be one of controlling pollution of the environment generally.[6]

The Heads of Nuisance

(a) *"Any premises in such a state as to be prejudicial to health or a nuisance"*   **23–005**

"Premises" is defined to include land and any vessel, with the exclusion of one "powered by steam reciprocating machinery".[7] Although the state of premises will not be a statutory nuisance if it only affects the occupants,[8] where the premises are such that the comfort of the occupants is disturbed by noise from outside, this may amount to a statutory nuisance.[9]

(b) *"Smoke emitted from premises so as to be prejudicial to health or a nuisance".*   **23–006**

There are a number of exceptions to this[10] to avoid overlap with the Clean Air Act 1993, the provisions of which will govern where it is applicable. Thus it does not apply to smoke emitted from a chimney of a private dwelling within a smoke control area, dark smoke emitted from a chimney of a building, or a chimney serving the furnace of a boiler or industrial plant either attached to a building or fixed to or installed on land, dark smoke emitted in any other circumstances from industrial or trade premises, and smoke emitted from a railway locomotive steam engine. "Smoke" is defined to include soot, ash, grit and gritty particles emitted in smoke; by implication from the definition of "dust" (see paragraph 23–008), smoke may also include "dust". It is specifically provided that expressions used in the definitions in E.P.A. s.79(7) are to have the same meaning as in the Clean Air Act 1993. Accordingly the definition of industrial or trade premises contained in section 2(6) of the Clean Air Act 1993[11] applies to

---

[6] Against this it may be noted that E.P.A. s.83 amends the statutory nuisance provisions of the Public Health (Scotland) Act 1897, and in that context at least, public health issues may perhaps be given greater weight.

[7] s.79(12).

[8] *National Coal Board v. Neath Borough Council*, disapproving *Betts v. Penge Urban District Council* [1942] 2 All E.R. 61; (1942) 2 K.B. 154.

[9] *Southwark London Borough Council v. Ince and Another*, (1989) 153 J.P. 597 (and see para. 18–013).

[10] Spelled out in s.79(3).

[11] *i.e.* premises used for any industrial or trade purposes; or premises not so used on which matter is burnt in connection with any industrial or trade process.

the exclusion from this head of nuisance, and not the E.P.A. definition of "industrial, trade or business premises". The effect of the exclusions in favour of the Clean Air Act 1993 means that the principal application of this statutory nuisance will be to fires burning on open ground.

23–007 (c) *"Fumes or gases emitted from premises so as to be prejudicial to health or a nuisance".*

"Fumes" means any airborne solid matter smaller than dust, while "gas" includes vapour and moisture precipitated from vapour. "Premises" for the purposes of this statutory nuisance is confined to private dwellings only. A private dwelling means any building, or part of a building, used or intended to be used, as a dwelling. The effect of all these definitions is to make a clear distinction between this statutory nuisance and that under (d) below.

23–008 (d) *"Any dust, steam, smell or other effluvia arising* ~~rising~~ *on industrial, trade or business premises and being prejudicial to health or a nuisance".*

In so far as "dust" is an ingredient of smoke emitted from a chimney, it is excluded from this head of statutory nuisance, and will be controlled under the provisions relating to smoke—in practice under the Clean Air Act 1993.[12] "Industrial, trade or business premises" are broadly defined as premises used for any industrial, trade or business purposes, or premises not so used on which matter is burnt in connection with any industrial, trade or business process; premises are used for industrial purposes where they are used for the purposes of any treatment or process as well as where they are used for the purposes of manufacturing. Steam from a railway locomotive engine is however excluded.[13]

23–009 Soya meal dust falling on cars was held to be outside the scope of the corresponding provision of the Public Health Act 1936 on the grounds that though it might cause inconvenience or diminish the value of the motor car, it did not interfere materially with the residents' personal comfort in the sense of materially affecting their well being.[14] This decision appears to have relied, to some extent at least, on the fact that the 1936 Act was concerned with public health; for the reasons given earlier, it must be open to question whether the corresponding statutory nuisance under the Environmental Protection Act should be regarded as limited in this way. Moreover, while every case depends

[12] Smoke from industrial or trade premises that is not dark smoke is potentially under head, though this seems unlikely to represent a problem in practice.
[13] s.79(5).
[14] *Wivenhoe Port v. Colchester Borough Council* [1985] J.P.L. 175 and [1985] J.P.L. 396.

on its facts, significant amounts of dust constantly falling on motor cars would appear to represent a public nuisance within the definition given in *National Coal Board v. Neath Borough Council*, namely "an act or omission which materially affects the material comfort and quality of life of a class of Her Majesty's subjects". In 1882 it was held that smells amounting to a nuisance would come within the 1875 Act, irrespective of any actual or potential injury to health.[15]

The definitions in section 79(7) distinguish between "industrial, **23–010** trade or business premises" on the one hand and a "private dwelling" on the other. In the case of a mixed hereditament, the definition of "private dwelling" clearly is applicable to such part as is used as a dwelling. The definition of "premises" does not necessarily require that the term apply to the entire structure of any building, and consequently given the evident intention of the legislature to distinguish between the two types of property use, it would be appropriate to regard only those parts of a mixed hereditament used for industrial, trade or business purposes as "industrial, trade or business premises" for the purposes of these statutory nuisance provisions.

(e) "Any accumulation or deposit which is prejudicial to health or a **23–011** *nuisance".*

This type of statutory nuisance dates from the 1875 Public Health Act. A mere accumulation or deposit on land that does not create any physical interference with the legitimate activities of anyone else is not likely to amount to a nuisance except in so far as there may be smells or noxious materials blowing or carried away by rain water on to other land, or where it attracts animals or birds that themselves represent a nuisance or risk to health. However, an accumulation of purely inert matter has been held not to amount to a statutory nuisance under this head, even though it may include broken glass and old tin cans liable to injure children from a nearby school.[16] Such a case is likely to be decided on the issue of whether the accumulation or deposit may properly be held to be prejudicial to health; as to that, much will depend on the particular evidence relating to the extent of danger and the risks posed to those who may have access to it.

[15] *Bishop Auckland Local Board v. Bishop Auckland Iron and Steel Company Limited*, see n.3 *supra*.
[16] *Coventry City Council v. Cartwright*, [1975] 1 W.L.R. 845, [1975] 2 All E.R. 99.

23–012   *(f) "Any animal kept in such a place or manner as to be prejudicial to health or a nuisance".*

This head is clearly appropriate to the keeping of animals in a manner that gives rise to smells or the risk of disease. It is open to question whether it applies to noise made by animals. The noise made by greyhounds was considered not to fall under this head in *Galer v. Morrissey,*[17] though this was disagreed with, *obiter*, in *Coventry City Council v. Cartwright.*

23–013   *(g) "Noise emitted from premises so as to be prejudicial to health or a nuisance".*

This type of statutory nuisance is considered in Chapter 18—see in particular paragraphs 18–008 to 18–013.

(ga) "Noise that is prejudicial to health or a nuisance and is emitted from or caused by a vehicle, machinery or equipment in the street".

23–014   This additional head of statutory nuisance was inserted by the Noise and Statutory Nuisance Act 1993. It is also considered in Chapter 18 — see paragraphs 18–033 to 18–036.

(h) "Any other matter to be declared by any enactment to be a statutory nuisance".

23–015   A number of matters have been declared to be statutory nuisances under this provision including:

— Any well, tank, cistern, or water-butt used for the supply of water for domestic purposes which is so placed, constructed or kept as to render the water therein liable to contamination prejudicial to health—P.H.A. 1936, s.141;

— Any pond, pool, ditch, gutter or watercourse which is so foul or in such a state as to be prejudicial to health or a nuisance; and any part of a watercourse, not being a part ordinarily navigated by vessels employed in the carriage of goods by water, which is so choked or silted up as to obstruct or impede the proper flow of water and thereby to cause a nuisance, or give rise to conditions prejudicial to health—P.H.A. 1936, s.259(1), and the Transport Act 1968, s.108;[18]

— A tent, van, shed or similar structure used for human habitation:
   (a) which is in such a state, or so overcrowded, as to be prejudicial to the health of the inmates; or

---

[17] [1955] 1 W.L.R. 110.
[18] As amended by E.P.A., Sched. 15, para. 10(1), (3).

(b) the use of which, by reason of the absence of proper sanitary accommodation or otherwise, gives rise, whether on the site or on other land, to a nuisance or to conditions prejudicial to health—P.H.A. 1936, s.268(2).

— Shafts and outlets of abandoned and discontinued mines, and quarries (whether being worked or not), where inadequately stopped up or without adequate barriers to protect the public—Mines and Quarries Act 1954, s.151(2).[19]

Though not "statutory nuisances" under the E.P.A., other statutes may adopt the same language to achieve essentially the same object. Thus section 59(1) of the Building Act 1984 provides that if a local authority considers that certain features of a building, for example, a cesspool, private sewer, drain, soil pipe or rain-water pipe, is in such a condition as to be prejudicial to health or a nuisance, then it must serve a notice on the owner or the occupier of the building requiring such work as may be necessary to be done.[20] In the case of a breach in a private sewer, it is sufficient to serve the notice on all those served by the sewer upstream of the breach; it is not necessary to serve it also on those connected downstream of it.[21]   **23–016**

The Duty to Inspect

An express duty is placed on every local authority to have its area inspected from time to time to detect any of these statutory nuisances. Where it is satisfied that one exists or is likely to occur or recur in its area, it is required to serve an abatement notice requiring the nuisance to be abated or prohibiting or restricting its occurrence or recurrence. The abatement notice may also require further action to be taken as may be necessary to achieve those ends. Additionally, if a complaint of a statutory nuisance is made to a local authority by any person in its area, it must take all reasonably practicable steps to investigate that complaint.[22] Exemption from the E.P.A. statutory nuisance provisions may however be granted by a local authority to enable the conduct of investigations or research into air pollution (see paragraph 10–053).   **23–017**

Local authorities have extensive powers of entry to any premises at any reasonable time to ascertain whether or not a statutory nuisance exists, as set out in Schedule 3, paragraph 2. At least 24 hours notice   **23–018**

---

[19] s.151(2) has been summarised here; it should be referred to for its full terms.
[20] ss.99 and 102 of the Building Act govern the procedures for service of notices and appeals.
[21] *Swansea City Council v. Jenkins, The Times*, April 1, 1994.
[22] s.79(1).

must be given where entry is required to premises used wholly or mainly for residential purposes, except in an emergency. In appropriate cases, a magistrate's warrant may be obtained to enter premises, if necessary by force.[23]

23–019　　If the Secretary of State considers that a local authority has failed to carry out its duty to have its area inspected to detect statutory nuisances, he may declare the authority to be in default, and give it directions for the purpose of remedying the default. If the authority fails to comply with the directions as well, the Secretary of State may himself take over the relevant functions of the authority to which the direction related.[24]

Abatement Notices and Orders

23–020　　An authority that has satisfied itself that a statutory nuisance either exists or is likely to occur or recur in its area must serve an abatement notice on "the person responsible" for the nuisance. If he cannot be found, or if the nuisance has not yet occurred, it is to be served on the owner or occupier of the relevant premises. (The special procedure for dealing with noise nuisances in the street is dealt with in chapter 18; the remainder of this chapter is therefore concerned only with that appropriate to the other heads of statutory nuisance). Also, where the nuisance arises from any defect of a structural character, the notice is to be served on the owner of the premises. The "person responsible" is defined, as regards statutory nuisances not involving vehicles or machinery or equipment, as the person to whose act, default or sufferance the nuisance is attributable.[25] This can include a person who has acquired or gone into occupation of premises and who has allowed a pre-existing nuisance on them to continue.[26]

23–021　　A separate procedure is available under section 82 to any person aggrieved by a nuisance, who may make a complaint to the magistrates court seeking an abatement order. The proceedings are taken against the same person or persons as a notice would be served on, as

---

[23] Sched. 3 para. 2(3).
[24] Sched. 3, para. 4.
[25] s.79(7).
[26] *Clayton v. Sale U.D.C.*, [1926] 1 K.B. 415; *cf. Sedleigh-Denfield v. O'Callaghan*, [1940] A.C. 880 as regards private nuisance. See also *Clydebank District Council v. Monaville Estates Ltd*, 1982 S.L.T. 2, as regards the corresponding provision applying in Scotland under the Public Health (Scotland) Act 1897, s.3, which defines the "author of a nuisance" as "the person through whose act or default the nuisance is caused, exists, or is continued, whether he be the owner or occupier or both".

just set out.[27] Not less than 21 days notice must be given of the intention to bring them, specifying what is complained of; however in the case of noise nuisances within head (g) or (ga) only three days notice is required.[28] If at the hearing of the complaint, it is proved that the alleged nuisance existed when the complaint was made, then the court must order the defendant(s) to pay the complainant his reasonable costs, whether or not at the date of the hearing the nuisance still exists or is likely to recur.

Where more than one person is responsible for a nuisance, an abatement notice or proceedings for an order may be served on any one or more of them individually, whether or not what the person served is responsible for would by itself amount to a nuisance.[29]   **23–022**

To avoid duplication of controls over processes that are registered   **23–023** under the Alkali, etc., Works Regulation Act 1906 (*i.e.* those not yet brought under the control of Part I of the E.P.A.), no summary proceedings may be brought by a local authority in respect of a nuisance falling within any of heads (b), (d) or (e) except with the consent of the Secretary of State, if proceedings in respect of it could be brought under the 1906 Act or section 5 of the H.S.W.A.[30] This does not prevent a person aggrieved applying for an abatement order in any such case. There is no comparable provision in respect of nuisances from processes controlled under Part I of the E.P.A. Part B processes are of course directly subject to local authority control, and HMIP and HMIPI will in practice be expected to initiate action in respect of Part A processes.

An abatement notice may require abatement of the nuisance or   **23–024** prohibit or restrict its occurrence or recurrence, and it may require the execution of any works and other appropriate steps as may be necessary to that end. Additionally it must specify the time or times within which these requirements are to be complied with.[31] An order may be made in respect of essentially the same matters, but since anticipatory action is not possible under section 82 there is no right to prohibit the occurrence of a nuisance, as opposed to its recurrence. Further, there is no power to order that recurrence of a nuisance be merely restricted, as opposed to prohibiting it outright.[32] A further distinction between the two procedures is that the magistrates may, when making their order, also impose a fine of up to £5000 — with an

[27] s.82(4).
[28] s.82(7).
[29] ss.81(1), 82(5).
[30] s.79(10).
[31] s.80(1).
[32] s.82(2).

abatement notice no penalties can be imposed unless the requirements of the notice are not observed.[33]

23–025   A person served with an abatement notice has a right of appeal to
the magistrates court within the 21 days following the date of service.
The appeals procedure is laid down by the Statutory Nuisance
(Appeals) Regulations 1990,[34] and there is a further right of appeal
from the magistrates to the Crown court at the instance of any party to
the proceedings.[35]

23–026   The Regulations set out[36] an extensive list of grounds of appeal
including:

- the abatement notice was not justified under the Act;
- there has been some informality, defect or error in or in
connection with the notice;
- the requirements of the notice are unreasonable or unnecessary, or the authority has unreasonably refused to accept
alternative requirements;
- times for compliance are not reasonably sufficient;
- in circumstances where use of best practicable means is a
legitimate defence, that such means were used to prevent or
counteract the effects of the nuisance;
- the notice should have been served on someone else;
- the notice might lawfully have been served on someone else
instead of or in addition to the appellant, and it would have
been equitable to do so.

23–027   In the last case the appellants must serve a copy of the notice of
appeal on the other person or persons referred to. The court hearing
the appeal may allow it and quash the abatement notice or dismiss it; it
may also vary the notice in such a manner as it thinks fit.[37] The court
may also, in its discretion, determine who should carry out any work
or contribute to its cost, and the proportions in which any recoverable
expenses are to be shared between the appellant and anyone else. In
making any such determination as between an owner and an occupier,
the court must have regard to the terms and conditions of any relevant

---

[33] This power to fine was inserted in the course of the legislation through Parliament, so
as to retain powers previously available under s.99 (taken with s.94) of the Public
Health Act 1936, which were frequently relied on by those occupying rented
property. Though compensation awards can be made following a conviction, they
could not be made in respect of damage suffered earlier, even after the making of an
abatement order. Criminal sanctions are in practice frequently more effective than
the prospect of having to pay a comparatively modest award of compensation.

[34] S.I. 1990 No. 2276, as amended by S.I. 1990 No. 2483.

[35] Sched. 3, para. 1(3).

[36] In reg. 2(2).

[37] reg. 2(5).

tenancy, and the nature of the works concerned; it must also be satisfied that any person that it makes subject to any requirement has received a copy of the notice of appeal.

An appeal does not automatically result in an abatement notice **23–028** being suspended, but it will ordinarily have that effect where compliance with it would require expenditure to be incurred on carrying out any works before the hearing of the appeal (whether by the appellant or anyone else).[38] However, suspension of the notice may be over-ridden if the notice says that it is to have that effect and the nuisance concerned is injurious to health, or is likely to be of so short a duration that suspension of the notice would mean that it had no practical effect, or if the expenditure that would be incurred before any appeal has been decided would not be disproportionate to the public benefit to be expected in that period from compliance with the notice.

Failure to comply with an abatement notice within the prescribed **23–029** time is an offence, subject to a maximum fine on summary conviction of £5000 with daily fines of up to £500 for so long as the non-compliance continues after conviction, save that where the non-compliance relates to action required on industrial, trade or business premises, the maximum fine is £20,000 (in this case, there is no provision for daily penalties in addition).[39] In the case of a failure to comply with an abatement order, no such distinction is made, and the maximum penalties are £5000 and daily fines of £500.

Where the local authority considers that taking proceedings against **23–030** a person who has failed to comply with an abatement notice would not provide an adequate remedy to the nuisance, it may take proceedings in the High Court for an appropriate injunction to abate, prohibit or restrict the nuisance.[40]

Unless otherwise stated, an abatement notice or order is of **23–031** unlimited duration. Thus, where a person who was served with a notice in respect of a noise nuisance, prohibiting its recurrence, created a further noise nuisance some three years later, he was convicted of breaching the original notice.[41] It has moreover been held by the House of Lords that a notice served under the corresponding

---

[38] reg. 3(1)(b). The notice will also be suspended in the case of a noise nuisance under s.79(1)(g) where the noise is caused in the course of the performance of some duty imposed by law on the appellant.

[39] s.80(5), (6).

[40] s.81(5). This is subject to s.81(6) which provides a defence in High Court proceedings in relation to a noise nuisance that the noise was authorised by a notice under C.O.P.A., s.60 or a s.61 consent.

[41] *Wellingborough District Council v. Gordon*, [1991] J.P.L. 874; also *R. v. Birmingham Justices, ex p. Guppy* (1988) 152 J.P. 159.

provision of C.O.P.A., namely section 58, remains in effect notwithstanding the repeal of that section, and despite the absence of
transitional provisions in Part III of the E.P.A.[41A] Whether the penalties
for relevant offences under the E.P.A. (see paragraph 23–029) can be
imposed in such a case, or only the lower amounts provided for by
C.O.P.A., remains an open question.[41B]

Defence of "Best Practicable Means"

23–032   It is a defence to an abatement notice, and to any proceedings for an
abatement order, to prove that "best practicable means" were used to
prevent, or to counteract the effects of, the nuisance in certain (only) of
the various heads.[42] The drafting of this head of defence is somewhat
convoluted, but the effect is that the use of best practicable means may
be pleaded as a defence:

> (i) where any of the following nuisances arise on industrial,
>   trade or business premises
>   — any premises in such a state . . .
>   — any dust, steam, smell or other effluvia . . .
>   — any accumulation or deposit . . .
>   — any animal kept in such a place or manner . . .
>   — noise emitted from premises . . .
> (ii) where noise is emitted from or caused by a vehicle, machi-
>   nery or equipment in a street, if the vehicle, machinery or
>   equipment is being used for industrial, trade or business
>   purposes.
> (iii) where smoke is emitted from premises, but only where it is
>   from a chimney.[43]

23–033   The use of best practicable means is not available as a defence in
relation to head (c) "fumes or gases emitted from premises (in fact
private dwellings), nor is it necessarily so in relation to head (h) "any
other matter declared by any enactment to be a statutory nuisance".
Additionally it is not available as a defence in proceedings for an
abatement order where the nuisance is such as to render the premises
unfit for human habitation.[44] There is no corresponding provision to
this last item in relation to abatement notices—it may be seen as aimed
particularly at housing departments of local authorities.

[41A] *Aitken v. South Hans District Council, The Times,* July 8, 1994.
[41B] See the comment on this case by R. Macrory, (1994) ENDS Report 234, pp.45, 46.
[42] s.80(7), (8) and 82(9), (10).
[43] In many circumstances smoke emitted from a chimney will not come under this head
of nuisance at all—see para. 23–006.
[44] s.82(10)(d).

The term "best practicable means" has a long statutory history, appearing in both the Alkali Act 1874 and the Public Health Act 1875. It was a requirement under the air pollution provisions of the H.S.W.A. 1974[45] to use the best practicable means for "preventing the emission into the atmosphere from premises of noxious or offensive substances, and for rendering harmless and inoffensive such substances as may be so emitted". The Guidance Note BPM 1 issued by HMIP (January 1988) in this context is of some assistance in establishing how the concept can be expected to be applied in practice.[46]

23–034

The expression is required[47] to be interpreted by reference to the following provisions:

23–035

(a) "practicable" means reasonably practicable having regard among other things to local conditions and circumstances, to the current state of technical knowledge and to the financial implications;

(b) the means to be employed include the design, installation, maintenance and manner and periods of operation of plant and machinery, and the design, construction and maintenance of buildings and structures;

(c) the test is to apply only so far as compatible with any duty imposed by law;

(d) the test is to apply only so far as compatible with safety and safe working conditions, and with the exigencies of any emergency or unforeseeable circumstances;

and, in circumstances where a code of practice under section 71 of the Control of Pollution Act 1974 (noise minimisation) is applicable (see paragraph 18–021), regard shall also be had to guidance given in it.

There is also a general defence of "reasonable excuse" for failure to comply with an abatement notice or order.[48] There is relatively little judicial authority on the applicability of this defence, save that it does not overlap with the statutory defence of using best practicable means,[49] nor extend to lack of money to carry out works.[50] The excuse is most likely to be available in connection with procedural matters, such as where the person served with a notice is for some reason physically incapacitated from complying with it or appealing against it (at least if there would have been good grounds for appealing), and possibly where there has been a genuine misunderstanding as to what

23–036

---

[45] s.5(1).
[46] See also the discussion on BPM and BATNEEC in para.9–047.
[47] By s.79(9).
[48] ss.80(4), 82(8).
[49] *A. Lambert Flat Management Company v. Lomas*, [1981] 2 All E.R. 280.
[50] *Saddleworth Urban District Council v. Aggregate and Sand* (1970) 114 S.J. 931.

was required, especially if brought about by officers of the local authority. Avoidable inadequacies in the apparatus or the management of the defendant are therefore unlikely to amount to a reasonable excuse.

Abatement

23–037   Where an abatement notice has not been complied with, the local authority has full powers to abate the nuisance itself and to do whatever may be necessary to give effect to its abatement notice, quite independently of whether or not it takes proceedings for the non-compliance.[51] Similarly, where a person subject to an abatement order has been convicted of contravening it, the magistrates court may direct the relevant local authority, having first given it an opportunity to be heard, to do anything which the person convicted was required to do by the order.[52] The court may also direct the local authority to do anything which the court might have ordered the person responsible for a nuisance to do, where neither he nor the owner or occupier of the relevant premises can be found,[53] subject to the authority's right to be heard before such a direction is made. In neither of these cases is the authority given any right of recourse against the person responsible for the nuisance to recover its costs.

23–038   In the case of an abatement notice, however, where an authority has undertaken the appropriate work itself, its reasonable expenses incurred in abating or preventing the recurrence of the nuisance may be recovered from the person by whose act or default the nuisance was caused.[54] The person liable to be charged is not necessarily the "person responsible", in that the latter expression includes a person to whose "sufferance" the nuisance is attributable. There will however be few circumstances in which a person may be said to have suffered or permitted a nuisance to be caused, but where he was not also in default in failing to make sure it did not happen. Where the person to be charged with the expenses is the owner of premises, and there is more than one owner, any one or more of them may be held liable. Further, where there are two or more persons whose acts or defaults cause the nuisance, the court may apportion the expenses between them as it thinks fair and reasonable.

---

[51] s.81(3).
[52] s.82(11).
[53] s.82(13).
[54] s.81(4).

For the purposes of these provisions, a definition of "owner" has **23–039** been has been inserted into the E.P.A.,[55] whereby it means, in relation to any premises:

> "A person (other than a mortgagee not in possession) who, whether in his own right or as trustee for any other person, is entitled to receive the rack rent of the premises or, where the premises are not let at a rack rent, would be so entitled if they were so let."[56]

"Premises" for this purpose does not include a vessel. Liabilities under these provisions may also affect a superior landlord whose immediate tenant, having sub-let the premises, is in arrears — if notice is given for rent to be paid by the under tenant direct to the superior landlord under section 6 of the Law of Distress (Amendment) Act 1908, the latter will become the owner and liable accordingly.

There is no definition of "occupier" in the statute. In *Southern Water* **23–040** *Authority v. Nature Conservancy Council*, where one issue was whether the water authority, which was temporarily present on land to carry out drainage work, was an occupier for the purposes of the Wildlife and Countryside Act 1981, Lord Mustill observed.[56A]

> "No useful progress can be made . . . by looking up in dictionaries the words "occupy" and "occupier" or by inquiring what meaning the Courts have given to them in reported caes, for they draw their meaning entirely from the purpose for which and the context in which they are used".

He noted that the term even has different meanings in different Parts of that one Act. Nevertheless he considered that, in view of the juxtaposition of "occupier" with "owner" in the provision in question, the occupier was for that purpose

> "someone who, although lacking the title of an owner, neverthe-less stands in a comprehensive and stable relationship with the land as to be, in company with the actual owner, someone to whom the [relevant mechanisms of the 1981 Act] can sensibly be made to apply."

A similar relationship is, it suggested, appropriate if a person is to be an "occupier" for the purposes of Part III of the E.P.A. This would nevertheless be likely to bring within the term a receiver who, although acting as agent for a company, has the power to manage and

---

[55] By the Noise and Statutory Nuisance Act 1993.
[56] s.81A(9).
[56A] [1992] 1 W.L.R., at 781; [1992] 3 All E.R. at 487. See also paras. 5–099, 5–100.

control it even though the directors have not been removed.[56B] It is this quality of control, in addition to a mere right to be present, that is generally necessary to be an "occupier", though it need not be exclusive.[56C]

23–041   Where expenses are recoverable from an owner, the local authority may create a charge on the relevant premises for the expenses concerned and accrued interest.[57] To create this charge, the authority must serve a notice on the owner of the premises, and also copies of it on every other person who to the knowledge of the authority has an interest in the premises who may be affected by the charge.[58] The charge takes effect after 21 days from the date of service of the notice or, where there is an appeal by either the owner or anyone served with a copy of the notice, the charge does not come into effect until the appeal is finally determined. Once it has come into effect, the charge continues until the expenses and accrued interest are recovered. Anyone served with such a notice or with a copy of it may appeal against it to the county court within 21 days; the court may confirm the notice or quash it, or vary the amount specified in it.[59]

23–042   In a case involving premises that were due to be demolished quite shortly[60] the position of the justices from whom an abatement order was sought was stated as follows:

> "Once they were satisfied that the house constituted a statutory nuisance they were bound to make a nuisance order under section 24 [of the P.H.A. 1936] but they have within the framework of this section a considerable tolerance as regards the precise terms which the nuisance order shall take. It must be directed, of course, to the abatement of the nuisance, that is the purpose of the order, but the section makes it clear that the justices have a discretion as to whether to require the owner to do the whole of that work referred to in the abatement notice as opposed to only part of it. Further the section expressly gives a discretion in regard to the time within which the work has to be done, and in my judgment would certainly enable the justices to divide the work into phases or programmes requiring some to be done quickly and others to be done at a later time . . . In deciding within that wide ambit of detailed discretion just what the terms of the

---

[56B] *Meigh v. Wickenden*, [1942] 2 K.B. 160.
[56C] *Wheat v. E. Lacon & Co. Ltd.*, [1966] A.C. 522; [1966] 2 W.L.R. 581; [1966] 1 All E.R. 582.
[57] s.81(A), inserted by the Noise and Statutory Nuisance Act 1993, reinstating provisions of the P.H.A. 1936, s.291.
[58] s.81A(3).
[59] s.81A(6), (7).
[60] *Nottingham City District Council v. Newton* [1974] 1 W.L.R. 923; [1974] 2 All E.R. 760 (*sub nom. Nottingham Corporation v. Newton*).

nuisance order should be, I have no doubt it is the duty of the justices, as common sense dictates, to look at the whole circumstances of the case and to try and make an order which is in its terms sensible and just having regard to the entire prevailing situation."[61]

This statement was referred to with approval by Lord Wilberforce in **23–043** *Salford City Council v. McNally*,[62] who said:

"[Magistrates] should in the first place, keep close to the wording of the Act and ask themselves, after they have found the condition of the premises, the questions (i) is the state of the premises such as to be injurious or likely to cause injury to health,[63] or, (ii) is it a nuisance? To consider these questions in terms of fitness or unfitness for human habitation is undesirable and is likely to confuse. And the magistrate should find specifically under which limb the case falls. If he answers either question in the affirmative he must make an abatement order, and he should, if possible, make this as specific as he can, rather than order in general terms to abate the statutory nuisance. That may lead to difficulties in cases like the present. In making the order the magistrate should take into account the circumstances in which the property is being occupied including, of course, the likely duration of the occupation. The shorter the period before probable demolition, the more severe must be the injury or likely injury to health or, as the case may be, the nuisance, to justify action by way of abatement."

His Lordship then referred to the decision in *Nottingham v. Newton* **23–044** quoted above, commenting that the keynote of the approach to be adopted by magistrates in making abatement notices is the need to use discretion and common sense.

Expenses due to a local authority under these provisions from a **23–045** person who is the owner of the relevant premises may carry interest, to be calculated at such reasonable rate as the authority may determine, and, with the accrued interest, be the subject of a charge on the premises.[64] To have this effect, the authority must serve notice on the owner specifying the expenses claimed, stating that these with accrued interest shall be a charge on the premises, and setting out the entitlement of the owner to appeal against the notice. The authority must also serve a copy of the notice on every other person who, to its knowledge, has an interest in the premises capable of being affected

---

[61] *per* Lord Widgery C.J.
[62] [1976] A.C. 379 at 390.
[63] This form of words found in the P.H.A. 1936 has of course now been replaced by "prejudicial to health".
[64] s.81A, inserted by the Noise and Statutory Nuisance Act 1993.

by the charge. The charge takes effect after 21 days from the date of service of the notice; the person served with the notice or with any copy of it has the same period within which to appeal against it. In the event of an appeal, the charge does not take effect until its determination. An appeal is made to the county court, which may confirm the notice as it stands, vary the amount specified in it, or quash the notice.

23–046   A local authority seeking to enforce a charge so made has the same powers and remedies as if it were a mortgagee by deed having powers of sale and lease, of accepting surrenders of leases and of appointing a receiver.[65]

23–047   Where expenses have been made subject to a charge on premises in this manner, the authority may by order declare them to be payable, with interest, by instalments within such a period of up to 30 years as may be specified in the order.[66] These instalments may be recovered from the owner or occupier for the time being of the premises, though where they are recovered from an occupier paying rent for them, he may deduct them from that rent.[67] Further, an occupier is not to be required to pay at any one time more than the rent due to his landlord. It follows that where premises are subject to such a charge, and the owner has leased them to someone who has in turn sublet them to an occupier subject to these provisions, while the occupier has the statutory right to make deductions from the rent payable by him, there is no corresponding statutory right benefitting the landlord leasing the premises from the owner, who must therefore ensure he is appropriately covered by contractual stipulations.

Scotland

23–048   The law of statutory nuisance in Scotland is still to be found largely in the Public Health (Scotland) Act 1897, requiring local authorities to inspect their areas of control and to take steps to abate any nuisances that come to light. The seminal case in this area is *Clydebank District Council v. Monaville Estates Limited*.[68] Here, the local authority served notice on the owner of a site to abate a nuisance caused by a deposit of asbestos at the hands of the previous owner. The identity of the former owner was well known but notwithstanding, the District Council successfully pursued Monaville as the "author" of the nuisance, defined as extending to "the person through whose fault the nuisance is caused, exists or is continued, whether he be the owner or occupier or both". Monaville was unable to pay the costs incurred by the District

[65] s.81A(8).
[66] s.81B(1).
[67] s.81B(4).
[68] 1982 S.L.T. (Sh.Ct.) 2.

Council in eradicating the nuisance and went into liquidation.

Part III of the Environmental Protection Act 1990 does not apply to Scotland, except to widen the definition of nuisances under the 1897 Act by including fumes, gases or vapours emitted from dwellings, and dust caused by any trade, business, manufacture or process.   **23–049**

With a view to removing some of the practical deficiencies experienced under the 1897 Act in taking action against the author of a nuisance and to bringing the 1897 Act into line with modern social and technical developments, the Scottish Office Environment Department has been reviewing nuisance legislation in Scotland, and issued a Consultation Paper in August 1994. The Environment Bill contains proposed clauses that would replace the 1897 Act provisions by others closely analogous to those of Part III of the E.P.A.   **23–050**

Chapter 24

ENVIRONMENTAL ISSUES IN TRANSACTIONS AFFECTING LAND

As has been described in earlier chapters, there are numerous **24–001** circumstances in which the occupier of land, and sometimes the owner where different, may be liable for any adverse consequences on third parties resulting from things or activities on that land, even though he was not primarily responsible for whatever acts or omissions may have led to those consequences. It follows, therefore, that anyone who acquires land either directly, or indirectly through purchase of the shares of a company that owns land, must take special precautions to avoid acquiring such liabilities unwittingly along with the land, and so far as practicable to minimise those that it does acquire. Similarly, those entering into leases, both the lessor and the lessee, must be aware of their potential exposure. Lenders need also to be aware of the potential exposure of their borrowers, and especially so where they have taken a charge or other security over the land and subsequently wish to enforce this.

The various liabilities that may arise under environmental legisla- **24–002** tion and at common law have been described in other chapters. The following is therefore merely a brief summary of the principal sources of liability that may be imposed on people other than those whose own actions or omissions have directly resulted in or risked causing pollution.

Waste

    (i)   E.P.A., s.33(1)(b) and (c) prohibit among other things the **24–003** keeping of controlled waste, except as licensed or in a manner likely to cause pollution of the environment or harm to human health, respectively. Clearly a deposit of waste may be acquired along with land and consequently be kept by the new owner.

    (ii) The duty of care under E.P.A., s.34(1) likewise extends to those who keep controlled waste, and is therefore capable of binding a new owner of land.

(iii) Where waste has been deposited in contravention of E.P.A., s.33(1), a waste regulation authority or waste collection authority may remove the waste under powers provided by E.P.A., s.59(7)(a) and charge the costs incurred on the occupier. The latter will be liable for them unless he can prove that he neither made nor knowingly caused nor knowingly permitted the deposit of the waste.

(iv) Section 61 of the E.P.A. (which will be replaced, without ever coming into force, by wider ranging provisions in the Environment Bill) imposes a duty on waste regulation authorities to clean-up any contaminated land liable to emit or discharge noxious gases or noxious liquids, and where they do so, they may recover the costs from the owner for the time being of the relevant land.

Statutory Nuisances

24–004   Any accumulation or deposit which amounts to a statutory nuisance must be dealt with by the relevant local authority by way of an abatement notice; other persons who are aggrieved may seek an abatement order in respect of it. The duty to respond to any such notice or order falls primarily on "the person responsible for the nuisance" but, where he cannot be found, on the owner or occupier of the relevant premises. The "person responsible" may include someone who merely permits a nuisance to continue, even though he did not create it; in Scotland this is the law.[1] Even where such steps have been taken prior to acquisition of land, any expenses recoverable from an owner may be the subject of a charge on those premises by virtue of amendments to the E.P.A. made by the Noise and Statutory Nuisance Act 1993, which will affect any subsequent owner, as well as anyone having an interest in the premises subject to the charge at the time it is imposed.

Radioactive Waste

24–005   In certain circumstances, the Secretary of State has power under R.S.A. 1993, s.30, to dispose of radioactive waste located on premises and to charge his costs on the occupier if there is one, and on the owner if the premises are unoccupied.

Water

24–006   Where an activity or deposit on or in land leads to pollution of, *e.g.* a neighbouring stream or groundwater, this is likely to constitute a

---

[1] *Clydebank District Council v. Monaville Estates Ltd.*, 1982 S.L.T. 2. See para. 23–048.

criminal offence under W.R.A., s.85. In addition, where any matter is likely to pollute controlled waters, or has already done so, the N.R.A. has powers under W.R.A., s.161 to take appropriate steps, either to prevent the pollution or to remove the potentially or actually polluting matter, and, where appropriate, to undertake remedial activities. Anyone who caused or knowingly permitted the actual presence of such matter in controlled waters or where it was likely to pollute them, is exposed to liability for all the remedial costs undertaken by the authority. A new owner of land may be held to be "knowingly permitting" continued pollution from what was on the land when he acquired it, and where this is so, made liable for such costs.

Common law

Where the condition of land or an activity on it causes damage to others, particularly those on neighbouring property, not only will the person who created that condition or initiated the activities be liable in nuisance, but also anyone who by taking reasonable steps can rectify the situation but fails to do so, at least where he either knows or should reasonably know of it. A new owner may therefore have to take action to prevent further pollution crossing the boundary of the acquired land on to that of neighbours, and may be liable for any further damage caused. Liability under *Rylands v. Fletcher* may possibly not apply to a new owner, where harmful substances on land have been acquired with property, on the grounds that the new owner has not "brought them on to his land", but the matter is by no means beyond doubt.

24–007

Numerous liabilities for continuing activities will inevitably arise as soon as a new owner takes control over them. These will include criminal liabilities under the relevant regulating statutes, any civil liability that may apply, the possibility of civil injunctions or prohibition orders under the various regulatory controls that may apply to ongoing activities, and enforcement of planning controls and those under the Planning (Hazardous Substances) Act 1990. Furthermore, a purchaser must have regard to the possibility, indeed the likelihood, that the effect of the Environment Bill will be to impose liability to clean-up contaminated land directly on the owner of that land, irrespective of who was responsible for the contamination, at least unless that owner can prove that he was not responsible for the creation of the contamination. He may be unable to produce any such evidence, unless before his acquisition the state of the land concerned was adequately investigated. Even where there is no immediate exposure to liability for enforced clean-up or damages to third parties, contamination of land is a "material consideration" to be taken into

24–008

account when considering any application for development of that land, and appropriate remediation may be made a condition of any planning consent. If these clean-up costs are substantial in relation to the benefits to be gained from development, the contamination may effectively render the site sterile.

24–009 For all these reasons, anyone considering acquiring any interest in land will wish to obtain as much information as possible on its current condition—not only on current activities, important though this is, but also on all past activities that might have caused pollution previously. The seller of land is under no obligation to make any disclosure of any of these matters by virtue of the rule of *caveat emptor*; he may not however take deliberate action to hide them from a prospective purchaser—if he does, he may be liable for the "fraudulent concealment" entailed.

24–010 The rule of *caveat emptor* was considered by the Conveyancing Standing Committee of the Law Commission which, in a preliminary consultation paper issued in November 1988, suggested that the rule be reversed, placing a burden on sellers to disclose material adverse matters of which they were aware. This provoked much opposition, and in the subsequent recommendations[2] the Committee concluded that if the rule were reversed there would be considerable difficulty in framing the extent of the duty of disclosure, and that, in any event, it is better that buyers should, by other means, ensure that they obtain property in a condition that is acceptable to them, rather than simply have a right to sue the seller, who may perhaps then be unavailable or have disposed of the purchase money. The final recommendation was therefore not to reverse the rule.

24–011 In so recommending the Committee was not specifically concerned with the existence of contamination, but with all potentially adverse aspects of a property. The considerations in favour of maintaining the rule generally have considerably less force in relation to the presence of contamination, albeit that there would still be some difficulty in defining what minimum threshold level of contamination would have to exist to trigger the duty to disclose. Most continental European jurisdictions impose such a duty of disclosure on sellers which, though not necessarily sufficient, does not create insuperable problems. In any event, a failure to disclose a comparatively trivial degree of contamination is likely to give rise to only a modest potential claim at most.

24–012 The Committee's considerations were moreover largely directed to the issue of disclosure in the context of domestic residential conveyancing. The types of environmental liability to which industrial

---

[2] "Let the Buyer be Well Informed", December 1989.

property owners may be exposed, though considered, were not the sole concern. Nevertheless, one of the particularly difficult issues is what should be done in relation to domestic residential property that has been built on an old landfill site without adequate precautions having been taken at the time of construction. As is reflected in the title of the Committee's report, its principal recommendation was that there should be public registers readily available that would enable purchasers in a single search to ascertain all relevant information. The inclusion of information as to possible contamination was specifically addressed.[3] Commenting in relation to contaminated land which is, or is potentially, contaminated "Clearly a prospective buyer needs to be forewarned" it was recommended that there should at least be a warning entered in a part of the local land charges register[4] that further enquiries are needed.

At much the same time as the Law Commission's Conveyancing **24-013** Standing Committee was drawing up its recommendations, the House of Commons Environment Committee was preparing its report on contaminated land[5]—a sequel to its report of the previous year on toxic waste. It also recommended the creation of registers of contaminated land, and that there should be express duties on local authorities to compile these. In so recommending, the Committee recognised both the problem of blight and the possibility that claims for compensation might be brought against authorities by those who find the value of their property reduced by its being placed on the register incorrectly. Additionally, the Committee reviewed the rule of *caveat emptor*. At the time it prepared its report, the Royal Commission's Standing Committee had not published its conclusions. Nevertheless the Environment Committee observed that the Law Commission inquiry was concerned with conveyancing practice as a whole, and went on to find that "in so far as the rule of *caveat emptor* relates to contaminated land, its effect is to discourage sound environmental practice and environmental responsibility. Its abolition would be a natural corollary to the compilation of local authority registers. We recommend that the Government bring forward legislation to place upon vendors a duty to declare information in their possession about contamination present on site".[6]

Both these reports were issued while the bill that was to become the **24-014** Environmental Protection Act was passing through Parliament. The Government's response to the Environment Committee's report was

---

[3] In para. 27.
[4] Kept under the Local Land Charges Act 1975.
[5] House of Commons Environment Committee session 1989–90, 1st report, "Contaminated Land", 3 Vols. January 24, 1990.
[6] para. 95.

firstly, to side with the Law Commission and retain the rule of *caveat emptor* in all respects, and so not reverse it for contamination of land, and, secondly, to propose registers that would give an indication to the public of *the possibility* of contamination on land. These registers, which were provided for by section 143 of the E.P.A. were not to be of land that was in fact contaminated, but of land that had at any time been put to a "contaminative use", this being defined as "any use of land which may cause it to be contaminated with noxious substances". Detailed proposals for the compilation of registers of this type were first put forward in May 1991. In an Annex were listed 42 separate potentially contaminating uses, as set out in Table 24/I. While minor criticisms may be made of the drafting of this list, it remains of value in its compilation of a wide variety of activities, awareness of which should alert a prospective purchaser to caution if any have been carried out on or near to land that he has in mind acquiring.

TABLE 24/I

24–015	Proposed Schedule of Contaminative Uses (May 1991)
1.	**Agriculture**
1.1	Burial of diseased livestock.
2.	**Extractive Industry**
2.1	Extracting, handling and storage of carbonaceous materials such as coal, lignite, petroleum, natural gas, or bituminous shale (not including the underground workings).
2.2	Extracting, handling and storage of ores and their constituents.
	Note: Handling includes loading, transport, sorting, forming and packaging and similar operations. Ore means any mineral, including non-metal bearing, except fuels.
3.	**Energy Industry**
3.1	Producing gas from coal, lignite, oil or other carbonaceous material (other than from sewage or other waste), or from mixtures of those materials.
3.2	Reforming, refining, purifying and odourising natural gas or any product of the processes outlined in 3.1 above.
3.3	Pyrolysis, carbonisation, distillation, liquefaction, partial oxidation, other heat treatment, conversion, purification, or refining of coal, lignite, oil, other carbonaceous material or mixtures and products thereof, otherwise than with a view to gasification or making of charcoal.

1056

3.4	A thermal power station (including nuclear power stations and production, enrichment and reprocessing of nuclear fuels).
3.5	Electricity sub-station.

4. **Production of Metals**

4.1	Production, refining or recovery of metals by physical, chemical, thermal or electrolytic or other extraction process.
4.2	Heating, melting or casting metals as part of an intermediate or final manufacturing process 7 (including annealing, tempering or similar processes).
4.3	Cold forming processes (including pressing, rolling, extruding, stamping, forming or similar processes).
4.4.	Finishing treatments, including anodising, pickling, coating, and plating or similar processes.
	Note: Metals are taken to include metal scrap.

5. **Production of Non-Metals and their Products**

5.1	Production or refining of non-metals by treatment of the ore.
5.2	Production or processing of mineral fibres by treatment of the ore.
5.3	Cement, lime and gypsum manufacture, brickwork and associated processes.

6. **Glass Making and Ceramics**

6.1	Manufacture of glass and products based on glass.
6.2	Manufacture of ceramics and products based on ceramics, including glazes and vitreous enamel.

7. **Production and Use of Chemicals**

7.1	Production, refining, recovery or storage of petroleum or petrochemicals or their by-products, including tar and bitumen processes and manufacture of asphalt.
7.2	Production, refining and bulk storage of organic or inorganic chemicals, including fertilisers, pesticides, pharmaceuticals, soaps, detergents, cosmetics, toiletries, dyestuffs, inks, paints, fireworks, pyrotechnic materials or recovered chemicals.
7.3	Production, refining and bulk storage of industrial gases not otherwise covered.

8.	**Engineering and Manufacturing Processes**
8.1	Manufacture of metal goods, including mechanical engineering industrial plant or steelwork, motor vehicles, ships, railway or tramway vehicles, aircraft, aerospace equipment or similar equipment.
8.2	Storage, manufacture or testing of explosives, propellants, ordnance, small arms or ammunition.
8.3	Manufacture and repair of electrical and electronic components and equipment.
9.	**Food Processing Industry**
9.1	Manufacture of pet foods or animal feedstuffs.
9.2	Processing of animal by-products (including rendering or maggot farming, but excluding slaughterhouses, butchering).
10.	**Paper, Pulp and Printing Industry**
10.1	Making of paper pulp, paper or board, or paper or board products, including printing or de-inking.
11.	**Timber and Timber Products Industry**
11.1	Chemical treatment and coating of timber and timber products.
12.	**Textile Industry**
12.1	Tanning, dressing, fellmongering or other process for preparing, treating or working leather.
12.2	Fulling, bleaching, dyeing or finishing fabrics or fibres.
12.3	Manufacture of carpets or other textile floor coverings (including linoleum works).
13.	**Rubber Industry**
13.1	Processing of natural or synthetic rubber (including tyre manufacture or retreading).
14.	**Infrastructure**
14.1	Marshalling, dismantling, repairing or maintenance of railway rolling stock.
14.2	Dismantling, repairing or maintenance of marine vessels, including hovercraft.
14.3	Dismantling, repairing or maintenance of road transport or road haulage vehicles.
14.4	Dismantling, repairing or maintenance of air or space transport systems.

15.	**Waste Disposal**
15.1	Treating of sewage or other effluent.
15.2	Storage, treatment or disposal of sludge including sludge from water treatment works.
15.3	Treating, keeping, depositing or disposing of waste, including scrap (to include infilled canal basins, docks or river courses).
15.4	Storage or disposal of radioactive materials.

16.	**Miscellaneous**
16.1	Premises housing dry cleaning operations.
16.2	Laboratories for educational or research purposes.
16.3	Demolition of buildings, plant or equipment used for any of the activities in this schedule.[7]

There was much opposition to the consultation paper, principally **24–016** directed to:

— The blight that would be caused to properties on the register even though they might in fact have no contamination whatsoever;[8]

— Even where contamination was present on land, there was no adequate guidance from government as to the standards to which it should be cleaned up, and hence the costs of remediation could not be adequately established;

— Inevitably, if a property had at any time been subject to a contaminative use, nothing could ever change that fact, and it would remain permanently on the register, even where it had been cleaned up to the highest possible standards (or exhaustive surveys had shown that it had never been contaminated at all);

— There was no adequate procedure for objecting to incorrect entries in the registers.

---

[7] Notes on this list of uses included the following:
    (c) A contaminative use is not to be taken to fall into the description if it is carried out as a domestic activity in connection with a private dwelling;
    (e) It is proposed that certain uses of land which may be contaminative are excluded from section 143 registers because the location of the use cannot be defined sufficiently precisely. For example, it would be impossible to establish all locations where asbestos products have been used.
[8] Had the registers been intended to list all uses of all land, whether considered contaminative or not, the issue of unwarranted blight would arguably have been far less serious. Depending on the number of further categories chosen, e.g. general agricultural or residential, the extra work entailed in compiling the registers would have been minimal.

24–017   In June 1992, a revised set of proposals was issued, containing a very much shorter list of contaminative uses and, among some procedural changes, provision for details of remedial work to be shown on the registers. However, the revised proposals did little to meet the main previous objections, while the truncation of the list of uses led to objections from those supporting the principle of a register that numerous contaminative uses would now not be made apparent, and so create a serious likelihood of misleading people that a property not on the register could be assumed to be free from risks of contamination. Following the further objections to the second document, the proposals for registers as provided for in section 143 were abandoned altogether, and the government promised to undertake a fundamental review of its policy towards historic contamination of land—a process that has led to Part II of the Environment Bill.

24–018   At much the same time there were being developed the European Commission's Green Paper on Civil Liability for Environmental Damage, and the Council of Europe 1993 Convention on Civil Liability for Damage Resulting from Activities Dangerous to the Environment. Both of these documents are primarily concerned with liability for future environmental damage, but necessarily also address the issue of liability for historic contamination. The House of Lords European Communities Committee issued a report on the EC Commission's Green Paper in December 1993.[9] Among its conclusions and recommendations is that "A new legal regime for future pollution should come into operation at a date, D-day, set some years in advance. Where pollution is cumulative over a period straddling D-day the onus should be on the defendant to prove that the damage resulted from acts or omissions prior to D-day".[10]

24–019   A purchaser must therefore, before committing himself in any case where there is a risk of his becoming subject to these various liabilities, seek to inform himself as far as he reasonably can as to the nature and extent of any there may be. It is unlikely that he will be able to obtain total certainty, but the seller may be prepared to give certain contractual stipulations that would reduce the impact of any such liabilities as might arise, and if the price is right, the purchaser may be willing to accept certain further risks as a matter of business judgment. Nevertheless, obtaining information on a potentially contaminated property will almost always be an essential step in seeking to avoid acquiring a liability of such a size as to destroy the commercial rationale of the deal. It is standard practice to undertake what is

---

[9] House of Lords, Select Committee on the European Communities, Session 1993–94, 3rd report, "Remedying Environment (*sic*) Damage", December 1993.
[10] paras. 48, 78.

sometimes termed a "Phase I" audit of the property, which will involve a survey and an inspection of records, but will not include any intrusive techniques such as taking core samples or analysing ground-water. Such further steps may well be called for where there is cause for concern, but determining the sampling methodology and the substances to be analysed for, and drawing relevant conclusions from the data, call for a different order of technical expertise that will not be required in every case.

A purchaser may well retain consultants to carry out the initial survey. He will need to establish whether he is thereby simply acquiring such additional information as they generate, or whether he is in fact transferring to the consultants the financial consequences of any contamination on the site that they fail to discover, whether due to their inadequacy or because it was not reasonably discoverable without employing intrusive techniques, and possibly not even then with any certainty.[11] Even where the consultant does not exclude liability, except perhaps for gross negligence, in his conditions of contract, he may in practice be only worth suing to the extent he has effective insurance, and in appropriate cases the purchaser may need to enquire as to this.

24–020

Privilege

Assuming no litigation is already commenced or in contemplation with regard to an allegation of pollution, privilege will only protect a document from disclosure in subsequent court proceedings in which it would otherwise be discoverable, if it is or forms part of a communication between a client and his lawyer, and is prepared for the purpose of giving or seeking legal advice. Privilege only attaches to documents that are confidential, and if any such document is or subsequently comes into the public domain, then privilege cannot be claimed for it. The privilege is not limited to the immediate exchange of letters or instructions to and opinions of counsel. A considerably wider range of documents will also be entitled to privilege provided they have been prepared for the purposes just stated; conversely, documents that are essentially commercial in character will not attract privilege, even though they may be sent to or from a solicitor or barrister, where the lawyer is not acting in his professional capacity, but is acting in a commercial role.[12] Surveys of sites to establish their

24–021

---

[11] A buried drum of toxic chemicals that has not yet started to leak will only be apparent if an attempt to make boreholes happens to hit it, unless a technique such as ground penetrating radar (GPR) is used.

[12] *Balabel v. Air India*, [1988] Ch.D. 317.

environmental condition may attract privilege in certain circumstances, but not in others. Where a survey is conducted directly by a solicitor with, if appropriate, a technical consultant for the purpose of giving legal advice as to potential liabilities, then the survey report should, provided these facts can be proved, which may not always be simple, be entitled to privilege. However if a similar survey were to be conducted either by a technical consultant on his own, or subsequently, as a management exercise to determine whether there had been improvements, for example in relation to compliance with applicable controls, privilege would almost certainly not attach even though a copy of this might be sent to the solicitor. There is no English case directly on the point, though in Canada privilege has been successfully claimed for the results of an environmental survey conducted by a company's outside lawyers.[13]

24–022   Privilege being an exception to the general rule for discovery, it is granted restrictively. In particular, in the absence of actual or contemplated litigation, documents prepared by third parties for a client will not be privileged, even though they may be prepared on his behalf to enable him to obtain legal advice. There is however an exception to this rule for accounting documents (which are not necessarily the same thing as documents prepared by accountants).[14]

24–023   Although privilege may to be potentially available in respect of environmental surveys to the extent that they are directly concerned with the giving or obtaining of legal advice, there may well be matters that could also usefully be investigated in any such survey which do not bear on legal liability. In so far as regard is to be had to any of such further matters, it would be imprudent to deal with them in the same document, since it will inevitably cast doubt on the legal character of the rest.

24–024   Protection of a document from disclosure is naturally only of importance where it contains material liable to affect adversely the person claiming it in subsequent litigation. In some cases, a document may serve to identify him, as opposed to any of his neighbours, as the source of a particular pollutant that has caused third party damage, but generally, if the existence of contamination is discovered in the course of a survey and is then dealt with in a satisfactory manner, it will be rare that an eventual disclosure of the survey will be harmful, when coupled with clear evidence that the problem is entirely past history. Privilege is likely to be of value principally where a person has discovered a problem that he is unwilling or unable to do anything

---

[13] *R. v. McCarthy Tétrault* (1993) 9 C.E.L.R. (N.S.) 12.
[14] *Gregory v. MNR* (1992) 82 D.T.C. 6518 (fed.C.T.TD), a further Canadian case, quoted in "Confidentiality and Environmental Audits", Stuart, Pugh and Oudkerk [1993] Env.Liability 137, which gives a valuable survey of the law in this area.

about. In the context of an acquisition, this is unlikely to be the purchaser's attitude. On the contrary, he may be expected to display enthusiasm for cleaning up any contamination present and effectively charging as much as possible of the costs to the seller.

Seller's Survey

A practice that is often of benefit is for a seller to commission his **24–025** own environmental survey by an independent consultant, and to make the results available to prospective purchasers. Provided the consultant is truly impartial, this saves both time and money in the pre-contract period, and allows tenders to be submitted on a consistent basis. A prospective purchaser should however stipulate in his purchase contract for the consultant to accept liability on his report in favour of the eventual purchaser, which the privity of the consultant's contract with the seller would otherwise preclude;[15] to ensure this is possible, which is of course in the seller's interest as well, the seller must also stipulate for this in his contract commissioning the consultant's survey.

Public Records

In addition to what is available from a physical examination of a site, **24–026** valuable information may also be found from public records where these show what activities may have been carried out either on or in the neighbourhood of the site in the past. Such records include old Ordnance Survey maps—the first of these were issued in the 1840s (for Yorkshire and Lancashire), with the whole country completed in the 25 inch series by 1883. These may often show the sites of old contaminating activities (notably gas works), including many, such as railway sidings that have since been re-developed, with varying amounts of attention being paid to past contamination. Other sources of information include the surveys of derelict and despoiled land, the publicly available registers of waste disposal site licences and licence applications, surveys of mineral workings carried out for the Department of the Environment and the Welsh Office, trade effluent

---

[15] Even without this the purchaser might be able to mount a case in tort on the basis of *Hedley Byrne & Co., Ltd. v. Heller & Partners, Ltd*, [1964] A.C. 465; [1963] 2 All E.R. 575, but there could be no certainty on the point.

consents held by the water companies, many inherited from the previous water authorities, and discharge consents, also inherited from the water authorities, that are now held by the NRA. Additionally, local street directories, which have been published since 1850, contain much information as to what has taken place on a particular site. Such historical surveys are of particular value where land is derelict and ripe for re-development, but all those who have ever been connected with activities on it have departed. There are of course now a variety of recently instituted registers of consents and authorisations issued under environmental legislation, in addition to those of consents for waste disposal and discharges to water and sewer. The relatively recent introduction of many of these registers means that they have as yet only slight value as a source of historical information; the information from these will mostly be relevant to questions of compliance by the operations on the site in question.

Remediation

24–027   Where pollution is found or seriously suspected, a purchaser will wish to protect himself so far as he can against, firstly, the costs of having to clean-up the contamination out of his own resources and, secondly, the costs of any claims that may be made against him by third parties in respect of the contamination and such damage as it may have caused or threatened. The second aspect can only be satisfactorily covered, if at all, by contractual stipulations. The costs of remediation may be reflected by a reduction in the purchase price, or indeed by refusal to proceed with the purchase at all. To assess the remediation costs necessarily entails an assessment of the clean-up standards that must be attained in the remediation. Relatively modest standards can be achieved at comparatively low cost, but any increase in the standards is liable to cause a disproportionate increase in the costs of achieving them. It is therefore of critical importance to be able to establish what standards are to be reached in any clean-up. Where a contract provides for a seller to pay the whole or any proportion of the clean-up costs, and these are required at some later date, it is of vital importance to establish whether the obligation on the seller relates to the clean-up standards applicable as at the date of sale or as at the date of clean-up, when higher standards may make the burden substantially greater.

24–028   In the United Kingdom, the Inter-departmental Committee on the Redevelopment of Contaminated Land (the ICRCL) has published a series of Guidance Notes on the remediation of various types of contaminated land as set out in Table 24/II.

Table 26/II

ICRCL Guidance Notes

ICRCL 59/83	Guidance on the assessment and redevelopment of contaminated land. (2nd ed.), July 1987.
ICRCL 17/78	Notes on the development and after-use of landfill sites. (8th ed.), December 1990.
ICRCL 18/79	Notes on the redevelopment of gasworks sites. (5th ed.) April 1986.
ICRCL 23/79	Notes on the redevelopment of sewage works and farms. (2nd ed.) November 1983.
ICRCL 42/80	Notes on the redevelopment of scrap yards and similar sites. (2nd ed.) October 1983.
ICRCL 61/84	Notes on the fire hazards of contaminated land. (2nd ed.) July 1986.
ICRCL 64/85	Asbestos on contaminated sites. (2nd ed.) October 1990.
ICRCL 70/90	Notes on the restoration and aftercare of metalliferous mining sites for pasture and grazing. (1st ed.) February 1990.

Many of these documents are however old and do not represent **24–029** current thinking on appropriate standards. Moreover, they are very largely concerned with the direct effect on people, plants and animals using the restored land, and comparatively little attention is paid to the effects of contamination on groundwater. Relatively small numbers of potential pollutants are considered — although these may be the most significant, there are many others that are highly undesirable in significant quantities. Soil standards are currently under consideration by the government and are also the subject of an inquiry by the Royal Commission on Environmental Pollution. In the absence of accepted British standards it has become common practice to have regard to those that have been developed in the Netherlands, on the basis that conformity with these will almost certainly meet any likely UK requirements. Indeed these Dutch standards may well in a number of cases go beyond what might be required in the United Kingdom, since they are determined on the basis of the geology of the Netherlands, with its sandy soil and high water tables. Such conditions do of course occur also in the United Kingdom, but there are many others, particularly those with clay strata at or near the surface, where contamination, once laid down, is likely to remain, without migrating through groundwater. In such cases there is little or no risk to neighbouring properties or of pollution of any abstracted ground-water. Accordingly, whether the pollutants need to be removed depends essentially on the use to which the land is to be put. "Soft" uses, such as residential housing with gardens, require substantial cleaning up if health risks to people and animals are to be avoided; "hard" uses, such as industrial development and car parking, are naturally far less sensitive to the presence of pollutants.

24–030   More up to date guidance has now been issued by the Department of the Environment in a series of Contaminated Land Research Reports, namely:

CLR Report No. 1	A Framework for Assessing the Impact of Contaminated Land on Groundwater and Surface Water (2 vols).
CLR Report No. 2	Guidance on Preliminary Site Inspection of Contaminated Land (2 vols).
CLR Report No. 3	Documentary Research on Industrial Sites.
CLR Report No. 4	Sampling Strategies for Contaminated Land.
CLR Report No. 5	Information Systems for Land Contamination.

The Contract

24–031   An environmental survey may establish that there is indeed actual contamination on the site, possibly coupled with a significant likelihood of other neighbouring land or aquifers having become contaminated, leading to the risk of potential third party actions against anyone who may conceivably be held liable, including a new owner and occupier. The parties will inevitably have conflicting interests with regard to such liabilities: the seller will wish to be rid of all problems associated with the site once he has sold it, while the purchaser will not wish to take on any liabilities arising from what may have happened before his acquisition. If the sale contract fails to allocate these risks adequately, any costs or damages that may subsequently arise from the historic contamination may fall arbitrarily on either the seller or the purchaser, depending on the choice made by a third party plaintiff. While the latter may choose to pursue both the seller and the purchaser, in the event of obtaining judgment in his favour, he may enforce it against one only, chosen on the basis of who has the greatest financial resources. It may be far from clear in that event whether the selected defendant will have a right to seek a contribution from the other.

Where potential liabilities are at all substantial, the parties will need **24–032** to review every potential head of liability, and determine in principle who should bear the risk of any proceedings in relation to that head. This may be quite straightforward, or it may prove to be extremely complex. The seller may have behaved relatively imprudently in relation to certain materials, but in other respects he may have been no worse than any purchaser might reasonably expect. In such a case the seller may have to accept some degree of liability in relation to particular types of claim relating to specified contaminants; the purchaser accepting all others. To achieve that, the seller will look for an indemnity from the purchaser against actions brought against the seller for any contamination other than that for which the seller has agreed to accept a degree of responsibility.

In other circumstances, the purchaser will seek to limit his liability to **24–033** certain known risks, on the basis that he is likely to address these in the near future in any event, and make the seller liable for all others that there may be. This may be unattractive for the seller, since he will retain an open-ended liability for an indeterminate period, but he may have little option or, alternatively, be prepared to take such risks if the price offered creates a sufficient inducement. Indeed, in certain transactions, particularly where several sites are being transferred simultaneously, the parties may agree that one or two highly contaminated sites should be excluded altogether from the deal and left with the seller, where the problems associated with them are excessive.

Of course, warranties and indemnities are only as good as the **24–034** person giving them. If there is a reasonable likelihood that the seller will go out of existence, or at least transfer his assets elsewhere leaving little more than an empty shell,[16] at any time while the purchaser may wish to make a claim under the contract, then the purchaser will not readily accept terms that do not properly reflect this lack of security.

In a conventional corporate acquisition a set of seller's warranties is **24–035** negotiated between the parties, but is subject to specific disclosures against the warranties. Environmental issues are usually dealt with separately in view of their relatively uncertain but potentially large financial implications. There will normally be provision for which party is to control any litigation that may be brought by third parties (including responding to action by regulatory authorities). Further, the purchaser may wish to stipulate for any contractual benefits in his

---

[16] In certain circumstances, such action would be open to challenge as a transfer at an undervalue or preference, or a breach of director's duty or *ultra vires*.

favour to be transferable to any person subsequently acquiring the site from him. The following discussion does not attempt to cover in detail the drafting techniques that may be employed, which would be out of place here, but is confined to the broad principles to be applied.[17]

24–036   Matters that are typically covered by environmental warranties—these are frequently stipulated to be also representations—are that:

(i)   the seller has complied with all relevant laws;

(ii)   the seller is in possession of and is in compliance with all necessary permits;

(iii) no notices have been served on the seller alleging any non-compliance of any applicable environmental laws;

(iv)   no remedial action has been ordered in respect of any contamination on the property;

(v)   there are no civil or criminal proceedings, whether actual or pending, in which it is alleged that there has been any breach of any applicable environmental laws or any pollution of the environment or harm to human health (as defined in the Environmental Protection Act 1990), nor has there been any within the past [six] years;

(vi)   there are no circumstances (for example impending new regulatory controls) that may lead to a requirement to undertake any remedial work in the future;

(vii) there are no circumstances that might require the purchaser to incur significant expense in order to be able to continue with the current activities on the property.

24–037   Some or all of these may well be qualified by "so far as the seller is aware", which inevitably transfers a considerable degree of risk across to the purchaser, particularly where the seller's competence in environmental management is not trusted.[17A] As in any other similar transaction, the purchaser will need precision as to whose knowledge is to be treated as relevant for the purposes of determining whether or not the seller was aware of any given facts.

24–038   The damages recoverable on a claim for breach of warranty are inevitably somewhat uncertain. The broad rule is that the damages should place the claimant in the position that he would be in if the facts warranted were true, and prima facie this is to be calculated on the basis of the "loss of bargain", *i.e.* the difference in value between that of the acquired asset in its actual condition in the light of the

---

[17] A useful article on this general topic is "Environmental Law in Transactions", Edward Keeble, PLC, June 1992, pp. 5–13.

[17A] Though it will be implied that the seller has made reasonable enquiries, *William Sindall plc v. Cambridgeshire County Council* [1994] 1 W.L.R. 1016; [1994] 3 All E.R. 932.

breach of warranty, and the value it would otherwise have had.[18] Where the asset is one of many similar that are marketed, and its particular identity is not of importance to the purchaser, the loss of bargain can be readily calculated and will represent a fair measure of actual damage. Nevertheless, this is only a *prima facie* approach, and not an absolute rule of law. In every case, the calculation must address the real commercial loss caused to a party by a breach of warranty, and where the asset has unique characteristics—a particular site or a specific business—the damage may be more appropriately measured by the cost of curing the breach by performing the warranty.[19]

Whether in any particular case damages should be assessed by reference to loss of bargain, as opposed to the cost of curing the breach will depend, among other things, on the relative importance of the subject matter of the warranty in question to the plaintiff party. Where during pre-contract negotiations the purchaser made clear his concern not to acquire environmental liabilities, and where these have been addressed in detail in the contract, this will favour damages being assessed by the cost of rectification. The full extent of such environmental liabilities is often inherently extremely difficult, if not impossible, to quantify at the time of the contract, and cannot therefore be sensibly taken into account in the price, even if a reasonable calculation of the risk of their arising is possible. The purchaser is thus forced to rely on contractual stipulations in order to cover such risks as there may be in this respect, which will also favour applying the cost of rectification as the proper measure of damages.

24–039

In many contracts, there may be a stipulation that the seller also represents to be true the matters warranted, thereby creating a liability to a claim in tort for misrepresentation in the event of a breach of warranty.[20] While such a claim will arise where it can be shown that the purchaser was induced to enter into the contract by the misrepresentation, this is not a necessary test for such a claim to succeed.[21] A legitimate approach in such a case is to consider the reduction in price that would have been made, had the truth been known and had there been no misrepresentation. However this may sometimes be an impossible figure to assess—indeed the sale might not have proceeded at all. As for breach of warranty there is also precedent for damages for

24–040

---

[18] *Livingstone v. Rawards Coal Co* (1880) 5 App.Cs. 25, 39; *Levison v. Farin* [1978] 2 All E.R. 1149.

[19] *Calabar Properties v. Stitcher* [1984] 1 W.L.R. 287; *Jones v. Herxheimer* [1950] 2 K.B. 106; *Tito v. Waddell* [1977] Ch.D. 106; *Radford v. de Froberville* [1977] 1 W.L.R. 1262; *Sunshine Exploration v. Dolly Varden Mines* (1970) 8 D.L.R. 441 (Canada) applying *Wertheim v. Chicoutimi Pulp Co* [1911] A.C. 301; *Ruxley Electronics and Construction Limited v. Forsyth* (C.A.) *The Times*, January 7, 1994.

[20] *Doyle v. Olby* [1969] 2 Q.B. 158.

[21] *Edgington v. Fitzmaurice* (1885) 29 Ch.D. 445.

misrepresentation to be assessed by reference to the cost of repair of a defective item rather than by reference to any diminution in value.[22]

24–041   Although in an appropriate case the damages for a breach of warranty as to the absence of contamination may be assessed by reference to the cost of cleaning up such contamination as is in fact present, the position of a purchaser will undoubtedly be stronger if there is also an appropriate indemnity. This may be triggered by facts amounting to the breach of warranty, or on the happening of certain other defined events. The value of an indemnity of course lies partly in the inherent possibility or risk that on any particular facts a court may hold that damages for breach of warranty should be assessed on the loss of bargain basis (in which event the purchaser may be unable to establish any figure to the satisfaction of the court). However, and additionally, an indemnity can spell out with precision the full extent of the parties' respective liabilities, in particular the heads of costs to be indemnified, and whether the relevant clean-up standards for the purpose of the indemnity are those applicable at the date of the contract or those at the date of the clean-up, and prescribe procedures for disposing of disputes, including those needed where the purchaser has himself contributed to contamination for part of which the seller is liable under the indemnity. It is normal for the benefit of an indemnity to extend to directors and other officers of the relevant company. An indemnity has the further advantage for the purchaser in that (in the absence of contractual stipulations to the contrary), it may be relied on at any time within six years from when a claim under it becomes due, whereas a claim for breach of warranty will ordinarily become time barred six years after the date of the contract containing the warranty breached. For this reason, among others, sellers will normally wish to limit the time during which they are exposed to the risk of claims under their indemnity; they will almost invariably place a maximum figure on their liability under it, and this maximum may reduce with time.

24–042   Frequently, where a seller is conscious of a substantial risk of there being a claim made against him, he will seek to ensure that this is not provoked by the purchaser deliberately encouraging a regulatory authority to require remedial action. While there may be a contractual stipulation to this effect, it may be hard to establish the facts given the necessary interchange between site owners and regulators in the ordinary course of business; a more effective control is to limit the recovery under the indemnity to a specific proportion of the total

---

[22] *Dodds v. Canterbury City Council* [1980] 1 All E.R. 928; *Dominion Mosaics and Tile Co v. Trafalgar Trucking Co.* [1990] 2 All E.R. 246.

outlays, thereby giving the purchaser a financial disincentive from inducing a clean-up that he would not undertake on his own account.

An element of the standard "due diligence" procedure is the making of disclosures by a seller against his warranties. A question that may arise is whether a purchaser may sue for breach of a warranty when he knows of the breach at the date of the contract, and so could have decided not to proceed, or to demand re-negotiation of the contract terms. The point remains arguable,[23] but at least in the case of environmental warranties as to the absence of contamination, it is suggested that a warrantor should quite properly be held to his warranty irrespective of the purchaser's knowledge. It seems self-evident that an indemnity would be enforceable in such circumstances, since its purpose is principally to address foreseeable and quite probable events. The whole complex of contractual terms resulting from detailed negotiations is inevitably a series of compromises, and it would be unconscionable for a party to deny that one term that he has agreed to have included that purports to benefit the other cannot be relied on, since this would destroy the balance of the agreement. Moreover, in many cases, even where contamination is known or suspected, its extent is not known, and cannot be without detailed and expensive sampling of soil and groundwater, and analysis of the samples. A seller is likely to have at least as good a knowledge as the purchaser of any contamination present, and if he is not prepared to stand by his warranties, then he should qualify them or not give them at all.

24-043

Where a seller warrants freedom from contamination, the legal effect of a disclosure against that warranty of the existence of some contamination may well prove contentious. Unless the disclosure is fully detailed, it will be uncertain what inferences may properly be drawn as to the presence of any further contamination beyond that expressly disclosed. In most cases it will be obvious that there is some additional contamination but of unknown extent; in view of the uncertainty as to the precise effect of such a disclosure, the purchaser should normally not be prepared to accept one made in this way.

24-044

Transfer of Consents, etc.

On taking over a business as a going concern otherwise than by acquisition of shares, the new operator must ensure that all authorisations, consents and licences that may have been issued to the seller under environmental legislation are, where necessary, either

24-045

---

[23] *Eurocopy plc v. Teesdale* (C.A.) [1992] B.C.L.C. 1067, where the issue was raised as a preliminary point on the pleadings, and allowed to stand. The case did not go to full trial.

transferred to him or renewed in his favour. Some of these are personal to the grantee, while others run with the land, and in the latter case the only action, if any, required will be to notify the relevant authority of the change of the grantee.

Discharge consents under the W.R.A. 1991

24–046   These run with the land, and relate to particular discharges at particular places. There is no requirement to inform the NRA of any change of owner or occupier of the land from which the discharge is made, though this is normal.[24]

Trade effluent consents and agreements

24–047   Trade effluent consents are granted on applications made by the owner or occupier of trade premises; in the event of a discharge either without or not in compliance with the trade effluent consent, it is the occupier who will be guilty of an offence.[25] Accordingly these consents run with the land, and a new occupier will have the benefit of any existing consent, though he will be required by his seller to notify the sewerage undertaker, to ensure appropriate transfer of the obligation to pay the sewerage charges.

24–048   A trade effluent agreement under W.I.A., s.129, on the other hand, would normally be a purely personal contract between a particular owner or occupier and the sewerage undertaker. Though this could be expressed to enure to the benefit of a subsequent occupier who agreed to pay the appropriate charges, or to be freely transferable by notice to the sewerage undertaker, in the absence of any such provisions a new occupier will need to obtain a fresh consent or agreement to dispose of his trade effluent. The terms of the agreement will always be decisive.

Waste management licences

24–049   Transfer of waste management licences is subject to the provisions of section 40 of the E.P.A. A formal application for the transfer must be made in accordance with that section to the waste regulation authority; provided the proposed transferee can satisfy the authority that he is a fit and proper person, it must transfer the licence to him.

Authorisations under E.P.A. Part I—Integrated Pollution Control/ Air Pollution Control

Transfer of authorisations under E.P.A., Part I is governed by section 9. In effect transfer is permitted without restriction, but the transferee

[24] W.R.A., Sched. 10, para. 2(6).
[25] W.I.A. 1991, ss.118(5), 121(5).

is required to notify the relevant enforcing authority in writing of   **24–050**
the transfer within the next 21 days. Failure to do so within this
prescribed period is an offence.

Hazardous Substances Consents

In general, a hazardous substances consent runs with the land to   **24–057**
which it relates and for the benefit of all persons interested in that
land.[26] Nevertheless, an application to continue a hazardous substances consent where there is a change of control over any part of the
land must be made before that change is made otherwise the consent
is automatically revoked.[27] Where any such application is made, the
hazardous substances authority has power to modify the consent or to
revoke it.

Abstraction Licences

Succession to abstraction licences is governed by sections 49 and 50   **24–052**
of the Water Resources Act 1991 and by the Water Resources
(Succession to Licences) Regulations 1969.[28] Where a person acquires
the whole of the land specified in the licence (being the land on which
the abstracted water is to be used) there are no restrictions on transfer,
but he must give notice to the NRA of the change in the occupation of
the relevant land within 15 months of his acquiring the land in
question or the licence will lapse. However, where he only succeeds to
part of the rights, both the previous licence holder and the successor
must apply for new licences if they both wish to abstract water. The
effect of this will be to share between them the amounts which might
be abstracted under the previous licence. The purchase contract will
need to include appropriate stipulations in such a case.

Lender Liability

Where a loan is made to finance a business operation, it is frequent   **24–053**
practice for the lender to take by way of security a charge on or other
interest in the borrower's assets, typically the property on which he
conducts his business and, in some cases, the totality of the business

---

[26] Planning (Hazardous Substances) Act 1990, s.6(2).
[27] s.17(1).
[28] S.I. 1969 No. 1976.

itself. In all cases, a prudent lender will be concerned with three distinct matters of potential concern to him:

(1) A borrower may (especially if he has no, or no adequate, environmental management system) incur significant fines or be subject to substantial civil claims; the trend of environmental legislation (or even the effect of current legislation if his equipment is relatively old) may also force him to make substantial investments in order to maintain compliance, and accelerate the writing down of existing asset values. A large outlay under any one or more of these heads may put the borrower's viability at risk, or at least his ability to service the loan and to repay it when due.

(2) The lender may become closely involved in the management of the borrower's business, particularly if it appears to be in need of management support to remain viable, or is otherwise dangerously close to insolvency. In any such case, especially where the lender has taken an equity stake and the borrower is (at least arguably) managed by its members, the lender may be criminally liable as a director or shadow director[29] of the company for any environmental offences that it may commit.

(3) Thirdly, and perhaps the most significantly, where a lender enforces his security and becomes a mortgagee in possession, he may find himself liable for any environmental acts or defaults of the company and responsible for the costs of remedial work on a contaminated site; even where an administrator or an administrative or Law of Property Act receiver is appointed, the lender may in practice assume similar liabilities through an indemnity given to the administrator or receiver.

24–054 The exposure of a lender under the first two heads requires little elaboration here; the legal requirements and the risks attached to them are set out elsewhere in this work. A lender wishing to maximise his protection against these eventualities will need to undertake an appreciably more thorough preliminary investigation into the environmental issues that may affect an applicant for a loan than has been usual in the UK. In doing this he should have regard to foreseeable changes in the law during the term of the loan that may affect the

---

[29] Defined in the Insolvency Act 1986, s.251, in relation to a company, as 'a person in accordance with whose directions or instructions the directors of the company are accustomed to act (but so that a person is not deemed a shadow director by reason only that the directors act on advice given by him in a professional capacity)'.

borrower's operations or the nature and extent of his liabilities.[30] After the loan has been made, the lender will continue to need to keep himself informed throughout its term as to any relevant developments in the law and the borrower's business, and provide as appropriate in the loan documents for certain events to be acts of default, at least where they are under the borrower's control and have not been previously authorised by the lender. These may include, for example, an acquisition of a seriously contaminated site, or a change in or an addition to the operations that involves the use or production of hazardous substances.

Ascertaining the exposure of a lender under the third head requires **24–055** consideration of the status of administrators, receivers and liquidators, and their personal exposure under applicable environmental laws. First, however, where a mortgagee has gone into possession, he will be an occupier of the relevant site and will normally be treated in law also as the owner of the property and the business concerned, and therefore liable accordingly. The Environmental Protection Act did not originally have any definition of "owner" (unlike the Public Health Act 1936) but, by virtue of the Noise and Statutory Nuisance Act 1993, this is now defined in section 81A(9) for the purposes of proceedings under section 81 for statutory nuisances, in the following terms:

"Owner", in relation to any premises, means a person (other than a mortgagee not in possession) who, whether in his own right or as trustee for any other person, is entitled to receive the rack rent of the premises or, where the premises are not let at a rack rent, would be so entitled if they were so let."

In the Water Resources Act 1991, the term is defined somewhat **24–056** differently[31] as a person who is for the time being receiving the rack rent of premises, whether on his own account *or as agent* or trustee for another person; or would receive the rack rent if premises were let at a rack rent—for the purposes of certain parts of the Act, the term excludes a mortgagee not in possession. The words "as agent" were also included in the Public Health Act 1936 definition, where they caused some difficulty; their omission from E.P.A., s.81A(9) may be seen as deliberate.

Though a bank may receive rent for a customer, it is not an agent for **24–057** the purposes of receiving rents if it merely acts as a conventional banker in relation to a private account.[32] However if it were to arrange

---

[30] For example, it is not uncommon in other jurisdictions for the closure of an industrial activity on a site to have to be accompanied by removal of any contamination on that site. It is at least possible that a similar obligation might be introduced into the UK.

[31] In s.221(1).

[32] *Midland Bank Ltd v. Conway Corporation* (1965) 1 W.L.R. 1165.

for rents to be paid into a special account in order to pay off some debt to a third party, then it would undoubtedly be acting as agent, and in that event would be potentially liable as owner where a definition including "as agent" applies. If it were to arrange to collect rents to pay off its own loan, it would be an owner within either definition, as it would be if it were entitled to receive that income by an assignment to support a charge on the lease or merely on the rent. In view of the narrower definition in the E.P.A. (albeit only for the purposes of Part III) it must be regarded as unlikely that the wider definition would apply to those sections elsewhere imposing liabilities on owners, though the matter must inevitably remain uncertain until the courts have had occasion to pronounce on it.

24–058   Although the E.P.A. does provide for liability to fall on owners in some circumstances, notwithstanding that they may not themselves have had any direct responsibility for the matters in question, a distinction can be drawn between a person who has a direct interest as freeholder or long leaseholder, and who has permitted others to go into occupation, and a bank which has merely financed certain activities. To enforce the law against a freeholder or long leaseholder would doubtless encourage such people to exert some additional control over those they have allowed to occupy their property, with few adverse consequences for the economy or society generally; whereas to place such liability on those whose business it is simply to make loans, and who have no natural wish or ability to exert constant control over their borrowers, may have as its principal consequence the inhibiting of lending, rather than resulting in any tighter controls. There are therefore cogent policy grounds for not classing lenders as "owners" unless the statute were expressly so to provide in a particular context.

24–059   A receiver is, by definition, appointed to receive the income of property, and hence he will be an owner, as will a mortgagee who has gone into possession. A receiver appointed by the court will not however normally be an agent for the company. He will act on behalf of the court, and will not have power in his own right to contract on behalf of the company. Administrative receivers, though appointed by a creditor are, in law, agents of the company borrower, as are administrators and also receivers appointed under the Law of Property Act 1925. They will all therefore be liable as agents and will also be potentially personally liable for offences committed by the company in their capacity as managers of it. They may also be liable as occupiers.[33] Additionally, if they act on instructions given by the appointing

---

[33] *Meigh v. Wickenden* [1942] K.B. 160; *Lord Advocate v. Aero Technologies (in receivership)* 1991 S.L.T. 134 (Scotland).

creditor, the creditor will be liable in tort to any third party injured in consequence.[34] Liquidators are likewise agents of the company, and though in the nature of their appointment they are unlikely to trade, they may nevertheless be at least temporarily responsible for on-going processes and the handling and disposal of dangerous substances and waste. Accordingly they also may become personally liable under environmental legislation. Further, even though it would be most unusual for a liquidator to give any express warranties or indemnities to a purchaser of an insolvent business or of any of its assets, liabilities arising out of environmental legislation may be inadvertently incurred in any such transactions. Trustees in bankruptcy are similarly exposed where they act in relation to a business previously operated by a sole trader or a partnership.

The personal liability of administrative receivers will frequently be **24–060** the subject of an indemnity given to them by their appointors—indeed except where the appointee is closely familiar with the nature of the processes and materials that he will be responsible for, in cases where these are hazardous or otherwise potentially polluting, it would be imprudent for him to take up his appointment in the absence of appropriate financial cover, whether from his appointor or through insurance, where available. Thus although the lender appointing such a person will not usually be directly exposed, he may nevertheless find himself liable under an indemnity for significant sums, conceivably greater than the amount of the original loan.

Before risking exposure under an indemnity or through taking **24–061** possession, a lender may well need to consider carefully whether the advantages of so proceeding outweigh the potential disadvantages; in some cases, the prudent decision might be to write off the loan and not to enforce the security. However, the lender may not have sufficient opportunity to ascertain all the facts needed to take an informed decision on this if he has not kept himself well aware of the circumstances and operations of the borrower, and of his performance in the light of the requirements of environmental legislation. Any accountant's report that may be made prior to the appointment of an administrative receiver, or before the court appoints an administrator, may be of some help if he has not done so, but he will need to consider the report very carefully to determine whether potential enviromental risks have been properly assessed. The terms of most banking loans in the UK still pay relatively little attention to environmental issues, particularly by comparison with those of comparable loans in the United States. While there are good reasons for some of the distinction, loan documentation should have regard to potential changes

---

[34] *American Express International Banking Corporation v. Hurley* [1985] 3 All E.R. 564.

during the period of the loan in the legal context in which it will operate. A prudent lender will take into account the general trend of liabilities and will consider including terms that allow him to keep himself informed of the borrower's environmental performance, and of any business developments that could affect this adversely, and in particular on the extent of any contamination of property over which security has been taken.

Leasehold Property

24–062   Many existing leases date from a time when land contamination was scarcely an issue for the vast bulk of those owning or occupying property, and accordingly do not spell out with clarity, as would today be prudent, the respective liabilities of the landlord and the tenant for contamination on the leased property, whether caused by activities on the property or elsewhere.

24–063   So far as contamination of the property itself is concerned, this may result from:

- The lessee's own activities;
- The activities of a previous lessee under the same lease;
- Contamination present at the site before the lease was granted;
- Contamination deriving from a third party outside the site.

24–064   Where the lessee has contaminated the property himself, this gives no legal difficulties, since he will usually be liable to the landlord under any reasonably well-drafted lease. This may address the point directly; a repairing clause may require the leased premises to be kept clean or cleansed (it must be doubted whether "repair" itself covers dealing with contaminated soil); there may be an obligation to comply with statutory requirements (which would at least include not disposing of any waste without a licence, not creating a statutory nuisance, and not allowing any polluting matter to enter groundwater or any stream); a right to carry on a specific permitted use may, expressly or by implication, prohibit any other activity that results in pollution; there may be a prohibition on activities amounting to a "nuisance" or "annoyance"; and, finally, the landlord may be in a position to rely on the tort of waste (see paragraphs 22–220 to 22–228), entitling him to damages and, where appropriate, an injunction against polluting activity.

24–065   Nevertheless, even where a lessee is in principle liable to the landlord for his action, if he has no funds to pay for any clean-up, becomes insolvent or otherwise defaults, the landlord will find himself left with a contaminated site that he must then restore at his own cost if he is to be able to make full commercial use of it thereafter. Moreover, as the owner and the occupier of a contaminated site, he will also be potentially liable to any third parties damaged by it. The landlord may therefore wish to provide in the lease for a system for keeping him aware of the tenant's activities, particularly where there is a substantial risk of causing significant contamination, for example ensuring that there are periodic surveys of the site to review the tenant's compliance with environmental legislation and also with accepted good practice. Where the activity is unquestionably dangerous, it would not be unreasonable to have regard to whether the tenant is complying with either BS 7750 or with the requirements for registration under the EC Eco-Management and Audit Scheme. Prevention is vastly better, and cheaper, than cure, and a prudent landlord will take an active interest in a tenant's activities on the leased property.

The catch however is that the more involved the landlord is with the   **24–066**
tenant's activities, the more likely he is to be held to be involved in the management of those activities, and hence directly liable, both criminally and for subsequent clean-up costs, in the event of any failure by the tenant to comply with the law. There is no easy answer to this, since the only reliable solution for the landlord would be to exclude his right to control the tenant at all, which is clearly not a realistic option. A line must therefore be carefully drawn between ensuring that the tenant is maintaining effective management systems, and actually joining in that management, which is to be avoided.

Where contamination has not been caused by the existing tenant,   **24–067**
but either by a previous lessee or before the grant of the lease, then the terms of the lease, and of any assignment, will be decisive. Almost invariably a lease will require the property to be surrendered at the end of the term in at least no worse condition than when the lease was granted, and the tenant at that time will therefore be potentially exposed to considerable liabilities. His concern will be to ensure that he has all appropriate evidence to establish the state of the property when he took an assignment of the lease (so that he may be able to recover from his assignor) and/or of the state of the property at the initial grant of the lease (which for older leases may be difficult if not impossible in practice). Site surveys to check for contamination are likely to become more frequent in the future, to protect tenants in this way. As yet, it is rare for grants of leases and assignments to be made subject to the kinds of environmental warranties and indemnities that are now relatively standard practice on outright sales of freehold property, but logically there is no reason for the distinction.

Where contamination has come on to a leased property from   **24–068**
elsewhere, the liability of the tenant will again depend on the terms of

his lease; almost as important is who should in those circumstances take action against whoever may be responsible for the contamination. Commercial leases commonly make some provision for joint participation in litigation, and this is highly desirable, preferably also covering how to allocate any awards of damages and liabilities for costs, and responsibility for clean-up operations.

24–069   The landlord and tenant must also consider how to handle liability for damage caused to third parties by activities on site. So far as the criminal law is concerned, in *National Rivers Authority v. Welsh Development Agency*[35] (see paragraphs 8–126 to 8–128) the landlord was held not to be criminally liable under section 85(1) of the W.R.A. where a tenant had allowed polluting matter to enter controlled waters. However that decision might have been different had the landlord been taking an active part in the tenant's operations, going beyond keeping himself informed, or had he deliberately developed the site with a view to its use for purposes inherently likely to cause pollution. The decision is moreover not readily reconcilable with *Taylor Woodrow Property Management Ltd. v. NRA*[36] (see paragraph 8–128); a landlord will unquestionably be at risk if any discharge or trade effluent consent is held in his name. Liability at common law depends on the actual or presumed ability of the owner of land to control the activities that occur on it, and again this will depend on the terms of the lease. In practice, any third party damaged may well sue both the tenant and the landlord, and whether or not the lease covers such a situation, the two parties will need to co-operate in any defence to the action, if they are not to be at risk of being played off against each other.

---

[35] [1993] Env L.R. 407.
[36] [1995] Env L.R. 52.

Chapter 25

INSURANCE

Accidents can happen in the best managed concerns, and the **25–001** prudent businessman would be negligent if he failed to seek insurance cover against any substantial liabilities that his business may incur as a consequence. As this book demonstrates, there are a multitude of potential liabilities, under both statute and common law, that may arise as a result of what may be broadly termed pollution of the environment, for example, property damage, contamination of land and water, personal injury, and injury to other living things, both owned and unowned. The purpose of this chapter is not to give a comprehensive review of insurance law, for which reference to the standard works should be made, but to indicate those aspects of it that are particularly relevant to liabilities arising under environmental law. Though the availability of insurance cover in this area is now markedly less than a few years ago, older policies with broad cover may still be of relevance in certain situations; some, very limited, cover is available under existing standard liability policies, while a variety of other policies are being developed providing more extensive cover, albeit at considerably greater cost and subject to fairly demanding pre-conditions.

The rights available under an insurance policy depend entirely on **25–002** its particular terms (applying where appropriate the *contra proferentem* rule). In the United Kingdom the relevant insuring clauses do not conform to any single standard precedent, unlike the position in the United States. Precedents from the case law necessarily deal with the particular facts and contract in issue, and in this area as much as any great care must be taken if attempting to apply them to other circumstances. There are, in any event, virtually no English cases directly relevant to the construction of environmental clauses, in notable contrast to the position in the United States where litigation in this area has been extensive. However, while the United States cases are instructive as to the issues that need to be considered, the decisions actually reached generally provide no reliable guide as to how a similar situation might be resolved in the United Kingdom. This is partly because the philosophy of insurance in the United States is distinctly different, in particular with its concern there for protecting the "legitimate expectations" of the insured. Further, cases in the USA are usually tried before a jury and, where local companies have been faced with massive clean-up claims under the Superfund legislation, juries may on occasion have been unduly inclined to find in favour of the insured, and against insurers with deep pockets.

25–003 Third party environmental liabilities have generally been covered by public liability policies, typically an employer's Comprehensive General Liability (CGL) policy. Such policies indemnify the insured against damages liabilities to others that he may have in respect of damage to property or personal injury. CGL policies have normally been written on an "occurrence" basis, providing cover for the consequences of an insured "event" that occurs in the period of the policy, irrespective of when a claim against the insured in respect of damage caused by that event may be made. In pollution cases, that may be many years, even decades, later, creating a "tail" of liability that may come to haunt an insurer long after he has settled his accounts for the policy period in question. Alternative "claims made" policies only provide cover for claims actually made in the policy period (or sometimes shortly after it, in respect of an occurrence of which the insured has, or should have, become aware during it), and for that reason are attractive to insurers, though less so to insureds. In practice, close analysis of the wording of a policy may be needed to establish which of these two bases it is written on.

25–004 In the past, the amount of remedial work required to respond to pollution damage was generally quite modest (though no doubt often relatively ineffective), and consequently not unduly expensive. However as standards have risen over recent years, the costs have also increased very substantially. Remediation costs in the United States have been notorious in this regard, and insurance of a large part of these costs has been placed on the London insurance market. The response of the market has been, firstly, to exclude pollution cover from CGL policies altogether, often, but not invariably, subject to an exception in relation to liability arising from an event that is both sudden and accidental (and/or "unintended and unexpected"), and secondly to try to re-write policies on a claims made basis. The issues that an insured must accordingly consider in relation to any CGL policy are:

(i) What event must occur, and when, to trigger liability?
(ii) Is it limited to "sudden and accidental" or similar events, and if so what does this mean?

1082

(iii) What liabilities are covered by the policy, and what are excluded, either by virtue of the contract terms or as a matter of general law?

Mention should be made also of Environmental Impairment Liabi-   **25–005**
lity (EIL) policies. As the standard CGL policies are concerned with liability to third parties, they provide no cover in respect of pollution damage to the insured's own property, at least where this does not in turn cause damage to any third party. Nevertheless, the consequences of leakage or a spill of a toxic substance on an insured's own site may well need to be dealt with, possibly at substantial expense, both to ensure that there is no polluting run-off to surface waters or pollution of groundwater, and also to avoid health risks to those on the site. EIL policies provide cover against such eventualities. However since the risk of a claim depends greatly on the activities undertaken on a site and the competence of the management in charge of it, and since the costs of dealing with a major problem are likely to be very large but nevertheless unpredictable, insurers are understandably reluctant to provide cover against them. Those that are offered are virtually all written on a claims made basis.

Though a number of insurers offer EIL policies, they are generally   **25–006**
subject to there being a satisfactory survey of a site in advance of it coming on cover, and the extent of cover is often subject to a maximum that may well be inadequate if a major problem were to occur. The premiums for these policies have been high, by historical standards at least; to a considerable degree, this is attributable to uncertainty as to the extent of clean up costs that might be required, due to the lack of any definitive clean up standards applying in the United Kingdom. Any new EIL policy will ordinarily specifically exclude liability for events occurring prior to the date of the policy—it will be a matter for interpretation as to whether this excludes from cover, for example, leaks that were in existence but unknown before the start of the policy.

The Duty of Disclosure

It is a cardinal feature of insurance that it is a contract of utmost good   **25–007**
faith (*uberrimae fides*), requiring a full disclosure by a person seeking insurance cover of all material facts relevant to the risk that the insurer is being asked to take on. Any material non-disclosure will entitle the insurer to avoid the entire policy *ab initio*. This requirement almost certainly extends to matters which, in the ordinary course of business ought to be known to the insured, whether he is in fact aware of them

1083

or not.[1] Given the degree of publicity and official concern now devoted to contaminated land and its avoidance, the efforts to locate and prevent pollution that would now be regarded as reasonable to expect as a matter of business prudence are likely to be quite substantial—the burden on a person seeking insurance to establish all material facts is correspondingly heavy. Accordingly if the insured has, or should reasonably have, knowledge of relevant facts, particularly where these are activities deliberately undertaken in the course of business, for example the dumping or storage of toxic wastes in circumstances that may give rise to a hazard, and has failed to disclose these, he may have no protection against the consequences of such activities. This obligation is a continuing one, and will apply in particular on each renewal; any relevant change in circumstances must always be promptly disclosed.

The Pollution Exclusion—"Sudden and Accidental" Events

25–008   Since April 1991, virtually all United Kingdom CGL policies have excluded liability for pollution damage except to the extent that it arises from events that are unintended, unexpected, sudden and accidental, though this particular form of words will not necessarily always be employed in full. Thus one Lloyds form of wording excludes cover in respect of:

> "Personal injury . . . or damage to . . . property directly or indirectly caused by seepage, pollution or contamination . . . [except] where such seepage, pollution or contamination is caused by a sudden unintended and unexpected happening during the period of this insurance".[2]

Another form[3] omits the exception and so is comprehensive in its exclusion of pollution cover.

25–009   It is trite law that insurance is only available in respect of fortuitous events, and not those that are intended. The difficulty with defining what is an "accident" is that in many cases the normal operation of a business inherently gives rise to some degree of risk that things will go wrong, even if this is in most cases quite small. In a leading Australian case[4] an insurer's liability to pay compensation "arising out of an

---

[1] *cf.* Marine Insurance Act 1906, s.18(1).
[2] N.M.A. 1685.
[3] N.M.A. 1686.
[4] *AFG Robinson v. Evans Bros. Pty Ltd*, (1969) VR 885.

accident" was held to be an indemnity for "unexpected and unintended damage occurring as a result of a deliberate act". Thus it was the quality of the damage that had to be unexpected and unintended, and not the act that caused it. The test was whether ordinary, reasonable and sensible men in the position of the responsible officers of the defendant would or would not have expected the occurrence.

In a subsequent case in the New Zealand Court of Appeal[5] it was held that there could be a category of cases falling short of the deliberate causing of damage by an insured, where his conduct was nevertheless so hazardous and culpable that the event the subject of the claim could not be called an accident. It was also held that it was not decisive that the risk may have been deliberately run or calculated, and that if what was done was reasonably seen as not a high risk, the occurrence might still be found to be an accident. (It is of note that in that case, it was doubted whether the test as to whether the defendant would or would not have expected the eventual outcome was a subjective rather than an objective one).

25–010

Much litigation in the United States has turned on whether, where an intentional act has led to damage, the damage itself can properly be said to be intended, and so outside the scope of the otherwise applicable policy insuring the ensuing liability. As always, the precise words of the policy are critical, but the general approach in environmental cases in the United States has been to exclude liability for damage where this is itself intended or expected, or is simply reasonably foreseeable from intended or conscious acts or omissions in the part of senior management which could reasonably have been expected by them, having regard to the nature and circumstances of such acts or omissions. In English cases, the line is usually drawn between giving cover for purely negligent acts, having regard to what is foreseeable as a consequence, and denying it for those that are reckless (or of course intentional).

25–011

What is properly "negligent", "unexpected and unintended" or "foreseeable" can be far from straightforward to establish. It will be a question of construction as to whether negligence by an insured's employee is to be regarded as negligence by the employer. In civil proceedings, the employer will ordinarily have vicarious liability; in criminal proceedings by contrast, the relevant state of mind must be that of those who are entrusted with the exercise of the powers of the company, ordinarily in practice the directors. One issue may be whether the negligence, if this can be shown, must necessarily be such as to lead to the kind of damage that is the subject of the claim, or

25–012

[5] *Mount Albert City Council v. NZ Municipalities Co-operative Insurance Co. Ltd.* [1983] N.Z. L.R. 190 at 194.

whether any negligence will suffice to exclude cover even though the damage that ensued was not reasonably foreseeable from a negligent act of that particular type. A further question is whether negligence is to be judged by some objective neutral standard, or whether it is to relate to the behaviour of the particular insured. An objective standard is in practice the more likely, but again all will depend on the policy wording.

25–013   "Foreseeability" raises very similar issues as regards who might be expected to foresee the consequences of an intended act, and the nature of the damage that this may give rise to. If it is not to be determined by the prescience of the person who performed the damaging operation, then whose ability to foresee is relevant? It might be that of the company's board if a subjective test is applied, or that of an independent man "skilled in the art" if the test is to be objective. A standard "known danger" clause in Australia excludes coverage for impairments "of which the Insured as a reasonable practitioner in the business activities conducted by it was or should have been aware at the inception date of the policy".

22–014   Although "sudden" and "accidental" are regularly bracketed to-gether in insurance language, these expressions relate to quite distinct concepts. In applying these concepts, it is of course essential to have regard to the nature of the insured "event" that must be sudden and accidental. The fracture of a pipe may be sudden but, if it is merely a crack rather than a break, any leakage from it may be quite slight and the resulting pollution essentially gradual. Conversely, the crack in a pipe may have become progressively more advanced over a consider-able time, but pollution resulting from liquids escaping through it may have first arisen seriously as a result of an abnormal amount of liquid being passed down the pipe, or maybe following an obstruction creating pressure within it.

25–015   The first question to be determined is what insured "events" are provided with cover. Policy wording may well treat as an "event" the occurrence of some physical defect, such as the fracture of a pipe, rather than the manifestation of this fracture, for example consequent pollution of a nearby stream, or any actual damage to property or personal injury of any third party. The "event" may therefore be completely unknown to the insured for many years—consequently it may be impossible to pin-point with any precision just when the event did occur, and hence which one of a series of policies applies to it.

25–016   What amounts to an insured "event", "occurrence" or "happening" may prove hard to determine. In a typical situation, an underground pipe or tank may spring a leak on a particular day, perhaps as a result of some mechanical shock such as a heavy vehicle passing over a pipe. The leak may not be observed however for a considerable period, and in the meantime may cause widespread contamination underground. Even after the problem has become apparent, there may not be any actual damage caused until a further period has elapsed, for example when the contamination reaches a stream or when a neighbour is impelled to incur expense to protect or clean up his property. The "event" within the cover of the policy may therefore be the initial, unobserved leak, or it may be when the problem is (or, arguably, should have been) first observed, or when actual damage of a type covered by the policy is suffered.[6] Where, as is common, the policy is part of a composite employer's liability insurance, covering, for example, product liability and employer's and occupier's liabilities, using the same insurance clause throughout, any construction of it must necessarily take into account its application to these other types of liability also. In some cases, the event and the damage are substantially simultaneous, but in others, such as in product liability, there can be many years between the relevant act (*e.g.* a sale or supply) by the insured and the subsequent damage.

One of the most relevant English cases in this regard is *Kelly v. Norwich Union Fire Insurance Society Ltd.*[7] In this case, a home insurance policy running from October 29, 1977 to October 28, 1978 provided for an indemnity in respect of loss or damage to the building caused by (*inter alia*) "bursting or overflowing of . . . pipes (forming part of the domestic fixed water system)" . . . and "landslip or subsidence of the site on which the building stands". It was found as a fact that the mains pipe leading to the house burst in the summer of 1977, before the insurance company was on risk. (There were also subsequent leaks which served to complicate the case, but the evidence as to their effect was inconclusive). This burst caused a prolonged discharge of water before it was repaired, which in turn led to "heave" (the opposite of subsidence) of the previously dried out clay subsoil, eventually causing damage to the house during the period of the insurance. The question before the court was whether there was an insured event during the period of cover—it was held that there was not. The indemnity was not in respect of damage caused during the policy term, but in respect of loss or damage caused by any "insured perils", such as bursting pipes or subsidence, that occur during the policy term. Since heave is not subsidence, the plaintiff could only rely on the reference to bursting of pipes, and this had occurred before the policy began. The fact that the resulting damage only manifested itself later, during the policy term, was irrelevant.

25–017

---

[6] These liability "triggers" are referred to as "exposure", "manifestation" and "injury-in-fact", respectively.
[7] C.A. [1989] 2 All E.R. 888.

The Meaning of "Damage"

25–018 Even where an insured peril is established to have occurred during the policy term, the insured is generally only entitled to recover under a CGL policy in respect of "damage" to third parties on their property for which he is liable. Depending on the precise wording of the policy, he may therefore not be able to recover in respect of remedial costs incurred by a regulatory authority, which are payable by him under statute, *e.g.* the statutory nuisance provisions of the E.P.A. or section 161 of the Water Resources Act 1991, even in situations where the standard "owned property" exclusion does not apply. *A fortiori*, he will not be able to recover in respect of costs incurred voluntarily by him in doing work that would otherwise be done by the regulatory authority and charged to him, at least in the absence of his insurer's consent. Where a policy is in respect of liabilities arising from damage to a third party, the issue may arise as to whether clean up costs incurred by the third party are properly "damages" suffered by him or merely economic loss, in the absence of any other physical injury to persons or property.[8]

25–019 "Damages", as used in collision clauses in marine insurance, has been held to be limited to a liability arising from a fault of some kind on the part of the ship insured (though not necessarily an act that would be an actionable tort in English law). Thus, in such clauses, "damages" does not include liabilities arising in contract[9] or under statute.[10] Nevertheless, the importance of construing a clause in its context is evident from the judgment of Sir Wilfred Greene M.R. in *Hall v. Young*. His analysis starts by saying:

> "Damages", to an English lawyer, imports the idea that the sums payable by way of damages are sums which fall to be paid by reason of some breach of duty or obligation, whether that duty or obligation is imposed by contract, by the general law, or by legislation." [11]

However, in the context of the clause in question, the term was to be understood much more restrictively, and excluded sums payable under contract or pursuant to legislation.

25–020 Even where clean up costs are recoverable under a policy, attention must be given to just which of these costs are recoverable. It may be that only the immediate costs of removing the contaminants or

---

[8] See, *e.g. Merlin et al. v. British Nuclear Fuels plc*, [1990] 2 Q.B. 557; [1990] 3 W.L.R. 383; [1990] 3 All E.R. 711.
[9] *Furness Withy & Co Ltd v. Duder* [1936] 2 K.B. 461; [1936] 2 All E.R. 119.
[10] *Hall Brothers SS Co. Ltd v. Young, The Trident* C.A. [1939] 1 All E.R. 809.
[11] [1939] 1 All E.R. at p. 814A.

contaminated soil off the site are covered, or the costs of treating the contamination *in situ*. Without express provision, the policy will not necessarily give cover for the actual transport of contaminated soil away from the site or for the eventual disposal or other treatment of the contaminated soil off-site.

Where pollution has resulted in damage to the unowned environ- **25–021** ment, most probably ground water, but also flora and fauna and other natural features, this will plainly not in itself be third party damage, unless the term has been so defined as to extend at least to the remedial costs incurred by a regulator. This may in practice prove to be highly unsatisfactory, given that the European Commission's Green Paper "Remedying Environmental Damage" canvassed the possibility of there being liability for damage to the unowned environment, and also that the Council of Europe Convention on environmental liability (which the United Kingdom has not ratified) expressly provides for there to be liability for damage to the unowned environment. Indeed one of the issues that the Green Paper discussed was the need for industrial operators to have some kind of insurance cover for the liabilities it was considering, since otherwise imposing them could turn out to be a waste of time.

Exclusion Clauses

Modern forms of policy are likely to contain a variety of express **25–022** exclusions, including the following:

(i) Gradual Pollution
As indicated above, cover for incidents that are not sudden and accidental is now in practice excluded from CGL policies—only certain EIL policies are designed to cover them. On the reasoning of *Kelly*, discussed in paragraph 25–017, the availability of cover may however turn, not on whether any pollution was itself gradual or sudden, but whether the event that caused it, such as the fracture of a pipe, was sudden and accidental.

(ii) Owned Property
A public liability policy will contain an "owned property" exclusion, since it is only designed to cover liabilities to third parties. Where the principal source of damage to a third party's property is contamination moving from the insured's own land, the most appropriate technical solution will usually be to clean up the source of pollution. However the costs of this will generally not be covered by a public liability policy, though of course if that were to

be the cheapest option it may well be possible to agree a deal with the insurers, having regard to the insured's duty to avert and minimise losses. A typical exclusion may relate to property "that has at any material time been owned or occupied by the insured" — given the multitude of ways in which one person may obtain a licence to or an easement over the property of another, this inevitably raises questions as to just what forms of ownership and occupation are covered.

Since there is no property in groundwater, it has been argued in a number of cases in the USA that pollution of the groundwater as it percolates through the insured's site is outside the "owned property" exclusion, with different results in different jurisdictions. While English courts might be expected to take the view that parties would not have intended to treat the groundwater percolating through a site differently from the site itself, applying the *contra proferentem* principle would normally result in an exclusion clause being construed narrowly against the insurer seeking to rely on it.

(iii) Fines

In English law, criminal penalties cannot, as a matter of public policy, be covered by insurance. Whether administrative penalties, as may be imposed in other jurisdictions, are covered may, on occasion, need to be reviewed.

(iv) Unlawful Acts

Where a policy excludes liability in respect of anything that represents non-compliance with the law, this may in practice deny the insured of virtually any effective cover, since almost certainly any pollution that has injured the property of a third party is likely to be an unlawful deposit of waste, a statutory nuisance (which is quasi-criminal in nature), or pollution of "controlled waters". Indeed, virtually any damage caused by waste is likely to be a breach of the duty of care imposed by section 34 of the E.P.A. An exclusion of this kind must therefore be treated with great caution.

To avoid this excessive restriction on cover, it is quite common for this exclusion to be framed by reference to the insured's "intentional, wilful or deliberate non-compliance with [relevant legislation]". In criminal proceedings for "knowingly permitting" a polluting activity, the question has arisen on occasion as to the exact extent of the knowledge that the defendant must have. For example, in *Ashcroft v Cambro Waste Products Limited*[12] it was held that it was only necessary for the prosecution to prove knowledge

---

[12] [1981] 1 W.L.R. 1349; [1981] 3 All E.R. 699, see para. 11–134.

1090

of the deposit, but not of the breach of condition. Thus an insurer seeking to argue that there had been deliberate non-compliance with relevant waste legislation might, arguably, find it sufficient to assert simply that a deposit had been deliberate, which in the event proved either to be unlicensed at all, or outside the terms of such licences there might be. Even if it were to be held that the exclusion only applied where the relevant company both knew of the deposit and that there was either no licence at all or such licence as there may have been had conditions which did not permit that deposit, the question arises as to whether that knowledge must be all in the mind of a single individual, or whether it is sufficient for the exclusion to apply for one person to know of the deposit and another to be aware of the licence issues. As with "accidental", the question also arises as to whether the relevant individuals, where an an exclusion requires an act that is intentional, wilful or deliberate must be a director or other person of comparable standing, or whether any employee, at least where he has some authority, will suffice.

(v) Professional Fees

Legal fees, at least those incurred by the insured, and similarly fees of technical consultants retained by the insured, will frequently be excluded, unless a specific extension to the policy is negotiated to cover these.

Claims against an Insolvent Insured

Where a person (including a company) has a claim made against **25–023** him that is within the scope of an insurance policy held by him, then if he subsequently becomes bankrupt or, in the case of a company, is wound up or has a receiver appointed, and in certain other circumstances, the claimant may proceed against the insurers directly, under the Third Parties (Rights against Insurers) Act 1930, s.1. This right is however not available if the claimant's right of action against the insured has not yet crystallised at the time of the insolvency.[13]

Directors' and Officers' Liability

Finally, as referred to in more detail in Chapter 21, directors and **25–024** other company officers may be held potentially liable, both criminally

---

[13] *Bradley v. Eagle Star Insurance Co. Ltd* H.L., [1989] All E.R. 961.

and civilly, for polluting acts of their companies. Likewise, administrators, receivers and liquidators may all be held legally liable for the
acts of companies with which they are involved in that capacity.
Personal insurance is generally available to protect them from civil
liabilities. However criminal penalties cannot generally be insured
against, though legal costs associated with defending a criminal
prosecution may be.[14] A company may pay for such insurance for its
directors by virtue of section 310(3)(a) of the Companies Act 1985. It
may also give certain indemnities in relation to liabilities arising in
legal proceedings, but only those in which the director is acquitted or
receives judgment in his favour.[15]

---

[14] The policy will usually exclude liability for legal costs of defending a charge on which
the insured is found guilty. Where a personal defendant needs legal costs to be
advanced to him in the course of litigation, this may lead to his being under an
obligation to pay them back if he is convicted. Nevertheless, the practice of insurers
appears to be not to require this.
[15] Companies Act 1985, s.310(3)(b)(i). If indemnities of any substantial width are to be
granted, care must be taken to avoid contravention of s. 310(1) of the 1985 Act.

Chapter 26

Environmental Management Systems and Audits

If a business operation is to be conducted in compliance with   **26–001**
environmental legislation, its management must, as a minimum, be
sufficiently aware of all the legislation that is relevant to it, and also of
all its activities that may (however remote the risk) give rise to a
breach. It is then a function of the management to institute suitable
systems, including education and training of the workforce, to extend
that awareness as comprehensively as may be necessary to ensure that
all appropriate precautions are taken to prevent a breach, and to
minimise the environmental consequences of any breach that may
nevertheless occur. For an increasing number of businesses, however,
an objective of mere legal compliance is simply a pre-requisite; many
have additionally found extensive scope for modifying the manner in
which their operations are conducted so as to reduce, and eventually
minimise, their impact on the environment, and at the same time save
money through eliminating wasteful practices.[1] The necessary first
step to achieve this is a review of the activities by reference to their
environmental impacts. Such reviews have been termed "audits" by
analogy with the audits of a firm's accounts, though the comparison is
not exact, in view of the impossibility of measuring environmental
impacts with the same degree of precision. Such audits are quite
distinct from those carried out when acquiring a property, which
are liable to be concerned solely with the condition of the land and
buildings, important though this information may be. They are
designed to provide information for a management that has devised
an environmental policy for its operations, so that it can assess the
extent to which its policy is being successfully implemented and
whether targets for environmental improvement are being met.

Audits may thus be carried out not only of compliance with   **26–002**
applicable legislation, but also in relation to such matters as raw

---

[1] One of the pioneers of this approach was the 3M Company that adopted the 3P
principle: Pollution Prevention Pays.

materials usage, energy consumption, waste production, packaging and transport. In addition, since the environmental impact of an organisation's operations is not confined to what it does directly, but also what it arranges for others to do on its behalf, similar audits may also be conducted of the activities of suppliers and of sub-contractors. In appropriate cases, an audit may also cover the environmental impacts of the products of an organisation, with a view to their redesign and/or re-formulation as appropriate. The considerations applicable to a product audit tie in very closely with those relevant to the grant of an eco-label, discussed in the next chapter.

26–003 There has been an increasing tendency for companies to refer in their annual reports to the responses that they have made to environmental concerns, but in the absence of any clear targets or of independent verification of the extent to which environmental objectives have been achieved, claims, however legitimate, of sound or improved environmental performance are liable to be met with some reservation.[2] There are thus two quite distinct needs. Firstly, a need for some consistent and independently verified system for assessing claims of environmental performance. Secondly, and probably more importantly, there would be a clear benefit to organisations in having clear guidelines to work to in setting up environmental management systems, so that they can establish and implement environmental policies in an effective manner, using the information as a management tool, quite independently of any publicity that the management may or may not choose to give to the organisation's environmental performance.

26–004 As part of its broad strategy to use other means in addition to command and control regulation to bring about improved environmental performance, the European Commission has devised what it now refers to as a "Community eco-management and audit scheme" (commonly known as "EMAS"), the subject of EC Regulation No. 1836/93.[3] The Regulation is expressed to come into force on July 13, 1993, but the substantive provisions described in this chapter first

---

[2] The significance of amounts of money said to be spent on environmental protection is notoriously open to dispute. Thus, a figure may be quoted that represents the entire capital cost of a new facility; while this may replace some, possibly more polluting operation, the expenditure may quite possibly have been prompted by other purely commercial considerations. Conversely, another organisation may refer to costs incurred on end-of-pipe pollution abatement facilities, but not include any sums in relation to a totally new, environmentally more desirable facility, that has no need for any end-of-pipe treatment at all. Figures for expenditure on effluent treatment on site may be quite properly claimed, but this may not lead to any better environmental performance overall, and possibly a worse return on assets, than a competitor who pays fees to the sewerage undertaker to treat trade effluent at the sewage treatment plant.

[3] [1993] O.J. L168.

apply on April 10, 1995.[4] Initially, the Commission intended that adoption of this scheme should be compulsory for a fairly wide range of industrial activities, so as to ensure that the managements concerned paid appropriate attention to environmental matters. However the argument prevailed that if the scheme was to be an effective management tool, and not merely an imposed procedural burden, it should be voluntary, albeit with incentives to encourage managements to seek to implement it. At essentially the same time as the EMAS Regulation was being developed, the United Kingdom British Standards Institution was developing a specification for environmental management systems as the basis for British Standard BS7750, this being itself a development from the quality systems standard BS5750 (also EN 29000, ISO 9000). A work on environmental law is not the place to treat in detail the management issues raised by the EMAS Regulation and BS7750, and the rest of this chapter accordingly briefly reviews the aims of and the rights available under the Regulation, and the procedures required if they are to be achieved.

The objective of the scheme established by the EMAS Regulation is to promote continuous improvements in the environmental performance of industrial activities by: **26–005**

    (a) the establishment and implementation of environmental policies, programmes and management systems by companies, in relation to their sites;

    (b) the systematic, objective and periodic evaluation of the performance of such elements; and

    (c) the provision of information of environmental performance to the public.[5]

The Regulation provides for the registration of sites on which industrial activities are carried out where these have in place the necessary elements of the scheme, including in particular an environmental policy, an environmental management system, and a periodic environmental audit. Where compliance with the scheme is established and independently verified, companies may use in relation to such sites as have been registered a formal statement of participation in the scheme (in prescribed terms and in a layout including the well known EC symbol of twelve stars in the form of a ring), as set out in Annex IV to the Regulation. Such a statement may not however be used to advertise products or on the products themselves or on their **26–006**

---

[4] Being 21 months after publication of the regulation in the Official Journal (Art. 21).
[5] Art. 1(2).

packaging.[6] It may of course be used to promote the reputation of the company itself, typically at the relevant site(s), and in the company's annual reports and other literature.

26–007   The scheme is open to companies undertaking an "industrial activity", a term that is defined as being any activity listed under sections C and D of the classification of economic activities in the European Community (NACE Rev.1). This classification, devised for statistical purposes, is set out in Regulation No. 3037/90.[7] Sections C and D relate to mining and quarrying and to manufacturing, respectively. Among the activities excluded are those concerned with agriculture, hunting, forestry and fishing (sections A and B), the production and distribution of electricity, the manufacture and distribution of gas and the collection, purification and distribution of water (section E), construction and demolition activities (section F), the wholesale and retail trades, and transport, storage and communications (sections G and I), and service activities generally, including in particular washing and dry cleaning of textile and fur products (in section O). Any member state may, however, apply the provisions of the scheme to sectors other than those of sections C and D on an experimental basis.[8]

26–008   The essential elements of the scheme are set out in Article 3 of the regulation, and consist of the following matters.

(1) A Company Environmental Policy

A company environmental policy must be adopted that includes as a minimum requirement compliance with all relevant regulatory requirements regarding the environment. It must further include commitments to reasonable continuous improvement of environmental performance, with a view to reducing environmental impacts to levels not exceeding those corresponding to the economically viable application of best available technology. The policy must be periodically reviewed at the highest management level, having regard in particular to the periodic environmental audits that have to be carried out, and revised as appropriate. The policy must be communicated to the company's personnel and be made publicly available.

Among the issues that must be addressed within the policy[9] are: the assessment, control and reduction of the environmental impacts of the activity; energy; raw materials; water usage; waste

---

[6] Art. 10(3).
[7] [1990] O.J. L293.
[8] Art. 14.
[9] Set out in Section C of Annex I to the Regulation.

(avoidance, recycling, re-use, transportation and disposal); noise; products (design, packaging, transportation, use and disposal); contractors, sub-contractors and suppliers; prevention and limitation of environmental accidents and contingency procedures; information and training for the workforce; and information to the general public, including the local community, on environmental issues.

The company's environmental policy must be based on good management practices (set out in section D of Annex I). These must include regular checking on the company's activities to establish that they are in fact consistent with these good management practices and with that of continual improvement in environmental performance. Among the measures that must be adopted are the fostering of a sense of responsibility for the environment amongst employees at all levels, assessing and monitoring the environmental impact of current and proposed future activities, the conservation of resources, monitoring procedures to check compliance with the environmental policy and action to be taken where non-compliance is shown, and ensuring that contractors working at the company's site on its behalf apply environmental standards equivalent to that of the company.

An essential part of the policy is the specifying of the company's environmental objectives at all relevant levels within the company. Wherever practicable there must be measurable targets devised to achieve the continual improvement in environmental performance over defined time-scales — the selection of appropriate measurable parameters, and setting suitable targets, is at the heart of any policy aimed at improvement in environmental performance.

(2) Environmental Review
An environmental review of the relevant site must be carried out that covers all the matters that the policy must address as set out in (1) above.

(3) Environmental Programme
An environmental programme for the site must be developed that has regard to the results of the environmental review, together with an environmental management system applicable to all activities at the site. The essential contents of an environmental management system are set out extensively in section B of Annex I to the regulation, and relate to the establishment and periodical review and revision of the environmental policy, and its objectives and programmes, at the highest management level, the definition

1097

and documentation of responsibilities within the company, including in particular (which in practice is a vital element) the appointment of a management representative who has authority and responsibility for ensuring that the management system is implemented and maintained. The management system must involve communication within the work force and training of it, evaluation of all the environmental effects of the company's activities and registering those that are identified as significant. Detailed operating procedures must be established of all activities that may affect the environment, including in particular appropriate planning and control of these, coupled with the setting of performance criteria. It is common experience that management systems are often set up with the best of intentions but fail over time, because attention to other matters that may appear more pressing in the short term, such as customer and cost considerations, leads to their neglect. It is therefore absolutely vital that an effective management system includes procedures for monitoring the performance of the company in meeting the requirements established by its policy and, equally important, the taking of corrective action where non-compliance is found. Finally, the management practices must include, in addition to the constant monitoring features, a system of periodic environmental audits of compliance of the activities and procedures with the company's environmental policy and programme.

(4) Periodic Environmental Audits

Environmental audits must be conducted on a regular basis in accordance with the requirements of Article 4. They may be handled either internally, by employees of the company, or by external advisors. The audits must address the policy matters referred to in (1) above, and comply with the requirements of Annex II to the Regulation. The audit must include in particular:

(a) an understanding of the management systems that are intended to be in operation;
(b) an assessment of the strengths and weaknesses of these;
(c) a gathering of relevant evidence;
(d) an evaluation of the audit findings;
(e) the preparation of audit conclusions;
(f) a report on the audit findings and the conclusions.

The report must go to the top company management, and among other things must provide it with information on the state of compliance with the company's environmental policy, and on the effectiveness and reliability of the arrangements for monitoring environmental impact at the relevant site. An essential element of the audit process is the preparation and implementation of a plan of appropriate corrective action, where needed, including mechanisms for ensuring that this corrective action is in fact effectively implemented. Audits must be carried out at intervals of at most three years. However shorter periods may be desirable, and must be set by top company management having regard to the potential overall environmental impact of the activities at the site, including in particular reference to the nature, scale and complexity of these activities, the nature and scale of emissions, waste, raw material and energy consumption, the importance and urgency of problems that have been detected in any initial review or the latest audit, and the history of environmental problems at the site.

(5) Objectives for Continuous Improvement
Objectives are to be set at the highest appropriate management level, aimed at continuous improvement of environmental performance in the light of the findings of the most recent audit. There must also be appropriate revision of the environmental programme as needed to enable the set objectives to be achieved.

(6) Environmental Statement
A distinctive feature of the Regulation is its requirement for an environmental statement specific to the site audited. This statement is to be made available to the public and must be designed for its use, and so be written in a concise and comprehensible form. The use of complex technical material is not excluded, but this is likely to be most appropriately included as an Annex. The statement is prepared on the basis of the initial environmental review of the site, and a new statement will be made following each audit of the site. Where there are several sites being audited in turn as part of an audit cycle, a full statement covering all the sites is required only once for each audit cycle. When audits are carried out at intervals of two or more years, simplified environmental statements are to be prepared in intervening years, summarizing figures on pollutant emissions, waste generation, consumption of raw material, energy and water, noise and other significant environmental aspects, as appropriate. The full details of information that must be included in these environmental statements are set out in Article 5; in addition, the first environmental statement must also cover the matters listed in Annex V to the Regulation.

(7) Verification
The environmental policy, programme, management system, review or audit procedure, and the environmental statement or

statements must all be verified by an accredited environmental verifier. The verifier must be independent both of the company operating the site and of the person carrying out the environmental audit of that site. The full requirements regarding the accreditation of environmental verifiers and their functions are set out in Annex III. Verifiers may be either individuals or organisations, and must be competent, in terms of qualifications, training and experience in relation to at least environmental auditing methodologies, management information and processes, environmental issues, relevant legislation and standards, including in particular guidance issued for the purposes of the regulation, and relevant technical knowledge of the activity carried out on the site concerned.

Verifiers must be accredited, and their activities supervised by a system established by each member state in accordance with Article 6. The United Kingdom government has announced that the National Accreditation Council for Certification Bodies (NACCB) will perform this role within the UK. The accreditation bodies in each of the member states are to establish, revise and update the list of accredited environmental verifiers in their respective countries, and provide this list to the Commission every six months. The Commission is required to publish an overall Community list of accredited environmental verifiers in the Official Journal.[10] Environmental verifiers accredited in any one member state may perform verification activities in any other. In that event, however they must give prior notice to the relevant accreditation body of the other Member State, and be subject to its supervision.

The environmental verifier must check on the following matters:[11]

(a) whether the environmental policy has been established and meets the requirements laid down in the regulation;
(b) whether an environmental management system and programme are in place and operation at the site, and whether they comply with the requirements of the regulation;
(c) whether the environmental review and audit have been carried out in accordance with the regulation;
(d) whether the data and information in the environmental statement are reliable, and whether the statement adequately

---

[10] Art. 7.
[11] Art. 4(5).

covers all the significant environmental issues of relevance at the site.[12]

Where the verifier is satisfied with regard to all the above matters, he will validate the environmental statement. Where he has any reservation only in relation to the statement itself (or in relation to an intervening statement made between audits), he must only validate the statement when it has been suitably amended or amplified by the company. Where the verifier is not satisfied in relation to the substantive matters of the environmental policy, the review or audit, the environmental programme or the environmental management system, the statement will not of course be validated, and he must make appropriate recommendations to the company's management on the improvements needed. It is only after the identified defects have been corrected and the procedures repeated so far as is necessary that the verifier will validate the then resulting statement.[13]

There has been considerable concern expressed as to the amount of work that a verifier will undertake, since the verification process could quite easily extend to a substantial repetition of the most recent audit. It is expressly stated[14] that the verifier will carry out his investigation without unnecessarily duplicating the environmental review audit or any other procedures carried out by the company, but it remains to be seen how far this can be done satisfactorily without what may be regarded by the companies concerned as excessive cost, leading to their deciding not to participate in the scheme.

(8) Registration of Site(s)
The validated environmental statement is submitted to the relevant competent body of the Member State where the site is located, and disseminated to the public in that State after registration of the site. In the United Kingdom, the Department of the Environment has been designated as the competent body for these purposes.[15] It will maintain a register of all sites that meet the requirements of the Regulation, and up-date it annually. Where there has been a breach of relevant regulatory requirements regarding the environment at any site, the competent body must, if it is informed of this

---

[12] By considering whether the company policy and programme are in compliance with the regulation, the verifier goes beyond what is required of him under BS7750, where the appropriateness of the company policy is a matter exclusively for the company's management.
[13] Annex III, s.B.4.
[14] In Annex III, s.B.1.
[15] DoE News Release 293, May 10, 1994.

by the relevant enforcement authority, either refuse registration of that site or, where it is already registered, suspend the registration. This action may be lifted, but only when the competent body has received satisfactory assurances from the enforcement authority that the breach has been rectified and that satisfactory arrangements are in place to ensure it does not recur.[16] The competent bodies of the various member states are required to inform the Commission for the end of each year of their lists of registered sites, together with any updating information, and the Commission is to publish all this information in the Official Journal.

To avoid unnecessary duplication of effort, where there are other standards for environmental management systems and audits and their certification, these standards and procedures may be recognised by the Commission in accordance with a procedure laid down by Article 19. Where this is the case, and the certification is undertaken by an accredited body in the relevant Member State, this will be treated as complying with the requirements of the Regulation. In all cases, however, the companies concerned must meet the requirements regarding the environmental statement and its validation as set out in Articles 3, 5 and 8 of the Regulation and described in outline above.[17]

26–009   Whether the scheme will be widely adopted remains very much an open question. Inevitably there is a risk that it may place excessive demands on a company's management such that only a very small percentage of all companies, being those already strongly committed to environmental protection, will consider it worthwhile. Unless there is relatively widespread take up of the scheme, a company that fails to register its sites under it will suffer no significant competitive disadvantage, and may well consider that it can handle its environmental concerns more cheaply and less publicly, for example, by following the procedures of the Regulation privately and on a more informal basis—possibly, but not necessarily, through complying with BS 7750. There are also considerable practical problems in establishing the scheme initially, in view of the need to create from a very small base a substantial body of accredited verifiers throughout the EC. Significant participation in the scheme seems likely to be gradual at best, and strongly dependent on the extent to which it is adopted by market leaders, so creating both social pressures on their competitors and also market pressures on the suppliers to and contractors with those in the scheme.

[16] Art. 8(4).
[17] Art. 12.

Chapter 27

Eco-Labelling

As consumers have become more environmentally conscious, they   27–001
have sought to discriminate between those products that are "environmentally friendly" and those that are less so or not at all. The
difficulty that they have had to face has been the tendency of some
manufacturers to try to capitalise on this market demand by claiming
that their products are environmentally friendly, without there being
necessarily any scientific basis for this, whether in absolute terms or by
comparison with other competitive products. A completely fictitious
claim of this nature would be likely to be actionable as a false trade
description under the Trade Descriptions Act 1968, but where there
are some beneficial properties, and all adverse properties are shared
with the great majority at least of competitive products, then as the
law currently stands it is unlikely that any offence would be
committed by an "environmentally friendly" claim. Indeed it is in the
consumers' interests (and those of the environment) that, where
products are genuinely to be preferred on environmental grounds,
this characteristic can be advertised.

A combination of approaches exist or are being developed to deal   27–002
with these concerns, namely:

— legally binding prohibitions on false, including misleading,
trade descriptions and advertisements;
— codes of advertising practice restraining unsubstantiated
claims;
— eco-label awards for products meeting prescribed standards;
— informative labelling.

The Trade Descriptions Act 1968

The Trade Descriptions Act 1968 makes it an offence to apply a false   27–003
trade description to any goods or to supply or to offer to supply any

goods to which a false trade description is applied.[1] A trade description is defined[2] as an indication, direct or indirect, and by whatever means given of any of the following matters with respect to any goods or parts of goods, that is to say:

(a) quantity, size or gauge;
(b) method of manufacture, production, processing or reconditioning;
(c) composition;
(d) fitness for purpose, strength, performance, behaviour or accuracy;
(e) any physical characteristics not included in the preceding paragraphs;
(f) testing by any person and results thereof;
(g) approval by any person or conformity with a type approved by any person;
(h) place or date of manufacture, production, processing or reconditioning;
(i) person by whom manufactured, produced, processed or reconditioned;
(j) other history, including previous ownership or use.

27–004 At least (b), (c) and (d) may well be matters that would be relevant to a claim that a product is "environmentally friendly". For a trade description to be false, it is sufficient that it is merely misleading, *i.e.* that it is likely to be taken for an indication of any of the matters just listed that would be false to a material degree.[3] However, except where an "environmental" claim is couched in terms that are plainly wrong, proof that it is false, within the meaning of section 3 of the Trade Descriptions Act would require the leading of a substantial amount of evidence that could itself be open to considerable challenge. Trading Standards Officers have reason therefore to be reluctant to prosecute such general claims under the Act, even though prosecutions might well be justified in certain cases.

27–005 The Control of Misleading Advertisements Regulations 1988[4] reinforce the powers available under the Trade Descriptions Act. They implement Directive 84/450[5] and provide for complaints regarding misleading advertisements to be made to the Director General of Fair

---

[1] s.1(1).
[2] In s.2(1).
[3] s.3(2).
[4] S.I. 1988 No. 915, amended by the Broadcasting Act 1990, Sched. 20, para. 51(3) and Sched. 21.
[5] [1984] O.J. L250.

Trading, the Independent Television Commission, the Welsh Authority and to the Radio Authority. All of these bodies have a duty to consider any such complaints unless a complaint appears to them to be frivolous or vexatious. The Director General of Fair Trading has the further power to apply to the court for an injunction to restrain publication of an advertisement that he considers to be misleading; the injunction may relate not only to a particular advertisement, but to any advertisement in similar terms or likely to convey a similar impression.[6] It is specifically provided that the court shall not refuse to grant an injunction for lack of evidence that publication of the advertisement has given rise to loss or damage to any person.[7]

The Department of Trade and Industry has issued guidance on **27–006** statements regarding the effects on the environment of operations, products or services, made otherwise than by advertising, and not controlled by existing regulatory or self-regulatory schemes.[8]

Advertising Codes of Practice

Advertising in the United Kingdom is also controlled by a number of **27–007** self-regulating systems, applicable to different media. The British Code of Advertising Practice (the BCAP), operated by the Committee of Advertising Practice, applies to virtually all advertising in Britain of any significance other than advertising on television and commercial radio. These latter are subject to separate, similar codes, operated respectively by the Independent Television Commission and the Radio Authority.[9] Though compliance with the BCAP is voluntary, reputable publishers of newspapers and other journals require advertisements they carry to comply with it. In the event of non-compliance, an advertiser may simply be asked to withdraw or amend his advertisement. The Committee may, by way of sanction, itself give publicity to the false or misleading nature of the advertisement, and in the last resort an advertiser may be asked to publish an apology or correction. One of the basic principles of all the codes is that all advertisements should be "legal, decent, honest and truthful". Consequently, an advertisement should not mislead, and if it is likely to be understood as dealing with facts capable of objective assessment,

---

[6] reg. 6(2).
[7] reg. 6(5)(a).
[8] "Guidelines for Non-Advertising Green Claims", DTI, March 1994.
[9] These various codes, and guidelines on how they apply to environmental claims in advertising, are the subject of a 10 page publication by the Incorporated Society of British Advertisers Ltd (ISBA)—"Environmental Claims in Advertising—A Single Guide to all the Applicable Codes".

the advertiser must himself have all documentary and other evidence necessary to substantiate the statement.

27–008   Claims to a product being "environmentally friendly" are not expressly referred to in the BCAP itself, but a "Briefing" issued by the Committee of Advertising Practice[10] states that:

> "Sweeping or absolute claims such as 'environmentally friendly', where the claim was not explained or qualified, were judged to be unacceptable under the Code. No product has yet proven to be totally harmless to the environment."

On this basis, an objection was sustained in respect of advertising cars as environmentally friendly because they were equipped with catalytic convertors. Even though this equipment helps to reduce harmful emissions, cars are nevertheless harmful to the environment in other ways. Similarly, claims to products being "recyclable" are required to be "authentic and realistic". The Briefing states that "even if a product can physically be recycled, it is of questionable advantage if no facilities exist to reprocess it." Both the ITC and Radio Authority Codes emphasise that any general claims to the environmental performance of a product are to be assessed on a "cradle to grave" basis, that is by reference to "the complete life cycle of the product and its packaging, taking into account any effects on the environment of its manufacture, use and disposal and other relevant aspects". They further make clear that categorical statements that a product is "environment friendly", "safe" or "green" are unlikely to be appropriate for any mass-produced product.

27–009   On the other hand, relative or qualified claims, for example that a product is more environmentally friendly than another, are regarded as legitimate, provided of course that there is appropriate substantiation, though it will usually be necessary to indicate in the advertisement the basis for any such claim. However where evidence for a claim is inconclusive, any advertisement containing it must make clear that this is part of an unresolved debate.[11] The ability to substantiate a claim remains fundamental in comparative advertising. Hence an advertisement reading "Be environmentally friendly—use uPVC not wood" (for conservatories) was disapproved. The advertiser maintained that using uPVC (a plastics material) resulted in benefits to the rain forests, but this ignored the effects of making the plastics material itself and also the fact that it, unlike wood, is not a renewable resource.

---

[10] July 1993.
[11] A case in 1992 concerning a claim for environmental advantages of towelling nappies over disposable ones was resolved in this way.

Eco-labelling—General Principles

The plethora of claims to the possession of "environmentally   27–010
friendly" properties, made in response to the growth of "green
consumerism" in the late 1980s, led to a degree of cynicism on the part
of the public, and a set of objective standards was called for, against
which such claims could be judged.[12] Once these were developed,
products meeting them could receive special recognition, by being
exclusively entitled to a distinctive logo or device, *i.e.* the eco-label. The
principle is simple; putting it into practice is however much more
complex.

The concept of a label denoting that the product to which it is   27–011
applied meets defined standards, is far from new.[13] Thus the British
Standards "kite" mark serves its purpose in relation to goods meeting
applicable British Standards, and similarly a distinctive label may be
applied to goods that have been given the approval of the Design
Council. These are technically "certification" trade marks which may
be registered under section 50 of the Trade Marks Act 1994. Certification marks are subject to regulations that must be approved by the UK
Trade Marks Registry for the purposes of registration, whereby they
may be used by anyone in relation to goods that meet the criteria laid
down by those regulations.[14] These are necessarily self-financing
schemes, and there is in principle no reason why a similar scheme
could not be organised by a body with relevant interests to award a
label representing good or high environmental standards.

One disadvantage of a purely private scheme, however, is the issue   27–012
of policing—ensuring that those who are not participants do not use
the same or a similar mark. While someone blatantly adopting
another's mark without an entitlement to do so may well be committing an offence under the Trade Descriptions Act in the United
Kingdom, and under similar legislation in other countries, anyone
using a mark that is merely "confusingly similar", to use trade mark
language, is likely to be faced with civil proceedings only, since public
authorities are reluctant to use their scarce enforcement resources to

---

[12] Friends of the Earth instituted "Green Con" awards for the most inappropriate
promotional statements. In 1990, the "winning" advertisement (for a car) read: "[It] is
capable of running on unleaded petrol. This means it is as ozone friendly as it is
economical.".
[13] Many trade mark proprietors, at least at the upper end of the market, will claim that
that is the function of their marks among other things, but this discussion is
concerned with marks available for use in relation to any goods or services meeting
the requisite standards, whatever their source.
[14] The regulations must comply with the requirements of Sched. 2, para. 6, of the Trade
Marks Act, and with any that may additionally be imposed by rules made under that
Act.

help police what they are liable to perceive as a largely private matter of which the outcome is uncertain.[15] Unless an organisation responsible for granting the right to use a certification mark is very well resourced, the costs of policing the mark, particularly across numerous countries, can assume daunting proportions.

27–013 Germany was the first country to introduce an eco-label;[16] the Canadians subsequently developed a similar scheme,[17] as have the Japanese. The European Commission was keen to respond to the consumer demand for an officially sponsored eco-labelling scheme, and to develop one that would be applicable throughout the EC, for two main reasons. First, it was in accordance with the EC's recognised strategy for harnessing social pressures and market forces to promote environmentally sound activities to reinforce conventional regulatory controls, and the eco-label is seen as one way of encouraging manufacturers to respond constructively. Secondly, the existence of the German eco-label, and proposals by the French, the British and others to introduce national schemes, was seen as a significant threat to the free movement of goods between Member States. If each Member State had its own national scheme, and if the public in that state could not or would not recognise eco-labels granted in other states, this would, at least where eco-labels had any significant impact on purchasing decisions, have a material effect on the ability of producers in one member state to export to another. They would tend to be forced to obtain eco-label awards in each of the countries having such schemes, which would be liable to lead to considerable duplication of effort and, no doubt, suggestions from time to time of unfair discrimination in favour of domestic producers.

27–014 In the United Kingdom, work commenced on developing an eco-labelling scheme in 1988, and public consultations took place from 1989. The Government's White Paper "This Common Inheritance"[18] stated its intention to introduce an eco-labelling scheme in the United

---

[15] The trade mark aspects of the new eco-label have yet to be fully worked out. Registration of a trade mark in EC member states generally does not require proof of distinctiveness. In the UK, certain well known marks such as the Red Cross and Royal coats of arms may not be registered by law, but as yet no such prohibition applies to the device chosen to be the EC eco-label. While it is unlikely any reputable person would apply in his own name for the identical mark, one can readily envisage marks that might be confusingly similar being developed, in perfectly good faith, for use in connection with a particular business; there may indeed be such marks already in use. Art. 16(2) of Reg. 880/92 prohibits the use of confusingly similar marks, though in different jurisdictions within the EC there are widely differing practices as to what is likely to be held confusingly similar to a registered mark.

[16] The Blue Angel, a device derived from the United Nations symbol.

[17] Using a stylised maple leaf symbol.

[18] Cm. 1200, para. 17.31.

Kingdom by the end of 1991. Nevertheless, the European Commission was developing its own proposals for an EC regulation at much the same time, and it rapidly became clear that if a satisfactory EC-wide scheme could be developed, that was to be preferred. Accordingly, proposals for an independent UK scheme were not actively proceeded with, but kept in reserve should the EC scheme either fail to materialise at all or only in a way that was felt in the United Kingdom to be unsatisfactory. In the event, the UK scheme has not proceeded, and it must now be highly unlikely that any independent Government-backed national scheme in the United Kingdom will emerge.

The House of Commons Environment Committee studied the issue, **27–015** and its 8th Report "Eco-Labelling" was published on July 24, 1991. This contains a valuable review of the various issues involved in an eco-labelling scheme. Among its conclusions were that:

> "Eco-labelling stands a good chance of assisting consumers to play their role in protecting the environment from the impact of contemporary lifestyles; that it need not be expensive; and that it will complement the government's existing portfolio of environmental policies. We recommend that the government proceed with its preparatory work on eco-labelling, with a view to being in a position to introduce it as soon as a practical and comprehensive scheme has been worked out."[19]

The European Commission first published its proposals for an eco- **27–016** labelling regulation in February 1991.[20] The original proposals involved a highly centralised bureaucratic procedure: these were substantially modified,[21] and the proposal was eventually adopted on March 23, 1992 as Regulation 880/92.[22] The Regulation came into force immediately and Member States were required to inform the Commission within six months of the measures they had taken to ensure compliance. Given the substantial administrative infrastructure needed to make the system work properly, this was, and has proved to be, an unrealistically short period for putting the Regulation into effect. Nevertheless, the scheme was eventually launched on June 28, 1993 with Commission Decisions 93/430 and 93/431 on ecolabelling criteria for washing machines and dishwashers.[23] Further progress

---

[19] 8th Report, p.ix.
[20] COM (91) 37 final: [1991] O.J. C75.
[21] In COM (91) 544 final, [1992] O.J. C12.
[22] [1992] O.J. L99.
[23] [1993] O.J. L198. Criteria have now also been established for soil improvers, toilet paper and kitchen rolls, [1994] O.J. L364.

has however proved painfully slow, due mainly to disagreements between several Directorates-General in the Commission.

Eco-labelling Criteria—Life Cycle Analysis

27–017   Before considering the elements of the EC eco-labelling scheme, it is as well to review the issues that arise in devising any scheme of this nature. Firstly the scheme should normally serve at least two distinct but connected purposes: (i) to inform the public of those products which, by comparison with competitive products, are preferable as regards their environmental impacts, and (ii) thereby encourage suppliers to do as much as they can to ensure that any harmful environmental impacts that their products and services may have are minimised. Indeed, unless effective commercial pressure on businesses to develop environmentally desirable products and services results, the ultimate purpose of eco-labelling is largely lost. These two purposes are not wholly compatible: in some product areas at least there is a very wide spectrum of items aiming to meet the same functional requirements and if what is sometimes referred to as the "beauty parade" approach is adopted, and an eco-label is only granted to the top one or two, in terms of environmental performance, representing perhaps less than 5 per cent of the market, then it may well be that producers of the other 95 per cent will not consider it commercially worthwhile to seek to adapt their products so as to meet the eco-labelling criteria. On the other hand, if too wide a range of products is able to obtain the eco-label, then it may be asserted that the whole scheme has been degraded and become largely meaningless, and that there is little incentive to make substantial improvements to the environmental performance of the products covered. Accordingly any effective scheme must try to strike a satisfactory balance between these two positions.

27–018   The determination of environmental impacts of a product is not considered purely in absolute terms, but also by reference to the impacts of competing products. Assessing whether a product scores sufficiently strongly to justify an eco-label award, accordingly first requires a definition of the scope of the product category it belongs to, thereby determining the products with which it is to be compared. If this category is too broad, then certain types of goods which consumers will still wish to continue buying will none of them justify an eco-label, which defeats the purposes of the scheme, so far as producers and consumers of those types of products are concerned. A classic example of this sort is comparing means of transport, where it would make no sense to exclude all cars from consideration on the ground that bicycles are environmentally preferable, true though that must be.[24] On the other hand, very narrowly defined product categories do not sensibly encourage consumers to choose, on environmental performance grounds, between products that are genuinely competitive with each other in the market place.[25] It follows that products should not be excluded from consideration merely because they are inherently environmentally unfriendly, but a judgment has to be made as to, for example, whether filament light bulbs could ever be given a label, given that low energy consumption lights represent an environmentally sounder alternative.[26]

This problem could in theory be resolved by setting up a more complex scheme in which products, for which an eco-label is sought, are not subjected to a simple pass or fail approach, but are given grades, with only the most environmentally desirable products receiving the top grade. No current scheme attempts this, however, and it would certainly add substantially to the complexity of the analysis of each product. The Environment Committee's conclusion on this point was that a pass/fail approach should be adopted initially at least, without prejudice to any future decision on the introduction of some graded system.

27–019

A separate issue that is logically extraneous, but nevertheless in practice important, is the actual ability of a product justifying an eco-label to perform satisfactorily the functions for which it is sold. In some cases, such as detergents, functional ability may directly affect the environmental performance of the product, since if significantly more of it is needed to do the same job, this must necessarily be taken into account in assessing its environmental impacts. Nevertheless, there are many other situations where that will not be a factor, but if the reputation of the eco-label is not to be harmed, it cannot afford to be seen to be largely given to products that do not work very well. The House of Commons Environment Committee agreed that "a test of fitness for purpose will be essential in maintaining the credibility of

27–020

---

[24] A horse might be better than either, and (bare) human feet best of all.

[25] The Environment Committee's 8th Report mentions (para. 27), as examples of excessively narrow groups in the German Blue Angel scheme, "sound-proofed glass collection bins for noise-sensitive areas" and "rapidly biodegradable chain lubricants for power saws".

[26] The argument on this point in the UK has resulted in proposals that would exclude conventional filament bulbs from ever receiving the eco-label. Highly contentious technical disputes may also prove intractable, *e.g.* whether use of phosphates in detergent compositions is harmful, through their ability to promote eutrophication, or whether it is beneficial, through less detergent being needed.

the eco-labelling scheme";[27] and this is reflected in the EC Regulation.[28]

27–021   A typical area where this problem may arise is if noise is regarded as a relevant criterion for the assessment of a product. This is the position under the German scheme and indeed particularly important in relation to, for example, assessment of lawnmowers and vacuum cleaners. However it is almost inevitable that reduced noise output will go hand in hand with reduced efficiency. The weighting that is attached to emitted noise levels cannot but be highly subjective: opinions could well vary widely within and between the different Member States of the EC.[29]

27–022   One subjective issue, that must nevertheless be determined and applied uniformly, is what is to be regarded as an "environmental" impact of the production, use and disposal of a product. Looking purely at emissions to air, water and land, and any human toxicity effects, would probably be regarded by most people as too narrow, since it would ignore impacts on the ozone layer, global warming and biodiversity, over which there is now international concern. For some people, it is essentially the long term impacts that they would wish to see addressed, since these may well be the most intractable to rectify, and also the effects that are most likely to be neglected by governments and regulators who are liable to be more strongly influenced by shorter term political questions. On the other hand, noise and smell are, where disagreeable, extremely important elements of the environment to those suffering them. In the case of cosmetics, objection was taken to proposed assessment criteria, because they took no account of whether there was any testing on animals.[30] Nevertheless, a line has to be drawn somewhere between issues that everyone would accept are "environmental", and those which represent social, political or ethical choices — the wider the net is drawn the more contentious the criteria are likely to become, and the more unworkable the entire scheme.

27–023   Having decided what matters should be taken into account in an assessment of the environmental impacts of any product the highly complex question remains how to weight the very different types of impact that competing products may have in terms of their environmental significance. A more durable product may place significantly

---

[27] 8th Report, para. 40.
[28] See Art.1: "without . . . significantly affecting the properties which make a product fit for use".
[29] In the case of cars and motorcycles, purchasers often have a very different attitude to the noise these may make from those who merely hear them go by.
[30] The Body Shop, an organisation with a reputation largely based on its commitment to natural products, threatened to boycott the scheme unless this criterion was included.

reduced demands on waste disposal facilities, but require a greater input of raw materials and/or energy at the manufacturing stage. A renewable resource, such as cotton or timber, may in principle be preferable to a plastic material made from non-renewable fossil fuel, but increased world demand for cotton or timber may lead to destruction of natural vegetation in order to cater for the demand, with consequent loss of biodiversity and, maybe, soil erosion.

The UK government's original approach was to consider only those 27–024 environmental impacts of a product that result from its use and disposal. Thus the impacts arising at the time of manufacture, and those involved in the production of the requisite raw materials were to be ignored. This approach would of course dramatically simplify the necessary impact analysis, but at the cost of, at best, misleading consumers as to the overall impact of a product, and, at worst, encouraging manufacturers to move towards products with good use and disposal characteristics, even if their overall environmental performance, including the manufacturing and raw materials aspects, were to be substantially worse. This proposal was abandoned, and forms no part of the EC eco-label system, which requires attention to be paid to the environmental impacts of a product throughout its entire life, from "cradle to grave". For each product, therefore, what is known as a "life cycle analysis" must be carried out, with a view to awarding grades to the product in terms of its environmental performance in all relevant respects. The approach to be adopted is illustrated in Annex I to the Regulation which sets out what is referred to as an "Indicative Assessment Matrix", reproduced as Table 27/I below.

When assessing the environmental impact of a manufacturing 27–026 process, this might be expected normally to consider the actual impacts of a particular process at the locality where it is carried on. However such site-specific criteria could in principle be seen as a restraint on trade from products imported from outside the EC, contrary to GATT, under which restrictions may not discriminate against imports unless the qualities of the product as imported differ in a relevant way from domestic products.[31] If process criteria are adopted for a particular product that are best for one location, they may quite conceivably be environmentally less satisfactory at another, for example in terms of their demands on water supplies or their contribution to the ambient air pollution. Consequently life cycle analysis will frequently omit site-specific, or even country-specific

---

[31] It was for this reason that the USA could not legitimately prevent imports of Mexican tuna that were caught by net rather than on a line, since the products were indistinguishable; for the purposes of GATT, the impact of the catching method on dolphins (not being endangered species) was irrelevant.

TABLE 27/I

Indicative Assessment Matrix

Environmental Fields	Product life-cycle				
	Pre-production	Production	Distribution (including packaging)	Utilisation	Disposal
Waste relevance					
Soil pollution and degradation					
Water contamination					
Air contamination					
Noise					
Consumption of energy					
Consumption of natural resources					
Effects on eco-systems					

issues, regarding these as matters that should properly be exclusively the province of the regulatory authorities.

Finally, any scheme must take account of the fact that new **27–027** manufacturing processes, and indeed altogether new products and materials, are liable to be developed from time to time. Where these and other technological advances can be adopted that would result in improved environmental performance, the criteria for awarding an eco-label will need to be adapted, if eco-labels granted on criteria fixed in the past are not to become misleading. The Regulation meets this by providing that the period of validity of the product groups themselves "shall be about three years", and further that the period of validity of the various ecological criteria used for assessing the products within that group may not exceed the period of validity of the product group itself.[32] The eco-label itself must be awarded for a fixed production period, which again may in no circumstances exceed the period of validity of the criteria.[33] Once the system is fully under way, therefore, there will be a constant review of old products as well as assessment of new ones. The costs that this entails must necessarily be kept within reasonable limits, if the scheme is to be commercially viable at all, and this is a further reason for avoiding great complexity, even if the end results are less than perfect.

Regulation No. 880/92

EC Regulation 880/92 provides for a decentralised system of **27–028** awarding an eco-label to goods. Services are not eligible for the eco-label. The label itself consists of a logo consisting of a stylised flower, in either black and white, or green and blue. The award of the label is to be made by national "competent bodies" set up under Article 9, subject to determination at European level in the event of objections. In the United Kingdom the UK Ecolabelling Board is constituted as the competent body by the United Kingdom Ecolabelling Board Regulations 1992.[34]

The Commission has set up a committee of representatives of the **27–029** Member States under Article 7, to which it must refer questions to relating to eco-label awards for determination. The national representatives have weighted voting rights corresponding to those of the members of the Council of Ministers under Article 148(2) of the Rome Treaty. The Committee (referred to here as the "Article 7 Committee)

[32] Art. 5(5).
[33] Art. 8(5).
[34] S.I. 1992 No. 2383.

does not itself have powers to initiate procedures, but only to vote on measures proposed by the Commission. If a Commission proposal is rejected, it must be submitted to the Council of Ministers for their determination. If the Council fails to act on this proposal within three months of the referral to it by the Commission, the Commission is entitled to adopt the measure as referred.

27–030   The Regulation confirms the dual purpose of the eco-label scheme as being intended to:

- promote the design, production, marketing and use of products which have a reduced environmental impact during their entire life cycle, and
- provide consumers with better information on the environmental impact of products, without, however, compromising product or workers' safety or significantly affecting the properties which make a product fit for use.[35]

27–031   Article 4 provides that the label can be awarded to products which meet the objectives just set out, and which comply with EC health, safety and environmental requirements. It may however not be awarded to products which are themselves dangerous substances or preparations classified as such under the Dangerous Substances and Dangerous Preparations Directives 67/548 and 88/379 (see paragraphs 12–008, 12–013 and 12–098 to 12–108). However products which merely *contain* such a substance or preparation may receive an eco-label if that product meets the objectives of Article 1.[36] The label may also in no case be awarded to products manufactured by processes "which are likely to harm significantly man and/or the environment". The quoted passage appears to qualify "processes" rather than "products".[37] If that is right, there would therefore be no bar to having, for example, a pesticides product group. The Regulation does not however apply to food, drink or pharmaceuticals.[38] It may nevertheless apply to the packaging used for such products, which has led to a debate as to whether the use of the eco-label on packaging would in practice be taken to apply to the contents of the packaging. No criteria have yet been established for packaging, though this is one of the product groups being worked on currently.

27–032   Determination of the product groups for which eco-labels will be awarded, and the ecological criteria to be used in assessing applications for the label in each group is the responsibility of the Article 7 Committee. In practice, to get the scheme under way, five of the

[35] Art. 1.
[36] Art. 4(2)(a).
[37] Art. 4(2)(b).
[38] Art. 2.

Member States took individual responsibility for particular product groups, and specifically for defining the groups with precision and setting appropriate criteria. Before the product groups and the criteria are determined, there must be consultation with interest groups representing industry, commerce, consumer organisations and environmental organisations, in accordance with Article 6.

Table 27/II shows the initial list of product groups, and the countries with responsibility for them.   **27–033**

TABLE 27/II

– paper (paper towelling, photocopying paper, writing paper, toilet paper) – textiles – insulation materials – dishwashing detergents (hand and machine)	Denmark
– washing machine detergents – household cleaning products – solar energy systems (photovoltaic and thermal)	Germany
– paints and varnishes – batteries and cells – shampoos	France
– packaging – construction materials (including ceramic tile) – refrigerators and cooling systems	Italy
– washing machines – dishwashers – hairsprays – light bulbs – organic fertilisers	United Kingdom

Each product group must be defined in such a way as to ensure that   **27–034**
all competing products which serve similar purposes and which have equivalence of use are included in the same group.[39] This approach thus is designed to avoid an unduly narrow definition. The Regulation does not in terms place any restriction on how wide the product groups might be, but it is to be hoped that the reference to products which "serve similar purposes and which have equivalence of use"

[39] Art. 5(3).

1117

will be taken as indicating where the outer limits should be drawn, though the text of the Regulation itself provides little help on the point.

27–036   The decision to bring a specific product group and its associated ecological criteria within the eco-label scheme is to be taken by the Article 7 Committee on the initiative either of the Commission or of any of the competent bodies. Where a competent body does not wish to act on its own initiative, it may request the Commission to take up the matter, provided it has undertaken appropriate consultation with interest groups.[40] The product groups, with their ecological criteria and periods of validity are to be published in the EC Official Journal.[41]

27–037   The ecological criteria to be applied to each product group are to reflect a "cradle to grave" approach,[42] defined to mean the life cycle of a product from manufacturing, including the choice of raw materials, distribution, consumption and use, to disposal after use.[43] There are only very general constraints placed on the selection of these criteria. They must however be based on the broad objectives of the Regulation as set out in Article 1 (see paragraph 27–030), the general principles set out in Article 4, and the parameters of the "Indicative Assessment Matrix" (reproduced in Table 27/I). The criteria are required to be "precise, clear and objective so as to ensure uniformity of application by the competent bodies".[44] This does not of course exclude the introduction of subjective assessments in the setting of the criteria: in relation to noise, in particular, this is virtually unavoidable. The criteria "must ensure a high level of environmental protection, be based as far as possible on the use of clean technology and, where appropriate, reflect the desirability of maximising product life".[45] The effect of these rules is that the system should set threshold values, and any product meeting those values will be entitled to an award. The scheme is thus not designed to operate on the "beauty parade" principle, entitling only the best one or two products to the eco-label.

Application Procedure

27–038   Applications for an eco-label may be made by manufacturers or importers; manufacturers must apply to the relevant body of the

[40] Art. 5(2).
[41] See Commission Decisions 93/430 and 93/431, [1995] O.J. L198, for the first such publication, in respect of washing machines and dishwashers.
[42] Art. 5(4).
[43] Art. 3(d).
[44] Art. 5(4).
[45] Art. 5(4).

country in which the product is manufactured or first marketed, and importers to the body of the country into which the product is imported from outside the EC. After assessing the product in the manner described above, if the relevant body decides to award a label it must notify the Commission of its decision, giving full results of the assessment and a summary in a prescribed format laid down by the Commission.[46] The Commission must then pass on copies of the decision and summary and, if so requested, full results of the assessment, to all the corresponding bodies in other Member States, who may raise reasoned objections to the proposed award. The original body may however proceed with the award if no reasoned objections have been received by it within 30 days after it sent its notice to the Commission of its decision. If reasoned objections are raised, it is clearly intended that there should be informal discussions to try to resolve any difficulties, but failing resolution in this manner, the Commission has power to take a decision on the matter itself.

The Commission is required to maintain separate registers of all applications received, of all those approved and of all that have been rejected. A competent body having received an application must consult these registers, and if it decides to award an eco-label to a product already rejected by the corresponding body of another Member State, it must mention this fact to the Commission. In such a case, it is for the Commission to decide whether or not the product should receive an eco-label, referring the question to the Article 7 Committee for determination. If the competent body decides to reject an application, it is required to inform the Commission of this, and to give the applicant the reasons for the rejection. Where the competent body decides that a product the subject of an application does not fall within a particular product category it is required to take a decision as to whether a proposal for the establishment of a new product group should be sent to the Commission for adoption.[47]

There is no appeals procedure provided in the Regulation, but there would appear to be nothing in it that would prevent a Member State from having rules of procedure for its competent body that would allow a review of a provisional decision by the competent body, before it came to a final determination. No such procedure has however been devised for the United Kingdom. Judicial review would be unlikely to be appropriate in most cases for challenging the decision of the UK Ecolabelling Board, in so far as the dispute is on the actual assessment

27–039

27–040

---

[46] Art. 10(3). The prescribed format is set out in Commission Decision 94/10, [1994] O.J. L7.
[47] Art. 10(8).

of the product. If, however, the Board were to construe a product category definition unduly narrowly, and thereby improperly exclude a particular type of product from consideration, this would be an appropriate matter to be subjected to judicial review, but on the face of the Regulation the application would be deemed to be refused, and it would appear that a new application would have to be made. If a failure by the Board to give correct effect to the Regulation, such as giving an improper construction to a product category definition, were to result in quantifiable damages to an applicant, the Ecolabelling Board or the UK government might be liable to pay compensation on the principles set out in *Francovich* (see paragraph 2–036).[48] However for any liability to arise, the applicable rules must be sufficiently precise, and this may normally prevent liability attaching, irrespective of any other grounds which may be available under EC law, where an administrative tribunal acts in good faith and without negligence.

27–041   For the reasons indicated above (see paragraph 27–037) an eco-label will normally be granted for at most three years, but it may be renewed, provided the criteria applied to assessing products for the label have not changed in the meantime.[49] The award of an eco-label is made by way of a contract between each applicant and the relevant competent body in the standard form contained in the Annex to Commission Decision 93/517.[50] The standard terms (in which the grantee of the right to use the eco-label is referred to as the "Holder") include:

—   the Holder is granted the right to use the eco-label for a defined period;

—   the relevant product must comply throughout the term of the contract with all the product group criteria and eco-label specifications annexed to the contract;

—   reference to the award of the eco-label must be made only in relation to the relevant product;

—   the competent body is entitled to obtain information from the Holder for the purpose of monitoring compliance with the terms of the contract;

—   where the Holder becomes aware that he has failed to meet the terms of use or other principal provisions, he must immediately refrain from using the eco-label;

---

[48] Whether there should be any such liability, and if so in what circumstances, would, it is submitted, be properly a matter of EC law, and English (or Scottish) law principles on the liability of administrative authorities should not be conclusive.

[49] Art. 8(5).

[50] [1993] O.J. L243.

- the eco-label is conditional upon all relevant fees being paid in good time;
- the Holder may be required to reply to any complaints concerning the product;
- if the European Commission amends or withdraws the relevant product group criteria, the competent body may terminate the right to use the eco-label;
- the contract may be terminated for breach by the Holder, or voluntarily by the Holder on one month's notice;
- following termination use may be made of the eco- label only in relation to products already supplied to the market, and then only for a maximum of six months from the date of termination;
- where the relevant product group criteria are extended without amendments beyond the period of the contract, if the awarding body has not terminated it on two months notice before expiry of the contract and of the product group criteria, the competent body will give the Holder at least two months advance notice that the contract will be automatically renewed for so long as the product group criteria remain in force.

The relevant competent body in any Member State may include in the contract additional provisions, so long as these are compatible with the Regulation; if it does so, it must forward the text of the contract to the Commission for assessment of their compatibility.[51]   **27–042**

Where an eco-label has been awarded to a product, this will be published in the Official Journal. The Commission is required to publish a list of all such products, together with the name of the manufacturer or importer and the expiration date of the label in each case; these lists must be published at least once a year.[52]   **27–043**

It is specifically prohibited to use the eco-label in any advertising except when a label has been awarded, and then only in relation to the specific product the subject of the award.[53] Further, there is an express ban on any false or misleading advertising or the use of any label or logo which leads to confusion with the EC eco-label.[54] Accordingly it is to be expected that the UK Trade Descriptions Act 1968 will be appropriately amended; it is also likely that it will be made impossible to register the eco-label or a mark confusingly similar with it as a trade mark.   **27–044**

[51] Decision 93/517, Art. 2.
[52] Art. 14(b).
[53] Art. 16(1).
[54] Art. 16(2). See also n. 15 to para. 27–012.

1121

Fees

27–045   Applicants for an eco-label must pay the costs of processing their applications, and further, where an eco-label is awarded, the conditions of use are to include payment terms in respect of that use. Although the national competent bodies are to fix the fees concerned, and variations are expressly permitted from one Member State to another, "indicative guidelines" on the fee levels are required to be established.[55] These are the subject of Commission Decision 93/326,[56] which sets the following guideline figures:

-   ECU 500 for the application fee;[57]
-   0.15 per cent of sales as a fee for use of the label, subject to
-   ECU 500 as a minimum annual fee.[58]

27–046   The extent to which there may be variations between Member States is limited by Article 3 of the Decision to at most 20 per cent either side of the guideline figures. If VAT is payable on the fees, the VAT-inclusive figure is to be used in assessing whether the amounts are within the 20 per cent range. Each Member State is required to keep its fee structure consistent, and accordingly any departure from the guideline figures must be in the same direction and by the same amount for all the fees it levies.[59]

27–047   The use fee is to be payable annually on the sales volume within the EC of the relevant product in each year, starting from the date of the award of the eco-label to it, and calculated on ex-factory prices. Presumably these prices should include the cost of any packaging taken into account when assessing the product for the award of the label, but no other, and be exclusive of VAT. The sales volume does not appear to be necessarily limited to that of those products that actually have the eco-label physically applied to them or to their packaging. Since the benefit of the label may also come to the manufacturer from associating it with the product through advertising, this is not unreasonable. There is no suggestion in the Regulation of reducing the total sales figure by the amount of any credits for damaged or returned goods, as is common in intellectual property licence agreements. However it is considered that this would be a legitimate provision to include in the contract terms, since it would merely lead to a more accurate figure for the true annual sales benefiting from the use of the

[55] Art. 11.
[56] [1993] O.J. L129.
[57] Art. 1.
[58] Art. 2.
[59] Art. 3(1).

label. Nevertheless there would need to be procedural terms defining when such credits may be claimed, to cover whether or not this would be possible several years after the original sale, perhaps following the outcome of lengthy litigation. Payment of the running fee on sales need not necessarily await calculation of the annual sales volume; a user may be required to pay the whole or part of an annual fee in advance on the basis of estimated sales, subject to adjustment when the actual figures are available.

Environmental Information Labels

In certain market sectors, promotional matter, such as an eco-label, that merely seeks to improve the image of a product, whether justifiably or not, will be insufficient for consumers who wish to be enabled to compare the environmental performance of competing products for themselves. Directive 92/75[60] thus provides for harmonising national rules on the giving of information in relation to the consumption of energy and other resources by household appliances. These are defined in Article 1 to consist of: **27–048**

- — Refrigerators, freezers and their combinations;
- — Washing machines, dryers and their combinations;
- — Dishwashers;
- — Ovens;
- — Water heaters and hot water storage appliances;
- — Lighting sources;
- — Air-conditioning appliances.

Appliances on the list are subject to the Directive even though they may be sold for non-household uses. Additional appliances may be added to the list by means of further directives.

Directive 92/75 is a framework directive setting out broad require-   **27–049**
ments only. Individual "daughter" directives are to be issued in respect of the various appliances which will provide specific detail on the labelling requirements. The first of these, Directive 94/2,[61] relates to household electric refrigerators, freezers and their combinations. It repeals and replaces Directive 79/530,[62] which had the same objectives but, since compliance with the labelling requirements by Member States was voluntary, proved unsatisfactory in practice, leading to

[60] [1992] O.J. L297.
[61] [1994] O.J. L45.
[62] [1979] O.J. L145.

only a single Directive 79/531,[63] in respect of electric ovens. This latter remains in effect, and Member States may make its requirements compulsory within their territories as though it were issued pursuant to Directive 92/75; however there is no compulsion on Member States to do this.

27–050   An essential feature of the new Directive is that, in relation to the appliances brought within its scope, the labelling requirements are mandatory. Nevertheless, it is intended that it should only apply to those appliances of which the aggregate energy use is significant and which afford adequate scope for increased energy efficiency. No implementing legislation has as yet been brought forward in the United Kingdom; this may well be deferred until adoption of the first daughter directive on a specific appliance type.

[63] [1979] O.J. L145.

INDEX

INDEX

1127

1133

POLLUTION — *cont.*
 water, of — *cont.*
  defences — *cont.*
   third party, unauthorised
    intervention of, 8–118, 8–119,
    8–132–8–134, 8–136
  discharge consent
   appeals, 8–163
   application for, 8–153
   compensation, payment of, 8–162
   conditions, subject to, 8–155,
    8–156
   contravention of, 8–090
   grant of, 8–154, 8–155
   objections to, 8–153, 8–154
   prescribed limits of discharge, 8–
    157, 8–158
   publicity, 8–153
   retrospective, 8–159
   review of, 8–161
   revocation or variation of, 8–161,
    8–162
   succession to, 8–160
  dumping at sea *See* DUMPING AT SEA
  sewerage undertaker, by *See*
   SEWERAGE UNDERTAKER
  statutory offences
   accumulated deposits, removal of,
    8–094
   "causing or knowingly
    permitting", meaning of
   "causing", 8–106–8–111
   "knowingly permitting",
    8–112–8–117
   "contravention", meaning of,
    8–090
   fish, injurious to, 8–093
   nature of, 8–090, 8–091
   permissive entry and discharge
    distinguished, 8–091
   "poisonous, noxious or polluting
    matter", meaning of
   discolouration of water, 8–100,
    8–101, 8–105
   "noxious", 8–099
   "poisonous", 8–097, 8–098
   "polluting", 8–100–8–105
   radioactive waste, 8–096
   "red list" substances, discharge
    of, 8–095
   strict liability for, 8–118
   trade or sewage effluent, 8–092
  trade effluent *See* SEWER
POLLUTION CONTROL REGISTERS, 8–173
POLYCHLORINATED BIPHENYLS (PCB's)
 regulation of, 12–155–12–160
 waste, as, 11–128, 11–129

POLYCHLORINATED TERPHENYLS (PCT's)
 regulation of, 12–155–12–160
 waste, as, 11–128, 11–129
PRIVATE NUISANCE
 action, requirements for
  defendant, liability of
   aggregation of small acts,
    contribution to, 22–070
   building contractors, 22–069
   land, possession and control of,
    22–053–22–055
   landlords and tenants/licensees,
    22–066–22–068
   nuisances initiated by others or by
    nature, 22–056–22–065
  land, interest in, 22–043–22–045
  plaintiff, qualification as,
   22–046–22–052
  reasonableness of use,
   22–072–22–087
   natural causes, arising from, 22–
    084–22–086
   object, duration or motive, 22–
    078–22–083
   third party actions, 22–084–22–086
 damage
  interference with character of
   neighbourhood, 22–108–22–117
  knowledge and forseeability, 22–
   094–22–104
  land, to
   types of, 22–092–22–093
   necessity for, 22–088–22–091
  physical
   standard and sensitivity, 22–105–
    22–107
  types of
   economic loss, 22–124–22–126
   land, to, 22–092–22–093, 22–118,
    22–119
   persons and chattels, 22–118, 22–
    120–22–123
 defences
  Act of God, 22–128
  care and skill, use of, 22–131
  consent, acquiescence or licence,
   22–136
  contributory acts by others, 22–132
  necessity, 22–128
  prescription, 22–137
  public benefit, 22–130
  self–protection, 22–128
  statutory authority, 22–123–22–135
  volenti non fit injuria, 22–129
 definition of, 22–016–22–028
 development of, 1–015–1–022

1160